MAINE

HILARY NANGLE

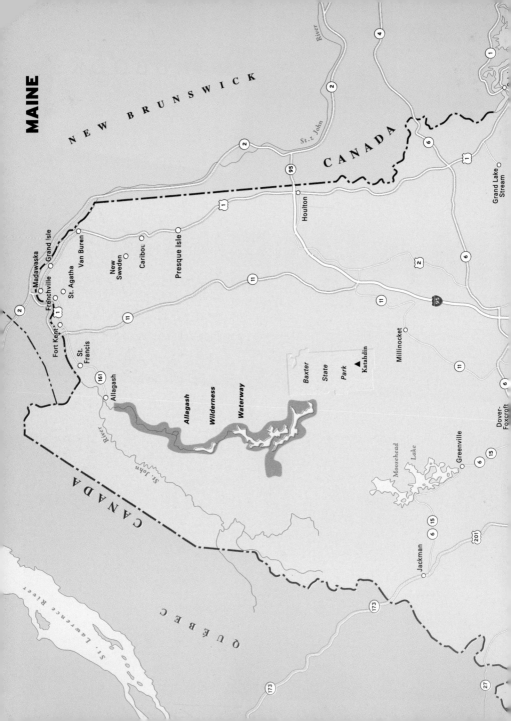

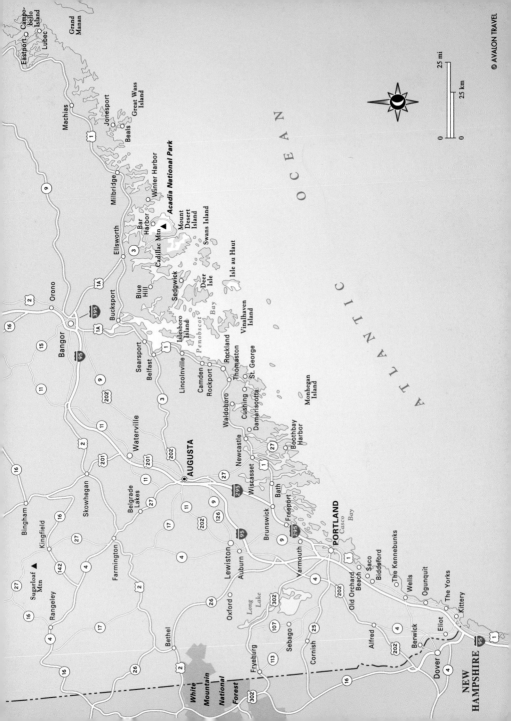

© AVALON TRAVEL

MOUNT DESERT ISLAND/ ACADIA NATIONAL PARK

Porcupine Islands

The Thrumcap

Schooner

SCHOON HEAD

Champlain Mountain

3

Frenchman

Bay

Bar Island

College of the Atlantic

Bar Harbor

INTERNATIONAL FERRY TERMINAL

COLLEGE OF THE ATLANTIC

3

SIEUR DE MONTS ★

Dorr Mountain

Cadillac Mountain

PARK LOOP RD

Bubble

Witch Hole Pond

HULLS COVE VISITOR CENTER

Acadia

Hulls Cove

Lake Wood

RD

233

Eagle Lake

The

Salisbury Cove

Aunt Betty Pond

National

NOR WAY

DR

Sargent Mountain

Somes

198

CROOKED

Eastern Bay

3

Lamoine State Park

Town Hill

102

198

Marlboro

Somesville

RD

OAK HILL

Somes Pond

Round Pond

102

Lamoine

Narrows

AIRPORT

102

198

RD

Indian Point

OAK HILL CROSS RD

102

3

To Ellsworth

Trenton

THOMPSON ISLAND INFORMATION CENTER

Desert

Mount

Blagden Preserve

INDIAN POINT

Squid Cove

Pretty Marsh

BETH MARSH

Alley Island

Green Island

Narrows

Bartlett

Black Island

Western

Bay

230

Union

River

Bay

Bartlett Island

Park Loop Road map — Acadia National Park

RD
Great Head
Sand Beach
THUNDER HOLE OVERLOOK
Beehive
Gorham Mountain
Otter Cliffs
Otter Creek
BLACKWOODS
Park
Pemetic Mountain
WILDWOOD STABLES
Day Mountain
Seal Harbor
Eastern Way
Penobscot Mountain
Jordan Pond
JORDAN POND HOUSE
ASTICOU AZALEA GARDEN
THUYA GARDEN
Little Long Pond
Parkman Mountain
Hadlock Ponds
Norumbega Mountain
198
3
SARGENT DR
Northeast Harbor
INFORMATION CENTER
Bear Island
Greening Island
Little Cranberry Island
Islesford
Sutton Island
Crow Island
Green Nubble
Baker Island
Acadia National Park
O C E A N
A T L A N T I C
Great Cranberry Island
Western Way
CLARK POINT RD
WENDELL GILLEY MUSEUM
Manset
SOUTHWEST HARBOR/TREMONT CHAMBER OF COMMERCE
Southwest Harbor
FERNALD POINT RD
Acadia Mountain
Hall Quarry
102
Sound
Echo Lake
Beech Mountain
LONG POND RD
National
Mansell Mountain
Bernard Mountain
WESTERN MOUNTAIN RD
Seal Cove Pond
SEAL COVE RD
Seal Cove
Acadia
Long Pond
Hodgdon Pond
Pretty Marsh Harbor
Folly Island
Moose Island
West Tremont
Tremont
Bernard
Bass Harbor
SWANS ISLAND FERRY TERMINAL
BASS HARBOR HEAD LIGHT
SEAWALL
102A
102
Park
Great Gott Island
Blue Hill Bay

2 mi
2 km

PARK LOOP ROAD
TWO-WAY
ONE-WAY
© AVALON TRAVEL

DISCOVER MAINE

Tucked into the northeasternmost corner of
the United States and comprising 33,215 square miles, Maine boldly
promotes itself as "The Way Life Should Be." Not to say that everything's perfect, mind you, but it is an extraordinarily special place.
There's a reason why more than eight million people visit yearly, why
longtime summer folk finally just pick up stakes and *settle* here. The
traditional Maine traits of honesty, thrift, frankness, and ruggedness
remain refreshingly appealing.

Maine is easy on the senses. The air is clean and clear, often
perfumed with pine, balsam, coastal rugosa rose or the earthy scent
of a flowing river. Even in cities, it's possible to escape into a preserve
or forest to hear birds sing, streams gurgle, and leaves rustle. Along
the coast, you can taste the salt in the air.

From the glacier-scoured beaches of the Southern Coast to the
rugged boulders Down East, Maine's coastline follows a zigzagging
route that would measure about 5,500 miles if you stretched it taut.

Lubec Landmarks is restoring the smokehouses lining Lubec's waterfront.

But taut it isn't – it's a wrinkled landscape whose countless bony fingers jut into the sea. Each of these peninsulas has its own character, as does each island offshore.

But don't stop there. Venture inland, where 6,000 lakes and ponds, 32,000 miles of rivers, and 17 million acres of timberlands await. Head north into Aroostook County, often compared with the big-sky country of the West. Segue over to northern Maine's wilderness – where on any state map, blue, indicating waterways, and green, indicating undeveloped lands, are the dominant colors. Thousands of miles of trails lure backpackers and mountain bikers in summer and fall, skiers and sledders in winter. Intrepid Appalachian Trail hikers finish at the summit of Mt. Katahdin, Maine's tallest peak; determined paddlers spend a week on the Allagash Wilderness Waterway, a water lifeline through the wilderness. Cross over to western Maine, where mountains cradle lakes, and hidden springs and snowmelt feed tumbling streams. Maine's mountains are especially spectacular in autumn, when brilliant reds, oranges, and yellows spike the slopes and reflect in the shimmering lakes and ponds below

Watch the sunset over Moosehead Lake from a high spot on the Lily Bay Road.

(and – *shhh* – Maine doesn't draw foliage crowds in numbers like other New England states).

If you get enough of natural highs, you can poke into manmade pleasures. Maine's inspired and inspiring scenery has drawn artists and artisans for generations. Studios and galleries are tucked on back roads and clustered in scenic locations, so searching for the perfect souvenir is as enjoyable as finding it.

Of course, lobster is king, seafood is fresh, and farmers markets are plentiful, which is why talented chefs are drawn here. You, too, can benefit from the bounty of cheesemakers, fish smokers, artisan bakers, microbrewers, and organic farmers, but balance that with classic Maine fare. Share a bean-hole or chowder supper with locals and, if you're lucky, hear a genuine Maine accent (here's a hint: "Ayuh" isn't so much a word as a sharp two-part intake of breath).

A student of Maine-born author Mary Ellen Chase once mused, "Maine is different from all other states, isn't it? I suppose that's because God never quite finished it." Maine may indeed be a work in progress, but it's a masterwork.

Candy-striped West Quoddy Head Lighthouse is a Down East coastal landmark.

Contents

MAP CONTENTS

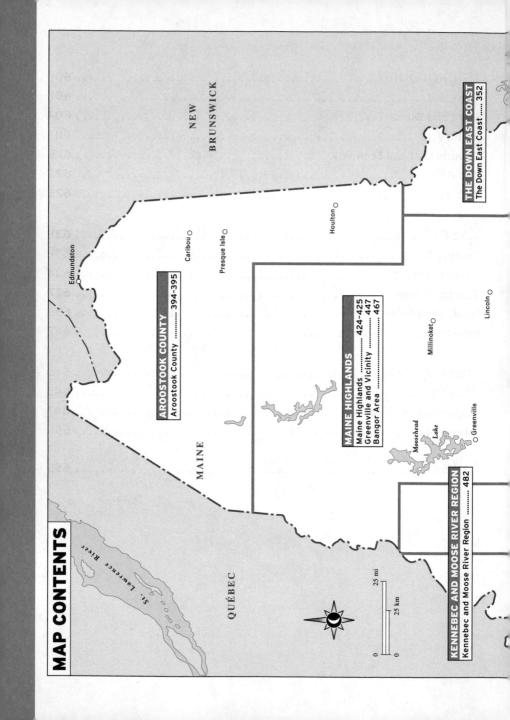

St. Lawrence River

QUÉBEC

NEW BRUNSWICK

MAINE

Edmundston ○

Caribou ○

Presque Isle ○

Houlton ○

Millinoket ○

Lincoln ○

Moosehead ○ Greenville
Lake

0   25 mi
0   25 km

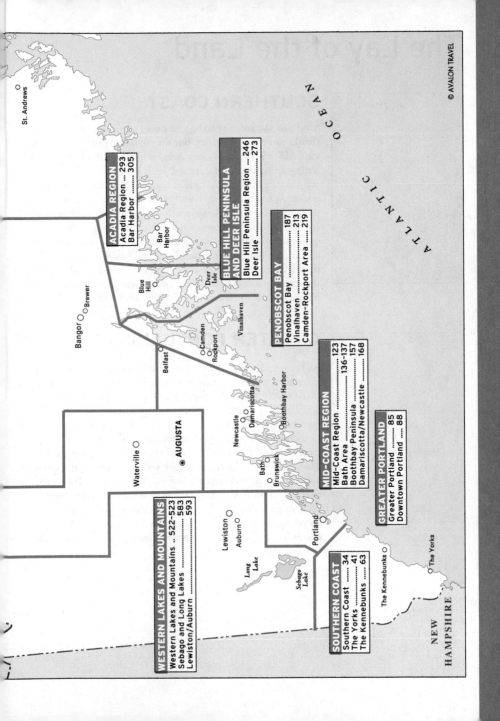

© AVALON TRAVEL

ATLANTIC OCEAN

St. Andrews

ACADIA REGION
Acadia Region ... 293
Bar Harbor 305

Bar
Harbor

BLUE HILL PENINSULA AND DEER ISLE
Blue Hill Peninsula Region ... 246
Deer Isle 273

Bangor ○ ○ Brewer

Blue
Hill

Deer
Isle

PENOBSCOT BAY
Penobscot Bay 187
Vinalhaven 213
Camden–Rockport Area 219

Belfast ○

Camden ○
Rockport ○

Vinalhaven

Waterville ○

● AUGUSTA

Damariscotta

Newcastle ○
Damariscotta ○

Boothbay Harbor

MID-COAST REGION
Mid-Coast Region 123
Bath Area 136–137
Boothbay Peninsula 157
Damariscotta/Newcastle 168

Bath ○
Brunswick ○

WESTERN LAKES AND MOUNTAINS
Western Lakes and Mountains .. 522–523
Sebago and Long Lakes 583
Lewiston/Auburn 593

Lewiston ○
Auburn ○

GREATER PORTLAND
Greater Portland 85
Downtown Portland 88

Long
Lake

Sebago
Lake

Portland ○

SOUTHERN COAST
Southern Coast 34
The Yorks 41
The Kennebunks 63

The Kennebunks ○

The Yorks ○

NEW
HAMPSHIRE

The Lay of the Land

SOUTHERN COAST

Sand and sun are the two biggest draws to this region of Maine, thanks to miles of beaches, but they're not the only reasons to visit. Maine's Southern Coast delights history buffs, with homes dating from the 17th century, such as those at **Old York;** architecture buffs, with scads of sea captains' and shipbuilders' homes in towns such as **Kennebunkport;** art connoisseurs, with its plentiful galleries and the **Ogunquit Museum of American Art;** outdoors-oriented folks, with numerous preserves for walking, hiking, and canoeing; maritime-heritage aficionados, with lighthouses, forts, and fishing villages; shoppers, with antiques shops and outlets galore; and families, with the state's best concentration of amusement parks and amusing places, such as the **Seashore Trolley Museum.**

GREATER PORTLAND

As far as cities go, Maine's largest is not overwhelming, and most of its must-see sights, including the **Portland Museum of Art, Victoria Mansion, Portland Observatory,** and **Old Port,** are within walking distance of one another on the downtown peninsula. A **Casco Bay Tour** will introduce you to the nearby islands, while a biking or driving tour to Cape Elizabeth will include **Portland Head Light.** Go on a **lobstering cruise,** and you might actually catch your dinner. Venture north to Freeport, and you'll find **L. L. Bean** and nearly 180 outlets to browse. But if what you really want to do is to go hiking, birding, deep-sea fishing, sea kayaking, or bicycling, all that's at your fingertips, too, thanks to plentiful preserves, a vibrant working waterfront, and miles of well-marked trails.

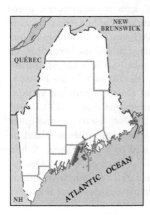

MID-COAST REGION

Between Brunswick and Waldoboro, long granite-tipped fingers of land are dotted with small fishing villages, sea captains' homes, lobster wharves, nature preserves, antiques and artisans' shops, and occasionally beautiful stretches of sand, such as **Popham Beach**. Brunswick is home to **Bowdoin College** and the Joshua Chamberlain Museum, which honors the Civil War hero. Maine's shipbuilding heritage is brought to life in Bath's **Maine Maritime Museum**. Wiscasset is famed for its antiques shops, while Boothbay is the departure point for many excursion boats, including one that takes in a living-history lighthouse tour of **Burnt Island**. The adjacent Pemaquid Peninsula is tipped by **Pemaquid Point Lighthouse**. And no place along the Maine Coast has as many places for enjoying al fresco **lobster in the rough**.

PENOBSCOT BAY

Island-studded Penobscot Bay is a sailor's dream. The rugged coastline hides protected harbors and links fishing villages with rather cosmopolitan towns. The jagged coastline is punctuated by beacons, such as **Owls Head Lighthouse** and **Rockland Breakwater Light**. Islands, including **Monhegan**, which is south of Penobscot Bay, frame the seaward background, while the **Camden Hills** are the inland backdrop. Lighthouses and lobster are two of the region's calling cards, but they're complemented by museums, such as **The Farnsworth Museum, Owls Head Transportation Museum**, and **Penobscot Marine Museum**. Throughout the region are antiques shops, art galleries, and artisans' studios. It's places such as **BlueJacket Shipcrafters,** where museum-quality ship models are handcrafted, that tie the seemingly diverse elements tidily together.

BLUE HILL PENINSULA AND DEER ISLE

Water, water everywhere. That's certainly how it feels in a region edged by a mapmaker-challenging coastline (a magnet for **sea kayakers**) that makes it possible to watch the sun both rise—and set—over the Atlantic. Flavoring the region is an odd mix of genteel retirees, back-to-the-landers, summer folk, traditional boatbuilders, rugged fishermen, and talented artists, many of whom join together to perform as the **Flash in the Pans Community Steel Band.** Equally eclectic are the dozens of artists, many first drawn here by the **Haystack Mountain School of Craft.** Well off the usual path is **Castine,** a peaceful and beautifully preserved village where historical markers throughout explain its turbulent past. From Stonington, it's a short boat ride to **Isle au Haut** and a remote and rugged section of **Acadia National Park.**

ACADIA REGION

Acadia National Park, the region's icon, is a miniature masterpiece, a gem of a natural and cultural resource. Get a taste with **The Park Loop** or the famed **Carriage Roads,** or go all out and hike rugged trails, kayak along undeveloped coastline, or canoe quiet ponds. Afterward, take part in a long-standing tradition, tea and popovers at the **Jordan Pond House.** Busy Bar Harbor anchors Mount Desert Island, but venture to Northeast Harbor's two fabulous gardens, **Asticou** and **Thuya,** and then loop around **Somes Sound** to the quiet side. Hop aboard an excursion boat to an offshore island or take an educational cruise narrated by a park ranger. While it's tempting to think that if you've been to Mount Desert, you've experienced Acadia, more parkland along with dozens of artists' studios and two scenic byways awaits on the quiet **Schoodic Peninsula.**

THE DOWN EAST COAST

East of Acadia the coastal geography changes, with blueberry barrens a frequent sight and huge tides ruling daily life. Traffic subsides, fast-food joints, shopping plazas, and chain motels all but disappear, and the stretch of road between towns gets longer. Artisans are plentiful. Fishing and lobstering are big business. But the biggest attraction is the wild expanse of coastline. Hiking and birding are renowned here and easy, thanks to a multitude of refuges, parks, and preserves, places such as **Maine Coastal Islands National Wildlife Refuge, Great Wass Preserve, West Quoddy Head State Park,** and **Shakford Head,** to name just a few. And offshore there's **Machias Seal Island,** a nesting ground for puffins, those clowns of the sea. Venture inland and find the Grand Lakes, ideal for fishing, boating, swimming, and lazy summer vacations.

AROOSTOOK COUNTY

When you really want to leave the tourists behind, Aroostook awaits. It's vast, rural, and undeveloped, and few folks make the effort to discover Maine's largest county. Those who do are rewarded for their efforts with a sense of plentiful elbow room and a down-home hospitality and friendliness that's all too rare in the world these days. Aroostook is Maine's original melting pot. The St. Jean River Valley is dotted with **Acadian** heritage sites. Just north of Caribou is **Maine's Swedish Colony.** And east of Houlton is an Amish settlement. Remnants of the bloodless Aroostook War with Canada dot the border, including the original 1839 **Fort Kent Blockhouse** and a replica in Fort Fairfield. In winter, world-class trails and training centers lure Nordic skiers, and more than 1,600 miles of groomed snowmobile trails connect to an international network.

MAINE HIGHLANDS

Here's where tar gives way to dirt, where it's possible to hike, paddle, and play undisturbed. The Maine Highlands are Maine's wilderness playground, home to **Baxter State Park,** with miles of hiking trails, including those on mile-high Mt. Katahdin, the official terminus of the Appalachian Trail; the Allagash Wilderness Waterway, a canoe route through the wilderness; the Penobscot River, a favorite for white-water fans and anglers; and Moosehead Lake, where you can cruise in historical fashion aboard the *Kate.* Hike the trails on **Kineo** or explore **Gulf Hagas,** nicknamed the Grand Canyon of the East. Go on a **moose safari** or dogsled into a remote sporting camp. When you're ready for a dose of civilization, visit Greenville or **Monson** for small shops or Bangor for a dose of city-style culture.

KENNEBEC AND MOOSE RIVER REGION

Route 201, which follows the Kennebec River, is the major thoroughfare between Québec City and the coast. Few people linger or mosey about, and that's a shame. It's a region where "Benedict Arnold Slept Here" signs are posted all along the **Old Canada Road National Scenic Byway,** which follows his famous march on Québec. In Augusta, Maine's capital, the **Maine State Museum** is an excellent introduction to the state, and **Old Fort Western** is the nation's oldest stockade fort. Discover the real Golden Pond with a cruise on the **Great Lakes Mail Boat.** View the extensive collection at the **Colby College Museum of Art,** and don't miss the quirky sights: **L. C. Bates Museum,** the Skowhegan Indian, and the **South Solon Meetinghouse.** Of course, a **white-water rafting** trip down the Kennebec is a must.

WESTERN LAKES AND MOUNTAINS

Generations of rusticators and summer campers have long favored the lakes pocketed in the mountains of western Maine. Take a cruise across Long Lake on the *Songo River Queen II,* fly above the Rangeley Lakes, hike the trails in **Grafton Notch State Park,** or spend a leisurely afternoon splashing in Sebago, and you'll understand why. At one time, giant summer hotels dotted the region; the largest was at **Poland Spring,** now famed for bottled water but also the site of a few intriguing museums. Nearby are the last inhabited **Shaker community** and the delightful **McLaughlin Garden.** Mosey the back roads through the idyllic Waterfords and up to **Paris Hill.** In autumn, the foliage is spectacular, and in winter, three of the East's best ski resorts, Sugarloaf, Saddleback, and Sunday River, keep things hopping.

Planning Your Trip

If you truly want to see *everything*, you'll need three weeks to a month, minimally, especially if you're someone who would rather do than just see. If your plans don't permit getting away for that long, the best strategy is to focus on a region or two or three, and immerse yourself in it.

WHEN TO GO

Maine has four distinct seasons: summer, fall, winter, and mud.

Spring

You might have to rethink your definition of spring, officially March 20 to June 21. It's an ill-defined season that arrives much too late and departs all too quickly. Melting winter snows combined with spring rains have earned March and April the well-deserved title Mud Season. March is the lowest month on the popularity scale (unless you're an alpine skier or snowboarder) with its mud-caked vehicles, soggy everything, irritable temperaments, tank-trap roads, and often the worst snowstorm of the year. Ice floes dot inland lakes and ponds until "ice-out," in early to mid-May; spring planting can't occur until well into May; lilacs explode in late May and disappear by mid-June. And just when you finally can enjoy being outside, blackflies stretch their wings and satisfy their hunger pangs, making outdoor activities pretty miserable. Along the coast, many smaller towns and villages don't even begin to wake up until mid-May and sometimes not even until mid-June.

Summer

Summer can be idyllic—with moderate temperatures, clear air, and wispy breezes—but it can also close in with fog, rain, and chills. Prevailing winds are from the southwest. Officially, summer runs from June 21 to September 22 or 23, but June, July, and August is more like it, with temperatures in the Portland area averaging 70°F during the day and in the 50s at night. The nor-mal growing season is 148 days. July and August are the peak season for visiting Maine and with good reason. These are the warmest months of the year and also when you'll have the greatest choice of recreation options. Of course, that means peak season rates, congested roads, and difficulty getting reservations at the best restaurants and accommodations unless you've planned well ahead.

Autumn

Ahhh, September. Maine heaves a collective sigh of relief after Labor Day. It is arguably the best time of the year to travel in the state. Days are warm and mostly dry, nights are cool, fog is rare, bugs are gone, and crowds are few. Foliage begins turning by mid-September in the northern regions, usually reaching its peak in southern and coastal areas by mid-October. Predictions are imprecise, so you'll need to allow some schedule flexibility to take advantage of the changes in different parts of the state. From mid-September to mid-October, check the state's Department of Conservation website (www.mainefoliage.com) for frequently updated maps, panoramic photographs, and reports on the foliage status. Or call the Foliage Hotline: 888/MAINE-45 (888/624-6345). Another resource for info on driving tours during foliage season is www.visitmaine.com, the official website of the Maine Office of Tourism.

A reminder: Fall-foliage trips are extremely popular and have become more so in recent years, so lodging can be scarce. Plan well ahead and make reservations, especially if you're headed for the Kennebunks, Boothbay Harbor, Camden, Bar Harbor, Greenville, Rangeley, or Bethel.

Winter

Winter, officially December 21 to March 20, means deep snow in the western mountains, deep cold in the North Woods, and an unpredictable potpourri along the coast. It also means great alpine skiing and snowboarding at Sugarloaf/USA, Sunday River, Shawnee Peak, Saddleback, and smaller peaks; splendid snowmobiling on a huge network of trails; and such other pursuits as cross-country skiing, ice fishing, snowshoeing, ice-skating, dog-sledding, ice-climbing, and winter trekking and camping. The Maine Coast slumbers in winter. While choices in lodging, dining, and activities are far fewer than in other months, the rates are at their lowest (except for special events). Instead of sunbathing on the sand, bundle up and take an invigorating walk or cross-country ski across a beach. In Camden, you can glide down alpine trails overlooking Penobscot Bay. In areas with solid year-round populations, life goes on full tilt, with an impressive array of cultural activities in cities such as Portland and in college towns, such as Brunswick, Waterville, and Lewiston.

WHAT TO TAKE

The adage "If you don't like the weather, wait a minute" certainly applies to Maine. I've seen June days that begin in the 70s and finish in the 30s. Similarly, it can be 80 degrees and sunny a mile or so inland and damp and foggy on the coast. A coastal breeze can make it feel much cooler than the temperature indicates. Layering clothing is the best option.

Do bring a fleece jacket or pullover, a windbreaker, a lightweight sweater, and rain gear. In spring and autumn, add a wool sweater and a microfleece top for cool, damp days. In the peak of summer, temperatures can range from the 60s to the 80s, with usually a handful of hot, muggy days that might reach into the 90s. Bring pants and shorts—I've found pants that convert to shorts to take me through a long day of touring, from foggy morning through hot afternoon to cool evening. If you're venturing inland or up north anytime after mid-September, bring a warm jacket, hat, scarf, and gloves, and in winter, don't forget good boots, ideally lined and with a surface that provides traction. Unless you're dining at the White Barn Inn or Arrows, you won't need fancy clothing.

Resort casual is the dress code in most better restaurants, with nice T-shirts and shorts being acceptable almost everywhere in beach communities and inland.

Good walking shoes are a must. If you're planning on getting afloat in a canoe or kayak, bring backup footwear.

A bathing suit, quick-drying shorts, a brimmed hat, and sunglasses are all useful. Either take or plan to buy on arrival sunscreen and, in late spring and early summer especially, bug dope. You can find Lewey's Eco-Blends, a bug repellent based on a Native American herbal recipe, in many shops. Unless you're heading into deep woods, it works well and has a pleasant scent. Or use a trick recommended by a Baxter State Park ranger: Tuck sheets of Bounce dryer sheets under a cap and into your waistband to create a force field that keeps bugs from biting.

If you're planning on going out on a windjammer, whale watch, puffin excursion, or kayak tour, check with the outfitter on appropriate gear for the outing. Many of these boats venture well offshore, where it can be significantly colder. Extra fleece, wool sweaters, gloves, and a hat can be worth their weight in gold, even in summer. If you're prone to motion sickness, pack appropriate precautions.

In winter and spring, add warm, waterproof boots, gloves, hat, and winter-weight clothing to your list and any necessary adventure-related clothing for skiing, snowshoeing, ice fishing, winter camping, and so on. If you're arriving by plane, it's best to leave the gear at home and rent it at your destination.

No matter when you come, bring a camera and plenty of film or memory cards (you can buy both here, and many photo shops in larger communities will download images onto a CD for a small fee) and binoculars. If you're planning to venture into Canada, make sure you have appropriate identification and paperwork.

Other handy items are a small backpack for day trips or light hiking and a small or collapsible cooler for picnics or storing food. You can greatly reduce the cost of eating by buying food at grocery stores instead of dining out.

Explore Maine

BEST OF MAINE

It's a tough job to single out Maine's sightseeing icons. It offers so many. Unless you have years to spend, such a big chunk of real estate needs some whittling to be made explorable. This itinerary exposes you to a good chunk of Maine while taking in many of the state's icons in 20 days.

The downside: You'll be doing a fair bit of driving primarily on two-lane roads, where speeds through towns are often 25 mph or below, and during a season when road construction is a fact of life. It's not exactly ideal for a speed trip through Maine. While this itinerary is planned as 20 days, if your schedule permits, you'll be rewarded if you spend longer in any of the locations.

Book your first two nights' lodging in Portland, nights three and four in Rockland or vicinity, nights five and six on Mount Desert Island, nights seven and eight in the Millinocket area, nights nine and 10 in the Moosehead region, nights 11 and 12 in The Forks, nights 13 and 14 in Rangeley, nights 15 and 16 spend in Bethel, and book nights 17 through 20 in Naples, Bridgton, or the Oxford Hills area as you see fit, as none of these sights is more than an hour's drive from another. You might consider booking your last night in or around Portland if you're flying home.

Day 1

Stretch your legs after your journey to Maine with a refreshing walk on **Ogunquit Beach,** one of Maine's prettiest and proof that there's plenty of sand along Maine's fabled rockbound coast. Afterward, head to **Kennebunkport** and indulge your passions: shopping in the boutiques and galleries that crowd Dock Square, taking a walking tour to view the historic homes, or enjoying a leisurely drive along the waterfront.

Day 2

Begin the day with a visit to **Portland Head Light,** a Cape Elizabeth landmark and Maine's oldest lighthouse (1791), at the edge of 94-acre Fort Williams Park. Spend the afternoon in the **Portland Museum of Art,** Maine's premier art museum, smack in the heart of the state's largest city. End the day with a sunset cruise on Casco Bay.

Day 3

Make a pilgrimage to gigunda sports retailer and outfitter **L. L. Bean,** hub of the hubbub in Freeport—Maine's outlet bonanza.

Either spend the morning shopping or taking a Walk-on Adventure class. In the afternoon, visit the **Maine Maritime Museum** in Bath, 10 acres of indoor and outdoor exhibits celebrating the state's nautical heritage.

Day 4

Take a day trip to **Monhegan Island** from Port Clyde. This car-free, carefree gem, about a dozen miles off the coast, is laced with hiking trails and has earned a place in art history books as the Artists' Island.

Day 5

Drive or hike to the top of **Mt. Battie,** in Camden Hills State Park on the northern fringe of Camden. The vistas are magnificent, with the broad sweep of Penobscot Bay for a backdrop. Then continue up the coast to Mount Desert Island, and begin your explorations of **Acadia National Park.** If you've arrived on the island before noon, pick up a picnic lunch and then drive the **Park Loop,** a perfect introduction to Acadia that covers many of the highlights.

Day 6

Welcome the day by watching the sunrise from the summit of **Cadillac Mountain.** Afterward, if you haven't either driven or bicycled the Park Loop, do so. If you have, then explore the park more in depth: Go hiking, bicycling, or sea kayaking, take a carriage ride, or book an excursion boat to Islesford or a whale-watching excursion.

Day 7

Depart Mount Desert Island and head inland to Millinocket, perhaps detouring to see **Katahdin Iron Works,** but arriving in time for a late-afternoon **moose safari.**

Day 8

Venture into **Baxter State Park** for a day of hiking or rent a canoe and paddle one of the many lakes and rivers.

Day 9

Drive across the Golden Road to Greenville and **Moosehead Lake.** If time permits, continue to Rockwood and take the shuttle over to **Kineo** for a hike.

Day 10

Take a cruise on *The Kate* and prowl around the area, perhaps driving to Pittston Farm or hiking.

Day 11

Drive to **Monson** for a browse-about before continuing to The Forks via the **Old Canada Road National Scenic Byway,** with a quick peek at the **South Solon Meeting House.** Stretch your legs on a hike into **Moxie Falls.**

Day 12

Go **white-water rafting** on the Kennebec River.

Day 13

Take the scenic drive to Rangeley via Route 16, keeping an eye out for moose along the way. Work out the driving kinks with either an afternoon paddle or hike.

Day 14

Take a lazy—or not—day: Hike, swim, paddle, explore, or simply sit and enjoy the environment.

Day 15

Head south on Route 17 over Height of Land, perhaps stopping in Coos Canyon to try your hand at panning for gold. Continue to **Grafton Notch State Park.**

Day 16

Prowl around Bethel's historic district and explore the Mahoosuc section of the White Mountains.

Day 17

Get a taste of the Oxford Hills with a visit to Perham's, **Paris Hill,** and the **McLaughlin Garden.**

Day 18

Spend the day in Bridgton and Naples, and perhaps take a cruise on the *Songo River Queen.*

Day 19

Visit the **Shaker Museum,** the world's last inhabited Shaker colony, and tour **Poland Spring;** there's a lot more here than bottled water.

Day 20

Head home after a dip in Sebago Lake.

LIGHTHOUSES, LOBSTER, AND L. L. BEAN

This six-day tour concentrates on the Southern Coast, Greater Portland, Mid-Coast, and Penobscot Bay regions. Book your first two nights' lodging in Portland, the second two in Damariscotta/Newcastle, and the final two in the Thomaston/Rockland area. If you're arriving by airplane, use Portland International Jetport. If you simply must stay in a lighthouse, real or close enough to fool most folks, add two nights on the Blue Hill Peninsula, at the First Light B&B, in East Blue Hill.

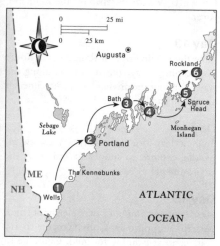

Have lunch at the Lobster Shack at Two Lights, overlooking **Cape Elizabeth Light.** Next, visit Maine's most-photographed lighthouse, **Portland Head Light,** and its museum in the keeper's house. Allow time for a late-afternoon cruise with **Lucky Catch Lobster Tours;** perhaps you'll catch your dinner. If not, you can still enjoy a lobster on the waterfront.

Day 3

Get an early start and begin at **L. L. Bean,** in Freeport. In the afternoon, visit the **Maine Maritime Museum,** in Bath, and, if time permits, take a lighthouse cruise on the Kennebec River.

Day 4

Take a morning **Burnt Island Tour** out of Boothbay Harbor. In the afternoon, loop over to the Pemaquid Peninsula and visit **Pemaquid Light** and the Fisherman's Museum at its tip. Afterward, feast on **lobster in the rough** in Round Pond.

Day 1

Begin in York and view **The Nubble,** and then head north to **The Lighthouse Depot,** in Wells, allowing plenty of time to shop. If time permits, veer down to East Point Sanctuary for distant views of Wood Island Light (bring binoculars).

Day 2

Begin at the **Portland Harbor Museum** and nearby **Spring Point Ledge Lighthouse.**

Day 5

Begin with **Marshall Point Light,** in Port Clyde, and then take the mail boat to **Monhegan Island.** Or take a lighthouse-themed cruise or sea-kayak tour out of Rockport or Rockland.

Either way, end with lobster in the rough at Waterman's Lobster in Spruce Head.

Day 6

Begin your day with a sunrise walk out the breakwater to **Rockland Breakwater Light.** Before heading home, tour the **Maine Lighthouse Museum** and, if time permits, take a short jaunt out to **Owls Head Light,** in Owls Head, before heading home.

MAINE OFF THE BEATEN TRACK

You've been there, done that, and seen all the icons. If you have a sense of adventure, consider getting to know some of the less touristed places.

Aroostook Loop

Few visitors make it to **Aroostook County,** and that's a pity, because it is a rural gem with great outdoor resources and intriguing heritage sites. Because of the sheer immensity of The County, you'll want to plan at least a full week.

While it's easy to loop through The County using Routes 1 and 11, be sure to explore the back roads for big views and surprises. For example, along Route 1 between Sherman Mills and Houlton is **Golden Ridge,** with panoramic views, a railroad museum, and an Amish colony. **Presque Isle** and **Caribou** are the center of most action that exists and have the most options for lodging and dining, as well as easy access to recreational facilities.

Be sure to stop at the state visitors information center in Houlton and pick up a map of the **Maine Solar System Model** so you can look for the planets along Route 1 as you drive north—it's a fun way to keep kids engaged.

Way Down East

Northeast of the Acadia region are spots that are less touristy and deliver a more authentic Maine experience. Here are a few yet-to-be-discovered places where it's usually not too hard to find a room for the night and where the sights are simply the natural scenery or the local character (or perhaps characters).

From **Milbridge** through **Calais,** the Maine Coast has a much different feel than points south. You'll pass through fishing villages that have yet to be gussied up or gentrified. Harbors are filled with lobster boats, not yachts. Fine restaurants are few; local spots serving good home cooking with an emphasis on fried fish are the rule. If you continue inland to **Grand Lake Stream,** you'll stumble upon an anglers' paradise and a not-too-shabby spot for an away-from-it-all family vacation, either.

Sporting Camp Adventure

There's no finer way to experience Maine's forested wilderness than to immerse yourself in it at a traditional sporting camp. Created more than a century ago to cater to the needs of sportspeople, namely hunters and anglers, today most are wonderful family destinations during the summer. You can hike, fish, paddle, swim, search for moose or other wildlife, or simple relax and enjoy the away-from-it-all experience.

Sporting camps dot Maine's North Country, with concentrations around the **Rangeley Lakes** and along the waterways in the **Katahdin/Moosehead region.** In almost all cases, they're on either a lake or a river. They can be either housekeeping style—you provide your own meals—or full service, meaning all meals are included in the per-person daily rate. Some have electricity; most have gas lamps. They might be just a few miles off a paved road, or they might best be reached by floatplane. Be sure to hire a Registered Maine Guide for at least part of a day to help you get the most out of the experience.

SPECIAL TRAILS FOR SPECIAL INTERESTS

Whether you are pining to view Maine's top art collections or hoping to smell the flowers, yearning to learn about native culture or the state's maritime heritage, or hoping to indulge passions for antiques or fiber art, Maine has mapped the route.

Maine Architecture Trail

Travelers in Maine pass through many small towns and villages, and it's not uncommon for them to stop and marvel at the wondrous architectural details. An informative brochure presents six specific routes, three emphasizing coastal sights, each explaining the connection between the landscape, the people, and the architecture by focusing on specific sights and putting it all in historical context. The brochure is available online from www.visitmaine.com.

Maine Art Museum Trail

An attractive brochure focuses on the state's seven significant art museums, containing more than 50,000 works of art—ancient to contemporary, painting and sculpture, furniture and textiles. Four of the seven are in coastal Maine. From south to north: Ogunquit Museum of Art (Ogunquit); Portland Museum of Art (Portland); Bowdoin College Museum of Art (Brunswick); and Farnsworth Art Museum (Rockland). (The museums inland are Bates College Museum of Art in Lewiston, the Colby Museum of Art in Waterville, and the University of Maine Museum of Art in Orono.) The trail website is www.maineartmuseums.org. The brochure is also available online from www .visitmaine.com.

Maine Garden and Landscape Trail

A handy foldout map lists and locates more than 50 gardens—a huge variety from pocket parks to city parks; formal, English, and experimental gardens; even a monastery and a cemetery. Although the trail covers the entire state, two-thirds of the sites are in coastal Maine. You'll find the finest displays in June and July, when garden tours are also on the agenda. Best of these tours

are in Camden, Damariscotta, the Kennebunks, and Mount Desert Island. The "trail" map also lists several dozen garden and plant centers with wonderful display gardens where you can indulge your horticultural habit. The brochure is available online from www.visitmaine.com.

Maine Maritime Heritage Trail

Any state that claims more than 5,000 miles of in-and-out coastline logically can also claim a rich maritime heritage. The Maritime Heritage Trail focuses on the sites that represent coastal Maine's rich history—maritime museums, boat-building schools, lighthouses, and sea captains' mansions. Also part of the story are maritime celebrations—windjammer and lobster boat races, lighthouse tours, and clam and lobster festivals. The special large-format, two-sided map serves as a handy reference as you travel the trail. The website www.maritimemaine.org has even more sights and information. The brochure is also available online from www.visitmaine.com.

Maine Outdoor Sculpture Guide

Three tours are highlighted in this handy and fun-to-read 64-page guidebook. The Seacoast Tour visits outdoor sculptures from Kittery to Machias, detailing each sculpture and explaining its history. The Sculpture Garden Tour highlights classic and whimsical coastal sculpture gardens in Ogunquit, Bath, Islesboro, and Mount Desert. The Civil War Tour explains coastal Civil War–related monuments in York and Calais. Noncoastal outdoor sculptures are also featured in the guide, which includes walking tours of outdoor sculpture in Portland and Bangor. Call 207/287-2724 to request a copy.

Native American Culture Guide

A Wabanaki Guide to Maine: A Visitor's Guide to

Native American Culture in Maine, a splendid 86-page spiral-bound booklet, published in 2001, is an excellent, if somewhat outdated, guide. The Wabanaki Trail is a go-at-your-own-pace route that leads you to museums, workshops, festivals, shops, significant landmarks, and even ancient canoe routes. Two trail sections are in the Acadia and Down East regions of coastal Maine, where two of Maine's four tribes' live. The guide is available for $10 (check or money order) from the Maine Indian Basketmakers Alliance (P.O. Box 3253, Old Town 04468, 207/827-0391). Consider planning a trip around one of two major Native American festivals sponsored by MIBA: one in early July in Bar Harbor, the other in early December in Orono.

Maine Fiber Arts

Craving cashmere? The *Maine Fiberarts Tour Map: Studios and Farms,* available from Maine Fiberarts (13 Main St., Topsham, mailing address P.O. Box 404, Brunswick 04011, 207/721-0678, www.mainefiberarts.org) lists well more than 100 fiber destinations statewide, including farms, studios, galleries, and festivals. Find a farm selling freshly shorn wool fleece, a garden where you can buy natural dyes, artisans selling handmade rugs or quilts, beautifully colored yarns and roving, and, well, the list goes on

and on. Most sites are open year-round, but the organization also hosts an **Open Studio and Farm Weekend** in early August.

The Antiques Trail

Maine is a favorite for antiques seekers and fans of all manner of country-cousin finds at juntiques shops and flea markets. Prime hunting grounds are strewn along the coast: Wells, Brunswick, Bath, Wiscassett, Damariscotta, and Searsport are all worth exploring, but shops dot the rest of the state, too. A couple of resources will help narrow the choices: *Maine Antiques Digest* (www.maineantiquedigest.com) is a monthly tabloid; the Maine antiques Dealers Association (www.maineantiques.org) lists members statewide by location and specialty. You'll often find directories of area shops in local information centers. Northern New England's largest show is the annual Maine Antiques Festival (Union, mid-August, 207/563-1013, www.maine antiquefest.com), which attracts dealers from across the country.

While there's no guarantee of *Antiques Road Show*–worthy finds, it's great fun to spend a Saturday morning shopping roadside yard sales for from-your-basement-to-my-attic finds. Best sources for yard-sale listings are local newspapers and bulletin boards at grocery stores.

RECREATION MILESTONES

Maine's a vast playground for outdoor sports fans, but while other people play, you hike, bike, kayak, or canoe with gusto. When the usual choices seem a bit too tame, consider these, some of which are definite ego-challenges. Most aren't for the faint of heart or weak of quad (or bicep), and almost all require planning well ahead to get the most out of the experience.

Kayaking the Maine Island Trail

Paddle along Maine's coast from **Cape Porpoise** to **Machias Bay** and beyond along the **Maine Island Trail.** The 350-mile-long waterway comprises islands and mainland sites available for leave-no-trace camping. Along

the way are sand beaches, protected saltwater rivers, more than 150 islands, plentiful capes and harbors, quiet bays, pocket beaches, and, of course, plenty of rockbound coastline. Waves, wind, tides, and commercial boats can all play havoc with the best of plans. If you don't want to plan all the logistics on your own, consider a planned itinerary with one of Maine's kayaking outfitters.

Too tame? Well, if you're a white-water hotshot, consider the Class III and IV **Kennebec River Gorge,** but only if you're ultra-experienced and have an ironclad roll. Check in with one of Maine's white-water rafting companies based in The Forks for know-how.

Canoeing Allagash Wilderness Waterway

The biggie of wilderness paddles, the **Allagash Wilderness Waterway** stretches 92 miles, from Telos Lake to East Twin Brook. Along the way, it flows through pristine lakes, tumbles down **Chase Rapids,** and requires a portage around **Allagash Falls.** The biggest challenges are the distance and the weather. Wind and rain can make progress across the big lakes incremental at best. Still, the rewards are magnificent scenery and plentiful wildlife. The biggest white-water stretch is the nine-mile Chase Rapids, but by the time you get here, you'll have plenty of paddling practice (and you can arrange for gear to be portaged). For the best experience, hire a Registered Maine Guide or join a planned, guide-led expedition.

Too tame? Pair it with a trip down the **St. John River,** from Baker Lake to Allagash village. Again, consider hiring a guide.

Climbing Mt. Katahdin

Mile-high **Katahdin,** terminus of the Appalachian Trail, is Maine's tallest peak; make that peaks: Although it tops out on **Baxter Peak,** it comprises several neighboring ones. The infamous and appropriately named **Knife Edge** provides the 1.1-mile connection between Baxter Peak and **Pamola Peak.** Katahdin is a full-day long and strenuous climb that requires planning and an early start.

Too tame? Ratchet up the difficulty by hiking to Katahdin along the **Appalachian Trail** from Monson. That section includes the 100-Mile Wilderness, one of if not the toughest sections along the entire Springer Mountain, Georgia, to Katahdin hiker's highway.

Bicycling Acadia's Carriage Trails

No, Acadia National Park's **Carriage Roads** aren't superchallenging, but they are plentiful, so you can link and loop the 45 miles of crushed gravel roadways to go as far as you wish. None are perfectly level, and many have significant hills—enough to deliver views that will take away any breath left after the uphill pedal. Another plus is the 17 handsome rough-stone bridges that accent the roads.

Too tame? Pedal the **Park Loop Road** at sunrise, culminating at the summit of **Cadillac Mountain** before heading to the Carriage Roads.

DESTINATION DINING TOUR

In recent years, Maine's restaurant scene has gained increasing national attention, with top awards and mentions in foodie magazines such as *Bon Appetit, Food and Wine, Gourmet,* and *Saveur.* If you want to dine your way through Maine, here's where to go to hit the biggies. You definitely want to plan well in advance for a summer visit, and even then, you might have to be flexible in your seating time.

SOUTHERN COAST
Arrows

A quiet, country farmhouse is the understated setting for this restaurant, named by *Gourmet*

as one of America's Top 50 Restaurants. Chefs Clark Frasier and Mark Gaier have twice been nominated for a James Beard award and have received accolades from magazines such as

Gourmet, Bon Appetit, and even *Time* magazines. They are renowned for their fresh flavorful cuisine, with many ingredients sourced from the restaurant's gardens. Jacket preferred for men.

White Barn Inn

Maine's only five-diamond restaurant regularly gets kudos from publications such as *Food and Wine, Travel and Leisure,* and *Condé Nast Traveler.* The dining room is an elegantly restored barn, where Chef Jonathan Cartwright's fixed-price, four-course menu, offering contemporary New England cuisine with European accents, is served by formally dressed waiters. Jackets are required for gentlemen.

And While You're Here...

Don't miss **Provence,** a fabulous country French Ogunquit restaurant, owned by Chef Pierre Gignac, that always wins top marks from local critics.

GREATER PORTLAND

For any of these three, you'll feel most comfortable in resort casual wear. There's no need for jackets, although you wouldn't feel out of place, either.

Fore Street

Ask any Maine foodie who the dean of Maine foods is, and likely the answer will be Sam Hayward. Here, Hayward has teamed with another highly regarded restaurateur, Dana Street, of Street and Co. The result won Hayward the "Best Chef in the Northeast" award from the James Beard Foundation in 2004.

Hugo's

Chef Rob Evans was named Best Chef in the Northeast by the Beard Foundation in 2007 and one of America's 10 Best New Chefs by *Food and Wine* in 2004. You'll learn why when you step into this fine restaurant, where Evans prepares New American cuisine.

Five Fifty-Five

Locals have been talking about Chef Steve Corry for years, but in 2007 he gained national attention when *Food and Wine* named him one of America's 10 Best New Chefs.

And While You're Here...

This one won't be a secret for long. Chef Krista Kerns has a skilled hand in the kitchen at tiny **Bresca.**

PENOBSCOT BAY

Primo

James Beard award–winning chef Melissa Kelly and her partner Price Kushner keep earning kudos for their farmhouse restaurant on the Rockland/Owls Head border. Resort casual is the preferred dress.

Waterman's Beach Lobster

What's a lobster-in-the-rough spot doing on this list? Well, the folks at the James Beard House thought it deserved an award, and we think you deserve a night when you can dress down and drink in the view (if you want anything more potent to drink, be sure to bring it with you). You'll be eating lobster on a picnic table, and jeans, shorts, and T-shirts are the dress code.

And While You're Here...

Don't miss **Francine,** chef/owner Brian Hill's lovely little bistro in a residential section of downtown Camden.

SOUTHERN COAST

Drive over the I-95 bridge from New Hampshire into Maine's Southern Coast region on a bright summer day and you'll swear the air is cleaner, the sky bluer, the trees greener, the roadside signs more upbeat: Welcome to Maine: The Way Life Should Be. (*Is* it? Or maybe the way life *used* to be?)

Most visitors come to this region for the spectacular attractions of the justly world-famous Maine coast—the inlets, islands, and especially the beaches, but it's rich in history, too.

Southernmost York County, part of the Province of Maine, was incorporated in 1636 (only 16 years after the *Mayflower* pilgrims reached Plymouth, Massachusetts) and reeks of history: ancient cemeteries, musty archives, and architecturally stunning homes and public buildings. Probably the best places to dive into that history are in the sites of the Old York Historical Society in York Harbor.

Geological fortune smiled on this 50-mile ribbon, endowing it with a string of sandy beaches—nirvana for sun worshipers, less enchanting to swimmers, who need to steel themselves to spend much time in the ocean (especially in early summer, before the water temperature has reached a tolerable level).

Complementing those beaches are amusement parks and arcades, fishing shacks turned chic boutiques, a surprising number of good restaurants (given the region's seasonality), and some of the state's prettiest parks and preserves.

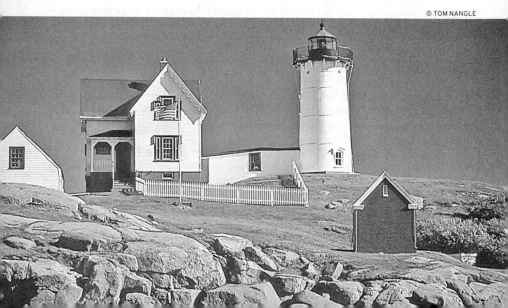

HIGHLIGHTS

《 Old York Historical Society: York dates from the 1640s, and on this campus of historic buildings, you can peek into early life (page 42).

《 Nubble Light/Sohier Park: You'll likely recognize this often-photographed Maine Coast icon, which is the easiest lighthouse to see in the region (page 43).

《 Ogunquit Museum of American Art (OMAA): It's hard to say which is more jaw dropping, the art or the view (page 51).

《 Marginal Way: Escape the hustle and bustle of Ogunquit with a stroll on this paved, shorefront path (page 51).

《 Wells Reserve at Laudholm Farm: Orient yourself at the visitors center, where you can learn about the history, flora, and fauna, and then take a leisurely walk to the seashore, passing through a variety of habitats (page 52).

《 Seashore Trolley Museum: Ring-ring-ring goes the bell...and zing-zing-zing go your heartstrings, especially if you're a trolley fan (page 62).

《 Dock Square: Busy, busy, busy is this heart of Kennebunkport, and with good reason. Brave the crowds and explore (page 65).

《 St. Anthony's Monastery: It's hard to believe this oasis of calm is just a short stroll

from busy-busy-busy Dock Square (page 66).

《 East Point Sanctuary: A must for birders, this coastal preserve provides dramatic views (page 78).

LOOK FOR **《** TO FIND RECOMMENDED SIGHTS, ACTIVITIES, DINING, AND LODGING.

Spend some time poking around the small villages that give the region so much character. Many have been gussied up and gentrified quite a bit but retain their seafaring or farming bones.

Some Mainers refer to the Southern Coast as northern Massachusetts. Sometimes it can seem that way, not only for the numbers of commonwealth plates in evidence but also because many former Massachusetts residents have moved here for the quality of life and commute to jobs in the Boston area. The downside is escalating real-estate prices that have forced families with deep roots off land that's been in their families for generations and pushed those in traditional seafaring occupations inland. Still, if you nose around and get off the beaten path, you'll find that real Maine is still here.

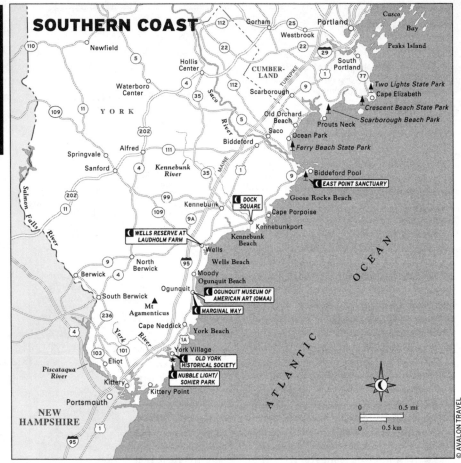

PLANNING YOUR TIME

The good news is that Maine's Southern Coast is a rather compact region. The bad news is that it's heavily congested, especially in summer. Still, with a minimum of four days, you should be able to take in most of the key sights, from beaches to museums, as long as you don't want to spend hours basking in the sun.

Route 1, the region's primary artery, is often bumper-to-bumper traffic. If you're hopscotching towns, consider using I-95, which has exits for York, Kennebunk, and

Saco/Biddeford/Old Orchard Beach. Parking, too, can be a challenge and expensive, but a trolley system operates in summer and connects most towns, making it easy to avoid the hassles and help the environment.

July and August are the busiest months. If you can avoid them, do. Spring and fall are lovely times to visit, and most attractions are open. In winter, you can walk the beaches without running into another soul, it's easy to get dinner reservations, and lodging prices plummet—the trade-off is that fewer businesses are open.

Kittery

Besides being a natural point of entry into the state, Kittery also competes with Freeport, farther up the coast, as an outlet-shopping mecca. Kittery boasts more than 120 factory outlets lining both sides of U.S. 1. But before or after you overdose on shoes, china, tools, toys, candles, and underwear, take time to explore the back roads of Maine's oldest town—settled in 1623 and chartered in 1647. Maine is home to a lot of well-kept secrets, Kittery being one of them. Parks, a small nautical museum, historic architecture, and lobster restaurants are only a few of the attractions in Kittery and its "suburb," Kittery Point. It was also on Kittery's Badger Island where the sloop *Ranger* was launched in 1777. The shipbuilding continues at Portsmouth Naval Shipyard, on Kittery's Dennet's Island, the first government shipyard in America.

To reach Kittery's shops and services from I-95 northbound take the Exit 3 cloverleaf, designated Kittery, Coastal Route 1 North, and continue to Route 1. From I-95 southbound, take the Yorks/Berwicks exit, and then take Coastal Route 1 South. Follow signs; the twists and turns can be confusing.

SIGHTS

Avoid the outlet sprawl and see the prettiest part of the area by driving along squiggly Route 103 from the Route 1 rotary in Kittery through Kittery Point (administratively part of Kittery) and on to Route 1A in York. You can even make a day of it, stopping at the sites mentioned here. Be very careful and watch for cyclists and pedestrians, as there are no shoulders and lots of blind corners and hills.

Kittery Historical and Naval Museum

Maritime history buffs shouldn't miss the small but well-stocked Kittery Historical and Naval Museum (Rogers Road Ext., near the junction of Rtes. 1 and 236, Kittery, 207/439-3080, 10 A.M.–4 P.M. Tues.–Sat. June–mid-Oct., $3 adults, $1.50 kids 7–15, family max. $6). A large exhibit hall and a small back room contain ship models, fishing gear, old photos and paintings, and an astonishing collection of scrimshaw (carved whale ivory).

Lady Pepperrell House

The 1760 Georgian Lady Pepperrell House (Pepperrell Rd., Rte. 103, shortly before the Fort McClary turnoff) is now privately owned and no longer open to the public, but it's worth admiring from afar. Nearby, across from the First Congregational Church, is the area's most-visited burying ground. Old-cemetery buffs should bring rubbing gear here for some interesting grave markers. The tomb of Levi Thaxter (husband of poet Celia Thaxter) bears an epitaph written for him by Robert Browning.

Fort McClary Historic Site

Since the early 18th century, fortifications have

Fort McClary has guarded Portsmouth Harbor since the early 18th century.

stood on this 27-acre headland, protecting Portsmouth Harbor from seaborne foes. Contemporary remnants at Fort McClary (Rte. 103, Kittery Point, 207/439-2845, $2 adults, $1 kids 5–11) are several outbuildings, an 1846 blockhouse, granite walls, and earthworks—all with a view of Portsmouth Harbor. Opposite are the sprawling buildings of the Portsmouth Naval Shipyard. Bring a picnic (covered tables and a lily pond are across the street) and turn the kids loose to run and play. It's officially open May 30–October 1, but the site is accessible in off-season. The fort is 2.5 miles east of Route 1.

Fort Foster

The only problem with Fort Foster (Pocahontas Rd., off Rte. 103, Gerrish Island, Kittery Point, 207/439-3800, 10 A.M.–8 P.M. Memorial Day–Labor Day and weekends May and Sept., $10 vehicle pass, $5 adult walk-in, $1 child walk-in) is that it's no secret, so parking can be scarce (and expensive) at this 90-acre municipal park at the entrance to Portsmouth Harbor. On a hot day, arrive early. Then you can swim, hike the nature trails, fish off the pier (no license needed), picnic, and investigate the tide pools. Bring your sailboard and a kite—there's almost always a breeze. From nearby **Seapoint Beach** (park in the small roadside lot and walk down to the beach; the lower lot is for residents only, no facilities) on a clear day, there's a wide-open view of the offshore Isles of Shoals, owned jointly by Maine and New Hampshire.

RECREATION
Brave Boat Harbor

One of the Rachel Carson National Wildlife Refuge's 10 Maine coastal segments is Brave Boat Harbor (207/646-9226), a beautifully unspoiled, 560-acre wetlands preserve in Kittery Point with a four-mile (round-trip) trail. Carry binoculars, wear rubberized boots to maneuver the squishy areas, and slather on the insect repellent. The habitat is particularly sensitive here, so be kind to the environment. Take Route 103 to Chauncey Creek Road, and continue past the Gerrish Island bridge to Cutts Island Lane. Just beyond it and across a small

bridge is a pullout on the left. You have a couple of options for hikes: a 1.8-mile loop trail, including a spur, or a half-mile loop. Bring binoculars to spot waterfowl in the marshlands.

Captain and Patty's Piscataqua River Tours

Take a spin around the Piscataqua River Basin with Captain and Patty's Piscataqua River Tours (Town Dock, Pepperrell Rd., Kittery Point, 207/439-8976 home or 207/451-8156 boat). The 80-minute historical tour departs seven times daily, including once in the evening for a two-hour twilight cruise for adults only. Along the way, Captain Neil Odams points out historic forts, lighthouses, and the Naval shipyard.

ENTERTAINMENT
Concerts in the Park

Kittery Recreation presents a free, summer concert series on Memorial Field, Old Post Road, 6:30–8 P.M. on Wednesday evenings mid-July–mid-August.

SHOPPING

No question, you'll find bargains at Kittery's 120-plus factory outlets (www.thekittery outlets.com)—actually a bunch of minimalls clustered along Route 1. All the household names are here: Bass, Calvin Klein, Eddie Bauer, J Crew, Mikasa, Esprit, Lenox, Timberland, Tommy Hilfiger, GAP, Villeroy and Boch, and a hundred more (all open daily). Anchoring it all is the **Kittery Trading Post** (301 Rte. 1, 207/439-2700 or 888/587-6246, www.kitterytradingpost.com), a humongous sporting-goods and clothing emporium. Try to avoid the outlets on weekends, when you might need to take a number for the try-on rooms. Most of the minimalls have telephones; several have ATMs; all have restrooms.

ACCOMMODATIONS

Put a little oooh and aaaah into your touring with a visit to the **Portsmouth Harbor Inn and Spa** (6 Water St., Kittery, 207/439-4040, www .innatportsmouth.com, $160–200 peak). The handsome brick inn, built in 1889, looks out over the Piscataqua River, Portsmouth, and the Portsmouth Naval Shipyard. Five attractive Victorian-style rooms (most with water views) are furnished with antiques and have air-conditioning, TV, and phones. There's an outdoor hot tub, and beach chairs are available. Breakfasts are multicourse feasts. Request a back room if you're noise sensitive, although air-conditioning camouflages traffic noise in summer. Rooms on the third floor have the best views, but these also have hand-held showers. Now for the aaaah part. The inn also has a full-service spa. The inn has lots of intriguing special packages. It's an easy walk across the bridge to Portsmouth for plentiful dining options.

Shopaholics take note: **Chicadee Bed and Breakfast** (63 Haley Rd., 207/439-0672 or 888/502-0876, www.chicadeebandb.net, $125 d) is within walking distance of Kittery's famed outlets. A full country breakfast should power you through a shopping spree. Afterward, return for a dip in the pool. Walter and Brenda Lawrence's family home is comfortably furnished with country flair. No pets—four dogs are in residence.

FOOD
Local Flavors
Kittery has an abundance of excellent specialty food stores that are perfect for stocking up for a picnic lunch or dinner. Most are along the section of Route 1 between the Portsmouth bridge and the traffic circle.

Three are within steps of each other. At **Beach Pea Baking Co.** (53 Rte. 1, 207/439-3555, 7:30 A.M.–6 P.M. Mon.–Sat.) you can buy fabulous breads and pastries. Sandwiches and salads are made to order 11 A.M.–3 P.M. daily. There's pleasant seating indoors and on a patio. Next door is **Golden Harvest** (7 A.M.–6:30 P.M. Mon.–Sat. and 9 A.M.–6 P.M. Sun.), where you can load up on luscious produce. Across the street is **Terracotta Pasta Co.** (52A, Rte. 1, 207/475-3025, 10 A.M.–6 P.M. Mon., 9 A.M.–6:30 P.M. Tues.–Sat., and noon–4 P.M. Sun.), where in addition to handmade pastas you'll find salads, soups, sandwiches, prepared foods, and lots of other goodies.

Just off Route 1 is **Enoteca Italiana** (20 Walker St., 207/439-7216, 10 A.M.–7 P.M. Mon. and Wed.–Sat. and noon–4 P.M. Sun.), which carries wine, an extensive selection of cured meats, fine cheeses, and other gourmet items.

What's a meal without chocolate? At **Cacao** (64 Government St., just off the town green, 207/438-9001, noon–6 P.M. Tues.–Fri. and 10 A.M.–4 P.M. Sat.), Susan Tuveson handcrafts outrageously decadent chocolate truffles and caramels. Flavors vary from the familiar to the exotic: Some are made with chilies (habanero lime!), some with cheeses. The strawberry balsamic vinegar with black pepper truffle and the fleur de sel caramel are particularly sublime.

Old World artisan breads made from organic ingredients are available at the company store for **When Pigs Fly** (447 Rte. 1, 207/439-3114, www.sendbread.com).

In Kittery Point, **Frisbee's Supermarket** (207/439-0014, 7 A.M.–8 P.M. Mon.–Sat., 8 A.M.–8 P.M. Sun.) is an experience in itself. Established in 1828, the store has marginally modernized but still earns its label as North America's oldest family store—run by the fifth generation of Frisbees.

At the **Sunrise Grill** (182 State Rd., Rte. 1, Kittery Traffic Circle, Kittery, 207/439-5748, 6:30 A.M.–2 P.M. daily), order waffles, granola, omelettes, or Diana's Benedict or at lunch, salads, sandwiches, and burgers. In downtown Kittery, **Crooked Lane Café** (Wentworth St., 207/439-2244), in a Victorian building with a tin ceiling and both indoor and outdoor seating, is a bit more polished and serves a full menu of espresso-style coffees along with breakfast and lunch fare.

Craving Mex? Some of the recipes in Luis Valdez's **Loco Coco's Tacos** (36 Walker St., Kittery, 207/438-9322, www.lococcos.com, 11 A.M.–3 P.M. and 4–8 P.M. Mon.–Fri., to 9 P.M. Sat.) have been passed down for generations, and the homemade salsas are fab. If you're feeling really decadent, go for the artery-busting California fries. There's a kids' menu, too. Nothing costs more than $9.

Casual Dining

Dining in Kittery took a bit of an upswing with the opening of ◖ **anneke jans** (60 Wallingford Sq., Kittery, 207/439-0001, www.anneke jans.net, 5–10 P.M. Tues.–Sat.). Charcoal walls, white-clothed tables with moss centerpieces, a wine bar, and windows that open to the street create an especially hip and stylin' atmosphere. The French/American bistro menu might include blue-corn-dusted sea scallops, herb-roasted chicken, or Angus strip sirloin, with prices ranging $14–31. The extensive wine list has more than 30 available by the glass. This is a local hot spot with a lively crowd; reservations are recommended.

Lobster and Clams

If you came to Maine to eat lobster, **Chauncey Creek Lobster Pier** (16 Chauncey Creek Rd., off Rte. 103, Kittery Point, 207/439-1030, www.chaunceycreek.com, 11 A.M.–8 P.M., to 7 P.M. after Labor Day, mid-May–Columbus Day) is the real deal. Step up to the window, place your order, take a number, and grab a table (you may need to share) overlooking tidal Chauncey Creek and the woods on the close-in opposite shore. It's a particularly picturesque—and extremely popular—place. Parking is a nightmare. BYOB and anything else that's not on the menu.

If clams are high on your must-have list, you can't do much better than **Bob's Clam Hut** (315 Rte. 1, Kittery 03904, 207/439-4233, www.bobsclamhut.com, 11 A.M.–9 P.M. Mon.–Thurs., to 9:30 P.M. Fri. and Sat., to 8:30 P.M. Sun.), next to the Kittery Trading Post. Using vegetable oil for frying, Bob's turns out everything from scallops to shrimp to calamari to, of course, clams—the tartar sauce is the secret weapon. Expect to pay market rates, but nothing is too pricey. Bob's is open all year.

The Berwicks

Probably the best known of the area's present-day inland communities is the riverside town of South Berwick—thanks to a historical and literary tradition dating to the 17th century, and antique cemeteries to prove it. The 19th- and 20th-century novels of Sarah Orne Jewett and Gladys Hasty Carroll have lured many a contemporary visitor to explore their rural settings—an area aptly described by Carroll as "a small patch of earth continually occupied but never crowded for more than three hundred years."

Also here is the 150-acre hilltop campus of **Berwick Academy,** Maine's oldest prep school, chartered in 1791 with John Hancock's signature. The coed school's handsome gray-stone William H. Fogg Memorial Library ("The Fogg") is named for the same family connected with Harvard's Fogg Art Museum. The highlight of the library is an incredible collection of dozens of 19th-century stained-glass windows, most designed by Victorian artist Sarah Wyman Whitman, who also designed jackets for Sarah Orne Jewett's books. Thanks to a diligent fundraising effort, the windows were recently restored to their former glory.

SIGHTS
Sarah Orne Jewett House

Don't blink or you might miss the tiny sign outside the 1774 Sarah Orne Jewett House (5 Portland St., Rtes. 4 and 236, South Berwick, 207/384-2454, www.historicnewengland.org, 11 A.M.–5 P.M. Fri.–Sun. June 1–Oct. 15, $8 adults, $7 seniors, $4 ages 12 and younger) smack in the center of town. Park on the street and join one of the tours—you'll learn details of the Jewett family and its star, Sarah (1849–1909), author of *The Country of the Pointed Firs,* a New England classic. Books by and about Sarah are available in the gift shop. House tours are at 11 A.M. and 1, 2, 3, and 4 P.M. The house is a Historic New England property.

© TOM NANGLE

Author Sarah Orne Jewett made her home in South Berwick.

Hamilton House

Dramatically crowning a bluff overlooking the Salmon Falls River and flanked by handsome colonial revival gardens, 18th-century Hamilton House (40 Vaughan's La., South Berwick, 207/384-2454, www.historicnewengland.org, 11 A.M.–5 P.M. Wed.–Sun. June 1–Oct. 15, $8 adults, $7 seniors, $4 ages 12 and younger) evokes history and tradition. Like the Jewett House, the 35-acre site is owned by Historic New England. Knowledgeable guides relate the house's fascinating history. Tours begin only on the hour—last one at 4 P.M. In July, the **Sunday in the Garden** concert series takes place on the lawn ($8 admission, including a free pass to come back and see the house). Pray for sun; the concert is moved indoors on rainy days. From Route 236 at the southern edge of South Berwick (watch for a signpost), turn left onto Brattle Street and take the second right onto Vaughan's Lane.

Vaughan Woods State Park

A path connects Hamilton House to adjoining Vaughan Woods State Park (28 Oldfields Rd., South Berwick, 207/384-5160, 9 A.M.–8 P.M. late May–early Sept., but accessible all year, $2 adults, $1 children 5–11, free over 65 or under 5), but it's not easy to find, and there's much more parking space at the main entrance to the 250-acre river's-edge preserve. Three miles of maintained trails wind through this underused park, and benches are scattered here and there. There's even a bench looking out over the river and Hamilton House.

Old Berwick Historical Society/ Counting House

Based in a onetime cotton-mill building known as the Counting House, the Old Berwick Historical Society (Liberty and Main Sts., Rte. 4, P.O. Box 296, South Berwick 03908, 207/384-0000, www.obhs.net, 1–4 P.M. Sat.–Sun. in July, Aug., and Sept.,), sees a steady stream of genealogists looking for their roots in one of Maine's oldest settlements. Books and documents are only part of the museum's collection, which includes old photos and tools, boat models and nautical instruments, plus special annual exhibits. Admission to the 19th-century Counting House is by donation.

ENTERTAINMENT

Theatergoers head to the Berwick area for the long-running (since 1972) **Hackmatack Playhouse** (538 School St./Rte. 9, Berwick, 207/698-1807, www.hackmatack.org), midway between North Berwick and Berwick. The popular summer theater, based in a renovated barn reminiscent of a past era, has 8 P.M. performances (comedies and musical comedies) Wednesday–Saturday and a 2 P.M. matinee Thursday. The ambience is relaxed and casual but quality is high, though it's a non-Equity house. The Hackmatack season runs late June–early September. Tickets are $20; discounts for seniors and students except Saturday.

ACCOMMODATIONS

Once the headmaster's residence for nearby Berwick Academy, the elegant, turn-of-the-20th-century **Academy Street Inn Bed and Breakfast** (15 Academy St., South Berwick, 207/384-5633) has crystal chandeliers, leaded-glass windows, working fireplaces, and high-ceilinged rooms full of antiques. Paul and Lee Fopeano's handsome home has five rooms with private baths ($84–94 d). Full breakfast or afternoon lemonade on the 60-foot screened porch is a real treat. Open all year.

FOOD

A local institution since 1960, **Fogarty's** (471 Main St., South Berwick, 207/384-8361, 11 A.M.–8 P.M., to 9 P.M. Sat.) has expanded through the years from a simple takeout to a local favorite for inexpensive, family-friendly dining. Ask for a river-view table in the back room.

Newer on the scene is **Pepperland Café** (279 Main St., South Berwick, 207/384-5535, 11 A.M.–11:30 P.M. Tues.–Sat., 9 A.M.–3 P.M. Sun.), a family-friendly pub-meets-bistro serving comfort food with pizzazz. Make a meal from smaller plates and salads ($5–10) or go big with the entrées ($16–19). Everything's prepared from scratch, and more than half of the waste is recycled.

Now here's a find: a cozy French bistro serving simple yet classic fare created from farm-fresh ingredients. **Margaux: Bistro Populaire** (404 Main St., South Berwick, 207/384-8249, 5:30–9 P.M. Tues.–Sat.) is an intimate, low-key neighborhood bistro, where Linda Robinson and Christine Prunier provide a warm welcome into the simple white house, with dining on the enclosed porch, one small dining room, and at the small bar. The frequently changing menu might include escargot au Pernod, braised lamb shank, duck confit, or seared sea scallops. Mix and match from small and large plates. Entrée range is $18–25.

The Yorks

Four villages with distinct personalities—upscale York Harbor, historic York Village, casual York Beach, and semirural Cape Neddick—make up the Town of York. First inhabited by Native Americans, who named it Agamenticus, the area was settled as early as 1624—so history is serious business here. Town high points were its founding, by Sir Ferdinando Gorges, and the arrival of well-to-do vacationers in the 19th century. In between were Indian massacres, economic woes, and

population shuffles. The town's winter population explodes in summer (pretty obvious in July and August, when you're searching for a free patch of York Beach sand or a parking place). York Beach, with its seasonal surf and souvenir shops and amusements, has long been the counterpoint to genteel York Village, but that's changing with the restoration and rebirth of downtown buildings and the arrival of tony restaurants, shops, and condos.

History and genealogy buffs can study the

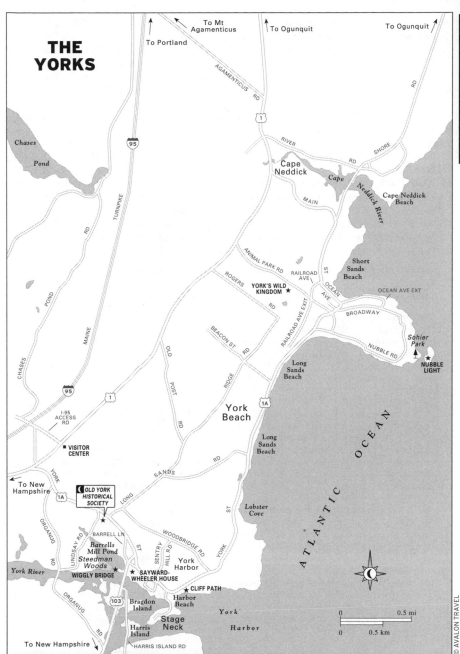

THE
YORKS

To Mt
Agamenticus
To Portland
To Ogunquit
To Ogunquit

AGAMENTICUS RD

Chases

Pond

95

RIVER RD

SHORE RD

Cape
Neddick

Cape

Neddick River

Cape Neddick
Beach

MAIN

TURNPIKE

RD

ANIMAL PARK RD

RAILROAD
AVE

ST

OCEAN AVE

Short
Sands
Beach

POND

ROGERS RD

YORK'S WILD
KINGDOM ★

OCEAN AVE EXT

MAINE

BEACON ST

RD

RAILROAD AVE EXT

BROADWAY

NUBBLE RD

*Sohier
Park*

★
NUBBLE
LIGHT

CHASES

95

1

OLD
POST RD

RIDGE RD

Long
Sands
Beach

York
Beach

1A

I-95
ACCESS
RD

Long
Sands
Beach

A T L A N T I C   O C E A N

■ VISITOR
CENTER

RD

SANDS

To New
Hampshire

1A

OLD YORK
HISTORICAL
SOCIETY

★

LONG

ST

*Lobster
Cove*

ORGANUG

BARRELL LN

WOODBRIDGE RD

RD

ST

LINDSAY RD

*Barrells
Mill Pond*

SENTRY HILL RD

York
Harbor

YORK

*Steedman
Woods*

★ SAYWARD-
WHEELER HOUSE

★
WIGGLY BRIDGE

York River

ORGANUG

103

*Bragdon
Island*

★ CLIFF PATH

*Harbor
Beach*

York

Harbor

*Harris
Island*

**Stage
Neck**

0   0.5 mi

0   0.5 km

To New Hampshire

HARRIS ISLAND RD

© AVALON TRAVEL

headstones in the Old Burying Ground or comb the archives of the Old York Historical Society. For lighthouse fans, there are Cape Neddick Light Station ("Nubble Light") and, six miles offshore, Boon Island. You can rent horses or mountain bikes on Mt. Agamenticus, board a deep-sea fishing boat in York Harbor, or spend an hour hiking the Cliff Path in York Harbor. For the kids, there's a zoo, a lobster-boat cruise, a taffy maker, or, of course, back to the beach.

SIGHTS
◖ Old York Historical Society
Based in York Village, the Old York Historical Society (207 York St., P.O. Box 312, York 03909, 207/363-4974, www.oldyork.org, museum buildings open 10 A.M.–5 P.M. Mon.–Sat. early June–early Oct., $10 adults or $5

one building, $8 seniors or $4 one building, $5 children 4–16 or $3 one building) is the driving force behind a collection of eight colonial and postcolonial buildings (plus a research library) open throughout the summer. Start at the Jefferds' Tavern Visitor Center (5 Lindsay Rd., York), where you'll need to pick up tickets for visiting. Don't miss the Old Burying Ground, dating from 1735, across the street (rubbings are a no-no). Nearby are the Old Gaol and the School House (both fun for kids), Ramsdell House, and the Emerson-Wilcox House. About one-half mile down Lindsay Road, on the York River, are the John Hancock Warehouse and the George Marshall Store Gallery (140 Lindsay Rd., operated in the summer as a respected contemporary-art gallery); across the river is the Elizabeth Perkins House. An-

---

SOUTHERN COAST LIGHTHOUSE TOUR

The lure of lighthouses is understandable. Legends tell of heroic keepers, prank-playing ghosts, and death-defying storms. Lighthouse lovers will find five in southern Maine, all viewable (binoculars will help) from land. Most of these were built in the 19th century on the wrecks of earlier lights that couldn't withstand winter storms.

Begin your journey by taking Route 103, off Route 1 in Kittery, and heading north. The best place to view **Whaleback Lighthouse,** which guards the Portsmouth Harbor and the mouth of the Piscataqua River, is from Fort Foster, on Gerrish Island, which is connected to the mainland via a bridge.

Continue on Route 103 until it merges with Route 1A, and then follow this north, bearing right, at the end of Long Sands Beach, on Nubble Road. The Cape Neddick Light, better known as **The Nubble,** stands just 200 yards or so off Cape Neddick Point and is easily seen from Sohier Park.

Sohier Park is also the best place to view the **Boon Island Light,** six miles offshore. The first three lighthouses constructed on this remote pile of rock were destroyed before the current light, dating from the

mid-19th century, was constructed of hand-hewn granite blocks.

Continue on 1A until it joins Route 1, and then head north. Break from viewing real lighthouses for a visit to the king of lighthouse emporia, **Lighthouse Depot,** on Route 1 in Wells.

After touring, browsing, buying, and learning everything there is to know about lighthouses, continue north on Route 1 until Route 9 East splits from it, just north of Wells. Follow Route 9 through the Kennebunks and on to the village of Cape Porpoise. The town pier, at the end of Pier Road, is the best place to view the **Goat Island Light,** which has the distinction of being the last manned lighthouse in the state. It was finally automated in 1990. There's also a great view from the Vaughn's Island Preserve, in Kennebunkport, but you'll have coordinate your visit with the tide.

Return to Route 9, and continue east until it merges with Route 208. You'll turn right, following signs for Biddeford Pool. The **Wood Island Light,** on the east end of Wood Island, marks the entrance to the Saco River. It can be seen from several points in Biddeford Pool and Hills Beach, but the best view is from the East Point Sanctuary.

© HILARY NANGLE

The Sayward-Wheeler House is one of many historical properties in York Harbor.

tiques buffs shouldn't miss the Wilcox and Perkins Houses. These two are open by guided tour; other buildings are self guided. Visit some or all of the buildings, at your own pace—no one leads you from one to another. In July and August, an architectural walking tour of York Village begins at 10 A.M. every Wednesday ($2 pp; meet at Jefferds' Tavern). At 196 York Street, across from the jail, is the well-stocked Museum Shop. Note: Some sites you can walk to from the tavern; others you'll need a car to reach and parking may be limited.

◖ Nubble Light/Sohier Park

The best-known photo op in York is the distinctive 1879 lighthouse known formally as Cape Neddick Light Station and familiarly as "The Nubble." Although there's no access to the lighthouse's island, Sohier Park Welcome Center (Nubble Rd., off Rte. 1A, between Long and Short Sands Beaches, York Beach, 207/363-7608, 10 A.M.–8 P.M. daily June–mid-Sept. and weekends in May and to early Oct.) provides the perfect viewpoint (and has restrooms). Parking

is limited, but the turnover is fairly good. Not a bad idea, however, to walk from the Long Sands parking area or come by bike, even though the road has inadequate shoulders. Weekdays this is also a popular spot for scuba divers.

Sayward-Wheeler House

Owned by the Boston-based Historic New England, the 1718 Sayward-Wheeler House (9 Barrell La. Ext., York Harbor, 207/384-2454, www.historicnewengland.org, $5) occupies a prime site at the edge of York Harbor. It's open with tours on the hour 11 A.M.–4 P.M. the first and third Saturday of the month, from June through mid-October. In the house are lots of period furnishings—all in pristine condition. Take Route 1A to Lilac Lane (Rte. 103) to Barrell Lane and then to Barrell Lane Extension.

York's Wild Kingdom

More than 250 creatures—including tigers, zebras, llamas, deer, lions, elephants, and monkeys—find a home at York's Wild Kingdom (102 Railroad Ave., off Rte. 1, York Beach,

207/363-4911 or 800/456-4911, www.yorkzoo
.com). It's not what you'd call a state-of-the-art
zoo, but it keeps the kids entertained. Elephant
shows and other animal "events" occur three
times daily in July and August—usually at noon,
2 P.M., and 4 P.M., but the schedule is posted, or
you can call ahead. Between the zoo and the
amusement-park rides, it's easy to spend a day
here—and there are snack bars on the grounds.
Admission (covering the zoo and some of the
rides) is in the neighborhood of $18 adults, $15
children 4–10, $4 age 3 and younger. Zoo-only
admission is $14 adults, $9 or $1 kids. The zoo's
open 10 A.M.–5 P.M., to 6 P.M. weekends and
July and August, from late May to late September; amusement park hours are noon–9:30 P.M.
late June through early September.

Spooky Sightseeing

Flickering candles and a black-hooded guide
get you right in the spirit of things during
imaginative evening candlelight walking tours
of historic York village. **Ghostly Tours** (250
York St., Rte. 1A, York, 207/363-0000, www
.ghostlytours.com) specializes in ghost stories
and 18th-century folklore during its 45-minute
meanders through burial grounds in the oldest
part of town. (Even the phone number is kinda
weird.) Cost is $10 pp. To continue the theme,
Gravestone Artwear (same address, 207/351-
1434 or 800/564-4310) carries wizard capes,
gravestone rubbing kits (but don't try them out
in the Old Burying Ground), notecards, T-shirts,
and lots of other cemetery-centered items.

RECREATION
Walk the Walks

Next to Harbor Beach, near the Stage Neck
Inn, a sign marks the beginning of the **Cliff
Path,** a walkway worth taking for its dramatic
harbor views in the shadow of elegant summer
cottages. On the one-hour round-trip, you'll
pass the York Harbor Reading Room (an exclusive club). The path is on private property,
traditionally open to the public courtesy of the
owners, but controversy surfaces periodically
about property rights, vandalism, and the condition of some sections of the walk. Note: It's

© TOM NANGLE

The Wiggly Bridge leads to Steedman Woods
preserve.

called the Cliff Path for a reason. It's not a good
choice for little ones.

A less strenuous route is known variously as the **Shore Path, Harbor Walk,** or
Fisherman's Walk, running west along the
harbor and river from Stage Neck Road (next
to Edwards' Harborside Inn) and passing the
Sayward-Wheeler House before crossing the
tiny, green-painted Wiggly Bridge leading into
the **Steedman Woods** preserve. Carry binoculars for good boat watching and birding in the
16-acre preserve, owned by the Old York Historical Society. A one-mile double-loop trail
takes less than an hour of easy strolling.

Mt. Agamenticus

Drive to the summit of Mt. Agamenticus ("The
Big A") and you're at York County's highest
point. It's only 692 feet, but on a clear day
you'll have panoramic views of ocean, lakes,
woods, and sometimes the White Mountains.
The preserve, comprising 7,000 acres of conservation land and 4,500 acres of water district
land, is considered among the most biologically
diverse wildernesses in Maine, and its landscape

includes vernal pools and ponds and it's home to rare and endangered species. At the top are a billboard map of the 40-mile trail network and a curious memorial to St. Aspinquid, a 17th-century Algonquian Indian leader. Also here are riding stables, offering trail rides Memorial Day to mid-September. Mountain biking is also hugely popular on Agamenticus. Take a picnic, a kite, and binoculars. In the fall, if the wind's from the northwest, watch for migrating hawks; in winter, bring a sled for the best downhill run in southern Maine. Contact the **York Parks and Recreation Department** (207/363-1040) for info about the trail rides and other activities at the mountain park. Fortunately, in recent years, conservationists have been particularly active here, saving thousands of acres from development. The efforts continue, with a goal of 14,000 acres. From Route 1 in Cape Neddick, take Mountain Road (also called Agamenticus Rd.) 4.2 miles west to the access road.

Golf

The **Ledges Golf Club** (1 Ledges Dr., off Rte. 91, York, 207/351-9999, www.ledgesgolf.com) is an 18-hole course with daily public tee times.

Swimming

Sunbathing and swimming are big draws in York, with four beaches of varying sizes and accessibility. Bear in mind that traffic can be gridlocked along the beachfront (Rte. 1A) in midsummer, so it may take longer than you expect to get anywhere. **Lifeguards** are on duty 9:30 A.M.–4 P.M. mid-June–Labor Day at Short Sands Beach, Long Beach, and Harbor Beach. Bathhouses at Long Sands and Short Sands are open 9 A.M.–7 P.M. daily in midsummer. The biggest parking space (metered) is at Long Sands, but that 1.5-mile beach also draws the most customers. Scarcest parking is at Harbor Beach, near the Stage Neck Inn, and at Cape Neddick (Passaconaway) Beach, near the Ogunquit town line.

Sea Kayaking

Kayak rentals are available for $30 a day, single, $45 double, from **Excursions: Coastal**

Maine Outfitting Company (1399 Rte. 1, Cape Neddick, 207/363-0181, www.excursions inmaine.com), owned by Mike Sullivan and Scott Leighton. Or sign up for one of their half-day tours: $55 (afternoon) or $60 (morning, with lunch). Kids 10–15 are $5 less. A four-hour basics clinic for ages 16 and older is $75; another for those comfortable with basics is also $75. Sea-kayak rental is $30/day or $45 for 24-hour period per double, $45/$60 for a single. Excursions is on Route 1 four miles north of the I-95 York exit.

Harbor Adventures (Harris Island Rd., York Harbor, 207/363-8466, www.harbor adventures.com) offers instruction and guided sea-kayaking trips from Kittery through Kennebunkport. Prices begin around $40 for a two-hour harbor tour.

Scuba and Surfing

York Beach Scuba (19 Railroad Ave., P.O. Box 850, York Beach 03910, 207/363-3330), a source for rentals, air, and trips, is conveniently situated not far from Sohier Park, a popular dive site. It also offers diving packages, including lodging and meals. For surfing information, lessons, or rentals, call **Liquid Dreams Surf Shop** (171 Long Beach Ave., York, 207/351-2545). It's open 10 A.M.–5 P.M. weekends, and it's right across from the beach.

Fishing

Local expert on fly-fishing, spin fishing, and conventional tackle is **Eldgrege Bros. Guide Service** (1480 Rte. 1, Cape Neddick, 207/373-9269, www.eldredgeflyshop.com). Four-hour guided trips for one or two anglers begin at $250 freshwater, $300 salt water. Kayak and rod and reel rentals are available.

ENTERTAINMENT

Live Music

Inn on the Blues (7 Ocean Ave., York Beach, 207/351-3221, www.inntheblues.com) has live music (acoustic, blues, reggae) every night but Monday during the summer. If you want to be close to both the music and the beach, consider booking one of the suites upstairs ($155–390).

The **Ship's Cellar Pub** in the York Harbor Inn frequently has live entertainment, too. Free concerts are often held at the **Ellis Park Gazebo,** usually 7–9 P.M. from early July to early September.

FESTIVALS AND EVENTS

Each year, the Old York Historical Society invites decorators to transform a local house for the **Decorator Show House,** culminating in an open house from mid-July to mid-August.

From late July into early August, the **York Days** festivities enliven the town for 10 days with concerts, dances, walking tours, a road race, sandcastle contests, antiques and art shows, a dog show, fireworks, a parade, and public suppers.

York Village's **Annual Harvestfest** takes place 10 A.M.–4 P.M. the weekend after Columbus Day in October and combines colonial crafts and cooking demonstrations, hayrides, museum tours, entertainment for adults and kids, and an ox roast with beanhole beans. This is one of the town's most popular events; most activities are free.

The annual **Lighting of the Nubble,** in late November, includes cookies, hot chocolate, music, and an appearance by Santa Claus. The best part, though, is seeing the lighthouse glowing for the holidays.

SHOPPING

Park in York Village and wander around the handful of small shops. **York Village Marketplace** (211 York St., Rte. 1A, York Village, 207/363-4830) is a three-level emporium based in a restored 1834 church. Lots of tasteful stuff, with an emphasis on antiques—bet you won't leave empty-handed. A model train shop occupies the entire third floor—go just to see the elaborate model set up in the shop.

Expect to wash your hands before examining any of the 400-plus, museum-quality antique quilts at Betsy Telford's **Rocky Mountain Quilts** (130 York St., York Village, 207/363-6800 or 800/762-5940, www.rockymountain quilts.com). This isn't a place for browsers.

Fans of fine craft shouldn't miss **Panache** (1949 Rte. 1, Cape Neddick, 207/646-4878).

It boasts of having New England's largest selection of fine contemporary art glass, but there's so much more here. It's a visual treat. Find it just south of the Ogunquit Playhouse, on the York-Ogunquit town line.

ACCOMMODATIONS
York Harbor

Bed-and-Breakfasts: Hosts Donna and Paul Archibald have turned Fannie Chapman's 1889 summer cottage into the elegant and romantic ◖ **Chapman Cottage** (370 York St., P.O. Box 575, York Harbor 03911, 207/363-2059 or 877/363-2059, www.chapmancottage bandb.com, $155–250), a truly special retreat. Rooms are huge and plush, with air-conditioning, Wi-Fi, TV, and spacious baths; most have whirlpool baths and fireplaces (some in the bathrooms), and a few have private decks and river views. The pampering includes a welcome fruit basket, fresh flowers, bathrobes, and fine linens. The inn also has a lovely dining room and an inviting lounge with tapas menu and martini/wine bar.

Inviting Adirondack-style chairs accent the green lawn rolling down to the harbor at **Edwards' Harborside Inn** (7 Stage Neck Rd., P.O. Box 866, York Harbor 03911, 207/363-3037 or 800/273-2686, www.edwardsharborside .com, $150–220 rooms, $150–320 suites). Many of the 10 rooms can be combined into suites, and most have water views. All have TV, phone, and air-conditioning. One suite has a party-size whirlpool tub facing the harbor, another a grand piano. Watch the sunset from the inn's 210-foot pier, stroll the adjacent shorefront paths, wander over to the beach, or just settle into one of those shorefront chairs and watch the world go by. A full lovely buffet breakfast is served in the water-view sunporch.

Bill and Bonney Alstrom, former innkeepers at Tanglewood Hall, weren't looking to downsize, but on a lark, they stumbled upon this woodland cottage, and they were smitten. After more than a year of renovations, they opened **Morning Glory Inn** (120 Seabury Rd., York, 207/363-2062, www.morninggloryinnmaine .com, $155–225 peak). A boutique B&B, catering to romantics, the Morning Glory has just three rooms, all very spacious and private, and all with doors to private patios or yards, air-conditioning, TV with DVD, fridge, Wi-Fi, and plentiful other little amenities. The living room, in the original section of the house, was a 17th-century cottage, barged over from the Isle of Shoals; the newer post-and-beam great room doubles as a dining area, where a hot breakfast buffet is served. The property is ultraquiet—listen to the birds singing in the gardens; it's truly a magical setting, far removed yet convenient to everything York offers.

Full-Service Inns: York Harbor Inn (Rte. 1A, P.O. Box 573, York Harbor 03911, 207/363-5119 or 800/343-3869, www.york harborinn.com, $99–349 d) is an accommodating in-town spot with a country-inn flavor and a wide variety of room and package-plan options throughout the year. The oldest section of the inn is a 17th-century cabin from the Isles of Shoals. Accommodations are spread out in the inn, adjacent Yorkshire building, and two elegantly restored houses, both with resident innkeepers: neighboring Harbor Hill, and 1730 Harbor Crest, about a half mile away. All have TV, phones, free Wi-Fi, and air-conditioning; some have four-poster beds, fireplaces, and whirlpools; many have water views. Rates include a generous continental breakfast.

You can't miss the **Stage Neck Inn** (100 Stage Neck Rd., P.O. Box 70, York Harbor 03911, 207/363-3850 or 800/340-9901, www .stageneck.com), occupying its own private peninsula overlooking York Harbor. Modern, resort-style facilities include two pools (one indoors), tennis courts, golf privileges, fitness center, and spectacular views from balconies and terraces. The formal Harbor Porches restaurant (no jeans; entrées $21–30) and the casual Sandpiper Bar and Grille are open to the public. Peak-season rates are $235–345 d mid-May–Labor Day (special packages and MAP are available). Open all year.

York Beach

Hotel and Motel: For more than 150 years, **The Union Bluff** (8 Beach St., P.O. Box 1860, York Beach 03910, 207/363-1333 or 800/833-0721, www.unionbluff.com, $159–329 peak) has stood sentry, like a fortress, overlooking Short Sands Beach. Many of the rooms have ocean views. All have TV, air-conditioning, and phone; some have fireplace, whirlpool bath, or ocean-view deck. Furnishings are modern motel-style. Also on the premises are the Beach Street Grill dining room and a pub serving lighter fare. Best deals are the packages, which include breakfast and dinner. The hotel and pub are open year-round; the restaurant is seasonal.

Bed-and-Breakfasts: Everything's casual and flowers are everywhere at the brightly painted **Katahdin Inn** (11 Ocean Ave. Ext., P.O. Box 193, York Beach 03910, 207/363-1824, www.thekatahdininn.com, $65–125 d), overlooking the breakers of Short Sands Beach. Longtime owners Rae and Paul LeBlanc appropriately refer to it as a "bed and beach." It was built in 1863 and has always been a guesthouse. Nine smallish first-, second-, and third-floor rooms (eight with water views) have lots of four-poster beds and mostly shared baths. Breakfast is not included, but coffee is always available, the rooms have refrigerators, and several eateries are nearby. It's open mid-May–October.

Not oceanfront, but offering ocean views from many rooms and just a short walk from Short Sands Beach, is Barbara and Michael Sheff's **Candleshop Inn** (44 Freeman St., P.O. Box 1216, York Beach 03910, 207/363-4087 or 888/363-4087, www.candleshopinn.com, $110–170 peak). The 10 guest rooms (private and shared baths) are decorated in a country cottage style, with area rugs, painted furniture, and florals; many are set up for families. The day begins with a vegetarian breakfast and a stretch-and-relaxation class. Spa services, including massage and Reiki, are available on-site by appointment.

Condominium Suites: Fabulously sited on the oceanfront and overlooking the Nubble Light, the high-end **ViewPoint** (229 Nubble Rd., York Beach, 207/363-2661, www.viewpoint hotel.com, $295 one bedroom–$575 three bedroom per night, $2,100–3,695 per week) comprises luxuriously appointed one-, two-, and three-bedroom suites. All have gas fireplace, fully equipped kitchen, washer/dryer, TV/VCR, phone, private patio, porch, or deck, Wi-Fi, and daily maid service. On the premises are an outdoor heated pool, grilling area, gardens, and playground.

Cape Neddick

A convenient location is the biggest selling point for the **Country View Motel and Guesthouse** (1521 Rte. 1, Cape Neddick, 207/363-7260 or 800/258-6598, www.countryviewmotel .com, $89–220 peak), a well-cared-for property with a variety of accommodations. Motel rooms vary from standard to ones with full kitchens; those in the 18th-century guesthouse have more of a B&B flair; all have air-conditioning, phone, and TV. On the premises are a pool and a picnic area with gas grills. Rates include continental breakfast. Pets are permitted in the motel.

Seasonal Rentals

Several companies manage week- or month-long rental properties, usually houses or condos. Weekly rentals begin and end on Saturday. Best is **Seaside Vacation Rentals** (Meadowbrook Plaza, 647 Rte. 1, P.O. Box 2000, York 03909, 207/363-1825, www.seasiderentals .com), a longtime family-operated firm with more than 500 properties in York, Ogunquit, Wells, Kennebunk, and Kittery.

CAMPING

Dixon's Coastal Maine Campground (1740 Rte. 1, Cape Neddick, 207/363-3626, www .dixonscampground.com, $30–36) has more than 100 well-spaced sites on 40 wooded and open acres. It can accommodate tents and small RVs. Electric and water hookups are available. Facilities include a playground and a good-size outdoor heated pool. It's also the base for Excursions Sea Kayaking.

FOOD
Seacoast Fine Dining Club

More than two dozen restaurants on Maine's Southern Coast participate in the Seacoast Fine Dining Club (P.O. Box 228, Newmarket, NH 03857, 603/292-5093, www.seacoastfinedining

.com). Membership costs $29.95 and entitles you to buy one entrée and get a second one of equal or lesser value free. It also provides discounts on some area attractions.

Local Flavors

Both *Gourmet* and *Saveur* know where to get dogs. Sometimes the line runs right out the door of the low-ceilinged, reddish-brown roadside shack that houses local institution **Flo's Steamed Dogs** (Rte. 1, opposite the Mountain Rd. turnoff, Cape Neddick). Founder Flo Stacy died at age 92 in June 2000, but her legend and her family live on. No menu here—just steamed Schultz wieners, buns, chips, beverages, and an attitude. The secret? The spicy, sweet-sour hot-dog sauce (allegedly once sought by the H. J. Heinz corporation, but the proprietary Stacy family isn't telling or selling). The cognoscenti know to order their dogs only with mayonnaise and the special sauce—nothing heretical such as catsup or mustard. It's open all year, 11 A.M.–3 P.M., and not a minute later, Thursday–Tuesday. Flo's has added stands in Kittery, Sanford, and Wells.

See those people with their faces pressed to the glass? They're all watching the taffy makers inside **The Goldenrod** (2 Railroad Ave., York Beach, 207/363-2621), where machines spew out 180 Goldenrod Kisses a minute, 65 tons a year—and have been at it since 1896. (The shop also accepts mail orders.) The Goldenrod is an old-fashioned place, with a tearoom, gift shop, old-fashioned soda fountain (135 ice-cream flavors), and casual dining room, with equally old-fashioned prices. It's open for breakfast (8 A.M.), lunch, and dinner daily late May–Columbus Day.

Tucked behind the York County Federal Credit Union is a delicious find, **Food and Co.** (1 York St./Rte. 1, York, 207/363-0900, www.foodnco.com, 7 A.M.–7 P.M. Mon.–Sat.). The combination gourmet food store and café does everything right: breakfast, lunch, and dinners to go (order by 3 P.M. and pick up after 5 P.M.). Prices are reasonable—most breakfast and lunch items are around $7—and the flavors creative and divine.

The *best* pies and other goodies come from **Pie in the Sky Bakery** (corner of Rte. 1 and River Rd., Cape Neddick, 207/363-2656, www.pieintheskymaine.com, 9 A.M.–6 P.M. Fri.–Mon.). You can pick up a slice for $4.50 or the whole pie for $25. Possibilities are numerous: apple crumb, blueberry, bumbleberry, jumbleberry, peach raspberry, and so on; all are handcrafted and made without preservatives or trans fats.

After viewing The Nubble, head across the road to **Brown's Ice Cream** (232 Nubble Rd., York Beach, 207/363-1277), where unusual flavors complement the standards.

Stop in at the **Gateway Farmers Market** (York Chamber of Commerce Visitor Center, Rte. 1, York, 9 A.M.–noon Sat., mid-June–mid-Oct.) and stock up for a picnic. If you still need more, head next door to Stonewall Kitchen.

Good Eats

The York Harbor Inn's **Ship's Cellar Pub** (11:30 A.M.–12:30 A.M. Mon.–Sat. and 4 P.M.–midnight Sun.) attracts even the locals. On the menu are soups, sandwiches, and salads as well as heftier entrées ($16–31), such as chicken scalopinne and pan lobster supreme. The food's good; the service is so-so. The pub doubles as a favorite local watering hole, with live music Wednesday–Sunday. Happy hour, with free munchies, is 4–6 P.M. and sometimes draws a raucous crowd.

Wood-fired pizza and finger-licking ribs are the best sellers at **Ruby's Genuine Wood Grill** (433 Rte. 1, a mile south of the I-95 exit, York, 207/363-7980, www.rubysgrill.com, 11:30 A.M.–10 P.M., to 11 P.M. Fri. and Sat.), but there's plenty more on the menu. Some of the pizzas are downright intriguing—pulled pork and barbecue sauce, for instance. Entrées vary from St. Louis ribs to fajitas to mahimahi, most priced in the low teens. Pastas, sandwiches, salads, and burgers fill out the menu. Lots of variety and flair here. In nice weather, opt for the enclosed deck, where there's often live music Saturday night.

Wild Willy's (765 Rte. 1, York, 207/3363-9924, www.wildwillysburgers.com, 11 A.M.–8 P.M. Mon.–Sat.) has turned burgers into an art form. More than a dozen hefty, mouthwatering burgers, all made from certified Angus beef, are available, from the classic Willy burger to the Rio Grande, with roasted green chiles from New Mexico and cheddar cheese. Don't miss the hand-cut fries. Chicken sandwiches, steak chili, and frappes are also served, as are beer and wine. Order at the counter before grabbing a seat in the dining area or out on the back deck; the servers will find you when it's ready. Cash only; burgers run about $6.

Locals swear by **Rick's All Seasons Cafe** (240 York St., York, 207/363-5584), where the food is good, and the gossip is even better. Go for breakfast or lunch—the fried clams earn raves. Have patience: Almost everything is cooked to order. It's worth the wait.

Casual to Fine Dining

It's hard to know whether Food or Shopping is the right category for **Stonewall Kitchen** (Stonewall La., York, 207/351-2712 or 800/207-5267, www.stonewallkitchen.com), a phenomenally successful company that concocts imaginative condiments and other food products, many of which have received national awards. The headquarters building—including a handsome shop with tasting areas and a "viewing gallery" where you can watch it all happen—is next to the Yorks Chamber of Commerce building, on Route 1. Go hungry: There are an espresso bar and an excellent café on the premises, open daily for breakfast and lunch and light fare in the late afternoon. Dinner may be served during peak season; call.

Don't let the forlorn and faded exterior deter you. Serving "food that loves you back," **Frankie and Johnny's Natural Foods** (1594 Rte. 1 N, Cape Neddick, 207/363-1909, www.frankie-johnnys.com, opens 5 P.M. Wed.–Sun., $17–26) is vibrant inside. Chef-owner John Shaw's eclectic menu varies from bean-curd satay, vegan delight, and Cajun crab cakes to toasted peppercorn-seared sushi-grade tuna, blackened pork Delmonico, and smoked mozzarella ravioli. It's the best vegetarian menu in York, and the house-made pastas are excellent. Reservations are recommended for summer weekends. Be forewarned: Portions are more than generous. No credit cards ("plastic is not natural"). BYOB. For a memorable meal, book a table at **◖ Chapman Cottage** (370 York St., P.O. Box 575, York Harbor 03911, 207/363-2059 or 877/363-2059, www.chapmancottage bandb.com). Dinner is served in two connected rooms, each with fireplace, and both are decorated in a style fitting the 1899 home. Nicely spaced tables, soft lighting, classical music, and comfortable chairs make it easy to settle in for a night of leisurely fine dining. Service is professional without being stuffy, and the menu is small but intriguing, with selections such as stuffed pork tenderloin, hazelnut ravioli, and duck ($18–27).

The glass-walled dining room at the **York Harbor Inn** (5:30–9:30 P.M. daily and 9:30 A.M.–2:30 P.M. Sun. brunch) gets high marks for creative cuisine (the head chef has been here since 1982), so reservations are essential. Entrées run $25–35. Ask about an early-bird special.

Renowned Boston chef Lydia Shire's new restaurant **Blue Sky on York Beach** (Rte. 1A, York Beach, 207/363-0050) is adding a new tone to downtown York Beach. Opened in late 2007, the second-floor restaurant in The Atlantic House is elegant yet welcoming, with gleaming wood floors, a see-through fireplace, white chairs, and big windows taking in the views. In summer, dinner also will be served on the oceanview porch. The dining room opens nightly at 5:30 P.M. The menu ranges from pizza to lobster, with most entrées around $20; a lounge menu is less pricey. For more casual eats, try Shire's first-floor cafe, **Clara's Cupcake Café,** named after her granddaughter and serving sandwiches, soups, and baked goods.

Lobster

Before heading for the **Cape Neddick Lobster Pound/Harborside Restaurant** (Shore Rd., Cape Neddick, 207/363-5471), check the tide calendar. The rustic shingled building dripping with lobster-pot buoys has a spectacular harbor view (especially from the deck) at high tide, a rather drab one at low tide, so plan accordingly. Entrées

are $15–24. Open at noon daily. It offers entertainment beginning at 10 P.M. Friday and Saturday in summer.

INFORMATION AND SERVICES

The Maine Tourism Association operates a Maine State Visitor Information Center (207/439-1319) in Kittery, between Route 1 and I-95, with access from either road. It's chock-full of brochures and has restrooms and a picnic area.

For York area information, head for the Shingle-style palace of the Yorks Chamber of Commerce (1 Stonewall La., off Rte. 1, York, 207/363-4422, www.gatewaytomaine.org), at I-95's York exit. Inside are restrooms. It's open daily in summer.

GETTING AROUND

The Maine Turnpike, a toll road, is generally the fastest route, if you're trying to get between two towns. Route 1 parallels the turnpike, on the ocean side. It's mostly two lanes and is lined with shops, restaurants, motels, and other tourist-oriented sites, which means stop-and-go traffic that often slows to a crawl. If you're traveling locally, it's best to walk or use the local trolley systems, which have the bonus of saving you the agony of finding a parking spot.

The **York Trolley** (207/748-3030, www.york trolley.com) provides a number of options for getting around the Yorks. A York tour departs hourly 10 A.M.–2 P.M. Monday and Friday with stops at Short Sands, York Village, York Harbor, York Beach, and Nubble Lighthouse. A day pass is $8 adult, $4 kids 3–10.

The company also operates a **York Beach Shuttle** from late June to early September. The service between Long and Short Sands beaches runs every 30 minutes 9:30 A.M.–10:30 P.M. ($1.50 one-way, $3 complete loop).

The **Shoreline Shuttle** operates hourly between York's Short Sands Beach and Ogunquit's Perkins Cove from late June through Labor Day. Fare is $1 each way; a 12-ride pass is $10; 18 and younger ride free.

Ogunquit and Wells

Ogunquit has been a holiday destination since the indigenous residents named it "beautiful place by the sea." What's the appeal? An unparalleled, unspoiled beach, several top-flight (albeit pricey) restaurants, a dozen art galleries, and a respected art museum with a view second to none. The town has been home to an art colony attracting the glitterati of the painting world starting with Charles Woodbury in the late 1880s. The summertime crowds continue, multiplying the minuscule year-round population of just under 1,400. These days, it's an especially gay-friendly community, too. Besides the beach, the most powerful magnet is Perkins Cove, a working fishing enclave that looks more like a movie set. The best way to approach the cove is via trolley-bus or on foot, along the shoreline Marginal Way from downtown Ogunquit—midsummer parking in the cove ($3 per hour) is madness.

Wells, once the parent of Ogunquit and since 1980 its immediate neighbor to the north, was settled in 1640. Nowadays, it's best known as a long, skinny, family-oriented community with about 10,300 year-round residents, seven miles of splendid beachfront, and heavy-duty commercial activity: lots of antiques and used-book shops, and a handful of factory outlets. It also claims two spectacular nature preserves worth a drive from anywhere. At the southern end of Wells, abutting Ogunquit, is **Moody,** an enclave named after 18th-century settler Samuel Moody and even rating its own post office.

If swimming isn't your top priority, plan to visit Ogunquit and Wells after Labor Day, when crowds let up, lodging rates drop dramatically, weather is still good, and you can find restaurant seats and parking spots.

SIGHTS
◖ Ogunquit Museum of American Art (OMAA)
Not many museums can boast a view as stunning as the one at the Ogunquit Museum of Ameri-

can Art (543 Shore Rd., P.O. Box 815, Ogunquit 03907, 207/646-4909, www.ogunquit museum.org), nor can many communities boast such renown as a summer art colony. Overlooking Narrow Cove, 1.4 miles south of downtown Ogunquit, the museum prides itself on its distinguished permanent collection. Works of Marsden Hartley, Rockwell Kent, Walt Kuhn, Henry Strater, and Thomas Hart Benton, among others, are displayed in five galleries. Special exhibits are mounted each summer, when there is an extensive series of lectures, concerts, and other programs. OMAA has a well-stocked gift shop, wheelchair access, and landscaped grounds with sculptures, a pond, and manicured lawns. Admission is $7 adults, $5 seniors, $4 students, and free for kids under 12. It's open 10:30 A.M.–5 P.M. Mon.–Sat., 2–5 P.M. Sunday July 1 to late October; closed Labor Day and for four days in mid-August for rehanging.

◖ Marginal Way
No visit to Ogunquit is complete without a leisurely stroll along the Marginal Way, the mile-long foot path edging the ocean from Shore Road (by the Sparhawk Resort) to Perkins Cove. It's been a must-walk since Josiah Chase gave the right-of-way to the town in the 1920s. The best times to appreciate this shrub-lined, shorefront walkway in Ogunquit are early morning or when everyone's at the beach. En route are tide pools, intriguing rock formations, crashing surf, pocket beaches, benches (though the walking's a cinch, even partially wheelchair-accessible), and a marker listing the day's high and low tides. When the surf's up, keep a close eye on the kids—the sea has no mercy. A midpoint access is at Israel's Head (behind a sewage plant masquerading as a tiny lighthouse), but getting a parking space is pure luck. Best advice is to stroll the Marginal Way to Perkins Cove for lunch, shopping, and maybe a boat trip, and then return to downtown Ogunquit via trolley-bus.

© TOM NANGLE

Most of Ogunquit's excursion boats leave from Perkins Cove.

Perkins Cove

Turn-of-the-20th-century photos show Ogunquit's Perkins Cove lined with gray-shingled shacks used by a hardy colony of local fishermen—fellows who headed offshore to make a tough living in little boats. They'd hardly recognize it today. Though the cove remains a working lobster-fishing harbor, several old shacks have been reincarnated as boutiques and restaurants, and photographers go crazy shooting the quaint inlet spanned by a little pedestrian drawbridge. In midsummer, you'll waste precious time looking for one of the three or four dozen parking places ($3 an hour), so take advantage of the trolley-bus service. In the cove are galleries, gift shops, a range of eateries (fast food to lobster to high-end dining—see *Ogunquit* under *Food*), boat excursions, and public restrooms.

Wells Reserve at Laudholm Farm

Known locally as Laudholm Farm (the name of the restored 19th-century visitors center), Wells National Estuarine Research Reserve (342 Laudholm Farm Rd., Wells, 207/646-1555, www.wellsreserve.org) occupies 1,690 acres of woods, beach, and coastal salt marsh on the southern boundary of the Rachel Carson National Wildlife Refuge, just one-half mile east of Route 1. Seven miles of trails wind through the property. The best trail is the Salt Marsh Loop, with a boardwalk section leading to an overlook with panoramic views of the marsh and Little River inlet. Another winner is the Barrier Beach Walk, 1.3-mile round-trip that goes through multiple habitats all the way to beautiful Laudholm Beach. Allow 1.5 hours for either; you can combine the two. Lyme disease ticks have been found here, so tuck pant legs into socks and stick to the trails (some of which are wheelchair-accessible). The informative exhibits in the visitors center (open 10 A.M. to 4 P.M. Mon.–Sat. and noon–4 P.M. Sun. May–Oct., weekdays Oct.–Mar., closed mid-Dec.–mid-Jan.) make a valuable prelude for enjoying the reserve. An extensive program schedule, April–November, includes lectures, nature walks, and children's programs. Reservations are required for some programs. Trails are accessible 7 A.M.–dusk. From late May to mid-October, admission is charged, $2 adult, $1 ages 6–16.

Rachel Carson National Wildlife Refuge

Ten chunks of coastal Maine real estate—now more than 4,700 acres, eventually 7,600 acres, between Kittery Point and Cape Elizabeth—make up this refuge (Rte. 9, 321 Port Rd., Wells, 207/646-9226, http://rachelcarson.fws.gov) headquartered at the northern edge of Wells, near the Kennebunkport town line. Pick up a *Carson Trail Guide* at the refuge office (parking space is very limited) and follow the mile-long walkway (wheelchair-accessible) past tidal creeks, salt pans, and salt marshes. It's a birder's paradise during migration seasons. As with the Laudholm Farm reserve, the Lyme disease tick has been found here, so tuck pant legs into socks and stick to the trail. Office hours are 8 A.M.–4:30 P.M. weekdays year-round; trail access is sunrise to sunset, year-round. Leashed pets are allowed.

Ogunquit Arts Collaborative Gallery

Closer to downtown Ogunquit is the Ogunquit Arts Collaborative Gallery (also known as the Barn Gallery, Shore Rd. and Bourne La., P.O. Box 529, Ogunquit 03907, 207/646-8400), featuring the works of member artists—an impressive group. The OAC is the showcase for the Ogunquit Art Association, established by Charles Woodbury, who was inspired to open an art school in Perkins Cove in the late 19th century. Special programs throughout the season include concerts, workshops, gallery talks, and an art auction. The gallery is open 11 A.M.–5 P.M. Monday–Saturday and 1–5 P.M. Sunday late May–Oct. 1. Admission is free.

Wells Auto Museum

More than 80 vintage vehicles, plus a collection of old-fashioned nickelodeons (bring nickels and dimes, they work), are jam-packed into the Wells Auto Museum (Rte. 1, Wells, 207/646-9064). From the outside, it just looks like a big warehouse, right on the highway. Admission is $5 adults, $2 children 6–12. It's open 10 A.M.–5 P.M. daily Memorial Day–Columbus Day.

Local History Museums

Ogunquit's history is preserved in the **Ogunquit Heritage Museum** (86 Obeds La., Dorothea Jacobs Grant Common, Ogunquit, 207/646-0296, www.ogunquitheritage museum.org, 12:30–4:30 P.M. Tues.–Sat. June–Sept.). The museum opened in 2002 in the restored Captain James Winn House, a 1785 cape listed on the National Register. Plans call for the construction of a fishing shack and boat shop to display appropriate exhibits, including an Ogunquit dory.

Right on the historic Post Road that once linked Boston with points north stands the **Historic Meetinghouse Museum** (938 Post Rd., Rte. 1, opposite Wells Plaza, P.O. Box 801, Wells 04090, 207/646-4775, 10 A.M.–4 P.M. Tues.–Thurs., to 1 P.M. Sat. June–mid. Oct, Wed. and Thurs. only in winter), a handsome steepled structure on the site of the town's first church (1643). Preserved and maintained by the Historical Society of Wells and Ogunquit, its displays include old photos, ship models, needlecraft, and local memorabilia. On the second floor is a genealogical library where volunteers will help you research your roots. Enter in the rear.

RECREATION

Beaches

One of Maine's most scenic and unspoiled sandy beachfronts, the 3.5-mile stretch of sand fringed with seagrass is a major magnet for hordes of sunbathers, spectators, swimmers, surfers, and sandcastle builders. Getting there means crossing the Ogunquit River via one of three access points. For Ogunquit's **Main Beach**—with a spanking new bathhouse and high crowd content—take Beach Street. To reach **Footbridge Beach,** marginally less crowded, either take Ocean Street and the footbridge or take Bourne Avenue to Ocean Avenue in adjacent Wells and walk back toward Ogunquit. **Moody Beach,** at Wells's southern end, technically is private property—a subject of considerable legal dispute. Lifeguards are on duty all summer at the public beaches, and there are restrooms in all three areas. The beach is free, but parking is not; parking lots charge by the hour ($4 an hour at the Main Beach) or the day ($15 per day at Main Beach, Footbridge Beach, and Moody Beach), and they fill up early on warm midsummer days. After 3 P.M., some are free. It's far more sensible to opt for the frequent trolley-buses.

Wells beaches continue where Ogunquit's leave off. **Crescent Beach,** Webhannet Drive between Eldredge and Mile Roads, is the tiniest, with tide pools, no facilities, and limited parking. **Wells Beach,** Mile Road to Atlantic Avenue, is the major (and most crowded) beach, with lifeguards, restrooms, and parking. Around the other side of Wells Harbor is **Drakes Island Beach** (take Drakes Island Road, at the blinking light), a less crowded spot with restrooms and lifeguards. Walk northeast from Drakes Island Beach and you'll eventually reach Laudholm Beach, with great birding along the way. Summer beach-parking permits are available from the town hall in Wells: it's $15 a day for nonresidents ($5 for a motorcycle, $25 for an RV); if you're staying longer, a $50 10-visit pass is a better bargain.

Bike, Kayak, and Surfboard Rentals

At **Wheels and Waves** (579 Post Rd., Rte. 1, Wells, 207/646-5774, www.wheelsnwaves .com), mountain-bike rentals begin at $20 a day; tandems are $40. Surfboards are $25.

Put in right at the harbor and explore the estuary from **Webhannet River Kayak and Canoe Rentals** (345 Harbor Rd., Wells, 207/646-9649, www.webhannetriver.com). Rates begin at $25 for two hours.

Boating Excursions

Depending on your interest, you can go deep-sea fishing or whale-watching or just gawking out of Perkins Cove, Ogunquit. Between April and early November, Captain Tim Tower runs half-day (departing 4 P.M.; $45 pp) and full-day (departing 7 A.M.; $70 pp) **deep-sea-fishing trips** aboard the 40-foot *Bunny Clark* (P.O. Box 837, Ogunquit 03907, 207/646-2214, www.bunnyclark.com). Reservations are necessary. Tim has a science degree, so he's a wealth of marine biology information. All gear is provided, and the crew'll fillet your catch for you; dress warmly and wear sunblock.

Perkins Cove (Barnacle Billy's Dock) is also home port for the Hubbard family's **Finestkind Cruises** (207/646-5227, www .finestkindcruises.com), offering 1.5-hour, 14-mile Nubble Lighthouse cruises (10 A.M., noon, 2 and 4 P.M. daily; $18 adults, $10 kids) and one-hour cocktail cruises (5:45 P.M. daily; two extra trips in July and Aug.; $12 adults, $7 kids; cash bar) in a sheltered powerboat. A 75-minute breakfast cruise, complete with coffee, juice, and muffin, departs at 9 A.M. daily ($15 adults, $10 kids). The family also does 50-minute lobster-boat trips, 4–6 cruises Monday–Saturday; look and listen—no helping; $12 adults, $7 kids) in a real lobster boat (no toilets). Also available are 1.75-hour sails aboard *The Cricket,* a locally

built wooden sailboat. It departs three times daily and costs $27.50 pp. High season runs July 1 through Labor Day; limited schedule May, June, September, October. Reservations are advisable but usually unnecessary midweek. No credit cards.

Golf

The 18-hole, Donald Ross–designed **Cape Neddick Country Club** (650 Shore Rd., 207/361-2011, www.capeneddickgolf.com) is a semiprivate 18-hole course with restaurant and driving range.

Sea Kayaking

World Within Sea Kayaking (746 Ocean Ave., Wells, 207/646-0455, www.worldwithin.com) has both tours and rentals. Rentals are available on the tidal Ogunquit River to experienced kayakers for $15/hour single, $25/hour double. Guided tours begin with one hour of land instruction followed by two hours on the water for $70 pp. World Within also has an outlet at Wheels and Waves.

ENTERTAINMENT
Theater

Having showcased top-notch professional theater since the 1930s, the 750-seat **Ogunquit Playhouse** (Rte. 1, P.O. Box 915, Ogunquit 03907, 207/646-5511, www.ogunquit playhouse.org) knows how to do it right: presenting comedies and musicals each summer, with big-name stars. The air-conditioned building is wheelchair-accessible. The box office is open daily in season, beginning in early May. Performances are at 8 P.M. Tuesday–Friday, 8:30 P.M. Saturday, matinees at 2:30 P.M. Wednesday and Thursday and 3:30 P.M. Sunday mid-June–Labor Day. Prices range $39–48. The playhouse also presents a children's series and a handful of Sunday night concerts. Parking can be a hassle; consider walking the short distance from the Bourne Lane trolley-bus stop.

Live Music

Ogunquit has several nightspots with good reputations for food and live entertainment.

Best known is **Jonathan's** (2 Bourne La., P.O. Box 1879, Ogunquit 03907, 207/646-4777 or 800/464-9934 in Maine), where national headliners often are on the schedule upstairs. Advance tickets are cheaper than at the door, and dinner guests get preference for seats. Reservations are essential at this popular spot. The well-respected downstairs restaurant has creative entrées for $18–30 and ethnic flavors at the oyster bar. Highlighting the dining room are contemporary artwork and a 600-gallon aquarium. It's open 5–9:30 P.M., to 10 P.M. Friday and Saturday.

Ogunquit Performing Arts (207/646-6170) presents a full slate of programs, including classical concerts, ballet, and theater.

The **Wells Summer Concert Series** runs from early July through early September at the Hope Hobbs Gazebo in Wells Harbor Park. A wide variety of music is represented, from sing-alongs to swing.

FESTIVALS AND EVENTS

The **Fourth of July** celebration on Ogunquit Beach includes fireworks and live music. **Harbor Fest,** a concert, craft fair, parade, chicken barbecue, and children's activities, takes place the second weekend of July in Harbor Park in Wells.

In mid-August, Ogunquit Beach hosts a **Sandcastle-Building Contest** and in late August is the annual **Sidewalk Art Show and Sale.**

Capriccio is a performing arts festival, with daytime and evening events as well as a kite festival, held during the first week of September. Then, the second weekend that month, Wells National Estuarine Research Reserve (Laudholm Farm) hosts the **Laudholm Nature Crafts Festival,** a two-day juried crafts fair with children's activities and guided nature walks. This is an especially fine event. And the *third* weekend of September, the **Annual Ogunquit Antiques Show** benefits the Historical Society of Wells and Ogunquit. It's held at the Dunaway Center, School Street, Ogunquit.

In late October is **OgunquitFest,** a family-oriented weeklong event with pumpkin

decorating, scarecrow contest, and other seasonal activities.

Christmas by the Sea, the second weekend of December, features caroling, tree lighting, shopping specials, Santa Claus, a chowderfest, and a beach bonfire in Ogunquit.

SHOPPING
Antiques and Antiquarian Books

Antiques are a Wells specialty. You'll find more than 50 shops, with a huge range of prices. The majority are on Route 1. **R. Jorgensen Antiques** (502 Post Rd., Rte. 1, R.R. 1, Box 1125, Wells 04090, 207/646-9444), is a phenomenon in itself, filling 11 showrooms in two buildings with European and American 18th- and 19th-century furniture and accessories. **MacDougall-Gionet Antiques and Associates** (2104 Post Rd., Rte. 1, Wells, 207/646-3531) has been here since the mid-1960s, and its reputation is stellar. The 65-dealer shop—in an 18th-century barn—carries American and European country and formal furniture and accessories.

If you've been scouring antiquarian bookshops for a long-wanted title, chances are you'll find it at **Douglas N. Harding Rare Books** (2152 Post Rd., Rte. 1, P.O. Box 184, Wells 04090, 207/646-8785 or 800/228-1398). Well cataloged and organized, the sprawling bookshop at any given time stocks upward of 100,000 books, prints, and maps, plus a hefty selection of Maine and New England histories. Don't count on leaving empty-handed—there are too many temptations.

Art Galleries

There's no scarcity of the spectacular scenery that drew artists to Ogunquit in the early 20th century, but it's not the artistic magnet it once was. Yet galleries have popped up here and there. After you've been to the art museum, do your art browsing along Shore Road and in Perkins Cove.

Lighthouse Extravaganza

Several minilighthouses stand watch over the **Lighthouse Depot** (Post Rd., Rte. 1, P.O.

Box 1690, Wells 04090, 207/646-0608 or 800/758-1444, www.lighthousedepot.com), a truly amazing mecca for lighthouse aficionados. Imagine this: two floors of lighthouse books, sculptures, videos, banners, Christmas ornaments, lawn ornaments, paintings, and replicas running the gamut from pure kitsch to attractive collectibles. Its *Maine Lighthouse Map and Guide* ($5.95) is particularly helpful for tracking down the state's sentinels. Depot owners Tim Harrison and Kathy Finnegan also publish the *Lighthouse Digest,* a monthly magazine focusing on North American lighthouses (annual subscription $28), and produce a large mail-order catalog. The shop is about 1.5 miles north of the junction of Routes 1 and 109.

ACCOMMODATIONS
Ogunquit

Motel-style accommodations are everywhere in Ogunquit, most along Route 1, yet finding last-minute rooms in July and August can be a challenge, so book well ahead if you'll be here then. Most properties are open only seasonally.

Hotels and Motels: You're almost literally within spitting distance of Perkins Cove at the 37-room **Riverside Motel** (159 Shore Rd., P.O. Box 2244, Ogunquit 03907, 207/646-2741, www.riversidemotel.com), where you can perch on your balcony and watch the action—or, for that matter, join it. Rooms with phone, air-conditioning, refrigerators, cable TV, and fabulous views are $130–160, with continental breakfast.

Juniper Hill Inn (336 Main St., Rte. 1, P.O. Box 2190, Ogunquit 03907, 207/646-4501 or 800/646-4544, www.ogunquit.com) is a particularly well-run motel-style lodging on five acres close to downtown Ogunquit and the beach. Amenities include refrigerators, cable TV, coin-operated laundry, fitness center, indoor and outdoor pools, and golf privileges. Rooms have all the amenities, plus free Wi-Fi. Peak rates are $149–219. Open all year.

You can't get much closer to the water than the **Above Tide Inn** (66 Beach St., P.O. Box 2188, Ogunquit 03907, 207/646-7454, www.abovetideinn.com, $170–250), which is built

on a wharf over the tidal Ogunquit River and has views to the open Atlantic. It's steps from the beach and downtown Ogunquit. Each of the nine rooms has air-conditioning, TV, and minifridge; a light breakfast is provided; no in-room phone.

Cottage Colony: It's nearly impossible to land a peak-season cottage at **The Dunes** (518 Main St., P.O. Box 917, Ogunquit 03907, 207/646-2612, www.dunesonthewaterfront.com), but it's worth trying. The property is under its third generation of ownership and guests practically will their weeks to their descendents. Tidy, well-equipped white housekeeping cottages and a handful of guest rooms are generously spaced on a shady, grassy lawns that roll down to the river, with the dunes just beyond. Facilities include a dock with rowboats, pool, and lawn games. It's all meticulously maintained. In peak season, one- and two-bedroom cottages require a one- or two-week minimum stay; guest rooms require three nights. Rooms begin at $105, cottages at $190 per night; weekly cottage rentals begin at $1,330.

Eclectic Properties: It's not easy to describe the **Sparhawk Oceanfront Resort** (41 Shore Rd., P.O. Box 936, Ogunquit 03907, 207/646-5562), a sprawling, one-of-a-kind place popular with honeymooners, sedate families, and seniors. There's lots of tradition in this thriving, six-acre complex—it's had various incarnations since the turn of the 20th century—and the Happily Filled sign regularly hangs out front. Out back is the Atlantic, with forever views, and the Marginal Way starts right here. It offers tennis courts, gardens, heated freshwater pool. No restaurant, but Ogunquit has plenty of options, and breakfast is included with your room. The 87 rooms vary in the different buildings—from motel-type rooms (best views) and suites to inn-type suites; rates run $170–300 (seven-night minimum July 4 to mid-August).

Nor is it easy to describe **The Beachmere Inn** (62 Beachmere Pl., Ogunquit, 207/646-2021 or 800/336-3983, www.beachmereinn.com, $150–390), a private, oceanfront property comprising a Victorian-style inn, an updated motel, and other buildings as well as its own beaches. All rooms have air-conditioning, TV, and phone; many rooms have kitchenettes; most have balconies, decks, or terraces; some have fireplaces. Morning coffee and muffins are provided. Reservations require three-night to one-week minimum in July and August; closed January–late March.

Bed-and-Breakfasts: Built in 1899 for a prominent Maine lumbering family, ((**Rockmere Lodge** (40 Stearns Rd., P.O. Box 278, Ogunquit 03907, 207/646-2985, www.rockmere.com, $160–225 peak), underwent a meticulous six-month restoration in the early 1990s, thanks to preservationists Andy Antoniuk and Bob Brown, and in 2006 the duo, along with Doug Flint, gave the inn and grounds a complete rejuvenation, lightening the decor. Near the Marginal Way on a peaceful street, the handsome home has eight very comfortable Victorian guest rooms, all with CD players and cable TV (a 1,000-title library of DVDs and VCR tapes and CDs is available) and most with ocean views. Rates

include a generous breakfast, with a hot entrée every other day. A wraparound veranda, a gazebo, and "The Lookout," a third-floor windowed nook with comfy chairs, make it easy to settle in and just watch the passersby on the Marginal Way. The woodwork throughout is gorgeous, and the grounds double as a public garden. Beach towels, chairs, and umbrellas are provided for guests. Closed March and April. No pets; four dogs in residence.

Floors glisten, brass gleams, and breakfast is served on the glass-walled porch at the **Hartwell House** (118 Shore Rd., P.O. Box 393, Ogunquit 03907, 207/646-7210 or 800/235-8883, www .hartwellhouseinn.com, $175–300), where the 13 rooms and three good-sized suites, all with air-conditioning, are divided between two buildings straddling Shore Road. Rooms are beautifully decorated with antiques and reproductions; try for a garden-view room in the main house. Rates include a full breakfast and afternoon tea.

Resorts: Founded in 1872, **The Cliff House Resort and Spa** (Shore Rd., P.O.

© TOM NANGLE

The Cliff House Resort and Spa is on the edge of Bald Head.

Box 2274, Ogunquit 03907, 207/361-1000), a self-contained Victorian-era complex, sprawls over 70 acres topping the edge of Bald Head Cliff, midway between the centers of York and Ogunquit. Third-generation innkeeper Kathryn Weare keeps updating and modernizing the facilities. Among the most recent additions are a spa building with oversize rooms with king-size beds, gas fireplaces, and balconies, as well as a full-service spa, indoor pool, outdoor vanishing-edge pool, and glass-walled fitness center overlooking the Atlantic. A new central check-in building with indoor amphitheater connects the main building to the spa building. The 150 room and suite styles and prices vary widely in decor, from old-fashioned to contemporary; all have cable TV and phones, some have gas fireplaces, most have a spectacular ocean view ($265–370). Packages are the way to go here. Other facilities include a dining room, lounge, family indoor and outdoor pools, games room, and tennis courts. Eight pet-friendly rooms ($25 per night) have bowl, bed, and treats, and there's a fenced-in exercise area. Open late March–early December.

Wells

Like Ogunquit, Wells has a long list of motel-type lodgings, mostly on Route 1, and everything fills up in late July and early August. If you're arriving then, don't count on finding last-minute space.

Once part of a giant 19th-century dairy farm, the **Beach Farm Inn** (97 Eldredge Rd., Wells, 207/646-8493, www.beachfarminn.com) is a 2.5-acre oasis in a rather congested area 0.2 mile off Route 1. Guests can swim in the pool, relax in the library, or walk one-quarter mile down the road to the beach. If you bring your own bikes, storage is provided; rentals are available within walking distance. Eight rooms (five with private baths, two detached) are $100–135 d, including a full breakfast; two cottages go for $650 and $950 a week. Third-floor rooms have air-conditioning. Open all year.

Even closer to the beach is **(Haven by the Sea** (59 Church St., Wells Beach, 207/646-4194, www.havenbythesea.com, $169–350), a lovely and modern B&B in a former church. Innkeepers John and Susan Jarvis have kept the original floor plan, which allows some surprises. Inside are hardwood floors, cathedral ceilings, and stained-glass windows. The confessional is now a full bar, and the altar has been converted to a dining area that opens to a marsh-view terrace—the bird-watching is superb. Guest rooms have sitting areas, and the suite has a whirlpool tub and fireplace. Guests have plenty of room to relax, including a living area with fireplace. Rates include a full breakfast and afternoon hors d'oeuvres. Also available are a three-bedroom, ocean-view cottage and an apartment.

FOOD
Ogunquit

Local Flavors: The Egg and I (501 Maine St., Rte. 1, 207/646-8777, www.eggandibreakfast .com) earns high marks for its omelettes and waffles. You can't miss it—there's always a crowd. Open 6 A.M.–2 P.M. daily for breakfast, with lunch choices also served after 11 A.M. No credit cards.

Equally popular is **Amore Breakfast** (178 Shore Rd., 207/646-6661, www.amorebreakfast .com, 7 A.M.–1 P.M. Fri.–Tues.). Choose from a baker's dozen omelettes, seven versions of eggs Benedict (including lobster and a spirited rancheros version topped with salsa and served with guacamole), as well as various French toast, waffles, and all the regulars and irregulars.

Eat in or take out from **Village Food Market** (Main St., Ogunquit Center, 207/646-2122, www.villagefoodmarket.com). A breakfast sandwich is less than $3; subs and sandwiches are available in three sizes, and there's even a children's menu.

Scrumptious baked goods, tantalizing salads, and panini sandwiches are available to go at Mary Breen's fabulous **(Bread and Roses** (28A Main St., 207/646-4227, www.breadand rosesbakery.com), a small bakery right downtown with a few tables outside.

Harbor Candy Shop (26 Main St., 207/646-8078 or 800/331-5856) is packed with the most outrageous chocolate imaginable. Fudge, truffles, and turtles are all made here in the shop. Fortunately (or maybe unfortunately), it also accepts mail orders. Open all year.

Lobster: Creative marketing, a knockout view, and efficient service help explain why more than 1,000 pounds of lobster bite the dust every summer day at **Barnacle Billy's** (Perkins Cove, 207/646-5575 or 800/866-5575, 11 A.M.–9 P.M. daily seasonally). For ambience, stick with the original operation; Barnacle Billy's Etc., next door (formerly the Whistling Oyster), is an upmarket version of the same thing with a broader menu. Full liquor license. Try for the deck, with a front-row seat on Perkins Cove.

Ethnic: The closest thing to an upscale-rustic French country inn is the dining room at **(Provence,** also referred to as 98 Provence (262 Shore Rd., 207/646-9898, www.98provence.com). Chef/owner Pierre Gignac produces the cuisine to match, turning out appetizers such as stewed pheasant in baked tomato and chevre gratin and superb entrées in the $26–33 range, but there are also three fixed menus (around $29–37). Duck, venison, seafood, veal, and lamb are all represented. Service is attentive and well paced. Don't miss it, and be sure to make reservations. Open for the season at 5:30 P.M. Wednesday–Monday beginning in mid-April.

Cross the street from Provence and you're in Italy—sort of. Vegetarians and pasta fanatics gravitate to **The Impastable Dream** (261 Shore Rd., 207/646-3011, www.impastabledream.com). Entrée range is $12–19; choices are predictable (ravioli, gnocchi, lasagna, Mediterranean tomato-based sauces over pasta, etc.) in this comfortable, casual spot. No reservations, so you may have to wait. It's open 5–9 P.M. daily, and a kids' menu is available until 6 P.M.

The best and most authentic Italian dining is at **Angelina's Ristorante** (655 Main St./Rte. 1, 207/646-0445), opened by popular local chef and owner David Giarusso in late 2005. Dine in the dining room or lounge or out on the deck, choosing from pastas, risottos (the house specialty), and main courses such as *rollantini di pollo,* a boneless chicken breast

stuffed with prosciutto, mozzarella, and basil and baked with a light spinach cream sauce, or a hand-cut filet mignon grilled and finished with a chianti-portobello-gorgonzola demi-glace. More than 30 wines are available by the glass. Most choices run $16–24. It opens nightly at 5 P.M.

Casual Dining: Gypsy Sweethearts (10 Shore Rd., 207/646-7021, www.gypsysweethearts.com, 5:30–9 P.M. Tues.–Sun.) serves in four rooms on the ground floor of a restored house, and on a rooftop deck, too. It's one of the region's most reliable restaurants, and the creative menu is infused with ethnic accents and includes vegetarian choices (entrées $17–30). Seating is both inside and out. Reservations advised in midsummer.

Equally reliable, and just south of it is **Five-O** (50 Shore Rd., 207/646-6365, www.five-oshoreroad.com, 5–10 P.M. daily), where executive chef Jonathan MacAlpine turns out classics with flair complemented by well-conceived inspirations. The menus changes frequently, but entrées such as pan-seared Atlantic salmon or Peking chicken are $25–33. Lighter fare ($9–16) is available in the lounge to 11 P.M., where martinis are a specialty. Service is excellent. In the off-season, multicourse regional dinners are held about once a month ($70). There's even valet parking.

The View's the Thing: There's not much between you and Spain when you get a window seat at **MC** (Oarweed La., Perkins Cove, Ogunquit, 207/646-6263, www.mcperkinscove.com), sister restaurant of the mega-high-end Arrows Restaurant. Actually, almost every table on both floors has a view, and the sophisticated decor doesn't compete with it. Service is extremely attentive, and the food is fab, creative, and in keeping with chefs Mark Gaier and Clark Frasier, ultrafresh. If you can't justify the splurge for Arrows, get a taste of their cuisine here. Reservations are essential for dinner. It's open 11:30 A.M.–2:30 P.M. for lunch (entrées $9–19) and 5:30–11 P.M. for dinner (entrées $22–34), with a bar menu served until 11 P.M. A jazz brunch is served beginning at 11 A.M. Sundays. Closed Tuesdays and January.

Equally if not more impressive are the views from the dining room at **The Cliff House** (Shore Rd., Ogunquit, 207/361-1000), open to the public for breakfast, lunch, and dinner daily. Try for the brunch buffet, 7:30 A.M.–1 P.M. Sunday. Service can be so-so. Reservations are required for dinner (no jeans, T-shirts, or sneakers); entrée range is $23–33. Before or after dining, wander the grounds. Open late March–early December.

Destination Dining: Restrain yourself for a couple of days and then splurge on an elegant dinner at **Arrows** (Berwick Rd., about 1.5 miles west of Rte. 1, Ogunquit, 207/361-1100, www.arrowsrestaurant.com), definitely one of Maine's finest restaurants. In a beautifully restored 18th-century farmhouse overlooking well-tended gardens (including a one-acre kitchen garden that supplies about 90 percent of the produce), co-owners/chefs Mark Gaier and Clark Frasier do everything right here, starting with the artistic presentation. Prices are stratospheric by Maine standards—with wine and all, count on paying at least $250 a couple—but well worth it. "Innovative" is too tame to describe the menu; entrées cost close to $50. Consider the six-course tasting menu ($95); serious foodies might splurge on the indulgence tasting menu, 10 courses for $135. A credit card is required for reservations—essential in midsummer and on weekends. Jackets are preferred for men; no shorts. It's open for dinner at 6 P.M. mid-April–early December: Tuesday–Sunday in July and August, Wednesday–Sunday in June and September–Columbus Day; mostly weekends other months. Off-season, ask about winemaker, regional, bistro nights, and specialty dinners and cooking classes (most $69–89 for a five-course meal).

Wells

Local Flavors: Best homemade doughnuts in Wells (and beyond), hands down, are at **Congdon's Doughnuts** (Rte. 1, Wells, 207/646-4219). Also try the strata. Open 6 A.M.–3 P.M. daily for breakfast and lunch year-round, closed Tuesday.

Bean suppers are held 5–7 P.M. on the first Saturday of the month, May–October, at the Masonic Hall on Sanford Road, and on the second Saturday at the Wells Congregational Church, on Route 1.

Flo's (Rte. 1, Wells, 11 A.M.–7 P.M. daily), an offspring of the York institution, has opened a stand in Wells. The famous hot dogs are served, but so are burgers and sandwiches. Order at the window, and then grab a picnic table under the pines.

For scrumptious baked goods and made-to-order sandwiches, head to **Borealis Bread** (Rte. 1, Wells, 8:30 A.M.–5:30 P.M. Mon.–Fri., 9 A.M.–4 P.M. Sat. and Sun.), in the Aubuchon Hardware plaza adjacent to the Wells Auto Museum. There are only two tables inside, so take it to the beach.

Pick up all sorts of fresh goodies at the **Wells Farmers Market** in the Town Hall parking lot, 3–6 P.M. Wednesdays.

Family Favorites: No eatery in this category qualifies as heart healthy, so don't say you weren't forewarned.

Longtime favorite **Billy's Chowder House** (216 Mile Rd., just off Rte. 1, 207/646-7558, www.billyschowderhouse.com) has a prime marsh-view location—with wall-to-wall cars in the parking lot. Seafood is the specialty here, but you can get just about anything. It's open 11:30 A.M.–10 P.M. July and August, to 9 P.M. other months, mid-January–early December.

The **Maine Diner** (2265 Post Rd., Rte. 1, Wells, 207/646-4441, www.mainediner.com) has a reputation built on lobster pie and award-winning seafood chowder. Beer and wine only. It's open 7 A.M.–9:30 P.M. (8 P.M. in winter) daily for breakfast, lunch, and dinner (breakfast available anytime). Prices run from less than $10 for diner food to $20 for surf and turf.

Newest among the family favorites is **Mainiax Restaurant** (Rte. 1, Wells, 207/646-0808, www.mainiaxrestaurant.com, 11:30 A.M.–8 P.M., to 9 P.M. Fri. and Sat.) The menu is huge—everyone in the family is sure to find something, the prices are moderate, and the decor is moosey. It's casual and fun.

Turf and Surf: A good steak in the land of lobster? You betcha. **The Steakhouse**

(1205 Post Rd., Rte. 1, 207/646-4200, www
.the-steakhouse.com, 4–9:30 P.M. Tues.–Sun.)
is a great big barn of place where steaks are
hand cut from USDA prime and choice, corn-
fed Western beef that's never been frozen.
Chicken, seafood, lobster (great stew), and
even a vegetarian stir-fry are also on the menu
(entreées $13–26); children's menu available.
Service is efficient. No reservations, so be prepared for a wait. This place is *very* popular.

Locals rave about the seafood chowder and the
lobster stew at **Lord's Harborside Restaurant**
(Harbor Rd., Wells Harbor, 207/646-2651,
www.lordsharborside.com, noon–9 P.M. Wed.–
Mon., to 8 P.M. spring and fall). They should
also rave about the view, a front-row seat on the
Wells working harbor. Sure, it's touristy, but
with these views, who cares? The menu has a
bit of everything, but the emphasis is on fish
and seafood, with most prices in the teens; lobster higher. Kids' menu available.

Fine Dining: Chef Joshua W. Mather
has brought true fine dining to Wells with
Joshua's (1637 Rte. 1, 207/646-3355, www
.joshuas.biz). Chef Joshua grew up on his family's organic farm, just six miles distant, and produce from the farm highlights the menu. In a
true family operation, his parents not only still
work the farm, but they also work in the restaurant, a converted 1774 home with many of
its original architectural elements. Everything is
made on the premises, from the fabulous bread
to the hand-churned ice cream. Entrées range
$19–29. The Atlantic haddock, with carmelized
onion crust, chive oil, and wild mushroom risotto is a signature dish and alone worth coming for. A vegetarian pasta entrée is offered
nightly. Do save room for the maple walnut pie
with maple ice cream. Yes, it's gilding the lily,
but you can always walk the beach afterward.
Reservations are essential for the dining rooms,
but the full menu is also served in the bar. It's
open 5–10 P.M. Monday–Saturday.

INFORMATION
AND SERVICES
At the southern edge of Ogunquit, right next
to the Ogunquit Playhouse, the Ogunquit

Chamber of Commerce's Welcome Center
(Rte. 1, Box 2289, Ogunquit 03907, 207/646-
2939, www.ogunquit.org), provides all the
usual visitor information, including restaurant menus. Ask for the *Touring and Trolley
Route Map,* showing the Marginal Way, beach
locations, and public restrooms. The chamber
of commerce's annual visitor booklet thought-
fully carries a high-tide calendar for the summer. It also has public restrooms.

Just over the Ogunquit border in Wells
(actually in Moody) is the Wells Information Center (Rte. 1 at Bourne Ave., P.O. Box
356, Wells 04090, 207/646-2451, www.wells
chamber.org). A touch-pad kiosk takes over
when the office is closed.

The handsome fieldstone Ogunquit Memorial Library (74 Shore Rd., Ogunquit,
207/646-9024) is the downtown's only National Historic Register building. Or visit the
Wells Public Library (1434 Post Rd., Rte. 1,
207/646-8181, www.wells.lib.me.us).

GETTING THERE
Amtrak's **Downeaster** (800/872-7245, www
.thedowneaster.com), which connects Boston's
North Station with Portland, Maine, stops in
Wells. The Shoreline Explorer trolley connects
in season.

GETTING AROUND
The Maine Turnpike, a toll road, is generally
the fastest route if you're trying to get between
two towns. Route 1 parallels the turnpike, on
the ocean side. It's mostly two lanes and is
lined with shops, restaurants, motels, and other
tourist-oriented sites, which means stop-and-
go traffic that often slows to a crawl. If you're
traveling locally, it's best to walk or use the local
trolley systems, which have the bonus of saving
you the agony of finding a parking spot.

Trolleys
The **Shoreline Explorer** (207/324-5762, www
.shorelineexplorer.com) trolley system makes it
possible to connect from York to Kennebunkport without your car. Each town's system is
operated separately and has its own fees.

Ogunquit Trolley Co. (207/646-1411, www.ogunquittrolley.com) operates seasonal service in Ogunquit, with 39 stops (signposted) weaving through Ogunquit. Each time you board, it'll cost you $1.50 (kids 10 and younger $1), exact fare, but for the same price you can go the whole route—a great way to get your bearings—in about 40 minutes. Hours are 8:30 A.M.–8 P.M. late May–late June and Labor Day to Columbus Day, and 8 A.M.–11 P.M. late June–Labor Day.

Wells's seasonal **Shoreline Trolley System** on Route 1 runs every 20–30 minutes, 9 A.M.–11 P.M. late June–Labor Day. Fare is $1 per trip or $3 for a day pass; family day passes are also available. It operates between Wells and Kennebunk's Lower village.

Another option is the **Hotel Shuttle** (800/696-2463, www.shorelineexplorer.com), which operates between the Amtrak station in Wells and lodging properties within the Shoreline Explorer communities. Fares vary by zone and day, and reservation is required.

The Kennebunks

The world may have first learned of Kennebunkport when George Herbert Walker Bush was president, but Walkers and Bushes have owned their summer estate here for three generations. Visitors continue to come to the Kennebunks (the collective name for Kennebunk, Kennebunkport, Cape Porpoise, and Goose Rocks Beach—combined population about 15,200) hoping to catch a glimpse of the former first family, but they also come for the terrific ambience, the B&Bs, boutiques, boats, biking, and beaches.

The Kennebunks' earliest European settlers arrived in the mid-1600s. By the mid-1700s, shipbuilding had become big business in the area. Two ancient local cemeteries—North Street and Evergreen—provide glimpses of the area's heritage. Its Historic District reveals Kennebunk's moneyed past—the homes where wealthy shipowners and shipbuilders once lived, sending their vessels to the Caribbean and around the globe. Today, unusual shrubs and a dozen varieties of rare maples still line Summer Street—the legacy of ship captains in the global trade. Another legacy is the shiplap construction in many houses—throwbacks to a time when labor was cheap and lumber plentiful. Closer to the beach, in Lower Village, stood the workshops of sailmakers, carpenters, and mastmakers whose output drove the booming trade to success.

While Kennebunkport draws most of the sightseers and summer traffic, Kennebunk feels more like a year-round community. It boasts an interesting, old-fashioned downtown and a mix of shops, restaurants, and attractions. Yes, its beaches, too, are well known, but many visitors drive right through the middle of Kennebunk without stopping to enjoy its assets.

The Kennebunks are communities with conscience—loaded with conservationists working to preserve hikeable, bikeable green space for residents and visitors. Be sure not to miss these trails, bikeways, and offshore islets. Gravestone rubbers will want to check out Evergreen Cemetery, and history buffs should pick up a copy of *Walking in the Port,* the Kennebunkport Historical Society's well-researched booklet of three self-guided historic walking tours. To appreciate the area another way, climb aboard the Intown Trolley, with regular summertime service and lots of entertaining tidbits from the driver.

SIGHTS
◖ Seashore Trolley Museum
There's nothing quite like an antique electric trolley to dredge up nostalgia for bygone days. With a collection of more than 250 transit vehicles (more than two dozen trolleys on display), the Seashore Trolley Museum (195 Log Cabin Rd., P.O. Box A, Kennebunkport 04046, 207/967-2800, www.trolleymuseum.org)

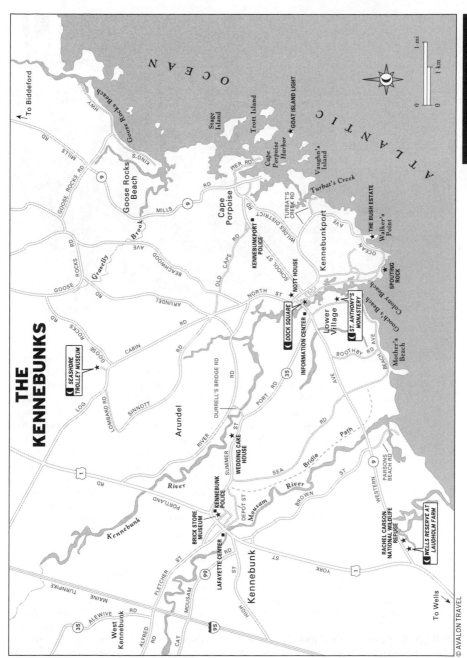

THE
KENNEBUNKS

To Biddeford

OCEAN

ATLANTIC

Goose Rocks Beach

Goose Rocks Beach

Cape Porpoise

Stage Island

Trott Island

★ GOAT ISLAND LIGHT

Cape Porpoise Harbor

Vaughn's Island

Turbat's Creek

THE BUSH ESTATE ■

Walker's Point

★ SPOUTING ROCK

Kennebunkport

KENNEBUNKPORT POLICE ■

NOTT HOUSE

WILDES DISTRICT RD

Colony Beach

Good's Beach

★ ST. ANTHONY'S MONASTERY

Lower Village

DOCK SQUARE ■

INFORMATION CENTER ■

Mother's Beach

SEASHORE TROLLEY MUSEUM ★

Arundel

WEDDING CAKE HOUSE ★

KENNEBUNK POLICE ■

BRICK STORE MUSEUM ■

LAFAYETTE CENTER ■

Kennebunk

Kennebunk River

RACHEL CARSON NATIONAL WILDLIFE REFUGE

WELLS RESERVE AT LAUDHOLM FARM

Bridle Path

Mousam River

West Kennebunk

MAINE TURNPIKE

To Wells

© AVALON TRAVEL

© TOM NANGLE

The Wedding Cake House was built by a local shipbuilder as a wedding gift for his wife.

verges on trolley-mania. Whistles blowing and bells clanging, restored streetcars do frequent trips (between 10:05 A.M. and 4:15 P.M.) on a 3.5-mile loop through the nearby woods. Ride as often as you wish, then check out the activity in the streetcar workshop, and go wild in the trolley-oriented gift shop. Bring a picnic lunch and enjoy it here. Special events are held throughout the summer, including Ice Cream and Sunset Trolley Rides at 7 P.M. every Wednesday and Thursday in July and August. Cost is $4 and includes ice cream. And here's an interesting wrinkle: Make a reservation, plunk down $50, and you can have a one-hour "Motorman" experience driving your own trolley (with help, of course). Museum tickets are $8 adults, $6 seniors, $5.50 kids 6–16, and free for kids 5 and under. The museum is 1.7 miles southeast of Route 1. It's open 10 A.M.–5 P.M. daily mid-June–Columbus Day, and weekends in May, late October, and Christmas Prelude.

Walker's Point: The Bush Estate

There's no public access to Walker's Point, but

you can join the sidewalk gawkers on Ocean Avenue overlooking George and Barbara Bush's summer compound. The 41st president and his wife lead a low-key, laid-back life when they're here, so if you don't spot them through binoculars, you may well run into them at a shop or restaurant in town. Intown Trolley's regular narrated tours go right past the house—or it's an easy, scenic family walk from Kennebunkport's Dock Square. On the way, you'll pass **St. Ann's Church,** whose stones came from the ocean floor, and the paths to **Spouting Rock** and **Blowing Cave**—two natural phenomena that create spectacular water fountains if you manage to be there midway between high and low tides.

Wedding Cake House

The Wedding Cake House (104 Summer St., Kennebunk) is a private residence, so you can't go inside, but it's one of Maine's most-photographed buildings. Driving down Summer Street (Rte. 35), midway between the downtowns of Kennebunk and Kennebunkport, it's hard to miss the yellow and white

Federal mansion with gobs of gingerbread and Gothic Revival spires and arches. Built in 1826 by shipbuilder George Bourne as a wedding gift for his wife, the Kennebunk landmark remained in the family until 1983.

Cape Porpoise

When your mind's eye conjures an idyllic lobster-fishing village, it probably looks a lot like Cape Porpoise—only 2.5 miles from busy Dock Square. Follow Route 9 eastward from Kennebunkport; when Route 9 turns north, continue straight, and take Pier Road to its end. From the small parking area, you'll see lobster boats at anchor, a slew of working wharves, and 19th-century **Goat Island Light,** now automated, directly offshore. In Cape Porpoise are a handful of B&Bs, restaurants, galleries, historic Atlantic Hall, and the extra-friendly Bradbury Bros. Market.

Local History Museums

Occupying four restored 19th-century buildings (including the 1825 William Lord store) in downtown Kennebunk, **The Brick Store Museum** (117 Main St., Kennebunk, 207/985-4802, www.brickstoremuseum.org, 10 A.M.–4:30 P.M. Tues.–Fri. and 10 A.M.–1 P.M. Sat.) has garnered a reputation for unusual exhibits: a century of wedding dresses, a two-century history of volunteer firefighting, life in southern Maine during the Civil War. Admission is by donation ($5 suggested). The museum encourages appreciation for the surrounding Kennebunk Historic District with hour-long **architectural walking tours,** mid-June to mid-October (call for current schedule). Cost is $5. If the schedule doesn't suit, the museum sells a walk-it-yourself booklet for $5.

Owned and maintained by the Kennebunkport Historical Society, **The Nott House** (8 Maine St., Kennebunkport) is a mid-19th-century Greek Revival mansion filled with Victorian furnishings. Be sure to visit the restored gardens. It's open 1–4 P.M. Tuesday–Friday and 10 A.M.–1 P.M. Saturday mid-June–ColumbusDay. Tour tickets are $5 adults, under 18 are free. Hour-long architectural walk-

ing tours of the Kennebunkport Historic District depart from the Nott House at 11 A.M. Thursday and Saturday in July and August, and Saturday only in September. Cost is $3 pp. At the house, you can buy a guidebook for a do-it-yourself tour for $4.

The Kennebunkport Historical Society also owns and maintains a five-building **History Center** (125–135 North St., Kennebunkport, 207/967-2751, www.kporthistory.org). The Town House School, dating from the turn of the 20th century, is the society's research center. The Pasco Exhibit Center, containing the society's offices, also has permanent and rotating exhibits of local memorabilia. It's open 10 A.M.–4 P.M. Tuesday–Friday all year. Admission is $3 adults, free for children under 18. If you call ahead for an appointment, a staff member will let you into the tiny old jail on the grounds.

◖ Dock Square

Even if you're not a shopper, make it a point to meander through the heart of Kennebunkport's shopping district, where one-time fishing shacks have been restored and renovated into upscale shops, boutiques, galleries, and dining spots. Some shops, especially those on upper floors, offer fine harbor views. If you're willing to poke around a bit, you'll find some unusual items that make distinctive souvenirs or gifts—pottery, vintage clothing, books, specialty foods, and, yes, T-shirts.

PARKS AND PRESERVES

Thanks to a dedicated coterie of year-round and summer residents, the foresighted **Kennebunkport Conservation Trust (KCT),** founded in 1974, has become a nationwide model for land-trust organizations. The KCT has managed to preserve from development several hundred acres of land (including 11 small islands off Cape Porpoise Harbor), and most of this acreage is accessible to the public, especially with a sea kayak. The trust has even assumed ownership of 7.7-acre Goat Island, with its distinctive lighthouse visible from Cape Porpoise and other coastal vantage points. Contact the KCT (P.O. Box 7028, Cape Porpoise

© TOM NANGLE

The sculpture on the St. Anthony's Monastery grounds was created for the 1964 World's Fair.

04014, www.thekennebunkportconservation trust.org) for information on its holdings or to volunteer for trail maintenance.

◖ St. Anthony's Monastery

Long ago, 35,000 Native Americans used this part of town for a summer camp. They knew a good thing. So did a group of Lithuanian Franciscan monks who in 1947 fled war-ravaged Europe and acquired the 200-acre St. Anthony's Franciscan Monastery (Beach St., Kennebunk, mailing address P.O. Box 980, Kennebunkport 04046, 207/967-2011). From 1956 to 1969, they ran a high school here. The monks occupy the handsome Tudor great house, but the well-tended grounds (sprinkled with shrines and a recently restored sculpture created by Vytautas Jonynas for the 1964 World's Fair) are open to the public sunrise–sunset. A short path leads from the monastery area to a peaceful gazebo overlooking the Kennebunk River. No pets or bikes. Public restrooms are available. The grounds are open 6 A.M.–8:30 P.M. in summer, closing at 6 P.M. in winter.

Vaughn's Island Preserve

Thanks to the Kennebunkport Conservation Trust, 96-acre Vaughn's Island has been saved for posterity. You'll need to do a little planning, tidewise, since the island is about 600 feet offshore. Consult a tide calendar and aim for low tide close to the new moon or full moon (when the most water drains away). Allow yourself an hour or so before and after low tide, but no longer, or you may need a boat rescue. Wear treaded rubber boots, since the crossing is muddy and slippery with rockweed. Keep an eye on your watch and explore the ocean (east) side of the island, along the beach. It's all worth the effort, and there's a great view of Goat Island Light off to the east. From downtown Kennebunkport, take Maine Street to Wildes District Road. Continue to Shore Road (also called Turbat's Creek Rd.), go 0.6 mile, jog left 0.2 mile more, and park in the tiny lot at the end.

Emmons Preserve

Also under the stewardship of the Kennebunkport Conservation Trust, the Emmons Preserve has two trails (blazed yellow and pink) meandering through 146 acres of woods and fields on the edge of Batson's River (also called Gravelly Brook). The yellow trail gives best access to the water. Fall colors here are brilliant, birdlife is abundant, and you can do a loop in half an hour. But why rush? This is a wonderful oasis in the heart of Kennebunkport. From Dock Square, take North Street to Beachwood Avenue (right turn) to Gravelly Brook Road (left turn). The trailhead is on the left.

Picnic Rock

About 1.5 miles up the Kennebunk River from the ocean, Picnic Rock is the centerpiece of the **Butler Preserve,** a 14-acre enclave managed by The Nature Conservancy. Well named, the rock is a great place for a picnic and a swim, but don't count on being alone. A short trail loops through the preserve. Consider bringing a canoe or kayak (or renting one) and paddle with the tide past beautiful homes and the Cape Arundel Golf Club. From Lower Village Kennebunk, take Route 35 west and hang a right onto Old Port Road. When the road gets close to the Kennebunk River, watch for a Nature Conservancy oak-leaf sign on the right. Parking is along Old Port Road; walk down through the preserve to Picnic Rock, right on the river.

RECREATION
Beaches

Ah, the beaches. The Kennebunks are well endowed with sand but not with parking spaces. Between mid-June and mid-September, you'll need to buy a **parking permit** ($10 a day, $20 a week, $50 a season) from the Kennebunk Town Hall (4 Summer St., 207/985-3675) or the Kennebunkport Police Station (101 Main St., 207/967-4243) or the chamber of commerce. (The police station is open 24 hours; other locations are not.) *You need a separate pass for each town.* Many lodgings provide free permits for their guests—be sure to ask when making room reservations. Or you can avoid the parking nightmare altogether by hopping aboard the Intown Trolley, which goes right by the major beaches.

The main beaches in **Kennebunk** (east to west, stretching about two miles) are 3,346-foot-long Gooch's (most popular), Kennebunk (locally called Middle or Rocks Beach), and Mother's (a smallish beach next to Lords Point, where there's also a playground). Lifeguards are on duty at Gooch's and Mother's Beaches July–Labor Day. Mother's Beach is the home of the Kennebunk Beach Improvement Association. Ask locally about a couple of other beach options.

Kennebunkport's claim to beach fame is three-mile-long Goose Rocks Beach, one of the loveliest in the area. Parking spaces are scarce and biking on Route 9 can be dicey, so if sun and sand are your primary goals, the best solution is to book a room nearby. You'll be about five miles east of all the downtown action, however. To reach the beach, take Route 9 from Dock Square east and north to Dyke

Road (Clock Farm Corner). Turn right and continue to the end (King's Hwy.).

The prize for tiniest beach goes to Colony (officially Arundel) Beach, near The Colony resort complex. It's close to many Kennebunkport lodgings and an easy walk from Dock Square.

Bicycling

A mandatory stop for anyone interested in bicycles and biking is **Cape-Able Bike Shop** (83 Arundel Rd., Town House Corners, Kennebunkport, 207/967-4382, www.capeable bikes.com), a local institution since 1974. The shop has all kinds of rentals and accessories, repairs your wounded gear, sponsors Saturday morning group rides, and provides a free area bike map and the best insider information. (The bike map is also available at the chamber of commerce.) One-day hybrid bike rental is $22. Road- or mountain-bike rental is $27 a day. Map, helmet, and lock are included. Delivery service is available, but the shop operates a seasonal outpost in Lower Village, next to the chamber of commerce.

Cape Abel also offers tours. The 10–15 mile Comfort Beach Tour lasts about 2.5–3 hours and costs $59 adults, $29 kids 15 and younger, including a snack. A Singletrack Adventure moderate to advanced mountain bike tour covers 6–8 miles and lasts about three hours and costs $59 adults, $29 kids, and includes a snack. Tours include rental bike, helmet, carry bag, and water bottle.

Golf

Three 18-hole golf courses make the sport a big deal in the area. **Cape Arundel Golf Club** (19 River Rd., Kennebunkport, 207/967-3494), established in 1897, and **Webhannet Golf Club** (8 Central Ave., Kennebunk, 207/967-2061), established in 1902, are semiprivate and open to nonmembers; call for tee times at least 24 hours ahead. At Cape Arundel, where George Bush plays, no jeans or sweatpants are allowed. In nearby Arundel, **Dutch Elm Golf Course** (5 Brimstone Rd., Arundel, 207/282-9850) is a public course with rentals, pro shop, and putting greens.

Whale Watches and Lobster-Boat Cruises

Whale sightings offshore include finbacks, minkes, and humpbacks, and the local cruise boats have had remarkable success. The 80-foot *Nick's Chance* (4 Western Ave., Lower Village, Kennebunk, 207/967-5507 or 800/767-2628, www.firstchancewhalewatch.com) departs twice daily in July and August for 4.5-hour whale watches to Jeffrey's Ledge, weather permitting. Cost is $40 adults, $25 children ages 3–12, $10 up to age 3. Departure is from Performance Marine in Kennebunk Lower Village (behind Bartley's Restaurant).

Under the same ownership and departing from the same location is the 65-foot open lobster boat *Kylie's Chance,* which departs four times daily in July and August for 1.5-hour scenic lobster cruses. A lobstering demonstration is given on most trips, but never on the evening one. Cost is $18 adults, $12 ages 3–12.

Boating Excursions

For day sailing, the 37-foot one-ton former racing yacht *Bellatrix* (95 Ocean Ave., Kennebunkport, 207/590-1125, www.sailing trips.com) charges $50 pp for a three-hour sail. The handsome 55-foot gaff-rigged schooner *Eleanor* (Arundel Wharf, 43 Ocean Ave., Kennebunkport, 207/967-8809, www.gwi .net/schoonersails) heads out for two-hour sails, weather and tides willing, 1–3 times daily during the summer. Cost is $40 pp.

Canoe and Kayak Rentals

Explore the Kennebunk River. *Kennebunkport Marina* (67 Ocean Ave., Kennebunkport, 207/967-3411) rents canoes and single kayaks for $25/two hours or $45 half day; double kayaks are $45/two hours or $60 half day. Hint: Check the tide before you depart, and plan your trip to paddle with it, rather than against it.

Sportfishing

Saltwater, light tackle, and fly sportfishing are the specialties of **Lady J Sportfishing Charters** (10 Kimball La., Kennebunk, 207/985-7304, www.ladyjcharters.com) aboard the *Rebecca Lynn*. Two-hour trips for kids ($175) include hauling lobster traps. Inshore trips for stripers and bluefish are $300 four hours, $400 six hours. Eight-hour specialty trips for shark or groundfish are $600. Trips leave from the Arundel Wharf Restaurant (Ocean Ave., Kennebunkport).

Surfing

If you want to catch a wave, stop by **Aquaholics Surf Shop** (166 Port Rd., Kennebunk, 207/967-8650, www.aquaholicsurf .com). The shop has boards, wetsuits, and related gear for both sale and rental, and it offers lessons and surf camps.

ENTERTAINMENT

Live entertainment is featured, mostly weekends, at Federal Jack's Brewpub and Windows on the Water, and at the Kennebunkport Inn and The Colony.

Kennebunk Parks and Recreation sponsors **Concerts in the Park,** a weekly series of free concerts 6:30–7:30 P.M. Wednesdays late June to mid-August, in Rotary Park on Water Street.

At 7 P.M. on Thursday evenings in July, the **River Tree Arts Summer Concert Series** brings music to the lawn of the South Congregational Church, Kennebunkport.

Live, professional summer theater is on tap at the **Arundel Barn Playhouse** (53 Old Post Rd., Arundel, 207/985-5552, www.arundel barnplayhouse.com), with productions staged in a renovated 1888 barn, June–September; tickets $19–24.

River Tree Arts (RTA)

The area's cultural spearhead is River Tree Arts (35 Western Ave., Kennebunk, 207/967-9120, www.rivertreearts.org), an incredibly energetic, volunteer-driven organization that sponsors concerts, classes, workshops, exhibits, and educational programs throughout the year.

FESTIVALS AND EVENTS

Concerts and kids' activities are part of the **Summer Solstice Festival** in June. Take the kids to the **Kennebearport Teddy Bear**

Show, usually the second Saturday in August, but watch the reactions of all the grown-ups.

The first two weekends of December mark the festive **Christmas Prelude,** during which spectacular decorations adorn historic homes, candle-toting carolers stroll through the Kennebunks, stores have special sales, and Santa Claus shows up in a lobster boat.

SHOPPING

Lots of small, attractive boutiques surround **Dock Square,** the hub of Kennebunkport, so gridlock often develops in midsummer. Avoid driving through here at the height of the season. Take your time and walk, bike, or ride the local trolley-bus.

Antiques and Art

English, European, and American furniture and architectural elements and garden accessories are just a sampling of what you'll find at **Antiques on Nine** (Rte. 9, Lower Village, Kennebunk, 207/967-0626). Another good place for browsing high-end antiques as well as home accents is **Hurlburt Designs** (Rte. 9, Lower Village, Kennebunk, 207/967-4110). More than 30 artists are represented at **Wright Gallery** (Pier Rd., Cape Porpoise, 207/967-5053).

Jean Briggs represents nearly 100 artists at her topflight **Mast Cove Galleries** (Maine St. and Mast Cove La., Kennebunkport, 207/967-3453), in a handsome Greek Revival house near the Graves Memorial Library. Prices vary widely, so don't be surprised if you spot something affordable. The gallery sponsors 2.5-hour Wednesday evening jazz concerts in July and August ($10 donation includes light refreshments). Call for the schedule. **The Gallery on Chase Hill** (10 Chase Hill Rd., Kennebunkport, 207/967-0049), in the stunningly restored Captain Chase House, next to the Windows on the Water restaurant, mounts rotating exhibits and represents a wide variety of Maine and New England artists. **Compliments** (Dock Sq., 207/967-2269) has a truly unique and fun collection of contemporary fine American crafts, with an emphasis on glass and ceramic wear.

Books, Clothing, and Gifts

The number of shops in this category in the Kennebunks is vast. You'll need to do your own exploring and discovering. Treasures are to be found all over the Kennebunks, but most are clustered around Dock Square (Kennebunkport) and in Lower Village (Kennebunk).

To appreciate the friendly, funky **Kennebunk Book Port** (10 Dock Sq., Kennebunkport, 207/967-3815 or 800/382-2710), climb to the second floor of the antique rum warehouse and read the shop slogan: "Ice cream, candy, children, bare feet, short, long, or no hair, cats, dogs, and small dragons are welcome anytime." This place has character.

Since 1968, **Port Canvas** (9 Ocean Ave., Kennebunkport, 207/985-9765 or 800/333-6788) has been turning out the best in durable cotton-canvas products. Need a new double-bottomed tote bag? It's here. Also here are golf-bag covers, belts, computer cases, day packs, and of course duffel bags.

Quilt fans should make time to visit **Mainely Quilts** (108 Summer St., Rte. 35, Kennebunk, 207/985-4250), behind the Waldo Emerson Inn. The shop has a nice selection of contemporary and antique quilts.

Most of the clothing shops clustered around Dock Square are rather pricey. Not so **Arbitrage** (28 Dock Sq., 207/967-9989), which combines designer consignment clothing with new fashions, vintage designer costume jewelry, shoes, and handbags.

Irresistible eye-dazzling costume jewelry, hair ornaments, handbags, lotions, cards, and other delightful finds fill every possible space at **Dannah** (123 Ocean Ave., Kennebunkport, 207/967-8640), in the Breakwater Spa building, with free customer-only parking in the rear.

Earth-Friendly Toiletries

Lafayette Center, a handsomely restored mill building housing boutiques and eateries, is also home to the **Tom's of Maine Natural Living Store** (Storer St., just off Main St., Kennebunk, 207/985-3874), an eco-sensitive local-turned-global firm that makes soaps, toothpaste, oils, and other products. "Factory seconds" are real bargains.

ACCOMMODATIONS

Rates listed are for peak season; most stay open through Christmas Prelude.

Inns and Hotels

Graciously dominating its 11-acre spread at the mouth of the Kennebunk River, **The Colony Hotel** (140 Ocean Ave. at King's Hwy., P.O. Box 511, Kennebunkport 04046, 207/967-3331 or 800/552-2363, www.thecolonyhotel.com/maine), springs right out of a bygone era, and its distinctive cupola is an area landmark. It's had a long-time commitment to the environment, with recycling, waste-reduction, and educational programs. There's a special feeling here, with cozy corners for reading, lawns and gardens for strolling, a beachfront swimming pool, room service, tennis privileges at the exclusive River Club, bike rentals, massage therapy, and lawn games. Doubles begin at $190, including breakfast, but not $5 pp daily service charge. Pets are $25 per night. Higher-priced rooms have ocean views, others have garden views. The hotel dining room is open to the public for breakfast, lunch, and dinner; reservations are advisable. Brunch is a big winner, 11 A.M.–2 P.M. Sunday mid-June–Labor Day. Open mid-May–late October.

The The White Barn Inn and its siblings have cornered the ultrahigh-end, boutique inn market, with four in this category. Most renowned is the **White Barn Inn** (37 Beach Ave., Kennebunk, mailing address P.O. Box 560, Kennebunkport 04046, 207/967-2321, www.whitebarninn.com, $340–780). Also part of the empire are **The Beach House Inn** (211 Beach Ave., Kennebunk, 207/967-3850, www.beachhseinn.com, $299–525), **The Breakwater Inn, Hotel, and Spa** (127 Ocean Ave., Kennebunkport, 207/967-3118, www.thebreakwaterinn.com, $290–345), **The Yachtsman Lodge and Marina** (Ocean Ave., Kennebunkport, 207/967-2511, www.yachtsmanlodge.com, $299–314), and three restaurants. Rooms in all properties have air-conditioning, phones,

satellite TV, VCR and CD players; bikes and canoes are available for guests. Rates include bountiful continental breakfasts and afternoon tea, but check out the off-season packages, especially if you wish to dine at one of the restaurants. All but the Beach House are within easy walking distance of Dock Square.

The White Barn Inn is the most exclusive, with five-diamond and Relais and Chateaux status. It's home to one of the best restaurants in the *country* (see *Food*). Many rooms have fireplaces and marble baths with separate steam showers and whirlpool tubs (you can even arrange for a butler-drawn bath). Service is impeccable, and nothing has been overlooked in terms of amenities. There's an outdoor heated European-style brimming pool, where lunch is available, weather permitting, and a full-service spa. For a truly away-from-it-all feeling, consider staying at one the inn's ultraprivate riverfront Wharf Cottages ($585–1,300—ouch!), which face Dock Square from across the river. The inn also has a Hinckley Talaria-44 available for charter.

The Beach House Inn faces Middle Beach and is a bit less formal than the White Barn, but the service is on par. The Breakwater, at the mouth of the Kennebunk River, comprises a beautifully renovated, historical inn with wraparound porches and an adjacent, more modern, newly renovated building that houses rooms and a full-service spa. The complex also is home to Stripers Restaurant (see *Food*). Finally, there's the Yachtsman, an innovative blend of a motel and B&B, with all rooms opening onto patios facing the river and the marina where George H. W. Bush keeps his boat.

Innkeeper (and restaurateur and artist) Jack Nahil seems to have a magic touch with everything he undertakes. Now he's rehabbed the ◖ **Cape Arundel Inn** (208 Ocean Ave., Kennebunkport, 207/967-2125, www.capearundelinn.com), making it (and its restaurant) a prime destination. The fabulous ocean view (all but two rooms overlook the Bush estate) doesn't hurt, either. The Cape Arundel compound comprises the Shingle-style main inn building (seven rooms, most with water view;

$295–375 peak), the Rockbound motel-style building (six rooms with sea-view balconies; $315–375 peak), and the Carriage House Loft, a large suite on the upper floor of the carriage house ($295 peak); an expanded continental breakfast buffet is included. Most rooms have fireplaces; Rockbound and Carriage House have TV. Open March–January 1. The inn's restaurant, where every table has an ocean view, earns raves for its intriguingly creative cuisine; entrées are $20–34.

If nonstop beaching is your vacation goal, book one of the 22 rooms at **Tides Inn by-the-Sea** (252 Kings Hwy., Goose Rocks Beach, Kennebunkport, 207/967-3757, www.tidesinnbythesea.com), directly across the street from superb Goose Rocks Beach. Decor at the John Calvin Stevens–designed Victorian inn is funky, whimsical (faux painting, costumed dummies, a resident ghost named Emma), and altogether fun. Next door is **Tides Too**, a modern, condo-type building with one- and two-bedroom efficiencies by the week ($3,500 for four people). Inn rooms, early June–Labor Day, go for $195–325 d, including continental breakfast. Open mid-May–mid-October. The inn's first-rate Belvidere Club is open to the public Wednesday–Sunday for breakfast and creative dinners with a small but select menu (entrées $22–25).

The sprawling, riverfront **Nonantum Resort** (95 Ocean Ave., P.O. Box 2626, Kennebunkport 04046, 207/967-4050 or 800/552-5651, www.nonantumresort.com, $189–439) complex, which dates from 1884, includes a bit of everything, from simple rooms with an old-fashioned, Victorian decor to modern family suites with kitchenettes. Some rooms have views to the open ocean. Facilities include a dining room, outdoor heated pool and whirlpool, and docking facilities—two tour boats are based here. All 115 rooms have air-conditioning, Wi-Fi, and TV; some have refrigerators. Rates include a full breakfast. The dining room is also open for dinner and, in July and August, lunch. Packages, many of which include dinner, are a good choice. Do note: Weddings take place here almost every weekend. Open April–early December.

Innkeepers and chefs Brian and Shanna O'Hea (they met at the Culinary Institute of America) have created a lovely escape at **The Kennebunk Inn** (45 Main St., Kennebunk, 207/985-3351, www.thekennebunkinn.com, $125–160 peak), a rambling 1799 inn in downtown Kennebunk. No two rooms are alike, and renovation is an ongoing process. Some have air-conditioning or antique claw-foot tubs or fireplaces, all have Wi-Fi, TV, and phone. The inn has both a dining room (5–9 P.M. Wed.–Sat., entrées $19–28) and pub (5–9 P.M. daily, $7–15). Rates include a continental breakfast. A few pet-friendly rooms ($20 per stay) are available.

Bed-and-Breakfasts

Three of Kennebunkport's lovliest inns are rumored to have been owned by brothers-in-law, all of whom were sea captains. Rivaling the White Barn Inn for service, decor, amenities, and overall luxury is the three-story **⊄ The Captain Lord Mansion** (P.O. Box 800, Kennebunkport 04046, 207/967-3141 or 800/522-3141, www.captainlord.com, $215–450), which is one of the finest B&Bs anywhere. And no wonder. Innkeepers Rick and Bev Litchfield have been at it since 1978, and they're never content to rest on their laurels. Each year the inn improves upon seeming perfection. If you want to be pampered and stay in a meticulously decorated and historical B&B with marble bathrooms (heated floors, many with double whirlpool tubs), fireplaces, original artwork, phones, and air-conditioning in all rooms and even a few cedar closets, then look no further. Even breakfast is a special affair, with fresh-squeezed orange juice made from oranges flown in daily. Bicycles and beach towels and chairs are available. Afternoon treats are provided.

The elegant, Federal-style **The Captain Jefferds Inn** (5 Pearl St., P.O. Box 691, Kennebunkport 04046, 207/967-2311 or 800/839-6844, www.captainjefferdsinn.com, $150–360), in the historic district, provides the ambience of a real captain's house. Each of the 15 rooms and suites (11 in the main house and four more in the carriage house) have plush linens, fresh flowers, down comforters, CD players, and air-conditioning; some have fireplaces, whirlpool tubs, and other luxuries. A three-course breakfast and afternoon tea are included. **The Captain Fairfield Inn** (8 Pleasant St., P.O. Box 3089, Kennebunkport 04046, www .captainfairfield.com, $225–340) is perhaps the most modest architecturally of the three, but it doesn't scrimp on amenities. Innkeepers Rob and Leigh Blood are slowly replacing traditional decor with a more contemporary style. All rooms have flat-screen TVs, air-conditioning, and Wi-Fi; some have gas fireplaces. The lovely grounds are a fine place to retreat for a snooze in the hammock or a game of croquet. Rates include a four-course breakfast.

Hidden in a woodsy, private residential neighborhood, the lovely **Old Fort Inn** (Old Fort Ave., P.O. Box M, Kennebunkport 04046, 207/828-3678, www.oldfortinn.com) is the kind of place that you might not want to leave, even for touring or shopping. Once part of a Colony-style grand hotel, the stable has been renovated into elegant, spacious guest rooms, many with fireplaces and/or jetted tubs, all with wetbars equipped with fridge and microwave. The main building houses a huge common room and a screened porch. On the 15-acre premises are a heated pool, tennis court, and antiques shop. Breakfast is a lavish hot-and-cold buffet. Rates are $160–375.

The inspiration for the **English Meadows Inn** (141 Port Rd., Lower Village, Kennebunk, 207/967-5766, www.englishmeadowsinn.com, $175–305 peak) came from those lovely English manor homes, elegant yet comfortable. The 1860s original Greek Revival architecture was married to the Victorian Queen Anne style later in the century. Inside, the woodwork gleams, the floors, scattered with Asian-style rugs, shine, and the antiques and country comfort pieces mix with an unusual collection of Asian and English antiques, collected by the owner when living abroad. Books fill the inn's many nooks and crannies. Rooms are split between the main house, carriage house (where children are welcome), and a pet-friendly, two-bedroom cottage, a good choice for young families. Breakfast is elaborate.

The low-key, turn-of-the-20th-century **Green Heron Inn** (126 Ocean Ave., Kennebunkport, 207/967-3315, www.greenheron inn.com) sees many repeat guests. Ten rooms and a two-story cottage have TV, phones, air-conditioning, private baths; some have fireplace, microwave, or refrigerator; and most have cove views. Prices are $145–175 d (cottage is $250). Children are welcome; some pets are accepted ($10 per night). Also included is breakfast—one of the best in town—served in the coveside breakfast room.

Neighboring the Wedding Cake House, **The Waldo Emerson Inn** (108 Summer St., Rte. 35, Kennebunk, 207/985-4250, www.waldo emersoninn.com) has a charming colonial feel—as it should, since the main section was built in 1784. Poet Ralph Waldo Emerson spent many a summer in this, his great-uncle's home. Six attractive rooms, three with working fireplaces, are $135–150 peak, including full breakfast. In-room massages are available. Quilters, take note: In the barn is Mainely Quilts, a well-stocked quilt shop, open daily in summer.

You'll awake to the drone of lobster-boat engines at **The Inn at Harbor Head** (41 Pier Rd., Cape Porpoise, Kennebunkport, 207/967-5564, www.harborhead.com), an idyllic spot on Cape Porpoise Harbor, 2.5 miles from Dock Square. Hand-painted murals, monogrammed bathrobes, flower bouquets, a superb library, hammocks in the yard, Wi-Fi, and outstanding views are just a few of the many pluses here. It offers three rooms and one good-size suite, some with whirlpool tub, fireplace, or private deck. Rates are $195–325 d.

Here's a bargain: The nonprofit **Franciscan Guest House** (28 Beach Ave., P.O. Box 980, Kennebunkport 04046, 207/967-4865, www .franciscanguesthouse.com), on the grounds of the monastery, has accommodations spread among two buildings, as well as three other Tudor-style cottages. Accommodations are basic, but they do have some nice amenities, including TV, air-conditioning, saltwater pool, and beach passes. A buffet breakfast is included in the rates, and a buffet dinner often is available. There is no daily mail service, but fresh towels are provided daily. Rooms are $92–154, and one- to three-bedroom suites are $149–279. No credit cards.

Motels and Cottages

Patricia Mason is the 12th-generation innkeeper at ❰ **The Seaside Motor Inn and Cottages** (80 Beach Ave., Kennebunk, mailing address P.O. Box 631, Kennebunkport 04046, 207/967-4461 or 800/967-4461 www.kennebunkbeach.com, $229–249), a property that has been in her family since the mid-1600s. What a location! The 22-room motel and 10 cottages sit on 20 acres bordered by the Atlantic Ocean, the Kennebec River, and Gooch's River. It's the only truly beachfront property in the area, with a private beach for guests. Motel rooms are spacious, with TV, air-conditioning, and refrigerators. A continental breakfast is included in the rates. The one- to four-bedroom cottages are rented by the week early and late season and by the month in July and August.

With indoor and outdoor heated pools and whirlpools and a good-size fitness center, the **Rhumb Line Motor Lodge** (Ocean Ave., P.O. Box 3067, Kennebunkport 04046, 207/967-5457 or 800/337-4862, www.rhumblinemaine.com) is a magnet for families. This well-managed two-story establishment in a quiet residential area three miles from Dock Square has easy access to the trolley-bus service. Fifty-nine large rooms have private balcony or patio, phones, air-conditioning, Wi-Fi, cable TV, and small refrigerators. Free continental breakfast. From late May to mid-September, weather permitting, there are nightly poolside lobster bakes. Rates are $155–185; kids 12 and under stay free. Closed in January.

Compared with other intown properties, the **Fontenay Terrace Motel** (128 Ocean Ave., Kennebunkport, 207/967-3556, www.fontenaymotel.com, $140–175 peak) is a bargain. Second-generation innkeepers David and Paula Reid keep the place spotless. It borders a tidal inlet and has a private grassy and shaded lawn, perfect for retreating from the hubbub of busy Kennebunkport. Each of the eight rooms has air-conditioning, minifridge, microwave,

Wi-Fi, cable TV, and phone; some have water views. A small beach is 300 yards away, and it's a pleasant one-mile walk to Dock Square.

The clean and simple **Cape Porpoise Motel** (12 Mills Rd., Rte. 9, P.O. Box 7218, Cape Porpoise 04014, 207/967-3370, www.capeporpoisemotel.com, $125–150 peak) is a short walk from the harbor. All rooms have TV and air-conditioning, some have kitchenettes; rates include a continental breakfast, with muffins, fruit, and other surprises. Also available by the week or month are efficiencies with full kitchens, phones, and one or more bedrooms.

FOOD

Hours are for peak season, when reservations are advised. Call ahead September–June.

Local Flavors

All Day Breakfast (55 Western Ave., Rte. 9, Lower Village, Kennebunk, 207/967-5132) is a favorite meeting spot, offering such specialties as invent-your-own omelettes and crepes, Texas French toast, and the ADB sandwich. ADB is open 7 A.M.–1:30 P.M. weekdays in summer (to 2 P.M. weekends). Closed mid-December–mid-January.

It's hard to choose the perfect pastry from the large selection at **Port Bakery and Café** (181 Port Rd., Kennebunk, 207/967-2263, opens at 7 A.M. daily). Hot breakfasts are also available, as are soups and sandwiches and other goodies. Eat in or outside on the deck or take it all to go.

Conveniently near the Kennebunk and Kennebunkport Chamber of Commerce, **H. B. Provisions** (15 Western Ave., Lower Village, Kennebunk, 207/967-5762) has an excellent wine selection, along with plenty of picnic supplies, newspapers, and all the typical general-store inventory. It also serves breakfast and prepares hot and cold sandwiches, salads, and wraps. It's open daily all year.

The name says it all at **The Bakery and Café** (50 Main St., Kennebunk, 207/985-7888, 6 A.M.–6 P.M. daily and 5–8 P.M. Fri.), a bright and airy downtown spot. Soups, salads, sandwiches, fancy coffees, and pastries are the usuals, but it's also open Friday nights for pizza and stromboli.

Equal parts fancy food and wine store and gourmet café, **Cape Porpoise Kitchen** (Rte. 9, Cape Porpoise, 207/967-1150, 7 A.M.–7 P.M. daily) sells sandwiches, salads, prepared foods, desserts, and everything to go with.

While away an afternoon with a traditional English tea at the **English Meadows Inn** (141 Port Rd., Lower Village, Kennebunk, 207/967-5766, 2–4 P.M. Thurs.–Sat.). Choose from a cream tea ($12.95), with tea, scones, and sweets, or a Queen's tea ($19.95), which adds petite sandwiches to the tray. It's beautifully presented, served in a lovely room or perhaps the garden. Reservations required.

The **Kennebunk Farmers Market** sets up shop mid-May–mid-October in the Grove Street municipal parking lot off Route 1 (behind the Mobil station). Hours are 8 A.M.–noon Saturday. Vendors sell crafts, condiments, fresh produce (including organic), flowers, breads, biscotti; special events (tastings, etc.) are sometimes on the agenda.

Family Favorites

The nearest thing to being afloat is sitting at a riverfront deck table at **Arundel Wharf** (43 Ocean Ave., Kennebunkport, 207/967-3444), where passing tour and lobster boats provide lunchtime entertainment. Captain's chairs and chart-topped tables complete the nautical picture. Burgers and fries are always on the menu for kids; adults might want to limit their choices to similar fare—dinner entrées are $14–30. Open at 11:30 A.M. daily for lunch and dinner mid-May–mid-December; reservations are wise for dinner.

A bit off the beaten track is **Lucas on 9** (62 Mills Rd./Rte. 9, Cape Porpoise, 207/967-0039, www.lucason9.com), a family-friendly, family-operated restaurant, and the Lane family knows food. Chef Jonathan Lane makes everything from scratch and delivers on his mother Deborah's mission of "Good American food at affordable prices." Jonathan's travels have infused his preparations with more than a bow toward his work on Southern riverboats (Louisiana

spicy crab soup, bread pudding with whisky). There are at least six specials nightly in addition to plenty of other choices ($13–30). The restaurant is named for Jonathan's brother Lucas, who died in 2005. It's open 11:30 A.M.–9 P.M., closed Tuesday and mid-December–early April.

Grab a stool at the counter, slip into a booth, or wait for a table at the **Wayfarer** (Pier Rd., Cape Porpoise, 207/967-8961), a casual restaurant that serves breakfast, lunch, and dinner to locals and in-the-know tourists (dinner entrées $10–19). It's open 7 A.M.–12:30 P.M. and 5–8 P.M. Tuesday–Saturday and 7 A.M.–noon Sunday. Good lobster stew; nightly dinner specials. Most choices are in the $10–19 range. No credit cards.

Casual Dining

Brian and Shanna O'Hea met at the Culinary Institute of America, and they've had a fine time creating **Academe** (The Kennebunk Inn, 45 Main St., Kennebunk, 207/985-3351, www.kennebunkinn.com), which they bill as a Maine brasserie and tavern. The choices vary from panini and pizzas to cashew-crusted wild salmon, which puts it within most budgets. The lunch menu, served Monday–Friday, comprises mostly soups and salads. A full dinner menu is served Tuesday–Saturday; a limited menu on Sunday and Monday. Children's menu selections are $4.50.

Just west of the junction of Routes 9 and 35 is the casually elegant **Grissini Trattoria** (27 Western Ave., Kennebunk, 207/967-2211, 5:30–9 P.M., Fri. and Sat. to 9:30 P.M.), a sibling of the White Barn Inn. Attentive service, an inspired Tuscan menu (entrées $15–33), and a bright, open-beamed space make it an appealing spot. In nice weather, try for the sunken patio.

The views complement the food at **Hurricane Restaurant** (29 Dock Sq., Kennebunkport, 207/967-9111, www.hurricane restaurant.com), where the dining room hangs over the river. A longtime favorite in Ogunquit, this is now the only location, but it continues to reel in the crowds, both for location and for quality and creativity. Dinner entrées begin at $19.

Eat well and feel good about it at **Bandaloop** (2 Dock Sq., Kennebunkport, 207/967-4994, www.bandaloop.biz, 5:30–9:30 P.M. daily), a hip, vibrant restaurant where chef/owner W. Scott Lee likes to push boundaries. Lee named the restaurant for author Tom Robbins's fictional tribe that knew the secret to eternal life. Lee believes the secret is fresh, local, organic, and cruelty free. Selections vary from meats and fish to vegetarian and vegan ($14–24); pair a "center of plate selection" with one of eight sauces, choose from nightly specials, or simply make a meal from the appetizers.

Fancy to Fine Dining

Every table at the **Cape Arundel Inn** (208 Ocean Ave., Kennebunkport, 207/967-2125, www.capearundelinn.com) has a knockout view of crashing surf, and the food matches the view. White-clothed tables topped with cobalt blue glassware add to the inn's casual yet elegant feel. Local artwork covers the walls. Chef Rich Lemoine's menu emphasizes fish and seafood in classic preparations, all prepared and served with care. Prices range from high $20s to mid $30s. Open for dinner daily (closed Mon. off season).

Floor-to-ceiling windows frame the Kennebunk River breakwater, providing perfect views for those indulging at **Stripers** (at the Breakwater Inn, 127 Ocean Ave., Kennebunkport, 207/967-5333), another White Barn Inn sibling. The emphasis on fish is also accented by a saltwater tank with coral reef and exotic fish. It's no surprise that fish and seafood are the specialties, with most entrées in the $18–28 range. Dress is casual. Valet parking is available. It's open 5:30–9 P.M., to 9:30 P.M. Friday and Saturday, April–late October, also 11:30 A.M.–2 P.M. Memorial Day–Labor Day.

Fusion cuisine reigns at **On the Marsh** (46 Western Ave./Rte. 9, Lower Village, Kennebunk, 207/967-2299, www.onthemarsh .com), a restored barn overlooking marshlands leading to Kennebunk Beach. Entrée range is $21–35. The decor here is astonishing, courtesy of owner Denise Rubin, an interior designer: raspberry exterior and art and antiques on both

floors of the interior. Dining choices include both an "owner's table" and a "kitchen table." Entrées might include grilled tuna with French bean salad and seared sea scallops with lobster risotto. Quiet piano music adds to the elegant but unstuffy ambience; service is attentive. Reservations are essential in midsummer. It's open for dinner 5:30–9:30 P.M. daily. Closed January.

Winner of a raft of culinary awards, **Windows on the Water** (12 Chase Hill Rd., Kennebunk 04043, 207/967-3313 or 800/773-3313, www .windowsonthewater.com, 11:30 A.M.–2:30 P.M. and 5:30–9:30 P.M., to 10:30 P.M. Fri. and Sat.) has been filling its screened porch, patio, and dining rooms since 1985. It's appropriately named, with big windows providing views over nearby shops to the busy harbor. Lunch entrées are $9–17; dinner entrées are $19–39, the high end for such dishes as lobster ravioli and Thai lobster; and the White Porch Bistro (opens for dinner at 5 P.M.) serves pub-style fare. Best deals are the five-course lunch for $15 and the three-course dinner for $33; add $10 for a bottle of wine. Reservations are advisable—essential in midsummer.

Both the view and the food are outstanding at ◖ **Pier 77** (77 Pier Rd., Cape Porpoise, 207/967-8500, 11:30 A.M.–2:30 P.M. and 5–9 P.M. daily). Chef Peter and his wife, Kate, have created an especially welcoming restaurant, where the menu varies from duck three ways to seafood mixed grill (entrées $16–30). Frequent live entertainment provides nice background and complements the views over Cape Porpoise Harbor, with lobster boats hustling to and fro. Reservations are advisable. Practically hidden downstairs is **The Ramp Bar and Grille** (11:30 A.M.–10 P.M. daily), with lighter fare and a sports-pub decor.

Destination Dining

One of Maine's biggest splurges is **The White Barn Inn** (37 Beach Ave., Kennebunkport, 207/967-2321, www.whitebarninn.com, 6–9 P.M. Mon.–Thurs., 5:30–9:15 P.M. Fri.–Sun.), with haute cuisine, haute prices, haute-rustic barn. In summer, don't be surprised to run into members of the senior George Bush clan (probably at the back window table). Soft piano music accompanies impeccable service and Chef Jonathan Carter's outstanding four-course fixed-price menu ($92 pp, excluding wine). Reservations are essential—well ahead during July and August—and you'll need a credit card (cancel 24 hours ahead or you'll have a charge). No jeans or sneakers—jackets are required. It's New England's only four-star, five-diamond, Relais Gourmand restaurant. Closed early–late January.

Lobster and Clams
Nunan's Lobster Hut (9 Mills Rd., Cape Porpoise, 207/967-4362, 5 P.M.–close daily) is an institution. Sure, other places might have better views, but this casual dockside eatery with indoor and outdoor seating has been serving lobsters since 1953.

Adjacent to the bridge connecting Kennebunkport's Dock Square to Kennebunk's Lower Village is another time-tested classic, the **Clam Shack** (Rte. 9, Kennebunkport, 207/967-2560, www.theclamshack.net). The tiny take-out stand serves perhaps the state's best lobster rolls, jam-packed with meat and available with either butter or mayo, and deelish fried clams. It opens at 11 A.M. daily May–October for lunch and dinner.

Bush-watchers often head to **Mabel's Lobster Claw** (Ocean Ave., Kennebunkport, 207/967-2562, 11:30 A.M.–3 P.M. and 5–9 P.M. daily), hoping to spot the former president (the little place is just around the corner from Walker's Point). Try Mabel Hanson's chowder or a lobster roll and see why the restaurant's a favorite (entrées top off around $30); reservations are wise.

INFORMATION AND SERVICES
Information
The Kennebunk and Kennebunkport Chamber of Commerce (17 Western Ave., Rte. 9, Lower Village, P.O. Box 740, Kennebunk 04043, 207/967-0857, www.visitthekennebunks.com) produces an excellent area guide to accommodations, restaurants, area maps, bike maps, tide calendars, recreation, and beach parking permits.

Check out Louis T. Graves Memorial Public Library (18 Maine St., Kennebunkport, 207/967-2778, www.graves.lib.me.us) or Kennebunk Free Library (112 Main St., 207/985-2173, kennebunklibrary.org).

Public Restrooms
Public toilets are at Gooch's and Mother's Beaches and at St. Anthony's Monastery, the chamber of commerce building (17 Western Ave.), and at the chamber's Dock Square Hospitality Center.

GETTING THERE AND AROUND
Amtrak's **Downeaster** (800/872-7245, www.thedowneaster.com) connects Boston's North Station with Portland, Maine, with stops in Wells, Saco, and Old Orchard Beach (seasonal).

Vermont Transit (800/552-8737, www.vermonttransit.com), a division of Greyhound bus lines, stops at the Wells Regional Transportation Center daily on the Boston–Portland–Bangor route. The trolley connects with the bus in season and stops in Kennebunk's Lower Village.

From Memorial Day to mid-October, the **Intown Trolley** (207/967-3686, www.intowntrolley.com) operates a 45-minute narrated sightseeing tour throughout Kennebunk and Kennebunkport, originating in Dock Square and making regular stops at beaches and other attractions. The entire route takes about 45 minutes, with the driver providing a hefty dose of local history and gossip. Seats are park bench–style. An all-day ticket is $13 adults, $6 children 3–14. You can get on or off at any stop. The trolley operates hourly 10 A.M.–5 P.M. in July and August, to 4 P.M. in spring and fall.

The free **Shoreline Explorer Kennebunk Shuttle** (www.shorelineexplorer.com) circulates hourly between Grove Street parking lot, Stop and Shop, Landing Store, Lower Village, and the beaches 10 A.M.–10:30 P.M. late June–Labor Day. It connects with the Shoreline and Intown trolleys.

Old Orchard Beach Area

Seven continuous miles of white sand beach has been drawing vacation-oriented folks for generations to the area stretching from Camp Ellis, in Saco, to Pine Point, in Scarborough. Cottage colonies and condo complexes dominate at the extremities, but the center of activity has always been and remains Old Orchard Beach.

In its heyday, Old Orchard Beach's pier reached far out into the sea, huge resort hotels lined the sands, and wealthy Victorian folk (including Rose Fitzgerald and Joe Kennedy, who met on these sands in the days when men strolled around in dress suits and women toted parasols) came each summer to see and be seen.

Storms and fires have taken their toll through the years, and the grand resorts have been replaced by endless motels, many of which display *Nous parlons Français* signs to welcome the masses of French Canadians who arrive each summer. They're accompanied by young families, who come for the sand and surf, and T-shirted and body-pierced young pleasure seekers, who come for the nightlife. (You'd better like people if you stop here, because this town welcomes tourists—the population expands from about 8,000 in winter to about 100,000 in midsummer.)

Although some residents are pushing gentrification, and a few projects are pushing it in that direction, Old Orchard Beach remains somewhat honky-tonk, and most of its visitors would have it no other way. French fries, cotton candy, and beach-accessories shops line the downtown, and as you get closer to the pier, you pass arcades and amusement parks. There's not a kid on earth who wouldn't have fun in Old Orchard—even if some parents might find it all a bit much.

Much more sedate are the villages on the fringes. The **Ocean Park** section of Old Orchard, at the southwestern end of town, was established in 1881 as a religious summer-cottage community. It still offers interdenominational services and vacation Bible school, but it also has an active cultural association

that sponsors concerts, Chautauqua-type lectures, films, and other events throughout the summer. All are open to the public.

South of that is **Camp Ellis.** Begun as a small fishing village named after early settler Thomas Ellis, Camp Ellis is crowded with longtime summer homes that are in a constant battle with the sea. A nearly mile-long granite jetty—designed to keep silt from clogging the Saco River—has taken the blame for massive beach erosion since constructed. But the jetty is a favorite spot for wetting a line (no fishing license needed) and for panoramic views off toward Wood Island Light (built in 1808) and Biddeford Pool. Camp Ellis Beach is open to the public, with lifeguards on duty in midsummer. Parking—scarce on hot days—is $10 a day.

As you head north from Old Orchard you'll pass **Pine Point,** another longtime community

Although storms have taken their toll over the years, the Old Orchard Pier still extends over the beach to the ocean's edge.

of vacation homes. Services are few and parking is $10 a day.

Most folks get to Old Orchard by passing through **Saco** and **Biddeford,** which have long been upstairs/downstairs sister cities, with wealthy mill owners living in Saco and their workers (and workplaces) in Biddeford. But even those personalities have always been split—congested, commercial Route 1 is part of Saco, and the exclusive enclave of Biddeford Pool is, of course, in below-stairs Biddeford. Saco still has an attractive downtown, with boutiques and stunning homes on Main Street and beyond.

Blue-collar Biddeford is working hard to change its milltown image. It's home to the magnificent Biddeford City Theater and the University of New England, and as a Main Street community, it's getting a much-needed sprucing up. New shops and restaurants are balancing the numerous thrift shops downtown, and artisans and woodworkers are filling vacant mills. Another Biddeford hallmark is its Franco American tradition—thanks to the French-speaking workers who sustained the textile and shoemaking industries in the 19th century. Never is the heritage more evident than during Biddeford's annual La Kermesse festival in late June.

SIGHTS

Founded in 1866, the **Saco Museum** (371 Main St., Saco, 207/283-3861, www.dyer librarysacomuseum.org, noon–4 P.M. Tues.–Sun., to 8 P.M. Thurs., $4 adults, $3 seniors, $2 students) rotates selections from its outstanding collection, including 18th- and 19th-century paintings, furniture, and other household treasures. Lectures, workshops, and concerts are also part of the annual schedule. Admission is free after 4 P.M. Thursday.

PARKS AND PRESERVES

Saco Bay Trails, a local land trust, has produced a very helpful trail guide that includes the Saco Heath, the East Point Sanctuary, and more than a dozen other local trails. The Cascade Falls trail, for example, is a half-mile stroll ending at a waterfall. Copies are available for $5 at a number of Biddeford and Saco locations

(including the Dyer Library) or from Saco Bay Trails (P.O. Box 7505, Ocean Park 04063). Trail information is also on the organization's website: www.sacobaytrails.org.

◖ East Point Sanctuary

Owned by Maine Audubon, the 30-acre East Point Sanctuary is a splendid preserve at the eastern end of Biddeford Pool. Crashing surf, beach roses, bayberry bushes, and offshore Wood Island Light are all features of the two-part perimeter trail here—skirting the golf course of the exclusive Abenakee Club. Allow at least an hour; even in fog, the setting is dramatic. During spring and fall migrations, it's one of southern Maine's prime birding locales, so you'll have plenty of company if you show up then, and the usual streetside parking may be scarce. It's open sunrise–sundown all year. It's poorly signposted (perhaps deliberately?), so here are the directions: From Route 9 (Main St.) in downtown Biddeford, take Route 9/208 (Pool Rd.) southeast about five miles to the Route 208 turnoff to Biddeford Pool. Go 0.6 mile on Route 208 (Bridge Rd.), and then left onto Mile Stretch Road. Continue to Lester B. Orcutt Boulevard, turn left, and go to the end. For further information, contact Maine Audubon (20 Gilsland Farm Rd., P.O. Box 6009, Falmouth 04105, 207/781-2330).

The Heath

Owned by The Nature Conservancy, 870-acre **Saco Heath Preserve** is the nation's southernmost "raised coalesced bog," where peat accumulated through eons into two above-water dome shapes that eventually merged into a single natural feature. For a bit of esoterica, it's the home of the rare Hessel's hairstreak butterfly. Pick up a map at the parking area and follow the mile-long, self-guided trail through the woods and then into the heath via a boardwalk. Best time to come is early–mid-October, when the heath and woodland colors are positively brilliant and insects are on the wane. You're likely to see deer and perhaps even spot a moose. The preserve entrance is on Route 112, Buxton Road, two miles west of I-95. Open all year, sunrise–sunset, it's also popular with snowshoers and cross-country skiers in winter.

Ferry Beach State Park

When the weather's hot, arrive early at Ferry Beach State Park (Bay View Rd., off Rte. 9, Saco, 207/283-0067, $3 adults, $1 children 5–11, free for seniors and kids under 5), a pristine beach backed by dune grass on Saco Bay. In the 117-acre park are changing rooms, restrooms, lifeguard, picnic tables, and five easy interconnected nature trails winding through woodlands, marshlands, and dunes. (Later in the day, keep the insect repellent handy.) It's open daily, late May–late September, but accessible all year. (Trail markers are removed in winter.)

RECREATION
Golf

Opened in 1922 as a nine-hole course, the

AMUSEMENT PARKS AND AMUSING PLACES

If you've got kids or just love amusement parks, you'll find Maine's best in the Old Orchard area, where sand and sun just seem to complement arcades and rides perfectly.

The biggie is **Funtown/Splashtown USA** (774 Portland Rd., Rte. 1, Saco, 207/284-5139 or 800/878-2900, www.funtownsplashtownusa .com). Ride Maine's only wooden roller coaster; fly down New England's longest and tallest log flume ride; free fall 200 feet on Dragon's Descent; get wet and go wild riding speed slides, tunnel slides, raft slides, and river slides or splashing in the pool. Add a huge kiddie ride section, games, food, and other activities for a full day or family fun. Funtown opens weekends in early May, Splashtown in mid-June; everything's up and running daily late June–Labor Day, when Funtown is open 10 A.M.–9 P.M., to 10 P.M. Saturday, and Splashtown 10 A.M.–6 P.M. Rates vary by height, with Big for those 48 inches and taller, Little for those 38-48 inches tall and seniors, and free for kids less than 38 inches tall. A Funtown USA Ride Pass provides two rides on the Grand Prix Racers and unlimited use of all other rides for $25 Big, $17 Little, and a night special valid after 5 P.M. is $18 Big and $12 Little. A Splashtown unlimited slide pass is $20 Big and $17 Little. Combo passes for two rides on the Grand Prix Racers and unlimited use of all other rides, slides, and pools, is $34 Big and $25 Little. Season passes also are available.

Three miles north of Funtown/Splashtown USA, **Aquaboggan Water Park** (980 Portland Rd., Rte. 1, Saco, 207/282-3112, www.aqua bogganwaterpark.com) is wet and wild, with such stomach turners as the Yankee Ripper, the Suislide, and the Stealth, with an almost-vertical drop of 45 feet – enough to accelerate to 30 mph on the descent. Wear a bathing suit that won't abandon you in the rough-and-tumble. Also, if you wear glasses, safety straps and plastic lenses are required. Besides all the water stuff, there are shuffleboard courts, minigolf, an arcade, picnic tables, and snack bars. Lots of ticket options cover varying numbers of attractions. You can pay as you go, one attraction at a time, but it adds up quickly; Mondays and Fridays are $10 for the day. It's open 10 A.M.–6 P.M. daily late June–Labor Day.

The biggest beachfront amusement park, **Palace Playland** (1 Old Orchard St., Old Orchard, 207/934-2001, www.palaceplayland .com) has more than 25 rides and attractions packed into four acres, including a giant water slide, fun house, bumper cars, Ferris wheel, roller coaster, and a 24,000-square-foot arcade with more than 200 games. For a bird's-eye view of the area, ride the 75-foot-high gondola Sunwheel. Get soaked riding the Log Flume. Rev up the action on two roller coasters, one with a five-story drop, both with high-speed twisting turns. Kiddie Land has more than a dozen rides, including a fun house and a splashing whale. An unlimited pass is $26.50 per day; a kiddie pass good for all two-ticket rides is $19.50; two-day, season, and per ride tickets ($2–4) are available. Open Memorial Day–Labor Day.

The Old Orchard Pier, jutting 475 feet into the ocean from downtown, is a minimall of shops, arcades, and fast-food outlets. Far longer when it was built in 1898, it's been lopped off gradually by fires and storms. The current incarnation has been here since the late 1970s.

Biddeford-Saco Country Club (101 Old Orchard Rd., Saco, 207/282-5883) added a back nine in 1987 (toughest hole on the par-71 course is the 11th). Tee times not usually needed. Fees are moderate.

Covering more than 300 acres is the challenging 18-hole, par-71 **Dunegrass Golf Club** (200 Wild Dunes Way, Old Orchard Beach, 207/934-4513 or 800/521-1029). Greens fees are a bit steep, but well worth a splurge. Tee times are essential. The sprawling modern clubhouse has a restaurant and pro shop.

Sea Kayaking
Gone with the Wind (Yates St., Biddeford Pool, 207/283-8446, www.gwtwonline.com) offers two tours, afternoon and sunset, with prices varying with the number of people on the tour (two people are about $85 pp). Wetsuits are supplied. The most popular trip is to Beach Island. Also available are rentals ($40 half day, $60 full day). Kids and seniors get a $10 pp discount.

Surfing
A seasonal branch of **Aquaholics Surf Shop** (www.aquaholicsurf.com) rents surfboards, bodyboards, wetsuits, and related gear from a kiosk next to the pier and Palace Playland.

ENTERTAINMENT
Biddeford City Theater
Designed by noted architect John Calvin Stevens in 1896, the 500-seat National Historic Register Biddeford City Theater (205 Main St., P.O. Box 993, Biddeford 04005, 207/282-0849, www.citytheater.org) has been superbly restored, and acoustics are excellent even when Eva Gray, the resident ghost, mixes it up backstage. A respected community theater group mounts a winter drama season and showcases other talent throughout the year. Check local papers or call for schedule.

Fireworks
Fireworks are set off by the pier in Old Orchard Beach at 9:45 P.M. every Thursday late June–Labor Day.

Live Music and Performances
You'll find plenty of it in Old Orchard Beach at places including **Pier Patio Pub, Village Inn, PICS Pizza,** and **Surf 6.** In Biddeford, there's live music at **Bebe's Burritos** (140 Main St., 207/283-4222, www.bebesburritos.com) 7–10:30 P.M. every Thursday, Friday, and Saturday.

Free concerts are staged by the pier at 7 P.M. every Monday and Tuesday in July and August.

Another option for family concerts and other performances is the **Old Orchard Beach Pavilion** (Union Ave. and 6th St., 207/934-2024, www.oobpavilion.org).

Ocean Park's **Temple,** a 19th-century octagon that seats 800-plus, is the venue for Sunday-night concerts (7:30 P.M., $8 adults) and many other programs throughout the summer.

EVENTS
La Kermesse (meaning the fair or the festival) is Biddeford's summer highlight, when nearly 50,000 visitors pour into town on the last full weekend in June (Thurs.–Sun.) to celebrate the town's Franco American heritage. Local volunteers go all out to plan block parties, a parade, games, carnival, live entertainment, and traditional dancing—most of it centered on Biddeford's Waterhouse Field. Then there's *la cuisine franco-américaine;* you can fill up on *boudin, creton, poutine, tourtière, tarte au saumon,* and crepes (although your arteries may rebel).

Generally scheduled for the Saturday of the same weekend, the **Saco Sidewalk Arts Festival** involves more than 150 artists exhibiting their work all along Saco's Main Street. Strolling musicians, kids' activities, and food booths are all part of the well-organized, day-long event.

In July, the parishioners of St. Demetrios Greek Orthodox Church (186 Bradley St., Saco, 207/284-5651) go all out to mount the annual **Greek Heritage Festival,** a three-day extravaganza of homemade Greek food, traditional Greek music and dancing, and a craft fair. Be sure to tour the impressive $1.5 million domed church building.

Football fans might want to watch the annual **Shriner's Lobster Bowl,** an all-star high school football game to benefit Shriner's Hospitals for Children.

The beaches come to life in July. Early July brings the annual **parade and Sandcastle Contest** to Ocean Park.

One weekend in mid-August, Old Orchard Beach's **Beach Olympics** is a family festival of games, exhibitions, and music benefiting Maine's Special Olympics program.

ACCOMMODATIONS

The area has hundreds of beds—mostly in motel-style lodgings. The chamber of commerce is the best resource for motels, cottages, and the area's more than 3,000 campsites. Only recently have a few B&Bs popped up.

The Old Orchard Beach Inn (6 Portland Ave., Old Orchard Beach, 207/934-5834 or 877/700-6624, fax 207/934-0782, www.old orchardbeachinn.com, $110–185) was rescued from ruin by owner Steve Cecchetti and opened in summer 2000. Built in 1730, and most recently known as the Staples Inn, the National Historic Register building seemed destined for the wrecker's ball in 1997. Now it's been transformed, with 18 antiques-filled rooms with air-conditioning, phones, and TV. Continental breakfast is included in the rates; a two-bedroom suite is $250–400. Open all year.

Practically next door is **The Atlantic Birches Inn** (20 Portland Ave., Rte. 98, P.O. Box 334, Old Orchard Beach 04064, 207/934-5295 or 888/934-5295), with 10 guest rooms with air-conditioning in a Victorian house and separate cottage. Breakfast is hearty continental, and there's a swimming pool. The beach is an easy walk. Rates run $101–131 d. It's open all year, but call ahead off-season.

Look out to sea from the porch or deck of **Cristina's Bed and Breakfast** (36 Main Ave., Camp Ellis Beach, Saco, 207/282-7483, trahan@prexar.com, $75–135), Cristina and Paul Trahan's vintage gingerbread-trimmed cottage with three pleasant guest rooms (one with private bath), all with Victorian furnishings. Rates include continental breakfast. No credit cards.

Brand spanking new and adjacent to the pier is the **Grand Victorian** (1 East Grand Ave., Old Orchard Beach, 207/934-0759, www.grandvictorianwaterfront.com), with oceanfront condominiums available for the week. Rates begin around $2,000 for a one-bedroom sleeping five. On-site are an indoor heated pool, fitness room, sauna, and spa.

FOOD
Old Orchard Beach

Dining is not Old Orchard's strong point. Nicest (although service and quality are inconsistent) is **Joseph's by the Sea** (55 W. Grand Ave., Old Orchard Beach, 207/934-5044, www.josephsbythesea.com, 7–11 A.M. and 5–9 P.M. daily), a quiet, shorefront restaurant amid all the hoopla. Request a table on the screened patio. The menu—French with a dash of Maine—has entrées in the $18–30 range. Reservations advisable in midsummer.

Immerse yourself in a Victorian manor at **Landmark** (28 E. Grand Ave., Old Orchard Beach, 207/934-0156, 5–8 P.M., to 9 P.M. Fri. and Sat.). Ornate tin ceilings, shining wood floors, and paintings distinguish the dining areas, which include an enclosed porch. Entrées ($19–22) vary from Parmesan haddock to lacquered duck; a kid's menu is available. Early-bird specials are served until 6 P.M.

Camp Ellis

Two well-seasoned family restaurants service Camp Ellis. **Wormwood's Restaurant** (16 Bay Ave., Camp Ellis Beach, Saco, 207/282-9679, 11:30 A.M.–9 P.M.), next to the stone jetty, still draws the crowds and keeps its loyal clientele happy with ample portions and $6–16 entrées. Cajun-style seafood is a specialty.

At **Huot's Seafood Restaurant** (Camp Ellis Beach, Saco, 207/282-1642, www.huots seafoodrestaurant.com, 11 A.M.–9 P.M. Tues.–Sun.), portions are large, prices are not.

Saco

Craving fast-ish food? The Camire family operates Maine's best home-grown option, **Rapid Ray's** (189 Main St., 207/283-4222, www.rapidrays.biz, 11 A.M. –12:30 A.M. Mon.–Thurs., to 1:30 A.M. Fri. and Sat., and noon–10 P.M. Sun.). Burgers, dogs, and fried foods are the specialty at the standing-room only joint.

Locals give a thumbs-up to **Mia's** (17 Pepperell Square, Saco, 207/284-6427, www.miasatpepperellsquare.com, 11 A.M.–2 P.M. and 5:30–9:30 P.M. Tues.–Sat., 9 A.M.–2 P.M. Sun.), a cheerful little place serving brunch (Maine lobster Benedict is $12) and dinner, BYOB. Make a meal from small plates ($7–10) or opt for entrées ranging from pan-seared scallops to braised short rib ($17–25). A three-course fixed-price menu, with several choices for each, is $30.

Biddeford/Biddeford Pool

For a town grounded in Franco American culture, Biddeford has an expanding array of ethnic choices, including a few that garner praise far beyond city limits: **Jewel of India** (26 Alfred St., 207/282-5600), the Vietnamese **Que Huong** (49 Main St., 207/571-8050), **Thai Siam** (144 Main St., 207/294-3300), and **Bebe's Burritos** (140 Main St., 207/283-4222), all serving lunch and dinner.

Buffleheads (122 Hills Beach Rd., 207/284-6000, www.buffleheadsrestaurant.com) is a family dining find with spectacular ocean views. Ray and Karen Wieczoreck opened the restaurant in 1994 and have built a strong local following through the years. The kids can munch on pizza, burgers, spaghetti, and other favorites while adults savor well-prepared seafood with a homestyle spin or landlubber classics. Lobster pie and a turkey dinner with all the trimmings are both perennial favorites here. Prices range $6–25. It's open 11:30 A.M.–2 P.M. and 5–8:30 P.M. daily, closed Monday offseason. Hills Beach Road branches off Route 9 at the University of New England campus.

Take your lobster or fried seafood dinner to an oceanfront picnic table on the grassy lawn behind **F. O. Goldthwaite's** (3 Lester B. Orcott Blvd., Biddeford Pool, 207/284-8872, 11 A.M.–7:30 P.M. daily), an old-fashioned general store. Salads, fried seafood, sandwiches (grilled salmon BLT!), and kid-friendly fare round out the menu ($3–15).

INFORMATION AND SERVICES

Sources of tourist information are Biddeford-Saco Chamber of Commerce and Industry (110 Main St., Saco 04072, 207/282-1567, fax 207/282-3149, www.biddefordsacochamber.org), Old Orchard Beach Chamber of Commerce (1st St., P.O. Box 600, Old Orchard Beach 04064, 207/934-2500 or 800/365-9386, www.oldorchardbeachmaine.com), and Ocean Park Association (P.O. Box 7296, Ocean Park 04063, 207/934-9068, www.oceanpark.org).

The Dyer Library (371 Main St., Saco 04072, 207/282-3031, www.sacomuseum.org), next door to the Saco Museum, attracts scads of genealogists to its vast Maine history collection. Also check out Libby Memorial Library (Staples St., Old Orchard Beach, 207/934-4351, www.ooblibrary.org).

GETTING THERE

Amtrak's **Downeaster** (800/872-7245, www.thedowneaster.com) connects Boston's North Station with Portland, Maine, with stops in Wells, Saco, and Old Orchard Beach (seasonal).

GETTING AROUND
Bus and Trolley

The **Biddeford-Saco-Old Orchard Beach Transit Committee** (207/282-5408, www.shuttlebus-zoom.com) operates three systems that make getting around simple. Between late June and Labor Day, the **Old Orchard Beach Trolley** operates on a regular schedule, connecting restaurants and campgrounds. Service begins at 10 A.M. and ends at midnight. Cost is $1 per ride; children under five ride free. **ShuttleBus Tri-Town Service** provides frequent weekday and less-frequent weekend service (except national holidays) between Biddeford, Saco, and Old Orchard Beach. One-way fare is $1.25 ages five and older, exact change required. **ShuttleBus InterCity Service** connects Biddeford, Saco, and Old Orchard with Portland, South Portland, and Scarborough. Fares vary by zones, topping at $5 for anyone over five.

GREATER PORTLAND

Whenever national magazines have articles highlighting the 10 best places to live, Greater Portland often makes the list. The very reasons that make the area so popular with residents make it equally attractive to visitors. Small in size, but big in heart, Greater Portland entices visitors with the staples—lighthouses, lobster, and L. L. Bean—but wows them with everything else it offers. It's the state's cultural hub, with performing arts centers, numerous festivals, and varied museums; a dining destination, with nationally recognized chefs as well as an amazing assortment and variety of everyday restaurants; and despite its urban environment, it has a mind-boggling amount of recreational opportunities.

Portland's population hovers around 65,000, but when the suburbs are included, it climbs to nearly a quarter of a million souls, making it Maine's largest, by far. Take a swing through the bedroom communities of Scarborough, Cape Elizabeth, and South Portland, and you'll better understand the area's popularity: easily accessible parks, beaches, rocky ledges, and lighthouses, all minutes from downtown. Then head north, passing through suburban Falmouth and Yarmouth and into Freeport, home of mega–sports retailer L. L. Bean. If you look carefully during your travels through suburbia, you'll still see the vestiges of the region's heritage: sailboats and lobster boats, traps and buoys piled on lawns or along driveways and, tucked here and there, farms with farmstands brimming with fresh produce.

Greater Portland also marks a transitional point on Maine's coastline. The long sand

© TOM NANGLE

GREATER PORTLAND

HIGHLIGHTS

◖ **The Old Port:** Plan to spend at least a couple of hours browsing the shops, dining, and enjoying the energy of this restored historic district (page 89).

◖ **Portland Museum of Art (PMA):** This museum houses works by masters such as Winslow Homer, John Marin, Andrew Wyeth, Edward Hopper, and Marsden Hartley, as well as works by Monet, Picasso, and Renoir (page 94).

◖ **Victoria Mansion:** This house is considered one of the most richly decorated dwellings of its period remaining in the country (page 94).

◖ **Portland Observatory:** Climb the 103 steps to the orb deck of the only remaining maritime signal tower on the Eastern Seaboard, and you'll be rewarded with views from the White Mountains to Casco Bay's islands (page 94).

◖ **Portland Head Light:** This lighthouse, commissioned by President George Washington, is fabulously sited on the rocky ledges of Cape Elizabeth (page 97).

◖ **Casco Bay Tour:** Take a three-hour tour on the mailboat, which stops briefly at five islands en route (page 97).

◖ **Lobstering Cruise:** Go out on a working lobster boat in Portland Harbor, see the sights, and perhaps return with a lobster for dinner (page 101).

◖ **L. L. Bean:** The empire's flagship store is in Freeport, and no trip to this shopping mecca is complete without a visit (page 114).

◖ **L. L. Bean Outdoor Discovery Schools:** Don't miss the opportunity for an inexpensive introduction to a new sport (page 117).

◖ **Atlantic Seal Cruises:** Cruise with Capt. Tom Ring to Eagle Island, once home to Arctic explorer Adm. Robert Peary (page 118).

LOOK FOR ◖ TO FIND RECOMMENDED SIGHTS, ACTIVITIES, DINING, AND LODGING.

beaches of the Southern Coast begin to give way to a different coastline, one dotted with islands and edged with a jumble of rocks and ledges interrupted by rivers and coves.

While it might seem tempting to dismiss Portland in favor of seeking the Real Maine elsewhere along the coast, the truth is, the Real Maine is here. And while Portland alone provides plenty to keep a visitor busy, it's also an excellent base for day trips to places such as the

Kennebunks, Freeport, Brunswick, and Bath, where more of that Real Maine flavor awaits.

PLANNING YOUR TIME

July and August are the most popular times to visit, but Greater Portland is a year-round destination. Spring truly arrives by mid-May, when most summer outfitters begin operations at least on weekends. September is perhaps the loveliest month of the year

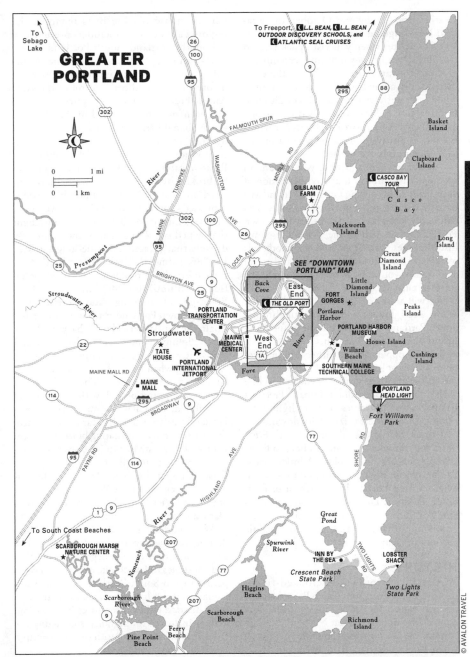

GREATER PORTLAND

To Sebago Lake

GREATER PORTLAND

26
100
95
302

0 ___ 1 mi
0 ___ 1 km

To Freeport, **L.L. BEAN**, **L.L. BEAN OUTDOOR DISCOVERY SCHOOLS**, and **ATLANTIC SEAL CRUISES**

9
295
88

FALMOUTH SPUR

MIDDLE RD

WASHINGTON

MAINE TURNPIKE

302
100
26
295

OCEAN AVE

GILSLAND FARM

CASCO BAY TOUR

C a s c o B a y

Basket Island

Clapboard Island

Mackworth Island

Long Island

Great Diamond Island

Little Diamond Island

Peaks Island

SEE "DOWNTOWN PORTLAND" MAP

25
Presumpscot River

95

BRIGHTON AVE

9
25

Back Cove

East End

FORT GORGES

THE OLD PORT

Portland Harbor

PORTLAND HARBOR MUSEUM

House Island

Cushings Island

Stroudwater River

PORTLAND TRANSPORTATION CENTER

Stroudwater

MAINE MEDICAL CENTER

West End

1A

Willard Beach

SOUTHERN MAINE TECHNICAL COLLEGE

22

TATE HOUSE

PORTLAND INTERNATIONAL JETPORT

Fore River

MAINE MALL RD

MAINE MALL

114

295

BROADWAY

9

PORTLAND HEAD LIGHT

Fort Williams Park

SHORE RD

95

114

PAYNE RD

HIGHLAND AVE

77

1
9

To South Coast Beaches

SCARBOROUGH MARSH NATURE CENTER

Nonesuch River

207

77

Spurwink River

Great Pond

INN BY THE SEA

Crescent Beach State Park

LOBSTER SHACK

TWO LIGHTS RD

Two Lights State Park

Higgins Beach

9

Scarborough River

207

Scarborough Beach

Richmond Island

Pine Point Beach

Ferry Beach

weatherwise, and by mid-October, those fabled New England maples are turning crimson. No matter when you visit, pack layered clothing. Damp, foggy mornings can quickly give way to warm sunshine. Truly, there are usually only a handful of days each summer when folks wish they had an air conditioner, but for those days, you'll want to dress accordingly. A light sweater, fleece, or windbreaker is always handy when a sea breeze kicks up or after the sun sets.

To do the region justice, you'll want to spend at least three or four days here, more if your plans call for using Greater Portland as a base for day trips to more distant points. You can easily kill two days alone in downtown Portland, what with all the shops, museums, historical sites, waterfront, and neighborhoods to explore. If you're staying in town and are an avid walker, you won't need a car to get to the in-town must-see sights.

You will need a car to reach beyond the city. Allow a full day for a leisurely tour through South Portland and Cape Elizabeth and on to Prouts Neck in Scarborough.

Rabid shoppers should either stay in Freeport or allow at least a day for L. L. Bean's and the 100 or so outlets nearby. If you're traveling with a supershopper, don't despair. Freeport has parks and preserves that are light-years removed from the frenzy of its downtown, and from the fishing village of South Freeport, you can take an excursion boat to Eagle Island, home of Arctic explorer Admiral Peary. Really, you simply must get out on the water, whether from Portland's waterfront or from South Freeport. Hop a ferry to one of the islands of Casco Bay, take an evening sail, an excursion to Eagle Island, or even a paddle around the islands in a kayak.

HISTORY

Portland's downtown, a crooked-finger peninsula projecting into Casco Bay and today defined vaguely by I-295 at its "knuckle," was named Machigonne (Great Neck) by the Wabanaki, the Native Americans who held sway when English settlers first arrived in 1632.

Characteristically, the Brits renamed the region Falmouth (it included present-day Falmouth, Portland, South Portland, Westbrook, and Cape Elizabeth) and the peninsula Falmouth Neck, but it was 130 years before they secured real control of the area. Anglo-French squabbles, spurred by the governments' conflicts in Europe, drew in the Wabanaki from Massachusetts to Nova Scotia. Falmouth was only one of the battlegrounds, and it was a fairly minor one. Relative calm resumed in the 1760s, only to be broken by the stirrings of rebellion centered on Boston. When Falmouth's citizens expressed support for the incipient revolution, the punishment was a 1775 naval onslaught that wiped out 75 percent of the houses—a debacle that created a decade-long setback. In 1786, Falmouth Neck became Portland, a thriving trading community where shipping flourished until the 1807 imposition of the Embargo Act. Severing trade and effectively shutting down Portland Harbor for a year and a half, the legislation did more harm to America's fledgling colonies than to the French and British it was designed to punish.

In 1820, when Maine became a state, Portland was named its capital. The city became a crucial transportation hub with the arrival of the railroad. The Civil War was barely a blip in Portland's history, but the year after it ended, the city suffered a devastating blow: exuberant Fourth of July festivities in 1866 sparked a conflagration that virtually leveled the city. The Great Fire spared only the Portland Observatory and a chunk of the West End. Evidence of the city's Victorian rebirth remains today in many downtown neighborhoods.

After World War II, Portland slipped into decline for several years, but that is over. The city's waterfront revival began in the 1970s and continues today, despite commercial competition from South Portland's Maine Mall; Congress Street has blossomed as an arts and retail district; public green space is increasing; and an influx of immigrants is changing the city's cultural makeup. With the new century, Portland is on a roll.

Portland

Often compared to San Francisco (an oft-cited, unchallenged, but never verified statistic boasts it has more restaurants per capita than any city but San Francisco), Portland is small, friendly, and easily explored on foot—although at times, it may seem that no matter which direction you head, it's uphill. The heart of Portland is the peninsula jutting into Casco Bay. It's bordered by the Eastern and Western Promenades, Back Cove, and the working waterfront. Salty sea breezes cool summer days and make winter ones seen even chillier. Unlike that other city by the bay, snow frequently blankets Portland from December into March.

Portland is Maine's most ethnically diverse city, with active refugee resettlement programs and dozens of languages spoken in the schools. Although salty sailors can still be found along the waterfront, Portland is increasingly a professional community, with young, upwardly mobile residents spiffing up Victorian houses and infusing new energy and money into the city's neighborhoods.

The region's cultural hub, Portland has a striking art museum housing three centuries of art and architecture and a world-class permanent collection, performing arts centers, active historical and preservation groups, an art school and a university, a symphony orchestra, numerous galleries, coffeehouses, and enough activities to keep culture vultures busy well into the night, especially in the thriving, handsomely restored Old Port and the up-and-coming Arts District.

Portland's also a sports- and outdoor-lovers' playground, with trails for running, biking, skating, and cross-country skiing, watersports aplenty, and a beloved minor league baseball team, the Sea Dogs. When city folks desire to escape, they often hop a ferry for one of the islands of Casco Bay or head to one of the parks, preserves, or beaches in the suburbs.

Still, Portland remains a major seaport. Lobster boats, commercial fishing vessels, long-distance passenger boats, cruise ships, and local ferries dominate the working waterfront, and the briny scent of the sea—or bait—seasons the air.

PORTLAND NEIGHBORHOODS

The best way to appreciate the character of Portland's neighborhoods is on foot. So much of Portland can (and should) be covered on foot that it would take a book to list all the possibilities, but several dedicated volunteer groups have produced guides to facilitate the process.

Greater Portland Landmarks (207/774-5561, www.portlandlandmarks.org) is the doyenne, founded in 1964 to preserve Portland's historic architecture and promote responsible construction. The organization has published more than a dozen books and booklets, including *Discover Historic Portland on Foot,* a packet of four well-researched walking-tour guides to architecturally historic sections of Portland's peninsula: Old Port, Western Promenade, State Street, and Congress Street. It's available for $5.95 at local bookstores, some gift shops, and the Visitor Information Center (245 Commercial St., 207/772-5800).

Also available at the Visitor Information Center is a map, $1, detailing 36 significant **antislavery sites** in Portland. It also includes stories and information about the slave trade and what life was like for blacks during the slavery era. Six significant sites, each marked, are included in a 1.6-mile walking tour.

The *Portland Women's History Trail* details four loops—Congress Street, Munjoy Hill, State Street, and the West End—with about 20 stops on each loop. Among the sites: a long-gone chewing-gum factory where teenage girls worked 10-hour shifts. The trail guide is available for $8.50 in selected bookstores and at the Maine History Gallery gift shop (489 Congress St., Portland, 207/879-0427).

Portland Trails (1 India St., Portland, 207/775-2411, www.trails.org), a dynamic membership conservation organization incorporated in 1991, continually adds to the mileage it has mapped out for hiking and biking around Portland. The group's accomplishments include the 2.1-mile Eastern Promenade Trail, a landscaped bayfront dual pathway

GREATER PORTLAND

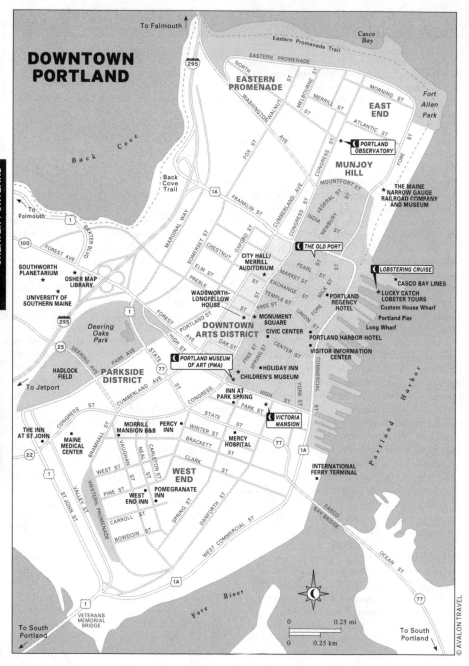

DOWNTOWN PORTLAND

© TOM NANGLE

GREATER PORTLAND

The revitalized Old Port, with its Victorian architecture, brick sidewalks, and boutiques, is the city's shopping neighborhood.

circling the base of Munjoy Hill and linking East End Beach to the Old Port, and a continuing trail connecting the Eastern Prom with the 3.5-mile Back Cove Trail, on the other side of I-295. Nearly two dozen trails are maintained, and the group also holds organized events—a great way to meet some locals. Contact Portland Trails for a colorful foldout map of Portland's entire trail and park system—including some proposed routes—a joint effort of Portland Trails and the Greater Portland Council of Governments' Kids and Transportation Program. Better still, join Portland Trails ($35 a year) and support its ambitious efforts.

(The Old Port

Tony shops, cobblestone sidewalks, replica streetlights, and a casual, upmarket crowd (most of the time) set the scene for a district once filled with derelict buildings. The 1970s revival of the Old Port has infused funds, foot traffic, and flair into this part of town. Scores of unusual shops, ethnic restaurants, and

spontaneous street-corner music make it a fun area to visit year-round. Nightlife centers on the Old Port, where a couple of dozen bars keep everyone hopping until after midnight. Police keep a close eye on the district, but it can get a bit dicey after 11 P.M. on weekends. Caveat emptor—or maybe caveat peregrinator!

At 10:30 A.M. daily July–September, knowledgeable guides from Greater Portland Landmarks (207/774-5561, www.portland landmarks.org) lead fascinating 90-minute **Old Port walking tours** in downtown Portland. No reservations needed. Buy tickets at the Visitor Information Center (245 Commercial St.), where the tours begin and end. Cost is $8 pp; kids under 16 with an adult are free.

Congress Street/Downtown Arts District

Bit by bit, once-declining Congress Street is becoming revitalized, showcasing the best of the city's culture. Artists, starving and otherwise, spend much of their time here, thanks

CASCO BAY ISLANDS

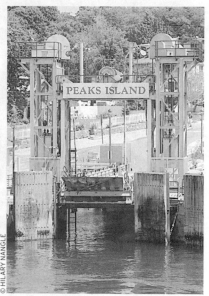

© HILARY NANGLE

The Casco Bay Lines ferry dock on Peaks Island requires precise maneuvering by the captain.

Casco Bay is dotted with so many islands that an early explorer thought there must be at least one for every day of the year and so dubbed them the Calendar Islands. Truthfully, there aren't quite that many, even if you count all the ledges that appear at low tide. No matter, the islands are as much a part of Portland life as the Old Port.

Casco Bay Lines is the islands' lifeline, providing car and passenger service daily in summer. Perhaps the best way to see the highlights is aboard the daily mail-boat run. Indeed, on hot days, it may seem as if half the city's population is hopping a ferry to enjoy the cool breezes and calming views.

PEAKS ISLAND

Peaks Island is a mere 20-minute ferry ride from downtown Portland, so it's no surprise that it has the largest year-round population. Historically a popular vacation spot – two lodges were built for Civil War veterans – it's now an increasingly popular suburb.

Although you can walk the island's perimeter in 3-4 hours, the best way to see it is to take a bike ($5 extra on the ferry) and pedal around clockwise. It can take less than an hour to do the five-mile island circuit, but plan on relaxing on the beach, savoring the views, and visiting the museums. Rental bikes are available on the island from Brad Burkholder at **Brad's and Wyatt's Bike Shop** (115 Island Ave., Peaks Island, 207/766-5631, about $20/day, hourly rental available, 10 A.M.-6 P.M.).

Another way to see the island is on a golf-cart tour with **Island Tours** (207/653-2549, islandtours@att.net, $15 adults, $12 seniors, $8 child), which offers a variety of 90-minute island tours as well as one-hour sunset tours ($10 adults, $8 seniors, $5 child). Admission to the Fifth Maine Regiment Museum is included in longer tours.

Civil War buffs have two museums worth a visit. The **Fifth Maine Regiment Center** (45 Seashore Ave., Peaks Island, 207/766-3330, www.fifthmainemuseum.org, 11 A.M.-4 P.M. daily July 1-Labor Day, to 5 P.M. weekends late May-July 1 and early Sept.-mid-Oct., $5 donation requested), a Queen Anne-style cottage built by Civil War veterans in 1888, now houses exhibits on the war and island history. Just a few steps away is the **Eighth Maine Regimental Memorial** (13 Eighth Maine Ave., Peaks Island, 207/766-5086, noon-3 P.M. Tues.-Sat. July 1-early Sept., $5 donation requested). Tours detail the building's fascinating history and its collection of artifacts pertaining to the Eighth Maine as well as material on the island, World War II, and more. Rustic lodging is available.

Another museum perhaps worthy of a visit just for its quirkiness is the **Umbrella Cover Museum** (207/766-4496), where owner Nancy 3. Hoffman (yes, 3) displays her collection.

Hungry? **The Cockeyed Gull** (78 Island Ave., 207/766-2880, www.cockeyedgull.com) is the best choice for either lunch or dinner.

GREAT DIAMOND ISLAND

Great Diamond is a totally different scene. In 1891, the U.S. government began building an Army post on Great Diamond, a quick ferryboat ride from the Portland harbor front. Completed in 1907, **Fort McKinley** (named after President William McKinley) became part of Portland Harbor's five-fort defense system during World Wars I and II. When peace descended, the fort's red-brick structures were left to crumble for nearly five decades. In 1984, developers stepped in, bought the derelicts, and began restoration – albeit not without financial setbacks and opposition from environmental organizations.

Today, the 193-acre **Diamond Cove** enclave boasts barracks-turned-townhomes, single-family houses, a general store (open daily late May–Labor Day), outdoor theater, a beach bar (open mid-June–mid-September), an art gallery, no cars (only bikes and golf carts), and the **Diamond's Edge Restaurant** (207/766-5850, www.diamondsedge.com).

GREAT CHEBEAGUE

Everyone calls Great Chebeague just "Chebeague" (shuh-BIG). Yes, there's a Little Chebeague, but it's a state-owned park, and no one lives there. Chebeague is the largest of the bay's islands – 4.5 miles long, 1.5 miles wide – and the relatively level terrain makes it easy to get around. Don't plan to bring a car; it's too complicated to arrange.

You can bike the leisurely 10-mile circuit of the island in a couple of hours, but unless you're in a hurry, allow time to relax and enjoy your visit. Pick up an island map at the Portland terminal or on the ferry; all the high points are listed, including two beach access points off North Road.

If the tide is right, cross the sandspit from The Hook and explore **Little Chebeague.** Start out about two hours before low tide (preferably around new moon or full moon, when the most water drains away) and plan to be back on Chebeague no later than two hours after low tide.

Back on Great Chebeague, when you're ready for a swim, head for **Hamilton Beach,** a beautiful small stretch of sand lined with dune grass, not far from the Chebeague Island Inn. Also on this part of the island is **East End Point,** with a spectacular panoramic view of Halfway Rock and the bay.

Chebeague Transportation Company, from Cousins Island, Yarmouth, also services the island.

EAGLE ISLAND

Seventeen-acre Eagle Island (207/624-6080, www.pearyeagleisland.org, 10 A.M.–5 P.M. mid-June–early Sept.) juts out of Casco Bay, rising to a rocky promontory 40 feet above the crashing surf. On the bluff's crest, Robert Edwin Peary, the first man to lead a party of fellow men to the North Pole without the use of mechanical or electrical devices, built his dream home. It's now a state historic site that's accessible via excursion boats from Portland or Freeport. The half-day trip usually includes a narrated cruise to the island and time to tour the house, filled with Peary family artifacts, and wander the nature trails. (Note: Trails are usually closed until approximately mid-July to protect nesting eider ducks).

Peary envisioned the island's rocky bluff as a ship's prow and built his house to resemble a pilot house. Wherever possible, he used indigenous materials from the island in the construction, including timber drift, fallen trees, beach rocks, and cement mixed with screened beach sand and small pebbles. From the library, Peary corresponded with world leaders, adventurers, and explorers, such as Teddy Roosevelt, the Wright Brothers, Roald Amundson, and Ernest Shackleton, and planned his expeditions. Peary reached the North Pole on April 6, 1909, and his wife, Josephine, was on Eagle when she received word via telegraph of her husband's accomplishment. After Peary's death, in 1920, the family continued to spend summers on Eagle until Josephine's death, in 1955. It was a unanimous family decision to donate the island to the state of Maine. Check the website for information on guided tours to the island led by Peary's grandson.

largely to encouragement from the energetic grassroots Downtown Arts District Association (DADA). Galleries, artists' studios, coffeehouses, cafés and bistros, craft shops, two libraries, the State Theatre, the Merrill Auditorium (in City Hall), the Portland Museum of Art, the Maine College of Art, and even

L. L. Bean and the Portland Public Market are all part of the ongoing renaissance.

West End

Probably the most diverse of the city's downtown neighborhoods, and one that largely escaped the Great Fire of 1866, the West End

LIGHTHOUSES AND PARKS TOUR

Whether in a car or on a bike, it's easy to loop through South Portland and Cape Elizabeth on a route that takes in lighthouses, forts, beaches, and parks.

Begin just over the Casco Bay Bridge from downtown Portland (Rte. 77), take Broadway and continue to the end at **Southern Maine Community College (SMCC),** overlooking the bay. (Best time to come here is evenings and weekends, when there's ample parking.) Unless it's foggy (when the signal is deafening) or thundering (when you'll expose yourself to lightning), walk out along the 1,000-foot granite breakwater to the **Spring Point Ledge Light,** with fabulous views in every direction. Also here are picnic benches, the remains of Fort Preble, and the Portland Harbor Museum. At the southern edge of the SMCC campus is the **Spring Point Shoreline Walkway,** a scenic three-mile pathway with views off to House, Peaks, and Cushings Islands. At the end of the shoreway, you'll reach crescent-shaped **Willard Beach,** a neighborhoody sort of place with lifeguards, a changing building, a snack bar, and those same marvelous views.

From the SMCC campus, return on Broadway to the major intersection with Cottage Road and bear left. Cottage Road becomes Shore Road at the Cape Elizabeth town line. Loop into Fort Williams Park and make a pilgrimage to **Portland Head Light** before continuing on Shore Road to its intersection with Route 77. Bear left and follow to Two Lights Road and follow signs to 40-acre **Two Lights State Park.** Almost a vest-pocket park, it has picnicking and restroom facilities, but its biggest asset is the panoramic ocean view from atop a onetime gun battery. Summer admission is $4.50 adults 12-64, $1 kids 5-11.

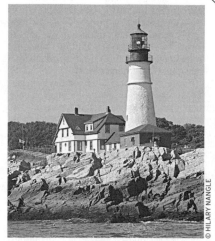

Portland Head Light guards the ledgy shores of Cape Elizabeth.

© HILARY NANGLE

Before or after visiting the park, take a left just before the park entrance (it's a continuation of Two Lights Road; the sign says Lighthouses). Continue to the parking lot at the end, where you'll see the signal towers for which Two Lights is named. (There's no access to either one; only one still works.) If you haven't brought a picnic for the state park, enjoy the food and the view at **The Lobster Shack.**

To eke out some beach time, return to Route 77 and continue to **Crescent Beach State Park,** a 243-acre park with changing rooms, lifeguard, restrooms, picnic tables, and a snack bar. Admission is $3.50 adults, 12-64, $1 kids 5-11. Directly offshore is Saco Bay's **Richmond Island,** a 200-acre private preserve with a checkered past dating to the 17th century.

includes the historically and architecturally splendid Western Promenade, Maine Medical Center (the state's largest hospital), the city's best B&Bs, a gay-friendly community with a laissez-faire attitude, a host of cafés and restaurants, as well as a few niches harboring the homeless and forlorn.

Munjoy Hill/East End

A once slightly down-at-the-heels neighborhood enclave with a pull-'em-up-by-the-bootstraps attitude, Portland's East End is rapidly gentrifying. Munjoy Hill is probably best known for the distinctive wooden tower that adorns its summit (see *Portland Observatory* under *Sights*).

Named for George Munjoy, a wealthy 17th-century resident, this district has a host of architectural and historic landmarks—well worth a walking tour. Fortunately, Greater Portland Landmarks (207/774-5561, www.portlandlandmarks.org) has produced a 24-page booklet, *Munjoy Hill Historic Guide* ($3), which documents more than 60 notable sites, including the National Historic Register Eastern Cemetery and, with spectacular harbor views, the Eastern Promenade and Fort Allen Park. From early June to early October, Landmarks also offers guided walking tours of the historic **Eastern Cemetery,** the oldest burial ground on the peninsula, at 10:30 A.M. on Thursdays, beginning at the Portland Observatory (138 Congress St.). Cost is $7 adult, free under 16.

Bayside and Parkside

A Babel of languages reverberates in these districts just below Portland City Hall. Bayside experienced the arrival of refugees—Cambodian, Laotian, Vietnamese, Central European, and Afghan families—from war-torn lands during the 1980s and 1990s. Nowadays, you'll hear references to Somali Town, an area named for all the resettled refugees from that shattered country. Others have come from Sudan and Ethiopia. Portland's active Refugee Resettlement Program has assisted all. Many have found employment with Barber Foods, a fantastically conscientious firm that

WINSLOW HOMER

Discovering Maine in his early 40s, Winslow Homer (1836–1910) was smitten – enough to spend the last 27 years of his life in Prouts Neck (Scarborough, south of Portland), a small fishing village gradually morphing into an exclusive summer enclave. Here, in a cluttered, rustic studio converted from a onetime stable (recently acquired by the Portland Museum of Art, which eventually plans to open it to the public on a limited basis), he produced his finest works, the seascapes that have become so familiar to us all. He painted the sea in every mood, the rocks in every light, the snow in all its bleakness, the hardy trees bent to the wind. Occasional forays to the Bahamas, the Adirondacks, and the Canadian wilderness inspired other themes, but Prouts Neck always lured him back. Homer's last work, an oil titled *Driftwood*, painted in 1909 when his health was in major decline, depicts once again the struggle of man against the roiling surf that Homer knew so intimately from his life on the coast of Maine.

hires many new immigrants in its processing plant and provides opportunities for employees to learn English and obtain social services. Many newcomers have also become entrepreneurs, opening restaurants and small markets catering to their compatriots but increasingly gaining customers among local residents. Real-estate pressures are contributing to changes in these neighborhoods, too. The city is working to relocate scrap-metal yards and replace them with housing and small businesses.

Beyond the Peninsula

At the western edge of Portland, close to the Portland Jetport, is the historic area known as **Stroudwater,** once an essential link in Maine water transport. The 20-mile-long **Cumberland and Oxford Canal,** hand-dug in 1828, ran through here as part of the timber-shipping route linking Portland Harbor, the

GREATER PORTLAND

Fore and Presumpscot Rivers, and Sebago Lake. Twenty-eight wooden locks allowed vessels to rise the 265 feet between sea level and the lake. By 1870, trains took over the route, condemning the canal to oblivion. Centerpiece of the Stroudwater area today is the historic 18th-century Tate House (see under *Beyond the Downtown Peninsula*).

SIGHTS
(Portland Museum of Art (PMA)
Three centuries of art and architecture: That's what you'll discover at Maine's oldest (since 1882) and finest art museum, the Portland Museum of Art (7 Congress Sq., Portland, 207/775-6148, recorded info 207/773-2787 or 800/639-4067, www.portlandmuseum.org, 10 A.M.–5 P.M., to 9 P.M. Fri., closed Mon. mid-Oct.–late May, $10 adults, $8 seniors and students, $4 ages 6–17, free admission 5–9 P.M. every Friday). The museum's topflight collection of American and impressionist masters and fine and decorative arts is displayed in three architecturally stunning, connected buildings: the award-winning Charles Shipman Payson building, designed by I. M. Pei and opened in 1983, the newly restored Federal-era McLellan House, and the beaux-arts L. D. M. Sweat Memorial Galleries, designed by noted Maine architect John Calvin Stevens. The museum also has a well-stocked gift shop and a pleasant café that's open for lunch daily (11 A.M.–4 P.M.) and for dinner Friday (to 7:30 P.M.). Call for information about family activities, lectures, and other events.

(Victoria Mansion
Jaws literally drop when their owners enter the Italianate Victoria Mansion, also called the Morse-Libby Mansion (109 Danforth St., Portland, 207/772-4841, www.victoria mansion.org, 10 A.M.–4 P.M. Mon.–Sat. and 1–5 P.M. Sun. May–Oct., special hours in Dec., $10 adults, $9 seniors, $3 6–17, holiday season $12 adults, $5 ages 6–17, $25 per family), widely considered the most magnificently ornamented dwelling of its period remaining in the country. The national Historic Landmark is rife with Victoriana—carved marble fireplaces, elaborate porcelain and paneling, a free-standing mahogany staircase, gilded glass chandeliers, a recently restored 6- by 25-foot stained-glass ceiling window, and unbelievable trompe l'oeil touches. It's even more spectacular at Christmas, with yards of roping, festooned trees, and carolers. (This is the best time to bring kids, as the house itself may not particularly intrigue them.) The mansion was built in the late 1850s by Ruggles Sylvester Morse, a Maine-born entrepreneur whose New Orleans–based fortune enabled him to hire 93 craftsmen to complete the house. The interior, designed by Gustave Herter, still boasts 90 percent of the original furnishings. Guided 45-minute tours begin every half hour (on the quarter hour) in season; tours are self-guided during the holidays.

(Portland Observatory
Providing a head-swiveling view of Portland (and the White Mountains on a clear day), the

Climb the 103 steps to the orb deck of the Portland Observatory for 360-degree views.

© TOM NANGLE

© TOM NANGLE

GREATER PORTLAND

Kids love riding the Narrow Gauge Railroad along the Eastern Prom waterfront.

octagonal red-painted Portland Observatory (138 Congress St., Portland, 207/774-5561, www.portlandlandmarks.org, 10 A.M.–5 P.M. late May–Columbus Day, last tour at 4:30 P.M., $6 adults, $4 ages 6–16) is the only remaining marine signal tower on the Eastern Seaboard. Built in 1807 at a cost of $5,000 by Captain Lemuel Moody to keep track of the port's shipping activity, the tower has 122 tons of rock ballast in its base. Admission in those days (only men were allowed to climb the 103 interior steps) was 12.5 cents. Today, admission includes the small museum at the tower's base and a guided tour to the top.

The Longfellow Connection

A few blocks down Congress Street from the PMA, you'll step back in time to the era of Portland-born poet Henry Wadsworth Longfellow, who lived in the accurately restored **Wadsworth-Longfellow House** (485 Congress St., Portland, 207/774-1822, www .mainehistory.org, 10 A.M.–4 P.M. Mon.–Sat., noon–4 P.M. Sun. May 1–Oct. 31, special hol-

iday hours Nov. and Dec., $7 adults, $6 seniors and students, $3 ages 5–17), as a child in the early 1800s—long before the brick mansion was dwarfed by surrounding high-rises. Wadsworth and Longfellow family furnishings fill the three-story house (owned by the Maine Historical Society), and savvy guides provide insight into Portland's 19th-century life. Don't miss the urban oasis—a wonderfully peaceful garden—behind the house (same hours, free admission). Buy tickets at the adjacent Center for Maine History, which also houses the **Maine History Gallery** (489 Congress St., 207/774-1822, www.mainehistory .org, 10 A.M.–5 P.M. Mon.–Sat., noon–5 P.M. Sun., $4 adults, $3 seniors, $2 children), where you can take in the Maine Historical Society's current exhibits and find an extensive collection of Maine history books in the gift shop.

Maine Narrow Gauge Railroad and Museum

A three-mile ride along Portland's waterfront is the highlight of a visit to the Maine Narrow

Gauge Railroad Company and Museum (58 Fore St., Portland, 207/828-0814, www.mngrr.org). The museum (10 A.M.–4 P.M. daily late May–late Oct., weekends only off-season, $2 adult, $1 seniors and ages 3–12 or free with train ticket) owns more than three dozen train cars and has others on long-term loan—most from Maine's five historic narrow-gauge railroads (the last one closed in 1943). You can board a number of the cars and see others undergoing restoration. For a fee, you can ride the two-foot rails aboard a multicar train. The schedule roughly follows museum hours, with rides on the hour ($10 adults, $9 seniors, $6 ages 3–12). The track edges Casco Bay along the Eastern Promenade—a short but enjoyable excursion that's a real kid pleaser. Years ago, hundreds of steam engines were built here, but steam locomotives now operate only for special occasions. Trains also operate during school vacation weeks; call for schedule. At the eastern end of Fore Street, turn at the railroad-crossing sign on the waterside; the museum is at the back of the complex.

Museum of African Culture

Founded in 1998, the Museum of African Culture (13 Brown St., Portland, 207/871-7188, www.museumafricanculture.org, 10:30 A.M.–4 P.M. Tues.–Sat., $5 donation) is the brainchild of Nigerian-born Oscar Mokeme (the director) and Arthur Aleshire. It's devoted to sub-Saharan African arts and culture. Among the museum's 300 or so treasures—not all on display at once—are Nigerian tribal masks and Benin lost-wax bronzes. The museum also has an ambitious outreach program, educating the community about African art and culture. Ask about Friday night programs.

Children's Museum of Maine

Here's the answer to parents' prayers—a whole museum in downtown Portland catering to kids. At the Children's Museum of Maine (P.O. Box 4041, 142 Free St., next to the Portland Museum of Art, Portland 04101, 207/828-1234, www.kitetails.com, 10 A.M.–5 P.M. Mon.–Sat., noon to 5 P.M. Sun., closed

Mon. early Sept.–late May, $7, children 1 and younger free, free admission 5–8 P.M. first Fri. of each month), lots of hands-on displays encourage interaction and guarantee involvement for a couple of hours. What's here? A submarine, computer lab, TV studio, L. L. Bean's Discovery Woods, a space shuttle, a supermarket, bank (with an ATM), lobster boat, a camera obscura (one of only three in the country, $3 for that exhibit only) and more than a dozen other activities. There's even an animal hospital. Call to check on the special-events schedule.

BEYOND THE DOWNTOWN PENINSULA
Seeing Stars

Under a 30-foot dome with comfy theater seats and a state-of-the-art laser system, the **Southworth Planetarium** (96 Falmouth St., Science Building, lower level, University of Southern Maine, Portland, 207/780-4249, www.usm.maine.edu/~planet, 7 and 8:30 P.M. Fri. and Sat., $5–6 adults, $4–6 seniors and children) presents astronomy shows. Computer-savvy kids will head for the interactive computers in the exhibit area; the gift shop stocks astronaut ice cream and other science-type stuff. For recorded information on moon and planet positions, eclipses, and other astronomical happenings, call the **Skywatch Hotline** (207/780-4719). Take Exit 6B off I-295 and go west on Forest Avenue to Falmouth Street (left turn). The Science Building is on the left, after the parking lot.

Tate House

Just down the street from the Portland International Jetport, in the Stroudwater district, is the 1755 Tate House (1270 Westbrook St., 207/774-6177, www.tatehouse.org, 10 A.M.–4 P.M. Tues.–Sat. 1–4 P.M. and first Sun. of each month June 15–Oct. 15, $7 adults, $5 seniors, $2 age 6–12), a National Historic Landmark owned by the Colonial Dames of America. Built by Captain George Tate, who was prominent in shipbuilding, the house has superb period furnishings and a lovely 18th-century herb garden (more than 70 varieties) overlooking the Stroudwater River. Tours last 40 minutes. Wednesdays mid-June–mid-September are "summer garden days," when tea and goodies follow tours of the garden (for an extra charge). Other special hour-long tours focusing on the architecture and the historic Stroudwater neighborhood can be arranged by appointment. Across the street, in the Means House, is the museum's gift shop. From downtown Portland, it's 3.2 miles; take Congress Street West (Rte. 22), under I-295, and out as far as Waldo Street, just after the Fore River. Turn left onto Waldo and then turn right onto Westbrook Street. If you find yourself with spare time at the Portland Jetport, Tate House is an easy walk from the terminal. Ask for directions at the airport information desk.

Portland Harbor Museum

The maritime history of Casco Bay and Maine is the focus of the small Portland Harbor Museum (Fort Rd., South Portland, 207/799-6337, www.PortlandHarborMuseum.org, 10 A.M.–4:30 P.M. daily late May–mid-Oct., and Fri.–Sun. spring and fall, $4 adults) on the waterfront campus of Southern Maine Community College (SMCC). To reach the museum, head over from downtown Portland (Rte. 77) and continue onto Broadway. Watch for SMCC signs. The museum now holds the title to the nearby Spring Point Ledge lighthouse, which is open for tours periodically during the summer. Call for the schedule. Also nearby are the remains of Fort Preble and the Spring Point Shoreline Walkway leading to Willard Beach.

(Portland Head Light

Just four miles from downtown Portland, Fort Williams, in Cape Elizabeth, feels a world away. This oceanfront town park, a former military base, is home to Portland Head Light (1000 Shore Rd., Fort Williams Park, Cape Elizabeth, 207/799-2661, www.portlandheadlight.com, open dawn–dusk). Commissioned by President George Washington and first lighted in 1791, it has been immortalized in poetry, photography, and philately. The surf here is awesome—perhaps too awesome. The

Annie C. Maguire was shipwrecked below the lighthouse on Christmas Eve, 1886. There's no access to the 58-foot automated light tower, but the superbly restored keeper's house has become **The Museum at Portland Head Light** (10 A.M.–4 P.M. daily late May–mid-Oct. and weekends late spring and late fall, but call first to confirm, $2 adults, $1 kids 6–18). It's filled with local history and lighthouse memorabilia. The 90-acre oceanfront park offers much else to explore, including ruins of the fort and the Goddard mansion. Walk the trails, play a game of tennis, dip your toes in the surf at the rocky beach, but be careful, as there's a strong undertow here. You might even catch the Portland Symphony Orchestra, which occasionally performs here in summer. The grassy headlands are great places to watch the boat traffic going in and out of Portland Harbor. Bring a picnic lunch, and don't forget a kite. From downtown Portland, take Route 77 and then Broadway, Cottage Road, and Shore Road.

TOURS
(Casco Bay Tour

Casco Bay Lines (Commercial and Franklin Sts., Old Port, Portland, 207/774-7871, www.cascobaylines.com), the nation's oldest continuously operating ferry system (since the 1920s), is the lifeline between Portland and six inhabited Casco Bay islands. What better way to sample the islands than to go along for the three-hour ride with mail, groceries, and island residents? The Casco Bay Lines mail boat stops—briefly—at **Long Island, Chebeague, Cliff,** and **Little** and **Great Diamond Islands.** Departures are 10 A.M. and 2:15 P.M. daily mid-June–Labor Day (plus 7:45 A.M. weekdays), 10 A.M. and 2:45 P.M. other months. Fares are $13 adults, $11.50 seniors, and $6.50 ages 5–9. The longest cruise on the Casco Bay Lines schedule is the five-hour, 45-minute narrated summertime trip (late June–Labor Day) to **Bailey Island,** with a two-hour stopover, departing from Portland at 10 A.M. daily ($18.50 adults, $16.50 seniors, $8.50 ages 5–9). Dogs (on leashes) and bicycles need separate tickets—$6 for bikes, $3.75 for animals.

Walking Tours

The best tours of the area are offered by **Greater Portland Landmarks** (207/774-5561, www.portlandlandmarks.org), which sponsors neighborhood walking tours as well as an annual **summer tour program,** featuring four or five walking trips and excursions to offshore islands, historic churches, revamped buildings, and gardens. Many of the destinations are private or otherwise inaccessible, so these are special opportunities. Registration is limited, and there's only one trip to each site. Tours run mid-July–mid-October, primarily on weekends.

Land and Sea Tours

Three commercial operators offer area land-and-sea tours, but frankly, none is first rate. On each, guides often present incorrect information. Still, such tours are a good way to get the city's general layout. The best of the lot is the 1.5-hour narrated sightseeing tour of Portland in a trolley-bus, by **Mainely Tours** (3 Moulton St., Old Port, Portland, 207/774-0808, www .mainelytours.com). Cost is $16 adults, $15 seniors, $9 ages 3–12. You can combine this tour with a 90-minute Lighthouse Lover's boat tour on Casco Bay. The combined price is $27 adult, $25 senior, and $16 kids.

An alternative, especially if you're traveling with kids, is the 60–70 minute **Downeast Duck Adventures** (office at Harbor View Gifts, 177 Commercial St., 207/774-3825, www.downeast ducktours.com, early June–early Oct., $22 adult, $19 senior, $17 ages 6–12, $5 age 5 and younger). Prepare to do a lot of quacking on the tour and to hear a lot of quackery regarding local history.

PARKS, PRESERVES, AND BEACHES

Greater Portland is blessed with green space, thanks largely to the efforts of 19th-century mayor James Phinney Baxter, who foresightedly hired the famed Olmsted Brothers firm to develop an ambitious plan to ring the city with public parks and promenades. Not all the elements fell into place, but the result is what makes Portland such a livable city.

Portland Peninsula

Probably the most visible of the city's parks, 51-acre **Deering Oaks** (Park and Forest Aves. and Deering St.) may be best known for the quaint little duck condo in the middle of the pond. Other facilities and highlights here are tennis courts, playground, horseshoes, rental paddleboats, a snack bar, the award-winning Rose Circle, a Saturday farmers market (7 A.M.–noon), and, in winter, ice skating. After dark, steer clear of the park.

At one end of the Eastern Promenade, where it meets Fore Street, **Fort Allen Park** overlooks offshore Fort Gorges (coin-operated telescopes bring it closer). A central gazebo is flanked by an assortment of military souvenirs dating as far back as the War of 1812. All along the Eastern Prom are walking paths, benches, play areas, even an ill-maintained fitness trail—all with that terrific view. Down by the water is **East End Beach,** with parking, token sand, and the area's best launching ramp for sea kayaks or powerboats.

West of Downtown

Just beyond I-295, along Baxter Boulevard (Rte. 1) and tidal **Back Cove,** is a skinny green strip with a 3.5-mile trail for walking, jogging, or just watching the sailboards and the skyline. Along the way, you can cross Baxter Boulevard and spend time picnicking, playing tennis, or flying a kite in 48-acre **Payson Park.**

Talk about an urban oasis. The 85-acre **Fore River Sanctuary,** owned by Maine Audubon, has two miles of blue-blazed trails that wind through a salt marsh, link with the historic Cumberland and Oxford Canal towpath, and pass near **Jewell Falls,** Portland's only waterfall, protected by Portland Trails. From downtown Portland, take Congress Street West (Rte. 22), past I-295. From here there are two access routes: either turn right onto Stevens Avenue (Rte. 9), continue to Brighton Avenue (Rte. 25), turn left and go about 1.25 miles to Rowe Avenue, and then turn left and park at the end of the road; or continue past Stevens Avenue, about one-half mile to Frost Avenue, take a hard right, and then left into the Maine Orthopedic Center parking lot. Portland Trails raised the funds for the handsome, 90-foot pedestrian bridge at this entrance to the sanctuary. Open sunup to sundown daily. No pets, free admission.

Bird-watchers flock to 239-acre **Evergreen Cemetery** (Stevens Ave.) in May to see warblers, thrushes, and other migratory birds that gather in the ponds and meadows. During peak periods, it's possible to see as many as 20 warbler species in a morning, including the Cape May, bay breasted, mourning, and Tennessee. Naturalists from Maine Audubon often are on-site helping to identify birds. For more info, check the events calendar at www.mainebirding.net.

Scarborough

Scarborough Beach Park (Black Point Rd., Rte. 207, 207/883-2416, www.scarborough beachstatepark.com, $4 adult, $2 child), a long stretch of sand, is the best beach for big waves. Between the parking area and the lovely stretch of beach, you'll pass Massacre Pond, named for a 1703 skirmish between resident Indians and resident wannabes. (Score: Indians 19, wannabes 0.) The park is open all year for swimming, surfing, beachcombing, and ice skating, but on weekends in summer, the parking lot fills early.

At 3,100 acres, **Scarborough Marsh** (Pine Point Rd., Rte. 9, 207/883-5100, www.maine audubon.org, 9:30 A.M.–5:30 P.M. June–Labor Day, and weekends in late May and Sept.), Maine's largest salt marsh, is prime territory for birding and canoeing. Rent a canoe ($15 an hour if you're not an Audubon member or $50 per half day) at the small nature center, operated by Maine Audubon, and explore on your own. Or join one of the daily 90-minute guided tours (call for the schedule, $11 adults, $9 children, subtract $1.50 pp if you have your own canoe). Guided full-moon tours ($12 per adult, $10 per child) June–September are particularly exciting; dress warmly and bring a flashlight. Other special programs, some geared primarily for children, include wildflower walks, art classes, and dawn birding trips; all require reservations and very reasonable fees. Also here is a walking tour trail of less than one mile. Pick up a map at the center.

Overlooking the marsh is 52-acre **Scarborough River Wildlife Sanctuary** (Pine Point Rd./Rte. 9), with 1.5 miles of walking trails that loop to the Scarborough River and by two ponds.

Falmouth (North of Portland)

Nearly a dozen of Falmouth's parks, trails, and preserves, official and unofficial, are described and mapped in the *Falmouth Trail Guide,* a handy little booklet published by the Falmouth Conservation Commission. Copies are available at Gilsland Farm, Falmouth Town Hall, and local bookstores. Two of the best options are described below.

A 65-acre wildlife sanctuary and environmental center on the banks of the Presumpscot River, **Gilsland Farm** (20 Gilsland Farm Rd., 207/781-2330, www.maineaudubon.org, dawn–dusk daily) is state headquarters for Maine Audubon. More than two miles of easy, well-marked trails wind through the grounds, taking in salt marshes, rolling meadows, woodlands, and views of the estuary. Observation blinds allow inconspicuous spying during bird-migration season. In the education center (9 A.M.–5 P.M. Mon.–Sat. and 1–4 P.M. Sun.) are hands-on exhibits, a nature store, and classrooms and offices. Fees are charged for special events, but otherwise it's all free. The visitors center is one-quarter mile off Route 1.

Once the summer compound of the prominent Baxter family, Falmouth's 100-acre **Mackworth Island,** reached via a causeway, is now the site of the Governor Baxter School for the Deaf. Limited parking is just beyond the security booth on the island. On the 1.5-mile, vehicle-free perimeter path (great Portland Harbor views), you'll meet bikers, hikers, and dog walkers. Just off the trail on the north side of the island is the late Governor Percival Baxter's stone-circled pet cemetery, maintained by the state at the behest of Baxter, who donated this island as well as Baxter State Park to the people of Maine. From downtown Portland, take Route 1 across the Presumpscot River to Falmouth Foreside. Andrews Avenue (third street on the right) leads to the island. Open sunup–sundown, all year.

RECREATION
Bicycling

The **Bicycle Coalition of Maine** (P.O. Box 5275, Augusta 04332, 207/623-4511, www.bikemaine .org) has an excellent website that lists nearly two dozen trails in Greater Portland. You'll also find info on events, organized rides, bike shops, and more. Another good resource is **Casco Bay Bicycle Club** (www.cascobaybicycleclub.org), a recreational cycling club with rides several times weekly. Check its website for details.

For rentals (hybrids are $25 a day) and repairs visit **Cycle Mania** (59 Federal St., 207/774-2933, www.cyclemania1.com).

The best locales for island bicycling—fun for families and beginners but not especially challenging for diehards—are Peaks and Great Chebeague Islands (see sidebar *Casco Bay Islands*), but do remember to follow the rules of the road.

Golf

You'll have no problem finding a place to tee off in Greater Portland. Some of the best courses are private, so if you have an "in," so much the better, but there are still plenty of public and semiprivate courses for every skill level. Free advice on helping you choose a course is offered by Maine's Golf Concierge (info@golfme.com).

Let's just consider Greater Portland's 18-hole courses. For all, it's a smart move to reserve tee times. **Sable Oaks Golf Club** (505 Country Club Dr., South Portland, 207/775-6257, www.sableoaks.com) is considered one of the toughest and best of Maine's public courses. Since 1998, **Nonesuch River Golf Club** (304 Gorham Rd., Rte. 114, Scarborough, 207/883-0007 or 888/256-2717, www.nonesuchgolf .com) has been drawing raves for the challenges of its par-70 championship course and praise from environmentalists for preserving wildlife habitat; full-size practice range and green, too. The City of Portland's **Riverside Municipal Golf Course** (1158 Riverside St., Portland, 207/797-3524) has an 18-hole par-72 course (Riverside North) and a nine-hole par-35 course (Riverside South). Opt for the 18-hole course.

Sea Kayaking

With all the islands scattered through Casco

© HILARY NANGLE

Maine Island Kayak Company operates from a beachfront location on Peaks Island, making it easy to tour the waters of Casco Bay.

Bay, Greater Portland has become a hotbed of sea-kayaking activity. The best place to start is out on Peaks Island, 15 minutes offshore via Casco Bay Lines ferry. **Maine Island Kayak Company (MIKCO)** (70 Luther St., Peaks Island, 207/766-2373 or 800/796-2373, www.maineislandkayak.com) is a successful tour operation that organizes half-day, all-day, and multiday local kayaking trips as well as national and international adventures. An introductory half-day tour in Casco Bay is $65 pp; a full day is $110, including lunch. Reservations are essential. MIKCO also does private lessons and group courses and clinics (some require previous experience). MIKCO's owner, Tom Bergh, has a flawless reputation for safety and skill. Send for the extensive trip schedule.

For a quickie intro, **L. L. Bean** (180 Commercial St., 207/400-4814) offers 90-minute Portland Harbor kayak tours three times daily late June–August, and then weekends into October. Cost is $29 adults, $19 ages 10–15.

ⓒ Lobstering Cruise

Learn all kinds of lobster lore and maybe even catch your own dinner with **Lucky Catch Lobster Tours** (170 Commercial St., 207/233-2026 or 888/624-6321, www.lucky catch.com, $22 adult, $20 seniors or juniors ages 13–18, $14 ages 12 and younger). Captain Tom Martin offers five different, 80–90-minute cruises on his 37-foot lobster boat. On each (except late Saturdays and all-day Sundays, when state law prohibits it), usually 10 traps are hauled and the process and gear explained. You can even help, if you're willing. Any lobsters caught are available for purchase after the cruise for wholesale boat price (and you can have them cooked nearby for a reasonable rate). Now wouldn't that make a nice story to tell the folks back home?

Sailboat and Powerboat Excursions

Down on the Old Port wharves are several excursion-boat businesses. Each has carved out a niche, so choose according to your interest and your schedule. Dress warmly and wear rubber-soled shoes. Remember that all cruises are weather-dependent.

Bay View Cruises operates the 66-foot *Bay View Lady* (184 Commercial St., Fisherman's Wharf, Old Port, 207/761-0496, www.bayview cruises-me.com, daily June–Sept., weekends May and June) and has five different cruises ranging from 40 minutes to two hours. On longer cruises, you can add a complete lobster bake, with notice. The main deck is enclosed and heated; the upper deck has the best views.

Cruise up to 20 miles offshore seeking whales with **Odyssey Whale Watch** (Long Wharf, 170 Commercial St., 207/775-0727, www.odysseywhalewatch.com, $40 adult, $35 ages 60-plus and 13–17, and $30 under 12). Five-hour whale watches aboard the *Odyssey* depart daily at 10 A.M. late June–early September, plus spring and fall weekends. (Don't overload on breakfast that day, and take preventive measures if you're motion-sensitive.)

Eagle Island Tours (Long Wharf, Old Port, 207/774-6498, www.eagleislandtours.com, no credit cards) offers several excursion options, but the best is the four-hour cruise, departing at 10 A.M., to 17-acre **Eagle Island** (Tues. and Thurs.–Sun. late June–early Sept., and some weekends June and September, $26 adults, $24 seniors, $14 ages 3–12) where Arctic explorer Admiral Robert Peary built his summer home. The cruise allows time on the island to visit the house and wander the grounds. Pack a picnic, or order a box lunch 24 hours in advance.

Sail quietly across the waters of Casco Bay aboard a windjammer with **Portland Schooner Company** (Maine State Pier, 40 Commercial St., 207/766-2500, www.portland schooner.com, late May–mid-Oct., $30 adult, $15 ages 2–12). Three or four two-hour sails are offered daily on two schooners, the 72-foot *Bagheera* and the 88-foot *Wendameen*, both historical vessels designed by John G. Alden and built in East Boothbay. Overnight windjammer trips also are available for $240 pp, including dinner and breakfast.

Spectator Sports

A pseudofierce mascot named Slugger stirs up

the crowds at baseball games played by the **Portland Sea Dogs** (Hadlock Field, 271 Park Ave., 207/879-9500 or 800/936-3647, www.portlandseadogs.com), a AA Boston Red Sox farm team. General-admission tickets are $6 adults, $3 seniors (62 and over) and kids 16 and under. Reserved seats are $7 adults, $6 all others.

For ice hockey action, the **Portland Pirates** (207/775-3458, www.portland pirates.com, $8–21), a farm team for the American Hockey League Anaheim Ducks, plays winter and spring home games at the 8,700-seat Cumberland County Civic Center.

ENTERTAINMENT AND NIGHTLIFE

The best places to find out what's playing at area theaters, cinemas, concert halls, and nightclubs are the *The Portland Phoenix* and the *Go* supplement in the Thursday edition of the *Portland Press Herald*. Both are available at bookstores and supermarkets; the *Phoenix* is free.

Merrill Auditorium

The magnificently restored Merrill Auditorium (20 Myrtle St., box office 207/874-8200) is a 1,900-seat theater inside Portland City Hall (on Congress Street) with two balconies and one of the country's only municipally owned pipe organs, the **Kotzschmar Organ.** A summer organ classical concert series with guest artists is held at 7:30 P.M. most Tuesdays mid-June–August, $10 donation. Call for more information on the Pops series (207/883-9525).

Special events and concerts are common at Merrill, and the auditorium is also the home to a number of the city's arts organizations. The **Portland Symphony Orchestra** (207/842-0800, www.portlandsymphony.org) and **PCA Great Performances** (207/773-3150, www.pcagreatperformances.org) have extensive, well-patronized fall and winter schedules; the PSO presents three summer Independence Pops concerts as well. The **Portland Opera Repertory Theatre** (437 Congress St., 207/879-7678, www.portopera.org) performs a major opera

each summer, usually in late July. In addition, there are films, lectures, and other related events throughout July. Tickets for the PSO, PCA, and PORT are available through PortTix (207/942-0800, www.porttix.com).

St. Lawrence Arts and Community Center

Proof of what enthusiastic, determined activists can accomplish is the new St. Lawrence Arts and Community Center (76 Congress St., 207/775-5568, www.stlawrencearts.org), formerly St. Lawrence Congregational Church. Built in 1897 in Queen Anne style, the church is a distinctive landmark with more than 90 stained-glass windows. On the same street as the Portland Observatory on Munjoy Hill, the center is a vibrant venue for professional and semiprofessional theater and concerts.

Drama

Innovative staging and controversial contemporary dramas are typical of the **Portland Stage Company** (Portland Performing Arts Center, 25A Forest Ave., 207/774-0465, www.portlandstage.com), established in 1974 and going strong ever since. Equity pros present a half dozen plays each winter season in a 290-seat performance space.

Live Music

The Portland Conservatory of Music presents the free, weekly **Noonday Concerts** at First Parish Church (425 Congress St., 207/773-5747) at 12:15 P.M. Thursdays October–early April (excluding late November). The music varies widely, from saxophone to Scottish fiddle and dance, a string quartet to Irish baroque.

Portland Parks and Recreation sponsors **Summer in the Parks** (207/7566-8275, www.ci.portland.me.us/summer.htm, July and Aug., free), a number of evening concert series, a noontime kids' series, and even movies, in downtown parks.

In summer, take the ferry to Peaks Island for sunset cocktails and often live entertainment on the deck at **Jones Landing** (at the ferry landing, Peaks Island, 207/766-4400).

Brewpubs and Bars

Not only is **Gritty McDuff's** (396 Fore St., Old Port, 207/772-2739, 11:30 A.M.–1 A.M. daily) one of Maine's most popular breweries, its brewpub was the state's first—opened in 1988. The menu includes pub classics such as fish-and-chips and shepherd's pie, as well as burgers, salads, and sandwiches. Among the Gritty's beers and ales on tap are Sebago Light and Black Fly Stout. Gritty's also books live entertainment fairly regularly. Tours by appointment. Gritty's also has a branch in Freeport.

Sebago Brewing Company (164 Middle St., Old Port, 207/775-2337, 11:30 A.M.–1 A.M. daily) is newer on the scene, but prolific, with brewpubs also in Gorham and at the Maine Mall. The Portland location has seating indoors and out and a menu that varies from munchies to steak and lobster. Tours on request.

A longtime favorite pub, **$3 Dewey's** (241 Commercial St., Old Port, 207/772-3310) is so authentic that visiting Brits, Kiwis, and Aussies often head here to assuage their homesickness. Inexpensive fare, 36 brews on tap, free popcorn, and live music on Sunday, Tuesday, Wednesday, and Thursday make it a very popular spot.

Especially popular in the late afternoon and early evening is **J's Oyster** (5 Portland Pier, 207/772-4828, 11:30 A.M.–1 A.M.), a longtime fixture on the waterfront known for its raw bar and for pouring a good drink.

Of all Portland's neighborhood hangouts, **Ruski's** (212 Danforth St., 207/774-7604, 7 A.M.–12:45 A.M. Mon.–Sat., 9 A.M.–12:45 A.M. Sun.) is the most authentic—a small, usually crowded onetime speakeasy that rates just as high for breakfast as for nighttime schmoozing. Expect basic, homemade fare for well under $10, darts and big-screen TV, too. Dress down or you'll feel out of place. No credit cards.

That said, it's **Rosie's** (330 Fore St., 207/772-5656) that *Esquire* named as one of America's best bars. **Blackstones** (6 Pine St., 207/775-2885, www.blackstones.com) claims to be Portland's oldest neighborhood gay bar.

West of I-295, **The Great Lost Bear** (540 Forest Ave., 207/772-0300, www.greatlost

bear.com, 11:30 A.M.–11:30 P.M. Mon.–Sat., noon–11 P.M. Sun.) has Portland's hugest inventory of designer beers, with 54 brews on tap, representing 15 Maine microbreweries and others from New England. The bear motif and the punny menus are a bit much, but the 15 or so varieties of burgers are not bad. It's a kid pleaser.

For more upscale tippling, head for **Top of the East** (157 High St., near Congress Sq., 207/775-5411), the lounge at the top of the Eastland Park Hotel, where all of Portland's at your feet. Happy hour is 4–6 P.M. weekdays; the lounge is open until 1 A.M. Thursday–Saturday, midnight other nights. Live jazz begins at 9:30 P.M. Friday and Saturday.

Bars with Entertainment

So many possibilities are in this category, but not a lot of veterans. The Portland club scene is a volatile one, tough on investors and reporters. The best advice is to scope out the scene when you arrive; the *Portland Phoenix* has the best listings. Most clubs have cover charges. A sampling of some Portland options follows. **Asylum** (121 Center St., 207/772-8274, www.portlandasylum.com) caters to a young crowd with dance jams, CD release parties, DJ nights, and live bands. **Geno's** (13 Brown St., 207/772-7891) has been at it for years—an old reliable for rock, with an emphasis on punk rock. **Brian Boru** (57 Center St., Old Port, 207/780-1506, www.bboru.com) is an Irish pub with live Irish music and $2 pints of Guinness on Sundays. Another venue for live music is **The Big Easy** (55 Market St., 207/871-8817, www.bigeasyportland.com).

Comedy

Portland's forum for stand-up comedy is the **Comedy Connection** (6 Custom House Wharf, 207/774-5554, www.maine comedy.com, open Thurs.–Sun. evenings), a crowded space that draws nationally known pros. Avoid the front tables unless you're inclined to be the fall guy/guinea pig, and don't bring anyone squeamish about the F-word. Reservations advised on weekends.

GREATER PORTLAND *(side tab)*

EVENTS

Pick up a free copy of the *Portland Area Arts and Events Calendar* at Portland shops and cafés, the Visitor Information Center, or City Hall (389 Congress St.).

June brings a host of events. The **Old Port Festival** (one of Portland's largest festivals), usually the first weekend, has entertainment, food and craft booths, and impromptu fun in Portland's Old Port. The **Greek Heritage Festival,** usually the last weekend, features Greek food, dancing, and crafts at Holy Trinity Church (133 Pleasant St., Portland).

Some of the world's top runners join upward of 500 racers in the **Beach to Beacon Race,** held in late July/early August. The 10K course goes from Crescent Beach State Park to Portland Head Light in Cape Elizabeth.

In mid-August, the **Italian Street Festival** showcases music, Italian food, and games at St. Peter's Catholic Church (72 Federal St.).

Artists from all over the country set up in 350 booths along Congress Street for the annual **Sidewalk Arts Festival,** in late August.

The **Maine Brewers' Festival,** the first weekend in November at the Portland Exposition Building, is a big event that expands every year, thanks to the explosion of Maine microbreweries. Samples galore. And from Thanksgiving weekend to Christmas Eve, **Victorian Holiday,** in downtown Portland, harks back with caroling, special sales, concerts, tree lighting, horse-drawn wagons, and Victoria Mansion tours and festivities.

SHOPPING

The Portland peninsula—primarily Congress Street and the Old Port waterfront district—is thick with non-cookie-cutter shops and galleries. This is just a taste to spur your explorations.

Antiquarian Bookstores

Carlson-Turner Books (241 Congress St., 207/773-4200 or 800/540-7323), based on Munjoy Hill, seems to have Portland's largest used-book inventory. Look for unusual titles and travel narratives. For good reads, contemporary fiction, and a big selection of cookbooks, visit **Cunningham Books** (199 State St., Longfellow Sq., 207/775-2246). Antique maps and atlases are the specialty at the Old Port's **Emerson Booksellers** (18 Exchange St., 207/874-2665), but it also has an excellent used-book selection.

Cookbook mavens will drool over the collection at **Rabelais Books** (86 Market St., 207/774-1044, www.rabelaisbooks.com), ideally situated in Portland's foodie neighborhood. Don and Samantha Hoyt Lindgren specialize in food and wine, carrying a delicious blend of thousands of current, rare, and out-of-print books covering culinary history, food lit, cookbooks, wine, and related topics.

Art Galleries

Intown Portland's galleries host a **First Friday Artwalk** on the first Friday evening of each month, with exhibition openings, open houses, meet-the-artist gatherings, and other such artsy activities.

A handful of galleries specializing in contemporary art are clustered in the Arts District. These include **Aucocisco** (613 Congress St., 207/553-2222, www.aucocisco.com), **June Fitzpatrick Gallery** (112 High St., 207/879-5742, www.junefitzpatrickgallery.com), and **Institute for Contemporary Art** (Maine College of Art, 522 Congress St., 207/879-5742), with walk-in tours at 12:15 P.M. every Wednesday. In the Old Port, find **Greenhut Galleries** (146 Middle St., 207/772-2693, www.greenhutgalleries.com), another well-respected gallery showing contemporary Maine art and sculpture.

Crafts

More than 15 Maine potters—with a wide variety of styles and items—market their wares at the **Maine Potters Market** (376 Fore St., 207/774-1633), an attractive shop in the heart of the Old Port. Established in 1980, the cooperative remains a consistently reliable outlet for some of Maine's best ceramic artisans.

Just around the corner is **Abacus** (44 Exchange St., 207/772-4880), where craft rises to a high art. Whimsy is the byword here; if you don't arrive smiling, you'll leave that way. Open all year. Abacus has branches in Kennebunkport and Freeport, and a seasonal shop in Boothbay Harbor.

Offbeat Shopping

Trustmi, you have to see **Suitsmi** (35 Pleasant St., 207/772-8285, www.suitsmi.com), which carries wearables (including jewelry) perfect for rock concerts, funky cafés, and, if you're dying to make a statement, your class reunion. Top it all off with a hat from **Queen of Hats** (560 Congress St., 207/772-2379, www.queenofhats .com). **Shipwreck and Cargo** (207 Commercial St., Old Port, 207/775-3057, www.shipwreck andcargo.com) stocks a wide assortment of marine-related items—boat models, barometers, navy surplus stuff, and more. Even more fun and offbeat is **China Sea Marine Trading Co.** (Wharf St., 207/773-0081, www.chinaseatrading .com), where Steve Bunker and his macaw Singapore sell his wild and eclectic finds.

Woof. The company outlet **Planet Dog** (211 Marginal Way, Portland, 207/347-8606, www .planetdog.com) is a barking good time for dogs and their owners. You'll find all sorts of wonderful products, and Planet Dog, committed to "think globally and act doggedly," has established a foundation to promote and serve causes such as therapy, service, search and rescue, bomb sniffing, and police dogs.

ACCOMMODATIONS
Downtown Portland

Portland's peninsula doesn't have an overwhelming amount of sleeping space, but it does have good variety in all price ranges. Rates reflect peak season.

Inns/Bed-and-Breakfasts: Railroad tycoon John Deering built **The Inn at St. John** (939 Congress St., 207/773-6481 or 800/636-9127, www.innatstjohn.com, $85–180) in 1897. The clean, comfortable, moderately priced 37-room hostelry has the feel of a European-style hotel. It welcomes children and pets and even has bicycle storage. Cable TV, air-conditioning, free local calls, free parking,

free airport pickup, and continental breakfast are provided. Most rooms have private baths (some are detached); some have fridge and microwave. The only downsides are the lack of an elevator and the lackluster neighborhood—in the evening you'll want drive or take a taxi when going out. It's about a half-hour walk to the Old Port or an $8 taxi fare.

Staying at **The Pomegranate Inn** (49 Neal St. at Carroll St., 207/772-1006 or 800/356-0408, www.pomegranateinn.com, $175–285) is an adventure in itself, with faux painting, classical statuary, art, antiques, and whimsical touches everywhere—you'll either love it or find it a bit much. The elegant 1884 Italianate mansion has seven guest rooms and a suite, all with private baths, air-conditioning, TV, and phones, some with fireplaces. Afternoon refreshments are served.

Take an 1830s townhouse, add contemporary amenities and a service-oriented innkeeper, and the result is the **Morrill Mansion Bed and Breakfast** (249 Vaughan St., 207/774-6900 or 888/566-7745, www .morrillmansion.com, $189–219), on the West End. Six rooms and one suite are spread out on the second and third floors (no elevator) in a carefully renovated town house. No frilly Victorian accents here—rather, the decor is understated, yet tasteful, taking advantage of hardwood floors and high ceilings. You'll find free Wi-Fi and local calls and TV/DVD in each room. A continental breakfast is included.

Built in 1835, **(The Inn at Park Spring** (135 Spring St., 207/774-1059 or 800/427-8511, www.innatparkspring.com, $149–175) is one of Portland's longest-running B&Bs. Current innkeepers Nancy and John Gonsalves are adding their own touches to make guests feel right at home. The location is just steps from most Arts District attractions. Six guest rooms are spread out on three floors (no elevator, steep stairs). All have air-conditioning and phones, some have Internet access; there's a guest fridge on each floor. Rates include a full breakfast.

Built in 1877, the handsome Georgian-style **The West End Inn** (146 Pine St. at Neal St., 207/772-1377 or 800/338-1377,

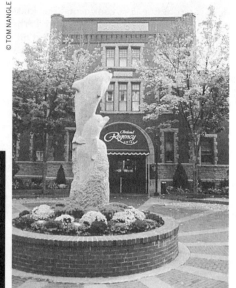

© TOM NANGLE

A former armory in the Old Port is now home to The Portland Regency, one of the city's finest accommodations.

www.westendbb.com, $159–209) has six nicely decorated second- and third-floor guest rooms with TV, and a first-floor room with private porch. A full breakfast is served. Pack light if you're on the third floor.

Full-Service Hotels: You might have trouble finding **The Portland Regency** (20 Milk St., 207/774-4200 or 800/727-3436, www.theregency.com, $199–249). That's because this lovely hotel is secreted in a renovated armory in the heart of the Old Port. Local calls are free, Wi-Fi and laptop rentals are available, and free shuttles are provided to all major Portland transportation facilities. Room configurations vary widely—some provide little natural window light or are strangely shaped. All have 27-inch TVs, minibars, and air-conditioning. A restaurant, spa, and fitness center are on-site.

Newest and most luxurious is the **⬤ Portland Harbor Hotel** (468 Fore St., 207/775-9090 or 888/798-9090, www.portlandharborhotel.com, $249–379), an upscale, bou-

tique hotel in the Old Port built around a garden courtyard. Rooms are plush, with chic linens, duvets, down pillows on the beds, Wi-Fi and digital cable TV, and bathrooms with separate soaking tubs and showers. Bike rentals are available for $15 per day, and the hotel offers a free local car service. The restaurant is excellent. The downside is that the neighborhood can be noisy at night, so request a room facing the interior courtyard, preferably on the upper floors.

Yes, it's a chain, and yes, it's downright ugly, but the **Holiday Inn by the Bay** (88 Spring St., 207/775-2311 or 800/345-5050, www.innbythebay.com, $176–188) provides a lot of bang for the buck. It's conveniently situated between the waterfront and the Arts District; rooms on upper floors have views either over Back Cove or Portland Harbor; Wi-Fi and parking are free as is a shuttle service. It also has an indoor pool, sauna, and fitness room and on-site laundry facilities, in addition to a restaurant and lounge.

Beyond Downtown

South of Portland are a number of inns and resorts, some right on the ocean, others within walking distance.

Just down the street from neighborhoody Higgins Beach is the informal **Higgins Beach Inn** (34 Ocean Ave., Scarborough, 207/883-6684 or 800/836-2322, www.higginsbeachinn.com, mid-May–mid-Oct., $125–165), what your mind's eye might conjure as a traditional, turn-of-the-20th-century summer hotel. It has 24 no-frills rooms, some with shared bath, a few with ocean views. The inn's **Garofalo's Restaurant** has a creative Italian slant, emphasizing seafood (entrées $18–26). In summer, the restaurant is open to the public for breakfast 7:30–10:30 A.M. and dinner 5–9 P.M.; reservations are advisable for dinner, especially on weekends.

In 2007, the **Black Point Inn Resort** (510 Black Point Rd., Prouts Neck, Scarborough, 207/883-2500 or 800/258-0003, www.blackpointinn.com, $190–289 pp, including breakfast, afternoon tea, and dinner) reopened after being dramatically downsized and upscaled. The historical shingle-style hotel sits at the tip of Prouts Neck, with views to Casco Bay from one side and down to Old Orchard from the other, and beaches out the front and back doors. Now owned by a local partnership, the inn has returned to its roots, catering to wealthy rusticators. The Point dining room is open to the public by reservation (6–9 P.M. daily, $19–38), but first, have cocktails on the porch at sunset. Staying here is splurge worthy. Guests have access to a private 18-hole golf course and tennis courts.

Seven miles south of downtown Portland, **Inn by the Sea** (40 Bowery Beach Rd., Rte. 77, Cape Elizabeth, 207/799-3134 or 800/888-4287, www.innbythesea.com, $399–789 d) is a well-managed modern complex with the stylishly casual feel of an upscale summerhouse. It underwent a major renovation and expansion (reopening June 2008) that added a full-service spa and cardio room. Guests stay in hotel rooms, spa suites, or two-bedroom garden cottages, all with spectacular water views. A boardwalk winds down through the salt marsh to the southern end of Crescent Beach State Park. Facilities include an outdoor pool and croquet lawn. By reservation, pets are honored guests here (they even have their own room-service menu). Make reservations early; the inn is incredibly popular. Priceless Audubon prints cover the walls in the appropriately named **Audubon Room** (207/767-0888), where moderate-to-expensive breakfasts, lunches, and dinners are served daily to guests—and to the public by reservation.

Peaks Island Lodging

The **Inn on Peaks Island** (33 Island Ave., www.theinnonpeaksisland.com, $250–300) overlooks the ferry dock and has jaw-dropping sunset views over the Portland skyline. No island roughing it here. The spacious cottage-style guest rooms have fireplaces, sitting areas, whirlpool baths, TV and VCR, refrigerators, and rates include a continental breakfast. Lunch and dinner are also served in the inn's Shipyard Brewhaus restaurant ($10–22). Access is via Casco Bay Lines or a water taxi.

On the other end of the Peaks Island luxury scale is the extremely informal and communal **Eighth Maine Living Museum and Lodge** (13 Eighth Maine Ave., 207/766-5086 mid-May–mid-Sept., 914/237-3165 off-season, $80–100), a shorefront, rustic, living history lodge overlooking White Head Passage. Shared baths and a huge shared kitchen (in which every room is allocated a two-burner gas stove, cabinet space, dining table, and access to full kitchen facilities) allow you to rusticate in much the same manner as did the Civil War vets who built this place, in 1891, with a gift from a veteran who had won the Louisiana Lottery. It has no housekeeping—you're responsible for stripping the linens and cleaning the room and your kitchen space before departing.

FOOD

Downtown Portland alone has more than 100 restaurants, so it's impossible to list even all the great ones—and there are many. The city's proximity to fresh foods, from both farms and the sea, makes it popular with chefs, and its Italian roots and growing immigrant population mean a good choice of ethnic dining, too. Below is a choice selection, by neighborhood, with open days and hours provided for peak season. Call in advance September–June. You'll note that some restaurants don't list a closing time; that's because they shut the doors when the crowd thins, so call ahead if you're heading out much after 8 P.M., just to be safe. Do make reservations, whenever possible, and as far in advance as you can, especially in July and August.

If you'll be in Maine for more than a few days, check out the **Portland Dine Around Club** (P.O. Box 15338, Portland 04112, 207/775-4711 or 877/732-2582, www.dine portland.com, $29.95). This discount card gets you two-for-the-price-of-one meals (usually dinner entrées) at more than 150 restaurants with a wide variety of menus, decor, and price ranges as well as discounts at numerous attractions, museums, performing arts venues, and even lodging, statewide. Check the website to see if the discounts are valid where and when you want them.

In addition to the many restaurant options

GREATER PORTLAND

listed here, check the *Community News* listings in each Wednesday's *Portland Press Herald.* Under "Potluck," you'll find listings of **public meals,** usually benefiting nonprofit organizations. Prices are always quite low (under $10 for adults, $2–4 for children), mealtimes quite early (5 or 6 P.M.), and the flavor quite local.

The Old Port and the Waterfront

All of these are east of the Franklin Street Arterial, between Congress and Commercial Streets. Be sure to ask about renowned Chef Erik Desjarlais's planned new restaurant **Evangeline** (190 State St.) on Longfellow Square. Expected are both three-course a-la-carte and seven-to-fifteen-course degustation menus, bar and table seating, a well-chosen wine menu, and artwork on view.

Local Flavors: You can usually get out for less than $10 from any of these, significantly less at most.

Best known for the earliest and most filling breakfast, **Becky's Diner** (Hobson's Wharf, 390 Commercial St., Old Port, 207/773-7070, 4 A.M.–9 P.M. daily) has more than a dozen omelette choices, just for a start. It also serves lunch and dinner, all at downright cheap prices.

The color's a lot more local just down the street at **The Porthole** (20 Custom House Wharf, Commercial St., Old Port, 207/774-6652, 7 A.M.–2 A.M. Mon.–Sat.), a onetime dive that's been gussied up a bit. The all-you-can-eat Friday fish fry pulls in *real* fishermen, in-the-know locals, and fearless tourists. Eat inside or on the wharf. I like it for breakfast or the Friday $5.95 all-you-can-eat fish fry.

Pizza with a view is on tap at **Flatbread Company** (72 Commercial St., 207/772-8777, www.flatbreadcompany.com, 11:30 A.M.–10 P.M. daily), part of a small, New England chain. The all-natural pizza is baked in a primitive, wood-fired clay oven and served in a dining room with a wall of windows overlooking the ferry terminal and Portland Harbor. Half- and whole-size pizzas include choices such as nitrate-free pepperoni, vegan

(dairy-free) flatbread, cheese and herb, and you-choose combos.

Healthful fast food? Stonyfield Farm CEO Gary Hirshberg proved it wasn't an oxymoron with **O'Natural's** (88 Exchange St., 207/321-2050, www.onaturals.com, 7:30 A.M.–8 P.M., to 8:30 P.M. Fri. and Sat., 10 A.M.–3 P.M. Sun.). The emphasis is on fresh, local, and organic, with choices including flatbread sandwiches, tossed salads, Asian noodles, soups, and even a kids' menu. Wheat-free, dairy-free, and veggie choices are available. It's all served in a historical bank building, where the huge safe is now a safe play area for kids.

For "gourmet goodies" don't miss **Browne Trading Market** (Merrill's Wharf, 262 Commercial St., 207/775-7560). Owner Rod Mitchell became the Caviar King of Portland by wholesaling Caspian caviar, and he's now letting the rest of us in on it. Ultimately fresh fish and shellfish fill the cases next to the caviar and cheeses. The mezzanine is wall-to-wall (literally) wine, specializing in French.

Sweet Treats: When you're craving carbs, want pastries for breakfast, or need to boost your energy with a sweet, follow your nose to **Standard Baking Company** (75 Commercial St., 207/773-2112), deservedly famous for its handcrafted breads and pastries. Chocoholics take note: When a craving strikes for scrumptious homemade chocolates or ice cream, head to **Fuller's** (Wharf St., 207/253-8010).

Fish and Seafood: Ask around, and everyone will tell you the best seafood in town is at **Street and Company** (33 Wharf St., Old Port, 207/775-0887, 5–9:30 P.M., to 10 P.M. Fri. and Sat.). Fresh, beautifully prepared fish (entrées begin about $18) is what you get, often with a Mediterranean flair. Tables are tight, and it's often noisy in the informal, brick-walled rooms.

If that's a little too limited, consider **Old Port Sea Grill and Raw Bar** (www.theold portseagrill.com, opens 11:30 A.M. daily), a sleek, modern spot near the waterfront, with a fabulous raw bar and 500-gallon aquarium inside. Entrées run $20–33, and no surprise, seafood is the specialty.

For lobster in the rough, head to **Portland Lobster Company** (180 Commercial St., 207/775-2112, 11 A.M.–9 P.M. daily). There's a small inside seating area, but it's much more pleasant to sit out on the wharf and watch the excursion boats come and go. Expect to pay in the low $20 range for a one-pound lobster with fries and slaw. Other choices ($8–23) and a kids' menu are available.

Ethnic Fare: Be forewarned: Your first foray into **◖ Bresca** (111 Middle St., 207/772-1004, opens 5:30 P.M. Tues.–Sat.) won't be your last. Chef Krista Kerns delivers big flavor in this small, Italian-flavored space next to Portland's police station. She shops each morning, buying just enough for that night's meal (yes, items do sell out). You'll need a reservation to land one of the 20 seats. Service is personal, the meal is leisurely, the food divine. Do save room for dessert: Krista initially made her name as a pastry chef.

Top-notch for northern Italian is **Cinque Terre Ristorante** (36 Wharf St., 207/347-6154, www.cinqueterremaine.com, 5–9 P.M. Sun.–Thurs., to 10 P.M. Fri. and Sat.). Chef Lee Skawinski is committed to sustainable farming, and much of the seasonal and organic produce used comes from the restaurant owners' Laughing Stock Farm and other Maine farms. The restaurant is housed in a former ship's chandlery that's been transformed into a comfortable, Tuscan-accented dining area, with an open kitchen and seating either on the main floor or a second-floor balcony that rims the open space. Choose from half- or full-size portions ranging $12–28. Do begin with the antipasto plate, and don't miss the handmade pastas or the lobster risotto. More than 100 Italian wines are on the award-winning list. Service can be iffy.

Cinque Terre's sister restaurant, **Vignola** (10 Dana St., 207/772-1330, www.vignolamaine.com, 11 A.M.–2:30 P.M. and 5 P.M.–midnight daily, opens 10 A.M. Sun. for brunch), is more casual and less pricey ($10–18) and wins points for late-night dining.

Ask locally about **Village Café**, an ever-popular family favorite for its respectable Italian food (entrées $10–23), healthful specials, and fried clams. In biz since 1936, it expected to reopen in a new Portland location in 2008.

Irish fare with a Maine accent fills the menu at **Ri-Ra** (72 Commercial St., Old Port, 207/761-4446, www.rira.com, 11:30 A.M.–10 P.M. daily). How about beef stew made with Guinness? Or grilled salmon with leeks? Entrées in the glass-walled second-floor dining room (overlooking the Casco Bay Lines ferry terminal) are $11–29. Appetizers and desserts are superb, too. The ground-floor pub, elegantly woody, with an enormous bar, is inevitably stuffed to the gills on weekends—a great spot for such traditional fare as corned beef and cabbage (pub entrées $8–16) as long as you can stand the din. No reservations, so be prepared to wait, especially on weekends.

Eclectic Dining: The people-watching can't be beat from the patio or deck of **Mims Brasserie** (205 Commercial St., Old Port, 207/345-7478, www.mimsportland.com, 8 A.M.–9:30 P.M. Mon.–Fri., 9 A.M.–10 P.M. Sat.–Sun.). The à-la-carte French-inspired menu features naturally raised meats. Dinner entrées are $12–25; side dishes are extra and designed to be mixed, matched, and shared. Create your own omelette at breakfast; Benedicts are the specialties during weekend brunch.

One of Portland's old reliables, **Walter's** (15 Exchange St., 207/871-9258, www.walterscafe.com, 11 A.M.–2:30 P.M. and 5–9 P.M., no lunch Sun.) has been serving creative fusion fare since 1990s, and despite the longevity, it's never tiresome. The two-level dining room can be noisy. Entrées run around $16–26.

Destination Dining: Plan well in advance to get a reservation at **◖ Fore Street** (288 Fore St., Old Port, 207/775-2717, www.forestreet.biz, 5:30–10 P.M. Sun.–Thurs., to 10:30 P.M. Fri. and Sat.). Chef Sam Hayward, a fixture on the Maine food scene who is well known for his creative use of Maine-sourced ingredients, won the James Beard Award for Best Chef in the Northeast in 2004 and has been featured in most of the foodie publications. Even though the copper-topped tables,

GREATER PORTLAND

open kitchen, and the industrial decor create a din in this ex-warehouse, no one seems to mind much. Game is roasted on a spit and seafood is grilled over apple wood or roasted in the wood oven. Appetizers are particularly imaginative. Entrées begin around $20. The restaurant is a joint project with Street and Company owner Dana Street.

Arts District

These restaurants are clustered from Danforth Street (an area sometimes referred to as the Studio District) up to and around Congress Street.

Local Flavors: Even the name **Norm's Bar and Grill** (617 Congress St., 207/828-9944, 11:30 A.M.–10 P.M., opens at 4 P.M. Sun.) is reminiscent of *Cheers*. Locals would prefer this neighborhood eatery were kept secret, but the food is too good not to share. One of the reasons Norm's is so popular is that you can cobble together a meal that meets your appetite from a menu that includes selections for tapas, sandwiches, salads, entrées, and sides in addition to chalkboard specials. Norm's doesn't take reservations, so you'll probably have to relax in the equally popular bar while waiting for a table. Norm also operates the tavern across the street and a barbecue joint in the Old Port.

Ole! Healthful Mexican is served at **Mesa Verde** (618 Congress St., 774-6089, 11:30 A.M.–9 P.M. Tues.–Thurs., to 9:30 P.M. Fri. and Sat., to 8:30 P.M. Sun.), a colorful restaurant and juice bar that also is rightfully famous for its margaritas.

If your sweet tooth is calling, answer it at **geo's patisserie café** (27 Forest Ave., 207/699-2655, www.geospatisserie.com, 7 A.M.–6 P.M. Mon.–Fri., 8 A.M.–5 P.M. Sat.), a European-style scratch bakery where chef George Gilfoil creates delicious pastries and also serves lunch.

Eclectic: Ever-popular **⬛ Local 188** (685 Congress St., 207/761-7909, www.local188 .com, 11 A.M.–3 P.M. and 5:30–10:30 P.M. daily) moved from its funky digs to a larger, more comfortable space, keeping its spirit but

maturing (a bit) in decor. This place serves fabulous Mediterranean-inspired food with a tapas-heavy menu. It doubles as an art gallery, with rotating exhibits. Spend lunch, Saturday or Sunday brunch (10 A.M.–3 P.M.), or an evening grazing through marinated mushrooms, vegetable salads, imaginative soups, mussel stew, even paella. Tapas selections are all under $10, heartier choices and entrées run $10–18. Free parking behind the building.

Be sure to have a reservation if you're going, pretheater, to **BiBo's Madd Apple Café** (23 Forest Ave., 207/774-9698, 11:30 A.M.– 2 P.M. Wed.–Fri., 5:30–9 P.M. Wed.–Sat., 11 A.M.–2 P.M. and 4–8 P.M. Sun.)—it's right next to the Portland Performing Arts Center. On the other hand, it's popular anytime, thanks to chef Bill Boutwell (BiBo). There's no way of predicting what will be on the bistro-fusion menu, although the sweet soy-marinated salmon is so popular that it's almost always available. Dinner entrée range is $15–25.

Well off most tourists' radar screens is **Artemesia Café** (61 Pleasant St., 207/761-0135, 11 A.M.–3 P.M. Mon.–Fri., 9 A.M.–2 P.M. Sat. and Sun., and from 5 P.M. Thurs.–Sat.), but it's another one of Portland's little surprises. It's a bright spot serving a creative menu that draws upon international influences.

Ethnic Fare: Portland has a number of good Japanese restaurants. **Yosaku** (1 Danforth St., 207/780-0880, 11:30 A.M.–2 P.M. and 5–9:30 P.M. Mon.–Thurs., to 10:30 P.M. Fri. and Sat., to 9 P.M. Sun., and noon–3 P.M. Sat. and Sun.) is an old standby serving delicious sushi along with noodle dishes, tempuras, and other Japanese favorites.

Newer on the scene is **Miyake** (129 Spring St., 207/871-9170, noon–2 P.M. Tues.–Fri., 5–9 P.M. Mon.–Thurs., to 9:30 P.M. Fri. and Sat.), which quickly established itself as a must-go; BYOB.

Destination Dining: Fun, whimsical, and artsy best describes most restaurants in the Arts District, but not **Five Fifty-Five** (555 Congress St., 207/761-0555, www.five fifty-five.com, 5–10 P.M. Mon.–Thurs., to

10:30 P.M. Fri. and Sat., 10:30 A.M.–2:30 P.M. (brunch) and 5–9:30 P.M. Sun.), where chef Steve Corry was named by *Food and Wine* as one of the top 10 best new chefs in the country. The bilevel dining area is bright and elegant. Fresh, local, and seasonal are blended in creative ways on his ever-changing menu, which is divided into small plates, green plates, savory plates, cheese plates, and sweet plates, with prices ranging about $8–30. A five-course tasting menu is available with 24-hour notice. If you can't afford to splurge in the main restaurant, Corry serves lighter fare in the lounge.

West End

Chef Abby Harmon's **Caiola's Restaurant** (58 Pine St., 207/772-1111, www.caiolas.com, 5:30–9:30 P.M. Tues.–Thurs., to 10 P.M. Fri. and Sat.) delivers a taste of Europe derived from local farms and gardens. It deserves its buzz as far more than a neighborhood spot. Harmon draws upon her experience at some of Maine's top restaurants, and her staff is well trained. Entrées begin around $14.

Superb, thin-crust pizzas in usual and unusual flavor combos emerge from the wood-fired oven at Chef Oliver Outerbridge's **Bonobo** (Pine and Bracket Sts., 207/347-8267, 11 A.M.–11 P.M. Mon.–Sat.). After the pizza, head to the ice-cream window, serving Maple's Organics gelato.

Have breakfast or lunch or pick up prepared foods at **Aurora Provisions** (64 Pine St., 207/871-9061, www.auroraprovisions.com, 8 A.M.–6:30 P.M. Mon.–Sat.), a combination market and café with irresistible goodies, most made on the premises.

Bayside

Fine Dining: For an elegant meal, look no farther than the (**Back Bay Grill** (65 Portland St., near the main post office, 207/772-8833, 5:30–9:30 P.M. Mon.–Thurs., to 10 P.M. Fri. and Sat.). The serene dining room is accented by a colorful mural, and arts-and-crafts wall sconces cast a soft glow on the white linen-draped tables. The menu, which highlights fresh, seasonal ingredients, ranks among the best in the city, and the wine list is long and well chosen. Service is professional. Entréees are $19–35 and worth every penny.

Casual Dining: In-the-know Portlanders have long favored **Bintliff's American Café** (98 Portland St., 207/774-0005, www.bintliffs cafe.com, 7 A.M.–2 P.M. daily and 5–9 P.M. Wed.–Sat.) for its fabulous brunches ($7–12); the menu is humongous. It also serves a much smaller dinner menu (entrées $17–25) to equally rave reviews. It takes no reservations for brunch, so expect to wait in line on weekends (it's worth it).

East End

These dining spots are all east of the Franklin Street Arterial, with most concentrated in the food-oriented neighborhood of India and Middle Streets.

Local Flavors: The most incredible fries come from (**Duckfat** (43 Middle St., 207/774-8080, www.duckfat.com, 11 A.M.–8 P.M. Mon.–Thurs., to 9 P.M. Fri. and Sat., noon–6 P.M. Sun.), an ultracasual, order-at-the-counter joint owned by Chef Rob Evans (of Hugo's fame), so you know it's not only good, but it has that spark, too. Fries, fried in duck fat, of course, are served in a paper cone and accompanied by your choice of sauce from six options; the truffle ketchup is heavenly. Want to really harden those arteries? Order the *poutine,* Belgian fries topped with Maine cheese curd and homemade duck gravy. In addition, Duckfat serves paninis, soups, salads, and really good milk shakes; wine and beer are available, too.

Mmmmm, mmmm. For finger-lickin' barbecued ribs and chicken, fried chicken, blackened catfish, and pulled pork or beef brisket sandwiches, it's **Norm's East End Grill** (37 Middle St., 207/253-1700, 11:30 A.M.–10 P.M. Mon.–Sat., 5–9 P.M. Sun.). All barbecue items are smoked on the premises with hickory and apple wood. Of course, this being Maine, clam and corn chowder, homemade fish cakes, and lobster stew are also available.

Mainers love their Italian sandwiches, and **Amato's** (71 India St., 207/773-1682, www .amatos.com, 6:30 A.M.–11 P.M. Mon.–Fri., opens 7 A.M. Sun.) is credited with creating this drool-worthy sub, made with ham, cheese, tomatoes, green peppers, black olives, and onions (or various other combinations), all wrapped in a doughy roll and drizzled with olive oil. Also available are calzones, salads, and other Italian-inspired foods. Amato's has outlets throughout southern Maine. This one has outdoor patio seating.

Micucci's Grocery Store (45 India St., 207/775-1854) has been servicing Portland's Italian community since 1949. It's a great stop for picnic fixings and a nice selection of inexpensive wines. It's also home to baker Stephen Lanzalotta's to-die-for breads and pastries, soups, little pizzas, and other healthful, delicious Mediterranean-style foods.

Huge portions at rock-bottom prices makes **Silly's** (40 Washington Ave., 207/772-0360, www.sillys.com, 11:30 A.M.– 9 P.M. Tues.–Sun.) an ever-popular choice among the young and budget minded; it has a huge menu, too, with lots of international flair and milk shakes in dozens of wacko flavors. And the decor? Vintage 1950s Formica and chrome.

Casual Dining: Blue Spoon (89 Congress St., 207/773-1119, 11 A.M.–3 P.M. and 5–9 P.M. Tues.–Sat.) was one of the first upscale eateries on Portland's gentrifying East End. Chef/ owner David Iovino, who studied at the French Culinary Institute, has created a warm, welcoming, and inexpensive bistro (entrées $9–13), where one of the best sellers is roast chicken that's pan seared and then roasted beneath a hot brick. Vegetarian and vegan selections are available.

Primo rustic Italian fare is the rule at **Ribollita** (41 Middle St., 207/774-2972, 5– 9 P.M. Tues.–Thurs., to 10 P.M. Fri. and Sat.). You'll want reservations at this small, casual restaurant that's justly popular for delivering fabulous food at fair prices ($12–20); just be in the mood for a leisurely meal. Handmade pastas, such as white bean and Romano ravioli or pan-seared gnocchi, and choices such as radicchio-wrapped salmon with pesto and roast pepper sauce are typical.

You never know what'll be on the menu (Indonesian chicken, North African stuffed peppers, maybe Caribbean shrimp cakes?) at funky **Pepperclub** (78 Middle St., 207/772-0531, www.pepperclubrestaurant.com, 5– 9 P.M. Sun.–Thurs., to 10 P.M. Fri. and Sat.), but take the risk. Vegetarian and vegan specials are always available, as are local and organic meats and seafood. If your kids are even vaguely adventuresome, they'll find food to like here—and prices to match (entrées $11– 15). In the mornings, it morphs into **The Good Egg** (7–11 A.M. Mon.–Fri., 8 A.M.–1 P.M. Sat. and Sun.), serving breakfast, including gluten-free foods.

Destination Dining: In 2004, *Food and Wine* named Rob Evans as one of America's 10 Best New Chefs, and in 2007 he was a Beard nominee for Best Chef in the Northeast, making ☾ **Hugo's** (88 Middle St., corner of Franklin St., 207/774-8538, www.hugos.net, 5:30–9 P.M. Tues.–Thurs., to 9:30 P.M. Sat. and Sun.) a destination unto itself. Not that savvy Portlanders hadn't already been beating a path to his door for his outstanding New American cuisine. In 2008, Evans and partner Nancy Pugh planned to change the formal fixed-price, multicourse menu to an à la carte one (most entrées $15–28) and present a more casual face. Evans will still draw from the freshest Maine ingredients available. Bar seating is available; for the dining room, reservations are essential.

The 'Burbs

Great sunset views over Portland's skyline, a casual atmosphere, and excellent fare have earned **Saltwater Grille** (231 Front St., South Portland, 207/799-5400, www.salt watergrille.com, 11 A.M.–3 P.M. and 5–9 P.M. daily) an excellent reputation. Dine inside or on the waterfront deck. Dinner entrées run $15–25.

Lobster in the Rough: Every Mainer has a favorite lobster eatery (besides home), but **The Lobster Shack** (222 Two Lights Rd., Cape Elizabeth, 207/799-1677, www .lobstershack-twolights.com, 11 A.M.–8 P.M. mid-Apr.–mid-Oct.) tops an awful lot of lists. Seniority helps—it's been here since the 1920s. Scenery, too—a panoramic vista in the shadow of Cape Elizabeth Light. Plus the menu—seafood galore (and hot dogs for those who'd rather). Choose a lobster from the tank; indulge in the lobster stew; grab a table on the ledges and watch the world sail by. Opt for a sunny day; the lighthouse's foghorn can kill your conversation when the fog rolls in.

INFORMATION AND SERVICES
Information
The Visitor Information Center of the Convention and Visitors Bureau of Greater Portland (245 Commercial St., Portland 04101, 207/772-4994, www.visitportland.com) has tons of brochures, plenty of restaurant menus, and public restrooms. The Portland Downtown District (94 Free St., 207/772-6828, www .portlandmaine.com) has a useful website.

Check out the Portland Public Library (5 Monument Sq., 207/871-1700, www .portlandlibrary.com).

For winter parking-ban information, call 207/879-0300.

Public Restrooms
In the Old Port area, you'll find restrooms at the Convention and Visitors Bureau Visitor Information Center (245 Commercial St.), the Spring Street parking garage (45 Spring St.), the Fore Street Parking Garage (419 Fore St.), and the Casco Bay Lines ferry terminal (Commercial and Franklin Sts.).

On Congress Street, find restrooms at Portland City Hall (389 Congress St.) and the Portland Public Library (5 Monument Sq.). In Midtown, head for the Cumberland County Civic Center (1 Civic Center Sq.). In the West End, use Maine Medical Center.

GETTING THERE AND AROUND
The best overall source for planning your transportation is the website www.transportme.org. It lists schedules, fares, and other information for airlines, buses, ferries, and trains.

The ultraclean and comfortable Portland Transportation Center (100 Thompson Point Rd., Portland, 207/828-3939) is the base for **Concord Trailways** (800/639-3317, concordtrailways.com) and **Amtrak's Downeaster** (800/872-7245, www.the downeaster.com). Parking is $3 per day, and the terminal has free coffee, free newspapers (while they last), and vending machines. The **Metro** (114 Valley St., P.O. Box 1097, Portland 04104, 207/774-0351, $1.25 exact change), **The Portland Explorer** (207/774-9891 or 800/377-4457, www.portland explorer.org, free), and the Zoom buses, with service from Biddeford/Saco, stop here and connect with **Portland International Jetport** (207/774-7301, www.portland jetport.org), **Vermont Transit Lines** (950 Congress St., 207/772-6587 or 800/552-8737), and **Casco Bay Lines ferry service** (www.cascobaylines.com). If you show your Trailways or Amtrak ticket stub to the Metro bus driver, you'll have a free ride downtown. Taxis charge $1.40 for the first plus $0.25 for each additional one-ninth mile.

Parking garages and lots are strategically situated all over downtown Portland, particularly in the Old Port and near the civic center. Unless you're lucky, you'll probably waste a lot of time looking for on-street parking (meters start at $0.25 a half hour), so a garage or lot is the best option. If you land in a garage or lot with a Park and Shop sticker, you can collect free-parking stamps, each good for an hour, from participating shops and restaurants. You could even end up parking for free. A day of parking generally runs $8–16. The Casco Bay Lines website (www .cascobaylines.com) has a very useful parking map, listing parking lots and garages and their hourly and daily rates. It's good for comparison shopping.

Freeport

Freeport has a special claim to historic fame—it's the place where Maine parted company from Massachusetts in 1820. The documents were signed on March 15, making Maine its own separate state.

At the height of the local mackerel-packing industry here, countless tons of the bony fish were shipped out of South Freeport, often in ships built on the shores of the Harraseeket River. Splendid relics of the shipbuilders' era still line the streets of South Freeport, and no architecture buff should miss a walk, cycle, or drive through the village. Even downtown Freeport still reflects the shipbuilder's craft, with contemporary shops tucked in and around handsome historic houses. Some have been converted to B&Bs, others are boutiques, and one even disguises the local McDonald's franchise.

Today, Freeport is best known as the mecca for the shop-till-you-drop set. The hub, of course, is sportswear giant L. L. Bean, which has been here since 1912, when founder Leon Leonwood Bean began making his trademark hunting boots (and also unselfishly handed out hot tips on where the fish were biting). More than 120 retail operations now fan out from that epicenter, and you can find almost anything in Freeport (pop. about 7,700)—except maybe a parking spot in midsummer.

When (or if) you tire of shopping, you can always find quiet refuge in the town's preserves and parks—Mast Landing Sanctuary, Wolfe's Neck Woods State Park, and Winslow Memorial Park—and plenty of local color at the Town Wharf in the still honest-to-goodness fishing village of South Freeport.

An orientation note: Don't be surprised to receive directions (particularly for South Freeport) relative to "the Big Indian"—a 40-foot-tall landmark at the junction of Route 1 and South Freeport Road. If you stop at the Maine Visitor Information Center in Yarmouth and continue on Route 1 toward Freeport, you can't miss it, just north of the Freeport Inn and the Casco Bay Inn.

SHOPPING

Logically, this category must come first in any discussion of Freeport, since shopping's the biggest game in town. It's pretty much a given that anyone who visits Freeport intends to darken the door of at least one shop.

☾ L. L. Bean

If it's *only* one, it's likely to be "Bean's." The whole world beats a path to L. L. Bean (95 Main St., Rte. 1, 207/865-4761 or 800/341-4341, www.llbean.com)—or so it seems in July, August, and December. Established as a hunting/fishing supply shop, this giant sports outfitter now sells everything from kids' clothing to cookware on its ever-expanding downtown campus. In 2007, it moved the hunting and fishing store into the expanded main store,

the boot that built an empire

© TOM NANGLE

MAINE WILDLIFE PARK

If you want to see where Maine's wild things are, venture a bit inland to visit the Maine Wildlife Park (Shaker Rd./Rte. 26, Gray, 207/657-4977, 9:30 A.M.-6 P.M. daily, gate closes 4:30 P.M. mid-Apr.-Veterans' Day, $6 ages 13-60, $4.50 seniors, $4 kids 4-12). Nearly 25 native species of wildlife can be seen at this state-operated wildlife refuge, including such ever-popular species as moose, black bear, white-tailed deer, and bald eagle. The park began in 1931 as a state-run game farm. For more than 50 years, the Department of Inland Fish and Game reared pheasants here for release during bird-hunting season. At the same time, wildlife biologists and game wardens with the state's Department of Inland Fisheries and Wildlife needed a place to care for orphaned or injured animals.

In 1982, the farm's mission was changed to that of a wildlife and conservation education facility. Today the park is a temporary haven for wildlife, but those who cannot survive in the wild live here permanently.

Among the wildlife that have been in residence at the park are lynx, deer, opossum, black bear, bobcat, porcupine, raccoon, red-tailed hawk, barred and great horned owl, mountain lion, bald eagle, raven, skunk, woodchuck, and coyote. Other frequent guests include wild turkey, fisher, gray fox, kestrel, turkey vulture, wood turtle, and box turtle. Most are here for protection and healing, and while they're in residence, visitors are able to view them at close range.

In addition to the wildlife, there are numerous interactive exhibits and displays to view, nature trails to explore, a nature store, snack shack, and even picnic facilities. Special programs and exhibits are often offered on weekends mid-May-mid-September.

The park is 3.5 miles north of downtown Gray and Maine Turnpike Exit 63. From the coast, take Route 115 from Main Street in downtown Yarmouth, continuing through North Yarmouth (with stunning old houses) to Gray, and then head north on Route 26 for 3.5 miles.

GREATER PORTLAND

and in 2008, the outlet store—a great source for deals on equipment and clothing—moved into the former hunting and fishing building, behind the main store. It's also partnered on a new parking and retail facility, expected to open in 2009, with as many as 40 shops. It's under construction on land behind Bow and Main Streets.

By 2010, Bean's aspires to have a new outdoor adventure center in full operation on its 700-acre property on Desert Road. Possibilities include a restaurant, lodging, a golf course, and opportunities for extended stay and participation packages for sports in its Walk-On Adventures and other programs, such as kayaking, canoeing, cross-country skiing, snowshoeing, shooting, and archery. Some opportunities may open prior to 2010.

Until the 1970s, Bean's remained a rustic store with a creaky staircase and a closet-size women's department. Then a few other merchants began arriving, Bean's expanded, and a

feeding frenzy followed. The Bean reputation rests on a savvy staff, high quality, an admirable environmental consciousness, and a no-questions-asked return policy. Bring the kids—for the indoor trout pond, the clean restrooms, and the "real deal" outlet store. The store's open-round-the-clock policy has become its signature, and if you show up at 2 A.M., you'll have much of the store to yourself, and you may even spy vacationing celebrities or the rock stars who often visit after Portland shows.

Outlets and Specialty Stores

After Bean's, it's up to your whims and your wallet. The stores stretch for several miles up and down Main Street and along many side streets. Pick up a copy of the *Official Map and Visitor Guide* at any of the shops or restaurants, at one of the visitor kiosks, or at the Hose Tower Information Center (23 Depot St., two blocks east of L. L. Bean). All the big names are here, as are plenty of little ones.

PARKS, PRESERVES, AND OTHER ATTRACTIONS
Mast Landing Sanctuary

More than two miles of easy, yellow-blazed trails wind through the 140-acre Mast Landing Sanctuary, an area that ages ago was the source of masts for the Royal Navy. Pick up a trail map at the parking area and start watching for birds. The best (and longest) route is the 1.6-mile Loop Trail, which passes fruit trees, hardwoods, and an old milldam. (Keep the kids off the dam.) The sanctuary is open sunrise–sunset, year-round, and is popular in winter with cross-country skiers. Admission is free. From downtown Freeport (Rte. 1), take Bow Street (opposite L. L. Bean) one mile east to Upper Mast Landing Road. Turn left (north) and go 500 feet to the parking area.

Wolfe's Neck Woods State Park

Five miles of easy to moderate trails meander through 233-acre Wolfe's Neck Woods State Park (Wolfe's Neck Rd., 207/865-4465, $3 ages 11–64, $1 children 5–11), just a few minutes' cycle or drive from downtown Freeport. You'll need a trail map, available near the parking area. The easiest route (partly wheelchair-accessible) is the Shoreline Walk, about three-quarters of a mile, starting near the salt marsh and skirting Casco Bay. Sprinkled along the trails are helpful interpretive panels explaining various points of natural history—bog life, osprey nesting, glaciation, erosion, and tree decay. Guided tours are offered at 2 P.M. daily mid-July–late August, weather permitting. Leashed pets are allowed. Adjacent **Googins Island,** an osprey sanctuary, is off-limits. From downtown Freeport, follow Bow Street (across from L. L. Bean) for 2.25 miles; turn right onto Wolfe's Neck Road (also called Wolf Neck Rd.) and go another 2.25 miles.

Wolfe's Neck Farm

The best time to visit Wolfe's Neck Farm (10 Burnett Rd., 207/865-4469, www.wolfes neckfarm.org) is March and April for the annual **Calf Watch,** when about 60 calves and 15 lambs join the herd on the 620-acre farm. During calving season, the farm is open 9 A.M.–5 P.M. daily, and kids can see the latest newborns as well as chickens, turkeys, pigs, and other creatures. Sustainable agriculture and environmental sensitivity are the overriding philosophies at this working farm owned and operated by the nonprofit Wolfe's Neck Farm Foundation. Nature trails lace the property, and a small retail shop in the farmhouse (open 9 A.M.–4:30 P.M. weekdays) sells naturally raised beef, lamb, pork, and eggs.

Winslow Memorial Park

Owned by the town of Freeport, Winslow Memorial Park (Staples Point, South Freeport, 207/865-4198, late May–late Sept., $1.50) is a spectacular 90-plus-acre seaside park, overlooking the islands of upper Casco Bay. Swim off the beach (changing house, restrooms, but no lifeguards), picnic on the shore, walk the three-quarters-mile nature trail and perch on the point, launch a canoe or kayak, or reserve one of the 100 inland or waterfront campsites ($22–29, no hookups, but some sites can take RVs). The boat landing and beach area are tidal, so boaters and swimmers should plan to be here two hours before and two hours after high tide; otherwise, you're dealing with mudflats. From the Big Indian on Route 1, take South Freeport Road one mile to Staples Point Road and continue to the end.

Bradbury Mountain State Park

Six miles from the hubbub of Freeport and you're in tranquil, wooded, 590-acre Bradbury Mountain State Park (Rte. 9, Pownal, 207/688-4712, $3 adults, $1 children 5–11), with facilities for picnicking, hiking, mountain biking, and rustic camping, but no swimming. Pick up a trail map at the gate and take the easy, 0.4-mile (round-trip) Mountain Trail to the 485-foot summit, with superb views east to the ocean and southeast to Portland. In fall, it's gorgeous. Or take the Tote Road Trail, on the western side of the park, where the ghost of Samuel Bradbury occasionally brings a chill to hikers in a hemlock grove. A playground keeps the littlest tykes happy. The nonresident camping fee is $14 per site per night ($11 for residents). The park season is May 15–October 15, but there's winter access for cross-country skiing. From Route 1, cross over I-95 at Exit 20 and continue west on Pownal Road to Route 9.

Pineland Farms

Once a home to Maine's mentally disabled citizens, 1,600-acre Pineland (15 Farm View Dr., New Gloucester, 207/688-4539, www.pineland farms.org) campus was closed in 1996. In 2000, the Libra Foundation bought it, and now the property comprises 19 buildings and 5,000 acres of farmland, and much of it is open for recreation. Walk or ski the trails, sight birds in the fields and woods, stroll through the garden, fish the pond or skate on it in winter, play tennis, go mountain biking or orienteering, or even take a horseback-riding lesson. It's a vast outdoor playground, but your first stop should be the visitors center (9 A.M.–5 P.M. daily) to see a list of any events (frequent ones include guided farm tours and family experiences), pick up maps, pay any necessary fees, shop for farm-fresh products, or even grab lunch or snacks at Foley's Bakery Coffee House or the Commons Caféteria. (Some activities, such as cross-country mountain-biking trail access and horseback-riding lessons require fees.) Also on the premises are a variety of accommodations, with rates beginning at $325–400 per night. No dogs.

Desert of Maine

Okay, so maybe it's a bit hokey, but talk about sands of time. More than 10,000 years ago, glaciers covered the region surrounding the Desert of Maine (95 Desert Rd., 207/865-6962, www.desertofmaine.com, early May–mid-Oct., $8.75 adults, $6.25 ages 13–16, $5.25 ages 6–12). When they receded, they scoured the landscape, pulverizing rocks and leaving behind a sandy residue that was covered by a thin layer of topsoil. Jump forward to 1797, when William Tuttle bought 300 acres and moved his family here, as well as his house and barn, and cleared the land. Now jump forward again to the present and tour where a once-promising farmland has become a desert wasteland. The guided, safari-style tram tours combine history, geology, and environmental science and an opportunity for children to hunt for "gems" in the sand. Decide for yourself: Is the desert a natural phenomenon? A man-made disaster? Or does the truth lie somewhere in the middle?

Harrington House

A block south of L. L. Bean is the Harrington House (45 Main St., Rte. 1, 207/865-3170, www.freeporthistoricalsociety.org, 10 A.M.–2:30 P.M. Tues., Thurs., and Fri. and 10 A.M.–7 P.M. Wed., free) home base of the Freeport Historical Society. You can pick up walking maps detailing Freeport's architecture for a small fee and tour the house. Exhibits pertaining to Freeport's history and occasionally ones by local artists are presented in two rooms in the restored 1830 Enoch Harrington House, a National Historic Register property.

RECREATION AND SPORTS
◖ L. L. Bean Outdoor Discovery Schools

Since the early 1980s, the sports outfitter's Outdoor Discovery Schools (888/552-3261, www.llbean.com) have trained thousands of outdoors enthusiasts to improve their skills in fly-fishing, archery, hiking, canoeing, sea kayaking, winter camping, cross-country skiing, orienteering, and even outdoor photography. Here's a deal that requires no planning. **Walk-On Adventures** provides 1.5–2.5-hour lessons in sports such as kayak touring, fly casting, archery, clay shooting, snowshoeing, and cross-country skiing for $15, including equipment. All of the longer fee programs, plus canoeing and camping trips, require preregistration, well in advance because of their popularity. Some are held in the mountains and on the rivers of western Maine, others are in Maryland and Virginia. Some of the lectures, seminars, and demonstrations held in Freeport are free, and a regular catalog lists the schedule. Bean's waterfront **Flying Point Paddling Center** hosts many of the kayaking, saltwater fly-fishing, and guiding programs and is home to the annual **PaddleSports Festival** in June, with free demonstrations, seminars, vendors, lessons, and more.

❰ Atlantic Seal Cruises

Atlantic Seal Cruises (Town Wharf, South Freeport, 207/865-6112 or 877/285-7325), owned and operated by Captain Tom Ring, makes two or three 2.5-hour cruises daily to 17-acre **Eagle Island,** a State Historic Site once owned by Admiral Robert Peary of North Pole fame. The trip includes a lobstering demonstration (except Sun., when lobstering is banned). Fee is $28 adult, $20 ages 5–12, $15 ages 1–4. Captain Ring also does daylong excursions once a week to **Seguin Island,** off the Phippsburg Peninsula, where you can climb the light tower and see Maine's only first-order Fresnel lens, the largest on the coast. (This trip, which costs $50 adult, $34 under 12, is not for the unsteady; you'll be offloaded from a small boat.) A Seal and Osprey Watch cruise is offered at twilight.

Kayak and Canoe Rentals

Ring's Marine Service (Smelt Brook Rd., South Freeport, 207/865-6143 or 866/865-6143, www.ringsmarineservice.com) rents single kayaks for $38, tandems for $60, and canoes for $28 per day, with longer-term rentals available.

ENTERTAINMENT

Shopping seems to be more than enough entertainment for most of Freeport's visitors, but don't miss the **L. L. Bean Summer Concert Series** (800/341-4341, ext. 37222). At

7:30 P.M. each Saturday early July–Labor Day weekend, Bean's hosts free big-name, family-oriented events in Discovery Park, in the Bean's complex. Arrive early (these concerts are *very* popular) and bring a blanket or a folding chair. Call for more info.

ACCOMMODATIONS

If you'd prefer to drop where you shop, Freeport has a large country inn, several motels, and more than two dozen B&Bs, so finding a pillow is seldom a problem, but it's still wise to have reservations. For camping, try Winslow Memorial Park and Wolfe's Neck Farm.

Downtown

One of Freeport's pioneering B&Bs is on the main drag yet away from much of the traffic, in a restored house where Arctic explorer Admiral Donald MacMillan once lived. The 19th-century **White Cedar Inn** (178 Main St., Freeport, 207/865-9099 or 800/853-1269, www.whitecedarinn.com, $145–200) has seven attractive guest rooms with antiques, air-conditioning, and Wi-Fi; some have gas fireplaces; one has a TV and accepts dogs ($20). The full breakfast will definitely power you through a day of shopping.

Two blocks north of L. L. Bean, the **❰ Harraseeket Inn** (162 Main St., Freeport, 207/865-9377 or 800/342-6423, www .harraseeketinn.com, $199–305 peak) is a splendid 84-room country inn with an indoor pool, cable TV, air-conditioning, phones, and Wi-Fi; many rooms have fireplaces and hot tubs. A few rooms are decorated with Thomas Moser furnishings, otherwise decor is colonial reproduction in the two antique buildings and a modern addition. Rates include a hot-and-cold buffet breakfast and afternoon tea—a refreshing break from power shopping—with finger sandwiches and sweets. Pets are permitted in some rooms. The $25/night fee includes a dog bed, small can of food, treat, and dishes. Ask about packages, which offer excellent value. Children 12 and younger stay free. If you're traveling solo, the nightly Innkeeper's Table (reservation required by 5:30 P.M. for 6:30 P.M.

seating, 207/865-1085) is a communal table hosted by an innkeeper and a great way to meet other guests. (See *Food* for information on its two excellent restaurants.)

Three blocks south of L. L. Bean, on a quiet side street shared with a couple of other B&Bs, is **The James Place Inn** (11 Holbrook St., Freeport, 207/865-4486 or 800/964-9086, www.jamesplaceinn.com, $155–185 peak). Innkeepers Robin and Tori Baron welcome guests to seven comfortable rooms, all with air-conditioning, Wi-Fi, and TV, a few with double whirlpool tubs, and one with a woodburning fireplace and private deck. If the weather's fine, enjoy breakfast on the deck. After shopping, collapse on the hammock for two.

Beyond Downtown

Here's a throwback. Three miles north of downtown is the **Maine Idyll** (1411 Rte. 1, 207/865-4201, www.maineidyll.com, $59–103), a tidy cottage colony operated by the Marstaller family for three generations. Twenty studio to three-bedroom pine-paneled cottages are tucked under the trees. All have refrigerators, fireplaces, and TV, and most have limited cooking facilities. Wi-Fi is available near the office. A light breakfast is included. There are two children's play sets, and well-behaved pets are $4.

The family-run **Casco Bay Inn** (107 Rte. 1, Freeport, 207/865-4925 or 800/570-4970, www.cascobayinn.com, $99–119 peak) is a bit fancier than most motels. It has a pine-paneled lounge with fieldstone fireplace and guest Internet station, with Wi-Fi throughout. The spacious rooms have double sinks in the bath area, and some have a refrigerator and microwave. A continental breakfast with newspaper is included.

Camping

Recompence Shore Campsites (134 Burnett Rd., Freeport, 207/865-9307, www.freeport camping.com, $21–32) is part of Wolfe's Neck Farm. It's an eco-sensitive campground with 175 wooded tent sites (a few hookups are available), many on the farm's three-mile-long Casco Bay shorefront. For anyone seeking peace, quiet, and low-tech camping in a spectacular setting, this is it. Amenities include a laundry and Wi-Fi. Ice, firewood, ice cream, and snacks are available at the camp store. Quiet, leashed, attended pets are welcome. Quiet time begins at 10 P.M. Swimming depends on the tides; check the tide calendar in a local newspaper. Take Bow Street (across from L. L. Bean) to Wolfe's Neck Road, turn right, and go 1.6 miles to Burnett Road, a left turn.

FOOD

Freeport has an ever-increasing number of places to eat, but nowhere enough to satisfy hungry crowds at peak dining hours on busy days. Go early or late for lunch, and make reservations for dinner.

Local Flavors

South of downtown, **Royal River Natural Foods** (443 Rte. 1, Freeport, 207/865-0046, www.rrnf.com) has a small selection of prepared foods, including soups, salads, and sandwiches, and a seating area.

At the Big Indian, **Old World Gourmet Deli and Wine Shop** (117 Rte. 1, 207/865-4477) is a great place to pick up sandwiches and salads for a picnic.

Craving a proper British tea? **Jacqueline's Tea Room** (201 Main St., Freeport, 207/865-2123, www.jacquelinestearoom.com, 10:30 A.M.–3 P.M.) serves a four-course tea by reservation for $20 pp in an elegant setting. Seatings for the two-hour indulgence are between 11 A.M. and 1 P.M. Tuesday–Friday, and every other weekend.

Casual Dining

The Harraseeket Inn's woodsy-themed **Broad Arrow Tavern** (162 Main St., 207/865-9377 or 800/342-6423, 11:30 A.M.–10 P.M., to 11 P.M. Fri. and Sat.), just two blocks north of L. L. Bean but seemingly a world away, is a perfect place to escape shopping crowds and madness. The food is terrific, with everything made from organic and naturally raised foods; prices run $10–23. Can't decide? Opt for the extensive,

GREATER PORTLAND

all-you-can-eat lunch buffet ($17) that highlights a bit of everything.

Ethnic Fare

Dine indoors or out on the tree-shaded patio at **Azure Italian Café** (123 Main St., 207/865-123, www.azurecafe.com, 11 A.M.–8 P.M., to 9 P.M. Fri. and Sat.). Go light, mixing selections from antipasto, *insalate,* and *zuppa* choices or savor the heartier entrées ($13–30), such as lasagna *formaggio,* Maine seafood risotto, or lemon-and-thyme roast chicken. The service is pleasant and the indoor dining areas are accented by well-chosen contemporary Maine artwork. Live jazz is a highlight some evenings.

Down the side street across from Azure is **Mediterranean Grill** (10 School St., Freeport, 207/865-1688, www.mediterraneangrill.biz, 11 A.M.–10 P.M.). Because it's off Main Street, the Cigri family's excellent Turkish-Mediterranean restaurant rarely gets the crowds. House specialties such as moussaka, lamb chops, and *tiropetes* augment a full range of kebab and vegetarian choices. Or simply make a meal of the appetizers—the platters are meals in themselves. Sandwiches and wraps are available at lunch. Entrées go for $16–25. Dine inside or on the streetside deck.

Two surprisingly good, easy-on-the-budget Asian restaurants share a building on the south end of town. **China Rose** (23 Main St., 207/865-6886, 11 A.M.–9:30 P.M., to 10 P.M. Fri. and Sat.) serves Szechuan, Mandarin, and Hunan specialties in a pleasant first-floor dining area. Upstairs is **Miyako** (207/865-6888, same hours), with an extensive sushi bar menu and it also serves other Japanese specialties, including tempura, teriyaki, *nabemono,* and noodle dishes. Luncheon specials are available at both.

Good food and attentive service has made **Thai Garden** (491 Rte. 1, Freeport, 207/865-6005, 11 A.M.–9 P.M. daily) an ever popular choice for Thai.

Fine Dining

Priciest and worth every penny is the Harraseeket Inn's cloth-and-candles **Maine Dining Room** (207/865-1085, 6–9 P.M., to 9:30 P.M. Fri. and Sat.). The service is excellent, and Chef Theda Lyden's commitment to natural and organic foods is impressive. Tableside preparations (for 2–7), such as Caesar salad, chateaubriand, and flaming desserts, add an understated note of theater. Dinner entrées are $24–38. Brunch (11:45 A.M.–2 P.M. Sun., $24.95) is a seemingly endless buffet, with whole poached salmon and Belgian waffles among the highlights.

Lobster

In South Freeport, order lobster in the rough at **Harraseeket Lunch and Lobster Company** (36 Main St., Town Wharf, South Freeport, 207/865-4888, 11 A.M.–8:45 P.M. daily summer hours, closes at 7:45 P.M. spring and fall). Grab a waterfront picnic table, place your order, and go at it. (There's also inside dining.) Be prepared for a wait in midsummer. Fried clams are particularly good here, and they're prepared either breaded or battered. Order both and decide for yourself which is better. Another option: If you're camping nearby, call ahead and order boiled lobsters to go. BYOB; no credit cards.

INFORMATION AND SERVICES

Freeport Merchants Association (Hose Tower, 23 Depot St., Freeport 04032, 207/865-1212 or 800/865-1994, www.freeportusa.com) produces an invaluable foldout map/guide showing locations of all the shops, plus sites of lodgings, restaurants, visitor kiosks, pay phones, restrooms, and car and bike parking. If you're serious about "doing" Freeport, send for one of these guides before you arrive so you can plan your attack and hit the ground running.

Just south of Freeport is the Maine Visitor Information Center (Rte. 1, at I-95 Exit 17, Yarmouth, 207/846-0833), part of the statewide tourism-information network. Staffers are particularly attuned to Freeport and Yarmouth, but the center has brochures and maps for the entire state. Also here are restrooms, phones, picnic tables, vending machines, and a dog-walking area.

MID-COAST REGION

In contrast to the Southern Coast's gorgeous sandy beaches, the Mid-Coast Region features a deeply indented shoreline with snug harbors and long, gnarled fingers of land. Even though these fingers are inconvenient for driving and bicycling, this is where you'll find picturebook Maine in a panorama format. Drive to the tips of the peninsulas and come upon lighthouses, fishing villages, country inns, and lobster wharves. The Mid-Coast, as defined in this chapter, stretches from Brunswick through Waldoboro.

Visitors come for Brunswick's Bowdoin College, Bath's marine museum, Wiscasset's historic homes, the jumbled shops of Boothbay Harbor, Pemaquid Point's lighthouse, and, of course, lobster. The Bath-Brunswick area is one of the least touristy areas of the coast.

Not that visitors don't come, but this area has a strong and varied economic base other than tourism, which means that no matter when you visit, you'll find shops, restaurants, and lodgings open and activities scheduled. Bowdoin College, Bath Iron Works, and the Brunswick Naval Air Station (slated for closure by 2011) also contribute to a population more ethnically diverse than in most of Maine and draw an active retiree population. Still, as you drive down the peninsulas that reach seaward from Bath and Brunswick, the vibrancy gives way to traditional fishing villages pressed by the hard realities of maintaining such lifestyles in a modern world and hanging on to waterfront properties in the face of rapidly rising real-estate prices.

Wiscasset still clings to the nickname of

© TOM NANGLE

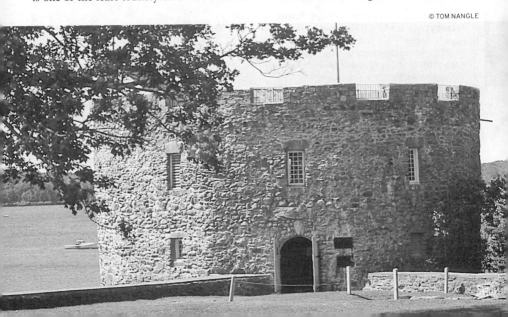

HIGHLIGHTS

◖ Bowdoin College: This beautiful, shady campus is home to the Bowdoin College Museum of Art, the Peary-MacMillan Arctic Museum, and the Maine State Music Theater (page 124).

◖ Maine Maritime Museum: It's easy to while away a half day touring the exhibits in the main and outer buildings and just enjoying the riverfront setting (page 135).

◖ Popham Beach: Often winning accolades as Maine's prettiest or best beach, Popham is a long stretch of sand, anchored by a fort at one end and seabird colonies at the other (page 139).

◖ Burnt Island Tour: Step back in history and visit with a lighthouse keeper's family circa 1952 on a living-history tour (page 156).

◖ Coastal Maine Botanical Gardens: This seaside garden comprises more than 125 acres of well-planned exhibits, trails, and art (page 158).

◖ Pemaquid Point Lighthouse: It's hard to say which is Maine's prettiest lighthouse, but Pemaquid's is right up there. It's also depicted on the Maine state quarter (page 169).

◖ Colonial Pemaquid/Fort William Henry: A beautiful setting overlooking John's Bay, a partially reconstructed fort, and remnants from archaeological digs researching one of the first English settlements in America make this well worth a visit (page 170).

◖ Lobster in the Rough: Lobster wharves abound in Maine, but the Pemaquid Peninsula has a concentration of scenic spots for lobster lovers (page 184).

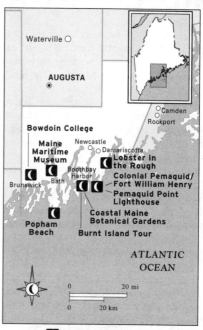

LOOK FOR ◖ TO FIND RECOMMENDED SIGHTS, ACTIVITIES, DINING, AND LODGING.

prettiest village in Maine, but for many travelers heading through it on Route 1, Wiscasset is nothing but an expletive deleted–producing headache. Traffic often backs up for miles, inching forward through the bottleneck village. Although many are just glad to get through it, those who take time to explore Wiscasset are rewarded with multitudes of antiques shops and lovely architecture.

The tempo changes northeast of Wiscasset. Traffic eases and there's less roadside development. Detour down the Boothbay and Pemaquid Peninsulas, and you'll be rewarded with the Maine of postcards. These two peninsulas appear unchallenged as home to more lobster-in-the-rough spots than elsewhere on the coast, and Maine's creative economy is blossoming here, as evidenced by the artists' and artisans' studios that pepper these peninsulas.

PLANNING YOUR TIME

Route 1 is the primary artery connecting all the points in the Mid-Coast Region, and

Wiscasset, a major bottleneck, is smack-dab in the middle. For this reason, it's best to split your lodging and explorations into two parts: south of Wiscasset and north of Wiscasset. Even then, driving down the long fingers of land requires patience. The towns south of Wiscasset are less touristy than those on the Boothbay or Pemaquid Peninsulas, with Orr's and Bailey's Islands and the Phippsburg Peninsula being the best places to sprout roots for old-time summer flavor.

To cover the region, you'll need 4–5 days.

Antiques mavens should concentrate their efforts in Bath, Wiscasset, and Damariscotta. Allow at least two days to appreciate the fine museums in Brunswick and Bath, and another day to tour Wiscasset's historical house museums and nearby fort. If you're an avid or even aspiring kayaker, you'll want time to puzzle through the nooks and crannies of the coastline in a boat, and if you value parks and preserves, this region offers plenty worth your time. For either, the Boothbay and Pemaquid Peninsulas are good bases.

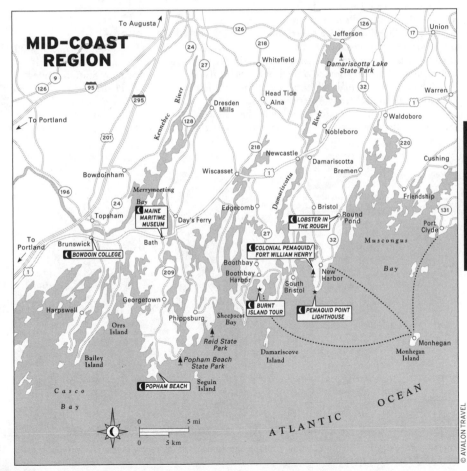

Brunswick Area

Brunswick (pop. 20,520), straddling Route 1, relies partly on modern defense dollars—but it was incorporated in 1738 and is steeped in history. The town is home to both prestigious Bowdoin College and the sprawling Brunswick Naval Air Station—an unusual and sometimes conflicting juxtaposition that makes this a college town with a difference. You'll find lots of classic homes and churches, several respected museums, and year-round cultural attractions.

Brunswick and Topsham face each other across roiling waterfalls on the Androscoggin River. The falls, which Native Americans knew by the tongue-twisting name of Ahmelahcogneturcook ("place abundant with fish, birds, and other animals"), were a source of hydropower for 18th-century sawmills and 19th- and 20th-century textile mills. Franco Americans arrived in droves to beef up the textile industry in the late 19th century (but lost their jobs eventually

in the Depression). Those once derelict mills now house shops, restaurants, and offices.

Brunswick is also the gateway to the stunning Harpswells, a peninsula/archipelago complex linked by causeways, several bridges, and a unique granite cribstone bridge. Scenic back roads on Harpswell Neck inspire detours to the fishing hamlets of Cundy's Harbor, Orr's Island, and Bailey Island, and once you're here, it's easy to want to linger.

SIGHTS
◖ Bowdoin College

Bowdoin College (Brunswick, 207/725-3000, www.bowdoin.edu) got its start here nearly 150 years before the Naval Air Station landed on the nearby Brunswick Plains. Founded in 1794 as a boys' college with a handful of students, Bowdoin (coed since 1969) now has 1,550 students. The college has turned out such noted

The new entry pavilion to the Bowdoin College Museum of Art is starkly modern when juxtaposed next to the original building.

graduates as authors Nathaniel Hawthorne and Henry Wadsworth Longfellow, sex pioneer Alfred Kinsey, U.S. President Franklin Pierce, Arctic explorers Robert Peary and Donald MacMillan, U.S. Senators George Mitchell and William Cohen, and a dozen Maine governors. Massachusetts Hall, oldest building on the 110-acre campus, dates from 1802. The stately Bowdoin pines, on the northeast boundary, are even older. The striking **David Saul Smith Union,** occupying 40,000 square feet in a former athletic building on the east side of the campus, has a café, pub, lounge, and bookstore open to the public. Call for information on admissions and campus tours (207/725-3100) and on campus concerts, lectures, and performances open to the public (207/725-3375).

Photos and artifacts bring Arctic expeditions to life at the small but fascinating **Peary-MacMillan Arctic Museum** (Hubbard Hall, 207/725-3416, http://academic.bowdoin.edu/arcticmuseum, 10 A.M.–5 P.M. Tues.–Sat., 2–5 P.M. Sun., free). Among the specimens are animal mounts, a skin kayak, fur clothing, snow goggles, and Inuit carvings—most collected by Arctic pioneers Robert E. Peary and Donald B. MacMillan, both Bowdoin grads. Permanent exhibits highlight the natural and cultural diversity of the Arctic. The small gift shop specializes in Inuit books and artifacts. Donations are welcomed.

An astonishing array of Greek and Roman artifacts is only one of the high points at the **Bowdoin College Museum of Art** (Walker Art Building, 207/725-3275, www.bowdoin.edu/art-museum, 10 A.M.–5 P.M. Tues.–Sat., 2–5 P.M. Sun., free). Designed in the 1890s by Charles McKim of the famed McKim, Mead, and White firm, it's a stunning neoclassical edifice with an interior rotunda and stone lions flanking the entry. In 2007, the museum was expanded and modernized for the 21st century, adding a striking bronze-and glass entry pavilion to preserve the facade while also achieving accessibility. The college's prized Assyrian reliefs, previously in the magnificent Rotunda, were moved to a glass-walled addition facing Brunswick's Park Row. The renovated museum is far more user friendly and a fitting setting for the impressive permanent collection of 19th- and 20th-century American art and its other works.

Pejepscot Historical Society Museums

Side by side in an unusual, cupola-topped duplex facing Brunswick's Mall (village green) are two museums operated by the Pejepscot Historical Society (159 and 160 Park Row, Brunswick, 207/729-6606), the **Pejepscot Museum** (159 Park Row, 10 A.M.–5 P.M. Tues.–Fri., free) and the **Skolfield-Whittier House** (161 Park Row, tours on the hour to 3 P.M. Thurs.–Sat. late May–late Oct., $5 adult, $2.50 child). Focusing on local history, the museum has a collection of more than 50,000 artifacts and mounts an always interesting special exhibit each year. The 17-room Skolfield-Whittier House, on the right-hand side of the building, looks as though the owners just stepped out for the afternoon. Unoccupied 1925–1982, the onetime sea captain's house has elegant Victorian furnishings and lots of exotic artifacts collected on global seafaring stints.

Also operated by the Pejepscot Historical Society, the **Joshua L. Chamberlain Museum** (226 Maine St., Brunswick, 207/729-6606, tours on the hour 10 A.M.–3 P.M. Tues.–Sat., $5 adult, $2.50 child), across from First Parish Church, commemorates the Union Army hero of the Civil War's Battle of Gettysburg, who's now gaining long-overdue respect. The partly restored house where Chamberlain lived in the late 19th century (and Henry Wadsworth Longfellow lived 30 years earlier) is a peculiar architectural hodgepodge with six rooms of exhibits of Chamberlain memorabilia, much of it Civil War–related. A gift shop stocks lots of Civil War publications, especially ones covering the Twentieth Maine Volunteers. A combination ticket for both historical houses is $8 adults, $4 kids.

Uncle Tom's Church

Across the street from the Chamberlain museum is the historic 1846 **First Parish Church**

(9 Cleaveland St. at Bath Rd., Brunswick, 207/729-7331), a Gothic Revival (or carpenter Gothic) board-and-batten structure crowning the rise at the head of Maine Street. Scores of celebrity preachers have ascended this pulpit, and Harriet Beecher Stowe was inspired to write *Uncle Tom's Cabin* while listening to her husband deliver an antislavery sermon here. If you're a fan of organ music, arrive here before noon any Tuesday early July–early August (or call ahead for details), when guest organists present 40-minute lunchtime concerts (12:10–12:50 P.M.) on the 1883 Hutchings-Plaisted tracker organ. Admission is free, but a $5 donation is requested. At other times, the church is open by appointment.

Brunswick's Noted Women

With more than 20 points of interest, the **Brunswick Women's History Trail** covers such national notables as authors Harriet Beecher Stowe and Kate Douglas Wiggin and lesser-known lights, including naturalist Kate Furbish, pioneering Maine pediatrician

JOSHUA L. CHAMBERLAIN, CIVIL WAR HERO

When the American Civil War began in 1861, Joshua Chamberlain was a 33-year-old logic instructor at Bowdoin College in Brunswick; when it ended, in 1865, Chamberlain earned the Congressional Medal of Honor for his "Daring heroism and great tenacity in holding his position on the Little Round Top." He was designated by Ulysses S. Grant to formally accept the official surrender of Confederate General John Gordon (both men represented the infantry). He later became governor of Maine (1867-1871) and president of Bowdoin College, but Chamberlain's greatest renown, ironically, came more than a century later – when 1990s PBS filmmakers focused on the Civil War and highlighted his strategic military role.

Joshua Lawrence Chamberlain was born in 1828 in Brewer, Maine, the son and grandson of soldiers. After graduating from Bowdoin in 1852, he studied for the ministry at Bangor Theological Seminary and then returned to his alma mater as an instructor.

With the nation in turmoil in the early 1860s, Chamberlain signed on to help, receiving a commission as a lieutenant colonel in the Twentieth Maine Volunteers in 1862. After surviving 24 encounters and six battle wounds and having been promoted to general (brigadier, then major), Chamberlain was elected Republican governor of Maine in 1866 – by the largest margin in the state's history – only to suffer through four one-year terms of partisan politics. In 1871, Chamberlain became president of Bowdoin College, where he remained until 1883. He then dove into speechmaking and writing, his best-known work being *The Passing of the Armies*, a memoir of the Civil War's final campaigns. From 1900 to 1914, Chamberlain was surveyor of the Port of Portland, a presidential appointment that ended only when complications from a wartime abdominal wound finally did him in. He died at the grand old age of 86.

Brunswick's Joshua L. Chamberlain Museum, in his onetime home at 226 Maine Street, commemorates this illustrious Mainer, and thousands of Civil War buffs annually stream through the door in search of Chamberlain "stuff." To make it easier, the Pejepscot Historical Society has produced a helpful map titled *Joshua Chamberlain's Brunswick*, highlighting town and college ties to the man – his dorm rooms, his presidential office, his portraits, even his church pew (number 64 at First Parish Church). Chamberlain's gravesite, marked by a reddish granite stone, is in Brunswick's Pine Grove Cemetery, just east of the Bowdoin campus.

Biennially, the museum celebrates **Chamberlain Days** with a symposium that concentrates on his roles in the war and in Maine. Typically, events include lectures by authors and scholars; field trips to places of interest connected with Chamberlain's life; tours of his home, concentrating on the most recent restoration work; musical or dramatic performances; and group discussions.

Dr. Alice Whittier, and the Franco American women who slaved away in the textile mills at the turn of the 20th century. Buy the walking-tour booklet at the Pejepscot Museum gift shop ($2). Then set out to follow the fascinating story. The museum offers guided tours lasting about one hour once a month in June, July, and August (donation requested).

Brunswick Literary Art Walk

Cast your eyes downward while walking along Maine Street. Four bronze plaques recognize Brunswick's most famous writers: Henry Wadsworth Longfellow, Nathaniel Hawthorne, Harriet Beecher Stowe, and Robert P. T. Coffin. Each plaque bears a quote from the author commemorated. The privately funded endeavor plans to produce a brochure with additional information on the writers along with a map. Look for it at stores, lodgings, and info bureaus.

Go, Fish!

If you're in town between mid-May and late June, plan to visit Central Maine Power's **Brunswick Hydro** generating station, straddling the falls on the Androscoggin River, Lower Maine Street, next to Fort Andross, Brunswick-Topsham town line (207/729-7644 or 207/623-3521, ext. 2116, weekdays, or 800/872-9937). A glass-walled viewing room lets you play voyeur during the annual ritual of anadromous fish heading upstream to spawn. Amazingly undaunted by the obstacles, such species as alewives (herring), salmon, and smallmouth bass make their way from salt water to fresh via a 40-foot-high, 570-foot-long man-made fish ladder. The viewing room, which maxes out at about 20 people, is open 1–5 P.M. Wednesday–Sunday during the brief spring spawning season.

RECREATION
Excursion Train

Ride in restored, vintage railcars on the scenic **Maine Eastern Railroad** (207/596-6725 or 800/637-2457, www.maineeasternrailroad.com), operating between Rockland and Brunswick, with stops in Wiscasset and Bath. The train operates late May–early November, with special holiday trains in December. Adult fares are $40 round-trip, $25 one-way; ages 5–15 pay $25/$15; seniors are $35/$25; family rate is $100/$75 covering two adults and two kids. Packages with lodging, meals, and theater are available.

Hiking and Biking

A good choice for family biking or a good walk in the Brunswick area is the 2.5-mile **Androscoggin River Bicycle Path** running between downtown Brunswick and Cooks Corner, meandering along the scenic Androscoggin River and paralleling Route 1. (Unfortunately, the traffic noise often makes the route less than tranquil.) The landscaped asphalt path is also popular with joggers, strollers, and in-line skaters. To reach the path from the lower end of Maine Street in downtown Brunswick, take Mason Street and then the next left onto Water Street. Continue about two blocks to the parking area (often very crowded) next to the boat-launching site. The path has no loop, so you'll need to return the way you came.

In the village of Bailey Island, there's a mini-walk to the **Giant Stairs,** a waterfront stone stairway of mammoth proportions. To get there, take Route 24 from Cooks Corner toward Bailey Island and Land's End, keeping an eye out for Washington Avenue, on the left about 1.5 miles after the cribstone bridge. (Or drive to Land's End, park the car with the rest of the crowds, survey the panorama, and walk 0.8 mile back along Route 24 to Washington Avenue from there.) Turn onto Washington Avenue, go 0.1 mile, and park at the Episcopal Church (corner of Ocean St.). Walk along Ocean Street to the shorefront path. Watch for a tiny sign just before Spindrift Lane. Don't let small kids get close to the slippery rocks on the surf-tossed shoreline. (The same advice, by the way, holds for Land's End, where the rocks can be treacherous.)

Thank the **Brunswick-Topsham Land Trust** (108 Maine St., Brunswick, 207/729-7694, www.btlt.org), founded in 1985, for access to 11-acre **Captain Alfred Skolfield Nature**

Preserve. One of its two blue-blazed nature-trail loops skirts a salt marsh, where you're apt to see egrets, herons, and osprey in summer. Adjacent to the preserve is an ancient Indian portage site that linked Middle Bay and Harpswell Coves when Native Americans spent their vacations here. (No dopes, they!) Take Route 123 (Harpswell Rd.) south from Brunswick about three miles; when you reach the Middle Bay Road intersection (on the right), continue on Route 123 for 1.1 miles. Watch for a small sign, and a small parking area, on your right.

The 103-acre **Cox Pinnacle,** owned by the town of Brunswick, comprises wooded hills, rocky ledges, and wetlands laced with about 1.5 miles of old logging and farming roads. The trails lead to Cox Pinnacle, the highest point of land in Brunswick (350 feet). Take the Durham Road, then turn right at the blinking light onto Hacker Road, and drive 0.3 mile to the parking lot on the left.

Center Street Bicycles (11 Center St., just off Maine St., Brunswick, 207/729-5309) does repairs and sells bikes and a good range of accessories. Prices vary with models, but figure about $35 for a one-day rental. The knowledgeable staff also act as a clearinghouse for route information. (For instance, they strongly urge every customer to avoid biking the Harpswells, especially Route 123; the scenic rewards are outstanding, but the risks are many on the shoulderless roads.)

Swimming

Thomas Point Beach (29 Meadow Rd., Brunswick, 207/725-6009 or 877/872-4321, www.thomaspointbeach.com) is actually 85 acres of privately owned parkland with facilities for swimming (lifeguard on duty, bathhouses), fishing, field sports, picnicking (500 tables), and camping (75 tent and RV sites at $20; no water or sewer hookups, but electricity and dump station available). No pets, skateboards, or motorcycles are allowed. The sandy beach is tidal, so the swimming "window" is about two hours before high tide until two hours afterward; otherwise, you're wallowing in mudflats. (The same rule holds

for kayakers or canoeists.) Toddlers head for the big playground; teenagers gravitate to the arcade and the ice-cream parlor. The park is also the site of several annual events, including the Maine Highland Games and the Bluegrass Festival. Parking is ample. At Cooks Corner, where Bath Road meets Route 24 South, go 1.5 miles on Route 24, then turn left, and follow signs for less than two miles to the park. It's open 9 A.M.–sunset mid-May–September. Admission to the park is $3.50 adults, $2 kids 3–12.

For freshwater swimming, head to town-owned **Coffin Pond** (River Rd., Brunswick, 207/725-6656), a man-made swimming hole with a sandy beach, lifeguards, water slide, picnic tables, playground, changing rooms, and snack bar. Kids' swimming lessons (ages 5–14) are held in August. It's a popular spot, so expect plenty of company. It's open 10 A.M.–7 P.M. mid-June–early September. Nonresident admission is $3.50 adult, $2 age 12 and younger. Heading west on Route 1 (Pleasant St.), turn right onto River Road and go about a half mile to the parking area (on the right).

Golf

Established in 1901 primarily for Bowdoin College students, the **Brunswick Golf Club** (River Rd., Brunswick, 207/725-8224) is now an especially popular 18-hole public course, so you'll need to call for a starting time.

Boating Excursions

Departing at noon from the Cook's Lobster House wharf (Cook's Landing) in Bailey Island (off Rte. 24), a large, sturdy **Casco Bay Lines ferry** does a 1.75-hour nature-watch circuit of nearby islands, including Eagle Island, the one-time home of Admiral Robert Peary (there are no stopovers on these circuits; for excursions to Eagle Island, see *Sailboat and Powerboat Excursions* under *Recreation* in the *Greater Portland* chapter). Reservations aren't needed. Cost is $12 adults, $10 seniors, $5.50 kids 5–9. To confirm the schedule when weather is iffy, call Casco Bay Lines (207/774-7871), or Cook's Landing (207/833-6641).

For a more intimate excursion in a smaller boat, Captain Les McNelly, owner of **Sea Escape Charters** (Box 7, Bailey Island 04003, 207/833-5531, www.seaescapecottages.com), operates two-hour on-demand sightseeing cruises throughout the summer (weather permitting) for $65 pp (two people) or $35 pp (four people). Or he'll take you out to Eagle Island for $140 a couple (lower rate if there are more passengers). He also offers fishing trips: $200 for four hours, including bait and tackle ($95 each additional person); no fishing license required; bring your own lunch. Call to schedule a trip. Trips operate out of Sea Escape Cottages, one- and two-bedroom well-equipped cottages, with full kitchens and oceanside decks that rent for $140–160 per night or $850–1,020 per week, including linens and one change of towels.

Sea Kayaking

H2Outfitters (P.O. Box 72, Orr's Island 04066, 207/833-5257 or 800/205-2925, www.h2outfitters.com) has been a thriving operation since 1978. Based in a wooden building on the Orr's Island side of the famed cribstone bridge, this experienced company organizes multiday trips, including island camping, for $395 pp and up; all gear is included.

Newer on the scene is **Seaspray Kayaking** (207/443-3646 or 888/349-7772, www.seaspraykayaking.com), with bases on the New Meadows River, in Brunswick, as well as at Sebasco, in Phippsburg, and Bay Point, in Georgetown. The New Meadows base is particularly good for those nervous about trying the sport, as it isn't open ocean and there are no waves. Rentals and tours are available. Rentals are $10–20 for the first hour, $5–10 for additional hours, $25–50 per day. Equipment options include solo and tandem kayaks, recreational kayaks, surf kayaks, and canoes. Tours, led by Registered Maine Guides, vary from sunset paddles to three-day expeditions and include moonlight paddles, island-to-island tours, and inn-to-inn tours. Rates begin at $50 adult, $25 child for shorter tours. A striper fishing kayak tour, including tackle

and instruction, is $75. Reserve early for the popular Moonlight Paddles ($40).

If you're an experienced sea kayaker, consider exploring Harpswell Sound from the boat launch on the west side of the cribstone bridge; kayaks can also put in at Mackerel Cove, near Cook's Lobster House. There's also a boat launch with plentiful parking at Sawyer Park on the New Meadows River, on Route 1, just before you cross the river heading north.

ENTERTAINMENT

The region's extremely active arts organization, **Five Rivers Arts Alliance** (108 Main St., Brunswick, 207/798-6964, www.fiveriversartsalliance.org), maintains a calendar of area concerts, gallery openings, art shows, lectures, exhibits, and other arts-related events and also sponsors a few key events. Listings also appear on www.midcoastmaine.com/events.

There's no lack of classical music in Brunswick each summer, but for lighter fare, **Maine State Music Theatre** (Pickard Theater, Bowdoin College, mailing/box office 22 Elm St., Brunswick 04011, 207/725-8769, www.msmt.org), has been a summer tradition since 1959. The renovated, state-of-the-art, air-conditioned theater brings real pros to its stage for four musicals (mid-June–late Aug.). Loyal subscribers book the same seats year after year, and performances tend to sell out, so call ahead for the schedule and reservations. (Nonsubscription tickets go on sale in early May.) Performances are at 8 P.M. Tuesday–Saturday; matinees are staged at 2 P.M. on an alternating schedule—each week has matinees on different days. (No children under four are admitted, but special family shows are performed during the season.) Ticket range is $30–49.

The **Bowdoin International Music Festival** (box office 12 Cleveland St., mailing address 6300 College Station, Brunswick 04011, 207/725-3895, www.summermusic.org) is a showcase for an international array of musical talent of all kinds late June–early August. The six-week festival, part of an international music school, presents a variety of concert opportunities—enough so that there's music almost every night of the week. Venues vary and tickets range free–$30. Call or check the website for the current schedule.

The First Paris Church sponsors a **Summer Organ Concert Series** (207/729-7331) at the church between noon and 1 P.M. on Tuesdays in July and August, suggested donation $5.

Second Friday Art Walks (207/725-4366) take place in downtown Brunswick 5–7:30 P.M. May–November. Gallery openings, wine tastings, light refreshments, and other activities are usually part of the mix.

Music on the Mall presents family band concerts at 7 P.M. Wednesdays (Thursdays if it rains) in July and August on the Brunswick Mall (the lovely park in the center of town).

FESTIVALS AND EVENTS

The first full week of August, the **Topsham Fair** is a weeklong agricultural festival with exhibits, demonstrations, live music, ox pulls, contests, harness racing, and fireworks at the Topsham Fairgrounds.

The third Saturday of August, the **Maine Highland Games,** sponsored by the St. Andrew's Society of Maine, mark the annual wearing of the plaids—but you needn't be Scottish to join in the games or watch the Highland dancing or browse the arts and crafts booths. (Only a Scot, however, can appreciate that unique concoction called haggis.) If you're seeking your clan roots, this is the place; lots of genealogical networking goes on here. It all happens at Thomas Point Beach in Brunswick.

Also at Thomas Point Beach, September's **Annual Bluegrass Festival** is a four-day event with nonstop bluegrass, including big-name artists. Kickoff is Thursday noon.

The **Family Arts Festival** (207/798-6964), in September, has hands-on workshops, music, dance, and storytelling for all ages under tents on the Mall.

SHOPPING

Downtown Brunswick invites leisurely browsing, with most of the shops concentrated on Maine Street. Do take special care when cross-

ing the four-lane wide street, and do so only at marked crosswalks.

Art, Craft, and Antiques Galleries

The **Bayview Gallery** (58 Maine St., Brunswick, 800/244-3007), mounts half a dozen superb shows annually, specializing in contemporary New England artists.

Facing the Mall, **Day's Antiques** (153 Park Row, Brunswick, 207/725-6959) occupies five rooms and the basement of the handsome historic building known as the Pumpkin House. Quality is high at David Day's shop; prices are fair.

More than 140 dealers show and sell their wares at **Cabot Mill Antiques** (14 Maine St., 207/725-2855), in the renovated Fort Andross mill complex next to the Androscoggin River.

Part gallery, part resource center, **Maine Fiberarts** (13 Maine St., Topsham, 207/721-0678, www.mainefiberarts.org) is a must-stop for anyone interested in fiber-related artwork: knitting, quilting, spinning, basketry. If you're really interested in finding artists and resources statewide, buy a copy of its resource book.

Nearly two dozen local artists exhibit their works in varied media at **Sebascodegan Artists Gallery** (Rte. 24, Great Island, Harpswell, 207/833-6260).

Bookstores

With an eclectic new-book inventory that includes lots of esoterica, **Gulf of Maine Books** (134 Maine St., Brunswick, 207/729-5083) has held the competition at bay since the early 1980s. The fiction selection is particularly good, as are the religion, health, and poetry sections. Poet/publisher/renaissance man Gary Lawless oversees everything.

Bookland (Cooks Corner Shopping Center, Bath Rd.d and Rte. 24 S, Brunswick, 207/725-2313), a thriving independent emporium, is also home to the very popular Hardcover Cafe.

ACCOMMODATIONS
Hotels, Motels, and Inns

Combining a Federal-style manse with a new hotel wing, **The Captain Daniel Stone Inn**

(10 Water St., Brunswick, 207/725-9898 or 877/573-5151, www.captaindanielstoneinn.com) has 34 guest rooms and suites furnished with antiques and reproductions and a country-inn feel, despite a location edging busy Route 1. It offers private baths, air-conditioning, phones, and cable TV. The inn is walking distance to downtown Brunswick, and it's close to the bike path (bikes are available to guests). A few rooms are pet friendly ($25 per night). In summer, rooms are $135–290, suites are $220–255, including expanded continental breakfast; rates are lower other months, and special packages are available. The inn's casually elegant restaurant, **Augustine's,** is open daily for lunch 11:30 A.M.–3 P.M. and dinner 5–10 P.M., serving both in a fine dining room and more casual tavern. Breakfast is available to guests.

A dozen miles down Route 24 from Cooks Corner is the turnoff for Jo Atlass's **Little Island Motel** (44 Little Island Rd., Orr's Island, 207/833-2392, www.littleislandmotel.com, $125–135 d peak), a nine-unit complex on its own spit of land with deck views you won't believe. Basic rooms have cable TV and small fridge. Rates include buffet breakfast and use of bikes, boats, and a little beach. No credit cards. Open mid-May–mid-October.

Continue another mile down Route 24, cross the cribstone bridge, and you'll come to Chip Black's **Bailey Island Motel** (Rte. 24, P.O. Box 4, Bailey Island 04003, 207/833-2886, www.baileyislandmotel.com, $95–215), a congenial, clean, no-frills waterfront spot with 11 rooms and wowser views. Kids under 10 are free; 10 and older are $15. Continental breakfast is included, and rooms have cable TV. A dock is available for boat launching. Open mid-May–late October.

Looking rather like an old-fashioned tear-jerker film set, the family-run **Driftwood Inn** (81 Washington Ave., Bailey Island, 207/833-5461, www.thedriftwoodinnmaine.com) has 25 very basic, pine-paneled rooms in four buildings (some with private toilet and sink; all with shared showers), six housekeeping cottages, a saltwater pool, a stunning view, a dining room (open to the public), and a determinedly rustic ambience. No frills, period,

but it has ocean-front porches, games, and an old-fashioned simplicity that you rarely find anymore, and you'll sleep at night listening to the waves crash on the rocky shore. It's all on three oceanfront acres near the Giant Stairs. The dining room, open to the public by reservation, serves a set, home-cooked meal nightly (usually with a fish-of-the-day alternative), late June–Labor Day for $16–19. Breakfast is $6.50. Rooms are $85–120 d; all meals are extra, but rates including breakfast and dinner are available ($450 pp/week). Cottages rent by the week in season, $645–680; off-season $115–125 per night. Dogs are allowed in the cottages. No credit cards. Open mid-May–October.

Bed-and-Breakfasts

Right downtown, facing the tree-shaded Mall, is the **Brunswick Inn on Park Row** (165 Park Row, Brunswick, 207/729-4914 or 800/299-4914, www.brunswickbnb.com, $125–190 d), a handsome, 30-room Greek Revival mansion built in 1849 and decorated with contemporary flair. Original works by Maine artists are displayed throughout the inn, including in the Cygnet Lounge Wine Bar. Fifteen elegant guest rooms are split between the main house and the newly renovated Carriage House (with two fully accessible rooms); all have Wi-Fi and phones, and Carriage House suites have TV. Breakfast is a treat. Open all year.

On the outskirts of town, in a rural location smack-dab on Middle Bay, is **◖ Middle Bay Farm Bed and Breakfast** (287 Pennellville Rd., Brunswick, 207/373-1375, www.middlebayfarm.com, $150–170) lovingly and beautifully restored by Phyllis Truesdell, who bought the property after it sat all but abandoned for a decade. Once the site of the Pennell Brothers Shipyard, the farmhouse and sail loft now house guests seeking an away-from-it-all, yet convenient, location. Four water-view guest rooms in the 1834 farmhouse are decorated with antiques and have TV/VCR. Also in the main house is a living room with fireplace and grand piano. Two suites in the sail loft each have a living room with kitchenette and two tiny bedrooms and share an open porch. All guests receive a full breakfast in the water-view dining room. Canoes and bicycles are available to guests. Bring a sea kayak to launch from the dock. Open all year.

At the 1761 **Harpswell Inn** (108 Lookout Point Rd., South Harpswell, 207/833-5509 or 800/843-5509, www.harpswellinn.com), innkeepers Anne and Richard Moseley operate a comfortable, welcoming, antiques-filled oasis on 2.5 secluded, water-view acres. It's tough to break away from the glass-walled great room, but Middle Bay sunsets from the porch can do it. And just down the hill is Allen's Seafood, where you can watch lobstermen unload their catches in a gorgeous cove. In fall, the foliage on two little islets in the cove turns brilliant red. The B&B has nine lovely rooms (most with private baths; $110–159 d), three suites ($235–249 d), and four cottages ($950–1,400 per week). Prices are slightly higher for one-night stays. From Bath Road, in Brunswick, take Route 123 eight miles to Lookout Point Road (on the right). Open all year.

After many years as an extremely popular dining destination 13 miles south of Cooks Corner, **The Log Cabin** (Rte. 24, P.O. Box 41, Bailey Island 04003, 207/833-5546, www.logcabin-maine.com) in 1996 added lodging to its repertoire, and now it serves meals only to guests. Nine nicely decorated rooms have phones, TV/VCR, private decks facing the bay, and, weather permitting, splendid sunset views to the White Mountains. Four rooms have kitchen facilities; some have gas fireplaces or whirlpool tubs. There's also an outdoor heated pool. Rates are $169–329 d in midsummer, lower early and late in the season. Full breakfast is included; dinner ($16–31) is available only to guests 6–6:30 P.M. Open April–October.

Seasonal Rentals

For weekly or monthly rentals in Great, Orr's, and Bailey Islands, try **Your Island Connection** (P.O. Box 300, Bailey Island 04003, 207/833-7779, www.mainerentals.com) or **Harpswell Property Management** (P.O. Box 6, Bailey Island 04003, 207/833-7795, www.baileyisland.com). The Bath-

Brunswick Chamber of Commerce also keeps a list of seasonal cottage rentals.

FOOD

Brunswick has an abundance of inexpensive cafés, delis, coffeehouses, and ethnic restaurants lining its main and side streets as well as seasonal vendors operating cart stands on the mall. At most, you order at the counter and then select your table.

Local Flavors

Wild O.A.T.S. Bakery and Café (149 Maine St., Tontine Mall, Brunswick, 207/725-6287, www.wildoatsbakery.com, 7:30 A.M.–5 P.M. Mon.–Sat., 8 A.M.–3 P.M. Sun.) turns out terrific made-from-scratch breads and pastries, especially the breakfast kind, in its cafeteria-style place. (Just so you know, the name stands for Original and Tasty Stuff.) It has inside and outside tables, moderate prices, good-for-you salads, and great sandwiches (try the Club Med or the curried chicken melt).

For food on the run—no-frills hot dogs straight from the cart—head for Brunswick's Mall, the village green where **Danny's on the Mall** (no telephone) has been cooking dirt-cheap tube steaks since the early 1980s.

Fat Boy Drive-In (Bath Rd., Old Rte. 1, Brunswick, 207/729-9431) is a genuine throwback—a landmark since 1955, boasting carhops, window trays, and a menu guaranteed to clog your arteries. Fries and frappes are specialties. If you insist, there are five booths indoors. No credit cards. It's open 11 A.M.–8:30 P.M. daily—get this—the third Tuesday in March to the second Sunday in October. The second Saturday in August, about 700 people show up, many in 1950s getups, for the annual sock hop. Only pre-1970 cars can park in the lot that night (if you have one, stop in ahead of time for a pass).

Afterward, stop by **Hattie's Ice Cream** (185 Park Row, Brunswick, 207/725-6139, www.hattiesicecream.com, noon–11 P.M. daily) for a scoop (or two, or three) of Maine-made organic ice cream, sorbet, or gelato in drool-worthy flavors that define creative (cardamon-ginger-infused gelato). Or how about a sundae atop a Simply Divine brownie?

Arguments rage endlessly about who makes the best chowder in Maine, but **The Dolphin Chowder House** (Dolphin Marina, 515 Basin Point Rd., South Harpswell, 207/833-6000, 11 A.M.–8 P.M. daily May 1–Nov. 1), heads lots of lists for its fish chowder, accompanied by a blueberry muffin. Equally famed is its lobster stew. Plus you can't beat the scenic 13-mile drive south from Brunswick and the spectacular water views, through two walls of windows at the tip of Harpswell Neck.

One of Maine's best farmers markets is the **Brunswick Farmers Market,** which sets up, rain or shine, on the Mall (village green) 8 A.M.–2 P.M. Tuesday and Friday May–November (Friday is the bigger day). The market moves to Crystal Spring Farm, Pleasant Hill Road, between 8:30 A.M. and 12:30 P.M. on Saturday. You'll find produce, cheeses, crafts, condiments, live lobsters, and serendipitous surprises—depending on the season.

Casual Dining

"Tis a gift to be local…" is the motto at Jessica Gorton's **Sweet Leaves Teahouse** (22 Pleasant St., Brunswick, 207/725-1376, 11:30 A.M.–9 P.M. Tues.–Sat.), a casual restaurant next to the post office just south of Maine Street that serves lunch, dinner, and afternoon tea. Chef Josh DeGroot has brought his immense talent here, shaping a menu that changes daily and honors local farmers, anglers, foragers, and fromage folks (that's cheesemakers). Just about everything is made on the premises except the bread, which comes from Standard Baking in Portland. Ice creams and sorbets are made in house, and don't miss DeGroot's signature chocolate goat cheese. After 5 P.M., "dinnerly plates" such as crab cakes, potato gnocchi, or hangar steak are served. Tuesdays feature an open mic 6:30–9 P.M.

At the upper end of the downtown drag is **Scarlet Begonias** (212B Maine St., Brunswick, 207/721-0403, 11 A.M.–8 P.M. Sun.–Wed., to 8:30 P.M. Thurs., to 9:30 P.M. Fri. and Sat., opens at noon Sat.), an especially cheerful place with a Mediterranean-influenced, bistro-type pizza-and-pasta menu. Order at the counter and look for a table. How could anyone resist a $10 pasta puttanesca dubbed Scarlet Harlot? You can't go wrong here; everything's a winner. No credit cards. BYOB.

An enticing selection of small plates, soups, salads, and sandwiches is served at the tiny **111 Maine Street** (111 Maine St., Brunswick, 207/729-9111, www.111maine.com, 11 A.M.–4 P.M. Tues.–Fri., to 9 P.M. Fri., 10 A.M.–2 P.M. Sat.–Sun.). Everything's ultrafresh and seasonally driven—the market veggie plate is delish in summer. Inside are a handful of tables and a window bar with stools; in summer, there usually are a few tables outside, too.

Just off Maine Street, **Renaissance Bistro and European Wine Bar** (25 Mill St., Brunswick, 207/721-0412, www.renaissance-bistro.com) is a find for European-influenced fare created from locally sourced ingredients and served in a casual, storefront bistro setting. Dinner choices ($18–26) vary from wild mushroom ravioli to rack of lamb to duck; brunch especially decadent. It's open for dinner beginning at 5 P.M. Tuesday–Saturday, and brunch beginning at 9 A.M. Saturday–Sunday.

Eclectic doesn't begin to describe **Frontier Cafe** (Mill 3, Fort Andross, 14 Maine St. at Rte. 1 overpass, Brunswick, 207/725-5222, www.explorefrontier.com, 9 A.M.–9 P.M. Mon.–Thurs., 11 A.M.–11 P.M. Sat.), a combination café, gallery, and cinema inspired by founder Michael Gilroy's world travels. The menu of soups, sandwiches, and salads changes weekly but usually includes wonderful market plates emphasizing the cuisine of a country or region—Maine, France, the Middle East, Italy. Desserts are homemade, and there's a kids' menu, too. Wine and beer are served. Films are screened ($7 adult), and there are frequent events, such as the monthly Knit and Fiddle, concerts, and other entertainment.

Ask a local to point the way to **Backstreet Bistro** (11 Town Hall Plaza, 207/725-4060, www.backstreetbistro.net, 5–9 P.M. daily, $15–26), an inconspicuous restaurant and wine bar that turns out well-prepared fare, such as lamb shank, stuffed quail, wild mushroom-encrusted bistro steak, and fresh-roasted fish and shellfish stew. It's tucked behind Maine Street, near the fire department. In summer there's deck dining.

Just over the bridge from Brunswick, in the renovated Bowdoin Mill complex overlooking the Androscoggin River, is the **Sea Dog Brewery** (1 Main St., Topsham, 207/725-0162, www.seadogbrewing.com, 11:30 A.M.–1 A.M. daily), with seating inside and on a deck overhanging the river. The menu ranges from burgers and sandwiches to full plate entrées ($11–18). It offers frequent acoustic entertainment, including karaoke on Thursdays. There are also games for kids and a games room with video arcade and pool tables. A jazz brunch is served until 1 P.M. Sundays.

Ethnic Fare

Generous portions, moderate prices, efficient service, and narrow aisles are the story at **The Great Impasta** (42 Maine St., Brunswick, 207/729-5858, www.thegreatimpasta.com, 11 A.M.–9 P.M. Mon.–Thurs., to 10 P.M. Fri.–Sat.), a cheerful, informal eatery where the garlic meets you at the door. No reservations, so expect to wait, although you can call ahead and add your name to the waiting list. Dinner entrées are $10–17. It has a small but varied wine list and a "bambino menu" for the kids.

Hip, funky, and full of personality are words often used to describe **El Camino** (15 Cushing St., Brunswick, 207/725-8228, 5–9 P.M. Wed.–Sat., to 10 P.M. Fri.–Sat.), which uses fresh, local, and often organic ingredients to create innovative Cal-Mex fare. Prices top out around $15.

Chef Richard Gnauck has been serving authentic German fare in the area for more than 20 years, and recently he's been joined by sons Erik and Wilhelm at his **Richard's Restaurant** (115 Maine St., Brunswick, 11 A.M.–2 P.M. and 5–9 P.M. Mon.–Sat., to 9:30 P.M. Fri. and Sat.). German favorites such as Wiener schnitzel and sauerbraten share the menu with American-style fare; heart-smart and petite portions are available; $12–20.

Lobster and Seafood

In late 2006, the Holbrook Community Foundation took ownership of Holbrook's Wharf, site of **Holbrook's Wharf and Grille** (984 Cundy's Harbor Rd., 207/729-0848, 11:30 A.M.–sunset daily), along with Holbrook's General Store and the Trufant mansion, preserving this slice of Maine-fishing-village life for future generations. The wharf lobster shack, under leased operation by the Morse family, is the real thing for authentic lobster in the rough, and the view's superb. Order at the window and then choose a picnic table on the wharf, some under cover. Seafood baskets, hot dogs, and burgers are also available. BYOB.

You want fresh? Fish doesn't get any fresher than that served at **Allen's Seafood** (119 Lookout Point Rd., Harpswell, 207/833-2828, 11 A.M.–7 P.M. daily), a seasonal take-out shack overlooking Middle Bay. Chowders, fried fish, lobster, and similar fare are prepared fresh from the bounty of the daily catch. Order and then grab a picnic table. Moorings and a dock are available if you arrive by boat.

INFORMATION AND SERVICES

The Southern Midcoast Chamber of Commerce (2 Main St., Topsham, 877/725-8797, www.midcoastmaine.com) publishes *Guide to Southern Midcoast Maine.*

For information on Harpswell, visit Harpswell Business Association (www.harpswellmaine.org).

Check the website of Curtis Memorial Library (23 Pleasant St., Brunswick, 207/725-5242, www.curtislibrary.com) for excellent local resources and guides.

Bath Area

One of the smallest in area of Maine's cities, Bath—with a population of about 9,920 in only nine square miles—has many similarities to Brunswick. It sits astride Route 1 and a river, relies on modern military funding, yet has centuries of historical and architectural tradition, enough distinction that the National Trust for Historic Preservation named it as one of a Dozen Distinctive Destinations in 2005. The defense part is impossible to ignore, since giant cranes dominate the riverfront cityscape at the huge Bath Iron Works complex, source of state-of-the-art warships—your tax dollars at work. Less evident (but not far away) is the link to the past: Just south of Bath, in Popham on the Phippsburg Peninsula, is the poorly marked site where a trouble-plagued English settlement, a sister colony to Jamestown, predated the Plymouth Colony by 13 years. (Of course, Champlain arrived before that, and Norsemen allegedly left calling cards even earlier.) In 1607 and 1608, settlers in the Popham Colony managed to build a 30-ton pinnace, *Virginia of Sagadahoc,* designed for transatlantic trade, but they lost heart during a bitter winter and abandoned the site. (A replica is under construction at the Maine Maritime Museum. For details, visit www.mainesfirstship.org.)

Bath is the jumping-off point for two peninsulas to the south—Phippsburg (of Popham Colony fame) and Georgetown. Both are dramatically scenic, with glacier-carved farms and fishing villages. Drive (bicycling is best left to experienced pedalers) a dozen miles down any of these fingers and you're in different worlds, ones where artists and photographers, hikers and historians go crazy with all the possibilities.

Across the soaring Sagadahoc Bridge from Bath is Woolwich, from which you can continue northeastward along the coast or detour northward on Route 128 to the hamlet of Day's Ferry. Named after 18th-century resident Joseph Day, who shuttled back and forth in a gondola-type boat across the Kennebec here, the picturesque village has a cluster of 18th- and 19th-century homes and churches—all part of the Day's Ferry Historic District. And the village's Old Stage Road saw many a stagecoach in its day; passengers would ferry from Bath and pick up the stage here to travel onward.

SIGHTS
Bath Iron Works

Only during one of its relatively infrequent launchings is Bath Iron Works (BIW) open to the public, and then it's a mob scene, with hordes of politicos, townsfolk, and military pooh-bahs in their scrambled eggs and brass. But the launchings are exciting occasions, with flags flying everywhere. BIW, under the umbrella of giant defense contractor General Dynamics, employs more than 8,500 in its Bath and smaller Brunswick sites. When BIW talks, everyone listens. And when BIW's afternoon shift changes, everyone from Brunswick to Wiscasset feels the gridlock. Avoid approaching Bath between 3:25 and 4 P.M. on a weekday; be forewarned and plan your schedule around the witching hour. Despite the construction of the brand-new Sagadahoc Bridge, which has definitely eased the situation, traffic still backs up at shift-change time.

◖ Maine Maritime Museum

Spread over 20 acres on the Kennebec River is the state's premier marine museum, the Maine Maritime Museum (243 Washington St., Bath, 207/443-1316, www.mainemaritimemuseum .org, 9:30 A.M.–5 P.M. daily, $10 adult, $7 ages 7–17, $9 over 65). On the grounds are relics of the 19th-century Percy and Small Shipyard (1897–1920) and a hands-on lobstering exhibit, but the first thing you see is the architecturally dramatic Maritime History Building, locale for permanent and temporary displays of marine art and artifacts and a shop stocked with nautical books and gifts. Bring a picnic and let the toddlers loose in the children's play area. Then join one of the three daily, hour-long guided shipyard tours or the special themed tours offered at 2 P.M. weekdays (all tours late May–mid-Oct.). Shipyard demonstrations are held on a rotating schedule, and brown-bag lectures are often given. In summer, weather permitting, the museum sponsors a variety of special river cruises; call for information. Percy and Small Shipyard is open all year as long as the weather holds.

Bath History Preserved
Sagadahoc Preservation (Box 322, Bath 04530, www.sagadahocpreservation.org), founded in 1971 to rescue the city's architectural heritage, has produced *Architectural Tours: Self-Guided Walking and Driving Tours of the City of Bath,* a terrific foldout brochure (with maps) to guide you—via car, ankle express, or bicycle—around Bath. Pick up a copy at a local business. It also offers an annual house tour, usually in June; check the website for details. Another free map and guide, *The Historic Architecture of Downtown Bath, Maine,* is sponsored by Main Street Bath (4 Centre St., Bath, 207/442-7291, www.mainstbath.com).

Phippsburg Peninsula
Thanks to an impressive map/brochure produced by the Phippsburg Historical Society and the Phippsburg Business Association, you can spend a whole day—or, better still, several days—exploring the peninsula that drops from Bath. Along the way are campgrounds, B&Bs, an updated traditional resort, restaurants, a unique state park, hiking trails, secluded coves, spectacular scenery, and tons of history.

About two miles south of Bath is a causeway known as **Winnegance,** an Wabanaki name usually translated as "short carry" or "little portage." Native Americans crossed here from the Kennebec to the New Meadows River. Early settlers erected nearly a dozen tide-powered mills to serve the shipbuilding industry, but they're long gone. Just before the causeway, on the Bath-Phippsburg boundary, is the **Winnegance General Store** (36 High St.,

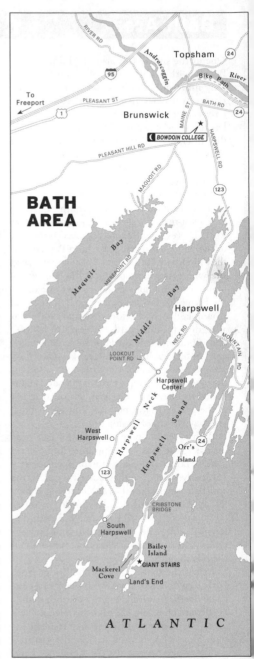

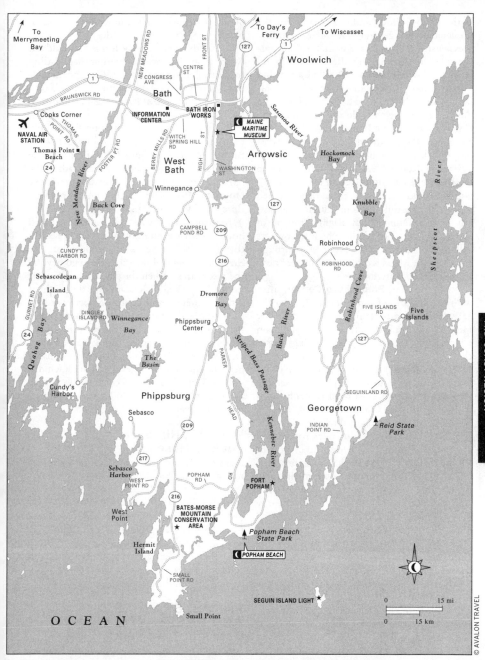

Bath, 207/443-9805), a local favorite for the miscellanea that general stores offer, including inexpensive sandwiches. About 1.5 miles farther is a left turn onto Fiddler's Reach Road, leading to the **Morse Cove Public Launching Facility,** one of the state's most scenic boat-launch sites. If you have a kayak, plan to go downriver on the ebb tide and return on the flow (otherwise, you'll be battling the strong Kennebec River current). There's plenty of paved parking here, plus a restroom.

Back on Route 209, it's another 1.3 miles to the **Dromore Burying Ground** (on the right), with great old headstones; the earliest is dated 1743. The next mile opens up with terrific easterly views of Dromore Bay. Right in the line of sight is 117-acre Lee Island (which the owners sold to the state in 1995). From May through mid-July, the island is off-limits to protect nesting eagles and waterfowl.

Next you're in **Phippsburg Center,** alive with shipbuilding from colonial days to the early 20th century. Hang a left onto Parker Head Road (but avoid this detour if you're on a bicycle; it's too narrow and winding). After the Phippsburg Historical Museum (in an 1859 schoolhouse) and the Alfred Totman Library, turn left onto Church Lane to see the **Phippsburg Congregational Church,** built in 1802. Out front is a "Constitution Tree," a huge English linden planted in 1774.

Parker Head Road continues southward and meets Route 209, which takes you to **Popham Beach State Park.** Continue to the end of Route 209 for **Fort Popham Historic Site,** where parking is woefully inadequate in summer (and costs an exorbitant $7 at nearby Percy's Store). The fort is accessible Memorial Day–September. Youngsters love this place—they can fish from the rocks, climb to the third level of the 1865 stone fortress, picnic on the seven-acre grounds, and create sand castles on the tiny beach next to the fort. Resist the urge to swim, though; the current is dangerous, and there's no lifeguard. Across the river is Bay Point, a lobstering village at the tip of the Georgetown Peninsula. **Percy's Store** (207/389-2010), by the way, with a handful

of tables, is the best place down here for pizza, picnic fare, and fishing tackle.

Across the cove from the fort is Fort Baldwin Road, a one-lane-wide, winding road leading to the shorefront site of the 1607 Popham Colony. Climb the path up Sabino Hill to World War I–era **Fort Baldwin,** the best vantage point for panoramic photos.

Backtrack about four miles on Route 209, turn left onto Route 216, and head toward **Small Point.** Go about 0.9 mile to Morse Mountain Road, on the left, which leads to the parking area and trailhead for **Bates-Morse Mountain Preserve.** Farther south are Head Beach and Hermit Island.

Returning northward on Route 216, you'll hook up with Route 209 and then see a left turn (Rte. 217) to Sebasco Harbor Resort (see *Accommodations*). Take the time to go beyond the resort area. When the paved road goes left (to the Water's Edge Restaurant), turn right at a tiny cemetery and continue northward on the Old Meadowbrook Road, which meanders for about four miles along the west side of the peninsula. About midway along is **the Basin,** regarded by sailors as one of the Maine coast's best "hurricane holes" (refuges in high winds). As you skirt the Basin and come to a fork, bear right to return to Route 209; turn left and return northward to Bath.

Woolwich Historical Society Museum

Next to a Route 1 flashing caution light, 2.5 miles north of Bath, the two-story Woolwich Historical Society Museum (Rte. 1 at Nequasset Rd., P.O. Box 98, Woolwich 04579, 207/443-4833, 10:30 A.M.–2:30 P.M. Tues.–Sat. July and Aug., $3 adults, $1 children over six), admirably well organized, has rooms full of early 19th- to early 20th-century quilts, clothing, tools, and tradesmen's wares. The oldest part of the building dates from the early 19th century.

PARKS, BEACHES, AND PRESERVES
Bath's In-Town Parks
An old-fashioned gazebo, just right for hanging

out with a book (bring a cushion), is the centerpiece of **Library Park,** the manicured space fronting the Patten Free Library, Summer and Washington Streets.

Waterfront Park, bordering the Kennebec on Commercial Street, has covered picnic tables, restrooms, and Friday-night concerts in summer.

At the end of High Street, at the tip of land where Whiskeag Creek meets the Kennebec River, is the **Thorn Head Preserve** (www.lkrlt.org/thornehead.html), maintained by the Lower Kennebec Regional Land Trust. Allow a half hour for the easy walk to the headland and its stone "picnic" table with views toward Merrymeeting Bay. Allow longer if you wish to explore any of the side trails.

Hamilton Sanctuary

Owned by Maine Audubon, Hamilton Sanctuary (Foster Point Rd., West Bath, no phone) is a peaceful site for walking and nature study on the New Meadows River, with 1.5 miles of trails winding through meadows and forests and along the Back Cove shoreline. From Route 1 between Bath and Brunswick, take the New Meadows Road exit. Head south on New Meadows. When it becomes Foster Point Road, go four miles to the sanctuary entrance. Open sunrise–sunset all year; free admission. For more information, contact Maine Audubon (20 Gilsland Farm Rd., Falmouth, 207/781-2330).

🌙 Popham Beach

On hot July and August weekends, the parking lot at Popham Beach State Park (Rte. 209, Phippsburg, 207/389-1335), 14 miles south of Bath, fills up by 10 A.M., so plan to arrive early at this huge crescent of sand backed by sea grass, beach roses, and dunes. Facilities include changing rooms, outside showers, restrooms, and seasonal lifeguards. Admission is $4 adults, $1 kids 5–11, free under 5 or over 65. It's officially open April 15–October 30, but the beach is accessible all year (no winter contact number).

© TOM NANGLE

Popham Beach, on the Phippsburg Peninsula, is one of Maine's best strands of sand.

© TOM NANGLE

Fort Popham guards the mouth of the Kennebec River.

Fort Popham Historic Site

A mile down the road, at the end of Route 209, is the seven-acre Fort Popham Historic Site, where kids of all ages can explore the waterfront tower and bunkers of a 19th-century granite fort. No swimming here—the current is dangerous—but there's fun fishing from the rocks (no license needed), plus picnic tables and restrooms.

Bates-Morse Mountain Conservation Area

Consider visiting the lovely, 600-acre Bates-Morse Mountain Conservation Area (Rtes. 209 and 216, Small Point, Phippsburg Peninsula, www.bates.edu/Morse-Mountain .xml) *only* if you are willing to be extraconscientious about the rules for this private preserve. A relatively easy four-mile round-trip hike takes you through marshland (you'll need insect repellent) and to the top of 210-foot Morse Mountain, with panoramic views, and then down to privately owned Seawall Beach. On a clear day, you can see

New Hampshire's Mt. Washington from the summit. No dogs or vehicles; no recreational facilities; stay on the preserve road and the beach path at all times (side roads are private). Least terns and piping plovers—both endangered species—nest in the dunes, so avoid this area, especially mid-May–mid-August. Birding hint: Morse Mountain is a great locale for spotting hawks during their annual September migration southward. Pick up a map (and the rules) from the box in the parking area, Morse Mountain Road, off Route 216 (just under a mile south of the Rte. 209 intersection). No admission fee; open sunrise–sunset.

Head Beach

Just off Route 216, about two miles south of the Route 209 turnoff to Popham Beach, is Head Beach, a sandy crescent that's open until 10 P.M. A day-use fee ($5) is payable at the small gatehouse; there's a restroom on the path to the beach and a store within walking distance.

Phippsburg Hiking Trails

The town of Phippsburg and the Phippsburg Land Trust (207/443-6309, www.phippsburg landtrust.org) have prepared a handy free brochure with map that describes nine preserves with trails. Three—Center Pond, Spirit Pond, and Ridgewell Preserve—have detailed maps and field guides available at trailhead boxes. The Land Trust also hosts guided walks mid-June–mid-September.

Reid State Park

Reid State Park, on the Georgetown Peninsula (Seguinland Rd., Georgetown, 207/371-2303), is no secret, so plan to arrive early on summer weekends, when parking is woefully inadequate. Highlights of the 765-acre park are 1.5 miles of splendid beach (in three distinct sections), marshlands, sand dunes, and tide pools. Kids love the tide pools, treasure troves left by the receding tide. Facilities include changing rooms (with showers), picnic tables, restrooms, and snack bars. Test the water before racing in; even in midsummer, it's breathtakingly cold. In winter, bring cross-country skis and glide along the shoreline. The park—14 miles south of Route 1 (Woolwich) and two miles off Route 127—is open daily all year. Admission is $4.50 adults, $1 kids 5–11, free for ages 5 and under and 65 and older.

Just half a mile beyond the Reid State Park entrance is **Charles Pond,** where the setting is unsurpassed for freshwater swimming in the long, skinny pond. You'll wish this were a secret, too, but it isn't. No facilities.

Josephine Newman Sanctuary

A must-see for any nature lover, the 119-acre Josephine Newman Sanctuary (Rte. 127, Georgetown, no phone) has 2.5 miles of blazed loop trails winding through 110 wooded acres and along Robinhood Cove's tidal shoreline. Josephine Oliver Newman (1878–1968), a respected naturalist, bequeathed her family's splendid property to Maine Audubon, which maintains it today. The 0.6-mile self-guiding trail is moderately difficult, but the rewards are 20 informative markers highlighting special

features: glacial erratics, reversing falls, mosses, and marshes. The easiest route is the 0.75-mile Horseshoe Trail, which you can extend for another mile or so by linking into the Rocky End Trail. The sanctuary is open sunrise–sunset daily all year,; free admission. No pets or bikes. The best way to appreciate it is to buy *Forests, Fields, and Estuaries,* a 60-page sanctuary guide ($3.50), with lots of natural-history information useful for other preserves. Contact Maine Audubon (20 Gilsland Farm Rd., Falmouth, 207/781-2330), or stop in at the society's environmental center in Falmouth. To reach the Newman sanctuary, take Route 127 from Route 1 in Woolwich (the road to Reid State Park) for 9.1 miles. Turn right at the sanctuary sign and continue up the narrow, rutted, dirt road (pray no one's coming the other way) to the small parking lot. A map of the trail system is posted at the marsh's edge and available in the box.

Robert P. Tristram Coffin Wildflower Sanctuary

The New England Wildflower Society owns this lovely 177-acre preserve bordering Merrymeeting Bay, with more than 100 species of wildflowers. Well-marked trails lace the sanctuary. To find it, take Route 127 north for 2.2 miles, then Route 128 for 4.5 miles, and look for a small parking area on the left.

RECREATION
Golf

The 18-hole **Bath Country Club** (Whiskeag Rd., Bath, 207/442-8411) has moderate greens fees, a pro shop, and a restaurant serving lunch and dinner. Starting times are needed on weekends.

The **Sebasco Harbor Resort** has a nine-hole course (expanding to 18 holes) open to nonguests on a space-available basis; call the resort's pro shop (207/389-9060) to inquire. Each hole has two sets of tees. Watch out for the infamous second hole, which gives new meaning to the term water hole, and be sure to say, "Morning, Sarah," on the sixth tee. If you look nearby, you'll find a gravestone inscribed "Sarah Wallace—1862." A local rhyme goes:

Show respect to Sarah
You golfers passing by;
She's the only person on this course,
Who can't improve her lie.

The course, called Shore Acres, is open early May–late October.

Bicycling

Bath-area headquarters for anything to do with bikes is **Bath Cycle and Ski** (Rte. 1, Woolwich, 207/442-7002 or 800/245-3626, www.bikeman.com). Rentals are $80/week, route maps are available, and the shop sponsors weekly rides on Tuesday nights and Saturday and Sunday mornings.

Excursion Boats

The 50-foot *Yankee* operates out of Small Point's Hermit Island Campground Monday–Saturday throughout the summer. You can go on nature cruises, enjoy the sunset, or visit Eagle Island; the schedule is different each day and rates vary widely by trip. Call for information and reservations (207/389-1788).

The M/V *Ruth,* a 38-foot excursion boat, runs cruises out of Sebasco Harbor Resort late June–Labor Day. You don't need to be a Sebasco guest to take the trips, but reservations are essential. The schedule changes weekly, but possible options are a nature cruise, Cundy's Harbor lunch cruise, lobstering demos, sunset cruise, and Pirate Island at lengths varying from one to two hours. Price for nonguests is $17 adults, $9 kids 3–12. Resort guests pay $13 adult, $6 child. Call the Sebasco Harbor Resort (207/389-1161) for the schedule, which is available a week in advance. Also sailing from Sebasco Harbor Resort is *Sail Magic* (207/650-3293, www.sailmagic.com), a Tartan 41 ocean racer built in 1974.

Long Reach Cruises (207/442-0092 or 888/538-6785, www.longreachcruises.com) offers a variety of one- to three-plus-hour cruises, departing from the Maine Maritime Museum. Options include narrated history, lighthouses, seal-watching, eagle-watching, and sunset cruises. Prices range $20–40 adult, $10–20 child, including museum admission.

The **Maine Maritime Museum** (see *Sights*) runs excursion boats to Seguin Island in summer, weather permitting, allowing you about three hours to explore the island, where you can climb the hill to the lighthouse and then climb the 53-foot light tower for a fabulous view from the deck. Afterward, visit the three-room **Seguin Museum,** loaded with lighthouse memorabilia. The nonprofit Friends of Seguin maintains the island's buildings and subsidizes the summertime caretakers, in residence Memorial Day–mid-September. The Coast Guard maintains the automated light, which has an 18-mile range. There's no dock, so you'll be offloaded by dinghy—not an experience recommended for the unsteady.

Canoeing and Kayaking

Close to civilization, yet amazingly undeveloped, 392-acre **Nequasset Lake** is a great place to canoe. You'll see a few anglers, a handful of houses, and near-wilderness along the shoreline. Personal watercraft and motors over 10 hp are banned. Take Route 1 from Bath across the bridge to Woolwich. Continue to the flashing caution light at Nequasset Road; turn *right* and go 0.1 mile. Turn left, and left again, into the parking area for the Nequasset Stream Waterfront Park, a popular swimming hole. Launch your canoe and head upstream, under Route 1, to the lake.

Paddle the relatively calm and safe waters of Winnegance Creek with a rental boat from **Up the Creak Kayak and Canoe Rentals** (Rte. 209, Phippsburg, 207/443-4845, www.rentkayaks.com). Canoe and kayak rentals are $10 pp for three hours.

Seaspray Kayaking (888/349-7774) operates from bases at the Sebasco Harbor Resort, in Sebasco Estates; Hermit Island Campground, on Small Point; and Bay Point Kayaking Center, in Georgetown. Hourly rentals begin at $10–20 the first hour plus $5–10 for each additional hour, up to $20–50 daily, with longer-term rates and delivery available. A variety of guided tours also are offered, with half-day options for $50 adult, $25 child, and specialty paddles, such as sunset or moonlight, for $40 pp.

Fishing Charters

For guided fishing trips for stripers, bluefish, pike trout, and smallmouth bass, contact **Kennebec Tidewater Charters** (207/737-4695, www .kennebectidewater.com). Captain Robin Thayer, a Master Maine Guide, offers freshwater and saltwater cruises, beginning at $300 for four hours. Tackle is provided and instruction is available. Catch-and-release is encouraged.

ENTERTAINMENT AND EVENTS

Bath's most diversified entertainment setting is the **Center for the Arts at the Chocolate Church** (804 Washington St., Bath, 207/442-8455, www.chocolatechurch.com), a chocolate-brown board-and-batten structure built in 1846 as the Central Congregational Church. Year-round activities at the arts center include music and dance concerts, dramas, exhibits, and children's programs.

At 7 P.M. every Tuesday and Friday mid-June–August, the **Gazebo Concert Series** brings live entertainment to Bath's Library Park.

Five Rivers Arts Alliances holds **3rd Friday Art Walks** (various locations, Bath, 207/798-6964, 5–8 P.M.) June–October.

Throughout the summer, the **Maine Maritime Museum** (207/443-1316) schedules special events, often hinging on visits by tall ships and other vessels. Some of the visiting boats are open to the public for an extra fee. Call the museum to check.

From November through April, 60 dealers show their wares at the monthly **Bath Antiques Shows** (207/443-8983, www.bathantiques shows.com, $4) at the Bath Middle School.

SHOPPING

Front and Center Streets are lined with fun, independent shops, including a number of antiques shops clustered on lower Front Street.

Bath's home to yet another good independent bookstore successfully bucking the megastore trend. The **Bath Book Shop** (96 Front St., Bath, 207/443-9338) has friendly, hometown service and a discerning taste in books.

Right in the shadow of the Route 1 overpass is an incredible resource for knitters and weavers. **Halcyon Yarn** (12 School St., Bath, 207/442-7909 or 800/341-0282, www.halcyon yarn.com), a huge warehouse of a place, carries domestic and imported yarns, looms, spinning wheels, how-to videos, kits, and pattern books.

About nine miles down Route 127, you'll come to **Georgetown Pottery** (Rte. 127, Georgetown, 207/371-2801), a top-quality ceramics studio/shop.

Anyone who appreciates fine woodworking tools *has* to visit the Shelter Institute's **Woodbutcher Tools** (873 Rte. 1, Woolwich, 207/442-7938) retail shop and bookstore, five miles north of Bath.

Flea Market

One of Maine's biggest and most enduring flea markets is right on Route 1 north of Bath, often creating near-accidents as rubbernecking motorists slam to a halt. **Montsweag Flea Market** (Rte. 1 at Mountain Rd., Woolwich, 207/443-2809) is a genuine treasure trove about seven miles northeast of Bath's Sagadahoc bridge. It's open weekends in May, September, and October and on Wednesday, Friday, Saturday, and Sunday June–August. Sales begin at 6:30 A.M.

Farmers Market

In Waterfront Park on Commercial Street, the **Bath Farmers Market** operates 8:30 A.M.–12:30 P.M. every Thursday and Saturday May 1–October, featuring crafts, plants, condiments, baked goods, and cheeses in addition to seasonal produce.

ACCOMMODATIONS
Bath

Most of Bath's in-town B&Bs and inns are in historic residences built by shipping magnates and their families, giving you a chance to appreciate the quality of craftsmanship they demanded in their ships and their homes alike.

The flamboyant pink and plum Italianate **Galen Moses House** (1009 Washington St., Bath, 207/442-8771 or 888/442-8771, www.galenmoses.com, $119–199) is a standout in the city's Historic District. Original architectural features—soaring ceilings, friezes, chandeliers, elaborate woodwork, stained-glass windows—and period antiques make it equally appealing inside, as do hosts Jim Haught and Larry Kieft. All rooms have air-conditioning and Wi-Fi. It has plenty of common rooms to relax, including one with TV and VCR. A fancy full breakfast and afternoon refreshments are included. Pets are allowed in one room for $15 per night.

Innkeeper Elizabeth Knowlton blends elegance and comfort at the **Inn at Bath** (969 Washington St., Bath, 207/443-4294 or 800/423-0964, www.innatbath.com, $165–185). Her culinary skills, honed as chef and co-owner of a Montana fly-fishing lodge, have garnered national attention. Guest rooms in the 1810 Greek Revival–style inn are decorated with antiques and each has air-conditioning, TV/VCR, Wi-Fi, and phone. Two have wood-burning fireplaces, and two have two-person whirlpool tubs. Kids over four and dogs are welcome. One room is ADA compliant.

Just a few miles from downtown Bath, yet feeling a world away, is the **Fairhaven Inn** (118 North Bath Rd., Bath, 207/443-4391 or 888/443-4391, www.mainecoast.com/fairhaveninn, $90–145). Antiques and country pieces furnish Dawn and Andrew Omo's truly rambling 1790 colonial, built on 16 country acres with views over the Kennebec River. It has eight rooms, all with Wi-Fi and air-conditioning; some share baths. The Omos grew up in Bath, so they know the area well. Open year-round.

Phippsburg Peninsula

The trouble with staying at the **❰ Sebasco Harbor Resort** (Rte. 217, Sebasco Estates, 207/389-1161 or 800/225-3819, www.sebasco.com), a self-contained resort on 575 waterfront acres, is that between the beautiful setting and the bountiful offerings, you might not set foot off the premises during your entire vacation. Situated at the mouth of the saltwater New Meadows River, 12 miles south of Bath, Sebasco has attracted families who return year after year—since 1930, when it opened. Many guests stay for a week. Sebasco changed hands in 1997, and owner Bob Smith has successfully brought the resort up to 21st-century standards, but he has kept the emphasis on families, and you'll have to look far and wide to find a better family resort. Scattered around the well-tended property are the main lodge and a variety of cottages (from 1–6 bedrooms; the two-bedroom units with shared living room are a great choice for families), a main lodge, a four-story cupola-topped lighthouse building edging the harbor, and two new suites buildings, Harbor Village and the waterfront Fairwinds Spa, with more contemporary amenities. All have private baths, phones, cable TV; many have water views, some have refrigerators or kitchenettes. Pets are allowed in a handful of cottages for $25. Most intriguing is The Lighthouse ($260–370 in July and Aug.); it's worth the splurge. Otherwise, in July and August, room rates range $199–399; suites are $349–479; cottage rates are $399–1,775; $15 per extra person; kids 10 and under are free. MAP rate, including breakfast and dinner, is an additional $48 pp (10 and younger no charge when dining with an adult and off the kids' menu), and special packages (and lower rates) are available spring and fall. The resort's **Pilot House** restaurant (7:30–9:30 A.M. and 6–9 P.M.), with a dramatic sunset water view, is also open to the public; dinner entrée range is $17–32. Below it, the patio at the casual Ledges Pub (11:30 A.M.–2 P.M. and 5–9 P.M., $8–23) is a late-day magnet, with indoor and outdoor seating. Weekly summer events include a Sunday evening reception and grand buffet, lobster bakes, family barbecues, bingo, live entertainment, and the free Camp Merrit children's program. Recreational facilities include two all-weather tennis courts, nine-hole championship golf course and a three-hole regulation course for beginners and families, the state's largest outdoor saltwater pool, boat tours aboard the *Ruth,* sailing trips, sea kayak excursions, mountain-bike tours, candlepin bowling, horseshoes, a playground, a well-equipped fitness center, and as much or as little organized activity as you want. In 2007, the resort opened an oceanfront spa. (See *Excursion Boats* under *Recreation* for info on cruises in the M/V *Ruth.*) Sebasco Harbor Resort is open early May–late October.

Right on the beach between Popham Beach State Park and Fort Popham is the **Popham Beach Bed and Breakfast** (4 Ocean View La., Popham Beach, Phippsburg, 207/389-2409, www.pophambeachbandb.com, $175–215 d), a unique hostelry in a restored 1883 Coast Guard station. Innkeeper Peggy Johannessen takes guests to the rooftop lookout tower and shares the building's history as a maritime lifesaving center. Inside are three rooms and a suite, two with gas fireplaces. A two-course breakfast is served in the dining room each morning, and guests can hang out in the large oceanfront living room. Open all year.

Magnificent gardens surround **Edgewater Farm Bed and Breakfast** (71 Small Point Rd./Rte. 216, Sebasco Estates, 207/389-1322 or 877/389-1322, www.edgewaterfarmbedand breakfast.com, $130–140 d), Carol and Bill Emerson's comfy, unfussy 19th-century farmhouse, just south of the turnoff to Popham Beach and close to the access for Morse Mountain. Families usually choose the carriage house, where kids can play in the huge recreation room. A brunch-size breakfast served in the many-windowed solarium benefits from lots of organic produce grown on the four-acre grounds. (The Emersons always plant extra to donate to the Bath food pantry each summer.) And then there's the four-foot-deep indoor lap pool, a hot tub outside on the deck, and the Benedictine labyrinth Bill created in a wooded grove. English, Spanish, a bit of French, and German are all spoken. Pets are possible.

Rock Gardens Inn (Rte. 218, Sebasco Estates, Phippsburg, 207/389-1339, www .rockgardensinn.com) hosts numerous artists' workshops, and no wonder. It sits on its own peninsula, and the pretty grounds are landscaped with wild and cultivated flowers. Guests stay in one of three inn rooms ($130–150 d, $175–190 s) or 10 cottages and have use of an outdoor heated pool and sea kayaks. Cottage rates begin at $140 d pp and include breakfast and dinner—and the weekly lobster cookout. After the minimum rate is reached per cottage, kids pay $50–110, depending upon age. Sebasco Harbor Resort is just steps away, and guests have access to its facilities, too. Ask about all-inclusive art retreats.

Joe and Debbie Braun have done a masterful job restoring **The 1774 Inn at Phippsburg** (44 Parker Head Rd., Phippsburg Center, 207/389-1774, www.1774inn.com, $125–185), a four-square Georgian Colonial National Historic Register property with an ell and barn. Many Colonial details have been preserved, including shutters with peepholes and strong bars to defend against attack, paneled wainscoting, ceiling moldings, fluted columns, and wide pine floors. Most of the eight rooms (all but two with private bath) have views of the Kennebec River. Rooms are furnished with antiques or tasteful reproductions. Also on the premises is the Riverside Guest House, a four-bedroom, two-bath cottage available for $1,800 per week.

Georgetown Peninsula

It'll be hard to tear yourself away from the scenery and sanctuary at **The Mooring Bed and Breakfast** (132 Seguinland Rd., Georgetown, 207/371-2790 or 866/828-7348, www .themooringb-b.com, $150–200), the original home of Walter Reid, who donated Reid State Park to the state. His great-granddaughter and her family have beautifully restored the house, situated on lovely, oceanfront grounds with island-studded views. Each room has a water view and air-conditioning. There's plenty of room to spread out, including the appropriately named Spanish room. A full breakfast is served.

Campgrounds

Plan to book a site in January if you want a waterfront campsite in midsummer at the Phippsburg Peninsula's **Hermit Island Campground** (6 Hermit Island Rd., Phippsburg, 207/443-2101, www.hermitisland.com, winter mailing address 42 Front St., Bath 04530, same phone). With 275 campsites (no vehicles larger than pickup campers; no hookups) spread over a 255-acre causeway-linked island, this is oceanfront camping at its best. The well-managed operation has a store, snack bar, seasonal post office, boat rentals, boat excursions, trails, and seven private beaches. The hub of activity (and registration) is the Kelp Shed, next to the campsite entrance. No washing machines, but dryers are available. Rules are strictly enforced (no visitors allowed in the camping area). Open and wooded sites run $34–56 (two adults and two kids) mid-June–Labor Day, $32 a site early and late in the season. Reservations for a week's stay or longer and Memorial and Labor Day Weekends can be made by mail beginning in early January and by phone in early February (call for exact date). Reservations for stays of less than one week accepted as of March 1. It's open mid-May–Columbus Day, but full operation is really June–Labor Day. The campground is at the tip of the Phippsburg Peninsula. No pets, no credit cards.

FOOD
Local Flavors

For breakfast, lunch, or sweets, drop into the **Starlight Café** (15 Lambard St., 207/443-3005, 7 A.M.–2 P.M. Mon.–Fri.), a too-cute and too-tiny daylight-basement space across a side street from the Customs House. It's bright and cheerful, and the food is fab.

Here's a wonderful, multifaceted find. Susan Verrier's **North Creek Farm** (24 Sebasco Rd., Phippsburg, 207/389-1341, 9 A.M.–6:30 P.M. daily, lunch served 11:30 A.M.–3:30 P.M.) is an 1850s saltwater farm with fabulous organic gardens, including ornamental display gardens and lots of rugosa roses (a specialty—Susan's written two books). Visitors can meander down by a waterfall, creek, and salt marsh. Inside the barn is a small store stocked with garden and gourmet goodies and a small café, where Susan makes delicious soups and sandwiches to order ($5–7). There are tables indoors, but there also are chairs and tables scattered in the

gardens. Pick up one of the illustrated catalogs—a fun read and you're almost guaranteed to find something you want.

On the Georgetown Peninsula, **Five Islands Farm** (13375 Rte. 127, Five Islands, 297/371-9383, www.fiveislandsfarm.com) is a fine stop for picnic fixings, with an excellent assortment of Maine cheeses, along with breads, meats, chips, salsa, and even wine.

Oh my! Patty Mains retired early from Bath Iron Works to pursue her passion, chocolate. Her handcrafted chocolates are made from the best ingredients and from traditional recipes—try the needhams, made with mashed potatoes. While chocolates are the centerpiece at **MainSweets** (Rte. 127, Georgetown, 207/371-2806), she also sells home-baked breads, cookies, brownies, fudge, and other sweet treats.

Bath's best pizza comes from **The Cabin** (552 Washington St., Bath, 207/443-6224, 10 A.M.–10 P.M., to 11 P.M. Thurs.–Sat.)—a local landmark since 1973. The white garlic sauce is outstanding, and the cheese steak is about the best outside of Philly. A large three-topping pizza is $15. Order food to go or eat in at this decidedly casual place across from Bath Iron Works.

Barbecue

Finger-licking, Memphis-style barbecue along with other Southern specialties are served in big quantities at **Beale Street Barbeque and Grill** (215 Water St., Bath, 207/442-9514, 11 A.M.–9 P.M. daily, to 10 P.M. in July and Aug.). Everything's made on the premises. Find it next to the municipal parking lot.

Casual Dining

Kate and Andy Winglass operate **Mae's Café and Bakery** (160 Centre St., at High St., Bath, 207/442-8577, www.maescafeandbakery.com), a longtime local favorite bakery and café, with seating indoors and on a front deck. It's *the* place to go for brunch (reservations essential on weekends). Breakfast and lunch are served 8 A.M.–3 P.M. daily; dinner, served to 8 P.M. Thursday–Saturday, is in the $14–20 range. Sunday brunch is served until 2 P.M.

The appealing menu has creative touches—the tarragon chicken salad croissant available for lunch is a winner. Rotating art shows enliven the open and airy dining rooms.

The Mediterranean theme at **Maryellenz Cafe** (15 Vine St., Bath, 207/442-0960, 11:30 A.M.–9:30 P.M. Tues.–Sat.) allows for some whiffs of Maine (crab cakes, for instance, and fresh fish); there's a good selection of creative pasta dishes. Or mix-and-match a meal from the tapas and meze selections. Entrée range is $10–25. The brightly colored dining rooms double as an art gallery.

The cool and contemporary Danish decor matches the food at **(Solo Bistro** (128 Front St., Bath, 207/443-3373, www.solobistro.com, opens at 5 P.M. Mon.–Sat.), a sophisticated storefront restaurant downtown, where the choices might range from a bistro burger to pan-seared wild salmon ($12–28). A nightly three-course fixed-price menu is usually around $23. The wine bar features jazz on Friday nights.

The View's the Thing

Even if you're not staying at **Sebasco Harbor Resort** (Rte. 217, Sebasco Estates, 207/389-1161 or 800/225-3819, www.sebasco.com), you can dine in either of its two waterfront restaurants, both with gasp-producing sunset views. Binoculars hang by windows in the **Pilot House** (5:30–9 P.M. Mon.–Sat.), the more formal of the two, so diners can get a better view of the boats or birds happening by. Dinner entrée range is $17–27. Below it is the casual Ledges Pub (11:30 A.M.–2 P.M. and 5–10 P.M. daily), with indoor and outdoor seating and a menu varying from kid-friendly burgers and fried foods to salmon salad ($6–18).

Gaze at seals playing in the Kennebec River, Fort Popham, and out to open ocean from **Spinney's Restaurant** (Rte. 209, Popham Beach, 207/389-2052, 8 A.M.–8:30 P.M. daily). Food varies in quality from year to year (best advice: Keep it simple; entrées run $10–30, but sandwiches and hot dogs are less than $5),

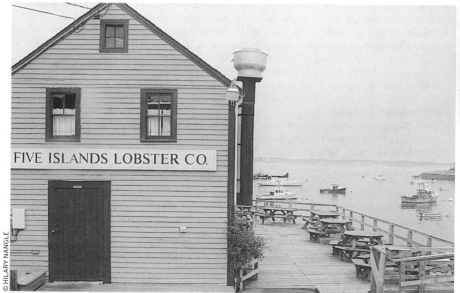

© HILARY NANGLE

It's worth the journey down the peninsula to reach Five Islands Lobster Company, for both the view and the food.

but you can't beat the view. Keep it budget friendly by coming for breakfast. Open mid-May–late October.

Lobster in the Rough

Phippsburg Peninsula: The rustic, buoy-draped **Lobster House** (395 Small Point Rd./Rte. 216, Small Point, 207/389-1596 or 207/389-2178, 5–9 P.M. Tues., noon–9 P.M. Wed.–Sun. late May–early Sept.) overlooks a scenic tidal cove; the view is best when the tide's in. No surprise that lobster and seafood are featured, but sandwiches, soups, salads, and a few grilled items make the menu wallet-friendly for anyone.

Georgetown Peninsula: Just over a mile beyond the turnoff to Reid State Park, you'll reach the end of Route 127 at Five Islands. Here you'll find **C Five Islands Lobster Company** (1447 Five Islands Rd., Five Islands, Georgetown, 207/371-2990, www.fiveislands lobster.com), known for its slogan: "Eat on the dock with the fishermen, but best avoid the table by the bait-shack door." Here you can pig out on lobster rolls, better-than-usual onion rings, crab cakes, and if you must, burgers and hot dogs 11:30 A.M.–8 P.M. daily mid-May–mid-October. It even takes credit cards, a rarity among lobster wharves. Dress down, BYOB, and enjoy the end-of-the-road ambience of this idyllic spot.

Destination Dining

The building alone is worth a visit to Chef Michael Gagne's **Robinhood Free Meetinghouse** (210 Robinhood Rd., HC 33, Box 1469A, Georgetown 04548, 207/371-2188, www.robin hood-meetinghouse.com, 5:30–9 P.M. daily in season), a multistar restaurant in a beautifully restored 1855 building on the Georgetown Peninsula. Most tables are on the main floor; overflow diners go to the second floor, where many of the pews remain. The enormous (more than two dozen entrées, a dozen appetizers) high-quality menu makes it even more enticing. Creativity is the menu byword for Gagne. If you're a chocoholic, save room for Gagne's swoon-worthy signature dessert: Obsession in Three Chocolates with chocolate sauce. Entrées are in the $22–28 range, and portions are large. This isn't a setting for children, but the kitchen can come up with chicken fingers or fettuccine if necessary. Reservations are essential. It's open 5:30–8 P.M. Thursday–Saturday mid-October–mid-May. In winter, ask about special "theme" nights. Gagne sells his famed 72-layer hand-cut cream cheese biscuits frozen, so take a half dozen or so home to enjoy with your leftovers. The restaurant is on the left, about a mile east of Route 127.

INFORMATION AND SERVICES
Information

The Southern Midcoast Chamber of Commerce (2 Main St., Topsham, 877/725-8797, www.midcoastmaine.com) publishes *Guide to Southern Midcoast Maine*. A visitor information center is located in Bath's renovated train station (restrooms available), adjacent to the Bath Iron Works main yard. It's open year-round with brochure racks, and staffed by volunteers from May into October. Request copies of the *City of Bath Downtown Map and Guide* and the *Bath-Brunswick Region Map and Guide*.

Main Street Bath (4 Centre St., Bath, 207/442-7291, www.visitbath.com) produces a guide and has an informative website.

Check out Patten Free Library (33 Summer St., Bath, 207/443-5141, www.patten.lib .me.us).

Public Restrooms

Public restrooms are at Bath City Hall (55 Front St.), Patten Free Library (33 Summer St.), Sagadahoc County Courthouse (752 High St.), and (summer only) Waterfront Park (Commercial St.).

GETTING AROUND

The Bath Trolley (443-9741, www.bathtrolley .org) circulates through the area, with each one-way trip costing $1. For a schedule, visit City Hall.

Wiscasset Area

Billing itself "The Prettiest Village in Maine," Wiscasset (pop. 1,200) works hard to live up to its slogan, with quaint street signs, well-maintained homes, and an air of attentive elegance. Behind the scenes, however, it's actually a rather workaday community—not overrun with deep-pocketed retirees. The interesting mix includes artists, antiques dealers, state government workers, worm diggers, and blue-collar types. And it seems to work.

Wiscasset ("meeting place of three rivers"), incorporated as part of Pownalborough in 1760, has had its current name since 1802. In the late 18th century, it became the shire town of Lincoln County and the largest seaport north of Boston. Countless tall-masted ships sailed the 12 miles up the Sheepscot River to tie up here, and shipyards flourished, turning out vessels for domestic and foreign trade. The 1807 Embargo Act and the War of 1812 delivered a one-two punch that shut down trade and temporarily squelched the town's aspirations, but Wiscasset yards soon were back at it, producing vessels for the pre–Civil War clipper-ship era—only to face a more lasting decline with the arrival of the railroads and the onset of the Industrial Revolution.

Just east of Wiscasset, across the Donald Davey Bridge, is Davis Island and Edgecomb, a tiny town that primarily serves as a funnel to the Boothbay Peninsula.

The Davey Bridge, built in 1983, is the most recent span over the Sheepscot. The earliest, finished in 1847, was a toll bridge that charged a horse and wagon $0.15 to cross, pedestrians $0.03 each, and pigs $0.01 apiece. Before that, ferries carried passengers, animals, and vehicles between Wiscasset and Edgecomb's Davis Island (then named Folly Island).

Wiscasset is notorious for midsummer gridlock. Especially on weekends, traffic backs up on Route 1 for miles in both directions—to the frustration of drivers, passengers, and Wiscasset merchants. The state Department of Transportation has tested traffic medians, stoplights, and other devices, but nothing seems to solve the problem. A bypass has been under discussion for years, but not-in-my-backyard opposition to every route has halted progress. (When you stop in town, try to park pointed in the direction you're going; it's impossible to make turns across oncoming traffic.)

SIGHTS

In 1973, a large chunk of downtown Wiscasset was added to the National Register of Historic Places, and a walking tour is the best way to appreciate the Federal, Classical Revival, and even pre-Revolutionary homes and commercial buildings in the Historic District. Below are a few of the prime examples. If you do nothing else, be sure to swing by the homes on High Street.

Castle Tucker

Once known as the Lee-Tucker House, Castle Tucker (Lee and High Sts., Wiscasset, 207/882-7169, www.historicnewengland.org, tours on the hour, 11 A.M.–4 P.M. Wed.–Sun. June–Oct. 15, $5) is a must-see. Built in 1807 by Judge Silas Lee, and bought by sea captain Richard Tucker in 1858, the imposing mansion has Victorian wallpaper and furnishings, Palladian windows, an amazing elliptical staircase, and a dramatic view over the Sheepscot River. In early 1997, Jane Tucker, Richard's granddaughter, magnanimously deeded the house to Historic New England.

Nickels-Sortwell House

Also owned by Historic New England, the three-story Nickels-Sortwell House (121 Main St., Wiscasset, 207/882-6218, www.historicnewengland.org, tours on the hour 11 A.M.–4 P.M. Fri.–Sun. June–Oct. 15, $5) looms over Route 1, yet it's so close to the road many motorists miss it. Don't. Sea captain William Nickels commissioned the mansion in 1807 but died soon after its completion. For 70 or so years, it was the Belle Haven Hotel, before Alvin

RURAL RAMBLINGS

Surrounding Wiscasset are the lovely rural inland communities of Dresden, Sheepscot, and Alna, definitely worth a detour.

Begin in Dresden at the 1761 **Pownalborough Court House** (River Rd./Rte. 128, Dresden, 10 A.M.–4 P.M. Tues.–Sat., noon–4 P.M. Sun. July and Aug., weekends only June and Sept., $4 adults, $2 children 7–17), a pre-Revolutionary riverfront courthouse listed in the National Register of Historic Places. President John Adams once handled a trial here – in a mid-18th-century frontier community (named Pownalborough) established by French and German settlers. During the 30-minute tour of the three-story courthouse, guides delight in pointing out the restored beams, paneling, and fireplaces, as well as the on-site tavern that catered to judges, lawyers, and travelers. Walk a few hundred feet south, and you'll find a cemetery with Revolution-era graves. Along the river is a nature trail developed by local Eagle Scouts. For more information, call or write **Lincoln County Historical Association** (Federal St., P.O. Box 61, Wiscasset 04578, 207/882-6817, www.lincolncountyhistory .org). From Route 1 in Wiscasset, take Route 27 about nine miles north to the junction with Route 128. Turn left (south) and go 2.5 miles to the courthouse sign. The courthouse is also an easy drive from Bath.

Return to Wiscasset, and follow Route 218 north for about eight miles to Head Tide Village, an eminently picturesque hamlet at the farthest reach of Sheepscot River tides. From the late 18th century to the early 20th, Head Tide (now part of the town of Alna) was a thriving mill town, a source of hydropower for the textile and lumber industries. All that's long gone, but hints of that era come from the handful of well-maintained 18th- and 19th-century homes in the village center.

Up the hill, the stunning 1838 **Head Tide Church,** another fine example of local prosperity, is usually open 2–4 P.M. Saturday in July and August. Volunteer tour guides point out the original pulpit, a trompe l'oeil window, a kerosene chandelier, and walls lined with historic Alna photographs.

Head Tide's most famous citizen was the poet **Edwin Arlington Robinson,** born here in 1869. His family home, at the bend in Route 194 and marked by a plaque, is not open to the public. Perhaps his Maine roots inspired these lines from his poem "New England":

Here where the wind is always north-
    north-east
And children learn to walk on frozen
    toes.

Just upriver from the bend in the road is a favorite swimming hole, a millpond where you can join the locals on a hot summer day. Not much else goes on here, and there are no restaurants or lodgings, so Head Tide can't be termed a destination, but it's a village frozen in time – and an unbeatable opportunity for history buffs and shutterbugs.

Also historic, but a bit more lively and fun for kids is the **Wiscasset, Waterville, and Farmington Railway** (97 Cross Rd., off Rte. 218, Sheepscot, 207/882-4193, www.wwfry .org, 9 A.M.–5 P.M. Sat. year-round and Sun. late May–mid-Oct.), a museum commemorating a two-foot gauge common carrier railroad that operated in the early part of the 20th century, from Wiscasset in the south, to Albion and Winslow in the north. On the grounds are a museum in the old station (free admission) and train rides along the mainline track running north from Cross Road, on the original roadbed ($6 adult, $4 kids 4–12). Trains depart Sheepscot hourly 10 A.M.–4 P.M. on weekends. From Route 1 in Wiscasset, take Route 218 north 4.7 miles to a four-way intersection and go left on the Cross Road to the museum.

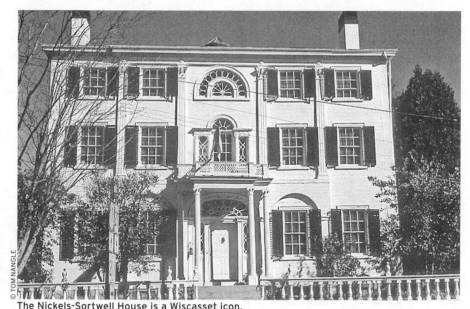

The Nickels-Sortwell House is a Wiscasset icon.

and Frances Sortwell's meticulous Colonial Revival restoration in the early 20th century.

Lincoln County Jail and Museum

Wiscasset's Old Jail, completed in 1811, was the first prison in the District of Maine (then part of Massachusetts). Amazingly, it remained a jail—mostly for short-termers—until 1953. Two years after that, the Lincoln County Historical Association took over, so each summer you can check out the 40-inch-thick granite walls, floors, and ceilings; the 12 tiny cells; and historic graffiti penned by the prisoners. Attached to the prison is the 1837 jailer's house, now the Lincoln County Museum, containing antique tools, the original kitchen, and various temporary exhibits. The complex is open 10 A.M.–4 P.M. Tuesday–Saturday and noon–4 P.M. Sunday in July and August, and weekends only June and September. Admission is $4 adults, $2 ages 7–17. A Victorian gazebo, overlooking the Sheepscot River, is a great spot for a picnic. From Route 1 (Main St.) in downtown Wiscasset, take Federal Street (Rte. 218)

1.2 miles. For more information, contact Lincoln County Historical Association (Federal St., P.O. Box 61, Wiscasset 04578, 207/882-6817, www.lincolncountyhistory.org).

Musical Wonder House

The treasures in the Musical Wonder House (18 High St., P.O. Box 604, Wiscasset 04578, 207/882-7163, www.musicalwonderhouse.com), an 1852 sea captain's mansion, are indeed astonishing, and eccentric Austrian-born museum founder Danilo Konvalinka delights in sharing them—for a price. The best way to appreciate the collection of hundreds of 19th-century European music boxes, player pianos, and musical rarities is to take a guided tour (available 10 A.M.–5 P.M. Mon.–Sat. and noon–5 P.M. Sun. late May–Oct., reduced schedule spring and fall), including two dozen player-piano and music-box demonstrations. A 35-minute tour is $10; 75-minute tour is $20; a three-hour tour, by appointment only, is $40. A web-order sideline, offering music-boxes and music box and player-piano cassettes and CDs, continues year-round.

Fort Edgecomb

Built in 1808 to protect the Sheepscot River port of Wiscasset, the Fort Edgecomb State Historic Site (Eddy Rd., Edgecomb, 207/882-7777, $2 adults, $1 kids 5–11) occupies a splendid, three-acre riverfront spread ideal for picnicking and fishing (no swimming). Many summer weekends, the Revolutionary encampments on the grounds of the octagonal blockhouse make history come alive with reenactments, period dress, craft demonstrations, and garrison drills. The fort officially is open 9 A.M.–5 P.M. daily late May–early September. It's off Route 1; take Eddy Road just north of Wicasset Bridge and go one-half mile to Fort Road.

FESTIVALS AND EVENTS

Wiscasset's daylong **Annual Strawberry Festival and Country Fair** (St. Philip's Episcopal Church, Hodge St., 207/882-7184) celebrates with tons of strawberries, plus crafts and an auction on the last Saturday in June. The church also is the site of **Monday-night fish-chowder suppers,** mid-July–mid-August. Reservations are advised (207/882-7184) for these very popular 5:30 P.M. suppers.

In early July, the daylong **Morris Farm Fair** takes place at the nonprofit community Morris Farm on Route 27, and includes animal exhibits, farm tours, crafts, games, and food.

A summer highlight at Watershed Center for the Ceramic Arts is its annual **Salad Days,** a fund-raising event held on a July Saturday. For a $25 donation, you choose a handmade pottery plate, fill it from a piled-high buffet of fruit and veggie salads, and be part of an old-fashioned picnic social—and you even get to keep the plate! Afterward, there's plenty of time to explore the center's 32 acres. Call ahead to confirm the date (207/882-6075).

SHOPPING
Antiques and Art

It's certainly fitting that a town filled end-to-end with antique homes should have more than two dozen solo and group antiques shops.

Right downtown, **Blythe House Antiques** (161 Main St., Wiscasset, 207/882-1280) has

Antiques and specialty shops line Wiscasset's streets.

© TOM NANGLE

multiple dealers exhibiting in room settings. Fine European antiques directly imported are the specialty at **Daybreak Manor** (106 Rte. 1, Wiscasset, 207/882-9786). Both fine art and antiques are sold at **French and Vandyke** (8 Federal St., Wiscasset, 207/882-8302).

European and American 19th- and 20th-century painters are the broad focus at **Wiscasset Bay Gallery** (67 Main St./Rte. 1, P.O. Box 309, Wiscasset 04578, 207/882-7682 or 888/622-9445) which schedules high-quality rotating shows throughout the season.

In the handsome open spaces of an early-19th-century brick schoolhouse, the **Maine Art Gallery** (Warren St., P.O. Box 315, Wiscasset 04578, 207/882-7511) was founded in 1954 as a nonprofit corporation to showcase contemporary Maine artists.

Two miles south of town is **Avalon Antiques Market** (563 Rte. 1, Wiscasset, 207/882-4239, www.avalonantiques market.com), a huge red barn of a place filled with more than 100 dealers showing on three floors.

Discount Shopping

Carving out a unique niche is **Big Al's Super Values** (Rte. 1, Wiscasset, 207/882-6423), a catchall emporium specializing in odd lots, closeouts, funky souvenirs, and half-priced birthday cards. Bargains galore, plus free coffee, restroom, and a gift shop. Some tourism brochures are also available here. It's three miles south of Wiscasset, across from the Sea Basket Restaurant.

ACCOMMODATIONS
Bed-and-Breakfasts

Wiscasset isn't loaded with B&Bs, but the choices are intriguing. As always, off-season rates are less expensive.

Named after a famous Maine clipper ship, Paul and Melanie Harris's **Snow Squall Inn** (5 Bradford Rd. at Rte. 1, P.O. Box 730, Wiscasset 04578, 207/882-6892 or 800/775-7245, www.snowsquallinn.com, $100–170 d) is a renovated mid-19th-century house with four lovely rooms and three suites, all with phone, air-conditioning, and Wi-Fi, and two with fireplace. Relax in two public rooms, both with TV and fireplace, on the porch or gazebo, and enjoy the landscaped grounds. Ask Melanie, a licensed massage therapist and a vinyasa yoga instructor, about scheduling a massage or taking a class. The suites, in the adjacent carriage house, each sleep four and are ideal for families. It's open all year, but only by reservation November–April.

Then there's a major getaway—**The Squire Tarbox Inn** (1181 Main Rd., Rte. 144, Westport Island, 207/882-7693 or 800/818-0626, www.squiretarboxinn.com, $135–195), an elegantly casual B&B/inn. Accomplished Swiss chef/owner Mario De Pietro and his wife, Roni, have continued the inn's reputation for dining excellence. Eleven lovely rooms, some with fireplaces, are divided between the late-18th-century main house and the early-19th-century carriage house; those in the main house are more formal. Rates include breakfast, and the dining room is open to the public by reservation for dinner (see *Food*). Also on the property are walking paths, a rowboat, mountain bikes,

a working pottery, and a working farm, with organic vegetable gardens, chickens, and goats. Open April–December. From downtown Wiscasset, head southwest four miles on Route 1 to Route 144. Turn left and go about 8.5 scenic miles to the inn.

Motels

Fairly close to Route 1 but buffered a bit by century-old hemlocks, the **Wiscasset Motor Lodge** (Rte. 1, R.R. 3, Box 911, Wiscasset 04578, 207/882-7137 or 800/732-8168, www.wiscassetmotorlodge.com, $62–108) is a comfortable, well-maintained motel. Rooms have phone, TV, and air-conditioning, and a light breakfast is included in summer. Ask for a room in the back building if you're sensitive to noise.

Resort

Stretching along the Sheepscot riverfront on Davis Island, **Sheepscot Harbour Village and Resort** (306 Eddy Rd., Edgecomb, 800/437-5503, www.midcoastresort.com) comprises beautifully renovated shingle-style buildings, including an inn, lodge, and cottages all adjacent to Bintliff's Ocean Grille restaurant. You can walk to Fort Edgecomb, across the bridge into Wiscasset, meander down the back roads to Boothbay Harbor, or simply stay put and enjoy the on-site amenities, including what must be one of the longest docks ever built, bicycles, canoes, kayaks, and planned walking paths, shops, and spa. In July and August, rates range $119–209 d with pets welcome for $15/night. Packages including breakfast and dinner are available. Owner and overall good guy Roger Bintliff is a strong supporter of military families; his Project Operation Recognition provides a free weeklong vacation each week to families of Maine National Guard soldiers.

FOOD

Across Federal Street from the Nickels-Sortwell House in downtown Wiscasset is the lovely **Sunken Garden,** an almost-unnoticed pocket park created around the cellar hole of a long-gone inn. It's a fine place for a picnic.

MID-COAST REGION

© TOM NANGLE

Red's Eats has earned national fame for its lobster rolls.

Local Flavors

Let's start with the obvious, **Red's Eats** (Main and Water Sts., Wiscasset, 207/882-6128, 11 A.M.–11 P.M. Mon.–Sat. and noon–6 P.M. Sun. early May–mid-Oct.). This simple take-out stand has garnered national attention through the decades for its lobster rolls stuffed with the meat from a whole lobster. It's easy to spot because of the line. Expect to wait. And wait. And wait, perhaps for an hour or more. Is it worth it? I don't think so, but others rave about the cold lobster rolls, the fried fish, the hot dogs, and the wraps. If you're planning on one of Red's lobster rolls, ask someone who's just bought one the price before you get in line and make sure you have enough cash (no credit cards). The few tables on the sidewalk and behind the building, overlooking the river, are seldom empty (except in bad weather), but it's only a quick walk across Main to picnic tables (and a public restroom) on the Town Wharf, where **Sprague Lobster** (22 Main St., Wiscasset, 207/882-2306) has set up a competing stand. Many locals prefer Sprague's. Lines are

rare and the lobster rolls also contain the meat from an entire crustacean.

Back up the street, across from the post office, is **Treat's** (80 Main St., Wiscasset, 207/882-6192, www.treatsofmaine.com, 10 A.M.–6 P.M. Mon.–Sat., noon–5 P.M. Sun.), a superb source of gourmet picnic fixings: sandwiches, soups, wine, cheese, condiments, and artisanal breads. You won't leave here empty-handed, even if you aren't hungry.

Family Friendly

Two miles southwest of downtown Wiscasset, **The Sea Basket Restaurant** (Rte. 1, Wiscasset, 207/882-6581, www.seabasket .com, 11 A.M.–8 P.M. Tues.–Sat.) has been serving hearty bowls of lobster stew and good-size baskets of eminently fresh seafood since 1981. There's always a crowd—locals eat here, too—so expect to wait. The fried fish is almost healthful, thanks to convection-style frying using trans fat–free oil. Closed January into February, with reduced hours and days in the off-season.

In a high-visibility location across Route

1 from Red's Eats, **Sarah's Cafe** (Main and Water Sts., Rte. 1, Wiscasset, 207/882-7504, www.sarahscafe.com, 11 A.M.–9 P.M., opens 7:30 A.M. Sat. and Sun.), is the home of huge "whaleboat" and "dory" sandwiches, homemade soups (self-serve), pizza, vegetarian specials, and an ice-cream fountain. Lobster meat shows up in salads, burritos, quesadillas, wraps, croissants, and more. The deck has front-row seats on the Sheepscot River. It has a beer and wine license and air-conditioning. Be forewarned that service sometimes is very sluggish, but crayons keep kids busy. It closes at 8 P.M. off-season.

Housed in a big red barn, about midway between Bath and Wiscasset, **Montsweag Roadhouse** (942 Rte. 1, Woolwich, 207/443-6563, www.montsweagroadhouse.com, 11 A.M.–9 P.M., to 10 P.M. Fri. and Sat.) gets two thumbs up for reasonably priced foods, from burgers and pizzas to steak and fried fish, and friendly service. The upstairs games room—pool and foosball tables and dart boards—keeps kids busy while the grown-ups chat. This is an especially casual place, with a strong local following. The bar remains open to 1 A.M., with live music both upstairs and down on weekends.

Casual Dining

Overlooking the Kennebec, and just two blocks off Route 1, is **Le Garage** (15 Water St., Wiscasset, 207/882-5409, www.legaragerestaurant.com, 11:30 A.M.–2:30 P.M. and 5–8:30 P.M. daily), an enduringly popular spot serving traditional fare with flair. Request a porch/deck table, and dine by candlelight. Lamb is a specialty, as is finnan haddie (entrée range is $10–25); light suppers are thrifty choices. Reservations are wise on weekends. It's closed January, and Mondays off-season.

Across the river, with fine views of Wiscasset, is **Bintliff's Ocean Grill** (318 Eddy Rd., corner of Rte. 1, Edgecomb, 207/882-9401, 8 A.M.–3 P.M. and 5–10 P.M. daily). Owner Roger Bintliff is renowned for his extensive and creative breakfast and brunch menus, with more choices for omelettes and eggs Benedict than you could imagine, never mind pancakes, French toast, and other egg dishes. Add sandwiches, salads, and soups, and a large dinner menu ($16–32), too. No one should complain about not finding something. In summer, there's nightly live music. Bintliff is well respected in the community for supporting local needs. On Thursday nights, he makes a contribution to a local charity for every purchase.

Well off the beaten path, on an island connected to the mainland by bridge, is **The Squire Tarbox Inn** (1181 Main Rd., Rte. 144, Westport Island, 207/882-7693 or 800/818-0626, www.squiretarboxinn.com), where Swiss chef Mario De Pietro serves memorable meals. Entrées, such as rack of lamb, Swiss-style veal, and a fish of the day run $25–29, and are served either on the porch or in an intimate dining room. It serves dinner nightly late May–late October, and Thursday–Saturday in April, May, November, and December, when Thursday nights are Swiss night, with appropriate cuisine served. Ask about cooking classes.

On the edge of town, **Mark Antony Italian Cuisine** (65 Gardiner Rd., Wiscasset, 207/882-9888, www.markantonysitaliancuisine.com, 5–8 P.M. Wed.–Sun., to 9 P.M. Fri. and Sat.) is a cozy spot that delivers more than its humble exterior promises. Chef/co-owner Mark Buscanera draws on his North End Boston roots to prepare classic Italian fare ($10–25), and he might even serenade your table.

INFORMATION AND SERVICES
Information

Since there's no official information center, the best place to find the annual WRBA booklet is the display rack at Big Al's Super Values, three miles southwest of downtown. Once you get into town, stop at Wiscasset Hardware for a free walking map of the downtown area.

Check out Wiscasset Public Library (21 High St., Wiscasset, 207/882-7161, www.wiscasset.lib.me.us).

Public Restrooms

The Town Wharf, Water Street, and the Lincoln County Court House, on Route 1 next to the sharp curve as you come down the hill from the south, have public restrooms.

Boothbay Peninsula

East of Wiscasset, en route to Damariscotta, only a flurry of signs along Route 1 in Edgecomb (pop. around 1,000) hints at what's down the peninsula bisected by Route 27. Drive southward down the Boothbay Peninsula between Memorial Day and Labor Day and you'll find yourself in one of Maine's longest-running summer playgrounds.

The four peninsula towns of Boothbay (pop. 2,675), Boothbay Harbor (pop. 2,165), East Boothbay (pop. 540), and, connected by a bridge, Southport Island (pop. 590) have sightseeing and whale-watching excursions, a first-rate small aquarium, an antique-railway museum, wall-to-wall shops, scads of restaurants and beds, and quiet preserves for escaping the inevitable midsummer crowds.

When Route 27 arrives at the water, having passed through Boothbay Center, you're at the hub, Boothbay Harbor ("the Harbor"), scene of most of the action. The harbor itself is a boat fan's dream, loaded with working craft and pleasure yachts. Ashore, you'll face one-way streets, traffic congestion, and pedestrians everywhere (avoid July and August, if you despise crowds). Parking areas are noted on the Boothbay Harbor Region Chamber of Commerce's walking map; just be prepared to shell out about $3–5 for the day. Better yet, stay in an intown accommodation and walk. Even in peak season, though, there are plentiful places to escape the hoards.

Try to save time for quieter spots: East Boothbay, Ocean Point, Southport Island, the Coastal Botanical Gardens, or even just over the 1,000-foot-long footbridge stretching across one corner of the harbor. Cross the bridge and walk down Atlantic Avenue to the Fishermen's Memorial, a bronze fishing dory commemorating the loss of hardy souls who've earned a rugged living here by their wits and the sea. Across the street is Our Lady Queen of Peace Catholic Church, with shipwright-quality woodwork and its own fishing icon—a lobster trap next to the altar.

In the 1870s, when many scenic coastal areas experienced an influx of steamboat-borne rusticators from the Boston area and beyond, the Boothbay region entered its tourism phase—an era that shows no indication of coming to a close.

SIGHTS
Boothbay Railway Village
Boothbay Railway Village (Rte. 27, Boothbay, 207/633-4727, www.railwayvillage.org, 9:30 A.M.–5 P.M. daily early June–mid-Oct., $8 adults, $4 ages 3–16) feels like a life-size train set. More than two dozen old and new buildings have been assembled here since the museum was founded, in 1964, and a restored narrow-gauge steam train makes a 1.5-mile, 20-minute circuit throughout the day. Among the structures are a toy shop, a one-room schoolhouse, a chapel, a barbershop, a 19th-century town hall, two railroad stations, and a firehouse. You'll also find more than four dozen antique cars and trucks. The gift shop stocks train-oriented items. During the summer, special events include an antique auto meet, Children's Day, and a fall foliage festival. The village is open daily; train rides also operate on Memorial Day weekend, early June weekends, and the last weekend in October (a ghostly Halloween ride). The village is 3.5 miles north of downtown Boothbay Harbor, 7.5 miles south of Route 1.

◖ Burnt Island Tour
Visit with a lighthouse keeper's family, climb the tower into the lantern room, and explore an island during a living- and natural-history program presented by the Maine Department of Marine Resources on Burnt Island (207/633-9580, www.maine.gov/dmr/education.htm, $22 adult, $12 kids under 12). The tour is offered twice daily in July and August. Travel via excursion boat from 21st-century Boothbay Harbor to Burnt Island, circa 1950, where actors portray the family of lighthouse keeper Joseph Muise, who lived here 1936–1951.

During the three-hour program, you'll spend time with the light keeper, his wife, and each of his children learning about their lifestyles and views on island life. Historical documents, photographs, and lenses, from 1821 to the present, are displayed in the 45-foot covered walkway between the house and tower. You may climb the spiral stairway up to the lantern room and see how the lighthouse actually functions. On an easy hike, a naturalist explains the island's flora, fauna, and geology and recounts legends, including one about a sea serpent. During free time, you may hike other trails, listen to a program on present-day lobstering and Maine fisheries, go beach-combing, fish for mackerel off the dock, or just relax and enjoy it all.

Marine Resources Aquarium

A 20-foot touch tank, with slimy but pettable specimens, is a major kid magnet at the Marine Resources Aquarium (McKown Point Rd., West Boothbay Harbor, 207/633-9559, www .maine.gov/dmr/education.htm, 10 A.M.–5 P.M. daily late May– early Sept., 10 A.M.–5 P.M. Wed.–Sun. in Sept., $5 adults, $3 seniors and kids 5–18), operated by the state Department of Marine Resources. Exhibits in the hexagonal aquarium include rare lobsters (oversize, albino, and blue) and other Gulf of Maine creatures, and new residents arrive periodically. Self-guiding leaflets are available. Consider bringing a picnic— it's a great setting. At the height

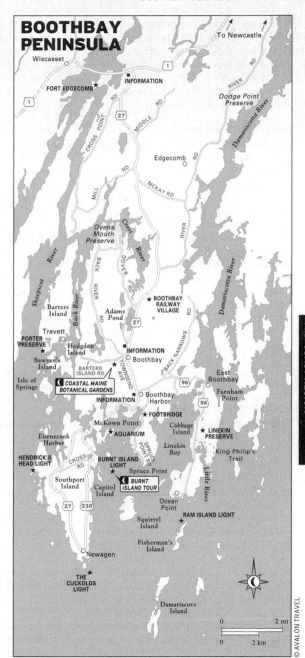

BOOTHBAY PENINSULA

MID-COAST REGION

© AVALON TRAVEL

of summer, parking is limited, and it's a long-ish walk from downtown around the west side of the harbor, so plan to take the free local trolley-bus, departing on the half hour from the Meadow Mall (many locals still call it the Small Mall, its former name) or from one of the downtown trolley-bus stops.

Southport Island

A historic 1810 Cape-style building, care-fully restored, is the 11-room home of the **Hendricks Hill Museum** (Rte, 27, West Southport, 207/633-4831, www.hendrickshill.org, 11 A.M.–3 P.M. Tues., Thurs., and Sat. July and Aug., donation appreciated), a community attic filled with all kinds of workaday tools and utensils and fascinating maritime memorabilia. The museum is about two miles south of the Southport Island bridge, on the right, in the center of West Southport.

Continuing down Route 27 toward Cape Newagen, stop at the **Southport Memorial Library** (207/633-2741). Here's a rare, surprising treat: a huge collection of beautifully mounted butterflies once owned by Dr. and Mrs. Stanley Marr. The library is open all year, 9–4 and 7–9 P.M. Tuesday and Thursday, plus 1–4 P.M. Saturday.

PARKS AND PRESERVES
Boothbay Region Land Trust

Courtesy of the very active Boothbay Region Land Trust (1 Oak St., P.O. Box 183, Boothbay Harbor 04538, 207/633-4818, www.bbrlt .org), an ever-increasing amount of acreage on the peninsula and nearby islands has been preserved for wildlife, residents, and visitors, with about 25 miles of trails available. Individual preserve maps, as well as a general brochure/map with driving directions, are available at the information centers or at the trust office. Kiosks at the trailheads hold preserve maps. There are no trash receptacles, so carry a litterbag and help the BRLT and everyone who follows you. To do even more, make a cash donation to the BRLT (any amount is welcome). The trust also offers a free series of summertime guided walks and paddles in the various preserves as well as talks. Here's just a sampling of the possibilities.

Most popular is the **Porter Preserve,** a 19-acre property bordering the Sheepscot River. Follow the moderately easy 0.86-mile loop trail and be rewarded with spectacular views, especially at sunset. You might even spy some seals lolling in the ledges at low tide. To get there, take Route 27 south to the monument in Boothbay Center. Bear right on Cory Lane and go 0.3 mile, bearing right again on Barters Island Road. Follow it 12.2 miles (perhaps stopping at the Barters Island General Store for lobster rolls or subs to go), and then go left on Kimballtown Road. Go 0.5 mile and turn left at the fork onto Porter Point Road. Park in the small lot just beyond the cemetery.

Also popular is the 146-acre **Ovens Mouth Preserve** with almost five miles of trails on two peninsulas linked by a 93-foot bridge (wear insect repellent). The 1.6-mile trail on the east peninsula is much easier than the 3.7 miles of trails on the west peninsula. To get there, from the monument in Boothbay Center, travel 1.7 miles north and then go left on Adams Pond Road. Bear right at the fork and then continue 2.2 miles. To get to the east peninsula, bear right at the junction onto the Dover Road Extension. Proceed to the end of the tarred road to the parking lot on the left. To get to the west peninsula, bear left at the junction and continue 0.15 miles to the parking area on the right.

In East Boothbay, on the way to Ocean Point, is the 94.6-acre **Linekin Preserve,** stretching from Route 96 to the Damariscotta River. The 2.3-mile, white-blazed River Loop (best done clockwise) takes in an old sawmill site, a beaver dam, and great riverfront views. You'll meet a couple of moderately steep sections on the eastern side, near the river, but otherwise it's relatively easy. To get there, take Route 96 3.8 miles and look for the parking area and trail head on the left.

▮ Coastal Maine Botanical Gardens

Masterful and magical, yet still in their youth,

are these shorefront gardens (Barters Island Rd., Boothbay, office Old Firehouse, Rte. 27, Boothbay, 207/633-4333, www.mainegardens .org, 9 A.M.–5 P.M. daily year-round, to 6 P.M. Sat. and Sun., to 8 P.M. Wed. in July and Aug., $10 adults, $8 ages 65-plus, $5 ages 5–17, $25 family of four). The nonprofit project, designed to preserve more than 125 acres of woodlands with a trail network and landscaped pocket "theme" gardens, has grown to encompass 248 acres, with formal gardens, paths, herb and kitchen gardens, woods walks, a fairy village, and nearly a mile of waterfront. Artwork is placed throughout. Plans include a five-senses and a children's garden. The visitors center has a café (10 A.M.–3 P.M. May 1–Oct. 15), library, and gift shop. Pick up a map and explore on your own, or ask whether a volunteer docent is available to provide a free tour. Allow at least two hours, although you could easily spend a full day here. A full slate of activities is offered, with more planned. Entrance to the preserve is on Barters Island Road, about 1.3 miles west of Boothbay Center.

RECREATION
Bicycling

When you're ready to take your bike on the road, head for one of the chamber of commerce information centers and pick up a copy of the bike route for the 31-mile Barters Island/Southport loop (also a fine driving itinerary). Pack a picnic. Allow a full day to bike it, including stops and detours. The terrain is mostly easy and relatively level, but many stretches are narrow and winding, with poor shoulders, so it's *essential* to follow biking rules and exercise caution.

An alternate loop route, about 15 miles long, follows only the Southport Island section, from downtown Boothbay Harbor. If you're biking with kids, opt for this itinerary—but make sure they know the rules of the road, too. Again, take a picnic, or plan to stop at the Southport General Store (Rte. 27, 207/633-6666), about two miles south of the bridge. Also check out the nearby historic cemetery, the Hendricks Hill Museum, and the Hendricks Head Light

(go west on Beach Road from the general store; the light is privately owned, so don't trespass).

When crossing the swing bridge that spans Townsend Gut, between West Boothbay Harbor and Southport Island, be especially cautious. The surface can be a bear trap for bike tires.

Another good biking (and driving) route begins at the junction of Routes 27 and 96, going through East Boothbay, then on down to Ocean Point, where the Shore Road loop skirts the rocky shoreline. (Ocean Point is about six miles from the Route 27/96 crossroads.) About halfway down Linekin Neck toward Ocean Point, hang a left onto King Philip's Trail, then left onto the loop road, clockwise, through the hamlet of Little River, returning to Route 96. As on the Southport Island route, the roads are narrow and winding along Linekin Neck, and traffic can be heavy at the height of summer. Early morning is a great time to bike here; park your car in the Hannaford supermarket lot, the Meadow Mall, or the YMCA, back on Route 27 at the entrance to Boothbay Harbor.

Excursion Boats

Two major fleet operators provide practically every type of sea adventure imaginable. Boothbay Harbor's veteran excursion fleet is **Cap'n Fish's Cruises** (Pier 1, Wharf St., Boothbay Harbor, 207/633-3244, 207/633-2626, or 800/636-3244, www.capnfishmotel.com/ boattrips.htm). In addition to whale-watching trips (see below), Cap'n Fish's 150-passenger boats do nine varied, mostly two- to three-hour cruises. There is bound to be a length and itinerary (seal-watching, lobster-trap hauling, lighthouses, Damariscove, puffin cruises, and more) that piques your interest. Pick up a schedule at one of the information centers and call for reservations.

The harbor's other big fleet is **Balmy Days Cruises** (Pier 8, Commercial St., Boothbay Harbor, 207/633-2284 or 800/298-2284, www.balmydayscruises.com), operating three vessels on a variety of excursions. The *Novelty* does about seven daily one-hour harbor tours daily late June–Labor Day; cost is $12 adults, $6 under 12. (The boat stops at Squirrel Island for dropoffs and pickups.) Reservations usually are unnecessary. The 31-foot Friendship sloop *Bay Lady* does five 90-minute sailing trips daily in summer. Cost is $20 pp. Reservations are wise for the *Bay Lady* as well as for the fleet's most popular cruise, a daylong trip to Monhegan Island on the *Balmy Days II,* departing at 9:30 A.M. and returning at 4:15 P.M. daily early June–September, plus weekends in late May and early October. The three-hour round-trip allows about 3.5 hours ashore on idyllic Monhegan Island. Cost is $32 adults, $18 ages 3–11. You're headed 12 miles offshore on the Monhegan trip, so be sure to dress warmly, wear sturdy walking/hiking shoes, and take a camera and binoculars.

Sailing

A trip aboard *Schooner Eastwind,* a 65-foot traditional wooden schooner built in 2004, with **Appledore Cruises** (20 Commercial St. Boothbay Harbor, 207/633-6598, www.fishermans wharfinn.com) is more than a day sail, it's an adventure. Herb and Doris Smith not only built this schooner, they've sailed around the world in their previous boats through the years, providing fodder for many tales. They take passengers on 2.5-hour cruises to the outer islands and Seal Rocks, up to four times daily, for $22. The boat departs from Fisherman's Wharf.

Whale- and Puffin-Watching Cruises

Variations in Gulf of Maine whale-migration patterns have added whale-watching to the list of Boothbay Harbor boating options as the massive mammals travel northeastward within reasonable boating distance. **Cap'n Fish's** (Pier 1, Wharf St., Boothbay Harbor, 207/633-3244, 207/633-2626, or 800/636-3244, www.maine whales.com) is the best choice. Three- to four-hour trips depart daily mid-June–mid-October. Cost is $35 adults, $22 kids 6–12, with a rain-check if the whales don't show up. Reservations are advisable, especially early and late in the season and on summer weekends. No matter what the weather on shore, dress warmly and carry more clothing than you think you'll need.

Motion-sensitive children and adults need to plan for appropriate medication.

Cap'n Fish's also runs 2.5-hour puffin-sighting tours to Easter Egg Rock, circling the island once or twice for the best views. Cruises are offered once weekly in June, then three times weekly through late August, for $24 adult, $12 kids.

Sea Kayaking

From Memorial Day weekend through September, **Tidal Transit** (18 Granary Way, Chowder House Building, Boothbay Harbor, 207/633-7140), near the footbridge, will get you afloat with two- to three-hour guided lighthouse, wildlife, or sunset tours for $35–40. No experience is necessary. Reservations are required. For do-it-yourselfers, Tidal Transit rents single kayaks for $15 an hour or $50 a day, tandems for $25 an hour, $75 a day; other time options are available.

On the other side of the harbor, **East Boothbay Kayak Co.** (Ocean Point Marina,

Kayaking is one way to get a closer look at the boats in Boothbay Harbor.

Rte. 96, East Boothbay, 207/633-7411 or 866/633-7411, www.eastboothbaykayaks.com) provides rentals and gives guided tours. Rentals range from $12 single to $20 tandem per hour; $50–75 per day. Delivery is available in the Boothbay region for $20, including pickup. Two- to four-hour guided tours are $40–60. The shop is next to the post office.

ENTERTAINMENT

The renovated 1894 **Opera House** (86 Townsend Ave., Boothbay Harbor, 207/633-6855, www.boothbayoperahouse.org) is now the site of concerts, lectures, dramas, and special events. An upstairs bar, in the former Knights of Pythias Hall, is open to adults before performances and for intermission, and often for special events.

The **Lincoln Arts Festival** (207/633-3913, www.lincolnartsfestival.org) presents half a dozen or more concerts—classical, pops, choral, and jazz—and other arts-related events at various locations on the Boothbay Peninsula late March–early October.

Early July through August is a great time for music in Boothbay Harbor. Free **band concerts** at 8 P.M. Thursdays are performed on the Memorial Library lawn. Bring a blanket or folding chair.

EVENTS

The **Fishermen's Festival** is a locally colorful early-season celebration, held the third weekend of April, beginning with a Friday Miss Shrimp Princess pageant. Saturday brings a lobster-crate race and afternoon contests such as trap hauling, scallop- and clam-shucking, fish-filleting, and net mending (plus a real steal—a lobster-eating contest you can enter for $5). Saturday night, church suppers feature fish and shellfish, and Sunday, a chowder luncheon precedes the blessing of the fleet to ensure a successful summer season.

June is the month for **Windjammer Days,** two days of festivities centering on traditional windjammer schooners. Highlights are the Windjammer Parade, harborfront concerts, plenty of food, and a fireworks extravaganza.

Huge sailboats arrive in the harbor in early September for the **Shipyard Cup** (www.shipyardcup.com), with racing on two days. Hop aboard an excursion boat for a close-up view or drive out to Ocean Point.

Columbus Day weekend marks the **Fall Foliage Festival,** featuring craft and food booths, a petting zoo, live entertainment, train rides, and more at Boothbay Railway Village.

SHOPPING

Artisans' galleries pepper the peninsula. Galleries, boutiques, T-shirt, and novelty shops crowd Boothbay Harbor, providing plenty of browsing for all budgets and tastes. Here's just a sampling.

Art and Craft Galleries

Gleason Fine Art (31 Townsend Ave., Boothbay Harbor, 207/633-6849) is one of Maine's top retail venues for 19th- through 21st-century painting and sculpture. Also downtown is the **Gold/Smith Gallery** (41 Commercial St., Boothbay Harbor, 207/633-6252), featuring intriguing gold jewelry and contemporary paintings.

The area's veteran craft shop is **Abacus** (12 McKown St., Boothbay Harbor, 207/633-2166 or 800/206-2166 outside Maine). It's great stuff—functional items, wearable art, and charming doodads—high-end American crafts from several hundred artisans.

It's hard not to stop at the wonderful **Edgecomb Potters Galllery** (Rte. 27, Edgecomb, 207/882-9493), filled with amazingly beautiful pottery as well as high-end crafts.

Juried works from 25 Maine artists are shown in **Boothbay Harbor Artisans** (11 Granary Way, Boothbay Harbor, 207/633-1152).

The working metalsmiths at **A Silver Lining** (17 Townsend Ave., Boothbay Harbor, 207/633-4103) create beautiful original jewelry in gold, sterling, brass, copper, and titanium.

A visit to the **Villiard Gallery** (57 Campbell St., Boothbay Harbor, 207/633-3507, www.villardstudios.com) is a must for fans of fine art crafts. Kim and Philippe Villiard split their lives between Boothbay Harbor and Southern

France, where they live in an abandoned village in the midst of a national park. Philippe is talented sculptor; Kim an equally talented painter. They collaborate on woodcuts and handmade books, and the results are in collections and museums. Call in advance if you want a demonstration of the process. They have works in all price ranges, from poster prints to the actual woodblocks themselves.

Take home a stoneware puffin, sandpiper, or seal from the **Anderson Studio** (Anderson Rd., East Boothbay, 207/633-4397 or 800/640-4397, www.andersonstudio.com).

Three miles south of Route 1 is the **Iron and Silk Forge and Gallery** (Rte. 27, Edgecomb, 207/882-4055), the 400-square-foot retail shop for Elizabeth Derecktor's hand-painted silk scarves and clothing and Peter Brown's high-end handwrought weathervanes, chandeliers, and fireplace tools.

Books, Music, and Gifts

You're bound to find something at the two-story **Sherman's Book and Stationery (and Music) Store** (5 Commercial St., Boothbay Harbor, 207/633-7262 or 800/371-8128). It offers cards and cassettes, games and gifts, books and more books, kitchenware and kitsch.

Antiques

Antique store or museum, you decide. The **Palabra Shop** (53 Commercial St., Boothbay Harbor, 207/633-4225) has 10 chock-full rooms of antiques and collectibles. It's also home to the world's largest collection of Moses bottles.

ACCOMMODATIONS

Boothbay Harbor's longevity as a holiday destination means beds galore—more than anyone cares to count. Even so, late June–mid-August, you'll meet a blur of No Vacancy signs. If that's when you decide to show up here, make reservations. Here's a hint: If you want to concentrate your time in downtown Boothbay Harbor, shopping or taking boating excursions, stay in town and avoid the parking hassles.

Although the town practically rolls up its sidewalks in the winter, a few businesses do stay open year-round. Lodgings that usually do so are noted; others are seasonal (usually mid-May–mid-October). You'll often find great rates before July and after August.

Classic Inns

To get away from it all, book in at the **Newagen Seaside Inn** (Rte. 27, Southport, 207/633-5242 or 800/654-5242 outside Maine, www.newagenseasideinn.com, $165–285), a full-service, unstuffy inn with casual fine dining and views that go on forever. Recently renovated rooms are split between the Main Inn, the Little Inn, where rooms have private decks, TV, and kitchenettes, and three cottages ($1,670 per week, with breakfast). Plus there are a long rocky shore, a nature trail, spa, tennis courts, heated oceanfront saltwater pool and hot tub, guest rowboats, game room, candlepin bowling, and porches just for relaxing. Rates include a generous buffet breakfast. The dining room is open to the public by reservation for dinner 5:30–9 P.M. daily; entrées run $18–28. There's also a pub serving lighter fare beginning at 4:30 P.M. It's open mid-May–September. The inn is six miles south of downtown Boothbay Harbor.

Families like the easygoing style of the **Lawnmere Inn** (Rte. 27, Southport Island, P.O. Box 505, West Boothbay Harbor 04575, 207/633-2544 or 800/633-7645, www.lawnmereinn.com, $115–189), only two miles from downtown Boothbay Harbor. Built in 1898 on Southport Island, overlooking Townsend Gut, the somewhat dated rooms are split between a traditional inn and two adjacent, motel-style wings. The grounds are lovely, but road noise can be a problem in some rooms. Guests have use of bicycles and kayaks. Rates include a full breakfast buffet. Pets are allowed in some rooms for $20 per night.

Over in East Boothbay, the oceanfront **Ocean Point Inn** (Shore Rd., P.O. Box 409, East Boothbay 04544, 207/633-4200 or 800/552-5554, www.oceanpointinn.com, $129–219) wows guests with spectacular sunset views and an easygoing ambience that keeps guests returning generation after generation. The sprawling complex includes numerous lodging buildings: an inn, lodge, motel, apartments, cottages, and others. All rooms have minifridge, phone, cable TV, and air-conditioning, and some have kitchenettes. Also on the premises are a well-respected dining room, a pier, an outdoor heated pool, and Adirondack-style chairs set just-so on the water's edge. The best deals are the packages.

For those who require luxury touches, the **Spruce Point Inn and Spa** (Atlantic Ave., P.O. Box 237, Boothbay Harbor 04538, 207/633-4152 or 800/553-0289, www.sprucepointinn .com) is the answer. Accommodations are traditional inn rooms and cottages and condos, all with private decks, minifridges, and TV; some have fireplaces, kitchenettes, and whirlpool tubs. Decor and prices vary widely. The inn holds big weddings on many weekends, so try for midweek. Rates begin around $315 d. Amenities at the 15-acre resort include a full-service spa and fitness center, freshwater and saltwater pools, tennis courts, rocky shorefront, and a shuttle bus to downtown (about 1.5 miles, although it seems farther). A children's program is available 9:30 A.M.–2:30 P.M. for $35 per day, including lunch and snack. Also available is an evening program for ages 4–12 6–9 P.M. Thursday–Sunday for $25. Dining choices range from poolside to pub-style to fine dining, with prices to match each setting. The inn is open late May–mid-October.

Bed-and-Breakfasts

Topping an intown hill with sigh-producing views over the inner and outer harbors and yet just a two-minute walk to shops and restaurants is ◖ **Topside Inn** (60 McKown St., Boothbay Harbor, 207/633-5404 or 877/486-7466, www .topsideinn.com, $120–185 d), a solid, 19th-century sea captain's home with two motel-style annexes. Innkeepers Brian Lamb and Ed McDermott have completely renovated the three-building complex with an emphasis on comfort. Rooms in the three-story main inn are mostly spacious (a small one under the eves is tight but inviting); most have nice views; some

have humongous bathrooms. Good books are everywhere, and the rockers on the wraparound porch and Adirondack chairs on the lawn are perfect places to read or relax. The annexes have motelish-type rooms done in B&B style; all have decks and most have at least glimpses of the ocean. All rooms have phone and TV, and there's Wi-Fi access in the main inn. Rates in all buildings include breakfast: a self-serve cold buffet with a hot entrée that's served to the table. Hot beverages are available all day; and some afternoons, home-baked cookies appear magically in the living room.

Next door is **The Welch House** (56 McKown St., Boothbay Harbor, 207/633-3431 or 800/279-7313, www.welchhouseinn.com, $135–205), with stunning 180-degree views from the third-floor deck (and not-shabby ones from the lower deck). This 14-room B&B (all private baths, but some are down the hall) is an elegant getaway in a 19th-century shipbuilder's home. All of the rooms have air-conditioning, cable TV/VCR, Wi-Fi, and phone; many have water views; some have fireplaces or whirlpool tubs. Breakfast in the solarium is a treat. It's open year-round with lower rates off-season.

In town and on the water, the **Blue Heron Inn** (65 Townsend Ave., Boothbay Harbor, 207/633-7020 or 866/216-2300, www.blue heronseasideinn.com, $185–240 peak) opened in 2003 and quickly made a name for itself. The Victorian vintage belies the clean, bright interior. Large rooms are accented with antiques and collectibles from Phil and Laura Chapman's years overseas. Each room has a waterfront deck, air-conditioning, fridge, microwave, TV, LCD-HDTV, microwave, Wi-Fi, and phone; some also have a fireplace and whirlpool tub. A dock with kayaks and a paddleboat is available. A full breakfast is elegantly served on Wedgwood china. It's open year-round.

On the east side of the harbor, up a side street but within walking distance of in-town shops and restaurants, is Mary Huntington's **Pond House** (7 Bay St., Boothbay Harbor, 207/633-5842, www.pondhousemaine.com, $80–1155). The 1920s barn-red home is just one block off the harbor, surrounded by beautiful gardens

MID-COAST REGION

and edging a pond. The five rooms, some with shared or detached baths, have beautiful oak woodwork and are decorated with a mix of antiques and country pieces, including quilts topping most beds. Rotating artwork covers the walls, and studio space is available to visiting artists. Wi-Fi is available throughout the inn. Mary's breakfasts are legendary.

Escape the hustle and bustle of Boothbay Harbor at the ◖ **Five Gables Inn B&B** (107 Murray Hill Rd., P.O. Box 335, East Boothbay 04544, 207/633-4551 or 800/451-5048, www.fivegablesinn.com, $150–225), which began life as a no-frills summer hotel in the late 19th century. It's gone steadily upmarket since then, and well-traveled innkeepers De and Mike Kennedy, owners since 1995, have added their unique touches, including wonderful murals throughout and window seats in the gable rooms. Fifteen of the light and airy 16 rooms have Linekin Bay views and some have fireplaces. The living room is congenial, the gardens are gorgeous, and the porch goes on forever. Rates include Mike's gourmet buffet breakfast. Book well ahead at this popular spot. The inn, on a side road off Route 96 in the traditional boatbuilding hamlet of East Boothbay, is 3.5 miles from downtown Boothbay Harbor. Arriving by boat? One mooring is available for guests.

Marti Booth and Larry Brown give guests a warm welcome to their **Linekin Bay Bed and Breakfast** (531 Ocean Point Rd., 207/633-9900 or 800/596-7420, www.linekinbaybb.com, $135–185 peak). No wonder, considering all the work they did to transform the 1878 home overlooking the bay into an inn. Begin the day with full breakfast on the deck, perhaps watching lobstermen pull their traps. Afternoon refreshments also are served. Guest rooms are spacious and beautifully decorated; all have fireplaces, air-conditioning, phone, TV/VCR, Wi-Fi, and bay views. It's open year-round.

Motels

A great location just 100 feet from the footbridge, a good dining room, a fun lounge, an indoor pool, and harbor views combine to make the **Rocktide Inn** (35 Atlantic Ave.,

Boothbay Harbor, 207/633-4455 or 800/762-8433, www.rocktideinn.com, $105–195) a popular spot. Rooms are spread out among four buildings, with rates varying according to the view. All have air-conditioning, cable TV, Wi-Fi, and phone, and a full buffet breakfast is included. Even if you don't stay here, pop over for a drink in the tastefully decorated tiki bar–style lounge (open 4–11 P.M. daily) or on the expansive decks overhanging the harbor. The dining room, open to the public for dinner (5:30–9 P.M. daily) has both casual and formal areas; men must wear jackets in the latter.

Since 1955, the Lewis family has owned and operated the **Mid-Town Motel** (96 McKown St., Boothbay Harbor, 207/633-2751, www.midtownmaine.com, $55–85), a spotless, no-frills, vintage motel that's within steps of everything. It's a classic: clean, convenient, and cheap, and the owners couldn't be nicer folks.

Here's another find for the budget bound. Spread out along 0.75-mile of 30 oceanfront acres, the **Ship Ahoy Motel** (Rte. 238, Southport, Box 235, Boothbay Harbor 04538, 207/633-5222, www.shipahoymotel.com, $49–79 d) has simple motel-style rooms, done in vintage 1960s decor, spread out in four buildings. All have TV and air-conditioning and most have private decks and spectacular views. Take a dip in the swimming pool, tie your small boat to the dock or fish from it, and munch on so-so breakfast pastries in the coffee shop. Do note: Walls are thin, so noise can be an issue.

Campgrounds

With 150 well-maintained wooded and open sites on 45 acres, **Shore Hills Campground** (Rte. 27, P.O. Box 448, Boothbay 04537, 207/633-4782, www.shorehills.com, $27–40) is a popular destination where reservations are essential in midsummer. Be sure to request a wooded site away from the biggest RVs. Leashed pets are allowed. Facilities include a laundry and free use of canoes. On the tidal Cross River, 7.5 miles south of Route 1 and close to the Boothbay Railway Village, Shore Hills is open mid-April–mid-October.

Much smaller and right on the ocean is the **Gray Homestead Oceanfront Camping** (21 Homestead Rd., Southport, 207/633-4612, www.graysoceancamping.com, $32–34), a family-run campground with 40 RV and tenting sites, as well as cottages and apartments. A stone beach, pier, laundry facilities, kayak rentals, and lobsters, live or cooked, are available. There's even a small sand beach. Rates cover two adults and two kids.

Seasonal Rentals

For a long-term rental, start with the **Cottage Connection of Maine** (P.O. Box 662, Boothbay Harbor 04538, 207/633-6545 or 800/823-9501, www.cottageconnection.com). The annual tourism booklet published by the Boothbay Harbor Region Chamber of Commerce includes cottage-rental listings.

FOOD
Local Flavors

Right in the center of all the action, **Village Market** (24 Commercial St., Boothbay Harbor, 207/633-0944) makes sandwiches and pizzas to order. Absolutely no atmosphere, but it's cheap and convenient.

It's worth the drive over to Trevett to indulge in a lobster roll from the **Barters Island General Store** (207/633-1140), just before the bridge connecting Hodgdon and Barters Islands.

"Free beer tomorrow" proclaims the sign in front of **Bets Famous Fish Fry** (Village Common, Rte. 27, Boothbay), a take-out trailer that's renowned for its ultrafresh haddock fish-and-chips. Picnic tables are available.

Far more upscale in offerings is the seasonal **Oak Street Provisions** (43 Oak St., Boothbay Harbor, 207/633-3622, 8 A.M.–7 P.M. daily), with a wide array of prepared foods as well as picnic fixings, sandwiches, and breakfast goodies.

On the east side, the **East Boothbay General Store** (255 Ocean Point Rd., Rte. 96, East Boothbay, 207/633-4503) has been serving locals since 1893. These days, it sells wine and specialty foods in addition to pizzas, sandwiches, and baked goods.

Lots of variety is the key at the seasonal **Boothbay Area Farmers Market** (Town Commons, Boothbay, 9 A.M.–noon Thurs.), with goat cheese, chicken, meats, preserves, breads, and of course fresh produce.

Here's a sleeper: **Bakers Way** (90 Townsend Ave., Boothbay Harbor, 207/633-1119), known locally as The Doughnut Shop. This hole-in-the-wall restaurant turns out the unusual combo of excellent baked goods and Vietnamese food. Go for breakfast: The breakfast sandwiches are good and the sticky buns are renowned, not only for size but taste. Then return for lunch or dinner, when a good variety of Vietnamese dishes are available, most for less than $10. While the inside dining area is purely functional, there's also seating in a pleasant garden in the backyard. Everything is also available to go.

Ask any local where to go for a reliably good and reasonably priced breakfast or lunch, and you'll be directed to the **Blue Moon Café** (54 Commercial St., Boothbay Harbor, 207/633-2349, www.bluemoonboothbayharbor.com, 7:30 A.M.–2 P.M. daily). Order at the counter and then grab one of the handful of tables inside or on the harbor-view deck or in the overflow garden seating behind the restaurant. Homemade soups and salads, great sandwiches, and sinful pastries ($4–10). If you're headed out for a picnic, the café will fix you up with a box lunch.

Another locals' favorite serving breakfast, lunch, and dinner is the unassuming **Ebb Tide Restaurant** (43 Commercial St., Boothbay Harbor, 207/633-5692, 6:30 A.M.–9 P.M. daily). Booths line the tiny pine-paneled dining area, where some mighty good homestyle cooking is served. The chowders are renowned, and breakfast is served all day. Friday night is the haddock fry and Monday night is the scallop fry, both about $12 with free seconds. Look for the red-and-white awning.

Casual Dining

Fresh fish expertly prepared has earned **93 Townsend** (93 Townsend Ave., Boothbay Harbor, 207/633-0777, www.93townsend.com,

11:30 A.M.–9:30 P.M. Mon.–Thurs., to 10:30 P.M. Fri. and Sat.) a strong local following. The menu also has steak, pasta, and kids' choices, but stick to fish and creative seafood renditions, including an award-winning lobster risotto and a decadent truffled mac and cheese; most choices are $15–25. No view, but the dining room is pleasant, and the martini options cover two pages.

Real Italian fare prepared by a real Italian chef is on the menu at **Ports of Italy** (47 Commercial St., Boothbay Harbor, 207/633-1011, 5–9:30 P.M. Mon–Thurs., to 10 P.M. Fri. and Sat., to 9 P.M. Sun.), an upper level restaurant with deck seating. This isn't a red-sauce place; expect well-prepared and innovative fare, with especially good seafood. Most choices are in the $20 range.

For spectacular sunset views and reliably good food, take a spin out to the **Ocean Point Inn** (Shore Rd., East Boothbay, 207/633-4200 or 800/552-5554, www.oceanpointinn.com, 6–8:30 P.M. daily). Every table in the two-tiered, pine-paneled dining room has a view. Most entrées are in the $20–28 range; a children's menu is available.

One of the most reliable dining experiences in town is at **The Thistle Inn** (55 Oak St., Boothbay Harbor, 207/633-3541, 5–9 P.M., to 10 P.M. Fri. and Sat.). Everything, from the salad dressings to the desserts, is prepared on-site. It would be easy to make a meal from the appetizers alone—crab cakes, brandied lobster, tempura banana salad, but then you wouldn't have room for the main event, perhaps lobster paella or port tenderloin ($18–30). On a cold night, ask for a table by one of the fireplaces; on a warm night, ask for one on the porch.

Lobster in the Rough

Boothbay Harbor and East Boothbay seem to have more eat-on-the-dock lobster shacks per square inch than almost anywhere else on the coast. If you're a lobster fanatic, you've reached nirvana, heaven, ground zero, whatever. On the Southport Island side of the harbor, overlooking Townsend Gut next to the swing bridge, **Robinson's Wharf** (Rte. 27, Southport Island,

207/633-3830, www.robinsonswharf.net, opens at 11:30 A.M. daily) is a sprawling place with tons of indoor and outdoor seating. Lobster dinners, lobster stew, fried seafood, steamed clams, mussels—it's all here. Plus burgers, dogs, fries, pasta salad, even BLTs and grilled cheese sandwiches. Save room for homemade pie.

Around the other side of the harbor, facing the Damariscotta River in East Boothbay, is the **Lobsterman's Wharf** (Rte. 96, East Boothbay, 207/633-3443, opens at 11:30 A.M. daily). Everything from ties to T-shirts adorns the clientele, usually a mix of locals and flatlanders. The lobsters are great; so are the baby-back ribs and the crab melt. It has nearly 200 seats inside and out. From the junction of Routes 27 and 96 in Boothbay Harbor, take Route 96 three miles to the wharf, on the left.

And then there's **The Lobster Dock** (49 Atlantic Ave., Boothbay Harbor, 207/635-7120, www.thelobsterdock.com, 11:30 A.M.–8:30 P.M.), where lobsters are delivered twice daily; now that's fresh. While there are a few choices for landlubbers—even PBJ for kids, lobster and fish are the prime attraction. It's right on the harbor, so the views are superb.

Cabbage Island Clambakes (Pier 6, Fisherman's Wharf, Boothbay Harbor, 207/633-7200, www.cabbageislandclambakes.com) deserves a category all its own. Touristy, sure, but it's a delicious adventure. You board the 126-passenger excursion boat *Argo* at Pier 6 in Boothbay Harbor; cruise for about an hour past islands, boats, and lighthouses; and disembark at 5.5-acre Cabbage Island. Watch the clambake in progress, if you like, explore the island, or play volleyball. When the feast is ready, pick up your platter, find a picnic table, and dig in. A cash bar is available in the lodge, as are restrooms. When the weather's iffy, the lodge and covered patio have seats for 100. For $50, you'll get two lobsters (or half a chicken), chowder, clams, corn, potatoes, dessert, beverage, and the boat ride. No credit cards. Clambake season is late June–early September. The 3.5-hour trips depart at 12:30 P.M. Monday–Friday, at 12:30 and 5 P.M. Saturday, 11:30 A.M. and 1:30 P.M. Sunday.

INFORMATION AND SERVICES

Information

The Boothbay Harbor Region Chamber of Commerce maintains one seasonal and one year-round information center. The seasonal center (May–mid-Oct.) is on Route 1, at the Route 27 junction. Down Route 27, 10.8 miles from Route 1, is the chamber's main office, next to Hannaford. It's open 8 A.M.–5 P.M. Monday–Friday all year. There's an information kiosk outside if the office is closed.

About eight miles south of Route 1, between the two centers above, is the Boothbay Chamber of Commerce Information Center (Rte. 27, Boothbay Center, 207/633-4743, daily mid-June–early Oct., weekends only the rest of the year).

All three centers stock brochures for the entire peninsula; wherever you stop, be sure to request the handy annual Boothbay Harbor walking map, the Boothbay Region Land Trust hiking brochure, and the tourism booklet covering the whole peninsula.

Check out Boothbay Harbor Memorial Library (4 Oak St., Boothbay Harbor, 207/633-3112, www.bmpl.lib.me.us). Thursday evenings in July and August, there are band concerts on the lawn.

Public Restrooms

At the municipal parking lot on Commercial Street (next to Pier 1), and at the municipal lot at the end of Granary Way, are public restrooms. Saint Andrews Hospital, the town offices, the library, and the Marine Resources Aquarium also have restrooms.

GETTING AROUND

The Rocktide Inn operates free trolley-buses on continuous scheduled routes during the summer.

Pemaquid Region

At the head of the Pemaquid Peninsula, the two riverfront towns of Damariscotta and her Siamese twin, Newcastle, anchor the western end of the Pemaquid Peninsula; Waldoboro anchors the eastern end. Along the peninsula are New Harbor (probably Maine's most photographed fishing village), Pemaquid Point (site of one of Maine's most photographed lighthouses), and historic ports reputedly used by Captain John Smith, Captain Kidd, and assorted less-notorious types. Here, too, are a restored fortress, Native American historic sites, antiques and craft shops galore, boat excursions to offshore Monhegan, and one of the best pocket-size sand beaches in Mid-Coast Maine.

On Christmas Day 1614, famed explorer Captain John Smith anchored on Rutherford Island, at the tip of the peninsula, and promptly named the spot Christmas Cove. And thus it remains today. Christmas Cove is one of three villages belonging to the town of South Bristol, the southwestern finger of the Pemaquid Peninsula. South Bristol and Bristol (covering eight villages on the bottom half of the peninsula) were named after the British city.

As early as 1625, settler John Brown received title to some of this territory from the Wabanaki sachem (chief) Samoset, an agreeable fellow who learned snippets of English from British codfishermen. Damariscotta (dam-uh-riss-COT-ta), in fact, is Wabanaki for "plenty of alewives [herring]." The settlement here was named Walpole but was incorporated, in 1847, under its current name.

Newcastle, incorporated in 1763, earned fame and fortune from shipbuilding and brickmaking—which explains the extraordinary number of brick homes and office buildings throughout the town. In the 19th century, Newcastle's shipyards sent clippers, Downeasters, and full-rigged ships down the ways and around the world.

On the other, northeastern end of the peninsula is Waldoboro. Route 1 cuts a commercial swath through Waldoboro without revealing the attractive downtown—or the lovely Friendship Peninsula, south of the highway. Duck into Waldoboro and then follow Route 220 south 10 miles to Friendship for an off-the-beaten-track drive.

Waldoboro's heritage is something of an anomaly in Maine. It's predominantly German, thanks to 18th-century Teutons who swallowed the blandishments of General Samuel Waldo, holder of a million-acre "patent" stretching as far as the Penobscot River. In the cemetery at the Old German Church, on Route 32, is a 19th-century marker whose inscription sums up the town's early history:

This town was settled in 1748, by Germans who emigrated to this place with the promise and expectation of finding a populous city, instead of which they found nothing but a wilderness; for the first few years they suffered to a great extent by Indian wars and starvation. By perseverance and self-denial, they succeeded in clearing lands and erecting mills. At this time [1855] a large proportion of the inhabitants are descendants of the first settlers.

(Sure makes you wonder why Waldo's name stuck to the town.)

After the mill era, the settlers went into shipbuilding in a big way, establishing six shipyards and producing more than 300 wooden vessels, including the first five-masted schooner, the 265-foot *Governor Ames,* launched in 1888. Although the *Ames*'s ill-supported masts collapsed on her maiden voyage, repairs allowed her to serve as a coal hauler for more than 20

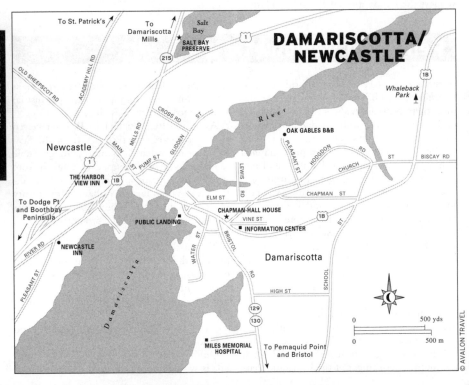

MID-COAST REGION

© AVALON TRAVEL

years, and many more five-masters followed in her wake. It's hard to believe today, but Waldoboro once was America's sixth-busiest port. At the Town Landing, alongside the Medomak River, a marker describes the town's shipyards and shipbuilding heritage.

SIGHTS

Pick up *A Walking Tour of the Early Dwellings of Damariscotta, Maine* at the chamber of commerce office. The book by the Damariscotta Historical Society (207/563-8441) covers sites in the Main Street Historic District and details their histories. Most are privately owned and not open for tours.

Chapman-Hall House

Damariscotta's oldest surviving building is the Cape-style Chapman-Hall House (270 Main St., 1–5 P.M. Tues.–Sun. July and Aug., $2), built in 1754 by Nathaniel Chapman, whose family tree includes the legendary John Chapman, a.k.a. Johnny Appleseed. Highlights are a 1754 kitchen and displays of local shipbuilding memorabilia. The National Historic Register house was meticulously restored by the Chapman-Hall House Preservation Society in the styles of three different eras. Don't miss the antique roses in the back garden.

☾ Pemaquid Point Lighthouse

One of the icons of the Maine Coast, Pemaquid Point's lighthouse has been captured for posterity by many photographers and even is depicted on the Maine state quarter. The lighthouse, adjacent keeper's house, and picnic grounds are a town park. Also on the premises is an art gallery. Admission to the grounds, payable at the gatehouse, is $2 for age 12 and older. The lighthouse grounds are accessible all year, even after the museum closes for the season, when admission is free. The point is 15 miles south of Route 1, via winding, two-lane Route 130.

Lighthouses are irresistible, and the setting here makes it even more so. Commissioned in 1827, Pemaquid Point Light (www.lighthouse foundation.org) stands sentinel over some of Maine's nastiest shoreline—rocks and surf

RETURN OF THE ALEWIVES

If you're in the Damariscotta area in May and early June, don't miss a chance to go to Damariscotta Mills to see the annual Alewife Run. More than 250,000 alewives *(Alosa pseudoharengus,* a kind of herring) make their way during this time from Great Salt Bay to their spawning grounds in freshwater Damariscotta Lake, 42 feet higher. Waiting eagerly at the top are ospreys, gulls, cormorants, and sometimes eagles, ready to feast on the weary fish. Connecting the bay and the lake is a man-made stone-and-masonry "fish ladder," a zigzagging channel where you can watch the foot-long fish wriggle their way onward and upward. The ladder was built in 1807 and restored in the early 1990s. A walkway runs alongside the route, and informative display panels explain the event. It's a fascinating historical ecology lesson. To reach the fishway, take Route 215 for 1.5 miles west of Route 1. When you reach a small bridge, cross it and take a sharp left down a slight incline to a small parking area. Walk behind the barn to follow the path to the fish ladder. Try to go on a sunny day – the fish are more active and their silvery sides glisten as they go.

that can reduce any wooden boat to kindling. Now automated, the light tower is licensed to the American Lighthouse Foundation and is managed by the Friends of Pemaquid Point Lighthouse. Volunteers *aim* to open the tower 9 A.M.–5 P.M. daily mid-May–mid-October, weather permitting. There is no charge for the tower, but donations are appreciated. Still can't get enough? Newcastle Square Vacation Rentals (207/563-6500, www.mainecoastcottages .com) manages a one-bedroom apartment available for weekly rental ($950) in the Keeper's House. Proceeds benefit preservation.

The adjacent **Fisherman's Museum** (207/677-2494), in the former light keeper's house, points up the pleasures and perils of the lobstering industry and also has some lighthouse memorabilia. The museum is open 9 A.M.–5 P.M. daily mid-May–mid-October. Museum admission is free (donations appreciated).

While here, you should also visit the **Pemaquid Art Gallery** (207/677-2752, 9 A.M.–5 P.M. Mon.–Sat., opens 1 P.M. Sun., mid-May–mid-Oct.). It's operated by the Pemaquid Group of Artists, which has displayed its juried members' works since 1928.

Bring a picnic and lounge on the rocks below the light tower, but don't plan to snooze. You'll be busy protecting your food from the dive-bombing gulls and your kids from the treacherous surf.

🄲 Colonial Pemaquid/ Fort William Henry

At the Colonial Pemaquid State Historic Site (end of Huddle Rd., 207/677-2423, www .friendsofcolonialpemaquid.org, 10 A.M.–7 P.M. daily late May–early Sept., $2 ages 12–65), visitors can gain a basic understanding of what life

was like in an English frontier settlement. The 19-acre complex, listed on the National Historic Register, comprises a museum/visitors center, Fort William Henry, the Fort House, the remnants of a village, an 18th-century cemetery, picnic area, a pier and boat ramp, and restrooms, all spread out on a grassy point sloping to John's Bay and bordered by McCaffrey's Brook, the Pemaquid River, and Pemaquid Harbor. Bring a picnic, bring a kite, bring a kayak, let the kids run, but do take time to visit the historic sites (a kids' activity book is available for $1). Demonstrations, tours, lectures, and reenactments are part of the site's summer schedule. Sadly, a monstrous McMansion, perhaps appropriate in another setting but built with no respect for the locale, now dominates the view across the river, lessening the historic feel of the experience.

Three national flags fly over the ramparts of Fort William Henry, a reconstruction of a fort dating from 1692, the second of three that stood here between 1677 and the late 18th century. The forts were built to defend the English

The Fort House at Colonial Pemaquid dates back to the late 1700s.

© TOM NANGLE

settlement of Pemaquid, settled between 1625 and 1628, from the French. From the rebuilt western tower, you'll have fantastic views of John's Bay and John's Island, named for none other than Captain John Smith; inside are artifacts retrieved from archaeological excavations of the 17th-century trading outpost.

The square, white Fort House, which dates to the late 1700s, houses a research library and archaeology lab as well as a gift shop.

Exhibits at the museum/visitors center focus on regional history, from early Native American life through the Colonial period. Selections from the more than 100,000 artifacts uncovered during archeological digs here are displayed along with a diorama of Pemaquid Village.

Take time to wander the village, 14 cellar holes of 17th- and 18th-century dwellings, a forge, trading post, jail, and other early buildings, all marked with interpretive signs. Also visit the burying ground. Note that no rubbings are permitted as they could damage the fragile old stones.

Historic Houses of Worship

One of the oldest houses of worship in Maine that still holds services, **The Old Walpole Meeting House** (Rte. 129, Bristol Rd., Walpole, 207/563-5554), built in 1772, remains remarkably unchanged, with original hand-shaved shingles and handmade nails and hinges. The balcony—where black servants once were relegated—is paneled with boards more than two feet wide. A nondenominational service is held 3 P.M. each Sunday in August, but better still is the annual candlelight concert, a dramatic occasion in this building with no electricity and splendid acoustics. It's at 7 P.M. on a Sunday in September (usually the second Sunday, but call ahead to confirm the date). It's always a sellout, but the acoustics are so good that attendees outside can hear every note. The meetinghouse is 3.5 miles south of Damariscotta and a quarter mile south of where Routes 129 and 130 fork.

The **Harrington Meeting House** (Old Harrington Rd., off Rte. 130, 2–4:30 P.M. Mon., Wed., and Fri. July and Aug., donations

© TOM NANGLE

Waldoboro's Old German Church was moved across the Medomak River in 1794.

© TOM NANGLE

Ice cutting is an annual event at the Thompson Ice House in South Bristol.

welcomed), begun in 1772 and completed in 1775, now serves as Bristol's local-history museum—town-owned and run by the Pemaquid Historical Association. Behind it is an old cemetery that's fascinating to explore—if you're a fan of that sort of thing.

A remnant of Waldoboro's German connection is the **Old German Church** (Rte. 32, Waldoboro, 207/832-5369 or 207/832-7742, 1–3 P.M. July and Aug.) and its cemetery. The Lutheran church, built in 1772 on the opposite side of the Medomak River, was moved across the ice in the winter of 1794. Inside are box pews and a huge hanging pulpit. One of the three oldest churches in Maine, it lost its flock in the mid-19th century, when new generations no longer spoke German.

Built in 1808, **St. Patrick's Catholic Church** (Academy Hill Rd., Damariscotta Mills, Newcastle, 207/563-3240, 9 A.M.–sundown daily), a solid brick structure with 1.5-foot-thick walls and a Paul Revere bell, is New England's oldest surviving Catholic church. Academy Hill Road starts at Newcastle

Square, downtown Newcastle; the church is 2.25 miles from there, and one mile beyond Lincoln Academy. The DaPonte String Quartet often performs here.

St. Andrew's Episcopal Church (Glidden St., Newcastle, 207/563-3533), built in 1883, is nothing short of exquisite, with carved-oak beams, stenciled ceiling, and, for the cognoscenti, a spectacular Hutchings organ.

The Thompson Ice House

On a Sunday morning in February (weather and ice permitting), several hundred helpers and onlookers gather at Thompson Pond, next to the Thompson Ice House (Rte. 129, South Bristol, 207/644-8551), for the annual ice harvest. Festivity prevails as a crew of robust fellows marks out a grid and saws out 12-inch-thick ice cakes, which are pushed up a ramp to the ice-storage house. More than 60 tons of ice are harvested each year. Sawdust-insulated 10-inch-thick walls keep the ice from melting in this National Historic Register building first used in 1826. In 1990, the house became part of a working museum (1–4 P.M. Wed., Fri., Sat. in July and Aug., donation), with ice tools and a window view of the stored ice cakes. The grounds are accessible free all year, including a photographic display board depicting a 1964 harvest. The site is on Route 129, 12 miles south of Damariscotta. Roadside parking is allowed.

The Gut

At the foot of a hill on Route 129 is the tiny community of **South Bristol,** the heart of the town that stretches along the western edge of the Pemaquid Peninsula. In the village center is a green-painted swing bridge (swinging sideways) spanning a narrow waterway quaintly named The Gut. Separating the mainland from Rutherford Island, The Gut is a busy thoroughfare for local lobster-boat traffic, so the bridge opens and closes often, very often. No one is in much of a hurry in this sleepy hamlet, so the frequent stoppages never seem to bother anyone, and the scenery is worth it all. So be patient.

Waldoborough Historical Society Museum

The Waldoborough Historical Society Museum (1164 Main St., Waldoboro, 207/832-4713, 1–4:30 P.M. July–Labor Day, free) is a three-building roadside complex just 0.1 mile south of Route 1, at the eastern end of town. On the grounds are the one-room 1857 **Boggs Schoolhouse,** the 1819 **Town Pound** (to detain stray livestock), and two buildings filled with antique tools, toys, and utensils, plus period costumes, antique fire engines, and artifacts from the shipbuilding era.

Maine Antique Toy and Art Museum

Indulge your inner child at the Maine Antique Toy and Art Museum (Rte. 1, Waldoboro, 207/832-7398, 10 A.M.–4 P.M. Thurs.–Mon. late May–mid-Oct., noon–4 P.M. Sat. and Sun. to Christmas, $4). The museum houses an extensive collection of antique toys and original comic art. See how Mickey Mouse first appeared. Browse a collection of Lone Ranger memorabilia. You'll find all the old favorites, from Popeye to Felix the Cat, Betty Boop to Snow White, Pogo to Yoda. Note: This museum is geared to nostalgic adults, not kids.

PARKS AND PRESERVES

Residents of the Pemaquid Peninsula region are incredibly fortunate to have several foresighted local conservation organizations, each with its own niche and mission: Damariscotta River Association, Pemaquid Watershed Association, Damariscotta Lake Watershed Association, and Medomak Valley Land Trust. In addition, The Nature Conservancy, Maine Audubon, and National Audubon all have holdings on the peninsula, a natural-resource bonanza. For good descriptions of trails throughout Lincoln county, buy a copy of Paula Roberts's *On the Trail in Lincoln County* ($15.75), which describes and provides directions to more than 60 area walking trails. It's available at Salt Bay Farm, which benefits from its sale.

Salt Bay Farm

Headquarters of the **Damariscotta River Association (DRA)** (P.O. Box 333, 109-110 Belvedere Rd., Damariscotta 04543, 207/563-1393, www.draclt.org, 9 A.M.–4 P.M. weekdays), founded in 1973, is the Salt Bay Farm Heritage Center, a late-18th-century farmhouse on a farm site. Here you can pick up maps, brochures, and other information on properties protected and managed by the DRA. It owns 40 conservation easements on 1,350 acres and owns 31 properties, preserving 700 acres, and it acts as a steward, managing another eight properties. Among these are the Dodge Point Preserve, Menigawum (Stratton Island) Preserve, and the Salt Bay Preserve. More than two miles of trails cover Salt Bay Farm's fields, salt marsh, and shore frontage and are open to the public sunrise–sunset daily year-round,. No camping or fires. DRA also has a healthy calendar of events, including birding tours, natural-history trips, concerts, and Trail Tamers, an opportunity to work on the trail system. To reach the farm from downtown Newcastle, take Mills

© TOM NANGLE

The Salt Bay Preserve Heritage Trail loops around Newcastle's Glidden Point.

Road (Rte. 215) to Route 1. Turn right (north) and go 1.4 miles to the blinking light (Belvedere Rd.). Turn left and go 0.4 mile.

Salt Bay Preserve Heritage Trail

Across Great Salt Bay from the DRA Salt Bay Farm is the trailhead for the Salt Bay Preserve Heritage Trail, a relatively easy three-mile loop around Newcastle's Glidden Point that touches on a variety of habitat and also includes remnants of oyster-shell heaps ("middens") going back about 2,500 years. This part of the trail is protected by the feds; do *not* disturb or remove anything. Better still, carry a litterbag and help maintain the path.

This is a super family hike, and leashed dogs are allowed. Along the trail, watch for eagles, osprey, herons, river otters, Indian pipes, several stands of rare white oaks, and open views of Great Salt Bay. Best time to come is close to low tide, as some parts of the trail require slight detours at high tide—especially during the new or full moon. In any case, rubberized shoes or boots are a good idea. To reach the

preserve from Newcastle Square, take Mills Road (Rte. 215) about two miles to the offices of the *Lincoln County News* (just after the post office). The newspaper allows parking in the northern end of its lot, but stay to the right, as far away from the buildings as possible, and be sure not to block any vehicles or access ways. Walk across Route 215 to the trailhead and pick up a brochure/map.

Whaleback Park

After a decade of push-me, pull-you struggling, the Damariscotta River Association, in conjunction with Maine's Bureau of Parks and Lands, finally acquired all the requisite permits in 2001 to create Whaleback Park, an eight-acre public preserve designed to highlight what remains of the "Glidden Midden," ancient oyster-shell heaps across the river from the park viewpoint. (The midden is also visible, but not as easily, from the Salt Bay Preserve Heritage Trail.) Informational signs explain the history of the midden, allegedly the largest such manmade artifact north of Florida. The "minimountain" of castoffs was even more vast until the 1880s, when a factory harvested much of it for lime. The trailhead and parking is on Business Route 1 opposite and between the Great Salt Bay School and the CLC YMCA. For information about the park, contact the DRA (207/563-1393).

Dodge Point Preserve

In 1989, the state of Maine acquired the 506-acre Dodge Point Preserve—one of the stars in its crown—as part of a $35 million bond issue. The Damariscotta River Association, which initiated its protection, helps manage and maintain the property. To sample what the Dodge Point Preserve has to offer, pick up a map at the entrance and follow the Old Farm Road loop trail, and then hook into the Shore Trail (Discovery Trail), heading clockwise, with several dozen highlighted sites. Consider stopping for a riverside picnic and swim at Sand Beach before continuing back to the parking lot. Hunting is permitted in the preserve, so November isn't the best time for hiking here (unless you hike on Sunday, when hunting is banned). Winter brings out ice-skaters and cross-country skiers. The Dodge Point parking area is on River Road, 2.6 miles southwest of Route 1 and 3.5 miles southwest of downtown Newcastle. It's open for day use only, closing at sunset, all year. Admission is free. For more information, contact the DRA.

Tracy Shore Preserve

Walk through a woodland wonderland that extends to ledgy shorefront along Jones Cove, in South Bristol. Old cellars, moss-covered trails, lichen-covered rocks, a vernal pool, old pasture grounds, and spectacular views highlight this little-known gem, owned by The Nature Conservancy. It has cliffs and lots of slippery rocks, so be extra watchful of children. You can connect to another preserve, the Library Preserve, on a link crossing busy Route 129. The trailhead and parking is at the intersection of Route 129 and the S Road, 8.7 miles south of the split from Route 130.

Rachel Carson Salt Pond

If you've never spent time studying the variety of sealife in a tidal pool, the Rachel Carson Salt Pond is a great place to start. Named after the famed author of *Silent Spring* and *The Edge of the Sea*, who summered in this part of Maine, the salt pond was a favorite haunt of hers. The whole point of visiting a tide pool is to see what the tide leaves behind, so check the tide calendar (in local newspapers, or ask at your lodging) and head out a few hours after high tide. Wear rubber boots and beware of slippery rocks and rockweed. Among the many creatures you'll see in this quarter-acre pond are mussels, green crabs, periwinkles, and starfish. Owned by The Nature Conservancy (14 Maine St., Fort Andross, Brunswick, 207/729-5181), the salt pond is on Route 32 in the village of Chamberlain, about a mile north of New Harbor. Parking is limited. Across the road is a trail into a 78-acre inland section of the preserve, most of it wooded. Brochures are available in the registration box.

Todd Wildlife Sanctuary

The mainland section of a 345-acre Audubon Society property, the Todd Wildlife Sanctuary (11 Audubon Rd., Bremen) includes a visitors center and gift shop (207/529-5148, open 10 A.M.–4 P.M. daily June–Aug.), and the **Hockomock Nature Trail,** winding through the woods and down to the shore (open year-round). Pick up a trail guide at the center and follow the informative signs. Allow about an hour. Don't forget a picnic so you can have lunch on the beach. Just offshore is 333-acre **Hog Island,** site of the summertime **Audubon Ecology Camp** for youth and adults. If you have your own boat, you can walk the island's beautiful perimeter trail (no camping). Allow about three hours for the hike. Just check in beforehand at the office near the dock at the north end of the island.

RECREATION
Golf

The nine-hole **Wawenock Country Club** (Rte. 129, Walpole, 207/563-3938), established in the 1920s, is a challenging and very popular public course about midway down the Pemaquid Peninsula from Damariscotta. The par-3 eighth hole features a treacherous bunker named Big Bertha. Starting times are needed on summer weekends.

Bicycling

As with so many other parts of Maine, bike lanes on the Pemaquid Peninsula are poor to nonexistent, so exercise the utmost caution. Roads are narrow, winding, and poorly shouldered.

Swimming

Best bet (but also most crowded) on the peninsula for saltwater swimming is town-owned **Pemaquid Beach Park,** a lovely, tree-lined sandy crescent. No lifeguard, but there are showers (cold water) and bathrooms, and the snack bar serves decent food. No alcohol is allowed on the beach. Admission is $2 for anyone over 12. At 7 P.M., the gates close (restrooms close at 5 P.M.). The beach is just off Snowball Hill Road, west of Route 130.

A much smaller beach is the pocket-size sandy area in **Christmas Cove,** on Rutherford Island. Take Route 129 around the cove and turn to the right, and then right again down the hill.

One of the area's most popular freshwater swimming holes is **Biscay Pond,** a long, skinny body of water in the peninsula's center. From Business Route 1 at the northern edge of Damariscotta, take Biscay Road (turn at McDonald's) three miles to the pond (on the right, heading east). On hot days, this area sees plenty of cars; pull off the road as far as possible.

Farther down the peninsula, on Route 130 in **Bristol Mills,** is another roadside swimming hole, between the dam and the bridge.

Boat Excursions

At 9 A.M. each day between mid-May and early October, the 60-foot powerboat *Hardy III* departs for **Monhegan,** a Brigadoon-like island a dozen miles offshore, where passengers can spend the day hiking the woods, picnicking on the rocks, birding, and inhaling the salt air. At 3:15 P.M., everyone reboards, arriving in New Harbor just over an hour later. Dress warmly and wear rubber-soled shoes. Cost is $29 adults, $17 kids under 12. Reservations are required, and they're held until 20 minutes before departure, but plan to arrive 30 minutes ahead of time (or 45 minutes if you have luggage). Trips operate rain or shine, but heavy seas can affect the schedule. Go light on breakfast beforehand, but there are restrooms aboard. From early June through late September, there's also a second Monhegan trip—used primarily for overnighters—departing New Harbor at 2 P.M. daily. Early and late season, Monhegan trips operate only Wednesday, Saturday, Sunday, and holidays. The *Hardy III* also operates daily 1.5-hour **puffin-watching tours** (5:30 P.M. mid-May–late Aug., $21 adults, $13 kids); one-hour **seal-watching tours** (noon daily mid-June–early Sept. and Sept. weekends, $11 adults, $9 kids); and one-hour evening **lighthouse cruises** (mid-June–early Sept., $12 adults, $8 kids). **Hardy Boat Cruises** (Rte. 32, New Harbor, 207/677-2026 or 800/278-3346, www.hardyboat.com) is 19 miles south of Route 1, based at Shaw's Fish and Lobster Wharf. Parking is $2/day, at the baseball field near Shaw's.

Cruise Muscongus Bay aboard the Friend-ship sloop *Sarah Mead* with **Sail Muscongus** (207/380-5460, www.sailmuscongus.com) on its morning, island, or sunset cruises. Most last about three hours, with rates ranging $30–50 pp; kids under 12 are half price. Bring water and snacks. Muscongus Road is off Route 32, north of Round Pond. Parking is $5/day.

Sea Kayaking and Canoeing

Pemaquid Paddlers, a local group, welcomes visitors to its weekly paddles, usually held beginning at 9 A.M. on Saturdays and lasting for about two hours. Check local papers for the schedule.

Midcoast Kayak (45 Main St., Damariscotta, 207/563-5732, www.midcoastkayak .com) has rentals and offers guided tours and lessons on Muscongus Bay and the Damariscotta River. Three-hour to full-day tours range $39–99, and include introductory, adventurer, sunset, night, and explorer tours. If you would rather do it yourself, sea recreational kayaks rent for $39/day, $29/half day, $22/two hours; sea kayaks (rescue experience required) rent for $49/day, $39/half day; and tandem sea kayaks rent for $65/full day, $49/half day, $39/two hours. Instruction also is available.

Operating from a base near Colonial Pemaquid is **Maine Kayak** (113 Huddle Rd., New Harbor, 866/624-6351, www.mainekayak.com). Guided options include sunset paddle, wildlife paddle, puffin paddle, paddle-and-sail, half- and full-day trips, and a variety of overnights. Rates begin at $40 for the shorter trips. Rentals begin at $25 single, $35 tandem for two hours, with free delivery in the New Harbor area.

Cane and Canvas (Bristol Mills, 207/563-1280) rents canoes and kayaks for use on the Pemaquid River. Paddle upstream from its launch site to Biscay, Pemaquid, and Duckpuddle Ponds or south to a recently restored, early 19th-century stone-arch bridge that was built without mortar. There's lots of wildlife to be seen in the area. Canoes rent for $30 half day, $45 full day; kayak rentals are $20–30 half day, $30–45 full day. Multiple day rates are available. Part of the fee supports the Pemaquid Watershed Association.

If you have your own canoe, or just want to paddle the three-mile length of **Biscay Pond,** you can park at the beach area and put in there (see *Swimming*). Another good launching site is a state ramp off Route 1 in **Nobleboro,** at the head of eight-mile-long **Lake Pemaquid.**

Two preserves are accessible if you have your own boat. Owned by the Damariscotta River Association, 30-acre **Menigawum Preserve (Stratton Island)** is also known locally as Hodgdon's Island. It's at the entrance to Seal Cove on the west side of the South Bristol peninsula. The closest public boat launch is at The Gut, about four miles downriver—a trip better done *with* (in the same direction as) the tide. The best place to land is Boat House Beach, in the northeast corner—also a great spot for shelling. Pick up a map in the small box at the north end of the island and follow the perimeter trail clockwise. At the northern end, you'll see osprey nests; at the southern tip are Native

American shell middens—discards from hundreds of years of marathon summer lunches. (Needless to say, do *not* disturb or remove anything.) You can picnic in the pasture, but camping and fires are not allowed. Stay clear of the abandoned homesite on the island's west side. The preserve is accessible sunrise–sunset.

Named for a 19th-century local woman dubbed "The Witch of Wall Street" for her financial wizardry, **Witch Island Preserve** is owned by Maine Audubon. The wooded, 19-acre island has two beaches, a perimeter trail, and the ruins of the "witch's" house. A quarter of a mile offshore, it's accessible by canoe or kayak from the South Bristol town landing, just to the right after the swing bridge over The Gut. Put in, paddle under the swing bridge, and go north to the island.

ENTERTAINMENT

Two struggling arts centers provide year-round concerts, plays, workshops, classes, and exhibits. **River Arts** (Business Rte. 1, P.O. Box 1316, Damariscotta 04543, 207/563-1507, www.riverartsme.org), previously Round Top Center for the Arts, is on 15 riverside acres, with performances held in the Darrows Barn. The neoclassic **Waldo Theatre** (916 Main St., P.O. Box 587, Waldoboro 04572, 207/832-6060, www.waldotheatre.org) was built as a cinema in 1936. Restored in the mid-1980s, it now operates as a nonprofit organization, presenting first-rate concerts, plays, films, lectures, and other year-round community events.

Lincoln County Community Theater (Theater St., Damariscotta, 207/563-3424, www.lcct.org) owns and operates the historic Lincoln Theater, dating from 1867. It also presents musicals and dramas, concerts, films, and more.

FESTIVALS AND EVENTS

July brings the annual **House and Garden Tour,** a peek into some lovely private homes and gardens, and the **St. Andrew's Lawn Party and Auction,** a fun event that always draws a crowd.

The second weekend in August, **Olde Bristol Days** features a craft show, a parade, road and boat races, live entertainment, and fireworks. At Fort William Henry, in Pemaquid, it's a summer highlight on the peninsula.

In August, hundreds of diehard shoppers turn out for the annual three-day **Miles Memorial Hospital League Rummage Sale,** held under tents on Business Route 1 (close to the junction with Rte. 1) in Damariscotta.

And in October, during the **Round Pond Round About,** local galleries hold open houses and demonstrations.

SHOPPING

Downtown Damariscotta is the region's hub, and it has a nice selection of independent shops, galleries, and boutiques. Downtown parking in summer is a major headache; the municipal lot, behind the storefronts, has a three-hour limit, and it's almost always full. You'll usually find spots on some of the side streets.

Antiques and Antiquarian Books

Antiques shops are numerous along the Bristol Road (Rte. 130), where many barns have been turned into shops selling everything from fine antiques to old stuff. Serous antiques aficionados will find plenty to browse and buy along this stretch of road.

The multidealer **Nobleboro Antique Exchange** (104 Atlantic Hwy., Rte. 1, Nobleboro, 207/563-6800) is housed in a light blue building that goes on and on, with more than 100 display areas on three levels. The selection is diverse, from period antiques to 20th-century collectibles.

Based in a screen-fronted antique carriage house just south of Round Pond Village, **Jean Gillespie Books** (1172 Rte. 32, Round Pond, 207/529-5555) has separate rooms and alcoves, all very user friendly. Specialties are cookbooks, nautical and Maine titles, and illustrated children's books; the "Royalty" category fills six shelves.

Art Galleries

Worth a visit for the building alone, the **Stable Gallery** (26 Water St., Damariscotta, 207/563-1991), just off Main Street, was built in the 19th-century clipper-ship era and still has original black-walnut stalls—providing a great foil for the work of dozens of Maine craftspeople. Lining the walls are paintings and prints from the gallery's large "stable" of artists.

In his **River Gallery** (Main St., Damariscotta, 207/563-6330), dealer Geoff Robinson specializes in 19th- and early-20th-century European and American fine art—a connoisseur's inventory.

Showing a high profile ever since it opened in the renovated antique fire station, **The Firehouse Gallery** (1 Bristol Rd., Damariscotta, 207/563-7299) has a tasteful, well-displayed selection of paintings, sculpture, prints, and jewelry. The gallery mounts half a dozen shows during its season (May–Oct.).

Betcha can't leave without buying something from **Pemaquid Craft Co-op** (Rte. 130, New Harbor, 207/277-2077), with 15 rooms filled with quality works by 50 Maine artisans. There's lots of stuff to see here: iron art, woodwork, needlework, quilts, bears, candles, jewelry, and much, much more.

Contemporary art is the focus at **Gallery 170** (170 Main St., Damariscotta, 207/563-5098), housed in a lovely 1803 downtown building and displaying works by artists both local and afar in rotating shows.

If you are especially interested in arts and crafts, make Round Pond part of your itinerary. The small village is home to about a dozen galleries and studios, many within walking distance of one another.

A delightful little off-the-beaten-path find is **Tidemark Gallery** (902 Main St., Waldoboro, 207/832-5109), showing fine arts and crafts from local artists.

Specialty and Eclectic Shops

The Pemaquid Peninsula is fertile ground for crafts and gifts, and many of the shop locations provide opportunities for exploring off the beaten path.

The inventory at the **Maine Coast Book Shop and Café** (158 Main St., 207/563-3207) always seems to anticipate customers' wishes, so you're unlikely to walk out empty-handed.

You'll find a superb children's section, large magazine selection, helpful staff, and always something tempting in the café.

Just off Main Street (turn at Reny's) is **Weatherbird** (72 Courtyard St., Damariscotta, 207/563-8993), a terrifically eclectic shop with an inventory that defies description. Housewares, wines, toys, cards, gourmet specialties, and intriguing women's clothing are all part of the mix. Above it is **Tin Fish Etc.** (207/563-8204). Dana Moses's shop features brilliantly hand-painted tin *objets* made from recycled roofing metal. She also accepts commissions.

All sorts of finds fill the **Walpole Barn** (Rte. 129, Walpole, 207/563-7050, www.walpole barn.com), Warren and Deb Storch's retirement fun. Browse home and garden products, whimsies, gourmet foods, even wines. Baked goods, tea, and other fare are sometimes available.

Down the peninsula, there's no question that the **Granite Hall Store** (9 Backshore Rd., off Rte. 32, Round Pond, 207/529-5864), is unique. Eric and Sarah Herndon's eclectic inventory is tough to describe but always fascinating. The first floor of this mid-19th-century emporium carries pottery, CDs, paper dolls, fudge, baskets, even catnip mice and cookie cutters. The "penny" candy, ice cream, and the old-fashioned peanut-roasting machine capture the kids. Upstairs, their parents usually succumb to books, antiques, and stunning handwoven Scottish and Irish woolens. Adding to the flavor are old ship models, hardwood floors, and a ship's bell that tolls the time. The shop is in "downtown" Round Pond, 11 miles south of Route 1.

Bells reminiscent of lighthouses, buoys, and even wilderness sounds are crafted by **North Country Wind Bells** (544 Rte. 32, Chamberlain, 207/677-2224).

A well-chosen selection of silver jewelry fills **Purple Cactus** (107 Huddle Rd., New Harbor, 207/677-2262), Elizabeth Gamage's seasonal shop on the road to Colonial Pemaquid.

Puzzle fans come from all over the country to shop at **I'm Puzzled** (246 Lower Cross Rd., Nobleboro, 207/563-5719), on the inland side of Route 1, stocked with nearly 2,000 jigsaw puzzles.

Reny's

Whatever you do, don't leave downtown Damariscotta without visiting Reny's (207/563-5757 or 207/563-3011), with stores on each side of Main Street; one sells clothing, the other everything else. This is Reny's hometown, so the selection is huge in both. If you can recognize the edges of cut-out labels, you'll find clothes from major retailers at very discounted prices. Stock up on housewares, munchies, puzzles, shoes, and whatever else floats your boat; the prices can't be beat.

ACCOMMODATIONS
Inns

Along a scenic side road and overlooking the Damariscotta River is **The Newcastle Inn** (River Rd., Newcastle, 207/563-5685 or 800/832-8669, www.newcastleinn.com, $175–255), an 1860s sea captain's home. Ideal for a romantic getaway, the lovely hostelry (main inn and carriage house) has 15 elegant guest rooms and suites (all with air-conditioning, some with fireplaces and whirlpool tubs), riverfront gardens, and an upscale country-inn ambience. Special packages are available off-season. Rates include a full breakfast. The inn's restaurant, **Lupines,** is open to the public by reservation. Guests gather for hors d'oeuvres at 6 P.M. Tuesday–Saturday and then move to the dining room for the four-course, fixed-price meal ($46).

Within easy walking distance of Pemaquid Light and 16 miles south of Route 1, **The Bradley Inn** (3063 Bristol Rd./Rte. 130, New Harbor, 207/677-2105 or 800/942-5560, www .bradleyinn.com, $165–325) is a beautifully restored, late-19th-century three-story building with rooms and a suite (with full kitchen and fireplace) in the inn and carriage house, a separate cottage, a spa, and lovely gardens—a great location for a quiet weekend getaway. The inn's restaurant, overlooking the gardens and open to the public, has an ambitious and pricey menu (entrées $25–32). Don't miss the granite bar in the adjoining pub. Room rates include full breakfast and afternoon tea.

Almost on top of Pemaquid Light is the rambling ⟨ **Hotel Pemaquid** (3098 Bristol

Rd., Rte. 130, New Harbor, 207/677-2312, www.hotelpemaquid.com, $85–155). Seventeen miles south of Route 1 but just 450 feet from the lighthouse (you can't see it from the inn, but you sure can hear the foghorn!), the hotel has been welcoming guests since 1900; it's fun to peruse the old guest registers. Hang out in the large, comfortable parlor or the wraparound veranda. The owners have gently renovated the property, updating and improving everything without losing the Victorian charm of an old seaside hotel. The inn building has rooms with private and shared baths and suites. Other buildings have motel-style units with private bath. Apartments in the annex rent for $140–200. A beautiful second-floor suite in the carriage house, with full kitchen and deck, is $200–240 per night or $1,200–1,500 per week. For the Victorian flavor of the place, request an inn room or suite. No restaurant, but The Bradley Inn and The Sea Gull Shop are nearby. No credit cards. It's open mid-May–mid-October.

Up the eastern side of the peninsula, in the middle of New Harbor, **The Gosnold Arms** (146 Rte. 32, New Harbor, 207/677-3727, off-season 561/575-9549, www.gosnold.com, $105–290) has been here since 1925 and remains deliberately old-fashioned, with pine-paneled rooms and a country-cottage common room. Customers return year after year. The family-owned operation includes the inn building and eight other buildings (with 14 units), so there's variety in layout, location, and decor. Many of the rooms include water views, but the loudspeaker at the lobster wharf across the street (Shaw's) can preclude an afternoon nap in front rooms. Rates include breakfast. It's open mid-May–mid-October.

Bed-and-Breakfasts

A lovely water-view living room with piano and harp sets the tone for **The Harbor View Inn** (Business Rte. 1, P.O. Box 791, Newcastle 04553, 207/563-2900, www.theharborview.com, $145–210 d). Another selling point is the huge deck overlooking the twin towns and the river. Joe McEntee's family antiques fill the three

beautifully decorated first- and second-floor suites. All rooms have phones, Wi-Fi, TV, comfortable chairs; two have fireplaces. Breakfast is a four-course extravaganza in the formal dining room with a printed menu, thanks to one of Joe's former careers as an executive chef (he was also a publishing executive). It's open all year.

Martha Scudder provides a warm welcome for her guests at **Oak Gables Bed and Breakfast** (Pleasant St., P.O. Box 276, Damariscotta 04543, 207/563-1476 or 800/335-7748, www.oakgablesbb.com, $95). At the end of a pretty lane, this 13-acre hilltop estate overlooks the Damariscotta River. Despite a rather imposing setting, everything's homey, informal, and hospitable. Four second-floor rooms, which can be joined in pairs, share a bath; a guest wing ($875 d) has a full kitchen, private bath, and separate entrance. The heated swimming pool is a huge plus, as is the boathouse deck, on the river. Guests can harvest blackberries from scads of bushes. Also on the grounds are a three-bedroom cottage ($1,200/week), a river-view studio apartment ($875/week), and a one-bedroom apartment ($980/week), usually booked up well ahead. It's open all year.

Wake up with a dip, after a restful sleep at the **Mill Pond Inn** (50 Main St., Rte. 215, Damariscotta Mills, Nobleboro, 207/563-8014, www.millpondinn.com, $130). The 1780 Colonial was restored and converted into an inn in 1986 by delightful owners Bobby and Sherry Whear. After a full breakfast, snooze in a hammock, watch for eagles and great blue herons, pedal a bicycle into nearby Damariscotta, or canoe the pond, which connects to 14-mile-long Damariscotta Lake. Bobby, a Registered Maine Guide, offers fishing trips and scenic tours of the lake in his restored, antique Lyman lapstrake (clinker-built) boat. Use of bicycles and canoe is free to guests. The inn is just a five-minute drive from downtown Damariscotta, but a world away. No credit cards.

The mansard-roofed **Inn at Round Pond** (1442 Rte. 32, Round Pond, 207/529-2004, www.theinnatroundpond.com, $150–190) commands a sea captain's view of the harbor as it presides over the pretty village of Round Pond.

It's an easy walk to a waterfront restaurant, two dueling lobster pounds, an old-timey country store, and a handful of galleries and shops. Bay Sail boat rentals is next door. Each of three good-size rooms has harbor views and sitting areas. A full breakfast is included. It's open all year.

You can walk to Christmas Cove from **Sunset Bed and Breakfast** (16 Sunset Loop, P.O. Box 91, South Bristol 04568, 207/644-8849, www.sunsetbnb.com). Kay and Dick Miller have two small rooms, one with full bed, the other with twins, sharing one bath in their modest Cape-style house with to-die-for views. Various rates are available, from one room with private bath ($120) to a family of four ($160). Rates include a hearty continental breakfast. Bring a kayak and launch it here. It's open May–October.

About three miles south of town is **Blue Skye Farm** (1708 Friendship Rd., Waldoboro, 207/832-0300, www.blueskyefarm.com), Jan and Peter Davidson's B&B in a gorgeous 18th-century farmhouse, set amid 100 acres, with trails, gardens, and lawns. Original wall stencils by Moses Eaton decorate the entry. Breakfast is provided, and guests have full use of the country kitchen, so you can prepare other meals. Other common roams include the dining room, screened-in sun room, and a sitting room, with fireplace, that's stocked with games. Five rooms, three with private baths, are meticulously decorated. Rates range $105–145.

Just up the hill from the Waldo Theatre, hospitable Libby Hopkins has been running the **Broad Bay Inn and Gallery** (1014 Main St., P.O. Box 607, Waldoboro 04572, 207/832-6668 or 800/736-6769, www.broadbayinn.com, $75–110) since 1984, and she's an energetic breakfast chef (she attended Le Cordon Bleu cooking school in Paris). Four antiques-filled rooms share three baths. Rates include afternoon tea or sherry. Guests can play the piano, browse through the huge art-book collection, or watch old films. The barn gallery—stocked with watercolors and some crafts—is open in July and August, when Libby also organizes art workshops run by professional teachers. It's open May–mid-October.

Motels and Cottage Colonies

You'll have to plan well in advance to snag one of the rustic **Ye Olde Forte Cabins** (18 Old Fort Rd., Pemaquid Beach, 207/677-2261, www.yeoldefortecabins.com, $80–126 per day, $410–595 per week). These simple cabins have edged a grassy lawn dropping to John's Bay since 1922. Each has at least a toilet and sink, but a shower house and a well-equipped cookhouse are part of the colony. Although guests are expected to clean up after themselves when using the kitchen, manager Julie Powell keeps the place spotless. No frills, unless you count the private small beach. It's a great place to bring a kayak. The cabins are less than 25 yards from Colonial Pemaquid and Fort William Henry. No credit cards.

Tony and Sally Capodilupo have restored four 19th- and 20th-century houses on a 22-acre hilltop, just steps from the village and overlooking the harbor, adding 21st-century amenities while retaining the original village appeal. **The Moorings** (P.O. Box 37, New Harbor 04554, 207/677-2409 summer, 617/731-4264 winter, www.themooringsnewharbor.com) comprises seven well-equipped weekly rental apartments, all with gas fireplace, TV/DVD, and heat, along with an indoor pool, tennis court, hot tub, laundry, cookout area, and billiards room. All sleep two and are restricted to adults. In-season rates begin at $1,200/week.

Just down the road, Dan Thompson is the third-generation innkeeper at **The Thompson House and Cottages** (95 South Side Rd., New Harbor, 207/677-2317, www.thompson cottages.net, $400–1,650/week), a low-key, old-timey complex of mostly waterfront rooms, apartments, and cottages split among two mini-peninsulas. Most have fireplaces. Rowboats are available, and there's a library with games, books, and puzzles.

Now here's a bargain. Up a long winding driveway behind Moody's Diner is **Moody's Motel** (Rte. 1, Waldoboro, 207/832-5362, www.moodysdiner.com, $44–52), in biz since 1927, and likely little has changed in the meantime. Nothing fancy here, but it's clean and well run. The motel and tourist cabins all have screened porches and TV, and a few have kitchenettes. It's open mid-May–mid-October.

Campgrounds

The area's best-run campground is 150-acre **Lake Pemaquid Camping** (off Biscay Rd., P.O. Box 967, Damariscotta 04543, 207/563-5202, www.lakepemaquid.com, $30–44), with 280 tent and RV sites, many right on the seven-mile-long lake. It's a lively operation, with tennis, pool and lake swimming, fishing (licenses available), playground, game room, store (lobsters available), snack room, laundry, sauna, whirlpool tub, and canoe, kayak, and boat rentals. There's also plenty of entertainment, including train and hay rides, dances, movies, and performances. Rustic cabins and cottages, with full baths, are $525–1,000 per week. The campground is open Memorial Day weekend–Columbus Day.

A favorite with kayakers is **Sherwood Forest Camping** (Pemaquid Trail, P.O. Box 189, New Harbor 04554, 800/274-1593, www.sherwoodforestcampsite.com, $29–35). Facilities include a playground, sundeck, and pool, but the campground is just 800 feet from Pemaquid Beach.

FOOD
Local Flavors
Damariscotta: For breakfast, look no farther than **The Breakfast Place and Bakery** (Business Rte. 1, Main St., Damariscotta, 207/563-5434, 7 A.M.–1 P.M. daily), a small place that turns out big breakfasts. Homemade breads, muffins, and biscuits, eggs, omelettes, pancakes, waffles, and more are all reasonably priced, most $4–6. A few specials, such as crabcakes and eggs or shimp creole omelette are closer to $8.

For baked goods, sandwiches, soups, and gourmet goodies to go, head to **Weatherbird** (1168 Elm St., Damariscotta, 207/563-8993, 8 A.M.–5:30 P.M. Mon.–Sat.). Eat at one of the handful of tables out front or take it to the waterfront.

In a barn-style building at the northern edge of Damariscotta is the area's best homemade ice cream—about four dozen flavors, including some unusual ones you'd never dream up.

Round Top Ice Cream (Business Rte. 1, Damariscotta, 207/563-5307) has been in business since 1924.

For pizza, subs, and pasta, the choice is **Romeo's Pizza** (Business Rte. 1, Damariscotta, 207/563-1563, 11 A.M.–9 P.M. daily). The gourmet pizzas are superb (try the Aegean). Dinners and pasta dishes, served with garlic bread and small tossed salad, are a steal at less than $10.

Rising Tide Natural Foods Market (Business Rte. 1, Damariscotta, 207/563-5556) has been a thriving co-op organization since 1978, and it keeps on growing. Bulk items are available, plus books, cosmetics, and all kinds of preservative-free organic food. A self-service deli section has soups, sandwiches, salads, and entrées; you may be lucky enough to snag one of the handful of tables in the dining area. At the northern end of town, the market is open 8 A.M.–7 P.M. Monday–Saturday all year.

The **Damariscotta Area Farmers Market** sets up 9 A.M.–noon on Friday mid-May–October at Salt Bay Heritage Center, on Belvedere Road, just off Route 1, Damariscotta. Condiments, baked goods, cheeses, local shellfish, and crafts are always available from about two dozen vendors, and you never know what else will turn up at this major market. A smaller market operates in the same location 9 A.M.–noon Monday late June–August.

Down the Peninsula: Great coffee and good home-style breakfasts and lunches are served at the retro **Bristol Diner** (1267 Bristol Rd., Bristol, 207/563-8000, 6 A.M.–2 P.M. Tues.–Sat., 7 A.M.–1 P.M. Sun.), which promises—and delivers—"Good grub, bub."

Homemade ice cream, delicious baked goods, prepared dishes, and sandwiches to go are just a few of the reasons to stop by the seasonal **Island Grocery** (12 West Side Rd., 207/644-8552, www.islandgrocery.net). It also has breads, cheese, and all kinds of gourmet goodies—stock up for a picnic. To find it, take the first right after the swinging bridge.

Just around the corner from Colonial Pemaquid, **The Cupboard Cafe** (137 Huddle Rd., New Harbor, 207/677-3911, 8 A.M.–7 P.M.

Tues.–Fri., to 3 P.M. Sat., to noon Sun.) is a homey cottage serving fresh-baked goods, breakfasts, and a nice choice of fresh salads, burgers, sandwiches, and specials.

Waldoboro: At the corner of Routes 1 and 220, opposite Moody's Diner, is the warehousey building that turns out superb **Borealis Breads** (1860 Atlantic Hwy., Rte. 1, Waldoboro, 207/832-0655). Using sourdough starters (and no oils, sweeteners, eggs, or dairy products), owner Jim Amaral and his crew produce baguettes, olive bread, lemon fig bread, rosemary focaccia, and about a dozen other inventive flavors (each day has its specialties). A refrigerated case holds a small selection of picnic fixings (sandwich spreads, juices). Great soups and salads, and excellent sandwiches are available to go. It's open 8:30 A.M.–5:30 P.M. Monday–Friday, 9 A.M.–4:30 P.M. Saturday and Sunday.

The **Waldoboro 5&10** (Friendship St., Waldoboro, 207/832-4624, 8 A.M.–5 P.M. Mon.–Sat.) is one of those old-fashioned, little-of-everything variety stores that disappeared ages ago. Inside are antiques, penny candy, and a deli serving excellent sandwiches and Round Top ice cream. It's a one-man operation, so service can be slow at peak times.

Pick up sandwiches, salads, and gourmet picnic fixings at **McKeen and Charles** (1587 Rte. 1, Waldoboro, 832-2221, 10 A.M.–6 P.M. Mon.–Sat., www.mckeanandcharles.com), and while you're there, ask about any scheduled wine tastings. The store also sells about 300 different beers.

Each fall, around mid-September, a tiny, cryptic display ad appears in local newspapers: "Kraut's Ready." Savvy readers recognize this as the announcement of the latest batch of ◖ **Morse's sauerkraut**—an annual ritual since 1918. The homemade kraut is available in stores and by mail order, but it's more fun (and cheaper) to visit the shop, the **Kraut House** (3856 Washington Rd., Rte. 220, Waldoboro, 207/832-5569 or 800/486-1605, www.morses sauerkraut.com, 9 A.M.–6 P.M. Thurs.–Tues.), which also has a small café (8 A.M.–4 P.M.) serving traditional German fare. Sandwiches, such as a classic Reuben, liverwurst, or Black Forest ham are $6; homemade pierogies are $5, a sausage plate is $7, and stuffed cabbage rolls are $8. Big serve-yourself jars of Morse's pickles are on the tables. The red-painted farm store also carries Aunt Lydia's Beet Relish, baked beans, mustard, maple syrup, and other Maine foods as well as a mind-boggling selection of hard-to-find and unusual northern European specialties. It's eight miles north of Route 1.

Truck drivers, tourists, locals, and notables have been flocking to **Moody's Diner** (Rtes. 1 and 220, Waldoboro, 207/832-7785, www .moodysdiner.com, 4:30 A.M.–11 P.M. Mon.–Fri., 5 A.M.–11 P.M. Sat., 6 A.M.–11 P.M. Sun.) since the early 1930s, when the Moody family established this classic diner on a Waldoboro hilltop. The antique neon sign has long been a Route 1 beacon, especially on a foggy night, and the crowds continue, with new generations of Moodys and considerable expansion of the premises. It's gone beyond diner-dom. Expect hearty, no-frills fare and such calorific desserts as peanut-butter or walnut pie. After eating, you can buy the cookbook.

Casual Dining

A reliable standby in downtown Damariscotta, next to the Damariscotta Bank and Trust, the **Salt Bay Café** (Main St., Damariscotta, 207/563-1666, 7:30 A.M.–9:30 P.M. Mon.–Sat., 8 A.M.–9 P.M. Sun.) has a loyal following—thanks to its imaginative, reasonably priced cuisine and cheerful, plant-filled setting. Vegetarians have their own menu, with two dozen–plus choices. Dinner entrées are $11–19; hearty lunch sandwiches run $6–8. It has a liquor license too.

An open kitchen and carefully prepared foods with an emphasis on ultrafresh seafood make **Damariscotta River Grill** (155 Main St., Damariscotta, 207/563-2992, 11 A.M.–8 P.M., to 9 P.M. Fri.–Sat., 9 A.M.–2:30 P.M. Sun.) a reliable favorite, with most entrées $14–24. The artichoke fondue is worth fighting over. Choose a table in the back with a river view, if available.

Pair fresh fish with a choice of sides and toppings, such as blue cheese merlot sauce or mango pepper relish, at **74 Maine Bistro**

(74 Main St., Damariscotta, 207/563-7444, www.74maine.com, 5–9 P.M. Tues.–Sat., $16–26), just off Main Street. Other possibilities include steaks, ribs, and pastas.

One of the best meal deals in the area is Rick and Jean Kerrigan's **Anchor Inn** (Harbor Rd., Round Pond, 207/529-5584, 11 A.M.–9:30 P.M. daily mid-May–mid-Oct.), tucked away on the picturesque harbor in Round Pond, on the eastern side of the peninsula. Informal and rustic, with a menu that'll surprise you (entrées $14–25), the place always attracts a crowd. Reservations are advisable on summer weekends. After Labor Day, the schedule can be a bit erratic; call to confirm. It's a sister property to the Damariscotta River Grill.

The view's even better at **Coveside Restaurant** (105 Coveside Rd., Christmas Cove, South Bristol, 207/644-8282, www.covesiderestaurant.com, 11 A.M.–9 P.M. daily, $10–28), based at a marina on Rutherford Island, just off the end of the South Bristol peninsula. It's open for lunch and dinner as well as light meals. Grab a seat on the deck and watch a steady stream of boaters and summer vacationers during the cruising season.

Location, location. Right next to Pemaquid Light is **The Sea Gull Shop** (3119 Bristol Rd., Pemaquid Point, 207/677-2374, 7:30 A.M.–7:30 P.M. daily mid-May–mid-Oct.), an oceanfront place with touristy prices, but decent food—pancakes and muffins, for instance, overflowing with blueberries.

Lobster in the Rough

The Pemaquid Peninsula must have more eat-on-the-dock places per capita than anyplace in Maine. Some are basic, no-frills operations, others are big-time commercial concerns. Each has a loyal following.

The biggest and best-known lobster wharf is **Shaw's Fish and Lobster Wharf** (Rte. 32, New Harbor, 207/677-2200 or 800/772-2209, 11 A.M.–9 P.M. daily), where you place your order, take a number, and wait for it to come booming back at you over the loudspeaker. (You can also order steak here. And margaritas. And oysters at the wharf raw bar.) Fried

seafood dinners run $8–17. It's open mid-May–mid-October, closing one hour earlier midweek off-season.

Facing each other across the dock in the hamlet of Round Pond are the **Round Pond Lobster Co-Op** (207/529-5725) and **Muscongus Bay Lobster** (207/529-5528). Both are good, and competition keeps prices low. Muscongus has enlarged in recent years, so it has a larger menu and covered seating, but tiny Round Pond Lobster keeps it simple and oh-so-fresh. Both usually open around 10 A.M. daily for lunch and dinner and close around sunset.

Other seasonal lobster wharves salting the peninsula are the **New Harbor Co-Op** (Rte. 32, New Harbor, 207/677-2791), **Pemaquid Fishermen's Co-Op** (Pemaquid Harbor Rd., Pemaquid Harbor, 207/677-2801), and **Broad Cove Marine Services** (off Rte. 32, Medomak, 207/529-5186), a low-key sleeper with a wowser view.

INFORMATION AND SERVICES

The Damariscotta Region Chamber of Commerce (P.O. Box 13, Damariscotta 04543, 207/563-8340, www.damariscottaregion.com) publishes a free annual information booklet about the area. Its office, just off Main Street, is open 9 A.M.–5 P.M. weekdays. The Pemaquid Area Association (Chamberlain, no telephone) produces a very useful annotated map covering the lower half of the Pemaquid Peninsula. Both publications are available by mail and at the information bureaus. Also ask for a copy of *The Upper River Region Field Guide,* a foldout map/brochure produced by the Damariscotta River Association and containing excellent information about the area's preserves and natural history.

Skidompha Library (Main St., Damariscotta, 207/563-5513, www.skidompha.org) also operates a used-book shop. (Incidentally, if you're puzzled by the name, it comes from the names of the members of a local literary society who founded the library at the turn of the 20th century.) Or check out Waldoboro Public Library (Main St., Waldoboro, 207/832-4484, www.waldoborolibrary.org).

PENOBSCOT BAY

Although considered part of the Mid-Coast, the region edging Penobscot Bay has a different feel and view. Coastal mountains in Camden and Lincolnville and an abundance of islands frame the view. These island-studded waters are renowned by sailors, so it's no surprise that Maine's famed windjammer fleet is based here.

From Thomaston through Searsport, no two towns are alike except that all are changing, as traditional industries give way to arts- and tourism-related businesses. Thomaston's Museum in the Streets, Rockland's art galleries, Camden's picturesque mountainside harbor, Lincolnville's pocket beach, Belfast's inviting downtown, Searsport's sea captains' homes, and Prospect's Fort Knox all invite exploration, as do offshore islands. From Port Clyde, take the ferry to Monhegan, an offshore idyll

known as the Artists' Island. From Rockland and Lincolnville Beach, car and passenger ferries head to Vinalhaven, North Haven, Matinicus, and Islesboro. All are occupied year-round by hardy souls and joined in summer by less-hardy ones. Except for Matinicus, they're great day-trip destinations. If what appeals to you about a ferry trip is traveling on the water, you can get a taste of the great age of sail by booking a three- or six-day cruise on one of the classic windjammer schooners berthed in Rockland, Rockport, and Camden (see the sidebar *Windjamming*). Or simply book a day sail or sea-kayak excursion.

PLANNING YOUR TIME

To hit just the highlights, you'll need at least four days. If you want to relax a bit and

HIGHLIGHTS

◖ Monhegan Museum: View an impressive collection of masters at this museum adjacent to the lighthouse, then visit contemporary studios and find their inspiration by hiking island trails (page 199).

◖ The Farnsworth Art Museum and the Wyeth Center: Three generations of Wyeths are represented in this recently expanded museum, which also boasts an excellent collection of works by Maine and American masters (page 203).

◖ Owls Head Transportation Museum: View a fabulous collection of vintage airplanes, automobiles, and even bicycles, many of which are flown, driven, or ridden during weekend special events (page 205).

◖ Rockland Breakwater: Take a walk on this nearly mile-long breakwater to the lighthouse at the end (open on weekends). It's an especially fine place to watch the windjammers sail in or out of Rockland Harbor (page 206).

◖ Owls Head Light State Park: The views of Penobscot Bay are spectacular, and it's a great place for a picnic lunch (page 207).

◖ Camden Hills State Park: If you have time, hike the moderate trail to the summit for a gull's-eye view over Camden Harbor and Penobscot Bay. If not, take the easy route and drive (page 220).

◖ Penobscot Marine Museum: Learn what life was *really* like during the Great Age of Sail in a town renowned for the number and quality of its sea captains (page 239).

◖ BlueJacket Shipcrafters: Even if you have no inclination whatsoever toward building a model ship, stop by and view some of the museum-quality models built at the oldest model company in the country (page 240).

◖ Fort Knox: A good restoration, frequent events, and secret passages to explore make this late-19th-century fort one of Maine's best (page 241).

◖ Penobscot Narrows Bridge and Observatory: On a clear day, the views from the 420-foot-high tower, one of only three in the world, extend from Mt. Katahdin to Cadillac Mountain (page 241).

LOOK FOR ◖ TO FIND RECOMMENDED SIGHTS, ACTIVITIES, DINING, AND LODGING.

enjoy the area, plan on 4–5 days. Make it a full week, if you plan on overnighting on any of the offshore islands. In general, lodging is less expensive in Rockland, Belfast, and Searsport than it is in Camden. In any case, head for Monhegan or Vinalhaven on a good day and save the museums for inclement ones.

Two-lane Route 1 is the region's central artery, with veins running down the peninsula limbs. Yes, traffic backs up, especially in Camden (and in Thomaston on the Fourth of July, when it's closed for a parade), but it rarely stops moving. If your destination is Rockland, take I-95 to Augusta and then Route 17 East; if it's Belfast or north, take I-95 to Augusta and then Route 3 East. Route 90 is a nifty bypass around Thomaston and Rockland, connecting Route 1 from Warren to Rockport. For moseyers, the **Georges River Scenic Byway** is a 50-mile rural, inland route, mostly along Route 131, between Port Clyde and Liberty. It parallels the coast, but it meanders through

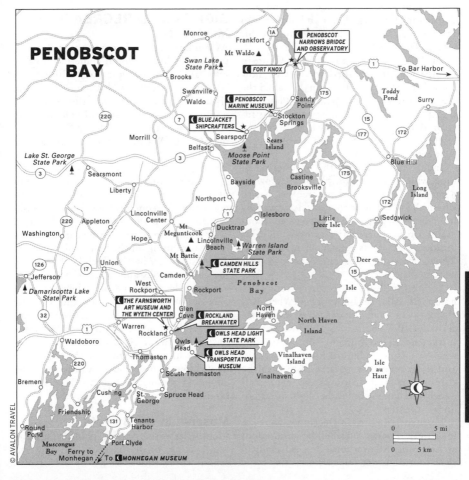

farmlands and tiny villages, and by lakes and rivers, with antiques shops and farm stands along the way. It's simply gorgeous in autumn.

In July and August, try to avoid arriving in this region without a reservation. Helpful chamber of commerce staffers in prime locations often can work last-minute miracles, but special events and festivals can fill up all the beds for miles around.

Thomaston Area

Thomaston is a little gem of a town, and getting more so each year thanks to the razing of the old Maine State Prison. It's also the gateway to two lovely fingers of land bordering the St. George River and jutting into the Gulf of Maine—the Cushing and St. George Peninsulas.

In 1605, British adventurer Captain George Waymouth sailed up the river now named after him (it was originally called the Georges River). A way station for Plymouth traders as early as 1630, Thomaston was incorporated in 1777 and officially named after General John Thomas, a Revolutionary War hero.

Industry began with the production of lime, which was used for plaster. A growing demand for plaster, and the frequency with which the wooden boats were destroyed by fire while carrying loads of extremely flammable lime, spurred the growth of shipbuilding and all its related infrastructure. Thomaston's slogan became "the town that went to sea."

Seeing the sleepy harborfront today, it's hard to visualize the booming era when dozens of tall-masted wooden ships slid down the ways. But the town's architecture is a testament and tribute to the prosperous past—all those splendid homes on Main and Knox Streets were funded by wealthy shipowners and shipmasters who well understood how to occupy the idle hands of off-duty carpenters.

If you're in the area in December, you're in for a treat: Thomaston's holiday decorations are stunning. All over town, but especially in the Historic District, huge wreaths, tiny white lights, and (usually) a blanket of snow create a scene lifted right out of a Currier and Ives print.

SIGHTS AND RECREATION
Montpelier
As you head out of Thomaston on Route 1, toward Rockland, you'll come face to face with an imposing colonial hilltop mansion at the junction with Route 131 South. (Behind it, unfortunately, is the rather ugly outline of a huge cement plant.) Dedicated to the memory of General Henry Knox, President George Washington's secretary of war, Montpelier (Rtes. 1 and 131, P.O. Box 326, Thomaston 04861, 207/354-8062, www.generalknoxmuseum.org) is a 1930s replica of Knox's original Thomaston home. The mansion today contains Knox family furnishings and other period antiques—all described with great enthusiasm during the hour-long tours, beginning on the hour and half hour. A gift shop run by the Friends of Montpelier carries books and other relevant items. Concerts, lectures, and special events occur here periodically throughout the summer; General Knox's birthday is celebrated with considerable fanfare in July. It offers tours on the half hour 10 A.M.–3 P.M. Tuesday–Saturday July and August, on the hour June, September, and October. Admission is $6 adults, $5 seniors, $3 kids 5–13, or $15 per family.

Museum in the Streets
Montpelier is the starting point for a walking, cycling, or, if you must, driving tour (about three miles) of nearly 70 sites in

Thomaston's National Historic District. Pick up a copy of the tour brochure at one of the local businesses. Included are lots of stories behind the facades of the handsome 19th-century homes that line Main and Knox Streets; the architecture here is nothing short of spectacular. Much of this history is also recounted in The Museum in the Streets, a walking tour taking in 25 informative plaques illustrated with old photos throughout town.

EVENTS

Thomaston's **Fourth of July,** an old-fashioned hometown celebration reminiscent of a Norman Rockwell painting, draws huge crowds. A spiffy parade—with bands, veterans, kids, and pets—starts off the morning (11 A.M.), followed by races, craft and food booths, and lots more. If you need to get *through* Thomaston on the Fourth of July, do it well before the parade or well after noon; the marchers go right down Main Street (Rte. 1), and gridlock forces a detour.

SHOPPING

Thomaston has a block-long shopping street (on Rte. 1), with ample free parking out back behind the stores.

If you arrive at Marti Reed's **Personal Book Shop** (78 Main St., Thomaston, 207/354-8058) at the right time, you're likely to run into local writers' groups that gather frequently to swap tips and gossip. That's just the kind of place this is—an independent bookstore with a warm, nurturing feel. Not to mention a dog in residence. Lots of unusual titles, too—you won't leave empty-handed. Just give Marti an idea of the type of books you enjoy, and she's bound to steer you toward winners. It's all part of her personal service. She also has a 100 percent success record, to date, for finding out-of-print books.

The **Maine State Prison Showroom Outlet** (Main St./Rte. 1, corner of Wadsworth St., Thomaston, 207/354-3131) markets the handiwork of inmate craftsmen. Some of the souvenirs verge on kitsch; the bargains are wooden bar stools, toys (including dollhouses), and chopping boards. You'll need to carry your purchases with you; prison-made goods cannot be shipped.

CAMPING

The best campground is on the Thomaston/ Cushing town line at **Saltwater Farm Campground** (Wadsworth St./Cushing Rd., Cushing, mailing address P.O. Box 165, Thomaston 04861, 207/354-6735, www .midcoast.com/~sfc), a 35-acre Good Sam park 1.5 miles south of Route 1. Thirty-seven open and wooded tent and RV sites ($30–39) overlook the St. George River. Cabins go for $60 a day. Facilities include a bathhouse, pool, hot tub, laundry facilities, store, and a play area. The river is tidal, so swimming is best near high tide; otherwise, you're dealing with mudflats. It's open mid-May–mid-October.

FOOD

Often overlooked by visitors (but certainly not by locals) is casual **Thomaston Café and Bakery** (154 Main St./Rte. 1, Thomaston, 207/354-8589, 7 A.M.–2 P.M. Mon.–Sat., 8:30 A.M.–1:30 P.M. Sun., and Fri. and Sat. 5:30–8 P.M.). German-born chef Herb Peters and his wife, Eleanor, produce superb pastries, breads, and desserts (eat here or take out). Everything's homemade, there are children's options, the café uses only organic poultry. Try the incredible wild mushroom hash. Beer and wine only. Dinner entrées are $16–22, reservations essential.

INFORMATION AND SERVICES

The Rockland-Thomaston Area Chamber of Commerce (Gateway Center, P.O. Box 508, Rockland 04841, 207/596-0376 or 800/562-2529, www.therealmaine.com) is open 9 A.M.–5 P.M. Monday–Friday and 10 A.M.–2 P.M. Saturday.

The Thomaston Public Library (42 Main St., Thomaston, 207/354-2453) occupies part of the Greek Revival Thomaston Academy.

Cushing Peninsula

Cushing's recorded history goes back at least as far as 1605, when someone named "Abr [maybe Abraham] King"—presumably a member of explorer George Waymouth's crew—inscribed his name here on a ledge (now private property). Since 1789, settlers' saltwater farms have sustained many generations, and the active Cushing Historical Society keeps the memories and memorabilia from fading away. But the outside world knows little of this. Cushing is better known as "Wyeth country," the terrain depicted by the famous artistic dynasty of N. C., Andrew, and Jamie Wyeth (and assorted talented other relatives).

Even though several Wyeths still spend time here, you're not likely to meet any members of the family (unless you hang out near Fales's Store for days on end). However, if

BEANHOLE BEANS

"To be happy in New England," wrote one Joseph P. MacCarthy at the turn of the 20th century, "you must select the Puritans for your ancestors...[and] eat beans on Saturday night." There is no better way to confirm the latter requirement than to attend a "beanhole" bean supper – a real-live legacy of colonial times, with dinner baked in a hole in the ground.

Generally scheduled, appropriately, for a Saturday night (check local newspapers), a beanhole bean supper demands plenty of preparation from its hosts – and a secret ingredient or two. (Don't even think about trying to pry the recipe out of the cooks.) The supper always includes hot dogs, cole slaw, relishes, home-baked breads, and homemade desserts, but the beans are the star attraction. (Typically, the suppers are also alcohol-free.) Not only are they feasts; they're also bargains, never setting you back more than about $8.

The beans at the Broad Cove Church's annual mid-July beanhole bean supper, served family-style at long picnic tables, are legendary – attracting nearly 200 eager diners. Minus the secrets, here's what happens:

Early Friday morning: Church volunteers load 10 pounds of dry pea and soldier (yellow-eye) beans into each of four large kettles and add water to cover. The beans are left to soak and soften for 6-7 hours. Two or three volunteers uncover the churchyard's four rock-lined beanholes (each about three feet deep), fill the holes with hardwood kindling, ignite the wood,

and keep the fires burning until late afternoon, when the wood is reduced to red-hot coals.

Early Friday afternoon: The veteran chefs parboil the beans and stir in the seasonings. Typical additions are brown sugar, molasses, mustard, salt, pepper, and salt pork (much of the secret is in the exact proportions). When the beans are precooked to the cooks' satisfaction, the kettle lids are secured with wire and the pots are lugged outdoors.

Friday midafternoon: With the beans ready to go underground, some of the hot coals are quickly shoveled out of the pits. The kettles are lowered into the pits and the coals replaced around the sides of the kettles and atop their lids. The pits are covered with heavy sheet metal and topped with a thick layer of sand and a tarpaulin. The round-the-clock baking begins, and no one peeks before it's finished.

Saturday midafternoon: Even the veterans start getting nervous just before the pits are uncovered. Was the seasoning right? Did too much water cook away? Did the beans dry out? Not to worry, though – failures just don't happen here.

Saturday night: When a pot is excavated for the first of three seatings (about 5 P.M.), the line is already long. The chefs check their handiwork and the supper begins. No one seems to mind waiting for the second and third seatings – while others eat, a sing-along gets under way in the church, keeping everyone entertained.

© TOM NANGLE

The Olson House inspired many of Andrew Wyeth's works.

you're an Andrew Wyeth fan, visiting Cushing will give you the feeling of walking through his paintings. The flavor of his Maine work is here—rolling fields, wildflower meadows, rocky tidal coves, broad vistas, character-filled farmhouses, and some well-hidden summer enclaves. The only retail businesses are a general store, a few farmstands, and a seasonal take-out—plus a campground on the Cushing/Thomaston town line.

SIGHTS

Cushing's town boundary begins 1.3 miles south of Route 1 (take Wadsworth St. at the Maine State Prison Showroom Outlet). Two miles farther, you'll pass giant wooden sculptures in the yard of the late artist **Bernard Langlais,** who died in 1977.

Six miles from Route 1 is the **A. S. Fales and Son Store** (locally, just "Fales's Store"), Cushing's heart and soul—source of fuel, film, gossip, and groceries. Built in 1889, the store has been in the Fales family ever since. Just beyond the store, take the left fork, continuing down the peninsula toward the Broad Cove Church and the Olson House.

Broad Cove Church

Andrew Wyeth aficionados will recognize the Broad Cove Church as one of his subjects—alongside Cushing Road en route to the Olson House. Most days, it's open, so step inside and admire the classic New England architecture. The church is also well known as the site of one of the region's best beanhole bean suppers, held on a Saturday mid-July and attracting several hundred appreciative diners. (See the sidebar *Beanhole Beans.*) Bear left at the fork after Fales's Store; the church is 0.4 mile farther, on the right.

The Olson House

Many an art lover makes the pilgrimage to the Olson House (11 A.M.–4 P.M. daily late May–mid-Oct., $4), a famous icon near the end of Hathorn Point Road. The early-19th-century farmhouse appears in Andrew Wyeth's 1948 painting *Christina's World* (which hangs in

PENOBSCOT BAY

New York's Museum of Modern Art), his best-known image of the disabled Christina Olson, who died in 1968. In 1991, two philanthropists donated the Olson House to the Farnsworth Art Museum in Rockland (an $11 combination ticket includes Farnsworth admission), which has retained the house's sparse, lonely, and almost mystical ambience. The clapboards outside remain unpainted, the interior walls bear only a few Wyeth prints (hung close to the settings they depict), and it is easy to sense Wyeth's inspiration for chronicling this place. From Route 1 in Thomaston, at the Maine State Prison Showroom Outlet, turn onto Wadsworth Street and go six miles to Fales's Store. Take the left fork after the store, go 1.5 miles, and turn left onto Hathorn Point Road. Go another 1.9 miles to the house.

St. George Peninsula

Even though the Cushing and St. George Peninsulas face each other across the St. George River, they differ dramatically. Cushing is far more rural, seemingly less approachable—with little access to the surrounding waters; St. George has a whole string of things to do and see, and places to sleep and eat—plus shore access in various spots along the peninsula.

The St. George Peninsula is actually better known by some of the villages scattered along its length: Tenants Harbor, Port Clyde, Wiley's Corner, Spruce Head—plus the smaller neighborhoods of Martinsville, Smalleytown, Glenmere, Long Cove, Hart's Neck, and Clark Island. Each has a distinct personality, determined partly by the different ethnic groups—primarily Brits, Swedes, and Finns—who arrived to work the granite quarries in the 19th century. Wander through the Seaview Cemetery in Tenants Harbor and you'll see the story: row after row of gravestones with names from across the sea.

A more famous former visitor was 19th-century novelist Sarah Orne Jewett, who holed up in an old schoolhouse in Martinsville, paid a weekly rental of $0.50, and wrote *The Country of the Pointed Firs,* a tale about "Dunnet's Landing" (Tenants Harbor).

Today the picturesque peninsula has saltwater farms, tidy hamlets, a striking lighthouse, spruce-edged tidal coves, an active yachting harbor, and, at the tip, a tiny fishing village (Port Clyde), which serves as the springboard to offshore Monhegan Island.

Port Clyde, in fact, may be the best-known community here. (Fortunately, it's no longer called by its unappealing 18th-century name—Herring Gut.) George Waymouth explored Port Clyde's nearby islands in 1605, but you'd never suspect its long tradition. It's a sleepy place, with a general store, an inn, a couple of galleries, and expensive parking.

SIGHTS
Marshall Point
Lighthouse Museum
Not many settings can compare with the spectacular locale of the Marshall Point Lighthouse Museum (Marshall Point Rd., P.O. Box 247, Port Clyde 04855, 207/372-6450, www.marshallpoint.org, 1–5 P.M. Sun.–Fri., 10 A.M.–5 P.M. Sat. late May–mid-Oct., free), a distinctive 1857 lighthouse and park overlooking Port Clyde, the harbor islands, and the passing lobster-boat fleet. Bring a picnic and let the kids run on the lawn (but keep them well back from the shoreline). The tiny museum, in the 1895 keeper's house, displays local memorabilia. The grounds are accessible year-round. Take Route 131 to Port Clyde and watch for signs to the museum.

Marine Education
Visitors are welcome to tour the facilities of **Herring Gut Learning Center** (59 Factory

In the keeper's house at Marshall Point Lighthouse, at the tip of the St. George Peninsula, is a small museum.

Rd., Port Clyde, 207/372-8677, www.herring gut.org, 8 A.M.–4 P.M. Sun.–Fri., $5 donation), a nonprofit marine education facility, with oyster and finfish hatcheries, touch tanks, exhibits, aquaponic greenhouse, and library. The center also hosts an evening lecture series in summer on topics such as sea urchins, climate change, and lobster. Enroll kids ages 5–13 in the one-day, field-based day camps ($35). Programs are organized by age groups and typically include crafts, activities, and specimen identification, collection, and examination.

RECREATION
Swimming and Beachcombing

Drift Inn Beach, on Drift Inn Beach Road (also called Candy's Cove Rd.), isn't a big deal as beaches go, but it's the best public one on the peninsula, so it gets busy on hot days. The name comes from the Drift Inn, an early-20th-century summer hotel. Drift Inn Beach Road parallels Route 131, and the parking lot

is accessible from both roads. Heading south on the peninsula, about 3.5 miles after the junction with Route 73, turn left at Drift Inn Beach Road. The sign frequently disappears; watch for an imposing square granite house and a red farm on your left. Go 0.2 mile from the turn.

Sea Kayaking

The St. George Peninsula is especially popular for sea kayaking, with plenty of islands to add interest and shelter. **Port Clyde Kayaks** (440 Glenmere Rd., Port Clyde, 207/372-8128, www.portclydekayaks.com) offers 2.5-hour ($55) and four-hour ($69) guided tours around the tip of the peninsula, taking in Marshall Point lighthouse and the islands. Other options include full moon, starlight, kayak fishing, and, for experienced paddlers only, a puffin tour. Ask about multiday camping or B&B tours.

If you've had experience, you can launch on the ramp just before the causeway that

PENOBSCOT BAY

links the mainland with Spruce Head Island, in Spruce Head (Island Rd., off Rte. 73). Parking is limited. A great paddle goes clockwise around Spruce Head Island and nearby Whitehead (there's a lighthouse on its southeastern shore) and Norton Islands. Duck in for lunch at Waterman's Beach Lobster. Around new moon and full moon, plan your schedule to avoid low tide near the Spruce Head causeway, or you may become mired in mudflats.

Boat Tours

The best boating experience on this peninsula is a passenger-ferry trip from Port Clyde to offshore **Monhegan Island**—for a day, overnight, or longer. (See *Monhegan Island* for more information on the island.) Perhaps because the private ferry company has a monopoly on this harbor, the trip isn't cheap, and parking adds to the cost, but it's a "must" excursion, so try to factor it into the budget. Port Clyde is the nearest mainland harbor to Monhegan; this service operates all year. **Monhegan-Thomaston Boat Line** (P.O. Box 238, Port Clyde 04855, 207/372-8848, www.monheganboat.com) uses two boats, the *Laura B.,* 70 minutes each way, and the newer *Elizabeth Ann,* 50 minutes. Round-trip tickets are $30 adults, $16 kids 2–12. (Leave your bicycle in Port Clyde; you won't need it on the island.) Reservations are essential in summer, especially for the 10:30 A.M. boat; a $5 pp fee holds the reservation until 75 minutes before departure, so you have to get to the dock early. No deposit is needed for other boats, but show up 30 minutes before departure. Parking in Port Clyde is $4 a day. If a summer day trip is all you can manage, aim for the first or second boat and return on the last one; don't go just for the boat ride.

During the summer, the Monhegan–Thomaston Boat Line also offers 2.5-hour sightseeing cruises, on a varied schedule, including a **Puffin/Nature Cruise and Lighthouse Cruise,** and mid-August–mid-September, a **Fall Fins and Feathers Cruise.** Each costs $24 adult, $10 child.

SHOPPING
Art

The St. George Peninsula has been attracting artists for decades, and galleries pepper the peninsula. Some have been here for years, others started yesterday; most are worth a stop, so keep an eye out for their signs. In early August, a number of renowned artists usually coordinate on an open-studio weekend.

The Drawing Room Gallery (863 River Rd., St. George, 207/372-6242) mounts several theme-based group shows each summer. Philip and Barbara Anderson's gallery is just north of the junction with Route 73, about five miles south of Route 1.

Overlooking the reversing falls in downtown South Thomaston, **The Old Post Office Gallery** (Spruce Head Rd., Rte. 73, South Thomaston, 207/594-9396, www.artofthesea.com) has 11 rooms filled with marine art and antiques: ship models, prints, paintings, sculpture, scrimshaw, and jewelry.

Since 1972, Tony Oliveri has been the inspiration and the artisan behind **Keag River Pottery** (Westbrook St., South Thomaston, 207/594-7915), a small shop attached to his home just 0.1 mile off Route 73 (or 2.2 miles east of Rte. 131). He produces brilliantly glazed functional wares, such as bowls, dishes, and lamps, and readily accepts commissions.

Newer on the scene is George Pearlman's **St. George Pottery** (1012 River Rd., St. George, 207/372-6464, www.stgeorge pottery.com). His work pushes the boundaries of traditional forms.

Used Books

Drive up to the small parking area at **Lobster Lane Book Shop** (Island Rd., Spruce Head, 207/594-7520), and you'll see license plates from everywhere. The tiny shop, in a crammed but well-organized shed that's been here since the 1960s, has 50,000 or so treasures for used-book fans. For a few dollars, you can stock up on a summer's worth of reading. The shop is just under a mile east of

Route 73, with eye-catching vistas in several directions (except, of course, when Spruce Head's infamous fog sets in).

General Store

Despite periodic ownership changes, **Port Clyde General Store** (Rte. 131, Port Clyde, 207/372-6543) remains a character-ful destination, a two-century-old country store with a few yuppie touches. Stock up on groceries, pick up a newspaper, order a pizza, or buy a sweatshirt (you may need it on the Monhegan boat). It's open 6 A.M.–9 P.M. daily in summer, shorter hours the rest of the year. Out back is the Dip Net Restaurant, a great place to eat on the dock (see *Food*).

ACCOMMODATIONS
Inns

The dreamy island-dotted, oceanfront setting complements **The East Wind Inn** (Mechanic St., P.O. Box 149, Tenants Harbor 04860, 207/372-6366 or 800/241-8439, www.eastwindinn.com, $109–201 peak), the perfect rendition of an old-fashioned country inn—some parts of it more old-fashioned than others. Built in 1860 and originally used as a sail loft, it has a huge veranda, a cozy parlor, harbor-view rooms, and a quiet dining room with a creditable New England menu. Rooms are divided between the main inn, some with shared bath, and the spiffed-up 19th-century Meeting House, a former sea captain's home, which also has one apartment. All rates include a full breakfast. The water-view dining room is open to the public daily for breakfast (7:30–9:30 A.M., to 10 A.M. in July and Aug.) and dinner (5:30–8:30 P.M., to 9:30 P.M. in July and Aug.). Dinner entrées are $17–26. Reservations are wise. Lunch is available in summer at a dockside take-out. Children are welcome; pets are $15 per visit. The inn is open all year; the dining room is open April–November.

Bed-and-Breakfasts

The oceanfront **Blue Lupin** (372 Waterman's Beach Rd., South Thomaston, 207/594-2673, www.bluelupinbandb.com, $88–155) has an out-of-this-world view in an off-the-beaten-track locale. Bring a sea kayak and launch it from the beach. Or bring a bicycle to explore the area. Or simply settle in with a book or a movie. Next door is Waterman's Beach Lobster (see *Food*). It's open all year, but call ahead off-season.

In the center of South Thomaston village but overlooking the reversing falls on the tidal Wessaweskeag River, the 1830 **Weskeag at the Water** (14 Elm St., Rte. 73, P.O. Box 213, South Thomaston 04858, 207/596-6676 or 800/596-5576, www.midcoast.com/~weskeag, $120–155) has nine rooms, of which four have private baths; one has a whirlpool tub. This place is especially relaxing; congenial innkeepers Gray and Lynne Smith provide guests with games, puzzles, books, a huge video library, a great deck, and a lawn stretching to the river. Bring your sea kayak and bicycles. It's 1.5 miles from the Owls Head Transportation Museum (the Smiths love vintage cars) and a few more miles from the restaurants of downtown Rockland. It's open all year.

Smack-dab in the middle of Port Clyde, the **Seaside Inn** (5 Cold Storage Rd., P.O. Box 215, Port Clyde 04855, 207/372-0700 or 800/279-5041, www.seasideportclyde.com, $109–149) is an unfussy 1850s sea captain's home with both private and shared baths. A first-floor library has books, puzzles, TV, and a fireplace. Rates include a full breakfast. On the premises is a gallery showing the works of more than a dozen artists.

Camping

The third generation now operates **Lobster Buoy Campsites** (280 Waterman's Beach Rd., South Thomaston, 207/596-7546, www.lobsterbuoycampsites.com, $20–27), an oceanfront campground, with 40 sites, 28 with water and electric, all with fire ring and picnic table. You can launch a canoe or kayak from the small, sand beach. Rates cover two adults, two kids under 12, and one vehicle; one dog is allowed per site. Most sites are open, but a few tenting sites are in the trees. Every evening in July and August, homemade pies are sold in the Day Room.

FOOD

All these restaurants are seasonal.

Picnic Fare

Don't be surprised to see the handful of tables occupied at the **Keag Store** (Rte. 73, Village Center, South Thomaston, 207/596-6810, 6 A.M.–9 P.M. Mon.–Sat. and 7 A.M.–8 P.M. Sun.), one of the most popular lunch stops in the area. (Keag, by the way, is pronounced GIG—short for "Wessaweskeag.") Roast-turkey sandwiches with stuffing ($4.50) are a big draw, as is the pizza, which verges on the greasy but compensates with its flavor—no designer toppings, just good pizza. Order it all to go and head across the street to the public wharf, where you can hang out and observe all the comings and goings.

Another good spot for picnic fare is the **Port Clyde General Store** (Rte. 131, Port Clyde, 207/372-6543).

Casual Dining

The decidedly old-fashioned **Craignair Inn Restaurant** (Clark Island Rd., off Rte. 71, Spruce Head, 207/594-7644, www.craignair .com), built in 1928 to house granite workers, serves dinner in its waterview dining room daily except Sunday, entrées $16–24. Seafood is the specialty. Also in the Main Inn and Vestry Annex are rooms, some with shared baths, $80–154 with breakfast.

Seafood is everything at **The Harpoon** (Drift Inn and Marshall Point Rds., Port Clyde, 207/372-6304, www.the-harpoon .com, 5–9 P.M., to 10 P.M. Fri. and Sat.) and it's about as fresh as it gets. Steaks are also on the menu, along with Cajun dishes ($17–23). Lobster's available, but save that for an outdoor deck (see *Lobster in the Rough*). Rebuilt from the ashes of an early 1990s fire, the in-formal restaurant is just over a low hill from the center of Port Clyde.

Lobster in the Rough

These open-air lobster wharves are the best places in the area to get down and dirty and manhandle a steamed or boiled lobster.

Out back behind the Port Clyde General Store, and overlooking the Port Clyde lobster-boat fleet, is the **Dip Net** (Rte. 131, Port Clyde, 207/372-6307, www.dipnetrestaurant .com, open 11 A.M.–10 P.M. daily mid-May–mid-Sept.) with indoor and outdoor seating. It's all quite casual. The menu emphasizes seafood, with a raw bar, light fare ($4.50–9) and more substantial choices ($9–20) available. It's a great place for a shore dinner: lobster, clams, mussels, corn, and bread, at market price.

Poking right into Wheeler's Bay, **Miller's Lobster Company** (Eagle Quarry Rd., off Rte. 73, Spruce Head, 207/594-7406, www .millerslobster.com, 11 A.M.–7 P.M. daily) is the quintessential lobster pound, a well-run operation that draws crowds all summer long. Lobster rolls, steamed clams, crabmeat rolls, homemade pies—the works. Even hot dogs if you need them. Several picnic tables are under cover for chilly or rainy weather. BYOB.

A broad view of islands in the Mussel Ridge Channel is the bonanza at ◖ **Waterman's Beach Lobster** (343 Waterman's Beach Rd., South Thomaston, 207/596-7819, 11 A.M.–7 P.M. Thurs.–Sun.). This tiny operation has a big reputation: It's won a James Beard Award. It turns out well-stuffed lobster and crabmeat rolls and superb pies. Step up to the window and place your order. Service can be slow, but why rush with a view like this? Choose a good day; there's no real shelter from bad weather. BYOB; no credit cards. Next door to the Blue Lupin B&B, the wharf is on a side road off Route 73 between Spruce Head Village and South Thomaston; watch for signs on Route 73.

Monhegan Island

Eleven or so miles from the mainland lies a unique island community with gritty lobstermen, close-knit families, a can-do spirit, a longstanding summertime artists' colony, no cars, astonishingly beautiful scenery, and some of the best birding on the Eastern Seaboard. Until the 1980s, the island had only radiophones and generator power; with the arrival of electricity and real phones, the pace has quickened a bit—but not much. Welcome to Monhegan Island.

But first a cautionary note: Monhegan has remained idyllic largely because generations of residents, part-timers, and visitors have been ultrasensitive to its fragility. When you buy your ferry ticket, you'll receive a copy of the regulations, all very reasonable, and the captain of your ferry will repeat them. *Heed them or don't go.*

Many of the regulations have been developed by The Monhegan Associates, an island land trust founded in the 1960s by Theodore Edison, son of the inventor. Firmly committed to preservation of the island in as natural a state as possible, the group maintains and marks the trails, sponsors natural-history talks, and insists that no construction be allowed beyond the village limits.

The origin of the name Monhegan remains up in the air; it's either a Maliseet or Micmac name meaning "out-to-sea island" or an adaptation of the name of a French explorer's daughter. In any case, Monhegan caught the attention of Europeans after English explorer John Smith stopped by in 1614, but the island had already been noticed by earlier adventurers, including John Cabot, Giovanni da Verrazzano, and George Waymouth. Legend even has it that Monhegan fishermen sent dried fish to Plimoth Plantation during the Pilgrims' first winter on Cape Cod. Captain Smith returned home and carried on about Monhegan, snagging the attention of intrepid souls who established a fishing/trading outpost here in 1625. Monhegan has been settled continuously since 1674, with fishing as the economic base.

In the 1880s, lured by the spectacular setting and artist Robert Henri's enthusiastic reports, gangs of artists began arriving, lugging their easels here and there to capture the surf, the light, the tidy cottages, the magnificent headlands, fishing boats, even the islanders' craggy features. American, German, French, and British artists have long (and continue to) come

TEN RULES FOR MONHEGAN VISITORS

1. Smoking is banned everywhere except in the village.
2. Rock climbing is not allowed on the wild headlands on the back side of the island.
3. Preserve the island's wild state – do not remove flowers or lichens.
4. Bicycles and strollers are not allowed on island trails.
5. Camping and campfires are forbidden islandwide.
6. Swim only at Swim Beach, just south of the ferry landing – if your innards can stand the shock. Wait for the incoming tide, when the water is warmest (and this warmth is relative). It's wise not to swim alone.
7. Dogs must be leashed; carry a pooper-scooper to remove their waste.
8. Be respectful of private property; stay on the trails. (As the island visitors guide puts it, "Monhegan is a village, not a theme park.")
9. If you're staying overnight, bring a flashlight; the village paths are very dark.
10. Carry the island trail map when you go exploring; you'll need it.

A strong suggestion: Carry a trash bag, use it, and take it off the island when you leave.

Monhegan's harbor is sheltered by Manana Island, once home to a renowned hermit.

here; well-known signatures associated with Monhegan include Rockwell Kent, George Bellows, Edward Hopper, James Fitzgerald, Andrew Winter, Alice Kent Stoddard, Reuben Tam, William Kienbusch, and Jamie Wyeth.

Officially called Monhegan Plantation, the island has about 75 year-rounders. Several hundred others summer here. A handful of students attend the tiny school through eighth grade; high-schoolers have to pack up and move "inshore" to the mainland during the school year.

For years, Monhegan's lobster-fishing season—a legislatively sanctioned period—perversely began on December 1 (locally known as Trap Day), but in 2007, that was moved forward to October 1, making it possible for visitors to view the action. An air of nervous anticipation surrounds the dozen or so lobstermen after midnight the day before as they prepare to steam out to set their traps on the ocean floor. Of course, with the lack of competition from mainland fishermen that time of year, and a supply of lobsters fatten-

ing up since the previous June, there's a ready market for their catch. But success still depends on a smooth "setting." Meetings are held daily during the month beforehand to make sure everyone will be ready to "set" together. The season ends on June 25.

Almost within spitting distance of Monhegan's dock (but you'll still need a boat) is whale-shaped **Manana Island,** once the home of an ex-New Yorker named Ray Phillips. Known as the Hermit of Manana, Phillips lived a solitary sheepherding existence on this barren island for more than half a century until his death in 1975. His story had spread so far afield that even *The New York Times* ran a front-page obituary when he died. (Photos and clippings are displayed in the Monhegan Museum.) In summer, youngsters with skiffs often hang around the harbor, particularly Fish Beach and Swim Beach, and you can usually talk one of them into taking you over, for a fee. (Don't try to talk them down too much or they may not return to pick you up.) Some curious inscriptions on Manana (marked with a yellow X near the boat landing) have led archaeologists to claim that Vikings even made it here, but cooler heads attribute the markings to Mother Nature.

When to Go

If a day trip is all your schedule will allow, visit Monhegan between Memorial Day weekend and mid-October, when ferries from Port Clyde, New Harbor, and Boothbay Harbor operate daily, allowing 5–9 hours on the island—time enough to do an extensive trail loop, visit the museum and handful of shops, and picnic on the rocks. Other months, there's only one ferry a day from Port Clyde (only three a week Nov.–April), so you'll need to spend the night—not a hardship, but definitely requiring planning.

Almost any time of year, but especially in spring, fog can blanket the island, curtailing photography and swimming (although usually not the ferries). A spectacular sunny day can't be beat, but the fog lends an air of mystery you won't forget, so don't be deterred. Rain, of course, is another matter; some island trails can be perilous even in a misty drizzle.

Other Points to Consider

Monhegan has no bank, but there are a couple of ATMs. Credit cards are not accepted everywhere. Personal checks, travelers checks, or cash will do. The few public telephones in the village require phone credit cards.

The only public restroom unconnected to a restaurant or lodging is on Horn Hill, at the southern end of the village (near the Monhegan House), and it will cost you $1 to use it. Outrageous, perhaps, but the restroom was installed to protect the woods and trails and deter day-trippers from bothering innkeepers. Unfortunately, the fee inspires some people to spurn these facilities and head for the woods. Please spend the dollar and preserve the island.

SIGHTS AND RECREATION

Monhegan is a getaway destination, a relaxing place for self-starters, so don't anticipate organized entertainment beyond the occasional lecture or narrated nature tour. Bring sturdy shoes (maybe even an extra pair in case trails are wet), a windbreaker, binoculars, a camera, and perhaps a sketchpad or a journal. If you're staying overnight, bring a flashlight for negotiating the unlighted island walkways, even in the village. For rainy days, bring a book. (If you forget, there's an amazingly good library.) In winter, bring ice skates for use on the Ice Pond.

◖ Monhegan Museum

The National Historic Register **Monhegan Lighthouse**—activated in July 1824 and automated in 1959—stands at the island's highest point, Lighthouse Hill, an exposed summit that's also home to the **Monhegan Historical and Cultural Museum** (207/596-7003, www.monheganmuseum.org, 11:30 A.M.–3:30 P.M. daily July and Aug., 12:30–2:30 P.M. daily June and Sept.) in the former keeper's house and adjacent buildings. Overseen by the Monhegan Historical and Cultural Museum Association, the museum contains an antique kitchen, lobstering exhibits, and a fine collection of paintings by noted and not-so-noted artists. Two outbuildings have tools and gear connected with fishing and ice-cutting, traditional island industries. The assistant lightkeeper's house, recently restored top to bottom as a handsome art gallery, provides a climate-controlled environment for the museum's impressive art collection. A volunteer usually is on hand to answer questions. Admission is technically free, but donations are encouraged.

Artists' Studios

Nearly 20 artists' studios are open to the public during the summer (usually July and Aug.), but not all at once. At least five are open most days—most in the afternoon (Mon. has the fewest choices). Sometimes it's tight timewise for day-trippers who also want to hike the trails, but most of the studios are relatively close to the ferry landing. An annually updated map/schedule details locations, days, and times. It's posted on bulletin boards in the village and is available at lodgings and shops.

PENOBSCOT BAY

Hiking/Walking

Just over a half mile wide and 1.7 miles long, barely a square mile in area, Monhegan has 18 numbered hiking trails, most easy to moderate, covering about 17 miles. All are described in the *Monhegan Associates Trail Map* (www .monheganassociates.org), available at mainland ferry offices and island shops and lodgings or on the website. (The map is not to scale, so the hikes can take longer than you think.)

The footing is uneven everywhere, so Monhegan can present major obstacles to those with disabilities, even on the well-worn but unpaved village roads. Maintain an especially healthy respect for the ocean here, and don't venture too close; through the years, rogue waves on the island's backside have claimed victims young and old.

A relatively easy **day-tripper loop,** with a couple of moderate sections along the backside of the island, takes in several of Monhegan's finest features starting at the southern end of the village, opposite the church. To appreciate it, allow at least two hours. From the Main Road, go up Horn Hill, following signs for the **Burnthead Trail** (no. 4). Cross the island to the **Cliff Trail** (no. 1). Turn north on the Cliff Trail, following the dramatic headlands on the island's backside. There are lots of great picnic rocks in this area. Continue to Squeaker Cove, where the surf is the wildest, but be cautious. Then watch for signs to the **Cathedral Woods Trail** (no. 11), carpeted with pine needles and leading back to the village.

When you get back to Main Road, detour up the **Whitehead Trail** (no. 7) to the museum. If you're spending the night and feeling energetic, consider circumnavigating the island via the **Cliff Trail** (nos. 1 and 1-A). Allow at least 5–6 hours for this route; don't rush it.

Birding

One of the East Coast's best birding sites during spring and fall migrations, Monhegan is a migrant trap for exhausted creatures winging their way north or south. Avid birders come here to add rare and unusual species to their life lists, and some devotees return year after year. No birder should arrive, however, without a copy of the superb *Birder's Guide to Maine* (see *Suggested Reading* under *Resources*).

Predicting exact bird-migration dates can be dicey, since wind and weather aberrations can skew the schedule. Generally, the best times are mid- to late May and most of September, into early October. If you plan to spend a night (or more) on the island during migration seasons, don't try to wing it—reserve a room well in advance.

ACCOMMODATIONS

The island has a variety of lodgings from rustic to comfortable; none qualify in the multistar category. Pickup trucks of dubious vintage meet all the ferries and transport luggage to the lodgings. For cottage renters, Monhegan Trucking charges a small fee for each piece of luggage.

Best lodging is the **◖ Island Inn** (P.O. Box 128, Monhegan 04852, 207/596-0371, www .islandinnmonhegan.com), an imposing three-story mid-19th-century building with an expansive veranda and lawns overlooking the ferry landing. The 32 harbor- and meadow-view rooms and suites (most with private baths) are $145–340 d, high season, including full breakfast, plus a $5 pp charge for a one-night stay. Cash, checks, or travelers checks are preferred. It's open late May–early October.

In the heart of the village, **Monhegan House** (P.O. Box 345, Monhegan 04852, 207/594-7983 or 800/599-7983, www.monheganhouse .com, $77–81 s, $129–185 d peak), built in 1870, is a large four-story building with 33 rooms. All have shared baths, not always on the same floor as your room. Don't miss the loose-leaf notebook in the lobby. Labeled *A Monhegan Novel*, it's the ultimate in shaggy-dog sagas, created by a long string of guests since 1992. Rates include breakfast. There's a $5 pp surcharge for one-night stays. Children are welcome. It's open late May–Columbus Day.

A more modernized hostelry, **Shining Sails** (P.O. Box 346, Monhegan 04852, 207/596-0041, www.shiningsails.com) lacks the quaintness of the other inns, but it's very comfortable, convenient to the dock, stays open all year, and has private baths. Breakfast (included only in season) is continental. Seven first- and second-floor rooms and efficiencies (some with water views) go for $115–180 May–mid-October; rates are lower for multiple nights and off-season stays. "Well-supervised" children are welcome. An additional four apartments are in a separate building and over a restaurant ($160–190). Shining Sails also manages more than two dozen weekly-rental cottages and apartments, with rates beginning around $750/week in season.

The funkiest lodging, and not for everyone, is **The Trailing Yew** (P.O. Box 98, Monhegan 04852, 207/596-0440 or 800/592-2520, www.trailingyew.com, $90 pp). Spread among five rustic buildings south of the village on the road to Lobster Cove are 35 rooms, most with shared baths (averaging five rooms per bath and not always in the same building) and lighted with kerosene (about 12 have electricity). Rates include breakfast and dinner; kids are $25 and up, depending on age. The old-fashioned, low-key 50-seat dining room is open to the public for dinner at 5:45 P.M., served family-style by reservation, and for breakfast at 7:45 A.M. Bring a sleeping bag in spring or fall; rooms are unheated. No credit cards. It's open late May–early October.

FOOD

Most visitors don't arrive on Monhegan expecting gourmet cuisine. Everything is quite casual, and food is hearty and ample. None of the eateries have liquor licenses, so buy beer or wine at the North End Market or the Barnacle Café, or bring it from the mainland. All of the restaurants and food sources are in or close to the village.

Prepared foods, varying from pastries to sandwiches to pizza, are available from **Barnacle Café** (207/596-0371), under the same ownership as the nearby Island Inn, **The Novelty,** behind and operated by The Monhegan House, and **North End Market** (207/594-5546). There's seating at **The Scruffy Dog** (207/594-0949).

If you're hankering for something fancier and more creative, both the **Island Inn** and the **Monhegan House** have restaurants open to the public for breakfast, lunch, and dinner, with prices beginning in the mid-teens for dinner entrées.

You can't get much rougher for lobster in the rough than **Shermie's Fish House** (on Fish Beach, 11:30 A.M.–2:30 P.M. and 4–6:30 P.M. daily). Lobster and crabmeat rolls, locally smoked fish, and homemade stews and chowders are on the menu as well as fresh lobster. Take it to the picnic table on the beach and enjoy.

INFORMATION AND SERVICES
Information

Several free brochures and flyers, revised annually, will answer most questions about planning a day trip or overnight visit to Monhegan. At the ferry ticket office in Port Clyde, pick up the 12-page *Visitor's Guide to Monhegan Island* and the *Monhegan Associates Trail Map.* Both are also available at island shops, galleries, and lodgings, and at the New Harbor and Boothbay Harbor ferry offices. To obtain copies beforehand, contact Monhegan–Thomaston Boat Line (P.O. Box 238, Port Clyde 04855, 207/372-8848, fax 207/372-8547, www.monheganboat.com) around mid-April. Also request a copy of the ferry schedule. For fastest service, send a self-addressed stamped envelope. The Rockland-Thomaston Area Chamber of Commerce also has some information about lodgings and other facilities on Monhegan. Monhegan info is also available online at www.monhegan.com and www.monhegan.info.

Monhegan's pleasant little library, the Jackie and Edward Library, was named after two children who drowned in the surf in the 1920s. The fiction collection is especially extensive, and it's open to everyone. At the head of Wharf Hill, it's usually open 1–4 P.M. Tuesday, Thursday, and Saturday, plus two or three evenings a week; check when you arrive.

Also check the Rope Shed, the community bulletin board next to the meadow, right in the village. Monhegan's version of a bush telegraph, it's where everyone posts flyers and notices about nature walks, lectures, excursions, and other special events. You'll also see the current *Monhegan Artists Studio Locations* map.

GETTING THERE AND AROUND

Ferries travel to Monhegan from Port Clyde year-round (see *Boat Tours* under *Recreation* in the *St. George Peninsula* section for details on cost and schedule). Seasonal service to the island is provided from New Harbor by Hardy Boat Cruises and from Boothbay Harbor by Balmy Days Cruises.

Part of the daily routine for many islanders and summer folk is a stroll to the harbor when the ferry comes in, so don't be surprised to see a good-size welcoming party when you arrive. You're the live entertainment.

Monhegan's only vehicles are a handful of pickup trucks owned by local lobstermen and li'l ol' trucks used by Monhegan Trucking. If you're staying a night or longer and your luggage is too heavy to carry, they'll be waiting when you arrive at the island wharf.

Rockland Area

A "Share the Pride" campaign—kicked off in the 1980s to boost sagging civic self-esteem and the local economy—was the first step in the transformation of Rockland. Once a run-down county seat best known for the aroma of its fish-packing plants, the city has undergone a sea change—most of it for the better. The expansion of the Farnsworth Museum of American Art and the addition of its Wyeth Center was a catalyst. Benches and plants line Main Street (Rte. 1), stores offer appealing wares, coffeehouses and more than a dozen art galleries attract a diverse clientele, and Rockland Harbor is home to more windjammer cruise schooners than neighboring Camden (which had long claimed the title "Windjammer Capital"). If you haven't been to Rockland in the last decade, prepare to be astonished.

Foresighted entrepreneurs had seen the potential of the bayside location in the late 1700s and established a tiny settlement here called "Shore Village" (or "the Shore"). Today's commercial-fishing fleet is one of the few reminders of Rockland's past, when multimasted schooners lined the wharves, some to load volatile cargoes of lime destined to become building material for cities all along the Eastern Seaboard, others to head northeast—toward the storm-racked Grand Banks and the lucrative cod fishery there. Such hazardous pursuits meant an early demise for many a local seafarer, but Rockland's 5,000 or so residents were enjoying their prosperity in the late 1840s. The settlement was home to more than two dozen shipyards and dozens of lime kilns, was enjoying a construction boom, and boasted a newspaper and regular steamship service. By 1854, Rockland had become a city.

Today, Rockland remains a commercial hub—with Knox County's only shopping plazas (not quite malls, but Wal-Mart and other big-box stores have arrived), a fishing fleet that heads far offshore, and ferries that connect nearby islands. Rockland also claims the title of "Lobster Capital of the World"—thanks to Knox County's shipment nationally and internationally of 10 million pounds of lobster each year. (The weathervane atop the police and fire department building is a giant copper lobster.)

With just more than 8,000 souls, Rockland is more year-round community than tourist town. But visitors pour in during two big summer festivals—the North Atlantic Blues Festival in mid-July and the Maine Lobster Festival in early August. Highlight of the Lobster Festival is King Neptune's coronation of the Maine Sea Goddess—carefully selected from a bevy of local young women—who then sails off with him to his watery domain.

© TOM NANGLE

Lobster boats and excursion boats crowd Rockland's harbor.

SIGHTS
⊂ The Farnsworth Art Museum and the Wyeth Center

Anchoring downtown Rockland is the nationally respected Farnsworth Art Museum (16 Museum St., Rockland, 207/596-6457, www .farnsworthmuseum.org), established in 1948 through a trust fund set up by Rocklander Lucy Farnsworth. With an ample checkbook, the first curator, Robert Bellows, toured the country, accumulating a splendid collection of 19th- and 20th-century Maine-related American art—the basis for the permanent *Maine in America* exhibition.

The 6,000-piece collection today includes work by Fitz Hugh Lane, Gilbert Stuart, Eastman Johnson, Childe Hassam, John Marin, Maurice Prendergast, Rockwell Kent, George Bellows, and Marsden Hartley. Best known are the paintings by three generations of the Wyeth family (local summer residents) and sculpture by Louise Nevelson, who grew up in Rockland. Sculpture, jewelry, and paintings by Nevelson form the core of the third-floor Nevelson-Berliawsky Gallery for 20th-Century Art. (The only larger Nevelson collection is in New York's Whitney Museum of American Art.) The new Wyeth Center, across Union Street in a former church, contains the work of Andrew, N. C., and Jamie Wyeth. In the summer of 2000, the Farnsworth opened its 6,000-square-foot Jamien Morehouse Wing, an elegant venue for rotating exhibits.

In the Farnsworth's library—a grand, high-ceilinged oasis akin to an English gentleman's reading room—browsers and researchers can explore an extensive collection of art books and magazines. The museum's hyperactive education department annually sponsors hundreds of lectures, concerts, art classes for adults and children, poetry readings, and field trips. Most are open to nonmembers; some require an extra fee. A glitzy gift shop stocks posters, prints, notecards, imported gift items, and art games for children.

Next door to the museum is the mid-19th-century Greek Revival **Farnsworth Homestead,** with original high-Victorian furnishings. Looking as though William Farnsworth's

WINDJAMMING

In 1936, Camden became the home of the "cruise schooner" (sometimes called "dude schooner") trade when Captain Frank Swift restored a creaky wooden vessel and offered sailing vacations to paying passengers. He kept at it for 25 years, gradually adding other boats to the fleet – and the rest, as they say, is history. Windjammers have become big business on the Maine coast, with Camden and Rockland sparring for the title of Windjammer Capital. Rockland wrested it from Camden in the mid-1990s and so far, has held onto it.

Named for their ability to "jam" into the wind when they carried freight up and down the New England coast, windjammers trigger images of the Great Age of Sail. Most are rigged as schooners, with two or three soaring wooden masts; their lengths range from 64 to 132 feet. Nine are National Historic Landmarks; four were built for the trade.

These windjammers head out for 3-6 days, late May–mid-October, tucking into coves and harbors around Penobscot Bay and its islands. The mostly engineless craft set their itineraries by the wind, propelled by stiff breezes to Buck's Harbor, North Haven, and Deer Isle. Everything's totally informal, geared for relaxing.

You're aboard for the experience, not for luxury, so expect basic accommodations with few frills, although newer vessels were built with passenger trade in mind and tend to be a bit more comfy. Down below, cabins typically are small and basic, with paper-thin walls – sort of a campground afloat (earplugs are often available for light sleepers). It may not sound romantic, but be aware that the captains keep track of postcruise marriages. Most boats have shared showers and toilets. If you're Type-A, given to pacing, don't inflict yourself on the cruising crowd; if you're flexible, ready for whatever, go ahead and sign on. You can help with the sails, eat, curl up with a book, inhale salt air, shoot photos, eat, sunbathe, bird-watch, eat, chat up fellow passengers, sleep, eat, or just settle back and enjoy spectacular sailing you'll never forget.

When you book a cruise, you'll receive all the details and directions, but for a typical six-day trip, you arrive at the boat by 7 P.M. for the captain's call to meet your fellow passengers. You sleep aboard at the dock that night and then depart midmorning Monday and spend five nights and days cruising Penobscot Bay, following the wind, the weather, and the whims of the captain. (Many of the windjammers have no engines, only a motorized yawlboat used as a pusher and a water taxi.) You might anchor in a deserted cove and explore the shore, or you might pull into a harbor and hike, shop, and bar-hop. Then it's back to the boat for chow – windjammer cooks are legendary for creating three hearty, all-you-can-eat meals daily, including at least one lobster feast! When the cruise ends, most passengers find it hard to leave.

On the summer cruising schedule, several weeks coincide with special windjammer events, so you'll need to book a berth far in advance for these: mid-June (Boothbay Harbor's Windjammer Days), July Fourth week (Great Schooner Race), Labor Day weekend (Camden's Windjammer Weekend), and the second week in September (WoodenBoat Sail-In).

Most windjammers offering three- to six-day sails out of Camden, Rockland, and Rockport are members of the **Maine Windjammer Association** (P.O. Box 1144, Blue Hill 04614, 800/807-9463, www.sailmainecoast.com), a one-stop resource for vessel and schedule information.

The majestic *Victory Chimes* windjammer homeports in Rockland.

© TOM NANGLE

At the Owls Head Transportation Museum, the airplanes really do fly.

family just took off for the day, the house has been preserved rather than restored.

The Farnsworth also owns the **Olson House,** 14 miles away in nearby Cushing, where the whole landscape looks like a Wyeth diorama. (See details in the *Cushing Peninsula* section.) Pick up a map at the museum to help you find the house—it's definitely worth the side trip.

The Farnsworth ($10 adults, $8 seniors and students 18 and older, free for kids under 18 and Rockland residents) is open year-round, including summer holidays. Farnsworth hours are 10 A.M.–5 P.M. daily (to 8 P.M. Wed.) in summer, 10 A.M.–5 P.M. Tuesday–Sunday in winter. Call the museum for its current definition of summer and winter. The Homestead (10 A.M.–5 P.M. daily) and the Olson House (11 A.M.–4 P.M. daily) are open late May–mid-October.

◖ Owls Head Transportation Museum

Don't miss this place, even if you're not an old-vehicle buff. A generous endowment has made the Owls Head Transportation Museum (Rte. 73, Owls Head, 207/594-4418, www.ohtm.org, 10 A.M.–4 P.M. daily Nov.–March, $8 adults, $7 seniors, $5 ages 5–17, $20 family, special events are extra), a premier facility for celebrating wings and wheels; it draws more than 75,000 visitors a year. Scads of eager volunteers help restore the vehicles and keep them running. On weekends May–October, the museum sponsors air shows (often including aerobatic displays) and car and truck meets for hundreds of enthusiasts. The season highlight is the annual rally and aerobatic show (early Aug.), when more than 300 vehicles gather for two days of festivities. Want your own vintage vehicle? Attend the antique, classic, and special-interest auto auction (third Sunday in Aug.). The gift shop carries transportation-related items. If the kids get bored (unlikely), there's a play area outside, with picnic tables. In winter, groomed cross-country-skiing trails wind through the museum's 60-acre site. (Ask for a map at the information desk.)

PENOBSCOT BAY

Maine Discovery Center

The headliner at the Maine Discovery Center (1 Park Dr., Rockland) is the **Maine Lighthouse Museum** (207/594-3301, www .mainelighthousemuseum.com, 9 A.M.–5 P.M. Mon.–Fri. and 10 A.M.–4 P.M. Sat. and Sun. late May–mid-Oct., closed Sun.–Wed. in winter, $5, under 12 free), home to the nation's largest collection of Fresnel lenses, along with a boatload-plus of lighthouse, Coast Guard, and maritime-related artifacts. On view are foghorns, ships' bells, nautical books and photographs, marine instruments, ship models, scrimshaw, and so much more.

Also exhibiting at the center are the Farnsworth Art Museum, Maine Lobster Festival, Penobscot Marine Museum, Owls Head Transportation Museum, Rockland Historical Society, Island Institute, and Knox Museum.

Project Puffin Visitor Center

If you can't manage a trip to see the puffins, Audubon's Project Puffin Visitor Center (311 Main St., Rockland, 207/596-5566 or 877/478-3346, www.projectpuffin.org, 10 A.M.–5 P.M. daily, to 7:30 P.M. Wed., June 1–Oct. 31; call for off-season hours) will bring them to you. Live videos of nesting puffins are just one of the highlights of the center, which also includes interactive exhibits, a gallery, and films, all highlighting successful efforts to restore and protect these clowns of the sea.

◖ Rockland Breakwater

Protecting the harbor from wind-driven waves, the 4,346-foot-long Rockland Breakwater took 18 years to build, with 697,000 tons of locally quarried granite. In the late 19th century, it was piled up, chunk by chunk, from a base 175 feet wide on the harbor floor (60 feet below the surface) to the 43-foot-wide cap. The Breakwater Light—now automated—was built in 1902 and added to the National Historic Register in 1981. The city of Rockland owns the keeper's house, but it's maintained by the Friends of the Rockland Breakwater Lighthouse (www .rocklandlighthouse.com). Member volunteers usually open the lighthouse to the

public 9 A.M.–5 P.M. Saturday and Sunday late May–mid-October and for special events. The breakwater provides unique vantage points for photographers, and a place to picnic or catch sea breezes or fish on a hot day, but it is extremely dangerous during storms. Anyone on the breakwater risks being washed into the sea or struck by lightning (ask the local hospital staff: it *has* happened!). Do not take chances when the weather is iffy.

To reach the breakwater, take Route 1 North to Waldo Avenue and turn right. Take the next right onto Samoset Road and drive to the end, to **Marie Reed Memorial Park** (tiny beach, benches, limited parking). Or go to the Samoset Resort and take the path to the breakwater from there.

Main Street Historic District

Rocklanders are justly proud of their Main Street Historic District, lined with 19th- and early-20th-century Greek and Colonial Revival structures, as well as examples of mansard and Italianate architecture. Most now house retail shops on the ground floor; upper floors have offices, artists' studios, and apartments. The district starts at the corner of Winter and Main Streets and runs north to the alley just after Kelsey's Appliances. The chamber of commerce has a map and details.

Flightseeing

Get a gull's-eye view of Coastal Maine riding in an R-44 Raven chopper with **Scenic Helicopters of Maine** (866/596-7006 or 207/596-7006, www.scenic-helicopters.com). Rates begin at $50 pp, minimum two people, for an introductory flight above Rockland and Thomaston covering 5–8 miles. Flights depart from a heliport on Route 1 at the Thomaston/ Rockland line.

For something a bit quieter, soar and swoop on a glider ride with **Spirit Soaring** (207/319-9514, www.spiritsoaring.org). Rates begin at $100 for a half-hour ride over coastal Penobscot Bay. It operates from Knox County Regional Airport in Owls Head, just south of Rockland.

Excursion Train

Ride in restored, vintage railcars on the scenic **Maine Eastern Railroad** (207/596-6725 or 800/637-2457, www.maineeasternrailroad .com), operating between Rockland and Brunswick, with stops in Wiscasset and Bath. The train operates late May–early November, with special holiday trains in December. Adult fares are $40 round-trip, $25 one-way; ages 5–15 pay $15; seniors are $35/$25; family rate is $100/$75 covering two adults and two kids. Packages with lodging, meals, and theater are available.

PARKS AND RECREATION
🄲 Owls Head Light State Park

On Route 73, about 1.5 miles past the junction of Routes 1 and 73, you'll reach North Shore Road in the town of Owls Head. Turn left, toward Owls Head Light State Park. Standing 3.6 miles from this turn, Owls Head Light occupies a dramatic promontory with panoramic views over Rockland Harbor and Penobscot Bay. Don't miss it. The keeper's house and the light tower are off-limits, but the park surrounding the tower has easy walking paths, picnic tables, and a pebbly beach where you can sunbathe or check out Rockland Harbor's boating traffic. (If it's foggy or rainy, don't climb the steps toward the light tower: The view evaporates in the fog, the access ramp can be slippery, and the foghorn is dangerously deafening.) Follow signs to reach the park. From North Shore Road, turn left onto Main Street, then left onto Lighthouse Road, and continue along Owls Head Harbor to the parking area. This is also a particularly pleasant bike route—about 10 miles round-trip from downtown Rockland—although, once again, the roadside shoulders are poor along the Owls Head stretch.

Swimming

Lucia Beach is the local name for **Birch Point Beach State Park,** one of the best-kept secrets in the area. In Owls Head, just south of Rockland—and not far from Owls Head Light—the spruce-lined sand crescent (free; outhouses but no other facilities) has rocks, shells, tide pools, and very chilly water. There's ample room for a moderate-size crowd, although parking and turnaround space can get a bit tight on the access road. From downtown Rockland, take Route 73 one mile to North Shore Drive (on your left). Take the next right, Ash Point Drive, and continue past Knox County Regional Airport to Dublin Road. Turn right, go 0.8 mile, then turn left onto Ballyhac Road (opposite the airport landing lights). Go another 0.8 mile, fork left, and continue 0.4 mile to the parking area.

If frigid ocean water doesn't appeal, head for freshwater **Chickawaukee Lake,** on Route 17, two miles inland from downtown Rockland. Don't expect to be alone, though; on hot days, **Johnson Memorial Park**'s pocket-size sand patch is a major attraction. A lifeguard holds forth; there are restrooms, picnic tables, a snack bar, and a boat-launch ramp. (In winter, iceboats, snowmobiles, and ice-fishing shacks take over the lake.) A signposted bicycle path runs alongside the busy highway, making the park an easy pedal from town.

Golf

The **Rockland Golf Club** (606 Old County Rd., Rockland, 207/594-9322, www.rockland golf.com, Apr.–Oct.), an 18-hole course 0.2 mile northeast of Route 17, ranks high on many a Maine golfer's list. In July and August, you'll need to reserve a starting time a day or so in advance if you plan to tee off anytime after 7 A.M. The modern clubhouse—rebuilt after a disastrous fire in the late 1980s—has a full bar and serves breakfast and lunch at reasonable prices. Parking is plentiful.

For an 18-hole course in an unsurpassed waterfront setting (but steep rental and greens fees), check out the links at the **Samoset Resort** (220 Warrenton St., Rockport, 207/594-2511 or 800/341-1650, www.samoset .com), technically in Rockport but most often reached via Rockland.

Sea Kayaking

Veteran Maine Guide and naturalist Mark Di-Girolamo is the sparkplug behind **Breakwater Kayak** (Rockland Public Landing, Rockland,

207/596-6895 or 877/559-8800, www.break waterkayak.com), which has a full range of tours, even multiday ones. A two-hour Rockland Harbor tour (usually offered three times a day at the height of summer) is $35, and the all-day Owls Head Lighthouse tour is $95, including lunch. Reservations are advisable. This outfit is particularly eco-sensitive—Mark has a degree in environmental science, definitely worth supporting. Maine Audubon often taps Mark to lead natural-history field trips. Dress warmly for these tours and be sure to bring a filled water bottle.

Boating Excursions

Marine biologist Captain Bob Pratt is the skipper of *A Morning in Maine* (207/594-1844 or 207/691-7245 seasonal boat phone, www .amorninginmaine.com), a classic 55-foot ketch designed by noted naval architect R. D. (Pete) Culler and built by Concordia Yachts. From June through October, *Morning* departs from the middle pier at the Rockland Public Landing three times daily for two-hour sails ($30), with plenty of knowledgeable commentary from Captain Pratt. A 6 P.M. sunset sail is available in July and August. Inquire about boat-and-breakfast overnights, which run $500 per couple and include a sail, lobster dinner, and continental breakfast.

Watch Captain Steve Hale set and haul lobster traps on a cruise aboard the *Captain Jack* (Rockland Harbor, 207/594-1048, www .captainjacklobstertours.com) during a 1.25-hour cruise aboard a 30-foot working lobster boat. Cruises depart five times daily, Monday–Saturday May–September; $25 adult, $15 kids under 12. Note: There are no toilets aboard. On Saturday and Sunday, Captain Jack offers a two-hour dinner cruise that includes a lobster feed with fixings for $50 pp. Reservation required; minimum two people for a trip.

Bicycling

Rentals, sales, repair, and twice-weekly group rides are provided by **Bikesenjava** (481 Main St., Rockland 207/596-1004, www.hay bikesenjava.com).

ENTERTAINMENT AND EVENTS

Stop by the **Lincoln Street Center for Arts and Education** (24 Lincoln St., Rockland, 207/594-6490, www.lincolnstreetcenter.org), a community arts center with exhibitions, performances, and classes, to see what's on the schedule.

The historic **Strand Theater** (339 Main St., 207/594-7266, www.rocklandstrand.com), opened in 1923, underwent an extensive restoration in 2005. Films as well as live entertainment are scheduled. It's also the venue for many **Bay Chamber Concerts** (207/236-2823 or 888/707-2770, www.baychamberconcerts .org) events.

The Farnsworth Museum and nearly two dozen galleries stay open until 8 P.M. every Wednesday June–mid-September for **Arts in Rockland** events, with art openings coordinated once each month.

In mid-July, the **North Atlantic Blues Festival** means a weekend of festivities featuring big names in blues. Thousands of fans jam Harbor Park for the nonstop music.

August's **Maine Lobster Festival** is a five-day lobster extravaganza, with live entertainment, the Maine Sea Goddess pageant, a lobster-crate race, craft booths, boat rides, a parade, lobster dinners, and megacrowds (the hotels are full for miles in either direction). Tons of lobsters bite the dust during the weekend—despite annual protests by the People for the Ethical Treatment of Animals. (The protests, however, seem only to increase the crowds.)

SHOPPING

Piggybacking on the fame of the Farnsworth Museum, or at least working symbiotically, art galleries line Rockland's main and many side streets. Ask around and look around. During the summer, many of them coordinate monthly openings (usually a Wednesday evening) so you can meander and munch (and sip) from one gallery to another.

Across from the Farnsworth's side entrance, the **Caldbeck Gallery** (12 Elm St., Rockland, 207/594-5935, www.caldbeck.com) has gained a top-notch reputation as a "must-see" (and "must-be-seen") space. Featuring the work of contemporary Maine artists, the gallery mounts more than half a dozen solo and group shows each year, May–September.

Eric Hopkins Gallery (21 Winter St., Rockland, 207/594-1996, www.erichopkins.com) shows the North Haven artist's colorful, aerial-view paintings.

Archipelago (Main St., Rockland, 207/596-0701), on the ground floor of the Island Institute (a nonprofit steward of Maine's 4,617 offshore islands), is an attractive retail outlet for talented craftspeople from 14 year-round islands.

Other eminently browsable downtown Rockland galleries are **Harbor Square Gallery** (374 Main St., 207/594-8700 or 877/594-8700), **Lucky Dog Gallery** (485 Main St., 207/596-0120), **Landing Gallery** (8 Elm St., 888/394-2787), and **Nan Mulford Gallery** (313 Main St., 207/594-8481). All are within steps of each other.

ACCOMMODATIONS

If you're planning an overnight stay in the Rockland area the first weekend in August, make reservations well in advance. Unless you're planning on attending the Lobster Festival, consider staying elsewhere then.

Samoset Resort

The 221-acre waterfront Samoset Resort (220 Warrenton St., Rockport, 207/594-2511 or 800/341-1650, www.samoset.com) straddles the boundary between Rockland and Rockport, the next town to the north. Most guests get to it via Rockland, from the south. Built on the ashes of a classic, 19th-century summer hotel, the Samoset is a top-of-the-line modern resort with knockout ocean views from most of its 178 rooms and suites, all refurbished in 2007, plus 72 separate town houses. Peak-season (early July–Labor Day) doubles go for $265–350, suites are $299–549. Room amenities include flat-screen TV, air-conditioning, and Wi-Fi. Conferences go on here throughout the year, but it's also a great family place, particularly off-season—with special package rates, indoor and outdoor swimming pools, fitness center, lighted tennis courts, cross-country skiing, children's day camp ($50, including lunch, ages 5–12), golf simulator, and a fabulous 18-hole waterfront golf course. On-site are a fine-dining restaurant and a casual lounge, serving light fare and with entertainment in summer.

Motel

Directly opposite the ferry terminal for boats going to the islands of Vinalhaven, North Haven, and Matinicus, the 81-room **Navigator Motor Inn** (520 Main St., Rockland, 207/594-2131 or 800/545-8026, www.navigatorinn.com, $95–155) is a five-story shingled place with TV, air-conditioning, phones, refrigerators, and laundry facilities. Rooms are basic motel-style, but upper-floor ones have plenty of space and great views of the harbor (be prepared for traffic noise from the parking lot and street). Pets are allowed in some rooms. The bright, modern Portsider Grill and Pub serves lunch and dinner year-round, and breakfast during summer, but you're just steps from Rockland's Main Street restaurants.

Bed-and-Breakfasts

These B&Bs are in Rockland's historic district, within easy walking distance of downtown attractions and restaurants, and are members of the **Historic Inns of Rockland Maine** (www.historicinnsofrockland.com), which coordinates such great off-season events as Pies on Parade and the Chocolate March.

Most elegant is **[The Berry Manor Inn** (81 Talbot Ave., P.O. Box 1117, Rockland 04841, 207/596-7696 or 800/774-5692, www.berrymanorinn.com, $155–255), on a quiet side street a few blocks from downtown. Cheryl Michaelsen and Michael LaPosta have totally restored the manse built in 1898 by wealthy Rocklander Charles Berry as a wedding gift for his wife (thoughtful fellow). High ceilings and wonderful Victorian architectural touches are everywhere, especially in the enormous front hall and two parlors. Eight second- and third-floor Victorian-decor rooms and four ultraluxurious suites in the adjacent Carriage

House have private baths, gas fireplaces, air-conditioning, hair dryers, dataports, journals, and more; many have whirlpools. In-room TV upon request. A guest pantry is stocked with free soda and juices and sweets, not that you'll be hungry after the extravagant breakfasts.

Opened in 1996, the **Captain Lindsey House Inn** (5 Lindsey St., P.O. Box 864, Rockland 04841, 207/596-7950 or 800/523-2145, www.lindseyhouse.com, $156–211) is more like a boutique hotel than a B&B. The Barnes family gutted the 1835 brick structure and restored it dramatically, adding such modernities as phones, air-conditioning, Wi-Fi, and TV. The décor is strikingly handsome, not at all fussy or frilly. Don't miss the 1926 safe in the front hall or the hidden-from-the-street garden patio—not to mention the antiques from everywhere that fill the nine comfortable rooms. It's smack downtown, and a few rooms have glimpses of the water. Rates include an extensive hot-and-cold breakfast buffet and afternoon refreshments.

Filled with reproduction furnishings and unusual touches, **The Limerock Inn** (96 Limerock St., Rockland, 207/594-2257 or 800/546-3762, $130–225, www.limerockinn.com) is a lovely painted lady. The 1890s Queen Anne mansion, with wraparound porch and turret, is listed on the National Historic Register and faces a quiet street in Rockland's historic district. Each of the eight rooms has its own distinctive flavor—such as the Turret Room with a wedding canopy bed and the Island Cottage Room with a private deck overlooking the back gardens. Some have whirlpool tubs, one a fireplace; there's Wi-Fi throughout. Breakfast is a treat.

FOOD
Local Flavors
A winner for creative breakfasts and lunches is **The Brown Bag** (606 Main St., Rockland, 207/596-6372 or 800/287-6372, bakery 207/596-6392, 6:30 A.M.–4 P.M. Mon.–Sat.). It's *the* place for breakfast, especially weekends, with fantastic baked goods and a full blackboard of other options. Lunches include a half-dozen veggie choices and imaginative salads. Order at the counter; no table service. The Brown Bag is at the junction of Routes 1 and 17.

Holding down the other end of Main Street is a relative newcomer, the **Brass Compass Café** (305 Main St., Rockland, 207/596-5960, www.brasscompasscafe.com, 5 A.M.–2 P.M. daily). A great choice for Maine fare, its portions are big, the prices are small, and most of the ingredients are locally sourced. Sit indoors or on the patio. If you're really hungry, try the Titanic omelette, made with "everything but the galley sink."

Lots of Rockland-watchers credit Maine's first bookstore/café, **Rock City Books and Coffee** (328 Main St., Rockland, 207/594-4123, www.rockcitycoffee.com, 7 A.M.–6 P.M. Mon.–Fri., 8 A.M.–6 P.M. Sat.) with sparking the designer-food renaissance in town. The menu has expanded greatly since the original coffee, tea, and treats to include frozen drinks, soups, salads, sandwiches, and wraps (including rockin' breakfast wraps, served until 11 A.M.), and plenty of vegetarian choices.

Scratch-made bread, pastries, and grab-and-go sandwiches have made **Atlantic Baking Co.** (351 Main St., Rockland, 207/596-0505, www.atlanticbakingco.com, 7 A.M.–6 P.M. daily) a popular spot for a quick, informal lunch. There are plenty of tables to enjoy your treats.

If you're craving a decent breakfast (or lunch or snack) and are up for a little foray "down the peninsula," head for the **Owls Head General Store** (2 S. Shore Dr., Owls Head, 207/596-6038), where the atmosphere is friendly and definitely contagious. If you get lost, the helpful staff will steer you the right way, and they will even take your photograph in front of the store. Despite all the competition from lobster-in-the-rough places, the lobster roll here is among the best around.

The **Rockland Farmers Market** gets under way 9 A.M.–1 P.M. each Thursday June–September at Harbor Park, on Rockland's Public Landing. Wares from more than a dozen vendors include produce, crafts, syrup, poultry, mushrooms, baked goods, and cheeses. Every week, there's a special event—music, dancers, lectures, special giveaways, and occasionally a llama or goat for the kids to pet.

Ethnic Fare

When you're *really* famished, the place to go (maybe) is **Conte's Fish Market and Restaurant** (Harbor Park, off Main St., Rockland, 207/596-5579), where portions are humongous and prices are not ($10–20). John Conte moved here from New York in 1995, bringing his family's century-old restaurant tradition. Specialties are pasta and seafood—Italian all the way, loaded with garlic. Beer and wine only. The decor is wildly funky—fishnets, marine relics, old books, even stacks of canned plum tomatoes—all with a terrific view of Rockland Harbor. Menus are handwritten on paper-towel rolls and in-your-face at the door (order before you sit down), table coverings are yesterday's newspapers, and Edith Piaf *chansons* or operatic arias sometimes play in the background. Eccentric, unpredictable, and definitely not for everyone. Bring your sense of humor and don't be put off by the exterior or the attitude; there's life behind the doors. No credit cards. It's open at 4 P.M. daily for dinner, all year (usually, but maybe not).

Amalfi (421 Main St., Rockland, 207/596-0012, 5–9 P.M. Tues.–Sat.) is a Mediterranean oasis. Originally downtown, in early 2008 it moved to a more spacious waterfront location in the old MBNA complex. Given the move, it's wise to call to verify hours. Most entrées are in the $16–22 range. An excellent wine list and hard-to-resist desserts round out the choices.

Sushi fans rave about Keiko Suzuki Steinberger's **Suzuki's Sushi Bar** (419 Main St., Rockland, 207/596-7447, 11 A.M.–2:30 P.M. and 5:30–8:30 P.M. Tues.–Sat.). The food matches the decor, simple yet sophisticated. Sashimi, nigiri, *maki,* and *temaki* choices range $6–10; hot entrées are $9–18. Both hot and cold sake are served, or try a saketume, made with gin or vodka, sake, and ume plum.

Casual Dining

Café Miranda (15 Oak St., Rockland, 207/594-2034, www.cafemiranda.com, 5:30–9 P.M. daily, 8:30 A.M.–1:30 P.M. Sun. brunch, and in summer, 11:30 A.M.–2 P.M. daily) is summed up in one of its slogans, "We do not serve the

food of cowards." This popular, casual place is terrific—and moderately priced—with a huge (make that overwhelming) and eminently adventurous (most choices work) menu. Lots of pastas, smoked items, veggies, olive oil, greens, and way-out combinations. Entrées are $15–26, but many of the appetizers ($6.50–12) are enough for a meal. Fresh-from-the-brick-oven focaccia comes with everything. If you sit at the counter, you can watch Chef Kerry Altiero's creations emerging from the oven. Beer and wine only. Reservations are essential throughout the summer and on weekends off-season.

At the end of a day exploring Rockland, relax at **In Good Company** (415 Main St., 207/593-9110, opens 4:30 P.M. Tues.–Sun.), a casual wine bar with a creative, tapas-style selection of small and large plates.

Destination Dining

Arriving in Rockland trailing a James Beard award–winning reputation, chef Melissa Kelly opened **◖ Primo** (Rte. 73, Rockland, 207/596-0770, www.primorestaurant.com, 5:30–10 P.M. daily in summer) in the spring of 2000 and hasn't had time to breathe. Since then, she's gone on to open two other restaurants and in 2007 expanded this one in an air-conditioned Victorian home. Fresh local ingredients (many from the restaurant's gardens) are a high priority, and unusual fish specials appear every day. Appetizers are especially imaginative; entrée range is $16–30. Kelly's partner Price Kushner produces an impressive range of breads and desserts. Reservations are essential, usually at least a week ahead on midsummer weekends—and you still may have to wait when you get there. That said, Primo slipped a notch during the renovations, so ask locally about its current reputation before making a special trip. Closed January–May.

INFORMATION AND SERVICES

Information

Check out the Rockland-Thomaston Area Chamber of Commerce (Gateway Center, P.O. Box 508, Rockland 04841, 207/596-0376

PENOBSCOT BAY

or 800/562-2529, www.therealmaine.com, 9 A.M.–5 P.M. Mon.–Fri. and 10 A.M.–2 P.M.) Sat.) or Rockland Public Library (80 Union St., Rockland, 207/594-0310, www.rockland library.org).

Public Restrooms

You'll find public restrooms at the Gateway Center; the Knox County Court House, Union and Masonic Streets; the Rockland Recreation Center, across from the courthouse, next to the playground, Union and Limerock Streets; the Rockland Public Library; and the Maine State Ferry Service terminal.

GETTING AROUND

All Aboard Trolley Co. (21 Limerock St., 207/594-9300 or 866/594-9300, www .aatrolley.com) offers 45-minute sightseeing tours of downtown Rockland ($8). It departs from Park Drive, next to the Maine Light-house Museum.

Vinalhaven and North Haven Islands

Vinalhaven and neighboring North Haven have been known as the Fox Islands ever since 1603, when English explorer Martin Pring sailed these waters and allegedly spotted gray foxes in his search for sustenance. Nowadays, you'll find reference to that name only on nautical charts, identifying the passage between the two islands as the Fox Islands Thorofare—and there's nary a fox in sight.

Each island has its own distinct personality. To generalize, Vinalhaven is the largest and busiest, while North Haven is sedate and exclusive.

VINALHAVEN

Five miles wide, 7.5 miles long, and covering 10,000 acres, Vinalhaven is 13 miles off the coast of Rockland—a 75-minute ferry trip. The shoreline has so many zigs and zags that no place on the island is more than a mile from water.

The island is famed for its granite. Vinalhaven granite first headed for Boston around 1826, and within a few decades, quarrymen arrived from as far away as Britain and Finland to wrestle out and shape the incredibly resistant stone. Schooners, barges, and "stone sloops" left Carver's Harbor carrying mighty cargoes of granite destined for government and commercial buildings in Boston, New York, and Washington, D.C. In the 1880s, nearly 4,000 people lived on Vinalhaven, North Haven, and Hurricane Island. After World War I, demand declined, granite gave way to concrete and steel, and the industry petered out and died. But Vinalhaven has left its mark—ornate columns, paving blocks, and curbstones in communities as far west as Kansas City.

With a full-time population of about 1,300 souls, Vinalhaven is a serious working community, not primarily a playground. Nearly 600 island residents depend on the lobster and fishing industry. Shopkeepers cater to locals as well as visitors, and increasing numbers of artists and artisans work away in their studios. For day-trippers, there's plenty to do—shopping, picnicking, hiking, biking, swimming—but an overnight stay provides a chance to sense the unique rhythm of life on a year-round island.

Sights

One Main Street landmark that's hard to miss is the three-story, cupola-topped **Odd Fellows Hall,** a Victorian behemoth with assorted gewgaws in the streetfront display windows. Artist Robert Indiana, who first arrived as a visitor in 1969, owns the structure, built in 1885 for the IOOF Star of Hope Lodge. It's not open to the public.

The unusually energetic **Vinalhaven Historical Society** (207/863-4410, 11 A.M.–3 P.M. daily July and Aug. or by appt., free), operates a museum in the onetime town hall on High Street, just east of Carver's Cemetery. The building itself has a tale, having been floated across the bay from Rockland, where it served as a Universalist church. The museum's documents and artifacts on the granite industry are particularly intriguing, and special summer exhibits add to the interest. Donations are welcomed. At the museum, request a copy of *A Self-Guided Walking Tour of the Town of Vinalhaven and Its Granite-Quarrying History,* a handy little brochure that details 17 in-town locations re-

lated to the late-19th and early-20th-century industry.

Built in 1832 and now owned by the town of Vinalhaven, **Brown's Head Light** guards the southern entrance to the Fox Islands Thorofare. To reach the grounds (no access to the light itself; the keeper's house is a private residence for the town manager), take the North Haven Road about six miles, at which point you'll see a left-side view of the Camden Hills. Continue to the second road on the left, Crockett River Road. Turn and take the

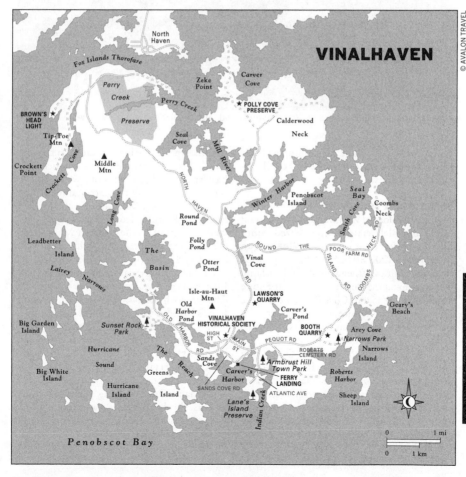

VINALHAVEN

© AVALON TRAVEL

PENOBSCOT BAY

Lobster fishing is big business on Vinalhaven Island, and the harbor is filled with working boats.

second road on the right, continuing past the Brown's Head Cemetery to the hill overlooking the lighthouse.

Parks and Preserves

Vinalhaven is loaded with wonderful hikes and walks, some deliberately unpublicized. Since the mid-1980s, the foresighted **Vinalhaven Land Trust** (207/863-2543) has expanded the opportunities. When you reach the island, pick up maps at the land trust's office at **Skoog Memorial Park** (Sands Cove Road, west of the ferry terminal) or inquire at the town office or the Paper Store. The trust also offers a seasonal series of educational walks and talks.

No, you're not on the moors of Devon, but you could be fooled in the 45-acre **Lane's Island Preserve,** one of The Nature Conservancy's most-used island preserves. Masses of low-lying ferns, rugosa roses, and berry bushes cover the granite outcrops of this sanctuary—and a foggy day makes it even more moor-like and mystical, a Brontë novel setting. The best (albeit busiest) time to come is early

August, when you can compete with the birds for blackberries, raspberries, and blueberries. Easy trails wind past old stone walls, an aged cemetery, and along the surf-pounded shore. The preserve is a 20-minute walk (or five-minute bike ride) from Vinalhaven's ferry landing. Set off to the right on Main Street, through the village. Turn right onto Water Street and then right on Atlantic Avenue. Continue across the causeway on Lane's Island Road and left over a salt marsh to the preserve. The large white house on the harbor side of Lane's Island is privately owned.

Just behind the Island Community Medical Center, close to downtown, is 30-acre **Armbrust Hill Town Park,** once the site of granite-quarrying operations. Still pockmarked with quarry pits, the park has beautifully landscaped walking paths and native flowers, shrubs, and trees—much of it thanks to late island resident Betty Roberts, who made this a lifelong endeavor. From the back of the medical center, follow the trail to the summit for a southerly view of Matinicus and other offshore islands. If you're with children, be especially careful about straying onto side paths, which go perilously close to old quarry holes. Before the walk, lower the children's energy level at the large playground off to the left of the trail.

Recreation

Swimming: Abandoned quarries are all over the island, and most are on private property, but two town-owned ones are easy to reach from the ferry landing. **Lawson's Quarry,** on the North Haven Road, is about a mile from downtown; **Booth Quarry** is on Pequot Road, 1.5 miles from downtown. Both are signposted. You'll see plenty sunbathers on the rocks and swimmers on a hot day, but there are no lifeguards, so swimming is at your own risk. There are no restrooms or changing rooms. *Note:* Pets and soap are not allowed in the water; camping, fires, and alcohol are not allowed in the quarry areas.

Down the side road beyond Booth Quarry is **Narrows Park,** a town-owned space looking out toward Narrows Island, Isle au Haut, and, on a clear day, Mount Desert Island.

For saltwater swimming, continue along Pequot Road about 1.5 miles beyond Booth Quarry. At the crossroads, you'll see a whimsical bit of local folk art—the Coke lady sculpture. Turn right (east) and go a half mile to **Geary's Beach** (also called **State Beach**), where you can picnic and scour the shoreline for shells and sea glass.

Bicycling: Even though Vinalhaven's 40 or so miles of public roads are narrow, winding, and poorly shouldered, they're relatively level, so a bicycle is a fine way to tour the island. Bring your own, preferably a hybrid or mountain bike or rent one at the **Tidewater Motel** (207/863-4618), on Main Street near the ferry landing ($10 a day or $5 a half day). A wide selection of rental bikes is available on the mainland in Rockport at **Maine Sport Outfitters** (Rte. 1, Rockport, 207/236-8797 or 888/236-8796), but you have to pay extra to bring one on the ferry.

A 10-mile, 2.5-hour bicycle route begins on Main Street and goes clockwise out the North Haven Road (rough pavement), past Lawson's Quarry, to Round the Island Road (some sections are dirt), then Poor Farm Road to Geary's Beach and back to Main Street via Pequot Road and School Street. Carry a picnic and enjoy it on Lane's Island; stop for a swim in one of the quarries; or detour down to Brown's Head Light. If you're here for the day, keep track of the time so you don't miss the ferry.

Sea Kayaking: By reservation, kayak tours and instruction are available through **SeaEscape Kayak** (15 Harbor View Dr., Vinalhaven, 207/863-9343, www.seaescapekayak.com). An Island Picnic Tour, $85, includes a gourmet picnic lunch on an island. If you're not that gung-ho, try the two-hour Harbor Tour, $45, which is a good introduction to sea kayaking.

Entertainment

No one visits Vinalhaven for nightlife, but concerts (Fox Island series and others), films, and lectures (most organized by the Vinalhaven Land Trust or the Vinalhaven Historical Society) are frequent. Check *The Wind* to see what's on the docket during your visit.

The Saturday morning flea markets are an island must, as much for the browsing and buying as for the gossip.

Shopping

Vinalhaven's shops change regularly, but here are a few that have withstood the test of time. **The Paper Store** (Vinal's News Stand; Main St., 207/863-4826) carries newspapers, gifts, film, maps, and odds and ends. **Port O' Call** (Main St., 207/863-2525) is much more than a hardware store. Poke around to see what you'll find. **New Era Gallery** (Main St., 207/863-9351, www.neweragallery.com) has a well-chosen selection of art in varied media representing primarily island artisans. Don't miss the sculpture garden. A few doors away is **Second Hand Prose,** run by the Friends of the Vinalhaven Public Library and carrying a nice selection of used books.

Accommodations

Don't even consider arriving in summer without reservations if you're planning on staying overnight.

Your feet practically touch the water when you spend the night at the ◖ **Tidewater Motel and Gathering Space** (12 Main St., Carver's Harbor, P.O. Box 546, Vinalhaven 04863, 207/863-4618, www.tidewatermotel .com, $125–256), a well-maintained motel in two buildings cantilevered over the harbor. Owned by Phil and Elaine Crossman (she operates the New Era Gallery down the street), the 19-room motel was built by Phil's parents in 1970. It's the perfect place to sit on the deck and watch the lobster boats do their thing. Be aware, though, that commercial fishermen are early risers, and lobster-boat engines can rev up as early as 4:30 on a summer morning—all part of the pace of Vinalhaven. Phil is practically a one-man chamber of commerce. He can recommend hikes and other activities and, since he maintains the island's calendar of events, he always knows what's happening and when. A continental breakfast and use of bicycles are included in the rates. Kids 10 and under are free; seven units are efficiencies. It's open all year.

Also convenient to downtown is **The Libby House** (Water St., Vinalhaven, 207/863-4696, $75–150, open summer only), with five rooms, three sharing one bath.

Food

Hours listed are for peak season. Expect reduced hours and fewer days of operation at other times.

Baked bean suppers are regularly held at a couple of island locations. Check *The Wind.*

Opposite the municipal parking lot is the **Harbor Gawker** (Main St., 207/863-9365, 10:30 A.M.–8 P.M. daily, to 9 P.M. July and Aug.), a local landmark since 1975, but now with a nice indoor dining area. On the menu are burgers, lobster rolls, sandwich baskets, fried seafood, terrific fish chowder (by the cup, pint, or quart), and soft ice cream. Dine in or take out.

The island's best dinner spot is the harborside room at **The Haven** (Main St., 207/863-4969, Tues.–Sat.), with a great view and a creative menu that changes nightly in summer. It has two reserved seatings—6 and 8:15 P.M. in the Harborside room. The restaurant's streetside room (6:30–9 P.M.) is more casual and less creative (it's called "pub style"), but the walls are lined with artwork on a rotating basis; no reservations, so you may need to wait, especially on summer weekends. The restaurant is a one-woman show, and Torry Pratt doubles as a local caterer and the girl's basketball coach, so hours can be sporadic.

The island's best breakfast place is **Surfside** (Harbor Wharf, 207/863-2767). Eat inside or out on the wharf.

Information and Services

For information on Vinalhaven, write the Vinalhaven Chamber of Commerce (P.O. Box 703, Vinalhaven 04863, www.vinalhaven.org). The chamber produces a helpful little flyer/map showing locations in the Carver's Harbor area. Also helpful for planning a trip to Vinalhaven is a guidebook published by Phil Crossman at the Tidewater Motel (207/863-4618, $3.50).

Getting Around

I can't emphasize this enough: Don't bring a car unless it is absolutely necessary. If you're coming over for a day trip, you can get to parks and quarries, shops, restaurants, and the historical society museum on foot. If you want to explore farther, a bicycle is an excellent option, or you can rent a car from the Tidewater Motel (207/863-4618), or Phil will meet you at the ferry landing. Call well ahead to reserve.

NORTH HAVEN

Eight miles long by three miles wide, North Haven is 12 miles off the coast of Rockland—an hour by ferry. The island boasts sedate summer homes, open fields where hundreds of sheep once grazed, about 350 year-round residents, a yacht club called the

Casino, and a village gift shop that's been here since 1954.

Originally called North Island, North Haven had much the same settlement history as Vinalhaven, but, being smaller (about 5,280 acres) and more fertile, it has developed—or not developed—differently. In 1846, North Haven was incorporated and severed politically from Vinalhaven, and by the late 1800s, the Boston summer crowd began buying traditional island homes, building tastefully unpretentious new ones, and settling in for a whole season of sailing and socializing. Several generations later, "summer folk" now come for weeks rather than months, often rotating the schedules among slews of siblings. Informality remains the key, though—now more than ever.

The island has two distinct hamlets—North Haven Village, on the Fox Islands Thorofare, where the state ferry arrives, and Pulpit Harbor, particularly popular with the yachting set.

North Haven doesn't offer a lot for the day visitor, and islanders tend not to welcome them with open arms.

North Haven Village

Fanning out from the ferry landing is a delightful cluster of substantial, year-round clapboard homes—a marked contrast to the weathered-shingle cottages typical of so many island communities. It won't take long to stroll Main Street's handful of shops.

Bicycling

North Haven has about 25 miles of paved roads, but, just as on most other islands, they are narrow, winding, and nearly shoulderless. Starting near the ferry landing in North Haven Village, take South Shore Road eastward, perhaps stopping en route for a picnic at town-owned Mullin's Head Park (also spelled Mullen Head) on the southeast corner of the island. Then follow the road around, counterclockwise, to North Shore Road and Pulpit Harbor. Be conscientious and obey the rules of the road and do carry out any trash (yours, or whatever you find along the way).

Accommodations and Food

Both beds and food are scarce on North Haven.

Within walking distance of the ferry is **Nebo Lodge** (11 Mullins La., P.O. Box 358, North Haven 04853, 207/867-2007, www.nebolodge .com, $125–225 peak), an artfully decorated B&B. Rates include a full breakfast and use of inn bikes.

Picnic fixings are available at **Brown's Market.** For a sit-down lunch head for the **Coal Wharf Restaurant** (Main St., 207/867-4739), next to Brown's Boatshop or **Sip Ahoy at H. J. Blake's** (29 Main St., 207/867-2060).

Information and Services

The best source of information about North Haven is the North Haven Town Office (Upper Main St., North Haven, 207/867-4433, www .northhavenmaine.org).

GETTING THERE

The Maine State Ferry Service (207/596-2202, www.exploremaine.com) operates six round-trips daily between Rockland and Vinalhaven (75-minute crossing) in summer and three round-trips between Rockland and North Haven (70-minute crossing). Round-trip tickets are $14.50 adults, $6.25 kids. Both ferries take cars ($41.50 round-trip, plus $14 reservation fee), but a bicycle ($13.75 round-trip per adult bike, $7 per child's bike) will do fine unless you have the time or inclination to see every corner of the island. Getting car space on the ferry during midsummer can be a frustrating—and complicated—experience, so *avoid taking a car to the island.* If you leave a car at the Rockland lot, space available, it's $7 per day or $35 per week. If you're not spending the night on the island, watch the clock so you don't miss the last boat back to Rockland.

Penobscot Island Air (207/596-7500, www.penobscotislandair.net) flies twice daily to Vinalhaven and North Haven, weather permitting, from Knox County Regional Airport in Owls Head, just south of Rockland. Seat availability is dependent on mail volume.

PENOBSCOT BAY

Camden-Rockport Area

Driven apart by a local squabble in 1891, Camden and Rockport have been separate towns for more than a century, but they're inextricably linked. They share school and sewer systems and an often-hyphenated partnership. On Union Street, just off Route 1, a white wooden arch reads Camden on one side and Rockport on the other. These days, this area is one of the Mid-Coast's—even Maine's—prime destinations.

Camden, the better known of the two, has a year-round population of about 5,300, but that triples during the summer; Rockport, with a much lower profile, doubles in summer from about 3,500 year-round. While Rockport's harbor is relatively peaceful—with yachts, lobster boats, and a single windjammer schooner—Camden Harbor is a summer-long madhouse, jammed with dinghies, kayaks, windjammers, megayachts, minor yachts, and a handful of fishing craft.

Much of Camden's appeal is its drop-dead-gorgeous setting—a deeply indented harbor with parks, a waterfall, and a dramatic backdrop of low mountains. It is views of Camden that typify Maine nationwide, even worldwide, on calendars and postcards, in photo books, you name it.

SIGHTS
Self-Guided Historical Tour

The Camden-Rockport Historical Society, supported by the Whitehall Inn, has produced a handy little flyer, *A Walking Tour and Bicycle or Car Tour,* detailing more than 50 significant historic sites (mostly private residences) in downtown Camden, Camden's High Street and Chestnut Street Historic Districts, and downtown Rockport. To cover it all, you'll want a car or bike; to cover segments and really appreciate the architecture, don your walking shoes. Pick up a copy of the flyer at the chamber of commerce.

© TOM NANGLE

Windjammers and pleasure boats crowd Camden's protected harbor.

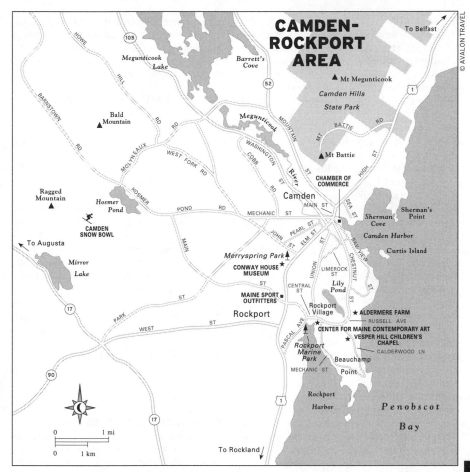

Old Conway Homestead and Cramer Museum

Just inside the Camden town line from Rockport, the Old Conway Homestead and Cramer Museum (Conway Rd., Camden, 207/236-2257, 10 A.M.–4 P.M. Mon.–Thurs. July–Aug., $5 adults, $2 kids) is a five-building complex owned and run by the Camden-Rockport Historical Society. The 18th-century Cape-style Conway House, on the National Register of Historic Places, contains fascinating construction details and period furnishings; in the barn are carriages and

farm tools. Two other buildings—a blacksmith shop and a 19th-century sap house used for making maple syrup—have been moved to the grounds and restored. In the contemporary Mary Meeker Cramer Museum (named for the prime benefactor) are displays from the historical society's collection of ship models, old documents, and period clothing. For local color, don't miss the Victorian outhouse. The museum and sap house are also open for maple-syrup demonstrations on Maine Maple Sunday (fourth Sunday in March).

Vesper Hill

Built and donated to the community by a local benefactor, the rustic, open-air **Vesper Hill Children's Chapel** is dedicated to the world's children. Overlooking Penobscot Bay and surrounded by gardens and lawns, the nondenominational chapel is an almost mystical oasis in a busy tourist region. Except during weddings or memorial services, there's seldom a crowd, and if you're lucky, you might have the place to yourself. From Central Street in downtown Rockport, take Russell Avenue east to Calderwood Lane (fourth street on right). On Calderwood, take the second right (Chapel St.) after the (private) golf course. If the sign is down, look for a boulder with Vesper Hill carved in it. From downtown Camden, take Chestnut Street to just past Aldermere Farm; turn left at Calderwood Lane and take the second right after the golf course.

Aldermere Farm (20 Russell Ave., Rockport, 207/236-2739, www.aldermere.org), by the way, is the home of America's original herd of Belted Galloway cattle—Anguslike beef cattle with a wide white midriff. First imported from Scotland in 1953, the breed now shows up in pastures all over the United States. The animals' startling "Oreo-cookie" hide pattern never fails to halt passersby—especially in spring and early summer, when the calves join their mothers in the pastures. Maine Coast Heritage Trust, a state conservation organization based in Brunswick, owns the 135-acre farm. Call for information on tours or other events.

Center for Maine Contemporary Art

Once a local firehouse, this attractive building has been totally rehabbed to provide display space for the work of Maine's best contemporary artists. The nonprofit Center for Maine Contemporary Art (62 Russell Ave., Rockport, 207/236-2875, www.artsmaine.org, 10 A.M.–5 P.M. Tues.–Sat., 1–5 P.M. Sun., $5), mounts as many as a dozen shows each summer, along with special lectures, a wildly popular art auction (early Aug.), an annual juried art exhibition featuring more than 100 selections, and an annual juried craft show (mid-Oct.) spotlighting several dozen artisans. An exceptional gift shop carries high-end crafts.

PARKS AND PRESERVES

For more than a century, the Camden-Rockport area has benefited from the providence of conscientious year-round and summertime conservationists. Thanks to their benevolence, countless acres of fragile habitat, woodlands, and scenic viewpoints have been preserved. Nowadays, the most active organization is the **Coastal Mountains Land Trust (CMLT)** (101 Mt. Battie St., Camden, 207/236-7091, www.coastalmountains.org), founded in 1986. It has protected nearly 6,000 acres. Maps and information about trails open to the public are available from CMLT. Check the website for guided hikes and other events.

A Rockland-based group, **The Georges River Land Trust** (207/594-5166, www.grlt.org), whose territory covers the Georges (St. George) River watershed, is the steward for The Georges Highland Path, a low-impact hiking trail that reaches Rockport and Camden from the back side of the surrounding hills. (See *Hiking* under *Recreation*.)

(Camden Hills State Park

A five-minute drive and a small fee gets you to the top of **Mt. Battie,** centerpiece of 5,650-acre Camden Hills State Park (Belfast Rd., Rte. 1, 207/236-3109, $3 adults, $1 kids 5–11) and the best place to understand why Camden is "where the mountains meet the sea." The summit panorama is, well, breathtaking, and reputedly the inspiration for Edna St. Vincent Millay's poem "Renascence" (a bronze plaque marks the spot); information boards identify the offshore islands. Climb the summit's stone tower for an even better view. The 20 miles of hiking trails (some for every ability) include two popular routes up Mt. Battie—an easy, hour-long hike from the base parking lot (Nature Trail) and a more strenuous 45-minute one from the top of Mt.

Battie Street in Camden (Mt. Battie Trail). Or drive up the paved Mt. Battie Auto Road. The park has plenty of space for picnics. In winter, ice climbers use a rock wall near the Maiden's Cliff Trail, reached via Route 52 (Mountain St.). The park entrance is two miles north of downtown Camden. Request a free trail map. The park is open mid-May–mid-October. Hiking trails are accessible all year, weather permitting.

Merryspring Park

Straddling the Camden-Rockport boundary, 66-acre Merryspring Park (Conway Rd., Camden, 207/236-2239, www.merryspring.org) is a magnet for nature lovers. More than a dozen well-marked trails wind through woodlands, berry thickets, and wildflowers; near the preserve's parking area are lily, rose, and herb gardens. Admission is free, but donations are welcomed. Special programs (fee charged) include lectures, demonstrations, and a summer Ecology Camp for youngsters. Most programs are held in the park's modern Ross Center, named for Merryspring founders Mary Ellen and Ervin Ross. The entrance is on Conway Road, 0.3 mile off Route 1, at the southern end of Camden. Trails are open dawn to dusk daily; the visitors center is open 9 A.M.–2 P.M. Tuesday–Friday.

Intown Parks

Just behind the Camden Public Library is the **Camden Amphitheatre** (also called the Bok Amphitheatre, after a local benefactor), a sylvan spot resembling a set for *A Midsummer Night's Dream* (which, yes, has been performed here). Concerts, weddings, and all kinds of other events take place in the park. Across Atlantic Avenue, sloping to the harbor, is **Camden Harbor Park**, with benches, a couple of monuments, and some of the best waterfront views in town. The noted landscape firm of Frederick Law Olmsted designed the park in 1931 and is listed on the National Register of Historic Places. Both the park and amphitheatre were restored to their original splendor in 2004.

Rockport's in-town parks include **Marine Park,** off Pascal Avenue, at the head of the harbor; **Walker Park,** on Sea Street, west side of the harbor; **Mary-Lea Park,** overlooking the harbor next to the Rockport Opera House; and **Cramer Park,** alongside the Goose River just west of Pascal Avenue. At Marine Park are the remnants of 19th-century lime kilns, an antique steam engine, picnic tables, a boat-launching ramp, and a polished granite sculpture of André, a harbor seal adopted by a local family in the early 1960s. André had been honorary harbormaster, ringbearer at weddings, and the subject of several books and a film—and even did the honors at the unveiling of his statue—before he was fatally wounded in a mating skirmish in 1986, at the age of 25.

Fernald's Neck

Three miles of Megunticook Lake shoreline, groves of conifers, and a large swamp ("the Great Bog") are features of 315-acre Fernald's Neck Preserve, on the Camden-Lincolnville line (and the Knox–Waldo County line). Shoreline and mountain views are stupendous, even more so during fall-foliage season. The easiest trail is the Blue and White Loop, at the northern end of the preserve; the longer Orange Loop begins at the same point, goes past the Great Bog, and loops around the southern end of the preserve. Yellow Trails connect the loops. While on the Blue and White Loop, take the Green offshoot for a great view of the lake and hills. Some sections can be wet; wear boots or rubberized shoes, and use insect repellent. From Route 1 in Camden, take Route 52 (Mountain St.) about 4.5 miles to Fernald's Neck Road, about 0.2 mile beyond the Youngtown Inn. Turn left and then bear left at the next fork. Go past the gray farmhouse at the road's end, continue into the hayfield, and park near the woods. Head into the woods (look for signs bearing The Nature Conservancy oak leaf) and pick up a map/brochure at the trailhead register. A map is also available at the chamber of commerce office.

PENOBSCOT BAY

Some trails at tiny Camden Snow Bowl have views to Penobscot Bay.

© TOM NANGLE

RECREATION
Recreation Centers

More than an alpine ski area, the **Camden Snow Bowl** (207/236-3438, www.camdensnowbowl.com) is a four-season recreation area with tennis courts, public swimming in Hosmer Pond, and hiking trails as well as alpine trails for day and night skiing and riding and the only toboggan chute in Maine.

Bicycling and Sea Kayaking

Local entrepreneurs Stuart and Marianne Smith have made **Maine Sport Outfitters** (Rte. 1, Rockport, 207/236-8797 or 888/236-8796, www.mainesport.com) a major destination for anyone interested in outdoor recreation. The knowledgeable staff can lend a hand and steer you in almost any direction, for almost any summer or winter sport. Nothing seems to stump them. The store sells and rents canoes, kayaks, bikes, skis, and tents, plus all the relevant clothing and accessories. A bicycle rents for $20 per day, calm-water canoes and kayaks are

$25–30 per day. Sea kayaks are $40 per day single, $50 per day tandem.

Maine Sport Outdoor School (800/722-0826, a division of Maine Sport) has a full schedule of canoeing, kayaking, and camping trips. A two-hour guided Camden Harbor tour departs at least three times daily in summer and costs $35 adult, $30 ages 10–15. A four-hour, guided harbor-to-harbor tour (Rockport to Camden) is offered once each day for $75 adult, $60 child, including a picnic lunch. Multiday instructional programs and tours are available. The store is a half mile north of the junction of Routes 1 and 90.

If you have your own canoe, kayak, rowboat, or whatever, there are a number of boat-launching sites, both saltwater (Eaton Point, at the end of Sea Street, in Camden; and, even better, Marine Park, in Rockport) and freshwater (Megunticook Lake, west and east sides; Bog Bridge, on Route 105, about 3.5 miles from downtown Camden; and Barrett's Cove, on Route 52, also about 3.5 miles from Camden).

Hiking

There's enough hiking in **Camden Hills State Park** to fill any vacation, but many other options exist. For instance, there's **Bald Mountain,** northwest of downtown Camden, for magnificent views of Penobscot Bay. From Route 1 at the southern end of town (between Subway and Exxon), take John Street for 0.8 mile. Turn left and go 0.2 mile to a fork. Continue on the left fork (Hosmer Pond Rd.) for two miles. Bear left onto Barnestown Road (passing the Camden Snow Bowl) and go 1.4 miles to the trailhead on the right, signposted Georges Highland Path Barnestown Access. Maps are available in the box; the parking lot holds half a dozen cars. The blue-blazed trail is relatively easy, requiring just over an hour round-trip; the summit views are spectacular, especially in fall. Carry a picnic and enjoy it at the top. Avoid this in late May and early June, however, when the blackflies take command. Depending on the season, you may encounter squishy areas, although trail stewards have installed some well-placed boardwalks.

The Georges Highland Path eventually will wind through the Georges (St. George) River watershed from the source in Liberty to the outlet in Port Clyde. Spearheaded by members of the Georges River Land Trust (207/594-5166, www.grlt.org), the blue-blazed trail now has access points on the outskirts of Camden and West Rockport. Contact the Rockland-based land trust for an up-to-date map, or pick it up from a trailhead box. The easiest access point is on Route 17 about 10 miles from downtown Rockland. Just past Mirror Lake (on your right) is a well-signposted parking area. The Ragged Mountain direction (north) is more strenuous than the Spruce Mountain/Mt. Pleasant section (south; across Rte. 17). The latter is a great three-hour round-trip. Views are spectacular in either direction; Ragged Mountain gets you closer to the ocean panorama.

Swimming

For freshwater swimming, head to **Barrett's Cove,** on Megunticook Lake, with restrooms, picnic tables, and grills, as well as a play area. Diagonally opposite the Camden Public Library, take Route 52 (Mountain St.) about three miles; watch for the sign on the left.

Camden and Rockport both have saltwater swimming but no major sandy beaches. In Camden, it's **Laite Beach Park,** on Bay View Street about 1.5 miles from downtown Camden. Right on Camden Harbor, the park has great views, a strip of sand, picnic tables, a playground, and children's musical events 1–3 P.M. every Wednesday in July and August. Check the local papers or contact Camden Parks and Recreation (207/236-3438) for the schedule. Rockport has **Walker Park,** tucked away on the west side of the harbor. From Pascal Avenue, take Elm Street, which becomes Sea Street. Walker Park is on the left, with picnic tables, a play area, and a small, pebbly beach.

Golf

On a back road straddling the Camden-Rockport line, the nine-hole **Goose River Golf Club** (50 Park St., Rockport, 207/236-8488) competes with the best for outstanding scenery. Starting times are needed on weekends and holidays. It has a snack bar, cart and club rentals, and moderate greens fees.

Day Sails and Excursions

Most day sails and excursion boats operate late May–October, with fewer trips in the spring and fall than in July and August. You can't compare a two-hour day sail to a weeklong cruise on a Maine windjammer (see sidebar *Windjamming*), but at least you get a hint of what could be—and it's a far better choice for most kids, who aren't allowed on most windjammer cruises. Several excursion boats operate out of Camden in summer. Most weekdays, you can just show up at the dock and find a space, but on weekends, you'd better call for a reservation. Several are based at Bay View Landing, formerly known as Sharp's Wharf.

A historic Camden day sailer is the 57-foot,

PENOBSCOT BAY

18-passenger schooner **Surprise** (207/236-4687, www.camdenmainesailing.com, $30) built in 1918 and skippered by congenial educator Jack Moore and his wife, Barbara. Between May and October, they do daily two-hour sails, departing from Camden's Public Landing. Minimum age is 12.

The 49-passenger **Appledore** (207/236-8353, www.appledore2.com), built in 1978 for round-the-world cruising, sails from Bay View Landing beginning around 10 A.M. 3–4 times daily June–October. Most cruises last two hours and cost $30. Cocktails, wine, and soft drinks are available.

Over in Rockport, the schooner **Heron** (207/236-8605 or 800/599-8605, www.woodenboatco.com) is a 65-foot, John Alden–designed wooden yacht launched in 2003. Sailing options include a lobster-roll lunch sail ($50), lighthouse sail ($38), and sunset sails with hors d'oeuvres ($50).

If the kids are bombarding you with FAQs about lobsters, here's the solution. Take a two-hour trip aboard Captain Alan Philbrick's **Lively Lady Too** (207/236-6672, $25 adults, $5 under 15), berthed at Camden's Bay View Landing. He hauls in a trap, takes out a lobster, explains all its parts, and generally provides all the answers. As a former biology teacher, he's a whiz at natural history, so there's also information about seabirds, seals, and lots more. Trips depart Monday–Saturday.

ENTERTAINMENT

At 8 P.M. Thursday and Friday in July and August, and once a month the rest of the year, **Bay Chamber Concerts** (207/236-2823 or 888/707-2770, www.baychamberconcerts .org) draw sell-out audiences to the beautifully restored (and air-conditioned) Rockport Opera House and Rockland's Strand Theatre. Founded in the 1960s as a classical series, the summer concerts feature a resident quartet, prominent guest artists, and outstanding programs. It has expanded to include world music, jazz, and dance. The first week in August ("Next Generation Week") is devoted to

classes and concerts for and by talented teenagers. Seats are reserved for summer concerts ($25–33 adults, $8 25 and younger); open seating is the rule in winter, when tickets are less expensive and programs vary from classical to pops to jazz. (Season tickets and flex passes are available.)

The beautifully renovated **Camden Opera House** (29 Elm St., Camden, 207/236-7963, box office 207/236-4884, www.camdenoperahouse.com) is the site of many performances by renowned performers.

FESTIVALS AND EVENTS

One weekend in February is given over to the **Camden Conference,** an annual three-day foreign-affairs conference with nationally and internationally known speakers. The first weekend in February marks the **National Toboggan Championships,** two days of races and fun at the nation's only wooden toboggan chute at the Camden Snow Bowl.

The third Thursday of July is **House and Garden Day,** when you can take a self-guided tour (10 A.M.–4:30 P.M.) of significant homes and gardens in Camden and Rockport. Proceeds benefit the Camden Garden Club. And the **HarborArts,** on the third weekend in July, draws dozens of artists and craftspeople displaying and selling their wares at the Camden Amphitheatre, Harbor Park.

Labor Day weekend is also known as **Windjammer Weekend** here, with cruises, windjammer open houses, fireworks, and all kinds of live entertainment in and around Camden Harbor. Twenty top artisans open their studios for the annual **Country Roads Artists and Artisans Tour** in September.

SHOPPING

Downtown Camden is a tough place to find socks or thread, but it's a boutique-shopper's paradise if gifts are your goal. Be sure to wander the side streets and back alleys. Rockport has a handful of unusual gift and antiques shops and galleries.

The **Owl and Turtle Bookshop** (32 Washington St., Camden, 207/236-4769 or 800/876-4769), one of Maine's best new-books stores, with thousands of books and a wonderful children's room, moved to spacious new digs in the Knox Mill Center in 2004. Replacing it in its old location is **Sherman's** (8 Bay View St., Camden, 207/236-2223), another excellent bookstore with shops up and down the coast.

For antiquarian books, **ABCD Books** (23 Bay View St., Camden, 207/236-3903 or 888/236-3903) maintains an excellent stock of rare books and first editions (prices are a bit steep). If you simply want a good read, **Stone Soup Books** (33 Main St., Camden, no phone), a tiny second-floor shop across from the Lord Camden Inn, is Camden's best source for contemporary used fiction.

A downtown Camden landmark since 1940, **The Smiling Cow** (41 Main St., Camden, 207/236-3351 or 800/646-6169) is as good a place as any to pick up Maine souvenirs—a few slightly kitschy, but most reasonably tasteful. Before or after shopping here, head for the rear balcony for coffee and a knockout view of the harbor and the Megunticook River waterfall.

For an excellent selection of Maine-made crafts, both traditional and contemporary, head to **Maine Gathering** (21 Main St., Camden, 207/236-9004).

Sturdy, well-designed, homemade (by knitting machine) wool and cotton sweaters are the specialty at **Unique One** (2 Bay View St., Camden, 207/236-8717). Or you can pick out yarn and make your own.

Follow West Street (Rte. 90) from Route 1 for almost three miles and you'll come to **Danica Candleworks** (Rte. 90, West Rockport, 207/236-3060), producers of the loveliest candle colors you've ever seen. Owner Erik Laustsen learned the hand-dipping trade from his Danish relatives, and Danica now ships its work all over the country. The Scandinavian-style shop also carries other gift items.

ACCOMMODATIONS

The Camden-Rockport area (including Lincolnville) is loaded with lodgings—from basic motels to cottage complexes to elegant inns and B&Bs. Many of Camden's most attractive accommodations (especially B&Bs) are on Route 1 (variously disguised as Elm St., Main St., and High St.), heavily trafficked in summer. If you're extrasensitive to nighttime noises, request a room facing away from the street.

Camden

One of Maine's most unusual (and priciest) B&Bs, **Norumbega** (61 High St., Rte. 1, Camden, 207/236-4646 or 877/363-4646, $300–475, www.norumbegainn.com) is an 1886 turreted stone castle overlooking Camden's outer harbor. Provided your wallet can stand the crunch, splurge for a night (or two) here—if only to feel like temporary royalty. Twelve rooms and suites, most named after European castles, are strikingly decorated, filled with antiques, and have all the expected amenities. Rates include a full breakfast.

Opened for guests in 1901, the **Whitehall Inn** (52 High St., Rte. 1, P.O. Box 558, Camden 04843, 207/236-3391 or 800/789-6565, www.whitehall-inn.com, $149–199) retains its century-old genteel air, right down to the telephone switchboard. Lovely gardens, rockers on the veranda, a tennis court, and attentive service all add to the appeal of this historic country inn. Ask to see the Millay Room, commemorating famed poet Edna St. Vincent Millay, who graduated from Camden High School and first recited her poem "Renascence" to Whitehall guests in 1912. Spread out between the main inn and the annex are 40 comfortable, unpretentious rooms, all with high-speed Internet access and imported linens; a few share baths. The dining room, Vincent's, is open to the public for breakfast (7–10 A.M. Mon.–Sat., to noon Sun.) and dinner (6–9 P.M. Wed.–Mon.). Also on the premises is Gossip, a bar serving pub fare. It's open mid-May–late October.

Innkeepers Bob and Juanita Topper, the hospitable hosts at **Camden Maine Stay** (22 High St., Rte. 1, Camden, 207/236-9636, www.mainestay.com, $135–250), do everything right, from the elegant decor to the delicious breakfasts to the welcoming window candles. The stunning residence, built in 1802, faces busy Route 1 and is just a bit uphill from downtown, but inside and out back, behind the carriage house and barn, you'll feel worlds away.

The ◖ **Hartstone Inn** (41 Elm St., Camden, 207/236-4259 or 800/788-4823, www.hartstoneinn.com, $125–265)is Michael and Mary Jo Salmon's imposing mansard-roofed Victorian close to the heart of downtown. In addition, there are rooms tucked in buildings behind the inn and in a separate location. All are elegant (Wi-Fi, air-conditioning), and some have fireplaces and whirlpools. Once inside, you're away from it all. Be *sure* to make reservations for dinner. And then, there's the incredible breakfast. If you get hooked, the Salmons organize culinary classes during the winter.

In the heart of downtown Camden, **The Lord Camden Inn** (24 Main St., Rte. 1, Camden, 207/236-4325 or 800/336-4325, www.lordcamdeninn.com, $179–289 peak) is a hotel alternative in a historic, four-story downtown building (with elevator). Decor is reproduction Colonial with exposed brick walls and scads of old framed photos in rooms and hallways. (The brick moderates the noise level.) All 31 rooms and suites have phones, air-conditioning, TV, and Wi-Fi; a full breakfast buffet is provided. In-room spa services are available. Top-floor rooms have harbor-view balconies. Pooches are pampered in pet-friendly rooms for $20 per night, including bed, biscuits, bowls, and local dog info.

A hybrid of an inn, B&B, motel, and cottage three miles north of town, **The High Tide Inn on the Ocean** (Rte. 1, Camden, 207/236-3724 or 800/788-7068, www.hightideinn.com, $95–220) has enough variety for every budget—all in an outstanding, seven-acre oceanfront setting with a private pebbly beach. The two-story, eight-unit "Oceanfront" motel unit is closest to the water and farthest from Route 1. Rates include continental breakfast on the water-view porch. Pets can be accommodated in some rooms.

It's a short stroll into Merryspring Gardens from the **Cedar Crest Motel** (115 Elm St., Rte. 1, Camden, 207/236-4839, www.cedarcrestmotel.com, $124–139), a nicely maintained property on 3.5 wooded and landscaped acres on the southern edge of downtown. Each of the 37 rooms has air-conditioning, Wi-Fi, phone, and TV. Some have minifridges. On the premises are a guest computer, outdoor heated pool, playground, laundry, and restaurant serving all meals.

Rockport

One of the area's spiffiest motels also has terrific Penobscot Bay views. In the Glen Cove section of Rockport (three miles south of downtown Rockport, three miles north of downtown Rockland, next door to Penobscot Bay Medical Center), the **Glen Cove Motel** (Rte. 1, P.O. Box 35, Glen Cove 04846, 207/594-4062 or 800/453-6268, www.glencovemotel.com, $129–209) sits on a 17-acre bluff with a lovely trail leading to the rocky shore. Many of the 34 units boast water views; all have air-conditioning, phones, cable TV, and refrigerators. The pool is heated. Request a room set back from Route 1.

Seasonal Rentals

The chamber of commerce maintains a lengthy list of seasonal rentals. Also handling private rentals is **Camden Accommodations** (43 Elm St., Rte. 1, Camden, 207/236-6090 or 800/344-4830, www.camdenac.com).

Camping

Camden Hills State Park (Belfast Rd., Rte. 1, 207/236-3109, $3 adults, $1 kids 5–11, $20 nonresident, $15 resident) has a 112-site camping area (no hookups) and is wheelchair-accessible. Pets are allowed, showers are free, and the sites are large.

Megunticook Campground by the Sea (Rte. 1, P.O. Box 375, Rockport 04856, 207/594-2428 or 800/884-2428, www.campgroundbythesea.com, $35–45) is the area's best-run commercial campground, a 17-acre facility with 87 wooded sites. Also on the premises are 10 camping cabins ($72). Amenities include a playground, snack bar, heated pool, laundry, and kayak rentals. Weekly lobster bakes (about $20) are held at the oceanfront picnic area. Noise rules are strictly enforced; pets are allowed. The only drawback is that the coin-op showers shut off too frequently. It's open mid-May–mid-October. The campground is three miles south of Camden, five miles north of Rockland.

FOOD

As always, make reservations.

Local Flavors

The best source for health foods, homeopathic remedies, and fresh, seasonal produce is **Fresh Off the Farm** (Rte. 1, Rockport, 207/236-3260, 8 A.M.–7 P.M. Mon.–Sat. and 9 A.M.–5:30 P.M. Sun.), an inconspicuous red-painted roadside place that looks like an overgrown farmstand (it is). Watch for one of those permanent/temporary signs highlighting latest arrivals (Native Blueberries, Native Corn, etc.). The shop is 1.3 miles south of the junction of Routes 1 and 90.

At the southern entrance to Rockport, a sprawling red building is the home of **The State of Maine Cheese Company** (461 Commercial St., Rte. 1, Rockport, 207/236-8895 or 800/762-8895), makers of a dozen varieties of cows'-milk hard cheeses, all named after Maine locations (Aroostook Jack, Allagash Caraway, St. Croix Black Pepper, and so on). Under the cheese company's umbrella (and roof) is the Maine-Made Products Center, covering 9,500 square feet. Among the items are blueberry chutneys, maple syrup, designer breads, great jams—a one-stop-shopping (and tasting) site.

The **Camden Farmers Market,** one of the best in the state, holds forth in a parking lot at Colcord and Limerock Streets, across from Tibbetts Industries. Temporary signs are posted on Route 1 on market days—4:30–6 P.M. Wednesday mid-June–mid-September; 9 A.M.–noon Saturday mid-May–October. The market goes on, rain

or shine. There's a winter market at Merry Spring November–May.

Good coffee is a draw at the **Camden Deli** (37 Main St., Camden, 207/236-8343, 6 A.M.–10 P.M. daily), in the heart of downtown, but its biggest asset is the windowed seating overlooking the Megunticook River waterfall. The view doesn't get much better than this (go upstairs for the best angle). Made-to-order sandwiches and wraps, homemade soups, veggie burgers, and subs all add to the mix. Beer and wine only for takeout.

Peek behind the old-fashioned facade at **Boynton-McKay Food Company** (30 Main St., Camden, 207/236-2465, 7 A.M.–6 P.M. Tues.–Sat. and 8 A.M.–4 P.M. Sun., kitchen closes 3 P.M.), and you'll see an old-fashioned soda fountain, early-20th-century tables, antique pharmacy accessories, and a thoroughly modern café menu. Restored and rehabbed in 1997, Boynton-McKay had been *the* local drugstore for more than a century. The new incarnation features bagels, creative salads, homemade soups, superb wrap sandwiches, an espresso bar, and the whole works from the soda fountain. It's open for breakfast and lunch.

Facing downtown Camden's five-way intersection, **French and Brawn** (1 Elm St., Camden, 207/236-3361, 6 A.M.–8 P.M. Mon.–Sat. and 8 A.M.–8 P.M. Sun.) is an independent market that earns the description *super*. Grab ready-made sandwiches, soups, and other goodies for a picnic.

Surprise! The best pizza in town comes from the **Elm Street Grille** (Cedar Crest Motel, 115 Elm St./Rte. 1, Camden, 207/236-4839, www .cedarcrestmotel.com), serving great breakfasts, lunch, and dinner Tuesday–Sunday. It's all very reasonably priced and served in a comfortable dining room, with a handful of seats on a deck. On Friday nights, there's live jazz.

In the heart of Camden, **Cappy's** (1 Main St., Camden, 207/236-2254, www.cappys chowder.com, 11 A.M.–midnight daily) is small, a bit cramped, reliably good (it's been here for more than 25 years), and very popular

PENOBSCOT BAY

with locals and out-of-towners alike. In summer, request a table in the second-floor Crow's Nest, where you'll be less squished; microbrew tastings are held here 5–7 P.M. daily in season. It's a burger-and-sandwich menu with some heartier seafood choices ($8–19); clam chowder is a specialty. During summer, Cappy's operates a bakery with take-out pastries, sandwiches, and other goodies underneath, facing on the alley that runs down to the public parking lot.

Casual Dining

Chef/owner Brian Hill has created one of the region's hottest restaurants with **℃ Francine Bistro** (55 Chestnut St., Camden, 207/230-0083, www.francinebistro.com, 5:30–10 P.M. daily). The well-chosen menu (entrées $24–30) is short and focused on whatever's fresh and usually locally available that day. In addition to the dining room, there's also seating at the bar and, when the weather cooperates, on the front porch.

Here's a sleeper: **Ephemere** (51 Bay View St., Camden, 207/236-4451, 5:30–9 P.M. Mon.–Sat.) is best known as a wine bar, but it also serves dinners that stretch the imagination, but that work. I mean, really, who would have paired lobster with gingerbread? The wine bar opens at 4:30 P.M. serving a light-fare menu.

Down on the harbor is the informal, art-filled **Atlantica** (1 Bay View Landing, Camden, 207/236-6011 or 888/507-8514, www.atlanticarestaurant.com, 5–9 P.M. daily), two floors of culinary creativity with an emphasis on seafood, entrées $25–36. Consider an onion-crusted halibut BLT or pan-seared dayboat scallops. In summer, try for a table on the deck hanging over the water.

The Waterfront Restaurant (Bay View St., Camden, 207/236-3747, 11:30 A.M.–2:30 P.M. and 5–9:30 P.M. daily) has the biggest waterside dining deck in town, but you'll need to arrive early to snag one of the tables. Lunches are the most fun, overlooking lots of harbor

action; at high tide, you're eye to eye with the boats. Most entrées run $16–25.

Food as art is the idea behind the **Gallery Café** (297 Commercial St., Rte. 1, Rockport, 207/230-0061, www.prismglassgallery .com, 11 A.M.–3 P.M. and 5–9 P.M. Wed.–Sat., 10 A.M.–3 P.M. and 4–8 P.M. Sun.), a restaurant that's part of **Prismglass**, a fine-art glass gallery and working studio representing more than 50 glass artists. The menu changes seasonally, with dinner entrées, many with Italian leanings, ranging $16–30; brunch is $8–18. It's on Route 1 across from Hoboken Gardens.

Fine Dining

Reservations are a must for Chef Michael Salmon's five-course fixed-price extravaganzas at the **Hartstone Inn** (41 Elm St., Camden, 207/236-4259 or 800/788-4823, www.hartstone inn.com, $45) Michael, named Caribbean chef of the year when they lived in Aruba, has cooked at the Beard House by invitation. Even Julia Child dined here. The menu changes weekly to use the freshest ingredients.

INFORMATION AND SERVICES
Information

The Camden-Rockport-Lincolnville Chamber of Commerce (P.O. Box 919, Camden 04843, 207/236-4404 or 800/223-5459, www.visit camden.com) is at the Public Landing. Request a copy of its map of area streets and businesses and the official chamber guide.

Check out Camden Public Library (Main St., Rte. 1, Camden, 207/236-3440, www.camden .lib.me.us) or Rockport Public Library (1 Limerock St., Rockport, 207/236-3642, www .rockport.lib.me.us).

Public Restrooms

Public restrooms are available at Camden's Public Landing, near the chamber of commerce, and at the Camden Public Library. In Rockport, there are restrooms at Marine Park.

Lincolnville

Since the early 1990s, the town of Lincolnville, in Waldo County just north of Camden, has outpaced all the surrounding communities in population growth. An influx of new residents has pushed the census to the 2,000 mark. Two distinct enclaves make up the town—oceanfront Lincolnville Beach ("the Beach") and, about five miles inland, Lincolnville Center ("the Center"). Lincolnville is laid-back and mostly rural; the major activity center is a short strip of shops and restaurants at the Beach, and few visitors realize there's anything else.

About a mile north of Lincolnville Beach is a part of town with the quaint name of Ducktrap. Near the mouth of the Ducktrap River, where shoreline trees screen the water, ducks used to gather as ducks do. During moulting season, when the ducks shed their feathers and were unable to fly, foraging Native Americans would sneak up on them and capture them for dinner. Or so the story goes.

Directly offshore from Lincolnville Beach, almost within spitting distance, is the island of Islesboro, a fine day-trip destination from Lincolnville and the Camden-Rockport areas. The car ferry departs from the southern end of Lincolnville Beach.

SIGHTS
Islesboro

Lying three miles offshore from Lincolnville Beach, via 20-minute car ferry, is 12-mile-long Islesboro, a year-round community with a population of about 600—beefed up annually by a sedate summer colony. Car ferries are frequent enough to make Islesboro an ideal day-trip destination—and that's the choice of most visitors, partly because both dining and lodging are pretty scarce. The only camping is on nearby **Warren Island State Park**—and you have to have your own boat to get there. If you're not spending the night, keep an eye on the time so you don't miss the last ferry (4:30 P.M.) back to the mainland.

The best way to get an island overview is to do an end-to-end auto tour. You won't see all

The only way to Warren Island State Park, on 700-Acre Island, off Islesboro, is by personal boat.

© TOM NANGLE

the huge "cottages" tucked down long driveways, and you won't absorb island life and its rhythms (that requires a longer stay), but you'll scratch the surface of what Islesboro is about. Drive off the ferry, which docks about a third of the way down the island, and go one mile to a stop sign. Turn right and go 1.2 miles to another stop sign. Turn right, onto Main Road, and go 4.3 miles south to the Town Beach at the bottom of the island. Then backtrack on Main Road, past the turnoff to the ferry dock, heading "up island" (as it's known locally) and covering 12 miles to northernmost Pripet and Turtle Head. En route, you'll pass exclusive summer estates, workaday homes, spectacular seaside vistas, and a smattering of shops. On the up-island circuit, watch for a tiny marker on the west side of the road (0.8 mile north of the Islesboro Historical Society building). It commemorates the 1780 total eclipse witnessed

PENOBSCOT BAY

here—the first recorded in North America. At the time, British loyalists still held Islesboro, but they temporarily suspended hostilities, allowing Harvard astronomers to lug their instruments to the island and document the eclipse.

Allow time before the return ferry to visit the **Sailors' Memorial Museum,** a town-owned museum filled with seafaring memorabilia and allegedly home to a benevolent ghost or two. It's in the keeper's house adjacent to **Grindle Point Light** (207/734-2253, http://lighthouse. cc/grindle), built in 1850, rebuilt in 1875, and now automated.

The car ferry *Margaret Chase Smith* departs Lincolnville Beach almost every hour on the hour, 8 or 9 A.M. to 5 P.M., and Islesboro on the half hour, 7:30 A.M.–4:30 P.M. Round-trip fares are $22.25 for car, $7.50 adults, $2.75 kids, $6.25 adult bicycles, and $3.50 kid's bikes. Reservations are $5 extra. A slightly reduced schedule prevails late October–early May. The 20-minute trip crosses a stunning three-mile stretch of Penobscot Bay, with views of islands and the Camden Hills. In summer, avoid the biggest bottlenecks: Friday afternoon (to Islesboro), Sunday afternoon and Monday holiday afternoons (from Islesboro). The *Smith* remains on Islesboro overnight, so don't miss the last run to Lincolnville Beach. For more information contact **Maine State Ferry Service** (P.O. Box 214, Lincolnville 04849, 207/789-5611, Islesboro 207/734-6935, www.exploremaine.org).

RECREATION
Sea Kayaking and Canoeing
Ducktrap Kayak (2175 Rte. 1, Lincolnville Beach, 207/236-8608) runs guided coastal tours, with rates beginning at $30 pp. Rentals are also available for $20–30, depending upon type and size, and delivery can be arranged. If you decide you need your own kayak, Ducktrap will even sell you one.

The best places to canoe are Norton Pond and Megunticook Lake, and you can even paddle all the way from the head of Norton Pond to the foot of Megunticook Lake. The only tricky part is navigating the drainage culvert between the pond and the lake.

Swimming
Penobscot Bay flirts with Route 1 at **Lincolnville Beach,** a sandy stretch of shorefront in the congested hamlet of Lincolnville Beach. This is about as close as the road gets to the ocean. On a hot day, the sand is wall-to-wall people; during one of the coast's legendary northeasters, it's quite a wild place. There's **freshwater swimming** at several area ponds (most people would call them lakes). On Route 52 in Lincolnville Center is Breezemere Park, a small town-owned swimming/picnic area on **Norton Pond.** The Lincolnville Band, one of the oldest town bands in the country, often plays in the park's Bicentennial Bandstand, built to commemorate the town's 200th birthday. Other swimming ponds are **Coleman Pond, Pitcher Pond,** and **Knight's Pond.**

Hiking
The boundaries of both Camden Hills State Park and Fernald's Neck extend into Lincolnville, where the major state-park hike follows the **Ski Shelter Trail** to the **Bald Rock Trail.** From Route 1 in Lincolnville Beach, take Route 173 west about 2.5 miles to the marked parking area just beyond the junction of Youngtown Road. The 1,200-foot summit—with great views of Penobscot Bay (weather permitting)—is about two miles one-way, easy to moderate hiking. The route links with the rest of the state-park trail network, but unless you've arranged for a shuttle, it's best to do Bald Rock as a round-trip hike.

SHOPPING
Art, craft, and souvenir shops are clustered along the Route 1 strip at Lincolnville Beach; just north of town are a couple of unusual shops and galleries worth a visit.

Handsome, dark wood buildings 0.2 mile north of the Beach are home to **Windsor Chairmakers** (Rte. 1, Lincolnville, 207/789-5188 or 800/789-5188). You can observe the operation, browse the display area, or order some of the well-made chairs, cabinets, and tables.

Professional boatbuilder Walt Simmons has branched out into decoys and wildlife carvings, and they're just as outstanding as his boats. Walt and his wife, Karen, run **Duck Trap Decoys** (Duck Trap Rd., Lincolnville, 207/789-5363), a gallery/shop that also features the work of nearly five dozen other woodcarvers.

ACCOMMODATIONS
Bed-and-Breakfasts
About four miles north of Camden and a mile south of Lincolnville, **The Victorian by the Sea** (Seaview Dr., Lincolnville Beach, mailing address P.O. Box 1385, Camden 04843, 207/236-3785 or 800/382-9817, www.victorianbythesea.com, $169–239) overlooks the bay at the end of a winding lane from Route 1. It's a dreamy Victorian with numerous fireplaces, clawfoot tubs, and a dining room in the turret, where a four-course breakfast is served.

Private, secluded, and surrounded by 22 acres of gardens, the oceanfront, Shingle-style **Inn at the Ocean's Edge** (Rte. 1, Lincolnville Beach, mailing address P.O. Box 704, Camden 04843, 207/236-0945, www.innatoceansedge.com, $245–405) is splurge-worthy. In 2004, Tim and Joan Porta, owners of the exclusive Migis Lodge, on Sebago Lake, bought it to complement their inland resort. Every room has a king-size bed, fireplace, and whirlpool tub for two, as well as TV, air-conditioning, Wi-Fi, and superb ocean views. The grounds are lovely, with a disappearing-edge pool, and chairs placed just so to take in the views. There's an excellent restaurant on the premises (see *Food*). Rates include breakfast.

Even more private and secluded is **The Inn at Sunrise Point** (Rte. 1, FR 9, Lincolnville, mailing address P.O. Box 1344, Camden 04843, 207/236-7716 or 800/435-6278, www.sunrisepoint.com, $235–545), an elegant retreat, with all the whistles and bells you'd expect at these rates. The three handsome rooms in the main lodge, four separate cottages, a loft, and two suites are all named after Maine authors or artists. Breakfast in the conservatory is divine.

Motel
The family-run ◖ **Mount Battie Motel** (2298

Atlantic Hwy., Rte. 1, Lincolnville, 207/236-3870 or 800/224-3870, www.mountbattie.com, $89–120) has 22 charming motel-style rooms with air-conditioning, TV, phone, fridge, and continental breakfast, including home-baked treats; Wi-Fi is available in the lobby.

FOOD
Local Flavors
More local than tourist-oriented, the **Whale's Tooth Pub and Restaurant** (2431 Atlantic Hwy./Rte. 1, 207/789-5200, www.whalestoothpub.com) is a fine choice for pub fare—try the fish-and-chips—in a cozy pub-style atmosphere. It serves lunch and dinner ($14–25) Wednesday–Sunday. In winter, snuggle by the fireplace.

French flair without the attitude is why **Chez Michel** (Rte. 1, Lincolnville Beach, 207/789-5600) is a perennial favorite, even for families. Try for one of the window tables with water views. Entrées begin around $10; it serves lunch and dinner Tuesday–Sunday.

Fine Dining
For a romantic, classic French experience, head a bit inland to **Youngtown Inn and Restaurant** (581 Youngtown Rd., Lincolnville, 207/763-4290 or 800/291-8438, www.youngtowninn.com, 6–9 P.M. Tues.–Sun.), where chef/owner Manuel Mercier draws on his Parisian heritage and European training; entrées are $22–28.

The food matches the view at **The Edge** (Inn at the Ocean's Edge, Rte. 1, Lincolnville Beach, 207/236-4430, www.innatoceansedge.com), where you can dine inside or on the deck, overlooking Penobscot Bay. The menu features familiar foods with creative touches and an emphasis on fresh and local; most entrées are in the $30–36 range. Service is attentive, and details are noticed. Sunday night is pizza night, with fancy pies.

Lobster in the Rough
Lincolnville's best-known landmark is **The Lobster Pound Restaurant** (Rte. 1, Lincolnville Beach, 207/789-5550,

www.lobsterpoundmaine.com, 11:30 A.M.–8 P.M. daily, to 9 P.M. in July and Aug.). About 300 people—some days, it looks like more than that—can pile into the restaurant and enclosed patio, so be sure to make reservations on summer weekends. Despite the crowds, food and service are reliably good. Lobster, of course, is king, but the huge menu includes other seafood, poultry, and steaks. Entrées are $12–35.

INFORMATION AND SERVICES

For planning, contact Camden-Rockport-Lincolnville Chamber of Commerce (P.O. Box 919, Camden 04843, 207/236-4404 or 800/223-5459, www.visitcamden.com). Also handy is a directory published by the Lincolnville Business Group (P.O. Box 202, Lincolnville 04849, www.lincolnville.org).

Belfast Area

With a population of about 6,400, Belfast is relatively small as cities go, but changes have been occurring at lightning speed—courtesy of gigantic credit-card company MBNA (the nation's largest in affinity cards), which established a major presence here in 1996, and later was bought out by Bank of America. Even before MBNA/BA arrived, Belfast was becoming one of those off-the-beaten-track destinations popular with tuned-in travelers. Chalk that up to its status as a magnet for leftover back-to-the-landers and enough artistic types to earn the city a nod for cultural cool. Belfast has a curling club, meditation centers, an increasing number of art galleries and boutiques, dance and theater companies, the oldest shoe store in America, and half a dozen different 12-step self-help groups. The city even has a poet laureate!

This eclectic city is a work in progress, a study in Maine-style diversity. It's also a gold mine of Federal, Greek Revival, Italianate, and Victorian architecture. Take the time to stroll the well-planned backstreets, explore the shops, and hang out at the newly gussied-up waterfront.

Separating Belfast from East Belfast, the Passagassawakeag River (Puh-sag-gus-uh-WAH-keg) fortunately is known more familiarly as "the Passy." The Indian name has been translated as both "place of many ghosts" and the rather different "place for spearing sturgeon by torchlight." You choose. No matter, you can cross it via a pedestrian bridge.

Many travelers make Belfast a day stop on their way between Camden and Bar Harbor. Truly, Belfast is worth more time than that. Spend a full day or two here, and it's likely you'll be charmed like many of the other urban refugees into resettling here.

SIGHTS
Historic Walking Tour
No question, the best way to appreciate Belfast's fantastic architecture is to tour by ankle express. At the Belfast Area Chamber of Com-

A pedestrian bridge across the river is a favorite fishing spot.

© HILARY NANGLE

merce, pick up the well-researched *Belfast Historic Walking Tour* map/brochure. Among more than 40 highlights on the mile-long, self-guided route are the 1818 Federal-style **First Church,** handsome residences on **High** and **Church Streets,** and the 1840 **James P. White House** (corner of Church St. and Northport Ave., now an elegant B&B), New England's finest Greek Revival residence. Amazing for a community of this size, the city actually has three distinct National Historic Districts: Belfast Commercial Historic District (47 downtown buildings), Church Street Historic District (residential), and Primrose Hill Historic District (also residential). Another walking tour is presented by the Belfast Historical Society's **Museum in the Streets,** comprising two large panels and 30 smaller ones highlighting historic buildings and people. Signs are in English and French.

Bayside

Continuing the focus on architecture, just south of Belfast, in Northport, is the Victorian enclave of Bayside, a neighborhoody sort of place with small, well-kept, gingerbreaded cottages cheek-by-jowl on pint-size lots. Formerly known as the Northport Wesleyan Grove Campground, the village took shape in the mid-1800s as a summer retreat for Methodists. In the 1930s, the retreat was disbanded and the main meeting hall was razed, creating the waterfront park at the heart of the village. Today, many of the colorfully painted homes are rented by the week, month, or summer season, and their tenants are more likely to indulge in athletic rather than religious pursuits. The camaraderie remains, though, and a stroll (or cycle or drive) through Bayside is like a visit to another era. Bayside is four miles south of Belfast, just east of Route 1.

Temple Heights

Continue south on Shore Road from Bayside to **Temple Heights Spiritualist Camp** (Shore Rd., Northport, mailing address P.O. Box 311, Lincolnville 04849 207/338-3029, www.temple heightscamp.org), yet another religious enclave—this one still going. Founded in 1882, Temple Heights has become a shadow of its for-

mer self, reduced primarily to the funky, 12-room Nikawa Lodge on Shore Road ($35 d, $25 s, shared bath, some with ocean view), but the summer program continues, thanks to prominent mediums from all over the country. Even a temporary setback in 1996—when the camp president was suspended for allegedly putting a hex on Northport's town clerk—failed to derail the operation. Camp programs, late June–Labor Day, are open to the public; a schedule is published each spring. Spiritualist church services and group healing sessions are free; Saturday-morning workshops are $20. Better yet, sign up for a 1.5-hour or longer **group message circle,** when you'll sit with a medium and a dozen or so others and receive insights—often uncannily on target—from departed relatives or friends. Message circles occur at 7:30 P.M. Wednesday and Saturday (arrive a half-hour early). Suggested donation is $15 pp and reservations are necessary. Private readings can be arranged for a donation of $30.

PARKS AND RECREATION

One of the state's best municipal parks is just on the outskirts of downtown. Established in

© HILARY NANGLE

PENOBSCOT BAY

A grassy park on the waterfront is a fine place for a picnic in Belfast.

1904, **Belfast City Park** (87 Northport Ave., 207/338-1661, free) has lighted tennis courts, an outdoor pool, a pebbly beach, plenty of picnic tables, an unusually creative playground, lots of green space for the kids, and fantastic views of Islesboro, Blue Hill, and Penobscot Bay. For more action, right in the heart of Belfast, head for **Heritage Park,** at the bottom of Main Street, with front-row seats on waterfront happenings. Bring a picnic, grab a table, and watch the yachts, tugs, and lobster boats.

Golf

Just south of Belfast is the nine-hole **Northport Golf Club** (581 Bluff Rd., Northport, Belfast, 207/338-2270), established in 1916. Operating out of a classic shingled clubhouse, the club is open mid-April–October. Snacks and carts are available; starting times usually aren't necessary.

Excursion Boats

Sail aboard the Friendship sloop *Amity* (evenings 207/469-0849, daytime 207/323-1443, www.friendshipsloopamity.com), based at the Belfast Public Landing for 90-minute morning ($20) or 2.5-hour afternoon ($30) sails; age 15 and younger are half price. The classic Friendship sloop, built in 1901 in Friendship, was originally used for lobstering. These days, it's been beautifully restored and carries up to six passengers. Home-baked cookies, hot coffee, and tea are served on all cruises. Captain Stephen O'Connell, a former journalist, explains the boat's history and its role in lobstering and regales passengers, when asked, with tales of his experiences living in exotic locations around the world.

Take a day trip to Castine aboard the *Good Return,* operated by Belfast Bay Cruises (207/322-5530, www.belfastbaycruises.com; ticket office 17 Main St., Belfast), departing from Thompson Wharf (between Belfast Maskers theater and the pedestrian bridge). Captain Melissa Terry, a fifth-generation descendent of a whaling captain from New Bedford, Massachusetts, is a Maine Maritime Academy graduate who enjoys sharing her love of the sea. The 4.5-hour Castine Lunch Cruise ($28 adults,

$15 kids 5–15) provides time for exploring Castine and lunch (on your own). Other options include a 1.5-hour educational lobstering cruise, during which traps are hauled ($22 adults, $12 kids), one-hour harbor cruises ($11 adults, $6 kids), two-hour full-moon ice-cream cruise ($25 adult, $13 kids), and a two-hour Penobscot Bay cruise ($22 adult, $12 kids).

If you don't have your own kayak, **Water Walker** (152 Lincolnville Ave., Belfast, 207/338-6424, www.kayak-tour-maine.com) has a full range of options. Owner Ray Wirth, a Registered Maine Guide and ACA-certified open-water instructor, will arrange customized trips from a few hours to multiple days, as well as provide instruction. Rates begin at $60 for one/$70 for two for 2–3 hours.

ENTERTAINMENT

It's relatively easy to find nightlife in Belfast—not only are there theaters and a cinema, but there usually are a couple of bars open at least until midnight, and sometimes later. Some spots also feature live music, particularly on weekends.

If you don't feel like searching out a newspaper to check the entertainment listings, just go to the **Belfast Co-op Store** (123 High St., 207/338-2532) and study the bulletin board. You'll find notices for more activities than you could ever squeeze into your schedule.

Just south of Belfast, the funky **Blue Goose Dance Hall** (Rte. 1, Northport, 207/338-3003) is the site for folk concerts, contra dances, auctions, and other events. Check local papers or the Belfast Co-op Store bulletin board.

About a dozen galleries participate in Belfast Arts' **Friday Gallery Walk,** held every Friday night in July and August, and every first Friday September–December.

Check local papers for the schedule of the **Belfast Maskers** (43 Front St., Belfast, 207/338-9668, www.belfastmaskerstheater .com), a community theater group that never fails to win raves for its interpretations of contemporary and classical dramas. In winter, wear an extra pair of socks; the floor is drafty.

Also worth checking out is the **Northport Music Theater** (851 Rte. 1, Northport,

OFF THE BEATEN PATH IN LIBERTY

You'll find practically every tool possible, and then some, at Liberty Tool.

Seventeen miles west of Belfast, off Route 3, is Liberty, a tiny town with a funky tool store, quirky museum, a bargain T-shirt shop, and a great state park. Everything is seasonal, running mid-May or so through mid-October or so. Call before visiting if you want to be sure everything's open.

It's a store! It's a museum! It's amazing! More than 10,000 "useful" tools – plus used books and prints and other tidbits – fill the three-story **Liberty Tool Company** (Main St., Liberty, 207/589-4771). Drawn by nostalgia and a compulsion for handmade adzes and chisels, thousands of vintage-tool buffs arrive at this eclectic emporium each year; few leave empty-handed. Nor do the thousands of everyday home hobbiests looking to pick up a hammer or find a missing wrench to fill out a set. Nor do the antiques-seekers, who browse the trash and treasures on the upper floors. The collection is beyond amazing, especially in its organization. Owner Skip Brack brings back vanloads of finds almost every week, and after sorting and cleaning, many make it into this store.

The best-of-the-best make it into Brack's

Davistown Museum (Main St., 207/589-4900, www.davistownmuseum.org), on the third floor of the building housing Liberty Graphics, across the street. The museum houses not only a history of Maine and New England hand tools, but also local, regional, Native American. and environmental artifacts and information and an amazing collection of contemporary art, highlighted by works by artists such as Louise Nevelson (who used to buy tools across the street), Melitta Westerlund, and Phil Barter.

Downstairs is **Liberty Graphics Outlet Store** (1 Main St., 207/589-4035), selling the eco-sensitive company's overstocks, seconds, and discontinued-design T-shirts. Outstanding silkscreened designs are done with water-based inks, and many of the shirts are organic cotton; prices begin at $5.

Just down Main Street is the old **Liberty Post Office,** a unique octagonal structure that looks like an oversize box. It was built in 1867 as a harnessmaker's shop and later used as the town's post office.

Two miles west of downtown, **Lake St. George State Park** (Rte. 3, 207/589-4255, $3 adults, $1 children 5-11) is a refreshing find. This 360-acre park has wooded picnic sites with grills along the lake, a beach, rental boats, playground, volleyball and basketball courts, and five miles of hiking trails. Also available are campsites, $20 for nonresidents. Afterward, head to **John's Ice Cream** (Rte. 3, 589-3700) for amazing flavors handcrafted (homemade is too pedestrian to describe it) on the premises.

If you're up for more inland exploring, weave your way along the **Georges River Scenic Byway,** a 50-mile auto route along the St. George River (a.k.a. Georges River) from its inland headwaters to the sea in Port Clyde. The official start is at the junction of Routes 3 and 220 in Liberty, but you can follow the trail in either direction, or pick it up anywhere along the way. Road signs are posted, but it's far better to obtain a map/brochure at a chamber of commerce or other information locale. Or contact the architects of the route, **The Georges River Land Trust** (328 Main St., Rockland, 207/594-5166, www.grlt.org).

PENOBSCOT BAY

207/338-8383, www.northportmusictheater
.com, $20–25), a 136-seat theater presenting
shows mid-June–late August.

EVENTS

Belfast is a hive of activity, but lots of the surrounding Waldo County communities also put
on some ambitious fairs, festivals, and public
suppers. Check the newspapers for schedules.

The Belfast Garden Club sponsors **Open
Garden Days** once a week mid-May–mid-September at the homes of club members and friends.
Gardens are open 10 A.M.–3 P.M., rain or shine; a
$3 pp donation is requested to benefit local beau-
tification projects. Check local newspapers or ask
at the chamber of commerce for the schedule.

In early July, soon after the Fourth of July,
the **Arts in the Park** festival gets under way at
Heritage Park, on the Belfast waterfront. It's a
weekend event, two days of music, juried arts
and crafts, children's activities, and lots of food
booths. The **Belfast Bay Festival,** usually the
third week of July, has music, carnival rides,
fireworks, food, and more.

SHOPPING

It's easy and fun to shop in downtown Belfast,
a town that has so far managed to keep the big
boxes away, providing fertile ground for entrepreneurs. Downtown shops reflect the city's
population, with galleries and boutiques, thrift
and used-goods stores, and eclectic shops.

Books

Belfast's independent bookstore is a friendly
place with good intentions but not a huge inventory. The quaintly named **Fertile Mind
Bookshop** (105 Main St., Belfast, 207/338-
2498) has a particularly good children's section
and also carries magazines.

Specialty Shops

Even if shoes aren't on your shopping list, stop in
at "the oldest shoe store in America." Founded
in the 1830s(!), **Colburn Shoe Store** (81 Main
St., Belfast, 207/338-1934 or 877/338-1934)
may be old, but it isn't old-fashioned—all the
latest brands and styles are here.

America's oldest shoe store is in Belfast.

Brambles (70 Main St., Belfast, 207/338-
3448) is a gardener's delight, with fun, whimsical, and practical garden-themed merchandise.

Perhaps it's not surprising in a city named
Belfast, but **Shamrock, Thistle and Rose** (39
Main St., Belfast, 207/338-1864) is a find for
lovers of Irish goods—clothing, jewelry, original art, and even music are found here.

About two miles east of Belfast's bridge, on
the right, is the small roadside shop of **Mainely
Pottery** (181 Searsport Ave., Rte. 1, Belfast,
207/338-1108). Since 1988, Jeannette Faunce
and Jamie Oates have been marketing the work
of more than two dozen Maine potters, each
with different techniques, glazes, and styles. It's
the perfect place to select from a wide range of
reasonably priced work. Peek into the adjacent
studio and you'll find Jamie, who specializes
in lamps (under the name of Pequog Pottery)
and is happy to answer questions. Don't miss
Jeannette's lovely garden out back.

The Green Store

Calling itself a "general store for the 21st

century," The Green Store (71 Main St., Belfast, 207/338-4045) carries a huge selection of environmentally friendly products. Whether you're thinking of going off the grid, need a composting toilet, want natural fiber clothing, or other natural-living products, this is the place. A very knowledgeable staff can answer nearly any question on environmentally sustainable lifestyles.

ACCOMMODATIONS
Bed-and-Breakfasts
On a quiet side street, **The Jeweled Turret** (40 Pearl St., Belfast, 207/338-2304 or 800/696-2304, www.jeweledturret.com, $105–159) is one of Belfast's pioneer B&Bs. Carl and Cathy Heffentrager understand the business and go out of their way to make guests comfortable. The 1898 Victorian inn is loaded with handsome woodwork and Victorian antiques—plus an astonishing stone fireplace. Carl can even fix your bike, if necessary, and he's up on all the local byways.

The White House (1 Church St., Belfast, 207/338-1901 or 888/290-1901, www.mainebb.com, $115–175), the handsomest manse in Belfast, is the star of the Church Street Historic District. Built in the mid-19th century, the Greek Revival building is elegant inside and out—parlors, library, and guest rooms are accented with plaster ceiling medallions; it features marble fireplaces and a magnificent stairway. A giant copper beech tree dominates the parklike grounds and gardens. Hosts Terry Prescott and Robert Hansen will lend you a tandem bike, pack you a picnic lunch, make dinner reservations—more than the comforts of home.

Motels and Suites
The 61 rooms at the oceanfront **Belfast Harbor Inn** (91 Searsport Ave., Belfast, 207/338-2740 or 800/545-8576, www.belfastharborinn.com, $79–149 d) have TV, air-conditioning, Wi-Fi, and phones, and there's an outdoor heated pool, a real plus for families, as is the laundry. Foxy's Steakhouse is next door. Pets are allowed in some rooms for $10 per night. Rates include a continental breakfast buffet. If you can swing it, request an ocean-view room.

Here's a nice spot with an artsy touch.

Phoenix Row (157 High St., Belfast, 207/338-0476, www.phoenixrow.com) is a restored 1924 three-story brick building downtown, with galleries on the lower floors and four one- and two-bedroom guest suites, each with kitchen, above. All have air-conditioning and TV; a few have decks with harbor views. Rates are $115–189/night or $650–1,000/week.

Campground
Every one of the 44 mostly open sites at the **Moorings Oceanfront RV Resort** (191 Searsport Ave., Rte. 1, Belfast, 207/338-6860, www.mooringscamp.com) has an ocean view and hookups. Views are fabulous, and the rocky beach has a pocket of sand; swimming is only for the hardy. The downsides: Many sites feel crowded, and there's often a wait for showers. Sites in midsummer are $40–48 (two adults plus three kids under 17). Coffee is available every morning, and special events are often held, including lobster shore dinners, barbecues, and deep-fried turkey fests. Facilities include laundry, play area, kayak launch, game room, Wi-Fi, and on-site restaurant.

Seasonal Rentals
Most of the Belfast area's seasonal rentals are in Northport, specifically the charming Victorian enclave of Bayside (see *Sights*). For info, contact **Bayside Cottage Rentals** (539 Bluff Rd., Northport, 207/338-5355, www.baysidecottagerentals.com).

FOOD
Local Flavors
Wraps are fast food at **Bay Wrap** (102 Main St., Belfast, 207/338-9757, www.baywrap.com, 11 A.M.–7 P.M. Mon.–Fri., to 4 P.M. Sat.). There's no limit to what the staff can stuff into various flavors of tortillas. Go for the adventure. Wraps are in the $6 range. Eat here or get them to go.

The **Belfast Co-op Store** (123 High St., Belfast, 207/338-2532, www.belfast.coop, 7:30 A.M.–8 P.M. daily) is an experience in itself. You'll have a good impression of Belfast after one glance at the clientele and the bulletin board. Open to members and non-members alike (with lower prices for members), the co-op store has local organic produce, fresh and frozen pesto, baked goods, teas and coffees, bulk grains and nuts, a great deli, meat and fish, dozens of cheeses, camping foods, wine and beer, and a deli-café serving lunches daily and weekend brunches.

The Belfast Farmers Market (Washington St. parking lot, downtown Belfast, 9 A.M.–1 P.M. Fri.) provides the perfect opportunity for stocking up for a picnic. In addition to plentiful veggies, you'll find honey, sweets, eggs, chicken pies, goat cheeses, breads, berries and apples in season, jams, medicinal and culinary herbs, jams, salsa, dillybeans, Asian vegetables, ready-to-eat Korean specialties, and even sushi.

Ethnic Fare

Don't be put off by the lackluster exterior of **Seng Thai** (160 Searsport Ave., Rte. 1, Belfast, 207/338-0010, 11 A.M.–9 P.M. Tues.–Sun.), a small, low building across from the Comfort Inn. Inside, the ambience is pleasant, the service is good, everything's available for takeout if you prefer, and best of all, it's really good Thai food (entrées $8–14).

Casual Dining

A longtime standby for creative (including vegetarian) world cuisine, **Darby's Restaurant and Pub** (155 High St., Belfast, 207/338-2339, 11:30 A.M.–3:30 P.M. and 5–9 P.M. daily) served tofu before tofu was cool. This place has been providing food and drink since just after the Civil War; the tin ceilings and antique bar are reminders of that. Entrées $11–20.

Fresh food prepared in creative ways has earned ❰ **Chase's Daily** (96 Main St., Belfast, 207/338-0555, 7 A.M.–5 P.M. Tues.–Sat., to 8 P.M. Fri, 8 A.M.–2 P.M. Sun.) a devoted local following. The emphasis is on vegetarian fare, with most of the vegetables coming from the Chase family farm in nearby Freedom. Most choices are in the $4–7 range; dinner entrées $15–18. The restaurant doubles as an art gallery, farmers market, and bakery. It's not the place for a quiet dinner, as the space is large and tends to be loud.

Industrial chic, casual, and laid-back best describe ❰ **Three Tides** (2 Pinchy La., on Marshall Wharf, Belfast, 207/338-1707, www.3tides.com, 4 P.M.–1 A.M. Tues.–Sat. and Sun. in summer). Grab a booth inside, a seat at the bar, or a table on the deck overlooking the working harbor, and then choose from the tapas-style menu ($3.50–12). You might even play a game of bocce while waiting. Beers and ales are brewed on the premises. Also part of the operation is **LB,** a lobster pound, so lobster is almost always on the menu.

It doesn't look like much from the outside, but **Papa J's and the Lobster Bar** (193 Searsport Ave., Belfast, 207/338-6464, www.3tides.com, 4–9 P.M. Tues.–Sat., to 10 P.M. Fri. and Sat.) is warm and welcoming inside, with nice water views, a casual style, and—most important—well-prepared food ($11–24) complemented by a surprisingly good wine list. Order the lobster and feta pizza; you won't be disappointed.

Lobster in the Rough

Young's Lobster Pound (2 Fairview St., Belfast, 207/338-1160, 8 A.M.–8 P.M. daily May–Nov.) is a classic eat-on-the-dock lobster place overlooking the bay. Dress down, relax, and pile into the crustaceans. BYOB. No credit cards. From downtown, cross the bridge to East Belfast and turn right at Jed's Restaurant. Continue to the end of the street.

INFORMATION AND SERVICES
Information

The Belfast Area Chamber of Commerce (17 Main St., P.O. Box 58, Belfast 04915, 207/338-5900, www.belfastmaine.org) has plenty of info about the region.

Check out Belfast Free Library (106 High St., Belfast, 207/338-3884, www.belfast.lib.me.us).

Public Restrooms

Facilities are at the waterfront Public Landing, in the railroad station, at the Waldo County Court House, and at the Waldo County General Hospital.

Searsport Area

Five miles northeast of downtown Belfast, you're in the heart of Searsport, a name synonymous with the sea, thanks to an enduring oceangoing tradition that's appropriately commemorated here in the state's oldest maritime museum. The seafaring heyday occurred in the mid-19th century, but settlers from the Massachusetts Colony had already made inroads here 200 years earlier. By the 1750s, Fort Pownall, in nearby Stockton Springs, was a strategic site during the French and Indian War (the American phase of Europe's Seven Years' War).

Shipbuilding was under way by 1791, reaching a crescendo between 1845 and 1866, with six year-round shipyards and nearly a dozen more seasonal ones. By 1885, 10 percent of all full-rigged American-flag ships on the high seas were under the command of Searsport and Stockton Springs captains—many bearing the name of Pendleton, Nichols, or Carver. Many of these were involved in the perilous China trade, rounding notorious Cape Horn with great regularity.

All this global contact shaped Searsport's culture, adding a veneer of cosmopolitan sophistication. Imposing mansions of seafaring families were filled with fabulous Oriental treasures, many of which eventually made their way to the Penobscot Marine Museum. Brick-lined Main Street is more evidence of the mid-19th-century wealth, and local churches reaped the benefits of residents' generosity. The Second Congregational Church, known as the Safe Harbor Church and patronized by captains and shipbuilders (most ordinary seamen attended the Methodist church), boasts recently restored Tiffany-style windows and a Christopher Wren steeple.

Another inkling of this area's oceangoing superiority comes from visits to local burial grounds: Check out the headstones at Gordon, Bowditch, and Sandy Point cemeteries. Many have fascinating tales to tell.

Today, with a population of just under 2,600, the Searsport area's major draws are the Penobscot Marine Museum, the still-handsome brick Historic District, several B&Bs, a couple of special state parks, and wall-to-wall antiques shops and flea markets.

The Maine Historic Preservation Commission considers the buildings in Searsport's Main Street Historic District the best examples of their type outside of Portland—a frozen-in-time, mid-19th-century cluster of brick and granite structures. The ground floors of most of the buildings are shops or restaurants; make time to stop in and admire their interiors.

SIGHTS
🕻 Penobscot Marine Museum

Exquisite marine paintings, ship models, and unusual China-trade *objets* are just a few of the 10,000 treasures at the Penobscot Marine Museum (5 Church St., at Rte. 1, Searsport, 207/548-2529, www.penobscotmarine museum.org, 10 A.M.–5 P.M. Mon.–Sat., noon–5 P.M. Sun., $8 adults, $3 kids 7–15, or $18 per family), Maine's oldest maritime museum—founded in 1936. Allow several hours to explore the 13 old and new buildings just east of downtown. For a start, you'll see one of the nation's largest collections of paintings by marine artists James and Thomas Buttersworth. And the 1830s Fowler-True-Ross House is filled with exotic artifacts from foreign lands. Check out the exhibits, have a picnic, and then visit the particularly well-stocked museum store on Main Street (Rte. 1). Pick up tickets at the Museum Admissions Building (restrooms are here, as well as in the museum store and the library), first building on your left on Church Street. Call or check the website for the schedule of lectures, concerts, and temporary exhibits. This isn't a very sophisticated museum, but it is a treasure. It's open late May–mid-October.

PENOBSCOT BAY

An inland lighthouse marks BlueJacket Shipcrafters, which builds museum-quality boat models.

© HILARY NANGLE

BlueJacket Shipcrafters

Complementing the collections at the museum are the classic and contemporary models built by BlueJacket Shipcrafters (160 E. Main St., Rte. 1, Searsport, 800/448-5567), which boasts Maine's largest selection of ship models and nautical gifts. Even if you're not a hobbiest, stop in to see the incredibly detailed models on display. Shipcrafters is renowned for building one-of-a-kind museum-quality custom models—it's the official modelmaker for the U.S. Navy—but don't despair, there are kits here for all abilities (and budgets). It's easy to find: Just look for the inland lighthouse on Route 1.

PARKS AND RECREATION
Moose Point State Park

Here's a smallish park with a biggish view—183 acres wedged between Route 1 and a dramatic Penobscot Bay panorama. Moose Point State Park (Rte. 1, Searsport, 207/548-2882, $2 adults, $1 kids 5–11) is 1.5 miles south of

downtown Searsport. Bring a picnic, let the kids hang out and play (there's no swimming, but good tide pooling at low tide), or walk through the woods or along the meadow trail. Moose-crossing signs are posted on the highway, but don't count on seeing one. It's open late May–October 1, but since it's alongside the highway, the park is accessible, weather permitting, all year.

Sears Island

After almost two decades of heavy-duty squabbling over a proposed cargo port on Searsport's 940-acre Sears Island, the state bought the island for $4 million in November 1997. Discussions are ongoing about the establishment of visitor facilities, but for now, the only improvement on this lovely, causeway-linked island is a road. It's a fine place for biking, picnicking, walking, fishing, and cross-country skiing. From downtown Searsport, continue northeast on Route 1 two miles to Sears Island Road (on your right). Turn and go 1.2 miles to the beginning of the island, where you can pull off and park before a gate (cars aren't allowed on the island). An easy 1.5-mile walk will take you to the other side of the island, overlooking Mack Point (site of a rather unattractive cargo port) and hills off to the left. Bring a picnic and binoculars—and a swimsuit if you're hardy enough to brave the water.

Fort Point State Park

Continuing northeast on Route 1 from Sears Island will get you to the turnoff for Fort Point State Park (Fort Point Rd., Stockton Springs, 207/567-3356, $2 adults, $1 kids 5–11) on Cape Jellison's eastern tip. Within the 154-acre park are the earthworks of 18th-century **Fort Pownall** (a British fortress built in the French and Indian War), **Fort Point Light** (a square, 26-foot, 19th-century tower guarding the mouth of the Penobscot River) and adjacent bell tower, shoreline trails, and a 200-foot pier where you can fish or bird- or boat-watch. (Birders can spot waterfowl—especially ruddy ducks, but also eagles and osprey.) Bring picnic fixings, but stay clear of the keeper's house—

it's private. At the Route 1 fork for Stockton Springs, bear right onto Main Street and continue to Mill Road, in the village center. Turn right and then left onto East Cape Road, then another left onto Fort Point Road, which leads to the parking area. Officially, the park is open late May–Labor Day, but it's accessible all year, weather permitting.

⟨ Fort Knox

Looming over Bucksport Harbor, the *other* Fort Knox (Rte. 174, Prospect, 207/469-7719, http://fortknox.maineguide.com, 9 A.M.–sunset May 1–Nov. 1, $3 adults, $1 kids 5–11) is a 125-acre state historic site, just off Route 1. Named for Major General Henry Knox, George Washington's first secretary of war, the sprawling granite fort was begun in 1844. Built to protect the upper Penobscot River from attack, it was never finished and never saw battle. Still, it was, as guide Kathy Williamson said: "very well thought out and planned, and that may have been its best defense." Begin your visit at the Visitor and Education Center, operated by the Friends of Fort Knox, a nonprofit group that has partnered with the state to preserve and interpret the fort. Guided tours are available Memorial Day–Labor Day, and well worth it, as guides point out some of the fort's distinguishing features, including two complete Rodman canons. In 2004, restoration of the Fort Knox Officers' Quarters was completed. Wear rubberized shoes and bring a flashlight to explore the underground passages; you can set the kids loose. The fort hosts Civil War reenactments several times a summer (check with the chamber of commerce). The Halloween Fright at the Fort is a ghoulish event for the brave. The grounds are accessible all year. Bring a picnic; views over the river to Bucksport are fabulous.

⟨ Penobscot Narrows Bridge and Observatory

Do not miss the Penobscot Narrows Bridge and Observatory (9 A.M.–5 P.M. late May–Nov. 1, $5 adults, $3 ages 5–11, includes fort admission), accessible via Fort Knox. The observatory tops the 420-foot-high west tower of the new bridge spanning the Penobscot River. It's one of only three such structures in the world and the only one in the States. You'll zip up in an elevator, and when the doors open, you're facing a wall of glass (yes, it's a bit of a shocker, downright terrifying for anyone with a serious fear of heights). Ascend two more flights (elevator available), and you're in the glass-walled observatory; the views on a clear day extend from Mt. Katahdin to Mount Desert Island. Even when it's hazy, it's still a neat experience.

Bicycling

Birgfeld's Bicycle Shop (184 E. Main St., Rte. 1, Searsport, 207/548-2916 or 800/206-2916), in business since the 1970s, is a mandatory stop for any cyclist, novice or pro. Local information on about 15 biking loops, supplies, maps, weekly group rides, sales (also skateboards and scooters), and excellent repair services are all part of the Birgfeld's mix.

An especially good ride in this area is the

© HILARY NANGLE

An observatory caps one tower of the new Penobscot Narrows Bridge.

PENOBSCOT BAY

Cape Jellison loop in Stockton Springs, even though it means biking from Birgfeld's about four miles along congested Route 1 (be extremely cautious). If you have your own bike or a car to transport the rental, park at Stockton Springs Elementary School and do the loop from there. Including a detour to Fort Point, the ride totals less than 10 miles from downtown Stockton Springs.

SHOPPING

The word "shopping" in Searsport usually applies to antiques—from 25-cent flea-market collectibles to well-used tools to high-end china, furniture, and glassware. The town has more than a dozen separate businesses—and some of *those* are group shops with multiple dealers. Searsport vies with Wiscasset as Maine's "Antiques Capital."

More than two dozen dealers supply the juried inventory for Bob and Phyllis Sommer's **Pumpkin Patch** (15 W. Main St., Rte. 1, Searsport, 207/548-6047)—with a heavy emphasis on Maine antiques. Specialties include quilts (at least 80 are always on hand), silver, paint-decorated furniture, Victoriana, and nautical and Native American items.

More than 70 dealers sell their antiques and collectibles at **Searsport Antique Mall** (149 E. Main St., Rte. 1, Searsport, 207/548-2640), making it another worthwhile stop for those seeking oldies but goodies.

Close to the highway in a farm stand–style building about a mile east of downtown Searsport, the **Waldo County Craft Co-op** (1778 E. Main St., Rte. 1, Searsport, 207/548-6686) features the work of about 30 Mainers: quilts, jams, bears, dolls, jewelry, baskets, pottery, floor cloths, and lots else.

Are you a hooker? Thirteen rooms full of hooked rugs, and supplies, fill **Searsport Rug Hooking** (396 E. Main St.,/Rte. 1, Searsport, 207/548-6100, www.searsportrughooking .com), in the midst of antiques shops and flea markets at the eastern end of town. Mother-daughter team of Christine Sherman and Julie Mattison, along with a talented staff, not only sell rugs, patterns, wool, and all the other supplies and necessities of the craft, they also design the patterns, dye the wools, teach, and, demonstrate.

Teddy bear fans must stop at **Cranberry Hollow** (157 W. Main St., Rte. 1, Searsport, 207/548-2647), a shop filled with stuffed bears, quilts, and other country folk items. You can also order a custom bear.

ACCOMMODATIONS
Bed-and-Breakfasts

The impressive **Carriage House Inn** (120 E. Main St., Searsport, 207/548-2167 or 800/578-2167, www.carriagehouseinmaine.com, $95–125), a National Historic Register sea captain's home, has been most recently restored by Marcia Mackwardt. Built in 1874 by Captain John McGilbery, it later became home to impressionist painter Waldo Pierce, whose friend Ernest Hemingway visited the inn often. The architectural detailing and 12-foot ceilings add elegance to this grand property. Each of the three guest rooms, as well as the public rooms, is decorated with Victorian-era antiques and family heirlooms. A multicourse breakfast and afternoon snacks are included.

Waving pennants mark the entrance to **1794 Watchtide** (190 W. Main St., Rte. 1, Searsport, 207/548-6575 or 800/698-6575, www.watchtide.com, $135–190), in a sprawling late-18th-century sea captain's home formerly known as The College Club Inn. Each of the three rooms and two suites has a historic-name connection; the Eleanor Roosevelt Suite acknowledges visits by former first ladies in decades past. Amenities are endless, from air-conditioning and white-noise clock radios (the inn is on a busy highway) to hot and cold drinks to unusual snacks. Two rooms have whirlpool tubs. Rooms in the back have the nicest views and are most quiet. Breakfasts are fabulous. Collapse on the 60-foot sun porch, overlooking the bay, and you may never want to leave.

Deb Bush and Cathy Keating are the über-enthusiastic hosts—and gardeners—at the **Wildflower Inn** (2 Black Rd. S/Rte. 1, Searsport, 207/548-2112 or 888/546-2112, www .wildflowerinnme.com, $85–140), an easy walk to downtown shops and the museum. Once home to a sailmaker and a sea captain, the extended Cape now has four guestrooms (Wi-Fi, air-conditioning, white-noise clocks, TV) along with plenty of shared living space, including double parlors. The decor is light, a mix of antiques and contemporary pieces. A full breakfast is served at 8:30 A.M., and there's a cookie jar should you get hungry later in the day.

Motel

The **Yardarm** (172 E. Main St., Rte. 1, P.O. Box 246, Searsport 04974, www.searsport maine.com, $80–120 peak), a small motel set back from the road, is next door to BlueJacket Shipcrafters. Each of the 18 pine-paneled units has TV, air-conditioning, and phone; suites (perfect for families) have a dinette, microwave, and small fridge. A continental breakfast is served in a cheery breakfast room in the adjacent farmhouse. It's open May–late October.

Campground

How can you beat 1,100 feet of tidal oceanfront and unobstructed views of Islesboro, Castine, and Penobscot Bay? **Searsport Shores Camping Resort** (216 W. Main St., Rte. 1, Searsport, 207/548-6059, www.campocean .com) gets high marks for its fabulous setting. About 120 good-size sites (including walk-in, oceanfront tenting sites) go for $36–53 a day. Facilities include a private beach, small store, free showers, laundry, play areas, recreation hall, nature trails, and volleyball court. Request a site away from organized-activity areas. Bring a sea kayak and launch it here. Leashed pets are allowed. In early September, the campground hosts Fiber Arts College, a weekend of classes, demonstrations, and camaraderie for spinners, hookers, weavers, and the like.

FOOD

The **⟨ Anglers Restaurant** (215 E. Main St., Rte. 1, Searsport, 207/548-2405, 11 A.M.–8 P.M. daily) is probably the least assuming and one of the most popular restaurants around. Expect hearty New England cooking, hefty portions, local color, no frills, and a bill that won't dent your wallet. Big favorites are the chowders and stews and lobster rolls. Dinner entrées are $9–14, although lobsters are higher. The "minnow menu" for smaller appetites runs $6–13. Desserts are a specialty: The gingerbread with whipped cream is divine; kids love the "bucket o' worms." If it's not too busy, and you've ordered a lobster, ask owner Buddy Hall if he'll demonstrate hypnotizing it. It's adjacent to The Bait's Motel, 1.5 miles northeast of downtown Searsport.

Good home cooking with an emphasis on fried food has made **Just Barb's** (Main St./Rte. 1, Stockton Springs, 207/567-3886) a dandy place for an unfussy meal at a low price. Fried clams and scallop stew are both winners; finish up with a slab of pie or shortcake. It's open for breakfast, lunch, and dinner daily—the $6.99 all-you-can-eat fish-and-chips platter is always available, and the Friday night prime rib special always draws a crowd.

The accent is Italian at **Abbracci** (225 W. Main St., Searsport, 207/548-2010, 11:30 A.M.–8 P.M., to 5 P.M. Sun.), a combination bakery, trattoria, and espresso bar south of downtown Searsport. Choose from sandwiches, salads, soups, and specialty pizzas at lunch, and a handful of traditional entrées ($12–18), such as eggplant parm and spaghetti and meatballs at dinner.

INFORMATION AND SERVICES

The Belfast Area Chamber of Commerce (P.O. Box 58, Belfast 04915, 207/338-5900, www .belfastmaine.org) and Waldo County Marketing Association (P.O. Box 139, Searsport 04974, 800/870-9934, www.waldocounty maine.com) have information about the Belfast area. The chamber operates a seasonal visitors information center (15 Main St.).

Searsport's small, self-serve info center is open on an unpredictable schedule. It's in a shedlike building on Route 1 (at Norris St.), across from the Pumpkin Patch antiques shop.

Check out Carver Memorial Library (Mortland Rd. at Union St., Searsport, 207/548-2303, www.carver.lib.me.us).

BLUE HILL PENINSULA AND DEER ISLE

The Blue Hill Peninsula, once dubbed "The Fertile Crescent," is unique. Few other Maine locales harbor such a high concentration of artisans, musicians, and on-their-feet retirees juxtaposed with top-flight wooden-boat builders, lobstermen, and umpteenth-generation Mainers. Perhaps surprisingly, the mix seems to work.

Anchored by the towns of Bucksport to the east and Ellsworth to the west, the peninsula comprises several enclaves with markedly distinctive personalities. Blue Hill, Castine, Orland, Brooklin, Brooksville, and Sedgwick are stitched together by a network of narrow, winding country roads. Thanks to the mapmaker-challenging coastline and a handful of freshwater ponds and rivers, there's a view of water around nearly every bend.

You can watch the sun set from atop Blue Hill Mountain; tour the home of the fascinating Jonathan Fisher; stroll through the village of Castine (charming verging on precious), whose streets are lined with dowager-like homes; visit *WoodenBoat* magazine's world headquarters in tiny Brooklin; and browse top-notch studios and galleries throughout the peninsula. Venture a bit inland of Route 1, and you find lovely lakes for paddling and swimming and another hill to hike.

After weaving your way down the Blue Hill Peninsula and crossing the soaring pray-as-you-go bridge to Little Deer Isle, you've entered the realm of island living. Sure, bridges and causeways connect the points, but the farther down you drive, the more removed from civilization you'll feel. The pace slows,

© HILARY NANGLE

HIGHLIGHTS

◖ The Parson Fisher House: More than just another historic house, the Parson Fisher House is a remarkable testimony to one man's ingenuity (page 251).

◖ Blue Hill Mountain: It's a relatively easy hike for fabulous 360-degree views from the summit of this local landmark (page 251).

◖ The Good Life Center: Remember the back-to-the-land movement of the 1960s? Refresh that memory and learn how to live a sustainable life as did founders Helen and Scott Nearing (page 258).

◖ Holbrook Island Sanctuary State Park: Varied hiking trails and great birding are the rewards for finding this off-the-beaten-path preserve (page 260).

◖ Flash in the Pans Community Steel Band Concerts: Close your eyes, and you might think you're on a Caribbean island rather than in Maine when you hear this phenomenal steel-pan band (page 262).

◖ Castine Historic Tour: A turbulent history detailed on signs throughout town make Castine an irresistible place to tour on foot or bike (page 266).

◖ Sea Kayaking: Hook up with "Kayak Karen" in Castine for a tour (page 268).

◖ Haystack Mountain School of Crafts: Arrange your schedule to visit the architect-designed campus of this renowned oceanfront school (page 275).

◖ Art and Craft Galleries: The Haystack crafts school has inspired dozens of world-class artisans to set up shop on Deer Isle (page 281).

◖ Acadia National Park: Tipping sparsely populated **Isle au Haut** is a remote section of the national park, perfect for a day trip or longer (page 288).

LOOK FOR ◖ TO FIND RECOMMENDED SIGHTS, ACTIVITIES, DINING, AND LODGING.

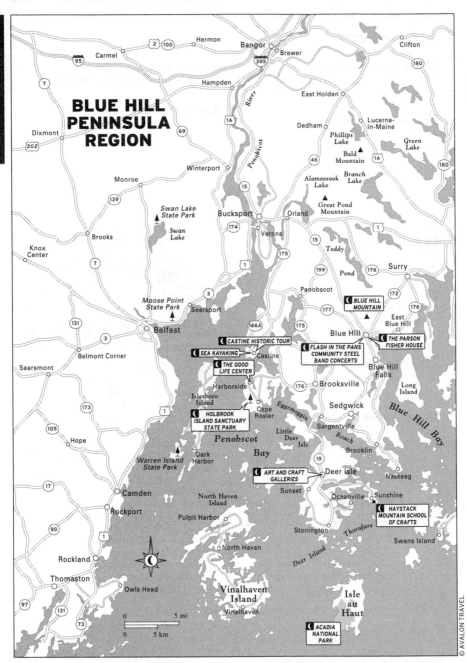

BLUE HILL PENINSULA REGION

© AVALON TRAVEL

the population dwindles. Fishing and lobstering are the mainstays, and lobster boats rest near many homes and trap fences edge properties. If your ultimate destination is the section of Acadia National Park on Isle au Haut, the drive down Deer Isle serves to help disconnect you from the mainland. To reach the park's acreage on Isle au Haut, after wending your way through Little Deer Isle and Deer Isle, you'll board the Isle au Haut ferryboat for the trip down Merchant Row to the island.

PLANNING YOUR TIME

To truly enjoy this region, you'll want to spend at least three or four days here, perhaps splitting your lodging between two or three locations. The region is designed for leisurely exploring; you won't be able to zip from one location to another. Traveling along the winding roads, discovering galleries and country stores, and lodging at traditional inns are all part of the experience.

Arts fans will want to concentrate their efforts in Blue Hill, Deer Isle, and Stonington. Outdoor-oriented folks should consider Deer Isle, Stonington, or Castine as a base for sea kayaking or exploring the area preserves. For architecture and history buffs, Castine is a must. Better yet, just settle into a cottage at one of the traditional lodges for a week, enjoying breakfast and dinner at the main inn and using your days to explore all that the region has to offer.

No visit to this region is complete without at least a cruise by if not a visit to Isle au Haut, an offshore island that's home to a remote section of Acadia National Park. Allow at least a few hours for a ride on the mail boat, but if you can afford the time, spend a full day hiking the park's trails. Don't forget to pack food and water.

Bucksport Area

The new Penobscot Narrows Bridge provides an elegant entry to the Bucksport area, a longtime rough-and-ready river port and papermaking town that's slowly gentrifying. Bucksport is no upstart. Native Americans first gravitated to these Penobscot River shores in summers, finding here a rich source of salmon for food and grasses for basketmaking. In 1764, it was officially settled by Colonel Jonathan Buck, a Massachusetts Bay Colony surveyor who modestly named it Buckstown and organized a booming shipping business here. His remains are interred in a local cemetery, where his tombstone bears the distinct outline of a woman's leg; this is allegedly the result of a curse by a witch Buck ordered executed, but in fact it's probably a flaw in the granite. Most townsfolk prefer not to discuss the matter, but the myth refuses to die—and it has immortalized a man whose name might otherwise have been consigned to musty history books. (The monument is across Route 1 from the Hannaford supermarket, on the corner of Hinks Street.)

Just south of Bucksport, at the bend in the Penobscot River, Verona Island is best known as the mile-long link between Prospect and Bucksport. Just before you cross the bridge from Verona to Bucksport, hang a left and then a quick right to a small municipal park with a boat launch and broad views of Bucksport Harbor (and the paper mill). In the Buck Memorial Library is a scale model of Admiral Robert Peary's Arctic exploration vessel, the *Roosevelt,* built on this site.

Bucksport really isn't considered part of the Blue Hill peninsula, but there are some sights here worth a look-see, a nice riverfront walkway, and area accommodations that are reasonably priced. Route 1 east of Bucksport leads to Orland, with an idyllic setting on the banks of the Narramissic River. It's also the site of a unique service organization called H.O.M.E. (Homeworkers Organized for More Employment). East Orland (officially part of Orland) claims the Craig Brook National Fish Hatchery and Great Pond Mountain (you can't miss it, jutting from the landscape on the left as you drive east on Route 1).

SIGHTS
Old-Time Flicks
Phoenixlike, the 1916 **Alamo Theatre** (85 Main St., Bucksport, 207/469-0924 or 800/639-1636, event line 207/469-6910, www .alamotheatre.org) has been retrofitted for a new life—focusing on films about New England produced and/or revived by unique **Northeast Historic Film (NHF),** which is headquartered here. Stop in, survey the restoration, visit the displays (donation requested), and browse the Alamo Theatre Store for antique postcards, T-shirts, toys, and reasonably priced videos on ice harvesting, lumberjacks, maple sugaring, and other traditional New England topics. One-half mile west of Route 1, it's open 9 A.M.–4 P.M. weekdays all year. The Alamo has also become an active cinema, screening classic and current films regularly in the 120-seat theater, usually weekends. Each summer there's also a silent film festival.

H.O.M.E.
Adjacent to the flashing light on Route 1 in Orland, H.O.M.E. is tough to categorize. Linked with the international Emmaus Movement founded by a French priest, H.O.M.E. (Homeworkers Organized for More Employment) was started in 1970 by Lucy Poulin, still the guiding force, and two nuns at a nearby convent. The quasireligious organization shelters refugees and the homeless, operates a soup kitchen and a car-repair service, runs a day-care center, and teaches work skills in a variety of hands-on cooperative programs. Seventy percent of its income comes from sales of crafts, produce, and services. At the Route 1 store (corner of Upper Falls Rd.; open 9 A.M.–4:30 P.M. daily), you can buy handmade quilts, organic produce, maple syrup, and jams—and support a worthwhile effort. You can also tour the crafts workshops on the property. To volunteer time in the workshops, store, or learning center, write P.O. Box 10, Orland 04472, or call 207/469-7961.

PARKS AND RECREATION
For a day of hiking, picnicking, swimming, canoeing, and a bit of natural history, pack a lunch and head for 135-acre **Craig Brook National Fish Hatchery** (306 Hatchery Rd., East Orland, 207/469-2803), on Alamoosook Lake. Turn off Route 1 six miles east of Bucksport and continue 1.4 miles north to the parking area just above the visitors center (open 8:30 A.M.– 3:30 P.M. weekdays and most weekends in summer; no charge; maps and restroom), with interactive displays on Atlantic salmon (don't miss the downstairs viewing area). The grounds are accessible all year, 6 A.M.–sunset daily. Established in 1871, the U.S. Fish and Wildlife Service hatchery raises sea-run Atlantic salmon for stocking seven Maine rivers, and each river has a different strain, so they're kept separate. The birch-lined shorefront has picnic tables, a boat-launching ramp, Atlantic salmon display pool, additional parking, and a spectacular cross-lake view. Watch for eagles, osprey, and loons. Also on the premises is the small Atlantic Salmon Museum, operated by the Friends of Craig Brook, with salmon and fly-fishing artifacts and memorabilia. Hiking options include nature trails through old-growth woods between Alamoosook and Craig Ponds and an easy-to-moderate two-hour (round-trip) hike up Great Pond Mountain.

Stroll the one-mile **Bucksport Waterfront Walkway,** from the Bucksport/Verona Bridge to Webber Docks. Along the way are historical markers, picnic tables, a gazebo, a restroom, and expansive views of the harbor and Fort Knox.

Canoeing
If you've brought a canoe, **Silver Lake,** just two miles north of downtown Bucksport, is beautiful place for a paddle. There's no development along its shores, and the birding is excellent. No swimming ($500 fine); this is Bucksport's reservoir. To get to the public launch, take Route 15 north off Route 1 after crossing the Verona-Bucksport Bridge. Go 0.5 mile and turn right on McDonald Road, which becomes Silver Lake Road, and follow it 2.1 miles to the launch site.

Hiking

The biggest rewards for the 1.8-mile easy–moderate hike up 1,038-foot **Great Pond Mountain** are 360-degree views and lots of space for panoramic picnics. On a clear day, Baxter State Park's Katahdin is visible from the peak's north side. In fall, watch for migrating hawks. Access to the mountain is via gated private property beginning about a mile north of Craig Brook National Fish Hatchery on Hatchery Road, East Orland. Roadside parking is available near the trailhead, but during fall-foliage season, you may need to park at the hatchery. Pick up a brochure from the box at the trailhead, stay on the trail, and respect the surrounding private property. The **Great Pond Mountain Conservation Trust** (P.O. Box 266, Orland 04472, 207/469-6772) acts as conscientious local steward for Great Pond Mountain and surrounding wild lands. It also hosts hikes and other activities.

River Cruise

See Fort Knox and the bridges from the water, on a narrated trip aboard *Lil' Toot* with **Bucksport Harbor Tours** (207/469-7498, www.littletoottours.com). Ninety-minute tours depart from the Bucksport Town Dock, five times Wednesday–Saturday late June–early September, four times Friday and Saturday through mid-October. Buy tickets, $15–20 adult, $8–10 children 16 and under, at **Dock Side Variety** (96 Main St., Bucksport).

ACCOMMODATIONS
Bed-and-Breakfasts

The most attractive B&B in this area is the 1820 **The Orland House** (10 Narramissic Dr., Orland, 207/469-1144, www.orlandhousebb .com, $85–105). Alvion and Cynthia Kimball's elegant, yet comfortable, Greek Revival home overlooks the Narramissic River. It's been beautifully restored with plenty of creature comforts.

Location, location, location. If only the six simple rooms at the **Alamoosook Lakeside Inn** (off Rte. 1, P.O. Box 16, Orland 04472, 866/459-6393 or 207/469-6393, www.alamoosook lakesideinn.com, $125 d) actually overlooked the lake, then it would be the perfect, rustic lakeside lodge. The property is gorgeous, the location well-suited for exploring the area, but the rooms are so-so, with tiny bathrooms. All have windows and doors opening onto a long sunporch overlooking the lake. A full breakfast is served. Alamoosook is great for wildlife-watching and fishing, and guests have access to canoes and kayaks. Paddle across the lake to the fish hatchery for a hike up Great Pond Mountain.

Motels

In downtown Bucksport, the award for best view goes to the **Fort Knox Inn** (64 Main St., P.O. Box 826, Bucksport 04416, 207/469-3113 or 800/528-1234, $99–159), a four-story Best Western motel nudged right up to the harbor's edge. Forty modern rooms have phones, air-conditioning, and cable TV. Be sure to request a water view, or you'll be facing a parking lot.

Campgrounds

The rivers, lakes, and ponds in the area between Bucksport and Ellsworth make it especially appealing for camping, and sites tend to be cheaper than in the Bar Harbor area. During July and August, especially weekends, reservations are wise.

Six miles east of Bucksport, across from Craig Pond Road, is Back Ridge Road, leading to **Balsam Cove Campground** (P.O. Box C, East Orland 04431, 207/469-7771 or 800/469-7771, www.balsamcove.com, $25–32). From Route 1, take Back Ridge Road 1.5 miles to the left turn for the campground, on the shores of 10-mile-long Toddy Pond. Facilities on the 50 acres include 60 wooded tent and RV sites, a one-room rental cabin ($60), on-site rental trailers ($75), dump station, store, laundry, free showers, boat rentals, and freshwater swimming. It's open late May–late September; dogs are $2/day.

The same season holds for 10-acre **Whispering Pines Campground** (Rte. 1, East Orland, 207/469-3443, www.whisperingpinesmaine.com, $26), also on Toddy Pond but with access directly from Route 1. Facilities include 50 tent and RV sites (request one close to the pond), canoes and rowboats, freshwater swimming, playground, free showers, and rec hall. Whispering Pines is 6.5 miles east of Bucksport.

FOOD

MacLeod's (Main St., Bucksport, 207/469-3963, opens at 4:30 P.M. daily) is Bucksport's most popular restaurant. Slip into a booth, and choose from a varied menu. Children are welcome, it has a liquor license, and it's air-conditioned. Dinner entrées are $9–16. Reservations are wise for Saturday dinner.

On Verona Island, just before you cross the bridge to Bucksport (if you're heading north), is **Kravings Bakery and Restaurant** (42 Rte. 1, Verona, 207/469-9900, 11 A.M.–close Tues.–Sat.), a bakeshop/café with seating indoors and on an outdoor patio. The interior is pleasant, homey, and accented with knickknacks. It's also air-conditioned. Outside, you're subject to the roar of traffic on Route 1. The dinner menu varies nightly ($9–12). Fajitas and nachos are big hits during lunch, but the sandwiches are excellent, too.

In what passes as downtown Orland (hint: Don't blink), **Orland Market and Pizza** (91 Castine Rd./Rte. 175, Orland, 207/469-9999, 7 A.M.–9 P.M. daily) is a delight. Established in 1860, the old-fashioned country store has a little of this and a bit of that along with breakfast sandwiches, hot and cold sandwiches, grilled foods, salad, and all kinds of pizza. Call or drop by to find out the day's homemade specials, perhaps lasagna or spaghetti and meatballs.

Pick up produce, Maine-made goods, and other finds at the **Bucksport Riverfront Market** (waterfront, behind Town Hall, 9 A.M.–3 P.M. Sat.).

INFORMATION AND SERVICES
Information

The Bucksport Bay Area Chamber of Commerce (52 Main St., P.O. Box 1880, Bucksport 04416, 207/469-6818, www.bucksport baychamber.com) is right next to the municipal office in downtown Bucksport. Office hours are 9 A.M.–5 P.M. weekdays, but the side door is always open for access to brochures, newspapers, and other publications, plus bulletin-board notices. Information is also available at the Gateway Mobil Station, at the traffic light on the corner of Route 1, between the bridge and the Hannaford supermarket.

Public Restrooms

In Bucksport, public restrooms next to the town dock (behind the Bucksport Historical Society) are open spring, summer, and fall. Restrooms are open year-round in the Gateway Mobil gas station (at the Rte. 1 traffic light next to the Bucksport bridge) and in the Bucksport Municipal Office (weekdays) on Main Street.

Blue Hill

Twelve miles south of Route 1 is the hub of the peninsula, Blue Hill (pop. 2,390), exuding charm from its handsome old homes to its waterfront setting to the shops, restaurants, and galleries that boost its appeal.

Eons back, Native American summer folk gave the name Awanadjo ("small, hazy mountain") to the minimountain that looms over the town and draws the eye for miles around. The first permanent settlers arrived after the French and Indian War, in the late 18th century, and established mills and shipyards.

More than 100 ships were built here between Blue Hill's incorporation, in 1789, and 1882—bringing prosperity to the entire peninsula.

Critical to the town's early expansion was its first clergyman, Jonathan Fisher, a remarkable fellow who's been likened to Leonardo da Vinci. In 1803, Fisher founded Blue Hill Academy (predecessor of today's George Stevens Academy), then built his home (now a museum), and eventually left an immense legacy of inventions, paintings, engravings, and poetry.

Throughout the 19th century and into the

20th, Blue Hill's granite industry boomed, reaching its peak in the 1880s. Scratch the Brooklyn Bridge and the New York Stock Exchange and you'll find granite from Blue Hill's quarries. Around 1879, the discovery of gold and silver brought a flurry of interest, but little came of it. Copper was also found here, but quantities of it, too, were limited.

At the height of industrial prosperity, tourism took hold, attracting steamboat-borne summer boarders. Many succumbed to the scenery, bought land, and built waterfront summer homes. Thank these summer folk and their offspring for the fact that music has long been a big deal in Blue Hill. The Kneisel Hall Chamber Music School, established in the late 19th century, continues to rank high among the nation's summer music colonies. New York City's Blue Hill Troupe, devoted to Gilbert and Sullivan operettas, was named for the longtime summer home of the troupe's founders.

SIGHTS
◖ The Parson Fisher House

Named for a brilliant renaissance man who arrived in Blue Hill in 1794, the Parson Fisher House (Rte. 15/176, 44 Mines Rd., Blue Hill, 207/374-2459, www.jonathanfisherhouse.org, 1–4 P.M. Thurs.–Sat. early July–mid-Oct., $5) immerses visitors in period furnishings and Jonathan Fisher lore. And Fisher's feats are breathtaking: He was a Harvard-educated preacher who also managed to be an accomplished painter, poet, mathematician, naturalist, linguist, inventor, cabinetmaker, farmer, architect, and printmaker. In his spare time, he fathered nine children. Fisher also pitched in to help build the yellow house on Tenney Hill, which served as the Congregational Church parsonage. Now it contains intriguing items created by Fisher, memorabilia that volunteer tour guides delight in explaining, including a camera obscura. Don't miss it.

Historic Houses

A few of Blue Hill's elegant houses have been converted to museums, inns, restaurants, even some offices and shops, so you can see them from the inside out. To appreciate the private residences, you'll want to walk, bike, or drive around town. Check with the Holt House about village walking tours.

In downtown Blue Hill, a few steps off Main Street, stands the **Holt House** (3 Water St., Blue Hill, 207/326-8250, 1–4 P.M. Tues. and Fri. and 11 A.M.–2 P.M. Sat. July–mid-Sept., $3 adults, free for children 12 and under), home of the Blue Hill Historical Society. Built in 1815 by Jeremiah Holt, the Federal-style building contains restored stenciling, period decor, and masses of memorabilia contributed by local residents. In the carriage house are even more goodies, including old tools, a sleigh, carriages, and so forth.

Walk or drive up Union Street (Rte. 177), past George Stevens Academy, and wander **The Old Cemetery,** established in 1794. If gnarled trees and ancient headstones intrigue you, there aren't many good-size Maine cemeteries older than this one.

Scenic Routes

Parker Point Road (turn off Rte. 15 at the Blue Hill Library) takes you from Blue Hill to Blue Hill Falls the back way, with vistas en route toward Acadia National Park. For other great views, drive the length of **Newbury Neck,** in nearby Surry, or head west on Route 15/176 toward Sedgwick, Brooksville, and beyond.

PARKS AND RECREATION
◖ Blue Hill Mountain

Mountain seems a fancy label for a 943-footer, yet Blue Hill Mountain stands alone, visible from Camden and even beyond. On a clear day, head for the summit and take in the wraparound view encompassing Penobscot Bay, the hills of Mount Desert, and the Camden Hills. Climb the fire tower and you'll see even more. In mid-June, the lupines along the way are breathtaking; in fall, the colors are spectacular—with reddened blueberry barrens added to the variegated foliage. Go early in the day; it's a popular easy-to-moderate hike. A short loop on the lower slopes takes only half an hour. Take Route 15 (Pleasant St.) to Mountain

GALLERY HOPPING IN BLUE HILL

Perhaps it's Blue Hill's location near the renowned Haystack Mountain School of Crafts. Perhaps it's the way the light plays off the rolling countryside and onto the twisting coastline. Perhaps it's the inspirational landscape. Whatever the reason, numerous artists and artisans call Blue Hill home, and top-notch galleries are abundant.

Judith Leighton knows contemporary art, and her **Leighton Gallery** (24 Parker Point Rd., 207/374-5001, www.leightongallery .com) is a real treat. The airy two-story-plus-basement space, in a converted barn on the Parker Point Road, is filled with a great selection. Be sure to visit the equally spectacular and extremely peaceful backyard sculpture garden. The **Liros Gallery** (14 Parker Point Rd., 207/374-5370 or 800/287-5370, www.lirosgallery.com) has been dealing in Russian icons since the mid-1960s. Prices are high, but the icons are fascinating. The gallery also carries Currier and Ives prints, antique maps, and 19th-century British and American paintings. From here, it's a short walk to **Blue Hill Bay Gallery** (Main St., 207/374-5773, www.bluehillbaygallery .com), which represents contemporary artists in various media.

Don't miss **Jud Hartmann** (Main St. at Rte. 15, 207/359-2544, www.judhartmann gallery.com). The spacious, well-lighted in-town gallery carries Hartmann's limited-edition bronze sculptures of the Woodland Tribes of the Northeast. Hartmann often can be seen working on his next model in the gallery – a real treat. He's a wealth of information about his subjects, and he loves sharing the fascinating – even mesmerizing – stories he's uncovered during his meticulous research.

Also on Main Street are three other fun, artsy gallery/shops. **Handworks Gallery** (Main St., 207/374-5613) sells a range of fun, funky, utilitarian and fine art crafts by more than 50 Maine artists and craftspeople, including jewelry, furniture, rugs, wall hangings, and clothing. Browse **North Country Textiles** (Main St., 207/374-2715, www .northcountrytextiles.com) for fine handwoven throws, rugs, clothing, and table linens as well as other fine crafts.

Pottery is abundant in Blue Hill. **Rowantrees Pottery** (Rte. 177, 207/374-5535) and **Rackliffe Pottery** (Rte. 172, 207/374-2297 or 888/631-3321, www.rackliffepottery .com) both have well-established reputations. Rowantrees Pottery's kiln was first fired in 1934. The handmade pottery is made from local marine clay accented by rich glazes derived from local sources. Rackliffe, noted for its vivid blue wares, also makes its own glazes and has been producing lead-free pottery since 1969.

About two miles from downtown is a another don't-miss. **Mark Bell Pottery** (Rte. 15, Blue Hill, 207/374-5881), in a tiny building signaled only by a small roadside sign, is the home of exquisite, award-winning porcelain by the eponymous potter. It's easy to understand why his wares were displayed at the Smithsonian Institution's Craft Fair as well as other juried shows across the country. The delicacy of each vase, bowl, or whatever is astonishing, and the glazes are gorgeous. Twice each summer he has kiln openings, must-go events for collectors and any fans. Call for details.

Functional porcelain pottery is Melody Lewis-Kane's specialty at **Clay Forms** (Rte. 15, 207/359-2321, www.clayformspottery .com), four miles south of Blue Hill. The pitcher plant and hummingbird pieces are especially graceful.

Also worth a look-see is **Rachel Raye** (13 Schoolhouse La., East Blue Hill, 207/374-5944), a master at depicting animals and capturing their personalities.

Road. Turn right and go 0.8 mile to the trailhead (on the left) and the small parking area (on the right). You can also walk (uphill) the mile from the village. The trail can be squishy, especially in the wooded sections, so you'll want rubberized or waterproof shoes or boots.

Blue Hill Heritage Trust

This fine organization (101 Union St., P.O. Box 222, Blue Hill 04614, 207/374-5118, www.bhht.org, 8 A.M.–5 P.M. weekdays) works hard at preserving the region's landscape. It also presents a Walks n Talks series, with offerings such as kayaking by preservation land along Eggemoggin Reach, a full-moon hike up Blue Hill Mountain, and walks through other trust properties, such as 700-acre Kingdom Woods Conservation Preserve and Cooper Farm at Caterpillar Hill. Many include talks by knowledgeable folks on complementary topics. Check the website, call, or stop by to see what's up when you're in town.

Blue Hill Town Park

At the end of Water Street is a small park with a terrific view. It has a small pebble beach, picnic tables, portable toilet, and a creative playground. It's a fine place for a picnic.

MERI Center for Marine Studies

A great way to raise kids' environmental consciousness is to enroll them in summer activities sponsored by the MERI Center for Marine Studies (55 Main St., Blue Hill, 207/374-2135, www.meriresearch.org). MERI (Marine Environmental Research Institute), a nonprofit marine-ecology organization, schedules daylong island boat trips, "eco-cruises," and island walks, plus a variety of naturalist-led morning and afternoon programs, each geared to different age groups or groupings ($20–50); cruises are limited to 12 passengers. The expanding MERI Center has a touch tank, a marine lending library, and exhibit space. At 10 A.M. on Fridays it hosts a story hour for preschoolers that concludes with a craft program. During fall, winter, and spring, MERI offers lectures and screens marine-related films. It's free, but a $3 donation is appreciated. MERI is open Monday–Saturday all year.

Boating

A favorite spot for *experienced* kayakers and canoeists is **Blue Hill Falls,** which churns with white water when the tide turns. Check for times of high and low tide. Roadside parking is illegal, but the law is too often ignored. The Route 175 bridge is narrow, and cars often stop suddenly as they come over the hill, so be particularly cautious here.

Unless you own a boat or know a member of the Kollegewidgwok Yacht Club in East Blue Hill (207/374-5581), there's no sailing out of Blue Hill. If you're trailing a boat, use the public boat launch down on the harbor. Kollegewidgwok, incidentally, is a Penobscot Indian word meaning "blue hill on shining green water."

Outfitters

Anna and Barry Snow's **Rocky Coast Outfitters** (Grindleville Rd., P.O. Box 351, Blue Hill 04614, 207/374-8866, rockycoast outfitters@verizon.net) delivers rental canoes, kayaks, and bicycles, along with the necessary helmets, paddles, and life vests, to your lodging. Delivery is free. Rates vary with equipment and rental period. Another source for rental canoes and kayaks is **The Activity Shop** (61 Ellsworth Rd., Blue Hill, 207/374-3500, www.theactivity shop.com).

SHOPPING

Boutiques, antiques, galleries, and even two downtown bookstores make shopping a pleasure in Blue Hill, especially if you're looking for the unusual. (See the sidebar *Gallery Hopping in Blue Hill.*)

Antiques

Historical and cottage goods are the specialty at **Salt Air Primitives** (5 Main St., Blue Hill, 207/374-8886). **Blue Hill Antiques** (8 Water St., Blue Hill, 207/374-2199 or 207/326-4973) specializes in 18th- and 19th-century French and American furniture—it attracts a high-end clientele. The same patrons seek out neighboring Brad Emerson's **Emerson Antiques** (33 Water St., Blue Hill, 207/374-5140), concentrating on early Americana, such as hooked rugs and ship models.

Books

Blue Hill's literate population manages to support two full-service, year-round, independent bookstores. The selection is excellent at **Blue Hill Books** (2 Pleasant St., Rte. 15, Blue Hill, 207/374-5632, www.bluehillbooks.com), thanks to knowledgeable owners Nick Sichterman and Mariah Hughs. The store organizes an "authors series" during the summer.

Around the corner, ever-helpful Bonnie Myers provides free advice on the region with a money-back guarantee at **North Light Books** (Main St., Blue Hill, 207/374-5422). It's a delight to browse, the children's book selection is terrific, and out back is Blue Hill Hearth, with all sorts of treats.

Eclectic

The Himalayas meet Blue Hill at Jeff Kaley's **Asian World Imports** (102 Pleasant St./ Rte. 15, Blue Hill, 207/374-2284, www.asianworldimports.com). A Nepal Peace Corps veteran, Kaley seeks out eco-sensitive suppliers using fair-trade practices, bringing back custom-made Nepalese, Tibetan, Indian, and Thai clothing, jewelry, and artifacts, as well as organic Himalayan tea. The shop is loaded with treasures. Jeff also leads small-group cultural tours and treks in Nepal and Tibet; contact him for details.

In downtown Blue Hill is Peter Stremlau's **New Cargoes** (49 Main St., Blue Hill, 207/374-3733), following somewhat in the Pier One/ Crate and Barrel tradition. Furniture, linens, notecards, candles, and on and on. The shop name is apt—new things arrive regularly.

Wine

Blue Hill Wine Shop (138 Main St., Blue Hill, 207/374-2161), tucked into a converted horse barn, carries more than 1,000 wines, plus teas, coffees, and blended tobaccos and unusual pipes for diehard, upscale smokers. Monthly wine tastings (2–5 P.M. last Saturday of the month) are always an adventure.

ENTERTAINMENT

Variety and serendipity are the keys here. Check local calendar listings and tune in to radio station WERU (89.9 and 102.9 FM, www.weru .org), the peninsula's own community radio; there might be announcements of concerts by local resident pianist Paul Sullivan or the Bagaduce Chorale, or maybe a contra dance or a tropical treat from Carl Chase's Atlantic Clarion Steel Band or Flash-in-the-Pans Community Band. The George Stevens Academy also has a weekly lecture series.

Music

Since 1922, chamber-music students have been spending summers perfecting their skills and demonstrating their prowess at the **Kneisel Hall Chamber Music School** (Pleasant St., Rte. 15, Blue Hill, 207/374-2811, www.kneisel.org). Faculty concerts run Friday evenings and Sunday afternoons late June–late August. The concert schedule is published in the spring, and reserved-seating tickets ($30 inside, $20 on the veranda outside, nonrefundable) can be ordered by phone. There is also unreserved tent seating ($10) for the Friday evening and Sunday afternoon concerts. Other opportunities to hear the students and faculty exist, including young artist concerts, children's concerts, open rehearsals, and more. Check the website or program for details. Kneisel Hall is about a half mile from the center of town.

Chamber music continues in winter thanks to the volunteer **Blue Hill Concert Association** (P.O. Box 140, Blue Hill 04614). Five concerts are performed between January and March at the Congregational Church, a handsome, traditional New England spired edifice on Main Street.

EVENTS

The first weekend in August, the **Academy Antiques Show** draws a huge crowd to the George Stevens Academy on Union Street in Blue Hill. Admission is $7, and lunch and tea are available.

WERU's annual Full Circle Fair is usually held in mid-August at the Blue Hill Fairgrounds (Rte. 172, north of downtown Blue Hill). Expect world music, good food, crafts, and socially and environmentally progressive talks.

On Labor Day weekend, the **Blue Hill Fair** (Blue Hill Fairgrounds, Rte. 172, Blue Hill, 207/374-9976) is one of the state's best agricultural fairs. Besides the food booths (good-for-you fare competes with fried dough), a carnival, fireworks, sheepdog trials, and live musical entertainment, you can check out the blue-ribbon winners for finest quilt, beefiest bull, or largest squash.

ACCOMMODATIONS
Inns and Bed-and-Breakfasts
On a quiet side street close to town, **◖ The Blue Hill Inn** (Union St., Rte. 177, P.O. Box 403, Blue Hill 04614, 207/374-2844 or 800/826-7415, www.bluehillinn.com, $158–195, mid-May–late Oct.) has been welcoming guests since 1840. If you're trying to imagine a classic country inn, this would be it. It came into new hands midsummer 2007, but new owner Sarah Pebworth planned few changes—still it's wise to inquire about particulars. Stay here if you enjoy antiques, warm hospitality, and classic New England inns; don't stay if you're on a tight budget or have small children. Ten rooms and a suite, all with air-conditioning, boast real chandeliers, four-posters, down comforters, fancy linens, and braided and Oriental rugs; three have wood-burning fireplaces. The third-floor garret suite is ideal for families with well-behaved children; a first-floor room is wheelchair-accessible. Rear rooms overlook the extensive cutting garden, with chairs and a hammock. The library, dominated by a Persian chandelier, has masses of local information. Refreshments are available all day; superb hors d'oeuvres are served 6–7 P.M. in two elegant parlors or the garden. Off-season, an adjacent suite in the elegant Cape House—the ground floor of a tiny dwelling—is $165. Twice each year, usually May and October, the inn puts on gala wine-dinner weekends; the multi-course gourmet dinners are outstanding. The

The Blue Hill Inn is a classic country inn.

innkeeper will arrange for Kneisel Hall tickets, kayak rentals, cruises, massages, and more.

What's old is new at **Barncastle** (125 South St., P.O. Box 1510, Blue Hill 04614, 207/374-2330, www.barncastlehotel.com, $125–175), a late-19th-century Shingle-style cottage that's listed on the National Register. It opens to a two-story foyer with a split stairway and balcony. Rooms and suites open off the balcony, and all are spacious, minimally decorated, and have contemporary accents, including flat-screen TVs, Wi-Fi, fridge, and microwave. Rates include a continental breakfast. Downstairs is a tavern, serving pizza, salads, and sandwiches.

Two miles north of town, at Marcia and Jim Schatz's **Blue Hill Farm Country Inn** (Rte. 15, P.O. Box 437, Blue Hill 04614, 207/374-5126, www.bluehillfarminn.com, $90–110 d peak), a huge refurbished barn serves as the gathering spot for guests. If the weather is lousy, you can plop down in front of the oversize woodstove and start in on cribbage or other games. Antique sleigh-runner banisters lead to the barn's seven second-floor rooms—all with private baths, skylights, hooked rugs, and quilts. A wing of the farm-house has seven more rooms with shared baths and more quilts. Breakfast is generous continental. During the summer, visiting jazz or classical musicians sometimes entertain in the barn, but it all eases off early. On the inn's 48 acres are well-cleared nature trails, an 18th-century cellar hole, and a duck pond. It's open year-round.

Okay, it's not a *real* lighthouse, but the wa-terfront **First Light B&B** (821 E. Blue Hill Rd., Blue Hill 04614, 207/374-5879, www .firstlightbandb.com, $110–200) is close enough to fool many folks. Huge windows frame views that, on a clear day, extend for five miles. Innkeeper Beverly Bartlett, a retired nursing professor, has three lighthouse-themed rooms. If you're a lighthouse buff, reserve the Lighthouse Suite, in the tower. Two other rooms share a bath or can be connected as a suite. Guests may climb the tower, built by an eccentric previous owner, for 360-degree views; it's the perfect place for seal-watching or birding. A comfortably cluttered common room, with fireplace, plentiful books, and a

grand piano, faces McHeard's Cove. Breakfast is served either in the dining room or on the patio. It's open year-round.

Seasonal Rentals

Weekly rentals (or longer) can pay off if you have a large family or are planning a group vacation. The Blue Hill Peninsula has lots of rental cottages, camps, and houses, but the trick is to plan well ahead. This is a popular area in summer, and many renters sign up for the following year before they leave town. For information, contact Sandy Douvarjo of **Peninsula Property Rentals** (Main St., P.O. Box 611, Blue Hill 04614, 207/374-2428, www.peninsulapropertyrentals.com).

FOOD
Local Flavors

Picnic fare is available at **Merrill and Hinckley** (Union St., Blue Hill, 207/374-2821, 7 A.M.–9 P.M. Mon.–Sat., 8 A.M.–9 P.M. Sun.), a quirky, family-owned grocery/general store dating from the mid-19th century.

The **Blue Hill Co-Op and Café** (Greene's Hill, Rte. 172, Blue Hill, 207/374-2165, café 207/374-8999, 8 A.M.–7 P.M. Mon.–Fri., to 6 P.M. Sat., 10 A.M.–5 P.M. Sun.) sells organic and hydroponic produce and grains, cheeses, organic coffee, and more. Breads are terrific here. Sandwiches, salads, and soups—many with ethnic flavors—are available in the café. The staff will pack it all up for a picnic, too.

Tucked behind First Light Books is **Blue Hill Hearth** (58 Main St., Blue Hill, 207/610-9090, 8 A.M.–7 P.M. Mon.–Fri., 10 A.M.–7 P.M. Sat., 10 A.M.–4 P.M. Sun.), operated by the for-mer owner of Pain de Famille. The breads are outstanding, but you can pick up ready-made sandwiches and other goods. It's wise to call ahead for the Friday Night Pizza Plus, when two sizes of pizza are offered with about two dozen possible toppings.

Just south of town is **Barncastle** (125 South St., Blue Hill, 207/374-2300, www.barncastle hotel.com), serving wood-fired pizzas as well as sandwiches and salads in a lovely shingle-style cottage. Everything is less than $10.

Local gardeners, farmers, and craftspeople peddle their wares at the **Blue Hill Farmers Market** (9–11:30 A.M. Sat.) It's a particularly enduring market, well worth a visit. Demonstrations by area chefs and artists are often on the agenda. The major effort is late June–September at the Blue Hill Fairgrounds (Rte. 172, just north of downtown).

Lobster and Fried Fish

For lobster, fried fish, and the area's best lobster roll, head to **The Fish Net** (Main St., Blue Hill, 207/374-5240, 11 A.M.–8 P.M. Mon.–Thurs., to 9 P.M. Fri. and Sat.). Dine outdoors on picnic tables or inside. Nothing's pricey.

Family-Friendly Casual Restaurants

First choice for families or anyone looking for a casual but very good meal is **The Blue Moose** (50 Main St., Blue Hill, 207/374-3274, www .thebluemooserestaurant.com, 10:30 A.M.–3 P.M. and 5–9 P.M. Mon.–Thurs., 10 A.M.–9:30 P.M. Fri., 7:30 A.M.–9 P.M. Sat.–Sun.), which has a wide-ranging menu and welcomes kids. Most choices are in the $8–12 range. Kids'/small appetite menu ranges $3–5.

Very popular with local folks is **Marlintini's Grill** (The Mines Rd., Blue Hill, 207/374-2500, 11:30 A.M.–9 P.M. daily, bar stays open until 1 A.M.). Inside, half is a sports bar, the other half a restaurant. You can sit in either, but the bar side can get raucous. Best bet: the screened-in porch. Expect burgers, salads, sandwiches, fried foods, and a kids' menu. The portions are big; the service is good; the food is reliable.

Casual to Fine Dining

Here's a doubleheader: **《 Arborvine and The Vinery** (Main St., Blue Hill, www.arborvine .com). For a light dinner, head to The Vinery (207/374-2441, 5:30–9 P.M. Wed.–Sun.), a piano and wine bar–style bistro in a beautifully renovated barn, where there's often evening entertainment, too. Entrées are $7–14. If you're up for something a bit more elegant, make reservations at Arborvine (207/374-2119, 5:30–9 P.M. Tues.–Sun. summer, Fri.–Sun. winter), a

conscientiously renovated two-century-old Cape-style house with four dining areas, each with a different feel and understated decor. Most entrées are in the $25–30 range; there's always at least one for vegetarians. The wine list is small but select. Chef/owner John Hikade and his wife, Beth, operate both.

Anneliese Riggall brought new life to the historical old forge building that hangs over the river downtown, reopening it as **《 The Wescott Forge** (66 Main St., Blue Hill, 207/374-9909, www.thewescottforge.com, 11:30 A.M.–2 P.M. Wed.–Sat. and 5:30–10 P.M. Mon.–Sat.). It's fabulous. The menu changes weekly but might include entrées such as seaweed-seared yellowfin tuna and Moroccan chickpea stew. Most run $16–25. The upstairs is a casual lounge, the downstairs has an easy elegance, all highlighted by beautiful forged accent pieces (check out the stairway railing). Request a table on the porch, and you'll be serenaded by the water rushing underneath as you dine.

INFORMATION AND SERVICES

Information

The Blue Hill Peninsula Chamber of Commerce (28 Water St., P.O. Box 520, Blue Hill 04614, 207/374-2281, www.bluehillpeninsula.org) is stocked with brochures, menus, and other information on Blue Hill and the surrounding area. You can also find information (although some is outdated) on www.bluehillme.com. One interesting feature on this site is a section on wildlife sightings.

At the Blue Hill Public Library (5 Parker Point Rd., 207/374-5515, www.bluehill.lib .me.us), ask to see the suit of armor, which *may* have belonged to Magellan. The library also sponsors a summer lecture series.

Public Restrooms

In season, there are portable toilets behind the chamber of commerce building and in the town park. Public buildings that have restrooms are the Blue Hill Town Hall (Main St.), Blue Hill Public Library (Main St.), and Blue Hill Memorial Hospital (Water St.).

Brooklin/Brooksville/Sedgwick

Nestled near the bottom of the Blue Hill Peninsula and surrounded by Castine, Blue Hill, and Deer Isle, this often-missed area offers superb hiking, kayaking, and sailing, plus historic homes and unique shops, studios, lodgings, and personalities.

The best-known town is Brooklin (pop. 841), thanks to two magazines: *The New Yorker* and *WoodenBoat*. Wordsmiths extraordinaire E. B. and Katharine White "dropped out" to Brooklin in the 1930s and forever afterward dispatched their splendid material for *The New Yorker* from here. (The Whites' former home, a handsome Colonial not open to the public, is on Route 175 in North Brooklin, 6.5 miles from the Blue Hill Falls bridge.) In 1977, *WoodenBoat* magazine moved its headquarters to Brooklin, where its 60-acre shoreside estate attracts builders and dreamers from all over the globe. Nearby Brooksville (pop. 911) drew the late Helen and Scott Nearing, whose *Living the Good Life* made them role models for back-to-the-landers. Their compound now verges on "must-see" status. Buck's Harbor, a section of Brooksville, is the setting for *One Morning in Maine,* one of Robert McCloskey's beloved children's books. Oldest of the three towns is Sedgwick (pop. 1,175, incorporated in 1789), which once included all of Brooklin and part of Brooksville. Now wedged *between* Brooklin and Brooksville, it includes the hamlet of Sargentville, the Caterpillar Hill scenic overlook, and a well-preserved complex of historic buildings. The influx of pilgrims continues in this area—many of them artists bent on capturing the spirit that has proved so enticing to creative types.

SIGHTS
WoodenBoat Publications
On Naskeag Point Road, 1.2 miles from downtown Brooklin (Rte. 175), a small sign marks the turn to the world headquarters of the *WoodenBoat* empire (Naskeag Point Rd., P.O. Box 78, Brooklin 04616, 207/359-4651, www.woodenboat.com). Buy magazines, books, clothing, and all manner of nautical merchandise at the handsome new store (www.woodenboatstore.com), stroll the grounds, or sign up for one of the dozens of one- and two-week spring, summer, and fall courses in seamanship, navigation, boatbuilding, sailmaking, marine carving, and more. Special courses are geared to kids, women, pros, and all-thumbs neophytes; the camaraderie is legendary, and so is the cuisine. School visiting hours are 8 A.M.–5 P.M. Monday–Saturday June–October.

Historical Sights
Now used as the museum/headquarters of the Sedgwick-Brooklin Historical Society, the 1795 **Reverend Daniel Merrill House** (Rte. 172, P.O. Box 171, Sedgwick 04676, 207/359-8086, 2–4 P.M. Sun. in July and Aug., or by appointment, donations welcomed) was the parsonage for Sedgwick's first permanent minister. Inside the house are period furnishings, old photos, toys, and tools; a few steps away are a restored 1874 schoolhouse, an 1821 cattle pound (for corralling wandering bovines), and a hearse barn. Pick up a brochure during open hours and guide yourself around the buildings and grounds. The **Sedgwick Historic District,** crowning Town House Hill, comprises the Merrill House and its outbuildings, plus the imposing 1794 Town House and the 23-acre Rural Cemetery (the oldest headstone dates from 1798) across Route 172.

◖ The Good Life Center
Forest Farm, home of the late Helen and Scott Nearing, is now the site of The Good Life Center (372 Harborside Rd., Box 11, Harborside, 207/326-8211, www.goodlife.org). Advocates of simple living and authors of 10 books on the subject, the Nearings created a trust to perpetuate their farm and philosophy. Resident stewards lead tours 1–5 P.M. Thursday–Tuesday in July and August (Thurs.–Mon. the rest of the year, but call ahead), $5 donation suggested. Copies of Nearing books are available for sale. From mid-June to mid-

September, Monday night meetings (7 P.M.) at the farm feature free programs by gardeners, philosophers, musicians, and other guest speakers. Occasional work parties, workshops, and conferences are also on the center's schedule. The farm is on Harborside Road, just before it turns to dirt. From Route 176 in Brooksville, take Cape Rosier Road, go eight miles, passing Holbrook Islands Sanctuary. At the Grange Hall, turn right and follow the road 1.9 miles to the end. Turn left onto Harborside Road and continue 1.8 miles to Forest Farm, across from Orrs Cove.

Four Season Farm

Almost next door to the Nearing's place is Four Seasons Farm (609 Weir Cove Rd., Harborside, 207/326-4455, www.fourseasonfarm.com, 1–5 P.M. Mon.–Sat.), the lush organic farm owned and operated by internationally renowned gardeners Eliot Coleman and Barbara Damrosch. Both have written numerous books and articles and starred in TV gardening shows. Coleman is a driving force behind the use of the word "authentic" to mean "beyond organic," demonstrating a commitment to food that is local, fresh, ripe, clean, safe, and nourishing. He's also successfully pioneered a "winter harvest," developing environmentally sound and economically viable systems for extending fresh vegetable production from October through May in cold-weather climates. After

E. B. WHITE: SOME WRITER

Every child since the mid-1940s has heard of E. B. White – author of the memorable *Stuart Little*, *Charlotte's Web*, and *Trumpet of the Swan* – and every college kid for decades has been reminded to consult his *Elements of Style*, but how many realize that White and his wife, Katharine, were living not in the Big City but in the hamlet of North Brooklin, Maine? It was Brooklin that inspired Charlotte and Wilbur and Stuart, and it was Brooklin where the Whites lived very full, creative lives.

Abandoning their desks at *The New Yorker* in 1938, Elwyn Brooks White and Katharine S. White bought an idyllic saltwater farm on the Blue Hill Peninsula and moved here with their young son Joel, who became a noted naval architect and yachtbuilder in Brooklin before his untimely death in 1997. Andy (as E. B. had been dubbed since his college days at Cornell) produced 20 books, countless essays and letters to editors, and hundreds (maybe thousands?) of "newsbreaks" – those wry clipping-and-commentary items sprinkled through each issue of *The New Yorker*. Katharine continued wielding her pencil as the magazine's standout children's-book editor, donating many of her review copies to Brooklin's Friend Memorial Library, one of her favorite "causes." (The library also has two original Garth Williams

drawings from *Stuart Little*, courtesy of E. B., and a lovely garden dedicated to the Whites.) Katharine's book, *Onward and Upward in the Garden*, a collection of her *New Yorker* gardening pieces, was published in 1979, two years after her death.

Later in life, E. B. sagely addressed the young readers of his three award-winning children's books:

Are my stories true, you ask? No, they are imaginary tales, containing fantastic characters and events. In real life, a family doesn't have a child who looks like a mouse; in real life, a spider doesn't spin words in her web. In real life, a swan doesn't blow a trumpet. But real life is only one kind of life – there is also the life of the imagination. And although my stories are imaginary, I like to think that there is some truth in them, too – truth about the way people and animals feel and think and act.

E. B. White died on October 1, 1985, at the age of 86. He and Katharine and Joel left large footprints on this earth, but perhaps nowhere more so than in Brooklin.

26 years, Coleman and Damrosch reopened their farm to the public in 2005. It's a treat for the eyes as well as the tastebuds—you've never seen such gorgeous produce. To find the farm, continue past The Good Life Center and look for a sign on the left.

Scenic Routes

No one seems to know how **Caterpillar Hill** got its name, but its reputation comes from a panoramic vista of water, hills, and blueberry barrens—with a couple of convenient picnic tables where you can stop for lunch, photos, or a ringside view of sunset and fall foliage. From the 350-foot elevation, the views take in Walker Pond, Eggemoggin Reach, Deer Isle, Swan's Island, and even the Camden Hills; interpretive signage puts it all in context. The signposted rest area is on Route 175/15, between Brooksville and Sargentville, next to a small, but excellent, gallery; watch out for the blind curve when you pull off the road. Between Sargentville and Sedgwick, Route 175 offers nonstop views of Eggemoggin Reach, with shore access to the Benjamin River just before you reach Sedgwick village.

Two other scenic routes are **Naskeag Point,** in Brooklin, and **Cape Rosier,** westernmost arm of the town of Brooksville. Naskeag Point Road begins off Route 175 in "downtown" Brooklin, heads down the peninsula for 3.7 miles past the entrance to *WoodenBoat* Publications; past Amen Farm (207/359-8982, call for hours), home of the late author Roy Barrette, where the gardens and 10-acre arboretum are open for viewing by appointment; to a small shingle beach (limited parking) on Eggemoggin Reach, where you'll find picnic tables, a boat launch, a seasonal toilet, and a marker commemorating the 1778 Battle of Naskeag, when British sailors came ashore from the sloop *Gage,* burned several buildings, and were run off by a ragtag band of local settlers. Cape Rosier's roads are poorly marked, perhaps deliberately, so keep your DeLorme atlas handy. The Cape Rosier loop takes in Holbrook Island Sanctuary, Goose Falls, the hamlet of Harborside, and plenty of water and island views.

PARKS, PRESERVES, AND RECREATION

◖ Holbrook Island Sanctuary State Park

In the early 1970s, foresighted benefactor Anita Harris donated to the state 1,230 acres in Brooksville that would become the Holbrook Island Sanctuary (207/326-4012, www.state.me.us/doc/parks, free). From Route 176, between West Brooksville and South Brooksville, head west on Cape Rosier Road, following brown-and-white signs for the sanctuary. Trail maps and bird checklists are available in boxes at trailheads or at park headquarters. The easy Backshore Trail (about 30 minutes) starts here, or go back a mile and climb the steepish trail to **Backwoods Mountain** for the best vistas. Other trails include one around a beaver flowage. Other attractions include shorefront picnic tables and grills, four old cemeteries, and super birding during spring and fall migrations. Leashed pets are allowed, but no bikes on the trails and no camping. Officially open May 15–October 15, but the access road and parking areas are plowed for cross-country skiers.

Or you can take a picnic to the **Bagaduce Ferry Landing,** in West Brooksville off Route 176, where there are picnic tables and cross-river vistas toward Castine.

A small, relatively little-known beach is Brooklin's **Pooduck Beach.** From the Brooklin General Store (Rte. 175), take Naskeag Point Road about half a mile, watching for the Pooduck Road sign on the right. Drive to the end. You can also launch a sea kayak into Eggemoggin Reach here.

Bicycling

Bicycling in this area is hazardous. Roads here are particularly narrow and winding, with poor shoulders. If you're determined to pedal, consider either the Naskeag scenic route or around Cape Rosier, where traffic is light.

Excursion Boats

Captain LeCain Smith sails *Perelandra* (Buck's Harbor, 207/326-4279), a 44-foot ketch, in the waters of Penobscot Bay. Rates begin at $40 pp for a two-hour trip and increase to $60 pp for a four-hour sail. The boat holds a maximum of six passengers.

Sail on a Maine windjammer with Captain Bill Brown on the **Summertime** (207/326-8485 or 800/562-8290, www.schoonersummertime .com), which sails from various locations on the peninsula, including Brooksville, Sedgewick, and Stonington in spring and fall. Six-hour sails are $40 per adult, $20 per child younger than 12; three-hour sails are $18 and $9. The schooner takes a maximum of 20 guests.

SHOPPING

Most of these businesses are small, owner-operated shops, which means they're often catch as catch can. If you want to be sure, call ahead.

Antiques

When you need a slate sink, a clawfoot tub, brass fixtures, or a Palladian window, **Architectural Antiquities** (52 Indian Point La., Harborside, 207/326-4938, www.archantiquities.com), on Cape Rosier, is just the ticket—a restorer's delight. Prices are reasonable for what you get, and it'll ship your purchases. Open all year by appointment; ask for directions when you call. Antiques dating from the Federal period through the turn of the 20th century are the specialties at **Sedgwick Antiques** (775 N. Sedgwick Rd./Rte. 172, Sedgwick, 207/359-8834). Early furniture, handmade furniture, and a full range of country accessories and antiques can be found at **Thomas Hinchcliffe Antiques** (26 Cradle Knolls La., off Rte. 176, W. Sedgwick, 207/326-9411). Painted country furniture, decoys, and unusual nautical items are specialties at Peg and Olney Grindall's **Old Cove Antiques** (106 Caterpillar Rd./Rte. 15, Sargentville 04673, 207/359-2031 or 207/359-8585), a weathered-gray shop, across from the Eggemoggin Country Store.

Artists' and Artisans' Galleries

Small studio-galleries pepper Route 175 (Reach Rd.) in Sedgwick and Brooklin; most are marked only by small signs, so watch carefully. First up is **Eggemoggin Textile Studio** (off Rte. 175/Reach Rd., Sedgwick, 207/359-5083, www.chrisleithstudio.com), where the incredibly gifted Christine Leith weaves scarves, wraps, hangings, and pillows with hand-dyed silk and wool; the colors are magnificent. You might catch her at work on the big loom in her studio shop, a real treat.

Continue along the road to find **Reach Road Gallery** (Reach Rd., Sedgwick, 207/359-8803), where Holly Meade sells her detailed woodblock prints as well as prints from the children's books she's illustrated.

Only a few doors down is **Mermaid Woolens** (Reach Rd., Sedgwick, 207/359-2747), source of Elizabeth Coakley's wildly colorful hand knits—vests, socks, and sweaters. They're pricey but worth every nickel. She also does seascape paintings. Clever woman.

Continue over to Brooklin, where Virginia G. Sarsfield's handcrafts paper products, including custom lampshades, calligraphy papers, books, and lamps at **Handmade Papers** (Rte. 175 at Center Harbor Rd., Brooklin, 207/359-8345, www.handmadepapersonline.com).

Just a bit farther is **Naskeag Gallery** (Rte. 175, Brooklin, 207/359-4619), a small shop that makes browsing an art form, especially if you appreciate meandering about antiques and art. The eclectic selection might include antique sweetgrass baskets and 19th-century furnishings and accent pieces mixed with works by local artists and artisans. Fun. Talented glass artist **Sihaya Hopkins** also has a shop here, as do a few other talented artisans.

In Brooksville, more treasures await on Route 176. You'll need to watch carefully for the sign marking the long drive to **Paul Heroux and Scott Goldberg Pottery** (2032 Coastal Rd./Rte. 176, Brooksville, 207/326-9062). The small gallery is a treat for pottery fans.

Continue southwest on Route 176 and watch closely for signs for **Bagaduce Forge** (140 Ferry Rd., Brooksville, 207/326-9676); this isn't easy to find. Joseph Meltreder is both blacksmith and farrier, and his small forge, with big views, is the real thing. He turns out whimsical pieces. Especially fun are the nail people—you'll know them when you see them.

Wine and Gifts

Three varieties of English-style hard cider are specialties at **The Sow's Ear Winery** (Rte. 176 at Herrick Rd., Brooksville, 207/326-4649), a minuscule operation in a funky, gray-shingled building. Winemaker Tom Hoey also produces sulfite-free blueberry, chokecherry, and rhubarb wines; he'll let you sample it all. Ask to see his cellar, where everything happens. No credit cards.

Nautical books, T-shirts, gifts, food (including homemade bread and key lime pie), and boat gear line the walls and shelves of the shop at **Buck's Harbor Marine** (on the dock, South Brooksville, 207/326-8839, www.bucks harbor.com).

ENTERTAINMENT AND EVENTS
(Flash in the Pans Community Steel Band Concerts

If you're a fan of steel-band music, check to see where and when Carl Chase's Flash-in-the-Pans Community Steel Band (207/374-2172, www .peninsulapan.org) is performing. It usually performs somewhere on the peninsula on Monday nights (7:30–9 P.M.) mid-June–early September. The musicians aren't professionals, but you'd never know it. Local papers carry the summer schedule for the nearly three-dozen-member band, which performs in various area locales and deserves its devoted following. Admission is usually a small donation to benefit a local cause. It's worth every penny to join the fun.

The Flye Point Music and Arts Festival

A relatively new event is getting excellent reviews. The Flye Point Music and Arts Festival at the Lookout (Flye Point Rd., off Rte. 175, North Brooklin, 207/359-2188, www.acadia .net/lookout) began in 2004. Held in late June, it features musicians such as Don McLean, Richie Havens, and Jonathan Edwards; check the website for details.

Eggemoggin Reach Regatta

Wooden boats are big attractions hereabouts, so when a huge fleet sails in for this regatta (usually the first Saturday in August, but the schedule can change), crowds gather. Don't miss the parade of wooden boats. Best locale for watching the regatta itself is on or near the bridge to Deer Isle, or near the Eggemoggin Landing grounds on Little Deer Isle. Contact *WoodenBoat* (207/359-4651) for details.

ACCOMMODATIONS
Cottage Colonies

The two operations in this category feel much like informal family compounds—where you quickly become an adoptee. These are extremely popular spots, where successive generations of hosts have catered to successive generations of visitors, and reservations are usually essential for July and August. Many guests book for the following year before they leave. We're not talking fancy; cottages are old-shoe rustic, of varying sizes and decor. Most of the cottages have cooking facilities, although both colonies include breakfast and dinner in July and August. Both also have hiking trails, playgrounds, rowboats, and East Penobscot Bay on the doorstep.

Jim and Sally Littlefield are the enthusiastic fourth-generation hosts at (**Oakland House Seaside Resort** (435 Herrick Rd., Brooksville, 207/359-8521 or 800/359-7352, www.oakland house.com), a sprawling 50-acre complex of 15 wooded and waterfront cottages, as well as Shore Oaks Seaside Inn. Much of this land, now threaded with hiking trails, was part of the original king's grant to Jim's ancestors, way back in 1765. The Homestead, where meals are served, dates from 1767. Jim is the eighth generation on the property; his daughter, Sally, is ninth, and she and her husband, Sean McGuigan, are fifth-generation hosts-in-training. Weekly rates for two people sharing a two-person cottage vary by date, but begin around $475 and top off about $1,255, plus service charge, including full breakfast and five-course dinner; lower rates for children. Thursday is lobster-picnic night on the beach. Biggest bargains are early May–mid-June and September–October, when meals and house-

The Homestead at Oakland House Seaside Resort dates from 1767, and the property has remained in the same family since it was awarded as a king's grant.

keeping aren't included. Rowboats are free for guests' use in season, and the staff organizes other boat excursions on request. Also ask about artist workshops—what a perfect location! And wait till you see the gorgeous gardens—enough to warrant a full-time gardener. Two cottages (Lone Pine and Boathouse) are winterized and available all year; the other cottages are closed in winter. Call to ask about last-minute specials and short-term getaway packages.

The fourth generation manages the **Hiram Blake Camp** (220 Weir Cove Rd., Harborside, 207/326-4951, www.hiramblake.com, Memorial Day–late Sept.), but with a difference: The second and third generations still pitch in and help with gardening, lobstering, maintenance, and kibitzing. Thirteen cottages and a duplex line the shore of this 100-acre complex. Don't bother bringing reading matter: The dining room has ingenious ceiling niches lined with countless books. There's a one-week minimum (beginning Sat. or Sun.)

July and August, when cottages go for $600–2,700 a week (including breakfast, dinner, and linens). Off-season rates (no meals or linens, but cottages have cooking facilities) are $600–850 a week. The best chances for getting a reservation are in June and September. No credit cards.

Bed-and-Breakfasts

A few steps up from the half-mile-long shorefront at the Oakland House Seaside Resort's cottage colony is **Shore Oaks Seaside Inn** (435 Herrick Rd., Brooksville, 207/359-8521 or 800/359-7352, www.oaklandhouse.com/inn.html), a handsome green-trimmed stone mansion carefully restored to its arts-and-crafts heritage. No in-room phones, no TV, no noise; just peaceful bliss. Hang out for too long in the common rooms or the veranda rockers and you might never leave; this place is magical and restorative. Ten first-, second-, and third-floor rooms (seven with private baths) top out at $105–265 d, $80–140 s, plus service charge, including breakfast; for an additional $25 pp, include a five-course dinner. Shoulder-season rates (May and late Oct.) are less expensive but still include breakfast.

In 2005, Joe Moore turned an 1874 mansard-roofed Victorian in what passes as downtown Brooklin into the **Dragonflye Inn** (Naskeag Point Rd., P.O. Box 220, Brooklin 04616, 207/359-808, www.dragonflyeinn.com, $135). It's a casual put-your-feet-up kind of place, with a special invitation issued to *WoodenBoat* school students, gallery fans (lots of work by local artisans), and kayakers. Moore's goal is sustainability: Towels and linens are made from organic cotton; soaps and shampoos are local and all natural; cleaning products are all natural, biodegradable, and earth friendly. Plans call for the roof to be replaced with faux slate comprising recycled auto tires, recycled bottle insulation, and power generated on-site from the sun or the wind. Breakfast is light continental. Wi-Fi available. Bicycles are available for guests. Kayak trips can be arranged, including local shuttles. An all-inclusive, three-hour guided sea-kayaking trip off Naskeag Point is available for $75 per person.

Best known for its restaurant and pub, **The Brooklin Inn** (Rte. 175, Brooklin, 207/359-2777, www.brooklininn.com, $105–125 with breakfast; add $10 for a one-night stay) also has four simple but comfortable bedrooms.

FOOD
Local Flavors
Competition is stiff for lunchtime seats at the **Morning Moon Café** (junction of Rte. 175 and Naskeag Point Rd., Brooklin, 207/359-2373, 7 A.M.–2 P.M. Tues.–Sun.), mostly because *WoodenBoat* staffers consider it an annex to their offices. "The Moon" is a friendly hangout for coffee, pizza, or great sandwiches and salads—or order it to go.

Across the street from the Morning Moon Café, the **Brooklin General Store** (1 Reach Rd., junction of Rte. 175 and Naskeag Point Rd., Brooklin, 207/359-8817, 5 A.M.–7 P.M. Mon.–Sat. and 7 A.M.–5 P.M. Sun.), vintage 1872, carries groceries, beer and wine,

newspapers, take-out sandwiches, and local chatter.

In North Brooksville, where Route 175/176 crosses the Bagaduce River, stands the **Bagaduce Lunch,** a popular take-out stand (outdoor tables only) open 11 A.M.–7 or 8 P.M. daily early May–mid-September. Check the tide calendar and go when the tide is changing; order a clam roll or a hamburger, settle in at a picnic table, and watch the reversing falls. The food is so-so, but the setting is tops.

Lunch is the specialty at **Buck's Harbor Market** (Rte. 176, South Brooksville, 207/326-8683, 7 A.M.–7 P.M. Mon.–Fri., 8 A.M.–7:30 P.M. Sat., 8 A.M.–6 P.M. Sun. all year), a low-key, marginally yuppified general store popular with yachties in summer. There's a small deli/lunch counter in the back room open 11 A.M.–2 P.M. Monday–Saturday, and for pizzas from 4:30 P.M. on Fridays and Saturdays. Behind the market is **Buck's Restaurant** (Rte. 176, South Brooksville, 207/326-8688, from 5 P.M. Mon.–Sat.), a quirky café with indoor and a few outdoor tables. The emphasis is on comfort food, with choices varying from sandwiches and pizza to nightly specials. With the café here at the market and summertime steel-band street concerts outside, this can be a busy corner.

Ethnic Fare
Okay, I know it's hard to believe, but **El El Frijoles** (41 Caterpillar Rd./Rte. 15, Sargentville, 207/359-2486, 11 A.M.–8 P.M. Wed.–Sun.) gets good marks for its empanadas, burritos, and tacos. It's a small, somewhat funky, mostly take-out operation with a few seats inside and out. It's housed in a barn behind Coast to Coast Fine Arts.

Country Inn Dining
An 1865 farmstead is the setting for the ◖ **Rusticator Restaurant** at the Oakland House Seaside Inn (435 Herrick Rd., Brooksville, 207/359-8521), open to the public by reservation mid-June–mid-September for its daily breakfast buffet, Sunday brunch, Thursday night shorefront lobster picnic, and superb

dinners, with seating beginning at 6 P.M. Entrée range is $11–17, a steal. The dining rooms are in the property's original farmstead, which dates from 1865. At dinner, families dine in a separate room from couples, keeping everyone happy.

Almost everything on the menu is local or organic at **The Brooklin Inn** (Rte. 175, Brooklin, 207/359-2777, www.brooklininn.com, 5:30–9 P.M. Wed.–Mon.). The chef tries to know "who raised, grew, picked, or caught all the food," and all the fish are wild, free swimming, and locally caught. Entrées are $18–32; a children's menu is available. Downstairs an **Irish Pub** (5:30–10 P.M. daily) serves burgers, Guinness stew, pizza, and on Fridays all the fresh baked haddock you can eat for $10.

INFORMATION AND SERVICES

The best source of information about the region is the Blue Hill Peninsula Chamber of Commerce (28 Water St., P.O. Box 520, Blue Hill 04614, 207/374-2281, www.bluehillpeninsula .org). Another possibility, although somewhat outdated when I checked, is the website of the East Penobscot Bay Association (www.penobscot bay.com). Request a copy of its handy flyer/ map. Once you've landed on Route 172 or 175, pop into one of the small roadside convenience stores and start asking questions. The clerks— often the owners—know it all cold, and these markets always have a fair share of local color. Of course, they won't object if you also buy something while you're there.

Castine

Castine (pop. 1,343) is a gem—a serene New England village with a tumultuous past. It's on the tip of a cape, surrounded by water on three sides, including the entrance to the Penobscot River, which made it a strategic defense point. Once beset by geopolitical squabbles, saluting the flags of three different nations (France, Britain, and Holland), its only crises now are local political skirmishes. This is an unusual community, a National Historic Register enclave that many people never find. The town celebrated its bicentennial in 1996. Today a major presence is Maine Maritime Academy, yet Castine remains the quietest imaginable college town. Students in search of a party school won't find it here; naval engineering is serious business.

What visitors discover is a year-round community with a busy waterfront, an easy-to-conquer layout, a handful of traditional inns and boutiques, wooded trails on the outskirts of town, an astonishing collection of splendid Georgian and Federalist architecture, and water views from nearly every which way you turn. If you're staying in Blue Hill or even Bar Harbor, spend a day here. Or book a room in one of the town's lovely inns, and use Castine as a base for exploring here and beyond. Either way, you won't regret it.

HISTORY

Originally known as Fort Pentagoet, Castine received its current name courtesy of Jean-Vincent d'Abbadie, Baron de St.-Castin. A young French nobleman manqué who married a Wabanaki princess named Pidiwamiska, d'Abbadie ran the town in the second half of the 17th century and eventually returned to France.

A century later, in 1779, occupying British troops and their reinforcements scared off potential American seaborne attackers (including Colonel Paul Revere), who turned tail up the Penobscot River and ended up scuttling their more than 40-vessel fleet—a humiliation known as the Penobscot Expedition and still regarded as one of America's worst naval defeats.

When the boundaries for Maine were finally set in 1820, with the St. Croix River marking the east rather than the Penobscot River, the last British Loyalists departed, some floating their homes north to St. Andrews, in New

MAINE MARITIME ACADEMY

The state's only merchant-marine college (and one of only seven in the nation) occupies 35 acres in the middle of Castine. Founded in 1941, the academy awards undergraduate and graduate degrees in such areas as marine engineering, ocean studies, and marina management, preparing a student body of about 825 men and women for careers as ship captains, naval architects, and marine engineers.

The academy owns a fleet of 60 vessels, including the historic research schooner *Bowdoin*, flagship of Arctic explorer Admiral Donald MacMillan, and the 499-foot training vessel TV *State of Maine*, berthed down the hill at the waterfront. In 1996-1997, the *State of Maine*, formerly the U.S. Navy hydrographic survey ship *Tanner*, underwent a $12 million conversion for use by the academy. It is still subject to deployment, and in 2005, the school had to quickly find alternative beds for students using the ship as a dormitory when it was called into service in support of rescue and rebuilding efforts after Hurricane Katrina in New Orleans. Midshipmen conduct free 30-minute tours of the vessel on weekdays in summer (about mid-July–late Aug.). The schedule is posted at the dock, or call 207/326-4311 to check; photo ID is required.

Weekday tours of the campus can be arranged through the Admissions Office (207/326-2206 or 800/227-8465 outside Maine, www.mainemaritime.edu). Campus highlights include three-story Nutting Memorial Library, in Platz Hall (open daily during the school year, weekdays in summer and during vacations); the Henry A. Scheel Room, a cozy oasis in Leavitt Hall containing memorabilia from late naval architect Henry Scheel and his wife, Jeanne; and the well-stocked bookstore (Curtis Hall, 207/326-9333, 8 A.M.-3 P.M. Mon.-Fri.).

Brunswick, Canada, where they can still be seen today. For a while, peace and prosperity became the bywords for Castine—with lively commerce in fish and salt—but it all collapsed during the California Gold Rush and the Civil War trade embargo, leaving the town down on its luck.

Of the many historical landmarks scattered around town, one of the most intriguing must be the sign on "Wind Mill Hill," at the junction of Route 166 and State Street:

> On Hatch's Hill there stands a mill. Old Higgins he doth tend it. And every time he grinds a grist, he has to stop and mend it.

In smaller print, just below the rhyme, comes the drama:

> Here two British soldiers were shot for desertion.

Castine indeed has quite a history.

◀ Castine Historic Tour

To appreciate Castine fully, you need to arm yourself with the Castine Merchants Association's visitors' brochure/map (all businesses and lodgings in town have copies) and follow the numbers on bike or on foot. With no stops, walking the route takes less than an hour, but you'll want to read dozens of historical plaques, peek into public buildings, shoot some photos, and perhaps even do some shopping.

Highlights of the tour include the late-18th-century **John Perkins House,** moved to Perkins Street from Court Street in 1969 and restored with period furnishings. It's open for guided tours 2–5 P.M. Sunday and Wednesday July and August; admission is $5.

Next door, **The Wilson Museum** (107 Perkins St., 207/326-8545, www.wilsonmuseum .org, 2–5 P.M. Tues.–Sun. late May–late Sept., free), founded in 1921, contains an intriguingly eclectic two-story collection of prehistoric artifacts, ship models, dioramas, baskets, tools, and minerals assembled over a lifetime by John Howard Wilson, a geologist/anthropologist who first visited Castine in 1891 (and died in 1936). Among the exhibits are Balinese masks, ancient oil lamps, cuneiform tablets, Zulu artifacts, pre-Inca pottery, and assorted local findings. Don't miss this, even though it's a bit musty, although that is changing thanks to a recent multimillion dollar bequest. (The only comparable Maine institutions are the Nylander Museum, in Caribou, and the L. C. Bates Museum, in Hinckley.) Open the same days and hours as the Perkins House are the **Blacksmith Shop,** where a smith does demonstrations, and the **Hearse House,** containing Castine's 19th-century winter and summer funeral vehicles. Both are free admission. The **Castine Scientific Society** (P.O. Box 196, Castine 04421), a private foundation, operates the five-building complex (the fifth being the Doudiet House, where the administrative offices are).

At the end of Battle Avenue stands the 19th-century **Dyce's Head Lighthouse,** no longer operating; the keeper's house is owned by the town. Alongside it is a public path (signposted) leading via a wooden staircase to a tiny patch of rocky shoreline and the beacon that has replaced the lighthouse.

Highest point in town is **Fort George State Park,** site of a 1779 British fortification. Nowadays, little remains except grassy earthworks, but there are interpretive displays and picnic tables.

Main Street, descending toward the water, is a feast for historic-architecture fans. Artist Fitz Hugh Lane and author Mary McCarthy once lived in elegant houses along the elm-lined street (neither building is open to the public). On Court Street between Main and Green stands turn-of-the-20th-century **Emerson Hall,** site of Castine's municipal offices. Since Castine has no official information booth, you may need to duck in here (it's open weekdays) for answers to questions.

Across Court Street, **Witherle Memorial Library,** a handsome early-19th-century building on the site of the 18th-century town jail, looks out on the Town Common. Also facing the Common are the Adams and Abbott Schools, the former still an elementary school. The **Abbott School** (10 A.M.–4 P.M. Tues.–Sat. and 1–4 P.M. Sun. July–Labor Day, reduced schedule spring and fall, free but donation welcome), built in 1859, has been carefully restored for use as a museum/headquarters for the **Castine Historical Society** (P.O. Box 238, Castine 04421, 207/326-4118, www.castinehistoricalsociety.org). A big draw at the volunteer-run museum is the 24-foot-long Bicentennial Quilt, assembled for Castine's 200th anniversary in 1996. The historical society, founded in 1966, organizes lectures, exhibits, and special events (some free) in various places around town.

On the outskirts of town, across the narrow neck between Wadsworth Cove and Hatch's Cove, stretches a rather overgrown canal (signposted British Canal) scooped out by the occupying British during the War of 1812. Effectively severing land access to the town of Castine, the Brits thus raised havoc,

Dyce's Head Lighthouse, in Castine, dates from the 19th century.

© TOM NANGLE

collected local revenues for eight months, and then departed for Halifax with enough funds to establish Dalhousie College (now Dalhousie University). Wear waterproof boots to walk the canal route; the best time to go is at low tide.

If a waterfront picnic sounds appealing, buy the fixings at Bah's Bakehouse and settle in on the grassy earthworks along the harborfront at **Fort Madison,** site of an 1808 garrison (then Fort Porter) near the corner of Perkins and Madockawando Streets. The views from here are fabulous, and it's accessible all year. A set of stairs leads down to the rocky waterfront.

PARKS, PRESERVES, AND RECREATION
Witherle Woods

This 96-acre preserve owned by Maine Coast Heritage Trust and managed by the Conservation Trust of Brooksville, Castine, and Penobscot is a popular walking area with a maze of trails and old woods roads leading to the water. The adjacent property is privately owned, so carry a trail map and stick to it. Many Revolutionary War–era relics have been found here; if you see any, do *not* remove them. Access to the preserve is via a shaded old woods road on Battle Avenue, between the water district property (at the end of the wire fence) and The Manor's exit driveway and diagonally across from La Tour Street. Several lodgings keep a supply of maps as does the nearby Adams Gallery, or contact (by phone or mail) the **Conservation Trust of Brooksville, Castine, and Penobscot** (P.O. Box 421, Castine 04421, 207/326-9711). The Trust has been protecting the natural resources of Castine, Penobscot, and Brooksville since the early 1980s. It also offers natural-history walks, canoe trips, and boat excursions. Also ask locally about the **Henderson Natural Area** and other preserves, some accessible only by boat.

Bicycling

Bicycling is an easy way to see Castine. The terrain is gentle and traffic in town is light. Rental bikes are available hourly, daily, and weekly from **Dennett's Wharf** (207/326-9045).

Sea Kayaking

Also based at Dennett's Wharf is **Castine Kayak Adventures** (15 Sea St., Castine, 207/326-9045, www.castinekayak.com), spearheaded by Maine Guide Karen Francoeur. Known locally as "Kayak Karen," she's particularly adept with beginners, delivering wise advice from beginning to end. All skill levels are accommodated. Three-hour half-day trips are $55; six-hour full-day tours are around $105 including lunch. Two-hour sunset tours are $40; the sunrise tour includes a light breakfast for $55. Friday nights, there are special two-hour phosphorescence tours, under the stars (weather permitting), for $55 pp. Longer trips are available for $110 per day. If you have your own boat, call Karen for advice; she knows these waters.

Swimming

Backshore Beach, a crescent of sand and gravel on Wadsworth Cove Road (turn off Battle Ave. at the Castine Golf Club) is a favorite saltwater swimming spot, with views across the bay to Stockton Springs. Be forewarned, though, that ocean swimming in this part of Maine is not for the timid. The best time to try it is on the incoming tide, after the sun has had time to heat up the mud. At mid- to high tide, it's also the best place to put in a sea kayak. Park along the road.

If a pool sounds more attractive, you can swim in the **Cary W. Bok indoor pool** at Maine Maritime Academy for $4. Call 207/326-4311, ext. 451, for open- and lap-swim times.

Golf

The **Castine Golf Club** (200 Battle Ave., Castine, 207/326-8844, www.castinegolfclub.com) dates to 1897, when the first tee required a drive from a 30-step-high mound. Redesigned in 1921 by Willie Park Jr., the nine-hole course is open May 15–October 15. Starting times are seldom required, and greens fees are reasonable.

Excursion Boat

On Fridays, Captain Melissa Terry's **Belfast**

Bay Cruises (207/322-5530, www.belfastbay cruises.com, $28 adult, $15 ages 5–15) reverses its usual Belfast to Castine course and offers an afternoon trip to Belfast aboard the *Good Return*. Whereas Castine is all white clapboard, Belfast is red brick. Spend a few hours shopping the intriguing Main Street shops or exploring the town's three National Historical Districts on foot—pick up a walking map at the chamber of commerce (15 Main St.) or wander along the Museum in the Streets, a series of markers highlighting historic buildings and people. Another option with Belfast Bay Cruises is a 45-minute **Castine Harbor Tour** ($10 adult, $8 child).

SHOPPING
Antiques and Galleries
Tucked into the back of the 1796 Parson Mason House, one of Castine's oldest residences, **Leila Day Antiques** (53 Main St., 207/326-8786, www.leiladayantiques.com) is a must for anyone in the market for folk art, period furniture, and quilts. Access is via a lovely, flower-lined walkway.

Traditional American craftwork is sold at **Castine Historical Handworks** (9 Main St., Castine, 207/326-4460, www.castinehistorical handworks.com). Among the selections are pottery, textiles, and folk art.

Oil paintings by local artists Joshua and Susan Adam are on view at **Adam Gallery** (140 Battle Ave., 207/326-8272, www.adam galleryonline.com).

Books
Driving toward Castine on Route 166, watch on your right for a small sign for **Dolphin Books and Prints** (314 Castine Rd., Castine, 207/326-0888, www.dolphin-book.com), where Pete and Liz Ballou have set up their antiquarian business with more than 10,000 books as well as framed prints and art.

In downtown Castine, a block up from the waterfront, **The Compass Rose Bookstore and Café** (3 Main St., 207/326-9366 or 800/698-9366, www.compassrosebooks.com) carries an ever-expanding selection of new books, cards, games, and prints chosen by owner Sharon Biggie. In the back of the shop is a café serving hot and cold drinks (espresso, too), soup, sandwiches, and tasty baked goods.

Furniture
Bench-made Windsor chairs are the specialty at **M&E Gummel Chairworks** (600 Shore Rd., P.O. Box 767, Castine 04421, 207/326-8122, www.gummelchairworks.com). The father-and-son team use 18th-century methods when handcrafting the chairs, Colonial dining tables, and bowls, one at a time in their late-19th-century barn workshop.

ENTERTAINMENT
Best place for live music is **Dennett's Wharf** (15 Sea St., 207/326-9045). Some performances require a ticket. Also head to **The Reef** (facing the waterfront parking lot), for pizza and entertainment, and to **Stella's Jazz Nocturnal** for jazz.

The Trinitarian Church often brings in high-caliber musical entertainment. The Castine Town Band often performs on the common. Check www.castine.org/band.htm for its schedule.

ACCOMMODATIONS
Inns
Castine is blessed with three fine traditional inns. This is not the place to come if you require in-room phones, air-conditioning, or fancy bathrooms. Rather, the pace is relaxed and the accommodations reflect the easy elegance of a bygone era.

The three-story, Queen Anne–style **Pentagöet Inn** (26 Main St., P.O. Box 4, Castine 04421, 207/326-8616 or 800/845-1701, www.pentagoet.com, May–late Oct., $115–245 peak) is the perfect Maine summer inn, right down to the lace curtains billowing in the breeze, the soft floral wallpapers, and the intriguing curiosities that accent, but don't clutter, the rooms. Congenial innkeepers Jack Burke, previously with the foreign service, and Julie Van de Graaf, a pastry chef, took over the century-old inn in 2000 and have given it new life, upgrading rooms and furnishing them with Victorian antiques, adding handsome gardens, and carving out a niche as a dining destination. Their enthusiasm for the area is contagious. The inn's 16 rooms are spread out between the main house (with Wi-Fi service) and the adjoining house. A hot buffet breakfast and afternoon refreshments are provided. Jack holds court in Passports Pub (chock-full of vintage photos and prints and exotic antiques) every afternoon, advising guests on activities and opportunities. Borrow one of the inn's bikes and explore around town or simply walk—the Main Street location is convenient to everything Castine offers. Better yet, just sit on the wraparound porch and take it all in.

The three-story **Castine Inn** (33 Main St., P.O. Box 41, Castine 04421, 207/326-4365, www.castineinn.com, May–late Oct., $105–300) earns a stellar rating for its stunning semi-formal gardens and extremely helpful staff. The 16 rooms and three suites, updated from their 1890s origins, vary in style, from simple Maine to simple elegance (if you're looking for bathrooms with whirlpool tubs, this is the place). Lots of interesting artwork is everywhere and there's a very simpatico and unpretentious air, encouraged by enthusiastic innkeepers Amy and Tom Gutow. In the small, English-style pub, hikers, bicyclists, kayakers, and less energetic guests mingle with a loyal local clientele. A full breakfast is included.

Once the summer "cottage" of Arthur Fuller, a South Boston Yacht Club commodore, **The Manor Inn** (Battle Ave., P.O. Box 873, Castine 04421, 207/326-4861 or 877/626-6746, www.manor-inn.com, $115–275) overlooks town and harbor from five mostly wooded acres elevated above Battle Avenue. Though the atmosphere is informal, there are lots of elegant architectural touches. Nancy Watson and Tom Ehrman took over in 1998, upgrading beds, linens, and furniture. They've expanded the dining room and continue to improve the inn each year. The 14 second- and third-floor rooms are an

eclectic mix—some with canopied beds and fireplaces, all with private baths. A separate guest building has a TV and games as well as Nancy's yoga studio; guests are welcome to join her morning Iyengear classes (Mon., Wed., Fri., $12 drop-in fee). Wi-Fi is available. The trailhead for Witherle Woods is close by. The inn is often the site of weddings and receptions; ask before you book unless you don't mind being the odd man out. It's open mid-February–late December.

Rental Cabins and Cottages

Perched in a field along the edge of Hatch's Cove, with terrific views, are the six two-bedroom, pine-paneled log cabins of **Castine Cottages** (33 Snapp's Way, Rte. 166, P.O. Box 224, Castine 04421, 207/326-8003, www.castinecottages.com), operated by Alan and Diana Snapp. Weekly rate is $625 late June–late September, $500 off-season; when available, cabins are rented nightly for $75–150. Well-behaved pets allowed. It's open May–October. You'll need to provide your own sheets and towels or pay an additional $10 per person.

FOOD
Local Flavors

Since 1920, locals have been buying lunch and ice cream at **Castine Variety** (1 Main St., Castine, 207/326-8625, 5 A.M.–10 P.M. daily in summer, to 7 P.M. the rest of the year). Go for the vintage feeling and the reasonably priced menu varying from sandwiches to pizza to lobster rolls, but don't expect anything approaching friendly service unless you're a local (although that attitude may be softening thanks to new owners).

Far more friendly are the folks at **The Breeze** (town dock, Castine, 207/326-9200), a waterfront take-out stand with reliably good basics—burgers, fried clams, ice cream. You can't beat the location or the view.

At **Eaton's Boatyard** (Sea St., P.O. Box 123, Castine 04421, 207/326-8579), a full-service marina renting moorings by the day or week, you can buy live lobsters May–October and have them cooked or order them shipped anywhere year-round.

Casual Dining

Here's a doubleheader: **Bah's Bakehouse** (26 Water St., Castine, 207/326-9510, 7 A.M.–6 P.M. Mon.–Sat., opens at 8 A.M. Sun.), and sharing the same location, **Stella's Jazz Nocturnal** (207/326-9710, opens at 4 P.M. Tues.–Sat., food service 5–9 P.M.). Upstairs is Bah's, a higgledy-piggledy eatery of three rooms and a deck at the end of an alleyway tucked between Main and Water Streets. Its slogan is "creative flour arrangements," and creative it is. Stop here for morning coffee, cold juices, interesting snacks and salads, homemade soups, wine or beer, and the best sandwiches in town. Be forewarned: If it's crowded, go elsewhere—the kitchen is quickly overwhelmed and service can be slow to frustrating. Underneath the deck is Stella's, an intimate lounge where live jazz is performed Thursday–Sunday. Listen while nibbling on a blue cheese burger, grilled lamb lollipops, pan-seared halibut, or other eclectic choices ($8.50–16).

On a warm summer day, it's hard to find a better place to while away a few hours than **Dennett's Wharf** (15 Sea St., 207/326-9045, www.dennettswharf.com, 11 A.M.–9 P.M. daily May–Columbus Day). Next to the town dock, it's a colorful barn of a place with outside deck and front-row windjammer-watching seats in summer. Kids are welcomed. The crayoned kids' menu includes all the usual favorites, such as mac-'n-cheese and gummy dinosaurs for dessert. Try attaching a dollar bill to the soaring ceiling; countless others have. Service is leisurely; don't dine here if you're in a hurry.

The Pine Cone Pub at The Manor Inn (76 Battle Ave., Castine, 207/326-4861) serves a light menu, with such choices as Caesar salad and fish-and-chips.

Fine Dining

Jazz music plays softly and dinner is by candlelight at the **(Pentagöet** (26 Main St., Castine, 207/326-8616 or 800/845-1701, www.pentagoet.com, opens at 6 P.M. daily July and Aug., Mon.–Sat. May, June, Sept., Oct.). In fine weather, you can dine on the porch. Choices vary from roasted *loup de mer* to slow-cooked lamb shank, or simply make a meal of small plates, such as lamb lollipops and crab cakes and a salad. Don't miss the lobster bouillabaisse or the chocolate *budino,* a scrumptious warm Italian pudding that melts in your mouth (a must for chocoholics). Can't make up your mind? Order the Taste of the Pentagöet sampling platter ($45), with tasting portions of the most popular dishes. Most entrées are in the $18–29 range.

The bilevel dining room at **The Manor Inn** (76 Battle Ave., Castine, 207/326-4861, 6–8:30 P.M. Tues.–Sat. in summer, Thurs.–Sat. off-season) overlooks the gardens and lawn. Dinner is served from an extensive menu accented with Asian flavors and Indian curries and other world flavors, accompanied by home-baked breads, and always including vegetarian choices (most entrées $16–24). Reservations are essential on weekends and for the annual Fourth of July pig roast. It's open Valentine's Day–late December.

INFORMATION AND SERVICES
Information

Castine has no local information office, but all businesses and lodgings in town have copies of the Castine Merchants Association's visitors' brochure/map. For additional information, go to the Castine Town Office (Emerson Hall, 67 Court St., Castine, 207/326-4502, www.castine.me.us, 8 A.M.–3:30 P.M. Mon.–Fri.).

Check out Witherle Memorial Library (41 School St., 207/326-4375, ww.witherle.lib.me.us). Also accessible to the public is the Nutting Memorial Library, in Platz Hall on the Maine Maritime Academy campus.

Public Restrooms

Castine has public restrooms on the town dock, at the foot of Main Street.

Deer Isle

"Deer Isle is like Avalon," wrote John Steinbeck in *Travels with Charley*—"it must disappear when you are not there." Deer Isle (the name of both the island and its midpoint town) has been romancing authors and artisans for decades, but it's unmistakably real to the quarrymen and fishermen who've been here for centuries. These long-timers are a sturdy lot, as even Steinbeck recognized: "I would hate to try to force them to do anything they didn't want to do."

Early-18th-century maps show no name for the island, but by the late 1800s, nearly 100 families lived here, supporting themselves first by farming, then by fishing. In 1789, when Deer Isle was incorporated, 80 local sailing vessels were scouring the Gulf of Maine in pursuit of mackerel and cod, and Deer Isle men were circling the globe as yachting skippers and merchant seamen. At the same time, in the once-quiet village of Green's Landing (now called Stonington), the shipbuilding and granite industries boomed, spurring development, prosperity, and the kinds of rough hijinks typical of commercial ports the world over.

Green's Landing became the "big city" for an international crowd of quarrymen carving out the terrain on Deer Isle and nearby Crotch Island, source of high-quality granite for Boston's Museum of Fine Arts, the Smithsonian Institution, a humongous fountain for John D. Rockefeller's New York estate, and less showy projects all along the Eastern Seaboard. The heyday is long past, but the industry did extend into the 20th century (including a contract for the pink granite at President John F. Kennedy's Arlington National Cemetery gravesite). Today, Crotch Island is the site of Maine's only operating island granite quarry.

Measuring about nine miles north to south (plus another three miles for Little Deer Isle), the island of Deer Isle today has a handful of hamlets (including Sunshine, Sunset,

The fishing village of Stonington, with its boat-filled harbor, tips Deer Isle.

© TOM NANGLE

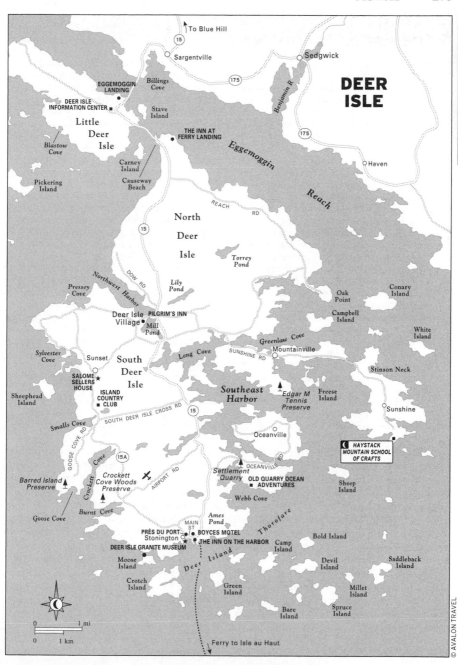

DEER ISLE

To Blue Hill

15

Sargentville

Sedgwick

175

Billings Cove

EGGEMOGGIN LANDING

DEER ISLE INFORMATION CENTER

Stave Island

Little Deer Isle

Benjamin R.

175

Blastow Cove

THE INN AT FERRY LANDING

Eggemoggin

Haven

Carney Island

Causeway Beach

Reach

Pickering Island

REACH RD

North Deer Isle

15

REACH RD

Torrey Pond

Oak Point

Conary Island

Pressey Cove

DOW RD

Northwest Harbor

Lily Pond

Campbell Island

White Island

Deer Isle Village

PILGRIM'S INN

Mill Pond

Greenlaw Cove

SUNSHINE RD

Mountainville

Sylvester Cove

Sunset

South Deer Isle

Long Cove

Stinson Neck

SALOME SELLERS HOUSE

ISLAND COUNTRY CLUB

Southeast Harbor

Edgar M Tennis Preserve

Freese Island

Sunshine

Sheephead Island

SOUTH DEER ISLE CROSS RD

15

HAYSTACK MOUNTAIN SCHOOL OF CRAFTS

Smalls Cove

Oceanville

GOOSE COVE RD

15A

Crockett Cove

Crockett Cove Woods Preserve

AIRPORT RD

OCEANVILLE RD

Settlement Quarry

OLD QUARRY OCEAN ADVENTURES

Sheep Island

Barred Island Preserve

Burnt Cove

Webb Cove

Goose Cove

Ames Pond

MAIN ST

PRÈS DU PORT

Stonington

BOYCES MOTEL

THE INN ON THE HARBOR

Thorofare

Bold Island

DEER ISLE GRANITE MUSEUM

Camp Island

Moose Island

Deer Island

Devil Island

Saddleback Island

Crotch Island

Green Island

Millet Island

Bare Island

Spruce Island

0   1 mi

0   1 km

Ferry to Isle au Haut

© AVALON TRAVEL

THE MAINE ISLAND TRAIL

In the early 1980s, a "trail" of coastal Maine islands was only the germ of an idea. By the end of the millennium, the **Maine Island Trail Association (MITA)** counted about 4,000 members dedicated to conscientious (i.e., low- or no-impact) recreational use of more than 100 public and private islands along 325 miles of Maine coastline between Portland and Machias.

More than a dozen of these islands (each year, new ones are added and others are subtracted) are in the Acadia region – between Isle au Haut and Schoodic Point. In fact, one of the best island clusters along the entire trail is in the waters off Stonington on Deer Isle.

Access to the trail is only by private boat, and the best choice is a sea kayak, to navigate shallow or rock-strewn coves. Sea-kayak rentals are available in Bar Harbor, Southwest Harbor, Blue Hill, and Stonington, and several outfitters offer island tours (see specific sections for details). The best source of information is the Maine Association of Sea Kayaking Guides and Instructors (MASKGI), whose members agree to adhere to the Leave No Trace philosophy.

The trail's publicly owned islands – supervised by the state Bureau of Public Lands – are open to anyone; the private islands are restricted to MITA members, who pay $45 a year for the privilege (and, it's important to add, the responsibility). With the fee comes the *Maine Island Trail Guidebook,* providing directions and information for each of the islands. With membership comes the expectation of care and concern. "Low impact" means different things to different people, so MITA experienced acute growing pains when enthusiasm began leading to "tent sprawl."

To cope with and reverse the overuse, MITA has created an "adopt-an-island program," in which volunteers become stewards for specific islands and keep track of their use and condition. MITA members are urged to pick up trash, use tent platforms where they exist, and continue elsewhere if an island has reached its assigned capacity (stipulated on a shoreline sign and/or in the guidebook).

A superb complement to the *Maine Island Trail Guidebook* is a copy of *Hot Showers!* by Lee Bumsted, a former MITA staff member (see *Suggested Reading* in the *Resources* section). Recognizing the need for alternating island camping and warm beds (and hot showers), she has almost singlehandedly alleviated island stress and strain. Some of the B&Bs and inns listed in her guide give discounts to MITA members.

Membership information is available from Maine Island Trail Association (P.O. Box C, Rockland 04841, 207/596-6456, www.mita.org).

Mountainville, and Oceanville) and two towns—Stonington and Deer Isle—with a population just under 3,000. Road access is via Route 15 on the Blue Hill Peninsula. A huge suspension bridge, built in 1939 over Eggemoggin Reach, links the Sargentville section of Sedgwick with Little Deer Isle; from there, a sinuous, 0.4-mile causeway connects to the northern tip of Deer Isle.

Deer Isle remains an artisans' enclave, anchored by the Haystack Mountain School of Crafts. Studios and galleries are plentiful, although many require noodling along back roads to find them. Stonington, a rough-and-tumble fishing port with an idyllic setting, is slowly being gentrified, as more and more galleries and upscale shops open for the summer each season. Locals are holding their collective breaths hoping that any improvements don't change the town too much (although most visitors could do without the car racing on Main Street at night). Already, real-estate prices and accompanying taxes have escalated way past the point where many a local fisherman can hope to buy, and in some cases, maintain a home.

SIGHTS

Sightseeing on Deer Isle means exploring back roads, browsing the galleries, walking the trails, hanging out on the docks, and soaking in the ambience.

opportunity to buy craftwork at often very reasonable prices.

Historic Houses and Museums

The 1830 **Salome Sellers House** (416 Sunset Rd./Rte. 15A, Sunset Village, 207/367-2629, 1–4 P.M. Wed. and Fri. July–mid-Sept., free), a repository of local memorabilia, is the headquarters of the **Deer Isle-Stonington Historical Society.** Volunteer guides love to provide tidbits about various items; seafarers' logs and ship models are particularly intriguing. It's just north of the Island Country Club and across from Eaton's Plumbing. Donations are appreciated.

Close to the Stonington waterfront, the **Deer Isle Granite Museum** (51 Main St., Stonington, 207/367-6331) was established to commemorate the centennial of the quarrying business hereabouts. Best feature of the small museum is a 15-foot-long working model of Crotch Island, center of the industry, as it appeared at the turn of the 20th century. Flatcars roll, boats glide, and derricks move—it all looks very real. The museum is open late May–early September, but it's best to call for current days and hours of operation. Recommended donation is $5 per family.

Another downtown Stonington attraction is a Lilliputian complex known hereabouts as the **"Miniature Village."** Some years ago, the late Everett Knowlton created a dozen and a half replicas of local buildings and displayed them on granite blocks in his yard. Since his death, they've been restored and put on display each summer in town—along with a donation box to support the upkeep. The village is set up on East Main Street (Rte. 15), below Hoy Gallery.

© TOM NANGLE

Tour the Haystack Mountain School of Crafts for the artwork, the campus architecture, and the views.

【 Haystack Mountain School of Crafts

The renowned Haystack Mountain School of Crafts (Sunshine Rd., P.O. Box 518, Deer Isle 04627, 207/348-2306, www.haystack-mtn.org) in Sunshine (see the sidebar *Getting Crafty*) is open to the public on a limited basis, but if it fits in your schedule, go. Tours of the campus ($5) are given at 1 P.M. every Wednesday. These include a video, viewing works on display, and the opportunity to tour some studios. Free slide programs, lectures, demonstrations, and concerts, presented by faculty and visiting artists, start at 8 P.M. on varying weeknights early June–late August. Perhaps the best opportunities are the End-of-Session auctions, held on Thursday nights every two or three weeks, when you can tour the studios free 4–6 P.M. and see the works the teachers and students have produced, then return for the auction preview at 7:30 P.M., followed by the auction at 8 P.M. It's a great

Pumpkin Island Light

A fine view of Pumpkin Island Light can be had from the cul-de-sac at the end of the Eggemoggin Road on Little Deer Isle. If heading south on Route 15, bear right at the information booth after crossing the bridge and continue to the end.

Penobscot East Resource Center

The purpose of the Penobscot East Resource Center, on the waterfront in Stonington (207/367-2708, www.penobscoteast.org) is "to energize and facilitate responsible community-based fishery management, collaborative marine science, and sustainable economic development to benefit the fishermen and the communities of Penobscot Bay and the Eastern Gulf of Maine." Bravo to that! It operates a **Lobster Hatchery** (Stonington Lobster Coop No. 1, 52 Indian Point Rd.), which was constructed by volunteers from the lobster industry in donated space with $25,000 raised locally and a matching grant. Lobster production began in 2006. Guided tours are offered ($10 adults, $5 children); call 207/367-2708 for the schedule.

The man behind both ventures is Ted Ames, who won a $500,000 MacArthur Fellowship "Genius Grant" in 2005 (see sidebar *Ted Ames, Genius*).

PARKS AND PRESERVES

Foresighted benefactors have managed to set aside precious acreage for respectful public use on Deer Isle. The Nature Conservancy owns two properties, **Crockett Cove Woods Preserve** and **Barred Island Preserve.** For information, contact The Conservancy (14 Maine St., Fort Andross, Brunswick 04011, 207/729-5181). The conscientious steward of other local properties is the **Island Heritage Trust** (3 Main St., at Rte. 15, P.O. Box 42, Deer Isle 04627, 207/348-2455, www.islandheritagetrust.org). When the office is open (usually 10:30 A.M.–3 P.M. weekdays July and Aug., 10 A.M.–2 P.M. Tues. and Thurs. off-season), you can pick up notecards, photos, T-shirts, and helpful maps and information on hiking trails and nature preserves. Proceeds benefit the IHT's efforts; donations are much appreciated.

Settlement Quarry

Here's one of the easiest, shortest walks in the area, leading to an impressive vista. From the parking lot on Oceanville Road (just under a mile off Rte. 15), marked by a carved granite sign, it's about five minutes to the top of the old quarry, where the viewing platform (a.k.a. the "throne room") takes in the panorama—all the way to the Camden Hills on a good day. In early August, wild raspberries are an additional enticement. Three short loop trails lead into the surrounding woods from here. A map is available in the trailhead box.

Edgar Tennis Preserve

The 145-acre Tennis Preserve, in particular, off the Sunshine Road, has very limited parking, so don't try to squeeze in if there isn't room; schedule your visit for another hour or day. But do go, and bring at least a snack if not a full picnic to enjoy on one of the convenient rocky outcroppings (carry in, carry out, though). Allow at least 90 minutes to enjoy the walking trails, one of which skirts Pickering Cove, providing sigh-producing views. Another trail leads to an old cemetery. Parts of the trails can be wet, so wear appropriate footwear. And do bring binoculars for bird-watching. The preserve is open sunrise–sunset. To find it, take the Sunshine Road 2.5 miles to the Tennis Road, and follow it to the preserve.

Shore Acres Preserve

The 38-acre preserve, a gift in 2000 from Judy Hill to the Island Heritage Trust, comprises old farmland, woodlands, clam flats, a salt marsh, and granite shorefront. Three walking trails connect in a 1.5-mile loop, with the Shore Trail section edging Greenlaw Cove. As you walk along the waterfront, look for the islands of Mount Desert rising in the distance and seals basking on offshore ledges. Do not walk across the salt marsh and try to avoid stepping on beach plants. To find the preserve, take the Sunshine Road 1.2 miles and then bear left at the fork onto the Greenlaw District Road. The preserve's parking area is just shy of one mile down the road. Park only in the parking area, not on paved road.

Crockett Cove Woods Preserve

Donated to The Nature Conservancy by benevolent, eco-conscious local artist Emily Muir, 98-acre Crockett Cove Woods Preserve is Deer

GETTING CRAFTY

Internationally famed artisans – sculptors and papermakers, weavers and jewelers, potters and printmakers – become the faculty each summer for the unique **Haystack Mountain School of Crafts.** Founded in 1950 by Mary Beasom Bishop (1885–1972) and a group of talented Maine artisans as a studio research and study program, Haystack has grown into one of the top craft schools in the country.

Under the direction of beloved former director Francis Merritt, the school opened its first campus near Haystack Mountain, in Montville, Maine, in 1951. Ten years later, when the state unveiled plans to build a new highway (Rte. 3) that would bisect that campus, the school moved to its present 40-acre oceanfront location at the end of the Sunshine Road in Deer Isle. Good move.

You would be hard-pressed to find a more artistically stimulating and architecturally stunning environment. Architect Edward Larrabee Barnes's award-winning campus perfectly complements its dramatic setting. The angular, cedar-shingled buildings are connected via walkways and teaching decks and a central staircase that cascades like a waterfall down the wooded hillside to the rocky coast below. The visual impression is one of spruce and ledge, glass and wood, islands and water.

One thing that makes Haystack work is its diverse student body. Students of all abilities, from beginners through advanced professionals, come from around the globe for the two- to three-week summer sessions, taking weekday classes and enjoying round-the-clock studio access to follow their creative muses. In a recent year, students ranged in age from 18 to 75, and in professions from a retired teacher to a physicist. What brings them all here, says current director Stuart Kestenbaum, is the "direct making experience." That experience draws not only those who make but those who collect. For a collector of fine craft, he says, taking a class is a "great way to get insight into the making process; it gives a different relationship with the craft being collected." Each session also includes a range of craft. These may include blacksmithing, drawing, metals, wood, beads, clay, fiber/design, printmaking, glass, weaving, mixed media, paper, and baskets.

© TOM NANGLE

Students come from throughout North America and beyond to study at Haystack Mountain School of Crafts.

TED AMES, GENIUS

Ted Ames, the man behind the Penobscot East Resource Center and the Lobster Hatchery, in Stonington, was in 2005 awarded a $500,000 MacArthur Fellowship. These prestigious "genius grants" are awarded to "talented individuals who have shown extraordinary originality and dedication in their creative pursuits and a marked capacity for self-direction." The foundation credited Ames with fusing "the roles of fisherman and applied scientist in response to increasing threats to the fishery ecosystem resulting from decades of over-harvesting." Criteria for selection are: exceptional creativity, promise for important future advances based on a track record of significant accomplishment, and potential for the fellowship to facilitate subsequent creative work. No question, they found the right guy in Ted Ames.

A humble, soft-spoken man with dogged determination, Ames found little time to bask in the limelight from the award. While he certainly appreciated the money and the attention paid to his causes, the numerous interviews with TV, radio, and newspaper reporters took up valuable time, time he would rather use researching fisheries, collecting data, and devising ways to develop community-based fisheries management.

Ames is a fascinating guy, a combination of fisherman, lobsterman, and research scientist with deep Maine roots. "My family were some of the original settlers of Vinalhaven," he said. His ancestors on his father's side arrived in 1757, on the island off Rockland in Maine's Mid-Coast Region. "My mother's side came from Mount Desert." They were the original settlers on Bartlett's Island. When King George told the family to leave, they refused and stayed put, he recalled. Ames grew up in a fishing family on Vinalhaven and went on to gain a master's degree in biochemistry from the University of Maine. But fishing was in his blood, and he eventually returned to the sea as a lobsterman and ground fisherman.

His years on the water gave him first-hand experience watching the changes in Maine's fisheries. He watched Maine's coastal economy change as fishing ports became more gentrified, commercial piers gave way to oceanfront homes, and marine-related businesses gave way to fancy boutiques. His education combined with his experiences gave him tools and the insight needed to work toward developing new fisheries management practices and supporting fishing communities. He studied fishing patterns in the Gulf of Maine, noting spawning and habitat, and he complemented his research with listening to the stories and experiences of aging fishermen. By doing so, he was able to establish a fishing timeline beginning with historical patterns and following their evolution to current ones.

The Penobscot East Resource Center, which he founded with his wife, Robin, a former marine resources commissioner, and the Lobster Hatchery both are designed as research facilities as well as places for community members and others to learn more about fishing, to meet commercial fishermen and women, and to learn about their lifestyles in order to help support them and preserve the tradition and the economy. Ames, a master at gaining community support (due perhaps to his impeccable Maine credentials), managed to raise $25,000 from local fishing families and local businesses and individuals in an area not known for wealth.

Ames plans to use the unrestricted MacArthur Fellows Program money to continue his fisheries research and to develop ways for "community-based groundfishing management to make it sustainable, so coastal fishing communities can survive into the next century. That's a challenge, but we're in the midst of it." There's no better person to be on the forefront than Ted Ames.

Isle's natural gem—a coastal fog forest laden with lichens and mosses. Four interlinked walking trails cover the whole preserve, starting with a short nature trail. Pick up the helpful map/brochure at the registration box. Wear rubberized shoes or boots and respect adjacent private property. The preserve is open sunrise–sunset daily all year. From Deer Isle Village, take Route 15A to Sunset Village. Go 2.5 miles to Whitman Road and then to Fire Lane 88. The local contact phone number is 207/367-2674.

Barred Island Preserve

Owned by The Nature Conservancy, but managed by the Island Heritage Trust, Barred Island Preserve was donated by Carolyn Olmsted, grandniece of noted landscape architect Frederick Law Olmsted, who summered nearby. A former owner of Goose Cove Lodge donated an additional 48 acres of maritime boreal fog forest. A single walking trail, one mile long, leads from the parking lot to the point. At low tide, and when eagles aren't nesting, you can continue out to Barred Island. Another trail skirts the shoreline of Goose Cove, before retreating inland and rejoining with the main trail. From a high point on the main trail, you can see more than a dozen islands, many of which are protected from development, as well as Saddleback Ledge Light, 14 miles distant. To get to the preserve, follow Route 15A to Goose Cove Road and then continue to the parking area on the right. If it's full, return another day.

Holt Mill Pond Preserve

The Stonington Conservation Commission administers this town-owned preserve, where more than 47 bird species have been identified (bring binoculars). It comprises four habitats: upland spruce forest, lowland spruce/mixed forest, freshwater marsh, and saltwater marsh. A self-guiding nature trail is accessible off the Airport Road (off Rte. 15 at the intersection with Lily's Café). Look for the Nature Trail sign just beyond the medical center. The detailed, self-guiding trail brochure, available at the trailhead registration kiosk, is accented with drawings by noted artist Siri Beckman.

Ames Pond

Ames Pond is neither park nor preserve, but it might as well be. On a back road close to Stonington, it's a mandatory stop in July and August, when the pond wears a blanket of pink and white water lilies. From downtown Stonington, take Indian Point Road east, just under a mile, to the pond. There's no official parking, so if you're shooting photos, pull off the road as far as possible, respecting private property.

Causeway Beach and Scott's Landing

If you're itching to dip your toes in the water, stop by Causeway Beach along the causeway linking Little Deer Isle to Deer Isle. It's popular for swimming and is also a significant habitat for birds and other wildlife. On the other side of Route 15 is Scott's Landing, with more than 20 acres of fields, trails, and shorefront.

RECREATION
Guided Walks

The Island Heritage Trust, along with the Stonington and Deer Isle Conservation Commissions, sponsors a Walks and Talks series. Guided walks cover topics such as Bird and Bird Calls for Beginners, Common Trees of Deer Isle, and Care and Culture of Your Small Woodlot. For information and reservations, call 207/348-2455.

Sea Kayaking

With lots of islets and protected coves, sea kayaking in the waters around Deer Isle, especially off Stonington, is extremely popular.

If you sign up with the **Maine Island Trail Association** (Box C, Rockland, www.mita.org, $45 a year), you'll receive a handy manual that steers you to more than a dozen islands in the Deer Isle archipelago where you can camp, hike, and picnic—eco-sensitively, please. Boat traffic can be a bit heavy at the height of summer, so to best appreciate the tranquility of this area, try this in September, after the Labor Day holiday. Nights can be cool, but days are likely to be brilliant. Do remember this is a working harbor.

The six-mile paddle from Stonington to Isle

au Haut is best left to experienced paddlers, especially since fishing folks refer to kayakers as "speed bumps."

For equipment rentals or guided trips, see *Sporting Outfitters and Guided Trips*. Old Quarry Ocean Adventures is especially helpful and provides many services for kayakers.

Swimming

The island's only major freshwater swimming hole is the **Lily Pond,** northeast of Deer Isle Village. Just north of the Shakespeare School, turn into the Deer Run Apartments complex. Park and take the path to the pond, which has a shallow area for small children.

Golf

About two miles south of Deer Isle Village, watch for the large sign (on the left) for the **Island Country Club** (Rte. 15A, Sunset, 207/348-2379), a nine-hole public course that's been here since 1928. Starting times are first-come, first-served, and greens fees are low; no credit cards. It's open early June–late September. Also at the club are three beautifully maintained tennis courts. Or just commandeer a rocking chair and watch the action from one of the porches. The club's cheeseburgers and salads are among the island's best bargain lunches.

Sporting Outfitters and Guided Trips

The biggest operation is **Old Quarry Ocean Adventures** (130 Settlement Rd., Stonington, 207/367-8977 or 877/479-8977, mobile 207/266-7778, www.oldquarry.com), with a broad range of outdoor-adventure choices. Bill Baker's ever-expanding enterprise rents canoes, kayaks, sailboats, bikes, moorings, platform tent sites, and cabins. Bicycle rentals are $20 a day or $100 a week. Canoes or rowboats are $42 half day, $52 full day, or $250 per week; sailboats are $80 or $100 half day, $100 or $150 full day. For all boat rentals, you must demonstrate competency in the vessel.

All-day guided tours in single kayaks are $105; tandems are $175. Half-day tours are $55 and $110, respectively. Plenty of other options are available, including sunset tours, family trips, and gourmet picnic paddles.

Sea-kayak rental rates are $57 per day for a single, $67 for a tandem. Half-day rates (based on a four-hour rental) are $42 and $52, respectively. Overnight rates (24-hour rental) are subject to a 10 percent surcharge. Weekly rentals are $300 single, $380 tandem.

A Registered Maine Guide leads overnight kayak-camping trips on nearby islands. Rates, including meals, begin at $285 adult for one night.

If you're bringing your own kayak, you can park your car ($6 per night for up to two nights, $5 per night for three or more nights) and launch from here ($5 per boat for launching), and Old Quarry will take your trash and any trash you find. Old Quarry is off the Oceanville Road, less than a mile from Route 15, just before you reach the Settlement Quarry preserve. It's well signposted.

Next to the restaurant of the same name and owned by the same family is **Finest Kind** (Center District Crossroad, about halfway between Rtes. 15 and 15A, 207/348-7714). Bicycle rentals are $15 per day or $75 per week. Kayak or canoe rentals are $35 per day solo, $45 per day tandem, including paddles, life jackets, spray skirts, delivery, and pickup.

EXCURSION BOATS
Isle au Haut Boat Company

If you're not up for self-propulsion, the *Miss Lizzie* or the *Mink* departs twice daily, morning and afternoon mid-June–early September, from the Isle au Haut Boat Company dock in Stonington for a narrated 75-minute trip among the islands before landing at Duck Harbor; on morning tours, the crew hauls a string of lobster traps. Cost is $32 adults, $16 kids, $8 bike. A 45-minute trip to the Isle au Haut town dock operates five times daily ($32 adult, $16 kids under 12, family fare available); you can rent a bike on Isle au Haut for $20. Reservations are advisable, especially in July and August. Parking is available at the pier for $9. The *Miss Lizzie* and the *Mink* are owned by the

Isle au Haut Boat Company (Seabreeze Ave., Stonington, 207/367-5193 or 207/367-6516, www.isleauhaut.com), the same company that operates the regular mail boat/passenger-ferry service to offshore Isle au Haut.

Guided Island Tours

Captain Walter Reed's Guided Island Tours (207/348-6789, www.guidedislandtours.com) aboard the *Gael* are custom designed for a maximum of four passengers. Walt is a Registered Maine Guide and professional biologist who also is steward for Mark Island Lighthouse and several uninhabited islands in the area. He provides in-depth perspective and the local scoop. The cost is $37.50 pp for the first hour plus $15 pp for each additional hour. Reservations are required; box lunches are available for an additional fee.

Old Quarry Ocean Adventures

Yet another aspect of the Old Quarry Ocean Adventures (Stonington, 207/367-8977 or 877/479-8977, mobile 207/266-7778, www .oldquarry.com) empire are sightseeing tours on the *Nigh Duck*. The three-hour trips, one in the morning (9 A.M.–noon) and one in the afternoon (1–4 P.M.) are $38 for adults and $22 for children under 12. Both highlight the natural history of the area, as Captain Bill navigates the boat through the archipelago. Lobster traps are hauled on both trips. The afternoon one features an island swimming break in a freshwater quarry. Also available is a 1.5-hour sunset cruise, departing one-half hour before sunset, for $30 adults and $20 kids under 12. And if that's not enough, Old Quarry also offers puffin, lighthouse, whale-watch, and island cruises, with rates beginning at $45 per adult, $305 for kids. Of course, if none of this floats your boat, you can also arrange for a custom charter for $175 per hour.

◖ ART AND CRAFT GALLERIES

Thanks to the presence and influence of Haystack Mountain School of Crafts, supertalented artists and artisans lurk in every corner of the island. Most are tucked away on back roads, so watch for roadside signs. Many have studios open to the public where you can watch the artists at work. First Friday open gallery nights are scheduled July–October (www.stonington galleries.com).

Little Deer Isle

On Little Deer Isle, don't miss **Morrow Wilson Studios** (455 Eggemoggin Rd., 207/348-6871, www.morrowwilsonstudios.com), Doug and Jennifer Morrow-Wilson's gallery. Doug has turned blacksmithing into an art form, while Jennifer makes paper by hand and then uses it in three-dimensional collages that often include internal lighting. Their collaborations are especially nice. Both often open their studios to visitors.

North End of Deer Isle

Although the artist has died, his innovative and beautiful jewelry lives on in his eponymous **Ronald Hayes Pearson studio and gallery** (29 Old Ferry Rd., 207/348-2535), where artisans continue to create his designs under the watchful eye of his wife.

The nearby **Greene Ziner Gallery** (73 Reach Rd., 207/348-2601, www.melissagreene.com) is a double treat. Melissa Greene turns out incredible painted and incised pottery (she's represented in the Renwick) and Eric Ziner works magic in metal sculpture and furnishings. Your budget may not allow for one of Melissa's pots (in the four-digit range), but I guarantee you'll covet them. The gallery also displays the work of several other local artists.

Deer Isle Village Area

One of the island's premier galleries is Elena Kubler's **The Turtle Gallery** (61 N. Deer Isle Rd., Rte. 15, 207/348-9977, www.turtlegallery .com), in a handsome space formerly known as the Old Centennial House Barn (owned by the late Haystack director Francis Merritt) and the adjacent farmhouse. Group and solo shows of contemporary paintings, prints, and crafts are hung upstairs and down in the barn; works by gallery artists are in the farmhouse; and there's usually sculpture in the gardens both in front and in back. It's just north of Deer Isle Village—across from the Shakespeare School, oldest on the island.

Although it's in a new location and craft queen Mary Nyburg is no longer at the helm, her **Blue Heron Gallery and Studio** (Main St., Deer Isle, www.blueherondeerisle.com) survives and continues to show the work of Haystack's internationally renowned faculty— printmakers, blacksmiths, potters, weavers, papermakers, glassworkers, and more.

Just a bit south is **Dockside Quilt Gallery** (33 Church St., 207/348-2531), where Nancy Knowlton, her daughter Kelly Pratt, and daughter-in-law Rebekah Knowlton stitch heirloom-quality quilts. Also here are Re-Bears, one-of-a-kind teddy bears handcrafted from vintage furs and fabrics by ninth-generation islander Heather Cormier. Custom quilts and bears are available.

The **Deer Isle Artists Association** (13 Dow Rd., 207/348-2330) is headquartered less than a mile northwest of the village. The co-op gallery features two-week exhibits of paintings, prints, drawings, and photos by local pros. Horse fans won't want to miss Penelope Plumb's upstairs gallery **Equine Art** (207/348-6892, www.penelopeplumb.com). The entrance is in the back of the building.

Just down the street, the **dowstudio** (Dow Rd., 207/348-6498, www.dowstudiodeerisle .com) shows pottery, metalwork, jewelry, prints, and drawings by Ellen Wieske, Carole Ann Fer, and Susan Webster.

Carol Scott Wainright's hand-woven **River Horse Rugs** (Deer Isle Village, 207/348-2589, www.riverhorserugs.net) are unmistakable. Her tapestry-like designs feature organic or geometric shapes on linen warp and hand-dyed wool in deep, vivid colors. Call for an appointment.

Sunshine Road

Now for a bit of whimsy. From Route 15 in Deer Isle Village, take the Sunshine Road east 2.9 miles to **Peter Beerits Sculpture** (600 Sunshine Rd., 800/777-6845, www.nervous nellies.com). The meadows and woods

surrounding the studio teem with whimsical wood and metal sculptures, including dragons, Huns on horseback, moose, and more (all for sale). The property is also home to Beerits's other enterprise, **Nervous Nellie's Jams and Jellies,** known for outstandingly creative condiments; sample the hot pepper jelly or blackberry peach conserve or ginger syrup. The promotional brochures are hilarious. Best time to come is 9 A.M.–5 P.M. May–early October, when the shop operates the ultracasual **Mountainville Café,** serving tea, coffee, and delicious scones—with, of course, Nervous Nellie's products. They're delicious; stock up, because they're sold in only a few shops.

Nearby is the **Pitcher Masters Studio Gallery** (Good Dog Run, 45 French Camp Rd., off Sunshine Rd., 207/348-2322, www.pitcher masters.com). Buzz Masters and Frank Pitcher show their paintings and pottery along with selected works by other megatalented artists.

Stonington

Cabinetmaker **Geoffrey Warner's Studio** (431 N. Main St., 207/367-6555, www.geoff warnerstudio.com) features his work as well as that of other local woodworkers in rotating shows. Warner mixes classic techniques with contemporary styles accented by Eastern, nature-based, and arts-and-crafts accents to create some unusual and rather striking pieces.

Bright and airy **Isalos Fine Art** (Main St., Stonington, 207/367-2700, www.isalosart .com) shows the work of local artists in rotating shows.

Jack and Harriet Rawle Hemenway's **Green Head Forge** (Old Quarry Rd., 207/367-2632) is a delight. Downstairs is Jack's forge and a gallery filled with his sculpted and forged metalwork; upstairs, you can watch Harriet create fabulous jewelry and small objects in gold and silver.

Debi Mortenson shows her paintings, photography, and sculptures at **D Mortenson Galley** (10 W. Main St., 207/367-5875, www .debimortenson.com) year-round.

The **d.Watson Gallery** (68 Main St., 207/367-2900) is a fine art gallery representing a number of artists working in varied media.

More paintings, many in bold, bright colors, can be found at Jill Hoy's **Hoy Gallery** (E. Main St., 207/367-2368).

OTHER SHOPPING

The greatest concentration of shops is in Stonington, where galleries, clothing boutiques, and eclectic shops line Main Street.

If you're looking for Maine pottery, weaving, metalwork, pewterware, imported tiles, or walking sticks, go directly to the **Harbor Farm Store** (Rte. 15, P.O. Box 64, Little Deer Isle 04650, 207/348-7755 or 800/342-8003, www .harborfarm.com), one of the state's best gift shops. Based in a mid-19th-century schoolhouse a mile south of the Deer Isle suspension bridge, the shop carries thousands of very unusual, high-quality items. The selection of tile—from around the world—is beyond amazing.

Three shops are in Deer Isle Village. **Old Fire House** (12 N. Deer Isle Rd./Rte. 15, Deer Isle, 207/348-9978), just north of Main Street, is chock-full of old furniture and collectibles.

Old buildings find new uses throughout Deer Isle.

© TOM NANGLE

Don't miss the downstairs. In "downtown" Deer Isle Village, you'll find **The Periwinkle** (8 Main St., Deer Isle, 207/348-2256), where Neva Beck carries a fine inventory of Maine books, as well as crafts, notecards, and gifts. Look for Neva's hand-braided rugs and chair pads and baby quilts. Just south off Main Street you'll come to Janice Glenn's **Old Deer Isle Parish House Antiques** (7 Church St., Rte. 15, Deer Isle, 207/348-9964), a funky shop heavy into vintage textiles, kitchenware, and other collectibles, with an especially nice collection of quilts, rugs, and samplers. For browsers, this place is heaven. No credit cards.

At the bottom of the island, **The Clown** (6 Thurlow's Hill Rd., Stonington, 207/367-6348) awaits. The imaginative owners came up with this combination of art, antiques, and... food and wine. Look, it works. Part of the key is the owners' farm in Tuscany, source of extra-virgin olive oil, wines, Deruta pottery, unusual furnishings, and other "necessities." Art openings double as wine tastings.

Dockside Books and Gifts (W. Main St., P.O. Box 171, Stonington 04681, 207/367-2652) carries just what its name promises, with a specialty in marine and Maine books. The rustic two-room shop is open May–November.

After all this browsing, you just might need a double-dip cone from **Harbor Ice Cream,** across the street from The Periwinkle, or **Island Cow Ice Cream,** on the main drag in Stonington.

ENTERTAINMENT AND EVENTS

Stonington's National Historic Landmark, the 1912 **Opera House** (207/367-2788, www .operahousearts.org), is home to Opera House Arts, which hosts films, plays, lectures, concerts, family programs, and workshops year-round. A café operates during programs.

In mid-June, when lupine in various shades of pink and purple seems to be blooming everywhere, is the **Lupine Festival** (207/342676 or 207/367-2420). The weekend festival includes arts openings and shows, boat rides, a private-gardens tour, and entertainment, varying from a contra dance to movies.

Seamark Community Arts (207/348-2333, www.seamarkcommunityarts.com) hosts arts workshops for children and adults in areas such as book arts, nature crafts, pottery, drawing and painting, film and video, printmaking, basketry, textile arts, and more. The summer highlight is the themed annual auction, in which dozens of artists contribute their interpretations. For example, in 2007, it was "Time."

Mid-July brings the **Stonington Lobsterboat Races** (207/348-2804), very popular competitions held in the harbor, with lots of possible vantage points. Stonington is one of the major locales in the lobster-boat race circuit.

In early October is **Peninsula Potters Open Studios** (207/348-5681), during which more than two dozen potters welcome visitors.

Want to meet locals and learn more about the area? **Island Heritage Trust** (207/348-2455) sponsors a series of walks, talks, and tours mid-June–mid-September. Call for information and reservations.

ACCOMMODATIONS
Inns and Bed-and-Breakfasts

Pilgrim's Inn (20 Main St., P.O. Box 69, Deer Isle 04627, 207/348-6615, www.pilgrimsinn .com, $109–249 d) is a beautifully restored Colonial building and newer cottages overlooking the peaceful Mill Pond. The National Historic Register inn began life in 1793 as a boardinghouse named The Ark; be sure to check out the fascinating guestbook, with names dating to 1901. A bit of a disconnect from the peacefulness is the recently added TV room (request a room far away from it, as the noise carries) and the downstairs tavern (formerly a fine-dining restaurant). It's open early May–mid-October.

◖ The Inn on the Harbor (Main St., P.O. Box 69, Stonington 04681, 207/367-2420 or 800/942-2420, www.innontheharbor.com, $130–215 peak) is exactly as its name proclaims. Its expansive deck hangs right over the harbor. Although recently updated, the 1880s complex still has an air of unpretentiousness. Most of the 14 rooms and suites, each named

after windjammers, have fantastic harbor views and private or shared decks where you can keep an eye on lobster boats, small ferries, windjammers, and pleasure craft. (Binoculars are provided.) Rooms on the street can be noisy at night. Rates include a continental buffet breakfast. An espresso bar is open 11 A.M.–4:30 P.M. Nearby are antique, gift, and craft shops; guest moorings are available. It's open all year, but call ahead off-season, when rates are lower.

In downtown Stonington, just up the hill from the Inn on the Harbor and convenient for walking to everything (even a small sandy beach a mile away) is **Près du Port** (W. Main St. and Highland Ave., P.O. Box 319, Stonington 04681, 207/367-5007, www.presduport .com, $125–150), a bright B&B run by amiable innkeeper Charlotte Casgrain. After many summers at a Deer Isle French summer camp, and a career as a Connecticut French teacher, she's settled here. Three rooms have detached baths, one has a private bath; there are vanity sinks in the rooms. Children are welcome; there's even a toy cupboard to entertain them. Adults can arrange for a Tuesday afternoon massage. No credit cards. It's open mid-June–mid-October. When Deer Isle beds are scarce at the height of summer, Charlotte is the best resource for dozens of last-minute overnight rooms in local homes. This location is ideal if you're en route to or returning from Isle au Haut.

Eggemoggin Reach is almost on the doorstep at **The Inn at Ferry Landing** (77 Old Ferry Rd., Deer Isle, 207/348-7760, www.ferry landing.com, $120–175), overlooking the abandoned Sargentville–Deer Isle ferry wharf. The view is wide open from the inn's "great room," where guests gather to read, play games, talk, and watch passing windjammers. Professional musician Gerald Wheeler has installed two grand pianos in the room; it's a treat when he plays. His wife, Jean, is the hospitable innkeeper, managing three water-view guest rooms and a suite. A harpsichord and a great view are big pluses in the suite. The Mooring, an annex that sleeps five, is rented by the week ($1,500, without breakfast). The inn is open all year except Thanksgiving and Christmas; Wi-Fi throughout.

Motels

Right in downtown Stonington, just across the street from the harbor, is **Boyces Motel** (44 Main St., P.O. Box 94, Stonington 04681, 207/367-2421 or 800/224-2421, www.boyces motel.com, $65–125). Eleven units all have TV, phones, and refrigerators; some have kitchens and living rooms, and one has two bedrooms. Across the street, Boyce's has a private harborfront deck for its guests. Ask for rooms well back from Main Street to lessen the noise of locals cruising the street at night. It's open year-round.

Seasonal Rentals

For house and cottage rentals by the week, month, or season, contact **Sargent's Rentals** (P.O. Box 115, Stonington 04681, 207/367-5156, www.sargentsrentalsinc.com). Plan well ahead, as the best properties get snapped up as much as a year in advance.

Campgrounds

Plan well ahead if you want to camp at **Old Quarry Ocean Adventures Campground** (130 Settlement Rd., Stonington, 207/367-8977, www.oldquarry.com). It has both oceanfront and secluded sites for tents and just three RV sites. Each site has a 12-by-12 platform, picnic table, deck chairs, and fire grill. Sites are $32–40 for two, plus $15–18 for each additional person. An overflow site, without platform, table, or fire ring, is $16 per night for two, plus $12 for each additional camper. Campground facilities include swimming pond, hiking trails, laundry, camp store (lobsters available), and kayak launch. Parking is designed so that vehicles are kept away from most campsites, but you can use a garden cart to transport your equipment between your car and your site. The campground is adjacent to Settlement Quarry Park.

FOOD
Local Flavors

Craving sweets? Head to **Susie Qu's Sweets and Curiosities** (40 School St., Stonington, 207/367-2415, 8 A.M.–4 P.M. Thurs.–Mon.).

Susan Scott bakes a fine selection of cookies and pies, offers a limited selection of breakfast and lunch choices, and also carries gifty items. It's a Wi-Fi hotspot.

Best pizza on the island? Head for **Burnt Cove Market** (Rte. 15, Stonington, 207/367-2681, 6 A.M.–9 P.M., opens at 9 A.M. Sun.). Besides pizza, you can get fried chicken and sandwiches, plus beer and wine.

In the May 2005 issue of the *Rosengarten Report,* the Hickory-Smoked Salmon, Unsliced of **Stonington Sea Products** (100 N. Main St., Stonington, 207/367-2400 or 888/402-2729, www.stoningtonseafood.com) was named one of the "25 Best Products" the noted food critic has ever recommended, describing it in terms including "Wow!" and "Bravo!" See for yourself, or try any of the company's other smoked products. If you don't visit in person, shop online.

Creativity defines the menu at **Lily's Café** (450 Airport Rd. at Rte. 15, Stonington, 207/367-5936, 7 A.M.–5 P.M. Mon.–Fri.) in a cute house at the corner of the Airport Road just over two miles from downtown. It's all very casual; order at the counter and find a table. (Some of the tables have fun windowpane shadowboxes.) Eat here or assemble a *haut gourmet* picnic: veggie and meat sandwiches, Mediterranean salads, cheeses, and homemade soups and breads. Upstairs is the Chef's Attic, with a smattering of antiques as well as works by local artists. Out back is an organic produce stand. Alas, it's open only for lunch (although you can pick up the fixings for a fine takeout-and-eat-later dinner) and closed on weekends. Occasionally it hosts wine-tasting dinners.

The Island Community Center (School St., Stonington) is the locale for the lively **Island Farmers Market,** selling smoked and organic meats, fresh herbs and flowers, produce, Asian foods, maple syrup, jams and jellies, crafts, and more 10 A.M.–noon every Friday May–October.

Family-Friendly Home Cooking

In July or August, don't show up at **Finest Kind Dining** (70 Center District Crossroad, Deer Isle, 207/348-7714, www.finestkindenterprises.com,

5–8:30 P.M. Mon.–Sat. mid-May–mid-Oct.) without a dinner reservation. This log-cabin family restaurant is no longer a secret. Expect home-style all-American food served conscientiously in a come-as-you-are setting. Pizza, pasta, prime rib, and seafood are all available, and there's a salad bar, too ($8–20). And save room for dessert. Wheelchair access; liquor license. The restaurant, owned by the Perez family, is halfway between Route 15 and Sunset Road (Rte. 15A). The enterprising Perezes also own the adjacent **Round the Island Mini Golf** (same phone, open the same months) and rent canoes, kayaks, and bicycles.

Harbor Café (Main St., Stonington, 207/367-5099, 6 A.M.–8 P.M. Mon.–Sat., often later Fri.–Sat., and to 2 P.M. Sun.) is *the* place to go for breakfast (you can eavesdrop on the local fisherfolk if you're early enough), but it's also reliable for lunch and dinner (especially on Friday nights for the seafood fry, with free seconds). Try to snag the front window table.

The views are top-notch from **Fisherman's Friend Restaurant** (5 Atlantic Ave., Stonington, 207/367-2442, 11 A.M.–9 P.M. Sun.–Thurs., to 10 P.M. Fri.–Sat.), which moved in 2005 from its longtime uptown digs to a harborfront location, complete with outdoor deck seating. The restaurant gets high marks for respectable food, generous portions, fresh seafood, and outstanding desserts, but it seems to have lost its soul in the move. Still, where else can you get lobster prepared 30 different ways? Prices are reasonable—the Friday night fish fry, with free seconds, is $7.99. It's open mid-May–October.

Casual Dining

Families are welcome at the **Whale's Rib Tavern** (20 Main St./Sunset Rd., Deer Isle Village, 207/348-5222, 5–9 P.M. daily), a comfy white-tablecloth tavern in the lower-level of the Pilgrim's Inn. Everyone can find something that appeals and is within budget on the menu, which varies from burgers to beef tenderloin, fish-and-chips to scampi.

You have a front seat—and a comfortable one at that—on all the harbor action at **Maritime Café** (27 Main St., Stonington, 207/367-2600, www.maritimecafe.com, 11:30 A.M.–3 P.M. and 5–8 P.M. daily). Big windows frame the harbor from the dining room, and there's also lunch seating on the harborside deck. The menu emphasis seafood (no surprise), but there are other choices and always a vegetarian selection. Entrées run $16–28.

Seafood in the Rough, or Not

When the weather's perfect, and you want seafood that's a bit different, in a fabulous setting, **Cockatu** (Carter's Seafood, 24 Carter La., off Oceanville Rd., Stonington, 207/367-0900, noon–8 P.M. daily late May–early Sept.) delivers. Fresh, fresh, fresh seafood, right out of the fish store, is cooked to order with some interesting, Portuguese-inspired preparations complementing the usual fried clams and lobster rolls. Most choices are $13–20, although lunch rolls (fish, crabmeat, scallop) begin at $8. It's takeout by definition: Order inside and then grab an outside table with serene views over idyllic Webb Cove and by the cockatoo, from which the operation gets its name. You won't find a finer place or better price for lobster, either. Do save room for the homemade but fancy European-style desserts. BYOB. While most folks arrive by car, you can also canoe or kayak here. A second location of the restaurant, **Cockatoo II** (Goose Cove Rd., Sunset, 207/348-2300, 11 A.M.–10 P.M. daily) opened in the lovely Goose Cove Lodge in 2007. The views are the best on the island, and there are both indoor and outdoor seating and a full bar; this menu is more extensive—and expensive, topping out at $40 for a 28-ounce porterhouse. Be forewarned: At either location, while the food earns raves, the service often is painfully sluggish—friends reported waiting more than two hours for their meal; if you're famished, go elsewhere.

INFORMATION AND SERVICES
Information

The Deer Isle–Stonington Chamber of Commerce (P.O. Box 459, Stonington 04681,

207/348-6124, www.deerislemaine.com) has a summer information booth, staffed by volunteers, on a grassy triangle on Route 15 in Little Deer Isle, a quarter of a mile after crossing the bridge from Sargentville (Sedgwick).

Across from the Pilgrim's Inn is the Chase Emerson Memorial Library (Main St., Deer Isle Village, 207/348-2899). At the tip of the island is the Stonington Public Library (Main St., Stonington, 207/367-5926).

Public Restrooms

Public restrooms are at the Atlantic Avenue Hardware pier and at the Stonington Town Hall, Main Street; at the Chase Emerson Library in Deer Isle Village; and behind the information booth on Little Deer Isle.

Isle au Haut

Eight miles off Stonington lies 4,700-acre Isle au Haut, roughly half of which belongs to Acadia National Park. Pronounced variously as "I'll-a-HO" or "I'LL-a-ho," the island has nearly 20 miles of hiking trails, excellent birding, and a tiny village.

About 60 souls call 5,800-acre Isle au Haut home year-round, most of them eking out a living from the sea. Each summer, the population temporarily swells with day-trippers, campers, and cottagers—then settles back in fall to the measured pace of life on an offshore island.

Samuel de Champlain, threading his way through this archipelago in 1605 and noting the island's prominent central ridge, came up with the name of Isle au Haut—High Island. Appropriately, the tallest peak (543 feet) is now named Mount Champlain.

More recent fame has come to the island thanks to island-based author Linda Greenlaw, of *Perfect Storm* fame, who wrote *The Lobster Chronicles*. Although that book piqued interest, Isle au Haut remains uncrowded and well off the beaten tourist track.

Most of the southern half of the six-mile-long island belongs to Acadia National Park, thanks to the wealthy summer visitors who began arriving in the 1880s. It was their heirs who, in the 1940s, donated valuable acreage to the federal government. Today, this offshore division of the national park has a well-managed 18-mile network of trails, a few lean-tos, several miles of unpaved road, and summertime passenger-ferry service to the park entrance.

In the island's northern half are the private residences of fisherfolk and summer folk, a minuscule village (including a market and post office), a five-mile paved road, and a lighthouse. The only vehicles on the island are owned by residents.

If spending the night on Isle au Haut sounds appealing (it is), you'll need to plan well ahead; it's no place for spur-of-the-moment

The Isle au Haut lighthouse is occasionally open to the public.

© TOM NANGLE

sleepovers. (Even spontaneous day trips aren't always possible.) The best part about staying overnight on Isle au Haut is that you'll have so much more than seven hours to enjoy this idyllic island.

C ACADIA NATIONAL PARK

Mention Acadia National Park and most people think of Bar Harbor and Mount Desert Island, where more than three million visitors arrive each year. The Isle au Haut section of the park sees maybe 5,000 visitors a year—partly because only 48 people a day (not counting campers) are allowed to land here. But the remoteness of the island and the scarcity of beds and campsites also contribute to the low count.

Near the town landing, where the year-round mail boat and another boat dock, is the **Park Ranger Station** (207/335-5551), where you can pick up trail maps and park information—and use the island's only public facilities. (Do yourself a favor, though: Make your plans by downloading Isle au Haut maps and information from the Acadia National Park website, www.nps.gov/acad.)

Hiking

Hiking on Acadia National Park trails is the major recreation on Isle au Haut, and even in the densest fog, you'll see valiant hikers going for it. A loop road circles the whole island; an unpaved section goes through the park, connecting with the mostly paved nonpark section. Walking on that is easy. Beyond the road, none of the park's 18 miles of trails could be labeled "easy"; the footing is rocky, rooty, and often squishy. But the park trails *are* well marked, and the views—of islets, distant hills, and ocean—make the effort worthwhile. Go prepared with proper footwear.

The most-used park trail is the four-mile, one-way **Duck Harbor Trail,** connecting the town landing with Duck Harbor. (You can either use this trail or follow the island road—mostly unpaved in this stretch—to get to the campground when the summer ferry ends its Duck Harbor runs.)

Even though the summit is only 314 feet, **Duck Harbor Mountain** is the island's toughest trail. Still, it's worth the 1.2-mile, one-way effort for the stunning, 360-degree views from the summit. Option: Rather than return via the trail's steep, bouldery sections, cut off at the Goat Trail and return to the trailhead that way.

For terrific shoreline scenery, take **Western Head** and **Cliff Trails** at the island's southwestern corner. They form a nice loop around Western Head. The route follows the coastline, ascending to ridges and cliffs and descending to rocky beaches, with some forested sections. Options: Close the loop by returning via the Western Head Road. If the tide is out (and *only* if it's out), you can walk across the tidal flats to the quaintly named Western Ear for views back toward the island. Western Ear is private, so don't linger. The **Goat Trail** adds another four miles (round-trip) of moderate coastline hiking east of the Cliff Trail; views are fabulous and birding is good, but if you're here only for a day, you'll need to decide whether there's time to catch the return mail boat. If you do have the time and the energy, you can connect from the Goat Trail to the **Duck Harbor Mountain Trail.**

OTHER RECREATION
Biking

Pedaling is limited to the 12 or so miles of mostly unpaved roads, and while it is a way to get around, frankly, the terrain is neither exciting, fun, nor view-worthy. Mountain bikes are not allowed on the park's hiking trails, and rangers try to discourage park visitors from bringing them to the island. If you're staying at the Inn at Isle au Haut, you can borrow a bike, which is handy around the "village" and for going swimming in Long Pond. You can also rent a bike ($18–20 per day) on the island from the Isle au Haut Ferry Service or Old Quarry Ocean Adventures. It costs $8 round-trip to bring your own bike aboard the Isle au Haut ferry. Both boats carry bikes *only* to the town landing, not to Duck Harbor.

Swimming

For superb **freshwater swimming,** head for Long Pond, a skinny, 1.5-mile-long swimming hole running north-south on the east side of the island, abutting national park land. You can bike over there, clockwise along the road, almost five miles, from the town landing. Or bum a ride from an island resident. There's a minuscule beachlike area on the southern end with a picnic table and a float. If you're here only for the day, though, there's not enough time to do this *and* get in a long hike. Opt for the hiking—or do a short hike and then go for a swim (the shallowest part is at the southern tip).

ACCOMMODATIONS AND FOOD

There are no restaurants serving breakfast or lunch on Isle au Haut, so if you're coming for a day trip, bring sufficient food and water.

On the east side of the island is **The Inn at Isle au Haut** (P.O. Box 78, Lighthouse Point, Isle au Haut 04645, off-island 207/335-5141, www.innatisleauhaut.com, $275–350 d), a mansard-roofed, waterfront Victorian home that Diana Santospago has turned into an inn. An accomplished cook, Diana whips up fabulous breakfasts, lunches, dinners for her guests; bring your own beer or wine. The downstairs room with private bath is most spacious. Three rather small rooms on the second floor share one bath; all but one have water views. Bikes are provided for guests, and it's an easy pedal to Long Pond for swimming or to connect with park trails. It's open June 1–Sept. 30.

Camping

The only camping on Isle au Haut is in lean-tos at the Acadia National Park campground. So you'll need to get your bid in early to reserve one of the five six-person lean-tos at **Duck Harbor Campground,** open May 15–October 15. Before April 1, contact the park for a reservation request form: Acadia National Park (P.O. Box 177, Bar Harbor 04609, 207/288-3338, www.nps.gov/acad). Anytime from April 1 on (*not before, or the park people*

will send it back to you), return the completed form, along with a check for $25, covering camping for up to six people for a maximum of five nights May 15–June 14, three nights June 15–September 15, and five nights again September 16–October 15. Mark the envelope: "Attn: Isle au Haut Reservations." Competition is stiff in the height of summer, so list alternate dates. The park refunds the check if there's no space; otherwise, it's nonrefundable and you'll receive a "special-use permit" (*do not* forget to bring it along). There's no additional camping fee.

Unless you don't mind backpacking nearly five miles to reach the campground, try to plan your visit mid-June–Labor Day, when the mail boat makes a stop in Duck Harbor. It's wise to call the Isle au Haut Company for the current ferry schedule before choosing dates for a lean-to reservation.

Trash policy is carry-in/carry-out, so pack a trash bag or two with your gear. Also bring a container for carting water from the campground pump, since it's 0.3 mile from the lean-tos. It's a longish walk to the general store for food—when you could be off hiking the island's trails—so bring enough to cover your stay.

The three-sided lean-tos are big enough (8 feet by 12 feet, 8 feet high) to hold a small (two-person) tent, so bring one along if you prefer being fully enclosed. A tarp will also do the trick. (Also bring mosquito repellent—some years, the critters show up here en masse.) No camping is permitted outside of the lean-tos, and nothing can be attached to trees.

Food

Isle au Haut is pretty much a BYO place—and that means BYO food. There is no restaurant. Unless you're staying at one of the two inns, the only source of food is the **Isle au Haut General Store,** not far from the town landing. Thanks to the store, you won't starve. The inventory isn't extensive, but it can be intriguing, which is due to the store manager, who travels worldwide and stocks the shop with her finds. On the other hand, food probably won't be your prime interest here—Isle au Haut is as good as it gets.

GETTING THERE

Until recently, unless you had your own vessel, the only access to Isle au Haut's town landing was the mail boat. That's still the only way to get there year-round, but two companies now offer transportation to and from the island. Use Isle au Haut Boat Company if your destination is the park, as it lands right at Duck Harbor twice daily during peak season.

Isle au Haut Boat Company

The Isle au Haut Boat Company (Seabreeze Ave., P.O. Box 709, Stonington 04681, 207/367-5193, www.isleauhaut.com) generally operates five daily trips Monday–Saturday, plus two on Sunday mid-June–early September. Other months, there are 2–3 trips Monday–Saturday. The best advice is to request a copy of the current schedule, covering dates, variables, fares, and extras.

Round-trips April–mid-October are $32 adults, $16 kids under 12 (two bags per adult, one bag per child). Round-trip surcharges: bikes ($16), kayaks/canoes ($30 minimum), pets ($8). If you're considering bringing a bike, be sure to inquire about on-island bike rentals ($20 per day). Weather seldom affects the schedule, but be aware that ultraheavy seas could cancel a trip.

There is twice-daily ferry service mid-June–Labor Day, from Stonington to Duck Harbor, at the edge of Isle au Haut's Acadia National Park campground. For a day trip, the schedule allows you 6.5 hours on the island Monday–Saturday and 4.5 hours on Sunday. No boats or bikes are allowed on this route, and no dogs are allowed in the campground. A ranger boards the boat at the town landing and goes along to Duck Harbor to answer questions and distribute maps. Before mid-June and after Labor Day, you'll be off-loaded at the Isle au Haut town landing, about five miles from Duck Harbor. The six-mile passage from Stonington to the Isle au Haut town landing takes 45 minutes; the trip to Duck Harbor is 1.25 hours.

Ferries depart from the Isle au Haut Boat Company dock (Seabreeze Ave., off E. Main St. in downtown Stonington). Parking ($9 outside, $11 indoors, per day) is available next to the ferry landing. Arrive at least an hour early to get all this settled so you don't miss the boat. Better yet, spend the night on Deer Isle before heading to Isle au Haut.

Old Quarry Ocean Adventures

The new kid on the block offering seasonal service to Isle au Haut, Old Quarry Ocean Adventures (Stonington, 207/367-8977 or 877/479-8977, mobile 207/266-7778, www.oldquarry.com) transports passengers on the recently renovated *Nigh Duck*. The boat usually leaves Old Quarry at 9 A.M. and arrives at the island's town landing one hour later. It departs from the same point at 5 P.M., arriving back at Old Quarry around 6 P.M. The fee is $34 round-trip for adults, $17 for children under 12. You can add an island bike rental for an additional $20. Old Quarry also offers a taxi service to Isle au Haut for $140/hour for up to six people.

ACADIA REGION

Summer folk have been visiting Mount Desert Island (MDI) for millennia. The earliest Native Americans discovered fabulous fishing and clamming, good hunting and camping, and invigorating salt air here. Today's arrivals find variations on the same theme: thousands of lodgings and campsites, hundreds of restaurant seats, dozens of shops, plus 40,000 acres of Acadia National Park.

It's no coincidence that artists were a large part of the 19th-century vanguard here: The dramatic landscape, with both bare and wooded mountains descending to the sea, still inspires everyone who sees it. Once the word got out, painterly images began confirming the reports, and the surge began. Even today, no saltwater locale on the entire Eastern Seaboard can compete with the variety of scenery on Mount Desert Island.

Those pioneering artists brilliantly portrayed this area, adding romantic touches to landscapes that really need no enhancement. From the 1,530-foot summit of Cadillac Mountain, preferably at an off hour, you'll sense the grandeur of it all—the slopes careening toward the bay and the handful of islands below looking like the last footholds between Bar Harbor and Bordeaux.

For nearly four centuries, controversy has raged about the pronunciation of the island's name, and we won't resolve it here. French explorer Samuel de Champlain apparently gets credit for naming it l'Ile des Monts Deserts, "island of bare mountains," when he sailed by in 1604. The accent in French would be on the second syllable, but today "Mount De-SERT" and "Mount DES-ert" both have their

© TOM NANGLE

HIGHLIGHTS

(Park Loop Road: If you do nothing else on Mount Desert, drive this magnificent road that takes in many of Acadia National Park's highlights (page 299).

(The Carriage Roads: Whether you walk, bike, or ride in a horse-drawn carriage, do make it a point to see Mr. Rockefeller's roads and bridges (page 300).

(Jordan Pond House: For more than a century, afternoon tea and popovers on the lawn of the Jordan Pond House have been a tradition. Do make reservations for an afternoon pick-me-up, perhaps after walking or biking the many carriage roads that lead here (page 303).

(Abbe Museum: The downtown Abbe Museum and its seasonal museum at Sieur de Monts Springs are fascinating places to while away a few hours and learn about Maine's Native American heritage (page 306).

(Oceanarium: A fabulous introduction to the coastal ecology is provided at this low-tech, kid-friendly site (page 306).

(Dive-In Theater Boat Cruise: Got kids? Don't miss this tour, where Diver Ed brings the undersea world aboard (page 309).

(Asticou Azalea Garden and Thuya Garden: "Magical and enchanting" best describes these two peaceful gardens. While Zenlike Asticou is best seen in spring, Thuya delivers color through summer and also has hiking paths (page 318).

(Wendell Gilley Museum: Gilley's intricately carved birds, from miniature shorebirds to life-size birds of prey, are a marvel to behold (page 323).

(Island Cruises: Kim Strauss shares his deep knowledge of island ways and waters on the lunchtime cruise that allows time to explore Frenchboro (page 325).

(Schoodic National Scenic Byway: Loop through the Schoodic region on this route highlighted by artisans' studios, mesmerizing views, and the pink-granite shores of Acadia National Park's only mainland section (page 338).

LOOK FOR **(** TO FIND RECOMMENDED SIGHTS, ACTIVITIES, DINING, AND LODGING.

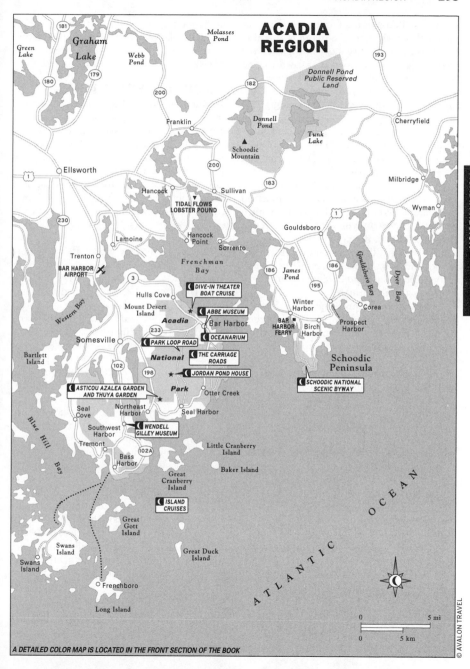

ACADIA REGION

© AVALON TRAVEL

advocates, although the former gets the accuracy nod. In any case, the island is anything but deserted today. Even as you approach the island, via the shiretown of Ellsworth and especially in Trenton, you'll run the gauntlet of a minor-league Disneyland, with water slides, bumper cars, and enough high-cholesterol eateries to stun the surgeon general. Don't panic. Acadia National Park lies ahead. Even on the most crowded days, if you venture more than a few steps into the park, you'll find you have it nearly to yourself.

As you drive or bike around Mount Desert—vaguely shaped like a lobster claw and indented by Somes Sound (the only fjord on the United States' east coast)—you'll cross and recross the national-park boundaries, reminders that Acadia National Park, covering a third of the island, is indeed the major presence here. It affects traffic, indoor and outdoor pursuits, and, in a way, even the climate.

The other major presence is Bar Harbor, largest and best known of the island's communities. It's the source of just about anything you could want (if not need), from T-shirts to tacos, books to bike rentals. The contrast with Acadia is astonishing as the park struggles to maintain its image and character.

Bar Harbor shares the island with Southwest Harbor, Tremont, and a number of small villages: Bass Harbor, Bernard, Northeast Harbor, Seal Harbor, Otter Creek, Somesville, and Hall Quarry. From Bass, Northeast, and Southwest Harbors, private and state ferries shuttle bike and foot traffic to offshore Swans Island, Frenchboro (Long Island), and the Cranberry Isles (and cars to Swans Island).

Stay on Route 1, instead of taking Route 3 to the island, and the congestion disappears. The towns lining the eastern shore of Frenchman Bay have some of the best views of all: front-row seats facing the peaks of Mount Desert Island. It's no wonder many artists and artisans make their homes here—for the inspiring scenery, no doubt. And at the tip of the Schoodic Peninsula, a stunning pocket of Acadia National Park sees only a fraction of the visitors who descend on the main part of the park.

PLANNING YOUR TIME

So much to do, so little time. That's the lament of most visitors. While you can circumnavigate Mount Desert Island in a day, hitting the highlights along the Park Loop with just enough time to oohhh and aahhh at each, to appreciate Acadia you need time to hike the trails, ride the carriage roads, get afloat on a whale-watching cruise or a sea kayak, visit museums, and explore an offshore island or two. A week or longer is best, but you can get a taste of Acadia in 3–4 days.

The region is very seasonal, with most restaurants, accommodations, and shops open mid-May–mid-October. May and June bring the new greens of spring and blooming rhododendrons and azaleas in Northeast Harbor's Asticou Garden, but mosquitoes and blackflies are at their worst, and weather is temperamental—perhaps sunny and hot one day, damp and cold the next, a packing nightmare. July and August bring summer at its best, along with the biggest crowds. September is a gem of a time to visit: no bugs, fewer people, less fog, and the golden light of fall. Foliage usually begins turning in early October, making it an especially beautiful time to visit (although the Columbus Day holiday weekend brings a spike in visitors). Winter is Acadia's silent season, best left for independent travelers who don't mind making do or perhaps making a meal of peanut-butter crackers if an open restaurant can't be found.

The only way onto Mount Desert Island is Route 3. Unless you're traveling in the wee hours of the morning or late at night, expect traffic. Avoid it during shift changes on island, 8–9 A.M. and 3–4 P.M. weekdays, when traffic slows to a crawl. On the island, use the Island Explorer bus system to avoid parking hassles.

Ellsworth

The punchline to an old Maine joke is "Ya cahn't get they-ah from he-ah." The truth is, you can't get to Acadia without going through Ellsworth and Trenton. Indeed, when you're crawling along in bumper-to-bumper traffic, it might seem as if all roads lead to downtown Ellsworth. And the truth is, many do. Route 1, the main thoroughfare along the coast, and Route 1A, which connects to Bangor, meet in downtown Ellsworth. Route 172 leads to the Blue Hill Peninsula and on to Deer Isle, Stonington, and the mail boat to Isle au Haut. Route 1 continues north, providing access to the Schoodic Peninsula and a remote section of the park. And the Bar Harbor Road (Rte. 3) is something of an Achilles heel—often a summertime bottleneck as it funnels all traffic to Mount Desert Island.

While there are ways to skirt around a few of the worst bottlenecks, the region does have its calling cards. Ellsworth, Hancock County's shire town, has mushroomed with the popularity of Acadia National Park, but you can still find handsome architectural remnants of the city's 19th-century lumbering heyday (which began shortly after its incorporation in 1800). Brigs, barks, and full-rigged ships—built in Ellsworth and captained by local fellows—loaded lumber here and carried it round the globe. Despite a ruinous 1855 fire that swept through downtown, the lumber trade thrived until late in the 19th century, along with factories and mills turning out shoes, bricks, boxes, and butter.

These days, Ellsworth is the region's shopping mecca. Antique shops and small stores line Main Street, which doubles as Route 1 in the downtown section; supermarkets, strip malls, and big-box stores line Routes 1 and 3 between Ellsworth and Trenton.

One more plus for the area is the new Bar Harbor Chamber of Commerce Information Center, which opened in 2006 in the former Acadia Information Center location on Route 3 in Trenton. If you're day-tripping to Mount Desert Island, you can leave your car here and hop aboard the free Island Explorer bus, eliminating driving and parking hassles.

SIGHTS
Woodlawn

Very little has changed at the Woodlawn Museum, the Colonel **Black House** (Surry Rd./ Rte. 172, Ellsworth, 207/667-8671, www .woodlawnmuseum.com, 10 A.M.–5 P.M. Tues.–Sat., 1–4 P.M. Sun. June–Sept., 1–4 P.M. Tues.–Sun. May and Oct., $7.50 adults, $3 children 5–12; grounds are free) since George Nixon Black donated it to the town in 1928. Completed in 1828, the Georgian house is a marvel of preservation, one of Maine's best, filled with Black family antiques and artifacts. Enthusiastic docents lead hour-long tours, beginning on the hour, to point out the circular staircase, rare books and artifacts, canopied

Ellsworth's city hall is just one of many buildings in the shire town with interesting architecture.

beds, a barrel organ, and lots more. Even kids appreciate all the unusual stuff. Afterward, plan to picnic on the manicured grounds and then explore two sleigh-filled barns, the Memorial Garden, and the two miles of mostly level trails in the woods up beyond the house. Restrooms are next to the parking area. On several Wednesday afternoons in July and August, there are elegant teas in the garden (or in the carriage house if it's raining). China, silver, linens, special-blend tea, sandwiches, pastries, and live music—for $15 a person; reservations are required. The grounds are accessible all year. In winter, there's cross-country skiing on the trails. On Route 172, a quarter mile southwest of Route 1, watch for the small sign and turn into the winding uphill driveway.

Birdsacre

En route to Bar Harbor, watch carefully on the right for the sign that marks Birdsacre (Rte. 3, Bar Harbor Rd., Ellsworth, 207/667-8460), a 185-acre urban sanctuary. Wander the trails in this peaceful preserve—spotting wildflowers, birds, and well-labeled shrubs and trees—and you'll have trouble believing you're surrounded by prime tourist territory. The sanctuary is open sunrise–sunset all year. At the sanctuary entrance is the 1850 **Stanwood Homestead Museum,** with period furnishings and wildlife exhibits. Once owned by noted ornithologist Cordelia Stanwood, the volunteer-operated museum is open for tours by chance or appointment, mid-May–mid-October. To be sure, call ahead for an appointment. Admission is free to the preserve and the homestead, but donations are needed and greatly appreciated. Birdsacre is also a wildlife rehabilitation center, so expect to see all kinds of winged creatures, especially hawks and owls, in various stages of rescue. Some will be returned to the wild, while others remain here for educational purposes. Stop by the Nature Center for even more exhibits.

The New England Museum of Telephony

What was life like before cell phones or touch-tone dialing? Find out at the New England Museum of Telephony (166 Winkumpaugh Rd., Ellsworth, 207/667-9491, www.ellsworthme .org/ringring, 1–4 P.M. Thurs.–Sun. July–Sept., $5 adult, $2.50 kids), a hands-on museum with the largest collection of old-fashioned switching systems in the East, including many from Maine. Place a call to see how these old systems work. To find the museum, head 10 miles north on Route 1A (toward Bangor) and then go left on Winkumpaugh Road for one mile.

Aerial Touring

Two businesses provide a variety of ways to get an eagle's-eye view of the area. Both are based on the Route 3 side of Hancock County/Bar Harbor Airport, just north of Mount Desert Island and 12 miles north of downtown Bar Harbor.

Scenic Flights of Acadia (Bar Harbor Rd., Rte. 3, Trenton, 207/667-6527, www.maine coastalflight.com) offers low-level flightseeing services in the Mount Desert Island region. Flights range 22–60 minutes and begin around $50 per person, with a two-passenger minimum.

Scenic Biplane, Helicopter and Glider Rides (968 Bar Harbor Rd./Rte. 3, Trenton, 207/667-7627, www.acadiaairtours.com) lets you soar in silence with daily glider flights. The one- or two-passenger gliders are towed to at least an altitude of 2,500 feet and then released. An FAA-certified pilot guides the glider. Rates begin at $179 for two, $129 for one, for a 20-minute flight. Or ride in a biplane: A 20-minute ride in an open-cockpit plane is $225 for two. Or go up in a chopper, with rates beginning at $230 for two; $345 for three. All flights are subject to an airport fee.

ENTERTAINMENT

Ace lumberjack "Timber" Tina Scheer has been competing around the world since she was seven, and she shows her prowess at **The Great Maine Lumberjack Show** (Rte. 3, 207/667-0067, www.mainelumberjack.com, 7 P.M. daily mid-June–late Aug., $8.50 adult, $6.50 ages 4–11). During the 75-minute "Olympics of the Forest," you'll watch two teams compete in 14 events, including ax throwing, cross-cut sawing, log rolling, speed climbing, and more. Some are open to participation. (Kids can learn log-rolling by appointment.) Performances are held rain or shine. Seating is under a roof, but dress for the weather if it's inclement. The ticket office opens at 6 P.M.

ACCOMMODATIONS

National chain (Comfort Inn, Holiday Inn, Travelodge) and independent motels line High Street (Rtes. 1 and 3), a densely commercial stretch in Ellsworth, and continue southward through Trenton toward Mount Desert Island.

Campgrounds

Equally convenient (or not) to the Schoodic Region and Mount Desert Island is the 55-acre **Lamoine State Park** (23 State Park Rd., Rte. 184, Lamoine, 207/667-4778), which is just off the shortcut route from Mount Desert Island to Schoodic. Park facilities include a pebble beach and picnic area with a spectacular view, a boat-launch ramp, and a children's play area. Day-use admission is $3 adults, $1 children 5–11. Camping (62 sites) is $20 per site per night for nonresidents ($15 for Maine residents), plus a $2-per-night fee for reservations; no hookups; two-night minimum, 14-night maximum. (Camping season is mid-May–mid-September. From January 2, reserve online at www.state.me.us/doc/parks/reservations using a credit card, or call 207/287-3824 weekdays.) Leashed pets are allowed, but not on the beach, and cleanup is required.

FOOD

Order breakfast anytime at **The Riverside Café** (151 Main St., Ellsworth, 207/667-7220, 6 A.M.–3 P.M. Mon.–Fri., opens at 7 A.M. Sat. and Sun., closes at 2 P.M. Sun.). The fresh-squeezed juices are fabulous, the buckwheat pancakes are outstanding, and there's even a vegetarian menu with vegan choices. Lunch menu includes homemade soups, salads, sandwiches, grilled sandwiches, and high-cal desserts. Sunday brunches are legendary. Break-

fast is served all day; lunch service begins at 11 A.M. And the café's name? It used to be down the street, overlooking the Union River.

Ice cream doesn't get much finer than that sold at **Morton's Ice Cream** (9 School St., Ellsworth, 207/667-1146, closed Sun.), a tiny shop with a deservedly giant reputation for homemade Italian gelato, sorbet, and ice cream. It's half a block off Main Street.

The area's best pizza is served at **Finelli Pizzeria** (12 Rte. 1, Ellsworth, 207/664-0230, 11 A.M.–8 P.M. Mon.–Thurs., to 9 P.M. Fri. and Sat.), where the pizza dough and focaccia bread are made fresh daily. The specialty is New York-style, thin-crust pizza, but other options include calzones, pastas, subs, and salads.

Cleonice Mediterranean Bistro (112 Main St., Ellsworth, 207/664-7554, 11:30 A.M.– 9 P.M. Mon.–Sat. and 5–9 P.M.Sun., but call ahead off-season) is named for chef/owner Richard Hanson's mother, Cleonice Renzetti. (It helps if you learn how to pronounce it: klee-oh-NEESE.) Gleaming woodwork and brass lighting fixtures combine for a golden glow in the long dining room, lined with wooden booths on one side, a 32-foot wooden bar, dating from 1938, on the other. The tapas and meze selection alone is worth the trip— covering the Mediterranean circuit (spanakopita, hummus, manchego cheese with pear sauce, and even *brandade de morue*); most are around $5. Dinner entrée range is $18–22.

Route 3 (Bar Harbor Rd.) is lined with eateries, including several lobster "pounds" that deserve a stop. One of the best known and longest running (since 1956) is **Trenton Bridge Lobster Pound** (Rte. 3, Bar Harbor Rd., Trenton, 207/667-2977, www.trentonbridgelobster .com, 11 A.M.–7:30 P.M. Mon.–Sat. late May– mid-Oct.), on the right, next to the bridge leading to Mount Desert Island. Watch for the "smoke signals"—steam billowing from the huge vats; the lobster couldn't be much fresher.

INFORMATION AND SERVICES

The Ellsworth Area Chamber of Commerce (163 High St., P.O. Box 267, Ellsworth 04605,

207/667-5584, www.ellsworthchamber.org) has information and an area guidebook.

En route from Ellsworth on Route 3, and shortly before you reach Mount Desert, you'll see (on your right) the Bar Harbor Chamber of Commerce (Rte. 3, Trenton, P.O. Box 158, Bar Harbor 04609, 207/288-5103 or 888/540-9990, www.barharbormaine.com). You'll find all sorts of info on the island as well as other locations, restrooms, phones, and a helpful staff.

Don't miss a chance to visit one of the state's loveliest libraries, the Ellsworth Public Library (46 State St., Ellsworth, 207/667-6363, www .ellsworth.lib.me.us). George Nixon Black, grandson of the builder of the Woodlawn Museum, donated the National Historic Register Federalist building to the city in 1897.

GETTING THERE AND AROUND

Route 1 of the **Island Explorer** bus system, which primarily serves Mount Desert Island with its fleet of propane-fueled, fare-free vehicles, connects the Hancock County/Bar Harbor Airport with downtown Bar Harbor. Operated by Downeast Transportation, the Island Explorer runs late June–Columbus Day.

Acadia National Park on Mount Desert Island

Rather like an octopus, or perhaps an amoeba, Acadia National Park extends its reach here and there and everywhere on Mount Desert Island. America's first national park east of the Mississippi River, and the only national park in the northeastern United States, was created from donated parcels—a big chunk here, a tiny chunk there—and slowly but surely fused into its present-day size of more than 46,000 acres. Within the boundaries of this splendid space are mountains, lakes, ponds, trails, fabulous vistas, and several campgrounds. Each year, more than two million visitors bike, hike, and drive into and through the park. Yet even at the height of summer, when the whole world seems to have arrived here, it's possible to find peaceful niches and less-trodden paths.

Acadia's history is unique among national parks and indeed fascinating. Several books have been written about some of the high-minded (in the positive sense) and high-profile personalities who provided the impetus (and wherewithal) for the park's inception and never flagged in their interest and support. Just to spotlight a few, we can thank the likes of George B. Dorr, Charles W. Eliot, and John D. Rockefeller Jr. for what we have today.

The most comprehensive guide to the park and surrounding area is *Moon Acadia National Park.*

NATIONAL PARK INFORMATION

Anyone entering the park by any means should buy a pass. Entrance fees, covering pedestrians, bicyclists, and motorized vehicles, are $20 late June–early October; $10 May 1–late June and most of October. That covers one vehicle for seven days. If you're traveling alone, an individual seven-day pass is $5. An annual pass to Acadia is $40, the America the Beautiful pass covering all federal recreation sites is $80, a lifetime senior pass is $10, and an access pass for disabled citizens is free. Passes are available at the visitors centers.

Hulls Cove Visitor Center

The modern Hulls Cove Visitor Center (Rte. 3, Hulls Cove, 207/288-3338, 8 A.M.–4:30 P.M. daily mid-April–late Oct. and to 6 P.M. July and Aug.) is eight miles southeast of the head of Mount Desert Island and well signposted. Here you can buy your park pass, make reservations for ranger-guided natural- and cultural-history programs, watch a 15-minute film about Acadia, study a relief map of the park, buy books, park souvenirs, and cassette guides, and use the restrooms. Pick up a copy of the **Beaver Log,** the tabloid-format park newspaper that lists the schedule of park activities, plus tide

WITH A LITTLE HELP FROM OUR FRIENDS...

As federal funding for national parks shrinks year after year, every park in America needs a safety net like **Friends of Acadia (FOA),** a dynamic organization headquartered in Bar Harbor. Historic stone bridges need repairs? FOA raises the funds. Propane-powered shuttle-bus service needs expanding? FOA finds a million-dollar donor. Well-used trails need maintenance? FOA organizes volunteer work parties. New connector trails needed? FOA gets them done. No vacuum seems to go unfilled.

FOA – one of Acadia National Park's greatest assets – is both reactive and proactive. It's an amazingly symbiotic relationship. When informed of a need, the Friends stand ready to help; when they themselves perceive a need, they propose solutions to park management and jointly figure out ways to make them happen. It's hard to avoid sounding like a media flack when describing this organization.

Founded in 1986 to preserve and protect the park for resource-sensitive tourism and myriad recreational uses, since 1995 FOA has contributed more than $6.5 million to the park and surrounding communities for trail upkeep, carriage-road maintenance, park

research, and other conservation projects. Plus it cofounded the Island Explorer bus system and instigated the Acadia Trails Forever program, a joint park-FOA partnership for trail rehabilitation. It's now working on establishing an off-island transportation hub, among other projects.

You can join FOA and support this worthy cause for $35 a year, or $100 for a family (43 Cottage St., P.O. Box 45, Bar Harbor 04609, 207/288-3340 or 800/625-0321, www .friendsofacadia.org). You can also lend a hand (or two) while you're here. FOA and the park organize volunteer work parties for Acadia trail, carriage-road, and other outdoor maintenance (8:30 A.M.–12:30 P.M. Tues., Thurs., Sat. June–Oct.). Call the recorded information line (207/288-3934) for the work locations, or 207/288-3340 or 800/625-0321 for answers to questions. The meeting point is Park Headquarters (Eagle Lake Rd., Rte. 233, Bar Harbor), about three miles west of town. This is a terrific way to give something back to the park, and the camaraderie is contagious. Be sure to take your own water, lunch, and bug repellent. Dress in layers and wear closed-toe shoes.

calendars and the entire schedule for the excellent **Island Explorer** shuttle-bus system, which operates late June–Columbus Day. The Island Explorer is supported by entrance fees (park pass required), as well as by Friends of Acadia and L. L. Bean. If you have children, enroll them for $2.25 in the park's **Junior Ranger Program.** They'll receive a booklet. To earn a Junior Ranger Patch, they must complete the activities and join one or two ranger-led programs or walks.

Thompson Island Visitor Center
As you cross the bridge from Trenton toward Mount Desert Island, you might not even notice that you arrive first on tiny Thompson Island, site of a visitors center (8 A.M.–6 P.M. daily mid-May–mid-Oct.), established jointly by the chambers of commerce of Mount

Desert Island's towns and Acadia National Park. In season, a park ranger usually is posted here to answer questions and provide basic advice on hiking trails and other park activities, but consider this a stopgap—be sure also to continue to the park's main visitors center.

Acadia National Park Headquarters
From November to April, information is available at Acadia National Park Headquarters (Eagle Lake Rd./Rte. 233, 8 A.M.–4:30 P.M. daily), about 3.5 miles west of downtown Bar Harbor. During the summer, it's open weekdays only.

SIGHTS
◖ Park Loop Road
The 27-mile Park Loop Road takes in most

of the park's big-ticket sites. It begins at the visitors center, winds past several of the park's scenic highlights (with parking areas), ascends to the summit of **Cadillac Mountain,** and provides overlooks to magnificent vistas. Along the route are trailheads and overlooks, as well as **Sieur de Monts Spring** (Acadia Nature Center, Wild Gardens of Acadia, Abbe Museum summer site, and the convergence of several spectacular trails), **Sand Beach, Thunder Hole, Otter Cliffs, Fabbri picnic area** (there's one wheelchair-accessible picnic table), **Jordan Pond House, Bubble Pond, Eagle Lake,** and the summit of **Cadillac Mountain.** Just before you get to Sand Beach, you'll see the Park Entrance Station, where you'll need to buy a pass if you haven't already done so. (If you're here during nesting/fledging season—April–mid-August—be sure to stop in the Precipice Trailhead parking area.)

Start at the parking lot below the Hulls Cove Visitor Center and follow the signs; part of the loop is one-way, so you'll be doing the loop clockwise. Traffic gets heavy at midday in midsummer, so aim for an early-morning start if you can. Maximum speed is 35 mph, but be alert for gawkers and photographers stopping without warning, and pedestrians dashing across the road from stopped cars or tour buses. If you're out here at midday in midsummer, don't be surprised to see cars and RVs parked in the right lane in the one-way sections; it's permitted.

Allow a couple of hours so you can stop along the way. You can rent an audio tour on cassette or CD for $12.95 (including directions, instruction sheet, and map) at the Hull's Cove Visitor Center. Another option is to pick up the drive-it-yourself tour booklet, ***Motorist Guide: Park Loop Road*** ($1.50), available at the Thompson Island and Hulls Cove Visitor Centers.

(The Carriage Roads

In 1913, John D. Rockefeller Jr. began laying out what eventually became a 57-mile carriage-road system, overseeing the project through the 1940s. Motorized vehicles have never been allowed on these lovely graded byways, making them real escapes from the auto world. Devoted

No two bridges are alike in the Carriage Road system.

© TOM NANGLE

now to multiple uses, the "Rockefeller roads" see hikers, bikers, baby strollers, horse-drawn carriages, even wheelchairs. Busiest times are 10 A.M.–2 P.M.

Pick up a free copy of the carriage-road map at any of the centers selling park passes. Fortunately, a $6 million restoration campaign, undertaken during the 1990s, has done a remarkable job of upgrading surfaces, opening overgrown panoramas, and returning the roads to their original 16-foot width.

The most crowded carriage roads are those closest to the visitors center—the Witch Hole Pond Loop, Duck Brook, and Eagle Lake. Avoid these, opting instead for roads west of Jordan Pond. Or go early in the morning or late in the day. Better still, go off-season, when you can enjoy the fall foliage (late September–mid-October) or winter's cross-country skiing.

If you need a bicycle to explore the carriage roads, you can rent one in Bar Harbor or Southwest Harbor. Be forewarned that hikers are allowed on the carriage roads that spill over onto private property south of the Jordan Pond House, but they are off-limits to bicyclists. The no-biking areas are signaled with Green Rock Company markers. The carriage-road map clearly indicates the biking/no-biking areas. *Bicyclists must be especially speed-sensitive on the carriage roads, keeping an eye out for hikers, horseback riders, small children, and the hearing impaired.*

To recapture the early carriage-roads era, take one of the horse-drawn open-carriage tours run by **Carriages in the Park,** based at Wildwood Stables (Park Loop Rd., P.O. Box 241, Seal Harbor 04675, 207/276-3622, www .acadia.net/wildwood), a mile south of the Jordan Pond House. Six one- and two-hour trips start at 9:30 A.M. daily mid-June–Columbus Day. Reservations are not required, but they're encouraged, especially in midsummer. Best outing is the two-hour **Sunset at the Summit** ($22 adults, $9 ages 6–12, $6 ages 2–5) to the top of Day Mountain. Other routes are $16–18 per adult, $8–9 children, $4.50–6 little kids. If you take the two-hour carriage ride to Jordan Pond House, departing at 1:15 P.M. daily ($18 adults, not counting food and beverage),

you're guaranteed a reserved lawn chair for tea and popovers.

Bass Harbor Light

At the southern end of Mount Desert's western "claw," follow Route 102A to the turnoff toward Bass Harbor Head. Drive or bike to the end of Lighthouse Road, walk down a steep wooden stairway, and look up and to the right. Voilà! Bass Harbor Head Light—its red glow automated since 1974—stands sentinel at the eastern entrance to Blue Hill Bay. Built in 1858, the 26-foot tower and lightkeeper's house are privately owned, but the dramatic setting is a photographer's dream.

Baker Island

The best way to get to—and to appreciate—wildlife-rich Baker Island is on the ranger-narrated Acadia National Park Baker Island Tour aboard the *Miss Samantha,* booked through **Bar Harbor Whale Watch Co.** (1 West St., Bar Harbor, 207/288-2386 or 888/942-5374, $32 adult, $18 ages 6–15, $8 5 and younger). The 4.5-hour tours depart Monday–Saturday late June–mid-September and include access via skiff to the 130-acre island with farmstead, lighthouse, and intriguing rock formations. The return trip provides a view of Otter Cliffs, Thunder Hole, Sand Beach, and Great Head from the water.

RECREATION
Hikes

If you're spending more than a day on Mount Desert Island, plan to buy a copy of *A Walk in the Park: Acadia's Hiking Guide,* by Tom St. Germain (see the *Suggested Reading* in the *Resources* section), which details more than 60 hikes, including some outside the park. Remember that pets are allowed on park trails, but only on leashes no longer than six feet. Four of the Island Explorer bus routes are particularly useful for hikers, alleviating the problems of backtracking and car-jammed parking lots. Here's a handful of favorite Acadia hikes, from easy to rugged.

These three easy trails are ideal for young

families. **Jordan Pond Nature Trail:** Start at the Jordan Pond parking area. This is an easy, one-mile, handicapped-accessible, wooded loop trail; pick up a brochure. Include Jordan Pond House (for tea and popovers) in your schedule. **Ship Harbor Nature Trail:** Start at the Ship Harbor parking area, on Route 102A between Bass Harbor and Seawall Campground, in the southwestern corner of the island. The easy, 1.3-mile loop trail leads to the shore; pick up a brochure at the trailhead. Ship Harbor is particularly popular among birders seeking warblers, and you just might spot an eagle while you picnic on the rocks. **Wonderland:** An even easier trail, with its parking area just east of the Ship Harbor parking area, Wonderland is 1.4 miles round-trip.

Great Head Trail: This moderately easy, 1.4-mile loop trail starts at the eastern end of Sand Beach, off the Park Loop Road. Park in the Sand Beach parking area and cross the beach to the trailhead. Or take Schooner Head Road from downtown Bar Harbor and park in the small area where the road dead-ends. There are actually two trail loops here, both of which have enough elevation to provide terrific views.

Beech Mountain: A moderate hike, Beech Mountain's summit has an abandoned fire tower, from which you can look out toward Long Pond and the Blue Hill Peninsula. A knob near the top is a prime viewing site for the migration of hawks (and other raptors) in September. Round-trip on the wooded route is about 1.2 miles, although a couple of side trails can extend it. You'll have less competition here, in a quieter part of the park. Take Route 102 south from Somesville, heading toward Pretty Marsh. Turn left onto Beech Hill Road and follow it to the parking area at the end.

Beehive Trail and **Precipice Trail:** These two are the park's toughest routes, with sheer faces and iron ladders; Precipice often is closed (usually mid-Apr.–late July) to protect nesting peregrine falcons. If challenges are your thing and these trails are open (check beforehand at the visitors center), go ahead. But a fine alternative in the difficult category is the **Beachcroft Trail** on Huguenot Head. Also

called the Beachcroft Path, the trail is best known for its 1,500 beautifully engineered granite steps. Round-trip is about 2.2 miles, or you can continue a loop at the top, taking in the **Bear Brook Trail** on Champlain Mountain, for about 4.4 miles. The parking area is just north of Route 3, near Sieur de Monts Spring, and just west of the Park Loop Road, near the Jackson Laboratory.

Rock Climbing

Acadia has a number of splendid sites prized by climbers: the sea cliffs at Otter Cliffs and Great Head; South Bubble Mountain; Canada Cliff (on the island's western side); and the South Wall and the Central Slabs on Champlain Mountain. If you haven't tried climbing, *never* do it yourself, without instruction. **Acadia Mountain Guides Climbing School** (198 Main St., Bar Harbor, 207/288-8186 or 888/232-9559, www.acadiamountainguides .com) and **Atlantic Climbing School (ACS)** (24 Cottage St., 2nd floor, P.O. Box 514, Bar Harbor 04609, 207/288-2521) both provide instruction and guided climbs. Costs depend upon the site, experience, session length, and number of climbers; call for details.

Swimming

Slightly below the Park Loop Road (take Island Explorer Rte. 3/Sand Beach), **Sand Beach** is the park's (and the island's) biggest sandy beach. Lifeguards are on duty during the summer, and even then, the biggest threat can be hypothermia. The salt water is terminally glacial—in mid-July, it still might not reach 60°F. The best solution is to walk to the far end of the beach, where a warmer, shallow stream meets the ocean. On a hot August day, arrive early; the parking lot fills up.

The park's most popular freshwater swimming site, staffed with a lifeguard and inevitably crowded on hot days, is **Echo Lake,** south of Somesville on Route 102 and well signposted (take Island Explorer Rte. 7/Southwest Harbor).

If you have a canoe, kayak, or rowboat, you can reach swimming holes in **Seal Cove Pond** and **Round Pond,** both on the western side of Mount Desert. The eastern shore of **Hodgdon Pond** (also on the western side of the island) is accessible by car (via Hodgdon Rd. and Long Pond Fire Rd.). **Lake Wood,** at the northern end of Mount Desert, has a small beach and auto access. To get to Lake Wood from Route 3, head west on Crooked Road to unpaved Park Road. Turn left and continue to the parking area, which will be crowded on a hot day, so arrive early.

PARK RANGER PROGRAMS

When you stop at the Hulls Cove Visitor Center and pick up the current issue of the park's *Beaver Log* newspaper (or download it ahead of time at www.nps.gov/acad), you'll find a whole raft of possibilities for learning more about the park's natural and cultural history.

The park ranger programs, lasting 1–3 hours, are great—and most are free. During July and August, there are about 100 programs each week, all listed in the *Log.* Included are early-morning (7 A.M.) birding walks; mountain hikes (moderate level); tours of the historic Carroll Homestead, a 19th-century farm; Cadillac summit natural-history tours; children's expeditions to learn about tide pools and geology (an adult must accompany kids); trips for those in wheelchair; and even a couple of tours a week in French. Some tours require reservations, some do not; a few, including boat tours, have fees.

Park rangers also give the evening lectures during the summer in the amphitheaters at Blackwoods and Seawall Campgrounds.

CAMPING

Mount Desert Island has at least a dozen private (commercial) campgrounds, but there are only two—Blackwoods and Seawall—within park boundaries on the island; neither has hookups. Both have seasonal restrooms (no showers) and dumping stations. Both also have seasonal amphitheatres, where rangers present evening programs.

Blackwoods Campground

With more than 300 campsites, Blackwoods,

just off Route 3, five miles south of Bar Harbor, is open all year. Because of its location on the east side of the island, it's also the more popular of the two campgrounds. Reservations are suggested May 1–October 31, when the fee is $20 per site per night. Call 877/444-6777; have your credit card handy. Or register online at www.recreation.gov. Reservations can be made up to six months prior. In April and November, camping is $10; December–March it's free.

Seawall Campground

Reservations are not accepted at Seawall Campground, on Route 102A in the Seawall district, four miles south of Southwest Harbor—it's first-come, first-served. But in midsummer, you'll need to arrive as early as 8:30 A.M. (when the ranger station opens) to secure one of the 200 or so sites. Seawall is open Memorial Day weekend–September. Cost is $20 per night for drive-up sites and $14 per night for walk-in sites.

RV length at Seawall is limited to 35 feet, with the width limited to an awning extended no more than 12 feet. Generators are not allowed in the campground.

((JORDAN POND HOUSE

The only restaurant within the park is the Jordan Pond House (Park Loop Rd., 207/276-3316, 11:30 A.M.–8 P.M. daily mid-May–late Oct., to 9 P.M. late June–early Sept.), a modern facility in a spectacular waterside setting. Jordan Pond House began life as a rustic 19th-century teahouse; wonderful old photos still line the walls of the current incarnation, which went up after a disastrous fire in 1979. Afternoon tea is still a tradition, with tea, popovers, and extraordinary strawberry jam, served on the lawn until 5:30 P.M. daily in summer, weather permitting. Not exactly a bargain at $8.75, but it's worth it. However, Jordan Pond is far from a secret, so expect to wait for seats at the height of summer. Jordan Pond House is on the Island Explorer's Route 5. *A health note:* Perhaps because of all the sweet drinks and jam served outdoors, patrons at the lawn

© HILARY NANGLE

Tea and popovers at Jordan Pond is an island tradition.

tables sometimes find themselves pestered by bees. They don't usually sting unless you pes-ter them back, but if you're hyperallergic to bee stings, or are with anyone who is, be alert.

Bar Harbor and Vicinity

In 1996, Bar Harbor celebrated the bicenten-nial of its founding (as the town of Eden). In the late 19th century and well into the 20th, the town grew to become one of the East Coast's fanciest summer watering holes.

In those days, ferries and steam yachts arrived from points south, large and small resort hotels sprang up, and exclusive mansions (quaintly dubbed "cottages") were the venues of parties thrown by summer-resident Drexels, DuPonts, Vanderbilts, and prominent academics, journal-ists, and lawyers. The "rusticators" came for the season, with huge entourages of servants, chil-dren, pets, and horses. The area's renown was such that by the 1890s, even the staffs of the Brit-ish, Austrian, and Ottoman embassies retreated here from summers in Washington, D.C.

The establishment of the national park in 1919 and the arrival of the automobile changed the character of Bar Harbor and Mount Desert Island; two World Wars and the Great Depres-sion took an additional toll in myriad ways; but the coup de grâce for Bar Harbor's era of elegance came with the Great Fire of 1947.

Nothing in the history of Bar Harbor and Mount Desert Island stands out like the Great Fire of 1947, a wind-whipped conflagration that devastated more than 17,000 acres on the eastern half of the island and leveled gorgeous mansions, humble homes, and more trees than anyone could ever count. Only three people died, but property damage was estimated at $2 million. Whole books have been written about the October inferno; fascinating scrapbooks in

ACADIA REGION

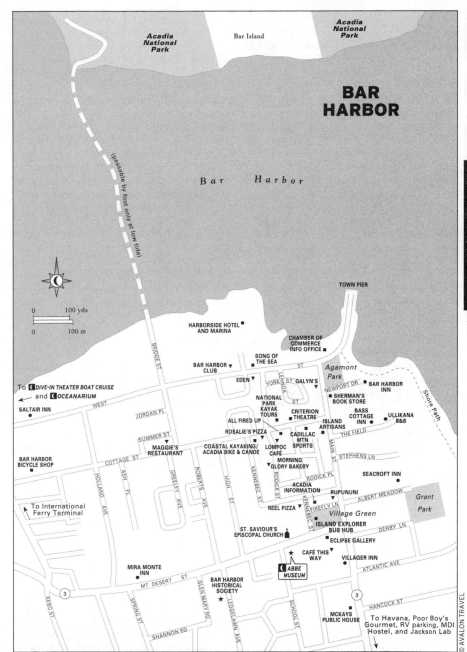

BAR HARBOR

Acadia National Park

Bar Island

Acadia National Park

Bar Harbor

(passable by foot only at low tide)

0   100 yds
0   100 m

TOWN PIER

HARBORSIDE HOTEL AND MARINA

CHAMBER OF COMMERCE INFO OFFICE

BAR HARBOR CLUB

SONG OF THE SEA

Agamont Park

EDEN

BRIDGE ST

GALYN'S

NEWPORT DR.

BAR HARBOR INN

YORK ST

LENNOX ST

ST

To DIVE-IN THEATER BOAT CRUISE
and OCEANARIUM

SALTAIR INN

WEST

JORDAN PL.

NATIONAL PARK KAYAK TOURS

ALL FIRED UP

ROSALIE'S PIZZA

CRITERION THEATRE

SHERMAN'S BOOK STORE

BASS COTTAGE INN

ULLIKANA B&B

ISLAND ARTISANS

Shore Path

THE FIELD

SUMMER ST

MAGGIE'S RESTAURANT

COASTAL KAYAKING/
ACADIA BIKE & CANOE

CADILLAC MTN SPORTS

BAR HARBOR BICYCLE SHOP

COTTAGE ST

LOMPOC CAFÉ

MORNING GLORY BAKERY

STEPHENS LN

SEACROFT INN

HOLLAND AVE

ASH PL.

GREELEY AVE

ROBERTS AVE

HIGH ST

KENNEBEC ST

RODICK ST

RODICK PL.

MAIN ST

ACADIA INFORMATION

RUPUNUNI

ALBERT MEADOW

Grant Park

To International Ferry Terminal

REEL PIZZA

FIREFLY LN

KENNEBEC ST

Village Green

ISLAND EXPLORER BUS HUB

DERBY LN

ST. SAVIOUR'S EPISCOPAL CHURCH

ECLIPSE GALLERY

CAFÉ THIS WAY

VILLAGER INN

MIRA MONTE INN

MT DESERT ST

GLEN MARY RD

LEDGELAWN AVE

ABBE MUSEUM

ATLANTIC AVE

BAR HARBOR HISTORICAL SOCIETY

3

KEBO ST

SPRING ST

SHANNON RD

SCHOOL ST

3

HANCOCK ST

MCKAYS PUBLIC HOUSE

To Havana, Poor Boy's Gourmet, RV parking, MDI Hostel, and Jackson Lab

© AVALON TRAVEL

Bar Harbor's Jesup Memorial Library dramatically relate the gripping details of the story. Even though some of the elegant cottages have survived, the fire altered life here forever.

SIGHTS
(Abbe Museum

The fabulous Abbe Museum is a superb place to introduce children (and adults) to prehistoric and historic Native American tools, crafts, and other cultural artifacts, with an emphasis on Maine's Micmac, Maliseet, Passamaquoddy, and Penobscot tribes. Everything about this privately funded museum, established in 1927, is tasteful. It has two campuses. The new main campus (26 Mt. Desert St., Bar Harbor, 207/288-3519, www.abbe museum.org, 10 A.M.–6 P.M. daily Apr.–Dec.—reduced days and hours before mid-May and after early Nov., $6 adults, $2 ages 6–15), built in 2001 and incorporating the former YMCA, is home to a collection spanning nearly 12,000 years. Museum-sponsored events include craft workshops, hands-on children's programs, archaeological field schools, and the **Native American Festival** (held at the College of the Atlantic usually the first Saturday after the Fourth of July). The museum's gift shop has an especially nice selection of Native American–made baskets.

Admission to the in-town Abbe also includes admission to the museum's original site in the park, about 2.5 miles south of Bar Harbor, at Sieur de Monts Spring, where Route 3 meets the Park Loop Road (9 A.M.–4 P.M. daily late May–early Oct., $2 adults, $1 children 6–15). Everything about this small, privately funded museum is tasteful, including the park setting, a handsome National Historic Register building, and displays from a 50,000-item collection.

While you're at the summertime Abbe Museum, take the time to wander the paths in the adjacent **Wild Gardens of Acadia,** a three-quarter-acre microcosm of more than 400 plant species native to Mount Desert Island. Twelve separate display areas, carefully maintained and labeled by the Bar Harbor Garden Club, represent native plant habitats; pick up the map/brochure that explains each.

St. Saviour's Episcopal Church

St. Saviour's (41 Mt. Desert St., Bar Harbor, 207/288-4215, 7 A.M.–dusk daily), close to downtown Bar Harbor, boasts Maine's largest collection of Tiffany stained-glass windows. Ten originals are here; an 11th was stolen in 1988 and replaced by a locally made window. Of the 32 non-Tiffany windows, the most intriguing is a memorial to Clarence Little, founder of the Jackson Laboratory and a descendant of Paul Revere. Images in the window include the laboratory, DNA, and mice. In July and August, volunteers regularly conduct free tours of the Victorian-era church (completed in 1878); call for the schedule or make an appointment for an off-season tour. The church is open for self-guided tours (8 A.M.–8 P.M.)—pick up a brochure in the back. If old cemeteries intrigue you, spend time wandering the 18th-century town graveyard next to the church.

(Oceanarium

At the northern edge of Mount Desert Island, 8.5 miles northwest of downtown Bar Harbor, is this understated but fascinating spot, also called the Maine Lobster Museum and Hatchery (1351 Rte. 3, Bar Harbor, 207/288-5005, 9 A.M.–5 P.M. Mon.–Sat. mid-May–mid-Oct.), one of the island's two related oceanariums. This low-tech, high-interest operation awes the kids, and it's pretty darn interesting for adults, too. David and Audrey Mills have been at it since 1972 and are determined to educate visitors while showing them a good time. At this facility (there's also a sister site in Southwest Harbor), visitors on tour view thousands of tiny lobster hatchlings, enjoy a museum, and meander along a salt-marsh walk, where you can check out tidal creatures and vegetation. All tours begin on the hour and half hour. Allow 1–2 hours to see everything. Tickets are $10 adults, $6 children 4–12 for a program with two talks; an expanded program includes a 45-minute Marsh Walk for $12 adults, $7 children; an all-access pass to both sites is $16 adults and $10.50 children.

Bar Harbor Whale Museum

Inside the Bar Harbor Whale Museum (52 West St., Bar Harbor, 207/288-0288, www.barharborwhalemuseum.org, 9 A.M.–9 P.M. daily July and Aug., noon–8 P.M. daily June, 10 A.M.–8 P.M. daily Sept. and Oct.) are a life-size model of a prehistoric walking whale, a pilot whale skeleton, seals, marine birds, a 22-foot-long minke porpoise, and exhibits on whales. There's also a mesmerizing video of whales in their habitat. Admission is free, but donations support marine mammal research and conservation.

Bar Harbor Historical Society

The Bar Harbor Historical Society (33 Ledgelawn Ave., Bar Harbor, 207/288-0000, 1–4 P.M. Mon.–Sat. mid-June–mid-Oct., free), in its own National Register building, has fascinating displays, stereopticon images, and a scrapbook about the 1947 fire that devastated the island. The photographs alone are worth the visit. Also here are antique maps, Victorian-era hotel registers, and much other local memorabilia. In winter, it's open by appointment. For a sample of Bar Harbor before the great fire, wander over to upper West Street, which is on the National Historic Register thanks to the remaining grand cottages that line it.

Mount Desert Island Biological Laboratory

Some of the world's top scientists work year-round or come to Bar Harbor in summer to work at Mount Desert Island Biological Laboratory (Old Bar Harbor Rd., Salisbury Cove, 207/288-3147, www.mdibl.org), one of the few scientific research institutions in the world dedicated to studying marine animals to learn more about human health and environmental health and the only comprehensive effort in the country to sequence genomes. Public tours are offered on Wednesdays (call for time) late June–late August, beginning at Maren Auditorium. The program begins with a presentation by a laboratory scientist about the lab's history and research, and a short video. Then a naturalist talks about animal life in Frenchman Bay and how it pertains to the lab's research. It includes a hands-on presentation at the touch tank, filled with marine animals from Frenchman Bay, a visit to a 15-foot glass tank with other marine creatures, and a stroll through the visitors center, where there are smaller tanks. The tour takes about 1.5 hours. To avoid crowds, go on a nice day. The lab also presents an evening lecture series. Most are serious scientific talks, but there's also usually a children's program.

Bar Harbor and Park Tours

The veteran of the Bar Harbor–based bus tours is **Acadia National Park Tours** (tickets at Testa's Restaurant, Bayside Landing, 53 Main St., P.O. Box 52, Bar Harbor 04609, 207/288-3327, www.acadiatours.com), operating May–October. A 2.5-hour, naturalist-led tour of Bar Harbor and Acadia departs at 10 A.M. and 2 P.M. daily from downtown Bar Harbor (Testa's is across from Agamont Park, near the Bar Harbor Inn). Reservations are wise in midsummer and during fall-foliage season (late September and early October); pick up reserved tickets 30 minutes before departure. Cost is $20 adults, $10 children under 12.

If there's a time crunch, take the one-hour trolley-bus tour operated by **Oli's Trolley** (P.O. Box 794, Bar Harbor 04609, 207/288-9899, www.acadiaislandtours.com), which departs downtown Bar Harbor five times daily (between 10 A.M. and 6 P.M.) in July and August, including Bar Harbor mansion drive-bys and the Cadillac summit. Starting point is the Oli's Trolley Ice Cream Shop (58 Cottage St.), across from the post office. (Tickets are also available at Harbor Place, the waterfront marketplace near the Bar Harbor Inn.) Dress warmly if the air is at all cool; it's an open-air trolley. Cost is $15 adults, $10 children under 12. Reservations are advisable. The trolley also does 2.5-hour park tours at 10 A.M. and 2 P.M. May–October. Tickets are $20 adults, $10 children under 12. The bus and trolley routes both include potty stops.

Note: While the Island Explorer buses do

ACADIA REGION

Bar Harbor's Shore Path edges the waterfront with views to the Porcupine Islands on one side and summer cottages on the other.

reach a number of key park sights, they are not tour buses. There is no narration, the bus cuts off the Park Loop at Otter Cliffs, and it excludes the summit of Cadillac Mountain.

Birding and Nature Tours

For private tours of the park and other parts of the island, contact Michael Good at **Down East Nature Tours** (P.O. Box 521, Bar Harbor 04609, 207/288-8128, www.downeast naturetours.com). A biologist with a special interest in birds, he'll take neophyte or advanced birders on two-hour and longer tours they won't forget. Good gives special attention to native and migrating birds, including bald eagles, osprey, peregrine falcons, shore birds, and warblers. He'll even take serious birders to spot the Nelson's sharptailed sparrow and other life-list birds. Prices begin at $50 pp for two hours and include transportation from your lodging; family rates available. Bring your own binoculars, but Michael supplies a spotting scope.

RECREATION
Shore Path

Be sure to stroll along downtown Bar Harbor's Shore Path, a well-trodden, granite-edged byway built around 1880. Along the craggy shoreline are granite-and-wood benches, town-owned **Grant Park** (great for picnics), birch trees, and several handsome mansions that escaped the 1947 fire. Offshore are the four Porcupine Islands. The path is open 6:30 A.M.–dusk, and leashed pets are okay. Allow about 30 minutes for the mile loop, beginning next to the town pier and the Bar Harbor Inn and returning via Wayman Lane.

Bicycle Rentals and Rides

With all the great biking options, including 45 miles of carriage roads (12 miles of which are off-limits to bicycles) and some of the best roadside bike routes in Maine, you'll want to bring a bike or rent one here. Expect to pay about $20 per day for a rental bike, including helmet, lock, and map. It's wise to make reservations.

The Minutolo family's **Bar Harbor Bicycle Shop** (141 Cottage St., Bar Harbor, 207/288-3886, www.barharborbike.com), on the corner with Route 3, has been in business since 1977 and has earned an excellent reputation (it's also known as Island Adventures). If you have your own bike, stop here for advice on routes—the Minutolos have cycled everywhere on the island and can suggest the perfect mountain-bike or road-bike loop based on your ability and schedule. The shop organizes free Sunday morning group road rides, usually 9 A.M.–noon, with a longer option for more experienced cyclists. Evening rides for various abilities, including a Ladies Ride, are also organized. The shop has rentals varying from standard mountain bikes to full-suspension models and even tandems as well as all the accessories and gear you might need. Hours in summer are 8 A.M.–8 P.M. daily, 9 A.M.–5:30 P.M. Tuesday–Saturday other months.

Sea Kayaking

National Park Kayak Tours (39 Cottage St., Bar Harbor, 207/288-0342 or 800/347-0940, www.acadiakayak.com) limits its Registered Maine Guide–led tours to a maximum of six tandem kayaks per trip. Four-hour morning, midday, afternoon, or sunset paddles are offered, including shuttle service, a paddle/safety lesson, and a brief stop, for $46 per person in July and August, $42 off-season. Most trips cover about six miles. Multiday camping trips also are offered. Try to make reservations at least one day in advance.

Golf

Duffers first teed off in 1888 at **Kebo Valley Golf Club** (100 Eagle Lake Rd., Rte. 233, Bar Harbor, 207/288-5000, www.kebovalleyclub.com, May–Oct.), Maine's oldest club and the eighth-oldest in the nation. The 17th hole became legendary when it took President William Howard Taft 27 tries to sink the ball in 1911. Kebo is very popular, with a gorgeous setting, an attractive clubhouse, and decent food service, so tee times are essential; you can reserve up to six days in advance. Greens fees are the highest on the island, but afternoon and twilight rates are available.

EXCURSION BOATS
(Dive-In Theater Boat Cruise

You don't have to go diving in these frigid waters; others will do it for you. When the kids are clamoring to touch slimy sea cucumbers and starfish at various touch tanks in the area, they're likely to be primed for Diver Ed's Dive-In Theater Boat Cruise (207/288-3483, www.divered.com), operating from the College of the Atlantic pier (105 Eden St.). Former Bar Harbor harbormaster Ed Monat heads the crew aboard the 46-passenger *Seal,* which goes a mile or two offshore and sends down two professional divers (including Ed) with video cameras. You and the kids stay on deck, all warm and dry, and watch the action on a TV screen. There's communication back and forth, so the kids can ask questions as the divers pick up urchins, starfish, crabs, lobsters, and other sea life. When the diver surfaces, he or she brings a bag of touchable specimens—another chance to pet some slimy creatures (which go back into the water after show-and-tell). Great concept. Watch the kids' expressions—this is a big hit. The two-hour trips depart three times daily Monday–Friday, twice daily Saturday, and once on Sunday in July and August, with fewer trips in spring and fall. Cost is $30 adults, $25 seniors, $20 children ages 5–11, $5 younger than 5; usually twice weekly there's a park ranger or naturalist on board and the tour lasts for three hours—check the park's *Beaver Log* newspaper or Diver Ed's website for the schedule and reservation information—these trips cost an additional $5.

Whale-Watching and Puffin-Viewing Excursions and Nature Cruises

Whale-watching boats go as much as 20 miles offshore, so no matter what the weather in Bar Harbor, dress warmly and bring more clothing than you think you'll need—even gloves, if you're especially sensitive to cold. Motion-sensitive children and adults should plan for appropriate medication, such as pills or patches.

Whale-watching, puffin-watching, and combo excursions are offered by **Bar Harbor Whale Watch Company** (1 West St., Bar Harbor, 207/288-2386 or 800/942-5374, www.barharborwhales.com), sailing from the town pier (1 West St.) in downtown Bar Harbor. The company operates under various names, including Acadian Whale Watcher, and has a number of boats. Most trips are accompanied by a naturalist (often from Allied Whale at the College of the Atlantic), who regales passengers with all sorts of interesting trivia about the whales, porpoises, seabirds, and other marine life spotted along the way. In season, some trips go out as far as the puffin colony on Petit Manan light. Trips depart daily late May–late October, but with so many options, it's impossible to list the schedule, so call. Tickets are $49 adults, $26 children 6–14, $8 children under 6. Part of the ticket price benefits Allied Whale, which researches and protects marine animals in the Gulf of Maine. Note: Trips often go longer than the 2.5–3 hours advertised. Don't plan anything else too tightly around the trip. Either before or afterward, be sure to visit the Whale Museum.

Scenic nature cruises (1.5–2 hours), lighthouse viewing, and kid-friendly lobster and seal-watch cruises (1.5 hours) also are offered. Rates for these are $22–32 for adults, $15–20 ages 6–14, $5–8 age 5 and younger.

Sailing

Captain Steve Pagels's **Downeast Windjammer Cruises** (207/288-4585 or 207/288-2373, www.downeastwindjammer.com, $32 adult, $22 kids under 12) offers 1.5–two-hour day sails on the 151-foot steel-hulled *Margaret Todd,* a gorgeous four-masted schooner with tanbark sails that he designed and launched in 1998. Trips depart three times daily mid-May–mid-October (weather permitting) from the Bar Harbor Inn pier, just east of the town pier in downtown Bar Harbor. You'll get the best wildlife sightings on the morning trip; better sailing on the afternoon trip; and live music on the sunset one. Some morning sails are narrated by a park ranger.

Sea/Venture Cruise

Captain Winston Shaw's custom boat tour by Sea/Venture (207/288-3355, www.svboattours.com) lets you design the perfect trip aboard *Reflection,* a 20-foot motor launch. Captain Shaw, a Registered Maine Guide and committed environmentalist, specializes in nature-oriented tours. He was involved in the inaugural Earth Day celebration in 1970. The founder and director of the Coastal Maine Bald Eagle Project, he's been studying Maine's coastal bald eagles since the late 1970s. You can pick from 10 recommended cruises lasting 1–8 hours or design your own. In any case, the boat is yours. Boat charter rate is $85 per hour for 1–2 passengers, $95 for 3–4, or $105 for 5–6. Captain Shaw can also arrange for picnic lunches. On longer trips, restroom stops are available.

Lobster Cruise

When you're ready to learn The Truth about lobsters, sign up for a cruise aboard Captain John Nicolai's *Lulu,* a traditional Maine lobster boat. *Lulu* departs 4–5 times daily May–September from the Harborside Hotel and Marina in Bar Harbor (55 West St., 207/963-2341 or 866/235-2341, www.lululobsterboat.com, $27 adult, $24 senior, $15 kids under 12). Captain Nicolai provides an entertaining commentary on anything and everything, but especially about lobsters and lobstering. He hauls a lobster trap and explains intimate details of the hapless critter. (Lobstering is banned on Sunday June–August; the cruises operate, but there's no hauling that day.) Reservations are required; six passengers maximum. No credit cards. There's free parking in the hotel's lot.

SHOPPING

Bar Harbor's boutiques—running the gamut from attractive to kitschy—are indisputably visitor oriented; many shut down for the winter.

Downtown Bar Harbor's best craft gallery is **Island Artisans** (99 Main St., Bar Harbor, 207/288-4214, www.islandartisans.com). More than 100 Maine artists are represented here, and the quality is outstanding. Don't miss it. You'll find basketwork, handmade paper, wood carvings, blown glass, jewelry, weaving, metalwork, ceramics, and more. **Eclipse Gallery** (12 Mount Desert St., Bar Harbor, 207/288-9048) specializes in handblown glass and complementary works and represents more than 100 contemporary American artists.

Toys, cards, and newspapers blend in with the new-book inventory at **Sherman's Book Store** (56 Main St., Bar Harbor, 207/288-3161). It's just the place to pick up maps and trail guides for fine days and puzzles for foggy days.

Souvenir shops are *everywhere* on Mount Desert Island, so why single out the Acadia Shops? If you need Maine-made mementos for Uncle Harry and Aunt Mary, if the kids need trinkets for friends back home, the Acadia Corporation has several shops in downtown Bar Harbor that can cover it all. Price range is broad, quality is fairly high, and clerks are especially friendly at **The Acadia Shop** (85 Main St., Bar Harbor, 207/288-5600, www.acadiashops.com). Another branch, **Acadia Outdoors** (45 Main St., Bar Harbor, 207/288-2422), features sportswear and outdoor accessories.

Most vacationers don't expect to shop for musical instruments, but everyone with an affinity for folkloric music gravitates toward **Song of the Sea** (47 West St., Bar Harbor 207/288-5653, www.songsea.com), a unique, jam-packed harborfront shop where you can find guitars, banjos, harmonicas, and tin whistles—but also such esoterica as hammered dulcimers, doumbeks, didgeridoos, psalteries, and Chilean rainsticks. Ed and Anne Damm are extremely knowledgeable and helpful, even to the point of playing instruments over the phone for call-in orders.

ENTERTAINMENT

At the height of the summer season, plenty of live entertainment varies from pub music to films to classical concerts.

The **Bar Harbor Town Band** performs free at 8 P.M. Monday and Thursday July–mid-August on the Village Green (Main St. and Mount Desert St., Bar Harbor).

Above Rupununi's restaurant, **Carmen Verandah** (119 Main St., Bar Harbor, 207/288-2766) is the weekend place to be and be seen. Everything gets rolling about 9:30 P.M.—blues, rock, salsa, funk, zydeco, ska, reggae, you name it—and there's lots of space for dancing. Other nights, there's a DJ. Darts and billiards round out the picture. It's open all year.

You never know quite what's going to happen at **Improv Acadia** (15 Cottage St., Bar Harbor, 207/288-2503, www.improvacadia.com, $15 adults, $10 kids 12 and younger). Every show is different, as actors use audience suggestions to create spots; the 8 P.M. show is family friendly.

The **Bar Harbor Music Festival** (207/288-5744 in July and Aug., 212/222-1026 off-season, www.barnharbormusicfestival.org), a summer tradition since 1967, emphasizes up-and-coming musical talent in a series of classical, jazz, and pops concerts, usually Fridays and Sundays, at various island locations, including local inns and an annual outdoor concert in Acadia National Park, early July–early August. A relatively new addition to the schedule is an opera, which received rave reviews in its debut season. Tickets begin at $25 adult, $15 student, available at the festival office building (59 Cottage). Preconcert dinners are also sometimes available at $30. Reservations are wise.

Cinemas

In 2001, new owners assumed the reins of the beautifully refurbished National Historic Landmark **Criterion Theatre** (35 Cottage St., Bar Harbor, 207/288-3441 for films or 207/288-5829 for concerts, www.criterion theatre.com), built in 1932. Now, in addition to screening films, the Criterion puts on concerts, plays, and other special events. You'll soak up the nostalgia in this art deco classic with nearly 900 seats (including an elegant floating balcony). Beer, wine, and light fare are available.

Combine pizza with your picture show at **Reel Pizza Cinerama** (33 Kennebec Pl., Bar Harbor, film 207/288-3811, food 207/288-3828, www.reelpizza.com). There are two showings nightly on each of two screens. All tickets are $6; pizzas are $13–20. Doors open at 4:30 P.M.; go early for the best seats.

EVENTS

Bar Harbor is home to numerous special events. Here's just a sampling. For more, call 207/288-5103 or visit www.barharbormaine.com.

In late May, the annual **Warblers and Wildflowers Festival** attracts birders and nature lovers. Events include morning birdsong walks, garden tours, art, lectures, and other events.

In late June **Legacy of the Arts** is a week-long celebration of music, art, theater, dance, and history, with tours, exhibits, workshops, concerts, lectures, demonstrations, and more.

The Abbe Museum, the College of the Atlantic, and the Maine Indian Basketmakers Alliance sponsor the annual **Native American Festival,** 10 A.M.–4 P.M. the first Saturday after the Fourth of July, featuring baskets, beadwork, and other handicrafts for sale, and Indian drumming and dancing. Free admission; it's held at College of the Atlantic, Bar Harbor.

In even-numbered years, the **Mount Desert Garden Club Tour** presents a rare chance to visit some of Maine's most spectacular private gardens the second or third Saturday in July (confirm the date with the Bar Harbor Chamber of Commerce).

The **Directions Craft Show** fills a weekend in late July or early August with extraordinary displays and sales of crafts by members of Directions. You'll find it at Mount Desert Island High School (Rte. 233, Eagle Lake Rd.). Hours are 5–9 P.M. Friday, 10 A.M.–5 P.M. Saturday and Sunday.

ACCOMMODATIONS

All are open seasonally, usually May into October, unless otherwise noted.

Hotels and Motels

One of the town's best-known, most-visible, and best-situated hotels is the **Bar Harbor Inn** (Newport Dr., P.O. Box 7, Bar Harbor 04609, 207/288-3351 or 800/248-3351, www.bar harborinn.com, $199–379), a sprawling complex on eight acres overlooking the harbor and Bar Island. Facilities include an outdoor pool, a spa, and two restaurants. The 153 rooms and suites, in three different buildings, vary considerably in style, from traditional inn to motel. Continental breakfast is included, and special packages, with meals and activities, are available—an advantage if you have children. Rooms in the Oceanfront Lodge are good choices, with reasonable rates and terrific views. The Main Inn rooms have seen the most recent upgrades. Service is attentive. It's open late March–late November.

The newest and fanciest hotel in town is **Harborside Hotel and Marina** (55 West St., Bar Harbor, 207/288-5033 or 800/238-5033, www.theharborsidehotel.com, $299–499), fronting on the water in downtown Bar Harbor. Almost all of the 185 rooms and suites have a water view and semiprivate balconies; some have whirlpool tubs; deluxe rooms have marble baths, and some have large outdoor hot tubs. Some of the one- to three-bedroom suites have whirlpools or fireplaces; penthouse suites have full kitchens. Rates include a continental breakfast buffet. Facilities include two restaurants, outdoor-heated pool and whirlpool, full-service spa, and fitness room.

At the opposite end of the budgetary scale are two neighboring motels: **Edenbrook Motel** (96 Eden St., Rte. 3, Bar Harbor, 207/288-4975 or 800/323-7819, www.acadia.net/ edenbrook, $70–130), with panoramic views of Frenchman Bay from some rooms, and the wee bit fancier **Highbrook Motel** (94 Eden St., Rte. 3, Bar Harbor, 207/288-3591 or 800/338-9688, www.highbrookmotel.com, $79–128). Both are about 1.5 miles from Acadia's main entrance, one mile from downtown, and 500 yards from the ferry servicing Canada.

Inns and Bed-and-Breakfasts

Few innkeepers have mastered the art of hospitality as well as Roy Kasindorf and Helene Harton, owners of the ◖ **Ullikana Bed and Breakfast** (16 The Field, Bar Harbor, 207/288-9552, www.ullikana.com, $180–330), a 10-room, Victorian Tudor inn, built by Alpheus Hardy, Bar Harbor's first "cottager" in 1885.

They genuinely enjoy their guests. Helene's a whiz in the kitchen; after one of her multicourse breakfasts, usually served on the water-view patio, you won't be needing lunch. She's also a decorating genius, blending antiques and modern art, vibrant color with soothing hues, folk art and fine art, with a result like a finely tuned orchestra. Roy excels at helping guests select just the right hike, bike route, or other activity. Afternoon refreshments provide a time for guests to gather and share experiences. Ten comfortable rooms all have private baths; many have working fireplaces, and some have private terraces with water views. Helene and Roy also own The Yellow House, next door, with six lovely rooms decorated in old Bar Harbor style and a huge living room filled with antique wicker. They're in a quiet downtown location close to Bar Harbor's Shore Path. French spoken.

Right next door is the fabulously renovated and rejuvenated **(Bass Cottage** (14 The Field, P.O. Box 242, Bar Harbor 04609, 207/288-1234 or 866/782-9224, www.bass cottage.com, $195–350). Corporate refugees Teri and Jeff Anderholm bought the 26-room 1885 cottage in 2003 and spent a year gutting it, salvaging the best of the old, and blending in new to turn it into a luxurious and stylish 10-room inn. It retains its Victorian bones, yet is most un-Victorian in style. Guest rooms are soothingly decorated with cream and pastel-colored walls and have phones and TV with DVD (a DVD library is available; a godsend on a yucky day); many rooms have fireplaces and whirlpool tubs. The spacious and elegant public rooms—expansive living rooms, cozy library, porches—flow from one to another. Teri puts her culinary degree to use preparing baked goods, fruits, and savory and sweet entrées for breakfast and evening refreshments. A guest pantry is stocked with tea, coffee, and snacks.

Much less pricey and a find for families is the **Seacroft Inn** (18 Albert Meadow, Bar Harbor, 207/288-4669 or 800/824-9694, www .seacroftinn.com, $99–139), well situated just off Main Street and near the Shore Path. All rooms in Bunny and Dave Brown's white,

multigabled cottage have air-conditioning, phone, TV, refrigerator, and microwave, and in season, continental breakfast (subtract $5 from the rate if you don't want it). Housekeeping is $10 per day. Some rooms can be joined as family suites. There's also an apartment, available by the week for $1,550.

Outside of town in a serene location with fabulous views of Frenchman Bay is Jack and Jeani Ochtera's **(Inn at Bay Ledge** (150 Sand Point Rd., Bar Harbor, summer 207/288-4204 or winter 207/875-3262, www.innatbay ledge.com, $150–475), an oasis of calm tucked under towering pines and atop an 80-foot cliff. A long veranda lined with wicker chairs and settees descends to decks, a pool, and on to the lawn, which stretches to the cliff's edge. Stairs descend to a private stone beach below. Almost all guest rooms have water views, some rooms have whirlpool tubs, some private decks. Breakfast is served on the water-view porch.

On a budget? Consider the pleasant but few-frills **Llangolan Inn and Cottages** (865 Rte. 3, Bar Harbor, 207/288-3016, www.llangolan .com), seven miles from downtown. The well-cared-for property includes a B&B and cottages. Five rooms, one with private bath and four sharing two baths, are comfortable and welcoming and go for a bargain $70–80, including a continental breakfast. Also available are basic housekeeping cottages sleeping 2–5, each with kitchenette, TV, and heat ($85–120 d). This property is right on Route 3, so expect traffic noise. Ask for rooms facing the back or for a cottage well away from the road. Even then, you'll probably hear the passing *vroom*.

Another budget choice is the **Otter Creek Inn** (Rte. 3, Otter Creek, 207/288-5151 or 800/845-5852, www.ottercreekme.com, $85–125), a well-maintained complex with a small motel-like inn, an apartment, and cottages. Rooms have minifridge, TV, and include continental breakfast. A two-bedroom apartment rents for $125–175; two housekeeping cabins are $95–125. There are laundry facilities, and all accommodations are adjacent to the Otter Creek Market, which has everything from camping supplies to lobster and wine.

Hostels

The **Bar Harbor/Mount Desert Island Hostel** (321 Main St., P.O. Box 32, Bar Harbor 04609, 207/288-5587, www.barharbor hostel.com), in a beautifully renovated building on the edge of town, has dorms for men and women ($25 pp), a family room ($80), and a well-equipped kitchen; outside are an organic garden (planted by College of the Atlantic students), where you can help yourself to the produce, and tent platforms ($10 pp). No smoking, no liquor, no credit cards, midnight curfew. Reservations (best by mail) are essential, as this is a popular location. It's open in winter by chance or reservation.

Seasonal Rentals

Contact **Lynam Real Estate** (227 Main St., P.O. Box C, Bar Harbor 04609, 207/288-3334, www.lynams.com) or **Maine Island Properties** (P.O. Box 1025, Mount Desert 04660, 207/244-4308, fax 207/244-0588, www.maineisland properties.com) for listings of houses/cottages available by the week or month.

FOOD

You won't go hungry in Bar Harbor, and you won't find chain fast-food places. The island's best collection of good, inexpensive restaurants, most open year-round, are along Rodick Street, from Reel Pizza down to Rosalie's, which actually fronts on Cottage Street. You'll find a good ethnic mix here, from Mexican to Thai to Italian. For sit-down restaurants, make reservations as far in advance as possible.

Local Flavors

Only a masochist could bypass **Ben and Bill's Chocolate Emporium** (66 Main St., Bar Harbor, 207/288-3281 or 800/806-3281), a long-running taste-treat-cum-experience in downtown Bar Harbor. The homemade candies and more than 50 ice-cream flavors (including a dubious lobster flavor) are nothing short of outrageous; the whole place smells like the inside of a chocolate truffle. It opens daily at 10 A.M., with closing dependent upon season and crowds, but usually late into the evening.

If ice cream is your passion, another must stop is **Mt. Desert Ice Cream** (325 Main St., and 7 Firefly Ln., Bar Harbor, 207/460-5515).

Probably the least-expensive lunch or ice-cream option in town is **West End Drug Co.** (105 Main St., Bar Harbor, 207/288-3318), where you can get grilled cheese sandwiches ($1.40), PBJ, and other old-fashioned white-bread basics as well as frappes (a Maineism—frappes are made with ice cream, milk shakes aren't) and sundaes at the fountain.

The **Eden Farmers Market** operates out of the YMCA parking lot off Lower Main Street in Bar Harbor 9 A.M.–noon each Sunday Mother's Day–late October. You'll find fresh meats and produce, local cheeses and maple syrup, bread, honey, preserves, even prepared Asian foods.

An unscientific but reliable local survey gives the best-pizza ribbon to **Rosalie's Pizza and Italian Restaurant** (46 Cottage St., Bar Harbor, 207/288-5666, opens 11:30 A.M. daily), where the Wurlitzer jukebox churns out tunes from the 1950s. This family-owned standard gets high marks for consistency with its homemade pizza (in four sizes or by the slice), calzones, and subs—lots of vegetarian options. If you need something a bit heartier, try the Italian dinners—spaghetti, eggplant parmigiana, and others—all around $7, including a garlic roll. Beer and wine are available.

Efficient, friendly, cafeteria-style service makes **EPI Sub and Pizza Shop** (8 Cottage St., Bar Harbor, 207/288-5853, 10 A.M.–8 P.M. daily, to 8:30 P.M. July and Aug.) an excellent choice for picnics or a quick break from sightseeing. The dozen-plus sub-sandwich choices at EPI's (short for epicurean) are bargains (try the Cadillac); it also serves salads, pizza, and Italian dinners. If the weather closes in, there are always the pinball machines in the back room. No credit cards.

For a light, inexpensive breakfast or lunch, you can't go wrong at **◖ Morning Glory Bakery** (39 Rodick St., Bar Harbor, 207/288-3041, 7 A.M.–4 P.M. Mon.–Fri., 8 A.M.–1 P.M. Sat.). Espresso and other fancy coffees, fresh-squeezed juices, smoothies, and fresh-baked goodies are all made from scratch. Planning a day in the park? Call ahead for a boxed lunch.

Brewpubs and Microbreweries

Bar Harbor's longest-lived brewpub is the **Lompoc Café** (36 Rodick St., Bar Harbor, 207/288-9392, www.lompoccafe.com, 11:30 A.M.–9 P.M. daily late Apr.–mid-Dec.), serving creative lunches and dinners ($8–19). How about a lobster and avocado quesadilla? After 9 P.M., there's just beer and thin-crust pizza until about 1 A.M. The congenial café has a beer garden, a bocce court, and open mic night Thursdays and live entertainment (blues, bluegrass, and jazz) Fridays and Saturdays May–October.

Lompoc's signature Bar Harbor Real Ale and five or six others are brewed by the **Atlantic Brewing Company** (15 Knox Rd., Town Hill, in the upper section of the island, 207/288-2337 or 800/475-5417, www.atlanticbrewing .com). Free brewery tours, including tastings, are given at 2, 3, and 4 P.M. daily Memorial Day–Columbus Day. Also based here is **Mainely Meat Bar-B-Q** (207/288-9200), offering daily specials and an all-you-can-eat barbecue on Saturdays.

Casual Family-Friendly Dining

Once a Victorian boarding house and later a 1920s speakeasy, **Galyn's Galley** (17 Main St., Bar Harbor, 207/288-9706, www.galynsbar harbor.com, 11:30 A.M.–10 P.M. daily March–Nov.) has been a popular eatery since 1986. Lots of plants, modern decor, reliable service, a great downtown location, and several indoor and outdoor dining areas contribute to the loyal clientele. The cuisine is consistently good (dinner entrées $15–25). Reservations advisable.

Set back from the road behind a garden is the very popular **McKays Public House** (231 Main St., Bar Harbor, 207/288-2002, www .mckayspublichouse.com, 11:30 A.M.–3 P.M. and 5–10 P.M. daily), a comfortable pub with seating indoors in small dining rooms or at the bar or outdoors in the garden. Classic pub fare includes Reubens, shepherd's pie with lamb, burgers, and

fish-and-chips ($8–10). At dinner, fancier entrées, such as coq au vin and seafood risotto, are also available, most in the $14–23 range.

Good food at a fair price reels them into **Poor Boy's Gourmet** (300 Main St., Bar Harbor, 207/288-4148, www.poorboysgourmet .com, opens at 4:30 P.M. daily). Until 6 P.M. it serves an Early Bird menu with about a half-dozen entrées as well as another 10 all-you-can-eat pasta choices for $8.95. The price jumps just a bit after that, with most entrées running $11–15. There's even a lobster feast for $21.

Eclectic Fare

Escape the humdrum at **Café This Way** (14 Mt. Desert St., Bar Harbor, 207/288-4483, www.cafethisway.com), where creativity reigns but isn't overdone—consider crab cakes with tequila-lime sauce or Thai-grilled salmon. The breakfast menu is a genuine wake-up call; try Green Eggs and Sam. Dinner entrées are in the $14–24 range; the wine list is very selective and the desserts are outstanding. It's open for breakfast (7–11 A.M. Mon.–Sat., 8 A.M.–1 P.M. Sun.) and for dinner (5:30–9 P.M. daily).

Another breakfast or lunch treat is **2 Cats** (130 Cottage St., Bar Harbor, 207/288-2808 or 800/355-2828, www.2catsbarharbor.com, 7 A.M.–1 P.M. daily), where you can dine inside or on the patio. Three upstairs rooms are $165–195, with breakfast, of course.

Town Hall Bistro (Rte. 102 and Crooked Rd., Bar Harbor, 207/288-1011, 5:30–9:30 P.M. Tues.–Sat.) promises interesting, creative cuisine served with a sense of humor, and it delivers. Possibilities include small and large plates, making it easy to please mixed appetites, and menu items fluctuate with what's fresh and available. The small dining area is simply adorned.

Ethnic and Vegetarian Fare

For Thai food, **Siam Orchard** (30 Rodick St., Bar Harbor, 207/288-9669, 5–9 P.M. daily, to 9:30 P.M. July and Aug.) gets the locals' nod. House specials run $14–17, curries and noodle dishes, such as pad thai, run $8–14 at dinner. There are plenty of choices for vegetarians. Beer and wine only. It's open all year.

ACADIA REGION

Sharing the same building is **Gringo's** (30 Rodick St., Bar Harbor, 207/288-2326, 11 A.M.–9 P.M. Mon.–Sat., noon–8 P.M. Sun.), a Mexican hole-in-the-wall specializing in take-out burritos, wraps, handmade salsas, and smoothies, with almost everything less than $7.50. For a real kick, don't miss the jalapeño brownies.

There's a good chance **Eden** (28 West St., Bar Harbor, 207/288-4422, www.barharbor vegetarian.com, 5–9:30-ish P.M. daily) could make a vegetarian out of even the most die-hard meat lover. This small restaurant is dedicated to using organic ingredients from area farms and preparing vegan entrées ($11–18).

For "American fine dining with Latin flair," head to [**Havana** (318 Main St., Bar Harbor, 207/288-2822, www.havanamaine .com, 5–10 P.M. daily May–late Oct., Wed.–Sat. the rest of the year), where the innovative, Cubanesque menu (entrées $16–35) changes almost daily to take advantage of what's locally available. Inside, bright orange walls and white tablecloths set a tone that's equally festive and accomplished.

It's back! Longtime favorite **Miguel's** (51 Rodick St., Bar Harbor, 207/288-5117, 4:30–9 P.M. daily) disappeared for a few years, but it's back serving the usual Mexican dishes along with a few surprises.

Italian with pizzazz is served in both half and full portions (yay!) at **Guinness and Porcelli's** (191 Main St., Bar Harbor, 207/288-0300, 4:30 P.M.–close daily). Unusual pizzas, such as lobster or wild boar, creative soups and salads, and entrées are a winning combo. The risotto *al arragosta,* made with lobster, sweet peas, and leeks, is a keeper, as is the butternut squash ravioli.

Fancy to Fine Dining

The view's the thing at the Bar Harbor Inn's **Reading Room Restaurant** (Newport Dr., Bar Harbor, 207/288-3351, www.barharbor inn.com); request a window seat. Once the stuffy Bar Harbor Reading Room, a gentlemen's club, the dining room still has a sweeping curve of windows overlooking Bar Island and Frenchman Bay. Dinner is available, but

opt for the Sunday brunch buffet (11:30 A.M.–2:30 P.M., $26 adults, $13 kids).

The stylish **Bar Harbor Club** (111 West St., 207/288-5033, 7–11 A.M. and 5–10 P.M. daily) was the playground of the Rockefellers, Pulitzers, Astors, Cornings, and other wealthy and famous residents during Bar Harbor's heyday. It survived the fire and hung on until 1989 and then sat abandoned and deteriorating for years. In 2005, after a multimillion dollar renovation, it reopened under the same ownership as the adjacent Harborside Hotel. Once again, it's providing elegant, harbor-view dining (as long as there isn't an events tent set up on the lawn; ask before you book if the view is important to you). Entrées, such as pan-roasted wild halibut and roast spring lamb, range $22–32. Ask for a table away from the large TV in the Vanderbilt Lounge.

Fresh, fresh, fresh seafood—that's what you'll find at **Maggie's Restaurant** (6 Summer St., Bar Harbor, 207/288-9007, www .maggiesbarharbor.com, 5–9:30 P.M. Mon.–Sat. June–Oct.). The restaurant grew out of owner Maggie O'Neil's experiences as a fishmonger, and much of the equally fresh produce comes from Maggie's own farm. Entrées, such as Maine seafood Provençal or bronzed cod with Latin lime tartar sauce, run $16–25. Hint: The lobster crepes are renowned. Soft music and good service complement the dining experience.

Five miles south of Bar Harbor in the village of Otter Creek (which itself is in the town of Mount Desert) is the inauspicious-looking [**Burning Tree** (Rte. 3, Otter Creek, 207/288-9331, 5–10 P.M. Wed.–Mon. late June–early Oct., also closed Mon. after Labor Day), which is anything but nondescript inside. Chef/owners Allison Martin and Elmer Beal Jr. have created one of Mount Desert Island's best restaurants. Bright and airy, with about 16 tables crowded in three areas, it serves a casually chic crowd. Reservations are essential in summer. Specialties are imaginative seafood entrées—such as curry pecan flounder, cioppino—and vegetarian dishes made from organic produce. Scallop kebabs have *lots* of scallops, the specialty crab cakes are 90 percent crabmeat, and edible flowers garnish the entrées ($18–25). The homemade breads and desserts are delicious. At the height of summer, service can be a bit rushed and the kitchen runs out of popular entrées. Solution: Plan to eat early; it's worth it.

Lobster

Lobster, lobster, and more lobster—that's what you'll find at **The Lobster Claw** (54 West St., Bar Harbor, 207/288-4489, 11 A.M.–8:30 P.M.), a take-out shack with a few tables. Sure there are other choices on the menu, including organic and vegetarian specials and a kiddie menu, but the lobster served here is fresh picked and never frozen. Lobster rolls come in four varieties, and there's always the lobsta-ka-bobsta, a grilled lobster meat kebab with accompaniments. Ask about local delivery.

INFORMATION AND SERVICES
Information

The Bar Harbor Chamber of Commerce (1201 Bar Harbor Rd./Rte. 3, Trenton, P.O. Box 158, Bar Harbor 04609, 207/288-5103 or 888/540-9990, www.barharbormaine .com) is open daily in summer, weekdays off-season. Late May–mid-October, you'll find a "branch" chamber office at Harbor Place, 1 West Street, next to the town pier. (Some

Bar Harbor information is also available at the Thompson Island Information Center, just after you cross the bridge from Trenton toward Mount Desert Island.) Bar Harbor's annual visitors information booklet usually is off the presses in January—a big help in making early plans for a summer vacation.

Check out Jesup Memorial Library (34 Mount Desert St., Bar Harbor, 207/288-4245, www.jesup.lib.me.us).

Public Restrooms

Downtown Bar Harbor has public restrooms in the Harbor Place complex at the town pier, in the municipal building (fire/police station) across from the village green, and on the School Street side of the athletic field, where there is RV parking. Restrooms are also at the Mount Desert Island Hospital and the International Ferry Terminal.

Parking

Make it easy on yourself and help improve the air quality and reduce stress levels by leaving your car at your lodging, or if day-tripping at the chamber's visitors center on Route 3 in Trenton, and taking the Island Explorer.

RVs are not allowed to park near the town pier; designated RV parking is alongside the athletic field, Lower Main and Park Streets, about eight blocks from the center of town.

ACADIA REGION

Northeast and Seal Harbors

Ever since the late 19th century, the upper crust from the City of Brotherly Love has been summering in and around Northeast Harbor. Sure, they also show up in other parts of Maine, but it's hard not to notice the preponderance of Pennsylvania license plates surrounding Northeast Harbor's elegant "cottages" mid-July–mid-August. (In the last decade or so, the Pennsylvania plates have been joined by growing numbers from Washington, D.C., New York, and Texas.)

Actually, even though Northeast Harbor

is a well-known name with special cachet, it isn't even an official township; it's a zip-coded village within the town of Mount Desert, which collects the breathtaking property taxes and doles out the municipal services.

The attractive boutiques and eateries in Northeast Harbor's small downtown area cater to a casually posh clientele, while the well-protected harbor attracts a tony crowd of yachties. For their convenience, a palm-size annual directory, *The Redbook,* discreetly lists owners' summer residences and winter addresses—but no phone numbers.

SIGHTS
Somes Sound

As you head toward Northeast Harbor on Route 198 from the northern end of Mount Desert Island, you'll begin seeing cliff-lined Somes Sound on your right. This glacier-sculpted fjord juts five miles into the interior of Mount Desert Island from its mouth, between Northeast and Southwest Harbors. Watch for the right-hand turn for Sargent Drive (no RVs allowed) and follow the lovely, granite-lined route along the east side of the sound. Half-way along, a marker explains the geology of this natural fjord, the only one on the Eastern Seaboard. There aren't many pullouts en route, and traffic can be fairly thick in midsummer, but don't miss it. An ideal way to appreciate Somes Sound is from the water—sign up for an excursion out of Northeast or Southwest Harbor.

◖ Asticou Azalea Garden and Thuya Garden

If you have the slightest interest in gardens (even if you don't, for that matter), allow time for Northeast Harbor's two marvelous public gardens. Information about both is available from the local chamber of commerce. If gardens are extra-high on your priority list, inquire locally about visiting the private Rockefeller garden, accessible on a very limited basis.

One of Maine's best spring showcases is the Asticou Azalea Garden, a 2.3-acre pocket where about 70 varieties of azaleas, rhododendrons, and laurels—many from the classic Reef Point garden of famed landscape designer Beatrix Farrand—burst into bloom. When Charles K. Savage, beloved former innkeeper of the Asticou Inn, learned the Reef Point garden was being undone in 1956, he went into high gear to find funding and managed to rescue the azaleas and provide them with the gorgeous setting they have today, across the road and around the corner from the inn. Oriental serenity is the key—with a Japanese sand garden, stone lanterns, granite outcrops, pink-gravel paths, and a tranquil pond. Try to visit early in the season, early in the morning, to savor

The Japanese-inspired Asticou Azalea Garden is fun to explore.

© HILARY NANGLE

the effect. The garden is on Route 198, at the northern edge of Northeast Harbor, immediately north of the junction with Peabody Drive (Rte. 3). Watch for a tiny sign on the left (if you're coming from the north) marking access to the parking area. Asticou is open sunrise–sunset daily May–November, and blossoming occurs here May–August, but prime time for azaleas is roughly mid-May–mid-June. A small pillar box suggests a $1 donation, and another box contains an attractively designed garden guide ($2). Pets are not allowed in the garden. Take Island Explorer Route 5/Jordan Pond or Route 6/Brown Mountain and request a stop.

Behind a carved wooden gate on a forested hillside not far from Asticou lies an enchanted garden also designed by Charles K. Savage and inspired by Beatrix Farrand. Special features of Thuya Garden are perennial borders, sculpted shrubbery, and Oriental touches. On a misty summer day, when few visitors appear, the colors are brilliant. Adjacent to the garden is **Thuya Lodge** (207/276-5130), former summer cottage of Joseph Curtis, donor of this awesome municipal park. The lodge, with an extensive botanical library and quiet rooms for reading, is open 10 A.M.–4:30 P.M. Monday–Saturday and noon–4:30 P.M. Sunday late June–Labor Day. The garden is open 7 A.M.–7 P.M. daily May 1–October 31. A collection box next to the front gate requests a $5 per adult donation. To reach Thuya, continue on Route 3 beyond Asticou Azalea Garden and watch for the Asticou Terraces parking area (no RVs, two-hour limit) on the right. Cross the road and climb the Asticou Terraces Trail (0.4 mile) to the garden. Or drive 0.2 mile beyond the Route 3 parking area, watching for a minuscule Thuya Garden sign on the left. Go half a mile up the steep, narrow and curving driveway to the parking area. Take Island Explorer Route 5/Jordan Pond and request a stop.

After you've visited Thuya Garden, open the back gate, where you'll see a sign for the **Eliot Mountain Trail,** a 1.4-mile moderately diffi-

cult round-trip (lots of exposed roots). Near the summit, Northeast Harbor spreads out before you. If you're here in August, sample the wild blueberries. Much of the Eliot Mountain Trail is on private land, so stay on the path and be respectful of private property.

Petite Plaisance

On Northeast Harbor's quiet South Shore Road, Petite Plaisance is a special-interest museum commemorating noted Belgian-born author and college professor Marguerite Yourcenar (pen name of Marguerite de Crayencour), the first woman elected to the prestigious Académie Française. From the early 1950s to 1987, Petite Plaisance was her home, and it's hard to believe she's no longer here; her intriguing possessions and presence fill the two-story house—of particular interest to Yourcenar devotees. Free, hour-long tours of the first floor are given in French or English, depending on visitors' preferences. (French-speaking visitors

ACADIA REGION

THE MAINE SEA COAST MISSION

Remote islands and other isolated communities along Maine's rugged coastline may still have a church, but few have a full-time minister; fewer yet have a health-care provider. Yet these communities aren't entirely shut off from either preaching or medical assistance.

Since 1905, the Maine Sea Coast Mission, nondenominational, nonprofit organization rooted in a Christian ministry, has offered a lifeline to these communities. The mission, based in Bar Harbor (127 West St., 207/288-5097 or 888/824-7258), serves nearly 2,800 people on eight different islands, including Frenchboro, the Cranberries, Swans, and Isle au Haut, as well as others living in remote coastal locations on the mainland. Its numerous much-needed services include a Christmas program; in-school, after-school, and summer-school programs; emergency financial assistance; food assistance; a thrift shop, ministers to island and coastal communities; scholarships; and health services.

Many of these services are delivered via the

mission's *Sunbeam V,* a 75-foot diesel boat that has no limitation on when it can travel and few on where it can travel. In winter, it even serves as an icebreaker, clearing harbors and protecting boats from ice damage.

A nurse and a minister usually travel on the *Sunbeam.* The minister may conduct services on the island, or on the boat, which also functions as a gathering place for fellowship, meals, and meetings. The minister also reaches out to those in need, marginalized, or ill, and often helps with island funerals. Onboard telemedicine equipment enables the nurse to provide much-needed health care, including screening clinics for diabetes, cholesterol, and prostate and skin cancer; flu and pneumonia vaccines; and tetanus shots.

During your travels in the Acadia region, you might see the *Sunbeam* homeported in Northeast Harbor or on its rounds. If you want to learn more about or support this worthwhile organization, visit www.seacoastmission.org.

often make pilgrimages here.) The house is open for tours daily June 15–August 31. No children under 12 are allowed. Call 207/276-3940 9 A.M.–4 P.M. at least a day ahead for an appointment and directions, or write: Petite Plaisance Trust, P.O. Box 403, Northeast Harbor 04662. Yourcenar admirers should request directions to Brookside Cemetery in Somesville, seven miles away, where she is buried.

Great Harbor Maritime Museum

Annual exhibits focusing on the maritime heritage of the Mount Desert Island area are held in the small, eclectic Great Harbor Maritime Museum (125 Main St., Northeast Harbor, 207/276-5262, 10 A.M.–5 P.M. Tues.–Sat. late June–Labor Day, plus weekends in Sept. and Oct., $3), housed in the old village fire station and municipal building. ("Great Harbor" refers to the Somes Sound area—Northeast, Southwest, and Seal Harbors, as well as the Cranberry Isles.) Yachting, coastal trade, and fishing receive special emphasis. Special programs and exhibits are held during the summer.

RECREATION

Northeast Harbor is the starting point for a couple of boat services headed for the Cranberry Isles. (Other boats depart from Southwest Harbor.) The vessels leave from the commercial floats at the end of the concrete municipal pier on Sea Street.

Sea Princess

The 75-foot *Sea Princess* (207/276-5352, www .acadiainfo.com/seaprincess.htm) carries visitors as well as an Acadia National Park naturalist on a 2.5-hour morning trip around the mouth of Somes Sound and out to Little Cranberry Island (Islesford) for a 50-minute stopover. The boat leaves Northeast Harbor at 10 A.M. daily mid-May to mid-October ($25). A narrated afternoon trip departs at 1 P.M. on the same route. A scenic 1.5-hour Somes Sound cruise departs at 3:45 P.M. daily late June–early September. The same months, two sunset cruises are offered. The three-hour sunset/dinner cruise departs for the Islesford

Dock Restaurant on Little Cranberry (Islesford) at 5:15 P.M. Dinner is on your own at the restaurant. A 1.5-hour sunset cruise of Somes Sounds departs at 7 P.M. Cost for all tours is $20–25 adult, $15 children 5–12, $5 for children under 5. Reservations are advisable for all trips, although even that provides no guarantee, since the cruises require a rather hefty 15-passenger minimum. Arrive at least one half hour before departure to buy tickets at the booth next to the harbormaster's office, at the head of the municipal pier.

SHOPPING

Upscale shops, galleries, and boutiques, with clothing, artworks, housewares, antiques, and antiquarian books, line both sides of Main Street, making for intriguing browsing and expensive buying (but be sure to check the sale rooms of the clothing shops for bona fide bargains). The season is short, though, with some shops open only in July and August.

One must-visit is **Shaw Contemporary Jewelry** (100 Main St., 207/276-5000 or 877/276-5001, www.shawjewelry.com). Besides the spectacular silver and gold beachstone jewelry created by Rhode Island School of Design alumnus Sam Shaw, the work of more than 100 other jewelers is displayed exquisitely. Plus there are sculptures, Asian art, and rotating art exhibits. It all leads toward a lovely, light-filled garden. Prices are in the stratosphere, but appropriately so. As one well-dressed customer was overhead sighing to her companion: "If I had only one jewelry store to go to in my entire life, this would be it." The gallery is open all year, with a varying schedule depending on the season.

ENTERTAINMENT
Mount Desert Festival of Chamber Music

Since 1964, the Mount Desert Festival of Chamber Music (207/276-3988, www.mt desertfestival.org) has presented concerts. Concerts are staged in the century-old Neighborhood House on Main Street at 8:15 P.M. Tuesdays mid-July–mid-August.

Past musicians have included the Borromeo String Quartet and the Miami String Quartet. Tickets ($20 general admission; $10 student section) are available at the Neighborhood House box office on Mondays and Tuesdays during the concert season or by phone reservation.

ACCOMMODATIONS

If money's no object and you're yearning for a classic, old-timey experience, spring for the **Asticou Inn** (Rte. 3, P.O. Box 337, Northeast Harbor 04662, 207/276-3344 or 800/258-3373, www.asticou.com). Do splurge; less-pricey rooms just don't make the grade. Built in 1883 and refurbished periodically, the classic harbor-view inn has 31 second-, third-, and fourth-floor rooms and suites in the main building, plus 16 rooms and suites in several more modern cottages. Facilities include an excellent restaurant, clay tennis courts, outdoor pool, and access to the Northeast Harbor Golf Club. The inn is open mid-May–late October. July and August rates are $225–240 d, including continental breakfast. Try to plan a late-May or early-June visit; you're practically on top of the Asticou Azalea Garden, Thuya Garden is a short walk away, and the rates are lowest ($130–215 d). The Asticou is a popular wedding venue, so if you're looking for a quiet weekend, check the inn's wedding schedule before you book a room.

In 1888, architect Fred Savage designed the two Shingle-style buildings that make up the three-story **Harbourside Inn** (Main St., P.O. Box 178, Northeast Harbor, 207/276-3272, www.harboursideinn.com, $125–295, mid-June–mid-Sept.). The Sweet family has preserved the old-fashioned feel by decorating the 17 spacious rooms and three suites with antiques, yet modern amenities include some kitchenettes and phones. Most rooms have working fireplaces. A continental breakfast is served. Trails to Norumbega Mountain and Upper Hadlock Pond leave from the back of the property. Do note that through the years, the waterfront property has been sold so

despite the inn's name, only glimpses of the harbor can be seen.

FOOD
Local Flavors

In the **Pine Tree Market** (121 Main St., Northeast Harbor, 207/276-3335, 7 a.m.–7 p.m. Mon.–Sat., 8 a.m.–6 p.m. Sun.), you'll find gourmet goodies, a huge wine selection, resident butcher, fresh fish, deli, homemade breads, pastries, sandwiches, and salads.

Pop into **Full Belli Deli** (Sea St., Northeast Harbor, 207/276-4299, 8 a.m.–4 p.m. Mon.–Sat., to 2 p.m. Sun.) for soups, fat sandwiches, and breakfast fare.

The **Northeast Harbor Farmers Market** is set up 9 a.m.–noon each Thursday from June well into October across from the Kimball Terrace Inn on Huntington Road. Look for the usuals, as well as cheeses, cider, maple syrup, breads and cookies, yarns and related fiber products, and prepared Asian foods.

Casual Dining

Real local color and crab cakes and crab sandwiches are *the best* at the **Docksider** (14 Sea St., Northeast Harbor, 207/276-3965, 11 a.m.–9 p.m. daily, summer only), a low-key, family-friendly, unassuming, hole-in-the-wall place inevitably jammed with devoted locals and summer folk. Just up the hill from the chamber office, the Docksider has an outside deck, plus a couple of veteran (since forever) waitresses, no view, and a reputation far and wide. Prices reflect market rates, with choices beginning around $8, and more popular ones in the $14–20 range. If you're smitten, buy one of the T-shirts, featuring an upright lobster announcing, "Frankly, I don't give a clam." Note: Early-bird specials and a 10 percent discount apply 4:30–6 p.m.

Tucked in a shady corner of a parking lot behind Shaw's Jewelry is a taste of the Mediterranean. **Bassa Cocina de Tapeo** (5 Old Firehouse La., Northeast Harbor, 207/276-0555, www.bassacocina.com), a perfect choice for a hot, sultry night, lets you pick and choose from a tapas menu ($3–12) or splurge on entrées ($15–35), all representing the flavors of the Mediterranean: Spain, France, Italy, and Morocco (hint: The paella is divine). A martini and wine bar serves grappas, sherries, and Mediterranean wines. Dine inside or on the patio. It's open for lunch and dinner daily in summer, dinner only spring and fall.

Casual, yet sophisticated, **Redbird Provisions** (11 Sea St., Northeast Harbor, 207/276-3006, 11:30 A.M.–2:30 P.M. and 6–9 P.M. Wed.–Sat., www.redbirdprovisions .com) is the perfect neighborhood restaurant— if your neighbors are the yachting type. Lunch and dinner ($10–26) are served in a renovated home that also houses Bella Spa.

Fine Dining

The elegant, mural-lined dining room at the **Asticou Inn** (Rte. 3, 207/276-3344 or 800/258-3373, 7–9 A.M., 11:30 A.M.–2 P.M., and 6–9 P.M. daily) is open to the public for breakfast, lunch, Sunday brunch, and dinner ($27–35). Lunch is served on the harborside deck, with serene views over Northeast Harbor. Jackets and ties are advised for dinner.

INFORMATION AND SERVICES
Information

The Chamber Information Bureau (also called the Yachtsmen's Building) of the Mount Desert Chamber of Commerce (18 Harbor Rd., P.O. Box 675, Northeast Harbor 04662, 207/276-5040, 8 A.M.–5 P.M. daily mid-June–mid-Oct.) covers the villages of Somesville, Northeast Harbor, Seal Harbor, Otter Creek, Pretty Marsh, Hall Quarry, and Beech Hill. Request a free copy of the annual *Mount Desert Chamber of Commerce Village/Island Guide and Northeast Harbor Port Directory*.

Public Restrooms

Restrooms are at the end of the building housing the Great Harbor Maritime Museum, in the town office on Sea Street, and at the harbor.

GETTING AROUND

Northeast Harbor is serviced by Route 5/Jordan Pond and Route 6/Brown Mountain of the Island Explorer bus system.

The Quiet Side

Southwest Harbor considers itself the hub of Mount Desert Island's "quiet side." In summer, its tiny downtown district is probably the busiest spot on the whole western side of the island (west of Somes Sound), but that's not saying a great deal. "Southwest" has the feel of a settled community, a year-round flavor that Bar Harbor sometimes lacks. And it competes with the best in the scenery department. The Southwest Harbor area serves as a very convenient base for exploring Acadia National Park, as well as the island's less-crowded villages and offshore Swans Island, Frenchboro, and the Cranberry Isles.

The quirky nature of the island's four town boundaries creates complications in trying to categorize various island segments. Officially, the town of Southwest Harbor includes only the villages of Manset and Seawall, but nearby

is the precious (really!) hamlet of Somesville. The Somesville National Historic District, with its distinctive arched white footbridge, is especially appealing, but traffic gets congested here along Route 102, so rather than just rubbernecking, plan to stop and walk around.

The "quiet side" of the island becomes even more quiet as you round the southwestern edge into Tremont, which includes the villages of Bernard, Bass Harbor, home of **Bass Harbor Head Light** and ferry services to offshore islands, and Seal Cove. Tremont occupies the southwesternmost corner of Mount Desert Island. It's about as far as you can get from Bar Harbor, but the free Island Explorer bus service, Route 7/Southwest Harbor, comes through here regularly.

Be sure to drive or bike these small villages.

© TOM NANGLE

Pretty Somesville is almost too precious to be real.

Views are fabulous, the pace is slow, and you'll feel as if you've stumbled upon "the real Maine."

SIGHTS
◖ Wendell Gilley Museum
In the center of Southwest Harbor, the Gilley Museum (Herrick Rd., corner of Rte. 102, Southwest Harbor, 207/244-7555, www.wendell gilleymuseum.org, 10 A.M.–4 P.M. Tues.–Sun. June–Oct., to 5 P.M. in July and Aug., Fri.–Sun. in May, Nov., and Dec., $5 adults, $2 kids 5–12) was established in 1981 to display the lifework of local woodcarver Wendell Gilley (1904–1983), a one-time plumber who had gained a national reputation for his carvings by the time of his death. The modern, energy-efficient museum houses more than 200 of his astonishingly realistic bird specimens carved over more than 50 years. Most days, a local artist gives woodcarving demonstrations. The gift shop carries an ornithological potpourri—books to binoculars to carving tools. Kids over eight appreciate this more than younger ones. If the carving bug catches you, workshops are

available varying from 90-minute introductory lessons for adults and children ($25) offered most weekdays during the summer to multiday classes on specific birds.

Southwest Harbor Oceanarium
Touching a sea cucumber or a starfish may not be every adult's idea of fun, but kids sure enjoy the hands-on experience at the Oceanarium (Clark Point Rd., Southwest Harbor, 207/244-7330, www.theoceanarium.com, 9 A.M.–5 P.M. Mon.–Sat. mid-May–late Oct., $10 adult, $7 ages 4–12), sister site to the Bar Harbor Oceanarium (combo tickets at 25 percent discount). A knowledgeable naturalist introduces creatures from a watery touch tank during a tour of the oceanarium. Twenty tanks hold a range of sea creatures. In addition, exhibits line the walls of the intriguing, low-tech museum. It's next to the Coast Guard station.

Mount Desert Island Historical Society Museum and Gardens
This tiny museum (Rte. 102, Somesville,

207/276-9323, 1–4 P.M. Tues.–Sat., seasonal) is adjacent to the gently curving white bridge in Somesville, so there's a good chance you're going to stop, if just for a photo. In season, the heirloom garden, filled with flowering plants and herbs of the 19th and early 20th centuries, is worth a photo or two in and of itself. The tiny one-room museum has local artifacts and memorabilia displayed in a themed exhibit that changes annually. You can buy a walking-tour guide to Somesville in the museum. If you're especially interested in history, ask about the museum's programs, which include speakers, demonstrations, and workshops.

Butterfly Garden

It's easy to miss the **Charlotte Rhoades Park and Butterfly Garden** (Rte. 102, Southwest Harbor), but that would be a mistake. This tiny, seaside, town-owned park was donated to the town in 1973 and is maintained entirely by volunteers. It's seldom busy, and it's a delightful place for a picnic. A kiosk is stocked with butterfly observation sheets. It's on the water side of Route 102 between the Causeway Golf Club and the Seal Cove Road.

The Seal Cove Auto Museum

On the westernmost side of the island, but easily accessible from Southwest Harbor, a nondescript blue building camouflages The Seal Cove Auto Museum (Pretty Marsh Rd., Rte. 102, Seal Cove, 207/244-9242, www.seal coveautomuseum.org, 10 A.M.–5 P.M. daily June–late Sept., $5 adults, $2 kids under 12), one of the largest collections of Brass Era (1905–1917) autos in the country comprising more than 100 antique autos and 35 antique motorcycles. All are in as-found condition; this varies from fresh-from-the-barn to meticulously restored. It's easy for kids of any age to spend an hour here, reminiscing and/or fantasizing. Among the highlights are a 1907 Chadwick Touring Car and a 1910 Chadwick Racer, two of only three Chadwicks still in existence; a 1915 F.R.P., the fifth of only nine built and the only one still in existence; an original 1903 Ford Model A, the first car commercially

produced by the Ford Motor Co., and a 1909 Ford Model T "Tin Lizzie," from the first year of production. The oldest car in the collection is an 1899 DeDion-Bouton, one of the earliest cars produced in the world. The museum is about six miles southwest of Somesville. Or, if you're coming from Southwest Harbor, take Route 102 North to Seal Cove Road (partly unpaved) west to the other side of Route 102 (it makes a giant loop) and go north about 1.5 miles. This is not on the Island Explorer route.

RECREATION

Acadia National Park, of course, is the recreational focus throughout Mount Desert Island; on the island's western side, the main nonpark recreational activities are bike, boat, and picnic related.

At the Southwest Harbor/Tremont Chamber of Commerce office, or at any of the area's stores, lodgings, and restaurants, pick up a free copy of the *Trail Map/Hiking Guide,* a very handy foldout map showing more than 20 hikes on the west side of Mount Desert Island. Trail descriptions include distance, time required, and skill levels (easy to strenuous).

Bicycle Rentals

A veteran business with a first-rate reputation, **Southwest Cycle** (Main St., Southwest Harbor, 207/244-5856 or 800/649-5856) rents bikes by the day and week and is open all year (hours are 8:30 A.M.–5:30 P.M. Mon.–Sat. and 10 A.M.–4 P.M. Sun. June–Sept.; shorter hours in winter). The staff at Southwest Cycle will fix you up with maps and lots of good advice for three loops (10–30 miles) on the western side of Mount Desert. (See *Islands near Mount Desert* for planning biking day trips to Swans Island or the Cranberry Isles.) Rentals are around $20. The shop also rents every imaginable accessory, from baby seats to jogging strollers.

Sea Kayaking

On the outskirts of Southwest Harbor's downtown, close to the chamber of commerce, is **Maine State Sea Kayak** (254 Maine St., Southwest Harbor, 207/244-9500 or 877/481-

9500, www.mainestatekayak.com). Staffed with experienced, environmentally sensitive kayakers (several are Registered Maine Guides), the company offers four-hour trips (8:30 A.M.–12:30 P.M., 10 A.M.–2 P.M., 2–6 P.M. and a sunset tour) with a choice of half a dozen routes (depending on tide, visibility, and wind conditions). The trip is for $46 pp ($42 late May–June and September) and it includes shuttle transportation, paddling equipment, and a guide. Most trips also include island or beach breaks. Maximum group is six tandems; minimum age is 12. Neophytes are welcome.

If you have your own boat, consider putting in at either the park's Pretty Marsh picnic area, off Route 102, in Pretty Marsh, or at the public boat launch at the end of Bartlett's Landing Road, off the Indian Point Road near the Route 102 end. From either put-in, you can paddle around privately owned Bartlett Island. For a longer trip, head north along the shoreline past Black and Green Islands, both privately owned, to Alley Island, which is open for day access.

Calm-Water Paddling

Just west of Somesville (take the Pretty Marsh Rd.), and across the road from Long Pond, the largest lake on Mount Desert Island, **National Park Canoe and Kayak Rental** (145 Pretty Marsh Rd., Rte. 102, Mount Desert, 207/244-5854 or 877/378-6907, www.acadia.net/canoe) makes canoeing and kayaking a snap. Just rent the boat, carry it across the road to Pond's End, and launch it. Be sure to pack a picnic. Half-day rate (8:30 A.M.–12:30 P.M. or 1–5 P.M.) for a canoe is $25, full-day rate is $45; solo kayak is $24 half day, $40 full day, $140 per week; tandem kayak is $27 half day, $52 full day, $185 per week. A do-it-yourself sunset canoe or kayak tour (from 5 P.M.–sunset) is $16 pp. Reservations are advisable and essential in July and August. It's open mid-May–mid-October.

Deep-Sea Fishing

Go fishing with the **Masako Queen Fishing Company** (Beal's Wharf, Clark Point Rd., Southwest Harbor, 207/244-5385, www.masakoqueen.com) aboard *The Vagabond,*

and you might return with a lobster. The boat goes 8–20 miles offshore for mackerel, bluefish, codfish, and more, but on each trip every passenger is assigned a lobster trap. When that trap is hauled, any legal-size lobster in your trap is yours. Trips last 5–7 hours, and all equipment is included. Dress warmly.

Boat Rentals and Lessons

Mansell Boat Rental Co. (135 Shore Rd., Manset, next to Hinckley, 207/244-5625, www.mansellboatrentals.com) rents sail- and powerboats, with rates varying by type of boat and duration, but expect to pay close to $200 for a day rental. Sailing lessons also are available.

Golf

Play a quick nine at the **Causeway Club** (Fernald Point Rd., 207/244-3780), which edges the ocean. Be forewarned: It's more challenging than it looks.

EXCURSION BOATS

Southwest Harbor is the starting point for a couple of boat services headed for the Cranberry Isles. (Other boats depart from Northeast Harbor; see the *Northeast and Seal Harbors* section; see the *Cranberry Isles* section for information on the regular ferry/mail-boat service between Northeast Harbor and the Cranberries—the ferries are slightly less expensive, but there's no narration.)

Island Cruises

High praise goes to Captain Kim Strauss's Island Cruises (Little Island Marine, Shore Rd., Bass Harbor, 207/244-5785, www.bassharborcruises.com) for its daily, narrated 3.5-hour lunch cruise to Frenchboro. The 49-passenger *R. L. Gott,* which Strauss built, departs at 11 A.M. daily during the summer. Kim has been navigating these waters for more than 55 years, and his experience shows not only in his boat handling but also in his narration. Expect to pick up lots of local heritage and lore about once-thriving and now-abandoned granite-quarrying and fishing communities, the sardine industry, and lobstering, and to see

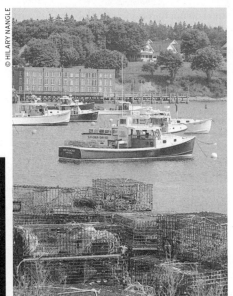

© HILARY NANGLE

ACADIA REGION

While other harbors share their waters with yachts, in Bass Harbor, lobster boats rule.

Friendship Sloop Cruises

Charter a traditional Friendship sloop with **Downeast Friendship Sloop Charters** (P.O. Box 1533, Southwest Harbor 04679, 207/266-5210, www.downeastfriendshipsloop.com). Private charters start at $125 per hour, including appetizer; shared trips are $50 for two hours, $75 for three hours. A sunset sail is a lovely way to end a day. One of the boats used is the oldest known Friendship sloop still sailing.

SHOPPING

The best shopping locale on this side of the island is Southwest Harbor. You'll also find a few (okay, very few) shops in Somesville. Mind you, there aren't *lots* of shops, but the small selection is interesting.

Art, Antiques, and Gifts

In the middle of Southwest Harbor's small shopping area is **Sand Castle Ocean and Nature Store** (360 Main St., Southwest Harbor, 207/244-4118), a delightful shop with a huge range of handcrafted items, most with a marine theme. Representing the work of several dozen artisans, the shop has wind chimes, jewelry, ceramics, ship models, and lots of other surprises.

Stop in at **E. L. Higgins** (Bernard Rd., Bernard, 207/244-3983, www.antiquewicker .com). In two onetime classrooms in an 1890s schoolhouse, Edward Higgins has the state's best collection of antique wicker furniture, about 400 pieces at any given time.

Right next door is **Linda Fernandez Handknits** (Bernard Rd., Bernard, 207/244-7224), with beautiful hand-knit sweaters, mittens, hats, socks, Christmas stockings, and embroidered pillowcases all handcrafted by the talented and extended Fernandez family. The kids' lobster sweaters are especially cute. It's a great place to stock up on mittens for holiday gift giving.

Fine art of the 19th and early 20th century is the specialty at **Clark Point Gallery** (46 Clark Point Rd., Southwest Harbor, 207/244-0920, www.clarkpointgallery.com). Most works depict Maine and Mount Desert Island.

seals, cormorants, guillemots, and often eagles, too. The trip allows enough time on Frenchboro for a picnic (or lunch at the summertime deli on the dock) and a short village stroll, and then a return through the sprinkling of islands along the 8.3-mile route. Kim also hauls a few traps and explains lobstering. He also earns major points for maneuvering the boat around so that passengers on both sides get an up-close view of key sights. It's an excellent, enthralling tour for all ages. Round-trip cost is $27 adults, $17 children 11 and younger. Be sure to reserve, and if the weather looks iffy, call ahead to confirm. Most of the trip is in sheltered water, but rough seas can put the kibosh on it. Island Cruises also does a two-hour afternoon nature cruise among the islands that covers the same topics but that spends a bit more time at seal ledges and other spots. On either trip, don't forget to bring binoculars. You'll find the Island Cruises dock by following signs to the Swans Island Ferry and turning right at the sign shortly before the state ferry dock.

Jewelry approaches fine art at **Aylen and Son Jewelers** (Main St., Rte. 102, Southwest Harbor, 207/244-7369, www.peteraylen.com). Since opening in 1979, Peter and Judy Aylen have been crafting and selling jewelry in 18-karat gold and sterling silver and augmenting it with fine gemstones or intriguing beads.

Potters Lisbeth Faulkner and Edwin Davis can often be seen working in their studio at **Seal Cove Pottery and Gallery** (Kelleytown Rd., Seal Cove, 207/244-3602). In addition to their functional hand-thrown or hand-built pottery, they exhibit Davis's paintings as well as crafts from other island artisans.

Books, Charts, and Music

The two-story **Port in a Storm Bookstore** (Main St., Rte. 102, Somesville, Mount Desert, 207/244-4114 or 800/694-4114, www.port inastormbookstore.com) is one of Maine's best independent bookstores. It's totally seductive, guaranteed to lighten your wallet. High ceilings, comfortable chairs, whimsical floor sculptures, open space, and Somes Cove views all contribute to the ambience. Inventory is not huge, but it's well selected—especially nature and children's books—and the staff is very knowledgeable. Especially in summer, noted authors often appear to lecture or sign their books. In the summer, the shop operates the **Port Side** outpost in the much-photographed, weathered faux lighthouse on Steamboat Wharf, in Bernard.

Don Gooding's **Mainely A Cappella** (11 Seal Cove Rd., Southwest Harbor, 800/827-2936, www.acappella.com) is the largest source of a cappella music in the world, with more than 3,000 a capella–related items. Available are CDs, sheet music, videos, songbooks, instructional materials, and more from all over the globe.

ENTERTAINMENT
Life Is a Cabaret

It's not too far to drive from Southwest Harbor to Bar Harbor for evening dinner and entertainment, but Southwest has a cabaret theater that even draws customers in the reverse direction for great entertainment and so-so food:

The Deck House Restaurant and Cabaret Theater (Great Harbor Marina, 11 Apple La., off Rte. 102, Southwest Harbor, 207/244-5044). Try to arrive for dinner by 6:30 P.M. to enjoy the spectacular harbor view and order your meal (entrées are $18–28). The cathedral-ceilinged dining room holds 140, and the table is yours for the evening for an additional $10 pp cover charge (reservations are essential in midsummer). About 8:15 P.M., the young waitstaff, chameleonlike, unveils its other talents—singing, dancing, even storytelling and puppetry. After hearing the dozen or so numbers, you won't be surprised to learn that many Deck House staff have moved on to Broadway and beyond. The performers aren't compensated, so be prepared to leave a tip.

Repertory Theater

Somesville is home to the **Acadia Repertory Theatre** (Rte. 102, Somesville, P.O. Box 106, Mount Desert 04660, 207/244-7260 or 888/362-7480, www.acadiarep.com, $22 adults, $16 seniors, students, and military, $10 kids under 16), which has been providing first-rate professional thespian summer stock on the stage of Somesville's antique Masonic Hall since the 1970s. Classic plays by Wilde, Goldsmith, even Molière, have been staples, as has the annual Agatha Christie mystery. Performances in the 144-seat hall run at 8:15 P.M. Tuesday–Sunday late June–late August, with 2 P.M. matinees on the last Sunday of each play. Special children's plays occur at 10:30 A.M. Wednesday and Saturday in July and August. Tickets for children's theater programs are $8 adults, $5 kids. (No credit cards; pay at the box office before the performance.)

EVENTS

In early October, Smuggler's Den Campground on Route 102 in Southwest Harbor is home to the annual **Oktoberfest International Food Festival and Craft Fair** (207/244-9264 or 800/423-9264, www.acadiachamber.com), a one-day celebration with crafts, food, games, music, and about two dozen Maine microbrewers presenting about 80 different brews.

ACADIA REGION

ACCOMMODATIONS

As the Asticou Inn is to Northeast Harbor, the Claremont is to Southwest Harbor. On the other end of the lodging scale, there are several commercial campgrounds in this part of the island, plus an Acadia National Park campground.

Inn

When you're ready to splurge, **The Claremont** (22 Claremont Rd., Southwest Harbor, 207/244-5036 or 800/244-5036, www.the claremonthotel.com) may well be your choice, but you'll have to plan a year ahead to land a room in July or August. The most popular time is the first week in August, during the annual Claremont Croquet Classic. An elegant grande dame, dressed in yellow clapboard, the Claremont dominates a six-acre hilltop overlooking Somes Sound and caters to honeymooners, yuppies, and gentrified folk. The views are stupendous. Guests have access to croquet courts, a clay tennis court, bikes, rowboats, and a library. Dating from 1884, the main building has 26 rooms (with bath and phones), most of them recently refurbished yet pleasantly old-fashioned and nonfancy. Other accommodations are in the six-room Phillips House, one-suite Clark House, and Cole Cottage, with two rooms and one efficiency. Rooms in these buildings are $185–245 including breakfast, early July–early September, plus a hefty 15 percent service charge and Maine sales tax. Also on the premises are 14 cottages ($205–300, early July–early Sept.); they can go as high as $3,500 a week in midsummer. No pets, no smoking, and, surprisingly, no credit cards. Children are welcome. The hotel and dining room are open early June–mid-October; cottages are open late May–mid-October.

Bed-and-Breakfasts

Many of Southwest Harbor's B&Bs are clustered downtown, along Main Street and the Clark Point Road.

Set on a corner, well back from the Clark Point Road, is ◖ **Harbour Cottage Inn** (9 Dirigo Rd., P.O. Box 258, Southwest Harbor 04679, 207/244-5738 or 888/843-3022, www

.harbourcottageinn.com), appealingly revamped in 2002, when Javier Montesinos and Don Jalbert took over the reins. Built in 1870, it was the "annex" for one of the island's original hotels and housed the increasing numbers of rusticators who patronized this part of the island. It has evolved into a lovely B&B with eight rooms ($159–175) and three suites ($205–259), decorated in a colorful and fun cottage style. Most rooms have whirlpool baths or steam-sauna showers, some have fireplaces, and all have telephones, TV, and Wi-Fi. Rates include a multicourse breakfast and use of beach bicycles. The inn stocks a nice selection of wine and beer. Also part of Harbour Cottage is **Pier One**, which offers five weekly waterfront suites ($1,260–1,575), including a studio cottage, all with kitchens, TV, and phone. Guests have private use of a 150-foot pier, and they can dock or launch canoes or kayaks or other small boats from right outside their doors; dockage is available for larger boats. It's all within walking distance of downtown.

The linden-blossom fragrance can be intoxicating in summer at the **Lindenwood Inn** (118 Clark Point Rd., P.O. Box 1328, Southwest Harbor 04679, 207/244-5335 or 800/307-5335, www.lindenwoodinn.com, $125–325). Jim King, the Australian owner, has imaginatively decorated the inn's nine rooms and poolside bungalow with artifacts from everywhere in a style that's sophisticated, yet comfortable. After you hike Acadia's trails, the heated pool and hot tub are especially welcome, and after that, perhaps the inn's full bar. Some rooms have harbor views. It's open all year.

At the Victorian **Inn at Southwest** (371 Main St., Rte. 102, P.O. Box 593, Southwest Harbor 04679, 207/244-3835, www.innat southwest.com, $135–185), guests gather for games, reading, conversation, and afternoon tea in a huge living room with fireplace and comfortable couches. Built in 1884 as the Freeman Cottage, the elegant building has 13 dormers and a wraparound veranda. Seven second- and third-floor guest rooms—named for Maine lighthouses and full of character—are fitted out with wicker furniture, ceiling fans, down comforters, and lots more. Some have gas stoves or limited water views. The inn is Wi-Fi wired. It's open May–October. Breakfast is a feast, with such treats as cheesecake crepes and eggs Florentine.

In Manset, adjacent to the Hinckley Yacht complex and with jaw-dropping views down Somes Sound, is **The Moorings** (Shore Rd., P.O. Box 744, Southwest Harbor 04679, 207/244-5523, 207/244-3210, or 800/596-5523, www.mooringsinn.com, $70–125), owned and operated by the King family since 1960. The oceanfront complex is part motel, part cottage rental, and part old-fashioned B&B, and the rates are terrific. Ten rooms in the Main House are named after locally built sailing vessels. Rates include juice, coffee, and doughnuts. The Lighthouse View Wing has motel-style rooms with refrigerator, microwave, waterfront decks, and incredible views (spend the afternoon counting the Hinckley yachts). Also on the property are cottage units, a combination of rooms and efficiencies ($115–175). Bikes, canoes, and kayaks are available for guests, so you can paddle around the harbor.

Motels and Cottages

Smack on the harbor and just a two-minute walk from downtown is the appropriately named **Harbor View Motel and Cottages** (11 Ocean Way, P.O. Box 701, Southwest Harbor 04679, 207/244-5031 or 800/538-6463, www.mainesunshine.com/harbview). The family-owned complex comprises motel rooms ($55–125) spread out in two older one-story buildings and a newish three-story one that fronts on the harbor. A continental breakfast is served to motel room guests July 1–Labor Day. Also on the premises are seven housekeeping cottages with kitchenettes varying from studios to two-bedrooms (weekly rentals only; $480–1,170).

Right across from the famed seawall and adjacent to the park is the **Seawall Motel** (566 Seawall Rd./Rte. 102A, Southwest Harbor, 207/244-9250 or 800/248-9250, www.seawallmotel.com, $75–110). The no-surprises, two-story motel (upstairs rooms have the best views) has free Wi-Fi, in-room phones, and cable TV. A continental breakfast is included mid-May–

October. Kids 12 and under stay free. The location's excellent for bird-watchers—there are a freshwater pond, pine forest, and the ocean. The motel is also home to the Acadia Workshop Center (207/244-3020 or 800/248-9250, www.acadiaworkshopcenter.com), which offers five-day art classes May–October. Packages are available that include lodging, meals, airport transportation, workshop, and park tour.

Campgrounds

On the eastern edge of Somesville, just off Route 198 at the head of Somes Sound, the 【 **Mount Desert Campground** (516 Somes Sound Dr., Rte. 198, Somesville, Mount Desert, 207/244-3710, www.mountdesertcampground.com) is especially centrally located for visiting Bar Harbor, Acadia, and the whole western side of Mount Desert Island. The campground has 152 wooded tent sites, about 45 on the water, spread out on 58 acres. Reservations are essential in midsummer— one-week minimum for waterfront sites, three days for off-water sites in July and August. (Campers book a year ahead for waterfront sites here.) This deservedly popular and low-key campground gets high marks for maintenance, noise control, and convenient tent platforms. Another plus is The Gathering Place, where campers can relax, play games, and buy coffee and fresh-baked treats or ice cream. Summer rates are $30–45 a night for two adults and two children younger than 18. Electrical hookups are available for $2 per night. No pets July– early September. No trailers longer than 20 feet. Kayak and canoe rentals are available. It's open mid-June–mid-September.

If staying at a quiet, no-frills campground in an outstanding setting appeals, head for Hall Quarry, a few miles south of Somesville. **Somes Sound View Campground** (86 Hall Quarry Rd., Mount Desert, 207/244-3890, www.ssvc.info), among the smallest campgrounds on the island, has 60 tight tent and RV (maximum 28 feet) sites on a hillside, with some on the ocean's edge. Facilities include hot showers (if you're camping on the lowest levels, it's a good hike up to the bathhouse), a pool, dock, and pond with paddleboats; nearest store is two miles. Canoe rentals are available, and you can swim in the sound (from a rocky beach). Leashed pets are allowed. Sites are $29–49 in July and August, less early and late in the season. No credit cards. It's open late May–mid-October. The campground is two miles south and east of Somesville and a mile east of Route 102.

Smuggler's Den Campground (Rte. 102, P.O. Box 787, Southwest Harbor, 207/244-3944, www.smugglersdencampground.com) is a midsize campground between Echo Lake and downtown Southwest Harbor. It's also the site of the annual Oktoberfest. Trails lead to back roads to both Echo Lake (1.25 miles) and Long Pond (one mile). Big-rig sites are grouped in the top third; pop-ups and small campers are in the middle third; tenting sites are in the lower third and in the woods rimming the large recreation field. Summer rates covering four adults vary from $28 (tent) to $49 (full hookups with concrete pads) for the 96 sites, 54 of which are designated for tents. Also available are four camping cabins that rent for $500 per week. Facilities include a heated pool and kiddy pool, laundry, free hot showers, lobsters and ice cream for sale, and entertainment. Well-behaved pets are a possibility.

Cottage Rentals

LSRobinson Co. (337 Main St., P.O. Box 1480, Southwest Harbor 04679, 207/244-5563, www.lsrobinson.com) has an extensive list of area rentals. The Southwest Harbor/Tremont Chamber of Commerce also keeps a helpful listing of privately owned homes/cottages available for rent. The chamber's annual summer guide usually contains a couple of pages of ads with photos.

FOOD
Local Flavors

Lots of goodies for picnics can be found at **Sawyer's Market** (Main St., Southwest Harbor, 207/244-7061, 5:30 A.M.–7:30 P.M. Mon.–Sat.); for wine and cheese head across the street to **Sawyer's Specialties** (Main St., Southwest Harbor, 207/244-3317), open daily.

Hot diggity dog! **Maddy's** (7 Clark Point Rd., Southwest Harbor, 207/244-0011, 7 A.M.–3 P.M., to 1 P.M. Sun.) welcomes kids with paper-topped, crayon- and game-stocked tables, and kid-pleasing basics and hot dog connoisseurs with gourmet tube steaks, all at reasonable prices. Soups, salads, sausages, chili, burgers, and even Mexican standards are on the menu, and breakfast is served all day.

The students at College of the Atlantic run **Beech Hill Farm** (Beech Hill Rd., Mount Desert, 207/244-5204, 8 A.M.–5 P.M. Tues., Wed., Fri., and Sat.), a five-acre MOFGA-certified organic farm that also has acres of heirloom apple trees and 65 acres of forestland. Visit the farmstand for fresh produce.

Ethnic Fare

◖ **XYZ Restaurant** (80 Seawall Rd., Rte. 102A, Manset, 207/244-5221, 5:30–9 P.M. daily) isn't easy to find, but it's well worth the effort. It's at the end of a dirt driveway rising slowly to a crest—look for the faux cacti marking the parking lot. There's dining inside and on the porch. No gloppy Mexican fare here; rather this popular spot (do make reservations) delivers the flavors of interior Mexico: Xalapa, Yucatán, and Zacatecas (hence XYZ). Most popular dish? *Cochinitas*—citrus-marinated pork rubbed with achiote paste (it's worthy of its reputation). Entrées are $21. The margaritas are classic—requiring, allegedly, 1,100 pounds of fresh limes each year. For dessert, try the exquisite XYZ pie.

From the outside, it doesn't look like much, but locals know you can count on ◖ **DeMuro's Top of the Hill** (Rte. 102, Southwest Harbor, 207/244-0033, 4:30 P.M.–close daily) for a really good meal at a very fair price. Dine in the country-style, pine dining room or on the weatherized patio. The Italian-influenced menu (try the excellent veal Italiano) has something in all price ranges ($9–18), but the real steal is the Lobster Paloozah special, including a cup of clam chowder, steamed mussels, a boiled lobster, pasta or potato, and vegetable, all for about $19. Early-bird specials are served 4:30–6:30 P.M.

Casual Dining

Some of the island's most creative sandwiches and pizza toppings emerge from Arthur and Kate Jacobs's **Little Notch Café** (340 Main St., Southwest Harbor, 207/244-3357, 11 A.M.–8 P.M. Mon.–Sat. May–Oct., 11 A.M.–7 P.M. weekdays Nov.–Apr.), next to the library in Southwest Harbor's downtown. How about a broccoli, sausage, and black olive pizza? Or a prosciutto sandwich with asiago and roasted peppers? All this plus Little Notch Bakery's famed breads, sinful desserts, a couple of pasta choices, and homemade soups, stews, and chowders make the café a winner.

By day, **Eat-a-Pita** (326 Main St., Southwest Harbor, 207/244-4344, www.eatapita-chef marc.com, 8 A.M.–9 P.M. daily) is a casual, order-at-the-counter restaurant, serving breakfast and lunch. At night, it morphs into **Café 2,** a tad more formal with full service. The dining room is furnished with old oak tables and chairs and an eclectic collection of stuff. Start the day with a Greek or Acapulco omelet. Lunch emphasizes pita sandwiches and salads (delicious! Call in advance for takeout); dinner choices ($8–22) include a half dozen pastas and entrées such as poached Atlantic salmon and boneless lamb loin. Desserts are homemade.

Good food, good coffee, and good wine mix with a Mediterranean-influenced menu at **Sips** (4 Clark Point Rd., Southwest Harbor, 207/244-4550, 6:30 A.M.–10 P.M. Mon.–Sat., 9 A.M.–2 P.M. Sun.). Small- and large-plate and tapas-style choices range $8–21.

Earning high praise for its internationally accented fare, good service, fabulous views over the harbor, and incredible martinis is **Fiddlers' Green** (411 Main St., Southwest Harbor, 207/244-9416, www.fiddlersgreenrestaurant .com, 11 A.M.–2:30 P.M. and 5:30 P.M.–close daily). House specialties, such as Asian vegetarian hot pot, pork *cubano,* and lobster pot pie, range $16–27.

Fine Dining

The dreamy views from **Claremont Dining Room** (22 Claremont Rd., 207/244-5036 or 800/244-5036, 6–9 P.M. daily) descend over the lawns and croquet courts, to the boathouse and dock, and beyond to the water backed by mountains. It's truly a special place for an elegant meal complemented by an old-fashioned grace. Unfortunately chefs seem to change annually, so it's hard to predict the quality; it's best to ask locally (jackets and ties requested for dinner, entrées $19–28). Dining-room reservations are wise in midsummer. In July and August, informal lunches and cocktails are served in the shorefront Boat House, also open to the public.

Red sky at night, diners delight. Gold walls, artwork, wood floors, and a giant hearth set a chic tone for **Red Sky** (14 Clark Point Rd., 207/244-0476, www.redskyrestaurant.com, 5:30–9:30 P.M. daily), one of the island's premier restaurants. The creative fare (entrées $19–30) emphasizes fresh seafood, hand-cut meats, and local organic produce, and there's always a vegetarian choice. Bread is baked daily and the desserts are homemade. The restaurant is open Valentine's Day–New Year's Eve.

Seafood and Lobster in the Rough

If you have a penchant for puns—or can tune them out—head for the family-run **Seafood Ketch Restaurant** (McMullin Ave., Bass Harbor, 207/244-7463, 11 A.M.–9 P.M. daily late May–mid-Oct.). The corny humor begins with "Please no fishing from dining room windows or the deck," and "What foods these morsels be," and goes up or down from there (depending on your perspective). But there's nothing corny about the seafood roll, an interesting change from the usual lobster or crab roll. There are a few "landlubber delights," but mostly the menu has fresh seafood dishes—including the baked lobster-seafood casserole (a recipe requested by *Gourmet).* Most entrées run $18–20, but sandwiches and lighter fare are available. This is a prime family spot (with a kids' menu), where the best tables are on the flagstone patio overlooking Bass Harbor. Follow signs for the Swans Island ferry terminal.

(Thurston's Lobster Pound (Steamboat Wharf Rd., Bernard, 207/244-7600, 11 A.M.– 8 P.M. daily early and late in the season, to 8:30 P.M. in July and Aug., open Memorial Day–Columbus Day) wins the award for the island's best lobster pound, with a screened dining room that practically sits in the water. Family-oriented Thurston's also has chowders, sandwiches, and terrific desserts. Beer and wine are available. Be sure to read the directions at the entry and order before you find a table on one of two levels.

INFORMATION AND SERVICES
Information
Near the public parking lots and fire station (behind Sawyer's Market) is the Southwest Harbor/Tremont Chamber of Commerce (P.O. Box 1143, Southwest Harbor 04679, 207/244-9264 or 800/423-9264, www.acadiachamber.com).

Check out Southwest Harbor Public Library (338 Main St., Southwest Harbor, 207/244-7065, www.swhplibrary.org).

Public Restrooms
In downtown Southwest Harbor, public restrooms are at the southern end of the parking lot behind the Main Street park and near the fire station. Across Main Street, Harbor House also has a restroom, and there are port-o-lets at the town docks. There's also a public restroom at the Swan's Island ferry terminal.

GETTING AROUND
Southwest Harbor, Tremont, and Bass Harbor are serviced by Route 7/Southwest Harbor of the Island Explorer bus system.

Islands near Mount Desert

Sure, Mount Desert is an island, but for a sampling of real island life, you'll want to make a day trip to one of the offshore islands. Most popular are the Cranberry Isles and Swans Island, but Frenchboro (see sidebar *Frenchboro, Long Island*) has begun seeing a steadier stream of visitors.

CRANBERRY ISLES
The Cranberry Isles, south of Northeast and Seal Harbors, comprise Great Cranberry, Little Cranberry (called Islesford), Sutton, Baker, and Bear Islands. Islesford and Baker include property belonging to Acadia National Park. Bring a bike and explore the narrow, mostly level roads on the two largest islands (Great Cranberry and Islesford), but *remember to respect private property.* Unless you've asked permission, *do not* cut across private land to reach the shore.

The Cranberry name has been attributed to 18th-century loyalist governor Francis Bernard, who received these islands (along with all of Mount Desert) as a king's grant in 1762. Cranberry bogs (now long gone) on the two largest islands evidently caught his attention.

Permanent European settlers were here in the 1760s, and there was even steamboat service by the 1820s.

Lobstering and other fishing industries are the commercial mainstay, boosted in summer by the various visitor-related pursuits. Artists and writers come for a week, a month, or longer; day-trippers spend time on Great Cranberry and Islesford.

Largest of the islands is **Great Cranberry,** with a general store, a small historical museum, and a gift shop, but not much else except pretty views.

The second-largest island is **Little Cranberry,** locally known as Islesford. It's easy to spend the better part of a day here exploring. Begin at **The Islesford Historical Museum** operated by the National Park Service (207/288-3338, 10 A.M.–noon and 12:30–4:30 P.M. Mon.–Sat. and 10:45 A.M.–noon and 12:30–4:30 P.M. Sun. mid-June–Labor Day, free). The exhibits focus on local history, much of it maritime, so displays include ship models, household goods, fishing gear, and other mem-

© TOM NANGLE

The Islesford Dock is the place to have lunch or dinner on Little Cranberry Island.

orabilia. Also on Islesford are public restrooms (across from the museum), a handful of galleries, and a general store. For lunch, bring a picnic or head to the **The Islesford Dock** (207/244-7494, 11 A.M.–3 P.M. and 5–9 P.M. Tues.–Sat., 10 A.M.–2 P.M. Sun. late June–Labor Day), where prices are moderate, the food is home-cooked, and the views across to Acadia's mountains are incredible. If you want to spend the night, reserve at the **Braided Rugs Inn** (Box 15, Islesford 04646, 207/244-5943, $100), with three shared-bath rooms. For **cottage rentals,** see www.islesford.com.

Getting There

Decades-old, family-run **Beal and Bunker** (P.O. Box 33, Cranberry Isles 04625, 207/244-3575) provides year-round mail-boat/passenger service to the Cranberries from Northeast Harbor. The ferries don't carry cars, but you can take a bike. Or just plan to explore on foot. The schedule makes it possible to do both islands in one day. The summer season, with more

ACADIA REGION

frequent trips, runs late June–Labor Day. The first boat departs Northeast Harbor's municipal pier at 7:30 A.M. Monday–Saturday; first Sunday boat is 10 A.M. The last boat for Northeast Harbor leaves Islesford at 6:30 P.M. and leaves (Great) Cranberry at 6:45 P.M. The boats do a bit of to-ing and fro-ing on the three-island route (including Sutton in summer), so be patient as they make the circuit. It's a people-watching treat. If you just did a round-trip and stayed aboard, the loop would take about 1.5 hours. Round-trip tickets (covering the whole loop, including intraisland if you want to visit both Great Cranberry and Islesford) are $16 adults, $10 kids under 12 (free for kids under 3). Bicycles are $5 round-trip. The off-season schedule runs early May–mid-June and early September–mid-October; the winter schedule runs mid-October–April. In winter, the boat company advises phoning ahead on what Mainers quaintly call "weather days."

The **Cranberry Cove Ferry** (upper town dock, Clark Point Rd., Southwest Harbor, 207/244-5882 or cell 207/460-1981, www.downeastwindjammer.com) operates a summertime service to the Cranberries, mid-May–mid-October, aboard the 47-passenger *Island Queen*. The ferry route begins at the upper town dock (Clark Point Rd.) in Southwest Harbor, with stops in Manset and Great Cranberry before reaching Islesford an hour later. (Stops at Sutton can be arranged.) In summer (mid-June–mid-September), there are six daily round-trips, with two additional evening trips Tuesdays, Thursdays, and Saturdays. The first departure from Southwest Harbor is 7 A.M.; last departure from Islesford is 6 P.M. Round-trip fares are $22 adults, $14 children, $6 bicycle.

The **MDI Water Taxi** (207/244-7312), a converted lobster boat, makes frequent on-demand trips to the Cranberries.

Captain John Dwelley (207/244-5724) also operates a water-taxi service to the Cranberries. His six-passenger *Delight* makes the run from Northeast, Southwest, or Seal Harbor for $55–70 per trip, depending upon time of day, early June–late September. Reservations are required for trips 6–11 P.M. and 6–8 A.M.

Custom cruises are available, including excursions to Baker's Island.

SWANS ISLAND

Six miles off Mount Desert Island lies scenic, 6,000-acre Swans Island (pop. 327), named after Colonel James Swan, who bought it and two dozen other islands as an investment in 1786. As with the Cranberries, fishing—especially lobstering—is the year-round way of life here; summer sees the arrival of artists, writers, and other seasonal visitors. The

FRENCHBORO, LONG ISLAND

Since Maine has more Long Islands than anyone cares to count, most of them have other labels for easy distinction. Here's a case in point – a Long Island known universally just as Frenchboro, the name of the village that wraps around Lunts Harbor. With a year-round population hovering at 50, Frenchboro has had ferry service only since 1960. Since then, the island has acquired phone service, electricity, and satellite TV, but don't expect to notice much of that when you get there. It's a very quiet place where islanders live as islanders always have – making a living from the sea and proud of it. In 1999, when more than half the island (914 acres, including 5.5 miles of shorefront) went up for sale by a private owner, an incredible fund-raising effort collected nearly $3 million, allowing purchase of the land in January 2000 by the Maine Coast Heritage Trust. Some of the funding has been put toward restoration of the village's church and one-room schoolhouse; islanders and visitors will still have full access to all the acreage, and interested developers will have to look elsewhere.

Frenchboro is a delightful day trip. A good way to get a sense of the place is to take the 3.5-hour lunch cruise run by Captain Kim Strauss of **Island Cruises** (Little Island Marine, Shore Rd., Bass Harbor, 207/244-5785, www.bassharborcruises.com; see *Island Cruises* under *Recreation* in *The Quiet Side* section). For an even longer day trip to Frenchboro, plan to take the passenger ferry *R. L. Gott* during her weekly run for the Maine State Ferry Service. The *Gott* departs Bass Harbor at 8 A.M. each Friday early April–late October, arriving in Frenchboro at 9 A.M. The return trip to Bass Harbor is at 6 P.M., allowing nine hours on the island. Round-trip cost

is $9 adults, $4.25 children (children under 5 are free).

Extra ferries operate for the island's annual **lobster festival,** usually the second Saturday in August, when islanders and hundreds of visitors gather in the village for lobster galore, games, and more. For info, call the Lunt and Lunt Lobster Company (207/334-2922).

When you go, take a picnic with you, or stop at **Lunt's Dockside Deli** (207/334-2922), open only in July and August. It's a very casual establishment – order at the window, grab a picnic table, and wait for your name to be called; lobster rolls and fish chowder are the specialties, but there are plenty of other choices, including sandwiches, hot dogs, and even vegetable wraps; of course, you can get lobster, too. It's inexpensive; the view is wonderful; and you might even get to watch lobsters being unloaded from a boat.

The **Frenchboro Historical Society Museum,** just up from the dock, has interesting old tools, other local artifacts, and a small gift shop. It's usually open afternoons late May–early September. The island has a network of maintained trails through the woods and along the shore, easy and not-so-easy; some can be squishy and some are along bouldery beachfront. The trails are rustic and most are unmarked, so proceed carefully. In the center of the island is a beaver pond. (You'll get a sketchy map on the boat, but you can also get one at the Historical Society.)

Frenchboro is the subject of *Hauling by Hand: The Life and Times of a Maine Island,* a fascinating, well-researched "biography" published in 1999 by eighth-generation islander Dean Lunt, now a journalist in Portland. (See *Suggested Reading*.) His website (www.islandportpress .com) has helpful info for visiting the island.

island has no campsites, few public rest-rooms (ferry dock and a port-o-let outside the museum), a tiny motel, and two small, traditional-style B&Bs. Visitors who want to spend more than a day tend to rent cottages by the week.

You'll need either a bicycle or a car to get around on the island, as the ferry comes in on one side, and the village center is on the other. Should you choose to bring a car, it's wise to make reservations for the ferry, espe-cially for the return trip. Bicycling is a good way to get around, but be forewarned that the roads are narrow, lacking shoulders, and hilly in spots.

If you can be flexible, wait for a clear day, pack a picnic, and catch the first ferry (7:30 A.M.) from Bass Harbor. At the ferry office in Bass Harbor, request a Swans Is-land map (and take advantage of the rest-room). Keep an eye on your watch so you don't miss the last ferry (4:30 P.M.) back to Bass Harbor.

The ferry arrives in the northeast corner of the island. Head off down the main road toward Burnt Coat Harbor. (The island has three villages—Atlantic, Minturn, and Swans Island.) First stop is the tiny **Seaside Hall Museum,** which describes itself as "The Is-land's Attic." It's usually open noon–3 P.M., but it's run by volunteers, so that's not a sure thing. Admission is a $1 donation.

Pedal around to the west side of the har-bor and down the peninsula to **Hockamock Head Light** (officially, Burnt Coat Harbor Light). From the ferry landing, Hocka-mock Head is 4.5 miles. The distinctive square lighthouse, built in 1872 and now automated, sits on a rocky promontory over-looking Burnt Coat Harbor, Harbor Island, lobster-boat traffic, and crashing surf. The keeper's house is unoccupied; the grounds are great for picnics.

If it's hot, ask for directions to one of two prime island swimming spots: **Fine Sand Beach** (salt water) or **Quarry Pond** (fresh water). Fine Sand Beach is on the west side of Toothacher Cove; you'll have to navigate

about a mile of unpaved road to get there, but it's worth the trouble. Be prepared for chilly water, however. Quarry Pond is in Minturn, on the opposite side of Burnt Coat Harbor from the lighthouse. Follow the one-way loop around, and you'll see it on your right as you're rounding the far side of the loop.

Overnight accommodations are available at **The Harbor Watch Motel** (111 Minturn Rd., Swans Island, 207/526-4563 or 800/532-7928, www.swansisland.com, $95–120). Dining choices are limited and include the **Swan's Island Store** (Minturn Rd.), the **Island Bake Shop** (73 Ferry Terminal Rd., 207/526-4123, 7 A.M.–2 P.M. Mon.–Sat.), and **The Boat House** (207/526-4201), a take-out restaurant and gift shop clinging to a cliff-side overlooking the harbor on the way to the lighthouse.

Getting There and Around

Swans Island is a six-mile, 40-minute trip on the state-operated car ferry *Captain Henry Lee.* The ferry makes 5–6 round-trips a day mid-April–late October, the first from Bass Harbor at 7:30 A.M. (9 A.M. Sun.) and the last from Swans Island at 4:30 P.M. Other months, the first and last runs are the same, but there are only 4–5 trips. For more infor-mation, contact **Maine State Ferry Service** (P.O. Box 114, Bass Harbor 04653, 207/244-3254; 303 Atlantic Rd., Swans Island, 207/526-4273; daily recorded info 800/491-4883, www.state.me.us/mdot/opt/ferry/ferry). Round-trip fares are $14.50 adults, $6.25 children 5–11. Bikes are $13.75 round-trip per adult, $7 per child. Round-trip ticket for vehicle and driver is $42 May–October. Res-ervations are accepted only for vehicles (be in line at least 15 minutes before departure or you'll risk forfeiting your space, reservation fee is $7 each way).

To reach the Bass Harbor ferry terminal on Mount Desert Island, follow the distinctive blue signs, marked Swans Island Ferry, along Routes 102 and 102A. Parking, when available, is $7 per day.

ACADIA REGION

Schoodic Peninsula

Slightly more than 2,366 of Acadia National Park's acres are on the mainland Schoodic Peninsula—the rest are all on islands (including Mount Desert). World-class scenery and the relative lack of congestion, even at the height of summer, are just two reasons to sneak around to the eastern side of Frenchman Bay. Others are abundant opportunities for outdoor recreation, two scenic byways, and, believe it or not, shopping. You can easily do your gift shopping for the year at the dozens of artists' and artisans' studios tucked throughout this region.

Still, the biggest attractions in this area are the spectacular vignettes and vistas—of offshore lighthouses, distant mountains, and close-in islands—and the unchanged villages. Winter Harbor (pop. 988), known best as the gateway to Schoodic, shares the area with an old-money, low-profile, Philadelphia-linked summer colony on exclusive Grindstone Neck.

Pots and buoys litter the wharves lining Corea's harbor.

© HILARY NANGLE

Gouldsboro (pop. 1,941)—including the not-to-be-missed villages of Birch Harbor, Corea, and Prospect Harbor—earned its own minor fame from Louise Dickinson Rich's 1958 book *The Peninsula,* a tribute to her summers on Corea's Cranberry Point, "a place that has stood still in time." Since 1958, change has crept into Corea, but not so's you'd notice. It's still the same quintessential lobster-fishing community, perfect for photo ops. A new section of the Maine Coastal Islands National Wildlife Reserve, the 431-acre **Corea Heath Unit,** has taken over former Navy lands along Route 195 in Corea. Plans call for developing trails, including one along the shorefront (call 207/546-2124 for updated information). In another initiative, the Frenchman Bay Conservancy is seeking to acquire the 600-acre Northern Corea Heath, across the highway, home to Grand Marsh and Grand Marsh Bay.

Between Ellsworth and Gouldsboro are Hancock, Sullivan, and Sorrento. Venture down the ocean-side back roads, and you'll discover an old-timey summer colony at Hancock Point, complete with library, post office, yacht club, and tennis courts.

Meander inland to find the lakes for boating and fishing and peaks for hiking.

SCHOODIC SECTION OF ACADIA NATIONAL PARK

The Schoodic section of Acadia has an entirely different feel from the main part on Mount Desert. It's much smaller, less busy, and provides fewer recreational opportunities, but it's still magnificent and well worth visiting. There's no official visitors center in this area, so you'll want to stop at the main Acadia Visitor Center on Mount Desert Island, or download Schoodic information before you come.

As with so much of Acadia's acreage on Mount Desert Island, the Schoodic section became part of the park largely because of the deft diplomacy and perseverance of George B. Dorr. No obstacle ever seemed too daunting to

Dorr. In 1928, when the owners objected to donating their land to a national park tagged with the Lafayette name (geopolitics being involved at the time), Dorr even managed to obtain congressional approval for the 1929 name change to Acadia National Park—and Schoodic was part of the deal.

There's no camping in this section of the park, but private camping and other lodging options are available in the area. There are no restaurants or other food sources in the park, but you won't need to go far.

To reach the park boundary from Route 1 in Gouldsboro, take Route 186 south to Winter Harbor. Continue through town, heading east, and then turn right and continue to the park-entrance sign, just before the bridge over Mosquito Harbor.

You can also tour the park using the free Island Explorer bus, which circulates through Winter Harbor, around the Schoodic Loop, and on to Prospect Harbor, with stops along the way. It's an efficient and environmentally friendly way to go.

Perhaps one of the best ways to get to know the park is to become involved with the **Friends of Schoodic** (P.O. Box 194, Prospect Harbor 04669, www.friendsofschoodic.org), which supports the park with clean-up projects, trail and building maintenance, and staffing the visitors information booth at the Gatehouse.

Schoodic Loop

The major sights of Acadia's Schoodic section lie along the six-mile one-way road that meanders counterclockwise around the tip of the Schoodic Peninsula. You'll discover official and unofficial picnic areas, the hiking trailheads, offshore lighthouses, and turnouts with scenic vistas. Also named the Park Loop Road, it's best referred to as the Schoodic Loop to distinguish it from the one on Mount Desert. From this side of Frenchman Bay, the vistas of Mount Desert's summits are gorgeous, behind islands sprinkled here and there.

The first landmark is **Frazer Point Picnic Area,** with lovely vistas, picnic tables, and wheelchair-accessible restrooms. Other spots are

fine for picnics, but this is the only official one. If you've brought bikes, leave your car here and do a counterclockwise 12.2-mile loop through the park and back to your car via Birch Harbor and Route 186. It's a fine day trip.

From the picnic area, the road becomes one-way. Unlike the Park Loop Road on Mount Desert, no parking is allowed in the right lane. There are periodic pullouts, but not many cars can squeeze in. Despite the fact that this is far from the busiest section of Acadia, it can still be frustrating in the summer to be unable to find a space. Best advice, therefore: Stay in the area and do this loop early in the morning or later in the afternoon, perhaps in May or June. (The late-September and early-October foliage is gorgeous, but traffic *does* increase then.) While you're driving, if you see a viewpoint you like (with room to pull off), stop; it's a long way around to return.

At 2.2 miles from the picnic area, watch for a narrow, unpaved road on the left, across from an "open" beach vista. It winds for a mile (keep left at the fork) up to a tiny parking circle, from which you can follow the trail (signposted "Schoodic trails") to the open ledges on 440-foot Schoodic Head. From the circle, there's already a glimpse of the view, but it gets much better. If you bear right at the fork, you'll come to a grassy parking area with access to the Alder Trail and the Schoodic Head Trail.

Continue on the Park Loop Road and hang a right onto a short, two-way spur to **Schoodic Point,** the highlight of this section of the park. Although crowds gather at the height of summer, especially when the surf is raging, the two-tiered parking lot, amazingly, seldom fills up. (There are restrooms here, too.) Check local newspapers for the time of high tide and try to arrive here then; the word *awesome* is overused, but it sure describes Schoodic Point's surf performance on the rugged pink granite. The setting sun makes it even more brilliant. This area is open 6 A.M.–10 P.M. only.

Caution: If you've brought children, keep them well back from the water; a rogue wave can sweep them off the rocks all too easily. It *has* happened. Picnics are great here (make sure you bring a litter bag), and so are the tide pools at mid- to low tide. Birding is spectacular during spring and fall migrations.

Just before the point is a small info center, staffed by volunteers and park rangers, on the site of a former top-secret U.S. Navy base that became part of the park in 2002. The campus is now the Schoodic Education and Research Center (locally called by its acronym, SERC); occasional lectures and programs are held here and it's the site of the biennial sculpture symposium.

From Schoodic Point, return to the Loop Road. Look to your right, and you'll see Little Moose Island, which is accessible at low tide. Be careful, though, and don't get stranded here. Continue to the **Blueberry Hill** parking area (about one mile from the Schoodic Point/Loop Rd. intersection), a moorlike setting where the low growth allows almost 180-degree views of the bay and islands. There are a few trails in this area—all eventually converging on **Schoodic Head,** the highest point on the peninsula. (Don't confuse this with Schoodic Mountain, which is well north of here.) Across the road and up the road a bit is the trailhead for the 180-foot-high **Anvil** headland. The Schoodic Head Loop hike comprises three connecting trails, and it can be hiked in either direction, or if time is tight, choose just one trail to hike (allow 2–3 hours for the full loop). Clockwise begins with the easiest terrain and ends with a downhill scramble over a steep and rocky hillside. As one ranger noted, it's tough on the knees and you have to be very careful with your footing in this direction. If you hike it counterclockwise, beginning with the Anvil Trail, you'll get the toughest terrain out of the way first.

As you continue along this stretch of road, keep your eyes peeled for eagles, which frequently soar here. There's a nest on the northern end of Rolling Island; you can see it with binoculars from some of the roadside pullouts.

From Blueberry Hill, continue 1.2 miles to a pullout for the East Trail, the shortest and most direct route to Schoodic Head. From here, it's about another mile to the park exit, in Won-

squeak Harbor. It's another two miles to the intersection with Route 186 in Birch Harbor. (If you didn't bring a picnic, Bunker's Wharf Restaurant is an excellent stop.)

SCENIC BYWAYS
Just how gorgeous is this region? Well, it has not one, but two scenic byways: one coastal and one inland. You can link the two together via Route 1 between Gouldsboro and Cherryfield.

◖ Schoodic National Scenic Byway
Beginning at the bridge on Route 1 in Sullivan, 27-mile Schoodic Byway (www.schoodic byway.org) passes a reversing falls and takes in vistas of Frenchman Bay and Acadia's peaks before looping down and around the Schoodic Peninsula via Route 186 and the Park Road, before ending in Prospect Harbor, with views of the boat-filled harbor and Prospect Harbor Lighthouse. Recent improvements have provided pullouts just where you want to stop and admire the views. Hint: Do yourself a favor and from Prospect Harbor, take Route 195 to Corea Harbor.

Maine Scenic Byway
A few miles east of Ellsworth, Route 182 veers northeast off Route 1 to Franklin and on to Cherryfield, a 25-mile stretch of sparkling ponds, brilliant colors, and no civilization. Schoodic Mountain, Donnell Pond, and Tunk Lake are just three of the natural treasures along the way. As you enter Washington County and land in Cherryfield, you're brought gently back to civilization by a whole town full of architectural treasures. This route is simply gorgeous in autumn.

RECREATION
Donnell Pond Public Reserved Land
More than 15,000 acres have been preserved for public access in Donnell Pond Public Reserved Land (Maine Bureau of Parks and Lands, 207/827-1818, www.state.me.us/doc/parks), a huge mountain-and-lake area north and east of

Sullivan. Developers had their eyes on this gorgeous real estate in the 1980s, but preservationists fortunately rallied to the cause. Outright purchase of 7,316 of the acres, in the Spring River Lake area, came through the foresighted Land for Maine's Future program. Hikers can climb Schoodic, Black, and Caribou Mountains; paddlers and anglers have Donnell Pond, Tunk Lake, Spring River Lake, Long Pond, Round Pond, and Little Pond, among others. Route 182, an official Scenic Highway, cuts right through the Donnell Pond preserve. The preserve encompasses lakes for boating and fishing, mountains for hiking, and primitive campsites. Do note: Hunting is permitted, so take special care during hunting season.

Schoodic Mountain, Donnell Pond Public Reserved Land

The hiking isn't easy here, but it isn't technical. And the options are many. The interconnecting trail system takes in Schoodic Mountain, Black Mountain, and Caribou Mountain. Follow the Schoodic Mountain Loop clockwise, heading westward first. To make a day of it, pack a picnic and take a swimsuit (and don't forget a camera and binoculars for the summit views). On a brilliantly clear day, you'll see Baxter State Park's Katahdin, the peaks of Acadia National Park, and the ocean beyond. And in late July/early August, blueberries are abundant on the summit. For such rewards, this is a popular hike, so don't expect to be alone, especially on fall weekends, when the foliage colors are spectacular.

The Black Mountain ascent begins easily enough and then climbs steadily through the woods, easing off a bit before reaching bald ledges. Continue to the true summit by taking the trail past Wizard Pond. Views take in forested lands, nearby lakes and peaks, and out to Acadia's peaks. You can piggyback it with Schoodic Mountain, using that trailhead base for both climbs. Another possibility is to add Caribou Mountain. That loop exceeds seven miles, making a full day of hiking.

Trailheads are accessible by either boat or vehicle. To reach the vehicle-access trailhead for Schoodic Mountain from Route 1 in East Sullivan, drive just over four miles northeast on Route 183 (Tunk Lake Rd.). Cross the Maine Central Railroad tracks and turn left at the Donnell Pond sign onto an unpaved road (marked as a jeep track on the USGS map). Go about 0.25 mile and then turn left for the parking area and trailhead for Schoodic Mountain, Black Mountain, Caribou Mountain, and a trail to Schoodic Beach. If you continue straight, you'll come to another trailhead for Black and Caribou Mountains. Water-access trailheads are at Schoodic Beach and Redman's Beach.

Shore Path

A pleasant and short shore path begins and ends at the **Dixon Memorial Rock** and follows the water's edge, rising through the woods and passing by cottages on eastern Grindstone Neck. The views are fabulous. To find it, take Beach Street to Club House Lane, proceed across the four-way intersection, and then go right on Steamboat Lane, following it to the oval at the end.

Bicycling

The best choices for cycling are the **Schoodic Loop** and the quiet roads of **Grindstone Neck** and **Corea.** Bike rentals ($15 per 24 hours) are available from **SeaScape Kayaking** (18 East Schoodic Dr., Birch Harbor, 207/963-7223, www.seascapekayaking.com), an ideal location for the Schoodic Loop.

Canoeing and Kayaking

Experienced sea kayakers can explore the coastline throughout this region. Canoeists can paddle the placid waters of Jones Pond, on the Schoodic Peninsula. In Donnell Pond Public Reserved Land, the major water bodies are **Donnell Pond** (big enough by most gauges to be called a lake) and **Tunk** and **Spring River Lakes;** all are accessible for boats (even, alas, powerboats).

To reach the boat-launching area for Donnell Pond from Route 1 in Sullivan, take Route 200 North to Route 182. Turn right and go about 1.5 miles to a right turn just before Swan

ACADIA REGION

Brook. Turn and go not quite two miles to the put-in; the road is poor in spots but adequate for a regular vehicle. The Narrows, where you'll put in, is lined with summer cottages ("camps" in the Maine vernacular); keep paddling eastward to the more open part of the lake. Continue on Route 182 to find the boat launches for Tunk Lake and Spring River Lake (hand-carry only). Canoeists and kayakers have access to Tunk Stream from Spring River Lake.

Still within the preserve boundaries, but farther east, you can put in a canoe at the northern end of Long Pond and paddle southward into adjoining Round Pond. In early August, Round Mountain, rising a few hundred feet from Long Pond's eastern shore, is a great spot for gathering blueberries and huckleberries. The put-in for Long Pond is on the south side of Route 182 (park well off the road), about two miles east of Tunk Lake.

Outfitters and Trips

Paddle around the waters of Schoodic or Flanders Bay with Ed and Cheryl Brackett's **SeaScape Kayaking** (18 E. Schoodic Dr., Birch Harbor, 207/963-7223, www.seascape kayaking.com). Guided three- to four-hour tours are $45 pp, including fortification: homemade blueberry scones for morning trips and blueberry-white chocolate chip cookies in the afternoon. Canoe rental for lake usage is $40 per day; kayaks are $40 double, $30 single.

Master Maine Guides Darrin Kelly and Megan Gahl are committed to sustainability and education—they not only talk the talk, they walk the walk, living off the grid in a yurt surrounded by protected lands. Their enthusiasm and knowledge come through on their trips. **Ardea Expeditions** (242 S. Gouldsboro Rd., Gouldsboro, 207/460-9731, www.ardea-ecoexpeditions.com) offers a wide range of sea kayaking options, from half- and full-day trips to camping or inn-to-inn overnights to research expeditions. Half-day coastal eco-adventures begin at $59 adult, $49 child; a full day of island hopping is $105, including lunch. Family trips are available as are instructional trips, a first-light sunrise tour geared to birders,

and a sunset tour that can be combined with a lobster bake. Custom overnights begin at $145 pp/day. Ask about voluntourism research expeditions, including island inventory and monitoring and seabird surveys. Ardea donates 1 percent of sales to local nonprofits—all the more reason to choose this outfitter.

Antonio Blasi, a Registered Maine Sea Kayak and Recreational Guide, leads guided tours of Frenchman or Taunton Bay and hiking and camping expeditions through **Hancock Point Kayak Tours** (58 Point Rd., Hancock, 207/422-6854, www.hancockpointkayak .com). A three-hour paddle, including all equipment, safety and paddling demonstrations, and usually an island break, is $45. You have a choice of single or double kayak. Minimum age is 9 for a double, 12 for a single. Overnight kayak camping trips are $150 per person. Antonio also leads overnight backpacking trips for $125 pp, and cross-country skiing and snowshoe tours are available in winter.

Swimming

The best freshwater swimming in the area is at **Jones Beach,** a community-owned recreation area on Jones Pond in West Gouldsboro. Here you'll find restrooms, a nice playground, picnic facilities, boat launch, swim area with a float, and a small beach. It's at the end of Recreation Road, off Route 195, which is 0.3 mile south of Route 1.

Two beach areas on Donnell Pond are also popular for swimming—**Schoodic Beach** and **Redman's Beach**—and both have picnic tables, fire rings, and pit toilets. It's a half-mile hike to Schoodic Beach from the parking lot. Redman's Beach is accessible only by boat. Other pocket beaches are also accessible by boat, and there's a rope swing (use at your own risk) by a roadside pullout for Fox Pond.

Golf

Play a nine-hole round at the **Grindstone Neck Golf Course** (Grindstone Ave., Winter Harbor, 207/963-7760, www.grindstonegolf .com, May–Oct.), just for the dynamite scenery and for a glimpse of this exclusive, late-19th-century summer enclave. Established in 1891, the public course attracts a tony crowd; 150-yard markers are cute little birdhouses.

SHOPPING
Art and Antiques

Browsers, dreamers, and collectors are welcome at **Art and Old Things** (70 Taunton Dr., Sullivan, 207/422-3551), a one-stop antiques and collectibles shop, art gallery, and sculpture garden that's just plain fun to visit. The eclectic gallery features the work of Joe Martell and other regional artists; the shop is filled with antiques, junktiques, and shabby chic furniture, decorative items, home accents, and architectural pieces; the garden is accented with granite and marble sculptures and unique functional artwork. The shop is just 500 yards off Route 1, just beyond Gazebo Park.

Winter Harbor Antiques and Works of Hand (424–426 Main St., Winter Harbor, 207/963-2547) is a double treat. Antiques fill one building and works by local craftspeople and artists fill the other. It's across from Hammond Hall and set behind colorful, well-tended gardens.

Barbara Noel makes most of the sea glass jewelry, mobiles, and other creations at **Harbor Treasures** (358 and 368 Main St., Winter Harbor, 207/963-7086).

Here's a nifty place: **Chapter Two** (611 Corea Rd., Corea, 207/963-7269) is home to the Corea Rug Hooking company and Accumulated Books Gallery. Spread out in three buildings are a nice selection of used and antiquarian books, locally made crafts, and Rosemary's hand-hooked rugs. Sip on tea or coffee while browsing. Yarn, rug-hooking supplies, and lessons are available.

Ever seen a palmara, durian jack, pangium edule, or dompaum? Even know what they are? **Coastal Antiques** (Rte. 186, Prospect Harbor, 207/963-5546) has the original nut collection from Perry's Nut House, which pulled in tourists from around the globe in Belfast until its demise. Some specimens are amazing to see. The shop, which also sells antiques, shares a building with DeMarco Realty at the intersection with the Corea Road/Route 195.

Food and Wine

German and Italian presses, Portuguese corks, and Maine fruit all go into the creation of Bob and Kathe Bartlett's award-winning dinner and dessert wines: apple, pear, blueberry, raspberry, blackberry, strawberry, and loganberry. Founded in 1982, **Bartlett Maine Estate Winery** (175 Chicken Mill Pond Rd., Gouldsboro, 207/546-2408, www.bartlettwinery .com, 10 A.M.–5 P.M. Mon.–Sat. late May–mid-Oct., or by appointment off-season) produces more than 20,000 gallons annually in a handsome wood-and-stone building designed by the Bartletts. No tours, but you're welcome to sample the wines, and you can buy single bottles and gift packages. Bartlett's is a half mile south of Route 1 in Gouldsboro.

Organic fruit and honey wines are produced at family-operated **Shalom Orchard Organic Winery and Bed and Breakfast** (158 Eastbrook Rd., P.O. Box 4, Franklin 04634, 207/565-2312, www.shalomorchard.com). The certified-organic farm is well off the beaten path but worth a visit not only for the wines, but also for yarns, pelts, fleece, and especially the views of Frenchman Bay from the hilltop orchard. The farm also has two simple rooms, sharing one bath and kitchenette. A full farm breakfast is included in the $55–65 rate. Pets and kids are welcome. To find it, take Route 182 to Route 200/Eastbrook Road, and go 1.6 miles.

This area has two excellent smokehouses. Defying its name, **Sullivan Harbor Smokehouse** (Rte. 1, Hancock, 207/422-3735 or 800/422-4014, www.sullivanharborfarm.com) has moved to spacious, modern new digs in Hancock. Big interior windows allow visitors to see into the production facility and watch the action. Among the offerings are Scottish-style smoked salmon, gravlax, smoked scallops, smoked trout, smoked Arctic char, smoked salmon pâté, and more.

The newer **Grindstone Neck of Maine** (311 Newman St., Rte. 186, just north of downtown Winter Harbor, 207/963-7347, or 866/831-8734, www.grindstoneneck.com) also earns high marks for its smoked salmon, shellfish, spreads, and pâtés, all made without preservatives or artificial ingredients. Also available are fresh fish, wine, and frozen foods for campers. Best seller: a can of Road Kill Stew; go figure.

This and That

You can find just about anything at the **Winter Harbor 5 and 10** (Main St., Winter Harbor, 207/963-7927, www.winterharbor5and10 .com). It's the genuine article, an old fashioned five and dime that's somehow still surviving in the age of Wal-Mart.

ENTERTAINMENT AND EVENTS

Winter Harbor's biggest wingding is the annual **Lobster Festival** (www.acadia-schoodic .org) the second Saturday in August. The gala day-long event includes a parade, live entertainment,

GALLERY HOPPING

Art and artisan studios and galleries are numerous, and it's easy to while away a foggy day browsing and buying. Begin by picking up copies of the *Artist Studio Tour Map,* which details and provides directions to about a dozen galleries in Franklin, Sullivan, and Hancock, and the *Schoodic Peninsula* brochure, which notes galleries and shops on the peninsula. Both are widely available and free. Hours and days of operation vary; it's best to call first if you really want to visit a gallery. Here's a sampling to get you started.

HANCOCK AND SULLIVAN

Take the Point Road 2.5 miles to find Russell and Akemi Wray's **Raven Tree Gallery** (536 Point Rd., Hancock, 207/422-8273). Russell specializes in wood sculpture, bronzes, prints, and jewelry; Akemi crafts pottery. Out front is a small sculpture gallery. Continue another two miles to the **Ragna Bruno Torkanowsky Studio and Gallery** (983 Point Rd., Hancock, 207/422-6252). Torkanowsky's home gallery is filled with her sculpture and paintings and selections from other artists.

Return to Route 1 and take Eastside Road, just before the Hancock–Sullivan Bridge, and drive 1.5 miles south to **Gull Rock Pottery** (325 Eastside Rd., Hancock, 207/422-3990), where Torj and Kurt Wray (Russell's parents) have a magical waterfront setting and sculpture gallery. Inside is wheel-thrown, hand-painted, dishwasher-safe pottery decorated with blue-and-white motifs representing local landscapes.

Cross the Hancock–Sullivan Bridge and then take your first left off Route 1 onto Taunton Drive to find the next three galleries. Drawing from her experiences as an oil painter and from her life in Japan, Peg McAloon creates masterful one-of-a-kind quilts at **Wildfire Run Quilt Boutique** (148 Taunton Dr., Sullivan, 207/422-3935, www.maineus.com/wildfirerun).

Nearby **Lunaform** (Cedar La., West Sullivan, 207/422-0923, www.lunaform.com) is in a class by itself. First there's the setting – the beautifully landscaped grounds surrounding an abandoned granite quarry. Then there's the realization that many of the wonderfully aesthetic garden ornaments created here look like hand-turned *pottery,* when in fact they're hand turned, but made of steel-reinforced concrete. It takes a bit of zigging and zagging to get here. Go right onto Track Road; after a half mile, go left onto Cedar Lane.

Bet you can't keep from smiling at the whimsical animal sculptures and fun furniture of talented sculptor/painter Philip Barter. His work is the cornerstone of the eclectic **Barter Family Gallery** (Shore Rd., Sullivan, 207/422-3190, www.barterfamilygallery.com). But there's more: Barter's wife and seven children have put their considerable skills to work producing hooked and braided rugs, jewelry, and other craft items. Follow Taunton Road 2.5 miles from Route 1.

Continue north on Taunton Road, and it will loop around Hog Bay and onto Route 200, for the next three stops. Charles and Susanne Grosjean's **Hog Bay Pottery** (245 Hog Bay Rd., Rte. 200, Franklin, 207/565-2282) is another double treat. Inside the casual, laid-back showroom are Charles's functional, nature-themed pottery and Susanne's stunning handwoven rugs.

lobster-boat races (a serious competition in these parts), crafts fair, games, and more crustaceans than you could ever consume.

Arts and Science

The **Pierre Monteux School for Conductors and Orchestra Musicians** (Rte. 1, Hancock, 207/422-3280, www.monteuxschool.org), a prestigious summer program founded in 1943, has achieved international renown for training dozens of national and international classical musicians. It presents two well-attended concert series starting in late June and running through July. The Wednesday series (7:30 P.M., $10 adults, $5 kids) features chamber music; the Sunday concerts (5 P.M., $15 adults, $5 students) feature symphonies. An annual children's concert usually is held on a Monday

Handwoven textiles are the specialty at **Moosetrack Studio** (388 Bert Gray Rd./Rte. 200, Sullivan, 207/422-9017), where the selections vary from handwoven area rugs to shawls woven from merino wool and silk. Camilla Stege has been weaving since 1969 and her work reflects her experience and expertise.

Paul Breeden, best known for the remarkable illustrations, calligraphy, and maps he's done for *National Geographic*, Time-Life Books, and other national and international publications, displays and sells his paintings at the **Spring Woods Gallery and Willowbrook Garden** (40A Willowbrook La., Sullivan, 207/422-3007, www.springwoodsgallery.com, www.willowbrookgarden.com). Also filling the handsome modern gallery space are paintings by Ann Breeden and metal sculptures and silk scarves by the talented Breeden offspring. Be sure to allow time to meander through the sculpture garden, where there's even a playhouse for kids.

SCHOODIC PENINSULA

From Route 1, loop down to Winter Harbor and back up on Route 186 through Prospect Harbor to find these galleries.

Architectural stoneware, with a specialty in sinks, is the drawing card at **Maine Kiln Works** (115 S. Gouldsboro Rd./Hwy. 186, Gouldsboro, 207/963-5819, www.waterstonesink.com), but you'll also find functional pottery in the shop. You might also see Dan Weaver at work on the wheel in the back room.

If you're lucky, you might catch Susan Dickson-Smith throwing a pot at **Stave Island Gallery/Proper Clay Stoneware** (Rte. 186, South Gouldsboro, 207/963-2040, www.properclay.com).

An old post office houses **Lee Art Glass** (679 S. Gouldsboro Rd./Rte. 196, Gouldsboro, 207/963-7280). Although Rod Lee has died, his works live on, thanks to Wayne Tucker and Sheldon R. Bickford, who bought the business after training with Lee. The fused-glass tableware is created by taking two pieces of window glass and firing them on terra-cotta or bisque molds at 1,500°F. What makes the end result so appealing are the colors and the patterns – crocheted doilies or stencils – impressed into the glass. The almost-magical results are beautiful, delicate-looking, yet functional.

Every piece handcrafted at **Gypsy Moose Glass Studio** (Main St., Winter Harbor, 207/963-2674, www.gypsymooseglass.com) is made from a single glass rod, which means no two are alike. You'll find glass beads, fused-glass earrings, swan weather predictors, and much more.

Visiting the **U.S. Bells Foundry and Watering Cove Pottery** (56 W. Bay Rd., Rte. 186, Prospect Harbor 04669, 207/963-7184, www.usbells.com) is a treat for the ears, as browsers try out the many varieties of cast-bronze bells made in the adjacent foundry by Richard Fisher. If you're lucky, he may have time to explain the process – particularly intriguing for children and a distraction from their instinctive urge to test every bell in the shop. The store also carries quilts by Dick's wife, Cindy, and wood-fired stoneware and porcelain by their daughter-in-law Liza Fisher. U.S. Bells is 0.25 mile up the hill from Prospect Harbor's post office.

(1 P.M.) in early to mid-July. Recently, it's been scheduling concerts in August, too. All concerts are held in the school's Forest Studio.

Concerts, art classes, coffeehouses, workshops, and related activities are presented year-round by the energetic **Schoodic Arts for All** (207/963-2569, www.schoodicarts.org), a volunteer organization. Many are held at historic Hammond Hall in downtown Winter Harbor. A summer series presents monthly concerts on Friday evenings May–October. In early August, the two-week **Schoodic Arts Festival** is jam-packed with daily workshops and nightly performances for all ages. Register early for any program that you don't want to miss.

Seeking to add more vibrancy and diversity to the peninsula's entertainment offerings and to indulge their own interests in music and the sciences, the owners of Oceanside Meadows Inn created the **Innstitute for Arts and Sciences** (207/963-5557, www.oceaninn.com), which presents a series of Thursday night events late June–late September, with a break during the Schoodic Arts Festival. The calendar includes lectures and concerts as well as art shows. Some are free, others are $10 in advance or $12 at the door.

Acadia Partners (P.O. Box 277, Winter Harbor 04693, 207/288-1326, www.acadiapartners.org) is working with Acadia National Park to create a scientific research center at **Schoodic Education and Research Center,** on the old Navy base on Schoodic Point, locally called SERC. In 2007, it launched a biennial international sculpture symposium, with the aim of creating granite sculptures to place within coastal communities throughout the region.

ACCOMMODATIONS

There are no lodgings in the Schoodic section of the park, but within less than a half hour of the Schoodic parkland, you'll have your choice of an impressive range of places to sleep—from an elegant French-style country inn with a fantastic restaurant to a rustic campground with lovely wilderness sites.

Country Inns
Buffered from the highway by a tall hedge,

Le Domaine (Rte. 1, HC 77, Box 496, Hancock 04640, 207/422-3395 or 800/554-8498, www.ledomaine.com) has gained a five-star reputation for its restaurant, founded in 1946—long before fine dining had cachet here. But that's only part of the story. Above the restaurant is a charming, five-room, country-French inn. The 80-acre inn property, nine miles east of Ellsworth, is virtual Provence, an oasis transplanted magically to Maine. On the garden-view balconies, or on the lawn out back, you're oblivious to the traffic whizzing by. Better yet, follow the lovely wooded trail to a quiet pond. Three guest rooms ($285 d, including breakfast and dinner; $200 B&B) and two suites ($370 d, MAP, $285 B&B) all are named after locales in Provence. Continental breakfast, usually including freshly made croissants and jams, can be served in your room or in the dining room. Alert the inn if you'll be arriving after 5:30 P.M., when the staff has to focus on dinner. The ultra-French restaurant is open to the public 6–9 P.M. Tuesday–Sunday. Reservations are essential, especially in July and August. Le Domaine's season is mid-June–early November.

Follow Hancock Point Road 4.8 miles south of Route 1 to the three-story, gray-blue **Crocker House Country Inn** (967 Point Rd., HC 77, Box 171, Hancock 04640, 207/422-6806, www.crockerhouse.com, $110–165), Rich and Liz Malaby's antidote to Bar Harbor's summer traffic. Built as a summer hotel in 1884, the inn underwent rehabbing a century later, but it retains a decidedly old-fashioned air, although Wi-Fi is now available. Breakfast is included. Guests can relax in the common room or reserve spa time in the carriage house. One kayak and a few bicycles are available. Nearby are clay tennis courts, quiet walking routes past Hancock Point's elegant seaside "cottages," and a unique octagonal public library. The Malabys will pack picnic lunches (extra charge) for day trips to Campobello Island, Acadia, or Lamoine State Park. If you're arriving by boat, request a mooring. The inn's dining room is a draw in itself.

Bed-and-Breakfasts
Overlooking the Gouldsboro Peninsula's only

sandy saltwater beach, ◖ **Oceanside Meadows Innstitute** (Rte. 195, Corea Rd., P.O. Box 90, Prospect Harbor 04669, 207/963-5557, www.oceaninn.com, $128–198, May–late Oct.) is a jewel of a place on 200 acres with fabulous gardens, wildlife habitat, and walking trails. The elegant 1860s Captain's House has seven attractive rooms, and the 1820 Shaw farmhouse next door has another seven. Each room has a copy of Louise Dickinson Rich's *The Peninsula*—a thoughtful touch. Breakfast is an impressive four-course event, usually featuring herbs and flowers from the inn's gardens. Energetic husband-and-wife team of Sonja Sundaram and Ben Walter seem to have thought of everything—hot drinks available all day, a guest fridge, beach toys, even detailed guides to the property's trails and habitats (great for entertaining kids). As if all that weren't enough, Sonja and Ben have totally restored the 1820 timber-frame barn out back—creating the **Oceanside Meadows Innstitute for the Arts and Sciences.** Local art hangs on the walls, and June–September, the 125-seat barn has a full schedule of classical concerts and lectures on natural history, Native American traditions, and more, usually on Thursday nights. Some are free, some require tickets; all require reservations. The inn's website is also a phenomenal resource on area activities. Oceanside Meadows is six miles off Route 1.

Watch lobster boats unload their catch at the dock opposite ◖ **Elsa's Inn on the Harbor** (179 Main St., Prospect Harbor, 207/963-7571, www.elsasinn.com, $105–155). Jeffrey and Cynthia Alley, their daughter, Megan, and her husband, Glenn Moshier, and grandsons Andrew and Emmett have turned Jeff's mother Elsa's home into a warm and welcoming inn. The Alley family roots in the area go back more than 10 generations, so you're guaranteed to receive solid information on where to go and what to do. Every room has an ocean view, and Megan, an experienced innkeeper whose career included positions at Ritz-Carlton and luxury boutique hotels, pampers guests with luxurious linens, down duvets, terry robes, and a hearty hot breakfast. After a day exploring, settle into

a rocker on the veranda and gaze over the boat-filled harbor out to Prospect Harbor Light. And afterward? Well perhaps a lobster bake. Upon request, Megan's dad will bring over some fresh lobster and Megan will prepare a complete lobster dinner—corn on the cob, cole slaw, homemade rolls, and a seasonal dessert, all for about $22 pp, depending upon market rates.

Set well back from Route 1, **Acadia View Bed and Breakfast** (175 Rte. 1, Gouldsboro, 207/963-7457 or 866/963-7457, www.acadiaview.com, $135–165) is built on a bluff with views across Frenchman Bay to the peaks of Mount Desert and a path down to the shorefront. Pat and Jim Close built the oceanfront house as a B&B, opening it in 2005. The building may be new, but it's filled with antique treasures from the Closes's former life in Connecticut. Each of the four guest rooms has a private deck. The Route 1 location, while next to nothing, is convenient for everything.

Off the beaten path is Bob Travers and Barry Canner's **Black Duck Inn on Corea Harbor** (Crowley Island Rd., P.O. Box 39, Corea 04624, 207/963-2689, www.blackduck.com, $140–170, May–mid-Oct.), literally the end of the line on the Gouldsboro Peninsula. Set on 12 acres in this timeless fishing village, the B&B has four handsomely decorated rooms and plenty of common space. Across the way, perched on the harbor's edge, are two little seasonal cottages, one rented by the day (three-night minimum) and one by the week ($825–900). The inn and Corea are geared to wanderers, readers, and anyone seeking serenity (who isn't?). Rocky outcrops dot the property and a nature trail meanders to a millpond; in early August, the blueberries are ready. If the fog socks in, the large parlor has comfortable chairs and loads of books.

Something of a categorical anomaly, **The Bluff House Inn** (Rte. 186, P.O. Box 249, Gouldsboro 04607, 207/963-7805, www.bluffinn.com, $65–100) is part motel, part hotel, part B&B—a seemingly successful mix in a contemporary building overlooking Frenchman Bay on the west side of the Gouldsboro Peninsula. Verandas wrap around the first and second floors, so bring binoculars for osprey and bald eagle sightings. Pine walls and flooring give a lodge feeling to the open first floor. Settle by the stone fireplace or grab a seat by the window. Breakfast, a generous continental with excellent baked goodies, is served here. The eight second-floor rooms are decorated "country" fashion, with quilts on the very comfortable beds. (In hot weather, request a corner room.) Also available is a two-bedroom housekeeping apartment ($120/day or $670/week) built above a garage. It's open all year.

The White Elephant Inn (25 Main St./Rte. 182, Franklin, 207/565-2020, $90) is anything but. Owner Dana Geel, a history teacher and lover of all things old and odd, has filled his circa 1830 Colonial farmhouse overlooking Hog Bay with antique treasures highlighted by his collection of 5,000 (!) elephants. Dana's owned a number of houses on Mount Desert and has amassed a collection of notable antiques in the process, including some furnishings from the estate of Evalyn Walsh McLean, one-time owner of the Hope diamond, and even a camel table—this you simply must see. Public rooms ramble from one to another, varying from formal ones to a cozy den. A full breakfast is served. Dana knows the region well and has even opened an info center in the barn.

Sustainable living is the focus of Karen and Ed Curtis's peaceful ❰ **Three Pines Bed and Breakfast** (HC 77, Box 349AA, Hancock 04640, 207/460-7595, www.threepinesbandb.com, $85–115, year-round), fronting on Sullivan Harbor, just below the Reversing Falls. Their quiet, off-the-grid, oceanfront farm faces Sullivan Harbor and is home to llamas, pigs, chickens, and ducks, as well as a large organic garden, berry bushes, a developing orchard, and greenhouses. Photovoltaics provide electricity; appliances are primarily propane powered; satellite technology operates the phone, TV, and Internet systems. Two inviting guest rooms have private entrances and waterviews. A full vegetarian breakfast (with fresh eggs from the farm available) is served. Bring kayaks or bikes. You can walk or pedal along an abandoned railway line down to the point or up to

the lobster pound, and you can launch your kayak from the back—or is it the front—yard. Children welcome; pets are a possibility.

Sorrento is such a low-key place that lots of people don't realize it has a B&B, an ultracasual homestay-style one at that. **Bass Cove Farm Bed and Breakfast** (312 Eastside Rd., Rte. 185, Sorrento, 207/422-3564, www.basscovefarm.com, $65–100) was opened in 1992 by spinner/weaver/gardener/editor Mary Ann Solet and her husband, Michael Tansey, a group-home supervisor whose résumé also includes the Harry S. Truman Manure Pitchoff Championship at the annual Common Ground Country Fair. The 1840s-era farmhouse uses solar-heated water; the cleaning is done with nontoxic products. Mary Ann can rattle off dozens of ideas for exploring the area, particularly in the craft department, and she raids her extensive vegetable garden daily to produce a hearty, healthful breakfast. Guest rooms have quilt-covered beds and other homey touches—some share baths. A one-bedroom apartment on the second floor rents for $375–395 a week.

Cottages

Roger and Pearl Barto, whose family roots in this region go back five generations, have four rental accommodations on their Henry's Cove oceanfront property, **Main Stay Cottages** (66 Sargent St., P.O. Box 459, Winter Harbor 04693, 207/963-2601, www.awa-web.com/stayinn, $80–115). Most unusual is the small, one-bedroom Boat House, which has stood since the 1880s. It hangs over the harbor, with views to Mark Island Light, and you can hear the water gurgling below you at high tide. Other options include a very comfortable efficiency cottage, a one-bedroom cottage, and a second-floor suite, with private entrance, in the main house. All have big decks and fabulous views over the lobster boat–filled harbor; watch for the eagles that frequently soar overhead. Main Stay is on the Island Explorer route and just a short walk from where the Bar Harbor Ferry docks.

Rustic, but charming in a sweet, old-fashioned way, are **Albee's Cottages** (Rte. 186,

Prospect Harbor, 207/963-2336 or 800/963-2336, www.theshorehouse.com, $73–114/night, May–late Sept.), a cluster of 10 somewhat ramshackle cottages, decorated with braided rugs, fresh flowers, and other homey touches. Two things make this place special: the waterfront location—and it's truly waterfront; many of the cottages are just a couple of feet from the high-tide mark—and the management. Owner Richard Rieth goes out of his way to make guests feel welcome. Pick up lobsters and say what time you want dinner, and they'll be cooked and delivered to your cottage. Richard sometimes brings home-baked sweets and other treats to cottages when he has the time and inclination. He's slowly fixing up the simple cottages, first tackling much-needed new roofs and exterior painting. Now he's updating the interiors. In peak season, cottages rent on a Saturday-to-Saturday basis, but shorter rentals are often available. Dogs allowed.

Campgrounds

On a wooded finger of land projecting eastward from the Schoodic Peninsula, **(Ocean Wood Campground** (P.O. Box 111, Birch Harbor 04613, 207/963-7194, early May–late Oct.) gets kudos for eco-sensitivity, noise control, and 17 fantastic wilderness sites, most on the ocean. Don't expect frills; nature provides the entertainment. The 70 campsites (20 with hookups) are $20–39, depending on location and services. Pets (leashed) and guests are allowed at regular sites, but not at the wilderness ones. No credit cards; free hot showers. The campground is a terrific base for exploring the Schoodic section of Acadia National Park. (Note, however, that the campground is at the *end* of the one-way Schoodic Loop Road. It's no problem hiking back into the park area the wrong way, but if you're driving or biking, you'll need to go around, about five miles, via Route 186, to do the loop.)

Donnell Pond Public Reserved Land

A handful of authorized, primitive campsites can be found on Tunk Lake (southwestern corner) and Donnell Pond (at Schoodic Beach and Redman's Beach), all accessible by foot or boat. Each has a table, fire ring, and nearby pit toilet. Many of the sites are lakefront. All are first-come, first-served (no fees or permits required), and are snapped up quickly on midsummer weekends. You can camp elsewhere within the unit, excepting day-use areas, but fires are not permitted on unauthorized sites.

FOOD
Local Flavors

Make a point to attend one of the many **public suppers** held throughout the summer in this area and so many other rural corners of Maine. Typically benefiting a worthy cause, these usually feature beans, chowder, or spaghetti and the serendipity of plain potluck. Everyone saves room for the homemade pies. Notices of such suppers are usually posted on public bulletin boards in country stores and in libraries, on signs in front of churches, and at other places people gather.

Delicious soups and sandwiches, baked goods, and a nice selection of prepared foods are available at **Mano's Market** (1517 Rte. 1, Hancock, 207/422-6500, 7 A.M.–6 P.M. Tues.–Sat.), a gourmet and prepared foods and wine market.

Pick up veggies, meats, eggs, cheeses, and handcrafted fiber products as well as jams, preserves, and baked goods at the **Winter Harbor Farmers Market** (parking lot, corner Newman St. and Rte. 186, Winter Harbor, 9 A.M.–noon Tues. late June–early Sept.).

Once a true, old-fashioned country store with a classic traditional soda fountain and penny candy, **J. M. Gerrish Provisions** (352 Main St., Winter Harbor, 207/963-2727, 8 A.M.–8 P.M. daily), known as Gerrish's Store, has undergone many changes in recent years. It's now an upscale specialty-foods store, coffee bar with Wi-Fi, ice-cream parlor, and café, but that might change under new ownership.

Craving curry? Call in your order before 3 P.M., and **Tandoor Downeast** (Eastbrook Rd., Franklin, 207/565-3598, www.tandoordowneast.com) will prepare authentic Indian cuisine for you to take away. The menu is extensive, and prices are reasonable, with most choices $6–8. A selection is usually also available at the Winter Harbor Farmers Market.

Family Fare

The best place for grub and gossip in Winter Harbor is **Chase's Restaurant** (193 Main St., Winter Harbor, 207/963-7171, 7 A.M.–8 P.M., to 2 P.M. Sun.), a seasoned, no-frills booth-and-counter operation that turns out first-rate fish chowder, fries, and onion rings, wraps, home-style dinners, and downright cheap breakfasts.

In "downtown" Prospect Harbor, the **Downeast Deli** (corner Rtes. 186 and 195, Prospect Harbor, 207/963-2700, 11 A.M.–7 P.M. Sun.–Thurs., to 8 P.M. Fri.–Sat.) will fix you right up with dozens of sandwich choices: hot or cold hoagies, hot dogs and burgers, Reubens, deli-style sandwiches, and good pizza with a wide array of mix-and-match choices.

Don't be put off by the lobster "sculpture" outside **Ruth and Wimpy's Kitchen** (792 Rte. 1, Hancock, 207/422-3723, 11 A.M.–9 P.M. daily Apr.–Dec.); you'll probably see a crowd as well. This family-fare standby serves hefty sandwiches, lobster prepared in 30 ways, pizza, pasta, and steak. Prices begin at less than $3 for a cheeseburger and climb to about $25 for a twin-tail lobster dinner. Locals praise the lobster roll as the cheapest and best around. Antique license plates and collections of miniature cars and trucks accent the interior. It's five miles east of Ellsworth, close to the Hancock Point turnoff.

Good food served by friendly folks is what pulls the locals into ◖ **Chester Pike's Galley** (2236 Rte. 1, Sullivan, 207/422-8200, 6 A.M.–2 P.M. Mon.–Sat., opens at 7 A.M. Sun., and 4:30–8:30 P.M. Fri. and Sat.). The prices are low, the portions big. If you're on a diet, don't even *look* at the glass case filled with fresh-baked pies, cakes, and cookies. Go early if you want to snag one of the homemade doughnuts (and order dessert first). It's also open Friday nights for a fish fry with free seconds, and Saturday nights for roast beef.

Casual Dining

Make it a point to find **Bunkers Wharf** (260 E. Schoodic Dr., Birch Harbor, 207/963-2244, www.bunkerswharfrestaurant.com, 11:30 A.M.–10 P.M. daily), just one mile from the end of the Schoodic loop. The dining room overlooks a working wharf, and there's a big stone fireplace to ward off the chill on inclement days. Crisp white linens and fresh flowers add a formal touch in the dining room, yet the feeling is unpretentious. You can also dine in the pub or on a patio that's practically in the harbor. Only drawback: Dinners are pricey: entrées are $18 and up. Open seasonally.

The Fisherman's Inn (7 Newman St., Rte. 186, Winter Harbor, 207/963-5585, 5–9 P.M. daily late May–mid-Oct.), established in 1947, has had a roller-coaster history, with good phases and bad ones. It's now under the ownership of Kathy Johnson and her award-winning chef/husband, Carl. The only remaining tradition seems to be the "gourmet cheese spread" served to every table—but you'll also have a sample of salmon pâté from Carl's latest venture, Grindstone Neck of Maine. Seafood is the specialty here, and there's a good chance that the guy at the neighboring booth caught your lobster or fish. Asian influences are evident, too. Entrée range is $14–25, although some dishes can top that given seasonal market rates.

It's easy to miss **Chipper's** (Rte. 1, Hancock, 207/422-8238, 5–9 P.M., closed Sun.–Mon.), a simple Cape-style building hard by Route 1, but that would be a mistake. Chip definitely knows his way around the kitchen. The wide-ranging menu includes rack of lamb and even chateaubriand, but the emphasis is on seafood; the crab cakes earn their rave reviews. Meals include a sampling of tasty haddock chowder and a salad, but save room for the homemade ice cream for dessert. Entrées are in the $16–30 range, but some appetizer/salad combo options provide budget options.

Fine Dining

The ultra-French restaurant ◖ **Le Domaine** (1515 Rte. 1, P.O. Box 519, Hancock 04640, 207/422-3395 or 800/544-8498, www.le domaine.com, Tues.–Sat. mid-June–early Nov.) has gained a five-star reputation.

Although ownership changed in 2005, the same crew is in the kitchen and the menu remains trés French. The restaurant is equally renowned for its 5,000-bottle wine cellar and lovely Provençal decor. Reservations are essential, especially in July and August. Opt for the five-course fixed-price menu for $35; otherwise the tab may dent your budget (entrées $22–31), but stack that up against plane fare to France.

The unpretentious dining rooms at the **Crocker House Country Inn** (967 Point Rd., Hancock Point, 207/422-6806, www.crocker house.com, 5:30–9 P.M.) provide a setting for well-prepared, continental fare with flair, crafted from fresh and local ingredients (entrées $22–32) and Sunday brunch (11 A.M.–2 P.M.); reservations are essential as this is one of the area's most consistent and popular dining spots. The dining room is open daily May 1–October 31 and Thursday–Sunday in April, November, and December.

Lobster in the Rough

Thank the Ellsworth-based Frenchman Bay Conservancy for buying the four-acre **Tidal Falls Preserve** (off Eastside Rd., Hancock), overlooking Frenchman Bay's only reversing falls (roiling water when the tide turns), and opening it to public access. When a half-century-old lobster pound went on the market a few years ago, the conservancy hastened into action, raised more than half a million dollars, and bought the property. Today, a dozen picnic tables on the lawn overlook the falls, and seals often haul out on nearby ledges. There's also a screened-in dining pavilion and free Wi-Fi. It's an idyllic spot. ◖ **Tidal Falls Lobster Pound** (207/422-6457, 11 A.M.–8:30 P.M. daily late May–early Sept.) leases the site. Come for the lobster (pricey for a lobster shack, but the view makes up for it); landlubbers will find a wood-fired barbecue smoker disguised as a train (really!). Order at the window and then grab a seat. BYOB. Eastside Road is off Route 1 (on your right, if you're heading north) just south of the Hancock–Sullivan bridge; follow it one mile and look for a sign on your left. Follow the gravel road to the end.

INFORMATION AND SERVICES

For advance information about the region, contact the Schoodic Peninsula Chamber of Commerce (P.O. Box 381, Winter Harbor 04693, 207/963-7658, www.acadia-schoodic.org) and request its handy map and brochure, revised annually. For information on the National and Maine Scenic Byways in this region, visit www .byways.org or www.exploremaine.org/byways.

Check out Dorcas Library (Rte. 186, Prospect Harbor, 207/963-4027, www.dorcas.lib .me.us) or Winter Harbor Public Library (18 Chapel La., Winter Harbor, 207/963-7556, www.winterharbor.lib.me.us). The octagonal Hancock Point Library (207/422-6400), formed in 1899, is a center for village activities. Check the bulletin boards by the entrance to find out what's happening when.

GETTING AROUND

The **Bar Harbor Ferry** (207/288-2984, www .barharborferry.com, round-trip $29.50 adult, $19.50 child, $6 bike), owned by Captain Steve Pagels (who also operates the four-masted schooner *Margaret Todd* and ferry service to the Cranberry Isles), runs his Bar Harbor–to–Winter Harbor, passenger-only ferry late June–late September. You can board the ferry with a bike in Bar Harbor (at the Bar Harbor Inn pier), disembark in Winter Harbor (at Winter Harbor Marine, on Sargent St.), pedal the short distance to Schoodic, then bike the Schoodic Loop Road, and return later to Bar Harbor on the ferry (last boat is 5 P.M.). The ferry departs Bar Harbor on even hours 8 A.M.–6 P.M., returning on odd hours from Winter Harbor 9 A.M.–5 P.M. (no ferry after 4 P.M. in Sept.).

Since the ferry's summer schedule is coordinated with the free **Island Explorer** (www .exploreacadia.com) bus's summertime Schoodic route, you can board the ferry in Bar Harbor, pick up the bus at the dock in Winter Harbor, and be shuttled along the Schoodic Loop. Stop where you like for a picnic and then board a later bus. Take the last bus back to the ferry and return to Bar Harbor. It's super car-free excursion!

THE DOWN EAST COAST

"Down East," people say, is the direction the wind blows—the prevailing southwest wind that powered 19th-century sailing vessels along this rugged coastline. But to be truly Down East, in the minds of most Mainers, you have to be physically here, in Washington County—a stunning landscape of waterways, forests, blueberry barrens, rocky shoreline dotted with islands and lighthouses, and independent, pocket-size communities, many still dependent upon fishing or lobstering for their economies.

At one time, *most* of the Maine coast used to be as underdeveloped as this part of it. You can set your clock back a generation or two while you're here; you'll find no giant malls and only a couple of fast-food joints. While there are a handful of restaurants offering fine dining, for the most part, your choices are limited to family-style restaurants specializing in home cooking with an emphasis on fresh (usually fried) seafood and lobster rolls. Nor will you find grand resorts or even not-so-grand hotels. Motels, tourist cabins, and small inns and B&Bs dot the region. The upside is that prices, too, are a generation removed. If you're searching for Maine of your memories or your imagination, this is it.

When eastern Hancock County flows into western Washington County, you're on the Down East Coast (also called the Sunrise Coast). From Steuben eastward to Jonesport, Machias, and Lubec—then "around the corner" to Eastport, and Calais—Washington County is twice the size of Rhode Island, covers 2,528 square miles, has about 35,000 residents, and stakes a claim as the first U.S.

© HILARY NANGLE

HIGHLIGHTS

◖ Maine Coastal Islands National Wildlife Refuge: More than 300 birds have been sighted at Petit Manan Point, but even if you're not a birder, come for the hiking and, in August, the blueberries (page 353).

◖ Great Wass Island Preserve: The finest natural treasure in this part of Maine is the Great Wass Archipelago, partly owned by The Nature Conservancy, with opportunities for hiking and birding (page 357).

◖ Machias Seal Island Puffin Tour: Excursion boats depart from Jonesport and Cutler for Machias Seal Island, home to Atlantic puffins (the clowns of the sea), as well as razorbill auks, Arctic terns, and common murres (pages 359 and 366).

◖ West Quoddy Head State Park: The candy-striped lighthouse is a Maine Coast icon and even a short hike along the paths edging the cliffs reaps big rewards (page 369).

◖ Roosevelt Campobello International Park: Make it an international vacation by venturing over to this New Brunswick park, home to the Roosevelt Cottage and miles of hiking trails, jointly managed by the United States and Canada (page 374).

◖ Shackford Head State Park: The reward for this easy hike are panoramic views over Cobscook Bay, from Eastport to Campobello (page 379).

◖ Downeast Heritage Center: Put your visit Downeast into perspective in one stop at this engaging museum that explores the people, history, economy, and environment of Washington County (page 386).

LOOK FOR ◖ TO FIND RECOMMENDED SIGHTS, ACTIVITIES, DINING, AND LODGING.

real estate to see the morning sun. The region also includes handfuls of offshore islands—some accessible by ferry, charter boat, or private vessels. (Some, with sensitive bird-nesting sites, are off-limits during the summer.) At the uppermost point of the coast, and conveniently linked to Lubec by a bridge, New Brunswick's Campobello Island is a popular day-trip destination—the locale of Franklin D. Roosevelt's summer retreat. Other attractions in this area include festivals, concert series, art and antique galleries, lighthouses, two Native American

reservations, and the great outdoors for hiking, biking, birding, sea kayaking, whale-watching, camping, swimming, and fishing. Hook inland to Grand Lake Stream to find a remote, wild land of lakes famed for fishing and old-fashioned family-style summer vacations.

One natural phenomenon no visitor can affect is the tide—the inexorable ebb and flow, predictably in and predictably out. If you're not used to it, even the six- to 10-foot tidal ranges of southern Maine may surprise you. But along this coastline, the tides are astonishing—as much as

THE DOWN EAST COAST

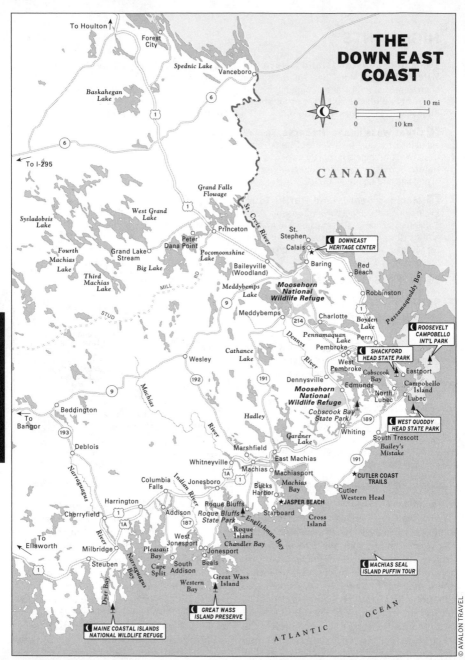

THE DOWN EAST COAST

CANADA

© AVALON TRAVEL

28 feet of difference in water level within six hours. Old-timers tell stories of big money lost betting on horses racing the fast-moving tides.

Another surprise to visitors may be how early the sun rises—and sets—on the Sunrise Coast. Keep in mind that if you cross into Canada in either Lubec or Calais, you enter Atlantic time, and you'll need to set your clock ahead one hour.

Yet another distinctive natural feature of Washington County is its blueberry barrens (fields). Depending on the time of year, the fields will be black (torched by growers to jump-start the crop), blue (ready for harvest), or maroon (fall foliage, fabulous for photography). In early summer, a million rented bees set to work pollinating the blossoms. By August, when a blue haze forms over the knee-high shrubs, bent-over bodies use old-fashioned wooden rakes to harvest the ripe berries. It's backbreaking work, but the employment lines usually form quickly when newspaper ads announce the advent of the annual harvest.

One bit of advice you might not receive from the tourism people is that warm clothing is essential in this corner of Maine. It may be nicknamed the Sunrise Coast, but it also gets plenty of fog, rain, and cool temperatures. Temperatures tend to be warmer, and the fog diminishes, as you head toward the inland parts of the county, but you can *never* count on that. Mother Nature is an accomplished curveball pitcher, and el Niño and la Niña periodically provide an assist.

PLANNING YOUR TIME

Downeast Maine is not for those in a hurry. Traffic ambles along. Towns are few and far between. Nature is the biggest calling card here, and to appreciate it, you'll need time to hike, bike, canoe, sea kayak, or take an excursion boat. Although Route 1 follows the coast in general, it's often miles from the water. You'll want to ramble down the peninsulas to explore the seaside villages, see lighthouses, or hike in parks and preserves, and perhaps wander inland to the unspoiled lakes. You'll need at least three days to begin to cover the territory, ideally five days or longer if you want to really explore it.

Milbridge

The pace begins to slow a bit by the time you've left Hancock County and entered western Washington County, the beginning of the Down East Coast. In this little pocket are the towns of Steuben, Milbridge, Cherryfield, and Harrington.

Life can be tough here nowadays, where once great wooden ships slid down the ways and brought prosperity and trade to shippers, builders, and barons of the timber industry. Cherryfield's stunning houses are evidence enough. The barons now control the blueberry fields, covering much of the inland area of western Washington County and annually shipping millions of pounds of blueberries out of headquarters in Milbridge (pop. 1,330) and Cherryfield (pop. 1,200). The big names here are Jasper Wyman and Sons and Cherryfield Foods.

Milbridge straddles Route 1 and the Narraguagus River (Nar-ra-GWAY-gus, a Native American name meaning "above the boggy place"), once the state's premier source of Atlantic salmon. Cherryfield is at the tidal limit of the Narraguagus. Even though Route 1A trims maybe three miles off the trip from Milbridge to Harrington (pop. 900), resist the urge to take it. Take Route 1 from Milbridge to Cherryfield—the Narraguagus Highway—and then continue to Harrington. You just shouldn't miss Cherryfield.

Steuben's claim to fame is the Petit Manan section of the Maine Coastal Islands National Wildlife Refuge.

SIGHTS
◖ Maine Coastal Islands National Wildlife Refuge

Occupying a 2,166-acre peninsula in Steuben with 10 miles of rocky shoreline (and three offshore islands) is the refuge's outstandingly scenic Petit Manan Point Division (Pigeon Hill Rd., Steuben, mailing address P.O. Box 279, Milbridge 04658, 207/546-2124, www.fws .gov/northeast/mainecoastal). The remote location means it sees only about 15,000 visitors a year, most of those likely birders, as more than 250 different birds have been sighted here. The refuge's primary focus is restoring colonies of nesting seabirds. Among the other natural highlights here are stands of jack pine, coastal raised peatlands, blueberry barrens, fresh- and saltwater marshes, granite shores, and cobble beaches. When asking directions locally, you'll hear it called 'tit Manan.

The moderately easy, four-mile round-trip Birch Point Trail and easy, 1.5-mile round-trip Hollingsworth or Shore Trail provide splendid views and opportunities to spot wildlife along the shore and in the fields, forests, and marshland. The Hollingsworth Trail, leading you to the shoreline, is the best. This is foggy territory, but on clear days, you can see the 123-foot lighthouse on Petit Manan Island, 2.5 miles offshore. The Birch Point Trail heads through blueberry fields to Dyer Bay and loops by the waterfront, with much of the trail passing through woods. If you arrive in August, help yourself to blueberries. The refuge is open sunrise–sunset daily all year; cross-country skiing is permitted in winter.

Milbridge Historical Society Museum

A group of energetic residents worked tirelessly to establish the Milbridge Historical Society Museum (S. Main St., Milbridge, 207/546-4471, www.milbridgehistoricalsociety.org, 1–4 P.M. Sat. and Sun. June and Sept., and Tues. July and Aug., donations accepted). Displays in the large exhibit room focus on Milbridge's essential role in the shipbuilding trade, but kids will enjoy such oddities as an amputation knife used by a local doctor and a re-created country kitchen.

Scenic Fall-Foliage Routes

In fall—roughly early September–early October

in this part of Maine—the postharvest blueberry fields take on brilliant scarlet hues, then maroon. They're gorgeous. The best barren-viewing road is Route 193 between Cherryfield and Beddington, via Deblois, the link between Routes 1 and 9—a 21-mile stretch of granite outcrops, pine windscreens, and fiery-red fields.

Cherryfield Historic District

Imagine a little town this far Down East having a 75-acre National Register Historic District with 52 architecturally significant buildings. If architecture appeals, don't miss Cherryfield. The **Cherryfield-Narraguagus Historical Society** (P.O. Box 96, Cherryfield 04622) has produced a free brochure/map, *Guide to the Cherryfield Historic District,* which you can obtain in advance or pick up once you get here. Architectural styles included on the route are Greek Revival, Italianate, Queen Anne, Colonial Revival, Second Empire, Federal, and Gothic Revival—dating from 1803 to 1940, with most being late 19th century. Especially

Cherryfield's National Historic District has 52 architecturally significant buildings.

impressive for such a small town are the Second Empire–style homes.

BOATING EXCURSIONS

Captain Jaime Robertson's **Robertson Sea Tours and Adventures** (Milbridge Marina, Fickett's Point Rd., 207/546-3883 or 207/461-7439, www.robertsonseatours.com, May 15–Oct. 1) offers a puffin and seabird cruise to Petit Manan Island, a scenic island cruise, a lobstering cruise, and others from Milbridge aboard the *Mairi Leigh,* a classic Maine lobster boat. The puffins and seabirds cruise lasts three hours and is $60 for adults, $45 for kids 12 and younger, with a $150 boat minimum. The island cruise ($50 for adults, $35 for kids, $125 boat minimum) lasts 2–2.5 hours, passes seven islands, and highlights the region's aquaculture industry. The lobstering cruise lasts 1.5–2 hours and costs $30 per adult, $20 per child, with an $80 boat minimum. An option includes a lobster lunch ($75 adult, $50 kids, boat minimum $200), complete with a steamed lobster served aboard. All cruises depart from the Milbridge Marina and require reservations.

Captains Harry "Buzzy" and Esther Shinn's **Downeast Coastal Cruises** (207/546-7720 or cell 207/598-7740, www.downeastcoastal cruises.com) depart from the Milbridge Landing aboard the comfortable *Alyce K.* for island cruises, lobster cruises (complete with meal), sunset cruises, and charters. Cruises last 2–4 hours and cost $45–75 per adult, $35–65 per child; boat minimums apply. Both Shinns have seawater flowing through their veins.

SHOPPING

Arthur Smith (Rogers Point Rd., Steuben, 207/546-3462) is the real thing when it comes to chainsaw carvings. He's an extremely talented folk artist who looks at a piece of wood and sees an animal in it. His carvings of great blue herons, eagles, wolves, porcupines, flamingoes, and other creatures are incredibly detailed, and his wife, Marie, paints them in lifelike colors. Don't expect a fancy studio; much of the work can be viewed roadside.

Also in Steuben, but on the other end of the spectrum, is **Ray Carbone** (460 Pigeon Hill Rd., Steuben, 207/546-2170), whose masterful wood, stone, and bronze sculptures and fine furniture are definitely worth stopping to see, if not buy. Don't miss the granite sculptures and bird baths in the garden.

ENTERTAINMENT AND EVENTS

The biggest event in this end of Washington County, and even beyond, is the **Milbridge Anniversary Celebration,** the last weekend in July, drawing hundreds of visitors. The Saturday-afternoon highlight is the codfish relay race—hilarious enough to have been featured in *Sports Illustrated* and on national television. The four-member teams, clad in slickers and hip boots, *really do* hand off a greased cod instead of the usual baton. Race rules specify that runners must be "reasonably sober" and not carry the codfish between their teeth or legs. Also on the schedule are blueberry pancake breakfasts, a fun parade, kids' games, auction, dance, beano and cribbage tournaments, craft booths, and a lobster bake. You have to be there. The relay race has been going since the mid-1980s; the festival has been going for a century and a half.

Check locally for the concert schedule of the **Cherryfield Band,** an impressive community group with about three dozen enthusiastic members. They're in demand May–December, but best of all are their concerts, usually Tuesday evenings, in the lovely downtown bandstand overlooking the Narraguagus River.

The Humboldt Field Research Institute (59 Eagle Hill Rd., Steuben, 207/546-2821, www.eaglehill.us, 7:30 P.M. Thurs. early July–late Aug., free) offers lectures, sometimes preceded by optional dinners (fee), by guest lecturers, authors, and scholars on wide-ranging, usually scientific topics. Call for the current schedule. The institute is four miles off Route 1. Take Dyer Bay Road off Route 1, bearing left at the fork onto Mogador Road for a total of 3.6 miles, then left on Schooner Point Road, then right on Eagle Hill Road. Programs take place in the dining hall lecture room. Most are free.

ACCOMMODATIONS
Bed-and-Breakfasts and Motels

One of Cherryfield's 52 Historic Register buildings, the 1793 Archibald-Adams House is now the **Englishman's Bed and Breakfast** (122 Main St., Cherryfield, 207/546-2337, www.englishmansbandb.com, $95–155). The magnificently restored Federal-style home borders the Narraguagus River and makes a superb base for exploring inland and Down East Maine. The lovely grounds have gardens and a screened-in gazebo. Owners Peter (the Englishman) and Kathy Winham are archaeologists and serious tea drinkers—they also sell fine teas online (www.teasofcherryfield.com) and in area specialty stores; afternoon tea is a treat (reservation required). Two guest rooms in the main house have river views. One has a private half bath but shares a full bath. A riverside guesthouse, built in the 1990s, melds beautifully with the inn's architecture and is self-catering; pets are allowed here for $7 per night.

Another B&B in a historic Federal-style house bordering the Narraguagus River is the 1803 **Ricker House** (49 Park St., Cherryfield, 207/546-9737, $75 d, $65 s), in one of the town's five oldest buildings. Jean and Bill Conway are enthusiastic hosts who welcome visitors into their comfy home and serve a full breakfast. Two guest rooms share one bath. Pore over the *Adventures* book in the living room or relax on the screened-in porch. It's a fine base for taking a stroll around the neighborhood of historical homes. No credit cards.

Campgrounds

Since 1958, the Ayers family has opened its quiet, well-off-the-beaten-path property on Joy Cove to campers. **Mainayr Campground** (321 Village Rd., Steuben, 207/542-2690, www.mainayr.com) has 35 tenting and RV sites, which go for $25–30, depending on type and hookups. Also on the premises are a playground, laundry, beach for tidal swimming, camp store, berries for picking, and fresh lobsters. If that's not enough, David Ayr enjoys regaling campers with stories.

Covering seven acres on the tidal Harrington River, Kurt and Patsy Petzold's small, low-key **Sunset Point Campground** (102 Marshville Rd., Harrington, 207/483-4412, www.sunsetpointcampground.com, May 15–Oct. 15) has 30 open sites ($16 tent sites, $22–26 RV sites), a playground, free Wi-Fi, laundry facility, and saltwater swimming. Lobster, clams, and clams usually are available, either live or cooked. Leashed pets are allowed. From Route 1, east of Harrington, take the road toward Marshville for 2.8 miles; the campground is on the right.

FOOD
Local Flavors

You can easily pick up enough goodies for a picnic lunch or to stock a cottage kitchen at the **Milbridge Farmers Market** (Milbridge Market parking lot, Main St., Milbridge, 9 A.M.–noon Sat. early June–early Oct.). Choose from fresh baked goods, goat cheese, organic veggies and meats, and eggs as well as wool products, soaps, and skin lotions. Go early for the best selection.

"Where rich espresso meets fattening pastries" is the motto at the artsy-themed and curiously named **Chicamoose Café** (1 N. Main St., Milbridge, 207/546-7495). Local artwork is featured, and open mic nights are occasionally held. A small selection of sandwiches is offered daily in this casual place—settle into a sofa or at a table. Free Wi-Fi.

Cinnamon doughnut muffins are just one reason to dip off Route 1 to **Wildflour Bakery** (314 Village Rd., Steuben, 207/546-0978, 8 A.M.–noon Wed., Thurs., and Sat.), a tiny bakery with some seating offering good breads, English muffins, and other goodies.

If you're heading out to Petit Manan Wildlife Refuge, trust me on this. Ignore the exterior and venture into **Country Charm** (336 Village Rd., Steuben, 207/546-3763, 5:30 A.M.–8 P.M., until 7 P.M. Sun.). The fried fish is fabulously fresh, crispy, light, and cheap, even by local standards. You easily can get out of here for less than $10 pp, far less if you're on a tight budget. The original dining room has, well, country charm (sit here if you want to listen in on the local gossip); the newer ones (added when a real kitchen replaced the original blue trailer) are purely functional. Hungry? Order the Charm Special: two eggs, bacon, sausages, pancakes, toast, and coffee all for a whopping $5; omelettes begin at $2.50.

Casual Dining

Best choice is **44 Degrees North** (17 Main St., Milbridge, 207/546-4440, www.44-degrees -north.com, 11 A.M.–8 P.M., Fri.–Sat. to 9 P.M.). The front room is family oriented, with booths, tables, and cheerful decor. The back room doubles as a bar and has a big-screen TV. Expect good home cooking, with a few surprises and, as is usually the case in this part of Maine, mouthwatering desserts. Prices top out at $15 for the house specialty, seafood lasagna. The pub side opens daily at 11 A.M. and stays open through "last call."

INFORMATION

The best source for area info is the Machias Bay Area Chamber of Commerce (207/255-4402, www.machiaschamber.org).

Jonesport/Beals Area

Between western Washington County and the Machias Bay area is the molar-shaped Jonesport Peninsula, reached from the west via the attractive little town of Columbia Falls, bordering Route 1. Rounding the peninsula are the picturesque towns of Addison, Jonesport, and Beals Island, and less scenic Jonesboro. First settled around 1762, Columbia Falls (pop. about 550) still has a handful of houses dating from the late 18th century, but its best-known structure is the early-19th-century Ruggles House.

On the banks of the Pleasant River, just south of Columbia Falls, Addison (pop. 1,150) once had four huge shipyards cranking out wooden cargo vessels that circled the world. Since that 19th-century heyday, little seems to have changed, and the town today may be best known as the haunt of painter John Marin, who first came to Maine in 1914.

Jonesport and Beals Island, with a combined population of about 2,185, are traditional hardworking fishing communities—old-fashioned, friendly, and photogenic. Beals, connected to Jonesport via an arched bridge over Moosabec Reach, is named for Manwarren Beal Jr. and his wife, Lydia, who arrived around 1773 and quickly threw themselves into the Revolutionary War effort. But that's not all they did—the current phone book covering Jonesport and Beals Island lists dozens of

Beal descendants (as well as dozens of Alleys and Carvers, other early names).

Even more memorable than Manwarren Beal was his six-foot, seven-inch descendent Barnabas, dubbed "Tall Barney" for obvious reasons. The larger-than-life fellow became the stuff of legend all along the Maine coast—and a popular Jonesport restaurant preserves his name.

Also legendary here is the lobster-boat design known as the Jonesport hull. People from away won't recognize its distinctive shape, but count on the fishing pros to know it. The harbor here is jam-packed with Jonesport lobster boats, and souped-up versions are consistent winners in the summertime lobster-boat-race series.

SIGHTS
◖ Great Wass Island Preserve

Allow a whole day to explore 1,579-acre Great Wass Island, an extraordinary preserve, even when it's drenched in fog—a not-infrequent event. Owned by The Nature Conservancy (Fort Andross, 14 Maine St., Brunswick, 207/729-5181), the preserve is at the tip of Jonesport's peninsula. Easiest hiking routes are the wooded, two-mile Little Cape Point and 1.5-mile Mud Hole Trails, retracing your path for each. (Making a loop by connecting the two along the rocky shoreline adds considerably to the time and difficulty, but do it if you have time; allow about six hours and wear waterproof

THE DOWN EAST COAST

footwear.) Expect to see beach-head iris (like a blue flag) and orchids, jack pine, a peat bog, seals, pink granite, pitcher plants, lots of warblers, and maybe some grouse. Carry water and a picnic; wear bug repellent. No camping, fires, or pets; no toilet facilities. Daytime access only. To reach the preserve from Route 1, take Route 187 to Jonesport (12 miles) and then cross the arched bridge to Beals Island. Continue across Beals to the Great Wass causeway (locally called "the Flying Place") and then go three miles on Black Duck Cove Road to the parking area (on the left). Watch for The Nature Conservancy oak-leaf symbol. At the parking area, pick up a trail map and a bird checklist.

Ruggles House

Behind a picket fence on a quiet street in Columbia Falls stands the remarkable Ruggles House (Main St., P.O. Box 99, Columbia Falls 04623, 207/483-4637, www.ruggleshouse .org, 9:30 A.M.–4:30 P.M. Mon.–Sat., 11 A.M.–4:30 P.M. Sun. June 1–Oct. 15, $5 adults, $2 children). Built in 1818 for Judge Thomas Ruggles—lumber baron, militia captain, even postmaster—the tiny house on a grand scale boasts a famous flying (unsupported) staircase, intricately carved moldings, Palladian window, and unusual period furnishings. Rescued in the mid-20th century and maintained by the Ruggles House Society, this gem has become a magnet for savvy preservationists. A quarter mile east of Route 1, it's open for hour-long guided tours.

At the house, pick up a copy of the Columbia Falls walking-tour brochure, which details the intriguing history of other houses in this hamlet.

Maine Central Model Railroad

Here's nirvana for model-train enthusiasts. Harold ("Buz") Beal and his wife, Helen, have created a fantastic model railroad layout—the Maine Central Model Railroad—covering about 900 square feet in a building next to their house. It features 4,000 trees, 396 train cars, 3,000 feet of track, 11 bridges and trestles, 200 switches.… The trains wind through

The Ruggles House is an architectural masterpiece.

towns modeled on real Maine places. Look for Stephen King's house in Bangor. Buz Beal, a 26-year Coast Guard veteran, figures railroading is in his blood; his grandfather was a Canadian Pacific engineer. Visitors are welcome any day of the year, but it's best to call ahead (207/497-2255) to be sure someone's home. On Route 187, about four miles northeast of downtown Jonesport, watch for the Church Enterprises sign on the right and then take the next left to the Beals' house. A railroad crossing sign marks the driveway. (Route 187 makes a loop through the peninsula; the Beals are on the easternmost side of the loop—7.7 miles south of Route 1.) There's no charge, but donations are welcomed. Buzz will usually run at least one train for visitors, but it takes three people to operate the full model. That usually occurs on Sunday evenings.

Downeast Institute for Applied Marine Research and Education

University of Maine at Machias professor Brian Beals founded the Beals Island Regional Shellfish Hatchery, now the Downeast Institute (Black Duck Cove, Great Wass Island, 207/497-5769, www.downeastinstitute.org), a marine field station for the University of Maine at Machias. Learn everything there is to know about shellfish, especially soft-shell clams, on this eight-acre property, with two natural coves. Tours are by appointment.

Wild Salmon Research Center

Established in 1922, the center (Columbia Falls, 207/483-4336, www.mainesalmon rivers.org, 8 A.M.–4 P.M. Mon.–Fri., free) has a few educational displays and a library. In the basement is a volunteer-run fish hatchery that raises 50,000 Atlantic salmon fry annually. Staff welcome visitors and explain the efforts to save Maine's endangered salmon. You might also ask about the status of the East Machias Aquatic Research Center, a new facility under development by the Downeast Salmon Federation. Planned are a fish hatchery, laboratories, resources center, and small museum.

EXCURSION BOATS
◖ Machias Seal Island Puffin Tour

A great-grandson of legendary local "Tall Barney" Beal, Captain Barna Norton began offering puffin-watching trips to Machias Seal Island (MSI) in 1940 in a 33-foot boat incautiously named *If.* Now his son, Captain John, has taken over the helm of **Norton of Jonesport** (118 Main St., Box 330, Jonesport 04649, 207/497-5933 or 207/497-5933, www.machiassealisland.com, $100). He captains *Chief,* heading 20 miles offshore to an island claimed by both the United States and Canada—a colorful saga. To preserve the fragile nesting sites of Atlantic puffins and arctic terns, access to the 15-acre island is restricted. Passengers are off-loaded into small boats, but sea swells sometimes prevent landing. (The captain supplies wristbands to queasy passengers.) The trip is *not* appropriate for small children or unsteady adults. The boat departs Jonesport around 7 A.M. and returns around noon. Wear waterproof hiking boots, take a hat, and pack some munchies.

Other Cruises

Operating as **Coastal Cruises** (Kelley Point Rd., R.R. 1, Box 1360, Jonesport, 207/497-3064 or 207/497-2699), Captain Laura Fish and her brother Harry Fish, a certified dive master, offer three-hour Moosabec Reach cruises in the 23-foot powerboat *Aaron Thomas.* Among the sights are Great Wass Island and Mistake Island. Cost is $45 pp, six-person maximum. Dive trips are a possibility. Reservations are required. Trips depart from Jonesport and operate May–mid-October.

ENTERTAINMENT AND EVENTS

For a taste of real Maine, don't miss the early April **Fried Smelt Dinner.**

The biggest annual event hereabouts is the wingding Jonesport **Fourth of July** celebration, with several days of special activities, including barbecues, beauty pageant, kids' games, fireworks, and the famed **Jonesport Lobsterboat Races** in Moosabec Reach.

The mid-August **Maine Wild Blueberry Festival,** in neighboring Machias, is an easy jaunt from the Jonesport/Beals area.

Peabody Memorial Library presents bi-monthly art shows and sponsors a summer music series.

SHOPPING

Flower-design majolica pottery and whimsical terra-cotta items are specialties at **Columbia Falls Pottery** (150 Main St., Columbia Falls,

PUFFINS

The chickadee is the Maine state bird, and the bald eagle is our national emblem, but probably the best-loved bird along the Maine coast is the Atlantic puffin *(Fratercula arctica),* a member of the auk (Alcidae) family. Photographs show an imposing-looking creature with a quizzical mien; amazingly, this larger-than-life seabird is only about 12 inches long. Black-backed and white-chested, the puffin has bright orange legs, "clown-makeup" eyes, and a distinctive, rather outlandish red-and-yellow beak. Its diet is fish and shellfish.

Almost nonexistent in this part of the world as recently as the 1970s, the puffin (or "sea parrot") has recovered dramatically thanks to the unstinting efforts of Cornell University ornithologist Stephen Kress and his Project Puffin. Starting with an orphan colony (of two) on remote Matinicus Rock, Kress painstakingly transferred nearly a thousand puffin chicks (also known fondly as "pufflings") from Newfoundland and used artificial nests and decoys to entice the birds to adapt to and reproduce on Eastern Egg Rock in Muscongus Bay.

In 1981, thanks to the assistance and persistence of hundreds of interns and volunteers, and despite the predations of great black-backed gulls, puffins finally were fledged on Eastern Egg, and the rest, as they say, is history. Within 20 years, more than three dozen puffin couples were nesting on Eastern Egg Rock, and still more had established nests on other islands in the area. Kress's methods have received international attention, and his proven techniques have been used to reintroduce bird populations in remote parts of the globe. In 2001, *Down East* magazine singled out Kress to receive its prestigious annual Environmental Award.

HOW AND WHERE TO SEE PUFFINS

Puffin-watching, like whale-watching, involves heading offshore, so be prepared with warm clothing, rubber-soled shoes, a hat, sunscreen, binoculars, and, if you're motion sensitive, appropriate medication.

Although the Maine Audubon Society undertakes evening excursions from New Harbor to Eastern Egg Rock 2-3 times a summer, and Hardy Boat Cruises has puffin-watching trips from New Harbor daily early June-mid-August, there are daily up-close-and-personal opportunities for puffin-watching along the Down East Coast – specifically, on Machias Seal Island, aboard boats departing from Cutler and Jonesport. Weather permitting, you'll be allowed to disembark on the 20-acre island.

Naturalist and skilled skipper Andy Patterson begins his puffin tours from Cutler in mid-May, departing each morning (about 7 A.M.) aboard the 40-footer *Barbara Frost.* The season wraps up in late August. Cost is $80 a person. Contact **Bold Coast Charters** (207/259-4484).

Captain John Norton – son of Barna Norton, the veteran of puffin-watching trips – departs from the waterfront in Jonesport at about 7 A.M. daily, late May-August. Cost is $100. Contact **Norton of Jonesport** (207/497-5933 or 888/551-4895).

ADOPT-A-PUFFIN PROGRAM

Stephen Kress's Project Puffin has devised a clever way to enlist supporters via the Adopt-a-Puffin program. For a $100 donation, you'll receive a certificate of adoption, vital statistics on your adoptee, annual updates, and a T-shirt. Email adoption requests to orders@projectpuffin.org.

207/483-4075 or 800/235-2512), an appealing shop in a rehabbed country store next to the Ruggles House. Veteran potter April Adams keeps the inventory fresh, and the company does a hefty mail-order business. A newly renovated, two-bedroom apartment is available for rent upstairs either as one unit by the week for $700 or, when available, by the room, for $120–150 per night.

Two adjacent antiques shops brighten Jonesport's waterfront: **Harbor House on Sawyer Cove** (32 Sawyer Sq., 207/497-5417) and **Moospecke Antiques** (Sawyer Sq., 207/497-2457).

ACCOMMODATIONS
Bed-and-Breakfasts

How about staying in a beautiful, modern farmhouse overlooking the water—with llamas llolling outside? At **(Pleasant Bay Bed and Breakfast and Llama Keep** (338 West Side Rd., P.O. Box 222, Addison 04606, 207/483-4490, www.pleasantbay.com, $50–135), Joan and Lee Yeaton manage to pamper more than 40 llamas and a herd of red deer as well as their two-legged guests. Three miles of trails wind through the 110 acres, and a canoe is available for guests. Three lovely rooms (private and shared baths) and one suite, with microwave and refrigerator, all have water views. Rates include a delicious breakfast. Arrange in advance for a llama walk ($15 per llama). It's open all year. The farm borders Pleasant Bay, 3.9 miles southwest of Route 1.

The fanciest digs in Jonesport are at **(Harbor House on Sawyer Cove** (P.O. Box 468, Sawyer Sq., Jonesport 04649, 207/497-5417, www.harborhs.com, $125), hospitably run by Maureen and Gene Hart—she an ex-nurse, he an ex-engineer. Relatively new to Jonesport, they've adopted it with a passion, enjoying sharing it with Harbor House guests. Two very comfortable and spacious second-floor rooms—named Beach Rose and Lupine and decorated accordingly—have incredible views of Moosabec Reach. Binoculars are provided so you can watch the action, including passengers embarking on the Norton puffin trip. The rooms also have TV and Wi-Fi, and a guest phone, fridge, and microwave are provided. The Harts operate an antiques shop, selling what they call "curiosities," on the first floor of this fascinating old building, once Jonesport's telegraph office. Maureen serves a great breakfast—early enough for birders—on the harbor-view porch. Harbor House is open all year.

Cottages and Apartments

Close to the best sandy beach on the peninsula, the **Church's Ocean Front Cottages** (49 Sandy River Beach Rd., Jonesport, 207/497-2886, www.oceancottagesmaine.com), managed by Linda Church, are three rustic, well-maintained cottages, all with Wi-Fi and direct TV/VCR, available by the week. Best view is from Sandpiper, which sleeps six and rents for $1,000 a week; the others (Linnet and Lemon Drop) are $700 a week. Bring your own sheets and towels. It's open May–October. The cottages are seven miles south of Route 1 and four miles northeast of downtown Jonesport. A fourth cottage, Harborview ($500/week or $100/day), an eccentric little place with a spectacular panoramic view, is on Main Street in downtown Jonesport.

Proprietor Dorothy Higgins's **Cranberry Cove Cottages** (56 Kelley Point Rd., Jonesport, 207/497-2139, ddhiggi@hotmail.com, $125) comprise two second-story cottage-style apartments, each distinctively furnished in cottage style and with TV, phone, and harbor view. Both have kitchenettes provisioned with all sorts of goodies, from fresh eggs to wine and cheese. Pets are welcome. Rates decrease with length of stay.

Abigail Oates-Alley has two two-bedroom units in an oceanfront duplex called **Moose-a-bec** (34 Old House Point, P.O. Box 557, Jonesport 04649, 207/497-2121, $125). Both have big views, full baths with laundries, TV, and phones with answer machines. It's adjacent to a working wharf, so expect to see and hear the boats going out and returning each day. The downstairs unit is handicapped-friendly. The upstairs unit has a tiny second bedroom.

Campgrounds

The town of Jonesport operates the low-key, no-frills **Jonesport Campground** (Henry Point, Kelley Point Rd., Jonesport) on two acres with fabulous views over Sawyer Cove and Moosabec Reach. Basic facilities include outhouses, picnic tables, and fire rings; three power poles provide hookups. Showers and washing machines are available across the cove at Jonesport Shipyard (207/497-2701). The campground is exposed to wind off the water, so expect nights to be cool. Sites are allocated on a first-come, first-served basis. It's open early May–Labor Day. Avoid the campground during Fourth of July festivities; it's jam-packed. From Route 187 at the northeastern edge of Jonesport, turn right onto Kelley Point Road and then right again to Henry Point.

FOOD

Craving carbs? Head for Lois Hubbard's home bakery, called **The Farm** (1561 Mason's Bay Rd., Rte. 187, R.R. 1, Box 3115, Jonesport, 207/497-5949). In addition to specialty breads, Lois produces 15 flavors of whoopie pies, including blueberry. The bakery, 3.3 miles south of the Jonesboro end of Route 1, is open all year.

For local color, start at **Tall Barney's** (52 Main St., Rte. 187, Jonesport, 207/497-2403, www.tallbarneys.com), where you'll find homemade baked beans and chowders, pizza, and more—and you won't break the bank. Sit back and watch the servers chat up the lobstermen regulars camped out at the big center table, known locally as the Liars' Table. Join them, if you dare. No credit cards. The restaurant is just before the bridge to Beals Island; watch for the statue of Barney. Days and hours of operation change frequently, so call.

INFORMATION AND SERVICES

The Machias Bay Area Chamber of Commerce (12 E. Main St., Machias, 207/255-4402, www.machiaschamber.org) handles inquires for the Machias area as well as Jonesport.

In downtown Jonesport, the best source of local information is Church's True Value (Main St., Rte. 187, Jonesport, 207/497-2778), open every day but Sunday. Another reliable source is Maureen Hart at Antiques on the Harbor (on Sawyer Cove, 207/497-5417).

Machias Bay Area

The only negative thing about Machias (Muh-CHY-us, pop. about 2,500) is its Micmac Indian name, meaning "bad little falls" (even though that's accurate—the midtown waterfall here *is* treacherous). A contagious local esprit pervades this shire town of Washington County, thanks to antique homes, a splendid river-valley setting, Revolutionary War monuments, and a small but busy university campus.

If you regard crowds as fun, an ideal time to land here is during the renowned annual Machias Wild Blueberry Festival, third weekend in August, when harvesting is under way in Washington County's blueberry fields and you can stuff your face with blueberry-everything—muffins, jam, pancakes, ice cream, pies. You can

also collect blueberry-logo napkins, T-shirts, magnets, pottery, and jewelry. The menu at the local McDonald's even lists blueberry pancakes and sundaes that weekend.

Among the other summer draws are a chamber-music series, art shows, and semi-professional theater performances. Within a few miles are day trips galore—options for hiking, biking, golfing, swimming, and sea kayaking.

Also included within the Machias sphere are the towns of Roque Bluffs, Jonesboro, Whitneyville, Marshfield, East Machias, and Machiasport. Just to the east, between Machias and Lubec, are the towns of Whiting and Cutler.

HISTORICAL SIGHTS

History is a big deal in this area, and since Machias was the first settled Maine town east of the Penobscot River, lots of enthusiastic amateur historians have helped rescue homes and sites dating from as far back as the Revolutionary War.

English settlers, uprooted from communities farther west on the Maine coast, put down permanent roots here in 1763, harvesting timber to ensure their survival. Stirrings of revolutionary discontent surfaced even at this remote outpost, and when British loyalists in Boston began usurping some of the valuable harvest, Machias patriots plotted revenge. By 1775, when the armed British schooner *Margaretta* arrived as a cargo escort, local residents aboard the sloop *Unity,* in a real David-and-Goliath episode, chased and captured the *Margaretta.* On June 12, 1775, two months after the famed Battles of Lexington and Concord (and five days before the Battle of Bunker Hill), Machias Bay was the site of what author James Fenimore Cooper called "The Lexington of the Sea"—the first naval battle of the American Revolution. The name of patriot leader Jeremiah O'Brien today appears throughout Machias—on a school, a street, a cemetery, and a state park. In 1784, Machias was incorporated; it became the shire town in 1790.

Museums

One-hour guided tours vividly convey the atmosphere of the 1770 **Burnham Tavern** (Main St., Rte. 192, Machias, 207/255-4432, www .burnhamtavern.com, 9 A.M.–5 P.M. Mon.–Fri. mid-June–Sept., or by appointment, $5 adults, $0.25 for kids under 12), where upstart local patriots met in 1775 to plot revolution against the British. Job and Mary Burnham's tavern/home next served as an infirmary for casualties from the Revolution's first naval battle, just offshore. Lots of fascinating history lies in this National Historic Site maintained by the Daughters of the American Revolution. Hanging outside is a sign reading, "Drink for the thirsty, food for the hungry, lodging for the weary, and good keeping for horses, by Job

Burnham." If you're here in early August, you can join in the museum's annual **lawn party,** including lunch, tours, and handicraft sales.

Headquarters for the Machiasport Historical Society and one of the area's three oldest residences, the 1810 **Gates House** (344 Port Rd., Machiasport, 207/255-8461, 12:30–4:30 P.M. Tues.–Sat. July and Aug., donation appreciated) was snatched from ruin and restored in 1966. The National Historic Register building overlooking Machias Bay contains fascinating period furnishings and artifacts, many related to the lumbering and shipbuilding era. The museum, four miles southeast of Route 1, has limited parking on a hazardous curve.

O'Brien Cemetery

Old-cemetery buffs will want to stop at O'Brien Cemetery, resting place of the town's earliest settlers. It's next to Bad Little Falls Park, close to downtown, off Route 92 toward Machiasport. A big plus here is the view, especially in autumn, of blueberry barrens, the waterfall, and the bay.

Fort O'Brien State Memorial

The American Revolution's first naval battle was fought just offshore from Fort O'Brien in June 1775. Now a State Historic Site, the fort was built and rebuilt several times—originally to guard Machias during the Revolutionary War. Only Civil War–era earthworks now remain, plus well-maintained lawns overlooking the Machias River. Steep banks lead down to the water; keep small children well back from the edge. No restrooms or other facilities, but there's a playground at the Fort O'Brien School, next door. Officially, the park is open Memorial Day weekend–Labor Day, but it's easily accessible all year. Admission is free. Take Route 92 from Machias about five miles toward Machiasport; the parking area is on the left.

UNIVERSITY OF MAINE AT MACHIAS

Founded in 1909 as Washington State Normal School, University of Maine at Machias (9 O'Brien Ave., Machias, 207/255-1200, www.umm.maine.edu) is now part of the state university system. The **UMM Art Galleries,** in Powers Hall, feature works from the university's expanding permanent collection of Maine painters—including John Marin, William Zorach, Lyonel Feininger, and Reuben Tam. Rotating exhibits occur throughout the school year. Hours are 1–4 P.M. Monday–Friday when school is in session, or by appointment.

RECREATION
Parks and Preserves

Just as dedicated as the historical preservationists are the hikers, birders, and other eco-sensitive outdoors enthusiasts who've helped preserve thousands of acres in this part of Maine for public access and appreciation.

At **Bad Little Falls Park,** alongside the Machias River, stop to catch the view from the footbridge overlooking the roiling falls (especially in spring). Bring a picnic and enjoy this midtown oasis tucked between Routes 1 and 92.

Thanks to a handful of foresighted year-round and summer residents, spectacular, crescent-shaped **Jasper Beach**—piled high with ocean-polished jasper and other rocks—has been preserved by the town of Machiasport. No sand here, just stones, in intriguing shapes and colors. Resist the urge to fill your pockets with souvenirs, maybe settling for just a single special rock. Parking is limited; no facilities. From Route 1 in downtown Machias, take Route 92 (Machias Rd.) 9.5 miles southeast, past the village of Bucks Harbor. Watch for a large sign on your left. The beach is on Howard's Cove, 0.2 mile off the road, and accessible all year.

Southwest of Machias, six miles south of Route 1, is **Roque Bluffs State Park** (Roque Bluffs Rd., Roque Bluffs, 207/255-3475). Saltwater swimming this far north is for the young and brave, but this park also has a 60-acre freshwater pond warm and shallow enough for toddlers and the old and timid. Facilities include primitive changing rooms, outhouses, a play area, and picnic tables (no food or lifeguards). Views go on forever from the wide-open, mile-long sweep of sand beach. Admission is $3 adults, $1 children 5–11. The fee box relies on the honor system. The park is open daily May 15–September 15, but the beach is accessible all year.

On Route 191, about 4.5 miles northeast of the center of Cutler, watch for the parking area (on the right) for the **Cutler Coast Public Preserve,** a 12,000-acre preserve with nearly a dozen miles of beautifully engineered hiking trails on the seaward side of Route 191. Allow 5–6 hours to do the shorter, 5.8-mile Black Point Brook Loop, providing an easy start for about 1.5 miles before getting to the Coastal Trail, a stretch of moderately rugged hiking southward along dramatic, tree-fringed shoreline cliffs. Then head back via the Black Point Brook cutoff and connect with the Inland Trail to return to your car (or bicycle). Bring binoculars and a camera; the views from this wild coastline are fabulous. Also bring insect repellent—inland boggy stretches are buggy. Carry a picnic and commandeer a granite ledge overlooking the surf. Precipitous cliffs and narrow stretches can make the shoreline section of this trail perilous for small children or insecure adults, so use extreme caution and common sense. There are no facilities in the preserve. If you're here in August, you can stock up on blueberries and even some wild raspberries. Another option, the 9.8-mile Fairy Head Loop, starts the same way as the Black Point Brook Loop but continues southward along the coast, leading to three primitive campsites (stoves only, no fires), available on a first-come, first-served basis. There's no way to reserve these, so you take your chances. Unless you have gazelle genes, the longer loop almost demands an overnight. Information on the preserve, including a helpful map, is available from the **Maine Bureau of Parks and Lands** (22 State House Station, Augusta 04333, 207/287-3821, www .state.me.us/doc/parks). Originally about 2,100 acres, this preserve was quintupled in 1997, when several donors, primarily the Richard King Mellon Foundation, deeded to the state 10,055 acres of fields and forests across Route 191 from the trail area, creating a phenomenal tract that now runs from the ocean all the way back to Route 1. Mostly in Cutler but

TWO SCENIC ROUTES

The drives described below can also be bike routes (easy to moderately difficult), but be forewarned that the roads are narrow and shoulderless, so caution is essential. Heed biking etiquette.

ROUTE 191, THE CUTLER ROAD

Never mind that Route 191, between East Machias and West Lubec, is one of Maine's most stunning coastal drives – you can still follow the entire 27-mile stretch and meet only a handful of cars. **East Machias** even has its own historic district, with architectural gems dating from the late 18th century along High and Water Streets. Farther along Route 191, you'll find fishing wharves, low moorlands, a hamlet or two, and islands popping over the horizon. The only peculiarly jarring note is the 26-tower forest of North Cutler's Naval Computer and Telecommunications Station, nearly 1,000 feet high – monitoring global communications – but you'll see this only briefly. (At night, the skyscraping red lights are really eerie, especially if you're offshore aboard a boat.) Off Route 191 are minor roads and hiking trails worth exploring, especially the coastal trails of the Cutler Coast Public Preserve. About three miles south of the Route 191 terminus, you can also check out **Bailey's Mistake,** a hamlet with a black-sand (volcanic) beach. And the name? Allegedly it stems from one Captain Bailey who, misplotting his course and thinking he was in Lubec, drove his vessel ashore here one night in the late 19th century. Unwilling to face the consequences of his lapse, he and his crew off-loaded their cargo of lumber and built themselves dwellings. Whether true or not, it makes a great saga. Even though it's in the town of **Trescott,** and the hamlet is really South Trescott, everyone knows this section as Bailey's Mistake.

ROUTE 92, STARBOARD PENINSULA

Pack a picnic and set out on Route 92 (beginning at Elm Street in downtown Machias) down the 10-mile length of the Starboard Peninsula to a stunning spot known as the Point of Maine. Along the way are the villages of Larrabee, Bucks Harbor, and Starboard, all part of the town of Machiasport. In Bucks Harbor is the turnoff (a short detour to the right) to **Yoho Head,** a controversial upscale development overlooking Little Kennebec Bay.

South of the Yoho Head turnoff is the sign for **Jasper Beach.** From the Jasper Beach sign, continue 1.4 miles to two red buildings (the old Starboard School House and the volunteer fire department). Turn left onto a dirt road and continue to a sign reading Driveway. Go around the right side of a shed and park on the beach. (Keep track of the tide level, though.) You're at **Point of Maine,** a quintessential Down East panorama of sea and islands. On a clear day, you can see offshore **Libby Island Light,** the focus of Philmore Wass's entertaining narrative *Lighthouse in My Life: The Story of a Maine Lightkeeper's Family* (see *Suggested Reading* in the *Resources* chapter).

also in Whiting, it was Maine's second-largest public-land gift—after Baxter State Park.

Next to the post office, on Route 1, in East Machias is the riverside **Eagle Watch picnic area,** which isn't much of a picnic area at all, but it is a great place to watch eagles soar in the spring and early summer.

Golf

With lovely water views, and tidal inlets serving as obstacles, the nine-hole **Great** **Cove Golf Course** (387 Great Cove Rd., off Roque Bluffs Rd., Jonesboro, 207/434-7200) is a good challenge. It has reasonable greens fees, carts, and a snack bar; you can also rent clubs. From Jonesboro (Rte. 1), go 3.5 miles east and south on Roque Bluffs Road. It's open May–October. You can play a quick nine at **Barren View Golf Course** (Rte. 1, Jonesboro, 207/434-6531, www.barrenview .com). A pro shop, snack bar, carts, and club rentals are available.

Canoeing, Sea Kayaking, and Bicycling

If you've brought your own sea kayak, there are public launching ramps in Bucks Harbor (east of the main Machias Rd.) and at Roque Bluffs State Park. You can also put in at Sanborn Cove, beyond the O'Brien School on Route 92, about five miles south of Machias, where there's a small parking area. Before setting out, be sure to check the tide calendar and plan your strategy so you don't have to slog through acres of muck when you return.

Sunrise Canoe and Kayak (0.02 mile off Rte. 1 on an unsigned road, behind Margaretta Motel, Machias, 207/255-3375 or 877/980-2300, www.sunrisecanoeandkayak.com) rents canoes and kayaks for $20 per day, sit-on-top kayaks for $15 per day, and offers half-day sea-kayak excursions on Machias Bay, including one to a petroglyph site ($48 pp). It also rents 24-speed mountain bikes for $15 per day. Pickup and delivery service is $25. It also offers fully outfitted, multiday canoeing and kayaking excursions on the Machias and St. Croix Rivers and along the Bold Coast.

The spectacular **Machias River,** one of Maine's most technically demanding canoeing rivers, is a dynamite trip mid-May–mid-June, but no beginner should attempt it. The best advice is to sign on with an outfitter/guide. The run lasts 4–6 days, the latter if you start from Fifth Machias Lake. Expect to see such wildlife as osprey, eagles, ducks, loons, moose, deer, beaver, and snapping turtles. Be aware, though, that the Machias is probably the buggiest river in the state, and blackflies will form a welcoming party. Bring khaki duds; the bugs are attracted to colors. The major portage is at Upper Holmes Falls; trying to run the half-mile-long rips would buy you a ticket to the morgue. In addition to Sunrise Canoe and Kayak, **Sunrise Expeditions** (4 Union Plaza, Ste. 2, Bangor, 207/942-9300 or 800/748-3730, www.sunrise-exp.com) also offers fully outfitted trips.

🄲 Machias Seal Island Puffin Tour

Andy Patterson, the skipper of the 40-footer *Barbara Frost,* operates the **Bold Coast Charter Company** (P.O. Box 364, Cutler 04626, 207/259-4484, www.boldcoast.com), homeported in Cutler Harbor. Andy provides knowledgeable narration, answers questions in depth, and shares his considerable enthusiasm for this pristine corner of Maine. He's best known for his five-hour puffin-sighting trips to Machias Seal Island (departing between 7 and 8 A.M. mid-May–Aug.). All trips are dependent on weather and tide conditions, and reservations are required. Cost is $80 (but don't bring small children or unsteady adults). No credit cards. Daily access to the island is restricted, and swells can roll in, so passengers occasionally cannot disembark, but the curious puffins often surround the boat, providing plenty of photo opportunities. A seabird tour, without an island visit, is available for $80 adult, $45 kids 14 and younger. No matter what the air temperature on the mainland, be sure to dress warmly, and wear sturdy shoes. The *Barbara Frost*'s wharf is on Cutler Harbor, just off Route 191. Look for the Little River Lobster Company sign; you'll depart from the boat-launching ramp.

ENTERTAINMENT, FESTIVALS, AND EVENTS

The University of Maine at Machias is the cultural focus in this area, particularly during the school year. **Stage Front: The Arts Downeast** puts on an annual series of concerts, plays, recitals, and other events in the Performing Arts Center at the university. The summer series, once a month, usually features classical and pops concerts, including at least one performance by the energetic Steuben-based Opera Maine organization. Contact UMM (207/255-1384) for schedule information.

Machias Bay Chamber Concerts (207/255-3849) occur at 7:30 P.M. Tuesday evenings early July–mid-August at the Centre Street Congregational Church. Art exhibits accompany concerts. Tickets are $12 for adults, $6 for students, and free for kids age 12 and younger. Call for a current schedule.

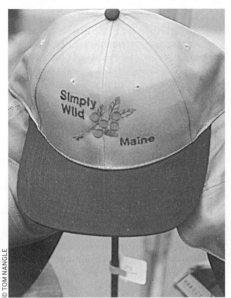

The Machias Wild Blueberry Festival celebrates the August harvest.

The **Machias Wild Blueberry Festival** (www.machiasblueberry.com) is the summer highlight, running Friday–Sunday the third weekend in August, featuring a pancake breakfast, road races, concerts, a craft show, a baked-bean supper, a homegrown musical, and more. The blueberry motif is everywhere. It's organized by Centre Street Congregational Church in downtown Machias.

SHOPPING

Influenced by traditional Japanese designs, Connie Harter-Bagley markets her dramatic ceramics at **Connie's Clay of Fundy** (Rte. 1, Box 345, East Machias, 207/255-4574, www.clayoffundy.com), on the East Machias River, four miles east of Machias. If she's at the wheel, you can also watch her work.

A number of regional artists and artisans show and sell their wares at **Unique Possibilities** (300 E. Main St./Rte. 1, Machias, 207/255-3337), in the Causeway Common building (same complex as Dunkin'

Donuts). Also here is **The Country Tea Room** (207/255-3337), a relaxing place to sip tea and snack on sweets.

ACCOMMODATIONS
Bed-and-Breakfasts and Inns

The first three B&Bs feature dining rooms open to the public (see *Food* for details).

The beautifully restored **[Chandler River Lodge** (654 Rte. 1, Jonesboro, 207/434-2540, $100–175) sits well off the highway and overlooks treed lawns that roll down to the Chandler River. It's an idyllic spot, with Adirondack-style chairs positioned just where you want to sit and take in the views. Or you might just want to sit on the porch. Upstairs are four guest rooms, three with private bath, one with detached bath. Downstairs is a fine-dining restaurant. Rates include a continental breakfast.

Victoriana rules at the **Riverside Inn** (Rte. 1, P.O. Box 373, East Machias 04630, 207/255-4134, www.riversideinn-maine.com, $95–130), a meticulously restored early-19th-century sea captain's home with two rooms and two suites (one with kitchenette). Relax on the deck overlooking the East Machias River and you'll forget you're a few steps from a busy highway. Sit in the lovely terraced perennial gardens and you'll feel the same way. There's also a popular dining room, where reservations are essential.

Fronting on the tidal Machias River, the barn-red **Inn at Schoppee Farm** (Rte. 1, Machias, 207/255-4648, www.schoppeefarm.com, $110) is earning fame as a dining and lodging destination. The 19th-century farm operated as a dairy for three generations before Machias natives David and Julie Barker returned home to operate it as a B&B. They welcome guests with two rooms, each furnished with antiques and such niceties as air-conditioning, Wi-Fi, whirlpool baths, and soft down comforters in addition to river views and a full breakfast. Also available is a two-bedroom suite with kitchen ($250 per night or $900 per week). The dining room is open for five-course dinners Thursday–Saturday, by

© TOM NANGLE

reservation. Just east of the causeway, it's a healthy walk to downtown diversions.

The second generation now operates **Micmac Farm Guesthouses** (Rte. 92, Machiasport, 207/255-3008, www.micmacfarm .com, $80–95/night, $495–595/week, May–late Oct.). Stay in one of Anthony and Bonnie Dunn's three comfortable, well-equipped cottages, and you'll find yourself relaxing on the deck overlooking the tidal Machias River and watching for seabirds, seals, and eagles. No breakfast is provided, but each wood-paneled cottage has a kitchenette and dining area. Pets and children are welcome. There's also a riverview room in the restored 18th-century Gardner House, with a private bath with whirlpool tub. Guests have use of the farmhouse, including a library. A light breakfast is provided for Gardner House guests. Micmac Farm, 2.5 miles south of Machias, is a lovely oasis.

Motels

The best feature of the two-story **Machias Motor Inn** (26 E. Main St., Rte. 1, Machias, 207/255-4861, www.machiasmotorinn.com, $70–110) is its location overlooking the tidal Machias River; sliding doors open onto decks with a view. Twenty-eight guest rooms and six efficiencies have extra-long beds, plus cable TV, air-conditioning, Wi-Fi, and phone. Next door is Helen's Restaurant—famed for seasonal fruit pies and an all-you-can-eat weekend breakfast buffet. Pets ($5 fee) are welcome at the motel. The motel is within easy walking distance to downtown; perfect if you're here for the Blueberry Festival. It's open all year.

For inexpensive digs, you can't beat the ◖ **Blueberry Patch** (550 Rte. 1, Jonesboro, 207/434-5411, $48–68), a clean and bright motel and tourist cabins, with three efficiency units. Nothing fancy here, but all rooms have satellite TV, air-conditioning, Wi-Fi, and phones, and there's even a pool and small playground. If you're taller than six feet, choose a motel room rather than a cabin (cabin bathrooms are tiny). Rates include coffee and pastry in the morning, but the Whitehouse Restaurant, next door, is open for breakfast, lunch, and dinner.

FOOD

Watch the local papers for listings of **public suppers, spaghetti suppers,** or **baked bean suppers,** a terrific way to sample the culinary talents of local cooks. Most begin at 5 P.M., and it's wise to arrive early to get near the head of the line. The suppers often benefit needy individuals or struggling nonprofits—always worth supporting—and where else can you eat nonstop for under $10?

Local Flavors

Fat Cat Deli (50 Main St., Machias, 207/255-6777, 11 A.M.–8:15 P.M. Mon.–Sat., 4–8:15 P.M. Sun.) makes the area's best pizzas and sandwiches and often has live music.

Craving something healthful? You can pick up breads and muffins as well as sandwiches and soups at **Whole Life Organic Market** (80 Main St., Machias, 207/255-8855, 9 A.M.–6 P.M. Mon.–Sat., 10 A.M.–2 P.M. Sun.). There's a small but pleasant seating area, too. It's open year-round.

Another source for fresh, healthful foods is the **Machias Valley Farmers Market** (8 A.M.–noon Sat. and often Wed. and Fri. May–Oct.). It's held on "The dike," a low causeway next to the Machias River. It's usually a good source for blueberries in late July and August.

Family-owned, and very popular all day long, is **The Blue Bird Ranch Family Restaurant** (3 E. Main St./Rte. 1, Machias, 207/255-3351, www.norumbegablue.com, 6 A.M.–8 P.M. daily), named for the Prout family's other enterprise, Blue Bird Ranch Trucking Company. Service is efficient, food is hearty, and portions are ample in the three dining rooms. The breakfast buffet, served 8–11 A.M., is $6.

Although pie aficionados say it's not what it used to be, **Helen's** (28 E. Main St./Rte. 1, Machias, 207/255-8423, 6 A.M.–8:30 P.M. daily) is renowned for its blueberry pie. It's also a source of inexpensive, family-style fare. The Sunday breakfast buffet, served 8–10:30 A.M., is $6, and the soup-and-salad bar is $6 anytime.

Casual Dining

Machias lucked out when Susan Ferro, owner,

artist, and chef—she claims she got her start garnishing mud pies as a kid—opened the **(Artist's Café** (3 Hill St., Machias, 207/255-8900, 11 A.M.–2 P.M. Mon.–Fri. and 5–8 P.M. Mon.–Sat.) in a small house across from the university. The dining rooms are decorated with paintings by Ferro and other local artists. Luncheon sandwiches—named The Impressionist, Garden of Eden, The Rococo, and so on, are always a reasonably priced adventure ($5–7). Dinner entrées, which change frequently and usually include a vegetarian option, are $22–28. Beer and wine are available. Be sure to reserve for dinner, especially on weekends.

Fine Dining

Reservations are essential at the popular dining room at the **Riverside Inn** (Rte. 1, East Machias, 207/255-4134, www.riversideinn-maine .com, open for dinner 5–8 P.M. Tues.–Sun. in peak season). The pricey menu might include entrées such as lobster and scallops in champagne sauce or Riverside Wellington as well as more budget-friendly main-course salads.

Machias's newest fine-dining restaurant, **Chandler River Lodge** (654 Rte. 1, Jonesboro, 207/434-2540, 5–8 P.M. Tues.–Sat.) has views over the Chandler River, and the grounds are perfect for a stroll either before or afterward. At dinner, entrées ($28–35) might include guava mango chicken, blueberry pork, or five-pepper steak. All include fresh baked breads and salad. If you don't want to splurge on dinner, lunch is served seasonally. Call for days and hours.

Far more intimate is the **(Inn at Schoppee Farm** (Rte. 1, Machias, 207/255-4648, www.schoppeefarm.com, 5–8 P.M. Mon.–Sat.), which serves five-course dinners ($36–44) in the Hannah Weston dining room by reservation. Seating is limited to 15, so call early. Usually the menu offers a choice of four entrées, varying from seafood, beef, chicken, duck, or lamb. The river-view dining room complements the farmhouse's Federal-style architecture—bright and airy, with pine floors, hand-hewn beams, and antiques. BYOB.

INFORMATION AND SERVICES

The Machias Bay Area Chamber of Commerce (12 E. Main St, Machias, 207/255-4402, www.machiaschamber.org) stocks brochures, maps, and information on area hiking trails. The office is generally open 10 A.M.–3 P.M. Monday–Friday.

Lubec and Vicinity

Literally the beginning of America—at the nation's easternmost point—Lubec (pop. 1,730) can serve as a base for exploring New Brunswick's Campobello Island, the Cutler coastline, and territory to the west. With a couple of appealing B&Bs and more than 90 miles of meandering waterfront, Lubec conveys the aura of realness: a hardscrabble fishing community that extends a welcome to visitors. Lubec residents love to point out that the closest traffic light is 50 miles away.

Settled in 1780 and originally part of Eastport, Lubec was split off in 1811 and named for the German port of Lübeck (for convoluted reasons still not totally clear). The town's most famous resident was Hopley Yeaton, first captain in the U.S. Revenue-Marine (now the U.S. Coast Guard), who retired here in 1809.

Along the main drag (Water St.), a number of shuttered buildings reflect the town's roller-coaster history. Once the world's sardine capital, Lubec no longer has a packing plant, but aquaculture has come to the forefront, and new businesses are slowly arriving.

(WEST QUODDY HEAD STATE PARK

Beachcombing, hiking, picnicking, and an up-close look at Maine's only red-and-white-striped lighthouse are the big draws at 480-acre

© TOM NANGLE

An easy mile-long boardwalk trail crosses a peat bog at West Quoddy Head State Park.

Quoddy Head State Park (West Quoddy Head Rd., Lubec, 207/733-0911, 9 A.M.–sunset May 15–Oct. 15, $2 adults, $1 kids), the easternmost point of U.S. land. Begin with a visit to the **Visitor Center** (Keeper's House, 207/733-2180, www.westquoddy.com, 10:10 A.M.–4 P.M. daily late May–mid-Oct., free), operated by the enthusiastic West Quoddy Head Light Keepers Association, a volunteer group. Inside are exhibits on lighthouse memorabilia, local flora and fauna, and area heritage; a gallery displaying local works; and a staffed information desk.

West Quoddy Head Light, towering 83 feet above mean high water, was built in 1808. (Its counterpart, East Quoddy Head Light, is on New Brunswick's Campobello Island.) Views from the lighthouse grounds are fabulous, and whale sightings are common in summer. The lighthouse tower is open annually for one day in June or early July, during Lighthouse Week, and other times when the Coast Guard is on-site.

The cliffs of Canada's Grand Manan Island are visible from the park's grounds. A 1.75-mile, moderately difficult trail follows the 90-foot cliffs to Carrying Place Cove, and an easy, mile-long boardwalk winds through a unique moss and heath bog designated as a National Natural Landmark. Be forewarned that the park gate is locked at sunset. In winter, the park is accessible for snowshoeing. From Route 189 on the outskirts of Lubec, take South Lubec Road (well signposted) to West Quoddy Head Road. Turn left and continue to the parking area.

SIGHTS
Mulholland Market and McCurdy Smokehouse

Lubec Landmarks (207/733-2068) is working to preserve these two local landmarks. The smokehouse complex, the last operating herring-smoking operation in the country, can be seen on the water side of Water Street. In 2007, after years of effort, it finally reopened to the public for tours. Mulholland Market is the organization's headquarters. Inside are displays about the smokehouses and exhibits of local art. It's volunteer operated, so hours change frequently.

Lubec Historical Society

The society's small museum in the **Old Columbian Store** (Main St., 207/733-4696, 9 A.M.–3 P.M. Mon., Wed., and Fri., free) doubles as a visitors information center. Among the historical and genealogical displays is a working model of the machine used in the infamous Gold from Seawater swindle of 1898. Volunteers will glad fill you in on that or you can pick up a brochure. While here, also pick up the *Lubec Historic Walking Tour* brochure, which highlights about a dozen historical sites in downtown Lubec. The museum is on the left as you're entering town, just beyond Uncle Kippy's restaurant.

Lubec Breakwater

Even the humongous tides and dramatic sunsets over Johnson Bay can get your attention if you hang out at the breakwater. Across the channel, on Campobello Island, is red-capped **Mulholland Point Lighthouse,** an abandoned beacon built in 1885. As the tide goes out—18 or so feet of it—you'll also see hungry harbor seals dunking for dinner. And if you're lucky, you might spot the eagle pair that nests on an island in the channel (bring binoculars).

RECREATION
Tours

Native Lubec residents, often with roots going back generations and with specialties as diverse as wildlife, birding, photography, and diving, deliver insights and share their knowledge on **Tours of Lubec and Cobscook** (24 Water St., P.O. Box 535, Lubec 04652, 207/733-2997 or 888/347-9302, www.toursoflubecandcobscook.com). Credit enthusiastic Lubec resident Ruta Jordans for creating the nonprofit Association to Promote and Protect the Lubec Environment (APPLE) to learn more about Lubec. APPLE sponsors personalized interpretive tours in areas covering area art, culture, the environment, history, and heritage. Rates range $20–40 pp. Call or visit the website to create an itinerary that works for you.

Hiking and Walking

Tag along with Lubec's **Pathfinders Walking Group** (207/733-4984 or 207/733-0988)—enthusiastic area residents who go exploring every Sunday year-round, usually meeting at 2 P.M. for a two-hour ramble. Nonmembers are welcome, there's no fee, and you'll see a Lubec (and more) that most visitors never encounter.

A fine place for a walk is the Maine Coast Heritage Trust's 376-acre **Hamilton Cove Preserve.** To find it, take Route 189 to the South Lubec Road toward Quoddy Head, but bear right at the fork and continue 2.4 miles to a small parking lot on the left. There's a kiosk with maps about 100 feet or so down the trail. The 1.5 miles of ocean frontage are highlighted by cobble beaches, rocky cliffs, and jaw-dropping views (on a clear day) of Grand Manan. It's about one mile to an observation platform and another half mile to the bench at the trail's end.

ENTERTAINMENT AND EVENTS

Classical music is the focus (for the most part) at **SummerKeys** (207/733-2316 or off-season 973/316-6220, www.summerkeys.com), a music camp for adults, no prior experience required, with weeklong programs in piano, voice, oboe, flute, clarinet, guitar, violin, and cello. Free concerts by visiting artists, faculty, and students are held at 7:30 P.M. Wednesday evenings late June–early September in the Congregational Christian Church, on Church Street.

Live music is usually on tap weekends at Cohill's Inn and Annabell's Pub, both on Water Street.

During summer, concerts are often held at the town bandstand on Main Street.

An ambitious, grassroots group has launched **Cobscook Community Learning Center** (207/733-2233, Timber Cove Rd., Trescott, www.thecclc.org). Two timber-frame buildings house CCLC's year-round programs, an open pottery studio, fiber-arts studio, and multiuse classrooms. Under construction are an outdoor amphitheater with dance floor, hiking and walking trails, and more on the center's 60-acre campus. The center's mission is "to enrich the lives of local community members through

THE DOWN EAST COAST

grassroots collaboration, using the arts, the rich social fabric, and the natural surroundings as the medium." Festivals, adult education, indigenous education, sustainable and value-added eco-ventures, youth programs, and more are planned. Open-jam music nights, held on the second, fourth, and fifth Mondays each month (7–10 P.M., donation appreciated), bring in as many as 20 musicians and a good crowd of listeners. Do call to see what's on the schedule.

Birding is big here, and spring brings **The Down East Spring Birding Festival** (P.O. Box 42, Whiting 04691, 207/733-2201, www.downeastbirdfest.org) to the Cobscook Bay Area, held annually in late May. Guided and self-guided explorations, presentations, and tours fill schedule, and participation is limited, so register early.

SHOPPING

Within strolling distance of each other downtown are **Dianne's Glass Gallery** (72 Water St., Lubec, 207/733-2458, www.diannesglass.com), where Dianne Larkin sells her handcrafted glass jewelry, plates, and other creations; **Northern Tides** (24 Water St., Lubec, 207/733-2500), with a nice selection of mostly local artwork; and **Downeast Artisans** (60 Washington St., Lubec, 207/733-8811), a collaborative gallery with works in varied media.

Lighthouse buffs must stop at **West Quoddy Gifts** (Quoddy Head Rd., one mile before the lighthouse, 207/733-2457). It's stocked with souvenirs and gifty items, most with a lighthouse theme.

ACCOMMODATIONS

Many visitors use Lubec as a base for day trips to Campobello Island, so it's essential to make reservations at the height of summer. Several lodgings are also available on Campobello.

Bed-and-Breakfasts

Built in 1860 by a British sea captain, **Peacock House Bed and Breakfast** (27 Summer St., Lubec, 207/733-2403 or 888/305-0036, www.peacockhouse.com, $90–130) has long been one of Lubec's most prestigious residences.

Among the notables who have stayed here are Donald MacMillan, the famous Arctic explorer, and U.S. Senators Margaret Chase Smith and Edmund Muskie. It has three rooms and four suites; suites have TV and sitting area; one has a gas fireplace and a refrigerator. One room is wheelchair-accessible.

Unusual antiques fill the guest and sitting rooms of the 19th-century **Home Port Inn** (45 Main St., Lubec, 207/733-2077 or 800/457-2077 outside Maine, www.homeportinn.com, mid-May–mid-Oct., $90–105), ensconced on a Lubec hilltop. Each of the seven rooms has a private bath, although some are detached; some have water views. Rates include a generous continental breakfast. The inn also serves dinner by reservation.

Piano students at SummerKeys often practice on the living room piano at **BayViews** (6 Monument St., Lubec, 207/733-2181, $50–80, May 1–Oct. 31), providing impromptu concerts for other guests. The 1824 Victorian house sits on two acres edging Johnson Bay. It's a relaxed B&B, filled with eclectic antiques, art, and books. (Owner Kathryn Rubeor has a master's in English literature.) It's an easy walk to town if you can tear yourself away from the back deck or lawn chairs or hammock. Breakfast is a bountiful continental, with fresh fruit and juice, home-baked bread, and homemade granola and toppings. One huge suite perfect for a family and one twin room, with a piano, have private baths; two doubles and one single share a bath. A five-bedroom, three-bath waterfront house also is available for $1,100 per week.

Motel

If you're traveling with small children, the lackluster **Eastland Motel** (County Rd., Rte. 189, R.R. 1, Box 6915, Lubec, 207/733-5501, www.eastlandmotel.com, $65–76) is Lubec's best bet. Four miles southwest of town, near the Lubec Municipal Airport (used infrequently), the motel has 20 rooms with cable TV and air-conditioning. Request one of the 12 rooms in the newer section. Free continental breakfast. Small pets possible ($10).

Rental Properties

The farmhouse on the Bell family's 200-year-old saltwater farm, **Tide Mill Farms** (40 Tide Mill Rd., Edmunds, two miles north of Rte. 189, 207/733-2110, www.tidemillfarm.com), is available for weekly rental. Ocean views are available from throughout the century-old farmhouse, which has five bedrooms and 1.5 baths. Amenities include a TV/VCR, washer/dryer, and gas grill. Linens are provided. Original settler Robert Bell built a tidal gristmill here, and one of the stones still lies on the point. Explore the farm's 1,600 acres, including six miles of shorefront as well as forest and mountain trails. Watch for eagles, seals, and loons. The property is home to the organic farm of the same name, and you'll see farm animals and operations.

Bill Clark has rescued the former Coast Guard Station at West Quoddy Head and restored, renovated, and reopened it as 🄲 **West Quoddy Station** (S. Lubec Rd., Lubec, Maine, 207/733-4452 or 877/535-4714, www.quoddy vacation.com), with five one-bedroom units (four in the lodge and one separate cabin), or opt for the five-bedroom, 2.5-bath Station House. All have kitchens, Wi-Fi, and DirecTV. Views are stupendous and extend to East Quoddy Head on Campobello; West Quoddy Head is about a half-mile walk. Rates begin at $75 per night, when available, but weekly rentals ($550–1,500) get first preference.

Campgrounds

A 3.5-mile network of nature trails, picnic spots, great birding and berry picking, hot showers, a boat launch, and wooded shorefront campsites make 888-acre **Cobscook Bay State Park** (Rte. 1, Edmunds Township, 207/726-4412) one of Maine's most spectacular state parks. It's even entertaining just to watch the 24-foot tides surging in and out of this area at five or so feet an hour; there's no swimming because of the undertow. Reserve well ahead to get a place on the shore. To guarantee a site in July and August, using MasterCard or Visa, call 207/287-3824 or visit www.campwithme .com; reservation fee is $2 per site per night,

two-night minimum. The park is open daily mid-May–mid-October; trails are groomed in winter for cross-country skiing, and one section goes right along the shore. Summer day-use fees are $3 adults, $1 children 5–11; under 5 or over 65 are free. The nonresident camping fee is $19 per site per night; the fee for Maine residents is $14.

The 80-acre **South Bay Campground** (591 County Rd./Rte. 189, R.R. 1, Box 6565, Lubec, 207/733-1037 or 877/733-1037, southbay@ midmaine.com, mid-May–mid-Oct.) has 74 RV and tent sites, a third on the shore of beautiful South Bay. Eight private island sites (accessible on foot at low tide) are also available. Noise regulations are strictly enforced. Facilities include a game room and a pool. Leashed pets are allowed. The campground is about seven miles from Route 1.

FOOD
Local Flavors

You can't go wrong with a stop at **Bold Coast Smokehouse** (224 County Rd./Rte. 189, 207/733-8912 or 888/733-0807, www.bold coastsmokehouse.com). Vinny Gartmayer is a master of the smoking process, creating delectable hot and cold smoked salmon, smoked fish spreads, smoked salmon sticks (great for picnics; try the garlic-pepper), and other goodies.

Oh my! 🄲 **Monica's** (56 Pleasant St., 866/952-4500, www.monicaschocolates.com) gives meaning to the term sinfully delicious. Monica Elliott creates sumptuous handmade gourmet chocolates using family recipes from her native Peru. Visitors can sample chocolates before buying (Smart move: You're guaranteed to buy after you taste.) Among the chocolates are scrumptious bonbons, blueberry wine and raspberry wine truffles, peanut butter cups made with homemade peanut butter, and other mouthwatering treats. Yum!

Stave off a midday hunger attack with home-baked goodies with an organic twist from **Sun Porch Industries** (99 Johnson St., 207/733-7587, 11 A.M.–5 P.M. Wed.–Sun.), a tiny natural and organic foods store.

The **Atlantic House Coffee Shop**

(52 Water St., Lubec, 207/733-0906, www
.atlantichouse.net, 7 A.M.–7 P.M. daily May–Oct.)
is one of the brightest spots on a rather forlorn
street. Breakfast pastries, tasty sandwiches, pizzas, great desserts, and decent coffee—load up
before you head out for a hike. Give yourself
time, though, as service can be slow.

Dining

Dining in Lubec is a bit of a crapshoot. It's wise
to ask locally about current reputations, although
often you'll find even mixed reviews then.

Depending on your source, **Uncle Kippy's**
(County Rd., Rte. 189, Lubec, 207/733-2400,
11 A.M.–8 P.M. Sun.–Thurs., to 9 P.M. Fri. and
Sat.) gets high and higher marks in Lubec
for wholesome cooking. A sign out front announces, "Stop in or we'll both starve."
Steak and seafood are specialties—at unfancy prices—and the pizza is the area's best
($7–29).

The nicest dining room in the area is at the
Home Port Inn (45 Main St., Lubec, 207/733-
2077 or 800/457-2077 outside Maine, www

.homeportinn.com, 5–8 P.M. daily). Reservations are advisable for this very popular restaurant—a sunken dining room with tables for 30.
The specialty is seafood (entrées run $12–24),
but the food often doesn't match the setting.
Open in summer only.

INFORMATION AND SERVICES

The Cobscook Bay Area Chamber of Commerce (P.O. Box 42, Whiting 04691, www
.cobscookbay.com) covers the Cobscook Bay
region, including Lubec. Local sources of information include: The Puffin Pines (240 Rte.
1, Whiting); the Old Columbian Store (Main
St., Lubec, 207/733-4696, limited hours Mon.,
Wed., and Fri.), home of the Lubec Historical
Society; and the Visitor Center (West Quoddy
Head Lighthouse, 207/733-2180, www
.westquoddy.com, 10:10 A.M.–4 P.M. daily late
May–mid-Oct.).

Lubec Memorial Library (corner of Water
and School Sts., Lubec, 207/733-2491) has a
public restroom.

Campobello Island

◖ ROOSEVELT CAMPOBELLO INTERNATIONAL PARK

Just over the Franklin D. Roosevelt Memorial Bridge from Lubec lies nine-mile-long
Campobello Island, in Canada's New Brunswick
province. Since 1964, 2,800 acres of the island
have been under joint U.S. and Canadian jurisdiction as Roosevelt Campobello International
Park, commemorating U.S. President Franklin
D. Roosevelt. FDR summered here as a youth,
and it was here that he contracted infantile pa-
ralysis (polio) in 1921. The park, covering most
of the island's southern end, has well-maintained
trails, picnic sites, and dramatic vistas, but its
centerpiece is the imposing Roosevelt Cottage,
a mile northeast of the bridge. Interesting to
note that before becoming a summer retreat for
wealthy Americans, Campobello was the feu-
dal fiefdom of a Welsh family. King George III

awarded the grant to Captain William Owen in
1767, and he arrived in 1770.

Roosevelt Cottage/Visitor Centre

Little seems to have changed in the 34-room
red-shingled Roosevelt "Cottage" overlooking
Passamaquoddy Bay since President Roosevelt
last visited in 1939. The grounds are beautifully
landscaped, and the many family mementos—
especially those in the late president's den—
bring history alive. It all feels very personal, far
less stuffy than most presidential memorials.

Stop first at the park's Visitor Centre, where
you can pick up brochures (including a trail
map, birding guide, and bog guide), use the restrooms, and see a short video setting the stage
for the cottage visit. Then walk across to the
house/museum (10 A.M.–6 P.M. Atlantic daylight time, 9 A.M.–5 P.M. eastern daylight time,

© HILARY NANGLE

Time seems to have stood still in the 34-room Roosevelt Cottage overlooking Passamaquoddy Bay.

last tour at 5:45 P.M., mid-May–mid-Oct., free). Guides are stationed in various rooms to explain and answer questions. Be sure to also visit the neighboring **Hubbard Cottage,** reopened to the public in 2006, and open July 1–early September whenever it isn't in use by conferences. Free outside walking tours of the estate and on-site presentations on local ecology are given, weather and staff permitting. For more information, contact Executive Secretary, Roosevelt Campobello International Park (P.O. Box 129, Lubec 04652, or 459 Rte. 774, Welshpool, Campobello, NB, Canada E5E 1A4, 506/752-2922 seasonal, www.fdr.net).

The Park by Car

If time is short, or you're unable to hike, at least take some of the park's driving routes— **Cranberry Point Drive,** 5.4 miles round-trip from the Visitor Centre; **Liberty Point Drive,** 12.4 miles round-trip, via Glensevern Road, from the Visitor Centre; and **Fox Hill Drive,** a 2.2-mile link between the other two main routes. Even with the car, you'll have access to beaches,

picnic sites, spruce and fir forests, and great views of lighthouses, islands, and the Bay of Fundy.

Just west of the main access road from the bridge is the **Mulholland Point picnic area,** where you can spread out your lunch next to the distinctive red-capped lighthouse overlooking Lubec Narrows.

Hiking/Picnicking

Within the international park are 8.5 miles of walking/hiking trails, varying from dead easy to moderately difficult. Easiest is the 1.2-mile (round-trip) walk from the Visitor Centre to **Friar's Head picnic area,** named for its distinctive promontory jutting into the bay. For the best angle, climb up to the observation deck on the "head." Grills and tables are here for picnickers. Pick up a brochure at the Visitor Centre detailing natural sights along the route.

The most difficult—and most dramatic— trail is a 2.4-mile stretch from **Liberty Point to Raccoon Beach,** along the southeastern shore of the island. Precipitous cliffs can make parts of this trail chancy for small

THE QUODDY LOOP

It's easy to make it a two-nation vacation and avoid backtracking along Route 1 by looping through Canada. In July and August, **East Coast Ferries** (Deer Island, New Brunswick, Canada, 506/747-2159 or 877/747-2159, www.eastcoastferries .nb.ca) operates funky, bargelike car ferries between Eastport and Deer Island, and then on to Campobello Island – and vice versa. The ferry schedule is in Atlantic time, so adjust for the one-hour time distance when planning, since Eastport is on eastern time and the two Canadian islands are on Atlantic time. Campobello departures are on the hour, beginning at 9 A.M. Atlantic time (8 A.M. eastern time). Eastport departures are on the half hour, beginning at 9:30 A.M. Atlantic time (8:30 A.M. eastern time). Check the schedule carefully to avoid missing the last boat back to Eastport. (If you take a car, you can drive back to Eastport from Campobello via Lubec. It's 1.5 miles by water and almost 50 miles by road.) The ferry landing in Eastport is just off Water Street, 0.3 mile north of Washington Street, next to the Eastport Chowder House Restaurant. Fees, in Canadian funds, for car and driver, are $15 for Deer Island/Campobello, $12 for Deer Island/Eastport, no charge for kids 12 and younger, and passengers without cars are $3 on each (no credit cards, fare collected on board). It all seems very informal, and the trip is an adventure, but remember that you're crossing the Canadian border. United States citizens need required identification; non-U.S. citizens need a passport; most non-Europeans also need a Canadian visa.

children or insecure adults, so use caution. Liberty Point is incredibly rugged, but observation platforms make it easy to see the tortured rocks and wide-open Bay of Fundy. Along the way is the SunSweep Sculpture, an international art project by David Barr.

At broad Raccoon Beach, you can walk the sands, have a picnic, or watch for whales, porpoises, and osprey. To avoid returning via the same route, park at Liberty Point and walk back along Liberty Point Drive from Raccoon Beach. If you're traveling with nonhikers, arrange for them to meet you with a vehicle at Con Robinson's Point.

A fascinating boardwalk, perfect for those in wheelchairs, is **Eagle Hill Bog,** 2.9 km down the Glensevern Road. Interpretive signs explain the lichens, scrub pines, pitcher plants, and other flora and fauna within the bogs. A spur trail leads to a trail that climbs quickly to an observation deck.

CAMPOBELLO BEYOND THE INTERNATIONAL PARK

Take a day or two and explore Campobello beyond the park; overnighters have several lodging and food options. You can also continue by ferry from here to New Brunswick's Deer Island and on to Eastport.

Herring Cove Provincial Park

New Brunswick's provincial government does a conscientious job of running Herring Cove Provincial Park (506/752-2396 or 800/561-0123), with picnic areas, 91 campsites (506/752-7010), a four-mile trail system, a mile-long sandy beach, freshwater Glensevern Lake, and the nine-hole championship-level **Herring Cove Golf Course** (506/752-2467). The park is open early June–September.

East Quoddy Head Light

Consult the tide calendar before planning your assault on East Quoddy Head Light (also known as Head Harbour Light), at Campobello's northernmost tip. It's an islet accessible only at low tide. The distinctive white light tower bears a huge red cross. (You're likely to pass near it on whale-watching trips out of Eastport.) From the Roosevelt cottage, follow Route 774 through the village of Wilson's Beach and continue to the parking area. A stern Canadian Coast Guard warning sign tells the story:

Extreme Hazard. Beach exposed only at low tide. Incoming tide rises 5 feet per hour and may leave you stranded for 8 hours. Wading or swimming are extremely dangerous due to swift currents and cold water. Proceed at your own risk.

So there. It's definitely worth the effort for the bay and island views from the lighthouse grounds, often including whales and eagles. Allow about an hour before and after dead low tide (be sure your watch coincides with the Atlantic-time tide calendar).

ACCOMMODATIONS AND FOOD

In midsummer, if you'd like to overnight on the island, be sure to reserve lodgings in advance; Campobello is a popular destination. The nearest backup beds are in Lubec, and those fill up, too. **The Owen House** (11 Welshpool St., Welshpool, Campobello Island, NB, Canada, 506/752-2977, www.owenhouse.ca, late May–mid-Oct., $107–210 Canadian), is the island's best address, a comfortably elegant early-19th-century inn on 10 acres on Deer Point overlooking Passamaquoddy Bay and Eastport in the distance. Nine guest rooms (two with shared baths) on three floors are decorated with antiques and family treasures along with owner Joyce Morrel's paintings (Joyce grew up in this house) and assorted handmade quilts. There's a first-floor room that's ideal for those with mobility problems. Joyce and innkeeper Jan Meiners are very active in the lighthouse preservation efforts. Just north of the inn is the Deer Island ferry landing.

The Lupine Lodge (610 Rte. 774, Welshpool, Campobello Island, NB, Canada, 506/752-2555, www.lupinelodge.com, early June–mid-Oct., $85–140 Canadian), a log lodge complex, is only a quarter mile from the Roosevelt cottage. Bay views from the 11-acre grounds and a few of the 11 rooms are terrific, but rooms are pretty basic. The adjacent restaurant serves breakfast, lunch, and dinner. Out the back door are the Adams Estate trails of the provincial park.

Campsites are available at **Herring Cove** **Provincial Park** (506/752-7010). Tent cabins also are available.

Don't expect culinary creativity on Campobello, but you won't starve—at least during the summer season. Best choice is **Family Fisheries** (1977 Rte. 774, Wilson's Beach, 506/752-2470, 10 A.M.–8 or 9 P.M. daily), a seafood restaurant and fish market toward the northern end of the island. Portions are huge, service is friendly, the fish is superfresh, and the homemade desserts are heavenly. BYOB. The only restaurant open year-round is **Sweet Time Bakery** (Rte. 774, 7 A.M.–8 or 9 P.M. daily), serving good home cooking and fresh-baked breads. The only island restaurant with a liquor license is Lupine Lodge.

INFORMATION AND SERVICES

To visit Campobello, you'll have to pass Customs checkpoints on the U.S. and Canada ends of the Franklin D. Roosevelt Memorial Bridge (Lubec, U.S., Customs 207/733-4331; Campobello, Canada, Customs 506/752-2091, fax 506/752-1080). Be sure to have required identification.

Be aware that crossing this short little bridge takes an hour, because there's a one-hour time difference between Lubec and Campobello. Lubec (like the rest of Maine) is on eastern standard time; Campobello, like the rest of Canada's Maritime Provinces, is on Atlantic time, an hour later. As soon as you reach the island, set your clock ahead an hour.

There is no need to convert U.S. currency to Canadian for use on Campobello; U.S. dollars are accepted everywhere on the island, but prices tend to be quoted in Canadian dollars.

Just after Canadian Customs waves you through from Lubec, stop at the Tourist Information Centre (44 Rte. 774, Welshpool, NB, 506/752-7043, May–Oct.), on your right. The staff can fix you up with an island map, trail maps of the international park, tide info for lighthouse visits, and New Brunswick propaganda, and then steer you toward the Roosevelt property.

For information on Campobello Island, contact Campobello Island Tourism Association (506/752-7010, www.campobello.com).

THE DOWN EAST COAST

Eastport and Vicinity

When you leave Whiting, and continue north on Route 1 around Cobscook Bay, it's hard to believe that life could slow down any more than it already has, but it does. The landscape's raw beauty is occasionally punctuated by farmhouses or a convenience store, but little else.

Edmunds Township's claims to fame are its splendid public lands—Cobscook Bay State Park and a unit of Moosehorn National Wildlife Refuge. Just past the state park, loop along the scenic shoreline before returning to Route 1.

Pembroke, once part of adjoining Dennysville, claims Reversing Falls Park, where you can watch (and hear) ebbing and flowing tides draining and filling Cobscook Bay.

If time allows a short scenic detour, especially in fall, turn left (northwest) on Route 214 and drive 10 miles to quaintly named Meddybemps, allegedly a Passamaquoddy word meaning "plenty of alewives (herring)." Views over Meddybemps Lake, on the north side of the road, are spectacular, and you can launch a canoe or kayak into the lake here, less than a mile beyond the junction with Route 191 (take the dead-end unpaved road toward the water).

Backtracking to Route 1, heading east from Pembroke, you'll come to Perry, best known for the Sipayik (Pleasant Point) Indian Reservation, a Passamaquoddy settlement, two miles east of Route 1, that's been here since 1822. Drop down Route 191 that cuts through the reservation's heart. If there's time, stop at the small Waponahki Museum. Or plan a visit around the reservation's August Indian Days celebration.

The city (yes, it's officially a city) of Eastport (pop. 1,900) is on Moose Island, connected by causeway to the mainland at Sipayik (Pleasant Point). Views are terrific on both sides, especially at sunset, as you hopscotch from one blob of land to another and finally reach this minicity, where the sardine industry was introduced as long ago as 1875. Five sardine canneries once operated here, employing hundreds of local residents who snipped the heads off herring and stuffed them into cans—one of those esoteric skills not easily translatable to other tasks. In the 1990s, the focus was on fish farming. In the new century, entrepreneurs and artisans seem to be leading the way.

Settled in 1772, Eastport has had its ups and downs, mostly mirroring the fishing industry. It's now on an upswing, as people "from away" have arrived to soak up the vibe of a small town with a heavy Down East accent. Artists, artisans, and antiques shops are leading the town's rejuvenation as a tourist destination, with The Tides Institute at the forefront. A big push came in 2001, when the Fox Network reality-TV series *Murder in Small Town X* was filmed here; the city morphed into the village of Sunrise, Maine, and local residents eagerly filled in as extras. The huge waterfront statue of a fisherman is a remnant of the filming.

The biggest controversy in these parts now is the possibility of a liquefied natural gas terminal on the coastline, something many locals on both sides of the border are fighting.

Until 1811, the town also included Lubec, which is about 2.5 miles across the water in a boat, but 40-something in a car. A ferry now shuttles passengers back and forth for Lubec's SummerKeys concerts, and locals hold out hope that a regular schedule will be established.

SIGHTS
Historic Walking Tour
The best way to appreciate Eastport's history is to pick up and follow the route in *A Walking Guide to Eastport,* available locally for $2. The handy map/brochure spotlights the city's 18th-, 19th-, and early-20th-century homes, businesses, and monuments, many now on the National Register of Historic Places. Among the highlights are historic homes converted to B&Bs, two museums, and a large chunk of downtown Water Street, with many handsome brick buildings erected after a disastrous fire swept through in 1886. A free walking map, with far fewer details, also is available.

Raye's Mustard Mill Museum
How often do you have a chance to watch mustard

being made in a turn-of-the-20th-century mustard mill? Drive by J. W. Raye and Co. (83 Washington St., Rte. 190, Eastport, 207/853-4451 or 800/853-1903, www.rayesmustard.com, 9 A.M.–5 P.M. daily), at the edge of Eastport, and stop in for a free 15-minute tour (call for schedule). You'll get to see the granite millstones, the mustard seeds being winnowed, and enormous vats of future mustard. Raye's sells mustard under its own label and produces it for major customers under their labels. The shop stocks all of Raye's mustard varieties (samples available), other Maine-made food, and gift items, and it also has a small café, where you can buy sandwiches, soups, and salads. Even Martha Stewart has discovered Ray's, which took home both gold and bronze medals from the 2007 World Wide Mustard Competition.

The Tides Institute and Museum of Art

One of the most promising additions to Eastport's downtown is The Tides (43 Water St., 207/853-4047, www.tidesinstitute.org, 10 A.M. to 4 P.M. Tues.–Sat., free), in a former bank that owner/director Hugh French, an Eastport native, is restoring. The institute's impressive goals are to build significant cultural collections and to produce new culturally important works employing printmaking, letterpress, photography, bookmaking, oral history, and other media. For its collection, the institute is focusing on works by artists and photographers associated with Maine and Maritime Canada. Already, it has significant works by artists such as John Marin and photographers such as Lewis Hine, a nice selection of baskets by Native Americans, and two organs made by the local Pembroke Organ Co. in the 1880s. These and others are displayed in rotating shows that also highlight contemporary area artists. The research and reference library has more than 4,000 volumes. The institute also offers workshops by visiting artists in printmaking and other topics. These are open to the public by reservation. Definitely stop in for a visit.

Passamaquoddy Indian Reservation

Baskets, tools, beadwork, a birch-bark canoe, and photo-lined walls are all part of the **Waponahki Museum** (Rte. 190, Perry, 207/853-4001, call for hours) on Sipayik (Pleasant Point Reservation). The small collection is dedicated to preserving the history and culture of Maine's Passamaquoddy Indians. The museum has spurred revival of the Passamaquoddy language, now being taught and written. The museum—two miles east of Route 1 and seven miles north of Eastport—is open all year. Admission is free, but donations are welcomed.

Ask at the museum or locally about basket makers who might sell from their homes. The fancy and work baskets are treasures, constantly escalating in price. It's a real treat to be able to buy one from the maker.

PARKS AND PRESERVES
◖ Shackford Head State Park

Ninety-acre Shackford Head (off Deep Cove Rd., Eastport, trailhead and parking area just

© TOM NANGLE

The Tides Institute houses an impressive and growing art collection.

TIDES

Nowhere in Maine is the adage "Time and tide wait for no man" more true than along the Washington County coastline. The nation's most extreme tidal ranges occur in this area, so the hundreds of miles of tidal shore frontage between Steuben and Calais provide countless opportunities for observing tidal phenomena. Every six hours or so, the tide begins either ebbing or flowing. The farther Down East you go, the higher (and lower) the tides. Although tides in Canada's Bay of Fundy are far higher, the highest tides in New England occur along the St. Croix River, at Calais.

Tides govern coastal life – particularly Down East, where average tidal ranges may be 10–20 feet and extremes approach 28 feet. Everyone is a slave to the tide calendar, which coastal-community newspapers diligently publish. Boats tie up with extra-long lines; clammers and wormdiggers schedule their days by the tides; hikers have to plan for shoreline exploring; and kayakers need to plan their routes to avoid getting stuck in the muck.

Tides, as we all learned in elementary school, are lunar phenomena, created by the gravitational pull of the moon; the tidal range depends on the lunar phase. Tides are most extreme at new and full moons – when the sun, moon, and Earth are all aligned. These are spring tides, supposedly because the water springs upward

(the term has nothing to do with the season). And tides are smallest during the moon's first and third quarters – when the sun, Earth, and moon have a right-angle configuration. These are neap tides ("neap" comes from an Old English word meaning "scanty"). Other lunar/solar phenomena, such as the equinoxes and solstices, can also affect tidal ranges.

The best time for shoreline exploration is on a new-moon or full-moon day, when low tide exposes mussels, sea urchins, sea cucumbers, starfish, periwinkles, hermit crabs, rockweed, and assorted nonbiodegradable trash. Rubber boots or waterproof, treaded shoes are essential on the wet, slippery terrain.

Caution is also essential in tidal areas. Unless you've carefully plotted tide times and heights, don't park a car or bike or boat trailer on a beach; make sure your sea kayak is lashed securely to a tree or bollard; don't take a long nap on shoreline granite; and don't cross a low-tide land spit without an eye on your watch.

A perhaps apocryphal but almost believable story goes that one flatlander stormed up to a ranger at Cobscook Bay State Park one bright summer morning and demanded indignantly to know why they had had the nerve to drain the water from her shorefront campsite during the night. When it comes to tides...you have to go with the flow.

© TOM NANGLE

Downtown Eastport fronts on the harbor, and water lines in the granite breakwater are evidence of the giant tides.

east of the Washington County Community College Marine Technology Center at the southern end of town, free) is on a peninsula that juts into Cobscook Bay. It has five miles of wooded trails, with the easiest being the one-mile round-trip to Shackford Head and its continuation onto the steeper Ship Point Trail, which adds another half mile, rising gently to a 175-foot-high headland with wide-open views of Eastport and, depending on weather, Campobello Island, Lubec, Pembroke, and even Grand Manan. This state preserve is a particularly good family hike. Use bug repellent and carry binoculars and a camera. There's a toilet near the parking area, but no other facilities. Also here is a memorial with plaques detailing the history of five Civil War ships that were decommissioned and burned on Cony Beach between 1901 and 1920 by the U.S. government. Eastport's huge tides allowed the ships to be brought in and beached and then taken apart as the tide receded. Of note is that 14 Eastport men served on four of the ships.

Reversing Falls Park

There's plenty of room for adults to relax and kids to play at the 140-acre Reversing Falls Park in West Pembroke—plus shorefront ledges and a front-row seat overlooking a fascinating tidal phenomenon. Pack a picnic and then check newspapers or information offices for the tide times, so you can watch the salt water surging through a 300-yard-wide passage at about 25 knots, creating a whirlpool and churning "falls." The park is at Mahar Point in West Pembroke, 7.2 miles south of Route 1. Coming from the south (Dennysville), leave Route 1 in West Pembroke when you see the Triangle Grocery Store. Turn right and go 0.3 mile to Leighton Point Road, where you'll see a sign saying, "Shore Access 5.5 miles." Turn right and go 3.8 miles, past gorgeous meadows, low shrubs, and views of Cobscook Bay. Turn right on Clarkside Road, at a very tiny Reversing Falls sign, posted high on a telephone pole. Go about 1.5 miles to the end and then turn left onto a gravel road and continue two miles to the park.

RECREATION

Whale-Watching and Scenic Cruises

Eastporter Butch Harris gave the waterfront a shot in the arm when he bought the sleek *Sylvina Beal,* a historic, 84-foot schooner built in 1911. His company, **Eastport Windjammers** (104 Water St. at the head of the breakwater, 207/853-2500, 207/853-4303 before 10 A.M. and 6–8 P.M., www.eastportwindjammers.com) offers a number of options to sail. The three-hour whale-watching cruise departs at 1:30 P.M. daily and heads out into the prime whale-feeding grounds of Passamaquoddy Bay—passing the Old Sow whirlpool (largest tidal whirlpool in the Northern Hemisphere), salmon aquaculture pens, and Campobello Island. En route, you'll see bald eagles, porpoises, possibly puffins and osprey, and more. Best months are July and August, when sightings are frequent, but Butch is a skilled spotter, so if they're there, he'll find them. The cost is $35 for adults, $18 for children 12 and younger. A two-hour sunset cruise departs the Eastport Pier at 7 P.M. and costs $25 for adults, $15 for children.

The newest addition to Captain Harris's fleet is the *Halie and Matthew,* a 92-foot schooner he built with John Bishop at Eastport's boat school. Each of the eight staterooms has double berths and private head with shower. Two- to five-day cruises range from $500 to more than $1,000 pp.

Deep-Sea Fishing

Eastport Windjammers also offers a four-hour fishing trip on the *Quoddy Dam,* with all equipment provided. No license is required for recreational saltwater fishing. Bring a cooler or fish container if you want to keep your catch. The trip costs $25 for adults and $15 for children. It leaves from the Eastport Breakwater at 8 A.M.

Sea Kayaking, Canoeing, and Hiking

Explore the region by sea kayak with **Cobscook Hikes and Paddles** (13 Woodcock Way, Robbinston, 207/726-4776 summer, 207/454-2130 winter, www.cobscookhikesandpaddles.com), which services the area between Whiting and

THE DOWN EAST COAST

Calais. Registered Maine Guides Stephen and Tessa Ftorek lead three-hour ocean or lake paddles, designed to meet your interests and ability, for $50 pp. Two-hour sunrise or sunset paddles are $40. On Friday nights, you can watch luminescent organisms sparkle in the water on a two-hour Phosphorescent Paddle, for $45. The Ftoreks also offer guided full-day ($80) and half-day ($40) hikes and snowshoeing adventures in winter. They opened an outpost in Eastport at Eastport Framing.

Quoss Boats (Rte. 1, Perry, 207/731-9595) rents lake kayaks for $40 per day, including paddle, life jacket, and portage. Renters must be swimmers, older than 21, and provide a major credit card for deposit. A half-day rental, when available, is $27. Kayaks are only for lake and estuary paddling, and introductory lessons are available. You can take them to one of the many pretty lakes on the inland side of Route 1.

Star-Gazing

The Downeast Amateur Astronomers' **Downeast Observatory** (356 Old County Rd., Pembroke, 207/726-4621, www.downeast aa.com), with eight-inch DE8 reflector and three- and five-inch refractors, is open to the public for free by appointment. Contact Charlie Sawyer at the number above for details.

ENTERTAINMENT

The **Eastport Arts Center** (36 Washington St., Eastport, 207/853-2358, www.eastport artscenter.com) is an umbrella organization for local arts groups, with headquarters and performing space in a former church. You can pick up a brochure with a complete schedule, which usually includes concerts, films, puppet shows, productions by local theater group **Stage East,** an Elderhostel program, and other cultural events. Also based here is **SummerArts** (207/853-6179, www.summerarts.com), a five-week series of classes and workshops.

The center works with Butch Harrison to provide a ferry to the free **SummerKeys** concerts, held Wednesday nights late June–early September in Lubec. Transportation is aboard the *Quoddy Dam,* departing Eastport at

6:30 P.M. and returning around 9:30 P.M. Ferry tickets are $14 in advance, $17 for walk-ons, space available, buy at the *Sylvina Beal* ticket office on Water Street or call 207/853-2500.

For **live music** in Eastport on weekends, try The Rose Garden (9 Dana St.).

FESTIVALS AND EVENTS

For a small community, Eastport manages to pull together and put on plenty of successful events during the year.

Eastport's annual four-day **Fourth of July–Old Home Week** extravaganza includes a parade, pancake breakfasts, barbecues, a flea market, an auction, races, live entertainment, and fireworks. This is one of Maine's best Fourth of July celebrations and attracts a crowd of more than 10,000. Lodgings are booked months in advance, so plan ahead.

Indian Ceremonial Days, a three-day Native American celebration, includes children's games, canoe races, craft demos, talking circles, fireworks, and traditional food and dancing at Sipayik, the Pleasant Point Reservation, in Perry, the second weekend in August.

The **Eastport Salmon Festival** celebrates the area's aquaculture industry. If you like salmon, you'll *love* this event, which combines a salmon barbecue, craft booths, live entertainment, and boat trips at the Eastport breakwater 11 A.M.–4 P.M. the Sunday after Labor Day.

SHOPPING
Art, Crafts, and Antiques

Eastport has long been a magnet for artists and craftspeople yearning to work in a supportive environment, but the influx has increased in recent years. Proof of this is **The Eastport Gallery** (74 Water St., Eastport, 207/853-4166, www.eastportgallery.com, mid-June–Sept.), a cooperative whose works in varied media line the walls of a downtown building. The gallery also sponsors the annual **Paint Eastport Day,** usually held the second Saturday in September, when anyone is invited to paint a local scene; a reception and "wet paint" auction follow.

Relatively new on Eastport's art scene is **The Commons** (51 Water St., 207/853-4123), a waterfront building that's been beautifully renovated by a gaggle of energetic women with local ties into a fabulous gallery displaying works by 60 area artists and artisans. The group has plans to renovate a nearby waterfront warehouse into more shops and perhaps a hotel.

Earth Forms (5 Dana St., Eastport, 207/853-2430, www.earthforms.biz) features potter Donald Sutherland's intriguing (and sometimes whimsical) wheel-thrown work—self-described as "functional, nonfunctional, and dysfunctional" pottery. You can often see him at work on his wheel. It's tough to walk out without buying one of these special pieces.

Next door to Earth Forms is **Rose Garden Antiques and Design** (9 Dana St., 207/853-9598), an eclectic collection of antiques, collectibles, and art. Owners Linda and Al Salleroli are renovating the building and have included an indoor garden, café, and space for independent vendors as well as public restrooms.

Woodworker Roland LaVallee's gallery **Crow Tracks** (11 Water St., 207/853-2336, www.crowtracks.com) is filled with his intricate carvings of birds and local fauna. The tiny garden entryway just doubles the pleasure of a visit.

It's a delight to wander through the sculpted mermaids, angels, goddesses, flora, and fauna in the garden at **Ostrander** (83 Clark St., corner of Brewster St., Eastport, 207/853-4342). Inside are more sculptures, paintings, and garden art by Elizabeth Ostrander.

A number of very talented artists and artisans are tucked along the back roads of the area. You might get lucky and find them open, but it's wise to call before making a special trip. These include the **Salt Meadow Gallery and Studio** (Hersey Rd., Pembroke, 207/726-5153), in a log cabin chock-full of hand-painted floorcloths and woodcuts by Beverly Runyan; **Done Roving Farm and Carding Mill** (20 Charlotte Rd., Charlotte, 207/454-8148), a working farm where fiber artist Paula Farra creates and sells handspun yarns and felts in a variety of fibers and displays the works of other area artisans; **Wrenovations** (84 Mill Stream Rd., Robbinston, 207/454-2382), stained art creations by Mark Wren; and **Susan Designs** (behind Loring's Body Shop on Gin Cove Rd., Perry, 207/853-4315), where gifted quilt artist Susan Plachy sells her creations.

Hand-Sewn Shoes

Shoemaking was once a major industry in Maine, although today only a couple of places still sew shoes by hand. One of them is **Quoddy Trail Moccasin Co.** (1041 Rte. 1, Perry, 207/853-2488, www.quoddytrail.com). The company was started by Harry Smith Shorey and is now run by his descendent Kevin Shorey and his wife, Kirsten. Overruns and seconds are sold at discounted prices at the Shoreys' store, the **Quoddy Wigwam** (Rte. 1 and Shore Rd., 207/853-4812), where you can also see a huge stuffed moose and buy Native American baskets and souvenirs. Call or ask at the store to arrange a tour of the low-key factory to see where the leather is cut and how it's sewn into moccasins, boat shoes, slippers, and other models, or to arrange for a custom pair ($70 and up; the best-selling model retails for $140) to be made.

Gifts and a Whole Lot More

Describing **45th Parallel: The Store** (Rte. 1, Perry, 207/853-9500) is a tough assignment. You really have to *go there* and see for yourself. The aesthetic displays are worth the trip to this eclectic emporium. Housed in a one-story log building two miles (in the Calais direction) from the junction of Routes 190 and 1, the 45th Parallel is part antiques shop, part gift shop, part global marketplace—and entirely seductive. Tiny white lights glimmer here and there, antique architectural remnants hang from the ceiling, and every little niche holds yet another fascinating treasure.

Do stop in, if only for a few minutes, at **S. W. Wadsworth and Son** (42 Water St., 207/853-4343), the oldest ship chandlery in the country and the oldest retail business in Maine. In addition to hardware and marine gear, you'll find nautical gifts and souvenirs.

ACCOMMODATIONS

Lodgings in Eastport can fill up in summer, and since it's literally the end of the road, it's wise to reserve ahead.

Bed-and-Breakfasts

In 1833, renowned artist John James Audubon stayed at the elegant **Weston House** (26 Boynton St., Eastport, 207/853-2907 or 800/853-2907, www.westonhouse-maine.com, $70–85), so one of the three second-floor guest rooms bears his name—and walls lined with Audubon bird prints. All rooms share 2.5 baths, but don't let that dissuade you from staying at this lovely home. Jett and John Peterson's family antiques and interesting art and crafts fill the beautifully decorated house on a quiet side street two blocks above the waterfront. Breakfast is outstanding (Jett is Eastport's favorite caterer), complete with candelabra and classical music. Outside are croquet and badminton facilities, plus lovely gardens with a gazebo, chairs, and table. Tea and sherry are available in the afternoon. With notice, Jett will prepare a private dinner and serve it in the formal dining room, a smart and delicious choice given Eastport's limited restaurants.

Pretty gardens surround the **❰ Chadbourne House** (19 Shackford St., Eastport, 207/853-2727 or 888/853-2728, www.chadbournehouse.com, $110–140), Eastport's most elegant B&B. Jill and David Westphal's antiques-filled, Federal-style home has four guestrooms, two with fireplaces and one that fills most of the third floor. The double living room has two fireplaces. Guests gather each morning at the dining room table for David's breakfasts, and they can arrange in advance for a seafood dinner feast to be served in the garden. It's walking distance to downtown. One caveat: You'll have to remove your shoes in the entryway. Wi-Fi throughout.

The comfortably furnished **Milliken House Bed and Breakfast** (29 Washington St., Eastport, 207/853-2955 or 888/507-9370, www.eastport-inn.com, $75–85) is a good choice for families, but be forewarned that you'll have to carry your luggage up at least one, and perhaps two, tall flights of stairs. Hosts Bill and Mary Williams welcome children and pets to their in-town home that's an easy walk to shops and restaurants. Breakfasts are huge and served family-style in the very-Victorian dining room. There's a big TV in the double parlor downstairs, Wi-Fi throughout, and a phone is available. Call ahead in winter.

Motel

Here's a motel with the spirit of a B&B. Enthusiastic about their adopted community, host Owen Lawlor and manager Deb Moore at **The Motel East** (23A Water St., Eastport, 207/853-4747, www.eastportme.info, $105–120) provide all kinds of advice and guarantee you'll enjoy the area. Got a problem or question? Owen or Deb can solve it or answer it. Guests have front-row seats on Passamaquoddy Bay, overlooking Campobello Island, and you can walk to everything downtown. Six good-size rooms and eight efficiency suites have Wi-Fi, phones, and cable TV, although the rooms could use freshening. Request a balcony room; avoid those on the basement level. Free coffee in the lobby. It's open all year. The separate Friar Roads Cottage is available for $150 d a day.

Apartments

On the second floor of **The Commons** (51 Water St., 207/853-4123, www.thecommons eastport.com), a newly renovated downtown building on the waterfront, are two nicely appointed, two-bedroom apartments, with decks and spectacular harbor views. Tide Watcher has two baths and rents for $950 per week; Water's Edge has one bath and rents for $900; either is $150 per night/three-night minimum, when available. Both are nicely decorated, have well-equipped kitchens and comfy living rooms, laundries, and big decks over the harbor, complete with gas grills.

Campground

On the outskirts of town is the quiet, well-maintained, waterfront **Seaview Campground** (16 Norwood Rd., Eastport, 207/853-4471, www.eastportmaine.com), just off Route 190, with 70 tent and RV open and semiwooded sites, nine cabins, and a four-unit motel. Shorefront sites on Harrington Cove have great views, but they're snapped up quickly. Cabins have excellent vistas. The camp store, open 7 A.M.–10 P.M., sells lobster live or cooked by the pound. There are also a recreation hall, dock, laundry, and a restaurant (open 7 A.M.– 8 P.M.) serving breakfast, lunch, and dinner. Leashed pets are allowed only at RV and tent sites. Campsites are based on a family of four. Tent sites are $14–20, RV sites are $25–40, depending upon location and season. One- to three-bedroom cabins are $70–145 per day or $425–800 a week; motel rooms are $55–80 a day. It's open mid-May–mid-October. Pets are $10 per day, with a two-pet limit.

FOOD

While you won't go hungry in Eastport, you won't be wowed by the food, either. As always in this region, ask locally about the current reputations.

Local Flavors

The best pizza in Eastport comes from **Bank Square and Deli** (34 Water St., Eastport, 207/853-2709, www.banksquarepizza.com, 11 A.M.–8 P.M. Mon.–Sat.), where you can also get subs, wraps, burgers, salads, chicken, and even pasta. It has only a few seats, so grab your stuff and eat it elsewhere. No credit cards.

The **Sunrise County Farmers Market** sets up its tables next to Raye's Mustard Mill (Washington St., Eastport) 11 A.M.–2 P.M. every Thursday late June–October.

Moose Island General Store (corner of Water and Washington Sts., 207/853-2622, 5 A.M.–10 P.M. daily) serves breakfast baked goods, pizza, and other foods and must-haves. Bonus points for the harborfront deck.

Here's something a bit different. **Blueberry Point Chefs** (Rte. 1, P.O. Box 58, Perry 04667, 207/853-4629, www.blueberrypointchefs.com) is a cooking school held on a 150-acre blueberry farm with panoramic views over Passamaquoddy Bay. Chef Audrey Patterson teaches two-day classes 5–8:30 P.M. Mondays and Tuesdays late May–late September for $80 pp or $50 for one night. Each evening concludes with a meal, and classes include opportunities for local culinary tours. Check the website for the specifics of each class. Also on the premises is the **Ice House Wine and Cheese Shop**

(10 A.M.–5 P.M. Tues.–Sat.), a gourmet food and wine shop.

Casual Dining

One of Eastport's dining secrets is Hilda and Sidney Lewis's **The Blue Iris** (31 Water St., Eastport, 207/853-2440, 6:30 A.M.–2 P.M. Tues.–Sat.), which shares space with a floral shop. Well-spaced indoor tables and outdoor ones on a bilevel deck all have water views. Breakfast is served all day; lunch is available beginning at 11 A.M., dinner is served on special occasions. With the exception of lobster and crabmeat rolls or clubs, a chicken Caesar, and perhaps daily specials, nothing on the menu is more than $5. It's all good, and the service is cheerful but, uhm, leisurely.

A popular roadside eatery with a well-deserved reputation, the aptly named **New Friendly Restaurant** (1014 Rte. 1, Perry, 207/853-6610, 11 A.M.–8 P.M. Mon.–Fri.) lays on home-cooked offerings for "dinnah" (a Maine-ism meaning lunch), specializing in steak and seafood, including what many label the area's best lobster roll. Don't be surprised to find it crowded.

A downtown Eastport institution since 1924, the **Wa-Co Diner and Dining Room** (47 Water St., 207/853-4046, 6 A.M.–9 P.M. daily), pronounced WHACK-o, short for Washington County *or,* the story goes, for Nelson Watts and Ralph Colwell, is a must-do local-color stop. Choose from the front diner, with counter and booths, the more refined dining room, or the waterfront deck. Expect diner fare with a dose of attitude; a few fancier items top out around $25, but most are inexpensive. New ownership took over in 2007, so ask locally as reviews have been mixed. No credit cards.

Time your meal right, and you can watch the Deer Isle ferry arrive and depart or view the windjammer *Sylvina Beal* sail by from the bilevel **Eastport Chowder House** (167 Water St., 207/853-4700, 11 A.M.–9 P.M. daily). Seafood, natch, is the specialty, with entrées in the $12–15 range. One drawback is the bar underneath—the jukebox is so loud that the tables in the dining room shake.

THE DOWN EAST COAST

INFORMATION AND SERVICES

Information

Brochures are available at the Quoddy Maritime Museum and Visitor Center (70 Water St., 10 A.M.–6 P.M. daily June–Sept.). In the museum section of the center is a huge model of the failed 1936 Passamaquoddy Tidal Power Project (an idea whose time hadn't come when it was proposed).

Information also is available from the Eastport Chamber of Commerce (207/853-3633, www.eastport.net) and online at www.cobscookbay.com/eastport.htm.

The handsome stone Peavey Memorial Library (26 Water St., Eastport, 207/853-4021), built in 1893, is named after the inventor of the Peavey grain elevator.

Public Restrooms

Restrooms are available at the library, and in summer, there are portable toilets on Eastport's breakwater.

Calais and Vicinity

Calais (CAL-us) is as far as you'll get on the coast of Maine; from here on, you're headed inland.

Europeans showed up in this area as early as 1604, when French adventurers established an ill-fated colony on St. Croix Island in the St. Croix River—16 whole years before the Pilgrims even thought about Massachusetts. After a winter-long debacle, all became relatively quiet until 1779, when the first permanent settler arrived.

The most interesting time to show up in Calais (pop. 3,890) is during the nine-day International Festival, the first or second week in August, when the city and neighboring St. Stephen, New Brunswick, go all out with dances, concerts, races, barbecues, and fireworks—reinforcing the transborder cooperation that has long benefited both communities. In late 2008, a third international bridge should open, connecting Route 1 north of downtown Calais to St. Stephen. It joins a downtown bridge, also connecting to St. Stephen, and a quieter, smaller crossing a few miles north, connecting with Mill Town.

Southeast of Calais is tiny Robbinston, a booming shipbuilding community in the 19th century but today little more than a 500-person blip on the map. Highlights nowadays are a wonderful chocolate shop and the Calais-Robbinston "milestones."

SIGHTS

C Downeast Heritage Center

The $6.5 million Downeast Heritage Cen-

ter (39 Union St., Calais, 207/454-7878 or 877/454-2500, www.downeastheritage.org, 10 A.M.–5 P.M. daily mid-May–mid-Oct., free) opened in the renovated Calais Train Station in May 2004 and now has three permanent, interactive, low-tech exhibits highlighting more than 12,000 years of regional cultural and natural history. These explain the region's shipbuilding, forestry, blueberrying, and fishing heritage; Passamaquoddy culture; and the St. Croix settlement. Among the highlights are a handmade Passamaquoddy canoe crafted using traditional tribal tools, a touch tank with marine creatures, and a riverfront walk, from which, if you're lucky, you might spot soaring eagles.

Walking Tour

Pick up a copy of the *Walking Tour Guide to Calais Residential Historic District* at the Maine Tourism Information Center, on the waterfront. The guide, produced by the St. Croix Historical Society, briefly covers the town's history and maps and describes the architecture and early owners of 23 historic houses, four of which are listed on the National Register of Historic Places.

St. Croix Island

Unless you have your own boat, you can't get over to 6.5-acre St. Croix Island, an International Historic Site under joint U.S. and Canadian jurisdiction (Rte. 1, Red Beach

Cove, eight miles south of Calais, www.nps
.gov/maac, free).

The island is the site of the pioneering colony established by French explorers Samuel de Champlain and Pierre du Gua (Sieur de Monts) in 1604. Doomed by disease, mosquitoes, lack of food, and a grueling winter, 35 settlers died; in spring, the emaciated survivors abandoned their effort and moved on to Nova Scotia. In 1969, archaeologists found graves of 23 victims, but the only monument on the island is a commemorative plaque dating from 1904.

The current in the St. Croix River is strong, and tidal ranges can be as high as 28 feet, so neophyte boaters shouldn't even attempt a crossing, but local residents often picnic and swim off the island's sandy beach on the southern end. For a better understanding of the historic colony, visit the Downeast Heritage Center. The attractive 16-acre roadside rest area on Route 1 at **Red Beach Cove** was greatly improved for the 400th anniversary of the settlement in 2004. A short heritage trail, with bronze statues depicting various key persona or cultures in the development of the colony, ends on the point with views of the island. Also here are picnic tables, restrooms, a gravel beach, and a boat launch. It's a great place to stop for a picnic.

Whitlock Mill Lighthouse

From the lovely Pikewoods Rest Area, beside Route 1, about four miles southeast of Calais, there's a prime view of 32-foot-high Whitlock Mill Lighthouse, on the southern shore of the St. Croix River. Built in 1892, the green flashing light is accessible only over private land, so check it out from this vantage point. Besides, you can also have a picnic break here.

Calais-Robbinston Milestones

A quirky little local feature, the Calais-Robbinston milestones are a dozen red-granite chunks marking each of the 12 miles between Robbinston and Calais. Presaging today's highway mileage markers, late-19th-century entrepreneur and journalist James S. Pike had the stones installed on the north side of Route 1

to keep track of the distance while training his pacing horses.

RECREATION
Parks and Preserves

More than 50 miles of trails and gravel roads wind through the 17,257-acre Baring Unit of the **Moosehorn National Wildlife Refuge** (Charlotte Rd., Baring, 207/454-7161, http://moose horn.fws.gov, sunrise–sunset daily, free), on the outskirts of Calais. Start with the 1.2-mile nature trail near the refuge headquarters, and get ready for major-league wildlife-watching: 35 mammal and 220 bird species have been spotted in the refuge's fields, forests, ponds, and marshes. Wear waterproof shoes and insect repellent. In August, help yourself to wild blueberries. During November deer-hunting season, either avoid the refuge Monday–Saturday or wear a hunter-orange hat and vest. Trails are accessible by snowshoes, snowmobile, or cross-country skis in winter. To reach refuge headquarters, take Route 1 north from downtown Calais about three miles. Turn left onto the Charlotte Road, and go 2.4 miles to the headquarters sign. The office is open 8 A.M.–4 P.M. Monday–Friday all year (except major national holidays); you can pick up free trail maps, bird checklists, and other informative brochures. If you want to help support the conservation of wildlife in eastern Maine and educational programs, you can join Friends of Moosehorn National Wildlife Refuge (R.R. 1, Box 202, Ste. 12, Baring, ME 04694). A check for a mere $10 will do the trick.

By the way, if you don't have time to walk the trails, watch for the elevated man-made nesting platforms—avian high-rises for bald eagles—outside of Calais alongside Route 1 North (near the junction with the Charlotte Road). Depending on the season, you may spot a nesting pair or even a fledgling. The chicks (usually twins but occasionally triplets) hatch around mid-May and try their wings by early August. A 400-square-foot observation deck across Route 1 is the best place for eagle-watching.

About six miles south of Calais, watch for signs pointing to **Devil's Head** and take the

THE DOWN EAST COAST

dirt road on the river side. The 315-acre site has a mile of frontage on the St. Croix River estuary and views to St. Croix Island. A road, with two parking areas, descends to the shoreline, and there are pit toilets and a marked hiking trail, approximately 1.5 miles looping from the road, leading to the highest point of coastal land north of Cadillac Mountain. According to locals, the headland was originally called d'Orville Head but it morphed into Devil's Head.

Calais has a lovely riverfront park at the foot of North Street. **Pike's Park** is the perfect place for a picnic. From here you have access to the **Calais Waterfront Walk,** which edges the river, running for 0.9 mile upriver and 0.6 downriver.

Golf

At the nine-hole **St. Croix Country Club** (River Rd., Rte. 1, Calais, 207/454-8875, late April–late Oct.), the toughest and most scenic hole is the seventh, one of five holes on the river side of Route 1.

River Tours

Captain Louis Bernardini shares his knowledge of the St. Croix River's tides, history, flora, and fauna on **Up Close Tours** (207/454-2844 day, 207/454-2285 night, www.upclosetours.com). Boat tours depart from the Robbinston boat landing 2–3 times daily Monday–Friday, and once on Saturday, and last for about two hours. The boat visits St. Croix Island, and lobstering is demonstrated. Adults are $25, children 12 and younger are $15. The boat carries a maximum of six passengers, and the minimum fee is $50. No credit cards.

ENTERTAINMENT AND FESTIVALS

First-run films show at the three-screen **State Cinemas** (79 Main St., Calais, 207/454-8830, $6). Sunday matinees are usually at 1:30 P.M.

Music on the Green is a series of free concerts presented at 6:30 P.M. Wednesdays at Triangle Park in downtown Calais. When the weather doesn't cooperate, concerts are moved to the Downeast Heritage Museum.

The **Brewer House** (Rte. 1, Robbinston, 12 miles south of Calais, 207/454-0333) sometimes hosts chamber music concerts featuring resident violinist Trond Saeverud.

Calais, Maine, and St. Stephen, New Brunswick, collaborate the first or second week of August for the nine-day **International Festival** of dinners, concerts, dances, a craft fair, ball games, and cross-border parade and road race. Newspapers carry schedules (just be sure to note which events are on eastern time and which are on Atlantic time).

SHOPPING

Downtown Calais has a few shops worthy of a look-see. **St. Croix Valley Antiques and Collectibles** (4 Monroe St., 866/420-1167) is a big shop with a wide range of furniture, quilts, baskets, and tableware. The **Urban Moose** (80 Main St., 207/454-8277) has an eclectic inventory that invites browsing. Perhaps most intriguing is Captain Craig Little's **Little Ships of the Maritimes** (32 North St./Rte. 1), which specializes in custom scale models. Nearly two dozen regional artists and artisans sell their works at **Cat's Eye Gallery** (272 North St., Calais, 207/454-2020). Books new, old, and rare are sold at the **Calais Book Shop** (405 Main St., 207/454-1110), which also sponsors a reading group.

If you stop in at **Katie's on the Cove** (Rte. 1, Mill Cove, Robbinston, 207/454-3297 or 800/494-5283, 10 A.M.–5 P.M. Tues.–Sat. late May–mid-Oct.), do it at your own risk. Chocoholics may need a restraining order. Joseph and Lea Sullivan's family operation, begun in 1982, has become a great success story. They now produce about four dozen varieties of homemade fudge, truffles, caramels, peanut brittle, even marzipan. The candies are available in Washington County gift shops and elsewhere in Maine (including Maine Black Bear Paws at L. L. Bean), and the Sullivans do mail orders, but the aroma alone is worth a trip to the source (call first, though, as days and hours are limited). The shop, 12 miles southeast of Calais and about 15 miles west of Eastport, is no place for unruly or demanding kids—space is limited and the candy is pricey.

You can't miss Katie's on the Cove, a chocolate shop in Robbinston.

ACCOMMODATIONS
Bed-and-Breakfasts

The classic, Greek Revival–style **(Brewer House** (Rte. 1, P.O. Box 88, Robbinston 04671, 207/454-0333, www.thebrewerhousebnb.com, $95–155 d) commands a knoll opposite the boat launch in Robbinston. Built by Captain John N. Marks in 1828, the house is distinguished by columns both in front and back, French nine-over-nine windows with carved Grecian moldings, Ionic pilasters, marble fireplaces, silver doorknobs, and an elliptical staircase—obviously the good captain was successful. The house also served as a stop on the Underground Railroad. The four guest rooms are furnished with antiques; some have ocean views, and some have shared baths. There's also a two-bedroom apartment ($125 d), where pets are welcome ($15 fee). A full breakfast is served. The B&B has an artsy feel, as the J. B. Siem Gallery is on the property, and chamber concerts featuring violinist Trond Saeverud are presented here. The innkeepers speak English, German, Danish, Norwegian, Swedish, and a little Japanese.

Within easy walking distance of downtown is **Greystone Bed and Breakfast** (13 Calais Ave., Calais, 207/454-2848, www.greystone calaisme.com, $80), Alan and Candace Dwelley's nicely restored, 1840 Greek Revival home. The property, listed on the National Historic Register, has two guest rooms (one of which can be paired with a third, smaller room), and the Dwelleys serve a full breakfast.

Motels/Cottages

The Gothic-styled, gingerbread-trimmed **Redclyffe Shore Motel and Dining Room** (Rte. 1, Robbinston, 207/454-3270, www.redclyffeshoremotorinn.com, $75) sits on a bluff jutting into the St. Croix River as it widens into Passamaquoddy Bay. The 16 motel units have cable TVs, phones, and sunset-facing river views. Redclyffe is locally popular for its greenhouse-style dining room, with ocean views, serving moderately priced entrées ($12–22) 5–9 P.M. daily. Dinner reservations are a good idea in July and August, especially during the International Festival. It's

12 miles south of Calais. The motel is open mid-May–October; the restaurant is open mid-May–December.

About 5.5 miles southeast of Calais, family-run **Heslin's Motel and Cottages** (Rte. 1, Calais, 207/454-3762, www.mainerec.com/heslins.html, May 1–late Oct.) has motel rooms ($62–70), cabins ($49–80), and rustic housekeeping cottages ($70–100 night, $420–600 week) on 60 acres alongside the St. Croix River. Some cottages are oceanfront. All units are heated and have TV; motel rooms have air-conditioning and phones; the more expensive cottages have kitchens. A big plus is a heated swimming pool. In the motel's informal river-view restaurant, steaks and fresh seafood ($12–20) are the specialties, served 5–9 P.M. daily. Small portions are available for kids and seniors. The cocktail lounge draws a loyal local clientele.

Campgrounds

High enough for a great view of the St. Croix River, **Hilltop Campground** (317 Ridge Rd., R.R. 1, Box 298, Robbinston, 866/454-3985 or 207/454-3985, www.hilltopcampgroundmaine.com, mid-May–mid-Oct.) has 84 tent and RV sites on 100 wooded and open acres, plus a pool, basketball court, a trout pond, a small store, Wi-Fi service, and laundry facilities. Sites are $22–32 a night.

FOOD
Local Flavors

If you're near downtown Calais, order picnic sandwiches to go at **Border Town Subz** (311 Main St., Calais, 207/454-8562, 10 A.M.–7 P.M. Mon.–Fri., 11 A.M.–3 P.M. Sat.), a reliable local favorite. It offers lots of choices, including vegetarian, and three sandwich lengths.

Another choice for picnic fixings, cottage staples, and other goodies is the **Sunrise County Farmers Market** (11 A.M.–3 P.M. Tues. late June–Oct.). Look for it in the downtown park.

Casual Dining

White Christmas lights brighten the ceiling of ◖ **Bernardini's** (257 Main St., Calais, 207/454-2237, 11 A.M.–8 P.M. Mon.–Sat.), a very popular downtown restaurant that has earned its repute with always-reliable Tuscany-inspired Italian cuisine, augmented by a few surprises, such as a crabmeat-stuffed avocado special that's a real winner; entrées are $10–15. The pleasant dining room is accented by woodwork salvaged from a local church. Save room for the tiramisu.

Calais's other restaurant is on a side street, off Route 1, just north of the center of town (and behind McDonald's). **The Chandler House** (20 Chandler St., Calais, 207/454-7922, 4–11 P.M. Tues.–Sun.) serves the usuals and is known for its prime rib.

INFORMATION AND SERVICES
Information

Sharing space with the Downeast Heritage Museum, near the Ferry Point Bridge just off Route 1 (Main St.) in downtown Calais, is a Maine Visitor Information Center (39 Union St., Calais, 207/454-2211), with clean restrooms and scads of brochures, including those produced by the St. Croix Valley Chamber of Commerce (207/454-2308 or 888/422-3112, www.visitcalais.com). The information center is open 8 A.M.–6 P.M. daily mid-May–mid-October, 9 A.M.–5:30 P.M. daily the rest of the year.

Check out Calais Free Library (Union St., Calais, 207/454-2758, www.calais.lib.me.us).

Public Restrooms

Restrooms are available at the Maine Visitor Information Center (39 Union St., Calais) and the St. Croix International Heritage Site, in Red Beach.

Crossing into Canada

If you plan to cross into Canada, you'll have to pass Customs checkpoints on both the Calais (U.S., 207/454-3621) and St. Stephen (Canada, 506/466-2363) ends of the bridges. Be sure to have the required identification and paperwork.

Pay attention to your watch, too—Calais is on eastern time, while St. Stephen (and the rest of Canada's Maritime Provinces) is on Atlantic time, one hour later.

Grand Lake Stream

For a tiny community of about 200 year-rounders, Grand Lake Stream has a well-deserved, larger-than-life reputation. It's the center of a vast area of rivers and lakes, ponds and streams—a recreational paradise, and more than 27,000 acres, including 62 miles of shore frontage, has been preserved by the **Downeast Lakes Land Trust** (www.downeastlakes.org). It's the literal town at the end of the world, remote in every sense of the word.

The famous stream is a narrow, three-mile neck of prime scenic and sportfishing water connecting West Grand Lake and Big Lake. A dam spans the bottom of West Grand, and just downstream is a state-run salmon hatchery. Since the mid-19th century, the stream and its lakes have been drawing fishing fans to trout and landlocked-salmon spawning grounds, and fourth and fifth generations now return here each year.

Canoe building has contributed to the area's mystique. The distinctive Grand Lake canoe (or "Grand Laker"), a lightweight, square-sterned, motorized 20-footer, was developed in the 1920s specifically for sport-fishing in these waters. In the off-season, several villagers still hunker down in their workshops and turn out these stable cedar beauties. (Interested? Call Bill Shamel, 207/796-8199).

RECREATION

The region has the greatest concentration of Registered Maine Guides in the state, which gives you an indication of the fishing, hunting, and canoeing opportunities here. Truly the best way to experience Grand Lake Stream is with a member of the **Grand Lake Stream Guides Association** (www.grandlakestreamguides.com). The website lists members and specialties. You can arrange for one of these skilled fellows to lead you on a fishing expedition, wildlife or photographic safari, or canoeing trip for a half day or longer.

Hiking

The 2.6-mile **Little Mayberry Cove Trail** edges the western shoreline of West Grand Lake. Pick up a trail map at the Pine Tree Store and then park at the dam.

EVENTS

A great time to visit the village is the last full weekend in July for the annual **Grand Lake Stream Folk Art Festival** (207/796-8199, 10 A.M.–5 P.M. Sat. and Sun., $5 one day, $8 both days), held on the town's grassy ballfield. Tents shelter approximately 50 top-notch, juried artisans. Nonstop bluegrass and folk music is another attraction. There's an exhibit highlighting the region's canoe-building tradition and another displaying antique and contemporary quilts. Breakfast, lunch, and snacks are available. Complementing the festival are lakeside barbecues by the guides; usually lobster on Friday evening, chicken on Saturday evening, with tickets available at the Pine Tree Store, across from the festival grounds. A contra dance takes place Saturday night, and a music jam, open to anyone, takes place Sunday morning. Leashed pets are welcome on festival grounds.

ACCOMMODATIONS

Cabin accommodations, with or without meals, are the lodgings of choice in Grand Lake Stream, and there's enough variety for every taste and budget. Few guests stay one night; most stay several days or a week. Rates quoted below are for two; many cabins can sleep more than that, and rates may be lower for extra people. Some housekeeping cabins require your own sheets and/or towels. Most camps have boat rentals for about $25 a day (motor brings the total to about $50).

Mike and Jean Lombardo's **Shore Line Camps** (P.O. Box 140, Grand Lake Stream 04637, 207/796-5539 or cell 703/300-8945, www.shorelinecamps.com) has eight one- to three-bedroom housekeeping cabins, most fronting right on Big Lake. All have spotless pine interiors and full kitchens. Base rate is $43 pp, kids under 2 are free, $20 kids under 12, but all cabins have a minimum rate per night ($86–129). Canoes, rowboats, and motorboats are available for rental. No credit cards.

Leen's Lodge (P.O. Box 40, Grand Lake Stream 04637, 207/796-2929 or 800/995-3367, www.leenslodge.com), on a spacious wooded shore and peninsula of West Grand Lake, has 10 small and large rustic cabins with baths. Rates, including breakfast, pack lunch, and dinner, are $135–155 pp. Children 12 and under pay $10 times their age, and kids 5 and under are free. Housekeeping rates are also sometimes available. Leashed pets are welcome, and kennels are provided. BYOB. Canoe and motorboat rentals should be arranged in advance. It's open May–October.

Grand Lake Lodge (P.O. Box 8, Grand Lake Stream 04637, 207/796-5584, www.grand lakelodgemaine.com, $35 d, $43 s pp), on the shore of West Grand Lake and two blocks from the village center, is a particularly good choice for families, with a safe swimming area. It's open ice-out–October. No credit cards.

FOOD

If you opt for housekeeping arrangements, you'll want to provision before you get here, but you can pick up pretty much anything at Kurt and Kathy Cressey's **Pine Tree Store** (3 Water St., P.O. Box 129, Grand Lake Stream 04637, 207/796-5027, pinetreestore@earth link.net), in the heart of the village. This mom-'n'-pop emporium is open daily, except in November and December, when the Cresseys concentrate on crafting handmade pack baskets (sold at L. L. Bean).

Both **Leen's Lodge** and **Weatherby's** (207/796-5558) open their dining rooms to guests by reservation. Expect to pay $25–35 for a full meal.

INFORMATION AND SERVICES

The volunteer-run Grand Lake Stream Chamber of Commerce (P.O. Box 124, Grand Lake Stream 04637, www.grandlakestream .com) produces a brochure listing accommodations, shops, and services. The Pine Tree Store (Water St., P.O. Box 129, Grand Lake Stream 04637, 207/796-5027, pinetreestore@ earthlink.net) is also a good source of local information, and it sells pizza, sandwiches, and general store merchandise.

GETTING THERE

To get to Grand Lake Stream, head north on Route 1 from Calais through Princeton. About two miles north of Princeton, turn left (west) onto Grand Lake Stream Road (also called Princeton Rd.). Continue about 10 miles to the village.

AROOSTOOK COUNTY

This is the Crown of Maine—at 6,500 square miles, Maine's largest county is larger than Connecticut and Rhode Island combined. When Mainers refer to "The County," this is the one they mean. Although Aroostook (a Micmac Indian word meaning "bright" or "shining") has plenty of wide-open space for its 76,085 residents, fully a quarter of them live in only two smallish cities, Presque Isle and Caribou.

Neat farmhouses and huge, half-buried potato-storage barns anchor vast, undulating patches of potatoes, broccoli, and barley. The sky seems to go on forever. Potato fields define The County—bright green in spring, pink and white in summer, dirt-brown and gold just before the autumn harvest.

Aroostook County, like the rest of Maine, has its share of hills, forests, and waterways, but the most significant hills here—Quaggy Jo, Mars, Debouillie, Haystack, Number Nine—are startling. Almost accidental, they appear out of nowhere—chunks the glaciers seem to have overlooked. Thanks to them, you'll find authentic vertical hiking, although Aroostook's trails are more often horizontal, through marshlands and woodlands, and along abandoned railbeds.

Winters are long, snowy, and cold. Snowmobiling is a big deal here (one national magazine ranked The County's snowmobile trails second best in the country), and a huge boost to the local economy. Legions of snowmobilers (often called "sledders" locally) crisscross The County every winter, exploring hundreds of miles of the incredible Interconnecting Trail System (ITS). More recently, Aroostook has embraced

© TOM NANGLE

a return to its Nordic skiing heritage, thanks to the Maine Winter Sports Center's mission and properties.

The County's agricultural preeminence sets it apart from the rest of Maine, but so does the Acadian culture of the northernmost St. John Valley, where the French dialect is unlike anything you'll ever hear in language classes (or even in France). It leads to some wonderfully whimsical street and road names—for instance, Brise Culotte Road, roughly translated as "Torn Trousers Road." Islands of Acadian or French culture exist in other parts of Maine, but it's in "the Valley" that you'll be tempted to pile on the pounds with such regional specialties as *poutine* (French fries smothered with cheese and gravy), *tourtière* (pork pie), and *tarte au saumon* (salmon tart).

As often occurs with remote rural areas, The County sometimes gets a bum rap (never from the snowmobiling crowd) among downstaters and others who've never been here. But it deserves notice—for the scenery if nothing else. Admittedly, it's a long haul—it's about as far as you can get from the rockbound coast—but you're guaranteed a totally different Maine experience. For many visitors, there's a sensation of traveling back 20 or 30 years, to an era when life was simpler, communities were small, and everyone greeted each other by name.

PLANNING YOUR TIME

Covering such a large expanse of geography takes time. While you can loop around Aroostook's periphery in 2–3 days, you'll need 4–5 days to explore the region and tease out its many charms.

Snowmobilers and cross-country skiers come January–March, when The County measures its snow in feet, not inches.

In June, newly planted potato fields resemble Ireland in their vibrant greens, although the blackflies and mosquitoes can be annoying, and two major festivals, Midsommar in mid-June and the Acadian Festival toward the end of the month mean lodging can be near to impossible to obtain without advance booking.

Most museums and historical sites are open

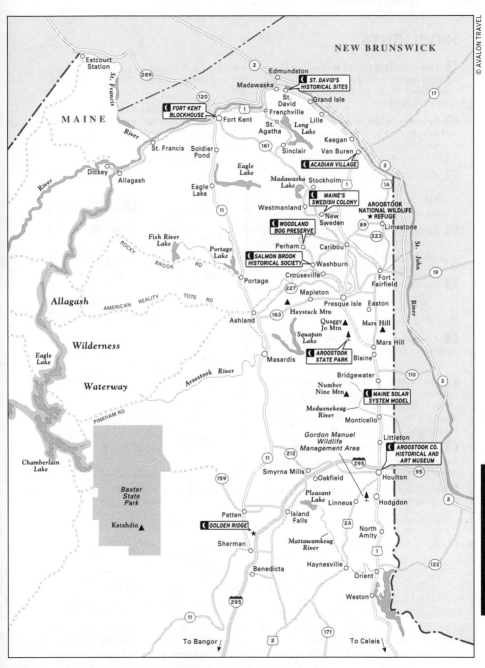

© AVALON TRAVEL

NEW BRUNSWICK

Estcourt Station

St. Francis River

MAINE

289

120

Madawaska

Edmundston

2

St. David's Historical Sites

St. David

Grand Isle

17

Fort Kent Blockhouse

Fort Kent

Frenchville

St. Agatha

Lille

Keegan

1

St. Francis

Soldier Pond

161

Sinclair

Long Lake

Van Buren

Acadian Village

2

Dickey

Allagash

Eagle Lake

Eagle Lake

Madawaska Lake

Stockholm

Maine's Swedish Colony

1A

1

11

Westmanland

New Sweden

Aroostook National Wildlife Refuge

Fish River Lake

Portage Lake

Woodland Bog Preserve

89

Limestone

ROCKY BROOK RD

Perham

Caribou

223

St. John River

Salmon Brook Historical Society

Washburn

Crouseville

Fort Fairfield

19

Allagash

AMERICAN REALITY

TOTE RD

Portage

227

Mapleton

Wilderness

163

Ashland

Haystack Mtn

Presque Isle

Easton

Eagle Lake

Quaggy Jo Mtn

Mars Hill

Waterway

Masardis

Squapan Lake

Aroostook State Park

Blaine

Mars Hill

Aroostook River

Bridgewater

110

2

PINKHAM RD

Number Nine Mtn

Maine Solar System Model

Meduxnekeag River

Monticello

Chamberlain Lake

Gordon Manuel Wildlife Management Area

Littleton

Aroostook Co. Historical and Art Museum

11

212

295

Houlton

95

159

Smyrna Mills

Oakfield

Baxter State Park

Pleasant Lake

Linneus

Hodgdon

2

Katahdin

Patten

Island Falls

Golden Ridge

2A

North Amity

Sherman

Mattawamkeag River

Haynesville

1

122

Benedicta

295

Orient

Weston

11

2

171

To Bangor

To Calais

AROOSTOOK COUNTY

HIGHLIGHTS

◖ **Maine Solar System Model:** Stretching 40 miles between Houlton to Presque Isle is a three-dimensional, scale model of the solar system (page 397).

◖ **Aroostook County Historical and Art Museum:** There are plenty of treasures for history buffs, including military artifacts dating from the Civil War (page 398).

◖ **Golden Ridge:** Route 2, between Sherman Mills and Houlton, passes along the ridge top, with panoramic views from Mt. Katahdin to distant lakes (page 399).

◖ **Salmon Brook Historical Society:** Learn about the traditional potato-farm lifestyle at this National Historic Register property and museum (page 405).

◖ **Maine's Swedish Colony:** It's an authentic touch of Sweden, and the best time to visit is during the annual June Midsommar Festival (page 406).

◖ **Aroostook State Park:** Maine's first state park has opportunities for hiking, swimming, and boating (page 407).

◖ **Woodland Bog Preserve:** In early summer, schedule a walk with Nature Conservancy steward Richard Clark to learn about the flora and fauna and see rare orchids (page 408).

◖ **Acadian Village:** Delve into Maine's Acadian history and heritage on a guided tour of 16 antique and replica buildings (page 414).

◖ **St. David's Historical Sites:** Learn about Acadian heroine Tante Blanche,

visit a typical homestead and school, and see where the Acadians first landed (page 415).

◖ **Fort Kent Blockhouse:** A relic of the bloodless Aroostook War, the 1839 blockhouse is being restored to its original design (page 415).

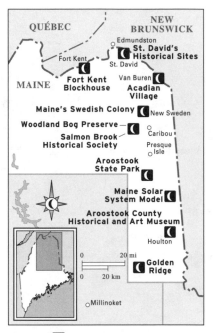

LOOK FOR ◖ TO FIND RECOMMENDED SIGHTS, ACTIVITIES, DINING, AND LODGING.

during the summer, so that's the best time for history buffs to visit. Days are long and temperatures moderate, making it also ideal for hikers, cyclists, and paddlers. In mid-July, the potato fields blossom, a gorgeous sight.

Autumn comes early, with leaves beginning to turn color as early as late August in the northern parts of The County.

Be sure to get off Route 1 and Route 11 and

mosey along some of the back roads that noodle through the farmlands and by lakes and rivers. Doing so will let you experience Maine's Big Sky Country, a landscape where endless fields meet expansive sky. And do make time to loop through the St. John Valley for a taste of Maine unlike any other. From Caribou or Presque Isle, you can drive up to the crown, visit Valley sites, and return in a long day.

Southern Aroostook County

Driving north on I-95, you find the interstate petering out at Houlton, about 120 miles northeast of Bangor. That sometimes makes this feel like the end of the earth, but it's actually just the beginning of Aroostook County.

Southern Aroostook, centered on Houlton, is a narrow north-south corridor, stretching from Sherman Mills, on I-95 to the Canadian border, and roughly straddling Route 1 from Danforth to Presque Isle. Among its communities are Island Falls, Oakfield, Smyrna, Monticello, and Bridgewater. It's in this region that the forests and mountains of the Maine Highlands begin to give way to the rolling farmlands characteristic of The County.

Hard by the New Brunswick border, Houlton (pop. about 6,300) has carved out its own niche as the shire town, and, according to the local historical society, "history's hiding place." Incorporated in 1834, Houlton is quiet and not often considered a "destination," but the county courts and other government offices are all here, so there's a fair amount of activity—at least midweek.

SIGHTS
Oakfield Railroad Museum
Housed in a 1910 Bangor and Aroostook Railroad station and run by the Oakfield Historical Society, the wheelchair-accessible Oakfield Railroad Museum (Station St., Oakfield, 207/757-8575, 1–4 P.M. Sat. and Sun. late May–early Sept., free) contains an impressive collection of iron-horse memorabilia—guaranteed to fascinate kids of any age. It's easy to get caught up in the enthusiasm of the railroad buffs who staff the museum. The gift shop carries all kinds of railroad-logo items. Donations are welcomed. The museum is 17 miles west of Houlton, off I-95 Exit 286.

Smyrna Amish Community
Many folks think they've stepped back in time when visiting The County, but that feeling intensifies in Smyrna, where horse-drawn carriages signal the presence of the Smyrna Amish community. Seeking a quiet place to work, raise their families, practice their faith, and interact with outsiders, five Midwestern families established a community in this rural farming town about 15 miles west of Houlton in 1996. Since then, the community has grown to 15 families. In addition to farming, the Smyrna Amish operate a number of businesses, open to the public, all of which are clustered along a short stretch of Route 2, one mile west of I-95 Exit 295. These include Sturdi-Bilt, which builds wooden sheds and outbuildings; Kauffman Metals, which fabricates metal roofing and building; Cedar Meadows Harness Shop; Northeastern Rustic Furniture; and Pioneer Place, a wonderful little general store; most businesses are closed on weekends. While the Amish welcome visitors to their businesses, please remember they're not a "tourist attraction." This is a living, breathing community that has opened a window to its lifestyle. Respect their personal and community property, and ask before taking photos of people.

◖ Maine Solar System Model
Space travel is possible in Aroostook County, where the three-dimensional Maine Solar System Model (207/764-6561 or 800/764-7420, www.umpi.maine.edu/info/nmms/solar) stretches 40 miles along Route 1. The model comprises the sun, nine planets, and moons for Earth, Saturn, Jupiter, and Pluto. All the planets, except Pluto, which is only one inch in diameter, are large enough to be seen while driving along Route 1, where one mile is equal to the distance between Earth and the sun.

The 93 million-to-one scale model was masterminded by Kevin McCartney, a geology professor at the University of Maine at Presque Isle, and implemented with the help of hundreds of local volunteers, varying from service and school groups to businesses to individuals. Local students built the planets.

Pluto (still a planet in this neck of the woods)

© HILARY NANGLE

It's easy to spot Venus in a field edging Route 1, south of Presque Isle.

is found at the Visitor Information Center, in Houlton, just off Route 1, north of the I-95 interchange. Other models are mounted on 10-foot-tall posts and dot parking lots and fields along the route. The project is detailed and mapped both in a brochure, available at the center, and on the Internet.

Market Square Historic District

A arced pedestrian bridge across the Meduxnekeag River links Gateway Park, on Route 1, with Market Square's 28 turn-of-the-20th-century National Historic Register buildings. Along the bridge and walkway (both wheelchair-accessible) are markers detailing Houlton's downtown history. A walking guide is available at the **Greater Houlton Area Chamber of Commerce** (109 Main St., Houlton), two blocks up Main Street.

◖ Aroostook County Historical and Art Museum

The 1903 White Memorial Building, the Colonial Revival residence that houses the chamber,

is also home to the Aroostook County Historical and Art Museum (207/532-6236, 1–4 P.M. Tues.–Fri. late May–early Sept. or by appointment), containing a fine collection of photos, books, vintage clothing, antique tools, and housewares. You can wander through on your own, but a guide will bring the collection to life. Of particular interest are military artifacts from the Hancock Barracks, the Civil War, and the Camp Houlton POW internment camp. Also on view are the ventilator cowl from the battleship *Maine,* which sank in Havana Harbor, and a Confederate battle flag captured by a Houlton member of the First Calvary Maine. Donations are appreciated.

Museum staff can also provide information about and direct you to a number of local historical sites. Frankly, there's not much to see at **Garrison Park,** but history buffs might want to visit the site of the **Hancock Barracks,** established in 1828 to protect American border settlements and garrisoned during the 1838–1839 Aroostook War. It provided frontier training for West Point graduates, and

General Robert E. Lee visited here. To find it, take Route 2 toward the airport and turn left onto Garrison Road, near the top of the hill.

Houlton Airport dates from the early 1940s. Neutrality laws prevented U.S.-built planes from flying directly from the States to Britain, so during the months before Pearl Harbor, planes were known to land in Houlton and then be towed across the border to Canada for takeoff. That all changed when the U.S. Army took over the airport during World War II and turned it into an airbase and Maine's largest **German POW camp**. About 4,000 prisoners lived here in barracks while laboring in lumber camps, canneries, potato farms, and paper mills. Sadly, there's not much left to see except for ruins of a barracks and a control tower. To see them, take Route 2 east from downtown. At the T intersection, bear right and follow it to the end. On your way to or from the airport, notice the pond near the U.S. Customs office—linger here a bit, especially early or late in the day, and you may spot a moose.

Watson Settlement Bridge

About six miles north of Houlton, amid typical Aroostook farmland in Littleton, stands Maine's northernmost (yes, and easternmost) covered bridge, built in the early 20th century and last used in 1985. The wood-truss bridge, straddling a branch of the Meduxnekeag River, feels quite forlorn, a remnant of the past just sitting here unused. Maine once had 120 or so covered bridges; only nine remain and this is the only one using the Howe truss system. For the prettiest route to the bridge from Houlton, take Foxcroft Road from Route 2 and continue 6.1 miles; turn left onto Carson Road. From Route 1 in Littleton, go right on the Carson Road, which winds its way down to the river (bear left at the fork). The quicker route is to head north on Route 1 four miles from the I-95 interchange and then go right on Carson Road for 2.9 miles.

Southern Aroostook Agricultural Museum

Farming memorabilia fills the Southern Aroostook Agricultural Museum (1664 Rte. 1, Littleton, 207/538-9300, w.ww.oldplow .org, 1–4 P.M. Thurs.–Sat. June–late Sept., $3 donation), started as a retirement project for Cedric and Emily Shaw. The collection grew, and in 2001 the museum moved from the Shaws' farm to the former Littleton Elementary School. Local support has allowed it to continue growing, adding a tool collection and a former one-room schoolhouse, building a model potato barn, and most recently a new barn.

SCENIC ROUTES
◖ Golden Ridge

The interstate is the fastest route to Houlton, but Route 2, from Sherman Mills through Oakfield and Smyrna, is the best choice for moseyers, and it really isn't that much longer. The far-less-traveled route passes through gorgeous countryside dotted with farms, lakes, and small villages. The views from Golden Ridge, a section between Island Falls and Oakfield, reach to Mt. Katahdin and beyond. Be sure to watch for potato barns, a unique barn built into the ground for cold potato storage. Most have a gambrel roof topping the landscape.

Million Dollar View Scenic Byway

South of Houlton and stretching eight miles along Route 1 between Danforth and Orient is an especially scenic drive that passes over Peekaboo Mountain and offers panoramic views over the Chiputneticook chain of lakes and to Mt. Katahdin. It's also prime moose-watching country.

PARKS AND PRESERVES
Houlton Town Parks

Near downtown Houlton, mystery surrounds the origins of **Pierce Park**'s quaint fountain with a centerpiece statue usually called *The Boy with the Leaking Boot*. Donated to the town in 1916, it's one of two dozen or so similar statues in the United States and Europe. Legends have it coming from Germany or Belgium or Italy, but no record exists. Benches surround the fountain, and lower- and upper-level troughs provide fresh water for pets and their owners.

© TOM NANGLE

Look for *The Boy with the Leaking Boot* statue in Houlton's Pierce Park.

The Houlton Garden Club maintains the flowers in the park—a popular local spot for photographs, picnics, and coffee breaks.

Also close to Houlton's downtown, **Civic Center Community Park** has a great playground, tennis courts, picnic tables, and plenty of space for kids to run. The park is the venue for major outdoor concerts and the Fourth of July fireworks extravaganza.

Forticor Farms Alpacas

Just south of Houlton is David and Judi Howard's Forticor Farms Alpacas (82 Ben Hill Rd., Hodgdon, 207/532-9696, www.forticorfarms .com, 10 A.M.–4 P.M. daily), where visitors are welcome to learn about alpaca farming and to shop for fleece and locally made items in the farm store.

A. E. Howell Wildlife Conservation Center and Spruce Acres Refuge

Art and Dot Howell and their family have dedicated their land (64 acres) and their lives to conservation and wildlife rehabilitation,

and their enthusiasm is contagious. Most creatures in the nonprofit refuge (Lycette Rd., HC 61, Box 6, North Amity, 207/532-6880, http://spruceacresrefuge.tripod.com) will be cared for and released, but permanent residents include a great horned owl, two bald eagles, and a bobcat. Frequent visitors include more than 65 species of birds, white-tailed deer, black bear, red fox, woodchucks, turkey vultures, and various hares. All visitors are taken through on guided tours, and appointments are required. Anyone older than 16 is charged $10, kids are free. If you have time, volunteer to lend a hand; there's always a need, and it's a rewarding experience. Membership in the organization is $25 a year, providing free admission and a quarterly newsletter. The season is 10 A.M.–4 P.M. Monday–Saturday mid-May–late October. Usually there also are one-day open houses with admission by donation in July and August; check the website. Do *not* bring pets; do bring binoculars. The refuge is just west of Route 1, on Lycette Road, 15 miles south of Houlton.

Gordon Manuel Wildlife Management Area

Just south of Houlton, in Hodgdon, the Gordon Manuel Wildlife Management Area (no phone) covers 6,488 acres of fields, woods, and marshland along the Meduxnekeag River. From Route 1, turn right (west) onto Hodgdon Road and watch for Layton's Dairy Bar. Take the first left after Layton's onto the unpaved Horseback Road. Continue 1.7 miles and turn left at a narrow dirt road. Wind through the trees, about 0.2 mile, to a small parking area on the Meduxnekeag River. Watch for osprey, green herons, even bald eagles. You can launch a canoe or kayak (no motors allowed) and explore the area. The setting is particularly gorgeous during the fall-foliage season, but be forewarned that hunting is allowed here, so wear a hunter-orange vest and/or hat mid-October–November.

If you don't have a canoe or kayak and just want to do some birding, this is a particularly relaxing bike ride, even from Houlton.

RECREATION
Golf

On a clear day, Baxter State Park's Katahdin is visible from **Va-Jo-Wa Golf Club** (142-A Walker Settlement Rd., Island Falls, 207/463-2128, www.vajowa.com), a particularly scenic 18-hole, par-72 course named after Vaughn, John, and Warren Walker. Call for a starting time; this course is popular. Greens fees are moderate. Facilities include a restaurant and bar, plus a driving range. Open May–October, Va-Jo-Wa is five miles north of I-95, off Route 2, between Pleasant and Upper Mattawamkeag Lakes.

Southwest of Houlton is the nine-hole **Houlton Community Golf Club** (Drew's Lake Rd., New Limerick, 207/532-2662, www .houltongolf.com), built on onetime potato fields in 1921. The setting is lovely, on the shores of Nickerson Lake; the lakefront clubhouse has a snack bar. Bring a swimsuit; a dip in the lake feels great after a round of golf. The course is open mid-May–mid-October. Take Route 2A (Bangor Rd.) west and south of Houlton about three miles to Drew's Lake

Road (also known as Nickerson Lake Rd.), continuing 2.5 miles to the club.

Horseback Riding

Saddle up for a trail ride at **Shiretown Livery Stables** (560 Rte. 1, Houlton, 207/532-0665). One-hour trail rides are $25, two hours are $45; rates are per person and rides are limited to five horses. Pony rides for children are a minimum of $10 or $25 per hour and take place in a supervised indoor arena. Riding lessons are $20 per hour. It's 1.5 miles north of I-95.

Winter Recreation

Houlton is at the fringe of prime **snowmobiling** country. The crowds tend to head up the road to Presque Isle, Caribou, and the St. John Valley, but there are plenty of trails here. For information on snowmobiling in the Houlton area, contact the chamber of commerce or the **Maine Snowmobile Association** (207/622-6983, www.mesnow.com), which can put you in touch with local snowmobile clubs. When snowmobiling in the Houlton area, you'll notice on trail maps that some routes cross into Canada. Be sure you are carrying valid identification when you are anywhere near the border. The Houlton border crossing is open 24 hours.

Also lacing the region are **cross-country ski trails.**

ENTERTAINMENT AND EVENTS

For canoeists and kayakers, the year's biggest event is the eight-mile spring-runoff **Meduxnekeag River Race,** held on a Saturday in late April or early May. Beginning in New Limerick, west of town, the route includes a short stretch of Class III rapids. For more information contact the Greater Houlton Chamber of Commerce (207/532-4216).

Check local listings and posters for the frequent outdoor **concerts** staged in local parks.

The annual **Soapbox Derby,** held in mid-June in Community Park, always attracts a big crowd.

The early July **Houlton Fair** (www.houlton fair.com) includes a carnival, a pig scramble,

AROOSTOOK COUNTY

truck pulling, pageants, entertainment, baking contests, and craft and agricultural exhibits.

Catch a flick at **Temple Theatre** (Market Sq., Houlton, 207/532-2200, www.temple movies.com), which has been screening films since 1918.

ACCOMMODATIONS

Occupying an idyllic and peaceful setting on the shores of five-mile-long Pleasant Lake, **Birch Point Cottages and Campground** (33 Birch Point La., Island Falls, 207/463-2515, www.birchpointcampground.com) is a well-maintained facility with campsites ($24–26) and lakefront housekeeping cottages ($90 d), as well as a lodge with bowling lanes downstairs and a lakefront restaurant, serving dinner Thursday–Sunday and breakfast on Sunday, a coin-op laundry, and a barbecue area. Motorboat rentals are $25 per hour or $85 per day; canoes, kayaks, and paddleboats are $5 or $25. Pets are $3 per day.

Clean and well maintained, **Ivey's Motor Lodge** (Rte. 1, P.O. Box 241, Houlton 04730, 207/532-4206 or 800/244-4206 in Maine, www.houlton.net/iveys, $80–110) wins folks over with good-size rooms, friendly service, and amenities unexpected in a small motel. All rooms have TV, DVD, fridge, and microwave. Rates include continental breakfast. On the premises is an Irish pub with big-screen TV. It's on Route 1, just north of I-95 Exit 302.

The **Shiretown Motor Inn** (282 North Rd./Rte. 1, Houlton, 207/532-9421 or 800/441-9421, www.shiretownmotorinn.com, $80–100), also at the interchange, lacks atmosphere and needs refurbishing, but it has an indoor pool as well as free Wi-Fi. Request a back-facing room if you're particularly noise sensitive.

FOOD
Island Falls

One of the brightest spots in downtown Island Falls is **Tiffany's** (Rte. 2, Island Falls, 207/463-2525, 6 A.M.–7 P.M. Mon.–Sat., to 2 P.M. Sun.). Expect everyone to give you the once-over upon entry: Strangers are rare here. Good home cookin' is the specialty, with little on the menu more than $10. Be sure to check out the huge muffins and gigunda whoopie pies.

For dinner, locals swear by **Horn of Plenty** (59 Houlton Rd., Island Falls, 207/463-2861, 11 A.M.–8 P.M. Tues.–Fri., 5–8 P.M. Sat.). Chef Bill Roderick's menu has an international accent, with European and Far East influences.

Houlton

Most of Maine's farmers markets operate one or maybe two days a week; the **Houlton Farmers Market** sets up shop daily early May–mid-October, next to McDonald's on Route 1, just south of I-95 Exit 62.

Craving something natural? **County Junction** (53 Main St., Houlton, 207/532-2218, 7 A.M.–4 P.M. Fri.–Wed.) is a good choice for terrific baked goods, coffees, a terrific tea selection, and a full range of natural foods and groceries. There's seating inside.

For humongous portions (even by County standards), home cooking, good service, and local color, **Grammy's Country Inn** (1687 Bangor Rd., Linneus, 207/532-7808) is Houlton's place to go. Nothing fancy, mind you, but a good spot to fill up the kids. Save room for dessert, and plan on having leftovers.

Hidden in the back of the small, downtown Fishman Mall and displaying the work of local artists, Joyce Transue's **The Courtyard Café** (61 Main St., Houlton, 207/532-0787, www.thecourtyardcafe.biz) is well worth finding. The café is open for lunch 11 A.M.–2 P.M. Monday–Friday and for dinner 5–8 P.M. Tuesday–Thursday, till 9 P.M. Friday and Saturday, closed Sunday. The menu changes daily, but dinner possibilities ($12–20) might include chicken parmesan or bourbon-glazed Norwegian salmon. Reservations recommended.

Across the street, occupying a former bank, is **The Vault** (64 Main St., Houlton, 207/532-2222, 5–8 P.M. Tues.–Sat.). Less pricey than the Courtyard, it serves simple, home-style meals. BYOB.

It's easy to spot **The Blue Moose** (Rte. 1, Monticello, 207/538-0991, 7 A.M.–8 P.M. Tues.–Thurs., to 9 P.M. Fri. and Sat., to 7 P.M. Sun.); just look for the, um, blue moose. Rather nondescript on the exterior, inside it's warm, inviting, and lodge-y. The family-operated restaurant serves home-style fare at better-than-reasonable prices, and there's a children's menu. As with most such restaurants in the region, the desserts are homemade and scrumptious.

INFORMATION AND SERVICES

The Greater Houlton Chamber of Commerce (109 Main St., Houlton, 207/532-4216, www.houlton.com), in the same 1903 Colonial Revival building as the Aroostook Historical and Art Museum, is open 9 A.M.–5 P.M. weekdays all year. Be sure to request the *Walking Guide to Market Square Historic District.*

Check out Cary Memorial Library (107 Main St., Houlton, 207/532-1302, www.carey.lib.me.us).

The Maine Visitor Information Center (28 Ludlow Rd., Houlton, 207/532-6346), with brochures and maps covering the entire state, is open 9 A.M.–5 P.M. weekdays all year, with weekend and extended weekday hours in summer. Restrooms are available

Aroostook County Tourism (888/216-2463, www.visitaroostook.com) has information on and links for the entire county.

Central Aroostook County

Ahhh. Sighs of contentment are common in a region where folks know their neighbors, crime is rare, and the only traffic jams are caused by slow-moving farm equipment.

Most of the 60,000 acres planted with spuds in Maine are found in the "Potato Triangle," the region framed by Presque Isle, to the south, Caribou, to the north, and Fort Fairfield, on the Canadian border, and tied together by the zigzagging course of the Aroostook River. Farmhouses, potato barns, and rolling fields dominate the landscape—and when those fields bloom in mid-July, it's one of the prettiest sights around. Northeast of Caribou is Limestone; south of Presque Isle is Mars Hill. Each is a day's stage ride from the others, about 13 miles, making it easy to explore the region from one base.

The economic impact caused by the closing of Limestone's Loring Air Force Base in the late 1990s devastated the region, and although the population erosion continues, the base is becoming a success story with the establishment of the Loring Commerce Centre and the creation of Aroostook National Wildlife Refuge.

Outdoor enthusiasts, especially, will find plenty: 577-acre Aroostook State Park, miles of multiuse trails, two small alpine areas, and impressive Nordic facilities that have hosted World Cup events. Nordic skiing was introduced to Maine by settlers of the Swedish Colony, the region northwest of Caribou anchored by New Sweden and Stockholm.

A handful of intriguing low-tech museums and heritage sites entertain history buffs. What you won't find here is much in the way of interesting shopping.

SIGHTS
University of Maine at Presque Isle

Established in 1903 as the Aroostook State Normal School for training teachers, UMPI (181 Main St., Rte. 1, Presque Isle, 207/768-9400) has more than 1,500 two- and four-year students on its 150-acre campus at the southern end of the city. The school is noted for its training in physical education and recreation.

In the Campus Center is the **Reed Art Gallery,** a one-room gallery that overflows into the hallway, where rotating exhibits spotlight Maine and Canadian artists. During the school year, the gallery is open 10 A.M.–5 P.M. Monday–Friday, 1–5 P.M. Saturday; the summer schedule tends to be less predictable.

Science wunderkind Kevin McCartney, a geology professor and the powerhouse behind the Maine Solar System scale model, also gets credit

AROOSTOOK COUNTY

ONE POTATO, TWO POTATO

Native to South America, the potato is king in Aroostook County, where 90 percent of Maine's spuds grow on more than 60,000 acres – Maine is America's fifth- to eighth-largest producer (depending on the harvest).

Aroostook County's potato heritage dates back more than 150 years, says fourth-generation potato farmer Keith LaBrie, of Labrie's Farms, in St. Agatha. "It became a staple on family farms generations ago. Back 50, 60 years ago, there were thousands of small growers, with 15- to 20-acre farms. Those have consolidated into 300- to 500-acre farms, and the harvesting is mechanized now for efficiency."

In the past, he says, Maine predominantly grew the round, white table stock variety. Recently, there's been more of a move toward russet types. While most of what Maine grows is used for processed French fries and potato chips, Maine potatoes are now being used to produce Cold River Vodka, made and sold in Freeport (www.coldrivervodka.com).

Potato fields are in full blossom in mid-July. Different varieties produce differently colored flowers, so there will be white in one field, red in another.

Annual festivals in Fort Fairfield and Houlton celebrate the blossoms and the harvest; potatoes appear on every restaurant menu and family table; and countless roadside stands peddle them by the bag. Although high schools still close for 2–3 weeks in September so students (and teachers) can assist with the harvest, most of the work is done mechanically these days.

Now if you don't get enough of this potato business while you're here in The County, there's always a membership in the **Maine Potato Sampler of the Month Club.** Eight months a year, Wood Prairie Farm (49 Kinney Rd., Bridgewater 04735, 800/829-9765 weekdays, www.woodprairie.com), an organic farm in Bridgewater, sends its members a 10-pound gift box of three different kinds of organic potatoes. The package comes with postcards and recipes, so you're all set. The base price for the eight-month club is $299; one month $39.95.

Information on the potato industry is available from the **Maine Potato Board** (744 Main St., Room 1, Presque Isle 04769, 207/764-4148, www.mainepotatoes.com).

Potato fields and a rolling countryside define central Aroostook's landscape.

© TOM NANGLE

The Aroostook Agricultural Museum is part of the Salmon Brook Historical Society complex.

for the **Northern Maine Museum of Science,** in Folsom Hall. Hallways in the three-story science building have been turned into a free teaching museum, where you can take a test to see if you're color blind, touch a real dinosaur bone, and take in all manner of scientific and mathematical exhibits explaining such hard-to-grasp concepts as DNA and the Fibonacci sequence and displays varying from bottle-nosed dolphins to fluorescent minerals. Also here is the sun, the epicenter of the Route 1 solar system model, as well as another scale model that extends the length of the second floor. Nothing is high tech, but it's enjoyable and well presented. Be sure to pick up a brochure that explains the exhibits—look for it on case tops. Also look for a guide to the **West Campus Woods Nature Trail,** protected by the museum. There are 10 interpretive stations, chosen to illustrate features of the northern forest.

◖ Salmon Brook Historical Society

Here's a worthwhile two-for-one deal, with lots

of charm and character: In tiny, downtown Washburn, across from the First Baptist Church, the Salmon Brook Historical Society (P.O. Box 71, Washburn 04786, 207/455-4339) operates the **Benjamin C. Wilder Homestead,** an 1852 National Historic Register farmhouse, and the **Aroostook Agricultural Museum** in the adjacent red barn. The well-restored 10-room house has period furnishings and displays; the barn contains old tools and antique cookware and pottery. The museums, on 2.5 acres at 17 Main Street (Rte. 164), are open 8–11 A.M. Wednesday and 1–4 P.M. Sunday mid-June–mid-September, other times by appointment. Admission is free, but donations are welcomed. Washburn is 11 miles northwest of Presque Isle and 10 miles southwest of Caribou.

Nylander Museum

If you were an eccentric, self-educated geologist and needed a place to display and store everything you'd accumulated, you'd create a place like the Nylander Museum (393 Main St., P.O. Box 1062, Caribou 04736, 207/493-4209,

AROOSTOOK COUNTY

www.nylandermuseum.org, 12:30–4:30 P.M. Tues.–Sat., donations welcomed). Swedish-born Olof Olssen Nylander traveled the world collecting specimens, settled in Caribou, and bequeathed his work, including 6,000 fossils and 40,000 shells, to the city. Since his 1943 death, the museum has acquired other collections: butterflies, mounted birds, and additional geological specimens. It's all displayed in two small galleries.

◖ Maine's Swedish Colony

New Sweden is eight miles northwest of downtown Caribou, via Route 161. At the **New Sweden Historical Museum** (Capitol Hill and Station Rds., New Sweden, 207/896-3018, www.geocities.com/maineswedish colony), three floors of memorabilia reflect the rugged life in this frontier community. An exact replica of the colony's "Kapitoleum" (capitol), the museum was built in 1971 after fire leveled the original structure. Check out the museum's guestbook: Visitors have come from all over Scandinavia to see this cultural enclave. The museum, 0.5 mile north and east of Route 161, is open 1–4 P.M. daily Memorial Day weekend–mid-September. Admission is free, but donations are welcome. Next door, in the **Capitol Hill School,** a gift shop carries Swedish items. Out back is a monument with the list of the original settlers.

Continuing east on Station Road, you'll pass **W. W. Thomas Memorial Park** on the left, a great spot for a picnic, with a play area for kids and a dramatic vista over the rolling countryside. Concerts occur periodically in the bandshell. About 0.2 mile farther are the circa 1870 **Larsson/Ostlund Log Home,** one of the colony's oldest buildings, and the shingled **Lars Noak Blacksmith and Woodworking Shop,** another remnant of the early settlers.

More exhibits await at the **Stockholm Historical Society Museum,** but hours for that aren't formal. Ask at the post office across the street, nearby Anderson Store, or simply call one of the names listed on the front door for access.

A fun time to visit New Sweden is during the **Midsommar** festival, on the closest weekend to Midsummer Day (June 21), when most sites are open for tours and residents don traditional Swedish costumes and celebrate the year's longest day. Activities include decoration of a maypole, Swedish dancing, a smorgasbord, concerts, and a prayer service. Non-Scandinavians are welcome to join in, but you'll need to plan way ahead; the smorgasbord's two seatings are usually sold out by mid-May.

Frontier Heritage Historical Society

Fort Fairfield's active historical society (20 Fort Hill St., Fort Fairfield, 207/472-3802) maintains a number of local properties. The **Fort Fairfield Blockhouse Museum** (Main St.) is a 1976 replica of the original, and it's filled with local memorabilia. The **Friends Church Museum** (Rte. 1A), built in 1858 as a Quaker meetinghouse, served as a station on the Underground Railroad during the Civil War. The **Railroad Museum** (Depot St.) comprises locomotives and cars and an 1875 Canadian-Pacific Railroad station. Industrious historical society volunteers plan eventually to offer train rides on eight miles of town-owned track. Also on the railroad site is the **Black/McIntosh One-Room School House,** built in 1848 and undergoing restoration. Plans call for moving a sawmill to the site, too.

SCENIC ROUTES

With so much open space in The County, particularly in the Potato Triangle, drivers and bicyclists can enjoy great long vistas. One route, a favorite of Senator Susan Collins, who ought to know, is **Route 164** between Caribou and Presque Isle, half of it along the Aroostook River. (Locals call it the Back Presque Isle Road; it's also the Washburn Road and the Caribou Road—just to make things totally confusing.) On the way, you can check out the museums in Washburn, detour on the multiuse trail, or loop out on Route 228 and visit the Woods Edge Gallery in Perham.

Another scenic drive is **Route 167,** between Presque Isle and Fort Fairfield; the 12-mile stretch is especially dramatic in mid-July, when the rolling fields are draped with pink and white potato blossoms and Fort Fairfield puts on its annual Potato Blossom Festival.

PARKS, FARMS, AND PRESERVES

◀ Aroostook State Park

Aroostook State Park (State Park Rd., Presque Isle, 207/768-8341, www.state.me.us/doc/parks) has the distinction of being Maine's first state park, created in 1939, when inspired citizens of Presque Isle donated 100 acres of land to the state. The park has grown significantly since then; it now comprises nearly 600 acres, encompassing Quaggy Jo Mountain and Echo Lake and providing plentiful opportunities for hiking, water sports, snow sports, camping, and more. Quaggy Jo comes from the MicMac word "quaquajo," which translates as "twin peaked." Allow 2–3 hours for the moderate (with steep sections) three-mile round-trip hike (clockwise) via the North Peak, North-South Peak Ridge, and South Peak Trails to take in both summits; the views, especially from North Peak, are superb. After hiking, have a lakeside picnic and then cool off with a swim or fish for brook trout. Public boat access is available as are canoe and paddleboat rentals ($3 per hour). Call it a night at one of 30 campsites. The park is equally inviting in winter, when a selection of trails are open for cross-country skiing. These range from the 1.6-km Novice Trail to the 6.4-km Quaggy Jo Mountain Trail, which is best for advanced skiers. Groomed snowmobile trails also pass through the park. Park admission is $2 adults, $1 children 5–11. The park is open daily mid-May–mid-October. The gate is 1.5 miles west of Route 1, five miles south of downtown Presque Isle.

Double Eagle Park

Just beyond the state park access road is a tiny park commemorating the launch (Spragueville Rd., Presque Isle) of the helium balloon *Double Eagle II*. A replica honors the first transatlantic balloon flight in August 1978, when a three-man crew made the Presque Isle–France passage in approximately 137 hours. (The first *solo* transatlantic balloon flight, six years later, took off from Caribou.)

Goughan's Farm

Almost qualifying as an amusement park, Goughan's (Rte. 161, 872 Fort Fairfield Rd., Caribou, 207/498-6565, 8 A.M.–5 P.M. daily Mar.–mid-Dec.) has a bit of everything, depending on when you show up. Goughan's (pronounced GAWNS) has maple syrup in spring; pick-your-own strawberries, raspberries, and veggies (string beans and peas) in summer; buy apples and choose-your-own pumpkins in fall; and Christmas wreaths and trees in winter. Kids can feed and pet the farm animals, ride the carousel, and get delicious homemade ice cream at the dairy bar in the granary. Also in the granary is a gift shop with Maine-made goodies. The farm is three miles southeast of Caribou, on the Fort Fairfield Road (Rte. 161).

Aroostook National Wildlife Refuge

Nearly 5,000 acres, encompassing grasslands, forests, 10 ponds, two brooks, and one stream, of the Cold War–era Loring Air Force Base have found new life as Aroostook National Wildlife Refuge (97 Refuge Rd., Limestone, 207/328-4634). Established in 1998, the refuge is still actively restoring habitat by removing buildings, railroad tracks, and fencing, and restoring wetlands. Seven trails, varying 0.12 mile–1.9 miles, provide excellent wildlife-viewing, especially early in the morning or late in the evening. According to the Friends of Aroostook National Wildlife Refuge (www.friendsofaroostooknwr.org), Aroostook County supports the largest density of moose and black bear in the lower 48 states, and sightings of each are a daily occurrence on the refuge. Migratory songbirds nest here in spring and summer, and various ducks, Canada geese, woodcock, and ruffled grouse are also frequently sighted. Stop at the visitors center on Refuge Road to pick up simple maps of the system. The refuge is off Route 89, eight miles east of Caribou, five miles west of Limestone. Trails are open sunrise–sunset daily; visitors center hours are limited, so call.

◖ Woodland Bog Preserve

About six miles west of Caribou, Woodland Bog Preserve, a 265-acre Nature Conservancy property, is home to several rare orchid species and dozens of bird species (nearly 90 have been banded here). Mid-May–mid-July, Perham resident Richard Clark—The Conservancy's on-site steward—leads fascinating free walks through this bog (technically, a calcareous fen surrounded by a cedar swamp) as well as the 200-acre **Perham Bog Preserve.** Clark also leads walks in **Salmon Brook Lake Bog,** 1,850 acres bought by the state under the Land for Maine's Future program. To set up a time, call him (207/455-8359 days or 207/455-8060 evenings and Mondays). Wear waterproof shoes and insect repellent. Dedicated environmentalists, Richard and his wife, Susan, have donated an easement on a 135-acre parcel that connects two sections of the state's land. Note: These preserves have extremely fragile ecosystems, so don't even consider visiting them on your own.

RECREATION
Multiuse Trails

In downtown Caribou, a 1.23-mile loop circles around **Collins Pond,** an old millpond and waterfall downtown. Walk or bike the path through a town park, with picnic area, by ballfields, and along city sidewalks. It passes through wetlands populated by muskrat, moose, red-winged blackbird, and other species; bring binoculars and head out early morning or before sunset for the best wildlife-spotting.

Bangor-Aroostook Valley Trails: Led by the Caribou Recreation Department, several volunteer groups have worked to open up more than 80 miles of abandoned railroad beds for year-round use by bikers, hikers, snowmobilers, and cross-country skiers. The trails are mostly packed gravel, so you'll want a mountain bike. Be forewarned: ATVs (all-terrain vehicles) are heavy users of the trails. The prettiest and most rural section of this impressive network begins in Washburn and ends in Stockholm (40 miles one-way), including a short stretch through the Woodland Bog. Park in downtown Washburn. Be sure to carry plenty of water. From Caribou, you can go to Stockholm and on to Van Buren (29 miles one-way). Or begin in Carson (just west of Caribou) and go to New Sweden (nine miles one-way).

Biking, Kayaking, and Roller-Skiing

Mojo (719 Main St., Presque Isle, 207/760-9500) rents bikes and kayaks. It also organizes a series of organized rides, from women's to family to ones for serious cyclists.

Twenty miles of marked, world-class mountain-biking trails are available free at the **Maine Nordic Heritage Center** (Nordic Heritage Access Rd., off Rte. 167, Presque Isle, 207/492-1444, www.mainewsc .org), part of the Maine Winter Sports Center. Also here is a one-kilometer paved roller-ski loop. Afterward, finish up with a sauna in the lodge.

Golf

The 18-hole **Presque Isle Country Club** (Rte. 205/Parkhurst Siding Rd., Presque Isle, 207/764-0430 or 207/769-7431, www.picountry club.com), established in 1958, was The County's first 18-hole course. Tee times usually aren't necessary; greens fees are $36 for 18 holes, $18 for nine. Facilities include a restaurant, driving range, cart and club rentals, and lessons. The course is open May–October.

Another easy-on-the-budget choice is the 18-hole **Mars Hill Country Club** (75 Country Club Rd., Mars Hill, 207/425-4802), where greens fees are $24 for 18, $12 for nine; with cart $40 or $20. It's open late April–late October.

Water Sports

Swim, fish, hike, bike, boat, picnic, camp, and

play at 85-acre **Trafton Lake Recreation Area** (Ward Rd., Limestone, 207/325-4025).

Fitness and Recreation Center

Weather not cooperating for outdoor fun? Inside **Caroline D. Gentile Hall** (University of Maine at Presque Isle campus, 207/768-9772, www.umpi.maine.edu) are a walking/running track, gym, 37-foot rock wall and bouldering wall, strength machines and free weights, cardio trainers, and a pool. A day pass is $5 per adult, $2 per child age 13 and younger; with climbing wall, it's $10.

Skiing

No surprise, given the Swedish ancestry prevalent in this area, that Nordic skiing is part of the region's heritage. Helping to keep it alive and grow is the **Maine Nordic Heritage Center** (Nordic Heritage Access Rd., off Rte. 167, Presque Isle, 207/492-1444, www.mainewsc.org), part of the Maine Winter Sports Center. The center is considered one of the world's best internationally licensed Nordic facilities, and it's hosted international biathlon and cross-country races. This is a full biathlon facility, with 30 shooting stations. Also on the premises is a lighted roller-ski loop and a sauna. Best of all, it's free.

If alpine skiing is your preferance, the center also operates the adjacent **Quaggy Joe Ski Area** (Rte. 167, Presque Isle, 207/764-3016) and the **Big Rock Ski Area** (Graves Rd., Mars Hill, 207/328-0991, www.bigrockmaine.com). Quaggy Joe is tiny, with only a T-bar servicing its 218-foot vertical, but the price is right: just $6 for an all-day ticket. Big Rock is a good-size community ski area with five lifts (a triple chair, a double chair, and three tows) and 28 trails and glades, a terrain park, and a tubing park on a 980-foot vertical. Although the area averages 160 inches of snow, 80 percent of the terrain is covered by snowmaking. About 55 percent is open for night skiing. Big Rock has a ski school, café serving grilled foods and homemade soups and sandwiches, and rental shop. Also on the premises are about

six miles of cross-country trails and a snowshoe trail. The area is open Wednesday–Sunday as well as holidays and school vacation periods. An adult weekend ticket is $25, age 65–74 and 6–17 are $18.

Snowmobile rentals are available at **The Sled Shop** (108 Main St., Presque Isle, 207/764-2900), next to the Presque Isle Inn.

ENTERTAINMENT AND EVENTS

The **Caribou Cinema Center** (66 Sweden St./ Rte. 161, Caribou, 207/493-3013) has four screens.

One of The County's biggest wingdings is the **Maine Potato Blossom Festival** held in Fort Fairfield in mid-July. Pagentry, potatoes, crafts, potatoes, entertainment, potatoes, fireworks, potatoes.

Agriculture exhibits, harness racing, live entertainment, and fireworks are all part of Presque Isle's **Northern Maine Fair,** the biggest country fair in this part of Maine, the first full week of August.

SHOPPING

About 11 miles west of Caribou, the **Woods Edge Gallery** (High Meadow Rd., P.O. Box 77, Perham 04766, 207/455-8359 or 455-8060) devotes almost 1,000 feet of exhibit space to watercolor and acrylic landscapes, plus photography—most by Aroostook County artists. The gallery, 1.25 miles west of Route 228, is open all year, 1–5 P.M. Tuesday–Saturday. Gallery owner Richard Clark, steward for The Nature Conservancy's nearby Woodland Bog, also leads seasonal nature tours there.

Sip a cup of cream Earl Grey while perusing the teas, imported condiments, teaware, and antiquarian books at **Heidi's Tea Shop** (769 Main St./Rte. 1, Presque Isle, 207/768-7900, www.heidisteashop.com).

ACCOMMODATIONS
Bed-and-Breakfasts

Convenient for skiers at Big Rock, the **Graham House B&B** (P.O. Box 131, 5 Church St., Mars Hill 04758, 207/429-8206, www.thegrahamhouse.com, $80–90 d) has two second-floor guestrooms, each with air-conditioning, fridge, microwave, deck, and private baths; one detached (robes supplied). The house is a two-minute walk from an in-town park and from Al's Diner.

Art professor Clifton Boudman and his wife, Judith, put out an unforgettable spread—a Scottish breakfast—when you stay at the **Rum Rapids Inn** (Rte. 164, Rum Rapids Dr., Crouseville, 207/455-8096, www.rum rapidsinn.com), a beautifully furnished 1839 house. By arrangement, he'll also produce an elegant multicourse candlelight dinner ($38–48; BYOB), served at 7 P.M. In summer, relax on the deck overlooking Rum Rapids; in winter, cross-country ski on the Boudmans' 15 acres and afterward soak in the whirlpool spa. Guests have free use of bikes, cross-country skis, and tennis rackets. Two rooms, with TV/DVD/VCR and Wi-Fi, are $89 d. The inn is five miles northwest of Presque Isle; watch for a tiny sign on the left.

Within walking distance of downtown Caribou sights and restaurants, the **◖ Old Iron Inn B&B** (155 High St., Caribou, 207/492-4766, www.oldironinn.com, $55–79) comes by its name honestly. Hundreds of antique irons are displayed through the in-town, 1913 arts and crafts–style house, and geology professor Kevin McCartney can recount the background of each one. Four rooms, two with private bath, are comfortably furnished with quilts and oak antiques. Also available is a two-bedroom guest cottage rented by the week ($350). A small office has fax, fridge, TV, and video collection; Wi-Fi is available. Settle into the living room with a choice from the extensive magazine selections or choose a good read—plenty of mysteries, along with Lincoln and aviation libraries—from the well-stocked bookcases. Known for her culinary talent, Kate McCartney serves a delicious breakfast in the Victorian dining room. Ask Kevin about the Maine Solar System or the Science Museum at UMPI, both of which he developed—clever and industrious fellow he.

Motels

University professors, snowmobilers, and traveling salespeople all gravitate to the 148-room **Presque Isle Inn and Convention Center** (Rte. 1, P.O. Box 270, Presque Isle 04769, 207/764-3321 or 800/533-3971, www.presqueisleinn.com, $80–145), atop a hill overlooking Presque Isle and beyond. Amenities include a restaurant, health club, indoor pool, on-site coin laundry, Wi-Fi, and cable TV. The bar is a popular local rendezvous spot, and there's live entertainment weekends in the lounge. Some rooms have kitchenettes. The motel is close to the University of Maine's Presque Isle campus. In winter, when the parking lot has more snowmobiles than cars, don't even think about arriving sans reservation. Pets are welcome.

Patronized primarily for its convenient downtown site, **The Northeastland Hotel** (436 Main St., Presque Isle, 207/768-5321 or 800/244-5321 in Maine, www.mainerec.com/eastland.shtml, $78–84), dating from 1934, has 50 oversize rooms with air-conditioning, TVs, Wi-Fi, and phones. The property could use a facelift, and noise from the bar can be a problem, but it's clean and inexpensive. No pets; children 12 and under stay free. The informal restaurant is a popular local breakfast and lunch spot, but you'll find better food and service at the Riverside, across the street.

Just south of town, the two-story **Caribou Inn and Convention Center** (Rte. 1, RFD 3, Box 25, Caribou, 207/498-3733, www.caribouinn.com, $98–150) has 73 large, comfortable rooms and suites with air-conditioning, cable TV, Wi-Fi, and refrigerators (suites have kitchenettes). Facilities include an indoor pool, health club, restaurant, and coin-op laundry. (Request a room away from the pool area.) Children 12 and under stay free.

Camping

Campsites at **Aroostook State Park** (State Park Rd., Presque Isle, 207/768-8341, www.state.me.us/doc/parks) are $15 per site per night. Sites are wooded and close to Echo Lake. Campers have a new shower house, with free hot showers, and new cookhouse, with cook stove, sink for washing dishes, picnic tables, and a cabinet of games. To be sure of a campsite on summer weekends, make reservations online (www.campwithme.com) or by phone (207/624-9950 out of state or 800/332-1501 in Maine; MasterCard or Visa needed) at least two weeks ahead; two-night minimum for reservations.

The 17 campsites at **Trafton Lake Campground** (Ward Rd., Limestone, 207/325-4025) have full hookups and are $15 per day, $95 per week for RVs, $8 per day or $50 per week for tents (four people). The campground, open late May–mid-September, is 2.5 miles off Route 89.

FOOD

As with other parts of Maine, Aroostook County has frequent **public suppers** throughout the summer. Visitors are welcome, even encouraged (most suppers benefit a good cause), so check the papers, line up early, and enjoy the local food and color.

Mars Hill

For a guaranteed dose of local color—and decent food besides—pull up at **Al's Diner** (87 Main St., Rte. 1, Mars Hill, 207/429-8186, 5 A.M.–8 P.M. Mon.–Thurs., 6 A.M.–9 P.M. Fri., Sat., and Sun.), a friendly village eatery that started as an ice-cream shop in 1937. The third generation is now running the place. For breakfast, try the Aroostook omelette, made with potatoes, of course.

Presque Isle

From the exterior, **[** **Heidi's Tea Shop** (769 Main St./Rte. 1, Presque Isle, 207/768-7900, www.heidisteashop.com) doesn't look too promising, given its location amid strip malls. Inside, however, it's a charming restaurant/gourmet shop/antiquarian bookstore, a winning combination complemented by fabulous food—and nothing is fried. Trained chef Heidi Samuel has passions for both tea

and baking, and everything is made from scratch. The dinner menu changes weekly, but usually includes 4–6 choices ($14–16) with an emphasis on fresh, local ingredients; or come for tea, choosing from a multipage menu of possibilities. The setting is intimate. Browse the books while waiting, or peruse the tea menu. It's open 10 A.M.–5 P.M. Tuesday and Wednesday, 10–3 and 6–8 Thursday and Friday, and 11 A.M.–4 P.M. Saturday. BYOB.

Where can you get an $18 bowl of gourmet lobster stew in February? At **Winnie's Restaurant and Dairy Bar** (79 Parsons St., Presque Isle, 207/769-4971). The restaurant's delicious lobster stew became so famous for being "the real thing" (no fillers) that then-owner Patty Leblanc made it into a business of its own in 1999 (Winnie was the first owner, in the 1940s), but the stew is still served here. Also known for its Winnie's burgers, this is a supercasual, call-your-number kind of place, with food served in plastic containers and carhops on summer evenings. It's always thronged with locals; in winter, snowmobilers arrive en masse, so be prepared to wait. Winnie's is open 10:30 A.M.–9 P.M. daily all year.

Despite its name, the **Riverside Inn Restaurant** (399 Main St., Presque Isle, 207/764-1447) doesn't have a river view. It's a cozy, neighborhoody place, with perhaps a dozen booths, a four-stool counter, and a glass case filled with home-baked goodies, including doughnuts and cookies. Breakfast is served all day (homemade white toast is available for an additional $0.25), along with the usual home-style fare. It's in downtown Presque Isle, close to Riverside Park and set back from the street. It opens at 5 A.M. Monday–Saturday, closing at 3 P.M. Monday–Wednesday, 8 P.M. Thursday and Friday, and 9 P.M. Saturday. Hours are 6 A.M.–3 P.M. Sunday.

Corned beef and cabbage, shepherd's pie, bangers and mash, and fish-and-chips are nightly dinner specials at the **Irish Setter Pub** (710 Main St., 207/764-5400, 11 A.M.–11 P.M.

daily, $7–13), a congenial and popular spot just north north of downtown.

Far more contemporary, and with a wide-ranging, something-for-every-taste-and-budget menu is **Slopes Northern Maine Restaurant and Brewing Co.** (150 Maysville St., Presque Isle, 207/769-2739, www.slopes restaurant.com, 11 A.M.–10 P.M. daily, food to 9 P.M.), a cavernous place just across from the Aroostook Mall. The tavern side, with glass windows to the brewing tanks, claims to have the longest bar in the state; it snakes across the back of the room. The dining room side opens at 4 P.M. Both sides serve from the same, extensive menu, and both have fireplaces and antique skis as accents on the walls. There's live entertainment in the tavern on Saturday nights.

Stock up on picnic goodies at the **Presque Isle Farmers Market,** held in the Sears parking area at the Aroostook Centre Mall. The market is The County's largest. A good-size crowd of vendors sets up shop 9 A.M.–1 P.M. every Saturday mid-May–mid-October.

Caribou

An extremely loyal clientele makes unpretentious **Frederick's Southside** (217 S. Main St., Caribou, 207/498-3464) busy most of the time. Inexpensive home cooking is the draw. It's open 5 A.M.–8 P.M. Monday–Saturday, 6:30 A.M.–8 P.M. Sunday all year.

Caribou's best pizza comes from **Napoli's** (6 Center St., Caribou, 207/492-1102, 11 A.M.–9 P.M. Mon.–Sat.).

Sandwiches, soups, and salads are available at **A Bite to Eat** (159 Bennett Dr., Caribou, 207/493-7858), a strip mall grab-and-go restaurant with some seating, open for breakfast and lunch Monday–Saturday. Be prepared for a wait.

Fort Fairfield

Wander well off the beaten path for an enchanted evening at **[Canterbury Royale** (182 Sam Everett Rd., Fort Fairfield, 207/472-4910), a destination-dining experience. Guests are immersed in an Old World Eu-

ropean setting for elegant six-course meals featuring haute French cuisine. They choose an entrée from a menu listing about a dozen choices and then half-sisters and classically trained chefs Barbara Boucher and Renee O'Neill choose the other courses. The setting, presentation, and food are sublime. Tables are set with crystal, silver, elaborate candelabras, and marble accents. Some furnishings and the elaborate, decorative woodwork were hand carved by Renee. Expect to pay around $45 pp, plus tax, tip, and wine. Plan far in advance, as only two parties are seated each evening. Reservations are required. No jeans, T-shirts, shorts, or sneakers. The restaurant also offers limited Victorian teas and European-style five-course brunches.

INFORMATION AND SERVICES

The Presque Isle Area Chamber of Commerce (3 Houlton Rd., Rte. 1, P.O. Box 672, Presque Isle 04769, 207/764-6561 or 800/764-7420, www.pichamber.com), on the southern outskirts of the city, has information in a greenhouse area.

The Caribou Chamber of Commerce (24 Sweden St., Caribou, 207/498-6156 or 800/722-7648, www.caribouchamber. com) is open 8:30 A.M.–4:30 P.M. Monday–Friday. Check out Caribou Public Library (30 High St., Caribou, 207/493-4214, www .caribou-public.lib.me.us). Both have public restrooms.

Aroostook County Tourism (888/216-2463, www.visitaroostook.com) has information on and links for the entire county.

GETTING THERE

US Airways Express/US Airways operates daily nonstop flights between Boston's Logan Airport and Northern Maine Regional Airport in Presque Isle (207/764-2550, www.fly presqueisle.com). While at the airport, check out the **Presque Isle Air Museum** (207/764-2542), which displays historical photos and memorabilia from Presque Isle's impressive aviation history in two corridors.

The St. John Valley

Settled by Acadians in 1785, the St. John Valley isn't quite sure whether it should be the 51st state or Canada's 11th province. Valley hallmarks are huge Roman Catholic churches, small riverside communities, unfancy but tidy homes, an eclectic French patois, and a handful of unique culinary specialties—all thanks to a twist of fate.

Henry Wadsworth Longfellow's immortal epic poem *Evangeline* relates a saga of *le grand dérangement,* when more than 10,000 French-speaking Acadians tragically lost their lease on Nova Scotia after the British expelled them for disloyalty in 1755—a date engraved ever since in the minds of their thousands of descendants now living on the American and Canadian sides of the St. John River. (Thousands more of their kin ended up in Louisiana, where Acadian-Cajun traditions also remain strong.)

In this part of Maine, Smiths and Joneses are few—countless residents bear such names as Cyr, Daigle, Gagnon, Michaud, Ouellette, Pelletier, Sirois, and Thibodeau. In Van Buren, Grand Isle, Madawaska, St. Agatha, and Frenchville, French is the mother tongue for 97 percent of the residents, who refer to the Upper St. John Valley as *chez nous* ("our house"), their homeland. Many roadside and shop signs are bilingual—even the nameboard for the University of Maine branch in Fort Kent.

Religion is as pervasive an influence as language. When a Madawaska beauty represented Maine in the Miss America contest in 1995, the local *St. John Valley Times* admonished its readers: "Keep your fingers crossed and your rosaries hot."

Since the 1970s, renewed local interest in and appreciation for Acadian culture has spurred cultural projects, celebrations, and genealogical research throughout the valley, with the eventual goal of a National Park Service Acadian culture center. "Valley French," a unique, archaic patois long stigmatized in Maine schools, has undergone a revival. Since the 1970s, several valley schools have established bilingual programs, and a 1991 survey estimated that 40 percent of valley schoolchildren speak both English and French.

Controversy erupts periodically over whose lineage is "true" Acadian (as opposed to Québécois—although many Acadians also fled to Québec), but valley residents all turn out en masse for the summer highlight: Madawaska's multiday Acadian Festival, centered on Acadian Day, June 28. It's a local festival unlike any other in Maine. If you plan to visit then, make lodging plans far in advance. Thousands of far-flung descendents of whichever founding family is being honored each year book every room on both sides of the border.

Between Madawaska and Fort Kent, detour off Route 1, via Route 162, into the lovely lake district, locally known as the "back settlements," through the town of St. Agatha (usually pronounced the French way: "Saint a-GAHT") and the village of Sinclair. T-shaped **Long Lake** is the northernmost of the Fish River Chain of Lakes, extending southwest to Eagle Lake.

West of Fort Kent are the tiny and tinier riverside communities of St. John, St. Francis, Allagash, and Dickey, the latter two serving as endpoints for two of Maine's most popular long-distance canoe routes: the St. John River and the Allagash Wilderness Waterway. The town of Allagash, curiously enough, was settled by Irish and English immigrants, so it's not unusual to find lots of Irish surnames in this part of the valley. Contemporary author Cathie Pelletier grew up in Allagash, called "Mattagash" in her entertaining novels of life in northern Maine. Pack up a picnic, allow a couple of hours, and take a jaunt out here in a car or on a bike. In mid-September, one of the best times to be here, the hills on your left are a riot of color all the way to Allagash. On your right, the river usually dribbles along this time of year, exposing gravel bars much of the way. It's a far cry from late winter and spring, when ice jams and spring runoff are the rule.

THE BLOODLESS AROOSTOOK WAR

Aroostook County's major brush with historic notoriety occurred in 1839, with the skirmish known as the Aroostook War. Always described by the adjective "bloodless" – since there were no casualties (other than a farmer accidentally downed by friendly fire) – the war was essentially a boundary dispute between Maine and New Brunswick that had simmered since 1784, when New Brunswick was established.

The 1783 Treaty of Paris had set the St. Croix River as the Washington County line, but loopholes left the northernmost border ill-defined. Maine feared losing timber-rich real estate to Canada, and matters heated up when 200 burly militiamen descended on the region in early 1839 to defend the young state's territory. About 3,000 troops ended up supporting the Maine cause, and legendary war hero General Winfield ("Old Fuss and Feathers") Scott was sent to Augusta for three weeks in March 1839 to negotiate the successful truce.

After the "war," Aroostook was incorporated as a county, and by 1842 the Webster-Ashburton Treaty (sometimes also called the Treaty of Washington), negotiated by Daniel Webster and Lord Ashburton, brought a long-awaited peace that opened the area for stepped-up settlement.

Among the remnants of the Aroostook War are two wooden blockhouses, one an original and a National Historic Site, on the banks of the St. John River in Fort Kent, the other a replica on the Aroostook River in Fort Fairfield.

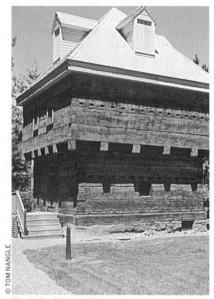

© TOM NANGLE

Fort Kent's blockhouse is a remnant from the Aroostook War.

SIGHTS
【 Acadian Village

In the hamlet of Keegan, about two miles northwest of downtown Van Buren, is a prominent reminder of the heritage in this valley. Begun as a small-scale bicentennial project in 1976, the Acadian Village (Rte. 1, Van Buren, 207/868-5042, www.connectmaine.com/acadianvillage, $5 adults, $3 kids) is a 2.5-acre open-air museum comprising 16 antique and replica buildings in an A-shaped layout. Included are a country store, forge, schoolhouse, chapel, and several residences. Tours by attentive guides vividly convey the daily struggles for 18th- and 19th-century Acadians in the valley. Kids particularly enjoy the schoolhouse and the barbershop; outside, there's plenty of letting-off-steam room. It's open mid-June–mid-September.

Le Musée et Centre Culturel du Mont-Carmel

As with the other religion-dominated communities in the valley, the most prominent landmark in the Lille village of Grand Isle (pop. 569) is the Catholic church, a twin, golden-domed building undergoing long-term restoration as a nonprofit bilingual museum/cultural center. Built in 1909, Our Lady of Mount Carmel Church had its first Mass on New Year's Day in 1910 and its last in 1978. Since historian/preservationist/renaissance man Don Cyr took over the wooden church in 1984, he's organized concerts and other events under the aegis of l'Association culturelle et historique du Mont-Carmel. The church is open noon–4 P.M. Sunday–Friday early June–mid-September. For information, contact Cyr (207/895-3339).

⟨ St. David's Historical Sites

As you reach the eastern edge of Madawaska, you can't help but notice the bell tower of the imposing brick **St. David Catholic Church,** established in 1871. The National Historic Register building, usually open, has a high arched ceiling, a domed altar, and stained-glass windows.

Just to the right (east) of St. David's is the one-room **Tante Blanche Museum** (Rte. 1, St. David Parish, Madawaska, 207/728-4518, free), containing Acadian artifacts. Run by the Madawaska Historical Society (P.O. Box 258, Madawaska 04756, www.madawaska

© TOM NANGLE

Woodcarvings in St. David's depict traditional Acadian culture.

historical.org), the log museum commemorates Marguerite Blanche Thibodeau Cyr ("Tante Blanche"), an Acadian heroine during a 1797 famine. The museum usually is open 11 A.M.–4 P.M. Wednesday–Sunday mid-June–early September; on-site volunteers answer questions and provide guidance. The museum's campus also includes the 1870 **School House #1** and the circa 1840 **Albert House.**

Continue down the 0.5-mile gravel road to the riverfront, where a 14-foot-high marble **Acadian Cross** marks the reputed 1785 landing spot of Acadians expelled by the British from Nova Scotia and New Brunswick. During the annual Acadian Festival, the landing is reenacted.

⟨ Fort Kent Blockhouse

Built in 1839 during the decades-long U.S.-Canada border dispute known as the Aroostook War, the National Historic Register Fort Kent Blockhouse (Blockhouse Rd., Fort Kent 04743) is the only remnant of a complex that once included barracks, a hospital, and an ammunition hoard. On the second floor are historic artifacts—unfortunately not well labeled—plus information about the curious "bloodless" border skirmish over timber rights. Bring a picnic and commandeer a table in the pretty little riverside park just below the fort. Early in the summer, before the river dwindles, you can also launch a canoe or kayak here. The Fort Kent Boy Scouts (207/834-3866) maintain and staff the blockhouse and the nearby log-cabin gift shop, which are open 9 A.M. to 7 P.M. daily Memorial Day weekend–Labor Day. Admission is free.

Fort Kent Railroad Station

The station, a National Historic Register site, was in service 1902–1979 and was part of the Bangor and Aroostook Railroad's Fish River division. It's now the home of the Fort Kent Historical Society and Gardens and is open 1–4 P.M. Tuesday–Friday in July or by appointment; call the chamber (207/834-5354).

Route 1 Terminus

In the middle of downtown Fort Kent, close to the bridge to Canada, is an almost offhand

AROOSTOOK COUNTY

roadside sign with an impressive message: This Site Marks the Northern Terminus of Historic U.S. Route 1 Originating in Key West, Florida. You're 318 miles north of Portland, 368 miles north of the New Hampshire border at Kittery, and 2,209 miles north of Key West.

University of Maine at Fort Kent

Founded in 1878 as a teacher-training school, the University of Maine at Fort Kent, UMFK (25 Pleasant St., Fort Kent, 207/834-7500, www.umfk.maine.edu) still prides itself on the quality of its teacher-education program. Because of its location in the Upper St. John Valley, UMFK also offers a BS degree in bilingual/bicultural studies, and the school's **Acadian Archives** (207/834-7535) are the state's best resource on Maine's Acadian heritage. The campus, just off Route 1, has a bucolic feel.

RECREATION
Golf

The Bangor and Aroostook Railroad line runs right through the first and ninth holes at the **Fort Kent Golf Club** (St. John Rd./Rte. 161, Fort Kent, 207/834-3149), but that never seems to bother anyone. The nine-hole hilly course has dynamite views of the St. John River. Call for a tee time on weekends; cart rentals are available. The attractive clubhouse has a bar and light meals. The club, three miles west of town (toward Allagash), is open May–October.

The ninth hole at the nine-hole **Birch Point Country Club** (Birch Point Rd., St. David, 207/895-6957) has the distinction of being New England's northernmost golfing hole. The clubhouse has a bar and basic menu; cart rentals are available. The course is open May–mid-October.

Swimming and Canoeing

Birch Point Beach (Chapel Rd., St. David, on the east side of Long Lake; turnoff to the beach at St. Michael's Chapel) has a small grassy area, plus picnic tables; the lake views are fantastic.

A lovely **picnic and recreation area** (Rte.

162 in St. Agatha) on the western shore of Long Lake has a boat launch, beach, grills, and restrooms.

Nordic Skiing

One of the top Nordic skiing facilities in the world, **The 10th Mountain Center** (Paradise Circle Rd., P.O. Box 541, Fort Kent 04743, 207/834-6203, www.10thmtskiclub.org, free) hosted the 2004 World Cup Biathlon. Another of the successful Maine Winter Sports Center facilities, this one has a biathlon and cross-country facility, with 12 km of trails, plus an additional 25 km of trails, a lighted roller-ski loop, wax building, stadium, and a full biathlon range with 30 shooting stations. Snowshoes and pets are permitted on 2.2 km Volunteer's Way, also known as the Pet Loop. The lodge, with sauna and fireplace, is a comfy place to relax after a day on the trails. The center's access road is off Route 1, 1.6 miles south of downtown Fort Kent.

Alpine Skiing

Just a couple of blocks off Main Street is **Lonesome Pine Trails** (Forest Ave., P.O. Box 372, Fort Kent 04743, 207/834-5202, www .skimaine.com/areas/lonesomepine), a volunteer-run community hill with a 500-foot vertical serviced by two tows and night skiing. Adult tickets are $18 full day, $13 half day.

Multiuse Trail

The 17-mile, crushed-stone **Saint John Valley Heritage Trail** edges the south bank of the St. John River between Fort Kent and St. Francis and connects with area ATV and snowmobile trails. It's also part of the National Park Service's Acadian interpretation efforts.

A 32-mile trail circles Long Lake.

Allagash and St. John Canoeing

Shuttles, pickups, food, and very basic lodgings are all available in Allagash and Dickey, the endpoints for many Allagash and St. John paddlers. (Information on outfitters, guides, and access appears in the *Maine Highlands* chapter, where these trips begin.)

PARKS AND PRESERVES
Fish River Falls

Getting to Fort Kent's Fish River Falls is an adventure in itself. There's not a sign in sight—perhaps deliberately. The optimum situation is having a local person lead you there. Otherwise, check with the chamber of commerce office. It's very near Bouchard Farm (which grows acres of buckwheat for *ployes,* a traditional Acadian pancake), and you can also ask for directions there. The falls are a 10-minute stroll slightly downhill once you get to the parking area. Carry a picnic and sit on the rocks, which have great wells formed by the grinding of boulders. It's a lovely setting, worth seeking out.

Deboullie Public Reserve Lands

Wildlife-watchers, hikers, anglers, campers, snowmobilers, and pretty much anyone who enjoys the great outdoors will appreciate the 22,000-acre Deboullie Public Reserve Lands (207/435-7963, www.maine.gov/doc/parks/programs/prl.html). Wildlife-watching is excellent throughout the reserve, thanks to varied habitats, including ponds, streams, marshes, and woodlands. Watch for deer and moose, beavers and snowshoe hares, loons and bald eagles. While the northern three-quarters of the preserve comprise gently rolling forested ridges, the southern quarter has mountains to climb and ponds for boating and fishing. Brook trout are abundant in most of the ponds; landlocked salmon can be hooked in Togue Pond. Hike Deboullie Mountain to the inactive fire station at the top for panoramic views of the region. Along the route, keep an eye out for ice caves, deep crevices in the rocks where ice can remain year-round. Allow at least four hours for the six-mile hike. Primitive, waterfront campsites dot the preserve, but for those who prefer a roof over their heads, Red River Camps (www.redrivercamps.com) is a traditional sporting camp on Island Pond. Debouillie gives meaning to the word remote. It's about 30 rugged miles southwest of Fort Kent. Access is via the North Maine Woods (www.northmainewoods.org) checkpoint, in St. Francis.

Deboullie, by the way, is a French derivation of a term meaning "rock slides."

EVENTS

Spectators crowd the snowy streets to watch Fort Kent's five-day March **Can Am Crown International Sled Dog Races** (http://can-am.sjv.net). Special locations offer vantage points for watching teams competing in 30-, 60-, and 250-mile races. A mushers' award ceremony is the finale.

Madawaska hosts the Franco American **Acadian Festival,** with a historical reenactment, tournaments, fishing derby, Acadian food, music, and dancing, a parade, and a featured family reunion late in June.

ACCOMMODATIONS

Lodging options are slim on this side of the border, and rates are low, generally less than $75 per room.

The **Long Lake Motor Inn** (596 Main St./Rte. 162, St. Agatha, 207/543-5006, www.stagatha.com/longlake) has 18 rooms with phones and cable TV, 11 with lake views (and great sunrises), two with kitchenettes. Continental breakfast is included. If you're here in winter, reserve well ahead or the snowmobilers will beat you to it.

Clean, comfortable, and inexpensive, the downtown **Northern Door Inn** (356 W. Main St., Fort Kent, 207/834-3133 or 866/834-3133, www.northerndoorinn.com) has a nice gathering area in the lobby, where a continental breakfast is served. Rooms have air-conditioning, phones, TV, and Wi-Fi. Pets are $5 each per night.

The Lakeview Camping Resort (9 Lakeview Dr., St. Agatha, 207/543-6331, www.lakeviewrestaurant.net) has 100 mostly wooded sites, with areas for RVs ($21–28 d) and tents ($19 d). Also on-site are a convenience store, shower house, and restaurant.

FOOD

Be sure to check local papers and bulletin boards for notices about **public suppers,** an inexpensive way to break bread with locals.

AROOSTOOK COUNTY

Frenchville

Eleven miles roughly west of Madawaska, on Route 1 North, you'll find Frenchville (pop. about 1,300). If you arrive in time for lunch or dinner, stop in at **Rosette's Restaurant** (240 Main St., Rte. 1, Frenchville, 207/543-7759), a valley favorite. Everything's homemade, prices are very reasonable, and the color is local. Rosette's is open 7 A.M.–9 P.M. Tuesday–Sunday all year.

St. Agatha

When it's time for a meal, head up the hill for the best panorama in town, at **The Lakeview Restaurant** (9 Lakeview Dr., St. Agatha, 207/543-6331, www.lakeviewrestaurant.net). An awning-covered deck overlooks Long Lake; indoor booths and tables have plenty of visibility. The wide-ranging menu has a choice and price for every taste and budget. The restaurant is open 11 A.M.–1 A.M. daily all year. A big surge occurs after 5 P.M. Mass lets out on Saturday, so don't plan to eat early; Lakeview doesn't take reservations.

For something a little different, the best view in the village of **Sinclair,** about six miles down the road from St. Agatha, is at the **Long Lake Sporting Club Resort** (Rte. 162, Sinclair, 207/543-7584 or 800/431-7584). In the middle of nowhere, this informal place is almost always crowded. In summer, guests come by boat or car, occasionally by floatplane; in winter, they arrive by snowmobile. The deck has a fabulous view over Long Lake. Huge steaks and giant lobsters are specialties, and all meals come with *ployes,* Acadian buckwheat pancakes typically served with an artery-clogging pâté called *creton.* Settle in the lounge, choose from six entrées ($10–19, except lobster), and you'll be ushered to your table when it's all ready. It's open 5–9 P.M. Monday–Saturday, noon–8 P.M. Sunday July–August; 5–9 P.M. Tuesday–Saturday, noon–8 P.M. Sunday the rest of the year. If you're ready to party, there's live music Saturday night, but be prepared for plenty of noise.

Madawaska

Michael Corbin's **【 Café de la Place** (285 Main St., Madawaska, 207/728-0944) is a cheerful place open for breakfast (homemade muffins) and lunch (superb homemade soups and sandwiches) 4:30 A.M.–2 P.M. Monday–Friday. The space doubles as a gallery, displaying the work of local artists.

Fort Kent

Rock's Family Diner (W. Main St., 207/834-2888), a local favorite since 1945, serves inexpensive sandwiches, burgers, and fried foods for lunch and dinner and the usuals for breakfast. It's open daily.

Walk into **Doris's Cafe** (345 Market St./Rte. 161, Fort Kent Mills, 207/834-6262, 6 A.M.–2 P.M. Mon.–Fri., to noon Sat.), and conversation ceases as every head in the place turns to see the stranger. Not to worry, chatter quickly resumes—and you can catch all the local gossip. If you've never had *poutine* (French fries smothered with gravy and cheese), you can order it here.

INFORMATION AND SERVICES

The Greater Madawaska Chamber of Commerce (356 Main St./Rte. 1, Madawaska, 207/728-7000, www.greatermadawaskachamber.com) is open 9 A.M.–5 P.M. weekdays.

The Greater Fort Kent Area Chamber of Commerce (76 W. Main St., Rte. 1, P.O. Box 430, Fort Kent 04743, 207/834-5354 or 800/733-3563, www.fortkentchamber.com) serves as a clearinghouse for much of the Upper St. John Valley. The downtown office is open 9 A.M.–5 P.M. weekdays. On weekends, stop in at the log cabin near the Fort Kent Blockhouse, where area brochures and maps are available.

Aroostook County Tourism (888/216-2463, www.visitaroostook.com) has information on and links for the entire county.

The 1994 National Park Service publication *Acadian Culture in Maine* is available online (http://acim.umfk.maine.edu).

GETTING AROUND

If you're planning to pass through one of the three U.S./Canada border stations, be sure to have the proper identification and paperwork. For crossings into the United States, see www.cbp.gov. For crossings into Canada, see www.cbsa-asfc.gc.ca. Remember, also, that New Brunswick is on Atlantic time, an hour later than eastern time.

The **U.S. Customs office** maintains offices in Madawaska (207/728-4376) and Fort Kent (207/834-5255). Both are open 24 hours.

South from the Peak of the Crown

The rolling farmlands of northern Aroostook give way to forests and mountains as you drive south on Route 11 from Fort Kent. If you took a poll among those who know, especially photographers, the stretch from Fort Kent through Eagle Lake to Portage probably would rank near the top as a favorite fall-foliage drive. What's so appealing along this 37-mile Scenic Highway? Brilliant colors, rolling hills, open vistas, and a smattering of lakes and ponds. It's really stunning, either by car or bike.

Through the years, Eagle Lake has benefited heavily from being the hometown of John Martin, one of Maine's most influential politicians, who served an unprecedented 10 terms as Speaker of Maine's House of Representatives. The town really looks as though someone has been paying attention. The official rest area, overlooking the lake, has picnic tables and plenty of parking. Many a photo has been snapped here. If it's a typically bright fall day, you'll see why: a prime hilltop with a pristine lake surrounded by multicolored foliage. Eighteen-mile-long, L-shaped Eagle Lake is a key link in the Fish River Chain of Lakes, starting at Long Lake in St. Agatha. In winter, the lake supports wall-to-wall ice-fishing shacks.

Portage is particularly popular as a summer playground, and many county residents have built or rented camps on the shores of Portage Lake.

Considered the "Gateway to the North Maine Woods," Ashland (pop. 1,535) is the home of **North Maine Woods** (P.O. Box 421, Ashland 04732, 207/435-6213, www .northmainewoods.org), a private organiza-tion charged with managing recreational use of more than three million acres of northern Maine's working timberlands. North Maine Woods publishes maps, newsletters, and serves as an information resource for camping, fishing, hunting, hiking trails, and logging roads. Call (weekdays only) for a free packet of regulations and list of outfitters, plus an order form for maps and other publications.

Route 11 continues southward and out of Aroostook County, to Patten, Medway, and Millinocket.

SIGHTS

The open-air **Ashland Logging Museum** (Garfield Rd., Ashland, 207/435-6679, www .townofashland.com) has six buildings containing a blacksmith shop, old woods rigs, and other gear—a taste of what the timber industry was like. The museum is open by appointment; call curator Ed Chase (207/436-6679). Just before Ashland, when Route 11 takes a sharp left, turn right onto Garfield Road and go a little less than a mile.

RECREATION
Swimming and Boating

Eagle Lake's **town park,** down at lake level, has shorefront picnic tables and grills. The wind kicks up wildly at times, but on a calm day, this is a fine place to launch a canoe. From Route 11, turn at Old Main Street and go 0.6 mile; there's plenty of parking.

From Route 11, turn west at West Cottage Road and go 0.5 mile to reach the Portage **town beach.** The view is fabulous and parking is ample; there are picnic tables, a grill, and a grassy "beach."

AROOSTOOK COUNTY

Roughly midway between Ashland and Masardis, in the town of Masardis, is an access road to the boat landing for **Squa Pan Lake,** probably the oddest-shaped lake in the state. One wag alleges the name comes from a squaw who married a French man named Pan, but if you believe that, there's this bridge…

Hiking

About eight miles south of Eagle Lake is the wooded **Hedgehog Mountain Rest Area,** trailhead for Hedgehog Mountain. It's not your most exciting climb, and the summit view is so-so, but it's easy exercise for an hour or so. The trail is just over a mile round-trip.

About 10 miles east of Ashland on Route 163 (Presque Isle Rd.) is the trailhead (on the left) for **Haystack Mountain,** a short, steep climb—easy to moderate—to a fairly bald summit. Pack a picnic so you can enjoy the almost 360-degree view.

Golf

Golfers may want to play a round at nine-hole **Portage Hills Country Club** (Portage, 207/435-8221), where the challenges come with the rolling terrain. Starting times aren't needed; the course is open Memorial Day weekend–Labor Day.

ACCOMMODATIONS

If you'd like to overnight along Route 11, opt for the immaculately maintained **Overlook Motel** (N. Main St./Rte. 11, Eagle Lake, 207/444-4535, www.overlookmotel.com), with the same dramatic view as the official rest area. Opened in 1995, it's become one of Route 11's most popular lodgings. Rooms include three singles ($58 s), two doubles ($67 d), four efficiencies ($73), and two hot-tub suites ($99 d, including free champagne). Amenities include phones, air-conditioning, TV, microwave, and fridge. Children 10 and under are free; pets are $5. In winter, snowmobilers pile in here.

Another choice is the **Eagle's View Bed and Breakfast** (1087 Sly Brook Rd., Eagle Lake, 207/444-2808, $60–80), a modern log chalet–style home with a fabulous lake view. Four rooms—one with deck and hot tub—share two baths. A full breakfast is served weekends; midweek it's continental. It's on the other side of the lake, so cross the Fish River in Soldier Pond and then head south on Sly Brook Road.

Right close by is the lakefront **Birch Haven Campground** (1165 Sly Brook Rd., Eagle Lake, 207/444-5102), with 80 sites for tents and RVs, a laundry, store, boat rentals, and swimming. It's open late May–early September.

Route 11 in Portage provides access to **Moose Point Camps** (Fish River Lake, P.O. Box 170, Portage 04768, 207/435-6156, www.moosepointcamps.com), an idyllic spot with 10 rustic, hewn-log cabins on the shore of five-mile-long Fish River Lake (a.k.a. Fish Lake). Rates are $395 a week pp ($85 per day), AP (all meals), $75 a week for children under 12. BYOB. Motorboat rentals are $35 a day, canoes are $12 a day. In the main lodge are games, books, and a huge fireplace. It's open for fishing and vacationers early May–late August. Watch for the sign on Route 11 and turn west. It's 17 miles over rugged logging roads to camp. About four miles from Portage, you'll reach the Fish River Checkpoint, the toll booth for entering the logging area. Round-trip fee is $7 per day for non-Maine residents; seniors and kids under 15 are free. **Note:** Don't expect to be alone with the moose and other wildlife out here; logging trucks legally own the road, and they know it, so give them a wide berth.

FOOD

Need a bite to eat? The dining room at **Dean's Motor Lodge** (Rte. 11, Portage, 207/435-3701 or 207/435-6840, www.deansmotorlodge .com) is a favorite with sportsmen and women. Breakfast is served 5–11 A.M. Monday–Saturday, 7–11 A.M. Sunday, and then the menu changes over, with steak and seafood as the house specialities. Burgers, sandwiches, and pizza are available. Expect to watch NASCAR or sports on the big-screen TV.

MAINE HIGHLANDS

Home to Maine's highest mountain and largest lake, the Maine Highlands region, covering all of Piscataquis County and the northern two-thirds of Penobscot County, typifies Maine's rugged North Woods. Within Piscataquis County are 40-mile-long Moosehead Lake, the appealing frontier town of Greenville, the headwaters of the Allagash Wilderness Waterway, and the controlled wilds of Baxter State Park.

Sport hunters and anglers have always frequented the North Woods, and they still do. But hunters, sport fishers, and back-to-the-landers increasingly have to share their untamed turf with a new generation of visitor. Sporting camps originally built for rugged anglers and hunters now welcome photographers, birders, and families; white-water rafting, canoeing, kayaking, and snowmobiling are all

big business; and hikers have found nirvana in a vast network of trails—particularly the huge, carefully monitored trail system in Baxter State Park.

In the 1970s, paper companies were forced by environmental concerns to halt the perilous river-run log drives that took their products to market. This cessation not only cleaned up the rivers but also spared the lives of the hardy breed of men who once made a living unjamming the logs in roiling waters. The alternative now is roads, lots of them, mostly unpaved—a huge network that has opened up the area to more and more outdoors enthusiasts. For generations, paper companies allowed public recreation on their lands and access via their roads, but as they sell off large chunks of wilderness, the patterns are changing. Some

© TOM NANGLE

HIGHLIGHTS

⟨ Patten Lumbermen's Museum: A visit to this replica of a lumberman's camp will cure any romantic notions about being a lumberjack (page 426).

⟨ Hiking in Baxter State Park: Explore Maine's gem, choosing from more than 200 miles of trails crowned by Mt. Katahdin, Maine's tallest peak (page 439).

⟨ Cruise on the *Kate*: See Moosehead Lake from the water on a historic vessel (page 448).

⟨ Kineo: It's worth the effort to get a close-up view of Kineo's icon cliffs and to hike to its summit (page 450).

⟨ Moose Safaris: You can't go home without spotting at least one moose, so go with a guide who knows where they hang out (page 451).

⟨ Monson: Artists, artisans, and hikers have made the pass-through village an engaging stop (page 460).

⟨ Gulf Hagas Reserve: Nicknamed the Grand Canyon of the East, the 3.5-mile-long gorge makes a spectacular hike (page 462).

⟨ University of Maine Museum of Art: Bangor lured the university's collection away from the Orono campus (page 469).

⟨ University of Maine: The Orono campus is home to a planetarium, gardens, museums, and a performing-arts venue (page 476).

⟨ Penobscot Nation Museum: Cross the bridge to Indian Island to see this engaging collection of artifacts, videos, and artwork from Maine's Penobscot Native Americans (page 477).

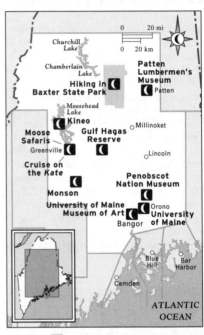

LOOK FOR ⟨ TO FIND RECOMMENDED SIGHTS, ACTIVITIES, DINING, AND LODGING.

new owners are discontinuing the open-road/open-land policies, and that's a cause for concern among many outdoor-oriented folks.

The area is rich in aquatic possibilities, too. Maine's best-known, classic canoe trips follow the Allagash and St. John Rivers northward, but no one can even begin to count the other lakes, rivers, and streams that have wonderful canoeing.

Stay at one of this region's primitive forest campsites and you'll really sense the wilderness—owls hoot, loons cry, frogs croak…and, oh yes, insects annoy. No matter how much civilization intrudes, it's still remote and wild. As one writer put it, "Trees grow, die, fall, and rot, never having been seen by anyone. They litter the shores of lakes, form temporary islands, block streams, and quickly eradicate paths."

Air gateway to the region is Bangor, Maine's second-largest city and home to horror maven Stephen King. Between Bangor and nearby Orono, a university town, there's enough "cultcha" to balance the wilderness.

© TOM NANGLE

Mile-high Katahdin is the centerpiece of Baxter State Park.

PLANNING YOUR TIME

If you merely want a taste of the wilderness, you can swoop from Bangor up to Millinocket on Route 11, segue over to Greenville on the Golden Road, and back down to Bangor via Monson, Guilford, and Dover-Foxcroft on Route 15 in two days, but if you want to experience it, you'll need time to paddle, hike, and explore—plan on at least a week. Greenville makes a fine base for exploring the region; it's on the edge of the wilderness, within striking distance of Baxter State Park and the Penobscot River, on the shore of Moosehead Lake, and surrounded by endless opportunities for outdoor recreation.

From mid-May–early July, the blackflies are more than annoying. When they begin to wane, the mosquitoes take up the charge. Arm yourself with bug dope. While DEET is the strongest, I've had excellent results with Lewey's Eco-Blends, an all-natural repellent available widely in Maine. The key is applying it liberally and often. One Baxter Park ranger I spoke with swore by Bounce dryer sheets—place one under a cap and the other under your shirt around the waistline to create a "force field" that keeps the bugs from biting.

Bangor's annual American Folk Festival, in August, is worth planning a visit around, and spending a day or so in Bangor lets you ease into the woods.

Autumn foliage comes early to these parts, with leaves often beginning to turn by early September. While this can be a beautiful time to be in the woods—bugs are few, color is gorgeous—it's also the beginning of hunting season, and it's wise to take precautions.

Winter is cold and usually very snowy, a real plus for cross-country skiing, snowshoeing, and especially snowmobiling.

Most timber-company throughways remain there for all to use, but never forget that the logging trucks *own* them—in more ways than one. As they barrel along, give them room—and some slack as well; you may even be glad they're there, especially if you get lost. The *DeLorme Atlas* is essential for exploring the area, but every time the loggers begin working a new patch, they open new roads, so the cartographers can barely keep up.

Finally, never underestimate the North Woods: Bring versatile clothing (more than you think you'll need), don't strike out alone without telling anyone, stock up on insect repellent and water, use a decent vehicle (4WD if possible), and carry a flashlight, maps, and a compass. Perhaps most important, be a conscientious, eco-sensitive visitor.

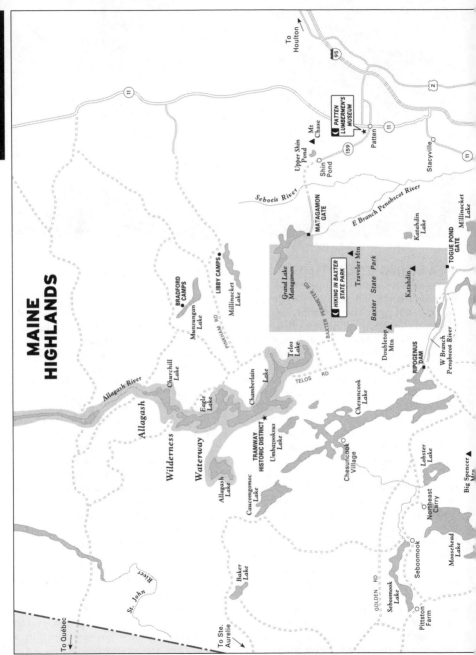

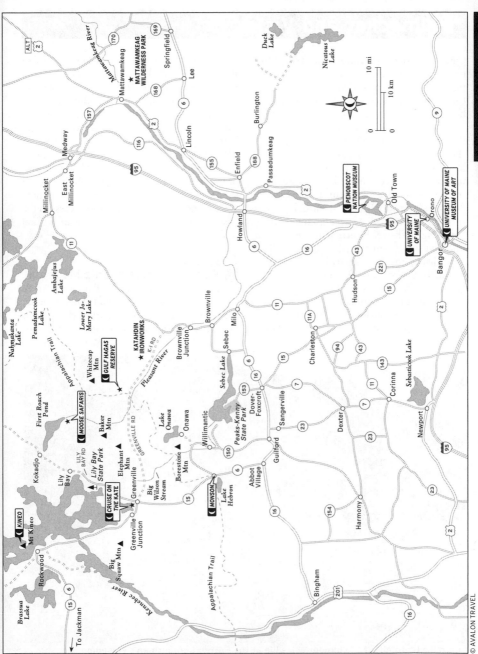

Millinocket and Vicinity

Once crucial to the timber industry, Millinocket is fighting for its future. For generations, paper mills provided the major support for the local economy, but major downsizings have left them a shadow of their former selves and have resulted in shrinking populations in the area's towns. Half the locals pray for the resurgence of the local mills and woods-based work; the other half are gung-ho for a tourism-based economy. The latter are pushing to re-create area towns as a recreation destination, and with the seemingly endless sporting opportunities—canoeing, rafting, kayaking, fishing, hunting, hiking, camping, and more—in the surrounding wilderness, that seems like a smart idea. Developers are circling—real estate here is a bargain—and plans are being filed for building major resorts that take advantage of the spectacular setting and the eco-vacation trend. Controversy is rampant and local politics are hot.

Millinocket is the closest civilization to Baxter State Park's southern entrance, so most Baxter visitors find themselves here at some time or other. Food, lodging, books, auto fuel, and other essentials are all available. But it's not a pretty downtown; giant, smoke-belching stacks dominate the skyline in Millinocket and adjoining East Millinocket.

The town of Medway links I-95 with the two mill towns; just to the north on Route 11 are the communities of Sherman, Sherman Station, Patten, and Shin Pond, providing access to the less-used northeast entrance (Matagamon Gate) of Baxter State Park.

SIGHTS
◖ Patten Lumbermen's Museum

About 40 miles northeast of Millinocket, 0.5 mile west of downtown Patten, and about 25 miles southeast of Baxter State Park's Matagamon Gate, is a family-oriented museum commemo-

Learn the truth about the lumberjack's life at the Patten Lumbermen's Museum.

© HILARY NANGLE

MAINE'S BIG DIG: THE GOLDEN ROAD

The era of nimble lumberjacks driving logs downriver ended in the early 1970s, when Maine's paper companies began building roads into the wilderness for access to their timberlands. The most famous of these, The Golden Road, runs from Millinocket around the top of Moosehead Lake to the Québec border. It took nearly 1,000 workers almost five years to build the private, 96-mile, mostly unpaved road.

Completed in 1975 and originally called the West Branch Haul Road, Maine's version of the Big Dig reputedly earned its current name from the megacost ($3.2 million) of construction.

The Golden Road is the most scenic link between Millinocket and Greenville, a 71-mile trip, two-thirds unpaved, through the wilderness. Red-and-white mile markers tacked to trees tick off the distance — if you can spot them. Driving this route is a true adventure, but it's not for everybody. If you're not used to driving back-woods dirt roads, this might not be the place to start. If you choose to do so, it's vital to ask about the road's condition — if there's been a lot of cutting going on along the route or it's been a while between gradings, it could be in uncomfortably rough shape. Remember, it's a private road built for trucks, not cars; logs, not people.

When driving from Millinocket, you'll exit the Golden Road after about 48 miles (watch for a fork in the road, with a crude sign denoting Greenville Road; if you make it to the North Woods checkpoint, you've overshot) and then drive paralleling Moosehead Lake's east shore to Greenville. Keep an eye peeled for moose, deer, and even black bear.

Do note: You are entering true wilderness. There are no gas stations, restaurants, lodgings or, well, anything but water, trees, and wildlife, and cell phone service is spotty at best. Go prepared with a full tank of gas, bottles of water, energy bars, bug dope, and a good spare tire. Bicycles, motorcycles, ATVs and horses are *not* allowed on the road. And one more note: Should you meet a logging truck along the way, pull way, way over and let it pass. If it's loaded, it might be carrying as much as 100,000 pounds of logs (and unlike Harry Chapin's song about bananas, it's you, not the logs, that will be mashed).

---

rating the lumberman's grueling life. The nine buildings at the open-air Patten Lumbermen's Museum (Waters Rd./Rte. 159, P.O. Box 300, Patten 04765, 207/528-2650, www.lumbermens museum.org, 10 A.M.–4 P.M. late May–mid-Oct., closed Mon. and Tues.–Thurs. spring and fall, $7 adults, $6 seniors, $2 kids 6–11) tell the tale of timber in the 19th and early 20th centuries: cramped quarters, hazardous equipment, rugged terrain, nasty weather. Lots of working gear and colorful dioramas appeal to children, and there are picnic tables, a snack bar, and room to roam. The reception center has a crafts shop and restrooms. Summer highlight is the annual **beanhole bean dinner** (beans baked underground overnight), held the second Saturday in August.

Ambajejus Boom House

You'll need either a boat or a snowmobile to get to the Ambajejus Boom House, a National Historic Register property on Ambajejus Lake, eight miles northwest of Millinocket, but once you get there, it's always open, and filled with incredible lumbering-era artifacts. Sign the register and jot down the weather conditions. The boom house, erected here in 1906, was used as a rest stop for 65 years by rugged river drivers, lumbermen who "boomed out" (collected with immense chains) and actually rode logs downstream to the sawmills. The meticulous restoration of the once-derelict house has been done as a personal project by Chuck Harris, a one-time river driver. Launch your boat in Spencer Cove, near Katahdin Air Service, on the west side of the Golden Road, and paddle or motor out and around to the right, to the head of the lake. Stay close to shore, as the wind can pick up unexpectedly. (If you need a canoe, you can rent one across the road at the Big Moose Inn.) Easiest way to get there is with Katahdin

Scenic Cruises (207/723-2020), which offers two-hour pontoon boat trips on the first and last Saturdays of June, July, and August for $40 pp (four-person minimum).

TOURS
Flightseeing

Based at Ambajejus Lake, about eight miles northwest of Millinocket, on the road to Baxter State Park, Jimmy Strang's **Katahdin Air Service (KAS)** (P.O. Box 171, Millinocket 04462, 207/723-8378 or 888/742-5527, www.katahdinair.com) provides access to wilderness locations in every direction, but even if you have no particular destination, the scenic floatplane flights are fabulous. Fall-foliage trips are beyond fabulous. Three short options, about 15–30 minutes each, cost $50–60 pp (two-person minimum). You'll

fly over Katahdin and the Penobscot River's West Branch, perhaps spotting moose en route. The best flight, though, is an hour-long one over Baxter State Park to the Allagash Wilderness Waterway and back along the West Branch. Cost is $105 pp (two-person minimum). Flights operate daily late May–October, weather permitting.

Katahdin Air Service is also a major link in the sporting-camp network, flying guests into and out of the remote camps via floatplane. When you contact a sporting camp for rate information, be sure to request the rates for floatplane access. It won't be cheap, but it's safe and fun. For a token sporting-camp experience without an overnight, sign up for one of KAS's "fly 'n' dine" trips. For $105 pp (two-person minimum, covering meals and transport), it'll fly you into a sporting camp

---

THE UNGAINLY, BELOVED MOOSE

Everyone loves Maine's state animal, *Alces alces americana*. The ungainly moose, bulbous-nosed and top-heavy, stops traffic and brings out the cameras. It also stops cars literally, usually creating a lose-lose situation. The moose's long legs put its head and shoulders about windshield level, and a crash can propel the animal headfirst through the glass. Human and animal fatalities are common.

State biologists estimate that Maine has nearly 30,000 moose, most in the North Woods, so it's pretty hard not to encounter one if you're driving the roads or hiking the trails in the Maine Highlands region.

Moose pay no heed to those yellow-and-black, diamond-shaped moose-crossing signs, but officials post them near typical moose hangouts, so *slow down* when you see them. During daylight hours, especially early and late in the day, keep your binoculars and camera handy. In late spring and early summer, pesky flies and midges drive the moose from the deepest woods, so you're more likely to see them close to the roadside. At night, be even more careful, as moose don't tend to focus in

on headlights (as deer do), and their eyes don't reflect at an angle that drivers can see.

Moose are vegetarians, preferring new shoots and twigs in aquatic settings, so the best places to see them are wetlands and ponds fringed with grass and shrubs. These spots are likely to be buggy, too, so slather yourself with insect repellent.

Moose hunting, officially sanctioned, is somewhat controversial, partly because the creatures seem to present little sporting challenge. But they are a challenge, not because of wile or speed but because of heft. Imagine dragging one of these fellows out of the woods to a waiting truck; it's no mean feat. In Maine's annual Moose Lottery – a herd-thinning scheme concocted by the Department of Inland Fisheries and Wildlife – hunters receive permits to shoot moose in specific zones in late September and early-mid-October. At official state weighing stations, the hapless moose are strung up, weighed, tested for parasites, and often butchered on the spot by freelance meat packagers. Moose meat is actually tasty.

for dinner and take you back afterward. A delicious adventure.

If you prefer your plane to have wheels, book a sightseeing flight with **West Branch Aviation** (Millinocket Municipal Airport, 16 Medway Rd., Millinocket, 207/723-4375, www.katahdingateway.com/wba/index.htm). Rate is $35 pp for a half hour, $60 pp for a full hour; two-person minimum on all flights.

Cruises

Katahdin Scenic Cruises (207/723-2020, www.katahdinsceniccruises.com), based at the Big Moose Inn, makes it easy to get out on the lakes and see the wildlife and Katahdin if you don't want to brave a canoe, kayak, or raft. The options are plentiful: Sunrise, Sunset, Afternoon Beach, One-Hour, and Ambajejus Boom House Cruises fill the schedule, with rates ranging $40–50 pp; most cruises have a two-person minimum. Three cruises are offered daily June–October; reservations are recommended.

Moose-Spotting

Want some assistance finding an elusive moose? Dale Stevens's **Maine-ly Moose and Photo Tour** (353 Penobscot Ave., Millinocket, 207/723-5465, www.mainelyphotos.com) provides van tours with guaranteed moose sightings. Tours are personalized and cost $45 pp for two, with a family rate of $35 pp.

SUMMER RECREATION
Mattawamkeag Wilderness Park

Talk about a well-kept secret that shouldn't be! Check out 1,000-acre, town-owned Mattawamkeag Wilderness Park (Rte. 2,

---

MOOSE TRIVIA

- Typical height for an adult bull moose is seven feet at the shoulders; typical weight is about 1,000 pounds, with 1,400-pounders also recorded. Cow moose run about 800 pounds.

- Moose usually lumber along, seemingly in no hurry, but they've been known to run as fast as 35 mph.

- The bull moose's rack of antlers can measure six feet across; the largest recorded was a hair under seven feet.

- Moose give birth in late May or early June, after a 35-week pregnancy; singles are normal, twins are less common, triplets are very rare. A newborn calf weighs 20-30 pounds, occasionally 35 pounds.

- Moose have extremely acute senses of hearing and smell, but their eyesight is pitiable. If you're utterly quiet and stay downwind of them, they probably won't spot you.

- Moose have no history of harming humans, but stay out of their way during "the rut," when they're charging around and out of the woods looking for females in heat. This usually occurs mid-September–mid-October, when the foliage is at its peak, hikers are out and about, and moose-lottery winners are in hot pursuit.

MOOSE-WATCHING HOT SPOTS

- Sandy Stream Pond, Baxter State Park

- Grassy Pond, Baxter State Park

- Russell Pond, Baxter State Park

- Sawtelle Deadwater, off Shin Pond Road, about seven miles northwest of Shin Pond

- Lazy Tom Bog, off Lily Bay Road, about 19 miles north of Greenville

- Route 6/15, between Greenville Junction and Rockwood, on the west side of Moosehead Lake

- The Golden Road, between Ripogenus Dam and Pittston Farm

P.O. Box 5, Mattawamkeag 04459, 207/736-4881 or 888/724-2465, www.mwpark.com), about an hour's drive southeast of Baxter State Park's southern gate. The park's well-managed facilities include 15 miles of trails, picnic tables, restrooms, free hot showers, recreation hall, playground, sand beach (on the Mattawamkeag River), and fishing for bass, salmon, and trout. There's also access to fine canoeing, including flat water and Class V white water, on one of northern Maine's most underused rivers. And you can stay the night at one of the 50 wooded campsites and 11 lean-tos. Entrance is about eight miles east of Route 2, on an unpaved logging road locally called "the park road"; it's signposted on Route 2. Day use is $3 pp, maximum $7 per car. Camping fees are $18–25 per site per night; seven sites have hookups. The park is open daily late May–October.

Canoeing and Kayaking

This part of Maine is a canoeist's paradise, well known as the springboard for Allagash Wilderness Waterway and St. John River trips.

Close to Millinocket, experienced canoeists and kayakers may want to attempt sections of the **East and West Branches of the Penobscot River,** but no neophyte should try them. We're talking Big Water. Refer to the *AMC River Guide* for details, or contact one of the local outfitters, such as New England Outdoor Center or Maine Quest Adventures.

A relatively gentle, early-summer canoe trip ideal for less-experienced paddlers is on the **Seboeis River,** between the Shin Pond/Grand Lake Road and Whetstone Falls, about 24 miles. Even easier, and a good family trip, is the flat-water run putting in below Whetstone Falls (west of Stacyville) and taking out before Grindstone Falls.

If you launch your canoe early in the day on **Sawtelle Deadwater,** near Shin Pond, west of Patten, you're bound to see moose. From Shin Pond, head northwest, crossing the Seboeis River at about six miles and then turn right onto the next unpaved road and continue less than two miles to the water. You can also reach the Deadwater off the parallel, paved Huber Road. Canoe rentals are also available at Shin Pond Village.

White-Water Kayak School: If you're itching to learn how to paddle in white water, **Maine Kayak** (866/624-6352, www.mainekayak.com) operates a white-water kayaking school with beginner courses costing about $350 for part one, $240 for part two. The program is based at the Big Moose Inn.

Outfitters: Most accommodations have canoes available for their guests, but if you need to rent, stop at **Maine Quest Adventures** (Rte. 157, P.O. Box 197, Medway 04460, 207/746-9615 or 207/290-1733, www.mainequestadventures.com). Daily canoe and kayak rentals are $25, fishing boats are $65, and a pontoon boat rents for $200; weekly rates available for all.

White-Water Rafting

Maine's biggest white-water rafting area is around The Forks, where the Kennebec and Dead Rivers meet, in the Kennebec Valley Region, but the second-largest area is along the West Branch of the Penobscot River, near Millinocket. About a dozen rafting companies operate on the Penobscot River. One-day trips pass through Ripogenous Gorge, a rip-roaring chasm of roiling Class IV and V white water, over nine-foot Nesoudnehunk Falls, through a few other Class IV rapids, and a few ponds, all in the shadow of Mt. Katahdin. It's a fabulous adventure, and a riverside lunch is included. Best source of information is **Raft Maine** (www.raftmaine.com).

The primary rafting outfitter here, as well as a major player in The Forks, is the **New England Outdoor Center (NEOC)** (Old Medway Rd., P.O. Box 669, Millinocket 04462, 207/723-5438 or 800/766-7238, www.neoc.com), based in a huge complex on the eastern outskirts of Millinocket. NEOC's Rice Farm headquarters organizes West Branch rafting trips ($79–119 pp, depending on day and month, minimum age 16). For lodging, NEOC has 40 campsites ($10–12 pp) and cabin tents ($20–23 pp) at its Rice Farm location and traditional sporting-camp log cabins at its Twin Pine Camps on Millinocket Lake, eight miles northwest of Millinocket; rates begin at $190 d per cabin. No pets at either Rice Farm or Twin Pines. Lots of special packages are available, covering lodging, breakfasts, and dinners. To reach the Rice Farm from I-95, take Exit 56 and head west on Route 157 toward Millinocket for eight miles. After the causeway over Dolby Pond, turn left (south) and go 1.2 miles to the NEOC.

Fishing

Water, water everywhere. That means primo fishing, including streams, rivers, walk-in and fly-in ponds for brook trout; ponds and lakes for splake and lake trout; rivers and lakes for landlocked salmon; brooks and streams for wild/native brook trout; lakes for brown trout; and streams and rivers for bass. The Maine Department of Inland Fisheries and Wildlife (www.mefishwildlife.com) produces "Fishing Opportunities in the Katahdin Region," a brochure detailing where to fish for what. Fishing licenses and other info also are available on the website.

Serious anglers should consider one of the sporting camps (see the *Accommodations* section). For info and supplies visit **Two Rivers Canoe and Kayak** (Rte. 175, Medway, 207/746-8181, www.tworiverscanoe.com), conveniently situated just west of the I-95 interchange.

Guided and outfitted fishing trips with **Maine Quest Adventures** (Rte. 157, P.O. Box 197, Medway 04460, 207/746-9615 or 207/290-1733, www.mainequestadventures.com) are $275 s, $300 d, full day with lunch; $175 d, $200 s half day.

Golf

An oasis in the wilderness, the nine-hole **Katahdin Country Club** (70 Park St., Milo, 207/943-2686) is open mid-May–early November.

WINTER RECREATION

The North Country gets socked with snow more often than not, so winter recreation provides a major boost for the local economy. Among the winter sports in the Millinocket area are snowmobiling, snowshoeing, cross-country skiing, and ice fishing. To accommodate winter-sports enthusiasts, several sporting camps in the area remain open all year.

Snowmobiling

Motels in Millinocket fill up fast in snow season, so you'll need to plan well ahead to try this sport. More than 350 miles of the Interconnecting Trail System (ITS) crisscross the Millinocket area, including some that run right through town. Local snowmobile clubs produce excellent trail maps available from the Katahdin Area Chamber of Commerce. Snowmobile enthusiasts might also want to visit the Northern Timber Cruisers Snowmobile Club's **Antique Snowmobile Museum** (Millinocket Lake Rd., Millinocket, 207/723-6203, www.northerntimbercruisers.com, weekends and by appointment), which contains about three dozen machines. The clubhouse also serves food.

Snowmobile rentals are available from **Katahdin Power Sports** (Rte. 157, Medway, 866/746-9977 or 207/746-9977), starting at $100 half day, $155 full day. The New England Outdoor Center, based near ITS-86 in Millinocket, rents snowmobiles and also offers guided all-day snowmobile trips.

If you've never tried snowmobiling, a one-day guided trip is the safest, sanest way to begin, even if it's not the cheapest.

SHOPPING

Unless you're looking for camping or sporting supplies, shopping choices are slim in the area, but **North Light Gallery** (256 Penobscot Ave., Millinocket, 207/723-4414 or 800/970-4278, www.artnorthlight.com) is well worth a stop. Owner Marsha Donahue specializes in art from the Katahdin-and-Lakes School, and she shows the works of numerous talented artists and artisans. You can't miss the building; Donahue has painted murals on the exterior.

ENTERTAINMENT AND EVENTS

Family fun is the specialty at **Magic City Mini Golf** (237 Penobscot Ave., Millinocket,

207/723-4404), an indoor fun center with an 18-hole miniature golf course, golf simulator, video games, and a pool table.

Millinocket is widely known for its week-long **Fourth of July** celebration (the fireworks display is outstanding). Every fifth year, there's also a giant homecoming celebration, bringing several thousand former residents back to their roots.

In August, the **Wooden Canoe Festival** has demonstrations, a white-water race, pig roast, music, and fireworks.

Patten's **Annual Bean-Hole Bean Dinner** is a great celebration featuring good food (and a fascinating culinary tradition) at the Patten Lumberman's Museum the second Saturday in August.

Labor Day weekend marks the **Olde Home Days Celebration** in Sherman with a parade, chicken barbecue, food booths, children's games, and lobster boil. Email info@katahdin maine.com for information on local festivals and events.

ACCOMMODATIONS

For years, Millinocket's lodging choices have been few, and many were well worn. That's changing, as new inns open and older ones refurbish.

Millinocket is also the springboard for a number of wilderness sporting camps, some of which are inaccessible, or nearly so, by road. Small planes equipped with skis or pontoons ferry clients to the remote sites—not an inexpensive undertaking, but a great adventure that's well worth the splurge.

Bed-and-Breakfasts

Whoo-eee! Millinocket's getting some fancy with the addition of ◖ **5 Lakes Lodge** (off Route 11, mailing address HC 74, Box 544, South Twin Lake, Millinocket 04462, 207/723-5045, www.5lakeslodge.com, $200–275). Area natives Rick and Debbie Levasseur built this eye-catching two-story log lodge on a spit of land extending into South Twin Lake. Soaring windows and a stone fireplace dominate the two-story living room, with wowser views of Katahdin over the chain of lakes out front.

Every guest room has a handcrafted, quilt-covered king-size bed, bath with double whirlpool tub, satellite TV, gas stove, fridge, data port, and that view. The Levasseurs provide canoes and kayaks for their guests on the pebble beach out front; pontoon and motorboats are available for rental at the dock out back. Rates include a full breakfast and afternoon refreshments. It's cushy, comfy, and a fine place for wildlife-watching: five pairs of eagles and 24 pairs of loons nest on the interconnecting lakes, and Rick has a few "guaranteed" moose-spotting sites.

Far simpler is the recently renovated **Keepridge Inn** (177 Central St., Millinocket, 888/723-6867, www.keepridgeinn.com, $65–95), just steps from downtown shops and restaurants. That's a good thing, since the inn doesn't serve meals. Rooms are pleasant and simply decorated; one has a whirlpool tub for two.

Just up the street is **The Young House Bed and Breakfast** (193 Central St., Millinocket, 207/723-5452, www.theyounghousebandb .com, $80). Each of the five smallish guest rooms has air-conditioning, TV/DVD, and Wi-Fi. Public rooms include a parlor with baby grand. A full breakfast is included.

Motels

The two-story, 48-room **Heritage Motor Inn** (935 Central St., Rte. 157, Millinocket, 207/723-9777, www.heritageinnmaine.com, $79–89 d) received a facelift in 2005 with the addition of a small indoor pool and the updating of its rooms (unfortunately, most face the highway or a parking lot). Other pluses are air-conditioning, free Wi-Fi, and continental breakfast. It's also right on ITS 83. Kids 12 and younger stay free; pets allowed with signed waiver.

Close to I-95, Exit 56, is the **Gateway Inn** (Rte. 157, P.O. Box 637, Medway 04460, 207/746-3193, www.medwaygateway.com), a 38-room/suite motel opened in 1995. Rooms on the west side have decks, great views of Katahdin (weather permitting), and higher rates. Rooms are $55–100 d July–August; eight suites are $80–100 d. Special rates are available for snowmobilers; pets are welcome. Continental breakfast is included; air-conditioning, phones, satellite TV, and an indoor pool are all available. There's even a guest kitchen with fridge and microwave.

Eclectic Properties

Hardest to characterize is the **Big Moose Inn** (Baxter State Park Rd., P.O. Box 98, Millinocket 04462, 207/723-8391, www.bigmoose cabins.com), on Millinocket Lake, midway between Millinocket and Baxter State Park's southern boundary. It's part inn, part sporting camp, part campground. Two white-water rafting companies, a boat tour company, and a kayak outfitter are based here. This is not the place to stay if you're seeking peace and quiet, but it is a great property steeped in Maine woods traditions. The main lodge is everything you'd expect: comfy antiques and country furniture, a big stone fireplace, moose head, and other woodsy accents, and a big screened-in porch. Traditional guest rooms ($45–49 pp) with shared baths are inviting but very small (if you're over six feet tall, don't even think about it as some have short beds); rate includes continental breakfast midweek/full breakfast on weekends. Three suites with private baths are $140 d. On the grounds are 36 tent sites ($10 pp) and six screened lean-tos ($13 pp), plus 14 cabins sleeping 2–16, all with screened porches ($42–45 pp; minimum varies by cabin; bring your own towels). Canoe or kayak rental is $5 per hour or $15 per day. The inn has a restaurant and pub, and next door is North Woods Trading Post, with pizza, sandwiches, and supplies. No smoking, no pets. The lodge, cabins, and campground are open May–Columbus Day.

Sporting Camps

Eight miles off the access road to Baxter's northern gate is **Bowlin Camps** (P.O. Box 251, Patten 04765, 207/528-2022, www.bowlincamps.com), a traditional fishing/hunting camp on the shore of the Penobscot's East Branch. It now also welcomes family groups, especially July–August. Kids love the suspension bridge across the river, and there are trails to ponds and two waterfalls. An easy, 16-mile

canoe run starts here (rentals are available), and someone will meet you at the other end. Cabins are rustic, heated with woodstoves; two have bathrooms and six share the clean bathhouse. Summer rates in cabins are about $500 pp a week for adults, $85 per night, including family-style meals served in the main lodge. Children under 16 are half price. There are three good-size housekeeping cabins (no meals provided, $105–165 per night). Snowmobiling is huge here, and there are 12 miles of cross-country trails; Bowlin is open all year.

Two excellent sporting camps off to the north, with longstanding reputations, are Libby Camps and Bradford Camps. Both require 60- to 90-minute drives on unpaved roads; it's worth the splurge to arrive by floatplane. July and August are the best times for families—when fishing is slow and hunting hasn't started.

About 150 miles north of Bangor, **Libby Camps** (Millinocket Lake, Township 8, Range 9, mailing address P.O. Box 810, Ashland 04732, 207/435-8274, www.libbycamps.com), on the east shore of a different Millinocket Lake than the one near Millinocket, is flanked by Baxter State Park and the Allagash Wilderness Waterway. Matt and Ellen Libby are the third generation to run this fishing and hunting camp, built in 1890; their son Matt and his wife, Jess, are next in line, and daughter Alison and her husband help out, too; it's a serious business. If you catch a trophy salmon or brook trout at this Orvis-endorsed fly-fishing lodge, they'll even ready it for the taxidermist. Eight comfortable cabins have flush toilets, propane lights, and quilt-topped beds. The basic daily rate, including three meals, boat, and cabin, is $155 pp d. Pets are allowed. Hearty meals are served in the handsome log-beamed lodge, close to an enormous stone fireplace. (Pray that Ellen will make her peanut-butter squares for dessert, and be sure to buy a copy of her cookbook.) Canoes, kayaks, and motorboats are available for guests, and there's a sandy beach. The Libbys also own 10 "outpost cabins" on wildly remote ponds. (Even more remote is their Riverkeep Lodge on the Atikonak River in Labrador.) Libby Camps

BE A SPORT

Although dozens of traditional sporting camps exist all over Maine, most of the veterans are in the Katahdin/Moosehead Region, with the Kennebec Valley and Western Mountains running a close second. Almost all are north of Bangor.

Sporting camps deliver an authentic, wilderness experience without camping. Noise and light pollution are nonexistent; on a clear night, the starscape is magnificent. They're so much more than a place to stay; they're an experience, often a throwback to the 19th century, or at least to the earlier 20th.

They're so varied that it's impossible to paint them with one broad brush. All but a few are accessible by road, but the "road" might be a rutted, muddy tank trap, making passengers yearn for a floatplane. All are rustic, no-frills operations, some much more so than others. (If you're a frill-seeker, forget it; seek elsewhere.) Some have electricity and flush toilets; others have kerosene lanterns and private or shared outhouses. All are on or close to fresh water, meant to be convenient for fishing.

Some offer American Plan (AP) rates, serving three meals a day, usually family-style; others have housekeeping facilities, where you're on your own; some let you choose.

Most camps have on-site guides available for hire – do so. Guides know the woods and water, and whether you want to find the fish or simply take a long walk in the woods, they know the best places and will point out hidden sights and wildlife.

With all the logging roads crisscrossing the region, there are only a few sporting camps now inaccessible by road, but most guests opt to fly in and out. As one guide put it, "People prefer flying over dying; those logging trucks run up and over a coupla cars every year." (See *Flightseeing* in this section for information about floatplane service.)

If all this sounds intriguing, request a brochure from the **Maine Sporting Camp Association** (P.O. Box 119, Millinocket 04462, 207/723-6622, www.mainesportingcamps .com), a group with more than 50 members founded in 1987.

The easiest way to get to remote sporting camps is via floatplane.

© TOM NANGLE

is open May–November. Both Matts are licensed pilots, and they'll fly you in on seaplane from the Presque Isle Airport or Matagamon Lake, near Patten, or you can arrange transport with other flying services.

The only sporting camp on a pristine, 1,500-acre lake,  **The Bradford Camps** (Munsungan Lake, P.O. Box 729, Ashland 04732, 207/746-7777, in winter P.O. Box 778, Kittery 03904, 207/439-6364, www.bradfordcamps .com), is owned by Igor and Karen Sikorsky. (If the name rings a bell, think helicopters). The scenery and sunsets are magnificent, the loons are mystical, and moose sightings are frequent. This is a special place. Eight good-size log cabins (with bathrooms and propane lamps), lined up along the lakefront, are $137 pp/day or $894/week; kids 1–16 pay $7 times their age/night; family rate for two adults and two kids under 17 is $2,150/week. Rates include excellent meals served family-style in the lake-view lodge. Most fascinating is the antique ice house, containing brilliantly clear ice cut arduously from the lake the previous winter. Canoes and kayaks are free for guests, boat with motor and gas is $50/day, and hiking trails await. A guide ($260/day, $230 for multiple days) is essential for fishing these waters—noted for rare blueback trout—and helpful for canoeing a nearby stretch of the Allagash. Open May–November (October–November most guests are hunters seeking deer, moose, and grouse). If you're an aviation fan, ask about the Skilorsky Seminar weekend, usually in early July. Karen and Igor can arrange flights from Millinocket Lake (about $180 pp round-trip) and Bangor (about $280 pp round-trip) or you can drive 60 miles over rough logging roads (trust me, fly).

Campgrounds and Campsites

Probably the closest you can get to Baxter's south gate with an RV is **Chewonki's Big Eddy Campground** (8027 Golden Rd., T3R11, Greenville, 207/350-1599, Oct. 15–Apr. 1, or 485 Chewonki Neck Rd., Wiscassett 04578, 207/882-7323, Oct. 16–Mar. 31, www.bigeddy.org). Many of the 75-acre

fly-fishing at Matagamon Wilderness Campground

© HILARY NANGLE

campground's 62 primitive sites edge the Penobscot River at the famed Big Eddy landlocked salmon pools. A few sites have electrical hookups; dumping station is available ($10). Rates are $10 pp for nonriver sites, $20 pp for river sites, plus $4 per day for electricity. Kids ages 13–17 are $6 per night; 12 and under are free. Showers are $1.50.

Closest campground to the north gate is the Christianson family's **Matagamon Wilderness** (P.O. Box 220, Patten 04765, 207/446-4635, www.matagamonwilderness.com), which is just a few miles from the Matagamon gate. On the premises and bordering the East Branch of the Penobscot River are 36 wilderness campsites that can accommodate up to a 42-foot RV ($18), housekeeping cabins ($22.50–$40 pp/day), a general store with food service, and boat rentals. Pets are allowed in campground, $10 per stay.

FOOD

While the local options are improving, this isn't a destination for foodies, not by a long shot. With few exceptions, most of what's available is good home cookin', and you're welcome anywhere in jeans.

Local Flavors

Given her last name, perhaps it's no surprise that Millinocket native Carla Portwine has made a name for herself in the specialty food business, and that one of her big sellers is a portwine cheese spread—it's delicious! In addition to specialty foods, **Portwine of Maine** (245 Aroostook Ave., Millinocket, 207/723-5343, www.portwineofmaine.com) also has soups, sandwiches, and ready-made dinners.

Sandwiches, salads, panini, and daily specials, most with an Italian accent, are the specialities at **Orvieto** (67 Prospect St., Millinocket, 207/723-8399, www.dicensiinc.com, 7 A.M.– 6 P.M. Mon.–Fri., to 2 P.M. Sat.).

For pizza, locals equally recommend **Millinocket House of Pizza** (Northern Plaza, 782 Central St., Millinocket, 207/723-4528) on the strip east of town, and **Angelo's** (118 Penobscot Ave., 207/723-6767) downtown. Both have way more than pizza on their menus, free local delivery, and are open 11 A.M. until at least 9 P.M. Monday through Saturday; Sunday hours vary.

While hikers tend to favor the **Appalachian Trail Café** (210 Main St., Millinocket, 207/723-6720, 6 A.M.–8 P.M. daily June–Nov.; 7 A.M.–6 P.M. daily, to 3 P.M. Sat.–Sun. in winter), locals prefer the **Downtown Restaurant** (53 Penobscot Ave., Millinocket, 207/723-9910, 5 A.M.–10 P.M. daily). They're within a block of each other downtown, so it's easy to compare the two and see which fits your yearnings. Both excel at the basics: breakfasts, burgers, and fried foods and both are extremely budget friendly. The Downtown has a full bar and serves dinner entrées as well as pizza; the ATC, recently purchased by a through-hiker, has been refurbished.

Casual Dining

When locals want to celebrate, they head to one of these restaurants.

Nicest downtown restaurant is the **Scootic**

In (70 Penobscot Ave., Millinocket, 207/723-4566, opens at 11 A.M. Mon.–Sat., at noon Sun., bar open to 1 A.M.), Millinocket's long-standing "Sunday dinnah" restaurant. The dining areas are pleasant, there's a full bar, and kids are welcome. The menu varies from pizzas, calzones, sandwiches, burgers, and fried foods to entrées such as broiled chicken ($9) and scallops Michelle ($17). Save room for homemade desserts.

Dine inside, on one of the antique oak tables in the airy, light-filled dining room, or outdoors on the screened-in porch at **Fredericka's** in the Big Moose Inn (Baxter State Park Rd., Millinocket, 207/723-8391, www.bigmoosecabins.com, 5–9 P.M. Tues.–Sat., and Sun. in July and Aug). The creative menu emphasizes fresh and local ingredients. Entrée choices ($16– 24) may include seared breast of Muscovy duck or oven-baked salmon. Lighter fare is served at the inn's **Loose Moose Bar and Grill** (5–11 P.M. Wed.–Sat., and Sun. in July and Aug.).

A tad more relaxed is **River Drivers Restaurant** at the New England Outdoor Center's Rice Farm campus (Old Medway Rd., Millinocket, 207/723-8475 or 800/766-7238, www.neoc.com, 5–9 P.M. Tues.–Sat.). The dining room and deck have glimpses of the Penobscot River through the trees, and the fare is well prepared. The Friday night special includes soup or salad, entrée special and dessert for $25; otherwise, most entrées are in the $18–24 range; children's menu available.

INFORMATION AND SERVICES
Information

The Katahdin Area Chamber of Commerce (1029 Central St., Rte. 157, Millinocket, 207/723-4443, www.katahdinmaine.com) is based in a small prefab building at the eastern edge of Millinocket.

Check out Millinocket Memorial Library (5 Maine Ave., Millinocket 04462, 207/723-7020, www.millinocket.lib.me.us).

Public Restrooms

Just east of Northern Plaza in Millinocket, Baxter State Park Headquarters, open weekdays, has public restrooms, as does Millinocket's municipal building (197 Penobscot Ave.) and the chamber of commerce.

Kennels

If you're headed with your pet for Baxter State Park, you'll need a kennel, as pets are not allowed in the park. Here are two places to park your pooch: K-9 Village (112 Main St., East Millinocket, 207/746-3434, www.katahdin k9.com) and Paw Prints (2211 Medway Rd., Medway, 207/746-3434, www.pawprints resort.com). Both offer day care and overnight boarding and pamper pets with services such as themed cabanas, spa services, ice-cream socials, and yappy hours. K-9 even operates the Bow-wow Bus, offering pickup and delivery.

GETTING AROUND

Katahdin Air Service (KAS) (P.O. Box 171, Millinocket 04462, 207/723-8378 or 888/742-5527, www.katahdinair.com) has an excellent half-century reputation, offering charter floatplane flights to remote campsites and sporting camps May–November.

A full-service shuttle provider, **Maine Quest Adventures** (Rte. 157, P.O. Box 197, Medway 04460, 207/746-9615, www.mainequest adventures.com) shuttles adventurers throughout the region. It also offers airport pickup.

Baxter State Park

Consider the foresight of Maine Governor Percival Proctor Baxter. After years of battling the state legislature to protect the area around Katahdin, Maine's highest mountain, he bade good-bye to state government in 1925 and proceeded on his own to make his dream happen. Determined to preserve this chunk of real estate for Maine residents and posterity, he pleaded the cause with landowners and managed to accumulate an initial 5,960-acre parcel—the nucleus of today's 209,501-acre Baxter State Park—and donated it to the state in 1931. From then on, he acquired and donated more and more bits and pieces (adding his last 7,764-acre parcel in 1962, just seven years before his death at the age of 90). The governor's prescience went far beyond mere purchases of land; his deed of gift carried stiff restrictions that have been little altered since then. And, thanks to interest from his final bequest, as well as small and large donations from park users and supporters, park authorities have been able to add even more acreage—including a splendid 4,119-acre parcel donated in 2006.

Today this fantastic recreational wilderness has 46 mountain peaks and about 200 miles of trails. One rough, unpaved road (20 mph limit) circles the park; no pets or radios are allowed; cell phones may be carried but used only for emergencies. No gasoline, drinking water, or food is available; camping is carry-in, carry-out.

Camping, in fact, is the only way to sleep in Baxter—at tent sites, lean-tos, bunkhouses, or rustic log cabins. Competition for sleeping space can be fierce on midsummer weekends; it's pure luck to find an opening, so you need to plan well ahead. Guaranteeing a spot, particularly one of the coveted 22 cabins, means reserving well in advance (no refunds). The rewards are rare alpine flowers, unique rock formations, pristine ponds, waterfalls, wildlife sightings (especially moose), dramatic vistas, and, in late September, spectacular fall foliage.

The hiking here is incomparable. Peakbaggers accustomed to 8,000-footers (or more) may be unimpressed by the altitudes, but no one should underestimate the ruggedness of Baxter's terrain or the vagaries of the weather in this unique microclime.

Percival Baxter was by no means the first to discover this wilderness. His best-known predecessor was author Henry David Thoreau, who climbed Katahdin in 1846 from what's now Abol Campground but who never reached the summit. He didn't even reach Thoreau Spring

(4,636 feet), named in his honor, but he *did* wax eloquent about the experience:

> This was that Earth of which we have heard, made out of Chaos and Old Night.... It was the fresh and natural surface of the planet Earth, as it was made forever and ever...so Nature made it, and man may use it if he can."

Locked in what he called "a cloud factory," Thoreau declined to approach the summit: "Pomola [Pamola, the Penobscot Indians' malevolent spirit of Katahdin] is always angry with those who climb to the summit of Ktaadn." And Native Americans traditionally stayed below the tree line, fearing the resident evil spirits. They all had a point. The current trail system didn't exist in the Native Americans' or Thoreau's days, of course (the first recorded summiteer was Charles Turner Jr., in 1804), so fatalities were probably more frequent, but even in the 21st century, climbers have died on Katahdin, and difficult rescues occur every year.

Regulations

The list of rules is long at Baxter (www.baxter stateparkauthority.com/rules/index.html), and park rangers make the rounds to ensure enforcement. In the end, the rules are what make Baxter so splendid. It's not unusual to hear grumbling about too much regimentation here, but longtime Park Director Irvin ("Buzz") Caverly, who retired in 2005, was often seen as a kind of one-man Supreme Court, interpreting Governor Baxter's stipulations. Caverly's dedication was legendary, and as one of the few surviving people who had known Percival Baxter, he had a leg up, with support from the Baxter State Park Authority, an autonomous board comprising three state officials who have ultimate park power.

- The park's **entrance gates** are staffed 6 A.M.–9 P.M. (Matagamon Gate) and 6 A.M.–10 P.M. (Togue Pond Gate) mid-May–mid-October; the gates open as early as 5 A.M. on midsummer weekends. Campers must arrive with their reservation forms at one of these two gates no later than 8:30 P.M. At the entry gates, rangers urge campers (as well as day hikers) to adhere to the seven outdoor-ethics guidelines of the national **Leave No Trace** organization (www.lnt.org). Since the park has no drinkable water, plan to boil your own, bring your own, or bring a small-pore filter (three microns or smaller).

- **No motorcycles, motorbikes, or ATVs** are allowed in the park; **bicycles** are allowed only on maintained roads, not on trails, but the narrow, rough Perimeter Road is not particularly bike friendly. When weather has been especially dry, bicyclists end up with mouthfuls of dust. **Snowmobiles** are restricted to certain areas; check with park rangers.

- As mentioned above, the park bans operation of **cell phones, TVs, radios, and CD or cassette players.** Noise levels in the park are strictly monitored by the rangers. There are no pay phones in the park, but all park rangers have radiophones.

Baxter in Winter

The roads aren't plowed, campgrounds are closed, and the lakes and ponds are frozen solid, but Baxter authorities allow winter use of the park—with a multipage list of rigid restrictions. If this sounds appealing, contact the Baxter State Park Authority for winter information.

DAY USE

Most day-use visitors are here to hike; on summer and fall weekends, you'll need to arrive early—even if you're not climbing Katahdin—because the day-use parking areas fill up. (There are only 284 day-use parking spots in the park.) On weekends, a long line forms before dawn at the Togue Pond Gate. A notice board at each gatehouse specifies which day-use parking areas are closed and which are open; there's almost always someplace to park (though *never* alongside the Perimeter Road or campground access roads), and zillions of trails to hike, even if it may not be what you had in mind. So plan to arrive early (no later than

7 A.M. to hike Katahdin) or be prepared to be totally flexible about your hiking choice.

Maine residents can take advantage of a special parking privilege by calling well in advance for free reservations (one site per month between April and October) for one of 16 daily parking spaces at three Katahdin trailheads. Call park headquarters, provide your Maine license-plate number, and be sure to show up at Togue Pond Gate to claim your reservation no later than 9 A.M.

The northern end of the park is much less used than the southern end, so consider entering via the northern Matagamon Gate and hiking the wonderful trails in that part of Baxter. Take I-95 Exit 264 (Sherman) and then drive another 33 miles west (via Patten and Shin Pond) to Matagamon Gate.

Picnicking

Picnic areas, some with only a single table, are spotted throughout the park; most of the vehicle-accessible campgrounds also have picnic areas where noncampers are welcome. At the campgrounds, park in the day-use parking area, not the campers' lots.

◖ HIKING

Baxter's 200 or so miles of trails could occupy hikers for their entire lives. There's no such thing as "best" hikes, but some are indeed better (for various reasons) than others. Below is a range of options; consult the most recent edition of Stephen Clark's *Katahdin: A Guide to Baxter State Park and Katahdin* for details and more suggestions.

Trails originating at campgrounds all have registration clipboards; sign-in is *required* for Katahdin hikes and encouraged for all other hikes. All trails are blue-blazed, except for white-blazed ones that are part of the Appalachian Trail. Carved brown signs appear at all major trail junctions. All hikers are required to carry a flashlight—which any hiker should know enough to do anyway.

Wear Polartec, polypropylene, Gore-Tex, or wool clothing, not cotton. Jeans can be a real drag (literally) if you get soaked in a stream,

waterfall, or rainstorm. If you're planning to hike Katahdin, bring more layers than you think you'll need. Bring plenty of insect repellent, especially in June, when the blackflies are on the rampage. In June, you'll probably be best off with 100 percent DEET bug dope, although the eco-friendly Lewey's Eco-Blends insect repellent is very effective and some outfitters (such as L. L. Bean) now feature clothing impregnated with it. Wear light-colored long pants and a long-sleeved shirt/sweater with tight-fitting wrists and a snug collar.

For a guided hike up Katahdin or other park peaks, call Master Maine Guide Jay Robinson, owner of **Katahdin Country Guide Service** (207/746-3488 or cell 207/249-4427, www.katahdincountry.com).

Nature Trails and Family Hikes

Baxter has three easy nature trails that make ideal hikes for families with a range of age and skill levels. Nature-trail maps are available at park headquarters, the park entrance gates, and the nearest ranger stations to the trailheads. The 1.8-mile **Daicey Pond Nature Trail,** beginning at Daicey Pond Campground, circumnavigates the pond counterclockwise, taking about an hour. In August, help yourself to the raspberries near the end of the circuit. Best of all, you can extend the hike at the end by renting a canoe ($1 an hour or $8 a day) at the campground's ranger station, in the shadow of Katahdin's west flank. After that, take the easy 1.2-mile round-trip hike from the campground access road to Big Niagara Falls.

The other nature trails are **South Branch Nature Trail,** a 0.7-mile walk starting at South Branch Campground, in the northern part of the park, and **Roaring Brook Nature Trail,** a 0.75-mile walk starting near Roaring Brook Campground, in the southeastern corner of the park, with dramatic views of Katahdin's east flank.

Other good family hikes, easy to moderate, are Trout Brook Mountain, Burnt Mountain, and Howe Brook Trail—all in the northern section of the park. Burnt Mountain has a fire tower at the top, and you'll need to climb the tower to see the view; the summit itself is quite overgrown. In the southern end of the park, a short, easy trail leads from Upper Togue Pond to **Cranberry Pond.** An easy, 5.2-mile round-trip from Daicey Pond Campground goes to **Lily Pad Pond** and then via canoe to **Windy Pitch Ponds.** Plan to picnic en route alongside Big Niagara Falls. (Before departing, stop at the Daicey Pond office and pick up the keys for the canoe locks at Lily Pad Pond.)

Howe Brook Trail, departing from South Branch Campground, requires fording the brook several times in summer, so wear waterproof footgear. The reward, higher up, is a series of waterfalls and little pools where the kids can swim (the water is frigid)—and flat boulders where you can picnic and sunbathe. In the fall, the foliage on this hike is especially gorgeous. For this six-mile hike, allow about four hours round-trip for lunch, a swim, and dawdling. Afterward, rent a canoe at the campground ($1 an hour or $8 a day) and paddle around scenic Lower South Branch Pond, in the shadow of North Traveler Mountain.

In 2006, after a multimillion-dollar fundraising campaign, the Trust for Public Land donated 4,119 acres on the park's eastern flank to the Baxter State Park Authority. Centerpiece of the parcel is spectacular Katahdin Lake—long coveted by Percival Baxter for inclusion in the park. Although work is ongoing on the century-old trail to the lake, the six-mile (round-trip) hike is relatively easy—via the trailhead at Avalanche Field, in the southeastern corner of the park. If you're inclined to linger longer at the lake, year-round accommodations (housekeeping and American Plan options) are available in the 10 lakeside log cabins managed by Holly and Bryce Hamilton at Katahdin Lake Wilderness Camps (P.O. Box 314, Millinocket 04462, www.katahdin lakewildernesscamps.com).

Moderate Hikes

Good hikes generally classified as moderate are Doubletop Mountain, Sentinel Mountain, and the Owl. If you decide to hike **Doubletop Mountain,** start at the Nesowad-

nehunk (Ne-SOWD-na-hunk) Field trailhead and go south to Kidney Pond Campground, an eight-mile one-way trek, up and over and down. It's much less strenuous this way. Allow about six hours.

Allow about six hours also for the **Sentinel Mountain Trail** from Daicey Pond Campground (6.6 miles round-trip) or Kidney Pond Campground (four miles round-trip). It's not difficult; the only moderate part involves a boulder field about midway up. Take a picnic and hang out at the top; the view across to Katahdin, the Owl, and Mt. OJI is splendid. With binoculars, you'll probably spot moose in the ponds below. Keep one eye on your lunch, however; a resident Canada jay at the summit has an acquisitive streak.

If weather has been rainy, *do not* hike the Owl. It verges on being strenuous even under normal conditions.

Katahdin

Mile-high Katahdin, northern terminus of the Appalachian Trail, is the Holy Grail for most Baxter State Park hikers—and certainly for Appalachian Trail through-hikers, who have walked 2,158 miles from Springer Mountain, Georgia, to get here. Thousands of hikers scale Katahdin annually via several different routes. The climb is strenuous, requires a full day, and is not suitable for small children; kids under six are banned above tree line. You'll be a lot happier and a lot less exhausted if you plan to camp in the park before and after the Katahdin hike.

Katahdin, by the way, is a Native American word meaning "greatest mountain"—hence there's no need to refer to it as *Mount* Katahdin. The Katahdin massif actually comprises a single high point (Baxter Peak, 5,267 feet) and several neighboring peaks (Pamola Peak, 4,902 feet; Hamlin Peak, 4,756 feet; and the three Howe Peaks, 4,734–4,612 feet).

Even though Thoreau never made it to Katahdin's summit (Baxter Peak), countless others have, and the mountain sees a virtual traffic jam in summer and fall, particularly late in the season, when most of the through-hikers are nearing the end of their odyssey. Some hikers make the summit an annual ritual; others consider it a onetime rite of passage and then opt for less-trodden paths and less-strenuous climbs.

Rangers post weather reports at 7 A.M. daily at all the campgrounds. Heed them. Katahdin has its own biome, and weather on the summit can be dramatically different from that down below. At times, especially in high-wind and blowing-snow conditions, park officials close trails to the summit. They don't do it frivolously; Katahdin is a killer, literally.

Besides the requisite photo next to the Baxter Peak summit sign, Katahdin's other "been there, done that" experience is a traverse of the aptly named **Knife Edge,** a treacherous, 1.1-mile-long granite spine (minimum width three feet) between Baxter and Pamola Peaks. If you can stand the experience, hanging on for all you're worth, next to a 1,500-foot drop, go for it; the views are incredible. But don't push beyond your personal limits; you're hours from the nearest hospital.

The most-used route to Baxter Peak is the **Hunt Trail,** a 10-mile round-trip that coincides with the Appalachian Trail from Katahdin Stream Campground; allow at least eight hours round-trip. Other routes start from Russell Pond, Chimney Pond, Roaring Brook, and Abol Campgrounds. See Stephen Clark's *Katahdin* guide for specific route information.

CAMPING

Facilities at 10 campgrounds vary from cabins to tent sites, lean-tos, and bunkhouses; there are also several wilderness campsites supervised by the nearest campground rangers.

All the campgrounds close October 15; they open at various times, beginning May 15. One hike-in campground (Chimney Pond) opens June 1. Fees range from $9 pp per night in lean-tos (two-person minimum) to $25 pp in cabins (minimums depend on cabin size). No charge for children age 1–6; kids age 7–16 are $15 each. Fees must be prepaid and are not refundable.

The park's only cabins are in the southwest corner—at **Daicey Pond Campground** (10 cab-

One of the pluses of staying at Daicey Pond Campground is the library.

ins) and **Kidney Pond Campground** (12 cabins). Daicey Pond has the best views—Katahdin from every cabin, and the sunrises are matchless. With two exceptions, Kidney Pond cabins overlook the pond and surrounding woods, but not the mountains; Doubletop Mountain is in back of the campground. All cabins have woodstoves (for heating only), gas lanterns, outhouses, outside fireplaces, and beds; bring your own linens, water, food, and whatever else you think you might need.

Chimney Pond and Russell Pond Campgrounds are hike-in campgrounds. Distance from the Roaring Brook parking area to Chimney Pond is 3.3 miles; to Russell Pond is seven miles. Chimney Pond has a bunkhouse and nine four-person lean-tos. Russell Pond has a bunkhouse, four lean-tos, and three tent sites—all arranged around the pond, where you can also rent canoes ($1 an hour or $8 a day).

South Branch Pond Campground, close to Matagamon Gate, has an eight-person bunkhouse, 12 lean-tos, and 21 tent sites in an especially idyllic setting; seven of the lean-tos are right next to the pond.

June–August, bring fabric screening if you're staying in a lean-to; a tarp may foil the black-flies, mosquitoes, and no-see-ums, but you don't want to suffocate.

Getting Reservations

Camping reservations must be made by mail or in person; no phone reservations (except at the last minute). July gets booked up first, then August; weekends are more crowded than weekdays.

In 2005, Baxter officials established a new reservation system in hopes of providing a more equitable allocation of space in the park's cab-ins, bunkhouses, tent sites, and lean-tos. Under this rather eccentric "rolling reservation sys-tem," campers can make reservations any time beginning four months before the desired camp-ing start date. For instance, to request a site or sites for July 14, you'll need to mail your reser-vation to arrive no earlier than March 14 (see www.baxterstateparkauthority.com/camping/chart.htm for the reservation schedule). Maximum length of stay is seven nights per campground, 14 nights total in the park.

Download the application form from the park website and mail it—along with pay-ment and a self-addressed, stamped legal-size envelope—to Baxter State Park Reservations (64 Balsam Dr., Millinocket, ME 04462). (If you'd prefer to hand deliver it, the office is open 8 A.M.–4 P.M. weekdays in spring, daily Memorial Day–Columbus Day. Do not try to send the reservation via email, as the website is not secure. Reservations are processed each day the office is open—applications from Maine residents are handled first.

If you can't plan four months ahead but can be fairly flexible, send in your request close to when you want to camp, or even take a chance on showing up at the last minute. Phone requests (207/723-5140; have your Visa or Mas-terCard handy) are accepted within 14 days of your visit—but there are no guarantees. Except on weekends July–mid-August, however, a tent

site can usually be found. But be sure to have a fallback plan. (It might have to be in Millinocket, 18 miles beyond the Togue Pond Gate.)

If you make a reservation and can't keep it, be considerate and call or email the park headquarters to cancel, even though you won't receive a refund. It will give someone else a chance to enjoy the beauty of Baxter.

PARK ACCESS, INFORMATION, AND SERVICES

Unless you're hiking the Appalachian Trail (AT), the only way to enter the park is via one of two gates. **Togue Pond Gate** (open 6 A.M.–10 P.M. Mon.–Fri., open 5 A.M. Sat.–Sun., May 15–Oct. 15), at the southern end of the park, is the choice for visitors from Greenville or Mil-linocket and the most-used gate. At the north-east corner of the park is **Matagamon Gate** (open 6 A.M.–9 P.M. Mon.–Fri., open 5 A.M. Sat.–Sun., May 15–Oct. 15), accessible via I-95, Patten, and Shin Pond Road.

Note: Before you enter the park, check your fuel gauge and fill up your tank; there are no fuel facilities in the park.

If you have camping reservations, be sure that you do not arrive at the park with more people than your receipt indicates; the rangers at the gate check this, and the campground rangers even do body counts to be sure you haven't stuffed extra people into cabins or lean-tos.

Appalachian Trail through-hikers are required to register at the Abol Stream kiosk (at the edge of the park), as well as at Katah-din Stream Campground, before ascending Katahdin.

Maine residents have free daytime use of the park—one of Governor Baxter's stipula-tions. At the gates, **nonresidents** pay $12 per vehicle for a day pass; a nonresident season pass is $37. (A rental car with Maine plates no lon-ger qualifies in the resident category.) Everyone must pay for camping.

There is no public transportation to or within Baxter State Park, so you'll need a car, truck, or bicycle. (The park's website lists a couple of enterprises that offer shuttle services.) RVs are also allowed, but maximum size is nine feet high, seven feet wide, and 22 feet long (or 44 feet for car-and-trailer). Baxter is not a drive-through park. The park's 43-mile unpaved **Perimeter Road,** connecting Togue Pond and Matagamon Gates, is narrow and corrugated, evidently deliberately so; it's designed for access, not joyriding.

A few trail loops include the Perimeter Road, but avoid walking on it if possible. In wet weather, you'll be splashed by cars navigating the potholes; in hot weather, the gritty dust gets in your teeth. Hitchhiking is discouraged, but you can usually get a ride if you need it.

Information
Books, maps, and information are available at Baxter State Park Headquarters (64 Balsam Dr., Millinocket 04462, 207/723-5140, www.baxterstateparkauthority.com, open 8 A.M.–5 P.M. Mon.–Fri. all year), at campground ranger stations, and at the Togue Pond Visitor Center. (Camping reservations must be made by mail or in person.)

Pick up a *Day Use Hiking Guide* at the visitors center or at park headquarters. The fold-out map, quite sketchy, also has basic info on major park trails.

Helping Hands
The Boston-based **Appalachian Mountain Club (AMC)** (www.outdoors.org), established in 1876, organizes a couple of summertime **trail-maintenance programs** (a.k.a. "volunteer vacations") at Baxter State Park. The one-week projects, including time to hike Katahdin, cost $145 for AMC members, $160 for nonmembers (food and lodging are included). No experience is necessary, but you need to be in reasonably good shape. For details and schedule, contact the AMC's White Mountains Trails Office (603/466-2721, ext. 192).

Baxter Park headquarters periodically puts out calls for volunteers (for trail repair, carpentry projects, etc.). If you have time to spare for a great cause, download a volunteer application form from www.baxterstateparkauthority.com.

The Allagash and St. John Rivers

ALLAGASH WILDERNESS WATERWAY
In 1966, the state established a 92-mile stretch of the Allagash River as the Allagash Wilderness Waterway (AWW), a collection of lakes, ponds, and streams starting at Telos Lake and ending at East Twin Brook, about six miles before the Allagash meets the St. John River. Also recognized as a National Wild and Scenic River, the waterway's habitats shelter rare plants, 30 or so mammal species, and more than 120 bird species. You'll spot plenty of wildlife along the way.

Arranging a flexible schedule to do the Allagash gives you enough slack to wait out strong winds on the three largest lakes. Such a schedule also allows time for a leisurely pace, side trips, and fishing along the way.

Highlights
Allagash Lake, one of the state's most pristine lakes, feeds into Chamberlain Lake from the west, via Allagash Stream. No motors are allowed on Allagash Lake, making it especially tranquil. The side trip is six miles one-way, and water levels (too high or too low) can make it a rough go. At Lock Dam, ask about conditions. Between Chamberlain and Eagle Lakes, on a narrow spit of land seemingly in the middle of nowhere, stand two of the waterway's oddities—two old **steam engines,** relics rusted out and long abandoned. Once linked to the Eagle Lake and Umbazooksus Railroad, the short-run Lombard Hauler locomotives operated around the clock, six days a week, between 1927 and 1933, hauling 125,000 cords of pulpwood annually for the timber industry.

An exhilarating white-water run is the reward for tackling **Chase Rapids,** a nine-mile stretch starting just below Churchill Dam. You can usually expect Class II white water—sometimes Class III—if you launch with the dam's water release schedule. Two hours after the dam's been closed, the route can get pretty "bony," so you're likely to be hung up temporarily several times along the way. In the afternoon, wear sunglasses (well secured) to protect yourself from glare. For a fee, the Churchill rangers will portage your gear to the end of the rapids, so you have to get only yourselves and your canoes to the end of the run. If you're at all hesitant about making the run, or the water is too low, the rangers will also carry passengers to the end of the run.

Allagash Falls, eight miles before the end of the waterway and 13 miles before the river meets the St. John, has a dramatic, 40-foot drop. Needless to say, you'll need to portage here (on the right)—but only a third of a mile.

When to Go

Canoeing season on the AWW usually runs late May (after "ice-out") to early October. Water and insect levels are high and water temperature is low in May and June; July and August are most crowded but have better weather; September can be chilly, but the foliage is fabulous. Average annual temperature in this area is 40°F; winter temperatures average 20°F. The AWW is accessible in winter for snowmobiling and ice fishing. Winter camping is permitted at the Chamberlain Thoroughfare Bridge parking lot, on a first-come, first-served basis.

Camping

There are 80 signposted campsites along the waterway; all are first-come, first served. July–August, when canoe traffic is fairly heavy, don't wait too late in the day to set up camp. Sites are $10 a night (including tax) for nonresidents, $8 a night for residents. Children under 15 are free. Fees are payable in advance at the ranger station where you enter the waterway. Theoretically, you're expected to stay only one night at any site, but an extension usually isn't a big problem.

Sporting Camp Along the Waterway

Close to one of the major waterway access points, and roughly 50 miles north of Millinocket, **Nugent's Chamberlain Lake Camps** (Chamberlain Lake, mailing address HC76, Box 632, Greenville 04441, 207/944-5991, www.nugent-mcnallycamps.com) is reachable only by boat, floatplane, or snowmobile. Built in 1936, the 12 clean cabins are determinedly rustic, all have privies, and there's a common shower. Although housekeeping rates are available (bring your own sleeping bags and towels; no meals; $33 pp a night), opt for the American Plan ($100 pp a day, including linens and meals) to save lugging victuals and to take advantage of the hearty family-style meals in the character-full main lodge. Cabin and dinner only is $60 pp. Boat rentals are $55 a day (plus gas). John Richardson and Regina Webster keep Nugent's open all year, catering to major clientele—a constant flow of snowmobilers and ice anglers in winter.

Information

The Maine Bureau of Parks and Lands, in the Department of Conservation (Northern Region, 106 Hogan Rd., Bangor 04401, 207/941-4014, www.state.me.us/doc/parks), manages operations on the Allagash Wilderness Waterway. During the season, rangers are stationed at key sites all along the route. Call or write the office for a useful free map and a list of outfitters. For seasonal water-level information, call the Forest Service (207/435-7963 8 A.M.–5 P.M. daily late Apr.–mid-Dec.).

Information also is available from North Maine Woods (NMW; P.O. Box 421, Ashland 04732, 207/435-6213, www.northmaine woods.org).

A particularly lovely pictorial overview of the waterway is naturalist Dean Bennett's excellent book, *Allagash: Maine's Wild and Scenic River.*

Getting There

The Allagash Wilderness Waterway is accessible by private logging roads at specified points. You'll need to pay the North Maine Woods gate fees when you cross onto timber-company land ($8 per day for residents, $10 for non-residents). You can get here from Greenville or Millinocket, or from the Aroostook County community of Ashland. Official access points with parking areas are Chamberlain Thoroughfare Bridge, Churchill Dam, Umsaskis Thoroughfare, and Michaud Farm. Winter access sites are different.

THE ST. JOHN RIVER

Like the Allagash, the St. John has long been associated with the timber industry—and the spring log drives when huge loads of giant logs were driven *upstream* and eventually to the mills. The history of the late-19th and early-20th-century lumbering era is especially colorful, loaded with tales of unbelievably rugged conditions and equally rugged characters. It's only a memory now that the log drives have ended, but you'll see remnants of the industry along the way.

When to Go

The prime season for canoeing the St. John River is May–early June, although many years there's enough water until late June. North Maine Woods monitors daily water levels on the river, so you'll need to call a day in advance (207/435-6213) to confirm that water flow is adequate, especially after mid-June. NMW suggests that 3,000 cfs (cubic feet per second) is the minimum for enjoyable canoeing—to avoid grounding out or extensive portaging—but experienced canoeists recommend a minimum of 2,000 cfs.

June brings out the blackflies at campsites, so be sure you are well prepared to combat them with high-powered (100 percent DEET) bug dope and tight-fitting, light-colored clothing.

Camping

Between Baker Lake and Allagash village, there are 28 riverside camping areas with a total of more than 60 sites. All are signposted. Most are on the left (west) side of the St. John; some require climbing the bank to reach level ground. Campsites are first-come, first-served. If a site is filled, you'll have to move on, anywhere from 2–5 more miles. Camping is allowed only at designated sites. About half of the sites have at least one sheltered picnic table, a real plus that saves rigging tarps for meals in rainy weather. Other facilities are outhouses and fire rings.

Note: Even though the St. John has no dams, a heavy rainstorm can swell the water level, causing the river to rise as much as three feet overnight. Keep this in mind when lashing your canoe for the night; secure it well, as high as possible.

Information

North Maine Woods (NMW; P.O. Box 421, Ashland 04732, 207/435-6213, www.north mainewoods.org) is the nonprofit recreational manager for this area. A guide for canoeing the river is available on its website. The Northwoods Maine Gate fee is $5 pp per day for residents, and $8 for nonresidents, plus a daily camping fee of $8 residents, $10 nonresidents pp per night. People over 70 have free day use, camping is $4; under 15 have free day use and camping.

Getting There

There are five main access points for the St. John, plus the final takeout point downriver at the top of Maine. From the southernmost point, **5th St. John Pond,** it's 143 miles to the town of Allagash. The easiest way to get here is via one of Greenville's two flying services. Downstream are **Baker Lake, St. Juste Road Bridge,** and **Moody Bridge,** the latter being best for low-water conditions; drive in via Ashland (about 3.5 hours on the American Realty Rd.). By the time you get to **Priestly Bridge,** you're more than halfway downriver—almost not worth the trip. Opt instead for starting at Baker Lake or Moody Bridge—or, if you're going with a guiding service, wherever your guides prefer to start. Shuttle arrangements can be complicated for St. John trips. If you're on your own hook, be sure all details are worked out in advance, and include access and camping fees in your budget.

GUIDES

Neophyte canoeists should think twice before setting out without a guide on multiday canoe trips. You should have experience with Class II white water before attempting either of these rivers. Even experienced paddlers who are unfamiliar with Maine's rivers ought to assess the pluses and minuses of a do-it-yourself expedition versus a guided trip. It's rare to find a deserted campsite. The costs of provisioning, arranging shuttles, camping fees, and gear rental can add up—and guides spare you from cooking and cleanup. Not a bad tradeoff.

Most guide services have their specialties, but few specialize in only one river. Some arrange trips all over the state; others go to Canada, Alaska, and beyond. Veteran guide services that offer trips on both the St. John and the Allagash include Mike Patterson and Edgar Eaton's **Wilds of Maine Guide Service** (192 Congress St., Belfast, 207/338-3932, www .wildsofmaine.com); the Cochrane family's **Allagash Canoe Trips** (P.O. Box 932, Green-

ville 04441, 207/237-3077, www.allagash canoetrips.com); and Blaine Miller's **Allagash Guide Inc.** (292 River Rd., Norridgewock, 207/634-3748, www.allagashguide.com).

If you're planning to visit a sporting camp within reasonable distance of the Allagash, check to see whether it arranges Allagash trips; a number of them do.

Two guide services well known for small groups and a special love of traditional woods lore and gear are Garrett and Alexandra Conover's **North Woods Ways** (2293 Elliottsville Rd., Willimantic, 207/997-3723, www .northwoodsways.com), and Ray and Nancy Reitze's **Earthways** (159 Earthways Rd., Canaan, 207/426-8138, www.earthways.net). The Conovers run the Allagash early and late in the season, and the St. John in mid-May, but they provide woodstove-heated tents to combat the chill.

Costs vary for guided trips, usually including everything except transportation to Maine; figure around $150–175 pp per day.

Greenville and Vicinity

Greenville (pop. about 1,500) is the jumping-off point for the North Woods—ground zero for float- and ski-planes maintaining contact with remote hamlets and sporting camps. It's the big city for tinier communities in every direction, but it's a bit like a frontier town itself. Greenville looks out over Moosehead Lake—Maine's largest—from its southern end. Moosehead is 40 miles long and covers 117 square miles, but counting all the niches and notches, its shoreline runs to more than 400 miles.

The origin of the lake's name *has* to be from the large number of antlered critters hereabouts, especially along the shore toward Rockwood or Kokadjo. In addition to moosewatching, you can wear yourself out with all the recreational choices: swimming, boating, fishing, camping, hiking, white-water rafting, golfing, picnicking, birding, skiing, snowshoeing, and snowmobiling. In spring, summer,

and fall, you can also cruise the lake aboard an antique steamer.

Moosehead has been attracting outdoors enthusiasts, primarily hunters and anglers, since the 1880s. The long haul from lower New England, ending with the passenger train from Bangor, apparently was worth it for the clean air, prime angling, and chance to rough it. That era has long passed, and the clientele has changed noticeably, but Greenville's downtown still has a rustic air, and the outlying hamlets even more so.

Greenville was incorporated in 1836, just before the timber industry began to take off. Steamboats hauled huge corrals ("booms") of logs down the lake to the East Outlet of the Kennebec River (East and West Outlets are both on the west side of Moosehead), where river drivers took over. All that ended fairly recently, in the 1970s. The steamer *Katahdin* is a relic of that colorful era.

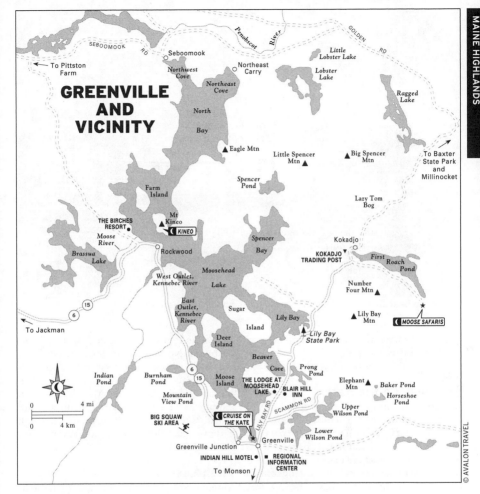

Greenville's lakeshore twin, Greenville Junction, once a busy rail crossroads, now has become one of those blink-and-you'll-miss-it places, but you can still eat and sleep there. Twenty miles northwest of Greenville, on Route 6/15, is the small and somewhat crowded hamlet of Rockwood, closest spot to Kineo, a lake icon marked by cliffs that plunge to the water. One of the best Kineo views is from the public boat landing, on a loop road just off Route 6/15. Route 6/15 then continues west, along Brassua Lake and the aptly named Moose River, to Jackman—a lovely 30-mile drive popular with moose-watchers.

Don't be surprised, when you make inquiries about the Moosehead area, to hear lots of references to "ice-out." It's almost a season—the time when winter's ice releases its grip on the lake and spring and summer activities can begin. Depending on the severity of the winter, ice-out occurs anywhere early–late May. Fisherfolk arrive, plumbing begins to work, and

© TOM NANGLE

One of the best ways to see Moosehead Lake is aboard the *Kate*.

a few weeks later, the blackfly larvae start to hatch. Spring is under way.

SIGHTS
Cruise on the *Kate*

A turn-of-the-20th-century wooden vessel once used in the lumber industry, the steamboat *Katahdin* (locally called the *Kate)* has been converted to diesel and now runs cruises on 40-mile-long Moosehead Lake from her base at the bottom of the lake, next to the **Moosehead Marine Museum** (12 Lily Bay Rd., P.O. Box 1151, Greenville 04441, 207/695-2716, www.katahdincruises.com). The best trip for children is the regular three-hour run, departing at 12:30 P.M. Tuesday, Thursday, Saturday, and Sunday. Tickets are $30 adults, $26 seniors, $15 kids 11–16; kids under 11 are free. A five-hour **Mount Kineo cruise** ($35 adults, $31 seniors, $18 kids, plus $6 for buffet lunch) is offered occasionally July–early October. An all-day head-of-lake trip (call for rates) operates the last Saturday of September, when it's chilly, but the fall foliage is fantastic ($60/56/30).

Indoor and outdoor seating; dinner available on board. No smoking or high-heeled shoes; the boat is wheelchair-accessible. Cruises operate on a regular schedule July–early September, but only on weekends late May–June and on a limited schedule through September. A full schedule resumes for foliage season, through early October. Reservations are advisable for the longer cruises.

Flightseeing

Moosehead Lake from the air during fall-foliage season is incomparable—you'll bank over Mount Kineo, survey a palette of autumn colors, and very possibly see a moose or two. (They're easiest to spot in the sad-looking tracts clear-cut by the timber companies.) Most fun is the lakefront takeoff and landing. **Currier's Flying Service** (Pritham Ave., Rte. 6/15, Greenville Junction, 207/695-2778, www.curriersflyingservice.com) flies a whole slew of on-demand trips over Mt. Kineo, Squaw Mountain, and Katahdin. Costs range $42–130 pp (two-person minimum). Moose-watching trips,

LITTLE FARM IN THE BIG WILDERNESS

Trust me. If you continue up Route 6/15 from Greenville, 20 miles to Rockwood, and then another 20 miles on an unpaved road, you're guaranteed to have an adventure at **Pittston Farm** (Seboomook Rd., T2 R4, mailing address P.O. Box 525, Rockwood 04478, 207/280-0000, www.pittstonfarm.com).

The South and North Branches of the Penobscot River wrap around Pittston Farm, which is truly an oasis in the wilderness. Once a working logging camp where teamsters were based, its two impressive barns and a three-story farmhouse remain relatively intact. New owners in late 2005, Bob and Jenny Mills, along with their son, grandkids, and parents, are investing in updating this National Historic Register property without losing its come-as-you-are hospitality. Although the frills are few, the welcome is warm, the price is right, and the experience is priceless. You'll likely spot a moose or two on the way; drive defensively.

A few miles before the farm, you'll need to stop at the timber-company checkpoint and pay the road fee, normally $5 for Maine plates, $8 for non-Maine plates, but Pittston Farm guests can pay $1 for a four-hour window to visit, and that's plenty of time for a meal; if you're staying overnight, the farm pays the fee.

This unincorporated territory, officially called the Pittston Academy Grant, once was a major center for timber operations along the Penobscot River. Now the 100-acre riverside farm is known as the place to go by car, flying service, or snowmobile for meals fit for lumberjacks. Dress down (suspenders will fit right in). All-you-can-eat breakfasts are served beginning at 8 A.M., lunch off a menu is available 11 A.M.–3 P.M., the huge dinner buffet is served 5–7 P.M.; BYOB. It's hearty home cooking, definitely meat-oriented, and you won't eat alone. The homemade pies and cookies alone are worth the trip. Reservations are advisable. No credit cards are accepted.

After eating, spend some time in the museum, blacksmith shop, and chapel (a former potato barn), stroll the grounds, and visit the horses, goats, and cattle. Canoe and kayak rentals are available, and there are plenty of hiking trails in the area.

A newer venture is horseback riding along marked, wooded trails. If you have your own horse, bring it. A $60 overnight fee includes horse accommodations and food; horse trailer parking is $25 per day. Horse-and-rider packages are available.

The main lodge is comfy, with a big wraparound porch and – surprise! – wireless Internet. Basic accommodations in the lodge (many rooms sharing few baths) go for $94 pp; renovated carriage house rooms (the name sounds fancy, but the rooms are extremely modest) have private baths, air-conditioning, and satellite TV and go for $99 pp. Also available are seven no-frills cabins, with newly added private baths, $99 pp. All lodging rates include the all-you-can-eat, home-style meals, bedding, and towels. RV sites in the field are $22/night, including electric hookups; water and dump station are nearby. Tent sites are $17 for two adults and three kids younger than 18.

If you're tentative about making the trip, call the Millses to see if they're offering any programs including transportation from Greenville.

© HILARY NANGLE

Take a day trip over the logging roads to remote Pittston Farm for lunch or dinner.

© HILARY NANGLE

The cliffs of Kineo are a Moosehead Lake landmark, accessible via launch from Rockwood.

depending on their length, are $65–130 pp. Call to arrange a flight schedule; planes depart from Greenville Junction, where the Currier family also operates a small gift shop, selling handmade wall hangings.

Kineo

Moosehead's most distinctive landmark, at the lake's "waistline," is Mt. Kineo, a 763-foot-high chunk of green-tinged rhyolite or felsite that erupted from the bowels of the earth about 425 million years ago. Smoothed by glacial activity on the west side, Kineo has sharp cliffs on its east side. The chertlike volcanic stone (not flint; Maine has no native flint) was a major reason Native Americans glommed on to the Moosehead area thousands of years ago; its hardness served them well for weapons and fishing and hunting tools. The surrounding woodlands yielded prime birch bark, supplying raw material for canoes, carryalls, and even shelters. Stone tools and arrowheads still turn up occasion-

ally, especially along the shore when the water level is low, but most have been carted off by amateur collectors. *Resist the urge to take home samples.* Once the site of a monumental summer resort hotel, Kineo is rather sleepy these days, with only a small B&B and no other services. But if your schedule permits, go. A hike up Mt. Kineo is a must.

Kineo is accessible by rough roads, via the east side of the lake, but just barely. It's far easier and better to rent a boat on the west side of the lake, in Rockwood (but beware of fluky lake winds), or take the Rockwood Village–Kineo shuttle service, which departs regularly from the village dock ($10 adult, $5 ages 6–11). Each Wednesday during the season, the steamboat *Katahdin* makes a 1.5-hour stop at the base of Mt. Kineo—not enough time for a major hike but ample for a sense of the site. Northwoods Outfitters offers private Kineo cruises ($275 for two) on its 23-foot boat *Angler Management*. The six-hour trip includes time to hike and explore as well as snacks and beverages.

From the dock, the Indian and Bridle Trails lead to the top, but signposting is a bit lax; keep an eye out for blue blazes. The Bridle Trail is easier. Allow about three hours round-trip for the hike; carry a picnic. In winter, when Moosehead Lake freezes solid, you can get to the Kineo peninsula by snowmobile (weather and common sense determine the schedule), but the trails are too full of snow for hiking.

Lily Bay State Park

Lining the eastern shore of Moosehead Lake, 925-acre Lily Bay State Park (Lily Bay Rd., HC 76, Box 425, Greenville, 207/695-2700, $3 adult, $1 children 5–11, over 65/under 5 free) is the place to go for moose-watching, fishing, picnicking, hiking, canoeing, swimming, birding, and camping at some of Maine's most desirable waterfront sites. The park is open 7 A.M.–11 P.M. daily May 1–October 15, but it's accessible in winter for cross-country skiing and snowmobiling. From Greenville, head north on Lily Bay Road for eight miles; the park is on the left.

RECREATION
Multisport Outfitters

The biggest and best outfitter in this neck of the woods is **Northwoods Outfitters** (Main St., P.O. Box 160, Greenville 04441, 866/223-1380 or 207/695-3288, www.maineoutfitter .com), in downtown Greenville, right across from the *Katahdin*. Northwoods should be your first stop, no matter what your choice of activity. These folks are the region's outdoor pros. Even if you have your own equipment and have no need of a guide, stop in for advice and information, maps, and perhaps a cup of java and final posting from the civilized world from its **Internet Café.** Northwoods does it all, offering rental equipment, shuttles, and guided trips: Moose safaris, Kineo cruises, mountain biking, hiking, sailing, canoeing, white-water rafting, fishing, snowmobiling, snowshoeing, and so on. It's open 9 A.M.–5 P.M. daily with extended hours during peak seasons.

◖ Moose Safaris

Ed Mathieu is the chief honcho of **Moose Country Safaris** (Rte. 1, Box 524D, Sangerville, 207/876-4907, www.moosecountry safaris.com), usually operating in the Greenville area. Reservations are essential. Moose safaris, lasting about four hours, go out at 5:45 A.M. and 2 P.M. mid-May–mid-October, by 4WD and canoe or kayak; there's a two-person minimum/maximum. Cost is $125–140 for two. Opt for the morning trip, which includes breakfast at West Branch Pond Camps.

The Birches Resort and Northwoods Outfitters also offer moose safaris; Currier's does its moose-watching from the air.

If you go on your own, swampy **Lazy Tom Bog** is one of the region's best moose-watching haunts. Plan to go soon after sunrise or just before sunset. From Greenville, take Lily Bay Road north to Kokadjo, 18 miles. A mile later, when the road forks, take the left fork (signposted Spencer Pond Camps). Continue 0.5 mile to a small bridge. Park on either side of the bridge and have your camera ready, preferably with a long lens. If you want to emerge from your car, or even stick your lens through the open window, you may need to douse yourself with insect repellent. And try to keep the kids quiet.

Hiking

Except for early June, when blackflies torment woodland hikers as well as moose, the Greenville area is sublime for hiking. The chamber of commerce has a list that includes hiking directions for **Number Four Mountain, Big and Little Squaw Mountains, Big and Little Spencer Mountains,** and **Elephant Mountain** (a B-52 wreck site). Ask at the chamber, too, for directions to **Moose Mountain,** off Route 6/16, topped with the first fire tower in the United States. It's a bit rickety but still there. The hike is moderate to difficult and takes about four hours round-trip.

Northwoods Outfitters offers **guided hikes** with Registered Maine Guides, but for a personalized, in-depth, educational experience, book a hike with Dr. Wendy Weiger of **Achor Guiding Service** (P.O. Box 131, Greenville Jct. 04442, 207/695-2707, www.achormaine.com). Dr. Weiger, a Registered Maine Guide, customizes itineraries for all ages—a great choice for those with children. She knows the flora, fauna, and natural history of the region and shares it along the trail. She provides round-trip transportation from lodging to trailhead. Full-day hikes are $150 for 1–2, $225 for 3–4, and include lunch. Half-day hikes are $80 or $120. In winter, she leads snowshoeing expeditions.

Mountain Biking

Given all the backwoods trails, mountain biking is very popular. You can bring a bike and strike out on your own, rent a bike, or go with a guide or group. Remember, however, that bicycles are *not* allowed on logging roads; the huge lumber trucks are intimidating enough for passenger vehicles, never mind bicycles.

Mountain bike rentals are available from **Northwoods Outfitters** for $25 a day. Also available are kids' bikes, child seats, and trail-a-bikes.

Twenty miles north of Greenville, **The Birches Resort** (P.O. Box 41, Rockwood 04478, 207/534-7305, www.birches.com)

rents mountain bikes and sends you off on its network of mountain-bike trails. It also has group rides, including an early-morning moose-watching pedal for $35 pp, including breakfast. Check the website for snowmobiling and cross-country skiing rates.

Canoeing and Kayaking

If you're not an experienced paddler, be cautious about canoeing or kayaking on Moosehead Lake. The sheltered bays and coves are usually safe, but you can have serious trouble in the open areas—*especially* the stretch between Rockwood and Kineo. Do *not* attempt it; even pros have been swamped by rogue winds on that route. At Lily Bay State Park, you can launch a canoe from the waterfront campsites and easily make it to Sugar Island.

At **Northwoods Outfitters** canoe or kayak rentals begin at $20/day; weekly rentals and deliveries are available as is shuttle service.

Sailing

Captains Bryan Pearce and Will Manion offer charter sails on Moosehead aboard their 30-foot catamaran *North Wind* (207/852-4203, www.sail-nw.com). For the best trip, book a minimum of 3–4 hours, which provides enough time to get out on the lake and sail, perhaps dive in the lake for a swim or two, and a snack. Minimum is two guests, maximum is six. Rates vary with the time chartered, but a $100 deposit is required to secure a reservation.

Swimming

In addition to Lily Bay State Park, there's fine swimming at **Red Cross Beach** in downtown Greenville. The parking area is near the Masonic Temple on Pritham Avenue, and a short path through the woods leads to the beach. You'll find lifeguards, picnic tables, and even floats.

White-Water Rafting

From Greenville, you're well positioned to raft either the Kennebec or the Penobscot Rivers. Check with Northwoods Outfitters.

Fly-Fishing

The best local resource for fly-fishing, hands down, is the **Maine Guide Fly Shop and Guide Service** (34 Greenville Rd., P.O. Box 1202, Greenville 04441, 207/695-2266, www.maineguideflyshop.com). This veteran operation, owned by Dan Legere, will set you up with a guide and all the equipment you need to do it right. Rates for a guided drift-boat experience, including lunch and gear, are $350 for one, $400 for two.

Golf

The most popular, scenic, and windswept course in the area is the nine-hole **Kineo Golf Club,** built for the 500 or so guests at the turn-of-the-20th-century Mount Kineo House. At every turn, you'll see Mt. Kineo or Moosehead Lake, or both. There are dynamite views. The course is open June–mid-October, and you'll need to get there by boat (see *Getting Around*).

Built in the 1920s, nine-hole **Squaw Mountain Village Golf Course** (Rte. 6/15, Greenville Junction, 207/695-3609) is now part of a modern condo complex. Greens fees are low and the pace is unhurried.

Dogsledding and Snowshoeing

Former Outward Bound instructor, Certified Wilderness Responder, and Registered Maine Guide Stephen Madera is the ideal guy to head into the Maine woods with via dogsled. His company, **Song in the Woods** (P.O. Box 127, Abbott 04406, 207/876-4736, www.songinthewoods.com), offers trips of all lengths into the wilderness around Gulf Hagas and the Roach Ponds. You can even mush your own team. Cost is $175 for two for two hours, daylight or moonlight, $230 half day, and $300 full day including lunch. Multiday trips are available. He also guides two-hour snowshoe tours for $30 pp including equipment.

Snowmobiling

The biggest winter pursuit hereabouts is snowmobiling, thanks to an average 102-inch annual snowfall and 300 miles of Greenville-area trails connecting to the entire state network.

It's pretty competitive trying to get a bed in winter if you don't plan well ahead; be forewarned. Incidentally, if you're curious about how people get around northern Maine in winter, check out the parking lot at the Greenville school complex (Pritham Ave.); the vehicle of choice is the snowmobile.

A particularly popular loop is the 160-mile **Moosehead Trail,** which circumnavigates Moosehead Lake: Greenville to Rockwood to Pittston Farm, Seboomook, Northeast Carry, Kokadjo, and back to Greenville. Or start at any access point along the route and go in either direction.

The chamber of commerce has snowmobile trail maps and can put you in touch with local snowmobile clubs. Thanks to these energetic clubs, trails are well maintained and signposted. Snowmobile rentals and guided tours are available from Northwoods Outfitters and the Birches Resort.

Cross-Country Skiing

The Birches Resort (Box 41, Rockwood 04478, 207/534-7305, www.birches.com) has miles of groomed cross-country ski trails winding through an 11,000-acre nature preserve. Call for rates and snow conditions. Ski rentals are available at The Birches Ski Touring Center. For lodging at the Birches, escape to one of its remote, heated trailside yurts for $35 pp in peak season (Jan.–Mar. and June–Sept.), $30 off-peak, two-person minimum both seasons. Skiers can use the hot tub and sauna, go on guided ski excursions, and avail themselves of ski packages.

West Branch Pond Camps grooms trails for snowshoe and cross country, but call ahead as days of operation are sporadic.

SHOPPING

The Greenville area, and especially downtown Greenville, is filled with shops selling moose-related merchandise and other goods with a woodsy theme.

If you're entering Greenville from the south, cresting the last hill you'll see on your right the **Indian Hill Trading Post** (Rte. 15, Green-

ville, 207/695-2104 or 800/675-4487, www .indianhill.com), one-stop shopping with camping gear, clothing, footwear, an ATM, fishing and hunting licenses, souvenirs, and a supermarket that sells ice, liquor, groceries, and even live lobsters. In short, if it doesn't have it, you don't need it.

On the main drag downtown is **Maine Mountain Soap and Candle Co.** (Main St., Greenville, 207/695-3926), with a huge array of flavors. The scents of blackberry, lemon, pine, and more all greet you at the door. It's hard to resist. Aromatherapy products are also available.

Just beyond the town offices, **Joe Bolf** (Minden St., Greenville, 207/695-3002, www .JoeBolf.com) works magic with a chainsaw; don't miss the "band."

Peter Templeton is keeping a family tradition of boatbuilding alive at **Ship Shape** (296 Pritham Ave., Greenville, 207/695-2402). Templeton specializes in building replica models of the steamships that used to ply Moosehead Lake, but he'll build other models too and takes commissions.

For reading material, **Gabriel's Studio** (Rte. 6/15, Greenville, 207/695-3968) has a good selection of inexpensive used books, while **From Away Books** (38 Main St., Greenville, 207/695-0266) has three rooms stocked with used and antiquarian books as well as a few other treasures, all at excellent prices.

ENTERTAINMENT AND EVENTS

Moosemainea, an annual, monthlong, moose-oriented festival sponsored by the Moosehead Lake Region Chamber of Commerce, combines canoe, rowboat, and mountain-bike races; a family fun day; moose safaris; even a best-moose-photo contest. Register your own moose sightings on a huge map at the chamber of commerce. Events take place in Greenville and Rockwood mid-May–mid-June.

The first full weekend in September, the **International Seaplane Fly-In Weekend** is a four-day event at Greenville and Greenville Junction drawing seaplanes from all over New England for public breakfasts, a two-day craft fair, flightseeing, and more. Beds are *very* scarce during the Fly-In, so either book well ahead to be part of it or wait for another time to visit.

The **Natural Resource Education Center at Moosehead Lake** (207/695-3705, www .naturalresourceeducationcenter.org) presents a summer series of lectures and field trips.

ACCOMMODATIONS

Lodging in the area varies from just a few grades above camping to exquisite country inns and lodges.

Country Inns

Wow! Combine a magnificent Victorian hillside manse, with eye-popping views of Moosehead Lake, with an English manor house decor and ambience, and the result is the **(Blair Hill Inn** (Lily Bay Rd., P.O. Box 1288, Greenville 04441, 207/695-0224, www.blairhill.com, $275–450), where Dan and Ruth McLaughlin (escapees from the software world) have created a relaxing, elegant retreat. Eight spacious second- and third-floor rooms in the magnificent 1891 home are furnished with comfy antiques and accented with ornate woodwork, fabulous lighting, and walls covered with fine paintings. Some have working fireplaces, room 6 has views down to Kineo from the window seat, and many of the bathrooms have separate soaking tubs and large showers. A truly gourmet, multicourse breakfast is included, and dinner is available weekends in peak season. Be sure to hike to the top of the hill for an even more expansive view; afterward, slip into the outdoor whirlpool tub or drink in the heady views while sipping a drink on the porch. The grounds include lovely gardens, greenhouses, a huge barn, and rolling lawns edged with stone walls. During summer, the inn hosts a concert series on the lawn; tickets $20.

Elegance and comfort are also bywords at Linda and Dennis Bortis's **The Lodge at Moosehead Lake** (Lily Bay Rd., P.O. Box 1167, Greenville 04441, 207/695-4400, www.lodge atmooseheadlake.com), which immerses guests in a chic version of a cabin in the woods. Perhaps the most astonishing feature is the furniture. Each of the five guest rooms in the main building has a theme—Trout, Loon, Moose, Totem, and Bear—and each has beds and mirrors hand-carved by local woodworking master Joe Bolf, plus lots of accessories, to carry it out. All but the Trout have dramatic views of Moosehead Lake. Whirlpool tubs, fireplaces, and camouflaged VCR/DVDs are in each room, as well as in the three bilevel, water-view carriage-house suites—Allagash, Baxter, and Katahdin. In Allagash and Baxter, lumber-era boom chains hold swaying queen-size beds with incredible lake views; Katahdin has a fireplace in the *bathroom.* In the guest pantry are a small gift shop with clever moose-themed items, snacks, and dozens of videos/DVDs for guests to borrow. Wi-Fi throughout. Latest addition is the two-bedroom Kineo suite, with kitchen, living/dining room, big deck, and jaw-dropping views, upstairs in the Carriage House. All of this, of course, comes with a price: Rooms and suites are $295–485 d in summer and fall, $225–385 off-season; Kineo is $680 per night. Breakfast is included all year; a three- or five-course menu ($40 and $55) is available Friday–Monday June–October, and Friday and Saturday in winter only; but call to be sure. A pub serves lighter fare until 9 P.M. Friday–Monday. Ask about the lodge's multiday packages that include a variety of area excursions. The inn, open all year, is 2.5 miles north of downtown Greenville. Visiting pooches ($40) are pampered in one suite.

Tucked on a side street in Greenville and just "300 steps" from the lake is **Pleasant Street Inn** (26 Pleasant St., P.O. Box 1261, Greenville 04441, 207/695-3400, www.pleasantstreetinn .com, $110–175), a lovely Victorian dating from 1889, with tiger oak woodwork throughout that's been burnished and polished to a soft glow. Guest rooms are spread on three floors, and all have private baths (although some are detached; robes provided). Be sure to check out the tower room, with views to the lake. Two other parlors and a wraparound porch mean there's plenty of room to spread out. Rates include a full breakfast and afternoon snacks. Kids over 14 are welcome.

Motels

The **Kineo View Motor Lodge** (Rte. 15, P.O. Box 514, Greenville 04441, 207/695-4470 or 800/659-8439, www.kineoview.com), three miles south of Greenville, sits on a prime hilltop with a dead-on view of Mt. Kineo and gorgeous sunsets. Opened in 1993, the chalet-style, three-story motel has 12 good-size rooms (phone, TV, fridge, microwave, and balconies) for $85–95 d, including free continental breakfast late May–mid-October; $59–69 d (no breakfast) other months. Two suites, with kitchenettes, are $169. This is a great place to bring kids—there's lots of acreage to run around, including nature trails. Outside are picnic tables and a grill; the windowed ground floor has a hot tub for guests' use. Some rooms accommodate pets, $10 by reservation.

Two miles closer to Greenville than Kineo View, with a fine hilltop view of Moosehead Lake itself, the **Indian Hill Motel** (127 Moosehead Lake Rd./Rte. 15, P.O. Box 327, Greenville Junction 04442, 207/695-2623 or 800/771-4620) is a vintage, one-story motel with 15 good-size rooms ($68 d summer, $53–73 d other months; air-conditioning, phones, cable TV) with tiny baths. All have a splendid view. In the commercial complex across Route 15 are a supermarket and the chamber of commerce.

You're practically *in* the lake at **Chalet Moosehead** (Birch St., P.O. Box 327, Greenville Junction 04442, 207/695-2950 or 800/290-3645, www.mooseheadlodging.com). A newish (spring 2000), two-story building is where you want to stay; first- and second-floor rooms have whirlpool tubs, fridges, TVs, phones, and private balconies with dynamite views, all for $116–136 in season (higher rates during September Fly-in). The older, two-story section has seven basic rooms for $92 d in season, $98 with kitchenette. Kids five and under stay free; pets ($10) are allowed in the older units. Dock space is free if you bring your own boat, and guests have free use of canoes, paddleboats, gas grills, and a private swimming area.

On a hillside with grand views over Kineo and Moosehead Lake is **Moosehead Motel and Condos** (Rte. 6/15, P.O. Box 235, Rockwood 04478, 207/534-7787, www.mooseheadmotel.org, $70–80). All units have equipped kitchenettes and air-conditioning.

Small Cottage Colonies

What a location! Smack-dab on Moosehead, adjacent to the East Outlet of the Kennebec River's dam, is ☾ **Wilsons on Moosehead Lake** (Greenville Junction, 207/695-2549 or 800/817-2549, www.wilsonsonmooseheadlake.com). Owners Scott and Alison Snell are updating this 1864 property and doing a fine job of it. The one- to five-bedroom housekeeping cottages are spotless, and all have screened porches as well as kitchens and fireplaces. Rates are $80–350 per night or $530–1,950 per week in July and August, less off-season. Canoe, motorboat, and paddleboat rentals are available. Pets are $10/day or $50/week with prior approval.

Fifty acres of woods etched with trails surround the new, nicely appointed **Moosehead Hills Cabins** (418 Lily Bay Rd., P.O. Box 936, Greenville 04441, 207/695-2514, www.mooseheadhills.com). Three hillside cabins have nice Moosehead views. A path and a road lead to the shoreline, where guests have use of a dock. Sunrise Lodge, a three-bedroom, two-bath cabin on seven-mile-long Wilson Pond. has a private dock and water frontage. Peak rates are $180–360/night, $1,170–2,500/week with a one-week minimum July and August, two- to three-night minimum the rest of the year.

Sporting Camps

Ease into sporting camp life at **Maynard's in Maine** (P.O. Box 220, Rockwood 04478, 207/534-7703 or 888/518-2055, www.maynardsinmaine.com), operated by Gail and William Maynard. Cross the Rockwood bridge, take a left, and you're on tarred road right to the property. Although it's not remote by most sporting camp standards, it's a rural gem. Meals are served in the central lodge; guests stay in the cabins, all with full bath and most with views over the Moose River to the Blue Ridge (a blaze of color during foliage season). The food is great, freshly made and home baked. Guests choose from two entrées each night. At first glance it may seem more run-down than rustic, but the cabins are comfy, the mattresses firm, and the plumbing is inside. Rates, including breakfast, dinner, and a packed lunch, are $65 adult, $32 kids ages 3–12; without meals, it's $35 pp. Cabins have 1–3 bedrooms. Pets are allowed for $20 per day. Motorboat rental is $55 per day; canoes are $10.

Eric Stirling is the fourth-generation host at **West Branch Pond Camps** Kokadjo (mailing address Box 1153, Greenville 04441, 207/695-2561, www.westbranchpondcamps.com). Lining the shore of First West Branch Pond, overlooking White Cap Mountain, are eight classically rustic (I'm being kind) cabins that have seen better days. Eric is slowly fixing them up, but staying here is just a few steps above camping, although it does have indoor plumbing and evening electricity. Some beds have new mattresses and box springs. Others, well, you just might want to drag that mattress onto the floor for support. And come after peak bug season—the screens are, well, a bit holey. So why come? This is the real thing, and the authenticity and peacefulness are all-encompassing. If you're hoping to spot a moose, well, the gangly mammals often stroll right through the property, even peeking in the kitchen window! Speaking of the kitchen: When the bell rings for meals, guests head to the 1890 lakeside lodge and vacuum up the hearty cuisine described in one upscale national magazine as "simple, soulful Yankee cooking." Thursday nights, the prime-rib dinner ($24 pp, including dessert) is open to the public by reservation. BYOB. Most guests stay for a week, and the many repeats make it tough to book space, but the daily rate is $90 pp American Plan, $50 for kids 5–11. Fly-fishing, hiking, and canoeing are the major pursuits here. Grouse and rabbit hunters come in fall, and cross-country skiers and snowshoers in winter. Take Lily Bay Road from Greenville 17 miles; turn right onto an unpaved road (signposted for West Branch Ponds) and go 10 more miles. It's open May–September and occasionally in winter.

Forty-three miles northeast of Greenville is **Nahmakanta Lake Camps** (P.O. Box 544, Millinocket 04462, 207/731-8888, www.nahmakanta.com), Don and Angel Hibbs's oasis in the wilderness on Nahmankanta Lake. Eight cabins right on the lake have screened porches, full kitchens, and woodstove. There is no electricity. Guests share three common bathhouses with showers and flush toilets, but each cabin also has a private privy. Choose from full American Plan, including all meals ($120 pp/day, plus $6 times age for kids 1–17); Modified American Plan, including supper ($95 pp/day adult, $4 times age for kid), or housekeeping ($75 pp/adult, $3 times age for kids); all rates are based on two-adult minimum and three-night stay, five nights mid-July–August 30. Canoes and kayaks are provided; boats and motors are $50 per day; guides are available. Summer access is via 25 miles of gravel roads or floatplane (call Folsom's, 207/695-2821). Now here's the really cool (okay, cold) part: Nahmakanta is open in winter. Access is by cross-country ski, snowmobile shuttle ($50 for two), or dog team. Relax in a wood-fired cedar sauna upon arrival, and yes, there are hot showers. Winter rates are slightly less. Ask about packages including dogsledding or visit the winter website (www.mainedogsledding.com).

Campgrounds and Campsites

The **Maine Forest Service** supervises and maintains free campsites, with fireplaces and outhouses, many on the shores of Moosehead Lake. Most are accessible only by boat—first come, first served. For information, contact the Maine Forest Service office (downtown Greenville, 207/695-3721).

At the northern end of Moosehead Lake, about 5.5 miles south of the Golden Road, **Seboomook Wilderness Campground** (Seboomook Village, mailing address HC85, Box 560, Rockwood 04478, 207/280-0555, www.seboomookwildernesscampground.us), has 84 wooded and open tent and RV sites, Adirondack shelters, and housekeeping cabins (no linens), many right on the water. Everything is very rustic, although there is a central bathhouse with flush toilets and free hot showers. Request a site on the eastern side, away from the long-term RV area. Facilities include a small, shallow beach and a grocery store/lunch counter. History buffs take note: This is the site of a World War II German POW camp. Camping sites are $18–30/day; shelters are $30 d; cabins are $50–100/day. Weekly rate available for both. Seboomook's store is open all winter for snowmobilers and cross-country skiers; campsites are open mid-May–November. Canoes, kayaks, and motorboat rentals are available. The campground is about 28 unpaved miles north of Rockwood; you'll need to pay a user fee ($8 for non-Maine plates, $5 for Maine plates) at the Twenty-Mile Checkpoint just before Pittston Farm.

You can't get much closer to the water than some of the primitive sites at **South Inlet Wilderness Campground** (Kokadjo, mailing address P.O. Box 542, Greenville 04441, 207/695-2474 evenings, 207/695-3954 winter). Although near a dirt road, many of the sites front on First Roach Pond. There's also a field for bigger RVs, but no hookups. Sites are in the $12 range. Facilities include beach, boat launch, privies, and picnic tables.

Plan well in advance to snag one of the primo waterfront sites at **Lily Bay State Park** (Lily Bay Rd., HC 76, Box 425, Greenville, 207/695-2700); on weekends July–August, campsite reservations are essential, with a two-night minimum (call 207/287-3824 and have a MasterCard, Visa, or Discover card ready or visit www.campwithme.com). Only the lucky will find a last-minute space, even though there are 93 sites in two clusters; no hookups. Nonresident camping fees are $19 per site per night ($14 residents), plus the reservation fee of $2 per site per night. The park's 91 sites are divided among two campgrounds.

FOOD

The range of dining experiences in and near Greenville is amazingly broad. From pure rustic to local color to upwardly mobile to gourmet cuisine, take your pick. One caveat: While choices are plentiful in summer, they're scanty at best in the off-season.

Local Flavors

Pick up sandwiches along with fine wines, cheeses, chocolates, and other gourmet goodies at **Lakeshore Provisions** (16 Pritham Ave., Greenville, 207/695-2400).

Extremely popular among local residents for breakfast and lunch is **Flatlanders** (38 Pritham Ave., Greenville, 207/695-3373). The best choice is the broasted chicken, which one waitress described as "kinda like fried chicken but cooked in a pressure cooker so it's more healthy." Whatever, everyone agrees it's tasty.

Buy pizza and subs, Ben and Jerry's, beer and wine coolers, and worms and crawlers at **Jamo's** (Pritham Ave., Greenville, 207/695-2201). Okay, skip the latter pairing, but the pizza's decent and the dagwood sandwiches, made on fresh-baked pita bread, earn raves.

The riverside **Moose River Country Store** (Rtes. 6/15, Rockwood, 207/534-7352, 6 A.M.–8 P.M. Sun.–Thurs., to 9 P.M. Fri. and Sat.) sells huge sandwiches (one large easily feeds two normal-size appetites) as well as burgers and pizza and, in the morning, breakfast fare. Eat in or take out.

Casual Dining

A dining bright spot in downtown Greenville, **Rod-N-Reel Cafe** (44 Pritham Ave., Greenville, 207/695-0388, 11 A.M.–9 P.M. Wed.–Sun.) reels them in for reliable home-style food with flair. Fish is the dominant theme, from the name to the decor to the menu, but you can get steaks, chicken, and pasta as well. Lunch for two won't set you back more than $16; dinner entrées are $8–21 (with extras), but lighter fare is available. Friday and Saturday are prime rib nights.

For upscale pub food, such as wraps and salads, as well as burgers and chili, detour into the **Stress-free Moose** (65 Pritham Ave., Greenville, 207/695-3100, 11 A.M.–10 P.M., to 11 P.M. Fri. and Sat). While you can sit inside, the big wraparound porch is the place to while away an afternoon or evening.

In Greenville Junction, with fantastic lake views, is **Kelly's Landing** (Rte. 6/15, P.O. Box 336, Greenville Junction 04442, 207/695-4438, kellysatmoosehead.com). Food's hit or miss, but you can't beat the location. If the weather's fine, dine on the deck; if not, the dining rooms have big windows on the lake. It's open daily all year for breakfast, lunch, and dinner. Entrées run $6–16, with a kids' menu available. The Sunday breakfast buffet is a megabargain at $10. There's always a crowd here, and boaters can tie up at the dock.

Downstairs in the Lodge at Moosehead, with fab lake views, a small bar, a big-screen TV, and a pool table, is **Sistah's Pub** (Lily Bay Rd., 207/695-4400, call for days and hours). The menu comprises upscale pub-style food and then some: lemon-garlic marinated shrimp, roast garlic Caesar salad, grilled flatbread pizza, seafood pasta, and the like, at prices in the $9–25 range.

Experience sporting-camp life and meals without getting too far into the woods at **Maynard's in Maine** (207/534-7703 or 888/518-2055, www.maynardsinmaine.com), an authentic main lodge and cabins overlooking the Moose River in Rockwood. Maynard's is open to the public (breakfast 7–8:30 A.M., dinner 6–7:30 P.M. daily, reservations required). There's a full menu for breakfast and a set menu, with a choice of two entrées, at dinner ($17), including soup or juice, salad, sides, dessert, and nonalcoholic beverage). Everything's homemade or baked and served family-style in the pleasant dining room.

Another good choice for a fine meal in a great setting is **Northern Pride Lodge** (3405 Lily Bay Rd., Frenchtown Township, 207/695-2890, www.northernpridelodge.com), 18 miles north of Greenville, overlooking First Roach Pond in Kokadjo. Entrées, such as port tenderloin medallions, baked salmon, and roast duckling, are around $20. Reservations are required by noon. If you don't want to drive the moose slalom back to Greenville, rooms are available for $59 s, $98 d, shared bath, including breakfast.

Fine Dining

Two inns open their dining rooms to nonguests by reservation.

The **Blair Hill Inn** (Lily Bay Rd., 207/695-

0224) serves a fixed-price ($59) five-course menu on Friday and Saturday evenings (6–8:30 P.M.) in the elegant dining room and adjacent glassed-in porch high on a hill with sweeping sunset views over Moosehead Lake. The inn has an indoor wood-burning grill, so meats and fish are grilled, and much of the produce comes from the inn's greenhouses and gardens. And almost everything is made from scratch—from sorbet and ice cream to breads to soups; special diets accommodated (vegan with notice). It's open mid-June–mid-October and Saturday nights in January and February.

Sharing much the same view, but serving in a more woodsy-themed dining room, is **The Lodge at Moosehead** (Lily Bay Rd.; call for days and hours, 207/695-4400). Choose from a three- or five-course menu ($40 or $55). Again, the fare is excellent.

INFORMATION AND SERVICES
Information

The regional information center is the Moosehead Lake Region Chamber of Commerce (Indian Hill, Rte. 15, P.O. Box 581, Greenville 04441, 207/695-2702, www.mooseheadarea.com), on a panoramic hilltop as you enter Greenville from the south. The modern office has public restrooms and a gift shop stocked with such moose-erie as T-shirts, moose magnets, bumper stickers, and boxer shorts. The chamber annually publishes a very helpful, free *Visitor's Guide*. The Greenville Downtown Merchants Association produces a map showing locations of shops, restaurants, and lodgings in the small downtown area.

DeLorme Mapping produces a widely available foldout *Map and Guide of Moosehead Lake,* with excellent detail and information on sightseeing and recreational pursuits.

The Shaw Public Library (N. Main St., Greenville, 207/695-3579, www.greenvilleme.com/library) has archives loaded with North Woods lore.

State agencies with offices in Greenville are the Maine Warden Service (MWS; 207/695-3756) and the Maine Forest Service (MFS; Lakeview St., Greenville, 207/695-3721). The

Greenville MWS office, with jurisdiction for all search-and-rescue missions of Maine's acreage, undertakes at least one search-and-rescue mission a week. The MFS, besides fire-spotting duty, also is responsible for a number of public campsites in the region.

Public Restrooms

In Greenville, the Indian Hill Trading Post has restrooms, as do the chamber of commerce office and the Moosehead Marine Museum, next to the *Katahdin* wharf. In Greenville Junction, there are restrooms at Junction Wharf; in Rockwood, there are restrooms at the public boat landing.

GETTING AROUND

Greenville flying services operating small pontoon- or ski-equipped planes act as the lifelines to remote North Woods sporting camps, campsites, rivers, lakes, and ponds inaccessible overland. In some cases, road access exists, but you'll jeopardize your vehicle, your innards, and maybe your life along the way. **Currier's Flying Service** (Pritham Ave., Rte. 6/15, Greenville Junction, 207/695-2778, www.curriersflyingservice.com) and **Jack's Air Service** (Pritham Ave., Greenville, 207/695-3020), based in downtown Greenville, provide on-demand charter service to remote locales. Both firms have flat hourly rates if you want to create your own itinerary.

You don't need a plane to get to Kineo, but you will need a boat. First, drive the 20 miles along Route 6/15 to Rockwood, where the lake is narrowest—about 4,000 feet across. The *Kineo Launch,* a sturdy transport vessel, has been operating since the spring of 1997. It runs back and forth continuously from the Rockwood public landing (on the village loop just off the highway) to Kineo. Just show up and climb aboard. Cost is $10 pp, round-trip. It is open Memorial Day–Labor Day.

Many of the **roads** in the Greenville area are unpaved; paper-company roads tend to be the best maintained, because access is essential for their huge log trucks and machinery. But others, especially roads leading to sporting camps, can become tank traps in spring—April–May—and after a heavy downpour. Before setting out during those times—especially if you don't have a 4WD vehicle—be sure to check on road conditions. Ask the chamber of commerce, the Maine Forest Service, the county sheriff, or the sporting camp owners.

Dover-Foxcroft Area

At the bottom of Piscataquis (Piss-CAT-uh-kwiss) County, Dover-Foxcroft is the county seat, hub for the surrounding towns of Milo, Brownville Junction, Sangerville, Guilford, Abbot, and Monson. Here's an area that's often overlooked, probably because Greenville, Moosehead Lake, and Baxter State Park are just up the road. But it's easy to spend a couple of exploring days here—notably for dramatic Gulf Hagas Reserve and Borestone Mountain Sanctuary, but also for a handful of out-of-the-way towns few visitors get to appreciate.

One town growing steadily in renown is Monson (pop. about 749), 20 miles northwest of Dover-Foxcroft and 15 miles south of Greenville. Incorporated in 1822, Monson has an old reputation and a new one. The old one comes from its slate quarries, first mined in the 1870s, which shipped slate around the nation for sinks, roof tiles, blackboards, and even urinals. A considerable Finnish community grew up here to work the quarries; their descendants still celebrate traditional holidays. Although the industry has declined, and only two companies still operate, Monson slate monuments adorn the gravesites of John F. Kennedy and Jacqueline Kennedy Onassis. You can still see an abandoned quarry pit on Pleasant Street, near Lake Hebron, on the western side of town.

Monson's current fame comes from Appalachian Trail through-hikers, whose energetic grapevine carries the word about the town's hospitality to the rugged outdoorsfolk nearing the end of their arduous trek from Springer Mountain, Georgia. The Monson stopover comes just before the AT leg known as the "100-Mile Wilderness," so it's a place to regroup, clean up, and rev up for the isolated week or 10 days ahead. It's also being reborn as a shopping town, with a handful of shops selling quality work by local artists and artisans and hodgepodge antiques.

Sangerville (pop. 1,324), incorporated in 1813, is the birthplace of the infamous Sir Harry Oakes, a colorful adventurer who acquired a fortune in Canadian gold mining. Murdered in bed in his Nassau (Bahamas) mansion in 1943, gazillionaire Oakes was interred in Dover-Foxcroft. His killer was never found. Also born in Sangerville was Sir Hiram Maxim, inventor of the Maxim gun. These days, it's the East Sangerville Grange that gets the attention, especially in winter, when there's entertainment accompanied by fantastic desserts.

Dexter and Corinna are actually in the Sebasticook Valley area, but since many visitors pass through them on Route 7, they're included here.

SIGHTS AND PARKS
◖ Monson

Most folks zip through this pretty little lakeside village, but Monson is worth a linger. A handful of antiques and artisans' shops lining Main Street and a good barbecue joint are reason enough to visit, but Monson is also a major stop on the Appalachian Trail, the last vestige of civilization before northbound hikers enter the infamous 100-Mile Wilderness on the way to Katahdin.

Low's Covered Bridge

In 1987, the raging Piscataquis River, swollen by spring rains, wiped out 130-foot-long Low's Covered Bridge, near Sangerville. Named after settler Robert Low, the original bridge was built in 1830 and replaced in 1843 and 1857. The current incarnation, a well-made replica, reopened in 1990 at a cost of $650,000. It's one of

© TOM NANGLE

The current Low's Covered Bridge was built after the 1857 bridge was lost to spring flooding.

only nine covered bridges now in Maine. Close to Route 16/6/15, the bridge is 3.7 miles east of Guilford and 4.5 miles west of Dover-Foxcroft. Across the street at the Covered Bridge Restaurant are photos of the 1987 flood.

Katahdin Iron Works

Only a lonely stone blast furnace and a charcoal kiln remain at Katahdin Iron Works, the site of a once-thriving 19th-century community where iron mining produced 2,000 tons of ore a year and steam trains brought tourists to the three-story Silver Lake House to "take the waters" at Katahdin Mineral Springs. Today most visitors drive down the unpaved 6.5 miles from Route 11 and stop just across the road, at the North Maine Woods **KI Checkpoint,** for hiking in Gulf Hagas Reserve. Entrance to the KI site (as it's known locally) is free.

Peaks-Kenny State Park

Get organized to arrive at Peaks-Kenny State Park (Sebec Lake Rd., Dover-Foxcroft, 207/564-2003, $4 adults, $1 ages 5–11, free for seniors and kids under 5) well before 11 A.M. on weekends in June, July, and August—after that, you may be turned away or have to wait. This particularly scenic park on 14-mile-long Sebec Lake has 50 picnic sites, a playground, lifeguard-staffed sand beach, nine miles of hiking trails, and 56 campsites. Canoe rentals are $3 an hour.

Lake Onawa

Four-mile-long Lake Onawa is the mountain-ringed setting for the charming hamlet of **Onawa,** once linked to civilization only by train. Then came the road, and passenger service ceased, leaving Onawa as a summer colony with a year-round population of three. A prime attraction is an incredible 126-foot-high wooden railroad trestle (pronounced "trussel" around here) that challenges even brave-hearted souls. Acrophobes, forget it. There's a walkway alongside, but it's still scary; don't attempt it on a windy day, and keep in mind that the tracks are still active. Bungee jumpers haven't yet discovered the trestle, but it *was* featured in one of Stephen King's films. During World War II, the trestle was protected by black security guards, among them Edward Brooke, the late U.S. senator from Massachusetts. The 1,400-foot-long trestle, officially the Ship Pond Stream Viaduct, soars over Ship Pond Stream, at the southern end of the lake, about 0.5 mile beyond the cluster of cottages. To reach Onawa, follow directions (see *Hiking* under *Recreation*) for Borestone Mountain, but turn right off Elliotsville Road at the Big Wilson Stream bridge and then take the next left onto Onawa Road. Continue about three miles to the settlement.

Historical Society Museums

Locals are proud of their history, and a handful of small museums are worthy of visits if you're a history buff.

The **Dexter Historical Society** (207/924-5721, www.dexterhistoricalsociety.com) operates three museums on its downtown Grist Mill campus (off Rte. 23, 10 A.M.–4 P.M. Mon.–Fri. and 1–4 P.M. Sat. mid-June–early Sept., 1–4 P.M. Mon.–Sat. Sept.): the one-room Carr Schoolhouse, the 1825 Miller's house, and the water-powered Grist Mill. The society's Abbott Museum headquarters (Rtes. 7/23, 10 A.M.–4 P.M. Mon.–Sat. late May–mid-Oct., noon–4 P.M. Wed., Thurs., Fri. and 10 A.M.–4 P.M. Sat. in winter) now doubles as a shop with works by local artisans. Admission is free, but donations are encouraged.

In downtown Monson, the old town hall has been reborn as the home of the **Monson Historical Society** (Main St., 207/876-3073, 10 A.M.–3 P.M. Sun. or by appt.), with a Scandinavian gift shop downstairs and exhibits upstairs (check out the birch shoes!).

RECREATION
Hiking
Owned and maintained by the Maine Audubon Society (www.maineaudubon.org), **Borestone Mountain Sanctuary** (Elliotsville Rd., Elliotsville Township, 207/631-4050, Oct.–May 207/781-2330, 8 A.M.–sunset May–Oct., $4 adults, $2 ages 6–18 and 60-plus) is a 1,600-acre preserve that provides a wonderful hiking

experience for all ages. The two-mile (each way), moderately difficult trail to the rocky, open summit delivers ample rewards at the top: full-circle views, including Lake Onawa below, and the mountains of the 100-Mile Wilderness. Foliage season is especially dramatic here. Allow 4–5 hours for the four-mile round-trip, including a halfway-up stop at the Sunrise Pond visitors center, with displays on local flora and fauna; don't miss it. No pets. From Route 6/16/15 at the northern edge of Monson, take the Elliotsville Road (partly unpaved) northeast 8.5 miles to the trailhead.

Sample the **Appalachian Trail** from the trailhead north of Monson on Route 6/15, just south of Spectacle Ponds.

For details on these or other hikes, consult *North Woods Walks* (Christopher Keene, 2003) or *Maine Mountain Guide* (AMC, ninth ed., 2005), available in local book stores.

Gulf Hagas Reserve

Hiking in and around Gulf Hagas Reserve, a spectacular 400-foot-high, 3.5-mile-long wooded, rocky gorge along the West Branch of the Pleasant River, requires registering first at the **KI Checkpoint** (207/965-8135) operated by North Maine Woods, the forest recreation-management association. (KI is short for Katahdin Ironworks.) The checkpoint is one of the entrances into the **KI Jo-Mary Multiple Use Forest,** a working forest of more than 200,000 acres. (Jo-Mary is the name of a legendary Indian chief.) The checkpoint is open 6 A.M.–9 P.M. (sometimes later on midsummer weekends) early May–Columbus Day. The staffers have maps of the reserve ($2) and KI Jo-Mary ($3); *do not* hike Gulf Hagas without the map. Access is $8 for nonresidents, $5 for Maine residents; seniors and kids under 15 are free. No bicycles, motorcycles, or ATVs can go beyond this point. Camping at one of the 60 scenic primitive sites in this area costs an extra $8 per night for residents, $10 for nonresidents, $4 for any senior. It's wise to call the checkpoint ahead of time to reserve one of the sites, which have outhouses, picnic tables, and fire rings. The policy is carry-in, carry-out. There's also a commercial campground here.

You'll need to drive about seven miles from the checkpoint to one of the two parking areas; remember that logging trucks have the right-of-way on this road. As you walk from your vehicle toward the gulf, you'll go through **The Hermitage,** a 35-acre Nature Conservancy preserve of old-growth pines. Gulf Hagas Reserve, a National Natural Landmark, is no cakewalk. Almost weekly, rangers have to rescue injured or lost hikers who underestimate the terrain. Ledges are narrow, with 100-foot drop-offs, and rain can make them perilous. Leave rambunctious children at home; the section beyond **Screw Auger Falls** is particularly dangerous for kids under 12. Wear waterproof hiking boots—you have to cross a stream to gain access to the reserve.

Caveats aside, the hike is fantastic—especially mid-September–early October, when the leaves are gorgeous and the bugs have retreated. Carry a compass and a flashlight and allow 6–8 hours for the 8.3-mile canyon circuit (although there are shortcuts if you tucker out before the end). Most hikers do the loop clockwise. North Maine Woods trails are blue-blazed; a spur of the AT is white-blazed. The trails are open mid-May–late October, but atypical weather can affect the schedule. The checkpoint is 11.5 miles northwest of Brownville Junction (6.5 miles northwest of Rte. 11).

Multiuse Trails

Stretching 27 miles, the **Newport/Dover-Foxcroft Rail Trail** is extremely popular, especially among horseback riders. From its Newport base, on the north side of Route 7, to its end near Fairview Street, in Dover-Foxcroft, the trail passes through towns and rural countryside, including farms, woods, and wetlands, and edges Sebasticook and Corundel Lakes, the east branch of the Sebasticook River, and the Piscataquis River.

The 10-mile Guilford Memorial River Walk edges the Piscataquis River from Guilford to Abbot. The trailheads are off Route 15 in

Guiford, east of the athletic fields, and at the Sangerville Station bridge, Route 23.

Canoeing and Kayaking

Lakes and rivers color much of the map blue in this region. If you have your own boat, quiet-water paddling options include the Sebec River, above Milo; the Piscataquis River, above the dam in Guilford; Lake Hebron, in Monson; and Branns Mill Pond, in Dover-Foxcroft.

Canoe and kayak rentals for three-mile-long Lake Hebron are available from **Lakeshore House** (9 Tenney Hill Rd./Rte. 5/15, Monson, 207/997-7069, www.lakeshore-house.com) for $15 generous half day, $25 full day.

Horseback Riding

Leaping Lippizanners! **Isaac Royal Farm** (849 Range Rd., Dover-Foxcroft, 207/564-3499, www.isaacroyalfarm.com) operates a renowned equestrian school (world-class instructors), holds dressage shows, and stages don't-miss, themed equestrian theatrical presentations, complete with music, choreography, and costumes. Check the website to see what's scheduled during your visit or to find out about lessons and camps.

Cross-Country Skiing

John Chase, a former U.S. biathlon team member, and Susan Fierce Chase operate **A Fierce Chase** (230 Elliotsville Rd., Monson, 207/997-3971, www.afiercechase.com), a 14-km center with primarily novice and intermediate groomed trails that are wide enough for freestyle and classic skiers to share. Ski and snowshoe rentals are available, as are lessons. In the off-season, the trails are open and free for hiking, walking, and running. Trails are open 9 A.M.–midnight daily. It's self-serve most weekdays, so call ahead if you need rentals or other info. Trail fee is $10 adult, $7 ages 9–18.

SHOPPING

Shopping isn't a big deal here, but you'll find a fine collection of arts-and-crafts shops in Monson and a growing number in Abbott.

Buy wonderful maple syrup, great dressings, and bison meat at **Breakneck Ridge Farm** (160 Mountain Rd., Blanchard Township, 207/997-3922, www.breakneckridgefarm.com). The farm has a few open houses each year; private tours are available year-round by reservation.

Fans of antiques and fine arts and handmade goods will find plenty in the shops along Monson's Main Street; most are open seasonally. **The Corner House** (207/997-3558) has a fine selection of locally made crafts, including quilts, jewelry, and pottery. In a side room is a model of Monson circa 1912 that's worth a look-see. You can also buy local guidebooks here. Just up the street is **Lake Hebron Artisans**, with an even more refined selection of fine crafts. Across the street, the **Hebron Gallery** (207/997-3950) is a small gallery showing fine art by local artists. **Violet's Everything Shop** (207/997-3945) delivers on its name with an eclectic selection of antiques and collectibles.

The **Maine Highlands Craft Guild** (207/564-0041, www.themainehighlands-guild.org) displays wares from its 20 or so talented members in the back of **Moosehead Manufacturing** (97 E. Main St., Dover-Foxcroft, 207/564-2600), which makes handsome wood furniture.

Angel Ginn sells her artwork along with the work of more than 20 other artisans at **Abbot Village Crafters** (Rte. 15, Abbot Village, 207/876-1087).

Bob Moore is the king of maple in these parts. At **Bob's Sugar House** (252 E. Main St./Rte. 15, Dover-Foxcroft, 207/564-2145, www.mainemaplesyrup.com), you'll find pure Maine maple syrup, maple butter, maple cream, maple popcorn, maple barbecue seasoning, and the list goes on and on.

ENTERTAINMENT AND EVENTS

October–May, the East Sangerville Grange Hall hosts its monthly, Saturday night **Winter Coffee House Series** ($12 adm., $2 per dessert), where the entertainment is fab and the desserts are beyond amazing, as local cooks vie to outdo each other.

Live music, community theater, movies, and other entertainment are regularly scheduled at the **Center Theatre for the Performing Arts** (Main St., Dover-Foxcroft, 207/564-8377, www.centertheatre.org), which opened in 2006 in a nicely renovated 300-seat movie theater. The Saturday Night Concert Series is presented on the third Saturday of the month June–December. Ask about the local doctor who was married on stage during a presentation by the Maine Hysterical Society, complete with reception line during intermission.

The last Saturday in April, the early-season **Piscataquis River Canoe Race** covers eight miles of mostly flat water between Guilford and Dover-Foxcroft. An hour-long, family-oriented race goes under Low's Covered Bridge. Starting time is 11 A.M., next to the Guilford Industries factory.

The **Piscataquis Valley Fair** takes place the fourth weekend in August. A family-oriented traditional county fair, it features agricultural exhibits, a pig scramble, a home-made ice-cream parlor, fireworks, and a carnival. It's at the Piscataquis Valley Fairgrounds, Fairview Avenue (just south of Rte. 6/15, east side of town), in Dover-Foxcroft.

Throughout the summer, Finn dances take place on Saturday nights at the **Finnish Farmers Club.** Look for the small sign hanging in front of the white frame building just south of the village on the west side of Route 6/15. Expect accordion music, dancing, perhaps traditional costumes, coffee, and dessert.

A decent community theater performs in summer at the **Wayside Theater** in North Dexter.

Snowy February brings the **Maine Highlands Sled Dog Championships.**

The Belvin family's **The Junction General Store and Entertainment Park** (197 Davis St./Rte. 11, Brownville Junction, 207/965-8876, www.thejunctiongeneral.com) is entertainment central in these parts. It sponsors a summer concert series with tribute concerts to bands such as Aerosmith, the Eagles, and others; has a drive-in theater; and operates a café serving big breakfasts, lunch, and ice cream.

Find out what's going on during your visit at www.deepinthemainewoods.org, an e-calendar with all sorts of local listings.

ACCOMMODATIONS
Bed-and-Breakfasts

On a prominent hilltop and surrounded by gardens, the dark-red-painted **⬛ Guilford Bed and Breakfast** (Elm St., Rte. 6/15/16, Guilford, 207/876-3477, www.guilfordbandb.com, $80–115), built by a woolen mill owner as a wedding gift for his daughter, exudes history, wealth, and prominence of a bygone era. A big screened porch wraps around the Queen Anne–style Victorian's front, leading into the formal hall and spacious public rooms, all filled with comfortable antiques. Four rooms on the second floor have private baths (two detached) and two on the third floor share one bath. Innkeepers Isobel and Harland Young, from Ohio, were long-time guests before buying the inn in 2006. They speak French.

Just beyond the Dover-Foxcroft area, but close enough, the **Brewster Inn** (37 Zion's Hill Rd., Dexter, 207/924-3130, www.brewster inn.com) is an attractive 19-room National Historic Register mansion designed by John Calvin Stevens and once owned by Maine Governor Ralph Brewster. The eight rooms and two suites ($59–129 d) all have phones, air-conditioning, TV, and stories to tell. The knotty-pine Games Room was the governor's private hideout, and guess who once slept in the Truman Room? In the aptly named Honeymoon Suite are a stained-glass window, four-poster bed, fireplace, and double whirlpool. Breakfast is a generous buffet. New English innkeepers Mark and Judith Stephens, who arrived in 2007, have big plans, including remodeling all rooms over the next few years (they need it) and bringing back the lovely gardens their mid-20th-century splendor. Two additional two-bedroom suites with full kitchens are in the farmhouse across the street ($100, two-night minimum). No pets; well-behaved children are welcome.

Leanne Pooler's **Down Home B&B** (51 Elm St., Milo, 207/943-5167 or 888/909-3422, www.downhomebnb.com) is a well-tended

Victorian on a quiet street, with three rooms sharing one bath ($65 d) and two with private baths ($75 d). Children are welcomed with a huge yard and a playground. Homemade quilts cover the beds. A big-screen TV dominates the comfy front parlor. Free Wi-Fi; huge breakfasts.

Neither hostel nor B&B, Jack and Rebekah Santagata's **Lakeshore House** (9 Tenney Hill Rd./Rte. 5/15, Monson, 207/997-7069, www .lakeshore-house.com) is a continually evolving lakeside business housing a launderette, guest rooms, pub, and canoe and kayak rentals on Lake Hebron. Options vary from from a bunk in a shared room for $25 to a lakeview room with two double beds for $80. All guests share two baths, a living room, and kitchenette. All rooms have TV.

Hostel

Headquarters for Appalachian Trail through-hikers, a home-away-from-home since 1977, is the legendary **Shaw's Boarding Home** (Pleasant St., Monson, 207/997-3597, www .shawslodging.com). To weary hikers, this welcoming, no-frills operation feels like the Hyatt Regency. Short-haul hikers are also welcome, as are snowmobilers in winter; couch potatoes will feel totally out of place. The home can accommodate nearly three dozen guests in varied arrangements—private rooms in the main house ($32 s, $54 d), bunkhouse beds ($22 pp), tent site ($10). A lumberjack-quality breakfast is $6.50 or all you can eat for $8.50. For small fees, shuttle and mail-drop service and laundry facilities are available; parking for short-haulers is $1 a day.

Campgrounds

Within the boundaries of the KI Jo-Mary Multiple Use Forest is a single commercial campground, the **Jo-Mary Lake Campground** (Upper Jo-Mary Lake, TB R10 WELS, mailing address P.O. Box 329, Millinocket 04462, 207/723-8117 or 800/494-0031, www.camp maine.com/jo-mary), on the southern shore of five-mile-long Upper Jo-Mary Lake. Despite being remote, the campground has 60 sites, flush toilets, hot showers, laundry facilities, a snack

bar, plenty of play space for kids, and a sandy beach. Sites are about $17 a night per family. There's a Wednesday night beanhole bean supper (beans baked underground) July–August. The campground, open mid-May–late September, is 15 miles southwest of Millinocket and 20 miles north of Brownville. From Brownville Junction, take Route 11 northwest about 15 miles, turn left onto an unpaved road, and stop at the Jo-Mary Checkpoint. After paying the user fee ($10/day for nonresidents, $8 for Maine residents; seniors and kids under 15 are free), continue six miles northwest to the campground.

Peaks-Kenny State Park (Sebec Lake Rd., Dover-Foxcroft, 207/564-2003) has 56 campsites. On weekends July–August, reservations are essential (two-night minimum; call 207/287-3824, using MasterCard or Visa). Nonresident camping fees are $20 per site per night; resident fees are $15 per site per night plus the reservation fee of $2 per site per night; no hookups. Leashed pets are allowed.

FOOD
Guilford

A popular local favorite, the family-friendly **The Covered Bridge Restaurant** (Rte. 15, Guilford, 207/564-2204, www.coveredbridge maine.com) is just across the street from Low's Covered Bridge, midway between Dover-Foxcroft and Guilford. The pleasant dining room has a full bar, and service is friendly and efficient. Dinner entrées emphasizing hearty home cooking run $6–16; the homemade lasagna is excellent. Breakfast is served only on weekends. Hours are 7 A.M.–7 P.M. Tuesday–Thursday and Sunday, 7 A.M.–8 P.M. Friday and Saturday in season. Also on the premises is a no-frills motel, where rooms go for $60 d.

Newer on the scene is **The Black Forest Restaurant and Biergarten** (42 Hudson Ave., Guilford, 207/876-2900), a taste of Bavaria just outside downtown Guilford. Don't let the exterior of the former garage building deter you; inside it's the real thing. Prices range $9–17; the Black Forest sampler platter is $15.

Just north of Guilford is the **Abbott Bakery** (Rte. 6/15, Abbott Village, 207/876-4243,

4:30 A.M.–9 P.M. daily), home of the "Skidder Doughnut," and the locals' choice for homemade doughnuts, breads, sweets, and sandwiches.

Dover-Foxcroft

Good home cooking with a few surprises packs **The Nor'easter Restaurant** (44 North St., Dover-Foxcroft, 207/564-2122, 11 A.M.–8 P.M. Sat.–Thurs., to 9 P.M. Fri.), a congenial place with country-style decor and seating both at the counter and tables. The service is warm and attentive. Prices range $4–16.

Named after Dover-Foxcroft's first settler, **Abel Blood's** (100 Main St., Dover-Foxcroft, 207/564-3177, 11 A.M.–2 P.M. Mon.–Tues., 11 A.M.–9 P.M. Wed.–Thurs., to 10 P.M. Fri., 4–10 P.M. Sat.) serves the region's best steaks as well as plenty of other choices, from quesadillas, burgers, and grilled pizzas to apricot-glazed salmon. Most entrées are available in small and regular sizes. Vegetarian and vegan options are available as are more than 50 beers. Prices are in the $7–13 range.

The favorite local farm market is **Stutzman's** (891 Doughty Hill Rd., 207/564-8596), on the back road between Sangerville and Dover-Foxcroft. Stock up on fresh produce and baked goodies and pick your own berries, peas, and so on in season.

Local caterer Tom Spencer operates a **takeout stand** in the small park adjacent to the chamber of commerce in Dover-Foxcroft. The chili is the area's best. Pick up a bowl and head for a riverside picnic table.

Monson

Mmmm, mmmm. Craving barbecue? You've come to the right place. Mike and Kim Witham's ☕ **Spring Creek Bar-B-Q** (Rte. 15, Monson, 207/997-7025) is the real thing. Prices and portions are geared to AT hikers, so you won't go hungry or poor. Tables inside and outside. No liquor license, no credit cards. It's open 10 A.M.–8 P.M. (or the food's gone) Thursday–Sunday all year, and other times when the porch light is on.

Reasonably priced pub fare is served at the **Lakeshore House** (9 Tenney Hill Rd., Rte.

5/15, Monson, 207/997-7069, www.lakeshore-house.com, 4–11 P.M. or so Tues.–Thurs., noon–midnight Fri. and Sat., noon–8 P.M. Sun.; kitchen closes at 9 P.M.), a casual spot overlooking Lake Hebron, with seating indoors and out. Salads, sandwiches, pizza, fried haddock, and daily specials provide plenty of choices, with most in the $7–12 range.

Corinna

Backing up to the East Branch of the Sebasticook River is the **Village Square** (Corinna Sq., Stetson Rd., Corinna, 207/278-2777, 7 A.M.–7 P.M. Mon.–Sat., to 2 P.M. Sun.), a stone's throw east of Route 11. At this combo bakery (peanut butter whoopie pies!), restaurant, and general store, the aroma of fresh baked breads greets you at the door. The pleasant dining area has a retro decor. Dine in or take out.

Milo

A bright spot downtown is **Valerie Jean's: An American Bistro** (26 Main St., Milo, 207/943-7470, 11 A.M.–2 P.M. and 5 P.M.–close Thurs.–Sun.), which opened in 2005 and quickly earned a reputation for excellent food with creative flair, with dinner entrées such as lobster risotto and roasted half duckling. The small restaurant has a side deck with tables overlooking the Sebec River.

INFORMATION AND SERVICES

Based in a riverside log cabin, the Southern Piscataquis County Chamber of Commerce (100 South St., Rte. 7, P.O. Box 376, Dover-Foxcroft 04426, 207/564-7533, www.spccc .org) is open 9 A.M.–4 P.M. daily June–August; weekdays only other months.

The Sebasticook Valley Chamber (Wal-mart Plaza, Rte. 2, Palmyra, 207/368-4698, www .ourchamber.org) has info on Corinna, Dexter, and other area towns.

For information about Gulf Hagas Reserve and the KI Jo-Mary Multiple Use Forest, contact North Maine Woods (P.O. Box 421, Ashland 04732, 207/435-6213, www.north mainewoods.org).

Bangor Area

Lumber Capital of the World in the 19th century, Bangor (BANG-gore), with a population of 31,500, is still northern Maine's magnet for commerce and culture—the big city for the northern three-quarters of the state. Chief draws now in this region are the Bangor Mall (and surrounding shops and minimalls), Bangor International Airport, and the academic, athletic, and artistic activities of the flagship University of Maine campus, in Orono, a few miles northeast.

The county seat for Penobscot County, downtown Bangor is awakening from a 1960s slump typical of many urban areas, and today you can stroll alongside Kenduskeag Stream, duck into shops and restaurants, and spend a comfortable night in the city's heart. The 2002–2004 waterfront National Folk Festivals brought excitement and major crowds to the city and dusted off its sense of possibility, and Bangor has continued the three-day late-August event as the American Folk Festival.

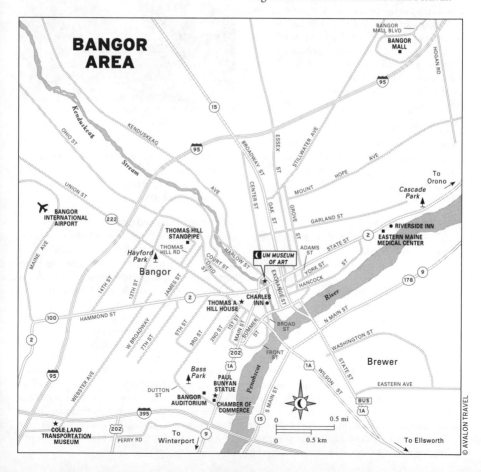

Bangor incorporated in 1791, but when explorer Samuel de Champlain landed here in 1604 (an event commemorated by a plaque downtown, next to Kenduskeag Stream), the Queen City bore the Native American name of Kenduskeag, meaning "eel-catching place."

In the late 19th century, when the lumber trade moved westward, smaller industries moved into greater Bangor to take up the slack, but a disastrous fire on April 30, 1911, leveled 55 acres of Bangor's commercial and residential neighborhoods, retarding progress for several decades.

Bangor highlights include a giant statue of legendary lumberjack Paul Bunyan and fine specimens of Victorian, Italianate, Queen Anne, and Greek Revival architecture—and who knows, you might see legendary author Stephen King in your travels. Part of what King enjoys about Bangor is that locals are used to him and accord him "normal-person" treatment.

Bangor claims legendary lumberjack Paul Bunyan as a native son.

SIGHTS

Downtown Bangor lends itself to walking, especially if hills don't intimidate you. A free, self-guided walking tour map is available at the **Bangor Historical Society** (25 Broad St., Bangor, 207/942-1900).

The Standpipe

A distinctive west-side landmark is the National Historic Register Thomas Hill Standpipe, a squat 1897 water tower on one of the city's highest points. It's open to the public about four times each year, which allows visitors access to the great view from the observation platform. For tour information, call the Bangor Water District (207/947-4516, www.bangorwater.org).

Paul Bunyan Statue

On Main Street, next to the chamber of commerce office and across from the Holiday Inn, stands a 31-foot-high statue of the mythical lumberjack Paul Bunyan, allegedly born in Bangor on February 12, 1834. Weighing 3,200 pounds, the colorful statue was erected in 1959 during the city's 125th anniversary. Inside the base is a time capsule due to be opened in 2084. Kids can run and play in adjacent **Paul Bunyan Park.**

Stephen King-dom

Maine native and naturalized hometown boy, horror honcho Stephen King is anything but a myth. Born in Portland, he's lived in Bangor since 1980, and you may spot him around town (especially at baseball and basketball games). His rambling mansion on West Broadway looks like a set from one of the movies based on his novels and stories—complete with a wrought-iron front gate and fence festooned with iron bats and cobwebs. Heed the No Trespassing sign; the best-selling author has had his share of odd encounters with off-the-wall devotees, not to mention his 1999 encounter with an out-of-control minivan. These days, even though he's back at work, it's best to keep up with him via his website (www.stephenking.com).

© TOM NANGLE

The Greater Bangor Convention and Visitors Bureau offers **Tommyknockers and More** bus tours about once a month. Advance registration and payment is required (800/916-6673, www.bangorcvb.org), and space is limited.

Best local sources for all things King are **Betts Bookstore** (584 Hammond St., Bangor, 207/947-7052, www.bettsbooks.com) and **BookMarc's** (78 Harlow St., Bangor, 207/942-3206), which both specialize in his works and collectibles.

Bangor Museum and Center for History

In downtown Bangor, near the Museum of Art and the Discovery Museum, the **Bangor Historical Society** (25 Broad St., Bangor, 207/942-1900, www.bangorhistorical.org, $5 adults, $4 seniors, kids free) offers a full schedule of tours, lectures, concerts, special events, and exhibits. The collection includes more than 10,000 images, historic clothing, and Civil War artifacts. Admission is free. Hours are 10 A.M.–4 P.M. Tuesday–Friday, noon–4 P.M. Saturday. You can buy Maine arts and crafts in the museum's Minerva Museum Store as well as books from a very comprehensive about-Bangor collection. The society also owns and manages the Greek Revival **Thomas A. Hill House** (159 Union St., Bangor, 207/942-1900). Built by a wealthy attorney in 1836, and listed on the National Register of Historic Places, the handsome brick building on the corner of High Street has been restored to Victorian elegance, with period furnishings, Maine paintings, and special exhibits. Tours are available noon–3 P.M. Tuesday–Friday, by appointment only.

◖ University of Maine Museum of Art

Bangor scored a coup when it lured UMMA (Norumbega Hall, 40 Harlow St., Bangor, 207/561-3350, www.umma.umaine.edu, 9 A.M.–5 P.M. Mon.–Sat., $3 pp) downtown. Winslow Homer, Goya, Kollwitz, and Picasso are just four of the painters in the collection, which includes more than 6,500 original works.

It's particularly strong in American, mid-20th century works on paper and Maine art.

Maine Discovery Museum

Opened in January 2001, after several years of planning, fund-raising, and construction, the Maine Discovery Museum (74 Main St., Bangor, 207/262-7200, www.mainediscovery museum.org, 9:30 A.M.–5 P.M. Tues.–Sat., noon–5 P.M. Sun., noon–5 P.M. Mon. in summer, $6.50 pp) occupies more than 22,000 square feet on three floors of the former Freese's Department Store. Seven permanent interactive exhibit areas feature nature, geography, art, science, anatomy, Maine children's literature, and music. It all awaits in this multimillion-dollar facility—the largest children's museum north of Boston. Kids can operate pulleys, open locks and dams, create a painting or sculpture, and explore a beaver dam from the underside. Most exciting are the global adventures in a Peruvian classroom, a Ghanaian market, and an Australian outback campsite. Special programs are scheduled for children and families throughout the year, and kids will like the museum store, called "Too Much Fun!"

Air and Fire Museums

On the grounds of Bangor International Airport, the **Maine Air Museum** is a fledgling museum operated by the Maine Aviation Historical Society (P.O. Box 2641, Bangor 04401, 877/280-6247 in Maine, www.maineair museum.org) and dedicated to the history of Maine aviation. Call for hours.

Kids get a kick out of the fire-fighting artifacts and fire trucks at the **Hose 5 Fire Museum** (247 State St., Bangor, 207/945-3229, free), in an 1897 fire station. Call for hours.

Cole Land Transportation Museum

Children *love* the Cole Land Transportation Museum (405 Perry Rd., P.O. Box 1166, Bangor 04401, 207/990-3600, www.colemuseum.org, 9 A.M.–5 P.M. daily May–mid-Nov., $6 adults, $4 seniors, free 19 and under), a sprawling facility founded by Bangor trucking magnate

Galen Cole. More than 200 19th- and 20th-century vehicles—just about anything that has ever rolled across Maine's landscape—fill the museum. Besides vintage cars, there are fire engines, tractors, logging vehicles, baby carriages, even a replica railroad station. And this being Maine, the museum believes it owns the largest collection of snow-removal equipment in America. A gift shop stocks transportation-related items. Outside are picnic tables and a covered bridge to walk over and under. The museum is near the junction of I-95 and I-395.

Winterport

In Waldo County, 12 miles downriver from Bangor, is Winterport, a pretty little sleeper of a town tucked along the Penobscot River. It earned its name as the limit of winter navigation for Bangor's lumber trade; ice blocked shipping traffic from proceeding farther upriver. The National Register **Winterport Historic District** includes splendid 19th-century Greek Revival homes and commercial buildings on Route 1A and the short side streets descending to the river. The **Winterport Winery** (279 S. Main St., Winterport, 207/223-4500, www.winterportwinery .com) has a tasting room for its fruit wines and a gallery for exhibiting local artists.

PARKS AND PRESERVES
Mt. Hope Cemetery

In a state where burial grounds usually command views to die for, the standout is Mount Hope (207/945-6589, www.mthopebgr.com, 7:30 A.M.–7:30 P.M. daily Apr. 1–Nov. 1, to 4 P.M. Nov. 1–Apr. 1), established in 1834, consecrated in 1836, and easily the state's loveliest. Among the prominent Mainers interred here is Civil War–era U.S. Vice President Hannibal Hamlin. Inspired by the design of Mt. Auburn Cemetery in Cambridge, Massachusetts, 264-acre Mount Hope is more park than cemetery—with gardens, ponds, bridges, paved paths, lots of greenery, a few picnic tables, and wandering deer. In-line skaters consider it paradise. The entrance to the green-fenced cemetery is at 1048 State Street (Rte. 2), about

0.25 mile east of Hogan Road. Cemetery tours are offered by the Bangor Historical Society (207/942-1900, www.bangormuseum.com, $5 adult, $4 senior, $2 students, under 12 free). Call or check the website for the schedule.

Fields Pond Audubon Center

South of Bangor/Brewer (although it feels as if you're heading east) is the Maine Audubon Society's Fields Pond Audubon Center (216 Fields Pond Rd., Holden, 207/989-2591). About four miles of footpaths wind through 192 acres of woods, fields, marshes, and lakeshore, all open sunrise–sunset daily year-round. (Wear waterproof shoes or boots; parts of the trail can be wet.) Canoe rentals are available to explore the pond. Headquarters is the L. Robert Rolde Nature Center (10 A.M.–5 P.M. Thurs.–Sat. and 1–5 P.M. Sun.), where you can pick up brochures and maps. A full schedule of programs occurs here throughout the year, including lectures, nature walks, slide talks, even a nature-book discussion group. Cost averages $4–5 per person. A nature store carries books, cards, and gifts.

Bangor City Forest and Orono Bog

Here's a double treat that's rich in flora and fauna.

About nine miles of trails and more than four miles of roads meander through this 650-acre working forest (http://cityforest.bangorinfo.com). It's a great place for a walk or bike ride and for wildlife-spotting.

Accessible through the Bangor City Forest, the mile-long **Orono Bog Boardwalk** (Tripp Dr., Bangor, 207/581-2850, www.oronobog walk.com), a National Natural Landmark, is wheelchair-accessible, has a restroom, benches every 200 feet, and interpretative signage. A series of guided nature walks are offered 9 A.M.–11 A.M. Saturday early June–late September. Most are free; reservations are recommended (207/989-2591). Hours are 7 A.M.–7 P.M. summer–August, 8 A.M.–5 P.M. September–November.

The forest and bog parking area are on Tripp Road, off Stillwater Avenue, about midway between the Bangor Mall and Kelly Road. Leashed pets are allowed in the forest, but not the bog.

RECREATION
Golf
Considered a standout among public courses, the **Bangor Municipal Golf Course** (280 Webster Ave., Bangor, 207/941-0232) has 18 holes dating from 1964 and a newer (and tougher) nine holes. Stretching over both sides of Webster Avenue, the course is also on the Bangor Airport flight path; don't flinch when a jet screams overhead. Tee times are needed for the newer nine, and on weekends for the 18, but plan to arrive early in midsummer (the course opens at 7 A.M.). Also on-site are a driving range and two practice greens.

Twelve miles southeast of Bangor, across from the Lucerne Inn, the nine-hole **Lucerne-in-Maine Golf Course** (Rte. 1A, Dedham, 207/843-6282), is worth a visit just for the spectacular view.

Bicycling
Bangor-area bike shops sponsor road and off-road group rides, most briskly paced. The **Bicycle Coalition of Maine** (www.bikemaine.org) maintains an online calendar listing rides by date and location.

For rentals, try **Ski Rack Sports** (24 Longview Dr., Bangor, 207/945-6474). Cost is $15–20 a day.

Hiking
In Dedham, 12 miles southeast of Bangor, a favorite hike climbs **Bald Mountain** (sometimes called Dedham Bald Mountain) to the disused fire tower on the bald summit. On a clear day, climb the tower for panoramic views to both Katahdin and Cadillac Mountain. Allow about two hours round-trip if you plan to picnic and climb the tower. To reach the trailhead from downtown Bangor, take Rte. 1A (Wilson St.) about 8.5 miles from the Penobscot River bridge to the Rte. 46 junction. Just beyond the junction, turn right onto Upper Dedham Rd. Go about 2.5 miles and, just after a stream, bear left

onto Dedham Rd. Continue about 3.5 miles to the parking area (on left). The trail leads up from here, over a few steep, ledgy spots. It's well worth the climb, especially during fall-foliage season.

Cruise
Explore the Penobscot on a narrated one-hour scenic cruise or 1.5-hour sunset cruise with **Bangor Harbor Cruises** (207/941-0952 or 207/546-2927, www.bangorharborcruises.com, $20–25 adult, $18–22 senior, $15–18 under 12) aboard the *Patience,* a replica 19th-century steam ferry. Some evening cruises have live music.

ENTERTAINMENT
More than a century ago, when cabin-feverish lumberjacks roared into Bangor for R&R, they were apt to patronize Fan Jones's "establishment" on Harlow Street. Adult entertainment is still available in the city, but so is higher-brow stuff. That said, nights in Bangor are pretty quiet for a city.

Bangor Symphony Orchestra (BSO)
Founded in 1896, Maine's BSO (207/942-5555 or 800/639-3221, www.bangorsymphony.com) has an enviable reputation as one of the country's oldest and best community orchestras. During the regular season, September–May, monthly concerts are presented weekends at the Maine Center for the Arts in Orono. The orchestra occasionally performs in summer, too.

Penobscot Theatre Company
Bangor's professional theater company, Penobscot Theatre (131 Main St., Bangor, 207/942-3333, www.penobscottheatre.org) performs classic and contemporary comedies and dramas, including the New Play Festival, September–early June in the 1920 Bangor Opera House. Ticket range is $12–24.

Summer Concerts
On Tuesday evenings, from late spring through summer, the **Bangor Band** performs free concerts in the Paul Bunyan Park

grandstand on Main Street, near the Bangor Auditorium.

Every Thursday evening in June and July, the **Cool Sounds of Summer** free outdoor concerts are held in Riverfront Park. Bangor Library also sponsors a summer concert series on its lawn.

FESTIVALS AND EVENTS

In April (usually the third Saturday), the **Kenduskeag Stream Canoe Race** is an annual (since 1969) 16.5-mile spring-runoff race sponsored by Bangor Parks and Recreation (207/992-4490). It draws upward of 700 canoes and thousands of spectators and finishes in downtown Bangor. The best location for spotting action is Six Mile Falls—take Broadway (Rte. 15) about six miles northwest of downtown.

Late July–early August, the **Bangor State Fair,** held in Bass Park, is a huge 10-day affair with agricultural and crafts exhibits, a carnival, fireworks, sinful food, and big-name live music. This is a big deal and attracts thousands from all over northern Maine.

Five stages of continuous music and dance by more than two dozen performing groups representing various cultures along with dozens of artisans, many demonstrating their crafts, bring in tens of thousands for the annual and free three-day **American Folk Festival** (207/992-2630, www.americanfolk festival.com), held on the Bangor waterfront. It's a fabulous event and one worth making an extra effort to attend.

SHOPPING
Antiques and More

Browse, eat, sip, and buy at the **Antique Marketplace and Cafe** (65 Maine St., Bangor, 207/941-2111 or 877/941-2111, www.antique marketplacecafe.com). Filling two floors are a wide range of antiques, along with used books and a café, serving breakfast and lunch daily.

Books

If you need a good read, Bangor's got plenty of sources.

If you can't decide between new or used, head to **BookMarc's Bookstore and Cafe** (78 Harlow St., Bangor, 207/942-3206), where you can peruse both and grab a cuppa joe. Just around the corner is **Lippincott Books** (36 Central St., Bangor, 207/942-4398), a longtime antiquarian-book resource, with more than 30,000 old and rare books. And practically next door is **Sarah's Used and Rare Books** (32 Central St., Bangor, 207/992-2080), where a fine collection of 5,000 mostly out-of-print hardcovers fill the second-floor.

Also in downtown Bangor is **Pro Libris** (10 3rd St., Bangor, 207/942-3019), billing itself as a "readers' paradise." With 30,000 used paperbacks and hardcovers, that's just about right.

New in town in the old-books department is a branch of island-based **Frenchboro Books, Art and Antiques** (46 Columbia St.), where in addition to books you'll find American furniture and decorative accessories, including more than 150 pairs of bookends.

Betts Bookstore (584 Hammond St., Bangor 04401, 207/947-7052, www.bettsbooks .com), in business since 1938, specializes in Stephen King. All of his books are here (and available by mail), including autographed copies and limited editions, plus King posters, T-shirts, magazines, and stickers. King groupies will love this place.

Gifts and Clothing

Believe it when **The Grasshopper Shop** (1 W. Market Sq., Bangor, 207/945-3132) claims to be the state's largest boutique—it sprawls over two floors in downtown Bangor.

Outdoor Market

Nearly 40 vendors, including artisans, farmers, and bakers, sell their products along the Kenduskeg Stream, behind Pickering Square Garage, on Thursday evenings mid-June–early August. It complements the Cool Sounds concert series in Pickering Square (www .downtownbangor.com).

ACCOMMODATIONS

New ownership has improved the **Charles Inn at West Market Square** (20 Broad St.,

Bangor, 207/992-2820, www.thecharlesinn .com, $89–159), a National Historic Register hostelry in downtown Bangor that doubles as an art gallery. Built in 1873, the four-story hotel now has air-conditioning and Wi-Fi, but frankly, it needs a major refurbishment. Still, you can't beat the walk-to-everything location. Rates include an expanded continental breakfast.

Many of the guests at the **Riverside Inn** (495 State St., Bangor, 207/973-4100 or 800/252-4044, www.riversidebangor.org, $79–129) have business at Eastern Maine Medical Center, next door, but the inn is open to everyone (as is the hospital's 24-hour cafeteria). Inn rooms—56 total, including 15 suites—are several notches above generic motel decor. Request one overlooking the Penobscot River; avoid rooms overlooking the hospital parking lot. Phones, air-conditioning, cable TV, and continental breakfast are all included; a coin-op laundry is available. Some pets allowed ($5).

Six miles north of downtown is **Nonesuch Farm Bed and Breakfast** (59 Hudson Rd., Bangor, 207/942-3631, www.bangorsfirst bedandbreakfast.com, $90–127), Jim and Mary Louis Davitt's 1865 farmhouse and working farm. Although much restoration and renovation has occurred, many of the original fixtures remain. Some of the welcome additions are an enclosed sunporch and an outdoor hot tub, as well as Wi-Fi and air-conditioning. Trails lace the property, and Six Mile Falls, a class IV drop, is a lure for expert paddlers. Laundry is available with notice. Children welcome. Rates include full breakfast June–November, continental breakfast off-season. No pets, because of farm animals on-site.

Route 1A runs between Winterport and Bangor, then turns southeast and returns to the coast at Ellsworth. Twelve miles southeast of Bangor (and 25 miles northwest of Ellsworth) is **The Lucerne Inn** (Bar Harbor Rd., Rte. 1A, RR 3, Box 540, Dedham, 207/843-5123 or 800/325-5123, www.lucerneinn.com, $99–199), a retrofitted early-19th-century stagecoach hostelry on a 10-acre hilltop overlooking Phillips Lake and the hills beyond. Despite the highway out front, noise is no problem in the antiques-

filled, rear-facing rooms (air-conditioning, phones, TV, and fireplaces). Rates include continental breakfast. Outside there's a pool. No pets. Also on-site is a dining room serving dinner and a popular Sunday brunch.

FOOD
Local Flavors

A downtown landmark since 1978, **Bagel Central** (33 Central St., Bangor, 207/947-1654, 6 A.M.–6 P.M. Mon.–Thurs., 6 A.M.–5:30 P.M. Fri., 6 A.M.–2 P.M. Sun.) is a cheerful spot to meet, greet, and grab some really good handmade bagels (try the blueberry), great deli sandwiches, soups, and more. It's operated under Orthodox rabbinical supervision.

A few doors down, **Friars Bakehouse** (21 Central St., Bangor, 207/947-3770) makes scrumptious baked goods at breakfast time—everything is made on the premises—and sandwiches for lunch, with daily specials. The breads are fabulous. Days and hours of operation change frequently—and it often sells out early; call or follow the advice on the door: If the light's on, it's open.

A branch of perennial Bar Harbor favorite **Epi Pizza and Subs** (128 Main St., Bangor, 207/942-3888, 10:30 A.M.–4 P.M. Mon.–Sat.) is across from the Opera House.

For New York–style, thin-crust pizza, no one does it better than **Finelli** (213 Ohio St., Bangor, 207/947-0900, 11 A.M.–9 P.M. daily). Even better, it delivers!

The menu changes daily at **Montes International Catering** (72 Columbia St., Bangor, 207/945-3990, www.downtownme .com/montes, 9 A.M.–5:30 P.M. Mon.–Fri.), but you can count on a mouthwatering selection of soups, salads, sandwiches, and perhaps quesadillas, fajitas, and pizza. After 3:30 P.M., you can even pick up gourmet dinners to go. The daily menu is posted online.

Convenient to I-95 Exit 180, **Dysart's** (Coldbrook Rd., Hermon, 207/942-4878, www.dysarts.com) is a truckers' destination resort—you can grab some grub, shower, shop, phone home, play video games, fuel up, and even sneak a bit of shut-eye. For real flavor, opt for the truckers' dining room, where the music is country and dozens of bleary-eyed drivers have reached the end of their transcontinental treks. If you're here with a carload, order an 18-Wheeler—18 scoops of ice cream with a collection of toppings. No question, Dysart's is unique, and it's open 24 hours every day all year.

Ethnic Fare

Everything is prepared to order at **Bahaar Pakistani Restaurant** (23 Hammond St., Bangor, 207/945-5979, www.bahaarpakistani .com, 11 A.M.–9 P.M. Tues.–Sat.). Vegetarians find lots of options among the 70-plus appetizers, *biryanis,* and curries, which you can order mild, hotter, and hottest. Most choices are around $10. Takeout available; full liquor license. Reservations are advisable weekend nights. Be advised that the restaurant doesn't stick to its promised hours.

Three blocks from Bahaar is **Taste of India** (68 Main St., Bangor, 207/945-6865, 11:30 A.M.–9 P.M. Mon.–Sat., 2–9 P.M. Sun.), an enduring South Asian favorite. Entrées range $7–12, but a lunch buffet is offered until 2 P.M. Wednesday–Friday for $7. Beer and wine only.

Long before sushi was mainstream, **Ichiban** (226 Union St., at 3rd St., Bangor, 207/262-9308, 11 A.M.–2:30 P.M. and 4:30–9 P.M. Mon.–Sat., to 10 P.M. Thurs.–Sat., 11 A.M.–9 P.M. Sun.) had introduced metro Bangor to it, along with a full menu of other Japanese specialties.

Casual Dining

A prime spot for view-and-brew is the riverfront **Sea Dog Brewing Co.** (26 Front St., Bangor, 207/947-8004, www.seadogbrewing .com, 11 A.M.–1 A.M. daily), part of a statewide chain, where you can dine on the deck in summer. The food can be uneven, but the award-winning lagers and ales are superb. Inside, it's attractively decorated with tongue-and-groove pine.

On the other side of the river with fine views of Bangor's waterfront is the **Muddy**

Rudder (5 S. Main St., Brewer, 207/989-5389, www.muddyrudder.com, 11 A.M.–10 P.M., to midnight Fri.–Sat.), a sister restaurant to Yarmouth's Muddy Rudder. Seafood's the specialty, but there are chicken, steak, sandwiches, and salads, along with a kids' menu; prices range $8–20. There's live jazz Friday and Saturday nights.

Reservations are essential at **Thistle's** (175 Exchange St., Bangor, 207/945-5480, www .thistlesrestaurant.com, 11 A.M.–2:30 P.M. and 4:30–9 P.M. Mon.–Sat.). Creative, moderately priced continental entrées ($16–25) with a Latin flair, plus excellent homemade breads and desserts, have drawn the crowds, especially at lunchtime. Paella is a specialty. A pianist plays quietly in the background Thursday and Saturday evenings and often during lunch.

Neighborhood chic describes the atmosphere of **Café Nouveau** (84 Hammond St., Bangor, 207/942-3336), but what distinguishes this wine bistro is attentive, friendly service, and imaginative, well-plated dishes at very reasonable prices. Among the appetizers are a *fromage* plate and lobster brioche. A vegetarian torte at $10 and lavender duck breast or tournedos of beef at $15 are among the entrées. Wine choices are extensive, as it's part of a wine store. Lunch is served 11 A.M.–3 P.M., dinner 5–9 P.M. Tuesday–Saturday. The wine bar is open till 11 P.M. Friday–Saturday. It takes reservations for parties of six or larger only.

Chef Roger Gelis's **Opus** (193 Broad St., Bangor, 207/945-5100, www.opusme.com, 5–9 P.M. Tues.–Sat.) offers a selection of small and big plates, making it easy to satisfy your hunger level. It's upstairs, with big windows taking in views of, well, an undistinguished parking lot and street. On Saturday nights, there's live music. About once a month, six-course wine dinners are offered ($65).

Behind City Hall, the stylish ◖ **New Moon Cafe** (47 Park St., Bangor, 207/990-2233, 5–9 P.M. daily) is widely considered Bangor's best fine-dining restaurant. Appetizers, perhaps Malay-style vegetable curry puffs or pan-seared foie gras, are $7–11; entrées, perhaps rabbit tenderloin, oven-roasted duck breast, or hearty polenta lasagna, are $18–28. Watch fresh ingredients—organic and from local producers in season—being transformed into dinner in the open kitchen. More than 200 wines are on the wine list, and the bar stocks nearly three dozen single-malt scotches.

INFORMATION AND SERVICES

The Bangor Region Chamber of Commerce (519 Main St., Bangor, 207/947-0307, www .bangorregion.com) is next to the Paul Bunyan statue. The office is open 9 A.M.–4 P.M. weekdays.

Two Maine Visitor Information Centers (8 A.M.–6 P.M. daily) are just south of Bangor on I-95, one on each side of the highway. The modern gray-clapboard buildings have racks of statewide information, agreeable staffers, clean restrooms, vending machines, and covered picnic tables. Northbound, the center is at mile 175 (207/862-6628); southbound, it's at mile 179 (207/862-6638).

If you plan far enough ahead, The Greater Bangor Convention and Visitors Bureau (40 Harlow St., Bangor 04401, 207/947-5205 or 800/916-6673, www.bangorcvb.org) will send information packets tailored to your needs.

Check out Bangor Public Library (145 Harlow St., Bangor, 207/947-8336, www.bpl.lib .me.us).

GETTING THERE AND GETTING AROUND

Bangor International Airport (BIA; 207/992-4600, www.flybangor.com) is serviced by major U.S. carriers.

Both **Concord Trailways** (1039 Union St./ Rte. 222, Bangor, 207/945-4000 or 800/639-3317, www.concordtrailways.com) and **Vermont Transit Co.** (158 Main St., Bangor, 207/945-3000 or 800/552-8737, www .vermonttransit.com) service Bangor, connecting with Portland and points south.

Cyr Bus Line (207/827-2335 or 800/244-2335, www.cyrbustours.com) operates one round-trip daily between Aroostook County and Bangor.

Operating once daily between Bangor and Calais is **West's Coastal Connection** (207/546-2823 or 800/596-2823, www.west busservice.com).

Servicing Bangor, Brewer, Old Town, Veazie, Orono, and Hampden is **BAT Community Connector** (207/992-4670, www.bangor maine.gov/cs_publictransit.php). The service operates 6:15 A.M.–6:15 P.M. Monday–Saturday, with no Hamden service on Saturday. Fare is $0.85, exact change required.

Orono and Vicinity

Home of the University of Maine's flagship campus, Orono is part college town, part generic Maine village, and a fine example of the tail wagging the dog. More than 11,000 university students converge on this Bangor suburb every year, fairly overwhelming the 8,600 year-round residents.

Called Stillwater when it was settled by Europeans in the 1770s, the town adopted the name of Penobscot Indian chief Joseph Orono and incorporated in 1806. By 1840, as with Bangor, eight miles to the southwest, prosperity descended, thanks to the huge Penobscot

River log drives spurring the lumber industry's heyday. A stroll along Orono's Main Street Historic District, especially between Maplewood Avenue and Pine Street, attests to the timber magnates' success; the gorgeous homes are a veritable catalog of au courant architectural styles: Italianate, Greek Revival, Queen Anne, Federal, and Colonial Revival. Contact Orono's municipal office for a free copy of *Orono Tree Walk,* describing the trees of the town.

Old Town (pop. 8,000) gained its own identity in 1840 after separating from Orono.

("Old Town" is the English translation of the settlement's Wabanaki name.) In those days, sawmills lined the shores of the town's Marsh Island, between the Stillwater and Penobscot Rivers—the end of the line for the log drives and the backbone of Old Town's economy. That all crumbled in 1856, though, when a devastating fire swept through the area. Occurring as residents exited from memorial services for Abraham Lincoln, it was called the "Lincoln Fire." Several decades later, Old Town finally regained its economic footing, thanks to factories making shoes, canoes, and paper products.

Under separate tribal administration and linked to Old Town by a bridge built in 1951, Indian Island Reservation is home to about 400 Penobscot Indians.

SIGHTS
◖ University of Maine

Orono's major sights are on the 660-acre campus of UMO, a venerable institution founded in 1868 as the State College of Agriculture and Mechanical Arts. It received its current designation in 1897 and now awards bachelor's, master's, and doctoral degrees. The oldest building on campus is North Hall, an updated version of the original Frost family farmhouse.

Information about the campus, including guided tours, is available from the **visitors center** (Buchanan Alumni House, University of Maine, 207/581-3740, www.umaine.edu, 8 A.M.–4 P.M. Mon.–Fri. and also 10 A.M.–2 P.M. Sat. during the academic year). Guided campus tours are offered daily.

One of the newest buildings, built in 1986, is the architecturally dramatic **Maine Center for the Arts,** scene of year-round activity. Cleverly occupying part of the center is the small **Hudson Museum** (207/581-1901, 9 A.M.–4 P.M. Tues.–Fri., 11 A.M.–4 P.M. Sat., and before Hutchins Hall performances, free), spotlighting traditional and contemporary world cultures in a series of well-designed galleries on three floors. Frequent special exhibits augment an eclectic ethnographic collection that includes Peruvian silver stick-

pins, African fetish dolls, Navajo looms, and the superlative Palmer Gallery of Pre-Hispanic Mexican and Central American Culture. An interactive corner lets visitors learn a few words in the Penobscot (Native American) language, and a small shop (207/581-1903) stocks unusual global gifts.

The Maine sky takes center stage at the **Maynard F. Jordan Planetarium** (5781 Wingate Hall, Munson Rd., University of Maine, Orono, 207/581-1341, www.galaxymaine.com), on the second floor of Wingate Hall. Multimedia presentations help explain the workings of our universe and bring astronomy to life. Comet collisions and rocketing asteroids keep the kids transfixed. Program scheduling is variable, so you'll need to call ahead to confirm the schedule and reserve space in the 45-seat auditorium. Admission to scheduled events is $3 across the board. The public is invited to view the sky though a telescope at the **Jordan Observatory** on many *clear* Friday and Saturday evenings.

At the eastern edge of the campus, the seven-acre **Lyle E. Littlefield Ornamental Trial Garden** (Rangeley Rd., 207/594-2948) contains more than 3,500 plant species, many being tested for winter durability. The best time to come is early June, when crabapples and lilacs put on their perennial show. The garden is open daily; bring a picnic. Horticulture fans will also enjoy the 10-acre riverside **Fay Hyland Arboretum,** on the western edge of campus.

In the last agricultural building on campus (the barn predating UMO), the **Page Farm and Home Museum** (207/581-4100) houses a collection of farm implements and home items; on-site are a one-room schoolhouse and heritage gardens. The museum presents an annual community picnic lunch at the end of July. Blacksmithing, old-fashioned games, and ice-cream making are part of the festivities. The museum's hours are 9 A.M.–4 P.M. Tuesday–Friday, 11 A.M.–4 P.M. Saturday–Sunday, except holidays.

Campus **parking** is a major sticking point at UMO, so you'll need a parking permit for most areas except the Maine Center for the

Arts and the sports complex when events are taking place. For other times and lots, you can obtain a free one-day permit either from campus security or the parking office. For more information call 207/581-4053.

Old Town Museum

In the former St. Mary's Catholic Church, the Old Town Museum (353 S. Main St., P.O. Box 375, Old Town 04468, 207/827-7256, www .old-town.org, 1–5 P.M. Wed.–Sun. early June–mid-Oct., donation accepted) has well-organized exhibit areas focusing primarily on Old Town's pivotal role in the 19th-century lumbering industry. Other displays feature woodcarvings by sculptor Bernard Langlais, an Old Town native, and an excellent collection of Native American sweetgrass baskets. Each year, temporary exhibits add to the mix. Ask about the Sunday afternoon (2 P.M.) programs— anything from carving, weaving, beadwork, and quilting demonstrations to hand-bell concerts and historical lectures.

C Penobscot Nation Museum

Don't be put off by the humble exterior of Indian Island's Penobscot Nation Museum (12 Downstreet St., Indian Island, 207/827-4153); inside it's jam-packed with tribal historical artifacts and artwork, including exhibits of baskets, beadwork, tribal dress, antique tools, and birch-bark canoes. Curator James Nepture brings the collection to life and will show videos of Penobscot life, including *Penobscot: The People and Their River.* Jewelry, dream catchers, and other handcrafted items are for sale in the small store. The museum is open 9 A.M.–2 P.M. Monday–Thursday and 10 A.M.–3 P.M. Saturday, other times by appointment, but be sure to call ahead.

In the island's Protestant cemetery is the grave of **Louis Sockalexis,** the best Native American baseball player at the turn of the 20th century. Allegedly, his acceptance onto Cleveland's baseball team spurred management to dub the team the Indians—a name that has stuck.

Leonard's Mills

Officially known as the **Maine Forest and Logging Museum** (off Rte. 9, Bradley, mailing address P.O. Box 456, Orono 04473, 207/581-2871, www.leonardsmills.com, $7 adult, $3 child), 400-acre Leonard's Mills re-creates a 1790s logging village, with a sawmill, blacksmith shop, covered bridge, log cabin, and other buildings. The site is accessible sunrise–sunset late April–October, but the best times to visit are during the museum's special-events days—variable schedule—when dozens of museum volunteers don period dress and bring the village to life. Demonstrations, beanhole bean dinners, hayrides, antique games, and kids dipping candles or making cider are all part of the mix. The season's biggest events are **Living History Days,** a two-day festival held in mid-July and the first weekend in October. An ongoing museum project is the restoration to working condition of one of the old Lombard Haulers, an important part of the North Woods story. The museum is on Penobscot Experimental Forest Road, in Bradley, 1.3 miles southeast of Route 178. It's directly across the river from Orono, but the only bridges are north (Old Town/Milford) and south (Bangor/Brewer).

RECREATION
University of Maine

Recreation resources are abundant at UMO. Campus Recreation (207/581-1082, www .umaine.edu/campusrecreation) oversees facilities including **Wallace Pool, Alfond Arena, Latti Fitness Center, Memorial Gym,** and the new **Student Recreation and Fitness Center.** Hours vary at each, and a small access fee may be required.

Ask at the campus recreation center or visitors center for a map of **University Forest,** with trails for biking, walking, snowshoeing, and cross-country skiing.

Sunkhaze Meadows National Wildlife Refuge

The best time to visit Sunkhaze Meadows National Wildlife Refuge (off Rte. 2,

Milford; mailing address 1168 Main St., Old Town 04468, 207/827-6138, ww.sunkhaze .org) is during the fall waterfowl migration, but hunting is allowed then, so wear a hunter-orange hat and/or vest. More than 200 bird species have been spotted here; moose and beaver are common. The best way to see them is to paddle the five-mile stretch of Sunk-haze Stream that bisects the refuge. Allow about six hours for this expedition, putting in on Stud Mill Road (park in the lot at the Ash Landing trailhead; do not park on the Stud Mill Road) and taking out on Route 2. (You'll need two vehicles for this.) Don't forget insect repellent. Access is via the unpaved Stud Mill Road or County Road, north of Milford. No staff or facilities are available at the 11,672-acre refuge; visit or call the Old Town office for information and a map. The office is open 7:30 A.M.–4 P.M. Monday–Friday. In winter, the refuge trails are open for cross-country skiing.

Golf

Play a quick round at **Hidden Meadows Golf Club** (240 W. Old Town Rd., Old Town, www .oldtowngolf.com). Nine holes is $12; 18 holes/all day is $20.

ENTERTAINMENT AND EVENTS

In early December, at the Hudson Museum on the Orono campus of the University of Maine, the **Maine Indian Basketmakers Sale** includes Maine Indian baskets, carvings, jewelry, and traditional arts. Demonstrations, drumming, and singing are all on the agenda. There's an admission fee for early-bird shopping 9–10 A.M. Free admission is 10 A.M.–3 P.M. For more information, contact the Hudson Museum (207/581-1904).

On the UMO campus, the **Maine Center for the Arts** is the year-round site of concerts, dramas, and other events with big-name performers. The box office for the 1,600-seat Hutchins Concert Hall is open 9 A.M.–4 P.M. weekdays, 207/581-1755 or 800/622-8499

(ticket orders), www.mainecenterforthe arts.org.

Catering to the college audience is the six-screen **Spotlight Cinemas** (6 Stillwater Ave., Orono, 207/827-7411, www.spotlightcinemas .com). Stadium-style seating was added in a recent renovation. Ticket price is $4.50 Mon-day–Thursday, for 12 and under at all times, and for matinees before 6 P.M. Friday–Sunday; after 6 P.M., adults pay $7. Spotlight is in University Mall, near I-95 Exit 193.

SHOPPING

Shopping at the **Wabanaki Arts Center Gallery** (240 Main St., Old Town, 207/827-0391, www.maineindianbaskets.org) is an art-ful experience. The gallery exhibits and sells the work of more than six dozen tribal artisans. It's on the banks of the Penobscot River, just around the corner from the Penobscot Nation Museum on Indian Island.

Next door to the Arts Center is a traveler's delight, **The Map Store** (240 Main St., Unit 5, Old Town, 207/827-4511), chock-full of maps, aerials, nautical charts, and GPS systems.

Native American art, jewelry, and musical instruments are the focus at **Penobscot Indian Art** (276 Main St., Old Town, 207/827-4725, www.penobscotindianarts.bizland.com).

The world's oldest continuously operating canoe manufacturer, **Old Town Canoe Company,** still has its big old factory on Middle Street, close to the Penobscot River in downtown Old Town. Incorporated in 1904, the company was turning out as many as 400 boats a month two years later. In 1915, the list of dealers included Harrod's in London and the Hudson's Bay Company in far northern Canada, and Old Town had supplied canoes to expeditions in Egypt and the Arctic. Quality is high at Old Town, so its boats are pricey, but you can visit the **Old Town Canoe Factory Outlet Store** (125 Gilman Falls Rd./Rte. 43, Old Town, 207/827-1530, www .oldtown-canoe.com), and look over the supply of "factory-blemished" canoe and kayak models. You may end up with a real bargain. There's also a full line of paddles, jackets, compasses, and other accessories. To find it, follow Main Street/Route 43 North.

ACCOMMODATIONS

Less than a mile from the university campus is **University Inn Academic Suites** (5 College Ave., Orono, 207/866-44921 or 800/321-4921, www.universityinnorono.com, $82–142), a somewhat dated motel overlooking the Stillwater River. Rates include an expanded continental breakfast. Also on site is The Starr Club, with foosball, darts, pool table, and jukebox; it's open weekend nights and serves light fare.

Even closer to the university is the three-story **Best Western Black Bear Inn** (4 Godfrey Dr., Orono, 207/866-7120 or 800/528-1234, www.blackbearinnorono.com, $99–130). Opened in 1990, it has 68 motel-style rooms, a coin-op laundry, Wi-Fi, exercise room, and sauna. Rates include continental breakfast. Pets accepted, $3.

In Milford is a real bargain for families. The **Milford Motel on the River** (154 Rte. 2, Milford, 800/282-3330, www.milfordmotelontheriver.com) has rooms with kitchenettes for $69 and two-bedroom suites, with living area and full kitchen, for $99. There's a coin-op laundry on the premises; pets are a possibility.

FOOD
Local Flavors

After visiting Leonard's Mills, head over to **Spencer's Ice Cream** (Rte. 178, Bradley, 207/827-8670) for homemade ice cream.

Orono's veteran restaurant is **Pat's Pizza** (11 Mill St., Orono, 207/866-2111, 7 A.M.– midnight Sun.–Thurs., to 1 A.M. Fri.–Sat.), a statewide family-owned chain founded in Orono in July 1931 by C. D. "Pat" Farnsworth. Then known as Farnsworth's Cafe, it became Pat's Pizza in 1953. Pizza toppings are endless,

even pineapple, sauerkraut, and capers. Subs, calzones, burgers, and "tomato Italian" entrées are also on the menu.

At the **Bear Brewpub** (36 Main St., Orono, 207/866-2739, 11:30 A.M.–1 A.M. daily, dinner to 10 P.M.), try a mug of Crow Valley Blonde, Midnight Stout, or I'll Be Darned Amber Ale. Brews are seasonal, made on the premises, with as many as seven on tap. Menu specials change daily, but Wednesday is "All You Can Eat Rib Night."

For natural foods, as well as baked goods and premade sandwiches at lunch, and cappuccino anytime, head to **The Store-Ampersand** (22 Mill St., Orono, 207/866-4110), just off Main Street.

Casual Dining

The views are pleasant and the choices plentiful at **City Park Grille** (170 Main St., Old Town, 207/827-3030, www.cityparkgrille.com, 11:30 A.M.–10 P.M. Sun.–Wed., to 12:30 A.M. Thurs.–Sat.), a combo pub and restaurant overlooking the Penobscot River. Choose from the full lunch or dinner menu, or from lighter fare on the pub menu.

The Mediterranean-inspired choices at the casual **Market Cafe** (827 Stillwater Ave., Old Town, 207/827-3663, 11 A.M.–9:30 P.M. daily) include pizzas, salads, strombolis, sandwiches, and a few entrées, with most items costing $8–12.

INFORMATION AND SERVICES

The best source of information on Orono and Old Town is the Bangor Region Chamber of Commerce (519 Main St., P.O. Box 1443, Bangor 04402, 207/947-0307, www.bangorregion .com). Also helpful is the Orono Town Office (59 Main St., P.O. Box 130, Orono 04473, 207/866-2556, www.orono.org, 8:30 A.M.– 4:30 P.M. Mon.–Fri.).

KENNEBEC AND MOOSE RIVER REGION

The mighty Kennebec, Maine's fourth-largest river, defines this region. It's part of the Kennebec-Chaudière corridor. For more than 3,000 years, the Kennebec and Québec's Chaudière Rivers have been the primary routes for trade and migration between Canada's St. Lawrence River and the Gulf of Maine, between Québec City and the sea. People and goods have moved through history along this corridor: farmers migrating north, hoping to profit from the Québec market; French, Irish, and British families moving south in search of opportunity; escaping slaves following the Underground Railroad north; antiprohibitionists smuggling alcohol south. The most famous traveler was Benedict Arnold, who followed the route on foot and in bateaux with a band of Colonial militia in 1775 in his ill-fated attempt to capture Québec City from the British.

The river wends its way through Somerset and Kennebec Counties from Indian Pond through The Forks, Bingham, Skowhegan, Waterville, Augusta, and Richmond, and then on toward the sea at Bath. Augusta, the state's capital, is rich in historical sights and balanced by the shops and restaurants in Hallowell. Waterville is home to Colby College, alone worth a visit for its Museum of Art. The region's lovely lakes districts—Belgrade Lakes, China Lakes, and Winthrop Lakes, have been favorite summer destinations for as long as anyone can remember. On the outskirts are rural farming communities, such as Unity, home to an annual organic-foods fair that's an equal draw for urbanites and back-to-the-landers.

© TOM NANGLE

HIGHLIGHTS

◖ **Maine State Museum:** Spend a few hours immersed in Maine's history and pick up all kinds of "Well, what-do-you-know?" trivia (page 486).

◖ **Old Fort Western:** The nation's oldest stockaded fort hosted Benedict Arnold on his march to Québec (page 486).

◖ **Great Pond Mail Boat:** Remember the movie *On Golden Pond*? Take a ride on the mail boat that inspired it (page 495).

◖ **Colby College:** Stroll the lovely grounds, visit the arboretum, and don't miss the Museum of Art (page 501).

◖ **L. C. Bates Museum:** View all sorts of eccentric natural-history relics and then walk the trails in the forest (page 508).

◖ **South Solon Meetinghouse:** From the exterior, it looks like just another New England meetinghouse – inside, however, wow! (page 508).

◖ **Moxie Falls:** It's a short hike into one of New England's tallest waterfalls (page 514).

◖ **Old Canada Road National Scenic Byway:** Benedict Arnold marched his troops along a good stretch of this National Scenic Byway along the Kennebec River (page 514).

◖ **White-Water Rafting:** For thrills, take a wild, guided ride down the Kennebec River (page 515).

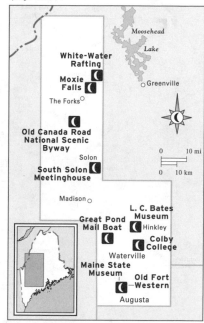

LOOK FOR ◖ TO FIND RECOMMENDED SIGHTS, ACTIVITIES, DINING, AND LODGING.

Many towns along the Kennebec had wood or textile mills. Locals called the rotten-egg stench emitted from the papermaking smokestacks "the smell of money." The region's mill-driven economy is dying, though, and dependent communities take a big hit with each closure or cutback. Many are finding new hope for the future in eco-tourism, especially from Skowhegan north, where the wilderness lakes, forests, and mountains provide endless opportunities for outdoors-oriented folks.

Traditional outdoor sports such as hunting, fishing, hiking, camping, and boating were joined, in 1976, by white-water rafting. That's the year timber companies stopped floating logs down the Kennebec to their lumber mills and gutsy outdoorsman Wayne Hawkmeyer decided to take a rubber raft through the Kennebec Gorge. He survived, and since then, white-water rafting has mushroomed, focusing long-overdue attention on the beautiful Upper Kennebec Valley and creating a whole new crowd of enthusiasts of this region. Now more than a dozen outfitters have bases in the region, and most are multisport outfitters, with canoeing, kayaking, sometimes hiking, and in winter snowmobiling.

KENNEBEC

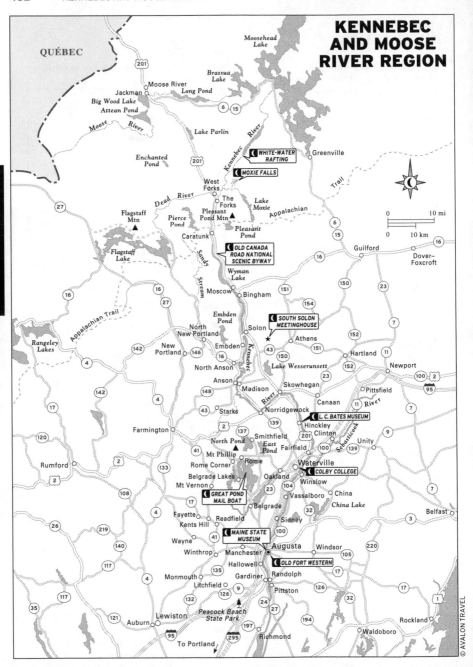

KENNEBEC AND MOOSE RIVER REGION

QUÉBEC

Moosehead Lake

201

Moose River
Jackman
Big Wood Lake
Attean Pond

Brassua Lake
Long Pond

6 15

Moose River

Lake Parlin

Kennebec River

Enchanted Pond

201

WHITE-WATER RAFTING

Greenville

MOXIE FALLS

Trail

West Forks

The Forks

Dead River

Flagstaff Mtn

Pierce Pond

Pleasant Pond Mtn

Lake Moxie

Appalachian Trail

27

Caratunk

Pleasant Pond

6

15

Flagstaff Lake

OLD CANADA ROAD NATIONAL SCENIC BYWAY

Guilford

16

Dover-Foxcroft

16

Sandy Stream

Wyman Lake

16

Appalachian Trail

16 27

Moscow

Bingham

151

150

23

Embden Pond

SOUTH SOLON MEETINGHOUSE

154

7

Rangeley Lakes

142

North New Portland

Solon

Athens

152

New Portland

146

Embden

43 150

151

Hartland

11

Newport

4

16

North Anson

Lake Wesserunsett

23

152

100 2

Anson

Kennebec River

Skowhegan

95

142

4

148

Madison

River

Pittsfield

Farmington

43

Starks

Norridgewock

139

Canaan

11

River

L. C. BATES MUSEUM

17

120

2

137

North Pond

Smithfield East Pond

Hinckley

201

Clinton

9

Rumford

133

Mt Phillip

Rome Corner

Rome

Fairfield

100

Unity

139

2

41

Belgrade Lakes

Oakland

104

Waterville

COLBY COLLEGE

108

Mt Vernon

GREAT POND MAIL BOAT

23

Winslow

Vassalboro

China

7

Belgrade

32

China Lake

26

219

Fayette

Readfield

Sidney

3

Belfast

Kents Hill

41

100

220

140

Wayne

MAINE STATE MUSEUM

Augusta

Windsor

105

117

Winthrop

Manchester

Hallowell

OLD FORT WESTERN

17

117

Monmouth

135

Gardiner

Randolph

126

32

17

35

121

Litchfield

126

9

Pittston

24 27

194

1

Auburn

Lewiston

95

Peacock Beach State Park

197

Richmond

Waldoboro

Rockland

295

To Portland

0 — 10 mi

0 — 10 km

© AVALON TRAVEL

PLANNING YOUR TIME

Depending upon your interests, you can swim, canoe, raft, hike, snowmobile, or cross-country ski; tour museums and historic sites; take walking tours; shop; or blend it all into one rich excursion, blending history, heritage, culture and adventure.

Getting around the region is easy: Route 201 parallels the Kennebec River from one end to the other. The downside is that Route 201 is also the major highway from Québec to the coast, and it may seem as if everyone else but you is simply trying to get from point A to point B in record time. Traffic generally isn't heavy, but it can be disconcerting to have a big rig on your bumper on the narrow and winding stretches of the road. Once you're above Skowhegan, moose too become a danger. Be wary, especially around dawn and dusk or in early spring, when moose often lick salt residue on roadsides.

Think of Route 201 as the region's spine, and Routes 2, 3, 16, 17, and 27 as crucial vertebrae linking it to Maine's Western Lakes and Mountains, Highlands, and Mid-Coast regions. There's a good chance you're going to pass through the region if you're gallivanting about the state. From Norridgewock, Route 201A parallels the river on its western banks, passing through Madison and the Ansons and pretty farm country before rejoining Route 201 in Bingham.

Unless you're a snowmobiler, May–October is the best time to appreciate this part of Maine. In May and June, blackflies are notorious and can make outdoor pleasures—with the exception of fishing—true misery. July–September, when both the air and water are warm, is the best time for white-water rafting, for recreating on the lakes, and for hiking. In late September–early October, when the foliage is at its peak, driving the northern stretch of Route 201, a National Scenic Byway, is glorious.

Outdoor enthusiasts will want to spend at least 2–3 days in and around The Forks or Jackman region, where rafting, canoeing, and hiking are plentiful. Plan on another 2–3 days to visit the cultural diversions clustered in Augusta and Waterville. If you want to loop out to Unity and Thorndike, add another half day or so (but don't even consider doing so during the third weekend

Attean Overlook, along the Old Canada Road National Scenic Byway, just south of Jackman

in September, unless you're ready to brave the crowds headed to the Maine Organic Farmers and Gardeners Association's annual Common Ground Fair). Of course, generations of folk spend a week or longer every summer in the lakes regions surrounding Augusta, but you can dip your toes in for a sample in a day or two.

If you're history minded—or just interested in "heritage touring"—consider following the **Kennebec-Chaudière International Corridor** (www.kennebec-chaudiere.com), a historic route that stretches from Bath, Maine, to Québec City. Benedict Arnold used it; Native Americans used it (on foot and by canoe); and enterprising 19th-century traders found it invaluable for moving their wares between the United States and Canada. Along the route are museums, churches, dramatic scenery, and French and American cultural centers. The heritage, people, and landscape are brought to life on a CD, *Deep Woods and River Roads,* narrated by Nick Spitzer, folklorist and host of Public Radio International's *American Routes.* Order it from the Mid-Maine Chamber of Commerce (207/873-3315) for $13.50 including tax and shipping; it's well worth it. You might also find it at an info center along the way.

© HILARY NANGLE

KENNEBEC

Augusta and Vicinity

As the state capital, Augusta is where everything is supposed to happen. A lot does happen here, but don't be surprised to find the imposing State House and lovely governor's mansion the centerpieces of a relatively sleepy city. With a population of only 20,280, Augusta is the seventh-largest city in Maine and no megalopolis, but it *is* the heart of state government and central Maine.

Pilgrims first settled here on the banks of the Kennebec River in the 17th century, and Boston merchants established Fort Western in the mid-18th century. Augusta was named state capital in 1827.

The three best-known communities south of Augusta—Hallowell, Gardiner, and Richmond—all scale down hillsides to the river, making their settings especially attractive. In Hallowell (pop. 2,600), settled in 1762, the main thoroughfare still retains the air of its former days as a prosperous port and source of granite and ice. The entire downtown, with brick sidewalks and attractive shops and restaurants, is a National Historic District.

Six miles south of Augusta, Gardiner (pop. 6,729), the "Tilbury Town" of noted author Edwin Arlington Robinson, claims more National Historic Register buildings than any of its neighbors. The Gardiner Historic District includes more than 45 downtown buildings. Main Street is a gem, and although still too many storefronts are empty, there's a bit of a buzz here. Besides Robinson, another prominent Gardiner resident was Laura Howe Richards, author of *Captain January* and daughter of Julia Ward Howe, who wrote "The Battle Hymn of the Republic." (The yellow Federal-style home where Richards and her husband raised seven children, at 3 Dennis Street, is not open to the public.) Most outstanding of Gardiner's mansions (also not open to the public) is Oaklands, a Gothic Revival home built in 1836 by the grandson of founding father Dr. Sylvester Gardiner, a wealthy land speculator.

Just over the border in Sagadahoc County,

Richmond (pop. 3,400), also flush with handsome buildings, was the site of a Russian émigré community in the 1950s. Here's a town that awaits rediscovery.

West of Augusta, the town of Monmouth (pop. 3,500) is the site of Cumston Hall, a dramatic, turn-of-the-20th-century structure that now houses the Theater at Monmouth as well as the municipal offices and public library.

SIGHTS
Maine State House

From almost every vantage point in Augusta, your eye catches the prominent dome of the Maine State House, centerpiece of the government complex on the west side of the Kennebec River. Occupying the corner of State and Capitol Streets, the State House dates originally

The Maine State House was designed by Charles Bulfinch.

from 1832, when it was completed to the design of famed Boston architect Charles Bulfinch, who modeled it on his Massachusetts State House design. Only a dozen years had passed since Maine had separated from Massachusetts, and Augusta became the state capital in 1827. Granite for the building came from quarries in nearby Hallowell; total construction cost was $145,000. Atop the oxidized copper dome stands a gold-gilded sculpture, *Lady Wisdom*. In the early 20th century, space needs forced a major expansion of the building, leaving only the eight-columned front portico as the Bulfinch legacy.

Visitors are welcome to wander around the State House, but check first to see whether the legislature is in session. If so, parking becomes scarce, the hallways become congested,

THE RUSSIANS WERE COMING

In the 1950s, the sleepy Kennebec River town of Richmond, 12 miles south of Maine's state capital, became the center of a unique and unlikely colony, as several hundred Russian-speaking refugee families settled among the area's villages and rolling farmland. The Kennebec Valley, economically depressed and remote from other Russian immigrant centers in the United States, seems an improbable choice for a Slavic enclave. Yet Richmond soon boasted a Russian restaurant, a Russian bootmaker's shop, and even onion domes – on St. Alexander Nevsky, Maine's first Russian Orthodox church. For the first time, Russian was heard on Richmond's streets, and Russian-speaking children enrolled in local schools.

The settlement was the brainchild of Baron Vladimir von Poushental, a swashbuckling veteran of the tsar's World War I air force. Fleeing the Bolshevik Revolution, he landed in New York, where his personality and family connections gained him entrée to a series of managerial jobs, if not to the wealth he had enjoyed as a Russian noble. An expert marksman and dedicated hunter, von Poushental in 1947 decided to retire to a modest cabin in the Kennebec Valley, where he had hunted and fished for many years. There he began buying up abandoned farms and promoting the valley's attractions to fellow Russian émigrés. The climate and countryside resembled Russia's, he said, and land was cheap. For a few thousand dollars, a refugee could buy a house and 30 acres. To create a nucleus for the settlers, the baron donated a 400-acre farm to the aging veterans of Russia's White armies, and he helped them establish a retirement home and an Orthodox chapel.

And so they came: Ukrainians, Russians, Byelorussians, and Cossacks; professors, farmers, artists, and carpenters. Some came directly from Europe's displaced-persons camps, others from homes and jobs in U.S. cities where they had lived for years. The settlers shared a common language, their Orthodox faith, a zest for life, and a hatred of the Soviet regime. The younger émigrés worked, raised families, and became part of the larger American community around them. Their elderly parents felt more comfortable associating with other Russian-speakers.

Today the bootmaker and restaurant are gone. Most of the elderly – the old émigrés from pre-Communist Russia – are dead, their Cyrillic gravestones dotting the Richmond cemetery. A few old-timers, still hardy, stand each Sunday through the long Orthodox service, and they bake *pirozhki* or sweets for church sales on special occasions, like the town's late-July celebration of Richmond Days.

Their grandchildren, Russian-Americans, have merged successfully into mainstream America. Most have married outside their ethnic group, and many have taken jobs outside the Kennebec Valley, not necessarily by choice. Yet a fair number still live and work in the area. In a way that might have surprised even von Poushental (who died in 1978), the colony he sponsored took root and flourished in a part of America he loved.

– Robert S. Jaster, author of *Russian Voices on the Kennebec: The Story of Maine's Unlikely Colony* and access may be restricted. The best place to enter the building is on the west side, facing the more modern state office building, and marked "Maine State House." Pick up the useful brochure for a self-guided tour, or, better still, take a free guided tour, usually available 9 A.M.–1 P.M. weekdays. Call ahead (207/287-2301; tours are organized by the Maine State Museum) to arrange it, or ask at the kiosk.

Maine State Museum

If the Smithsonian is the nation's attic, welcome to Maine's attic—and a well-organized one at that. At the Maine State Museum (State House Complex, 83 State House Station, Augusta, 207/287-2301, www.mainestatemuseum .org, 9 A.M.–5 P.M. Mon.–Fri., 10 A.M.–4 P.M. Sat., 1–4 P.M. Sun., $2 adults, $1 for ages 6–18 and seniors, free under 6, $6 family maximum), gears and tools spin and whir in the intriguing *Made in Maine* industrial exhibits, focusing on quarrying, ice harvesting, fishing, agriculture, lumbering, and shipbuilding. A spiraled archaeological exhibit covers the past 12 millennia of Maine's history. Some displays are interactive, and all exhibits are wheelchair-accessible. During the winter, the museum sponsors a free lecture series, and special programs occur throughout the year. A small gift shop stocks historical publications and Maine-related gifts and toys. The museum is part of the state government complex that includes the State House and the Maine State Library. The museum and library share a building, separated by a parking lot from the State House.

The Blaine House

In 1833, a year after the State House was ready for business, retired sea captain James Hall finished his elegant new home across the street. But it was not until 29 years later, when prominent politico James G. Blaine assumed ownership, that the house became the hotbed of state and national political ferment. No underachiever, Blaine was a Maine congressman and senator, Speaker of the U.S. House, U.S. Secretary of State under two presidents, and Republican candidate for the presidency. Two

decades after his death, Blaine's widow donated the family home to the state of Maine; it's been the governor's mansion ever since.

Free, half-hour guided tours of the ground-floor public areas of the Blaine House (State and Capitol Sts., Augusta, 207/287-2121), occur 2–4 P.M. Tuesday–Thursday all year. A special event occasionally cancels the tour schedule, so it's wise to call ahead to avoid being disappointed.

Old Fort Western

Built in 1754 for the French and Indian Wars and restored as recently as 1988, Old Fort Western (16 Cony St., Augusta, 207/626-2385, www .oldfortwestern.org), reputedly the nation's oldest remaining stockaded fort, has witnessed British, French, and Native Americans squabbling over this Kennebec riverfront site. Benedict Arnold and his troops camped here during their 1775 march on Québec. Today, costumed interpreters help visitors travel through time to the 18th century; hands-on demonstrations—butter churning, musket drill, barrel building, weaving, even vinegar making—occur daily Fourth of July–Labor Day. Admission is $5 adults, $4 seniors (55 and over), $3 children 6–16. It's open 1–4 P.M. daily Memorial Day weekend–Labor Day, 1–4 P.M. weekends only Labor Day–Columbus Day, 1–3 P.M. first Sunday of month November–January, 1–3 P.M. Maple Syrup Day, fourth Sunday of March. The museum is on the east bank of the Kennebec in downtown Augusta, next to Augusta City Hall.

Children's Discovery Museum

"Small is beautiful" fits the Children's Discovery Museum (265 Water St., Vickery Building, Augusta, 207/622-2209, www.childrensdiscovery museum.org, 10 A.M.–4 P.M. Tues.–Thurs., 10 A.M.–5 P.M. Fri. and Sat., 11 A.M.–4 P.M. Sun., $5 adult, $4 kids 1 and older), with interactive activities and imaginative playthings for kids to age 10. Adults must accompany all children.

Tours

Many of Hallowell's distinctive homes have stories to tell. Stop by Hallowell City Hall

(1 Winthrop St., 207/623-4021, www.govoffice .com) to buy a copy of *Historic Old Hallowell Walking Tour* or download it. Available free is *The Maine of Martha Ballard: A Self-Guided Tour,* which details sites pertinent to famed midwife Martha Ballard's era.

Fans of poet Edgar Arlington Robinson will find a map of Gardiner-area (Tilbury town) sites at www.earobinson.com.

PARKS AND PRESERVES

On the east side of State Street, between the State House and the river, is 10-acre **Capitol Park,** a great place for a picnic after visiting the Maine State Museum, the State House, and the Blaine House. In the park is the **Maine Vietnam Veterans Memorial,** a dramatic, you-are-there, walk-through monument erected in 1985.

On the east side of the Kennebec River is a wonderful oasis. The **Pine Tree State Arboretum** (153 Hospital St., Rte. 9, P.O. Box 344, Augusta 04332, 207/621-0031, www.pine treestatearboretum.org) devotes 224 acres to more than 300 varieties of trees and shrubs. Bring a picnic (carry-in, carry-out) and wander the nearly six-mile trail network. If you're a birder, bring binoculars. Well-designed planting clusters include hosta and rhododendron collections, a rock garden, an antique apple orchard, and the Governors Grove, with a white pine dedicated to each Maine governor. Stop first at the Viles Visitor Center to pick up a trail map. The grounds are open sunrise–sunset daily all year; the visitors center is open 8 A.M.–4 P.M. Monday–Friday. Leashed pets are allowed; no smoking on the grounds. During the winter, the trails are groomed for cross-country skiing. Admission is free; donations are appreciated.

Next to the arboretum parking lot is **Cony Cemetery** (also known as Knight Cemetery), one of Augusta's oldest, with gravestones dating from the late 18th century. Old-cemetery buffs will want to check it out, but rubbings are not permitted.

Escape shopping hubbub at the **Kennebec Valley Garden Club Park,** an oasis of tranquility at the Augusta Civic Center. Designed in 1974 by Lyle Littlefield, a professor of horticulture

at the University of Maine, it's now maintained by club members. Within the two-acre park's borders are a water-lily pond rimmed with cattails, two formal gardens, and trails edged by perennials. Nearby are children's butterfly and hummingbird gardens and woodlands with wildflowers.

About 12 miles south of Augusta, 100-acre **Peacock Beach State Park** (Rte. 201, Richmond, 207/582-2813, $3 adult, $1 ages 5–12), on long, narrow Pleasant Pond, is an underused pocket park great for swimming and picnicking; a lifeguard is on duty in summer.

Swan Island

The Maine Department of Inland Fisheries and Wildlife (IF&W) has established a byzantine reservation system to limit visitors to its **Steve Powell Wildlife Management Area** on 1,755-acre, four-mile-long Swan Island (207/547-5322, www.state.me.us/ifw/education/ swanisland), in the middle of the Kennebec River. Don't be daunted; it's worth the effort. The entire island is on the National Register of Historic Places. Well-marked trails are everywhere; one trail takes 30 minutes, another takes three hours and goes the length of the lovely wooded island. Plan to take the free, hour-long ranger-guided tour. No license is needed for fishing, but even private boats need permission to land here (near the campground); small boats are not recommended because of 10-foot tidal variations; bikes are permitted on the center main road only; cars and pets are not allowed.

Getting here requires taking a small ferry the very short distance from a dock in Richmond, next to the town-owned Waterfront Park on Route 24. The boat operates May 1–Labor Day. Call for reservations and an informational brochure 7:30–11:30 A.M. Monday–Friday. Day-use admission is $5 adults, $4 seniors, and $3.50 for kids 4–12. Pack a picnic lunch; fireplaces at the campground are available for day use if no campers are using them, but bring tinfoil for cooking. Alcohol is *not* allowed on the island.

The island, settled in the early 1700s, once

KENNEBEC

had as many as 95 resident farmers, fishermen, ice cutters, and shipbuilders. Now there are derelict antique houses, a herd of white-tailed deer, wild turkeys, nesting bald eagles, plenty of waterfowl and other birds, and the primitive campground.

Swan Island's campground has 10 well-spaced lean-tos (each sleeping six) with picnic tables, fireplaces, and outhouses; firewood and potable water are provided. Cost is $8 a night for adults, $7 for seniors, and $6.50 for children. (Add the state's 7 percent lodging tax to those rates.) Kids 3 and under are free. There's a two-night maximum. The policy is carry-in, carry-out, so bring trash bags. A rickety flat-bed truck with benches meets campers at the island dock and transports them the 1.5 miles to the campground. The same truck does the island tour.

RECREATION
Bicycling
You can walk, bike, ski, or run the **Kennebec River Rail Trail,** keeping an eye peeled for bald eagles, salmon, and just the general flow of the Kennebec. The Friends of KRRT (P.O. Box 2195, Augusta 04338, www.KRRT.org) are building the 6.5-mile riverside trail connecting Augusta to Gardiner. Much of it is already open. Call for information, or pick up maps at local businesses and tourism offices.

Bicycle rentals are available from **Kennebec Bike and Ski** (276 Whitten Rd., Hallowell, 207/621-4900, www.kennebecbikeski.com) and **Au Clair Cycle and Ski** (64 Bangor Rd., Augusta, 207/623-4351).

Golf
Ten miles north of Augusta and 12 miles south of Waterville, the highly rated **Natanis Golf Club** (Webber Pond Rd., Vassalboro, 207/622-3561, www.natanisgc.com) has been the site of many a Maine golf tournament. Named after a trusted Indian guide, the Natanis club has two separate 18-hole courses.

Paddling
Take a look at a map of the region, and you'll find plenty of blue, indicating lakes, ponds, rivers and streams. **Farmingdale Kayak and Canoe** (27 Northern Ave., Farmingdale, 207/582-1916, www.farmingdalekayak rentals.com) rents Old Town canoes and double kayaks for $30 and single kayaks for $25 per 24-hour period, with the daily rate decreasing with longer rentals. It also offers guided trips ranging from three hours ($45 pp) to six hours with lunch ($75 pp); kids 15 and younger are half price.

Richmond Corner Sauna
Meriting a recreational category of its own—or maybe it should qualify as entertainment—the clothing-optional Richmond Corner Sauna (81 Dingley Rd., Richmond, 207/737-4752 or 800/400-5751, www.richmondsauna.com) is one of those funky places you either like or you don't. But it's been here since 1976. And maybe you'll like it. Finnish-American owner Richard Jarvi has built up a loyal clientele for his authentic, wood-heated sauna house with six private rooms and a group one. In between and afterward, there's a pool and a hot tub. If nudity bothers you, don't come, but no one seems to gawk. If you're too relaxed to drive after the sauna, the casual main house, built in 1831, has five B&B rooms at $80 d (shared baths; sauna and continental breakfast included). The sauna is open 5–9 P.M. in winter, 6–10 P.M. in summer Tuesday–Sunday all year. Cost is $20 pp. From downtown Richmond, take Route 197 west about five miles and turn left (south) onto Route 138. Take an immediate left onto Dingley Road, where you'll see the sign.

ENTERTAINMENT
The **Gaslight Theater,** a talented community-theater group, performs periodically throughout the year at the **Hallowell City Hall Auditorium** (Winthrop St., Hallowell, 207/626-3698, www.gaslighttheater.org). Call for the schedule or stop in at Hallowell's town office.

Six miles south of Augusta, the 1864 **Johnson Hall Performing Arts Center** (280 Water

St., P.O. Box 777, Gardiner 04345, 207/582-7144, www.johnsonhall.org) is the year-round site of just about anything anyone wants to present—plays, lectures, art camps, after-school programs, classes, concerts, and more.

Maine's enduring Shakespearean theater is the **Theater at Monmouth** (Main St., Rte. 132, P.O. Box 385, Monmouth 04259, box office 207/933-9999 or 800/769-9698 in Maine, www.theateratmonmouth.org, $10–26), based in Monmouth's architecturally astonishing Cumston Hall. Completed in 1900, the Romanesque Victorian structure has columns, cutout shingles, stained glass, and a huge square tower. The interior is equally stunning, with frescoes and a vaulted ceiling. The theater's summer season, performed by professionals in rotating repertory, runs early July–August. Shakespeare gets the nod for at least two of the four plays.

On the northern edge of Augusta, across from the Augusta Civic Center (Rte. 27), is the 10-screen **Regal Theaters** (23 Marketplace Dr., Augusta, 207/623-3698).

Late June–mid-August, free concerts are offered at the **New England Music Camp** (Lake Messalonskee, Sidney, 207/465-3025, www.nemusiccamp.com). Students perform at 3 P.M. Saturday and Sunday, with chamber-music recitals by students and faculty at 8 P.M. Wednesday and 7:30 P.M. Friday. Weekend concerts are at the outdoor "Bowl-in-the-Pines" (bring a blanket or folding chair); Wednesday and Friday performances take place in Alumni Hall.

During the school year, the **University of Maine at Augusta** campus schedules lectures, concerts, and other performances. Check with the school (student activities 207/621-3000, ext. 3442, or information center 877/862-1234) for current information.

FESTIVALS AND EVENTS

The Augusta area seems to claim more country fairs than any other part of the state; don't miss an opportunity to attend at least one. Each has a different flavor, but there are always lots of animals, games, and junk food, often a carnival, and sometimes harness racing.

In June, the Maine Alpaca Association sponsors the **Maine Fiber Frolic,** a celebration of fiber, fiber animals, and fiber arts at the Windsor Fairgrounds. Expect llamas, alpacas, angora rabbits, sheep, goats, and other livestock, as well as demonstrations, workshops, and exhibits.

The small, four-day **Pittston Fair** features agricultural exhibits, a carnival, and even a woodsman contest at the Pittston Fairgrounds, East Pittston, in mid-July. The third Saturday in July, **Old Hallowell Day** includes a craft fair, a parade, food booths, and a road race in downtown Hallowell. The **Monmouth Fair** fills four days with agricultural exhibits, a carnival, and crafts in early August.

The last week of August, the Windsor Fairgrounds come alive with the weeklong **Windsor Fair,** with agricultural exhibits, harness racing, demolition derby, beauty pageant, and carnival.

The three-day **Litchfield Fair** has farm exhibits, animal pulling, a carnival, and more the second weekend in September.

SHOPPING

One mile south of Augusta is **Hallowell,** where boutiques, restaurants, and nearly a dozen antiques shops line historic Water Street.

Art, Crafts, and Antiques

Brahms Mount Textiles (19 Central St., 207/623-5277 or 800/545-9347) is an honest-to-goodness factory outlet, delivering significant savings on the luxurious linen and cotton blankets and throws woven on the premises. **David-Brooks Goldsmiths** (190 Water St., 207/622-9895) sells contemporary, unique and limited-production jewelry; for antique jewelry, shop **Johnson-Marsano Antiques** (172 Water St., 207/623-6263). **Kennebec River Artisans** (144 Water St., 207/623-2345) shows and sells the wares for more than three dozen craftspeople. Studio? Gallery? **Hallowell Clay Works** (100 Water St., 207/626-7687) is both, featuring work from about a dozen potters.

The **Harlow Gallery** (160 Water St.,

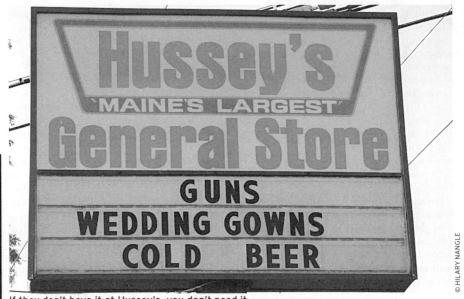

If they don't have it at Hussey's, you don't need it.

Hallowell, 207/622-3813), headquarters for the Kennebec Valley Art Association, serves as a magnet not only for its member artists but also for friends of art. One of Maine's best sources for vintage lighting is **Brass and Friends Antiques** (154 Water St., 207/626-3287). Goods varying from antique china to felted bowls fill the appropriately named **Potluck Shop** (109 Water St., 207/622-8992).

Books
The apt slogan at **Merrill's Bookshop** (134 Water St., 2nd Floor, Hallowell, 207/623-2055) is "Good literature from Edward Abbey to Leane Zugsmith." John Merrill has an eye for unusual rare and used books, so you may walk out with a personal treasure.

General Store
"Guns. Wedding Gowns. Cold Beer." The sign outside **Hussey's General Store** (510 Ridge Rd., corner of Rtes. 32 and 105, Windsor, 207/445-2511) says it all. With merchandise spread out on three floors, there isn't

much that Hussey's doesn't have, and that bridal department does a steady business. Its slogan: "If we don't have it, you don't need it." From Augusta, take Route 105 about 11 miles east to Route 32; Hussey's is on the corner. If you're at the Windsor Fairgrounds, the store is only about two miles farther north on Route 32.

ACCOMMODATIONS
On the western side of the city, close to I-95 but convenient to downtown and the Capitol complex, is the **Best Western Senator Inn and Spa** (284 Western Ave., Augusta, 207/622-5804 or 877/772-2224, www.senatorinn.com, $140–270 d). Recent upgrades—including a good restaurant (great Sun. brunch), full-service spa, and indoor and outdoor heated pools—have made this the area's most upscale lodging; some rooms have fireplaces and/or whirlpool tubs. A full cooked breakfast is included in the rates. Pets are allowed in certain rooms with security deposit and pet fee.

Bed-and-Breakfasts

On a back road only 10 minutes from the State House, 130-acre **Maple Hill Farm Bed and Breakfast Inn and Conference Center** (11 Inn Rd., off the Outlet Rd., Hallowell, 207/622-2708 or 800/622-2708, www.maple bb.com, $95–195) feels like worlds away. Eight rooms (all with Wi-Fi, phones, cable TV, VCR, air-conditioning, and individual heat control) in the informal, renovated 1890s farmhouse overlook woods, fields, gardens, and even the Camden Hills. Room amenities may include double whirlpool tubs, gas fireplaces, and private decks. Breakfast is a custom-cooked affair off a menu and features the inn's own fresh eggs as an option. Coffee, tea, and baked goodies are available any time in the inn's common guest kitchen. Call if you are bringing children. No pets are permitted because of the delightful farm animals, including llamas, cows, and goats. The eco-aware inn has a wind-generating turbine and energy-saving methods in place. Maple Hill Farm is three miles west of downtown Hallowell, next to an 800-acre wildlife preserve with an extensive trail network.

About 10 miles southwest of Augusta but a world removed is **A Rise and Shine B&B** (19 Moose Run Dr./Rte. 135, Monmouth, 207/933-9876, www.riseandshinebb.com), the former Woolworth family estate overlooking Lake Cobbosseeconte, in Monmouth. Restoring the main house after it had been empty for five years has been ongoing for partners Lorette Comeau and Tom Crocker, but they're turning it into a real gem, with Lorette's hand-painted murals in a few of the eight guest rooms. The overall atmosphere is a tad feminine, with many pastels and soft colors, but it's very inviting, with plenty of shared public rooms—great room, living room, dining room, TV room—to spread out and relax. Rates ($125–180) include a full breakfast; Wi-Fi and computer access are provided. Two first-floor rooms connect through a bath for a family suite. In the evenings, Tom, a professional singer, often entertains guests—a real treat, as is the outdoor hot tub. Also on the premises is a small rental cottage with two bedrooms and full kitchen. Now here's a twist on pets: The property previously was a race-horse farm, so horses can be accommodated by arrangement.

West of Augusta, in the Winthrop Lakes Region, is **Maple Tree Inn** (P.O. Box 281, 34 High St., Winthrop 04364, 207/377-5787, maple treeinn@att.net, $85), a renovated 1900 farmhouse with a decidedly natural bent. Owners Lloyd and Ann Lindholm also operate Annie's Naturals, a line of aromatherapy products such as soap, sachets, oils, and bath products, with a shop in the barn. The inn comprises one suite, with private entrance, parlor, kitchen, and bedroom, all with air-conditioning and decorated with vintage collectibles and family pieces. It's within walking distance of the lake. Breakfast features organic foods, some sourced from the Lindholm's gardens. Victorian tea served by reservation. It's open May–November or by appointment.

FOOD
Local Flavors

The yummy aromas of Old World–style baking are reason enough to venture off the beaten path to find **Black Crow Bakery** (232 Plains Rd., Litchfield, 207/268-9927, 7 A.M.–7 P.M. Tues.–Sat.), where the specialty, a Tuscan loaf, is as pretty as it is tasty. Almost all the breads baked in the brick oven are sourdough based, and every day features a different loaf, perhaps Sicilian, olive herb, focaccia, the fantastic apricot almond, or Greek cheese. A modern mixer is Mark and Tinker Mickalide's only high-tech tool; they operate a very traditional bakery in their 1810 farmhouse's former summer kitchen, even grinding their own grains on Maine granite. The shop, which operates on the honor system, is across from the Legion Hall, between I-495 and the Litchfield Fairgrounds.

Great breads, delish cookies, and other treats come from **Slates Bakery** (169 Water St., Hallowell, 207/622-4104, 7 A.M.–6 P.M. daily, to 4 P.M. Sun.).

Another source of fabulous baked goods is

Blue Sky Bakery (339 Water St., Gardiner, 207/582-5450, www.blueskybakery.net, 6 A.M.–5 P.M. Thurs. and Fri., 7 A.M.–4 P.M. Sat.), an artisan bakery using ultrafresh and ultragood ingredients and making pastries and other goodies from scratch. On Saturday, you can pick up beans and brown bread.

Maine's best bagels come from **Bagel Mainea,** with shops in Augusta (190 Western Ave., 207/626-5581) and Gardiner (242 Water St., 207/582-1125). Pick up bagels, bagel sandwiches, even soups and salads and dine or take them to go. Both shops are open 6 A.M.–4 P.M. Monday–Friday, 7 A.M.–2 P.M. Saturday, and 8 A.M.–1 P.M. Sunday.

Webber's (Rte. 201, Farmingdale) and **Hamilton's** (Water St./Rte. 201, downtown Hallowell) dish out homemade ice cream.

If you're noodling around the back roads and make it as far as Readfield Center, duck into **The Emporium** (corner of Rtes. 41 and 17) for an ultracasual dinner. Pizza's the big draw, but with options such as pizza spanokopita or pizza piccata, it's no ordinary pie shop. It also doubles as an art gallery and import shop. The Emporium is open 5–9 P.M. Wednesday–Sunday in summer only; pizza jams on the second and fourth Sundays pack the house with both musicians and listeners.

At the Turnpike Mall on Western Avenue, the **Augusta Farmers Market** operates 10 A.M.–noon Wednesday and Saturday. It's a large market with produce, syrup, crafts, chicken, eggs, and such exotica as rabbit meat. There's also an **Augusta River Market,** at the old Edwards Mill site on the north end of Water Street, operating 2–6 P.M. Tuesday, selling produce, baked goods, jams, some crafts, and more. West of Augusta, the **Winthrop Farmers Market** is set up in the municipal building parking lot (Main St. in Winthrop) 9 A.M.–1 P.M. Tuesday and Saturday.

Quick Meals

In downtown Gardiner, on the corner by the A-1 Diner, is **A-1 to Go Community Market and Café** (347 Water St., Gardiner, 207/582-5586, http://a1-to-go.a1diner.com,

7 A.M.–7 P.M. Mon.–Sat.), a stylish café cum bakery/deli counter serving both breakfast and lunch, and with plentiful—and very enticing—fresh and frozen takeout selections. Soup, salad, wrap, and panini lunches run $5–10; takeout dinners such as chicken Marbella or tofu with Korean garlic sauce cost about $8–10/pound.

Expanding from its original Belfast store to a location near the State House, **Bay Wrap** (1 Hitchborn St., Augusta, 207/620-9727, 7 am.–5:30 P.M. Mon.–Fri.) fills tortillas with all kinds of concoctions.

Local Favorites

It's the 20-ounce pint glass, not politics, that helped christen **The Liberal Cup** (115 Water St., Hallowell, 207/623-2739, 11:30 A.M.–10 P.M., noon–9 P.M. Sun.), a brewpub and restaurant where owner Geoffrey Houghton, who studied in Britain, makes six different great beers. Homemade is true of the food, too; the place is packed with diners sampling the salads, salmon, steak, fish-and-chips, and shepherd's pie. Even the salad dressings are made on the premises. Lunch and dinner are served year-round.

Hard by the Kennebec River in downtown Gardiner, adorned with flower boxes, is the first-rate ◖ **A-1 Diner** (3 Bridge St., Gardiner, 207/582-4804, www.a1diner.com, 7 A.M.–8 P.M. Mon.–Sat., to 9 P.M. Fri.–Sat., 8 A.M.–1 P.M. Sun.). The building's the real thing, a gen-u-ine classic diner, with moderate prices and some added attractions, such as air-conditioning. The menu, however, goes well beyond diner fare. How about tilapia with pesto? Or Transylvania eggplant casserole? Or wild mushroom ragout? Board specials are $9–13. It makes great soups, too. (There's also a regular diner menu.) Sunday brunch draws a big crowd.

When you have a hankering for finger-lickin', Memphis-style barbecue, **Riverfront Barbeque and Grill** (300 Water St., 207/622-8899, www.riverfrontbbq.com, noon–9 P.M. Sun., 11 A.M.–9 P.M. Mon.–Wed., 11 A.M.–10 P.M. Thurs.–Sat., closes earlier Oct.–Apr.)

delivers, serving big portions of slow-smoked goodness—and a few surprises, such as veggie risotto—at affordable prices ($8–18).

Downriver from Augusta, the **Railway Café** (64 Main St., Richmond, 207/737-2277) has been the favorite local gathering spot since 1984. Looking at the original 19th-century woodwork and tin ceiling, who'd guess it had once been a funeral parlor? If you're here on Friday (and sometimes other days), order the lobster stew, *loaded* with lobster meat. Dinner entrées—steak, seafood, grilled chicken, pizza—run $6–14. The café is open all year for breakfast, lunch, and dinner.

Ethnic Fare

Café de Bangkok (272 Water St., 207/622-2638, 11 A.M.–9:30 P.M. Mon.–Sat., to 10 P.M. Fri. and Sat., and 4–9 P.M. Sun.) deserves its rep as one of Maine's best Thai restaurants. Not only is the food excellent—great sushi—but the setting on the Kennebec River is lovely.

Casual Dining

Ask anyone where to eat in the Augusta area, and chances are high that the answer will be (**Slates** (167 Water St., Hallowell, 207/622-9575), the Energizer bunny of local restaurants. Founded in 1979, it just keeps improving. Destroyed by fire in early 2007, it rose anew from the ashes, revitalized. Dinner entrées—mostly creative seafood and chicken, and a few token tournedos—are in the $11–19 range. The Saturday and Sunday brunches are fabulous: grilled fish and meats, unique omelettes and Benedicts, huevos rancheros, stuffed croissants, homemade granola, salads. Reservations only for six or more, except dinner, when reservations are taken for any size party. It's open for breakfast 7:30–11 A.M. Monday–Friday; for lunch 11:30 A.M.–2:30 P.M. Monday–Friday; for dinner 5:30–9 P.M. Monday–Saturday, to 8 P.M.on Monday, to 9:30 P.M.Friday–Saturday); and for brunch 9 A.M.–2:30 P.M. Saturday and 9:30 A.M.–2 P.M. Sunday. Don't let the location inside a hotel deter

you from **Cloud 9** (at the Senator Inn and Spa, 284 Western Ave., Augusta, 207/622-5804, 6:30 A.M.–10 P.M. daily). The chefs are committed to using local ingredients and take great care in preparing the fare. Choices vary from wood-oven pizzas to handmade pastas, burgers and fries to filet mignon. The brunch buffet, served 11 A.M.–2 P.M. Sunday, brings them in from points far and wide.

INFORMATION AND SERVICES

The information center of the Kennebec Valley Chamber of Commerce (21 University Dr., P.O. Box 676, Augusta 04332, 207/623-4559, www.augustamaine.com) is open 8:30 A.M.–5 P.M. Monday–Friday all year (answering machine on weekends). It's in the Augusta Civic Center complex at the northern edge of the city.

The Hallowell Board of Trade maintains a website (www.hallowell.org) with information on local businesses and attractions and an info phone (207/620-7477).

The Romanesque Revival Lithgow Public Library (Winthrop and State Sts., Augusta, 207/626-2415, www.lithgow.lib.me.us), one of Maine's handsomest libraries, was built in 1896 of Maine granite. Do not miss the gorgeous reading room, with a Tiffany clock, stained-glass windows, and French-inspired decor.

The Maine State Library (Maine State Cultural Building, Augusta, 207/287-5600, www.maine.gov/msl), in the State House complex, includes the Maine State Museum and the State Archives (207/287-5790) within its walls.

GETTING THERE AND AROUND

US Airways Express (800/428-4322, www.usairways.com) operates flights all year between Boston's Logan Airport and the Augusta State Airport, a distance of 148 miles.

Vermont Transit, connected with Greyhound (207/772-6587 or 207/622-1601), operates bus service between Portland and Augusta.

KENNEBEC

Belgrade Lakes Area

The Belgrade Lakes area is one of those Proustian memories-of-childhood places, where multi-generational family groups return year after year for idyllic summer visits full of nothing but playing, going for hikes or swims, fishing, listening for the loons, watching sunsets, and dreading the return to civilization. Today's boomer generation, recalling carefree days at one of the many Belgrade-area summer camps, now send their own kids to camp here, or they rent lakefront cottages and devote their energies to re-creating those youthful days.

Water, water everywhere: Mosey along the back roads, and it seems as if there's yet another body of water around every other bend or so. Belgrade's chain of lakes comprises seven major lakes and ponds: Long Pond, North Pond, Great Pond, East Pond, Salmon Pond, McGrath Pond, and Messalonskee Lake (also known as Snow Pond), as well as numerous smaller ones, and as you continue south, so

do the lakes and ponds. Camps and cottages are sprinkled around their shores—you might even spot Elizabeth Arden's once-famed Maine Chance Farm. Roadside put-ins and boat-launch ramps, from which you can put in a canoe, kayak, or powerboat, can be found on every lake. This is a great area to just strap a canoe or kayak on the car and wander about, stopping wherever seems interesting for a paddle. Incidentally, the village of Belgrade Lakes, heart of the region, has its own post office but is part of the towns of Belgrade and Rome.

Since the Belgrade Lakes area is tucked in between Waterville and Augusta, those cities serve as the easily accessible commercial and cultural hubs for Belgrade visitors.

Directly west of Belgrade Lakes village is the charming, out-of-the-way hamlet of Mount Vernon (pop. 1,430), founded in 1792 and worth a visit by car or bike. North of that is Vienna (VI-enna), and south is lovely Kent's

Mosey over to Mount Vernon to the old mill stream.

© TOM NANGLE

Hill, home to a prep school, and just beyond that, Readfield.

SIGHTS
◖ Great Pond Mail Boat

Remember the movie *On Golden Pond?* Well, author Ernest Thompson found his inspiration summering on the shore of Great Pond. (He's still here, although Hollywood's version was filmed in New Hampshire.) You can join the real-life postman on his rounds, feeding the 100-plus lakefront mailboxes—but you'll be in a pontoon boat instead of a Chris-Craft. Bring binoculars, a camera, a jacket, and a sandwich, and settle in aboard the stable boat. Reservations are essential—only four passengers per trip, so call well ahead, especially in July and August. Occasionally, you can luck out and find space available without a reservation. If your kids can behave for the duration of the up to four-hour excursion, by all means try this one. But leave them ashore if they're restless types (there's only an emergency Porta-Potti on board). Operated by Great Pond Mail Boat (207/215-7520, $20), the mail boat departs at 10 A.M. Monday–Saturday mid-June–mid-September from Great Pond Marina, off Route 27 just south of Belgrade Lakes village.

D. E. W. Animal Kingdom

Lions, and tigers, and bears, oh my! And monkeys, camels, wallabies, ostriches, a binturong, a hyena, and, well, the list goes on and on. Allow at least an hour to visit the 42-acre D. E. W. (Domestic/Exotic/Wild) Animal Kingdom (9918 Pond Rd., Rte. 41, Box 2820, Mount Vernon, 207/293-2837), west of Belgrade Lakes village. Kids love the hands-on stuff at Julie and Bob Miner's innovative nonprofit zoo, where they raise and rehabilitate exotic and not-so-exotic animals, enhancing rare and endangered breeds, and educate visitors about them. Bob, a disabled Vietnam vet, has rescued animals from zoos and shows and even New York City apartments. Julie and Bob have hand raised and bottle fed many of these animals from infancy, and they will enter every cage. Bob kisses the bears and the lions, and Julie

nuzzles the panther, but visitors watch from behind a double fence; trust me, it's plenty close enough, especially when you learn such facts as the hyena has the strongest jaw pressure of any land mammal. The zoo, on Route 41, is in West Mount Vernon, midway between Mount Vernon village and Kents Hill. It's open 10 A.M.–5 P.M. Tuesday–Sunday and on holidays May 1 through late September; it's open 10 A.M.–5 P.M. weekends and midweek by appointment April and October; other times, it's open weather permitting and by appointment. Admission is $8 per person, except for "infants and over 100," who are free. Note: Whining children are strongly discouraged.

Flightseeing

Take off from the water and cruise by air over the lakes with **Airlink** (Great Pond Marina, 207/859-0109, www.airlinkconnection.com). A 20-minute flight over Great and Long Pond is $120 for up to three passengers. A 35-minute flight is $180.

RECREATION
Parks and Views

Just north of Day's Store in Belgrade Lakes village is a cute little picnic area on Long Pond, **Belgrade Peninsula Park,** open 5:30 A.M.–10:30 P.M., next to an old dam. Late in the day, it's a great spot for sunset watching and fishing; no camping or fires permitted. The Belgrade Lakes Conservation Corps restored it in 1996, and there is space for five (carefully parked) cars.

Another scenic standout, with a super photo op of Long Pond and Belgrade Lakes village, is the state-maintained overlook at **Blueberry Hill,** on the west side of Long Pond. From Route 27, just south of Belgrade Lakes village, take Castle Island Road west about three miles to Watson Pond Road. Turn right (north) and continue about 1.5 miles. (Another 2.8 miles north of Blueberry Hill is the trailhead for French's Mountain.)

Golf

Golf has taken center stage here ever since

the opening of the splendid **Belgrade Lakes Golf Club** (West Rd., P.O. Box 500, Belgrade Lakes 04918, 207/495-4653, www.belgrade lakesgolf.com) in 1998. Designed by noted British expert Clive Clark, the course is an 18-hole standout, and the view from the elegant clubhouse is dazzling. Caddies are available to encourage walking. Tee times are necessary; greens fees are high.

Swimming

Good places for swimming are **Long Pond Public Beach** on Lakeshore Drive in Belgrade Lakes Village (near Sunset Grille) and at the Belgrade Community Center, Route 27, just south of the village. In addition to the lakefront, the center also has a pool open to nonresidents for $2 during community swim hours.

Hiking

Proactive in protecting much of the region's beautiful land for hiking and responsible enjoyment, the **Belgrade Regional Conservation Alliance (BRCA)** (P.O. Box 250, Belgrade Lakes 04918, www.belgradelakes.org, 207/495-6039) has a terrific trail map and hiking guide to the Kennebec Highlands available—although it doesn't show every protected acre, since the alliance is managing to protect land faster than it can print maps.

The two good hikes listed here are included on the map, which can also be obtained at local general stores, such as Day's. Both hikes are just north of Belgrade Lakes village in the town of Rome. Neither is particularly high, but their summits are isolated enough to provide panoramic vistas.

For lots of gain and little pain and a good family hike, head for **French's Mountain,** on the west side of Long Pond. To reach the trailhead from Route 27, go about 4.2 miles north of Belgrade Lakes village and turn left onto Watson Pond Road. Go less than a mile; the trail (signposted) begins on the left. Allow about 20 minutes to reach the summit, with fantastic views of Long Pond, the village, and Great Pond. Take a picnic (and a litter bag) and stretch out on the ledges.

A marginally tougher yet still-easy hike is **Mt. Phillips,** a 755-footer with summit views of Great Pond. Allow about 20 minutes to reach the top from the Route 225 trailhead. From Route 27, north of Belgrade Lakes village, turn right onto Route 225 at Rome Corner (Logan's Country Antiques is at the fork). Continue another 1.5 miles to the trailhead (on the left), across from a Hemlock Trail sign. Park as far off the road as possible. Head on up the blue-blazed trail to the summit.

Fishing

Fishing is a big deal here, particularly in May, June, and September (the season runs Apr. 1–Oct. 1). Among the 20 species in the seven major lakes and ponds are landlocked salmon, brown trout, black bass, pickerel, white perch, and eastern brook trout. You'll have to stick to bag, weight, and length limits. Pick up tackle and nonresident fishing licenses at Day's Store (Main St., Belgrade Lakes, 207/495-2205 or 800/993-9500).

Boating

About five miles south of Belgrade Lakes village (across from the turn to Oakland), Ralph Ardito's **Belgrade Canoe and Kayak** (Rte. 27, Belgrade, 207/495-2005 or 888/226-6311) has a hefty inventory of Old Town kayaks, canoes, and accessories for sale and rents canoes and kayaks. You can try them outside in the store's demo pond or on a local streams tour.

At Mike and Louise Pooler's **Belgrade Boat Rentals and Storage** (Foster Point Rd. on Great Pond in Pinkham's Cove, P.O. Box 471, Belgrade 04917, 207/495-3415 or 888/226-6311), either Old Town lake kayaks or 16-foot canoes can be rented for three days for $75, $110 for a week, $200 deposit required. Also available are 14-foot motorboats, $175 for three days, $295 for one week, $500 deposit. Free local pickup and delivery.

Here's a tasty choice: **Maine Wilderness Tours** (207/465-4333, www.mainewilderness tours.com) leads paddle trips down Belgrade Stream that conclude with a lobster picnic. The half-day trip is $50 pp unguided, $100 pp guided. Other trips are available; call for details.

Roller Skating

Here's a throwback: When the windows are open, it feels as if you could dive out and into the water at **Sunbeam Roller Rink** (Rte. 8, Smithfield, 207/362-4951), an old-fashioned roller-skating rink that's right on North Pond. It's open evenings in summer; call for the schedule.

Belgrade Community Center

Belgrade's spiffy recreation center (Rte. 27, Belgrade, 207/495-3481, www.belgrademaine .com) fronts on Great Pond and has a beach as well as an outdoor pool. Inside are the town library and a full-size basketball court. Everything's open to visitors, although if you want to borrow a book or two, you'll have to join the library as a nonresident for $10 (well worth it if the weather isn't cooperating and you're in a camp or cottage for the week). The center offers a full range of programs, from pick-up basketball and volleyball to a summer kids' camp to a knitting/crafts club.

SHOPPING

Mosey and poke around the back roads, and you'll be rewarded with a handful of galleries and what-not shops.

You-Name-It

Cars and canoes are about the only things you can't buy at **Day's Store** (Main St., Rte. 27, Belgrade Lakes, 207/495-2205 or 800/993-9500, www.go2days.com), a legendary institution since 1960. From firewater to fishing tackle, sandwiches (including the Long Pond Grinder) to souvenirs, and more than a dozen kinds of homemade fudge, it's a general store par excellence. Don't expect fancy; the local flavor provides its character. Long Pond is at its back door, providing access by boat or car. Day's is in the center of the village; you can't miss it.

Gifts and Crafts

A few doors south of the Village Inn in Belgrade Lakes is the seasonal branch of Waterville's **Maine Made and More Shop** (Main St., Rte. 27, Belgrade Lakes, 207/495-2274), a summer landmark since 1980. Here's the place to stock up on tasteful gifts and crafts: jams and maple syrup, cards and guidebooks, T-shirts and sweatshirts, stuffed moose, and even shoes.

Delivering what its name promises, **Maine Bone Carving** (Rte. 41, Mt. Vernon, 877/562-6637, www.mainebonecarving.com) sells hand-carved moose bone and also sells the works of Maine and New Zealand artisans.

ENTERTAINMENT AND EVENTS

The big entertainment here is shared family time on the lakes, but there are a few nearby venues worth exploring.

The **New England Music Camp** (207/465-3025, www.nemusiccamp.com) in Sidney stages faculty and student performances during camp sessions.

ACCOMMODATIONS
Inns and Bed-and-Breakfasts

Practically hidden on a hillside just steps from downtown Belgrade Lakes is the ◖ **Wings Hill Inn and Restaurant** (Rte. 27, P.O. Box 386, Belgrade Lakes 04918, 866/495-2400, www .wingshillinn.com, $140–210 peak). Built around the turn of the 18th century, the rambling farmhouse-turned-inn houses six rooms and the area's best fine-dining restaurant (see *Food,* thanks to hands-on chef/owners Christopher and Tracey Anderson. The downstairs Sage Suite sleeps three and has a private entrance, TV with DVD, and small fridge. All of the second-floor rooms have balconies, some shared. The best room is Moonlight, a spacious room with large private deck and lake views. Relax on the screened, wraparound porch or snag an Adirondack-style chair on the lawn or a patio seat or, in winter, inside by the fire. TV and guest phone are in the living room; Wi-Fi throughout. Rates include a sumptuous full breakfast and fresh-baked treats with afternoon tea.

Relax in a natural environment at the **Yeaton**

Farm Inn (298 West Rd., Belgrade, 207/495-7766, www.yeatonfarminn.com, $150 d), a historical 1826 stagecoach stop set upon 40 quiet, aahhh-inspiring country acres. Each of the three antiques-filled guest rooms has a woodburning fireplace and an air-conditioner, but don't mistake this for a chi-chi inn—this is creaky and cluttered, with funky bathrooms wedged in where possible and antique rope beds fitted with good mattresses (some are authentic trundle beds—a real hit with kids). Loyal guests would have it no other way. Innkeeper Connie Parker and her mother, Connie, are warm, welcoming, and eager to help you get the most out of your stay. Follow an old woods trail to a brook and watch for wildlife along the way; moose and deer sightings aren't unusual. There's even an outpost on the lake. A full breakfast and afternoon tea are served. There are a resident dog and cat, but friendly dogs are allowed with notice for $25 per night. No minimum stay except during two Colby College event weekends. The inn also rents a four-bedroom, lakeside cottage for $1,200–1,500 per week, depending upon the season. A one-bedroom apartment in the main inn is $950 per week.

On the eastern side of Great Pond is the aptly named **Among the Lakes Bed and Breakfast** (58 Smithfield Rd., Belgrade, 207/465-5900, www.amongthelakes.com, $120–140). Although it doesn't have a lake view, Great Pond is about a one-mile stroll. Each of the five guest rooms has air-conditioning; some share baths. Rates include a full breakfast.

Just west of Waterville, on the eastern edge of the Belgrade Lakes region, is **The Pressey House Lakeside Bed and Breakfast** (32 Belgrade Rd., Oakland, 207/465-3500, www.presseyhouse.com), Lorne and Lorie McMillan's mid-19th-century octagonal house with ell and barn at the head of nine-mile-long Messalonskee Lake (also known as Snow Pond). Five good-size rooms, one with a balcony overlooking the lake, another with a fireplace, are $115–195 d mid-May–mid-October, $100–150 d other months, including a full breakfast; the inn is family friendly, and suites sleep as many as five. No smoking, no pets. Relax in the Gallery great room, with a huge brick fireplace dividing it in two, or on the patio or borrow the canoe, paddleboat, or motorboat to explore the lake. The Pressey House, a five-minute drive from I-95 Exit 127, is open all year.

Cottage and Rooms

Smack downtown, wedged between Route 27 and Long Pond, is **Partridge Cottage and Rooms** (174 Main St., Belgrade Lakes, 207/495-3864, www.balloonsandthingsmaine.com). Jan Partridge has been vacationing here since childhood and married into a family with deep roots. She knows the area's history and readily shares it. A trained balloon artist, she operates a balloon and gift shop and a hair salon on the first floor of the family's lakefront home. Up a steep stairway are two guest rooms ($75–85), the pricier one with a lake view. Both have TV and air-conditioning. No breakfast, but the rooms share a microwave and refrigerator, and Day's Store is next door. Guests also share a dock. Adjacent to the main house is a two-bedroom guest cottage (once a chicken coop transported to its location over the ice) with a screened-in porch built over the lake and its own dock. The rate is $695 per week.

Sporting Camps

Distant from most of Maine's sporting camps, two classic Belgrade-area operations nonetheless retain the flavor of those much farther north. And it's a heck of a lot easier to reach when driving from the south.

Established in 1910, and still operated by the same family, **Bear Spring Camps** (60 Jamaica Point Rd., Rome, www.bearspringcamps.com) is one of the state's largest sporting camps, with 32 rustic cottages on 400 wooded acres. All have baths and Franklin stoves and overlook the North Bay of nine-mile-long Great Pond; each has its own dock, and rental motorboats, kayaks, canoes, even a pontoon boat are available. Other facilities include a sandy beach, tennis court, and hiking trails. Cabins, one- to four-bedroom, are $755–2,680 a week, including all meals, served in the main lodge. In traditional style, lunch (a.k.a. dinner) is the main meal of the day, while supper comprises lighter fare. (The staff will even cook the fish you catch.) Cabins are available only by the week mid-June–Labor Day, and reservations are tough to come by; off-season, when they're available, daily rates are $65 pp d. Some guests stay a month, and they book a year ahead. No pets. Open mid-May–September (it's not open during hunting season). Bear Spring Camps is a quarter mile off Route 225, four miles east of Route 27.

Founded in 1909, **Alden Camps** (3 Alden Camps Cove, Oakland, 207/465-7703, www.aldencamps.com) has an incredibly loyal following, unto fourth-generation guests (again, getting reservations is tough but not impossible). The 18 rustic cottages face great sunrises across three-mile-long East Pond (a.k.a. East Lake). Most guests spend a week. Each no-frills cottage has a screened porch, electricity, bath, fridge, and daily maid service. The crew of college kids aims to please, and former staffers now show up as guests. Meals are hearty and surprisingly creative with about a dozen or so entrée choices nightly (limited reservations for nonguests, $18 entrée, including salad course). The Friday-night lobster bake/clam bake—open to the public, call for reservations—is a longstanding tradition. BYOB. The 40-acre spread on Route 137 has a clay tennis court, sand beach, waterskiing boat, boat rentals, and a kids' play area. Rates, which include all meals, vary with cottage size and occupancy and range from $105 pp/night or $630 pp/week for a one-room cottage to $130 pp/day or $780/week for two adults with children. Children are $17–73/day or $102–438/week, depending on age. Spring and late summer rates are lower. After Labor Day–late September, cottages are available without meals for $81–163/day or $486–978/week. Rates do not include gratuities. Note: Low-season midweek specials are a real steal. Pets are allowed for $25/day. Boat rentals are $20/day or $120/week; canoes and kayaks are free. Alden Camps is seven miles off I-95 Exit 127. It's open mid-May–late September.

Occupying all of tiny Castle Island, a blip on the causeway, is **Castle Island Camps** (P.O. Box 251, Castle Island Rd., Belgrade Lakes 04918, 207/495-3312 or winter 207/293-2266, www.castleislandcamps.com). What a location! The 12 rustic cabins are geared to anglers, but they're popular with families in summer who want a simple, old-style lake-based holiday. Each cabin fronts on the lake, and home-style meals, served in the lodge, are included in the rates ($80 s, $150 d night, $546 s, $1,025 d per week; kids' rates begin at $25 for ages 1–2 and increase with age). Rental boats ($50 with gas/day) and kayaks ($20/day or $15 for four hours) are available, and there's a swimming dock. It's open May 1–September 30. No credit cards.

Seasonal Rentals
Seasonal rentals are the preferred lodging in the Belgrade Lakes area. It must relate to the children's summer camps in this area—you may not be able to go home again, but you *can* spend a week or two trying to recapture the aura. The **Belgrade Reservation Center** (262 Augusta Rd./Rte. 27, P.O. Box 284, Belgrade Lakes 04918, 207/495-2104, www.belgraderental.com), based in the Day's Real Estate building on the southern outskirts of Belgrade Lakes Village, has the best selection of rentals. Cottages with 1–5 bedrooms are $350–3,750 per week, mid-May–mid-October.

FOOD
Local Favorites
If you're looking for picnic fare or a quick bite, stop in at **Day's Store** (Main St./Rte. 27, Belgrade Lakes, 207/495-2205 or 800/993-9500, www.go2days.com) and pick up pizza, sandwiches, and/or baked goodies.

Two Wendys with two Labs and too many other similarities operate **The Lazy Lab Café** (81 Main St./Rte. 27, Belgrade Lakes, 207/495-2872, www.lazylabcafe.com, 7:30 A.M.–3 P.M. daily), a combination Internet café and bookstore, serving breakfast, lunch, and sweets.

Detour down by the old millstream to **The Olde Post Office Café** (366 Pond Rd.-Village Center, Mount Vernon, 207/293-4978). The café overlooks Minnehonk Lake and is open 7 A.M.–2 P.M. Monday–Friday, 8 A.M.–2 P.M. Saturday–Sunday and also once a month for

Saturday night dinners with music. Sandwiches, salads, paninis, and wraps fill the menu, along with baked goodies. Grab a seat inside or on the screened porch overlooking the stream. Don't miss the old wheel-driven mill across the street. There are occasional music nights in July and August.

Reliability is the biggest selling point for the **Sunset Grille** (4 West Rd., Belgrade Lakes, 207/495-2439, 7 A.M.–10 P.M. Sun.–Thur., to midnight Fri.–Sat.). The local grub and gossip spot is open daily for breakfast, lunch, and dinner, and it has a full bar. Stick to the basics and the chili.

Fancier Fare

Who'd a thunk a sporting camp would serve fare such as beef chimichurri or Thai sizzling snapper? You'll have to call in advance to book one of the few seats on the porch available to nonguests at ◖ **Alden Camps** (3 Alden Camps Cove, Oakland, 207/465-7703, www.aldencamps.com). Even though you'll hear the passing whiz of traffic, the experience is worth it. The menu, posted nightly on the blackboard, lists more than a dozen choices, from rack of lamb to smoked mozzarella ravioli. The chef obviously knows his way around the kitchen. Entrées are $18, and that includes a loaf of fresh baked bread and a salad with homemade dressing choice. BYOB. On Friday nights, it's an outdoor lobster and seafood bake—a very popular choice. Open for dinner daily late May–early September.

Fine Dining

Innkeepers Tracey and Christopher Anderson, at **Wings Hill Inn and Restaurant** (Rte. 27, P.O. Box 386, Belgrade Lakes 04918, 866/495-2400, www.wingshillinn.com) met while attending culinary school, fortunately for diners at the inn. The five courses on their $50 fixed-price menu, with seatings at 6 and 8 P.M. Thursday–Sunday (and Wed. in July and Aug.), change weekly, but provide appetizers, choices of soup, salad, main courses such as grilled pork or slow-roasted Cornish hen, and desserts such as brown sugar crème brûlée. On Thursday and Sunday in winter, there might be a three-course option for $40. BYOB. Reservations strongly recommended.

INFORMATION

The self-serve Belgrade Lakes Region Information Center (P.O. Box 72, Belgrade 04917, 207/495-2744, www.belgradelakesmaine.com) is on the east side of Route 27, about 10 miles north of Augusta.

Summertime in the Lakes, a free tabloid with ads, features, and calendar listings, is an especially helpful local publication that appears weekly during the summer. Copies are available at the information center and at most of the restaurants and shops in the region.

Check out the Belgrade Public Library (Belgrade Community Center, Rte. 27, Belgrade, 207/495-3481, www.belgrademaine.com).

Waterville and Vicinity

The second-largest community in Kennebec County, the city of Waterville boasts a population of 16,000. When you throw in its sister town of Winslow, the head count jumps to nearly 24,000. A key player in Waterville life today is prestigious Colby College, whose students and faculty give a college-town flavor to this mill town incorporated in 1802.

As early as 1653, Europeans set up a trading entrepôt here, calling it Teconnet—the earlier version of today's Ticonic Falls, on the Kennebec—and commerce with the Indians thrived until the onset of the Indian Wars two decades later. In the late 19th century, a contingent of Lebanese immigrants arrived, finding employment in the town's mills, and many of their descendants have become respected community members. Best known of these is favorite son and former U.S. Senate Majority Leader George J. Mitchell, who still returns to spend time with his many relatives here.

Waterville has long been overshadowed by Augusta, the Kennebec County seat 20 miles to the south, but commercial turnarounds and communal efforts such as Waterville Main Street have led to rising optimism about the city's prospects.

SIGHTS

◖ Colby College

Crowning Mayflower Hill, two miles from downtown Waterville, Colby College (Mayflower Hill, Waterville, 207/872-3000, www.colby.edu) is a must-see. Colby's 1,800 students attend a huge variety of liberal-arts programs on a 713-acre campus noted for its handsome Georgian buildings. Founded by Baptists in 1813 as the all-male Maine Literary and Theological Institution, Colby received its current name in 1867 and went coed in 1871. Campus tours are available by arrangement through the Admissions Office (207/859-4828 or 800/723-3032, open 8:30 A.M.–4:30 P.M. weekdays).

The **Colby College Museum of Art** (207/859-5600), in the Bixler Art and Music Center, has earned an especially distinguished reputation for its remarkable permanent collection of 18th-, 19th-, and 20th-century American art. Colby's museum is a stop on the Maine Art Museum Trail, which highlights the state's seven major art museums. In 1996, the museum opened its $1.5 million Paul J. Schupf Wing to house 415 paintings and sculptures created by artist Alex Katz during a 50-year period. In July 1999, the architecturally stunning $1.3 million Lunder Wing opened, expanding the museum's exhibit space to 28,000 square feet. Other significant holdings include works by Gilbert Stuart, Winslow Homer, and John Marin; special solo and group shows are mounted throughout the year. And don't miss the tasteful gift shop. Museum hours are 10 A.M.–4:30 P.M. Tuesday–Saturday, noon–4:30 P.M. Sunday. Admission is free. The museum is on the east side of the campus's main quadrangle, just north of Mayflower Hill Drive.

Also on the campus is the 128-acre **Perkins Arboretum and Bird Sanctuary,** with three nature trails. Bring a picnic and blanket and stretch out next to Johnson Pond. In winter, there's ice-skating on the pond.

Fort Halifax

Left over from a fort built in 1754, the two-story Fort Halifax (Bay St., Winslow) stands sentinel where the Sebasticook River meets the Kennebec. Oldest blockhouse in the nation, it was built of doweled logs during the French and Indian Wars. In 1984, after rampaging Kennebec floodwaters swept away the building, more than three dozen of the giant timbers were retrieved downstream. Energetic fund-raising allowed the blockhouse to be meticulously restored. The surrounding park is a great place for a picnic, with tables dotting shaded, grassy lawns rolling to the river's edge and a free Tuesday evening concert series in summer.

Fort Halifax, the nation's oldest blockhouse, was rebuilt from original timbers after floodwaters carried it away.

KENNEBEC

© TOM NANGLE

Two-Cent Bridge

Spanning the Kennebec from Benton Avenue in Winslow to Front Street in Waterville (walk down Temple Street in Waterville), the 700-foot-long Two-Cent Bridge (officially the Ticonic Footbridge) was built in 1903 for pedestrian commuters to the Scott Paper mill in Winslow, who paid two cents to cross. Closed in 1973, the bridge was recently reopened and is the forerunner of a Head of Falls waterfront redevelopment effort. Possibly the only toll pedestrian bridge left in the United States, its replica tollbooth is a "stand still" museum. A stroll over the bridge gives a good view of "Empire Falls."

Redington Museum

Home of the Waterville Historical Society, the Redington Museum and Apothecary (62 Silver St., Waterville, 207/872-9439, $3 adults, $2 children under 12) has a particularly intriguing 19th-century pharmacy, as well as Native American artifacts. The Federal-style Redington House was built in 1814 by early settler Asa Redington for his son, Silas. The museum is open 10 A.M.–3 P.M. Tuesday–Saturday Memorial Day week–Labor Day (closed holidays); tours are at 10 and 11 A.M. and 1 and 2 P.M.

Off the Beaten Path

The gentle farming communities northwest of Wateville have a few sites worth a detour.

Since 1867, the **Belfast and Moosehead Lake Railroad Company** (207/948-5500, www.unitytrainmuseum.org) is one of the oldest continuously operated railroads in the country and one of the best-preserved rural branch lines in the Northeast. Trains depart most Fridays, Saturdays, and Sundays June–October for two-hour round-trip excursions to Burnham Junction. The trip crosses two trestles and passes through rural countryside and alongside a lake. There's a café on board. Depending on the train operated, tickets are $20–23 adult, $18–21 senior, $10–12 ages 3–15. Special-event trains are also frequently scheduled, including a Santa Express during the holiday season. Some artifacts are displayed at the station.

Sometimes you really do have to see it to believe it. That's the case with the **Bryant Stove and Music Museum** (27 Stovepipe Alley, Thorndike, 207/568-3665, www.bryantstove .com, $4), a labor of love collected, created, repaired, and assembled by Joe and Bea Bryant. Begin with the Doll Circus. Flip a switch, and the room comes alive with dolls dancing, marching, swinging, turning, twisting to music. Airplanes fly, a Ferris wheel turns, stuffed animals swing. There's a Barbie Doll fashion show and a hula show and a line of Barbies and Kens marching to the altar. No matter which you way look, dolls and stuffed animals are actively positioned in creative scenes. It's a jaw-dropping marriage of lights and music and movement. And that's just the first room. Beyond it are a small engine room with miniature working steam engines; a music section with player pianos, Nickelodeons, juke boxes, organs, barrel pianos, hurdy-gurdys, and more. In summer, Joe might be the one who shows you around—just be ready to spend some time as he explains each instrument and brings it to life, often singing along with it. The museum is very hands-on, and visitors are encouraged to push buttons and play the instruments and learn about the mechanisms. If that's not enough, there are also antique stoves and automobiles that Joe has lovingly repaired. A separate part of the business specializes in antique stoves, and Joe might even tell you about some of the celebrities who have bought the restored beauties from him.

PARKS AND RECREATION

Golf

Public access is limited at the semiprivate 18-hole **Waterville Country Club** (Country Club Rd., Oakland, 207/465-9861), so you'll need to call for a starting time. The course, covering both sides of Country Club Road, is particularly well maintained, and facilities include a pro shop and driving range. There's a certain degree of stuffiness here; greens fees are moderate. Open mid-April–October, the course is a mile from I-95 Exit 127.

Hiking

Kennebec Messalonskee Trails (207/873-

6443, www.kmtrails.org) is busy, busy, busy constructing a riverside trail network in the region. For descriptions of finished trails, check the website.

ENTERTAINMENT

One of Maine's premier art-film houses is in downtown Waterville. The two-screen **Railroad Square Cinema** (17 Railroad Sq., Waterville, 207/873-6526, www.railroad squarecinema.com) is the home of the Maine International Film Festival (MIFF, www.miff .org), which has brought such luminaries as Sissy Spacek and Peter Fonda to town to receive Mid-Life Achievement Awards. For festival passes, call 207/873-7000. The festival takes place in the summer, but a MIFF in the Morning series takes place January–March. Shows change weekly; there are matinees most weekends and occasional weekdays.

About City Hall is the refurbished turn-of-the-20th-century **Waterville Opera House** (93 Main St., 207/873-5381, ticket hotline 207/873-7000, www.operahouse.com). Once the haunt of vaudevillians, the Opera House is now the site of plays, dance performances, and concerts throughout the year.

About 20 minutes northeast, in rural Unity, is **Unity Centre for the Performing Arts** (42 Depot St., 207/948-7469, www.unitymaine .org/theater), a 200-seat theater built by Bert and Coral Clifford and donated to Unity College in 2007.

Flagship Cinemas (247 Kennedy Memorial Dr., Shaw's Plaza, movie hotline 207/873-0033, www.flagshipcinemas.com) has eight screens, Internet ticketing, and a "Super Bargain Tuesday."

The downtown **Midnight Blues Club and Restaurant** (2 Silver St., Waterville, 207/877-8300, www.midnightbluesclub.net, 11–1 A.M.) has entertainment nightly.

FESTIVALS AND EVENTS

During the academic year, and less often in summer, Colby College (207/859-4353, or visit www .colby.edu/news) is the venue for exhibits, lectures, concerts, performances, and other events.

At various locations between Waterville and Jackman the first Saturday in June, **National Trails Day** features organized noncompetitive biking, hiking, and canoeing.

In mid-June, the annual **Blistered Fingers Family Bluegrass Music Festival** (www .blisteredfingers.com) takes place at the Silver Spur Riding club, in Sidney.

A gathering of New England's best fiddlers, the **East Benton Fiddlers' Convention** draws close to 2,000 enthusiasts to open-air performances at the Littlefield farm in East Benton. The convention happens noon–dusk the last Sunday in July. Call 207/453-2017 for directions.

Downtown Waterville is the site of late July's **Taste of Greater Waterville.** The food-focused one-day festival, usually held on a Wednesday, is organized by more than two dozen restaurants. In Castonguay Square and surrounding streets, there's alfresco dining, plus music for kids and adults.

During the third weekend in September, sleepy Unity comes alive with the **Common Ground Fair,** a celebration of organic foods and country life sponsored by the Maine Organic Farmers and Gardeners Association.

SHOPPING

Unlike so many former mill towns, Waterville's downtown has life, with shops and restaurants and plenty of free parking in The Concourse, the triangle framed by Elm, Main, and Spring Streets.

New, Used, and Children's Books

Conveniently situated downtown (facing the square), **Re-Books** (25 E. Concourse, Waterville, 207/877-2484) is a basement-level shop with a fairly extensive selection of hardcovers and paperbacks. Amiable proprietor Robert Sezak's specialties include poetry, philosophy, mysteries, Judaica, photography, sci-fi, and language titles. Directly above it (despite the name), facing Main Street, is the **Children's Book Cellar** (207/872-4543), a super-kid-friendly space with a great selection of books and toys.

Colby College's **Seaverns Bookstore**

(Roberts Union, Colby College, Waterville, 207/872-3609 or 800/727-8506) has general books and lots of Colby-logo sweatshirts, T-shirts, and other wearables. Roberts Union is on the northern side of the campus.

Crafts and Gifts

Paula and George Gordon's **Maine Made and More Shop** (93 Main St., Waterville, 207/872-7378) spotlights the work of Maine individuals and companies, but you'll find far more than crafts, and everything's high quality.

Johnny's Selected Seeds

If you're a gardener, farmer, horticulturalist, or just plain curious, take a 15-minute drive east of Waterville to visit the research farm of Johnny's Selected Seeds (Foss Hill Rd., Albion). Pick up a map and then take a self-guided tour of the 40 acres of trial gardens 9 A.M.–4 P.M. Monday–Friday in July and August. Or visit the store (207/861-3999) and headquarters (955 Benton Ave., Winslow, 207/861-3900, www.johnnyseeds.com). The eponymous seed source has a national reputation. More than 2,000 varieties of herbs, veggies, and flowers are grown in the trial gardens, which were started in 1973. Known for high-quality seeds and service, the company makes good on anything that doesn't sprout.

ACCOMMODATIONS

Chains dominate the lodging in this region, but The Pressey House, in the Belgrade Lakes area, is convenient to Waterville.

About 20 minutes northeast of Waterville is **The Copper Heron** (130 Main St., Unity, 207/948-9003, www.copperheron.com, $95 d), with four rooms in an in-town Greek Revival house built in 1842. Common areas include a library with a TV/VCR and a dining room, where full breakfasts (and dinners by arrangement) are served. You can walk to the Unity Centre for the Performing Arts, Unity College, and lovely Unity Pond (there's a boat put-in, but you'll want to drive to that). Unity is also home to the Maine Organic Farmers and Gardeners Association and its annual Common Ground Fair, in September. Children are welcome.

FOOD
Local Flavors

In a local twist on the traditional Maine public suppers—thanks to Waterville's substantial Lebanese community—**St. Joseph Maronite Church** (3 Appleton St., Waterville, 207/872-8515) puts on a Lebanese supper at least once a year (the second Sunday after Easter). If you enjoy Eastern Mediterranean home cooking, be there. Call the church for details.

Nothing's finer on a hot summer day than a banana or peanut butter-chocolate chip ice cream from **North Street Dairy Cone** (127 North St., Waterville, 207/873-0977).

Jorgensen's Café (103 Main St., Waterville, 207/872-8711, 7 A.M.–6 P.M. Mon.–Fri., to 5 P.M. Sat., 8 A.M.–4 P.M. Sun.) is a downtown institution, with a French-language club meeting there on Saturday mornings. But you can hear French spoken at other times, too, while sipping one of what seem to be hundreds of kinds of coffee set out on a center counter and enjoying a bagel, muffin, or breakfast sandwich. Lunch consists of a unique variety of specialty sandwiches, with every kind of deli meat available, plus quiche, salads, and soups. There's also an unusually interesting selection of gourmet gifts, implements, wine, and sweets.

An extremely popular hangout, **Big G's Deli** (Benton Ave., Winslow, 207/873-7808, www.big-g-s-deli.com, 6 A.M.–7 P.M. daily) began as a sandwich shop in 1986 and now seats 200. It's renowned for enormous "name" sandwiches such as the Miles Standwich (nearly a whole turkey dinner), all on thick slices of homemade bread (half sandwiches are available). In fact, all breads and pastries are house made. You can enjoy breakfast until 1 P.M. Order at the counter and try for a seat; or get it to go for the mother of all picnics. No credit cards. On the east side of the Kennebec, Big G's is about a mile north of the Route 201 bridge to Waterville.

The **Grand Central Café** (10 Railroad Sq., 207/873-9135) is a local favorite for fancy brick-oven pizza. Very popular are the buffets, with all-you-can-eat pizza, soup, and salad for $7.95 at lunch and $11.95 at dinner, with kids under 12 charged $4.95. It's open 11 A.M.–2 P.M. and 5–close Monday–Thursday, 11 A.M.–close Friday–Saturday, noon–close Sunday.

If you are waiting to ride the train, **Crosstrax** (215 Depot St., Unity, 207/948-3663, www.crosstrax948food.com, 7 A.M.–6 P.M. Mon.–Wed., 7 A.M.–8 P.M. Thurs.–Sat.) is a comfy place to do so. It's part deli, part market; simply order at the counter, choosing from a huge range of sandwich possibilities, along with soups and daily specials.

Here's a spot worth seeking out. The **C Riverside Farm Market** (291 Fairfield St., Oakland, 207/465-4439, 9 A.M.–6 P.M. Mon.–Sat., 10 A.M.–2 P.M. Sun.) doubles as a casual café, serving fabulous sandwiches, soups, and salads with a Mediterranean bent, scrumptious baked goods, and designer coffees for breakfast, lunch, and Sunday brunch, with plans to expand to dinner, perhaps when an addition is completed in 2008. There's seating inside and on the porch. Order scones or muffins, or lunch—soups, salads, quiche, and sandwiches—at the deli/baked goods counter. And if you have a cottage, pick up one of the homemade pies—the *tortierre,* a traditional Franco American meat pie, is delicious. Closed late December–early April.

The **Downtown Waterville Farmers Market** (2–6 P.M. Thurs.) sets up in the concourse along Appleton Street downtown. Breads, organic meats and cheese, veggies galore, even handcrafted items and wrought-iron work, are sold.

Ethnic Fare

Food to soothe the Southern soul is served at **The Freedom Café** (141 College Ave., Waterville, 207/859-8742, 5–9 P.M. Wed.–Sat.). Owners James and Janice Swinton—she's the chef—might be serving barbecue bourbon pork ribs, creole-fried tilapia with pineapple salsa, jambalaya, or Caribbean chicken breasts, perhaps accompanied by succotash, candied yams, hopping John, or collard greens. Everything is freshly made daily in small batches, so don't be surprised if they run out of an item. There are two seatings nightly, and reservations are essential in this tiny place. Full meals range $19–22 and include beverage and dessert; ages 6–10 are $6.95, under five eat 5.

Linked like a Siamese twin to the Railroad Square Cinema, **Buen Apetito** (4 Chaplin St., Railroad Sq., Waterville, 207/861-4649, 5–8 P.M. Sun.–Mon., 11 A.M.–8 P.M. Tues.–Thurs., 11 A.M.–9 P.M. Fri.–Sat.) serves popular Mexican fare accented by fresh salsas and homemade tortillas.

It doesn't look like much from the outside—or on the inside for that matter, but the little **Lebanese Cuisine** (34 Temple St., Waterville, 207/873-7813) serves authentic and delicious homemade spinach and meat pies, hummus, tabbouleh, and kibbee. Prices range from less than $2 to about $10. The baklava is heavenly—not the sticky, overly sweet stuff that masquerades as baklava, but a flavorful treat. Eat here or get it to go. The bakery is open 9 A.M.–4 P.M. Monday–Friday, 9 A.M.–1 P.M. Saturday all year.

The area has numerous Asian restaurants, and one that's stood the test of time is **Asian Café** (53 Bay St., Winslow, 207/877-6688), serving Japanese, Korean, Thai, and Vietnamese cuisine 11 A.M.–9:30 P.M. daily. Don't overorder appetizers. They're huge!

Family Friendly

Just across the Waterville/Winslow bridge, with deck tables overlooking the Kennebec, is the **Lobster Trap and Steakhouse** (25 Bay St., Rte. 201, Winslow, 207/872-0529, www.lobstertrap-seafood.com, 11 A.M.–9 P.M. daily). Frankly, you'll find better food and service elsewhere, but if you're craving a lobster, this is the place to come. Most entrées are $10–16; light appetite choices are less, lobsters are more. When the weather turns sour, there's plenty of room inside this casual place.

Casual Dining

Fresh, flavorful cuisine with varied ethnic inspirations makes dining at **The Last Unicorn**

KENNEBEC

(98 Silver St., Rte. 201, Waterville, 207/873-6378, 11 A.M.–10 P.M. daily) a delicious adventure. Creative appetizers, an extensive wine and cocktail list, and Saturday and Sunday brunch are other pluses of this friendly place, with patio dining in summer. Soups and desserts are made daily, most dressings and spreads are made on the premises, and the house dressings, sauces, and *boursin* are sold retail. Lunch and brunch specials range $6–12; dinner entrées $16–22.

Lunch is excellent at **The Bread Box Café** (137 Main St., Waterville, 207/873-4090, 11 A.M.–10:30 P.M. Tues.–Sat.), but dinner is pricey (most choices in the low $20s) and service is iffy. The bistro-style menu favors creative American cuisine with an emphasis on fresh and local.

Fancier Fare

Up a steep flight of stairs, on the second floor of a Victorian home that also houses a spa, is **Apollo's Bistro** (91 Silver St., Waterville, 207/872-2242, www.apollosalonspa.com, 5:30–10 P.M. Tues.–Sat.), an elegant choice for a creative meal. Given that it's connected to the spa, it's no surprise that the emphasis is on fresh, local, and organic foods. Entrées ($18–33) might include Moroccan lamb tagine, butter-poached Maine lobster, or pan-roasted East Coast halibut. Expect a leisurely meal, as all meals are prepared to order. If you're in the mood to be pampered, ask about specials that combine spa treatments with lunch or dinner.

INFORMATION AND SERVICES

The Mid-Maine Chamber of Commerce (1 Post Office Sq., Elm and Main Sts., Waterville, 207/873-3315, www.midmainechamber.com) has its headquarters in an elegant 1911 Greek Revival building. The office is open 9 A.M.–5 P.M. Monday–Friday.

Check out Waterville Public Library (73 Elm St., Waterville, 207/872-5433, www.waterville.lib.me.us). Miller Library (Colby College, Waterville, 207/859-5100) has a huge Irish literature collection and a room dedicated to poet Edwin Arlington Robinson.

Skowhegan Area

The Wabanaki named Skowhegan (skow-HE-gun) "the place to watch for fish," because that's just what the early Native Americans did at the Kennebec River's twin waterfalls here. Their spears were ready when lunch came leaping up the river. The island between the falls later formed the core for European settlement of Skowhegan (pop. 9,000), largest town and county seat in Somerset County. Named for England's Somersetshire, the county was incorporated in 1823 and covers 3,633 square miles.

Favorite daughter Margaret Chase Smith, one of Maine's preeminent politicians, put Skowhegan on the map, and even since her 1995 death, admirers and historians have made pilgrimages to her former home. During her years in the U.S. Congress and Senate, "The Lady from Maine" would return to her constituents—and she was never too busy to autograph placemats at her favorite local restaurant or to wave from her chair in her house's streetside solarium. Older local residents still recall the day President Dwight D. Eisenhower and his entourage visited Mrs. Smith, in 1955, when "Ike" spoke to an enthusiastic crowd at the Skowhegan Fairgrounds.

Another local institution is the nationally and internationally renowned Skowhegan School of Painting and Sculpture, founded in 1946 as a summer residency program. One of America's few art schools offering workshops in fresco painting, Skowhegan provides 65 artists with a bucolic, 300-acre lakeside setting for honing their skills and interacting with peers and prominent visiting artists. Acceptance is highly competitive for the nine-week program. Skowhegan's annual summer lecture series, featuring big names in the art world, is open to the public.

In the early 18th century, the town of Norridgewock (NORE-ridge-wok) was a French and Indian stronghold against the British. A century earlier, French Jesuit missionaries had moved in among the Norridgewock Indians at their settlement here and converted them to Catholicism. Best known of these was Father Sebastien Râle, beloved of his Indian parishioners. In 1724, taking revenge for Indian forays against them, a British militia detachment marched in and massacred the priest and his followers, a major milestone during what was known as Dummer's War. Today, a granite monument to Father Râle stands at the crime scene, Old Point, along the Kennebec about two miles south of downtown Madison, close to the Madison/Norridgewock town boundary.

Meaning "smooth water between rapids," Norridgewock (pop. 3,340) was the last bit of civilization for Benedict Arnold and his men before they headed into the Upper Kennebec wilderness on their March to Québec in 1775. Stopping for almost a week, they spent most of their time caulking their leaky bateaux. Today the town has a slew of handsome 18th- and 19th-century homes.

More recently, some of the scenes in the movie *Empire Falls* were shot in Skowhegan. That was one of the bright spots in a town that's fighting for its economic survival. It recently received grants to spruce up its architecturally rich main street, which unfortunately doubles as Route 201, the major thoroughfare between Québec and the coast. Take care crossing the street.

SIGHTS
Margaret Chase Smith Library
Beautifully sited on Neil Hill, high above the Kennebec River, the Margaret Chase Smith Library (56 Norridgewock Ave., Skowhegan, 207/474-7133, www.mcslibrary.org, 10 A.M.–4 P.M. Mon.–Fri., donation welcome) bulges with fascinating memorabilia from the life and times of one of Maine's best-known politicians, who spent 32 years in the U.S. House and Senate and died in 1995. Over the entrance door is her signature red rose; inside is a 20-minute video

describing her career. In 2000, the library held a special commemoration of the 50th anniversary of Senator Smith's "declaration of conscience" speech, in which she courageously castigated Senator Joseph McCarthy for his "Red Scare" witch-hunting tactics. Ask if a staff member is available to show you Senator Smith's house, connected to the library on the 15-acre estate. (She was born at 81 North Ave. in Skowhegan.) The library is closed the week between Christmas and New Year's Day. The complex is 0.5 mile west of Route 201 (Madison Ave.).

Skowhegan History House
When you enter the handsome red-brick Skowhegan History House (40 Elm St., Skowhegan, 207/474-6632, 1–5 P.M. Tues.–Fri. early June–late Sept., $2 adults, $1 kids and seniors), with only a half dozen rooms, you'll find it hard to believe that blacksmith Aaron Spear built it in 1839 for his family of 10 children. Must have been mighty cozy sleeping. Skowhegan treasures—antique clocks, china, and other furnishings—now fill the two-story structure, which has a commanding view over the Kennebec River and lovely gardens. The house is just west of Route 201, at the junction of Elm and Pleasant Streets.

The Skowhegan Indian Monument
On High Street, next to a parking lot just east of Madison Avenue (Rte. 201), stands the giant wooden Skowhegan Indian. Rising 62 feet above its pedestal and weighing 24,000 pounds, the statue was carved in 1969 by Maine sculptor Bernard Langlais, who died in 1977. Nationally known for his work, Langlais dedicated the monument to the Native Americans who first settled this area. One hand holds a spear, the other holds a stylized fishing weir.

Skowhegan Historic District
Bounded roughly by Water and Russell Streets and Madison Avenue, the Skowhegan Historic District, close to the Kennebec River, contains 38 turn-of-the-20th-century buildings from the town's heyday as a commercial center. After trains arrived in 1856, the wireless telegraph in

KENNEBEC

© TOM NANGLE

The exterior of the L. C. Bates Museum provides no clue about the eclectic artifacts within it.

1862, and telephones in 1883, Skowhegan saw incredible prosperity. It's worth a walkabout to admire the architectural details of a bygone era, although sad to say, many of the buildings need maintenance.

(L. C. Bates Museum

Offbeat doesn't begin to describe this treasure chest. In a Romanesque National Historic Register building on the Good Will-Hinckley School campus, established in 1889 as a school for disadvantaged children, the L. C. Bates Museum (Rte. 201, Hinckley, 207/238-4250, www.gwh.org, 10 A.M.–4:30 P.M. Wed.–Sat., 1–4:30 P.M. Sun. Apr. 1–Nov. 30, or by appointment, $2 adults, $1 ages 12–17, and $0.75 children) is a way-cool, way-retro museum, with a broadly eclectic collection focusing on natural history. Among the treasures in the dozen or so rooms are hundreds of mounted rare birds, priceless Native American artifacts, and a trophy marlin caught by Ernest Hemingway.

Behind the museum, visit the arboretum and nature trails, open dawn–dusk. "Forest Walking Trails" maps are available in the museum. Alongside the trails are monuments to prominent conservationists. For a small fee, kids can attend Saturday-morning natural-history workshops May–November. While on campus, stop at the visitors center to view a small gallery of memorabilia relating to Senator Margaret Chase Smith. The turreted brick and granite building is five miles north of I-95 Exit 133, between Fairfield and Skowhegan, and is visible from Route 201 at the southern end of the campus.

(South Solon Meetinghouse

This place is nothing short of amazing. As you drive out the East Madison Road from Skowhegan, headed north, you'll pass Lake Wesserunsett and soon come to the hamlet (little more than a crossroads) of South Solon. Here you'll find a serene white clapboard building, a traditional mid-19th-century New England meetinghouse. Inside, it's *totally* frescoed with interdenominational religious scenes. One of the founders of the Skowhegan School of Painting and Sculpture rescued the church from ruin in the 1930s; in the 1950s, fresco artists selected in a stiff competition were given a free hand to have a go at the place. The riot of color followed until every square inch of walls and ceiling was covered. (A fresco program still continues at the Skowhegan School.) Fund-raising is under way to restore the building and the frescoes. If the door is locked when you get there, call Andy Davis (207/643-2555); better still, call ahead. The meetinghouse is on the corner of the South Solon and Meetinghouse Roads, north of Route 43 and east of Route 201.

PARKS AND RECREATION

Skowhegan is the base for **Kennebec Valley Trails (KVT)** (P.O. Box 144, Skowhegan 04976, 207/474-9606), an energetic membership organization promoting an ambitious long-range plan for multiuse recreational trail systems throughout the Kennebec Valley. KVT publishes *The Kennebec River: A Guide for Paddlers and Friends,* an extensive guide to the river, its history, and its environs, and *Take a Ride: Road and Mountain Biking Guide to the Upper Kennebec Valley.* The organization annually sponsors **National Trails Day** events the first Saturday in June. If you'd like to order a guidebook or become a member, contact KVT.

Coburn Park

Donated to the town by Abner Coburn, 13-acre Coburn Park, a wonderful riverside oasis, has a lily pond, memorial gardens (including a hospice garden and a Margaret Chase Smith rose garden), a summer concert series at the gazebo, pagodas, and more than 100 species of trees and shrubs. Bring a picnic, grab a table, and enjoy. The park is on Water Street/Route 2, at the eastern edge of town.

Lake George Park

Eight miles east of Skowhegan is 3320-acre state-owned Lake George Regional Park (Rte. 2/Canaan Rd., 207/474-1292, 8 A.M.–sunset seasonally, $3 adults, $1 children 5–11, children under 5 and seniors over 65 free), with facilities for swimming and picnicking, plus a boat launch, restrooms, ball fields, hiking trails, and cross-country trails. No pets, alcohol, or camping.

Pedestrian Bridges

Spanning the South Channel of the Kennebec River, the **Swinging Bridge** connects Skowhegan Island (from behind the ice-cream stand) to Alder Street, off West Front Street. First built in 1883, floods in 1888, 1901, 1936, and 1987 damaged or destroyed the wire footbridge. Its latest incarnation was unveiled in 2006, when the town completely renovated it. The views are terrific, and the island park is a jewel.

The **Skowhegan Walking Bridge** spans the river about a block below the dam, opposite where Route 201 North and Route 2 split downtown. This one traces its history back to 1856, when it was constructed for the Somerset and Kennebec Railroad. The following year, it was carried away by floodwaters. A wooden bridge followed, and then a steel one, also destroyed by floodwaters. The current bridge was built in 1988. Like the Swinging Bridge, it's worth a stroll just for the views.

Arnold's Way Rest Area

About three miles north of Solon, close to the Solon/Bingham town line and just north of the area known as Arnold's Landing, is this especially attractive state rest area with covered picnic tables, grills, and an outhouse. Interpretive panels here mark the beginning of two dozen along the Old Canada Road Scenic Byway at Moscow, The Forks, Parlin Pond, and Attean, helping motorists get a feel for area history and pursuits such as logging.

Traditional Skills Courses

In Canaan, east of Skowhegan, Master Maine Guide Ray Reitze Jr. and his wife, Nancy, operate **Earthways Guided Canoe Trips and School of Wilderness Living** (159 Earthways Rd., Canaan, 207/426-8138, www.earthways .net), with an extensive schedule of canoe trips on the St. John, Allagash, Poland Pond, and classes on traditional skills such as basket-making, flint knapping, snowshoe lacing, and traditional medicine. Primitive campsites are available on their "campus" in Canaan. Ray, who learned woods lore as a youth from a Native American elder, has written a book about his spiritual philosophy, *And We Shall Cast Rainbows upon the Land.*

Golf

The 18-hole **Lakewood Golf Course** (Rte. 201, Madison, 207/474-5955), five miles north of Skowhegan, dates from 1925. The trickiest hole is the eighth, with a good-size pond between you and the green. Tee times are advisable here, especially in fall when the foliage is spectacular; carts are available.

ENTERTAINMENT
Theaters

A blast from the past is the refurbished **Strand Cinema** (19 Court St., Skowhegan, 207/474-3451, www.mainecinemas.com), which opened in late 1929 as the Strand Theater, and now has one of the, if not the, largest screens in the state.

For another dose of nostalgia, plan to catch a flick at the 350-car **Skowhegan Drive-In** (Waterville Rd., Rte. 201, Skowhegan, 207/474-9277, www.skowhegandrivein.com), a landmark since 1954. Nightly double features start at dusk or whenever the sun disappears. Gates open at 7:30 P.M. The drive-in, at the southern end of town, is open Thursday–Sunday late May–late June and then daily until Labor Day. The show goes on, rain or shine, except in fog.

Built in 1901, the **Lakewood Theater** (Rte. 201, Madison, 207/474-7176, mailing address P.O. Box 331, Skowhegan 04976, www.lakewoodtheater.org), on the shores of Lake Wesserunsett six miles north of Skowhegan, has had a roller-coaster history, but it's now in a decidedly "up" phase. Maine's oldest summer theater presents nine musicals, comedies, and light dramas each season. Performances are at 8 P.M. Thursday–Saturday, plus matinees at 2 P.M. every other Wednesday and at 4 P.M. Sunday late May–mid-September. On matinee Wednesdays, there is also a 7 P.M. evening

performance. Tickets are in the low $20s for adults, midteens for ages 4–17. For about $5 more, you can have cabaret seating on the side balconies. Special children's plays ($5 adult, $3.50 ages 10 and younger) are performed at 10 A.M. on four summer Saturdays. You'll find food just steps from the theater at the Lakewood Inn Restaurant.

Lectures and Concerts

Performing-arts events are sometimes scheduled in Skowhegan's **Opera House** inside the circa 1909 City Hall, where Booker T. Washington spoke in 1912.

Mid-June–early August, the evening **Barbara Fish Lee Lecture Series** draws nationally and internationally noted artists to participate in its lecture/presentation series at the Old Dominion Fresco Barn, Skowhegan School of Painting and Sculpture. Contact the school (207/474-9345) for dates and times.

A concert series is held at Skowhegan's Coburn Park at 5 P.M. on Sundays during July and August.

ENTERTAINMENT AND EVENTS

Megaomelettes made in the world's largest omelette pan, a parade, a craft fair, live entertainment, a carnival, and fireworks are among the features of the **Central Maine Egg Festival.** The biggest day is Saturday. It's held at Manson Park in Pittsfield mid-–late July.

Billed as America's oldest country fair, going back more than 175 years, and Maine's largest outdoor event, the **Skowhegan State Fair** is a 10-day extravaganza with agricultural exhibits galore, live entertainment, harness racing, food booths, a carnival, and a demolition derby at the Skowhegan Fairgrounds, Route 201, Skowhegan, early–mid-August.

On the Fourth of July, the **In Spite of Life Players** stage a performance at the gravel pit in West Athens.

SHOPPING
Factory Outlet

Discounts of up to 50 percent are typical for

athletic-shoe seconds at the **New Balance Factory Store** (12 Walnut St., Skowhegan, 207/474-6231). The store also carries sportswear, socks, sports bags, and such. The outlet is just off Route 201 (W. Front St.), south of the Kennebec. The turn is next to Skowhegan Savings Bank.

Antiques

The **Fairfield Antiques Mall** (382 Rte. 201, Fairfield, 207/453-4100) boasts that it's the state's largest antiques mall. Judge for yourself. It's 2.5 miles north of the I-95 interchange.

ACCOMMODATIONS
Bed-and-Breakfasts

Helen Lamphere and her daughter Charlene run **Helen's Bed and Breakfast** (165 Madison Ave., Rte. 201, Skowhegan, 207/474-0066, www.helensbandb.com, $65–95 d), a lovely 19th-century brick Victorian with four air-conditioned rooms. Antiques, country pieces, and Helen's hand-braided rugs create a comfy retreat. Helen also sells her rugs. Guests share the large deck and yard. It's open April–December.

The sunset views over the western mountains win over newly arriving guests at Al and Cindy Laiho's **⟨ Mountains View Bed and Breakfast** (243 Hilton Hill, Skowhegan, 207/858-0946 or 866/267-8181, www .mountainsviewbandb, $90 d). The rural hilltop location is private yet just five minutes from downtown. Two spacious guest rooms are tastefully decorated, air-conditioned, and have sitting areas with TV, toaster oven, microwave, minirefrigerator, and coffeemaker. The downstairs living room has a powerful telescope trained on Sugarloaf Mountain. On the grounds are a pretty pond and walking trails. A continental breakfast is served the first morning. No credit cards.

Just west of Skowhegan is the **Norridgewock Colonial Inn** (15 Upper Main St., P.O. Box 932, Norridgewock 04957, 207/634-3470), innkeepers Nancy and Lincoln Fickett's Victorian with fireplaces, cable TV, air-conditioning, and an outside area for smokers. Rates range

$65 off-season–$95 in season, d, and include a full breakfast and afternoon tea. Some pets are allowed.

Sleep where the stars slept at **The Colony House Inn Bed and Breakfast** (P.O. Box 251, Madison 04950, 207/474-6599 or 888/268-2853, $75 d), a lovely, lakefront historical B&B adjacent to the Lakeside Theater. The shingle-style inn is wrapped in old-style elegance, with comfy public rooms, a nice screened porch, and a many-windowed dining room, where a full breakfast is served. The ultrareasonable prices reflect the old-fashioned baths. One room has a private bath, two lake-facing rooms are connected by a bath, and two other rooms share a bath. Also on the premises are two cottages ($400–500/week or $75 d/night), one lakefront, the other lake facing. Within walking distance are the theater, golf course, and a spiritualist camp that's been running for more than 125 years. Rent a boat. Or simply settle into one of the Adirondack chairs on the lawn and gaze out at Lake Wesserunsett. Heaven!

Motel

Also convenient to downtown, the **Towne Motel** (172 Madison Ave., Rte. 201 N, Skowhegan, 207/474-5151 or 800/843-4405, www .townemotel.com) has 33 rooms, all with phones, air-conditioning, cable TV, high-speed Internet access, and some have kitchenettes. Continental breakfast is included. The large outdoor pool is great for kids. Pets are welcome in some rooms. Rates are $84–108 July–mid-October, $64–75 other months.

Campgrounds

How often do you find a campground on the National Historic Register? That's the case at **The Evergreens Campground and Restaurant** (Rte. 201A, P.O. Box 114, Solon 04979, 207/643-2324, www.evergreens campground.com), upon a prehistoric site used by Native Americans about 4,000 years ago. Many stone tools and weapons excavated here are now in the Maine State Museum in Augusta; a small collection is displayed at the campground. The campground has mostly wooded sites ($7.50 pp for tent sites, $24 d for RV sites; children under eight are free), some right on the Kennebec River. Cottages are $30 pp. Pets are allowed; rental canoes, kayaks, and tubes are available by the day; and shuttle service is available. There is a small launch fee for people bringing their own boats, and a guest fee. The restaurant, open 5–p.m. Friday and Saturday for dinner and 7–11 A.M. Saturday and Sunday for all-you-can-eat breakfast, has a bar and a riverfront deck. Directly across the river (technically in Embden) is a huge outcrop covered with ancient Indian petroglyphs; eagles can often be seen on this shore. The campground, a mile south of the center of Solon, is open all year, except mud season, catering to snowmobilers in winter.

FOOD
Local Flavors
Just south of downtown, the **Snack Shack** (100 Waterville Rd./Rte. 201, Skowhegan, 207/474-0550, 11 A.M.–8 P.M. Tues.–Wed., to 10 P.M. Thurs.–Sat., noon–8 P.M. Sun.) never disappoints for fried foods or sandwiches. It has a few tables, but most folks get takeout.

More than two dozen fat sandwiches, as well as good salads and a soup of the day, draw locals into **Kel-Matt Café** (112 Madison Ave./Rte. 201, Skowhegan, 207/474-0200, 11 A.M.–4 P.M. Mon.–Wed., 6:30 P.M. Fri. to, to 3 P.M. Sat.), in a Victorian house just north of downtown across from Bangor Savings Bank. Order at the counter and then grab a table in one of the small dining rooms, both spotless, or out on the front porch. Service is friendly and efficient. Be careful to park only in the restaurant's designated lot and not in that of the insurance agency next door.

I scream, you scream, in Maine, everyone screams for **Gifford's Ice Cream** (307 Madison Ave./Rte 1, Skowhegan). At this roadside institution, you can lick whoopie pie, Maine tracks, Denali peanut butter Iditarod, or Maine wild blueberry flavors while playing a game of miniature golf.

The **Skowhegan Farmers Market** sets up in the Skowhegan Savings Bank parking lot, corner of Route 201 and Pleasant Street, 9 A.M.–1 P.M. Saturday early July–October. About 15 vendors sell baked goods, produce, and meats, much of it organic. There usually are children's activities and music.

Family Fare
The parking lot's always busy at **Ken's Family Restaurant** (414 Madison Ave., Rte. 201, Skowhegan, 207/474-3120, 10:30 A.M.–8 P.M. Mon.–Thurs., 5:45 A.M.–9 P.M. Fri.–Sat., 8 A.M.–8 P.M. Sun.), in its second generation of Dionne family ownership. Seafood's the specialty, and seconds are on the house when you order either the jumbo fish fry ($10) or fried fantail shrimp ($13). The Italian menu is equally popular; select a pasta and pair it with a sauce for $7. Families know they can count on good home cooking, and there's always the all-you-care-to-eat breakfast, served weekends. The children's menu lists about a dozen choices for $3.49, and of course there's the kid-pleasing dirt pudding. Afterward you can bowl at Ken's Family Bowling Center, across the street.

The downtown **Empire Grill** (105 Water St., Skowhegan, 207/474-3440, 6 A.M.–9 P.M. Sun.–Thurs., to 3 A.M. Fri.–Sat.) is so ultra-retro it seems like a movie scene. That's because it was created during the filming of *Empire Falls,* the movie based on Richard Russo's Pulitzer Prize–winning novel. Breakfast is served all day, but sandwiches, burgers, dogs, pizza, and even a few dinners are available, and nothing on the menu is more than about $12. Ask locally about its current reputation—new owners were trying to turn it around.

Casual Dining
Right on the river, the **Old Mill Pub and Restaurant** (39 Water St., Skowhegan, 207/474-6627), in a handsome antique brick building, gets high marks for its buffalo wings. Weather permitting, you can drink and dine on the deck. Prices are moderate. It's open all year, 11:30 A.M.–9 P.M. Monday–Thursday (to 10 P.M. Fri.–Sat.) and noon–8 P.M. Sunday. It's closed Sunday and Monday November–March. Friday night there's live music; it gets pretty noisy.

Two doors from the Towne Motel, in a renovated 19th-century home, the **Heritage House Restaurant** (182 Madison Ave., Skowhegan, 207/474-5100) is Skowhegan's best dining choice. Dinner entrées run $10–20. Apricot mustard chicken breast is a specialty. Reservations are advisable on weekends. The Heritage House is open Tuesday–Friday for the lunch buffet (11:30 A.M.–2 P.M.) and nightly for dinner (5–9 P.M., to 10 P.M. Fri.–Sat.) all year.

Elegance is the byword at the restored **Lakewood Inn Restaurant** (Rte. 201, P.O. Box 331, Skowhegan 04976, 207/858-4403, www.lakewoodtheater.org), open to theatergoers and the public. There's a "Bette Davis table," and Lana Turner and John Travolta have also frequented the premises. It's open at 5 P.M.

Wednesday, Thursday, Friday, and Saturday, at 6 P.M. Sunday, and on show days. There's a two-for-one entrée special on Wednesday, and a brunch buffet 11:30 A.M.–2 P.M. on show Wednesdays, and an evening buffet after the 4 P.M. Sunday matinee.

INFORMATION AND SERVICES

The Skowhegan Area Chamber of Commerce (23 Commercial St., Skowhegan, 207/474-3621 or 888/772-4392, www.skowhegan chamber.com) has info, as does the town's website (www.skowhegan.org).

Check out Skowhegan Free Public Library (9 Elm St., Skowhegan, 207/474-9072, www .skowhegan.lib.me.us).

Bingham to Jackman

Route 201, from Solon north to Jackman, is a National Scenic Byway that's a treat for the eyes. Until the arrival of white-water rafting in the late 1970s, the Upper Kennebec Valley was best known to anglers, hunters, timber truckers, and families who'd been summering here for generations. And long before that, long before dams changed the river's flow patterns, Native Americans used the Kennebec as a convenient chute from the interior's dense forests to summer encampments on the coast. In 1775, Colonel Benedict Arnold led more than 1,000 men up this river in a futile campaign to storm the ramparts of Québec City.

Midway between Skowhegan and The Forks, 23 miles in each direction, Bingham (pop. 989 in the 2000 census) is also right on the 45th parallel and thus equidistant between the North Pole and the equator (3,107 miles in each direction). This quiet valley town is a low-key commercial center with attractive, manicured homes and is a stopping point for many white-water rafters en route to Caratunk and The Forks. The town was named for William Bingham, an influential Colonial-era banker and land speculator who made a fortune in pri-

vateering. Roscoe Vernon ("Gadabout") Gaddis, TV's pioneering Flying Fisherman, built Bingham's funky grass airfield, the Gadabout Gaddis Airport, site of an annual September fly-in with plane rides and aerobatics.

Just north of Bingham is Moscow, home of the 155-foot-high Wyman Dam, harnessing the Kennebec River for hydroelectric power. Backed up behind the dam is gorgeous Wyman Lake, lined with birches, evergreens, frequent pullouts (great for shutterbugs), and a small lakeside picnic area on the west side of Route 201.

Appropriately named, The Forks stands at the confluence of the Kennebec and Dead Rivers, making it obvious why rafting companies have set up shop here. The tiny year-round population of 35 supports an ever-expanding transient population for the white-water rafting trade late April–mid-October.

Surrounded by mountains, Jackman (pop. 718) is the valley's frontier town, the last outpost before the Québec provincial border, 16 miles northward. In the middle of town, the Moose River links Jackman to the town of Moose River (pop. 219), just to the north.

KENNEBEC

THE BENEDICT ARNOLD TRAIL

"A tragic masterpiece of bad timing, bad maps, and bad luck" is author Ogden Tanner's summation of Colonel Benedict Arnold's March on Québec. Even though Arnold's expedition has been little more than a footnote to history, it's an incredible story, and one best appreciated during a visit to this region.

Arnold marched his troops up the Kennebec River Valley, before crossing it and veering inland and up along the Carrabasset River. From Pittston to the Carrying Place (10 miles north of Bingham) and along Route 27, between Kingfield and the border, Arnold Trail historical markers note the expedition's rest stops, obstacles, and other details.

When you see the terrain, you'll begin to understand some of the awful rigors endured by Arnold (before his change of heart and alliance) and his men when they chose a route through the Kennebec Valley to attack the British in Québec City in 1775. Although he later betrayed the Revolutionary cause, Arnold was in good graces when he set out that fall with 1,100 adventurers to remove the English from their Québec stronghold.

In Pittston (six miles south of Augusta), the expedition assembled 220 locally made bateaux and then continued up the Kennebec River to Augusta (camping at Old Fort Western), Skowhegan, and Norridgewock – cutting a swath through the Kennebec River Valley, before portaging westward at Carrying Place Township to the Western Lakes and Mountains region and on into Canada. Afflicted by disease, hunger, cold, insects, and unforgiving terrain, the group was devastated before dragging into Québec City in December 1775.

If you're interested in Arnold, pick up a copy of *Following Their Footsteps: A Travel Guide and History of the 1775 Secret Expedition to Capture Quebec*, by Stephen Clark. The 160-page book (Clark Books, Shapleigh, Maine, 2003) includes history, maps, canoe routes, and an appendix of places to visit along the way.

Wander into local businesses, and you'll likely hear a French lilt to conversation.

From Bingham to Jackman, Route 201 is better known as "Moose Alley." Even though state transportation officials have built rumble strips into the road and littered the roadsides with flashing yellow lights and cautionary Moose Crossing signs, drivers still barrel along, and every year fatalities occur. Those who drive carefully, though, have a treat in store: Moose sightings are relatively frequent, especially early and late in the day. If you notice a car or two pulled off the road, it's likely someone has spotted a moose. (Another Moose Alley in this area—a pretty sure bet for spotting one of the behemoths—is Route 6/15 from Jackman east to Rockwood.)

SIGHTS

◖ Moxie Falls

Here's a big reward for little effort. One of New England's highest waterfalls, Moxie Falls, with drops of as much as 100 feet, is one of the easiest to reach. From Route 201, just south of the Kennebec River bridge in The Forks, drive 1.8 miles east on Lake Moxie Road to the sign-posted parking area. From here, via an easy, wide trail, plus steps and a boardwalk, it's 0.6 mile to the falls in Moxie Stream. Allow a relaxed hour for the round-trip; if it's hot, cool off in the stepped pools. Avoid the falls in June, when blackflies will have you for lunch.

◖ Old Canada Road National Scenic Byway

High on everyone's list of "best roads to drive in fall" is **Route 201,** the 78-mile officially designated Old Canada Road Scenic Byway between Lakewood and the Canadian border. Every curve in the winding, two-lane road reveals a red, gold, and green palette any artist would die for. But truly, it's gorgeous in any season.

It's also a historic stretch of route. Benedict Arnold marched his troops along the Kennebec to north of Moscow, before crossing the river turning inland. Rest stops along the route have interpretive signage and picnic tables. Two of the prettiest are **Wyman Lake Rest Area,** about midway between Bingham and

The Forks, and **Attean View Rest Area,** just south of Jackman (climb the Owl's Head Trail for an even more spectacular view). The rest area in The Forks, just before the bridge, is a great place to watch rafts float by at the end of their thrilling trip down the Kennebec River. Detour into the neat little hamlet of **Caratunk** (pop. 108), a smidgen east of Route 201 on the way to Pleasant Pond.

RECREATION

Recreation is The Big Focus in this part of Maine. Among the opportunities in the Upper Kennebec Valley are hiking, canoeing, kayaking, bicycling, fishing, and snowmobiling—just for a start—but the big business is white-water rafting, headquartered in and around The Forks.

White-Water Rafting

Carefully regulated by the state, the rafting companies have come a long way since the sport really took off in the early 1980s. Most have sprawling base-camp complexes and have

diversified year-round into such other adventure sports as mountain biking, canoeing, kayaking, camping, rock climbing, horseback riding, snowmobiling, and cross-country skiing. The state strictly monitors the number of rafts allowed on the rivers; on midsummer weekends, there's a near-capacity crowd.

The focus of white-water rafting in this region is the **East Branch of the Kennebec River,** a 12-mile run from the Hydro Harris Station hydroelectric dam, below Indian Pond, to The Forks. The dam's controlled water releases produce waves of up to eight feet, and the trip begins with a bang in the Alleyway. Highlight is Magic Falls, a Class IV drop that appears as nothing more than a horizon line when approaching it but that has the punch to flip rafts. The excitement is concentrated in the first half of the trip; by the end of it you're just floating along, but that provides opportunities for swimming, water fights between rafts, and perhaps kayaking. Some companies also break for a riverside lunch. Kennebec trips operate early May–mid-October.

KENNEBEC

© TOM NANGLE

White-water rafting is the big attraction in The Forks.

Most of the rafting companies also organize trips on the more challenging and oddly named **Dead River,** but serious water releases occur only half a dozen times during the season, mostly on spring weekends. Competition is stiff for space on the infrequent Dead River trips, an exhilarating 16-mile run through Class III to Class V white water from below Grand Falls to The Forks. Biggest thrill is Poplar Hill Falls. In July and August, the Dead River lives up to its placid name, and outfitters organize moderately priced Sport-Yak and family rafting trips.

Cost of a one-day Kennebec River trip ranges $80–130 pp, depending on whether it's a weekday, weekend, or midsummer. Prices include a hearty cookout or lunch either along the river or back at base camp. Cost of the one-day Dead River trip ranges $90–140 pp. Scads of economical package rates are available—covering lodging, meals, and other activities—especially early and late in the season. Be forewarned that all outfitters have age minimums: usually 10 on the upper Kennebec and 15 on the Dead. Some also impose a weight minimum.

If you want to make more than a day of it—definitely a good plan, since trips start early in the morning and you'll be exhilarated but dog-tired at the end of the day—spend a night or two, maybe one night before and one night afterward. Most of the outfitters have accommodations and dining for every budget. The camaraderie is contagious when everyone around you is about to go rafting or has just done it.

About a dozen outfitters operate on the Kennebec and Dead Rivers. The best source of information is **Raft Maine** (P.O. Box 78, West Forks 04985, 800/723-8633, www .raftmaine.com), which provides info, sends out brochures, and fields reservation requests; the website has direct links and phone numbers for member companies—check out a few before booking as each company tends to have a slightly different approach or niche.

Canoeing and Kayaking

If you're a neophyte canoeist, or you have never done a multiday trip, or you want to go *en fa-mille,* your baptismal expedition probably ought to be the three-day **Moose River Bow Trip,** an easy, 45-mile loop (ergo, "bow") with mostly flat water. Of course, you can do this yourself, and you don't even need to arrange a shuttle, but a guided trip has its advantages—not the least of which is that the guides provide the know-how for the beginners, they do the cooking and cleanup, and they're a big help for portaging.

Experienced guides Andy and Leslie McKendry operate **Cry of the Loon Kayak Adventures** (P.O. Box 238, Jackman 04945, 207/668-7808, www.cryoftheloon.net), mid-May–early October. Lots of options are available, including a three-day Moose River Bow ($325 pp, with only one portage). Maximum group is eight, minimum four. Leslie's gourmet meals are included in the cost. Andy and Leslie will also do one-day guided trips ($60 pp with lunch), or they'll customize a multisport trip for you, with kayaking, rafting, rock climbing, and hiking. If you want to be on your own, they rent Old Town kayaks for $25 a day and Old Town canoes for $20 a day. Avoid June, when the blackflies descend; water level can be a problem in August for the bow trip. Cry of the Loon's base is on Route 15, 6.5 miles east of Jackman.

A number of white-water rafting outfitters also offer white-water canoeing and kayaking lessons and trips. Visit www.raftmaine.com and click on Outdoor Adventures for a chart detailing which ones offer instruction, rental boats, and guided trips.

Hiking

The **Appalachian Trail,** extending 2,158 miles from Springer Mountain, Georgia, to the summit of Maine's Katahdin, crosses the Upper Kennebec Valley near Caratunk, just south of The Forks. The *Appalachian Trail Guide to Maine* provides details for reaching several sections of the white-blazed trail accessible to short-haul hikers. Crossing the 70-yard-wide Kennebec at this point would be a major obstacle were it not for the seasonal, free ferry service operated for AT hikers by Rivers and Trails Northeast. The designated boatman is Steve Longley (207/663-4441 or 888/356-2863, www.riversandtrails.com). Since the mid-1980s, he's been one of the "old reliables" along the AT. The ferry schedule tends to be two hours in the morning late May–mid-July, four hours a day mid-July–September, and two hours in the morning in early October.

Not up for the AT? Other hikes abound, but access is often through a maze of logging roads or through territory where active logging may change landmarks. Ask locally for directions to the trailheads to **Sally Mountain, Number 5** (topped with a fire tower), **Coburn Falls,** and **Kibby Mountain** (with an observation deck).

If you're spending any time in the woods mid-October–November, *do not go out* without at least a hunter-orange cap to signal your presence to hunters; a hunter-orange vest is even better. Even though some properties are posted No Hunting, don't take a chance; one scofflaw can make a life-and-death difference. If you're skittish, or don't have the proper clothing, hike on Sunday, when hunting is banned.

Mountain Biking

The **Kennebec Valley Trail** is an easy 12-mile multiuse loop trail that follows an old railroad bed (no tracks) from between the Williams Dam public landing, alongside the Kennebec in Solon, and Gaddis Airport, on the southern outskirts of Bingham. The route roughly parallels the river and Route 201.

In the Jackman area, an easy-to-moderate 10-mile trip is the **Sandy Bay Loop,** beginning seven miles north of downtown Jackman. Jackman's chamber office has a recreational map detailing this route and others in the area.

Snowmobiling

The region is a snowmobiling hotbed, with hundreds of miles of groomed snowmobile trails that connect east to the Moosehead Lake area, west to the Sugarloaf/USA area, and north into Canada.

Most of the rafting companies exchange white-water helmets for snowmobiling ones in winter and operate under the umbrella Sled Me

(877/275-3363, www.sledme.com). Information on lodging, rentals, guide trips, snow conditions, and trails is available via the website.

Flightseeing

See the rivers and mountains or spot moose from above with James Schoenmann's **Jackman Air** (Newton Field, Jackman, 207/668-4461). Flights, by appointment only, are $75 per half hour and cover three people.

ACCOMMODATIONS

Most of the white-water rafting companies have lodging, and it's convenient to stay where you play. But if you aren't rafting, staying at these places can be a bit overwhelming, especially with the après-raft party atmosphere. If you're planning to be in this area during snowmobiling season, especially in Jackman, be sure to book well in advance; the lodgings get chockablock full of sledders.

Bingham

The appropriately named **Riverside Inn** (178 Main St., Bingham, 207/672-3215, riverside inn1@verizon.net, $60–80) is sandwiched between Route 201 and the Kennebec River. The rambling white inn is being renovated, with good results. Four guest rooms in the main inn share one bath, although two others are available if necessary. The annex is a two-room suite with one bath. Guests have use of the kitchen, living room, porch, and a backyard that edges the river. Also here is a seasonal dairy bar.

Jackman

◖ **Attean Lake Lodge** (Birch Island, P.O. Box 457, Jackman 04945, 207/668-3792, www.atteanlodge.com) has certain trappings of a traditional sporting camp, but it's more like an upscale rustic cottage colony geared to families. Owned by the Holden family since 1900, it's on Birch Island in the center of island-and-rock-sprinkled Attean Lake (also called Attean Pond). Brad and Andrea Holden now make it all work—flawlessly. Fourteen well-maintained log cabins (some old, some new, 2–6 beds) have bathrooms, fireplaces, gas or kerosene lamps, and porches with fantastic views of the lake and surrounding mountains. Guests tend to collect in the new main lodge, with its cathedral ceiling, stone fireplaces, and window-walled dining room. Kids love the sandy beach. Meals have plenty of creativity (swordfish with ginger sauce, for instance). Motorboats are $30 a day; canoes, kayaks, paddleboats, and a sailboat are free. July–Labor Day, rates for two adults are $300 per day, including three meals (wine and beer are available), but nobody stays just one night. (Early and late in the season, rates are $240 d per day; children's rates are much lower.) Book well ahead; this is a popular getaway, and many families have been coming for years. Some guests barely leave the island the whole time they're here, but be sure to paddle across the pond and climb **Sally Mountain** (about 1.5 miles round-trip) for views that stretch as far as Katahdin. (In fall, the foliage vistas are fabulous.) Access to the island is via the lodge launch, a five-minute run. It's open Memorial Day–September.

The nicest motel in town is **Bishop's Country Inn Motel** (P.O. Box 158, 461 Main St., Jackman 04945, 207/668-3231 or 888/991-7669, www.bishopsmotel.com, $85–90 d), a newish, two-story building with free Wi-Fi and HBO, air-conditioning, and continental breakfast. All rooms also have a microwave and coffeemaker, and there's a coin-op laundry on the premises. It's directly across Route 201 from Bishop's Store, where you can get everything else you might possibly want or need.

Here's a different twist on a B&B. **Big Wood Lake Bed and Breakfast** (19 Forest St., Jackman, 207/668-4461, www.bigwoodlake bedandbreakfast.com) is a private house just a two-minute walk from its namesake lake. The kitchen is stocked with breakfast fixings, including bagels, muffins, OJ, fruit, and cereals. Also available are kayaks, a washer/dryer, outdoor hot tub, and outdoor grill. Rate is $45 pp for 1–2, plus $28 for each additional. Spend a week, and the rate is $28 pp/night.

Campgrounds

Indian Pond Campground (HC 63, Box 52,

The Forks, 800/371-7774), next to Harris Station on the East Branch of the Kennebec, where Upper Kennebec rafting trips begin, has 27 tent and RV sites (no hookups), including picnic tables and fire rings. There also are 21 water-access primitive sites. Other facilities include showers, restrooms, RV dump station, laundry machines, and boat launch. Cost is $17 a site (for two); kids under 10 stay free. Leashed pets are allowed. You can hike from here to Magic Rock and watch Kennebec rafters surging through Magic Falls. If hydroelectric plants pique your interest, ask at the gatehouse about a tour of Harris Station. To reach the campground from Route 201 in The Forks, take Lake Moxie Road (also Moxie Pond Rd.) about five miles east; turn left (north) onto Harris Station Road and continue eight miles to the campground gatehouse. It's open mid-April–mid-October.

On Heald Stream in Moose River, a mile east of downtown Jackman, the 24-acre **Moose River Campground and Cabins** (P.O. Box 98, Jackman 04945, 207/668-3341, www.moose rivercampground.net) has 51 tent and RV sites close to a picturesque old dam site. Now crumbling from disuse, the dam once was part of a thriving, turn-of-the-20th-century lumber mill that employed more than 700 workers to turn out 35 million board feet annually. Open and wooded campsites are $18–25 per family. Housekeeping cabins are $25–28 pp (minimum $75–85/night), kids 5–12 half price, dogs welcome. Canoe rentals are available. Facilities include a snack bar, swimming pool, trout pond, laundry room, and children's play area. Also on site are three year-round cabins. It's open mid-May–mid-October.

For a totally peaceful camping experience, book one of the 15 Lake Parlin waterfront sites (no hookups) at **Loon Echo Campground** (Lake Parlin, P.O. Box 711, Jackman 04945, 207/668-4829, www.campmaine.com/ loonecho), 14 miles north of The Forks and 12 miles south of Jackman. Former teachers Bill and Holly Erven can provide all kinds of information on hiking, rafting, fishing, and more. Kayaks, canoes, and fishing gear are available for rent. Quiet time is strictly enforced. If you're here in late July, you can even help with the annual loon count on Lake Parlin.

FOOD

Fine dining simply doesn't exist in this region, but you'll find plenty of good home cooking with a few surprises. It's always wise to ask locally about current reputations, as they do seem to change with the wind as cooks blow in and out of town or head downriver.

Bingham

It's easy to find **Antlers Inn and Restaurant** (Upper Main St., Rte. 201, Bingham, 207/672-3006, 11 A.M.–10 P.M. daily); just look for the moose. Area residents are hopeful that Antlers, which opened its restaurant midsummer 2007, will be a bright spot in the struggling riverside town. The restaurant is large and comfortable, with tables in one room and booths in another, and a menu with just enough to satisfy most folks. Plans call for adding a bakery, microbrewery, 18 guest rooms upstairs, and a gift shop next door.

The Forks

Most of the rafting companies also operate restaurants.

Of course, there's always **Berry's Store** (Rte. 201, The Forks, 207/663-4461), an institution in these parts. Gordon Berry provides everything the sports-minded person might want or need. Or you might just want to sit down a spell in one of the rockers by the register and catch up on the local gossip.

Jackman

When Jim and Karen Hewke's kids left home, the Hewkes turned their house into **Bigwood Steakhouse** (1 Forest St., Jackman, 207/668-5572, www.bigwoodsteakhouse.com, 4–8:30 P.M. Wed.–Sun., to 9 P.M. Fri.–Sat.). The decor is purely functional, but the portions are big, and the food—home-style steak and seafood preparations—is good. You can't say the same about the service; if you're in a hurry, go elsewhere. Most choices are $10–20.

Home cookin' is also the specialty at **Mama Bear's** (420 Main St., Jackman, 207/668-4222, 4 A.M.–8 P.M. Mon.–Thurs., to 9 P.M. Fri., 6 A.M.–9:30 P.M. Sat., 6 A.M.–8 P.M. Sun.). You can't miss it: It's pinkish purple with teal trim.

Part coffee shop, part craft store, **Jackman Java** (466 Main St., Jackman, 207/669-2090, www.jackmanjava.com, 6 A.M.–2 P.M. Wed.–Fri., 7 A.M.–3 P.M. Sat.–Sun.) is cozy and casual, with comfy seating by a fireplace, free Wi-Fi, TV, and a selection of games. Breakfast, lunch, ice cream, and coffee/tea are available, but it's a one-woman operation, so browse the local crafts or catch up on the news while waiting.

INFORMATION AND SERVICES

Request information in advance, as local centers are staffed by volunteers, so hours are irregular.

The Upper Kennebec Valley Chamber of Commerce (Murray St., P.O. Box 491, Bingham 04920, 207/672-4100, www.upperkennebecvalley.com) covers the Bingham area.

If your aim is to go rafting, The Forks Area Chamber of Commerce (The Forks, 207/663-4430, www. forksarea.com) is a good source of info.

The Jackman/Moose River Region Chamber of Commerce (Lakeside Town Park, Main St., Rte. 201, P.O. Box 368, Jackman 04945, 207/668-4171 or 888/633-5225, www.jackmanmaine.org) publishes the *Jackman/Moose River Region Recreational Map,* showing canoeing, biking, hiking, and snowmobile trails, plus driving routes and good moose-watching spots.

The umbrella organization for most white-water rafting companies is Raft Maine (P.O. Box 3, Bethel 04217, 207/824-3694 or 800/723-8633, www.raftmaine.com), which provides info, sends out brochures, and fields reservation requests. The toll-free number rotates like Russian roulette, connecting you to the next-in-line rafting outfitter. If you prefer, contact individual outfitters directly—check the website for individual listings.

KENNEBEC

WESTERN LAKES AND MOUNTAINS

When I tire of the summertime coastal crowds or I'm ready to hit the slopes, I head for Maine's Western Lakes and Mountains—about 4,500 outstandingly scenic square miles of Franklin, Oxford, Androscoggin, and Cumberland Counties. The recreational variety is astonishing. In winter, the state's two alpine powerhouses—Sunday River and Sugarloaf/USA—entice skiers and riders from throughout the Northeast and even abroad. Six smaller, family-oriented ski areas—Saddleback, Shawnee Peak, Mt. Abram, Black Mountain, Titcomb, and Lost Valley—deliver fewer on-mountain amenities but offer more wallet-friendly prices. Cross-country and snowshoeing trails also lace the region, dogsledding is increasingly popular, and snowmobiling is big business.

Still, winter is the off-season in much of this region. The multitude of lakes, ponds, rivers, and streams satisfy recreational boaters and anglers, while the mountains attract hikers. One of the most rugged stretches of the 2,158-mile Appalachian Trail, which runs from Georgia to Maine, passes through this area.

Major "urban" destinations in the region are Bethel, Lewiston/Auburn, and Farmington. Of Maine's nine covered bridges (seven originals and two carefully built replicas), five are in the Western Lakes and Mountains—including the picturesque "Artist's Covered Bridge," near Sunday River, my favorite because you can ski through the forest and suddenly come upon it.

Sprawling, mountainous Oxford County, with its back to New Hampshire, has fabulous trails for hiking and rivers for canoeing. There's gold—and all kinds of other minerals—

© HILARY NANGLE

HIGHLIGHTS

◖ **Sugarloaf/USA:** The summit snowfields are the only lift-accessible above-treeline skiing and riding in the East (page 531).

◖ **Wilhelm Reich Museum:** You don't have to agree with the controversial scientist to enjoy the views from the estate (page 539).

◖ **Grafton Notch State Park:** This is a spectacular chunk of real estate, with hiking trails, waterfalls, and picnic areas (page 554).

◖ **Paris Hill:** Take a walk around this hidden hilltop National Historic District (page 567).

◖ **McLaughlin Garden:** A community effort preserved this in-town oasis (page 569).

◖ **Songo River Queen II:** Take in views to Mt. Washington and pass through a hand-turned lock (page 582).

◖ **Saints Peter and Paul Basilica:** New England's only basilica has a magnificent rose window (page 594).

◖ **Shaker Museum:** Visit the world's last inhabited Shaker community (page 594).

◖ **Poland Spring:** The story behind the bottled water is fascinating (page 595).

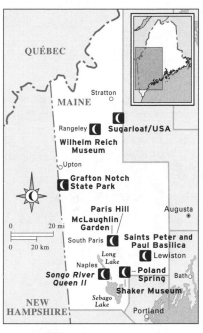

LOOK FOR ◖ TO FIND RECOMMENDED SIGHTS, ACTIVITIES, DINING, AND LODGING.

WESTERN LAKES

in the Oxford Hills; the official state gemstone, tourmaline (an intriguing stone that turns up in green, blue, or pink), is most prevalent in western Maine. Grab a digging tool or gold pan and have a go at amateur prospecting. You're unlikely to find more than a few flakes or some pretty specimens of sparkly pyrite ("fool's gold"), but the fun is in the adventure anyway.

East of Oxford County, Franklin County comprises Sugarloaf/USA and the lovely Rangeley Lakes recreational area. Farmington is the county seat. Mostly rural Androscoggin, fourth-smallest of the state's 16 counties, takes its commercial and political cues from Lewiston and Auburn, the state's second-largest population center.

Directly west of Portland, and partly in Cumberland County, are Sebago and Long Lakes, surrounded by towns and villages that swell with visitors throughout the summer. Also here are most of the state's youth summer camps—some many generations old. During the annual summer-camp parents' weekend in July, Bridgton's tiny, besieged downtown feels like Times Square at rush hour.

PLANNING YOUR TIME

If you're coming for warm-weather recreation—boating, swimming, hiking, and simply playing in the great outdoors, you'll find it here in abundance. And in July and August, you won't be alone in the Route 302 corridor stretching

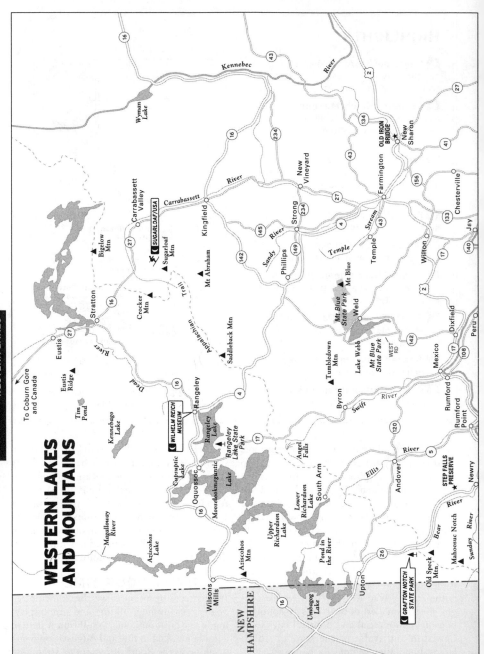

WESTERN LAKES

WESTERN LAKES AND MOUNTAINS

NEW HAMPSHIRE

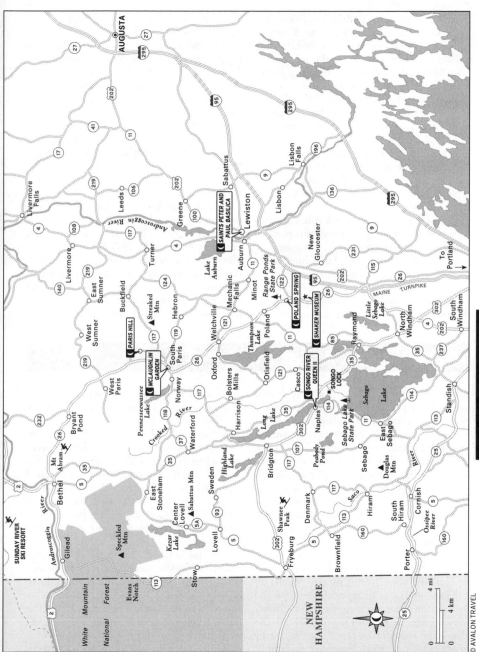

WESTERN LAKES

from Windham through Bridgton. Skip north to the Oxford Hills, Bethel, and the Kingfield region, and the crowds diminish. Bethel, home to Sunday River, and Kingfield, nearest big town to Sugarloaf, come to life during the ski season, but otherwise are quiet places to escape, recreate, and especially to enjoy fall's foliage. If winter sports are your priority, late February–mid-March usually brings the best combination of snow and temperatures.

While you can loop through this region in 3–4 days, to get the most out of the summer recreational opportunities, pick one spot and explore from there. Good hubs are Rangeley, Bethel, Bridgton, and Naples.

If you're interested in Franco American culture, plan on spending the better part of a day in the Lewiston/Auburn area. For antiquing, be sure to slip over to Cornish. For fishing, make Rangeley your base. No matter where you stay, don't overplan. The region's riches demand that you get off the highways and byways and onto the back roads. Noodle around and you'll stumble upon spectacular views, great hikes, country stores, and swimming holes.

For tackling the many miles of trails in this region, you may find several guidebooks helpful—especially *AMC Maine Mountain Guide, 50 Hikes in the Maine Mountains, Guide to the Appalachian Trail in Maine,* and *Hikes in and Around Maine's Lake Region.* If you can afford only one, pick up the *Hikes* booklet, a handy, inexpensive publication written by a local resident (available locally or through REI.com).

An excellent resource for exploring the historical/cultural/natural resources in this region is a foldout map/brochure produced by a consortium led by the Maine Mountain Counties Regional Heritage Program (P.O. Box 508, Farmington 04938, 207/778-3885, www.discovermainemountains.com). The "Franklin Heritage Loop" brochure includes information on museums, hikes, historic sites, events, and visitor services in the areas around Farmington, Sugarloaf, and Rangeley Lakes.

Farmington Area

Farmington (pop. 6,880) is a sleeper of a town—home to a respected University of Maine campus, an excellent art gallery, and an unusual opera museum. What's more, mountain towns and scenery stretch out and beyond in every direction. Less than an hour's drive north of town is the stunning Carrabassett Valley, made famous by the year-round Sugarloaf/USA alpine resort. Off to the northwest are the fabled Rangeley Lakes, and a drive southwest leads to Bethel, home of Sunday River Ski Resort, mineral quarries, and the White Mountain National Forest. Farmington itself is surprisingly thin on lodgings, but otherwise it's an ideal base for exploring western Maine.

Farmington was incorporated in 1794 and became the county seat for Franklin County 44 years later. It remains the judicial hub but also is the commercial center for the nearby towns of Wilton, Weld, New Sharon, Temple, and Industry. To the south and west are Jay, Livermore Falls, Livermore, Dixfield, Mexico, and Rumford.

In Rumford and Jay, your nose will tell you it's paper-mill territory, part of Maine's economic lifeline; locals call the sulfuric odor "the smell of money." Residents have become inured to the aroma, but visitors may need a chance to adjust. Livermore is the site of the Norlands Living History Center, a unique participatory museum that rewards you with a real "feel" for the past.

And, lest we forget, Farmington's leading candidate for favorite son is Chester Greenwood, who, in 1873, rigged beaver fur, velvet, and a bit of wire to create "Champion ear protectors"—earmuffs to you—when he was only 15. The clever fellow patented his invention and then went on to earn 100 more patents for such things as doughnut hooks and shock absorbers.

His early-December birthday inspires the quirky annual Chester Greenwood Day celebration in downtown Farmington.

SIGHTS
Nordica Homestead Museum

Gem-encrusted gowns, opera librettos, lavish gifts from royalty, and family treasures fill the handful of rooms in the Nordica Homestead Museum (116 Nordica La., Farmington, 207/778-2042, 10 A.M.–noon and 1–5 P.M. Tues.–Sat. June–Labor Day, $2 adults, $1 children over five), birthplace of Lillian Norton (1857–1914), better known as Madame Lillian Nordica, the legendary turn-of-the-20th-century Wagnerian opera diva. Her influence still pervades the house, where scratchy recordings play in the background and newspaper clips line the walls. No opera buff should miss this. A caretaker is on hand to answer questions. Even the kids get a kick out of the costumed mannequins, and there's lots of space on the grounds for letting off steam. Take Route 4/27 north from Farmington and turn right (east) onto Holley Road; the farm is half a mile down the road.

Ski Museum of Maine

Established in 1995, the Ski Museum (Church St. Commons, 109 Church St., Farmington, 207/491-5481, www.skimuseumofmaine. org, 1–4 P.M. Wed.–Sat.) began exhibiting its collection of Maine-related ski artifacts and memorabilia in late 2006. It's worth a stop for skiers of any age.

Weld Historical Society Museum

Three carefully preserved 19th-century buildings and a reconstructed Grange Hall in the village center are the domain of the Weld Historical Society Museum (Rte. 156, P.O. Box 31, Weld 04285, 207/585-2542 or 207/585-2542, 1–4 P.M. Wed. and Sat. May–Sept.). Among the local memorabilia are old photos, antique tools and furniture, vintage clothing, even medical paraphernalia. The museum is just east of the Route 142 junction. Donations are encouraged.

Mainely Critters Museum

Far from your typical museum, if "museum" is the correct term, Mainely Critters (1563 Main St./Rte. 2, R.R. 1, Box 510, Dixfield, 207/562-8231, 9 A.M.–5 P.M. Mon–Fri. or by appointment), is a quirky place (about seven miles east of downtown), the brainchild of taxidermists Vance and Diane Child. The museum houses their collection of road-killed and other Maine creatures, all restored and displayed in lifelike settings. Among the specimens are raccoons, skunks, black bears, foxes, even a bull moose. Friends and motorists drift in regularly with future exhibits. Admission is free, but donations are welcome.

PARKS AND RECREATION
Mt. Blue State Park

Mount Blue State Park (299 Center Hill Rd., Weld, 207/585-2261, www.maine.gove/doc/ parks, campground 207/585-2261, www .campwithme.com), covering 5,021 acres, is one of Maine's best-kept secrets. Yes, it's crowded in summer, but mostly with Mainers. It offers multilevel hiking, superb swimming, wooded campsites, mountain scenery, and daily interpretive natural-history programs in summer. There are movies on weekends, guided hikes, weekly guest speakers, even gold-panning expeditions—you'll never be bored. The park is split into two sections; swimming and camping are on Lake Webb's west side; the Center Hill section, including the trail to Mt. Blue itself, is on the lake's east side. The main entrance, with a two-mile access road, is eight miles from Weld, on the lake's west side. Day-use admission is $3 adults, $1 children 5–11. Canoe rentals are $3 an hour. Winter activities include showshoeing, snowmobiling, and more than a dozen miles of groomed cross-country-ski trails. There is also an ice rink.

Swimming and Paddling

Five miles northeast of downtown Farmington is the hamlet of Allens Mills (officially the town of Industry), where you can swim or paddle in aptly named **Clearwater Lake.** To get there from Farmington, follow Broadway

(Rte. 43) until you reach the T junction and boat landing at the lake.

Another local swimming hole is at the Route 4 bridge, in Fairbanks, just north of Farmington.

Hiking

You're getting into western Maine's serious mountains here, so there are plenty of great hiking opportunities, running the gamut from a cakewalk to a workout.

In Weld, a deservedly popular hiking route goes up 3,187-foot **Mt. Blue,** in the eastern section of Mt. Blue State Park. From Route 142 in Weld village, follow signs and take Maxwell Road and then Center Hill Road about 2.5 miles to the parking area for Center Hill itself. (There's no fee in this part of the park.) You can stop for a picnic (sweeping views even at this level, plus picnic tables and outhouses), follow the mile-long self-guided nature-trail loop (pick up a brochure here), and then go on. (It's also a great spot for sunset-watching.) Continue up the unpaved road 3.5 miles to the parking lot for the Mt. Blue trailhead. Allow about three hours for the steepish three-mile round-trip (easy, then moderately difficult). In midsummer, carry plenty of water. Pray for clear air on the summit; vistas of the Longfellows and beyond are awesome. Climb the stanchions of the old fire tower, now used for cellular-phone communications.

Other good hikes around Weld, on the west side of Lake Webb, are **Tumbledown Mountain** (3,068 feet via several route options; nesting peregrines can restrict access in early summer) and **Little Jackson Mountain** (3,434 feet). Tumbledown, moderately strenuous, attracts the been-there-done-that set. A much easier hike, but likely to be more crowded, is 2,386-foot **Bald Mountain,** with a scoured summit fine for picnics if it's not too blustery. Allow about two hours for the three-mile round-trip, including lunch break. To reach the trailhead from Weld, take Route 156 southeast about 5.5 miles. There's limited parking on the right; watch for the sign.

Multiuse Trail

The trailhead and parking for the 14-mile **Jay Farmington Rail Trail** is on Oak Street (off Rte. 2 and 4 at Rite-Aid), across from the post office in West Farmington.

Golf

Nine-hole **Wilson Lake Country Club** (Weld Rd., Rte. 156, Wilton, 207/645-2016, www .wilsonlakecc.com), established in 1931, is a sleeper of a course, not as well known as it should be. Tee times are a good idea. Facilities include a pro shop and snack bar.

Fitness Center

A rainy-day godsend is the $4.5 million University of Maine at Farmington **Health and Fitness Center** (152 Quebec St., corner of Quebec and Lincoln Sts., Farmington, 207/778-7495). It's open to the public for weight training, indoor jogging, tennis, and swimming in a six-lane heated pool. Call for current hours and fees.

ENTERTAINMENT

Throughout the year, something is always happening at the **University of Maine at Farmington:** lectures, concerts, plays, you name it. Contact the college for schedule and details (207/778-7000).

At Meetinghouse Park, on Main Street in downtown Farmington, **band concerts** are held at 7:30 P.M. periodically throughout the summer; take a folding chair or a blanket. The Old Crow Band holds forth in a green and white octagonal bandstand. Check locally for the schedule.

FESTIVALS AND EVENTS

The second weekend in August, the two-day **Wilton Blueberry Festival** is (obviously) a blueberry-oriented celebration (always crowded), including a parade, road races, games, craft booths, a book sale, a museum open house, live entertainment, lobster-roll lunch, chicken barbecue, and a pig roast in downtown Wilton.

The third week of September is given over to

the **Farmington Fair,** a weeklong country fair (one of the last of the season) with agricultural exhibits, a parade, harness racing, and live entertainment at the Farmington Fairgrounds.

The first Saturday in December, Farmington honors a native son on **Chester Greenwood Day.** Festivities commemorating the inventor of earmuffs include a road race, an oddball earmuff parade, a polar-bear swim, and other activities.

SHOPPING

Downtown Farmington has just enough options to entertain shoppers of all budgets.

Fans of fine craft simply must visit **SugarWood Gallery** (248 Broadway, Farmington, 207/778-9105), which features the work of western Maine artisans. Furniture, pottery, weaving, art quilts, handmade teddy bears, and more fill this cooperative gallery.

It's hard to resist the cheerful, welcoming ambience at **Devaney Doak and Garrett Booksellers** (193 Broadway, Farmington, 207/778-3454, www.ddgbooks.com), not to mention the upholstered chairs, classical background music, and a children's corner piled high with books, toys, and games. Cookbooks are a specialty, along with literary journals, lots of Maine books, unusual cards, and even designer coffees. Owner Kenny Brechner does the ordering (and the website book reviews); his eclectic taste is evident. And how many independent bookshops have a website with hilarious parody reviews?

Around the corner, **Twice-Sold Tales** (155 Main St., Farmington, 207/778-4411) has a well-chosen and well-organized selection; Maine titles are a specialty, and prices are reasonable (paperback mysteries are only $1). Ask owner Jim Logan, an avid outdoorsman, about hiking options in Farmington and beyond.

I always introduce visiting friends to **Reny's** (24 Broadway, Farmington, 207/778-4641), and they always leave with at least a bag or two. From clothing to cleaning supplies to electronics to food, Reny's has it all. Part of a small, statewide chain, this one is spread out on three floors—be sure to wander everywhere; even the back corners have finds.

ACCOMMODATIONS

The **Farmington Motel** (489 Farmington Falls Rd., Farmington, 207/778-4680 or 800/654-1133 outside Maine, www.farmingtonmotel.com, $50–80) gets the nod for inexpensive, clean lodging in the area, but don't expect lots of amenities. All 37 rooms and two suites have phones, air-conditioning, and cable TV. No pets. The biggest plus is behind the motel: a nature trail leading down to the Sandy River, where you can launch a canoe or just sit on the shore. The motel, 1.5 miles southeast of downtown Farmington, is open all year.

Just west of Farmington on Wilson Lake, **The Whispering Pines Motel and Gift Shop** (P.O. Box 649, 183 Lake Rd., Wilton 04292, 207/645-3721 or 800/626-7463) is a well-maintained, two-story property with 29 rooms and suites, nine with kitchens. All have free HBO, air-conditioning, minifridge, data port, and phone, and there's a laundry on the premises. Pets are welcome in some rooms. Guests have free use of a canoe, paddleboat, and rowboat as well as outdoor grills. Rates are $60–90 for a room, $130 for a two-bedroom suite.

In Weld village, west of Farmington and northwest of Wilton, you'll find Fred and Cheryl England's **Lake Webb House Bed and Breakfast** (19 Church St., Weld, 207/585-2479, www.lakewebbhouse.com, $85–95 d), a cheerful sight with a wraparound porch and lovely gardens. Three second-floor rooms share a full bath; a fourth, available in summer only, has a private half bath. Children are welcome. The full breakfast might include goodies from the family's seasonal **Morning Glory Bake Shop** (207/585-2479), with sandwiches and goodies. In part of the garage is a seasonal gift shop, with quilts, carvings, and other handmade items.

About a mile south of the center of Weld, on the east shore of Lake Webb, is the **Kawanhee Inn** (12 Ann's Way, Rte. 142, Weld, 207/585-2000, www.maineinn.net). Rooms in the classic, rustic-style lodge and the adjacent cabins are being freshened. Sunsets in this mountain-and-lake setting are spectacular; loons' cries add to the magic. Ten second-floor rooms in the large

WESTERN LAKES

main lodge rent for $85–140 per day (shared and private baths) with a two-night minimum stay on weekends. Cabins ($850–1,150/week; nightly rates, when available, begin at $165) vary in size and facilities; eight have fieldstone fireplaces and screened porches facing the lake; one is on two acres of land and has a full kitchen. A deluxe continental breakfast is included for all lodgers, as is use of canoes, kayaks, and paddleboats. The sandy beach is great for kids, and superb hiking is close by. The lodge's lake-view dining room is open to the public nightly late May–early September ($15–25). With a day's notice, box lunches can be ordered, starting at $8. No smoking in the lodge. Kawanhee Inn is open late May–mid-October. Devotees keep returning here, so book well ahead for midsummer (when the dining room is open). In mid-September, nights are coolish and it's pretty quiet, but the foliage is incredible.

Campgrounds

Mount Blue State Park (299 Center Hill Rd., Weld, 207/585-2261, www.maine.gov/doc/parks; campground 207/585-2261, www.campwithme.com) has 136 wooded sites. Camping fees are $20 per site/night for non-residents, $15 for Maine residents. Reservations are handled through the state-park reservation system; from out of state call 207/287-3824 at least two weeks ahead, and have your Visa or MasterCard handy. You can book reservations online as of February 1 at www.campwithme.com. The reservation fee is $2 per site per night; two-night minimum. No hookups. Camping is available May 15–September.

FOOD
Local Flavors

In downtown Farmington, **Up Front and Pleasant Gourmet** (157 Front St., Farmington, 207/778-5671) has all kinds of condiments, cheeses, homemade pasta, plus a decent wine selection. Be sure to try the locally made York Hill Farm goat cheese. No credit cards.

The **Sandy River Farmers Market** sets up its tables in the parking lot of the Better living Center (Front St., Farmington, 9 A.M.–2 P.M. Fri.

May–Oct.). You'll find herbs, homemade bread, cheeses, and organic meats and produce.

If you'll be camping or staying in a condo or cottage with cooking facilities, swing by **Whitewater Farm** (28 Mercer Rd./Rte. 2, Mercer, 207/778-4748) for local, naturally raised meats (beef, lamb, chicken, turkey, rabbit, pork), cheeses, eggs, and produce.

There's always a line at **Gifford's Ice Cream** (Intervale Rd., Rte. 4/27, Farmington, 207/778-3617), a longtime take-out spot. Besides about four dozen terrific ice-cream flavors, it also has foot-long hot dogs. It's open 11 A.M.–10 P.M. daily in summer, to 9 P.M. in spring and fall, mid-March–early November.

Craving chocolate? Don't miss **Mountain View Chocolate Shop** (248 Wilton Rd., Farmington, 207/778-2500, www.mainechocolates.com). Hand-dipped chocolates, handmade peanut butter cups, and all sorts of fabulous truffles make it hard to leave without something.

Soup for You! Café (222 Broadway, Farmington, 207/779-0799, 10 A.M.–7 P.M. Mon.–Sat., 11 A.M.–5 P.M. Sun.) is funky little spot with about two dozen named sandwiches and the opportunity to create your own from two dozen or so ingredients. Soups are made daily, and smoothies and coffee drinks are very popular here. Vegetarians will find plenty of choices, and kids can get PB&J. Nothing on the menu is more than $6.

Casual Dining

Tucked away on a side street, with a deck overlooking the Sandy River, **The Granary** (147 Pleasant St., Farmington, 207/779-0710, www.thegranarybrewpub.com, 11 A.M.–10 P.M. daily) packs them in, especially when the university is in session. The extensive menu of dinner entrées, many with creative fare, ranges $14–29. Lunch, vegetarian, and kids' menus are available, as is inexpensive pub food. Early-bird specials are offered from 4–5:30 P.M. daily except Wednesday, which features a "two-fer" dinner special. Sunday brunch, with its own huge menu in addition to the regular offerings, is served 11 A.M.–3 P.M.

Most weekends, there's live music; Tuesday is open-mike night. Dine inside, on the deck, or on the screened porch. Next to the bar is a games room.

Farmington's most creative menu is at **The Homestead Bakery Restaurant** (186 Broadway, Farmington, 207/778-6162, www .thehomesteadbakery.com, 7 A.M.–2 P.M. Mon.–Fri., 11 A.M.–2 P.M. Sat.–Sun., and 5–9 P.M. Mon.–Sat.), where there's plenty of ethnic variety—Mediterranean, Mexican, Thai, fancy pizzas, even vegetarian. A mar-tini and wine bar, with couches by a fireplace, provides cozier seating.

INFORMATION AND SERVICES

The Franklin County Chamber of Commerce (407 Wilton Rd./Rtes. 2 and 4, Farmington, 207/778-4215, www.farmingtonchamber.org) publishes *Franklin County Maine Visitors' Guide.*

Check out Cutler Memorial Library (117 Academy St., Farmington, 207/778-4312, www.farmington.lib.me.us.

Sugarloaf Area

The thread tying together the Sugarloaf area is the lovely Carrabassett River, which winds its way through the smashingly scenic Carrabassett Valley from the area more or less around Sugarloaf/USA to North Anson, where it tumbles over treacherous falls and flows into the mighty Kennebec. On both sides of the valley, the Longfellow and Bigelow Ranges boast six out of 10 of Maine's 4,000-footers—a hiker's paradise.

Flanking the west side of the valley is the huge Sugarloaf/USA resort—only a germ of an idea little more than half a century ago. In 1951, Kingfield businessman Amos Winter and some of his pals, known locally as the "Bigelow Boys," cut the first ski trail from the above-treeline snowfields atop Sugarloaf Mountain, dubbing it "Winter's Way." A downhill run required skiing three miles to the base of the trail and then strapping on animal skins for the uphill trek. Three runs on wooden skis would be about the max in those days. By 1954, the prophetically named Winter and some foresighted investors had established the Sugarloaf Mountain Ski Club...and the rest, as they say, is history.

Sugarloaf/USA is the megataxpayer in the relatively new town of Carrabassett Valley (year-round population 367). It bills itself as a year-round resort, which is true, but winter is definitely the peak season, when the head count is highest and so are the prices. Everything's open and humming November–late April; in 1997, spring skiing extended even into June. More than 350,000 skiers hit the slopes here each winter.

Before Amos Winter brought fame and fortune to his hometown and the valley, Kingfield was best known as a timber center and the birthplace of the Stanley twins (designers of the Stanley Steamer). Today it's an appealing slice-of-life rural town (pop. 1,245), with handsome old homes and off-mountain beds and restaurants.

Farther up the valley, old-timers reminisce over the towns of Flagstaff and Dead River—already historic two centuries before they were consigned to the history books in the 1950s. That's when the Long Falls Dam, built on the Dead River, backed up the water behind it, inundated the towns, and created 20,000-acre Flagstaff Lake. The hydroelectric dam now controls the water flow for spring white-water rafting on the Dead River. In Stratton village, the Dead River Historical Society's museum contains fascinating memorabilia from the two submerged villages.

Flagstaff owes its name to Colonel Benedict Arnold, whose troops en route to Québec in 1775 flew their flag at the site of today's Cathedral Pines Campground. After struggling up the Kennebec River to the spot known as The Carrying Place, the disheartened soldiers turned northwest along the Dead River's North Branch at Flagstaff and then on through the Chain of Ponds to Canada.

WESTERN LAKES

Route 27, from Kingfield to the Canadian border at Coburn Gore, is an officially designated Scenic Highway, a 54-mile stretch that's most spectacular in mid–late September. But there's no pot of gold at the end—not much to Coburn Gore except a customs outpost, a convenience store (with fuel), and a few unimpressive dwellings.

SIGHTS
Stanley Museum

Children of all ages love antique cars, so this museum is a must. The small but captivating Stanley Museum (40 School St., Kingfield, 207/265-2729, www.stanleymuseum .org, 1–4 P.M. Tues.–Sun. June–Oct., 1–4 P.M. Tues.–Fri. Nov.–Apr. and by appointment, $4 adults, $3 seniors, $2 under 12) has two meticulously restored Stanley Steamers, designed at the turn of the 20th century by the Kingfield-born Stanley twins, Francis Edgar and Freelan Oscar. These versatile overachievers also gained fame with the invention of the photographic dry plate, eventually selling out to George Eastman. Freelan Stanley, the first to climb Mt. Washington by car, later became a noted violinmaker. Also in the museum, based in the yellow, Georgian-style Stanley School, are hundreds of superb photographs (and glass-plate negatives) by the twins' clever sister, Chansonetta Stanley Emmons, and work by Chansonetta's artist-daughter, Dorothy. The museum gift shop contains auto-related books, pamphlets, and other specialty items.

Nowetah's American Indian Museum

A bold, in-your-face sign announces the driveway to Nowetah's American Indian Museum (Rte. 27, Box 40, New Portland, 207/628-4981, 10 A.M.–5 P.M., free), an astonishing repository of hundreds of Maine Indian baskets and bark objects—plus porcupine-quill embroidery, trade beads, musical instruments, soapstone carvings, and other Native American esoterica. Susquehanna-Cherokee owner Nowetah Timmerman loves explaining unique details about the artifacts she's displayed here since 1969; be forewarned: She's a talker. In the museum's gift shop are many craft items made by Nowetah and her seven children (one daughter is now a lawyer), and she runs a thriving mail-order

---

LARRY WARREN'S DREAM TRAIL

Inch by inch, mile by mile: Imagine a 180-mile-long highway through the wilderness. Not one for motorized vehicles, but rather for hikers, mountain bikers, snowshoers, and cross-country skiers. Larry Warren, a former Sugarloaf/USA manager and preservation advocate, had the vision, and in 2008, after years of arm twisting, persuasion, and major fundraising, the first section of the **Maine Huts and Trails system** (office 375 N. Main St., Kingfield, 207/265-2400, www .mainehuts.org) opened in Carrabassett Valley (access is near the town recreation center off Rte. 27).

When finished, the easygoing 12-foot-wide corridor through the wilderness will stretch from Newry, in the Mahoosuc Mountains, to Rockwood, on Moosehead Lake, and in winter it will be groomed for cross-country skiing. Here's the best part. A comfortable backwoods lodge, where guests can expect a bed (but not bedding) and hot meals, is planned approximately every 12 miles along the trail.

Phase I of trail construction runs 36 miles from Carrabassett Valley to The Forks. The first hut opened in early 2008 by Poplar Falls, on the (not-so) Dead River, in the shadow of Little Bigelow Mountain. Later in 2008, two more huts, one on the shores of Flagstaff Lake and the other at Grand Falls on the Dead River, were expected to open. This is absolutely gorgeous territory, and the trail's design makes it welcoming to beginning hikers and mountain bikers (as well as skiers and snowshoers). Call or check the website for current information on the trail, huts, and pricing for overnight stays.

© TOM NANGLE

The Wire Bridge spanning the Carrabassett River is on the National Historic Register.

business. It's 16 miles north of Farmington and just south of New Portland village.

Bridge to the Past

Now here's a most unusual landmark—about seven miles south of Kingfield and not far from Nowetah's museum. Twenty-five-foot-tall shingled towers announce the entrance to the **Wire Bridge** suspended over the Carrabassett River in New Portland. Built in 1841–1842 at a cost of $2,000, with steel supports imported from England, the bridge is on the National Historic Register. Locals often refer to it as the "Rustproof Wire Bridge," for its stainless-steel construction, or "Floodproof Wire Bridge," for its longtime survival despite nasty spring floods. To find the bridge from Route 146 in New Portland, turn north onto Wire Bridge Road and follow signs for less than a mile.

PARKS
Picnic and Rest Areas

Several riverside and viewpoint rest areas on or near Route 27 make picnicking almost manda-

tory in the Carrabassett Valley—especially in September, when the leaf colors are fabulous. The mountains, the foliage parade, the rock-clogged river—all really splendid. On Route 27, roughly halfway between Kingfield and the Sugarloaf access road, a lovely picnic area is sandwiched between the highway and the Carrabassett River, just north of Hammond Field Brook.

About 12 miles north of the Sugarloaf access road, turn left (west) onto Eustis Ridge Road and go two miles to the **Eustis Ridge picnic area,** a tiny park with an expansive view of the Bigelow Range.

Finally, on Route 27, about 23 miles north of Sugarloaf, there's another scenic picnic area, this one alongside the Dead River (east side of the highway).

◖ SUGARLOAF/USA

Best known as the king of alpine resorts in Maine, Sugarloaf (Carrabassett, 207/237-2000 or 800/843-5623, www.sugarloaf .com) is a four-season destination resort with alpine skiing and snowboarding, snowshoeing,

© TOM NANGLE

Sugarloaf/USA has the East's only above-treeline, lift-serviced skiing.

cross-country skiing, and ice skating December–late April, and golf, hiking, and mountain biking the rest of the year. A compact base village has a hotel, inn, and gazillions of condos as well as restaurants, chapel, a handful of shops, and a huge base lodge, housing snow-school and rental operations. The separate Outdoor Center, linked via shuttle and trails, houses Nordic operations and has an ice-skating rink and café.

Winter Sports

At 4,237 feet, Sugarloaf is not only Maine's highest skiing mountain, but it also has the only above-treeline, lift-serviced terrain in the East. That's just one highlight of 1,400 skiable acres, 94 percent covered with snowmaking. Well more than 100 named trails and glades, served by 15 lifts, ranging from a T-bar to detachable high-speed quads, ribbon its 2,820 vertical. Even beginners can ski from the summit, a 3.5-mile descent via the longest run. Although the resort has produced national and international ski and snowboard champions

(2006 Olympic gold snowboard cross medalist Seth Wescott calls it home), Sugarloaf has always been especially family-friendly, with day care, reduced kids' rates, and all kinds of children's ski and entertainment programs. Adult full-day lift tickets are about $60 for adults, $55 for teens, and $40 for kids 6–12; children 5 and under ski free. Most lodging packages include lift tickets; multiday tickets are less expensive, as are "midmountain" tickets, which are restricted to the lower slopes.

On Route 27, about a mile south of the Sugarloaf access road, is the entrance to the **Sugarloaf Outdoor Center** (207/237-6830), geared in winter toward cross-country skiing, snowshoeing, and ice-skating. Some sections of the 63-mile Nordic trail network are on Maine Public Reserve Land and some are on Penobscot Indian Nation land. Also at the Outdoor Center is an Olympic-size outdoor ice-skating rink, lighted on weekend nights and holiday weeks. The renovated, glass-walled lodge looking out on Sugarloaf Mountain has ski, snowshoe, and skate rentals, plus a casual café. Cross-country lessons are available. Call for current hours and fees for all programs, and ask about special events, such as guided moonlight tours and snowshoe tours.

Summer Activities

Summer activities for Sugarloaf/USA include guided hikes, canoe trips, moose-spotting tours, and wilderness cookouts, but the big draw is golf.

Designed by Robert Trent Jones Jr., and regularly ranked in national golf magazines as Maine's top course, the 18-hole, par-72 **Sugarloaf Golf Club and Golf School** meanders through woods and alongside the Carrabassett River in the shadow of the Longfellow Range. It's actually a town-owned course but is managed by Sugarloaf. An active bug-suppression program makes golfing pleasant even in June, when blackflies normally could dampen the fun. You get what you pay for; greens fees are steep. Tee times are essential; book a week or two in advance for weekends. Sugarloaf's golf school offers multiday programs all summer, with special weeks designed for Women's Golf School and Junior Golf Camp. Club rentals and private lessons are available; carts are mandatory. A driving range, a pro shop, and a café round out the facilities.

Antigravity Center

A partnership between Sugarloaf, the town, and CVA (Carrabassett Valley Academy, a ski preparatory school at the mountain's base that's produced many Olympians), the Antigravity Center is the answer to a parent's prayers when the weather doesn't cooperate. Tucked between Mountainside Grocery and the base of the Access Road, inside the AGC are a gym, climbing wall, skate park, trampolines, weight room, and more. Call 207/237-5566 for current hours and programs.

RECREATION
Multisport Trails

The town-owned **Narrow Gauge Trail,** begins on the east side of Route 27 at the foot of the Sugarloaf access road and continues seven miles, gradually downhill, to Riverside Park in Carrabassett Valley. The trail follows the abandoned narrow-gauge railway bed along the river. Pack a picnic and wear a bathing suit under your biking duds; you'll be passing swimming holes along the way. In winter, it's groomed weekly for cross-country skiing.

Hiking

An easy family hike, combining a picnic and swim, goes to the twin cascades of **Poplar Stream Falls.** On Route 27 in Carrabassett Valley, leave your car at Valley Crossing and walk northeast 1.5 miles to the falls. Pack a picnic and let the kids have a swim.

Just east of Stratton (eight miles northwest of Sugarloaf) is the dedicated hiker's dream: 35,000-acre **Bigelow Preserve**—all public land, thanks to conservationists who organized a statewide referendum and yanked it from developers' hands in 1976. Within the preserve are the multiple peaks of the **Bigelow Range**— the Horns Peaks (3,810 and 3,831 feet), West Peak (4,150 feet), Avery Peak (4,088 feet), and Little Bigelow (3,040 feet), as well as 3,213-foot Cranberry Peak. In the fall, when the hardwoods all change colors, the vistas are incomparable. In winter, snowmobilers crisscross the preserve, and cross-country skiers often take advantage of their trails, especially along the East Flagstaff Road, where you can stop for hot chocolate at volunteer-staffed Bigelow Lodge. The trailhead for Cranberry Peak (6.6 miles round-trip, moderate to strenuous) is next to Route 27 at the southern end of Stratton village.

About five miles southeast of Stratton, the **Appalachian Trail** crosses Route 27 and continues north and then east across the Bigelow Peaks, the spine of the Bigelow Range. You can get to the AT here, or drive back northwest half a mile on Route 27 and go 0.9 mile on the rugged, unpaved Stratton Brook Road to another AT trailhead. In any case, if you do the whole AT traverse, 16.5 miles from Route 27 to East Flagstaff Road, you'll probably want to arrange a shuttle at East Flagstaff Road (via the Long Falls Dam Rd. from North New Portland), or opt for the Round Barn camping area on

Flagstaff Lake, to save a retraverse. The white-blazed AT route is strenuous; four free campsites with lean-tos are spotted along the way. (The most-used campsite is Horns Pond; space can be tight there.)

Depending on your enthusiasm, your stamina level, and your time frame (and maybe the weather), there are lots of options for short hikes along the AT or on a number of side trails. Preserve maps usually are available at the Sugarloaf Area Chamber of Commerce, but for planning your hikes, request a copy of the Bigelow Preserve map/brochure from the Maine Bureau of Parks and Lands (22 State House Station, Augusta, 207/287-3821), or the regional office of the Bureau of Public Lands (207/778-8231). Also helpful is the *Appalachian Trail Guide to Maine.*

Swimming

Along the Carrabassett River between Kingfield and the Sugarloaf access road are half a dozen swimming holes used by generations of local residents. Several spots have natural waterslides and room for shallow dives. They're not all easy to find, and parking is limited, but a refreshing river dip on a hot day is hard to beat. Look for roadside pullouts with parked cars.

On mountain-rimmed Flagstaff Lake in Eustis, about 11 miles north of Sugarloaf, the town-owned beach next to the Cathedral Pines Campground has a playground and changing rooms. There are no lifeguards, but there's also no admission fee. (Do not use the campground's beach unless you're staying there.)

Paddle Sports

If you want to paddle across Flagstaff Lake, rent a canoe or kayak from **Arnold Trail Sports Center** (108 Main St., Stratton, 207/246-2244). The Old Town boats rent in the $25–30 range per day, and free local delivery is available to area boat landings on a set schedule. If you want a guide, that can be arranged, too.

Moose-Watching

Head up Route 27 to Route 16 and go west. Early or late in the day, perhaps en route to

dinner in Rangeley, you're almost guaranteed to see a moose in the boggy areas or near the sand and salt piles stored for winter use. Just remember to drive slowly and watchfully. No one wins when you hit a moose.

ENTERTAINMENT

Sugarloaf is entertainment central in these parts. Every night in winter, there's live music somewhere at Sugarloaf, so you can hopscotch from The Bag to Geppetto's to The Rack (owned by Olympic snowboard cross gold medalist Seth Wescott) and back again.

Every Tuesday evening, local artist Karen Campbell's **KC's Kreativity Center** (Old Huse Mill Rd., Carrabassett Valley, 207/235-3000, www.kcskreativitycenter.com) offers an open pottery studio for all ages and skill levels. The $20 fee covers everything: materials, instruction, firing, and more. She also offers classes in all manner of arts-related media.

EVENTS

The last full week in January is **White White World Week,** Sugarloaf's winter carnival, with discount lift tickets, reduced lodging rates, ski races, fireworks, a torchlight parade, and other special events.

Sugarloaf meets the Caribbean during **Reggae Ski Week,** with spring skiing, reggae bands day and night, and lots of boisterous fun the second week of April. Bring earplugs.

In early July, the annual **Kingfield POPS** concert features the Bangor Symphony Orchestra, an arts-and-crafts festival, garden tour, and more.

ACCOMMODATIONS

When you've had a long day on the slopes, a bed close by can be mighty tempting—plus you can be upward bound quickly in the morning. But such convenience doesn't come cheaply, so your budget may dictate where you decide to stay. Basically, the choices are on the mountain at Sugarloaf/USA, in Carrabassett Valley near the Sugarloaf access road, or farther afield in Kingfield, Stratton, Eustis, and beyond. On weekends and holiday periods, on-mountain beds are scarce to nonexistent, so reservations well in advance are necessary.

Many of the lodgings in the region around Sugarloaf provide discount passes for Nordic skiing out of the Sugarloaf Outdoor Center. It's a nice little perk, so if you're planning any cross-country skiing, be sure to ask when you're inquiring about a room.

Sugarloaf/USA

Accommodations are available all year at the resort, and prices vary widely depending upon property and dates (call 800/843-5623). Possibilities include condominiums and two hotels. The **Sugarloaf Inn** (207/237-6837), conveniently situated in front of the Sawduster double chairlift, has 42 rooms (some in need of a facelift) with rates in the same ranges as the condos. It's home to the Shipyard Brew Haus, open daily for breakfast, lunch, and dinner. The imposing **Grand Summit Resort Hotel** (207/237-2222 or 800/527-9879) with 119 rooms and suites and two penthouses is in the village center. Amenities include microwave, refrigerator, and VCR. Guests have use of a small health club. No pets, no smoking. All reservations booked by Sugarloaf include use of the **Sugarloaf Sports and Fitness Club** (207/237-6946), in the Sugartree condo complex on Mountainside Road.

Kingfield

The renovated **Herbert Grand Hotel** (246 Main St., Rte. 27, P.O. Box 67, Kingfield 04947, 207/265-2000 or 800/843-4372, www.herbert grandhotel.com, $80–190) is a three-story Victorian hotel completed in 1918, where you can meet kindred spirits in the lobby. Rates include a light continental breakfast and Wi-Fi access. Dogs are welcome at $10 each per night.

Another historic property is **The Inn on Winter's Hill** (33 Winter Hill St., Kingfield, 207/265-5421, www.wintershill.com, $95–150), a mansion designed by the Stanley Steamer twins for Amos Winter, who cut the first trail on Sugarloaf. It was the first home in Maine with central heat; now it has both outdoor and indoor pools, a hot tub, and clay tennis court. The nicest rooms are in the main house; motel-style rooms are in a newer wing. Rates include a light continental breakfast. The inn is the site of Julia's Restaurant, a fine-dining experience, entrées $20–25.

Next door to One Stanley Avenue restaurant and under the same ownership, **Three Stanley Avenue** (3 Stanley Ave., P.O. Box 169, Kingfield 04947, 207/265-5541, www.stanley avenue.com, $65–75 d) has been a B&B since the early 1980s. The antiques-filled yellow Victorian (built by Bayard Stanley, younger brother of the famed Steamer twins) has three first-floor rooms with private baths and three second-floor rooms sharing two baths. It's all very welcoming, with comfortable wicker chairs on the front porch and a traditional gazebo (ex-bandstand) in the backyard.

Stratton and Eustis

You can launch a canoe or kayak into Flagstaff Lake from the backyard of **Tranquility Lodge** (Rte. 27, P.O. Box 600, Stratton 04982, 207/246-2122, www.tranquillitylodge.com, $72–85), an especially peaceful bed-and-breakfast in a converted 19th-century post-and-beam barn just north of Stratton village. Old farming tools decorate the walls, and there's a carriage, too, which keeps the feel rural and rustic. Rates include a continental breakfast.

A wonderful, old-time traditional sporting camp, **Tim Pond Camps** (Box 22, Eustis, 207/243-2947, in winter P.O. Box 89, Jay 04239, 207/897-4056, www.timpond camps.com) has been operating since 1877, when guests took so long to get here that they stayed the whole summer. Harvey and Betty Calden have owned this idyllic lakeside retreat since 1980. Eleven rustic log cabins (all with full baths and maid service) are nestled in the woods on either side of a modern-rustic lodge (the original lodge burned), where everyone gathers three times a day for great comfort food; the dinner bell rings promptly at 5:30 P.M. (BYOB). Daily rates are $155 pp, including all meals and use of a classic Rangeley boat, with motor and gas, and a canoe; half price for children 5–12. Pet fee is $10/visit. Be forewarned, though, that it's worth your life to get a reservation here—about 90 percent of the guests are repeats, and most stay at least a week. Fly-fishing for brook trout is the prime pursuit (every spring, a fly-fishing school is offered), but it's just a fine place to relax and listen to the loons. Here's how one avid fisherman describes the schedule: "Fish, eat breakfast, fish, eat lunch, fish, eat supper, fish, sleep." July is the best month for families, but August offers a family discount. Cabins have bathrooms, electricity (until 10 P.M.), daily maid service, and fascinating guest journals. Tim Pond Camps is at the northern end of mile-long Tim Pond, on a dirt road about 10 miles west of Route 27 in Eustis. It's open mid-May–mid-October, then again in November. The dining room is open to the public in July, August, and September by reservation.

CAMPGROUNDS

Right on the 45th parallel, 40-acre **Deer Farm Campground** (495 Tufts Pond Rd., Kingfield, 207/265-2241 or 207/265-4599, www.deer farmcamps.com) has 47 well-maintained sites and camping cabins. Facilities include laundry, a small store, and a playground. Tufts Pond is close enough for swimming, and canoe rentals are available. Easy hiking trails fan out from the campground. Pets are allowed. No credit cards. Take Route 27 north of Kingfield about a mile; turn left onto Tufts Pond Road and continue another two miles northwest to the campground.

With 115 wooded sites (most with hookups) on 300 acres, nonprofit **Cathedral Pines Campground** (Rte. 27 N, P.O. Box 146, Eustis 04936, 207/246-3491, www.eustismaine.com/pines) has one of Maine's most scenic locations. It's set amid gigantic red pines and surrounded by mountains on the shore of Flagstaff Lake. Look for the marker that designates this site as one of Benedict Arnold's stops during his march to Québec City in 1775. Facilities include a recreation hall, bathhouse, laundry, swimming beach, basketball, playground, canoe rentals, and paddleboat rentals. Pets are allowed. The campground is 26 miles south of the Québec border.

FOOD

You can bounce around to different Sugarloaf-area restaurants in the winter season and even catch a two-fer night here and there. You certainly won't starve if you stick with the food at one of the resort-based restaurants, and the range of choices means you won't bust your budget, but do yourself a favor and explore the dining options in Carrabassett Valley, Stratton, Eustis, and Kingfield. During holidays and winter weekends, be sure to make dinner reservations.

Sugarloaf Resort

Bullwinkle's Grill (207/237-2000), off Tote Road, on the mountain's western side, is the resort's only on-mountain restaurant. In 2007 it was mercifully expanded with a spacious restaurant in addition to the cafeteria fare. On Saturday nights, and sometimes on midweek nights during peak periods, it morphs into a rustically elegant restaurant, accessed via snowcat. The adventure includes the snowcat transportation and a five-course meal.

In the base village are two extremely popular sit-down restaurants, **Gepetto's** (207/237-2192) and **The Bag** (207/237-2451). Hard to say which is better. The Bag, which doubles as a brewpub, is famous for its burgers, soups, and wood-fired-oven pizzas, although the menu is much broader than that; Blues Monday features live music. Gepetto's is a bit fancier, with seating areas including a plant-filled atrium warmed by a gas stove, and it's open during the summer season for dinner; Tuesday is two-fer night. Truly, you can't go wrong with either.

For ample sandwiches, homemade soups, salads, and hearty breakfasts, **D'Ellies** (207/237-2490) is one of Sugarloaf Village's most popular eateries. It's open daily, during summer and ski seasons, for breakfast and lunch. Seating is extremely limited—this is more of a to-go kind of place. To avoid the swarming noontime rush, call in your sandwich order in the morning before heading for the lift line. Name a time, and it'll be ready for you to pick up at the express register. You can also grab drinks, soups, and baked goods at the express.

Carrabassett Valley

Reservations are a good idea at **Hug's** (Rte. 27, Carrabassett Valley, 207/237-2392, 5–9:30 P.M. Tues.–Sun.), a northern Italian restaurant that's always jam-packed. Be forewarned: Tables are tight and there's little place to wait for a table. But who cares! The food is good, the atmosphere festive, the pesto breadsticks are addictive, and the family-style salad is delicious. Entrées run $11–20; kids' portions are available. Hug's is a mile south of the Sugarloaf access road.

Six miles south of the Sugarloaf access road is **Tufulio's** (Rte. 27, Valley Crossing, Carrabassett Valley, 207/235-2010, 5–9:30 P.M. daily), another Italian-accented family favorite and producers of the valley's best pizza. The shrimp-and-artichoke-pesto pie is tops. Also on the menu are seafood, chicken, and plenty of pasta dishes. Go on Sunday for the two-for-one specials. In summer, you can eat on the deck. The wine list is ambitious, and there's plenty of beer on tap. It opens at 4 P.M. for a popular happy hour.

Kingfield

The Orange Cat Café (329 Main St., Kingfield, 207/265-2860), in the "brick castle" and open for breakfast and lunch, serves breakfast sandwiches and pastries, homemade soups, creative sandwiches, salads, and other goodies.

Locally popular **Longfellow's Restaurant** (247 Main St., Kingfield, 207/265-4394, 11 A.M.–9 P.M. daily) serves better-than-average home-style fare in two rooms decorated with plaid, plants, and pine. The rear dining room overlooks the falls on the Carrabassett River; the front one doubles as a bar. The menu has a bit of everything, and prices range $6.50–16, with most pastas around $8 and entrées about $14. Tuesday is two-fer night.

Everyone eventually shows up at the **Kingfield Woodsman** (Rte. 27, Kingfield, 207/265-2561, 5 A.M.–2 P.M. Mon.–Fri., 7 A.M.–2 P.M. Sat., and 7 A.M.–1 P.M. Sun.), usually just referred to as the "Woodsman." It's the best choice in the area for local color, especially at breakfast, which starts early. The rustic eatery has been a local landmark since the mid-1970s. Don't be surprised if the staff gives you the once-over and proclaims that you shouldn't order the tall stack of pancakes 'cause it's too big.

The best and priciest restaurant in the entire area is **One Stanley Avenue** (1 Stanley Ave., Kingfield, 207/265-5541, www.stanleyavenue.com, 5–9:30 P.M. Tues.–Sun.), a Kingfield magnet since 1972. Cocktails in the Victorian lounge precede a dining experience: unobtrusive service, understated decor, and entrées ($21–35) such as roast duck with rhubarb glaze, chicken with fiddleheads, and saged rabbit. Reservations are essential on winter weekends; the restaurant attracts Sugarloaf's higher-end ski crowd. It's closed April–December.

Eustis

Although it's way out in the back of beyond, the **◖ Porter House Restaurant** (Rte. 27, Eustis, 207/246-7932, 5–9 P.M. Tues.–Sun.) is no secret, and it's wise to make reservations before making the trip. This simple 1908 farmhouse along the highway to Canada serves excellent fare, drawing folks from as far away as Rangeley and even Canada. Downstairs is a leisurely fine-dining experience, with tables spread out in three rooms. Upstairs is the cozy **Blue Heron Pub,** with a less fussy and less pricey menu and faster service. Cobble together a meal from the tasty appetizers, such as Thai-style mussels, Maine crab cakes, and steamed pork dumplings. Hint: Many of the entrée choices ($20–28) come bathed in sauces—if you're not a sauce fan, ask for it on the side. Tuesday features two-fer specials, and Friday is the night for prime rib. Dress is casual or formal, your choice.

INFORMATION AND SERVICES

The Sugarloaf Area Chamber of Commerce (Rte. 27, R.R. 1, Box 2151, Carrabassett Valley, 207/235-2100, www.sugarloafarea chamber.com) handles information requests for the whole valley, including Sugarloaf/USA, and publishes a helpful map/guide as well as annual dining and lodging brochures. The office, across the road from Ayotte's Country

Store, also handles reservations for lodging in the valley as well as on the mountain (800/843-2732).

Sugarloaf/USA (5092 Access Rd., Carrabassett Valley, 207/237-2000, www.sugarloaf .com) provides information on anything and everything on the mountain. During the ski season, the free tabloid *Sugarloaf This Week,* published biweekly, carries comprehensive information about on-mountain activities. It's available everywhere on the mountain and throughout the valley and beyond.

The recorded Snowphone hotline (207/237-6808) has up-to-the-minute info on snow conditions and special events at Sugarloaf/USA. If you're staying hereabouts (on the mountain or in the valley) and have cable TV, tune to channel 17 (WSKI) for weather, snow, trail, and lift updates, plus an entertainment rundown.

The Flagstaff Area Business Association (P.O. Box 134, Eustis 04936, 207/246-4221, www.eustismaine.com) has information about the Stratton–Eustis region.

GETTING AROUND

The free **Sugarloaf Shuttle** operates 8 A.M.–midnight daily; it's on an on-call basis midweek (207/237-6853) and on a set schedule on weekends and during holiday periods. Various routes pick up at the condos frequently on the mountain, with condo and parking lot pickups 8 A.M.–midnight daily, during the ski season.

Rangeley Lakes Area

Incorporated in 1855, the town of Rangeley (pop. 1,075) and the surrounding Rangeley Lakes region have seen ups and downs in the past century or so—grand hotels and great fires, regression and renewal. The uncrowded streets, slower pace, and countless recreational opportunities are changing the face of western Maine. Centerpiece of a vast system of lakes and streams, and surrounded by mountains, Rangeley is loaded with potential for year-round activities. Summer sees swimming, golf, tennis, canoeing, biking, hiking, fishing, even panning for gold; in winter there's snowmobiling, ice fishing, snowshoeing, and downhill and Nordic skiing. But there's more—Rangeley Friends of the Arts cultural events, old-fashioned annual festivals and fairs, the unique Wilhelm Reich Museum, a flightseeing service, and shops that carry antiques, books, sportswear, and crafts.

And then there's history, even prehistory—excavations have revealed evidence of human habitation in this area as long ago as 9000 B.C. More than 8,000 stone tools and other artifacts were uncovered at the Vail site, on the edge of Aziscohos Lake. Native Americans certainly left their linguistic mark here, too, with tongue-twisting names applied to the lakes and other natural features. Mooselookmeguntic means "where hunters watch moose at night"; Umbagog means "shallow water"; Mollychunkamunk (a.k.a. Upper Richardson Lake) means "crooked water"; Oquossoc means "landing place"; and Kennebago means "land of sweet water." The town's more prosaic name comes from 19th-century landowner Squire James Rangeley.

Rangeley is a catchall name. First applied to the town (formerly known as the Lake Settlement), it now also refers to the lake and the entire region. "I'm going to Rangeley" could indicate a destination anywhere in the extensive network of interconnecting lakes, rivers, and streams backing up to New Hampshire. The Rangeley Lakes make up the headwaters of the Androscoggin River, which technically begins at Umbagog Lake and flows seaward for 167 miles to meet the Kennebec River in Merrymeeting Bay, near Brunswick and Topsham.

Southeast of Rangeley, the town of Phillips was the birthplace of fly-fishing legend Cornelia T. ("Fly Rod") Crosby (1854–1946), recipient of the first Registered Maine Guide license issued by the state—the imprimatur

© HILARY NANGLE

The views are fabulous from controversial scientist Wilhelm Reich's home, now a museum and parkland.

for outdoors professionals. Crosby, who wrote columns for the local paper, was a fanatic angler and hunter who always kept a china tea set neatly stowed in her gear.

While most visitors reach Rangeley via Route 4 from the Farmington area, another popular route is Route 17 from the Rumford/Mexico area. When you reach Byron on the Swift River, you enter the 35-mile Rangeley Lakes Scenic Byway, stretching from Byron north to Oquossoc and then southward down Route 4 through Rangeley to Madrid. The label is unquestionably deserved, especially in autumn, when the vibrant colors are unforgettable. The two-lane road winds through the rural woods of western Maine, opening up periodically to reveal stunning views of lakes, streams, forested hillsides, and the Swift River. You might even see a moose. Highlights are two signposted viewpoints—Height of Land and the Rangeley Scenic Overlook—surveying Mooselookmeguntic and Rangeley Lakes, respectively. Height of Land, 11 miles south of Oquossoc,

adjoins the Appalachian Trail. Have your camera handy; it's a photogenic standout.

Along Route 17 (about 23 miles south of Oquossoc) is Coos Canyon, in the town of Byron, where gold was found in the early 1800s on the East Branch of the Swift River. Amateur prospectors still flock to the area, but don't get your hopes up—it's more play than profit.

SIGHTS
◖ Wilhelm Reich Museum

Controversial Austrian-born psychoanalyst/ natural scientist Wilhelm Reich (1897–1957), noted expert on sexual energy, chose Rangeley for his residence and research. Hour-long guided tours of The Wilhelm Reich Museum (Dodge Pond Rd., P.O. Box 687, Rangeley 04970, 207/864-3443, www.wilhelmreich museum.org), his handsome fieldstone mansion, include a slide presentation covering Reich's life, eccentric philosophy, experiments, and inventions such as the orgone accumulator and the cloudbuster. Reich is buried on the estate grounds. Views are spectacular from the roof of the museum, also known as Orgonon, so bring binoculars and a camera. A nature-trail system, including a bird blind, winds through the wooded acreage. Museum hours are 1–5 P.M. Wednesday–Sunday in July and August, and Sunday only in September. The museum hosts free outdoor-oriented, natural-science programs 2–4 P.M. on Sundays. Admission to the museum (no charge for being on the grounds) is $6 adults, children 12 and under free. Private tours are available by appointment and cost $100 for up to 10 people. The museum is west of Rangeley, 0.8 mile north of Route 4.

Rangeley Lakes Region Logging Museum

The three-story Rangeley Lakes Region Logging Museum (Rte. 16, Rangeley, 207/864-7311) and its grounds are home to an eclectic assortment of lumberjack paraphernalia, artifacts, and samples of traditional artwork created in the camps. The museum is open 11 A.M.–2 P.M. weekends in July and August and by appointment. Donations are welcomed. Every year, on the last Friday and Saturday in July, the museum sponsors Logging Festival Days, complete with beanhole beans, music, and a woodsmen's competition.

Bennet-Bean Covered Bridge

Spanning the Magalloway River beneath Aziscohos Mountain, the 92-foot-long Bennett Covered Bridge (also known as the Bennett-Bean Bridge), built in 1898–1899, sees far fewer visitors than most of Maine's eight other covered bridges. The setting, in the hamlet of Wilsons Mills, makes for great photos, so it's worth detouring on the unpaved road next to the Aziscoos Valley Camping Area, 0.3 mile west of Route 16 and 28 miles west of Rangeley.

Narrow Gauge Railroad

The **Sandy River and Rangeley Lakes Railroad** (Mill Hill Rd., Phillips, 207/788-3621, www.srrl-rr.org) dates to 1879, when the first section was constructed to connect northern Franklin County with Farmington,

the terminus of the Maine Central Railroad. Since 1969, volunteers have been working to restore and reopen a section of the original two-foot narrow gauge track. Visit the small museum and then board a restored 1884 passenger car for a 50-minute excursion through the countryside. The train operates June–mid-October on an erratic schedule. Adult fares are $4–6, kids under 13 are $1. Call or check the website for current season info and schedule; even then, it's all dependent upon availability of equipment and manpower.

Moose-Spotting

Do-it-yourself moose-spotting is a favorite pastime in this area. The likelihood of spotting one of these gangly critters can be quite high, depending if conditions are ripe. Route 16, between Rangeley and Stratton, is well known as "Moose Alley," especially in the boggy areas close to the road. Sunrise and sunset are the best times for sighting moose. Keep your camera handy, and drive slowly; no one wins in a moose-car collision, and fatal accidents are not uncommon on this unlighted stretch.

TOURING
Flightseeing

The best way to put the region in perspective is from the air. **Lake Region Air** (2602 Main St., Rte. 4, P.O. Box 1313, Rangeley 04970, www.lakeregionair.com, 207/864-5307) does on-demand tours via floatplane, an adventure in itself. A 20-minute flight is $100 for up to three people. Longer flights can be arranged, based on a $300-per-hour charge. Reservations aren't always needed, but call ahead to be sure.

PARKS AND PRESERVES
Rangeley Lake State Park

With 1.2 miles of lake frontage and panoramic views toward the mountains, nearly 1,000-acre Rangeley Lake State Park (S. Shore Dr., HC 32, Box 5000, Rangeley, 207/864-3858, www.maine.gov/doc/parks) gets high marks for picnicking, swimming, fishing, birding, boating, and camping. The swimming "beach" is a large patch of grass. None of the 50 campsites is at water's edge, but a dozen have easy shore access. (For camping reservations, visit www .campwithme.com; from out of state call 207/287-3824 at least two business days in advance—MasterCard and Visa only. Maine residents should call 800/332-1501.) If you're doing any boating, stay close to shore until you're comfortable with the wind conditions; the wind picks up very quickly on Rangeley Lake, especially in the south and southeast coves near the park. Day-use admission is $3 adults, $1 children 5–11. For those under 5 and over 65, admission is free. Nonresident camping is $20 per site per night (plus $2 per site per night for a reservation); no hookups, but there are hot showers. The park, four miles off Route 17, is open mid-May–September, but it's accessible in the winter for cross-country skiing and snowmobiling.

Lakeside Park

In downtown Rangeley, overlooking both lake and mountains, is this lovely, grassy town park with a tiny beach with safe swim area, grills and covered picnic tables, tennis courts, a playground with plenty of swings, lots of lawn for running, and a busy boat-launching ramp. Restrooms are open when a lifeguard is on duty. The park is open 5 A.M.–10 P.M. Access is from Main Street (Rte. 4), near the Parkside and Main Restaurant and the chamber of commerce office.

Rangeley Lakes Heritage Trust

These foresighted conservationists have helped set aside recreational land for everyone to enjoy. Rangeley Lakes Heritage Trust (RLHT; Rte. 4, P.O. Box 249, Oquossoc 04964, 207/864-7311, www.rangeley.org/rlhthome), an energetic membership organization, oversees thousands of acres of protected land, including 10 islands and more than 20 miles of lake and river frontage. The RLHT office, in the Stony Batter Station building, across from The Gingerbread House in Oquossoc, is open all year. Summer hours are 9 A.M.–4:30 P.M. Monday–Friday, plus 9 A.M.–noon Saturday; call for winter hours.

Hunter Cove Wildlife Sanctuary

Loons, ducks, and other waterfowl are the principal residents of Hunter Cove Wildlife Sanctuary, a small preserve previously owned by the Maine Audubon Society, transferred to the Rangeley Lakes Heritage Trust in July 2004. While walking the three miles of easy blazed trails, best in a clockwise direction, keep an eye out for blue-flag iris, which blossoms throughout the summer. You may even spot a moose. If you launch a canoe into Hunter Cove and paddle under the Mingo Loop Road bridge early in the season, you'll come face-to-face with nesting cliff swallows. To reach the sanctuary, take Route 4 west of downtown Rangeley for about 2.5 miles, turning left into the preserve across the road from Dodge Pond. It's signposted. The preserve is open sunrise–sunset daily. Admission is free.

Smalls' Falls Rest Area

One of Maine's most accessible cascades, Smalls' Falls is right next to Route 4, at a state rest area, 12 miles south of Rangeley. Pull into the parking area and walk a few steps to the overlook. Bring a picnic. For more of a challenge, ascend a bit farther to Chandler's Mill Stream Falls. The rest area is officially open mid-May–October, but it's easy to park alongside the highway early and late in the season.

SUMMER RECREATION
Hiking

Hiking in this region is plentiful, and indeed there are numerous hiking guidebooks that provide details on more serious endeavors. Here's a sampling of a few hikes that reap big rewards for not-quite-so-big efforts. Be sure to wear appropriate footwear and carry water, snacks or lunch, and bug repellent.

Centerpiece of a 1,953-acre parcel of Maine Public Reserve Land, **Bald Mountain** is a relatively easy two-hour round-trip hike that ascends less than 1,000 feet, yet the minimal effort leads to stunning views of Mooselook-meguntic and Upper Richardson Lakes—not to mention the surrounding mountains. Even three-year-olds can tackle this without terrorizing their parents. Pack a picnic. The trailhead is on Bald Mountain Road in Oquossoc, about a mile south of Route 4 and roughly across from the entrance to Bald Mountain Camps. Park well off the road.

Dropping 90 feet straight down, dramatic **Angel Falls** is one of New England's highest cascades, reached after a fairly short easy-to-moderate hike. Even in midsummer, you'll be fording running water, so wear rubberized or waterproof shoes or boots. Best time to come is autumn, when most of the rivulets have dried up and the woods are brilliantly colorful. Allow an hour to 1.5 hours for the 1.5-mile round-trip hike. The trail is mostly red-blazed, with the addition of orange strips tied at crucial points. From Oquossoc, take Route 17 South 17.9 miles to the unpaved Bemis Track, on the right. Follow the road along Berdeen Stream about 3.6 miles until you see a steep road descending to a gravel pit on the left. Park alongside the Bemis Track and walk down the hill. This is a popular hike, so you should see other cars. The trail leads off to the left.

A distinctive landmark on the western slope of Saddleback Mountain, **Piazza Rock** is a giant cantilevered boulder 600 feet off the Appalachian Trail. The hike up is easy to moderate, not a cakewalk but fine for families, along the white-blazed AT from Route 4. From downtown Rangeley, go seven miles southeast on Route 4 and park in the new lot on the south side of the highway. Piazza Rock is 1.2 miles northeast of the highway.

If you continue on the AT from Piazza Rock, it's another four miles to the summit of 4,116-foot **Saddleback Mountain,** but most hikers take the shorter route up the mountain from the ski area's Base Lodge. To get there from Rangeley, go south on Route 4 to Dallas Hill Road and then go 2.5 miles to Saddleback Mountain Road. From the lodge, follow the orange trail markers. Expect a stiff breeze and 360-degree vistas. A trail map is available at the lodge.

Other excellent hikes west and north of Rangeley are **Aziscohos Mountain** and **West Kennebago Mountain.** Both are easy to moderate, have terrific views from their summits,

and require 3–4 hours round-trip from their trailheads. West Kennebago has a fire tower.

Fishing

The Rangeley Lakes area earned its vaunted reputation from world-class fishing, and die-hard anglers will always show up in May and early June, lured by landlocked salmon and brook trout. The region boasts of being the birthplace of contemporary fly-fishing, and indeed many famous flies originated here. Best fly-fishing correlates with waves of fly hatches late May–early July. Both the **Kennebago River** and **Upper Dam** on Mooselookmeguntic are hot spots for fly-fishing. If you're super-serious about fishing, arrange to be flown into a wilderness pond.

Best local source of information on fly-fishing is **Rangeley Region Sport Shop** (2529 Main St., Rangeley, 207/864-5615), where the enthusiastic owners will get you outfitted, point you in the right direction, or help you find a guide.

Note that many waters are restricted to fly-fishing and catch-and-release is mandated on some bodies of water at certain times of the year. For the best advice, hire a local guide. Registered Maine Guide Larry Guile's **Westwind Charters and Guide Service** (P.O. Box 1092, Rangeley 04970, 207/864-5437, www.westwind-charters.com) has been fishing these waters for more than 35 years. He provides the tackle for half- and full-day salmon or trout fishing expeditions about his 17.5-foot Sea Nymph Sportfisher. For advice or equipment, head to **Rangeley Region Sport Shop** (2529 Main St., Rangeley, 207/863-5615).

Combine fly-fishing with literary heritage. Maine Guide Aldro French's **Rapid River Fly Fishing** (Middle Dam, P.O. Box 355, Andover 04216, cell 207/650-3890, www.rapidriver flyfishing.com) is based at Forest Lodge, made famous by noted author Louise Dickinson Rich in *We Took to the Woods*. Aldro knew Rich, which makes the experience all the more authentic. You can even stay in Rich's Winter House ($175 d), a magical setting on the Rapid River. Spend the day wading into the

Rapid's pools with Aldro; $250 s, $350 d includes lunch. Buy any necessary gear, including proven flies, along with Rich's book at Aldro's Bare Bones Fly Shop, a shed in the woods. Be sure to ask Aldro how his efforts to preserve the property as a historical site are progressing.

Canoeing and Kayaking

Canoeing and kayaking are splendid throughout this region. Be forewarned, though, that Rangeley and Mooselookmeguntic Lakes are much larger than they look, and they have wide-open expanses where flukey winds can kick up suddenly and mightily and swamp boats. Fatalities have occurred in just such circumstances. Check on wind conditions before you head out. Do not take chances.

If you're looking for pristine waters where motorboats are banned, opt for **Saddleback Lake, Loon Lake, Little Kennebago Lake,** or **Quimby Pond,** all fairly close to Rangeley.

Choices for canoeing near Rangeley are Rangeley Lake (especially around Hunter Cove), the Cupsuptic River, the lower Kennebago River, and Mooselookmeguntic Lake. Slightly farther afield are Upper and Lower Richardson Lakes, both wonderfully scenic, as is Umbagog Lake (um-BAY-gog), straddling the Maine-New Hampshire border. The Cupsuptic, Kennebago, and Magalloway Rivers are all easy Class I waters. The Rangeley Lakes Area Chamber of Commerce has produced a suggested canoeing itinerary for the Rangeley Lakes chain, including information about wilderness campsites en route. Some of the campsites require reservations and fire permits.

Besides being a fishing-gear supplier and a place that has camping, fishing, and hunting gear, water toys, outdoor clothing, and unique gifts, **River's Edge Sports** (Rte. 4, P.O. Box 347, Oquossoc 04964, 207/864-5582, www.riversedgesports.com) also rents canoes and kayaks. Rates start at $25 a day or $125 per week, canoe or single kayak. Double kayaks are $40/day and $200/week. For $45, including canoe rental, it'll shuttle you and the canoe up the Kennebago River to the start of an idyllic two- to three-hour downstream paddle to

PADDLE ACROSS MAINE

You can paddle an ancient, Native American route through the mountains and wilderness of northern New England and Québec. The 740-mile **Northern Forest Canoe Trail** (P.O. Box 565, Waitsfield, VT 05673, 802/496-2285, www.northernforestcanoetrail.org) begins in Old Forge, New York, and passes through 35 communities in Vermont, Québec, New Hampshire, and Maine, following lakes, rivers, and streams, both flat water and white water, before finishing in Fort Kent. While some dedicated paddlers have completed the trek from start to finish, most folks dabble in various areas.

More than 350 miles of the waterway are in Maine. The trail enters the state via Lake Umbagog in section eight and then progresses through the Rangeley Lakes and across Flagstaff Lake to Spencer Stream before crossing into the Kennebec River Valley region, following the Moose River, and finishing section 10 in Moosehead Lake. Sections 11 through 13 pass from the lake to the West Branch of the Penobscot and on to Chesuncook Lake. From here, it follows the Allagash Wilderness Waterway to its confluence with the St. John River at the tip of Maine.

If you get serious about paddling it, the trail is mapped in 13 sections (sections 8-13 are in Maine, maps are $9.95 each, available online or in local shops). The maps detail the waterways, portages, dams, communities en route, and natural sights. Much information is available online, with even more available to those who join Northern Forest Canoe Trail; membership is $35.

Route 16 and your car; go at sunrise for the best chance of spotting a moose.

Ecopelagicon (7 Pond St., P.O. Box 899, Rangeley 04970, 207/864-2771, www.ecopelagicon.com) rents kayaks for use on Haley Pond for a short paddle or to take to your camp. Single kayaks rent for $29 per day, $21 half day, or $10 per hour for use on Haley Pond; doubles are $32, $24, and $12. Long-term rates are available. Delivery and pickup are available for a fee.

Mookwa, at Ecopelagicon, specializes in guided kayak tours. The four-hour, half-day tours are $60–75 pp. Fees include paddling gear and a snack. Six-hour trips include lunch and cost an additional $15. Trips are offered on Thursdays, and usually depart the store at 8 A.M. Minimum age is 12. By the way, Mookwa is a Cree word for loon.

Maine Professional Guide **Rich Gacki, Recreation Resources** (P.O. Box 695, Rangeley 04970, 207/864-5136) has 20-plus years' experience as a guide. He leads guided canoe trips on the Kennebago River in search of moose and other wildlife and also leads nature hikes and sailing excursions.

Motorboating

Of course, the easiest way to explore these massive lakes is by motorboat. Most lakes have public access points, but these may be busy. Put-ins for Rangeley Lake include the state park, Lakeside park, and off Route 4 in Oquossoc. The best one for Mooselookmeguntic is Haines Landing, at the end of Route 4. There's another ramp off Route 16 west, approximately four miles from the intersection with Route 4. Also off Route 16 is the Mill Brook access for Lake Richardson and the Black Cove Campground access for Aziscohos (careful; it's extremely shallow in places). Maine has strict rules about boating. For information, contact the Maine Department of Inland fisheries and Wildlife (www.maine.gov/ifw) or a local outfitter.

The best place to rent a sturdy motorboat is **Oquossoc Cove Marina** (Rte. 4, Oquossoc, 207/864-3463, www.oquossocmarine.com). Prices begin at $100 per day; half-day rates begin at $60; hourly rental is $35; gas and oil are extra. Oquossoc Cove Marina is owned by the same owners of Oquossoc Marine, whose fine reputation means their boats are much in demand, so reserve well ahead. Restroom and picnic facilities are available. **Haines Landing Marina** (end of Rte. 1, Oquossoc, 207/864-2393, 207/864-5040 in winter) on Mooselookmeguntic Lake also has motorboat, canoe, and kayak rentals.

Biking

Mountain biking is popular here. Road biking is best left to experienced cyclers who know how to share the highway with RVs, trucks, and gawking drivers. For rental bikes and general advice, head to **Seasonal Cycles** (2593 Main St., Rangeley, 207/864-2100). Mountain bikes rent for $22 per day and include a helmet and "all the free advice you can stand." The shop also sponsors weekly group rides; call for details.

In downtown Rangeley, the multiuse **Railroad Trail Loop** begins on Depot Street (not far from Seasonal Cycles). The 12.5-mile circuit travels over mixed terrain, including paved and unpaved roads and an abandoned railroad bed, and has some steep sections.

In 2006, **The Rangeley Lakes Trails Center** (207/864-4309) opened a 45-kilometer groomed trail network on lower Saddleback Mountain, with the base facility just before the alpine ski lodge. Trails are open for hiking, biking, and, in winter, for cross-country skiing.

Golf

Noted golfers have been teeing off at **Mingo Springs Golf Course** (Country Club Rd., P.O. Box 399, Rangely 04970, 207/864-5021) since 1925, when the course started with nine holes. Today's 18-hole, par-70 course boasts panoramic vistas of lakes and mountains—and sometimes an annoying breeze. Facilities include lessons, a pro shop, and cart rentals. Tee times are advisable, particularly on weekends. Golf-and-lodging packages are available at the adjacent Country Club Inn. Take Route 4 west of Rangeley and turn left onto Mingo Loop Road; follow the signs.

A bit off the beaten track is the nine-hole **Evergreen Golf Course** (Dallas Hill Rd., Rangeley, 207/864-9055).

Gold Panning

"Gold bought, sold, and lied about here!" proclaims the sign outside **Coos Canyon Rock and Gift Shop** (472 Swift River Rd., Byron, 207/364-4900), which has been in business since 1956. Check out the exhibits of some of the nuggets found in the Swift River and then rent a plastic pan and try it yourself. A plastic pan rents for $2 per day, a fancier sluice box for $20. It's a relatively inexpensive lesson in patience.

WINTER RECREATION
Alpine Skiing and Snowboarding

Saddleback (P.O. Box 490, Rangeley 04970, 207/864-5671 or 866/918-2225, www.saddlebackmaine.com) is the yin to nearby Sugarloaf's yang. Although its reputation is as a low-key, wallet-friendly, family-oriented area (resort is too high-falutin' a word), Saddleback delivers big-mountain skiing, with a 2,000-foot vertical drop, but the only way to reach its 4,116-foot summit—and its very challenging expert trails—is via an ancient T-bar, but that will soon change. A new 10-year plan is under way that will add new lifts, trails, accommodations, and more. Already there's a fabulous post-and-beam lodge, a new beginner area serviced by a fixed-grip quad, new intermediate trails, and expanded capacity on another chair. Over the next several years, the improvements and expansion will continue. The sun-drenched base lodge welcomes brown-baggers; try to snag a seat by the massive stone fireplace.

Daily lift tickets for adults are $40, with weekday specials at $25. Children 13–18 years old are $31; 7–12 years old are $29. Children 6 and younger are free, as are ages 70 and older. Inside the base lodge are a cafeteria, espresso bar, pub, ski school, rentals, inexpensive day care (six months–eight years).

Cross-Country Skiing and Snowshoeing

The volunteer-operated, nonprofit Rangeley Lakes Cross Country Ski Club (524 Saddleback Mountain Rd., 207/864-4309, www.rangeleyxcski.com) operates the **Rangeley Lakes Trails Center,** with 35 kilometers of

© TOM NANGLE

Saddleback is renowned for its old-style New England trails.

groomed trails lacing through the Saddleback preserve on lower Saddleback Mountain. It opened in 2006 and is still a work in progress. Maps are available at the center. Trails are open 8:30 A.M.–4:30 P.M. daily. Full-day trail passes are $13 adults, $4 kids midweek, $16 and $6 weekends/holidays. Half-day passes are available. The summer nature trails at **Orgonon, the Wilhelm Reich Museum** (207/864-3443), west of downtown Rangeley, are accessible for free Nordic skiing or snowshoeing 9 A.M.–4 P.M. weekdays.

Maine Guide Rich Gacki of **Recreation Resources** (P.O. Box 695, Rangeley 04970, 207/864-5136) leads guided cross-country-skiing and snowshoeing tours. He's a certified ski instructor, so lessons can be part of the deal.

For cross-country ski or snowshoe rentals, visit **The Alpine Shop** (2504 Main St., Rangeley, 207/864-3741). **River's Edge Sports** (Rte. 4, P.O. Box 347, Oquossoc 04964, 207/864-5582) rents cross-country skis.

Snowmobiling

Snowmobiling is big business in Rangeley, and in winter most accommodations and lodgings cater to it. The Rangeley area, linked to the state's interconnected trail system (ITS) via ITS 84, 89, and 117, has its own well-marked, 150-mile groomed network, thanks to the diligent efforts of the local Rangeley Lakes Snowmobile Club (P.O. Box 950, Rangeley 02970, www.rangeleysnowmobile.com). A family club membership is $40; individual $25. The club's monthly social hour and dinner for members is a good way to get the local scoop. The club also operates a conditions hotline (207/864-7336). Popular rides include a 65-mile lake loop; all or part of the 300-mile Black Fly Loop, which circles through Franklin and Somerset Counties; Kennebago Mountain; and even into Canada on the 12,500-mile international circuit. There are no local trail fees, but support at local fund-raisers is appreciated.

For advice, rentals, or a guided tour, check with **River's Edge Sports** (Rte. 4, Oquossoc 04967, 207/864-5582, www.riversedge sports.com).

ENTERTAINMENT

The great outdoors is the Rangeley region's biggest source of entertainment, but there are some options for rainy days and evening fun.

Rangeley Friends of the Arts (RFA) (P.O. Box 333, Rangeley 04970, 207/864-2958, www.rangeleyarts.com) is a local cultural organization that promotes the arts in the region through concerts, events, scholarships, and school programs. Call for event information.

Stop by **Mojo's** (2473 Main St., Rangeley, 207/864-5557) for a schedule of arts-and-crafts classes. Enthusiastic owneer Tami Wentworth offers classes daily during summer and school vacation periods, less frequently other times. Many classes, such as thumbprint art, felt finger puppets, and little clay monsters are geared to children. Open studio time is also offered. Most classes are less than $10. Reservations are recommended.

Once a month, avid readers gather for a book discussion hosted by **Hooks, Line and Thinkers** (Main St., Rangeley, 207/864-4355, bltbooks@rangeley.org). Discussions are usually held at 5:30 P.M. Thursdays at the Rangeley Inn. Call the shop for the schedule or to buy that month's book.

Lakeside Theater (Main St., Rangeley, 207/864-5000) screens major films year-round (weekends only off-season). On Thursday and Sunday nights during summer, independent films are shown.

The Club House (Main St., Rangeley, 207/864-9955) draws a crowd starting at 9 P.M. Friday–Saturday, when there's live music or a deejay. On winter weekends, there's frequently après-ski entertainment at **Saddleback.**

Natural-science programs are held at the **Wilhelm Reich Museum** (207/864-3443) 2–4 P.M. every Sunday during the summer.

FESTIVALS AND EVENTS

Hardly a day goes by in July and August without something scheduled. Other times, events are less frequent.

Avid snowmobilers shouldn't miss the annual Jaunary **Snodeo.** Events at the family-oriented festival include competitions, food, games, an auction, raffles, live entertainment, radar runs, children's events, a snowmobile parade, antique snowmobile displays, fireworks, and more.

The third Sunday in July, the **Old-Time Fiddlers' Contest** draws great musicians and includes a barbecue. Bring your own chair or blanket and expect lots of foot-stomping fun. The last weekend in July, **Logging Museum Festival Days** includes a parade, beanhole bean supper, lumberjack events, and the Little Miss Woodchip contest. It's held on the Rangeley Logging Museum grounds, Route 16.

On the first Thursday in August, the **Sidewalk Art Show** is an all-day street festival featuring dozens of artists displaying a wide range of talents along Rangeley's Main Street. Downtown Rangeley comes alive the third Thursday in August for the **Annual Blueberry Festival,** a daylong celebration of the blueberry harvest, with sales of blueberry-everything.

In even-numbered years, **Quilts in the Garden** is an outdoor quilt show in the colorful gardens behind Threads Galore Quilt Shop.

Held the first Saturday in October, the **Logging Museum Apple Festival** is a daylong, apple-theme celebration including cider pressing. It's held on the Rangeley Logging Museum grounds, Route 16.

SHOPPING

The new-book selection is distinguished at **Books, Lines, and Thinkers** (Main St., P.O. Box 971, Rangeley 04970, 207/864-4355, bltbooks@rangeley.org), thanks to owner Wess Connally, a former high-school English teacher in Rangeley. The small, user-friendly shop has lots of great reading. The schedule is a bit unpredictable, with Wednesdays and Thursdays by chance, so call ahead. Wess organizes and leads a book-discussion group year-round, and visitors are welcome.

Ecopelagicon: A Nature Store (3 Pond St., Rangeley, 207/864-2771) is a kind of miniaturized (and less expensive) Nature Company, emphasizing eco-oriented gifts, books, toys, games, and cosmetics. Don't miss it.

In downtown Rangeley, you can't miss the house and shop of **Rodney Richard, the Mad Whittler** (123 Main St., Rte. 4, P.O. Box 183, Rangeley 04970, 207/864-5595) behind all the wood shavings and works in progress. If Rodney's performing his magic with the chainsaw and jackknife, you can stand by and watch, or perhaps buy one of his woodcarvings. His son, Rodney Jr., a chip off the old block, has earned his own reputation as an accomplished woodcarver, specializing in loons. Rodney Sr. has achieved national and international renown as a folk artist and master carver. His work has traveled to dozens of museums and appears in collections as far afield as Archangel in Russia. He's also the prime mover behind Rangeley's Logging Museum. Look for the Open pennant outside his shop in July and August; other times, call ahead to make sure someone is home.

ACCOMMODATIONS
Inns

Entering Rangeley from the south, you can't miss the rambling, three-story **Rangeley Inn and Motor Lodge** (2443 Main St., P.O. Box 160, Rangeley 04970, 207/864-3341 or 800/666-3687, www.rangeleyinn.com), on the edge of downtown's Haley Pond. Thirty-five Victorian-style rooms in the turn-of-the-20th-century main section and 15 modern rooms in the motel annex (overlooking the pond) are $84–139. All have private baths; some rooms have whirlpools and/or fireplaces or woodstoves. The main building also houses a dining room and tavern.

Next to the stunning Mingo Springs Golf Course, the **Country Club Inn** (56 Country Club Rd., P.O. Box 680, Rangeley 04970, 207/864-3831, www.rangeleyme.com/ccinn) claims the same fabulous lake-and-mountain panorama as the golf course. Nineteen '60s-style lake-view rooms go for $122 d, including breakfast ($99 off-season), or $182 d, with breakfast and dinner. A room-only rate ($104 d) is also available, as is a two-night all-inclusive golf package. Decor is woodsy: two huge fireplaces in the living room accented by wildlife trophies, lots of pine paneling everywhere. The inn is superbly maintained and run, and there's an outdoor pool. Pets are $10 per night. The inn, 2.2 miles west of downtown Rangeley, is open mid-May–mid-October and late December–March.

Bed-and-Breakfasts

On a quiet hillside, less than a half mile from downtown, Rob Welch, a retired principal, and his wife, Jan, a schoolteacher, are the enthusiastic hosts at (**Pleasant Street Inn B&B** (104 Pleasant St., Rangeley, 207/864-5916, www.pleasantstreetinnbb.com, $125–145 d). The Welches have completely renovated and expanded a traditional Maine farmhouse to include five good-size rooms, all with Wi-Fi and satellite TV, and two with whirlpool tubs. It's all bright, airy, and comfy. Guests have plenty of room to spread out in the guest parlor with TV, comfy living room, and dining area, where a full breakfast is served. Guests also have access to a pantry, stocked with afternoon refreshments, and a guest computer. The inn is on the in-town snowmobile route, and there's plenty of parking for snowmobile trailers. No children younger than 12, no pets.

Right downtown, with views over Rangeley Lake, is the **North Country Inn B&B** (2541 Main St., Rangeley, 800/295-4968, www.northcountrybb.com, $96–116). The two front guest rooms have the best views, but the two in back are quieter. All have queen beds and cable TV. The front porch is an inviting place to relax and watch the parade and fireworks during special events. Rates include a full breakfast. No pets, no kids under six.

Cabin Colonies

On a quiet cove about four miles west of town, **Hunter Cove on Rangeley Lake** (334 Mingo Loop Rd. office, Hunter Cove Rd. cabins, Rangeley, 207/864-3383, www.huntercove.com) has eight rustically modern waterfront cabins on six acres. Each has 1–2 bedrooms, screened porch, woodstove, phone, and TV. Rates are $150–210, two-night minimum. Weekly rates (required July–Aug.) are $900–

1,160. Rates cover up to four people; pets are $10 per day. The pricier cabins have hot tubs in the living room. It's open all year, with lower rates off-season and midweek. From here, it's an easy paddle to the western edge of the Hunter Cove Wildlife Sanctuary, and Mingo Springs Golf Course is nearby.

Far more remote is **Nioban Camps** (P.O. Box 770, Rangeley 04970, 207/864-2549, www.niboban.com), on South Shore Drive near the state park. Although the sporting camp is historical, the original cottages were replaced in 2001 with nice two-bedroom, lakefront cabins, each with a screened porch and well-equipped kitchen. A Ping-Pong table, phone, TV, and games are available in the main lodge. Moose and deer sightings are frequent; beaver and ducks swim along the shore; and eagles fly overhead. The camps are open year-round for snowmobiling, snowshoeing, and skiing. Rates are $800 per week, mid-June–early September. The rest of the year (closed Apr.), it's available with a two-night minimum stay for $135–170 per night. Pets are $15 per day. A one-bedroom honeymoon cabin is $115–135 per night or $575 per week.

Sporting Camps

Stephen Philbrick is the third-generation owner of (**Bald Mountain Camps** (Bald Mountain Rd., P.O. Box 332, Oquossoc 04964, office 207/864-3671, 207/864-3778, or 888/392-0072, www.baldmountaincamps.com), a family-oriented traditional sporting camp on the shore of Mooselookmeguntic Lake. Established in 1897 and now run by Steve and his wife, Fernlyn, the superb operation has more than 90 percent repeat guests, some of whom have been returning since the 1930s. It's tough to get a reservation, especially in peak summer. Fifteen rustic, waterfront log cabins can accommodate 2–8 people. Cabins are completely furnished, each offering a private porch, fireplace, living room, individual bedrooms, full housekeeping services, and porter service. Three meals a day are served daily in the lake-view lodge. No alcohol is served, so BYOB. A highlight is the Friday-night cookout, with lobster, ribs, corn, steamed clams, and blueberry pancakes for dessert. The informal dining room is open to the public for dinner (book well ahead) by reservation only (see *Food*). Among the activities are swimming (sandy beach), fishing, tennis, canoeing, motorboating, sailing, and waterskiing. There's a playground for kids. Rates range $125–145 per day, per person, depending on the season. Kids' rates vary with age and month. Pets are $12 per day. It's open mid-May–late September.

More rustic and remote than Bald Mountain Camps, **Grant's Kennebago Camps** (P.O. Box 786, Rangeley 04970, 207/864-3608 or 800/633-4815, www.grantscamps.com) is a classic sporting camp built in 1905 on remote, five-mile-long Kennebago Lake. Expect to hear lots of loons and see plenty of moose—*if* you can get a reservation. Seriously dedicated fly-fishers fill up the beds in May and September; families take their places July–August, when a boat, motorboat, mountain bikes, sailboat, hiking packs, and sailboard are included in the cabin price. Daily rates for the 18 rustic cabins, with private bathrooms and hot showers, are $155 pp (three or more nights) to $175 pp (for two nights or fewer); all include three meals a day in the dining room overlooking the water. Children under 12 are $60 a night; however, children under 4 are free. Pets are $15 a night, per pet. The main lodge's lake-view dining room is open to the public for all meals by reservation (BYOB), but the hearty cuisine makes it a popular place, so call well ahead. Canoe rentals are $15 a day. July–August, Grant's arranges a daily moose run on the Kennebago River for $30 per person. (Nonguests can also go on the moose run, for a higher fee; call for details.) Access is via a gated nine-mile road from Route 16, west of Rangeley. The gate is open 7 A.M.–6 P.M. only; if you're coming just for dinner, Grant's will arrange for access. It's open mid-May–mid-October.

Avid fly fishermen and women have been heading to **Lakewood Camps** (P.O. Box 1275, Rangeley 04970, 207/243-2082, www.lakewoodcamps.com) for more than 150 years.

The camps are by Middle Dam, which separates Lower Richardson Lake from the famed Rapid River, and are accessible only by boat. The cold and wild Rapid River, which falls nearly 1,100 feet in fewer than eight miles, is restricted to fly-fishing. Landlocked salmon and brook trout are found in both the lake and river, but the lake also is home to togue (or lake trout). Much of this area is protected Maine Public Reserve Land. Walk the Carry Road, which parallels the river, and you'll pass the home where Louise Dickinson Rich lived when she wrote *We Took to the Woods*. The daily per-person rate ($155–175 pp d, $60 per child 3–12) includes all meals and boat transportation, but not boat usage. Guest stay in simple lakeside cabins, which have Franklin fireplaces, electricity, and full baths. Pets are $15 per night.

Campgrounds and Campsites

In addition to the nonprofit and commercial campgrounds described here, the Rangeley Lakes Region Chamber of Commerce maintains a list of no-fee and low-fee **remote wilderness campsites** throughout the Rangeley Lakes.

The **Maine Forest Service** (Rte. 16, P.O. Box 267, Oquossoc 04964, 207/864-5545), responsible for more than a dozen no-fee primitive campsites, will provide a copy of its list upon request. The office also issues fire permits.

The **Stephen Phillips Memorial Preserve Trust** (P.O. Box 21, Oquossoc 04964, 207/864-2003) oversees 70 primitive tent sites on both the east and west shores of Mooselookmeguntic Lake and on Students, Toothaker, and other islands, all part of a 400-acre charitable preserve that includes more than four miles of lakefront. Many sites are lakefront; island sites and those on the west shore are accessible only by boat. Nightly cost is $16 per site (for two), teens or extra adults are $8, kids 6–12 are $5, dogs are $5 each. Two nature trails cross and circle Students Island. The campsites are open May–September.

At the southeast corner of Aziscohos Lake,

Black Brook Cove Campground (Lincoln Pond Rd., P.O. Box 319, Oquossoc 04964, 207/486-3828, www.blackbrookcove.com) provides three different kinds of camping experiences. The main campground has 30 tent and RV sites with hookups; the secluded east shore area has 26 wooded waterfront sites for small, self-contained units and tents. These wooded waterfront sites are 3.5 miles from the main campground and 100 feet from the water. Twenty-acre, boat-accessible Beaver Island, out in the lake, has nine wilderness sites, with another seven wilderness sites around the lake. The remote sites include outhouses. Rates are $20 per family per site, plus a hookup fee. The main campground facilities include coin-operated hot showers, a private beach, a convenience store, and rental boats and canoes.

Hardy folks can camp year-round at **Cupsuptic Family Campground** (Rte. 16, P.O. Box 326, Oquossoc 04964, 207/864-5249, www.cupsupticcampground.com). The lakefront campground has a full range of sites in summer, with rates beginning at $18 for a wilderness site. Site fees cover two adults and two children. Rental boats are available, and dogs are permitted ($3/day). Also on-site are a recreation hall, sandwich shop, bakery, bandstand, playground, and sand beach. The winter rate for sites with electricity is $25; hot showers and flush toilets are available. A three-mile trail connects snowmobilers with ITS 84.

Seasonal Rentals

The **Morton and Furbish Agency** (P.O. Box 1209, Rangeley 04970, 207/864-5777 or 888/218-4882, www.rangeleyrentals.com) has a wide selection of daily, weekly, and monthly rental cottages, camps, houses, and condos for winter and summer use.

The chamber of commerce can assist with seasonal rentals.

FOOD

Check the local newspaper for announcements of **public suppers,** featuring chicken, beans, spaghetti, or just potluck. Most suppers benefit charitable causes, cost under $10 pp, and provide an ample supply of local color.

Local Flavors

While bagels are the specialty at **Moosely Bagels** (2588 Main St., Rangeley, 207/864-5955), there's plenty more on the menu. For breakfast, choose from a full range of baked goods and simple to fanciful egg concoctions; lunch options include sandwiches, wraps, soups, and hot specials. There's seating inside or on the back, lake-view deck. It's open 5:30 A.M.–2:30 P.M. Monday–Saturday for breakfast and lunch (closed Wed.) and 6–11:30 A.M. Sunday for breakfast only.

"Meet me at the Frosty" is Rangeley's summertime one-liner, a ritual for locals and visitors. **Pine Tree Frosty** (Main St., Rangeley, 207/864-5894, noon–10 P.M. daily seasonal), a tiny take-out near Haley Pond and the Rangeley Inn, serves ever-popular Gifford's ice cream, in dozens of flavors, plus good-size lobster rolls and superb onion rings.

Far more than the usual produce is available at **The Farmer's Wife** (corner Rte. 17 and Rangeley Ave., Oquossoc, 207/863-2492), a farmstand that also sells gourmet foods, fresh-baked breads and pies, salads, and wine. Nearby **Oquossoc Grocery** (Rte. 4, Oquossoc, 207/864-3662) has fresh-baked doughnuts, hot and cold sandwiches, and pizza.

Watch the game while chowing down on good burgers, nachos, hand-cut fries, and similar fare at ever-popular **Sarge's Sports Pub and Grub** (Main St., 207/864-5616). More substantial entrées ($10–17) are served after 5 P.M., and there's even a kids' menu. Weekends there's often live entertainment.

Ethnic Fare

Sam Sriweawnetr, the owner of Rangeley's fabulous Thai restaurant, is a real-life hero. A former chef in the U.S. embassy in Iran, he was instrumental in helping lead five hostages to freedom. He spent years in hiding and then eventually escaped to the United States. He opened an acclaimed restaurant in Boston, later relocating to Maine's Western Mountains. **Thai Blossom Express** (2473 Main St., Rangeley, 207/864-9035, 11 A.M.–9 P.M. Thurs.–Tues.) serves some of the state's best Thai food. There's some seating, but it's more of a to-go place. No restrooms.

Family Friendly

Several sporting camps in the Rangeley area open their dining rooms to the public, primarily for dinner, during the summer. Grab the opportunity to sample the sporting-camp ambience and the retro comfort food that brings guests back from one generation to the next.

A notable exception to the retro comfort-food theme is **Bald Mountain Camps** (Bald Mountain Rd., Oquossoc, 207/864-3671, www.baldmountaincamps.com). Choose from an à la carte menu (entrées $13–25) or the regular house menu, which includes a full meal for $24–30. Especially popular is the Friday night cook-out, with lobster, spare ribs, chicken, burgers, dogs, and all the go-withs). Make reservations well in advance.

The Red Onion (Main St., Rte. 4, Rangeley, 207/864-5022) is a barn of a place where you can also get award-winning chili and pizza made on homemade dough. Portions are large. The "Onion" is open 11 A.M.–9:30 P.M. daily all year, unless, as the staff say, "High winds, low humidity, and plain laziness" inspire them to close the doors.

Try to snag a table on the deck overlooking the park and lake at **Parkside and Main** (2520 Main St., Rte. 4, Rangeley, 207/864-3774), a family-friendly restaurant known for its homemade soups and salads. The menu varies from burgers to steak; stick with the simpler preparations. It's open 11:30 A.M.–11 P.M. daily in summer, when there's often entertainment on the deck; call for winter hours.

Casual to Fine Dining

Huge windows frame dramatic views of Rangeley Lake from the dining room of the hilltop 【 **Country Club Inn** (56 Country Club Rd., Rangeley, www.rangeleyme.com/ ccinn). White tableclothes drape the well-spaced tables, and the food complements the view. Entrées ($20–30) include choices such as veal gruyere, filet mignon, and haddock Provençal. If the weather's fine, begin with cocktails on the deck overlooking the lake. The restaurant is open to the public by reservation for dinner, 6–8:30 P.M. Wednesday–Sunday, but tables for the public can be scarce when the inn is fully booked. Call well ahead, especially for summer weekends.

The Gingerbread House (Rte. 4, Oquossoc, 207/864-3602) underwent an incredible transformation in early 1997, going from a chummy, old-fashioned place to a casually upmarket, bright, open restaurant. The only hints of the former incarnation are the exterior gingerbread and the gussied-up antique soda fountain. On the menu are regional American items varying from turkey pot pie to beef Wellington (dinner entrées $14–28). Ask for a fireside table in winter, a porch one in summer. Breakfast is especially popular, as is the ice-cream takeout (Annabelle's Ice Cream). It opens at 6 A.M. daily for breakfast, lunch, and dinner.

The sunset views are the best reasons to reserve a table at **Loon Lodge** (16 Pickford Rd., Rangeley, 207/864-5666, www.loonlodgeme .com, 5–9 P.M. Tues.–Sat.), where pub and casual dining menus vary from burgers to rack of lamb.

INFORMATION AND SERVICES

The Rangeley Lakes Region Chamber of Commerce (Lakeside Park, P.O. Box 317, Rangeley 04970, 207/864-5364 or 800/685-2537, www .rangeleymaine.com, 9 A.M.–5 P.M. Mon.–Sat. and 10 A.M.–2 P.M. Sun. July and Aug.) produces annual guides to lodgings and services; the useful *Maine's Rangeley Lakes Map* costs $4.

The Rangeley Public Library (Lake St., Rangeley, 207/864-5529, 10 A.M.–4:30 P.M. Tues.–Fri. and 10 A.M.–2 P.M. Sat.) is housed in a wonderful old stone building just off Main Street.

Bethel and Vicinity

WESTERN LAKES

Bethel (pop. 2,380) is a sleeper. It's a classic New England village, tucked in the folds of the White Mountains. White-steepled churches, an ivy-covered brick prep school (Gould Academy), lovely antique homes, a main street dotted with shops and restaurants, and a sprawling inn on the common are all easily explored on foot. Six miles away, Sunday River, one of New England's hottest alpine resorts, draws skiers and snowboarders to its modern slopes and lodges. The Ellis, Bear, and Androscoggin Rivers wind through the region, and in the river valleys are two covered bridges, a handful of ponds, and many working farms. Framing the region on two sides are two spectacular notches, Evans Notch, part of the White Mountain National Forest, and Grafton Notch, a state park, as well as the city of Rumford, with a paper mill that emits the "smell of money," as locals like to say. Rumfort Point, Center Rumford, and Hanover are

don't-blink villages between Rumford and Bethel, and each has its calling cards.

Thanks to Sunday River, winter is peak season here. In addition to skiing and riding, there's snowshoeing, snowmobiling, dogsledding, skijoring, ice-skating, ice fishing, even ice climbing. Spring brings canoeists and anglers. Summer is lovely, with hiking for all abilities, biking, boating, fishing, rockhounding in local quaries, golfing, even llama trekking.

Autumn is still surprisingly undiscovered. It's perhaps the region's prettiest season, one when visitors can take advantage of all the summer activities and do so under a canopy of blazing crimsons, golds, and oranges backed by deep evergreens.

But let's back up a bit. Bethel's "modern" history dates from 1774, when settlers from Sudbury, Massachusetts, called it Sudbury Canada, a name reflected in the annual August Sudbury Canada Days festival. Another present-

Gould Academy's ivy-covered brick buildings are an integral part of Bethel.

© TOM NANGLE

© TOM NANGLE

Travel a bit off the beaten path to find the Lovejoy covered bridge, spanning the Ellis River, in South Andover.

day festival, Mollyockett Day, commemorates one of the area's most intriguing historical figures, a Pequawket Indian woman named Mollyockett. She practiced herbal medicine among turn-of-the-19th-century settlers, including a baby named Hannibal Hamlin. Her remedies proved effective in snatching from death in 1809 Abraham Lincoln's future vice president. (The incident actually occurred in the Hamlin home on Paris Hill, southeast of Bethel.) Mollyockett died August 2, 1816, and is buried in the Woodlawn Cemetery on Route 5 in Andover.

Meanwhile, the name Bethel surfaced in 1796, when the town was incorporated. Agriculture sustained the community for another half a century, until the Atlantic and St. Lawrence Railroad connected Bethel to Portland in 1851 (and later to Montréal) and access to major markets shifted the economic focus toward timber and wood products, which remain significant even today.

North of Bethel, Andover (pop. 945) has become a word-of-mouth favorite among through-hikers and section hikers on the Appalachian Trail, which snakes by about eight miles to the west. It's Maine's southernmost town near the AT, and the hikers pile into Andover for a break in August and September after negotiating the Mahoosuc Range, one of the toughest parts of the AT.

East of Bethel are the communities of Locke Mills (officially in the town of Greenwood, pop. 725) and Bryant Pond (in the town of Woodstock, pop. 1,240), both with summer and winter recreational attractions. Northeast of Bethel is Rumford (pop. 6,750), a paper-manufacturing center whose favorite son was former Secretary of State Edmund Muskie.

SIGHTS
Covered Bridges
Often called the **"Artist's Covered Bridge"** because so many artists have committed it to canvas, an 1872 wooden structure stands alongside a quiet country road north of the Sunday River Ski Resort. Kids love running

© TOM NANGLE

WESTERN LAKES

Bethel's downtown historic district includes two Bethel Historical Society properties.

back and forth across the unused bridge, and in summer they can swim below in the Sunday River. The bridge is 5.7 miles northwest of Bethel; take Route 2 toward Newry, turn left at the Sunday River Road, and then bear right at the fork. The bridge is well signposted, just beyond a small cemetery.

About 20 miles north of Bethel, the **Lovejoy Bridge,** in South Andover, built in 1867, is one of the lesser-visited of Maine's nine covered bridges. It's also the shortest. Spanning the Ellis River, a tributary of the Androscoggin, the 70-foot-long bridge is 0.25 mile east of Route 5 but not visible from the highway; it's about 7.5 miles north of Rumford Point. In summer, local kids use the swimming hole just below the bridge.

Dr. Moses Mason House

Listed on the National Historic Register, the 1813 Federal-style Dr. Moses Mason House not only is a beautifully restored eight-room museum but also serves as the headquarters

of the very active **Bethel Historical Society** (Bethel Common, 14 Broad St., P.O. Box 12, Bethel 04217, 207/824-2908, www.bethel historical.org). Particularly significant are the hall murals painted by noted itinerant muralist Rufus Porter or his nephew Jonathan Poor. Dr. Moses Mason, a local physician, was elected to the U.S. Congress a dozen years after Maine statehood and served two terms as a Maine congressman. The museum is open 1–4 P.M. Tuesday–Sunday July–early September and by appointment other months. Admission is $3 adults, $1.50 children.

Bethel Historic District

At the Dr. Moses Mason House, or at the chamber of commerce, pick up a copy of the Bethel Historical Society's *Walking Tour of Bethel Hill Village,* detailing information on 29 buildings and monuments in the downtown area's Historic District. Officially, more than 60 structures are included in the district. Follow the self-guided route (allow about an hour) to appreciate the 19th- and 20th-century architecture that gives real cachet to Bethel's heart.

PARKS AND PRESERVES
Step Falls Preserve

The Nature Conservancy's first Maine acquisition (in 1962), 24-acre Step Falls Preserve (Rte. 26, Newry, mailing address The Nature Conservancy, Maine Chapter, Fort Andross, 14 Maine St., Brunswick 04011, 207/729-5181) is ideal for family hiking—an easy, one-hour round-trip through the woods alongside an impressive series of cascades and pools. Pick up a trail map at the box in the parking area. Bring a picnic and have lunch on the rocks along the way. The waterfalls are most dramatic in late spring; the foliage is most spectacular in fall; the footing can be dicey in winter. Trailhead for the preserve is on Route 26, eight miles northwest of Route 2 and 10 miles southeast of the New Hampshire border. Watch for The Nature Conservancy oak-leaf sign on the right, next to Wight Brook.

◖ Grafton Notch State Park

Nestled in the mountains of western Maine,

3,192-acre Grafton Notch State Park (Rte. 26, Grafton Township, mailing address HC 61, Box 330, Newry 04261, 207/824-2912, 207/624-6080 off-season, $2 adults, $1 children 5–11; payment is on the honor system) boasts splendid hiking trails, spectacular geological formations, and plenty of space for peace and quiet. It's hard to say enough about this lovely park, a must-visit. Bring a picnic. Highlights include **Screw Auger Falls, Mother Walker Falls,** and **Moose Gorge Cave.**

The best (but not easiest) hike here is the **Table Rock Loop,** a 2.4-mile, moderate-to-strenuous two-hour circuit from the main trailhead (signposted Hiking Trails) at the edge of Route 26. The trailhead parking area is four miles inside the park's southern boundary and 0.8 mile beyond the Moose Cave parking area. Part of the route follows the white-blazed Appalachian Trail; otherwise the trail is orange-and blue-blazed. Some really steep sections are indeed a challenge, but it's well worth the climb for the dramatic mountain views from aptly named Table Rock.

Another favorite hike, moderate to strenuous, goes up **Old Speck Mountain** (4,180 feet), third highest of 10 Maine 4,000-footers and part of the Mahoosuc Range. The 28-foot-high viewing platform on the recently restored fire tower gets you above the wooded summit for incredible 360-degree views of the White Mountains, the Mahoosuc Range, and other mountains and lakes. Allow a solid seven hours for the 7.8-mile round-trip from the trailhead on the west side of Route 26 in Grafton Notch. The route follows the white-blazed Appalachian Trail most of the way; the tower is about 0.25 mile off the AT. Although there's a route map at the trailhead (same location as for the Table Rock hike), the best trail guide for this hike is in John Gibson's *50 Hikes in Southern and Coastal Maine* (2nd ed.).

If you're driving along Route 26 early or late in the day, keep a lookout for moose; have your camera ready and exercise extreme caution. You'll usually spot them in boggy areas, munching on aquatic plants, but when they decide to cross a highway, watch out—unlike the rest of us, they don't look both ways. And their eyes don't reflect headlights, so be vigilant after dark. Moose-car collisions are too often fatal to both moose and motorists.

The Mahoosuc Range
South and east of Grafton Notch State Park is a 27,253-acre chunk of Maine Public Reserve Land known as The Mahoosucs, or the Mahoosuc Range, where the hiking is rugged and strenuous but the scenic rewards are inestimable. The Appalachian Trail traverses much of the reserve, and AT hikers insist that the mile-long Mahoosuc Notch section, between Old Speck and Goose Eye Mountains, is one of their biggest challenges on the 2,158-mile Georgia-to-Maine route, requiring steep ascents and descents, with insecure footing, gigantic boulders, and narrow passages. If you're an experienced hiker, go for it, and use reliable guidebooks and maps, preferably USGS maps. The best overview of the reserve is *Recreational Opportunities in the Mahoosuc Mountains,* a free foldout map/brochure available from the Bureau of Parks and Lands (22 State House Station, Augusta 04333, 207/287-3821) or the Western Region Office, Bureau of Parks and Lands (129 Main St., P.O. Box 327, Farmington 04938, 207/778-8231). The helpful brochure lists and characterizes trails, lists campsites, and provides info on wildlife, vegetation, and water supplies.

White Mountain National Forest
Just under 50,000 acres (49,800 to be exact) of the 770,000-acre White Mountain National Forest (www.fs.fed.us/r9/white) lie on the Maine side of the New Hampshire border. Route 113, roughly paralleling the border, bisects the **Caribou-Speckled Mountain Wilderness,** the designated name for this part of the national forest. It's all dramatically scenic, with terrific opportunities for hiking, camping, picnicking, swimming, and fishing.

A drive along Route 113, north to south between Gilead and Stow, is worth a detour. It takes about 30 minutes nonstop, but bring a picnic and enjoy the mountain views from the tables at the Cold River Overlook, about a mile south of the Evans Notch highpoint. Route 113 is too narrow for bikes in midsummer, when logging trucks and visitor traffic can be fairly dense. Save this bike tour for a fall weekday, and take it south to north for a good downhill run from Evans Notch. The road is closed in winter. If you plan on stopping or hiking, Evans Notch requires a parking permit. It's $5 for seven days. Some locations have an "iron ranger" allowing payment of $3 per parking place per day. Permits, along with more information on hiking, camping, and other recreational opportunities in this section of the WMNF, are available at the **Evans Notch Ranger District** (18 Mayville Rd., Rte. 2, Bethel, 207/824-2134). It's on Route 2, next to the Crossroads Diner, just before the bridge across Route 26. Sheets detailing hiking trails also are available at the chamber office.

A good family hike is the **Albany Brook Trail,** an easy one-mile hike each way between the Crocker Pond Campgound (at the end of Crocker Pond Road) and the northern shore of Round Pond.

WARM-WEATHER RECREATION
Sporting Outfitters and Guide Services

These two companies provide rentals, guide services, and support for many of the sports detailed below. They're also great resources if you've brought your own equipment.

The Maine Guides at **Bethel Outdoor Adventures (BOA)** (121 Mayville Rd., Rte. 2, Bethel, 207/824-4224 or 800/533-3607, www.betheloutdooradventure.com) are pros at canoeing, kayaking, and bicycling. They also offer snowmobiling tours and rent machines. On the riverside premises are a campground and café.

Rocky and Lisa Freda of **Sun Valley Sports and Guide Service** (129 Sunday River Rd., Bethel, 207/824-7533 or 877/851-7533, www.sunvalleysports.com) provide Orvis-endorsed wading/driftboat trips, fly-fishing instruction, wildlife safaris, and guided snowmobile and

ATV tours, in addition to renting canoes, kayaks, snowmobiles, and ATVs. They also provide shuttle services for those with their own boats.

Hiking and Walking

Much of the hiking in this area is within the various parks and preserves, but a fun family hike not in that category is the easy-to-moderate ascent of **Mt. Will** in Newry, on the outskirts of Bethel. The Bethel Conservation Commission has developed a 3.2-mile loop trail that provides mountain and river views; allow about 2.5 hours to do the loop. At the chamber of commerce information center, pick up a Mt. Will trail-map brochure, which explains three different hiking options. There also may be maps at the trailhead, which is on the west side of Route 2/26, 1.9 miles north of the Riverside Rest Area—a terrific spot, incidentally, for a posthike picnic next to the Androscoggin River.

The wheelchair-accessible **Bethel Recreational Path** is about a mile long and parallels the Androscoggin River. It begins at Davis Park (on the corner of Rte. 26 and the Intervale Rd.), where there's also a skateboard park, picnic tables, boat launch, and playground, and ends near Bethel Outdoor Adventure, on Route 2. Expect to share it with joggers, in-line skaters, and cyclists. The **Androscoggin River Recreational Walking Trail** covers 1.5 miles, beginning at the lovely Riverside Rest Area, on Route 2, just east of the Sunday River access road, and continuing to the River View Resort.

Boating

The rivers in the Bethel area are a paddler's dream, varying from beginner/family stretches to white-water sections for intermediate and advanced canoeists. Fortunately, the major artery, the **Androscoggin River,** seldom has low-water problems, and you'll see lots of islands, as well as eagles, moose, and a beaver dam. West of Bethel, there's even an old cable from a onetime ferry crossing.

The best source of information on the Androscoggin is **Bethel Outdoor Adventures (BOA)** (121 Mayville Rd., Rte. 2, Bethel,

207/824-4224 or 800/533-3607, www.bethel outdooradventure.com). It offers canoe rentals, maps, shuttle service, and trip-planning advice. In addition, the BOA staff, especially owners Jeff and Pattie Parsons, can advise on canoeing the Ellis, Little Androscoggin, and Sunday Rivers. Kayak rentals are $35 full day.

The annual Androscoggin River Source to the Sea Canoe Trek is a celebration of the river's revival from years of unbridled pollution caused primarily by paper-mill runoff (see *Events*).

Just east of Locke Mills, before the Littlefield Beaches Campground (207/875-3290, www .littlefieldbeaches.com), you can put in at **Round Pond,** on the south side of Route 26, and continue into North and South Ponds. Bring a picnic and before you head out, enjoy it across the road at the lovely state rest area, with grills and covered picnic tables in a wooded setting.

Veteran professional guides Polly Mahoney and Kevin Slater of **Mahoosuc Guide Service** (1513 Bear River Rd., Newry, 207/824-2073, www.mahoosuc.com) lead wilderness canoe trips not in the Bethel area but on the Allagash, Penobscot, and St. John Rivers, as well as in Québec. With extensive wilderness backgrounds in such locales as Labrador and the Yukon Territory, management experience with Outward Bound, a flair for camp cooking, and a commitment to Native American traditions, Polly and Kevin are ideal trip leaders. Request a brochure with their schedules and rates.

Fishing

The 26-mile stretch of the Upper Androscoggin River, between the New Hampshire border and Rumford Point, its tributaries, the Wild, Pleasant, Sunday, and Bear Rivers, and local brooks are popular with anglers seeking rainbows, brookies, browns, and land-locked salmon. Even during the peak of summer, it's possible to catch smallmouth bass on the Andro.

Pick up a copy of *A Guide to Local Fishing* at the Bethel Area Chamber of Commerce.

Rocky and Lisa Freda of **Sun Valley Sports** (129 Sunday River Rd., Bethel, 207/824-7533 or 877/851-7533, www.sunvalleysports.com) provide Orvis-endorsed Master Maine Guide

services for fly-fishing, wading, river and pond fishing, and drift-boat fishing ($225 half day, $350 full day), as well as canoe and kayak rentals ($25–35 for two hours, including local shuttle), shuttles, and more. Their full-service fly shop has thousands of flies, as well as all the other gear anglers need or crave. Ask about their rental cabin or about golf and fishing packages with The Bethel Inn.

Master Maine Guide **Sandy MacGregor** (2094 Rt. 2, Rumford, 207/364-2506, www .mountainranger.com) grew up fishing the Androscoggin River. He knows where to find rainbows, browns, and smallmouth bass, and fly-fishing is his passion. Half-day float trip is $250, full day is $375.

Wildlife, Scenic, and Recreational Safaris

Steve White describes himself as a "Registered Maine Guide, Storyteller, and Aspiring Eccentric." He's also president of the local land trust, first selectman of the town of Newry, on the board of Maine's Land Use Regulatory Commission, and owner of a 1934 Chevy pickup awaiting restoration. It would be difficult to find a more fun, personalized, and customized adventure than those offered by his **Steve's Scenic Safaris to Exotic Places** (207/824-2410). Call him, and you won't be disappointed.

Explore the Androscoggin River with Maine Guide Sandy MacGregor on a late-afternoon **Wine and Dine Naturalist Float Trip** (207/364-2506, www.mountainranger .com). MacGregor guides a maximum of four guests in the *Molly Alexis,* a 17-foot handcrafted wooden drift boat with swivel bucket seats. You bring the wine, but he'll customize a menu for you. Bring a camera and binoculars: You'll see all types of waterfowl, maybe river otters, muskrat, or beaver, perhaps even osprey, eagle, or a moose. Sandy also offers other recreational tours, including gold panning in the Swift River, a moose safari-hike, boating on Richardson Lake and Aziscohos Lake, one of the Rangeley Lakes, where, he believes, God lives. Basic fee for a daylong float trip is

WESTERN LAKES

$375, excluding meals; a 15 percent discount is granted on additional days.

Explore the Lake Umbagog Wilderness Park on a sunset pontoon boat tour with **Bethel Outdoor Adventures** (121 Mayville Rd., Rte. 2, Bethel, 207/824-4224 or 800/533-3607, www.betheloutdooradventure.com). Moose sightings are almost guaranteed, and you'll see a bald eagle nest. The rate is $35 per person, including drinks and a light snack.

Biking

The Bethel Area Chamber of Commerce has sheets detailing about a dozen rides in the region, with lengths varying from a five-mile Village Restaurant Ride (don't be deceived; it takes in Paradise Hill, a killer for Sunday cyclists) to the 53-mile covered bridge cruise. For an easy pedal, follow the Sunday River Road as it continues out past Artist's Covered Bridge. It's mostly level and winding, paralleling the river and providing beautiful mountain views. No matter where you ride, do follow the rules of the road, keeping right and riding single file.

Mountain-bike rentals are available for $27/day from **Bethel Outdoor Adventures** (121 Mayville Rd., Rte. 2, Bethel, 207/824-4224 or 800/533-3607, www.betheloutdoor adventure.com).

Golf

Thanks to its spectacular setting, the 18-hole championship course at the **Bethel Inn and Country Club** (Bethel Common, Bethel, 207/824-2175, www.bethelinn.com) wows every golfer who plays here. Starting times are definitely needed, and caddies are available. If you want to improve your game, consider the **Guaranteed Performance School of Golf** (800/654-0125, www.gpgolfschool.com). It includes five hours of on-course instruction and video analysis with PGA professionals, maximum of three students per instructor.

Newest course in the area is the spectacular Robert Trent Jones Jr.–designed 18-hole course at **Sunday River Ski Resort** (207/824-3000, www.sundayriver.com), which opened in 2005.

Horseback Riding

No matter what your experience, you can enjoy a trail ride at **Sparrow Hawk Mountain Ranch** (120 Fleming Rd., Bethel, 207/836-2528, www.maineranch.com), a 160-acre property bordering White Mountain National Forest lands. Reservations are required for the rides, which vary from one hour to full day with lunch. Customized two-night getaway packages, with lodging, are available.

Rockhounding

Here's a great family experience. Maine's Western Mountains are filled with gems and minerals.

Take a one-hour guided digging tour of the Bumpus Maine, in Albany, with **Maine Mineralogy Expeditions,** which operates from Bethel Outdoor Adventures (121 Mayville Rd., Rte. 2, Bethel, 207/824-4224 or 800/533-3607, www.rocksme.biz or www.bethel outdooradventure.com). You'll learn about the mine's history of producing feldspar, mica, and beryl, and have the opportunity to search for rose quartz or beryl in mine dump areas. The fee is $25 adult, $9 kids 12 and under, or a maximum of $55/family, with a minimum of eight per trip.

WINTER RECREATION
Alpine Skiing and Riding

Sprawling octopuslike over eight mountains, **Sunday River Ski Resort** (Sunday River Rd., Newry, mailing address P.O. Box 450, Bethel 04217, 207/824-3000 or 800/543-2754, snow phone 207/824-6400, www.sundayriver.com) defines the winter sports scene in this area, with world-class downhill skiing and snowboarding, ice-skating, access to Nordic skiing, phenomenal snowmaking capability, slopeside lodging, and every possible amenity. The megaresort has nine quads (five high speed), four triples, two doubles, and three surface lifts serving 127 trails and glades.

Sunday River's trademarked Perfect Turn ski clinics, pegged as "skier development," have created hordes of enthusiastic new skiers and smoothed the style of intermediate skiers. And the resort's Learn-to-Ski-in-One-Day Program is more than just a slogan. It works. Sunday River also is home to **Maine Handicapped Skiing** (207/824-2440, www.skimhs.org), which provides free lessons and tickets for alpine and Nordic skiing and snowboarding for people with physical disabilities. Reservations are required.

Sunday River has day-care facilities in three locations (reservations advised), ski school for kids, an excellent inventory of top-of-the-line rental skis and snowboards, free on-mountain trolley-bus service, and plenty of places, with a wide range of prices, to grab a snack or a meal. Call or check the Internet for current ticket prices.

The ski season usually runs mid-October–early May, weather permitting (average annual snowfall is 155 inches). Lift hours are 9 A.M.–4 P.M. weekdays, 8 A.M.–4 P.M. weekends and holidays. Especially on weekends and during school vacations, make every effort to avoid the opening and closing hours for buying lift tickets, renting skis, or heading home; the congestion can be maddening. There's only one road on and off the mountain, so expect delays early and late in the day.

Nordic Skiing

The **Sunday River Cross Country Ski Center** (23 Skiway Rd., R.R. 2, Box 1688, Bethel, 207/824-2410, www.sundayriverinn.com), based at the independent Sunday River Inn, is not officially part of the Sunday River operation, but it's conveniently only 0.5 mile away. Nearly 25 miles of lovely, well-groomed wooded trails extend from the center. The best one leads from the lodge to the Artist's Covered Bridge. A clever innovation is the free *Kids' Trail Map,* showing locations of special surprises along the trails (totem pole, wind chimes, and more). Trail passes range from $8 for a child under 12 to $16 for an adult; ski rentals, for $10–16, are available in the small lodge, which also has a snack bar. Dogsledding trips are available.

Right in downtown Bethel, the **Bethel Inn Touring Center** (Bethel Common, P.O. Box 49, Bethel 04217, 207/824-6276, www.caribou recreation.com) uses its scenic golf course for nearly 25 miles of novice-to-advanced cross-country trails. The ski shop has a wax room and snack bar with seating areas. Ski rentals are available ($16 for the day) as are private and group lessons. Trail passes are $16 adults, $11 children.

About 30 miles of trails wind through 1,000 acres at **Carter's Cross-Country Ski Center** (Middle Intervale Rd., Bethel, 207/539-4848, www.cartersxcski.com), owned and managed by Carter's Cross-Country Ski Center in Oxford (207/539-4848). In winter, the Bethel location operates a lodge, a ski shop, and snack bar and rents skis and snowshoes. Daily rates are $12 adults, $8 for children, and $20 for racing skis.

Free cross-country skiing and snowshoeing are allowed on Duane's Nordic Retreat at **Mt. Abram** (Howe Hill Rd., off Rte. 26, Locke Mills, 207/875-5002, www.skimtabram.com). Duane's is the alpine area's former beginner mountain. Pick up a free trail pass at the alpine ticket window.

Ice-Skating

Picture an old-fashioned Currier and Ives winter landscape, with skaters skimming a snow-circled pond, and you'll come close to the scene on Bethel Common in winter. Bring a camera. The groomed ice-skating area, in the downtown Historic District, usually is ready for skaters by Christmas vacation. Sunday River Ski Resort (see *Alpine Skiing and Riding*) and Mt. Abram (see *Nordic Skiing*) both have ice-skating rinks.

Dogsledding

When they're not off leading three- or four-day dogsledding trips in the Mahoosucs or on Umbagog Lake ($450–525 pp), or even with the Inuit in Nunavut (formerly Baffin Island; $4,500 pp), or the Cree in Québec ($2,900 pp), Kevin Slater and Polly Mahoney of **Mahoosuc Guide Service** (1513 Bear River Rd., Newry, 207/824-2073, www.mahoosuc.com) will bundle you in a deerskin blanket and take you on

WESTERN LAKES

a one-day dogsled trip on Umbagog Lake, beyond Grafton Notch State Park. Wear goggles or sunglasses; the dogs kick up the snow. A campfire lunch and warm drinks are included in the $225 pp fee. Trips are limited, and they're *very* popular; book well in advance.

Snowmobiling

Rentals and guided snowmobile tours are available from **Sun Valley Sports** (129 Sunday River Rd., Bethel, 207/824-7533, www .sunvalleysports.com).

ENTERTAINMENT

The **Mahoosuc Arts Council (MAC)** (P.O. Box 534, Bethel 04217, 207/824-3575, www .mahoosucarts.org) sponsors more than a dozen performances throughout the year, plus about a dozen art residencies and other cultural events in local schools. An additional source of MAC schedule information is the Bethel Area Chamber of Commerce.

At **Sunday River Ski Resort,** there's live entertainment in several locations weekends and during school vacations. The resort also runs the Black Diamond Family Entertainment series, with performances such as vaudeville, marionettes, storytelling, and circus acts.

When the weather doesn't cooperate—and even if it does—and the kids need to let off steam, **BIG Adventure Center** (12 North Rd., Bethel, 207/824-0929, www.bigadventure.com) is just the ticket. Outdoor activities include two giant waterslides and an 18-hole miniature golf course; indoor possibilities are rock climbing, bowling, laser tag, and video games.

Two hot spots for après-ski into the night are **Suds Pub,** at the Sudbury Inn, where the Thursday open-mike night is legendary, and **The Matterhorn,** on the Sunday River access road, which books Boston bands on weekends. Both also serve food.

EVENTS

On the nearest March or April Saturday to April Fools' Day, Bethel's **April Fools' Pole, Paddle, and Paw Race** pits two-person triathlon teams against one another in Nordic skiing, canoeing, and snowshoeing. Events begin at the Sunday River Cross-Country Ski Center.

The first or second weekend of June, the annual three-day **Trek Across Maine: Sunday River to the Sea** draws nearly 2,000 cyclists for the 180-mile bike expedition from Bethel to Rockland, proceeds from which benefit the Maine Lung Association. Registrations are accepted on a first-come, first-served basis, and the trek usually is fully booked by April. Pledges are required, and there's a registration fee. Call 800/458-6472 for details. Don't like cycling? Perhaps the **Androscoggin River Source to the Sea Canoe Trek** is more your style: The annual 19-day paddle (last weekend in June–mid-July) from the New Hampshire headwaters to Fort Popham, near Bath—about 170 miles—is open to all canoeists, who can participate on any leg of the journey. A contribution is requested to benefit the Androscoggin Land Trust (207/527-2918, www.androscogginriver.net).

Bethel's **Annual Gem, Mineral, and Jewelry Show** is a long-running event with exhibits, demonstrations, and sales of almost everything imaginable in the rock and gem line—even guided field trips to nearby quarries. Hours are 9 A.M.–5 P.M. Saturday and 10 A.M.–4 P.M. Sunday; admission is $2. It takes place at Telstar Regional High School the second weekend in July. The third Saturday in July, on Bethel Common in downtown Bethel, **Mollyockett Day** commemorates a legendary turn-of-the-19th-century Native American healer with a parade, children's activities, a craft fair, food booths, and fireworks. There's also usually an oddball race—a couple of years it was wheeled beds; another year it was spouse-carrying.

Andover presents a parade, live entertainment, children's games, art and flower shows, antique cars, a barbecue, and a beanhole bean supper the first weekend in August as part of **Andover Old Home Days.** The second weekend that month at the Moses Mason House in Bethel, **Sudbury Canada Days** commemorates Bethel's earliest settlers with traditional crafts, an art show, parade, croquet, bean supper, and contradance.

Maine artisans take center stage in the annual

display and sale at the **Blue Mountains Arts and Crafts Festival,** held the second weekend in October at the Sunday River Ski Resort, Newry.

SHOPPING

While Bethel doesn't have tons of shops, the ones it has are not the run-of-the-mill variety.

Books-N-Things of Bethel (130 Main St., 207/824-0275 or 800/851-3219) provides the kind of personal service that no chain bookstore could ever achieve.

Check out the strikingly unusual designs and glazes at **Bonnema Potters** (146 Main St., 207/824-2821), in a handsomely restored studio across the street from the Sudbury Inn. Best of all are the earth colors used on tiles, dishes, vases, and lamps.

If something a bit more offbeat appeals, stop in for Moose-Drop earrings, allegedly the genuine article, at **Maine Line Products** (23 Main St., 207/824-2522), source of whimsical souvenirs for your whimsical friends. In the same vein is the "Lobsta Parts Jewelry," but Maine Line also carries serious gifts, such as jams, syrup, fudge, buckets, and wind chimes.

At **Mt. Mann Jewelers** (57 Main St., 207/824-3030, www.mtmann.com), Jim Mann wears the hats of owner, miner, gem cutter, and jeweler, and he's full of information in every category. Here's the Bethel area's best place to see Maine's special gems: tourmaline (the official state mineral), aquamarine, amethyst, and morganite. The shop also has a basement "crystal cave," where kids can "discover" minerals and learn to identify them. For $0.50, Jim has free maps to area mines and quarries open to the public. Inquire about guided quarry tours. (Also see *Oxford Hills* for information on Perham's of West Paris, Maine's mother of all rock shops.)

Shoppers entering **Linda Clifford–Scottish and Irish Merchant** (91 Main St., 207/824-6560, www.lindaclifford.com) are almost always overwhelmed by the quality and selection. Pottery, chrystal, clothing, jewelry, tartans, and more are all elegantly displayed. Be prepared to drool or part with some serious bucks.

Shaker-reproduction furniture and a home store filled with decorative items and accessories and woodware can be found at **Timberlake Home Store** (158 Rt. 2, Bethel, 207/824-6545 or 800/780-6681, www.stimberlake.com). Ask about lectures, demonstrations, and workshops.

Handcrafted wood products fill **Maine Artisans Wood Gallery** (1180 Rte. 2, Rumford, 207/364-7500), which sells hardwood goods, including furniture and accent pieces.

A section of the store at **Pooh Corner Farm** (Bog Rd., off Rt. 2, West Bethel, 207/836-3276, www.poohfarm.com), western Maine's largest greenhouse and florist, is dedicated to Pooh-related merchandise and Pooh, Piglet, Rabbit, Roo, and Eyeore are in residence on the farm. You'll find fun garden items, too.

If you're serious about antique shopping, pick up a copy of *Antiques in Western Maine* at the chamber of commerce office. The map and guide is published annually and includes Bethel and nearby communities. Local treasures, including vintage clothing, books, baskets, and quilts, dominate the stock at **Playhouse Antiques** (46 Broad St., Bethel, 207/824-3170). Glass, china, books, furniture, textiles, and much more fill two floors of a five-story barn at **The Lyons Den** (2034 Rt. 2, Bethel, 207/364-8634). **Top Hat Antiques and Collectibles** (Rt. 2, Hanover, 207/364-8321), a one-story warehouse-style barn, is filled with a lot of this and more of that.

ACCOMMODATIONS

Conveniently, the **Bethel Area Chamber of Commerce Reservations Service** (800/442-5826, www.bethelmaine.com) provides toll-free lodging assistance for more than 1,000 member beds in B&Bs, motels, condos, and inns in Bethel, at Sunday River Ski Resort, and farther afield. If you're planning a winter visit, however, particularly during Thanksgiving and Christmas holidays, February school vacation, or the month of March, don't wait until the last minute. Procrastination will put you in a bed 40 miles from the slopes.

Keep in mind that peak season (ergo highest room rates) in this part of Maine is in *winter,* not summer. Some lodgings also have higher rates for fall foliage in September and October.

Sunday River Lodging

On-mountain lodging options at Sunday River Ski Resort include 425 rooms and suites in two full-service hotels—the **Grand Summit** and the **Jordan Grand Hotel**—as well as more than hundreds of slope-side condos and town houses in seven different clusters. Nicest (and priciest) of the latter are the Locke Mountain Townhouses. Both hotels have restaurants and cafés, indoor/outdoor heated pool, tennis courts, video game room, and lots of extra amenities; the Jordan Grand is in an isolated location. Most rooms have full kitchen facilities. Except for dorm rooms, lodging packages include lift tickets. Prices for accommodations and activity packages vary widely (207/824-3000, reservations 800/543-2754, www.sundayriver.com).

Country Inns

The Bethel Inn and Country Club (Bethel Common, P.O. Box 49, Bethel 04217, 207/824-2175 or 800/654-0125, www.bethelinn.com) fronts on the Bethel Common in the historical district; out the back door is the golf course. It's the centerpiece of a classic New England village scene. Rooms are spread out between the traditional main inn and outbuildings and modern one- to three-bedroom condominiums. Rooms vary widely in decor and quality; upgrading is an ongoing process here. If you can afford it, spring for a room in the new wing of the main inn. This is a full-service resort, and amenities include golf, tennis, a health club with pool and sauna, game room, a lakeside outpost for swimming and boating, and a summer children's program. Best of all, it's all included in the rates. Per person inn rates, including breakfast and dinner, begin at around $80 d midweek/$100 d weekend and holiday for a standard and increase to $210 d midweek/$239 weekend and holiday for a deluxe suite. Children 11 and younger stay free in the same room, but those 4–11 pay $20 per night for the meal plan. Kids 12 and older pay $65 per night, including the meal plan. Condo rates, which do not include meals, begin at

about $275 per night, for a one-bedroom condo sleeping four, and increase to nearly $1,000 for a three-bedroom sleeping 10. A 15 percent service charge is added to all rates. Some accommodations permit dogs for $10 night. Numerous packages are available. It's open all year, but the restaurant may be closed some nights in April and November (see *Food*).

Since buying **The Sudbury Inn** (Main St., P.O. Box 369, Bethel 04217, 207/824-2174 or 800/395-7837, www.sudburyinn.com) in 2000, enthusiastic owners Bill and Nancy White have turned the white elephant into a lovely and homey country inn with an exceptional dining room and the region's best pub. The Whites have deep roots in this area and are eager to help guests plan their adventures. Rooms and suites (and even a three-bedroom apartment with full kitchen and fireplace) are spread out between the main house and the dog-friendly carriage house ($15 per dog/day, including bed and bowls). The two-bedroom suites are especially good for families. All are comfortably furnished and have cable TV, air-conditioning, and phone. A full breakfast is included in the rates, which begin at $89–120 for a standard.

New owners have breathed new life into the grand **Victoria** (32 Main St., P.O. Box 249, Bethel 04212, 207/824-8060 or 888/774-1235, www.thevictoria-inn.com, $99–179 d), a downtown landmark with its turret and elegant carriage house. All rooms are decorated with antiques and have TV, air-conditioning, and phone; some have a whirlpool tub. The carriage house suites with sleeping loft are a good choice for families ($149–309). Rates include a full breakfast, and the dining room is open for dinner, too (see *Food*).

Bed-and-Breakfasts

Richard and Jenni Fredericks give an English accent to the **Briar Lea B&B** (150 Mayville Rd., Rte. 2/26, Bethel, 207/824-4717 or 877/311-1299, $90–160), a mid-19th-century, Georgian Colonial farmhouse with restaurant and authentic English pub just east of downtown Bethel. They've freshened the rooms with fancier linens and accents without losing the homespun charm the floral wallpapers and antique furnishings provide. All have TV/DVD, Wi-Fi, and air-conditioning. A "full English" breakfast is included. In summer, request a back-facing room if highway noise bothers you.

Innkeepers Tom and Marcey White are only the third owners of the farmhouse and magnificent barn they've christened (A **Prodigal Inn and Gallery** (162 Mayville Rd., Rte. 2, Bethel, 207/824-8884 or 800/320-9201, www.prodigalinn.com, $150–160). They've redone the long-established inn into one of the loveliest B&Bs in the area. Tom's bronze sculptures accent many of the public rooms, and guests can watch him at work in his barn studio-gallery. Rates include a multicourse breakfast and homemade goodies for afternoon tea or snack.

Tucked well off Route 2, on a quiet road that meanders through woods and farm country, is **The Perennial Inn** (141 Jed Martin Rd., Rumford Point, 207/369-3039, www.perennialinn.com), a homey B&B with a put-your-feet-up-and-relax attitude. The sprawling Victorian farmhouse, built in 1884, has a pool room, living room, family room with fireplace and TV/DVD, and dining room, where a family-style full breakfast is served. The six guest rooms (some with shared bath) are decorated in simple, country style: a bit of this and a touch of that. Rates range $125–165 d, including breakfast and afternoon refreshments. Attached to the inn is a large red barn, where innkeepers and animal lovers Darlene and Jenna Ginsberg breed chocolate, black, and yellow Labrador retrievers (www.killingworthlabs.com). Also in residence are three cats. Well-behaved pets are welcome ($20) and provided with ceramic bowls, bed or crate, and a treat. Outside the farmhouse are acres of fields and woods, streams and ponds, laced with trails; snowshoes are available. Bring a bike and explore the back roads.

Architect Stuart Crocker designed the lovely, Shingle-style **Crocker Pond House** (917 North Rd., Bethel, 207/836-2027, www.crockerpond.com, $95–105) so that it fits naturally into its setting on 50 mostly wooded acres. It's a lovely spot that blends contemporary amenities, such

as Wi-Fi and in-room phones, with traditional cottage design in a restorative atmosphere (no TV). Crocker and his wife, Ellen, welcome guests in seven rooms, all south-facing with mountain views; one is wheelchair-accessible with a roll-in shower. Begin the morning with Stuart's blueberry pancakes, and return after hiking, relaxing by the pond, or exploring for afternoon tea and cookies. No pets; two cats are in residence. Norwegian, French, and German are spoken at the inn. Children are welcome (the room with the loft is especially good for families). Children younger than 14 sharing a room are $15 each; older children are $25 each.

Motel

The **The Inn at the Rostay** (186 Mayville Rd./Rt. 2, Bethel, 207/824-3111 or 888/754-0072, www.rostay.com) isn't your typical motel. Rather, it's an inn-type experience. The rooms are decorated with homey touches, and many have themes, such as duck, goose, or cat. Most have refrigerators and microwaves, all have phones, cable TV/VCR (video library available), and air-conditioning or ceiling fans. Wi-Fi is provided, and there's a quilt shop on the premises. Guests can have a full breakfast, served in a dining room adjacent to a guest parlor, for $7. Rates begin at $68 d midweek and vary greatly. Winter holiday weeks are priciest, at $112–120.

Lodge

Here's a property with a twist: In 1988, Steve Crone introduced llama trekking to Maine, and he's still at it, even more enthusiastically, offering half-day and multiday trips in the White Mountain National Forest from his casually rustic **Telemark Inn Wilderness Lodge** (591 King's Hwy., Mason Township 04217, 207/836-2703, www.telemarkinn.com, $125, including breakfast), open spring, summer, and fall. Be forewarned, though: You'll be hiking *with* the llamas, not *on* them; they tote the gear. A Half-Day Llama Trek, lasting about three hours, is $75 adults, $65 children under 14, including a stop for swimming and snacks. It departs from the inn at 9 A.M. and noon. Better yet, book a lodging/trekking package incorporating nature hikes, mountain biking, canoeing, or llama treks. Two- to five-day activity packages are $390–875 per adult, $300–675 for kids, including breakfasts and lunches and guided day activities; five-day packages include family-style dinners. Three-day overnight llama treks are $600 per adult, $525 per child.

Campgrounds

Riverside Campground (121 Mayville Rd., Rte. 2, Bethel, 207/824-4224) is closest to downtown Bethel and has 48 RV ($22 with full hookup) and tent sites ($16) on the banks of the Androscoggin River north of downtown Bethel. The family-oriented campground is under the same ownership as **Bethel Outdoor Adventures (BOA)** (www.betheloutdoor adventure.com), a recreational backup operation providing gear rentals and guided tours. Rent a canoe, kayak (day rate $52 canoe, $35 kayak, including shuttle service) or mountain bike ($27/day); BOA will shuttle you upriver on the Androscoggin for a leisurely downstream paddle. Both the campground and BOA are open daily May–October.

Well-maintained **Littlefield Beaches Campground** (13 Littlefield La., Greenwood, 207/875-3290, www.littlefieldbeaches .com, $29–34) has minigolf, horseshoes, playgrounds, canoe/kayak rentals, general store, laundry, weekly cottage rental, and more; it caters primarily to the RV trade with 130 sites and has a terrific 40-acre location with a sandy beach on South Pond. Rules are enforced, including the campground's ban on water scooters. Pets are allowed, but not on the beach; the store has pooper-scoopers you can borrow.

Thirteen miles west of Bethel is the seven-acre **Hastings Campground** (800/280-2267 for credit-card reservations), one of four campgrounds along Route 113 in the White Mountain National Forest. The 24-site campground is primitive, with no hookups or showers, but it does have vault toilets, hand pump for water, fishing and hiking, and is wheelchair-accessible. Route 113 is especially scenic, so this is a prime location for extensive hiking in the national forest. Trail information and maps are

available from the Evans Notch Ranger District office (see *Information and Services*). The campground is in Gilead, three miles south of Route 2. Base rate for a campsite is $16. It's open mid-May–mid-October.

Seasonal Rentals

For weekly or monthly seasonal rentals, winter or summer, contact **Maine Street Realty and Rentals** (20 Railroad St., Bethel, 207/824-2114, www.mainestreetrealty.com).

FOOD
Local Flavors

You can feel good when eating at the **Good Food Store** (Rte. 2, Bethel, 207/824-3754 or 800/879-8926, www.goodfoodbethel.com). The combination store and take-out sells both good food and food that's good for you and stocks a huge array of natural foods. Create an instant picnic with sandwiches, salads, and soups ($3–6), even beer and wine. If you're renting a condo and don't feel like cooking or eating out, you can pick up homemade soups, stews, and casseroles to go. The barn-based shop is open 8 A.M.–8 P.M. daily all year. Operating from Graceland, a bright-orange trailer outside the store, is **BBQ Bob's Real Pit BBQ** (207/824-4744, 11:30 A.M.–7 P.M. Thurs.–Tues.). A local transplanted Texan gives it an enthusiastic thumbs-up. Choices include pulled pork, beef brisket, ribs, chicken, and sides such as barbecue beans, slaw, and corn bread. Yum.

Baked goods made daily from scratch from all-natural ingredients have earned **DiCocoa's Bakery** (119 Main St., Bethel, 207/824-5282, www.cafédicocoa.com) a solid following. Go for the fabulous baked goods, but don't miss the lunch specials, including panini and soup. The bakery doubles as a market selling fancy foods and take-home meals. It also makes scrumptious gelato. It opens at 7 A.M. daily for breakfast and lunch.

The **Bethel Farmers Market** sells good-for-you produce and other items 9 A.M.–noon each Saturday mid-June–mid-October, on Route 26, Railroad Street, next to Bethel Family Health Care at the southern edge of town.

On-Mountain Dining

Sunday River has always suffered from a lack of choice and quality, but it's slowly improving. Best choices on the mountain are two independent restaurants, both seasonal. **Phoenix House and Well** (Skiway Rd., across from the South Ridge base complex, Newry, 207/824-2222, www.phoenixhouseandwell.com, 11 A.M.–midnight daily during ski season) is a modern, chalet-style building with a nice view of the slopes. Fine dining at Phoenix House varies from tuna steaks to filet mignon ($18–28), and the restaurant has earned a *Wine Spectator* Award of Excellence; it's also a good choice for Sunday brunch. The Well is the best bet for lunch, with sandwiches, soups, and stews.

For upscale Tex-Mex, slide into **Gringo Harry's** (Fall Line condominiums, Sunday River Rd., Newry, 207/824-4000), serving dinner only.

Pubs and Pizzas

Also open only in winter, but farther down the access road, is **Great Grizzly/Matterhorn** (292 Sunday River Rd., Newry, 207/824-6271), an immensely popular restaurant and with good reason. This barn of a place is *the* après-ski spot in Bethel, with entertainment on weekends. You have to see it to believe the decor. It's filled with co-owner Roger Beaudoin's finds, many from his travels and climbing expeditions in Switzerland (The Matterhorn, of course). Antique mountain-climbing gear is in one room; a village motif complete with a real-estate office and old Sunoco pumps is in another; classic skis are everywhere. Be sure to check out the bar, made from 120 skis. The wideranging menu includes the best pizzas in the region, cooked in a wood-burning oven ($12) as well as steaks, seafood, salads, and sandwiches. There's even a kids' menu. On weekend nights, there's often family-style entertainment 6–8 P.M. On Tuesday–Friday and Sunday nights, bring your skis and have them sharpened and waxed while you eat for just $10. No reservations, so it's wise to dine early on weekends or expect to wait. Live entertainment, usually rock bands, begins at 9:30 P.M. on Friday and Saturday; a cover is charged unless you're already seated and have had dinner.

On the lower level of the Sudbury Inn is the **Suds Pub** (151 Main St., Bethel 207/824-2174 or 800/395-7837, www.sudburyinn.com), a very relaxing hangout. The moderately priced menu includes appetizers, burgers, soups, salads, pizza, and a few entrées, most in the $7–15 range. The full bar has 29 beers on tap. Thursday night is Hoot Night, a open-mike tradition since 1987 and a great chance to mingle with locals. There's also live music on Friday and Saturday nights.

For an authentic English pub experience, head to **The Jolly Drayman English Pub and Restaurant** (at the Briar Lea Inn, 150 Mayville Rd./Rt. 2, Bethel, 207/824-4717 or 877/311-1299, www.briarleainn.com). Owners Richard and Jenni Fredricks remodeled the space based on the 15th-century pub they owned in England years ago and named it for the drayman, the driver of the beer wagon. How good is it? Well, it was noticed by *Bon Appetit*. The tiny pub is a treat, with fine ales and stouts. The restaurant is open for lunch Wednesday–Sunday and dinner Tuesday–Sunday. The menu includes pub-style favorites, such as Thatcher's shepherd's pie and bangers-and-mash along with a few surprises, such as Mrs. Balbir Singh's Indian Korma and beef Vindaloo. There are sandwiches, salads, soups, and a children's menu, too. Most choices are $7–15.

Ethnic and Vegan Fare

Café DiCocoa Restaurant (125 Main St., Bethel, 207/824-5282, www.cafédicocoa.com) is open Saturday evenings (6:45 P.M.) during winter for "Gentle Dining," a candlelight-dinner experience during ski season. The five-course, fixed-price dinner (BYOB) is by reservation only, and usually features Mediterranean foods. About once a month during winter, the restaurant also hosts Mediterranean Tasting Workshops or cooking classes ($20). The 90-minute evening workshops include an overview of the history and culture of the featured region, explanations of ingredients, cooking demonstrations, and plentiful samples. The restaurant's name is cleverly derived from that of co-owner Cathy diCocco.

Taste of Eden (188 Mountain View Mall, Bethel, 207/824-8939), a vegan café and bakery, concentrates on food from scratch. Everything is homemade from whole foods, even condiments, and wheat-free dishes are usually on the menu. Breakfast and lunch are served all day; a typical price is $4.99 for an entrée, $3.50 for a soup. It's open 7 A.M.–7 P.M. Sunday–Thursday.

Hard to believe, but you can even get authentic—and truly delicious—Japanese and Korean food in Bethel. **Cho Sun** (141 Main St., Bethel, 207/824-7370, www.chosunrestaurant .com) is in a lovely New England Victorian house decorated with Asian art and antiques. Sushi is a specialty, but owner Pok Sun Lane's South Korean fare draws on her heritage. Most entrées are $15–24.

Fine and Fancy Dining

For an upscale dining experience, head to ◖ **The Sudbury Inn** (151 Main St., Bethel, 207/824-2174 or 800/395-7837, www.sudbury inn.com, 5:30–9 P.M. Tues.–Sun.), a warmly retrofitted 1873 Victorian inn with several separate dining areas. Entrée range is $18–32 (more if you order lobster), but there's no surcharge for sharing; the rack of lamb and the cioppino are superb. Reservations are essential, especially on weekends and holidays.

A homey atmosphere, excellent food, and good service have made chef-owned **S. S. Milton** (43 Main St., Bethel, 207/824-2589, 11:30 A.M.–2:30 P.M. and 5–9 P.M. daily summer, 5–9 P.M. Wed.–Sun. winter) a popular destination. Dinner entrées, such as Maine lobster casserole, roast duckling, and New Zealand lamb, are in the $16–24 range. Kid-pleasing choices such as mac and cheese, hot dogs, and pasta, are on the children's menu ($3–5). You can dine on the porch in summer.

The dining room at **The Bethel Inn** (on the common, Bethel, 207/824-2175, www.bethel inn.com) is open to the public for breakfast (7:30–9:30 A.M. weekdays and 7–10 A.M. weekends/holidays) and dinner (5:30–8:45 P.M.

nightly). The dining rooms overlook the golf course to the mountains beyond. Dinner entrées may include veal jagar Schnitzel, lobster and scampi, or New York sirloin and range $18–26. Ask about the early-seating, dinner-for-two special, which includes four courses and a bottle of wine; reservations required.

The desserts are to die for at **The Victoria Inn Restaurant** (32 Main St., Bethel, 207/824-8060 or 888/774-1235, 11:30 A.M.–4 P.M. Wed.–Sat., 5:30–9 P.M. Mon.–Sat.), so plan well in advance. Dining is in three intimate rooms, set with white tablecloths, china, and crystal and accented with chandeliers, wall murals, and the architectural niceties of a beautifully restored Victorian. Afternoon tea is served.

INFORMATION AND SERVICES

The Bethel Area Chamber of Commerce (Cross St., P.O. Box 1247, Bethel 04217, 207/824-2282 or 800/442-5826, www.bethelmaine.com) is open all year; hours are 9 A.M.–6 P.M. Mon.–Fri., 9 A.M.–5 P.M. Sat., noon–5 P.M. Sun. in summer). The building has public restrooms.

Just north of downtown Bethel is the Evans Notch Information Center for the Evans Notch Ranger District of the White Mountain National Forest (18 Mayville Rd., Rte. 2, R.R. 2, Box 2270, Bethel, 207/824-2134, www.fs.fed.us/r9/white). Trail maps, campsite information, bird checklists, and other helpful wildlife brochures are all available here. Even in summer, the office may be closed at unexpected times; call for hours.

GETTING AROUND

The free **Bethel Explorer** bus service operates between Bethel and Sunday River. It runs 6:30–1 A.M. weekends Thanksgiving–mid-December and then daily through early April (but check the schedule).

At Sunday River, the free **Sunday River Trolley** (207/824-3000) circulates throughout the resort, operating weekends Thanksgiving–Christmas and then daily until early April. It runs on a 30-minute cycle, 8–1 A.M. weekdays and 7–1 A.M. weekends and holidays.

Oxford Hills

Sandwiched between the Lewiston/Auburn area and the Bethel area, with Sebago and Long Lakes off to the south, the Oxford Hills region centers on Norway and South Paris. The town of Norway (pop. 4,740) shares the banks of the Little Androscoggin River with the community of South Paris, the major commercial center for the town of Paris.

From here it gets really complicated, although it's unlikely to affect a visitor. Oxford County's official seat is Paris (pop. 4,360), but all the relevant county offices are in South Paris. Next, throw into the mix the town of West Paris (pop. 1,620), which is, in fact, mostly *north* of Paris and South Paris. Within the boundaries of West Paris is the hamlet of North Paris. Fortunately, there's no East Paris, but there is the tiny enclave of Paris Hill, a pocket paradise many people never discover.

West Paris gained its own identity when it separated from Paris in 1957, but its traditions go way back. The Pequawket Indian princess Mollyockett, celebrated hereabouts as a healer, supposedly buried a golden treasure under a suspended animal trap, hence the name of Trap Corner for the junction of Routes 26 and 219. No such cache has been uncovered, but the corner is the site of the incredible gemstone collection at Perham's of West Paris. More recent traditions in West Paris come from Finland, home of many 19th- and early-20th-century immigrants who gravitated to a new life in this area. Finnish names are common on the town's voting registers.

Norway, fortunately, is far less complicated. The name, incidentally, comes not from Europe, or Norwegian settlers, but rather from a variation on a Native American word for waterfalls—cascades on the town's Pennesseewassee (PENN-a-see-WAH-see) Lake (called Norway Lake locally), which powered 19th-century mills. European settlement began in 1786.

Norway was the birthplace of C. A. Stephens (1844–1931), who for 55 years wrote weekly stories for a 19th-century boys' maga-

zine, *Youth's Companion*. Colorfully reflective of rural Maine life, the entertaining tales were collected in *Stories from the Old Squire's Farm,* published in 1995.

Waterford (pop. 1,460) is a must-see, especially the National Historic District known as Waterford Flat or Flats—too pretty to believe, with classic homes and tree-lined streets alongside Keoka Lake in the shadow of Mt. Tire'm. It's a 19th-century village frozen in time.

SIGHTS
(Paris Hill

On Route 26, just beyond the northern edge of **South Paris,** a sign on the right marks one end of Paris Hill Road, a four-mile loop that reconnects farther along with Route 26. As you head uphill, past an old cemetery, you'll arrive at a Brigadoon-like enclave of elegant 18th- and 19th-century homes—a National Historic District with dramatic views off to the White Mountains and the lakes below. Centerpiece of the road is Paris Hill Common, a pristine park in front of the birthplace (not open to the public) of former Vice President Hannibal Hamlin (1809–1891). South of the green stands the **Hamlin Memorial Library** (P.O. Box 43, Paris Hill, Paris 04271, 207/743-2980, www.hamlin.lib .me.us), the only Paris Hill building open to the public, where you can bone up on the history of this pocket paradise. Visit the library's website to download a copy of the Paris Hill walking tour.

Most children (and adults) get a kick out of entering a public library that once was a town jail. This one, built in 1822, held as many as 30 prisoners until 1896. Three prisoners somehow escaped in the 1830s, abandoning one of their pals stuck in the wall opening they had created. In 1902, the jail became the library, retaining the telltale signs of jail-bar hinges in the granite walls. Admission is free to the library's upper-level museum section, but donations are welcomed. The library has no heat, so be sure

© TOM NANGLE

The public library for Paris Hill was previously a jail.

to dress warmly if you're here early or late in the season. Hours vary with the season.

If you're in the area on the first December weekend in an even-numbered year, inquire about the **Biennial Holiday House Tour,** when a dozen of these elegant homes, decorated exquisitely for Christmas, are open to the public, all to benefit the Paris Hill Community Club.

Perham's of West Paris

And now for something completely different. Welcome to rockhound heaven! Perham's of West Paris (194 Bethel Rd., Rte. 26, P.O. Box 280, West Paris 04289, 207/674-2342 or 800/371-4367) is part museum, part shop, and part counseling service. You can admire shelf after shelf of spectacular rare gems, buy cut and uncut gems and minerals, and get do-it-yourself advice for a family outing in the mineral-rich quarries of the Oxford Hills. Established in 1919 at the Trap Corner crossroads, Perham's sells books, videos, rock tumblers, metal detectors, gold pans, and all the tools you'll need for treasure hunting. Request a

free map of the five quarries it owns. And good luck! You may keep anything you find.

Global Maine

Posted almost casually on an undistinguished corner in western Maine is a roadside landmark that inevitably appears in any travel book or slide show with a sense of the whimsical. Nine markers direct bikers, hikers, or drivers to Maine communities bearing the names of international locales: **Norway, Paris, Denmark, Naples, Sweden, Poland, Mexico, Peru,** and **China.** All are within 94 miles of the sign, which stands at the junction of Routes 5 and 35 in the burg of Lynchville (part of Albany Township), about 14 miles west of Norway. If you approach the sign from the south on Route 35, you're likely to miss it; it's most noticeable when coming from the north on Route 35 or the west on Route 5.

Beech Hill Farm and Bison Ranch

I know you came to Maine to see a moose, but did you know that you can see buffalo,

Woodland gardens are just one aspect of the McLaughlin Garden, an intown oasis in South Paris.

© TOM NANGLE

too? Usually associated with Western ranges, buffalo are increasingly finding a home in Maine, and at the Beech Hill Farm and Bison Ranch (Rte. 35, North Waterford, 207/583-2515; www.beechhillbison.com), you can have a close encounter with the beasts. The farm has been in the Hersey family for four generations, first as a dairy farm and later as a vacation home. Paul and Marcia Hersey decided to return it to its family farm glory, but with a Western accent. The Herseys are aiming to produce one of the finest-quality herds of buffalo in the East, and they're well on their way. In 2003, they produced a national champion heifer calf, and they've won numerous awards. You're also welcome to take walking tours of the farm. After you've met the buffalo, visit the store, where you can buy bison meat and fabulous bison jerky as well as other products and souvenirs, such as buffalo hides.

◖ McLaughlin Garden

In 1997, a little miracle happened in South Paris. For more than 60 years, Bernard McLaughlin had lovingly tended his two-acre perennial garden alongside Route 26, eventually surrounded by commercial development, and he'd always welcomed the public into his floral oasis. In 1995, at the age of 98, McLaughlin died, stipulating in his will that the property be sold. Eager developers eyed it, but loyal flower fans dug in their heels, captured media attention, created a nonprofit foundation, and managed to buy the property—the beginning of the little miracle. The McLaughlin Garden (97 Main St., Rte. 26 and Western Ave., South Paris, mailing address the McLaughlin Foundation, P.O. Box 16, South Paris 04281, 207/743-8820, www.mclaughlin garden.org) lives on, with its 98 varieties of lilacs, plus lilies and irises and so much more. The gardens are open daily May–late October for self-guided tours. Admission is free, but donations are welcomed. Check the website for special events and programs. The **Garden Café** (207/739-2228, 11 A.M.–3 P.M. Wed.–Sun. late May–early Sept.) serves soups, salads, and sandwiches. A gift shop (10 A.M.–5 P.M.) in the house's front parlor carries gardening items and high-end crafts and gifts, mostly Maine made.

Snow Falls
A 300-foot gorge on the Little Androscoggin River is the eye-catching centerpiece of Snow Falls rest area, an easy-off-easy-on roadside park where you can commandeer a table alongside the waterfall. What better place for a relaxing picnic (no grills, some sheltered tables)? Trucks whiz by on the highway, but the water's noise usually drowns them out. The rest area is on Route 26, about six miles north of the center of South Paris.

RECREATION
The most popular Oxford Hills hikes are particularly family friendly—no killer climbs or even major ascents, no bushwhacking, just darned good exercise and some worthwhile views. July–mid-August, don't be surprised to encounter clusters of summer campers, since camp counselors all over this region regularly gather up their kids and take them out on the trail or paddling the ponds. If you're spending more than a day hiking in this area, pick up a copy (at bookstores and gift shops) of *Hikes in and around Maine's Lake Region,* by Marita Wiser; it's the best available advice on this area.

Hiking
It's hard to resist a hike up **Mt. Tire'm** (1,104 feet)—if only to disprove its name. Actually, it's supposedly a convolution of a Native American name. The only steep section is at the beginning, after the memorial marker dedicated to 19th-century Waterfordite Daniel Brown, for whom the trail (unblazed) is named. Allow an hour or so for the 1.5-mile round-trip, especially if you're carrying a picnic. Allow time on the summit ledges to take in the views—all the way to Sebago on a clear day. From downtown Waterford (Rte. 35), take Plummer Hill Road about 300 feet beyond the community center; the trailhead is on the west side of the road; watch for the marker.

Straddling the Paris-Buckfield-Hebron town boundaries, **Streaked** (STREAK-ed) **Mountain** (1,770 feet) has a moderate and then easy trail to an expansive summit with an abandoned fire tower, wireless towers, and vistas as far as Mt. Washington. Pack a picnic. If you're here in early August, take along a small pail to collect wild blueberries. Late September–early October, it's indescribable, but remember to wear a hunter-orange hat or vest once hunting season has started—or tackle the trail on a Sunday, when there's no hunting. Allow about 1.5 hours for the one-mile round-trip, especially if you're picnicking and blueberrying. To reach the trailhead from South Paris, take Route 117 west to Streaked Mountain Road, on the right (south). Turn and go about 0.5 mile. Park well off the road. (You can also climb Streaked from the east, but it's a much longer hike that requires waterproof footwear.)

Golf
At nine-hole **Paris Hill Country Club** (355 Paris Hill Rd., Paris, 207/743-2371), founded in 1899, you'll find a low-key atmosphere, reasonable greens fees, cart rentals, and a snack bar. No tee times are needed. The rectangular course has all straight shots; the challenges come from slopes and unexpected traps.

It's not just golfers who patronize the nine-hole **Norway Country Club** (Lake Rd., Rte. 118, P.O. Box 393, Norway 04268, 207/743-9840); this is a popular spot to have lunch or kick back on the club porch. The mountain-lake scenery, especially in the fall, is awesome. Starting times are not required; first-come, first-served. Established in 1929, the club is a mile west of Route 117.

Spectator Sports
If you're partial to guerrilla warfare on wheels, the place to be is **Oxford Plains Speedway** (Rte. 26, P.O. Box 208, Oxford 04270, 207/539-8865, www.oxfordplains .com), Maine's center for stock-car racing. Late April–mid-September, souped-up high-performance vehicles careen around the track

in pursuit of substantial money prizes. All races begin at 6:30 P.M.

Winter Sports

The best Oxford Hills locale for **cross-country skiing** is Carter's Cross-Country Ski Center (420 Main St./Rte. 26, Oxford, 207/539-4848, www.cartersxcski.com/oxfordtrails.html), with about 40 km of groomed novice, intermediate, and advanced trails amid lovely frozen-lake scenery in the Welchville section of Oxford. Facilities include ski and snowshoe rentals, a well-equipped ski shop, plus snack bar, solarium, and sauna. Trail pass is $12 adults, $10 seniors, $8 students under 18. Kids under 6 are free.

ENTERTAINMENT

Marcel Marceau wannabes come to study at the nationally famed **Celebration Barn Theater** (190 Stock Farm Rd., South Paris, 207/743-8452, www.celebrationbarn.com), established in 1972 by the late mime master Tony Montanaro. Mime, juggling, dance, clowning, storytelling, and improv comedy performances are open to the public in the 125-seat barn at 8 P.M. on assorted Fridays and Saturdays July–August. Reservations are required. Ticket prices are $12 adults, $8 students and seniors. Pack a picnic supper and arrive early. The theater also offers residential workshops for aspiring mimes, storytellers, comedians, and the like. Check the website for details. The theater (signposted) is just off Route 117.

Another place to catch a wide variety of shows is the **Oddfellow Theater** (P.O. Box 127, Rte. 117, Buckfield 04220, 207/336-3306, www.oddfellow.com).

FESTIVALS AND EVENTS

Wall-to-wall paintings are for sale along Main Street in downtown Norway for the **Sidewalk Art Festival,** the second Saturday in July, in which nearly 100 artists participate. **Founders' Day** brings craft and antiques exhibits, music, and an antique-car open house on Paris Hill Common, Paris Hill, the third Saturday in July. A special highlight is a one-day showing of a private car collection. The name of North Waterford's **World's Fair** seems sort of cheeky for this three-day country medley of egg-throwing contests, talent show, live music, dancing, and more the fourth weekend in July.

The family-oriented, four-day agricultural **Oxford County Fair,** "The Horse-Powered Fair," held in mid-September, features 4-H exhibits, a beauty pageant, a pig scramble, live entertainment, an apple-pie contest, and plenty of crafts and food booths at the Oxford County Fairgrounds.

SHOPPING

Books-N-Things (430 Main St., Norway, 207/743-7197, www.bntnorway.com) is one of those full-service bookstores that inspires you to buy more than you ever planned. A few doors away is **The Irish Ewe** (446 Main St., Norway, 207/743-6263, www.theirishewe.com), a paradise for knitters and fans of hand-crafted Irish goods. A knit-and-spin group meets 4–8 P.M. Wednesdays. You can even arrange to adopt an Irish ewe.

Just beyond the Celebration Barn Theater, **Christian Ridge Pottery** (210 Stock Farm Rd., South Paris, 207/743-8419, www.applebaker.com) produces functional ceramic designs and *objets,* including a trademarked apple baker and a bagel cutter. You can see the work in progress at the shop.

ACCOMMODATIONS
Sumner

For a complete change of pace, back in time and back of beyond, **Morrill Farm Bed and Breakfast** (85 Morrill Farm Rd., Sumner, 207/388-2059, www.bbonline.com/me/morrillfarm, $75 d) is a late-18th-century farm with three rustic second-floor rooms sharing one bath in the ell connecting the house and the barn. On the 217-acre spread are nature/cross-country skiing trails, river fishing, and a menagerie of domestic farm animals. Pets are kenneled on-site for $15 a day. The farm is north and east of Norway/South Paris, a mile from Route 219 (West Sumner Road). Turn north on Greenwoods

WESTERN LAKES

Road at Roll-In Variety and continue a mile to Morrill Farm Road.

Norway/South Paris

Clean, convienient, and cheap summarizes the **Inn Town Motel** (58 Paris St., Norway, 207/743-7706 or 800/227-8770, $62–69). Rooms are boring motel style, with faux paneling, but all have air-conditioning, TV, phone, and high-speed Internet access. The location at the intersection of Routes 117 and 26 makes it easy to get just about anywhere in the Oxford Hills region.

The 200-year-old expanded Cape that now houses the **King's Hill Inn** (56 King Hill Rd., South Paris, 207/744-0204, www.kingshillinn .com, $95–160) was the birthplace of Horatio King, who served as postmaster general under President Buchanan. Inside are three rooms and three suites, all with a range of comfortable touches, perhaps a gas stove, microwave and dining area, deck entrance, whirlpool tub, or antiques. The quiet, rural location is convenient to hiking trails and the Celebration Barn Theatre. Rates include a *seven-course* breakfast.

Waterford

Waterford—that lovely little enclave flanked by Norway/South Paris, Bridgton/Naples, and the Lovells—has a couple of fine places to put your head.

Barbara and Rosalie Vanderzanden's traditionally elegant **Waterford Inne** (258 Chadbourne Rd., Box 149, Waterford, 207/583-4037, www.waterfordinne.com, $100–175), an antiques-filled 19th-century farmhouse on 25 open and wooded acres, is a prime getaway spot. A delicious breakfast is included; children are welcome, pets are allowed for $15 extra. No credit cards. The inn is close to East Waterford, 0.5 mile west of Route 37. It's open all year.

You have to love bears (and who doesn't?) if you stay at the **⟪ Bear Mountain Inn** (Rte. 35, South Waterford, 207/583-4404, www .bearmtninn.com), a beautifully updated 1820s B&B on 53 acres overlooking Bear Pond (it's really a lake). This is one of those places that's hard to leave, especially after you settle in on the pond-view terrace or the beach. Enthusiastic innkeeper Lorraine Blais, a professional decorator, has created five bear-themed rooms, with Wi-Fi, private and shared baths, for $120–160 d, plus luxury and family suites for $220–325, including breakfast. The self-contained Sugar Bear cottage, with fireplace and kitchenette, is pet friendly. Across the road from the inn is a trail up Bear Mountain, and Hawk Mountain is just around the corner. Lorraine can set you up with all kinds of special activities—trail riding, fishing, mountain biking in summer; snowmobiling, dogsledding, and ice-fishing in winter. No children under eight.

Quilt lovers will think they've arrived in heaven at the **Kedarburn Inn** (Rte. 35, Box 61, Waterford, 207/583-6182 or 866/583-6182, www.kedarburn.com, $71–125), in an 1858 streamside home where Margaret Gibson also has Kedar Craft, a quilt and fabric shop filled with her handmade quilts and stocked with quilters' supplies. Of course, the house is filled with quilts, and Margaret also offers quilters' retreat weekends. Walk down the road to town and Lake Keoka. Seven rooms, and two share a bath. Rates include a full breakfast.

FOOD
Local Flavors

Fare Share Market and Natural Foods Co-op (443 Main St., Norway, 207/743-9044, www .fairesharecoop.org, 9 A.M.–6 P.M. Mon.–Sat., to 7 P.M. Fri.), in a rehabbed building downtown, is a great place for natural and organic goods, including fresh-baked breads and muffins, wraps, and soup. There's a seating area inside. It's also home to the **Commons Art Collective,** a collaborative galley.

Local produce, honey, organic meat, perennials, preserves, syrup, cheese, and baked goods are all part of the stock at **Norway Farmers Market,** which sets up downtown at Main and Deering Streets in the parking lot of L. M. Longley's, 2–6 P.M. Thursday late May–October.

Many people flock to **The Lake Store** (14 Waterford Rd., Rtes. 117 and 118, Norway

Lake, Norway, 207/743-6562, 6 A.M.–9 P.M. daily) just to check out the crazy collection of Coca-Cola memorabilia, but you can also load up with picnic fixings, pizza, liquor, groceries, and videos.

What's the most intriguing short-order menu item at **Melby's Market and Eatery** (Rte. 35, North Waterford, 207/583-4447 or 800/281-4437)? The buffalo burger, made from bison raised right down the road at the Jones farm. A popular item, especially in summer, is Maine-made Gifford ice cream. Melby's has all the usual general-store stuff, plus plenty of seating.

Don't blink, or you'll miss **Rising Sun Café and Bakery** (74 Main St./Rte. 26, South Paris, 207/743-7046). Although the name sounds big, the place is tiny, with only one table. Still, it's one popular place, thanks to the the baking and sandwich-making talents of owners Jennifer Liby and Sarah Colby. It's open 6 A.M.–4 P.M. Tuesday–Friday, 6 A.M.–2 P.M. Saturday.

Casual Dining

An unassuming exterior on a busy in-town thoroughfare camouflages the pleasant interior at **Maurice Restaurant Français** (109 Main St./Rte. 26, South Paris, 207/743-2532, www.mauricerestaurant.com, 11 A.M.–2 P.M. Sun. and 4:30–8:30 P.M. daily (to 9 P.M. Fri.). A veteran in this area, the popular restaurant serves creditable French cuisine in the $14–24 price range. Reservations are a good idea, especially on weekends.

By reservation, the Vanderzandens will prepare a four-course dinner for guests and the public at the peaceful ☾ **Waterford Inne** (258 Chadbourne Rd., Waterford, 207/583-4037, www.waterfordinne.com). The leisurely meal is $75 per couple; spring for it, they do a wonderful job. No credit cards; BYOB.

INFORMATION AND SERVICES

The information center for the well-organized Oxford Hills Chamber of Commerce (4 Western Ave., South Paris, 207/743-2281, www.oxfordhillsmaine.com) is open 9 A.M.–4 P.M. weekdays. It produces an annual magazine that's actually an interesting read, far less promotional than the usual CC material.

Check out Norway Memorial Library (258 Main St., Norway, 207/743-5309, www.norway.lib.me.us).

Fryeburg Area

Fryeburg (pop. 3,000), a crossroads community on busy Route 302, is best known as the funnel to and from the factory outlets, hiking trails, and ski slopes of New Hampshire's North Conway and the White Mountains. Except during early October's annual extravaganza, the giant Fryeburg Fair, Fryeburg seldom ends up on anyone's itinerary. Too bad. The mountain-ringed community has lots of charm, historic homes, the flavor of rural life, and access to miles of Saco River canoeing waters.

Incorporated in 1763, Fryeburg is Oxford County's oldest town; even earlier, it was known as Pequawket, an Indian settlement and trading post—until skirmishes with white settlers routed the Native Americans in 1725 during Dummer's War (also known as Lovewell's War). Casualties were heavy on both sides; Lovewell and the Pequawket chief were among the fatalities.

In 1792, Fryeburg Academy, a private school on Main Street, was chartered; the school's Webster Hall is named after famed statesman Daniel Webster, whose undistinguished teaching career at the school began and ended in 1802. Among the students at the time was Rufus Porter, who later gained renown as a muralist, inventor, and founder of *Scientific American* magazine. Today the school is one of a handful of private academies in Maine that provide public secondary education, a uniquely successful private/public partnership.

© HILARY NANGLE

The Presidential Range of the White Mountains is the backdrop for Fryeburg's farmlands.

Just north of Fryeburg is the town of Lovell, with three hamlets—known collectively as "The Lovells"—strung along Route 5, on the east side of gorgeous Kezar Lake. Anyone who has discovered Kezar Lake yearns to keep it a secret, but the word is out. The mountain-rimmed lake is *too* beautiful.

SIGHTS
Covered Bridges
Two of Maine's nine covered bridges are within striking distance of Fryeburg. In the hamlet of East Fryeburg, just west of Kezar Pond, 116-foot-long **Hemlock Bridge** was built in 1857. Beneath the bridge runs the "Old Saco," or "Old Course," a former channel of the Saco River. The best time to visit is July–October; mud or snow can prevent car access other months, and June is buggy. From the Route 5/302 junction in Fryeburg, take Route 302 East 5.5 miles to Hemlock Bridge Road. Turn left (north) and go about three miles on a paved and then unpaved road to the bridge. Or paddle under the bridge on a detour from canoeing on the Saco River.

A bit farther south, 183-foot-long **Porter Covered Bridge,** linking Oxford and York Counties and the towns of Porter and Parsonsfield, spans the Ossipee River. Officially known as the **Parsonsfield-Porter Historical Bridge,** it was built in 1798 and then rebuilt once or twice between 1858 and 1876. The bridge is just east of Route 160, about 0.5 mile from the center of Porter. From Fryeburg, take Route 5/113 to East Brownfield and then Route 160 to Kezar Falls and Porter.

Hopalong Cassidy Memorabilia
When he died in 1956, longtime Fryeburg resident Clarence Mulford, author of the Hopalong Cassidy books, left his extensive collection of Western Americana, including models, copies of his books, research materials, and more to the Fryeburg Women's Club, along with enough money to build an addition onto the Fryeburg Public Library (98 Main St., Fryeburg, 207/935-2731) for their display. The library is

open 9 A.M.–7 P.M. Monday, 9 A.M.–5 P.M. Tuesday–Thursday, and 9 A.M.–2 P.M. Saturday.

RECREATION
Canoeing

The **Saco River,** headwatered in Crawford Notch, New Hampshire, meanders 84 miles from the Maine border at Fryeburg to the ocean at Saco and Biddeford. Its many miles of flat water, with intermittent sandbars and a few portages, make it wonderful for canoeing, camping, and swimming, but there's the rub: The summer weekend scene on the 35-mile western Maine stretch looks like bumper boats at Disneyland and it can be quite raucous—with large parties towing canoes filled with beer. Aim for midweek in late September and early October, when the foliage is spectacular, the current is slower, noise levels are lower, and the crowds are busy elsewhere. For a relaxing trip, figure about two miles an hour and you can do the Fryeburg-to-Hiram segment with two overnight stops, including a couple of interesting side-trip paddles to Hemlock Bridge, Pleasant Pond, and Lovewell's Pond. If you put in at Swan's Falls in Fryeburg, you won't have to deal with portages between there and Hiram. For multiday trips, you'll need to get a **fire permit** (free), or stay at one of the commercial campgrounds. Fire permits are available at some local stores.

Saco River Canoe and Kayak (Rte. 5, P.O. Box 111, Fryeburg 04037, 207/935-2369, www.sacorivercanoe.com), close to the convenient put-in at Swan's Falls, rents canoes and tandem kayaks ($42 a day Fri.–Sun. July and Aug., $30 midweek and off-season) and provides delivery and pickup service along a 50-mile stretch of the Saco River. Shuttle costs range $6–16 per canoe (depending on location). Safety-conscious owners Fred and Prudy Westerberg know their turf—they've been in biz since the 1970s—and provide helpful advice for planning short and extended canoe trips. They're open mid-May–late October.

If crowds on the Saco become a bit much, head east or north with your canoe or kayak to the area's lakes and ponds, even to **Brownfield**

Bog. Prime canoeing spots are **Lovewell Pond** and **Kezar Pond** in Fryeburg; **Kezar Lake** in Lovell; and **Virginia Lake** in Stoneham. (If a north wind kicks up on Kezar Lake, stay close to shore.) Most spectacular is mile-long Virginia Lake, nudged up against the White Mountain National Forest. A house on the wooded shoreline is a rarity. The access road (off Rte. 5 between North Lovell and East Stoneham) is a mechanic's delight, but persevere; tranquility lies ahead.

The best way to see beautiful Kezar Lake is by renting a boat from **Kezar Lake Marina** (W. Lovell Rd., Lovell, 207/925-3000, www.kezarlake.com). Canoes and kayaks rent for $10 per hour or $25 per day. A 13-foot Boston Whaler is $50/half day, $90/full day.

Hiking

The easiest (and therefore busiest) trail in the area is the 20-minute stroll up (barely up) **Jockey Cap,** named for a cantilevered ledge that's long since disappeared. At the top of the trail, with a 360-degree view of lakes and mountains, is a monument to Admiral Robert Peary, the Arctic explorer who once lived in Fryeburg. The metal edge of the monument is a handy cheat sheet—profiles and names of all the mountains you're seeing, more than four dozen of them. The trail is fine for kids, but keep a close eye on the littlest ones; the drop-off is perilous on the south side. Jockey Cap is also popular with rock climbers and boulder mavens. The trailhead is on Route 302, about a mile east of downtown Fryeburg, on the left, between the Jockey Cap Country Store and the Jockey Cap Motel. And here's a bit of trivia: Jockey Cap was the site of Maine's first ski tow.

Allow about half an hour to reach the summit of **Sabattus Mountain** in Lovell, north of Fryeburg. This is an especially good family hike, easy and short enough for small children. Carry a picnic and enjoy the views at the top—on the ledges of the more open second summit. You'll see the White Mountains, Pleasant Mountain, and skinny Kezar Lake; in fall, it's fabulous. To reach the trailhead from Fryeburg, take Route 5 North to Center Lovell. About 0.8

mile after the junction of Routes 5 and 5A, turn right onto Sabattus Road. Go about 1.6 miles, bearing right at the fork onto an unpaved road. Continue another half mile to a parking area on the left; the trailhead is across the road. The round-trip hike is about 1.5 miles.

Other good hikes in this area are **Mt. Tom** (easy, about 2.5 hours round-trip; just east of Fryeburg), **Burnt Meadow Mountain** (moderately difficult, about four hours round-trip to the north peak, good views of the Presidential Range; near Brownfield); and **Mt. Cutler** (moderately difficult, about two hours round-trip; near Hiram).

Swimming

Fryeburg has two public beaches that double as canoe put-ins. **Weston's Beach** (on River St./Rte. 5 N, just off Rte. 302) is a swath of sand extending into the Saco River that gets wider as the summer progresses and the river level drops. Another sand beach is adjacent to **Canal Bridge Campground,** just off Route 5 heading toward Lovell.

Snowmobiling

More than 600 miles of groomed trails are accessible from Fryeburg. For information and sled rental, try **Fryeburg Snowmobile Rentals** (103 Main St./Rte. 302, Fryeburg, 207/935-1220 or 800/458-1838, www .sledandbed.com), which rents environmentally friendly snow machines. Rates begin at $119 for a half day. Full clothing, including boots, pants, jacket, and gloves, is $25. Guided tours are available by request.

ENTERTAINMENT AND EVENTS

Anything happening in Bethel and vicinity, Oxford Hills, or Sebago and Long Lakes is also within easy reach of the Fryeburg area, especially in the daytime.

Singer/songwriter Carol Noonan has created a phenomenal 200-seat performing arts center on her hilltop farm. **Stone Mountain Arts Center** (695 Dug Way Rd., Brownfield, 866/227-6523, www.stonemountainartscenter.com) brings in nationally renowned performers such as Leon Kottke, The Capitol Steps, Livingston Taylor, Richie Havens, Paula Poundstone...just to name a few. The calendar is jam-packed. All events take place in the barn, and preshow dinners, pizzas and salads ($10–16), are available by reservation. Credit cards are taken for reservations, but cash or check is required for actual payment. Be sure to print out a copy of the directions—this place is in the boonies.

The **Ossipee Valley Fair** is an old-fashioned, four-day agricultural fair with tractor pulling, animal exhibits, live entertainment, food booths, games, and a carnival. It's in South Hiram the second weekend in July.

The Big Event in these parts is the **Fryeburg Fair,** the last country fair of the season (first week of Oct., sometimes including a few days in Sept.), Maine's largest agricultural fair and an annual event since 1851. A parade, a carnival, craft demonstrations and exhibits, harness racing, pig scrambles, children's activities, ox pulling, and live entertainment are all here, as are plenty of food booths (it's sometimes called the "Fried-burg" Fair). More than 300,000 turn out for eight days of festivities, so expect traffic congestion. The fair runs Sunday–Sunday, and the busiest day is Saturday. No dogs are allowed on the 180-acre site. Spectacular fall foliage and mountain scenery just add to the appeal. Find it at the Fryeburg Fairgrounds (officially the West Oxford Agricultural Society Fairgrounds) on Route 5, Fryeburg.

In summer, **outdoor concerts** are held Tuesday nights at the gazebo (or in the fire barn, if it's raining).

SHOPPING

It's hard to believe that the jewelry and crafts inside the **Harvest Gold Gallery** (Rte. 5, Center Lovell, 207/925-6502, www.harvest goldgallery.com) are more stunning than the setting overlooking Kezar Lake. Magnificent gold jewelry, much of it accented with Maine gemstones, is made on the premises. Also here is a very well-chosen selection of high-end crafts, with an emphasis on fine glasswork. It's definitely not a place to bring young kids.

Less high-end, but no lower in quality, are the crafts at **Weston's** (48 River St./Rte. 113 N, Fryeburg, 207/935-2567, www.westonsfarm .com). The mostly locally made selection includes baskets, bears, pillows, candles, and more.

ACCOMMODATIONS

If you're planning to be in the area during the Fryeburg Fair, you'll need to reserve beds or campsites months ahead, in some cases a year in advance. Don't procrastinate.

Bed-and-Breakfasts

Named after the famed polar explorer who lived here in the late 19th century, the **Admiral Peary House** (9 Elm St., Fryeburg, 207/935-3365 or 877/423-6779, www.admiralpeary house.com, $139–189) has seven Peary-themed rooms with air-conditioning and Wi-Fi. Some rooms have gas stoves and/or whirlpool tubs. You'll have the run of several comfortable first-floor rooms, including a living room with pool table, a quiet parlor, and a huge three-season porch. No small children, no pets; cats are in residence. It's open all year, but reservations are preferred.

In the center of town, **The Oxford House Inn** (548 Main St., Rte. 302, Fryeburg, 207/935-3442 or 800/261-7206, www.oxford houseinn.com, $125–175 d) is better known for its dining room. Although modern conveniences include TV, air-conditioning, and Wi-Fi, comfy antiques and old-fashioned wallpapers provide a Grandma's-house atmosphere. Breakfasts, served in the mountain-view porch/dining room, are every bit as creative as the inn's dinner menus (see *Food*).

The comments in one of the in-room guest books say everything you need to know about **Peace With-Inn** (254 W. Fryeburg Rd./Rte. 113 N, Fryeburg, 207/935-7563 or 877/935-7322, www.peacewithinn.com, $95–165): "peaceful," "cozy," "restorative." The truly rambling, circa 1750 farmhouse on the winding road that climbs from the Saco River Valley farmlands up through Evans Notch is an ideal base for exploring the notch or other parts of the White Mountain National Forest or to retreat to after a shopping foray into nearby North Conway, New Hampshire. Each of the five rooms has air-conditioning and TV, and a few have big whirlpool tubs. There's Wi-Fi, and for true bliss, a massage room with sauna. A living room, den, book nook, games room, porch, and patio provide plenty of room to spread out. A full breakfast is served family style. Do note: The inn's owners live out of state but employ daytime innkeepers and resident caretakers. Guests who do not arrive by a specified time are instructed how to find their room.

Cottage Colony

The *New York Times* once headlined a story on **Quisisana** (Kezar Lake, Center Lovell, 207/925-3500, www.quisisanaresort.com, winter address P.O. Box 142, Larchmont, NY 10538, 914/833-0293) as "Where Mozart Goes on Vacation." Amen. By day, the staff at this elegantly rustic 47-acre retreat masquerades as waiters and waitresses, chambermaids, boat crew, and kitchen help; each night, presto, they're the stars of musical performances worthy of Broadway and concert-hall ticket prices. Since 1947, it's been like this at "Quisi"—with a staff recruited from the nation's best conservatories. (The resort was founded in 1917.) Veteran managers literally attuned to guests' needs keep it all working smoothly.

The frosting on all this culture is the setting—a beautifully landscaped pine grove on the shores of sandy-bottomed Kezar Lake, looking off to the White Mountains and dramatic sunsets. No wonder that reservations for the 38 neat white cottages are hard to come by. The New York–heavy clientele knows to book well ahead, often for the same week, and new generations have followed their parents here. In July and August, lodge rooms are $175–180 pp/night and cottages are $185–2220 pp/night (all require one week minimum, Sat.–Sat. only), including meals, musical entertainment, tennis, and nonmotorized boats. Mid-June–July, lower rates and occasionally shorter stays are available. No credit cards; beer and wine only. Quisisana's season begins in mid-June and ends in late August.

Campgrounds

Canoeing is the major focus at **Woodland Acres Campground** (Rte. 160, R.R. 1, Box 445, Brownfield, 207/935-2529, www.woodland acres.com), with a 100-canoe fleet available for rent ($45 a day, including shuttle service to one location; reduced rates for additional days). The staff makes it all very convenient, even suggesting more than half a dozen daylong and multiday canoe trips for skill levels from beginner to expert. This well-maintained campground on the Saco River has 109 wooded tent and RV sites ($30–36 a night per family; two-night weekend minimum). Riverfront sites are the best, but you'll need to stay a week in July and August unless you luck out with a cancellation. Facilities include a rec hall, beach, camp store, and free hot showers. Leashed pets are allowed ($2.50/day). From Fryeburg, take Route 5/13 southeast to Route 160. Turn left (north) and go a mile to the campground. It's open mid-May–mid-October.

Also in Brownfield, and also geared toward canoeists, is **River Run** (Rte. 160, P.O. Box 90, Brownfield 04010, 207/452-2500, www.river runcanoe.com), with 22 large primitive tent sites on 100-plus acres next to the Saco River's Brownfield Bridge; no hookups. Sites are $10 pp. Canoe rentals and shuttle service are available—canoes run about $21 a day Monday–Thursday, and $40 on weekends and holidays, with the shuttle price about $9–15. At the end of the season, River Run sells its rental canoes at greatly reduced rates; call to find out when the bargains begin. The campground is open mid-May–mid-October; after Labor Day, reservations are required.

The Appalachian Mountain Club maintains a wilderness campground on the Saco River. The **AMC Swan's Falls Campground** (Rte. 5, P.O. Box 378, Fryeburg 04037, 207/935-3395, www.outdoors.org), just north of Fryeburg, has 20 campsites and one lean-to, picnic tables, and toilets. Nightly rate is $20 per site for nonmembers. Reservation requests, including numbers of people and equipment in your party, dates, and arrival time, are processed starting May 15, and need to be mailed attention of the campground manager. The AMC has volunteers and staff stationed at the campground to answer questions and provide info about river conditions. This is a very busy canoe and kayak access point on the Saco River. It's open late May–mid-October.

FOOD
Local Flavors

Two general stores serve the Lovell area, providing staples and more. The upscale-ish **Center Lovell Store** (Rte. 5, Center Lovell, 207/925-1051, opens 6 A.M. Mon.–Sat. and 8 A.M. Sun., closes at 7 P.M. Sun.–Thurs. and 8 P.M. Fri. and Sat.) serves pizza and sandwiches and has premade items as well as a full deli and even seating. More simple is the **Lovell Village Store and Restaurant** (Rte. 5, Lovell 207/925-1235, 5 A.M.–8 P.M., opens at 6 A.M. on Sun.), which serves breakfast all day.

Casual Dining

Fronting on the golf course, yet hidden on a back road, is a local secret with a big reputation, **Ebenezer's Restaurant and Pub** (44 Allen Rd., off the W. Lovell Rd., Lovell, 207/925-3200, noon–9 P.M. daily, fewer hours off-season). Most folks come for the Belgian beer selection—easily the best in New England, perhaps in the entire country. And if you're not a fan of Belgian brews, there are dozens of other beer choices. Complementing that is good pub fare, burgers, sandwiches, salads, pizzas ($6–12) as well as heartier entrées, most $15–20. Dine on the screened-in porch or inside the tavern and bar.

Grab and go or snag a booth at **D's Pizza, Pasta and Subs** (Fryeburg Plaza, Rte. 302, Fryeburg, 207/935-4447, www.dspizza.com). Add to the descriptive name fresh salads served with homemade pita bread. It's in the plaza opposite Jockey Cap, so take the short hike before or after your meal or get picnic fare for the summit.

Weston's Farm, established by the Weston family in 1799 and now operated by the sixth generation, edges the Saco River and is across from Weston's Beach. Stop at **Weston's**

Farm Stand (48 River St./Rte. 113 N, Fryeburg, 207/935-2567, www.westonsfarm.com, 9 A.M.–6 P.M. mid-April–Dec. 24) for all kinds of picnic and cottage fixings, from fresh produce and local meats to cheese and maple syrup.

Fine Dining

Chef/co-owner John Morris's creative menu (entrées $26–32) at **The Oxford House Inn** (548 Main St., Fryeburg, 207/935-3442, www.oxfordhouseinn.com) has earned the inn's restaurant a first-rate reputation. The back porch/dining room (where B&B guests have breakfast) has wonderful mountain views. Dinner reservations are wise, especially July–August and during the Fryeburg Fair. It's open for dinner 6–9 P.M. daily July–October and Thursday–Sunday the rest of the year.

What do you do for an encore when you've won a country inn in an essay contest and become a cover story in the *New York Times Magazine*? You prove you deserved it, and that's what's happened at the **Center Lovell Inn and Restaurant** (1107 Main St., P.O. Box 261, Center Lovell 04016, 207/925-1575 or 800/777-2698, www.centerlovellinn.com).

Janice Sage has been here since 1993, serving an enthusiastic clientele drawn to the wide-ranging continental menu, which changes weekly (entrées average $25–30). Save room for one of the pastry chef's incredible desserts. The best tables are on the glassed-in porch, where you can watch the sun slip behind the mountains. The inn serves dinner 6–9 P.M. daily May–October; reservations are advised, especially in midsummer. Dinner is served Friday–Saturday December–March, as well as daily during school vacation weeks. The inn has five second-floor rooms (private and shared baths) in the 1805 main building, plus five more (private and shared baths) in the adjacent Harmon House. Room rates are $115–145 d without meals (breakfast is $7.50). Suites are $240 triple, $265 quad. The inn and its restaurant are open May–October and December–March.

INFORMATION

Check with the Fryeburg Town Office (2 Lovewell's Pond Rd., Fryeburg, 207/935-2805, www.fryeburgmaine.org) 7:30 A.M.–4 P.M. Tuesday–Friday, 7:30 A.M.–noon Saturday. On the website, you can download a bike tour.

Cornish

Well off the radar screen of most tourists, Cornish is a charming little town (pop. about 1,300) incorporated as Francisborough in 1791. Local historians boast that in the 1850s many of the splendid homes on the main drag were moved by oxen from other parts of town to be close to the stagecoach route. Many of those homes now house antiques and crafts shops.

WILLOWBROOK MUSEUM VILLAGE

Plan a day trip to tiny Newfield, probably best known for the fascinating 19th-century museum/village known as Willowbrook Museum Village (Main St., just north of Rte. 11, Newfield, 207/793-2784, www.willowbrookmuseum.org, late 10 A.M.–5 P.M. Thurs.–Mon.

May–late Oct., $9 adults, $4 children 6–18, $7.50 65 and older, free kids under 6). Spend several hours here exploring the 37 buildings listed on the National Register of Historic Places in this country village created by Don King (not the music guy) and his wife, Pan. What's to see? A carriage house, firehouse, country store, schoolhouse, a magnificently restored carousel, and incredible collections of farm tools, toys, sewing machines, and musical instruments. Bring a picnic (or visit the café and ice cream shop) and camera and soak up the history.

SHOPPING

Antiques and artisans' shops dominate the genuinely quaint downtown and beyond. **Cornish Trading Company** (19 Main St., Rte. 25,

Cornish, 207/625-8387) is a terrific group antiques shop in the handsome Masonic building. **Cottage Treasures** (47 High Rd., 207/625-2301) specializes in porcelain, glass, and vintage linens. For American folk art, visit **Plain and Fancy** (30 Main St., Cornish, 207/625-3577). For vintage commercial signage and memorabilia, visit **Smith Company Antiques** (Main St., Cornish, 207/625-6030). Ice cream, Maine-made crafts, and a yarn shop are all under one roof at **Rosemary's Gift Shop** (22 Main St., Cornish, 207/625-8550).

ENTERTAINMENT AND EVENTS

Every summer, the **Saco River Festival Association** (P.O. Box 610, Parsonfield 04047, 207/625-7116, www.sacoriverfestival.org) sponsors a concert series at the Cornish Elementary School.

A great time to visit Cornish is the last Saturday in September, when the annual **Apple Festival** (207/625-7447, www.cornish-maine.org), held in downtown Cornish, celebrates the area's major crop with music, a crafts fair, and even an apple-pie contest. You can overdose all day on apples and stock up for winter, and do it just as fall foliage is starting to appear. For a spectacular panorama of fall colors along the Ossipee and Saco River Valleys, drive up Towles Hill Road (left turn, just west of town).

ACCOMMODATIONS

Smack-dab downtown is the decidedly old-fashioned **Cornish Inn** (2 High St., Cornish, 207/625-8501 or 800/352-7235, www.cornish inn.com, $85–145), a three-story classic with a wraparound porch. The 16 rooms are simple yet comfortable. Rates include a light breakfast midweek or a coupon toward brunch on weekends.

The barn-red **Midway Country Lodging** (712 S. Hiram Rd., Cornish, 207/625-8835, www.mainemidwaylodging.com, $59–89) is a motel-like inn, or maybe an innlike motel. Whatever. Country is the theme, and all rooms have TV, Wi-Fi, fridge and microwave, and phone; some have a whirlpool, VCR, or balcony. The outdoor

If the weather's fine, snag a porch seat at Krista's Restaurant.

pool has a nice mountain view, and the landscaped grounds even have a fountain.

FOOD

Fresh and seasonal are the hallmarks at the **Cornish Inn** (2 High St., Cornish, 207/625-8501 or 800/352-7235, www.cornishinn.com, 8 A.M.–2 P.M. Sat. and Sun and 5–9 P.M. Wed.–Sun.). The menu changes weekly to reflect what's locally available, varying from shepherd's pie to wild sea bass ($13–22).

Locals rave about **Krista's Restaurant** (2 Main St., Cornish, 207/625-3600, www.kristas restaurant.com), a cheerful downtown spot open for breakfast, lunch, and dinner Wednesday–Monday (closed Wed. in winter), with choices for all budgets.

Ultrafresh seafood is served at **Bay Haven Lobster Pound Two** (Maple St., Cornish, 207/625-7303, 11 A.M.–8 P.M. daily), operated by a fishing family. Portions are very generous; prices are reasonable.

INFORMATION

The Cornish Association of Businesses (P.O. Box 573, Cornish 04020, 207/625-8856, www.cornish-maine.org) is the best source of info.

Sebago and Long Lakes

Maine's Lakes region, the area along the shores of Sebago and Long Lakes, includes the two major hubs of Bridgton (pop. 4,900) and Naples (pop. 3,170) as well as the smaller communities of East Sebago and Harrison and the larger communities of Raymond, Casco, and Windham. All are in Cumberland County.

Settled in 1768, Bridgton was incorporated in 1794; Naples was not incorporated until 1834. When the summer-vacation boom began in the mid-19th century, and then erupted after the Civil War, visitors flowed into this area via stagecoach, the Cumberland and Oxford Canal, and later the Bridgton and Saco Railroad.

The 28-lock canal, opened in 1830 and shut down in 1870, connected the Fore River in Portland with Sebago and Long Lakes. Its only working remnant is the Songo Lock in Naples, on the Songo River between Brandy Pond and Sebago Lake.

Sebago is an apt Native American word meaning "large, open water"; it's the state's second-largest lake (after Moosehead), and flukey winds can kick up suddenly and toss around little boats, so be prudent. Now a major water source for Greater Portland, the lake reportedly served as the crossroads for major Native American trading routes, and artifacts still occasionally surface in the Sebago Basin area.

Engage in a heart-to-heart with an adult vacationing in this area and you're likely to find someone trying to recapture the past—the carefree days at summer camp in the Sebago and Long Lakes region. The shores of Sebago, Long, and Highland Lakes shelter dozens of children's camps that have created several generations of Maine enthusiasts—"people from away" who still can't resist an annual visit. Unless your own kids are in camp, however, or you're terminally masochistic, do *not* appear in Bridgton, Naples, or surrounding communities on the last weekend in July. Parents, grandparents, and surrogate parents all show up then

for the midseason summer-camp break, and there isn't a bed or restaurant seat to be had in the entire county, maybe beyond. Gridlock is the rule.

The rest of the time, congestion can occur regularly in the center of Naples, where traffic backs up half a mile when the drawbridge on the Route 302 causeway opens for boat traffic passing between Brandy Pond and Long Lake. Openings are on even-numbered hours 8 A.M.–8 P.M. daily June 15–early September, 8 A.M.–4 P.M. May 1–June 15 and early September–October 15. Plan accordingly.

Aside from those minor glitches, this mountain-lake setting has incredible locales for canoeing, swimming, hiking, fishing, golfing, camping, biking, ice-skating, snowshoeing, and skiing. (Maine's first ski lift opened in 1938 on Pleasant Mountain, now the Shawnee Peak ski area—see the sidebar *Family-Size Alpine Areas*).

These lakes are terribly convenient to Portland—Sebago is the large body of water you'll see to the west as you descend into the Portland Jetport.

SIGHTS
Narramissic, The Peabody-Fitch Farm

Built in 1797 and converted to Federal style in 1828, the Peabody-Fitch Farm is the crown jewel of the Bridgton Historical Society. Still undergoing restoration—now to the pre-Civil War era—the homestead includes a carriage house, ell, barn, blacksmith shop, and historic gardens. The barn has its own story: It's known as the "Temperance Barn" because the landowners were avowed teetotalers, so the volunteer barn-raisers earned only water for their efforts. Narramissic is a relatively recent name, given to it by the 20th-century owner who donated it to the historical society in 1986. The name is a Native American word meaning "hard to find," reflecting her lengthy search for a family

© HILARY NANGLE

The 90-foot Mississippi stern-wheeler replica *Songo River Queen II* cruises Long Lake, Brandy Pond, and the Songo River.

summer home. But it also suits the circuitous route, fortunately signposted, to the South Bridgton farm from downtown Bridgton (Main St. to Rte. 117 to Rte. 107 to Ingalls Rd.). A season highlight is the Woodworkers' Show in July. The farm is open July–August; call ahead for hours and admission prices. Contact the **Bridgton Historical Society** (P.O. Box 44, Bridgton 04009, 207/647-3699) for more information.

◖ *Songo River Queen II*

Berthed in downtown Naples, Maine, is a 90-foot Mississippi stern-wheeler replica that operates narrated cruises throughout the summer: the *Songo River Queen II* (Bay of Naples Causeway, Rte. 302, P.O. Box 1226, Naples 04055, 207/693-6861, www.songoriverqueen .net). Opt for the 2.5-hour Songo River trip, which departs at 9:45 A.M. and 3:45 P.M.; you'll cross Brandy Pond and head downriver, transiting the 19th-century **Songo River Lock** via a hand-turned swing bridge that raises and low-

ers the river level by five feet. Kids love it, and the lockkeeper plays to his audience. Cost is $15 adults, $10 children. The other option is a one-hour Long Lake cruise ($8 adults, $6 kids), at 1, 2:30, and 7 P.M. Cruises operate daily, rain or shine, July–Labor Day (two Songo cruises, three Long Lake trips). In June and September, the boat operates weekends only, making one Songo Lock cruise at 9:45 A.M. daily. On a clear day, you can even spot Mt. Washington, centerpiece of the White Mountains; bring binoculars and a camera. Onboard are restrooms and a snack bar.

Presidential Maine

Inspired by a famous western Maine signpost giving directions to nine Maine towns named for foreign cities and countries, Boy Scouts in Casco decided to create some competition—a directional sign for 10 Maine towns named for U.S. presidents. The marker stands next to the village green in **Casco,** at the corner of Route 121 and Leach Hill Road, pointing to towns such as Washington (76 miles), Lincoln (175 miles), Madison, and Monroe. There's even a Clinton (84 miles).

If you're here in the fall, take time to detour briefly to Casco's "million-dollar view." Continue south from the signpost less than two miles on Route 121 to Route 11 (Pike Corner), turn right (west) and go about half a mile to Quaker Ridge Road and turn left (south). Views are spectacular along here, especially from the Quaker Hill area.

Rufus Porter Museum

The early 19th-century itinerant artist's murals and paintings are the focus at the Rufus Porter Museum and Cultural Heritage Center (67 N. High St., Bridgton, 207/647-2828, www.rufusportermuseum .org, $5 adults, $4 seniors and students, 6 and under free, 1–4 P.M. Thurs.–Sun. in July and Aug., then weekends until mid-Oct., $5 adult, $4 seniors and students). Porter, the founder of *Scientific American* magazine, painted landscapes on the walls of homes throughout New England. Most were unsigned. Some of Porter's murals are displayed in the front hall of the house. Plans call for creating a teaching facility concentrating on the arts and sciences of the 19th and 20th centuries. During one week in July, the museum hosts a **Cultural Heritage Series** with classes, workshops, and lectures. The museum is in a barn-red house on the northern edge of downtown Bridgton.

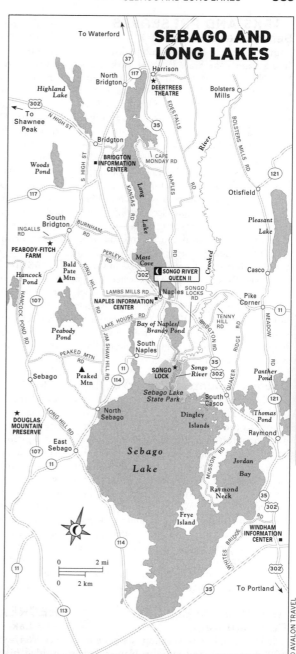

WESTERN LAKES

© AVALON TRAVEL

PARKS AND PRESERVES
Sebago Lake State Park

Fourth-largest of Maine's state parks, 1,400-acre Sebago Lake State Park (11 Park Access Rd., Naples, 207/693-6613 late June–Labor Day, 207/693-6231 off-season, www.state.me.us/doc/parks, $4 adults, $1 children 5–11) is one of the most popular—so don't anticipate peace and quiet here in July and August. Swimming and picnicking are superb, fishing is so-so, personal watercraft are an increasing hazard. During the summer, park officials organize lectures, hikes, and other activities; the schedule is posted at the gate. The park is open mid-May–October, but there's winter access to 4.5 miles of groomed cross-country skiing trails—mostly beginner terrain. It's ideal, too, for snowshoeing.

You can reach the park's separate picnicking and camping areas from Route 302 in Casco. Take State Park Road to the fork, where you go left to the picnic area or right to Songo Lock and the camping area. (Both sections have sandy beaches, now slightly diminished after major storms in 1996.) Or, from downtown Naples, take Route 11/114 to Thompson Point Road and follow the signs.

Douglas Mountain Preserve

The Douglas Mountain Preserve was formerly owned by The Nature Conservancy and was deeded to the town of Sebago in 1997. Fortunately or unfortunately, Douglas Mountain (also called Douglas Hill) is one of southern Maine's most popular hikes, so you probably won't be alone. Park in the lot on the left. Walk farther up, take a brochure from the registration box, and follow the easy Woods Trail to the 1,415-foot summit—30 minutes maximum. At the top is a 0.75-mile nature-trail loop, plus a 16-foot stone tower with a head-spinning view. In the fall, the vistas are incomparable. Be eco-sensitive and stick to the trails in this 169-acre preserve. No pets. The trails are accessible dawn–dusk.

Holt Pond and Bald Pate Mountain

The Holt Pond Preserve comprises more than 400 mostly wetland acres in Naples and is owned by the Lakes Environmental Association (207/647-8580, www.mainelakes.org). A trail with boardwalks makes it easy to spot the flora and fauna in the wetlands and bogs. The Town Farm Brook Trail connects to twin-peaked Bald Pate Mountain, part of a 468-acre preserve in South Bridgton maintained by the Loon Echo Land Trust (207/647-4352, www.loonecholandtrust.org). Bald Pate's trail network is open year-round, and there's a kiosk with trail maps at the parking lot (signposted off Rte. 107). The first peak has views to Pleasant Mountain and the summit peak is bald, with panoramic views. Pack a lunch and plan for a full day if you decide to connect the two preserves. If you come in winter, some of Bald Pate's trails are groomed for cross-country skiing.

Pleasant Mountain

A preserve in the making borders the northern and eastern sides of the Shawnee Peak alpine resort on Pleasant Mountain, in Bridgton. Six interconnecting trails provide access to the main summit—at 2,000 feet, it's the highest mountain in southern Maine and a landmark for pilots. The most popular—and relatively easiest for kids—is the Ledges (or Moose) Trail. In late July, allow four hours for the 3.5-mile round-trip, so you can pick blueberries on the open ledges midway up. At the top is a disused fire tower—and plenty of space for spreading out a picnic overlooking panoramic vistas of woods, lakes, and mountains. The mountain straddles the Denmark/Bridgton town line, as well as the Cumberland/Oxford County line. From Bridgton, drive 5.75 miles west on Route 302 to Mountain Road (just after the causeway over Moose Pond). Turn left (south) at signs for Shawnee Peak ski area and go 3.3 miles to the trailhead for the Ledges (or Moose) Trail; parking is limited. An alternative access route, from the west side of the mountain, is via the Wilton Warren Road, also south of Route 302.

RECREATION

The **Lakes Environmental Association** (207/647-8580, www.mainelakes.org) hosts guided hikes, birding programs, talks, and other events throughout the year; check the website for current listings.

Swimming

Besides two sandy beaches at Sebago Lake State Park, other swimming locations are the **Naples Town Beach; Crystal Lake Beach** in Harrison; **Salmon Point** and the **Town Beach on Highland Lake** in Bridgton; and **Tassel Top Beach** in Raymond (where the local Boy

---

FAMILY-SIZE ALPINE AREAS

Maine's big resorts get most of the attention, but for young families or anyone on a budget, the smaller resorts provide not only a fun experience, but also a good value. Perhaps the vertical isn't as grand, but really, how often do you ski 2,000 feet straight? All of these little guys have night skiing, most have tubing parks, and some have Nordic trails, too. If you're searching for areas with soul, for friendly faces, and places where kids matter, head to these slopes.

Lost Valley (200 Lost Valley Rd., off Young's Corner Rd., Auburn, 207/784-1561, www.lostvalleyski.com) is a vest-pocket ski area secreted in the barely rolling countryside outside Auburn. Don't be deceived by the hill's diminutive size. Although the vertical drop is only 240 feet, it was enough to produce four Olympians: Karl Anderson and Anna, Julie, and Rob Parisien. This is an especially family-friendly area; the base lodge doubles as the local baby-sitting service – parents just naturally watch out for one another's kids. According to Julie Parisien, who has coached local youth, you may be able to make only 10 turns from top to bottom, but that's 10 good turns. And that's what matters.

Maine's oldest ski area is **Shawnee Peak** (Rte. 302, Bridgton, 207/647-8444, www.shawneepeak.com), an increasingly popular destination given its proximity to Portland (45 miles). I have a soft spot for the area where I spent my youth – bring your family, and you'll likely understand why. The setting is rural and undeveloped, and Pleasant Mountain appears to rise out of Moose Pond. The views, which take in Mt. Washington and the Presidential Range of the White Mountains, are calming, almost inspirational. It's the largest night-skiing facility, acreage-wise, in New England. Arrive at night, and you'll notice that the trails spell out the word LOV in 1960s-block-style lettering. The mountain skis bigger than its

1,300-foot vertical indicates, as it has two faces, with open slopes on one and squiggly trails ribboning the other.

For anyone weak in the wallet or overawed by megaresorts, **Mt. Abram** (Howe Hill Rd., off Rte. 26, Locke Mills, 207/875-5002, www.skimtabram.com) is the solution. This longtime family favorite is something of a sleeper. Most folks drive right by on their way to glitzy Sunday River, just up the road. A savvy few turn off Route 26 in Locke Mills, drawn by this resort's commitment to family skiing. The segregated learning area, tubing park, night lights, cross-country loop, low-key atmosphere, and lack of crowds make it a real gem.

A real success story is **Black Mountain of Maine** (39 Glover Rd., Rumford, 207/364-8977, www.skiblackmountain.org), where prices are low and spirit is high. It's owned and operated by the Maine Winter Sports Center, which is committed to reestablishing skiing as part of the local lifestyle. MWSC has invested heavily in the 1,150-foot vertical hill, putting in new lifts, cutting new trails, adding snowmaking, and making it smoke free. Another plus is the Nordic trail system, designed by two-time Olympian Chummy Broomhall.

The Farmington Ski Club operates **Titcomb Mountain Ski Area** (Morrison Hill Rd., West Farmington, 207/778-9031, www.titcombmountain.com), an all-volunteer operation with a modest 340-foot vertical. It's the hill where Olympic gold medalist Seth Wescott played as a youth. In addition to the alpine terrain, there are nine miles of groomed trails for cross-country skiing and snowboarding (a potential solution for mixed marriages or partnerships). The operating schedule coincides with school hours, so it's open late afternoon and evenings, weekends, and daily during vacation weeks. Yes, it's a club, but nonmembers are welcomed.

WESTERN LAKES

Scout troop maintains a nature trail through the woods bordering the beach.

Golf

The 18-hole **Bridgton Highlands Country Club** (Highland Ridge Rd., R.R. 3, Box 1065, Bridgton, 207/647-3491, www.bridgton highlands.com) course is outstandingly scenic and very popular, especially at the height of summer. Starting times are needed. Also here are a handsome clubhouse, tennis courts, a pro shop, and a snack bar. The course, about two miles from downtown Bridgton, is open mid-April–October.

Less expensive but also scenic is the **Naples Golf and Country Club** (Rte. 114, Naples, 207/693-6424, www.naplesgolfcourse.com), established in 1922. Light meals are available at the clubhouse, and there's a pro shop. On midsummer weekends, call for a starting time. The course, across from the Naples Golf Driving Range, adjoins Bay of Naples Family Camping. It's open mid-April–October.

The championship-level **Point Sebago Golf Club** (Rte. 302, R.R. 1, Box 712, Casco, 207/655-2747, www.pointsebago.com) is part of a once low-key campground transformed into the 800-acre, family-oriented, Club Med–style Point Sebago Resort. Call for starting times at the 18-hole course, which is open to the public. Golf-and-lodging packages are available. It's open May–mid-October.

Boating

In addition to cruises on the *Songo River Queen II,* and the mail-boat rides, you can rent your own pontoon boat, powerboat, or, if you must, a water scooter (officially, a personal watercraft, PWC, often referred to by the trademark-name Jet Ski). Water scooters have become a major itch on huge Sebago Lake, as well as many other Maine lakes, and there's no gray area in the opinion department. Biggest objections are noise pollution and excessive speed. The state requires PWCs to be licensed as powerboats, but regulations are weak, the state legislature has taken little action, and inadequate funding has led to inadequate enforcement. Each year,

fatalities occur, spurring towns to try (usually unsuccessfully) to ban or limit PWCs. If you *do* rent one, play by the rules, exercise caution, and operate at sensible speeds.

The best source for boats and info on paddling local waters is **Complete Paddler** (188 Bushrow Rd., off Rte. 117, Denmark, 207/452-8001, www.completepaddler.com). Jim and Leslie Stanicki's operation (well, actually, it belongs to the chickens—you'll have to get the story from them) offers canoes and kayaks ranging $21–48 per day, with discounts for multiday rentals.

Naples Marina (Rtes. 302 and 114, Naples, 207/693-6254), behind Rick's Café, rents pontoon boats, runabouts, and fishing boats. **Causeway Marina** (Rte. 302, Naples, 207/693-6832, www.causewaymarina.com) rents canoes, kayaks, powerboats, pontoon boats, water-skiing boats and gear, and PWCs. Both marinas are open daily during the summer.

Other sources for rental canoes and kayaks are **Sebago Outfitters** (Rte. 115, North Windham, 207/892-9228), which also rents mountain bikes; **Sports Haus** (103 Main St., Bridgton, 207/647-5100), which will deliver canoes, kayaks, and sailboats within 10 miles for $30, for a three-day minimum rental; and **Sebago Lake Lodge and Cottages** (White's Bridge Rd., North Windham, 207/892-2698), which rents canoes, kayaks, and motorboats by the half day, full day, and week. Sportshaus also offers water-ski, wakeboard, and kneeboard demos for $20 per day.

If you've brought a **canoe or kayak,** don't launch it into Sebago Lake; save it for the smaller lakes and ponds, where the winds are more predictable and the boat traffic is less congested. Long Lake is also a possibility if you put in at Harrison, on the east side.

Flightseeing

The best way to figure out the lay of the lakes and land is on a scenic plane ride with **Naples Seaplane Rides** (Rte. 302, Causeway, Naples, 207/693-3736, www.naplesseaplanerides.com, daily late May–early Sept., weekends to mid-Oct.). Pilot Jacki Rogers takes off from the

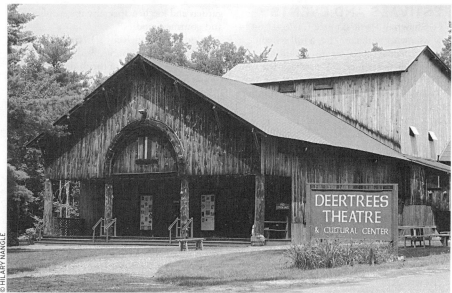

© HILARY NANGLE

The stars have been coming to Deertrees Theatre and Cultural Center in Harrison since 1936.

western end of the causeway on 25- and 50-mile flights (rates begin around $60 pp, two-person minimum/five-person maximum).

ENTERTAINMENT

Tucked away on a back road in Harrison, east of Long Lake, dramatic-looking 278-seat **Deertrees Theatre and Cultural Center** (Deertrees Rd., P.O. Box 577, Harrison 04040, 207/583-6747, www.deertreestheatre.org) is a must-see even if you don't attend a performance. The acoustically superior National Historic Register building, constructed of rose hemlock in 1936, has seen the likes of Rudy Vallee, Ethel Barrymore, Tallulah Bankhead, and Henry Winkler; restoration of the rustic building in the 1990s has given it an exciting new life. During the summer season, there's something going on nearly every night—musicals, plays, comedy, folk, jazz, blues, and weekly children's performances. The theater is off Route 117 (signposted) in the Harrison woods. Tours are available (wheelchair-accessible); contact the box office in advance if possible. Also here is the **BackStage**

Gallery, open 1–6 P.M. Tuesday–Saturday and one hour before all performances.

Mid-July–early August, the **Sebago-Long Lake Chamber Music Festival** (207/583-6747, www.sebagomusicfestival.org) brings 8 P.M. Tuesday chamber-music concerts to Harrison's Deertrees Theatre. Advance booking is essential for this popular series, founded in 1975. Single adult tickets cost $20, $10 for students and children.

Sunday evening **band concerts** around the gazebo behind the Naples Information Center are free mid-July–mid-August. Bring a chair or blanket to the Village Green, Routte 302, Naples.

Live entertainment is scheduled most weekends at **Bray's Brewpub and Eatery** (Rtes. 302 and 35, Naples, 207/693-6806, www.braysbrewpub.com).

One of a dying species, **Bridgton Drive-In** (Rte. 302, Bridgton, 207/647-8666) screens a double feature beginning at dusk each night July–August. Sound comes via the FM radio in your car. The drive-in is 2.5 miles south of downtown Bridgton.

FESTIVALS AND EVENTS

The **Shawnee Peak** ski area (207/647-8444, www.shawneepeak.com) has a full schedule of family-oriented special events, including races, throughout the winter; call or check the website for information.

Nearly 100 teams compete in the **Mushers Bowl Winter Carnival** (www.mushersbowl.com), two days of dogsled and skijoring races on Highland Lake, a great spectator event along with activities, in West Bridgton in late January or early February. Be sure to leave your own pets at home.

The third Saturday in July, Bridgton is the scene of the **Annual Art in the Park** exhibition and sale, a mad success since its inception. Also in July is Bridgton's annual **Chickadee Quilters Show** (www.quiltguilds.com/maine.htm), with exhibits and sales of magnificent quilts and wall hangings at the Bridgton Town Hall.

In late September, the **Brewers Festival** (www.lakesbrewfest.com) brings meisters from all over Maine to the Point Sebago Resort in Casco to display their art.

SHOPPING

Interesting shops fill historic buildings along the main drag in downtown Bridgton, best source in this region for crafts, gifts, and more—especially the work of Maine artisans.

Art, Craft, and Antiques

Art central—**Gallery 302** (112 Main St., Bridgton, 207/647-2787), in yet another example of adaptive reuse, has turned a former hardware store into the home of the nonprofit Bridgton Art Guild. More than 60 member artists exhibit their work. The co-op sponsors the town's annual Art in the Park, and the gallery hosts exhibits, monthly receptions, and classes and workshops.

A onetime Unitarian church and its church hall make terrific settings for the carefully chosen and superbly eclectic inventory at **Craftworks** (53 Main St., Bridgton, 207/647-5436), a Bridgton landmark since the early 1970s. In the church building are clothing, jewelry, and pottery; in the church hall are

garden and kitchen specialty items, plus wine and gourmet goodies.

Hidden behind Reny's is **Bridgton Arts and Crafts** (10 Depot St., Bridgton, 207/647-8781), where members of the Bridgton Arts and Crafts Society sell their wares, which include pillows, quilts, place mats, and an especially fine selection of handmade baby items.

The Sheep Shop (2056 N. High St., Rte. 302, Bridgton, 207/647-3548) is the ultimate source for sheepskins in six colors, washable wool blankets, sheepskin vests and jackets, sheepskin toys, Christmas ornaments, and wool and wool/mohair yarns.

Cry of the Loon (Rte. 302, P.O. Box 40, South Casco 04077, 207/655-5060) has three floors of gifts, a tasteful, eclectic mix of gourmet condiments, Maine crafts, furniture, and much more. It's definitely worth a stop.

Since the 1970s, **Hole in the Wall Studioworks** (1544 Roosevelt Trail/Rte. 302, Raymond, 207/655-4592) has been selling an especially fine selection of American-made art and craft. Don't miss the sculpture garden.

Books

Bridgton Books (140 Main St., Bridgton, 207/647-2122), an independent bookstore, carries an excellent selection of books (20,000 titles, including new, selected used, and a large bargain-book section), cards, and bargain music CDs—a browser's (and buyer's) delight.

Winery

Yes, there's even a winery in the region. **Blacksmiths** (Rte. 302, South Casco, 207/655-3292) produces more than a dozen wines on the premises and offers tastings 11 A.M.–5 P.M. daily.

ACCOMMODATIONS
Bed-and-Breakfasts

Bridgton: On a busy corner in downtown Bridgton, convenient to all the shops, **The Bridgton House Bed and Breakfast** (2 Main Hill, Bridgton, 207/647-8175 or 866/779-3335, www.bridgtonhouse.com), built in 1815, has been tastefully updated with five rooms, three with private baths. If you're highly noise sensitive, request a back-facing room. Rates of $115 d private bath, and $95 d shared bath, include full breakfast and afternoon tea or snacks. Pets only by arrangement. Innkeepers Bill and Tina Berghof have young children and make a specialty of catering to visiting families. It's open mid-June–Labor Day and then weekends in fall by appointment.

Just around the corner from the Bridgton House and off the main road, Rick and Julie Whelchel's **(The Noble House** (81 Highland Rd., P.O. Box 180, Bridgton 04009, 207/647-3733, www.noblehouse.com) is a turn-of-the-20th-century Victorian with nine warmly decorated rooms (six with private baths). Guests have use of a comfortable sitting room with TV and VCR, living room with grand piano and organ, and a great veranda. A short walk brings you to Bridgton's Highland Park on the lake, with swimming, picnicking, and boating access. Peak rates are $135–260 d (the latter for the honeymoon suite), including a full breakfast. It's open all year.

Naples: Front and center on the action, yet set off the highway just enough to provide privacy, the three-story, brick **Augustus Bove House** (corner Rtes. 302 and 114, Naples, 207/693-6365, www.naplesmaine.com, $125–200 peak) has been welcoming guests for more than a century. Rooms in the main house are Victorian in style, although Arlene Stetson's quilts lighten things up quite nicely. All have air-conditioning and TV. Rooms in the front have lake views, but everyone can enjoy the views from the porch and gardens. A full breakfast is served.

Stroll up a short hill, and you'll arrive at **The Inn at Long Lake** (Lakehouse Rd., P.O. Box 806, Naples 04055, 207/693-6226 or 800/437-0328, www.innatlonglake.com). Innkeeper Buddy Marcum displays his collection of more than 100 antique clocks throughout the Victorian-style inn. Sixteen meticulously decorated rooms on three floors are decorated with antiques and named after boats that used to ply the lakes. All have Wi-Fi, some have lake views. Wicker furniture on the veranda, a

gazebo, and a garden makes this an ideal retreat from the business of downtown Naples. Rates are $160–200 d, mid-June–early September, less other seasons. It's open year-round.

Cottage Colonies and Resorts

Generations upon generations of families summer at the traditional lakeside cottage colonies so prevalent in this region. Many return to find the next generation of ownership running the resort but with little else changed. Some are housekeeping cottages; others provide all meals and more.

Ray and Cheryl Nelson are third-generation owners of **Sebago Lake Cottages** (774 Sebago Rd., Sebago, 207/787-3211, www.sebagolake cottages.net), a colony of 16 cottages ringing a grassy recreation lawn, just across the street from Nason's Beach. The well-equipped cottages vary from one to three bedrooms, and all have knotty pine interiors and screened porches. A grocery store is just steps away, and boat, canoe, and kayak rentals and boat moorings are available. The cottages, which rent for $475–1,030 per week, or when available, $80–169 per night, are on Routes 114 and 11 in North Sebago. No dogs in July or August.

Another multigeneration operation is **Sebago Lake Lodge and Cottages** (White's Bridge Rd., P.O. Box 110, Windham 04062, 207/892-2698, www.sebagolakelodge.com), which sits on a point of land with 700 feet of lake frontage adjacent to White's Bridge. Swimming, picnic and cookout facilities, free canoes, kayaks, and rowboats, rental motorboats, boat slips and moorings, and an adults-only fitness room are just a few of the amenities that make this spot special. Guest rooms in the main lodge, with its wonderful wraparound porch, have kitchenettes or kitchen privileges and nice screened porches. A continental breakfast is served in the gathering room, which also has a fireplace and TV. The lake-view cottages have 1–2 bedrooms (guests provide their own linen and paper products); most have screened porches. Pets are allowed in the cottages by arrangement for $15, but not in the lodge. Lodge rooms ($68–185) rent by the night or week; cottages are available

Saturday–Saturday ($750–1,300); deluxe cottages, one wheelchair-accessible, rent Sunday–Sunday ($1,800). Discounts apply early and late in the season.

At **Migis Lodge** (Migis Lodge Rd., P.O. Box 40, South Casco 04077, 207/655-4524, www.migis.com), on the east side of Sebago Lake, guests often confirm their next year's July or August booking before they depart for home. The rustic elegance of 100-acre Migis, along with attentive service and a fabulous lakeside setting, have drawn big-name guests through the years—ever since the resort was established in the early 20th century as lodging for the parents of summer campers. Men wear jackets for dinner, and there is a supervised meal and playtime for children during dinner hours. All this comes at a price, which includes almost everything but tax and tips: sailboats, island cookouts, waterskiing, tennis courts, even a cinema. Daily rates for the 35 lake-view cottages (1–6 bedrooms) are $290–345 d summer, $210–245 d fall per person, per night, AP; one-week minimum. In the main lodge, six rooms have private baths, private balconies, and lake views, and are $295 summer, $240 fall d per person, per night, also AP. Shorter stays are allowed at the fringes of the season. No credit cards, no pets. It's open mid-June–mid-October. Migis is down an unpaved road off Route 302.

Campgrounds

Camping is especially popular in this part of Maine, and many campgrounds have long-term RV or "immobile" home rentals (also known as "seasonal sites"), so you'll need to plan well ahead and reserve sites well in advance. Be forewarned, though, that if you're looking for a wilderness camping experience, especially in midsummer, you probably ought to head for the hills. Many of the campgrounds in this area feature nonstop organized fun, which is fine for enthusiastic families, but the intense activity can be overwhelming for those seeking a quiet respite.

It's crucial to book well ahead to land one of the 250 sites at **Sebago Lake State Park** (11 Park Access Rd., Naples, 207/693-6613

late June–Labor Day, www.state.me.us/doc/parks; reservations in state 800/332-1501, out of state 207/624-9950 or www.campwithme.com). Despite its popularity, well-spaced sites provide some privacy. No hookups. Rate is $20 per night for nonresidents, $15 for residents. Reservation fee is $2.

All 135 sites at the Mason family's **Loon's Haven Family Campground** (Rte. 11/114, Box 557, Naples, 207/693-6881, www.loonshaven.com, May 15–Oct. 15, $23–42) have water and electric hookups, and about 20 front on Trickey Pond. The campground has three sand beaches as well as a boat ramp, boat and canoe rentals, a rec hall, playground, basketball court, laundry, and other facilities. Plenty of planned activities keep everyone busy. Quiet hours are enforced at night. The campground is 1.4 miles off Route 302.

Practically a self-contained village, **Lakeside Pines Campground** (Rte. 117, P.O. Box 182, North Bridgton 04057, 207/647-3935, www.lakesidepinescamping.com, $39–49/family), on the shores of Long Lake, has 185 sites as well a trailer rentals, housekeeping cottages, and bunkhouses, spread out on 50 acres with towering pines, a gurgling stream, and 3,500 feet of shore frontage. Facilities include two beaches, boat rentals, playground, rec hall, snack bar and general store, laundry, and even mosquito control.

Seasonal Rentals

Krainin Real Estate (Rte. 302, P.O. Box 464, South Casco 04077, 207/655-3811 or 800/639-2321, www.krainin.com) handles weekly and monthly rentals for cottages on Sebago and Long Lakes as well as many of the surrounding smaller lakes and ponds. Krainin also arranges rentals on **Frye Island,** a 1,000-acre summer community in the middle of Sebago Lake that's accessible only by car ferry.

FOOD
Local Flavors

For **public suppers,** see listings in *The Bridgton News* (www.bridgtonnews.com) for details on chicken barbecues, potluck buffets, baked-bean suppers, and public breakfasts—all to benefit good local causes and usually well under $10 (less for kids).

The **Naples Farmers Market** sets up on the Naples village green, off Route 302, 8 A.M.–1 P.M. each Thursday early May–mid-September, bringing to market organic vegetables and fruits, herbs, flower arrangements, shellfish and crabmeat, baked goods, preserves, and other gifts of the earth and sea.

The **Bridgton Farmers Market** is open 8 A.M.–1 P.M. Saturday mid-May–September on Depot Street, in front of the community center. Pick up veggies, lamb, goat cheese, baked goods, crabmeat, shellfish, flowers, jams, relishes, and more, all locally produced.

Conveniently situated across from a lakeside picnic area, **The Good Life Market** (1297 Roosevelt Trail/Rte. 302, corner of Rte. 85, Raymond, 207/655-1196, 7 A.M.–7 P.M. daily) is a great place to pick up sandwiches, salads, fresh baked treats, wine, and specialty foods. There's even a very inexpensive kids' menu.

Just south of downtown Bridgton, at the Route 117 intersection, is a terrific natural-foods store and café, **Morning Dew** (19 Sandy Creek Rd., Bridgton, 207/647-4003, 9 A.M.–6 P.M. Mon.–Fri., to 5:30 P.M. Sat., 10 A.M.–5 P.M. Sun.). The menu goes far beyond usual natural-foods fare, with sandwiches, grilled items, burritos, salads, soups, and bagels.

Breakfast is an all-day affair at **Chute's Café and Bakery** (Rte. 302, South Casco, 207/655-7111, 6 A.M.–2 P.M. Mon.–Sat., to 1 P.M. Sun.), an always popular local choice for good home cooking. Prices are low, portions ample, and some choices even have two sizes.

Family Favorites

Sandy's at the Flight Deck (Rte. 302, on the Causeway, Naples, 207/693-3508) is practically *in* Long Lake, so you can watch floatplane takeoffs and all the boating traffic. An especially kid-friendly spot, the Flight Deck is open 7 A.M.–8 P.M. daily mid-May–Labor Day, with shorter hours when schools are open. Most dinner choices are in the $8–18 range.

Casual Dining

One of Naples's newer restaurants, the **Freedom Café and Publick House** (932 Roosevelt Trail/Rte. 302, on the Causeway, Naples, 207/693-3700, noon–9 P.M. Mon.–Wed., to 11 P.M. Thurs.–Sat., to 8 P.M. Sun.) has a prime lakeside location on the western edge of the causeway. The dining rooms are nicer than most in the region, and the food is very good. The service, however, can be s-l-o-w. Tables on the back deck overlook the lake.

In a Victorian farmhouse, **Bray's Brewpub and Eatery** (Rtes. 302 and 35, Naples, 207/693-6806, www.braysbrewpub.com, 11:30 A.M.–10 P.M. daily) is the pioneer brewpub in this part of Maine. Dinner specialties are steaks, seafood, and ribs—$15–20; a pub menu with lighter fare is served all day. If the brewmaster can spring free, he'll give a brewery tour on request—a 15-minute "quickie" or a 30-minute in-depth explanation of the process.

Although it doesn't look like much from the outside, **Sydney's Restaurant and Pub** (Rte. 302, Naples, 207/693-3333, 4–9 P.M. daily, closed Nov.–Apr.) is widely regarded as the region's most dependable and best restaurant. The menu has a little bit of everything, from salads and sandwiches to roast maple leaf duck breast and stuffed veal scallopini; most entrées are in the $16–22 range. An early-bird menu is served 4–6 P.M., with a choice of four entrées each night ($9–12, including dessert).

North of downtown Bridgton, **Venezia Ristorante** (corner Rtes. 302 and 93, Bridgton, 207/647-5333, 5–9 P.M. Tues.–Sun., Thurs.–Sat. in winter) is a funky little spot that's been dishing out okay Italian fare ($15–20) since the late 1980s.

INFORMATION AND SERVICES

The Greater Bridgton Lakes Region Chamber of Commerce (Portland Rd., Rte. 302, P.O. Box 236, Bridgton 04009, 207/647-3472, www.mainelakeschamber.com) has an attractive information center (with public restrooms) half a mile south of downtown Bridgton. It's open 9 A.M.–5 P.M. daily, 9 A.M.–4 P.M.

WESTERN LAKES

Saturday–Sunday Memorial Day–beginning of October. It's open 9 A.M.–5 P.M. Monday–Friday, 9 A.M.–4 P.M. Saturday other months.

In Naples, the Sebago Lakes Region Chamber of Commerce (Rte. 302, Naples, 207/693-3285, www.sebagolakeschamber.com) operates a small brick information center on the village green, next to the 1831 Naples Town Hall on Route 302. It's open 10 A.M.–3:30 P.M. weekends in June and then 10 A.M.–3:30 P.M. daily July–Labor Day.

The Sebago Lakes Region Chamber of Commerce (816 Roosevelt Trail, Rte. 302, P.O. Box 1015, Windham 04062, 207/892-8265, www.sebagolakeschamber.com) has a small seasonal information booth along the Route 302 commercial strip. It's open 9 A.M.–5 P.M. daily Memorial Day weekend–Labor Day. Off-season, call the chamber for info on Naples, Windham, and other Sebago Lakes region towns.

Of interest is a good general website for the area, the "Maine Mountain Heritage Area" (www.visitmainemountains.com).

Lewiston/Auburn Area

A river runs through the heart of Lewiston and Auburn—the Androscoggin River, headwatered in the Rangeley Lakes and coursing southeastward until it joins the Kennebec in Merrymeeting Bay, near Brunswick. Surging over Great Falls, the mighty Androscoggin spurred 19th-century industrial development of the Twin Cities, where giant textile mills drew their power from the river and their hardworking employees from the local community of Yankees, then Irish, French Canadian, and other immigrants. The Québécois and Acadian French, who flocked to mills in Lewiston, Biddeford, Sanford, Augusta, and Brunswick, today constitute Maine's largest ethnic minority. In Lewiston and Auburn, the French-accented voting registers reveal long lists of Plourdes and Pomerleaus, Carons and Cloutiers, and the spires of Catholic churches still dominate the skyline.

Long before white men harnessed the falls of the Androscoggin, Native Americans recognized the area for its prime salmon fishing and set up seasonal campsites and year-round settlements. Nowadays, their artifacts occasionally turn up along the riverbanks.

European settlers began putting down roots around 1770, earning their keep from small water-powered mills. Quakers established a community as early as 1773. By 1852, the giant Bates Mill (of bedspread fame) began manufacturing cotton, expanding by that century's end to an annual output of more than 10 million yards. During the Civil War, Bates was a prime supplier of fabric for soldiers' tents. In 1861, Lewiston was incorporated as a city; Auburn was incorporated in 1869.

By the early 20th century, with a dozen more mills online, taking advantage of the convenient hydropower, the lower reaches of the Androscoggin became polluted, a stinky eyesore until the 1980s, when environmental activists took up the cause. Now you can stroll the banks, fish the waters, paddle a canoe, and get up close on the walkways, bridges, and plazas linking the two cities.

LA also has quite a sporting heritage in boxing and, believe it or not, skiing. World-class boxer Joey Gamache emerged from the local clubs here, and the controversial world title fight between Sonny Liston and Muhammad Ali took place here. Olympic skiers Karl Anderson and Julie Parisian (and her siblings Anna and Rob) are also local products.

Natural gems are found in the region. Auburn's Mt. Apatite has produced record-setting tourmalines, Maine's state gemstone, as well as quartz and feldspar. Now owned by the city, the mountain is open to the prospecting public.

Lewiston (pop. 35,776) and Auburn (pop. 23,551)—locally known as "the *other* LA"—still are not typical vacation destinations, but

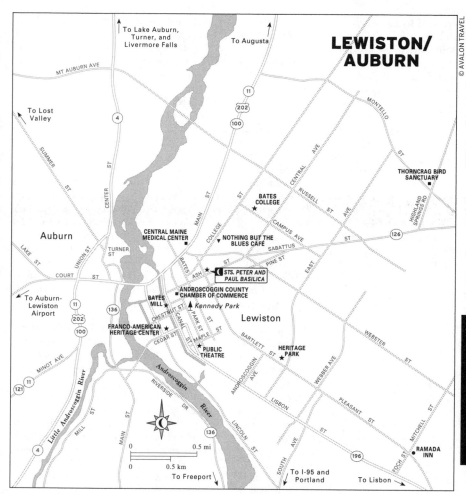

they deserve more than a drive-through glance. Lewiston is the state's second-largest city and home to Bates College, a highly selective private liberal-arts school and a magnet for visiting performers, artists, and lecturers.

Auburn, the Androscoggin County seat, began its industrial career with a single shoe factory in 1836, expanding swiftly in those heady days. By the turn of the 20th century, Auburn's shoe factories were turning out six million pairs a year.

Lewiston and Auburn occupy a pivotal location in southern Maine, with easy access to Portland (35 miles away) and Freeport (28 miles), the western mountains, and the state capital (30 miles).

SIGHTS
Bates College

Founded in 1855 on foresighted egalitarian principles, Bates College (2 Andrews Rd., Lewiston, 207/786-6255, www.Bates.edu)

received its current name after major financial input from Benjamin Bates of the Bates Mill. On a lovely wooded, 109-acre campus in the heart of Lewiston, the college earns high marks for small classes, a stellar faculty, a rigorous academic program, and a low faculty-to-student ratio. The student body of 1,700 comes from almost every state and about four dozen foreign countries; diversity has always been evident and a point of honor. The oldest campus building is red-brick **Hathorn Hall,** built in 1856 and listed on the National Historic Register; one of the newest buildings, the Olin Arts Center, built in 1986, is an award-winning complex overlooking man-made Lake Andrews.

Within the **Olin Arts Center** (Russell and Bardwell Sts., 207/786-6135) are the **Bates College Museum of Art** (75 Russell St., 207/786-6158) and the 300-seat **Olin Concert Hall.** Most college-sponsored exhibits, lectures, and concerts at the Arts Center are free and open to the public (other organizations also use the concert hall). At 6 P.M. each Thursday mid-July–mid-August, free **lakeside concerts** are presented outside the Arts Center; bring a picnic and a blanket or chair. The **Bates College Museum of Art** (10 A.M.–5 P.M. Tues.–Sat., free), with rotating exhibits, is open all year. A significant stop on the Maine Art Museum Trail, the Bates museum is best known for its holdings of prints, drawings, and paintings by Lewiston-born Marsden Hartley.

The college has won national and international acclaim for the summertime (mid-July–mid-Aug.) **Bates Dance Festival,** featuring modern-dance workshops, lectures, and performances. Sell-out student and faculty programs, most presented in 300-seat Schaeffer Theater, are open to the public. Call well ahead for tickets (207/786-6161).

Bates is the repository of the **Edmund S. Muskie Archives** (70 Campus Ave., 207/786-6354), containing the papers of the Bates graduate (1936) and former Maine governor, U.S. senator, and U.S. secretary of state who died in 1996. The archives are open 9 A.M.–noon and 1–4 P.M. weekdays.

At the western edge of the campus, at the corner of Mountain Avenue and College Street, walk up **Mt. David,** actually a grandly named hill, for a surprisingly good view of the Lewiston/Auburn skyline.

Bates Mill

Thanks to a progressive public/private partnership, the 19th-century Bates Mill complex, on Canal Street in downtown Lewiston, is being revitalized for a variety of new uses. Occupying 1.2 million square feet in 12 buildings spread over six acres, the mill once produced nearly a third of the nation's textiles. Maine Heritage Weavers now turns out the popular Bates bedspreads in one of the original buildings of the Bates Manufacturing Company here (41 Chestnut St., 207/782-2184). Since 1992, much of the hulking brick complex has been undergoing a long-term makeover—offices, studios, shops, and restaurants have moved in, ever so slowly, helping the mill to reinvent itself.

𝄐 Saints Peter and Paul Basilica

Most distinctive of Lewiston/Auburn's churches is the Gothic Revival Roman Catholic Saints Peter and Paul Basilica (27 Bartlett St., corner of Bartlett and Ash Sts., Lewiston, 207/777-1200), listed on the National Register of Historic Places. Noteworthy is a rose window replica of the one at Chartres. It's the second-largest church in New England and capable of seating more than 2,000 for its separate services in English and French. Dedicated in 1938, the recently designated basilica is the only one in New England.

Museum L-A

Appropriately situated inside the Bates Mill Complex, Museum L-A (35 Canal St., Lewiston, 207/333-3881, $3 adults, $2 seniors and students, $1 ages 6–12, call for hours) documents the region's industrial heyday, with exhibits of equipment, photos, textiles, and other artifacts.

𝄐 Shaker Museum

Twelve miles southwest of Lewiston/Auburn, only a handful of Shakers remain in the world's last inhabited Shaker community. Nonethe-

Crowning a hillside, with gardens and farmlands and views over Sabbathday Lake, is the last living Shaker community in existence.

© TOM NANGLE

less, the members of the United Society of Shakers, an 18th-century religious sect, keep a relatively high profile with a living-history museum, craft workshops, store, publications, mail-order herb and gift business, and even a music CD released in 1995. (See their website for the wonderful herb and herbal tea catalogue.) Each year, more than 8,000 visitors arrive at the 1,800-acre **Sabbathday Lake Shaker Community** (707 Shaker Rd., Rte. 26, New Gloucester, 207/926-4597, www.shaker .lib.me.us) to glimpse an endangered lifestyle, and the Shakers welcome the public to their 10 A.M. Sunday service (men and women enter through separate doors and sit separately). The 75-minute basic guided tour costs $6.50 adults, $2 children 2–12. Tours begin at 10:30 and are then given every hour on the half hour, with the exception that the last tour of the day is at 3:15 P.M. The village is open Monday–Saturday late May–mid-October.

Twice each year, on Saturdays in late May and mid-October, the Friends of the Shakers

at Sabbathday Lake, a nonprofit group (annual membership for an individual is $15, a family $25), organizes **Friends' Work Day,** when three or four dozen volunteers show up at 10 A.M. to do spring and fall cleanup chores. The all-day work party includes a communal dinner. If you'd like to help, call the number above for exact dates.

◖ Poland Spring

Take a tour through the history of one of the world's most famous waters. It was Poland Spring Water (now owned by Perrier) that built Hiram Ricker's family empire, and a visit to Poland Spring should include Poland Spring Preservation Park (207/998-4142, www.polandspringps .org, 8 A.M.–4 P.M. Tues.–Sun., free), home of the Poland Spring Museum and Spring House, and learn about the legendary healing power of the water. Also here are the the Maine State Museum and All Souls Chapel, remnants of one of the world's largest resort hotels.

Begin at the museum, where exhibits detail

Poland Spring Preservation Park tells the story of the famous bottled water.

the history of the famed water and explain its origins. The water won the Medal of Excellence at the 1893 Chicago World's Fair, and the Grand Prize at the 1904 St. Louis World's Fair. After touring the exhibits, be sure to visit the Spring House. Nature trails lace the grounds and connect to the other sites.

It was the water's fame that helped the Ricker family grow their small hotel into the Poland Spring House, a 300-room hotel that was an architectural and technological marvel on a 5,000-acre property that included the world's first resort golf course and one of the first courses designed by Donald Ross. During its heyday in the early 20th century, the richest and most powerful people in the country gathered here to play golf and discuss world policy. Almost every American president from Ulysses S. Grant to Theodore Roosevelt stayed here. Other guests and visitors of note include Babe Ruth, Alexander Graham Bell, Mae West, Betty Grable, Judy Garland; Charles Lindberg flew over the hotel on July 25, 1927, but he was unable to land because of the crowds. The

Poland Spring House was destroyed by fire in 1975, but the Maine State Building and the All Souls Chapel remain.

The three-story, octagonal Maine State Building (9 A.M.–4 P.M. Tues.–Sat.) was built as the state pavilion for the 1893 Chicago World's Fair. Afterward, Ricker bought it for $30,000 and moved it to Maine aboard a special freight train and then via horse-drawn wagon to Ricker Hill, where it was reassembled, piece by piece. One year later, it reopened as a library and art museum as part of the Ricker family's centennial celebration of their settlement at Poland Spring. Although it suffered years of neglect in the mid-20th century, it's been restored and is now operated by the Poland Spring Preservation Society as a museum and art gallery. Guided tours cover the resort's history.

The adjacent All Souls Chapel was built in 1912 by the Ricker Family with donations from guests and staff of the Poland Spring House. The 1926 Skinner pipe organ and a set of Westminster chimes are still in working order. The chapel is home to a summer concert series (7 P.M. Mon., $5). For more information, call or visit the website.

PARKS AND PRESERVES
Thorncrag Bird Sanctuary
Imagine being able to bird-watch, hike, cross-country ski, and snowshoe on 312 acres within the city limits of Lewiston in one of New England's largest bird sanctuaries. At the Thorncrag Bird Sanctuary (Montello St., Lewiston, mailing address Stanton Bird Club, P.O. Box 3172, Lewiston 04240, 207/782-5238, www .avcnet.org/stanton/thorncrg.htm, free), pick up a trail map at the gate and head out on the three miles of well-maintained, color-coded, easy-to-moderate trails—past ponds, an old cellar hole, stone memorials and benches, and through stands of beech, hemlock, white pine, and mixed hardwoods. Bicycles are banned in the preserve, which is open dawn–dusk daily year-round. Bring a picnic. A 32-page guide to the sanctuary's flora and fauna is available at the customer service desk at Hannaford Supermarket. Throughout the year, the **Stanton Bird Club** sponsors close to three dozen lectures and free, open-to-the-public field trips; call or see its website for the schedule. The club also sponsors an excellent junior naturalist program. From downtown Lewiston, take Sabattus Street (Rte. 126) east about three miles to Highland Springs Road. Turn left (north) and continue to the end (Montello St.). You'll be facing the entrance to the sanctuary.

Range Ponds State Park
Brimming with swimmers when the temperature skyrockets, 777-acre Range (pronounced RANG) Ponds State Park (Empire Rd., Poland, mailing address P.O. Box 475, Poland Spring 04274, 207/998-4104) has facilities for swimming (including lifeguard and bathhouse) and picnicking, plus a playground and two miles of nature trails. (Part of the trail verges on a marsh; be prepared with bug repellent.) The beach, parking, restrooms, and picnic tables are wheelchair-accessible. Most of the park's acreage once was the estate of Hiram Ricker, owner of Poland Spring Water (now owned by Perrier). Bring a canoe or kayak and launch it into Lower Range Pond. Admission is $4.50 adults, $1 children 5–11; the park is open mid-May–mid-October. From Lewiston/Auburn, take Route 202/11/100 South to Route 122. Turn right (east) and continue to the Empire Road in Poland Spring; the turnoff to the park is well signposted.

RECREATION
Golf
The 18-hole **Poland Spring Country Club** (41 Ricker Rd., Rte. 26, Poland Spring, 207/998-6002) was first laid out in 1893 on the grounds of the long-gone Poland Spring House, a health spa. In 1912, Donald Ross added the second nine. Call for tee times. Incredibly inexpensive golf packages, including buffet-style meals, are available with a rustic—bring your own sheets, towels, and soap—motel. Not for everyone, but a reliable, unfussy cheap sleep.

Bicycling
The countryside in this area is mostly gentle, not much of a challenge for gonzo bikers but a decent workout for anyone looking for an average challenge. Although Route 202 between Lewiston and Augusta is a well-traveled highway, it has good, broad shoulders for biking—a rarity in Maine. Distance is about 30 miles one-way; a shorter pedal, as far as Greene or Monmouth and return, makes a good day trip. One of the best vistas along Route 202 is from the hilltop near Highmoor Farm, just north of Route 106 near the Androscoggin/Kennebec County line.

Rockhounding
For sheer fun, spend a few hours searching for apatite, tourmaline, and quartz at **Mount Apatite Park** (dawn–dusk), a 325-acre park that's been popular with rockhounds for more than 150 years. For a detailed map contact Auburn Parks and Recreation Department (48 Pettingill Park, Auburn, 207/784-0191).

ENTERTAINMENT

Throughout the year, **Bates College** (207/786-6255 weekdays, www.bates.edu) presents a full schedule of concerts, lectures, exhibits, sporting events, and other activities.

The former St. Mary's Church, considered one of the finest examples of Renaissance architecture in the country, has found new life as the **Franco-American Heritage Center** (46 Cedar St., Lewiston, 207/783-1585, box office 207/689-2000, www.francoamericanheritage.org), a performing arts center that presents symphonic, chamber, and choral music concerts as well as other events.

Since 1973, **L/A Arts** (221 Lisbon St., Lewiston, 207/782-7228 or 800/639-2919, www.laarts.org), a respected nonprofit arts-sponsorship organization, has been bringing a whole range of cultural events to the area, including films, concerts, family events, and more. The group sponsors **Music in the Parks,** with free concerts on Thursdays in Lewiston's Fountain Park and Auburn's Festival Plaza. It also operates **Gallery 5 at Lyceum Hall** (49 Lisbon St., Lewiston), with rotating shows. Area arts activities are listed in the *Area Arts Calendar* link.

Lewiston/Auburn's Professional Theatre Company, **The Public Theatre** (31 Maple St., Lewiston, mailing address 2 Great Falls Plaza, Box 7, Auburn 04210, box office 207/782-3200) has been presenting musicals and dramas for more than a decade, leading the way in the Twin Cities cultural scene and receiving recognition for the quality of its performances. Adult ticket prices are about $16, less for students and seniors.

The Maine Music Society (P.O. Box 711, Auburn 04212, 207/782-1403, www.mainemusicsociety.org) is the overlord of the 40-voice Androscoggin Chorale and the Maine Chamber Ensemble, which usually accompanies the chorale but also performs on its own. Concerts for both are held in various locations.

Auburn's Festival Plaza is the venue for **Auburn Community Band Concerts,** at 7 P.M. Wednesday July–August.

Each summer, **Poland Spring Preservation Society** hosts a series of weekly concerts in the All Souls Chapel. The music varies from acoustic guitar to jazz.

FESTIVALS AND EVENTS

The second weekend in July brings the **Moxie Festival,** a certifiably eccentric annual celebration of the obscure soft drink Moxie, invented in 1884 and still not consigned to the dustbin of history. Among the activities: a huge offbeat parade, food booths, a Moxie recipe contest, Chief Worumbo's Androscoggin Fun Race, a pancake breakfast, games, a carnival, live entertainment (including an appearance by Elvis), a chicken barbecue, a bubble-gum contest, a road race, and collectibles exhibits and sales. The biggest day is Saturday. It all happens in downtown Lisbon.

The acclaimed annual **Bates Dance Festival,** at Bates College, Lewiston, mid-July–mid-August, features behind-the-scenes classes and workshops, as well as performances, which are open to the public.

August brings the **Festival Franco Fun,** at the Franco-American Heritage Center, and the **Great Falls Balloon Festival,** with food, entertainment, a carnival, fireworks, and, of course, balloon launches.

Greek food, music, and dance highlight the schedule at the annual **Greek Festival** at the Greek Ortodox Church, in September.

ACCOMMODATIONS

At the popular **Ware Street Inn** (52 Ware St., Lewiston, 207/783-8171 or 877/783-8171, www.warestreeetinn.com, $75–180), guests have the best of both worlds, an in-city accommodation right across the street from Bates, but surrounded by more than an acre of gardens and trees. Innkeeper Jan Barrett pampers guests, providing concierge services, afternoon snacks, and evening turndown. Guest rooms have Wi-Fi, TV/VCR, and comfortable seating; common areas include a library, terrace, and living room. Jan's husband, Mike, is an avid cyclist who can help you plan routes. Breakfast is a hot buffet.

Out in the country, on the shores of Tripp Lake about 13 miles from Lewiston, the **Wolf**

Cove Inn Bed and Breakfast (5 Jordan Shore Dr., Poland, 207/998-4976, www.wolfcoveinn .com) is a delightful spot to recoup. Ten rooms (eight with private baths, three with fireplaces) are named after flowers, from Sweet Alyssum and Hollyhock at $85 d up to the Calla Lilly suite at $250 d. Off-season rates are $75–200 d. Paddle around in one of the inn's canoes or go for a swim in the lake, or both. Sunsets are magnificent here. No pets, no smoking. It's open all year.

Campground

On the shore of Lower Range Pond, 40-acre **Poland Spring Campground** (Rte. 26, P.O. Box 409, Poland Spring 04274, 207/998-2151, www.polandspringcamp.com) has 130 wooded tent and RV sites ($20–34 for two adults, three children, and one dog). Facilities include an outdoor pool, coin-operated showers, a general store, laundry, play areas, and rental canoes, kayaks, and rowboats. There's plenty of organized fun; be prepared for campfires, ice-cream parties, hay rides, barbecues, and other activities, although noise rules are monitored. The campground is about 10 miles west of Auburn.

FOOD
Local Flavors

Look for the **Auburn Mall Farmers Market** at 550 Center Street/Route 4, 9 A.M.–3 P.M. each Saturday in season.

Named for the river running through town, **⟨ Nezinscot Farm Store** (284 Turner Center Rd./Rte. 117, Turner, 207/225-3231, www .nezinscotfarm.com, 6 A.M.–6 P.M. Mon.–Fri., 8 A.M.–5 P.M. Sat.) is worth the detour. Besides organically grown produce, the farm makes its own organic baked goods, cheeses, and cream products. There's a café that makes meals to order and a tea shop, serving both light and full teas. The shop sells all-natural wool yarns from the farm's sheep, llamas, alpacas, and goats. The farm is five miles east and north of the junction of Routes 4 and 117 (about 16 miles north of downtown Auburn). Call ahead if you're making a special trip.

Locals rave about **Italian Bakery Products**

Co. (225 Bartlett St., Lewiston, 207/782-8312, 7 A.M.–5:30 P.M. Mon.–Sat.). It's a great little place to pick up baked goods such as cannoli or Bismarck doughnuts, as well as sandwiches for lunch.

Eclectic Fare

Breakfast, lunch, and tapas selections are available at **Holly's Own Deli** (84 Court St./Rte. 202, Auburn, 207/333-3041, www.hollysown .com, 7 A.M.–9 P.M. Mon.–Fri., to 10 P.M. Fri., 9 A.M.–10 P.M. Sat.), a casual spot with an upstairs wine and martini bar. The deli serves salads, soups, and sandwiches varying from build-your-own to paninis, along with a few house specialties, including burgers and lasagne. The upstairs evening menu has traditional favorites such as artichoke-spinach dip and bacon-wrapped scallops, as well as antipasto platters, French bread pizza, and crab cakes ($7–11). There's often entertainment Thursday–Saturday.

The college crowd beats a path to **Nothing but the Blues Cafe** (81 College St., Lewiston, 207/784-6493, www.nbtbcafe.com, 11:30 A.M.–2 P.M. and 5–8 P.M. Tues.–Fri., 5–9 P.M. Sat. all year), a casual, 32-seat restaurant not far from Bates. Entrées on the eclectic menu, emphasizing vegetarian and changing daily, are all under $12. Lunch portions are smaller, designed for speedy service. No liquor license; don't bring any.

Family Friendly

In the retrofitted Bates Mill, **DaVinci's Eatery** (150 Mill St., Lewiston, 207/782-2088, www .davinciseatery.com, 11 A.M.–9 P.M. Sun.– Thurs., to 10 P.M. Fri.–Sat.) specializes in pasta and brick-oven pizza but has a variety of other regional American and Italian entrées in the $10–17 range. Weekdays it features a luncheon pizza buffet.

A few miles southeast of Lewiston is **Graziano's Casa Mia Restaurant** (Lisbon Rd., Rte. 196, Lisbon, 207/353-4335, 11 A.M.– 9 P.M. Tues.–Thurs., to 10 P.M. Fri., 4–9 P.M. Sat., 4–9 P.M. Sun.), a locally colorful eatery lined floor to ceiling with classic autographed

WESTERN LAKES

boxing portraits and a few ringers: Edmund Muskie, Frank Sinatra, Jimmy Carter, and the pope. Even if boxing is your least-favorite sport, you'll get a kick out of this traditional "tomato Italian" spot owned by Joe Graziano since 1968. The atmosphere in the sprawling, six-room restaurant is funky and friendly, average entrées range $10–14, with a couple of outliers, and the pasta and sauces are homemade, with some upscale touches. If you're into veal, eat it here. Children are welcome (the booths are convenient); the menu even has a "bambino corner," although there's pizza on the regular menu.

Well known for steaks, **Mac's Grill** (1052 Minot Ave., Auburn, 207/783-6885, www .macsgrill.com, 11 A.M.–9 P.M. Tues.–Thurs., to 10 P.M. Fri. and Sat., to 8 P.M. Sun.) has a wide variety of other menu items, from wraps and burgers to a seafood pasta bake, lots of salads, and stuffed chicken pomodoro.

Casual Dining

If you're heading to a show, **Fish Bones American Grill** (70 Lincoln St., Auburn, 207/333-3663, www.fishbonesag.com, 4–9 P.M. Tues.–Sat., to 10 P.M. Fri. and Sat.), in a renovated mill with handsome brick-accented decor, serves a theater menu nightly for $22.50, including entrée (with about five choices) and either appetizer or dessert as well as coffee, tea, and soft drinks. Otherwise, the entrée options expand to more than a dozen choices, with an emphasis on fish (entrées begin at $20), or simply mix and match appetizers, salads, and flatbreads. Reviews are mixed about dinner, but fall–spring, Fish Bones also serves a killer brunch—hint: Go hungry.

Warm up on a cool evening at jazzy **Fuel** (49 Lisbon St., Lewiston, 207/333-3835, www .fuelmaine.com, 4–9 P.M. Tues.–Thurs., to 10 P.M. Fri. and Sat., $10–30), a country French–inspired bistro and wine bar that opened in 2007 in historic Lyceum Hall. Owner Eric Agren calls the decor "urban cozy," and that seems about right. The menu is ambitious, and choices don't always hit the mark, but that might be due to the newness of the venture; do ask locally. You might begin with a charcuterie plate, move onto coq au vin or duck cassoulet or perhaps the vegetarian choice of the day. If you're feeling adventuresome, Chef Justin Oliver offers a four-course degustation menu for the table or a custom tasting menu (reservation required) at a chef's table, in the kitchen. Service is friendly; portions are large.

And then there's a country inn standby. Dining is by reservation only at **The Sedgley Place** (54 Sedgley Rd., P.O. Box 517, Greene 04236, 207/946-5990 or 800/924-7778, www.sedgley place.com, seatings on the hour beginning at 5 P.M. Tues.–Sun.), in a lovely Federal-style homestead a mile southwest of Route 202 (six miles north of Lewiston). The menu changes weekly, but always includes prime rib, fresh fish, and poultry ($26.95, request vegetarian and children's portions ahead). Every week features a five-course special for $21. The restaurant makes it a point to support local growers. Occasionally, there are wine tastings.

INFORMATION AND SERVICES

The Androscoggin County Chamber of Commerce (179 Lisbon St., P.O. Box 59, Lewiston 04240, 207/783-2249, www.androscoggin county.com, www.laitshappeninghere.com, 8 A.M.–5 P.M. Mon.–Thurs. and 8 A.M.–noon Fri. in summer, to 3 P.M. in winter) serves as the tourism information center for the entire county. Parking can be a problem in this part of Lewiston, so use the Canal Street parking garage and take the fourth-floor walkway; you'll be right on the chamber's level. (Parking is cheap, and the chamber office will validate your ticket so you can park for free.) The website includes details on an exceptional historical walking tour, with photos of local landmarks.

Housed in a handsome granite Romanesque Revival building (1903), the Lewiston Public Library (105 Park St., Lewiston, 207/784-0135, www.lplonline.org) is one of the sponsors of the Great Falls Forum, presenting monthly lunches with expert speakers on various thought-provoking topics. It's also home to the Marsden Hartley Cultural Center, a meeting and performance venue.

BACKGROUND

The Land

IN THE BEGINNING...

Maine is an outdoor classroom for Geology 101, a living lesson in what the glaciers did and how they did it. Geologically, Maine is something of a youngster; the oldest rocks, found in the Chain of Ponds area in the western part of the state, are only 1.6 billion years old—more than two billion years younger than the world's oldest rocks.

But most significant is the great ice sheet that began to spread over Maine about 25,000 years ago, during the late Wisconsin Ice Age. As it moved southward from Canada, this continental glacier scraped, gouged, pulverized, and depressed the bedrock in its path. On it continued, charging up the north faces of mountains, clipping off their tops and moving southward, leaving behind jagged cliffs on the mountains' southern faces and odd deposits of stone and clay. By about 21,000 years ago, glacial ice extended well over the Gulf of Maine, perhaps as far as the Georges Bank fishing grounds.

But all that began to change with meltdown, beginning about 18,000 years ago. As the glacier melted and receded, ocean water moved in, covering much of the coastal plain and working its way inland up the rivers. By 11,000 years ago, glaciation had pulled back from all but a few minor corners at the top of Maine,

© TOM NANGLE

Glaciers contributed to the formation of the Desert of Maine in Freeport.

revealing the south coast's beaches and the unusual geologic traits—eskers and erratics, kettleholes and moraines, even a fjord—that make the rest of the state such a fascinating natural laboratory.

Today's Landscape

Three distinct looks make up the contemporary Maine coastal landscape. (Inland are even more distinct biomes: serious woodlands and mountains as well as lakes and ponds and rolling fields.)

Along the **Southern Coast,** from Kittery to Portland, are fine-sand beaches, marshlands, and only the occasional rocky headland. The **Mid-Coast** and **Penobscot Bay,** from Portland to the Penobscot River, feature one finger of rocky land after another, all jutting into the Gulf of Maine and all incredibly scenic. **Acadia** and the **Down East Coast,** from the Penobscot River to Eastport and including fantastic Acadia National Park, has many similarities to the Mid-Coast (gorgeous rocky peninsulas, offshore islands, granite everywhere) but, except

on Mount Desert Island, takes on a different look and feel by virtue of its slower pace, higher tides, and quieter villages.

GEOGRAPHY

Bounded by the Gulf of Maine (Atlantic Ocean), the St. Croix River, New Brunswick Province, the St. John River, Québec Province, and the state of New Hampshire (and the only state in the Union bordered by only one other state), Maine is the largest of the six New England states, roughly equivalent in size to the five others combined—offering plenty of space to hike, bike, camp, sail, swim, or just hang out. The state—and the coastline—extends from 43° 05' to 47° 28' north latitude, and 66° 56' to 80° 50' west longitude. (Technically, Maine dips even farther southeast to take in five islands in the offshore Isles of Shoals archipelago.) It's all stitched together by 22,574 miles of highways and 3,561 bridges.

Maine's more than 5,000 rivers and streams provide nearly half of the watershed for the Gulf of Maine. The major rivers are the

Penobscot (350 miles), the St. John (211 miles), the Androscoggin (175 miles), the Kennebec (150 miles), the Saco (104 miles), and the St. Croix (75 miles). The St. John and its tributaries flow northeast; all the others flow more or less south or southeast.

CLIMATE

Whoever invented the state's oldest cliché—"If you don't like the weather, wait a minute"—must have spent at least several minutes in Maine. The good news, though, is that if the weather is lousy, it's bound to change before too long. And when it does, it's intoxicating. Brilliant, cloud-free Maine weather has lured many a visitor to put down roots, buy a retirement home, or at least invest in a summer retreat.

The serendipity of it all necessitates two caveats: *Always pack warmer clothing than you think you'll need.* And *never arrive without a sweater or jacket—even at the height of summer.*

The National Weather Service assigns Maine's coastline a climatological category distinct from climatic types found in the interior.

The **coastal** category, which includes Portland, runs from Kittery northeast to Eastport and about 20 miles inland. Here, the ocean moderates the climate, making coastal winters warmer and summers cooler than in the interior (relatively speaking, of course). From early June through August, the Portland area—fairly typical of coastal weather—may have three to eight days of temperatures over 90°F, 25–40 days over 80°, 14–24 days of fog, and 5–10 inches of rain. Normal annual precipitation for the Portland area is 44 inches of rain and 71 inches of snow (the snow total is misleading, though, since intermittent thaws clear away much of the base).

FALLING FOR FOLIAGE

The timing of Maine's fall foliage owes much to the summer weather that precedes it, and so does the quality (although the annual spectacle never disappoints). In early September, as deciduous trees ready themselves for winter, they stop producing chlorophyll, and the green begins to disappear from their leaves. Taking its place are the spectacular pigments – brilliant reds, yellows, oranges, and purples – that paint the leaves and warm the hearts of every "leaf-peeper," shopkeeper, innkeeper, and restaurateur in the region.

The colorful display begins slowly, reaches a peak, andd then fades – starting in the north in early to mid-September and working down to the southwest corner by mid-October. Peak foliage in far-north Aroostook County usually occurs in late September, about three weeks after the colors have begun to appear there. Along the South Coast and Mid-Coast, the peak can occur as late as the middle of October, with the last bits of color hanging on even beyond that.

Trees put on their most magnificent show after a summer of moderate heat and rainfall; a summer of excessive heat and scant rainfall means colors will be less brilliant and disappear more quickly. Throw a September or October northeaster or hurricane into the mix and estimates are up for grabs.

So predictions are imprecise, and you'll need to allow some schedule flexibility to take advantage of the changes in different parts of the state. From mid-September to mid-October, check the state's Department of Conservation website (www.mainefoliage .com) for frequently updated maps, panoramic photographs, and reports on the foliage status (this is gauged by the percentage of leaf drop in every region of the state). Or call the Foliage Hotline: 888/MAINE-45 (888/624-6345). Another resource for info on driving tours during foliage season is www.visitmaine.com, the official website of the Maine Office of Tourism.

A reminder: Fall-foliage trips are extremely popular and have become more so in recent years, so lodging can be scarce in some areas (although often you'll find beds in adjacent towns). Plan well ahead and make reservations, especially if you're headed for the Kennebunks, Boothbay Harbor, Camden, Bar Harbor, Greenville, Rangeley, and Bethel.

Northeasters and Hurricanes

A northeaster is a counterclockwise, swirling storm that brings wild winds out of—you guessed it—the northeast. These storms can occur any time of year, whenever the conditions brew them up. Depending on the season, the winds are accompanied by rain, sleet, snow, or all of them together.

Hurricane season officially runs June–November but is most prevalent late August–September. Some years, the Maine coast remains out of harm's way; other years, head-on hurricanes and even glancing blows have eroded beaches, flooded roads, splintered boats, downed trees, knocked out power, and inflicted major residential and commercial damage. Winds—the greatest culprit—average 74–90 mph. A **hurricane watch** is announced on radio and TV about 36 hours beforehand, followed by a **hurricane warning,** indicating that the storm is imminent. Find shelter, away from plate-glass windows, and wait it out. If especially high winds are predicted, make every effort to secure yourself, your vehicle, and your possessions. Resist the urge to head for the shore to watch the show; rogue waves, combined with ultrahigh tides, have been known to sweep away unwary onlookers.

Sea Smoke and Fog

Sea smoke and fog, two atmospheric phenomena resulting from opposing conditions, are only distantly related. But both can radically affect visibility and therefore be hazardous. In winter, when the ocean is at least 40°F warmer than the air, billowy sea smoke rises from the water, creating great photo ops for camera buffs but especially dangerous conditions for mariners.

In any season, when the ocean (or lake or land) is colder than the air, fog sets in, creating perilous conditions for drivers, mariners, and pilots. Romantics, however, see it otherwise, reveling in the womblike ambience and the muffled moans of foghorns. Between April and October, Portland averages about 31 days with heavy fog, when visibility may be a quarter mile or less.

Storm Warnings

The National Weather Service's official daytime signal system for wind velocity consists of a series of flags representing specific wind speeds and sea conditions. Beachgoers and anyone planning to venture out in a kayak, canoe, sailboat, or powerboat should heed these signals. The flags are posted on all public beaches, and warnings are announced on TV and radio weather broadcasts, as well as on cable TV's Weather Channel and the NOAA broadcast network.

Flora and Fauna

From this elevation, just on the skirts of the clouds, we could overlook the country, west and south, for a hundred miles. There it was, the State of Maine, which we had seen on the map, but not much like that. Immeasurable forest for the sun to shine on…. No clearing, no house. It did not look as if a solitary traveler had cut so much as a walking stick there. Countless lakes…and mountains. The forest looked like a firm grass sward, and the effect of these lakes in its midst has been well compared…to that of a mirror broken into a thousand fragments, and widely scattered over the grass, reflecting the full blaze of the sun.

– Henry David Thoreau, *The Maine Woods*

Looking out over Maine from Katahdin today, as Thoreau did in 1857, you get a view that is still a mass of green stretching to the sea, broken by blue lakes and rivers. Although the forest has been cut several times since Thoreau saw it, Maine is proportionately still the most forested state in the nation.

It also is clearly one of the best watered. Receiving an average of more than 40 inches of precipitation a year, Maine is abundantly endowed with swamps, bogs, ponds, lakes, streams, and rivers. These, in turn, drain from a coast deeply indented by coves, estuaries, and bays.

In this state of trees and water, nature dominates more than most—Maine is the least densely populated state east of the Mississippi River. Here, where boreal and temperate ecosystems meet and mix, lives a rich diversity of plants and animals.

The Alpine Tundra

Three continental storm tracks converge on Maine, and the state's western mountains bear the brunt of the weather they bring. Stretching from Katahdin in the north along most of Maine's border with Québec and New Hampshire, these mountains have a far colder climate than their temperate latitude might suggest.

Timberline here occurs at only about 4,000 feet, and where the mountaintops reach above that, the environment is truly arctic—an alpine-tundra habitat where only the hardiest species can live. Beautiful, pale-green "map" lichens cover many of the exposed rocks like shapes cut from an atlas, and sedges and rushes take root in the patches of thin topsoil. As many as 30 alpine plant species—typically found hundreds of miles to the north—grow in crevices or hollows in the lee of the blasting winds. Small and low-growing to conserve energy in this harsh climate, such plants as **bearberry willow, Lapland rosebay, alpine azalea, diapensia, mountain cranberry,** and **black crowberry** reward the observant hiker with white, yellow, pink, and magenta flowers in late June and July.

Areas above tree line are generally inhospitable to most animals other than secretive **voles, mice,** and **lemmings.** Even so, summer or winter, a hiker is likely to be aware of at least one other species—the **northern raven.** More than any of the 300 or so other bird species that regularly occur in Maine, the raven is the bird of the state's wild places, its mountain ridges, rocky coasts, and remote forests. Solid black, like a crow, but larger and stockier and

Pitcher plants can often be sighted in the peat bogs along the Maine Coast.

with a wedge-shaped tail and broad wings, the northern raven is a magnificent flyer—soaring, hovering, diving, and often turning loops and rolls as though playing in the wind. Known to be among the most intelligent of all animals, ravens are quite social, actively communicating with one another in throaty croaks as they range over the landscape in search of carrion and other available plant and animal foods.

At tree line and below, where conditions are moderate enough to allow black spruce and balsam fir to take hold, fauna becomes far more diverse. Among the wind- and ice-stunted trees, called *krummholz* (crooked wood), forage **northern juncos** and **white-throated sparrows.** The latter's plaintive whistle (often mnemonically rendered as "Old Sam Peabody, Peabody, Peabody") is one of the most evocative sounds of the Maine woods.

The Boreal or Northern Forest

Mention the Maine woods and the image that is likely to come to mind is the boreal forests of

spruce and **fir.** In 1857, Thoreau captured the character of these woods when he wrote:

> It is all mossy and moosey. In some of those dense fir and spruce woods there is hardly room for the smoke to go up. The trees are a standing night, and every fir and spruce which you fell is a plume plucked from night's raven wing. Then at night the general stillness is more impressive than any sound, but occasionally you hear the note of an owl farther or nearer in the woods, and if near a lake, the semi-human cry of the loons at their unearthly revels.

Well adapted to a short growing season, low temperatures, and rocky, nutrient-poor soils, spruce and fir do dominate the woods on mountainsides, in low-lying areas beside watercourses, and along the coast. By not having to produce new foliage every year, these evergreens conserve scarce nutrients and also retain their needles, which capture sunlight for photosynthesis during all but the coldest months. The needles also wick moisture from the low clouds and fog that frequently bathe their preferred habitat, bringing annual precipitation to more than 80 inches a year in some areas.

In the lush boreal forest environment grows a diverse ground cover of herbaceous plants, including **bearberry, bunchberry, clintonia, starflower,** and **wood sorrel.** In older spruce-fir stands, mosses and lichens often carpet much of the forest floor in a soft tapestry of greens and gray-blues. Maine is extraordinarily rich in **lichens,** with more than 700 species identified so far—20 percent of the total found in all of North America. **Usnea** is a familiar one; its common name, old man's beard, comes from its wispy strands, which drip from the branches of spruce trees. The **northern parula,** a small blue, green, and yellow bird of the wood warbler family, weaves its ball-shaped pendulum nest from usnea.

The spruce-fir forest is prime habitat for many other species that are among the most sought-after by birders: **black-backed** and **three-toed woodpeckers,** the audaciously bold **gray jay** (or camp robber), **boreal chickadee, yellow-throated flycatcher, white-winged crossbill, Swainson's thrush,** and a half-dozen other gemlike wood warblers.

Among the more unusual birds of this forest type is the **spruce grouse.** Sometimes hard to spot because it does not flush, a spruce grouse is so tame that a careful person can actually touch one. Not surprisingly, the spruce grouse earned the nickname "fool hen" early in the 19th century, and no doubt it would have become extinct long ago but for its menu preference of spruce and fir needles, which render its meat bitter and inedible (you can get an idea by tasting a few needles yourself).

Few of Maine's 56 mammal species are restricted to the boreal forest, but several are very characteristic of it. Most obvious from its trilling, far-carrying chatter, is the **red squirrel.** Piles of cone remnants on the forest floor mark a red squirrel's recent banquet. The red squirrel itself is the favored prey of another coniferous forest inhabitant, the **pine marten.** An arboreal member of the mustelid family—which in Maine also includes **skunk, weasel, fisher,** and **otter**—the pine marten is a sleek, low-slung predator with blond to brown fur, an orange throat patch, and a long, bushy tail. Its beautiful pelt nearly led to the animal's obliteration from Maine through overtrapping, but with protection, the marten population has rebounded.

Nearly half a century of protection also allowed the population recovery of Maine's most prominent mammal, the **moose.** Standing 6–7 feet tall at the shoulder and weighing as much as 1,200 pounds, the moose is the largest member of the Cervidae or deer family. A bull's massive antlers, which it sheds and regrows each year, may span five or more feet and weigh 75 pounds. The animal's long legs and bulbous nose give it an ungainly appearance, but the moose is ideally adapted to a life spent wading through deep snow, dense thickets, and swamps.

Usually the best place to observe a moose is at the edge of a body of water on a summer afternoon or evening. Wading out into the water, the animal may submerge its entire head to browse on the succulent aquatic plants below the surface. The water also offers a respite from the swarms of biting insects that plague moose (and people who venture into these woods without bug repellent). Except for a limited hunting season, moose have little to fear from humans and often will allow close approach. Be careful, however, and give them the respect their imposing size suggests; cows can be very protective of their calves, and bulls can be unpredictable, particularly during the fall rutting (mating) season.

Another word of caution about moose: When driving, especially in spring and early summer, be alert for moose wandering out of the woods and onto roadways to escape the flies. Moose are dark brown, their eyes do not reflect headlights in the way that most other animals' do, and they do not get out of the way—of cars or anything else. Colliding with a half-ton animal can be a tragedy for all involved. Pay particular attention while driving in Oxford, Franklin, Somerset (especially Route 201), Piscataquis, and Aroostook Counties, but with an estimated 25,000–30,000 moose statewide, they can and do turn up anywhere and everywhere—even in downtown Portland and on offshore islands.

Protection from unlimited hunting was not the only reason for the dramatic increase in Maine's moose population; the invention of the chain saw and the skidder have played parts, too. In a few days, one or two men can now cut and yard a tract of forest that a whole crew of lumbermen with saws and horses formerly took weeks to harvest. With the increase in logging, particularly the clear-cutting of spruce and fir (whose long fibers are favored for papermaking), vast areas have been opened up for regeneration by fast-growing, sun-loving hardwoods. The leaves of these young **white birch, poplar, pin cherry,** and **striped maple** are a veritable moose salad bar.

The Transition Zone: Northern Hardwood Forest

Although hardwoods have replaced spruce and fir in many areas, mixed woods of **sugar maple, American beech, yellow birch, red oak, red spruce, eastern hemlock,** and **white pine** have always been a major part of Maine's natural and social histories. This northern hardwood forest, as it is termed by ecologists, is a transitional zone between northern and southern ecosystems and rich in species diversity.

Dominated by deciduous trees, this forest community is highly seasonal. Spring snowmelt brings a pulse of life to the newly exposed forest floor as herbaceous plants race to develop and flower before the trees overhead leaf out and limit the available sunlight. (Blink and you can practically miss a Maine spring.) **Trout lily, goldthread, trillium, violets, gaywing,** and **pink lady's slipper** are among the many woodland wildflowers whose blooms make a walk in the forest so rewarding at this time of year. Deciduous trees, shrubs, and a dozen species of ferns also must make the most of their short (four-month) growing season. In the Maine woods, the buds of mid-May unfurl into a full canopy of leaves by the first week of June.

Late spring and early summer in the northern hardwood forest is also a time of intense animal activity. Runoff from the melting snowpack has filled countless low-lying depressions throughout the woods. These ephemeral swamps and vernal pools are a haven for an enormous variety of aquatic invertebrates, insects, amphibians, and reptiles. Choruses of spring **peepers,** Maine's smallest—but seemingly loudest—frog, alert everyone with their high-pitched calls that the ice is going out and breeding season is at hand. Measuring only about an inch in length, these tiny frogs with X-shaped patterns on their backs can be surprisingly difficult to see without some determined effort. Look on the branches of shrubs overhanging the water—males often use them as perches from which to call prospective mates. But then why stop with peepers? There are eight other frog and toad species in Maine to search for, too.

Spring is also the best time to look for **salamanders.** Driving a country road on a rainy night in mid-April provides an opportunity to witness one of nature's great mass migrations, as salamanders and frogs of several species emerge from their wintering sites and make their way across roads to breeding pools and streams. Once breeding is completed, most salamanders return to the terrestrial environment, where they burrow into crevices or the moist litter of the forest floor. The movement of amphibians from wetlands to uplands has an important ecological function, providing a mechanism for the return of nutrients that runoff washes into low-lying areas. This may seem hard to believe until one considers the numbers of individuals involved in this movement. To illustrate, the total biomass of Maine's **redback salamander** population—just one of the eight salamander species found here—is heavier than the combined weight of all the state's moose!

The many bird species characteristic of the northern hardwood forest are also most in evidence during the late spring and early summer, when the males are engaged in holding breeding territory and attracting mates. For most passerines—perching birds—this means singing. Especially during the early-morning and evening hours, the woods are alive with choruses of song from such birds as the **purple finch, white-throated sparrow, solitary vireo, black-throated blue warbler, Canada warbler, mourning warbler, northern waterthrush,** and the most beautiful singer of them all, the **hermit thrush.**

Providing abundant browse as well as tubers, berries, and nuts, the northern hardwood forest supports many of Maine's mammal species. The **red-backed vole, snowshoe hare, porcupine,** and **white-tailed deer** are relatively abundant and in turn are prey for **fox, bobcat, fisher,** and **eastern coyote.** Now well established since its expansion into Maine in the 1950s and 1960s, the eastern coyote has filled the niche at the top of the food chain once held by wolves and mountain lions before their extermination from the state in the late 19th century. **Black bears,** of which Maine has an estimated 25,000, are technically classified as carnivores and will take a moose calf or deer on occasion, but most of their diet consists of vegetation, insects, and fish. In the fall, bears feast on beechnuts and acorns, putting on extra fat for the coming winter, which they spend sleeping (not hibernating, as is often presumed) in a sheltered spot dug out beneath a rock or log.

Autumn is a time of spectacular beauty in Maine's northern hardwood forest. With the shortening days and cooler temperatures of September, the dominant green chlorophyll molecules in deciduous leaves start breaking down. As they do, the yellow, orange, and red pigments (which are always present in the leaves and which serve to capture light in parts of the spectrum not captured by the chlorophyll) are revealed. Sugar maples put on the most dazzling display, but beech, birches, red maple, and poplar add their colors to make up an autumn landscape famous the world over.

Ecologically, one of the most significant mammals in the Maine woods is the **beaver.** After being trapped almost to extinction in the 1800s, this large swimming rodent has recolonized streams, rivers, and ponds throughout the state. Well known for its ability as a dam builder, the beaver can change low-lying woodland into a complex aquatic ecosystem. The impounded water behind the dam often kills the trees it inundates, but these provide ideal nest cavities for **mergansers, wood ducks, owls, woodpeckers,** and **swallows.** The still water is also a nursery for a rich diversity of invertebrates, fish, amphibians, and Maine's seven aquatic turtle species, the most common of which is the beautiful but very shy **eastern painted turtle.**

The Aquatic Environment

Small woodland pools and streams are, of course, only a part of Maine's aquatic environment. The state's nearly 6,000 lakes and ponds provide open-water and deep-water habitats for many additional species. A favorite among them is the **common loon,** symbol of North cCountry lakes across the continent. Loons impart a sense of wildness and mystery with their haunting calls and yodels resonating off the surrounding pines on still summer nights. Adding to their popular appeal are their striking black-and-white plumage, accented with red eyes, and their ability to vanish below the surface and then reappear in another part of the lake moments later. The annual census of Maine's common loons since the 1970s indicates a relatively stable population of about 3,200 breeding pairs.

Below the surface of Maine's lakes, ponds, rivers, and streams live 69 freshwater fish species, of which 17 were introduced. Among these exotic transplants are some of the most sought-after game fish, including **smallmouth** and **largemouth bass, rainbow trout,** and **northern pike.** These introductions may have benefited anglers, but they have displaced native species in many watersheds.

Several of Maine's native fish have interesting histories in that they became landlocked during the retreat of the glacier. At that time, Maine was climatically much like northern Canada is today, and **arctic char** ran up its rivers to spawn at the edges of the ice. As the ice continued to recede, some of these fish became trapped but nevertheless managed to survive and establish themselves in their new landlocked environments. Two remnant subspecies now exist: the **blueback charr,** which lives in the cold, deep water of 10 northern Maine lakes, and the **Sunapee charr,** now found only in three lakes in Maine and two in Idaho. A similar history belongs to the **landlocked salmon,** a form of Atlantic salmon that many regard as the state's premier game fish and now widely stocked throughout the state and around the country.

Atlantic salmon still run up some Maine rivers every year to spawn, but dams and heavy commercial fishing at sea have depleted their numbers and distribution to a fraction of what they once were. Unlike salmon species on the Pacific coast, adult Atlantic salmon survive the fall spawning period and make their way back out to sea again. The young, or parr, hatch the following spring and live in streams and rivers for the next two or three years before migrating to the waters off Greenland. Active efforts are now under way to restore this species, including capturing and trucking the fish around dams. Salmon is just one of the species whose life cycle starts in fresh water and requires migrations to and from the sea. Called anadromous fish, others include **striped bass, sturgeon, shad, alewives, smelt,** and **eels.** All were once far more numerous in Maine, but fortunately pollution control and management efforts in the past three decades have helped their populations rebound slightly from their historic low numbers.

Estuaries and Mudflats

Maine's estuaries, where fresh- and salt water meet, are ecosystems of outstanding biological importance. South of Cape Elizabeth, where the Maine coast is low and sandy, estuaries harbor large salt marshes of **spartina** grasses that can tolerate the frequent variations in salinity as runoff and tides fluctuate. Producing an estimated four times more plant material than an equivalent area of wheat, these spartina marshes provide abundant nutrients and shelter for a host of marine organisms that ultimately account for as much as 60 percent of the value of the state's commercial fisheries.

The tidal range along the Maine coast varies 9–26 vertical feet, southwest to northeast. Where the tide inundates sheltered estuaries for more than a few hours at a time, spartina grasses cannot take hold, and mudflats dominate. Although it may look like a barren wasteland at low tide, a mudflat is also a highly productive environment and home to abundant marine life. Several species of tiny primitive worms called **nematodes** can inhabit the mud in densities of 2,000 or more per square inch. Larger worm species are also very common. One, the **bloodworm,** grows up to a foot in length and is harvested in quantity for use as sportfishing bait.

More highly savored among the mudflat residents is the **soft-shelled clam,** famous for its outstanding flavor and an essential ingredient of an authentic Maine lobster bake. But because clams are suspension feeders—filtering phytoplankton through their long siphons, or "necks"—they can accumulate pollutants that cause illness, including hepatitis. Many Maine mudflats are closed to clam harvesting because of leaking septic systems, so it's best to check with the state's Department of Marine Resources or the local municipal office before digging a mess of clams yourself.

For birds—and birders—salt marshes and mudflats are an unparalleled attraction. Long-legged wading birds such as **glossy ibis, snowy egret, little blue heron, great blue heron, tricolored heron, green heron,** and **black-crowned night heron** frequent the marshes in great numbers throughout the summer, hunting the shallow waters for mummichogs and other small salt-marsh fish, crustaceans, and invertebrates. From mid-May to early June, and then again from mid-July until mid-September, migrating shorebirds pass through Maine to and from their subarctic breeding grounds. On a good day, a discerning birder can find 17 or more species of shorebirds probing the mud-flats and marshes with pointed bills in search of their preferred foods. In turn, the large flocks of shorebirds don't escape the notice of their own predators—**merlins** and **peregrine falcons** dash in to catch a meal.

The Rocky Shoreline and the Marine Environment

On the more exposed rocky shores—the dominant shoreline from Cape Elizabeth all the way Down East to Lubec—where currents and waves keep mud and sand from accumulating, the plant and animal communities are entirely different from those in the inland aquatic areas. The most important requirement for life in this impenetrable, rockbound environment is probably the ability to hang on tight. **Barnacles,** the calcium-armored crustaceans that attach themselves to the rocks immediately below the high-tide line, have developed a fascinating battery of adaptations to survive not only pounding waves but also prolonged exposure to air, solar heat, and extreme winter cold. Glued in place, however, they cannot escape being eaten by **dog whelks,** the predatory snails that also inhabit this intertidal zone. Whelks are larger and more elongate than the more numerous and ubiquitous **periwinkle,** accidentally transplanted from Europe in the mid-19th century.

Also hanging onto these rocks, but at a lower level, are the brown algae—seaweeds. Like a marine forest, the four species of **rockweed** provide shelter for a wide variety of life beneath their fronds. A world of discovery awaits those who make the effort to go out onto the rocks at low tide and look under the clumps of seaweed and into the tidal pools they shelter. Venture into these chilly waters with mask, fins, and wetsuit and still another world opens for natural-history exploration. Beds of **blue mussels, sea urchins, sea stars,** and **sea cucumbers** dot the bottom close to shore. In crevices between and beneath the rocks lurk **rock crabs** and **lobsters.** Now a symbol of the Maine coast and the delicious seafood it provides, the lobster was once considered "poor man's food"—so plentiful that it was spread on fields as fertilizer. Although lobsters are far less common than they once were, they are one of Maine's most closely monitored species, and their population continues to support a large and thriving commercial fishing industry.

Sadly, the same cannot be said for most of Maine's other commercially harvested marine fish. When Europeans first came to these shores four centuries ago, **cod, haddock, halibut, hake, flounder, herring,** and **tuna** were abundant. No longer. Overharvested, their seabed habitat torn up by relentless dragging, these groundfish have all but disappeared. It will be decades before these species can recover—and then only if effective regulations can be put in place soon.

The familiar doglike face of the **harbor seal,** often seen peering alertly from the surface just offshore, provides a reminder that wildlife populations are resilient—if given a chance. A century ago, there was a bounty on harbor seals because it was thought they ate too many lobsters and fish. Needless to say, neither fish nor lobsters increased when the seals all but disappeared. With the bounty's repeal and the advent of legal protection, Maine's harbor seal population has bounced back to an estimated 15,000–20,000. Scores of them can regularly be seen basking on offshore ledges, drying their tan, brown, black, silver, or reddish coats in the sun. Though it's tempting to approach for a closer look, avoid bringing a boat too near these haulout ledges, as it causes the seals to flush into the water and imposes an unnecessary stress on the pups, which already face a first-year mortality rate of 30 percent.

Positive changes in our relationships with wildlife are even more apparent with the return of birds to the Maine coast. Watching the numerous **herring gulls** and **great black-backed gulls** soaring on a fresh ocean breeze today, it's hard to imagine that a century ago, egg collecting had so reduced their numbers that they were a rare sight. In 1903, there were just three pairs of **common eiders** left in Maine; today, 25,000 pairs nest along the coast. With creative help from dedicated researchers using sound recordings, decoys, and prepared burrows, **Atlantic puffins** are recolonizing historic offshore nesting islands. **Osprey** and **bald eagles,** almost free of the lingering vestiges of DDT and other pesticides, now range the length of the coast and up Maine's major rivers.

Looking into the Future

Many Maine plants and animals, however, remain subjects of concern. Listed or proposed for listing as endangered or threatened species in the state are 178 vascular plants and 54 vertebrates. Too little is known about most of the lesser plants and animals to determine what their status is, but as natural habitats continue to decline in size or become degraded, it is likely that many of these species will disappear from the state. It is impossible to say exactly what will be lost when any of these species cease to exist here, but, to quote conservationist Aldo Leopold, "To keep every cog and wheel is the first precaution of intelligent tinkering."

It is clear, however, that life in Maine has been enriched by the recovery of populations of pine marten, moose, harbor seal, eider, and others. The natural persistence and tenacity of wildlife suggests that such species as the Atlantic salmon, wolf, and mountain lion will someday return to Maine—provided we give them the chance and the space to survive.

Flora and Fauna *written by William P. Hancock, director of the Environmental Centers Department at the Maine Audubon Society and former editor of* Habitat Magazine.

History

Prehistoric Mainers: The Paleoindians

As the great continental glacier receded northwestward out of Maine about 11,000 years ago, some prehistoric grapevine must have alerted small bands of hunter-gatherers—fur-clad Paleoindians—to the scrub sprouting in the tundra, burgeoning mammal populations, and the ocean's bountiful food supply. Because come they did—at first seasonally and then year-round. Anyone who thinks tourism is a recent Maine phenomenon needs only to explore the shoreline in Damariscotta, Boothbay Harbor, and Bar Harbor, where heaps of cast-off oyster shells and clamshells document the migration of early Native Americans from woodlands to waterfront. "The shore" has been a summertime magnet for millennia.

Archaeological evidence from the Archaic period in Maine—roughly 8000–1000 B.C.—is fairly scant, but paleontologists have unearthed stone tools and weapons and small campsites attesting to a nomadic lifestyle supported by fishing and hunting (with fishing becoming more extensive as time went on). Toward the end of the tradition, during the late Archaic period, emerged a rather anomalous Indian culture known officially as the Moorehead phase but informally called the Red Paint People; the name is due to their curious trait of using a distinctive red ocher (pulverized hematite) in burials. Dark red puddles and stone artifacts have led excavators to burial pits as far north as the St. John River. Just as mysteriously as they had arrived, the Red Paint People disappeared abruptly and inexplicably around 1800 B.C.

Following them almost immediately—and almost as suddenly—hunter-gatherers of the Susquehanna Tradition arrived from well to the south, moved across Maine's interior as far as the St. John River, and remained until about 1600 B.C., when they, too, enigmatically vanished. Excavations have turned up relatively sophisticated stone tools and evidence that they cremated their dead. It was nearly 1,000 years before a major new cultural phase appeared.

The next great leap forward was marked by the advent of pottery making, introduced about 700 B.C. The Ceramic period stretched to the 16th century, and cone-shaped pots (initially stamped, later incised with coiled-rope motifs) survived until the introduction of metals from Europe. Houses of sorts—seasonal wigwam-style dwellings for fishermen and their families—appeared along the coast and on offshore islands.

The Europeans Arrive

The identity of the first Europeans to set foot in Maine is a matter of debate. Historians dispute the romantically popular notion that Norse explorers checked out this part of the New World as early as A.D. 1000. Even an 11th-century Norse coin found in 1961 in Brooklin (on the Blue Hill Peninsula) probably was carried there from farther north.

Not until the late 15th century, the onset of the great Age of Discovery, did credible reports of the New World (including what's now Maine) filter back to Europe's courts and universities. Thanks to innovations in naval architecture, shipbuilding, and navigation, astonishingly courageous fellows crossed the Atlantic in search of rumored treasure and new routes for reaching it.

John Cabot, sailing from England aboard the ship *Mathew,* may have been the first European to reach Maine, in 1498, but historians have never confirmed a landing site. No question remains, however, about the account of Giovanni da Verrazzano, an Italian explorer

commanding *La Dauphine* under the French flag, who reached the Maine coast in May 1524, probably at the tip of the Phippsburg Peninsula. Encountering less-than-friendly Indians, Verrazzano did a minimum of business and sailed onward. His brother's map of the site labels it "The Land of Bad People." Esteban Gomez and John Rut followed in Verrazzano's wake, but nothing came of their exploits.

Nearly half a century passed before the Maine coast turned up again on European explorers' itineraries. This time, interest was fueled by reports of a Brigadoon-like area called Norumbega (or Oranbega, as one map had it), a myth that arose, gathered steam, and took on a life of its own in the decades after Verrazzano's voyage.

By the early 17th century, when Europeans began arriving in more than twos and threes and getting serious about colonization, Native American agriculture was already under way at the mouths of the Saco and Kennebec Rivers, the cod fishery was thriving on offshore islands, Indians far to the north were hot to trade furs for European goodies, and the birch-bark canoe was the transport of choice on inland waterways.

In mid-May 1602, Bartholomew Gosnold, en route to a settlement off Cape Cod aboard the *Concord,* landed along Maine's southern coast. The following year, merchant trader Martin Pring and his boats *Speedwell* and *Discoverer* explored farther Down East, backtracked to Cape Cod, and returned to England with tales that inflamed curiosity and enough sassafras to satisfy royal appetites. Pring produced a detailed survey of the Maine coast from Kittery to Bucksport, including offshore islands.

On May 18, 1605, George Waymouth, skippering the *Archangel,* reached Monhegan Island, 11 miles off the Maine coast, and moored for the night in Monhegan Harbor (still treacherous even today, exposed to the weather from the southwest and northeast and subject to meteorological beatings and heaving swells; yachting guides urge sailors not to expect to anchor, moor, or tie up there). The next day, Waymouth crossed the bay and scouted the mainland. He took five Indians hostage and sailed up the St. George River, near present-day Thomaston. As maritime historian Roger Duncan has put it:

> The Plimoth Pilgrims were little boys in short pants when George Waymouth was exploring this coastline.

Waymouth returned to England and awarded his hostages to officials Sir John Popham and Sir Ferdinando Gorges, who, their curiosity piqued, quickly agreed to subsidize the colonization effort. In 1607, the *Gift of God* and the *Mary and John* sailed for the New World carrying two of Waymouth's captives. After returning them to their native Pemaquid area, Captains George Popham and Raleigh Gilbert continued westward, establishing a colony (St. George or Fort George) at the tip of the Phippsburg Peninsula in mid-August 1607 and exploring the shoreline between Portland and Pemaquid. Frigid weather, untimely deaths (including Popham's), and a storehouse fire doomed what's called the Popham Colony, but not before the 100 or so settlers built the 30-ton pinnace *Virginia,* the New World's first such vessel. When Gilbert received word of an inheritance waiting in England, he and the remaining colonists returned to the Old World.

In 1614, swashbuckling Captain John Smith, exploring from the Penobscot River westward to Cape Cod, reached Monhegan Island nine years after Waymouth's visit. Smith's meticulous map of the region was the first to use the "New England" appellation, and the 1616 publication of his *Description of New-England* became the catalyst for permanent settlements.

The French and the English Square Off

English dominance of exploration west of the Penobscot River in the early 17th century coincided roughly with French activity east of the river.

In 1604, French nobleman Pierre du Gua, Sieur de Monts, set out with cartographer Samuel de Champlain to map the coastline, first reaching Nova Scotia's Bay of Fundy and then sailing up the St. Croix River. In midriver, just west of present-day Calais, a crew planted gardens and erected buildings on today's St. Croix Island while de Monts and Champlain went off exploring. The two men reached the island Champlain named l'Isle des Monts Deserts and present-day Bangor before returning to face the winter with their ill-fated compatriots. Scurvy, lack of fuel and water, and a ferocious winter wiped out nearly half of the 79 men. In spring 1605, de Monts, Champlain, and other survivors headed southwest, exploring the coastline all the way to Cape Cod before heading northeast again and settling permanently at Nova Scotia's Port Royal (now Annapolis Royal).

Eight years later, French Jesuit missionaries en route to the Kennebec River ended up on Mount Desert Island and, with a band of French laymen, set about establishing the St. Sauveur settlement. But leadership squabbles led to building delays, and English marauder Samuel Argall—assigned to reclaim English territory—arrived to find them easy prey. The colony was leveled, the settlers were set adrift in small boats, the priests were carted off to Virginia, and Argall moved on to destroy Port Royal.

By the 1620s, more than four dozen English fishing vessels were combing New England waters in search of cod, and year-round fishing depots had sprung up along the coast between Pemaquid and Portland. At the same time, English trappers and dealers began usurping the Indians' fur trade—a valuable income source.

The Massachusetts Bay Colony was established in 1630 and England's Council of New England, headed by Sir Ferdinando Gorges, began making vast land grants throughout Maine, giving rise to permanent coastal settlements, many dependent on agriculture. Among the earliest communities were Kittery, York, Wells, Saco, Scarborough, Falmouth, and Pemaquid—places where they tilled the acidic soil, fished the waters, eked out a barely-above-subsistence living, coped with predators and endless winters, bartered goods and services, and set up local governments and courts.

By the late 17th century, as these communities expanded, so did their requirements and responsibilities. Roads and bridges were built, preachers and teachers were hired, and militias were organized to deal with internecine and Indian skirmishes.

Even though England yearned to control the entire Maine coastline, her turf, realistically, was primarily south and west of the Penobscot River. The French had expanded from their Canadian colony of Acadia, for the most part north and east of the Penobscot. Unlike the absentee bosses who controlled the English territory, French merchants actually showed up, forming good relationships with the Indians and cornering the market in fishing, lumbering, and fur trading. And French Jesuit priests converted many a Native American to Catholicism. Intermittently, overlapping Anglo-French land claims sparked locally messy conflicts.

In the mid-17th century, the strategic heart of French administration and activity in Maine was Fort Pentagoet, a sturdy stone outpost built in 1635 in what is now Castine. From here, the French controlled coastal trade between the St. George River and Mount Desert Island and well up the Penobscot River. In 1654, England captured and occupied the fort and much of French Acadia, but, thanks to the 1667 Treaty of Breda, title returned to the French in 1670, and Pentagoet briefly became Acadia's capital.

A short but nasty Dutch foray against Acadia in 1674 resulted in Pentagoet's destruction ("levell'd with ye ground," by one account) and the raising of a third national flag over Castine.

The Indian Wars (1675-1760)

Caught in the middle of 17th- and 18th-century Anglo-French disputes throughout Maine were the Wabanaki (People of the Dawn), the collective name for the state's major Native American tribal groups, all of whom spoke Algonquian languages. Modern ethnographers label these groups the Micmacs, Maliseets, Passamaquoddies, and Penobscots.

In the early 17th century, exposure to European diseases took its toll, wiping out three-quarters of the Wabanaki in the years 1616–1619. Opportunistic English and French traders quickly moved into the breach, and the Indians struggled to survive and regroup.

But regroup they did. Less than three generations later, a series of six Indian wars began, lasting nearly a century and pitting the Wabanaki most often against the English but occasionally against other Wabanaki. The conflicts, largely provoked by Anglo-French tensions in Europe, were King Philip's War (1675–1678), King William's War (1688–1699), Queen Anne's War (1703–1713), Dummer's War (1721–1726), King George's War (1744–1748), and the French and Indian War (1754–1760). Not until a get-together in 1762 at Fort Pownall (now Stockton Springs) did peace effectively return to the region—just in time for the heating up of the revolutionary movement.

Comes the Revolution

Near the end of the last Indian War, just beyond Maine's eastern border, a watershed event led to more than a century of cultural and political fallout. During the so-called Acadian Dispersal, in 1755, the English expelled from Nova Scotia 10,000 French-speaking Acadians who refused to pledge allegiance to the British Crown. Scattered as far south as Louisiana and west toward New Brunswick and Québec, the Acadians lost farms, homes, and possessions in this *grand dérangement*. Not until 1785 was land allocated for resettlement of Acadians along both sides of the Upper St. John River, where thousands of their descendants remain today. Henry Wadsworth Longfellow's epic poem *Evangeline* dramatically relates the sorry Acadian saga.

In the District of Maine, on the other hand, with relative peace following a century of intermittent warfare, settlement again exploded, particularly in the southernmost counties. The 1764 census tallied Maine's population at just under 25,000; a decade later, the number had doubled. New towns emerged almost overnight, often heavily subsidized by wealthy investors from the parent Massachusetts Bay Colony. With almost 4,000 residents, the larg-

© TOM NANGLE

A cross marks the spot where Acadians landed in 1785.

est town in the district was Falmouth (later renamed Portland).

In 1770, 27 Maine towns became eligible, based on population, to send representatives to the Massachusetts General Court, the colony's legislative body. But only six coastal towns could actually afford to send anyone, sowing seeds of resentment among settlers who were thus saddled with taxes without representation. Sporadic mob action accompanied unrest in southern Maine, but the flashpoint occurred in the Boston area.

On April 18, 1775, Paul Revere set out on America's most famous horseback ride—from Lexington to Concord, Massachusetts—to announce the onset of what became the American Revolution. Most of the Revolution's action occurred south of Maine, but not all of it.

In June, the Down East outpost of Machias was the site of the war's first naval engagement. The well-armed but unsuspecting British vessel HMS *Margaretta* sailed into the bay and was besieged by local residents angry about a Machias merchant's sweetheart deal

with the British. Before celebrating their David-and-Goliath victory, the rebels captured the *Margaretta,* killed her captain, and then captured two more British ships sent to the rescue.

In the fall of 1775, Colonel Benedict Arnold—better known to history as a notorious turncoat—assembled 1,100 sturdy men for a flawed and futile "March on Québec" to dislodge the English. From Newburyport, Massachusetts, they sailed to the mouth of the Kennebec River, near Bath, and then headed inland with the tide. In Pittston, six miles south of Augusta and close to the head of navigation, they transferred to a fleet of 220 locally made bateaux and laid over three nights at Fort Western in Augusta. Then they set off, poling, paddling, and portaging their way up-river. Skowhegan, Norridgewock, and Chain of Ponds were among the landmarks along the grueling route. The men endured cold, hunger, swamps, disease, dense underbrush, and the loss of nearly 600 of their comrades before reaching Québec in late 1775. In the Kennebec River Valley, Arnold Trail historical signposts today mark highlights (or, more aptly, lowlights) of the expedition.

Four years later, another futile attempt to dislodge the British, this time in the District of Maine, resulted in America's worst naval defeat until World War II—a little-publicized debacle called the Penobscot Expedition. On August 14, 1779, as more than 40 American warships and transports carrying more than 2,000 Massachusetts men blockaded Castine to flush out a relatively small enclave of leftover Brits, a seven-vessel Royal Navy fleet appeared. Despite their own greater numbers, about 30 of the American ships turned tail up the Penobscot River. The captains torched their vessels, exploding the ammunition and leaving the survivors to walk in disgrace to Augusta or even Boston. Each side took close to 100 casualties, three commanders—including Paul Revere— were court-martialed, and Massachusetts was about $7 million poorer.

The American Revolution officially came to a close on September 3, 1783, with the signing of the Treaty of Paris between the United States and Great Britain. The U.S.-Canada border was set at the St. Croix River, but, in a massive oversight, boundary lines were left unresolved for thousands of square miles in the northern District of Maine.

Trade Troubles and the War of 1812

In 1807, President Thomas Jefferson imposed the Embargo Act, banning trade with foreign entities—specifically, France and Britain. With thousands of miles of coastline and harbor villages dependent on trade for revenue and basic necessities, Maine reeled. By the time the act was repealed, under President James Madison in 1809, France and Britain were almost unscathed, but the bottom had dropped out of New England's economy.

An active smuggling operation based in Eastport kept Mainers from utter despair, but the economy still had continued its downslide. In 1812, the fledgling United States declared war on Great Britain, again disrupting coastal trade. In the fall of 1814, the situation reached its nadir when the British invaded the Maine coast and occupied all the shoreline between the St. Croix and Penobscot Rivers. Later that same year, the Treaty of Ghent finally halted the squabble, forced the British to withdraw from Maine, and allowed the locals to get on with economic recovery.

Statehood

In October 1819, Mainers held a constitutional convention at the First Parish Church on Congress Street in Portland. (Known affectionately as "Old Jerusalem," the church was later replaced by the present-day structure.) The convention crafted a constitution modeled on that of Massachusetts, with two notable differences: Maine would have no official church (Massachusetts had the Puritans' Congregational Church), and Maine would place no religious requirements or restrictions on its gubernatorial candidates. When votes came in from 241 Maine towns, only nine voted against ratification.

For Maine, March 15, 1820, was one of those good news/bad news days: After 35 years of separatist agitation, the District of Maine broke from Massachusetts (signing the separation allegedly, and disputedly, at the Jameson Tavern in Freeport) and became the 23rd state in the Union. However, the Missouri Compromise, enacted by Congress only 12 days earlier to balance admission of slave and free states, mandated that the slave state of Missouri be admitted on the same day. Maine had abolished slavery in 1788, and there was deep resentment over the linkage.

Portland became the new state's capital (albeit only briefly; it switched to Augusta in 1832), and William King, one of statehood's most outspoken advocates, became the first governor.

Trouble in the North Country

Without an official boundary established on Maine's far northern frontier, turf battles were always simmering just under the surface. Timber was the sticking point—everyone wanted the vast wooded acreage. Finally, in early 1839, militia reinforcements descended on the disputed area, heating up what has come to be known as the Aroostook War, a border confrontation with no battles and no casualties (except a farmer who was shot by friendly militia). It's a blip in the historical timeline, but remnants of fortifications in Houlton, Fort Fairfield, and Fort Kent keep the story alive today. By March 1839, a truce was negotiated, and the 1842 Webster-Ashburton Treaty established the border once and for all.

Maine in the Civil War

In the 1860s, with the state's population slightly more than 600,000, more than 70,000 Mainers suited up and went off to fight in the Civil War—the greatest per-capita show of force of any northern state. About 18,000 of them died in the conflict. Thirty-one Mainers were Union Army generals, the best known being Joshua L. Chamberlain, a Bowdoin College professor, who commanded the Twentieth Maine regiment and later became president of the college and governor of Maine.

During the war, young battlefield artist Winslow Homer, who later settled in Prouts Neck, south of Portland, created wartime sketches regularly for such publications as *Harper's Weekly.* In Washington, Maine Senator Hannibal Hamlin was elected vice president under Abraham Lincoln in 1860 (he was removed from the ticket in favor of Andrew Johnson when Lincoln came up for reelection in 1864).

Maine Comes into Its Own

After the Civil War, Maine's influence in Republican-dominated Washington far outweighed the size of its population. In the late 1880s, Mainers held the federal offices of acting vice president, Speaker of the House, secretary of state, Senate majority leader, Supreme Court justice, and several important committee chairmanships. Best known of the notables were James G. Blaine (journalist, presidential aspirant, and secretary of state) and Portland native Thomas Brackett Reed, presidential aspirant and Speaker of the House.

In Maine itself, traditional industries fell into decline after the Civil War, dealing the economy a body blow. Steel ships began replacing Maine's wooden clippers, refrigeration techniques made the block-ice industry obsolete, concrete threatened the granite-quarrying trade, and the output from Southern textile mills began to supplant that from Maine's mills.

Despite Maine's economic difficulties, however, wealthy urbanites began turning their sights toward the state, accumulating land (including islands) and building enormous summer "cottages" for their families, servants, and hangers-on. Bar Harbor was a prime example of the elegant summer colonies that sprang up, but others include Grindstone Neck (Winter Harbor), Prouts Neck (Scarborough), and Dark Harbor (on Islesboro in Penobscot Bay). Vacationers who preferred fancy hotel-type digs reserved rooms for the summer at such sprawling complexes as Kineo House (on Moosehead Lake), Poland Spring House (west of Portland), or the Samoset Hotel (in Rockland). Built of wood and catering to long-term visitors, these and many others all eventually succumbed to altered vacation patterns and the ravages of fire.

As the 19th century spilled into the 20th, the state broadened its appeal beyond the well-to-do who had snared prime turf in the Victorian era. It launched an active promotion of Maine as "The Nation's Playground," successfully spurring an influx of visitors from all economic levels. By steamboat, train, and soon by car, people came to enjoy the ocean beaches, the woods, the mountains, the lakes, and the quaintness of it all. (Not that these features didn't really exist, but the state's aggressive public relations campaign at the turn of the 20th century stacks up against anything Madison Avenue puts out today.) The only major hiatus in the tourism explosion in the century's first two decades was 1914–1918, when 35,062 Mainers joined many thousands of other Americans in going off to the European front to fight in World War I. Two years after the war ended, in 1920 (the centennial of its statehood), Maine women were the first in the nation to troop to the polls after ratification of the 19th Amendment granted universal suffrage.

Maine was slow to feel the repercussions of the Great Depression, but eventually they came, with bank failures all over the state. Federally subsidized programs, such as the Civilian Conservation Corps (CCC) and the Works Progress Administration (WPA), left lasting legacies in Maine.

Politically, the state has contributed notables on both sides of the aisle. In 1954, Maine elected as its governor Edmund S. Muskie, only the fifth Democrat in the job since 1854. In 1958, Muskie ran for and won a seat in the Senate, and in 1980 he became secretary of state under President Jimmy Carter. Muskie died in 1996.

Elected in 1980, Waterville's George J. Mitchell made a respected name for himself as a Democratic senator and Senate majority leader before retiring in 1996, when Maine became only the second state in the union to have two women senators (Olympia Snowe and Susan Collins, both Republicans). After his 1996 reelection, President Bill Clinton appointed Mitchell's distinguished congressional colleague and three-term senator, Republican William Cohen of Bangor, as secretary of defense, a position he held through the rest of the Clinton administration. Mitchell spent considerable time during the Clinton years as the U.S. mediator for Northern Ireland's "troubles" and subsequently headed an international fact-finding team in the Middle East. Both Mitchell and Cohen have retired to the private sector, but no one will be surprised to see them on the national stage again.

Government and Economy

STATE GOVERNMENT

Politics in Maine isn't quite as variable and unpredictable as the weather, but pundits are almost as wary as weather forecasters about making predictions. Despite a long tradition of Republicanism dating from the late 19th century, Maine's voters and politicians have a national reputation for being independent-minded—electing Democrats, Republicans, or independents more for their character than their political persuasions.

Four of the most notable recent examples are Margaret Chase Smith, Edmund S. Muskie, George J. Mitchell, and William Cohen—two Republicans and two Democrats, all Maine natives. Republican Senator Margaret Chase Smith proved her flintiness when she spoke out against McCarthyism in the 1950s. Ed Muskie, the first prominent Democrat to come out of Maine, won every race he entered except an aborted bid for the presidency in 1972. George Mitchell, as mentioned, has gained a stellar reputation, as has William Cohen. In a manifestation of Maine's strong tradition of bipartisanship, Mitchell and Cohen worked together closely on many issues to benefit the state and the nation (they even wrote a book together).

In the 1970s, Maine elected an independent governor, James Longley, whose memory is still respected (Longley's son was later elected to Congress as a Republican, and his daughter to the state senate as a Democrat). In 1994, Maine voted in another independent, Angus King, a relatively young veteran of careers in business, broadcasting, and law. The governor serves a term of four years, limited to two terms.

The state's Supreme Judicial Court has a chief justice and six associate justices.

Maine is ruled by a bicameral, biennial citizen legislature comprising 151 members in the House of Representatives and 35 members in the state senate, including a relatively high percentage of women and a fairly high proportion of retirees. Members of both houses serve two-year terms. Along with the governor, they meet at the State House in Augusta to pass legislation and administer an annual state budget of around $2 billion. In 1993, voters passed a statewide term-limits referendum restricting legislators to four terms.

Whereas nearly two dozen Maine cities are ruled by city councils, about 450 smaller towns and plantations retain the traditional form of rule: annual town meetings. Town meetings generally are held in March, when newspaper pages bulge with reports containing classic quotes from citizens exercising their rights to vote and vent. A few examples: "I believe in the pursuit of happiness until that pursuit infringes on the happiness of others"; "I don't know of anyone's dog running loose except my own, and I've arrested her several times"; and "Don't listen to him; he's from New Jersey."

Nonresidents are welcome to attend town meetings. Although, of course, you can't vote, a town meeting is a great way to experience true local government. Refreshments are usually available—typically, proceeds benefit some local cause—and sometimes there's even a potluck lunch or supper. The meeting provides the live entertainment.

ECONOMY

When the subject of the economy comes up, you'll often hear reference to the "two Maines," as if a line bisected the state in half, east to west. There's much truth to the image. Southern Maine is prosperous with good jobs (although never enough), lots of small businesses, and a highly competitive real estate market. Northern Maine struggles along, suffering from its immensity and lack of infrastructure as much as from its low population density.

Maine's relatively uninhabited, mostly rural and coastal land mass lends the state its renowned scenic beauty, but the lack of large urban centers also makes for a patchwork economy. In this sprawling state—as big as the rest of the New England states put together—small businesses and independent work dominate.

Many Mainers, especially in the less-populated northern regions, often hold two or three jobs to meet their families' needs. Perhaps they will cut a little firewood, make wreaths in the fall, or rake blueberries in season, sometimes to supplement factory wages. Younger, more mobile workers may move from ski instructing on the slopes in the winter to working as lifeguards or waiters in summer resorts.

A few large companies employ significant numbers of residents, but some of them have cut their work forces in recent years. Once the paper industry was the largest overall employer of Mainers, but as paper companies have shut down or reduced their work forces, tourism has stepped into first place.

Tourism

Summer, defined as July and August, was once the only significant time of year for tourism. If the weather were bad on Fourth of July weekend or Labor Day, seasonal businesses suffered losses of up to half their annual income. Now more of the millions of tourists who arrive by plane, boat, and car annually visit increasingly in fall and winter, not only to enjoy the many delights of sailing, swimming and fishing, but activities such as leaf-peeping, skiing, snowmobiling, and ice fishing.

Tourism jobs are harder to track because they cut across many areas such as transportation, meals, lodging, entertainment, other services, and retail. Yet by 2001, estimates showed tourism supports roughly 58,000 Maine jobs, and conservatively, pumped $6.2 billion into the state economy. On a per-capita basis, the concentration of tourism-related jobs in Maine is nearly double that of other states.

If the state's natural resources—the evergreen woods, the convoluted 5,300-mile coastline, and the wild Atlantic Ocean—attract tourists, they also underpin Maine's traditional industries of fishing, farming, and timber. The woods provided the timber for Maine's healthy shipbuilding industry in the days of sail while the ocean provided the means of launching the ships, which carried more wood and other products, including ice and lime, around the world.

Paper and Other Forest Products

A combination of spruce and fir, the best woods for making paper, comprise 35 percent of the Pine Tree State's forests. Maine also boasts one of the finest white birch resources in the world. Nearly 89 percent of the state is covered by 17 million acres of woods, making Maine the most heavily forested state in the country. While paper is still the second-largest industry paying the highest average wage in the state, the paper companies, primary users of the resource, have been shutting down or cutting back for a number of years now. Still, Maine is the second-highest producer of paper, after Wisconsin, and a recent industry report predicted a rebound in paper sales, perhaps to be followed by an upsurge in paper manufacturing.

More than 96 percent of Maine timberlands are privately owned, giving Maine the lowest percentage of national forest land, with only 0.19 percent, compared to the national average of 46 percent. Only one million acres of Maine woods are publicly owned. Besides paper, other Maine forest products include firewood, hardwood and softwood sawlogs, and biomass for wood-burning energy plants. Secondary processing, from clothespins and golf tees to decking and furniture, is on the increase.

In recent years, forest products pumped $5.6 billion into the state economy, or 40.5 percent of the state's manufacturing sales. Maine's forests may assume more importance to the U.S. industry if national forests are restricted for cutting, and attempts are being made to ensure the future of the Maine resource through widespread "green" programs that certify loggers and companies for sustainable practices.

Fishing

Commercial fishing throughout New England has suffered ups and downs in the past decade because of downtrends in traditional stocks such as cod, haddock, and scallops, followed by stringent federal regulations. Maine coastal communities have depended for hundreds of years on fishing, and although the fleet has been reduced, anglers still harvest groundfish, shrimp, clams, mussels, and other seafood in mostly seasonal fisheries. Sea urchins were not harvested at commercial levels until the mid-'80s, when they commanded high prices to Japanese markets. Urchin landings peaked at above 40 million pounds worth, or more than $37 million, in 1993. Since then, the resource has declined and catches have fallen to around five million pounds per year.

Lobster, for years Maine's most valuable sea-

© HILARY NANGLE

Lobster is Maine's most valuable seafood product.

food product, has also proven to be the state's most enduring fisheries resource. Along the convoluted 5,300-mile coastline, more than 7,000 residents hold lobster licenses. Nearly 1,200 lobstermen (and most women prefer to be called lobstermen) are considered full time, dependent on their lobstering income for their livelihood. Some fish nearly year-round, weather permitting. Others are considered part time, lobstering only in the summer when their other jobs, such as teaching or working in winter fisheries, are done.

It's easy to spot lobstering communities, their docks usually piled high with the colorful wire mesh traps. When traps are all in the water, colorful buoys, each with the owner's trademark color scheme and pattern, mark their location. Lobster boats come and go at the docks, refueling, offloading, or just sitting and facing the wind in the harbor, waiting for the next haul.

Maine lobstermen and women, rugged individualists all, rightly claim some credit for protecting the lobster resource through voluntary conservation measures. In 2004, Maine lobstermen harvested 63.2 million pounds of *Homarus americanus,* the favorite crustacean of tourists. Lobster landings continue to set records with recent catches of nearly 73 million pounds valued at around $300 million, beating out the previous record set in 2002, valued conservatively at $254 million. In 1990, the record catch totaled 28 million pounds, and in 1999, it soared to 52.3 million. Maine lobsters are enjoyed by diners in the shell, and, by those who don't want to work so hard, in lobster rolls up and down the coast all summer. However, lobsters are shipped live all over the country and the world to tanks in stores and restaurants.

Aquaculture

If fishing has gone down, aquaculture seemed poised to fill in the gaps, but the industry has been plagued by problems. Farming of Atlantic salmon started slowly in Penobscot and Cobscook Bays in the 1980s with a handful of independent farms, later consolidated by fewer but larger owners, some from Canada, Norway, and Chile. Harvests peaked at around 37 million pounds in 2000 and have declined steadily since. Several years ago a worldwide glut of farmed salmon depressed prices everywhere and strict environmental regulations governing escapes and other biological aspects of farming increased costs. Competition from the newer but fast-growing industry in Chile, where production costs are lower, offers a major challenge to the survival of North American salmon farming. But salmon is now recognized as one of the heart-healthiest foods on the market and worldwide sales are on the rise, offering hope for Maine's Down East salmon industry.

Shellfish such as oysters and clams are also farmed in Maine's tidal rivers, and seaweed for food and nutraceuticals is harvested wild and cultivated in Cobscook Bay. Wild blue mussels are plentiful along the shore and on the bottom, and many mussel beds are seeded by harvesters to increase the yield. Now mussels are also being raised on ropes to provide a cleaner, high-quality product.

Agriculture

A meal composed of Maine's primary seafood and agricultural products would be a tasty and nutritious one. A delicious banquet composed of lobster, salmon, mussels, and clams, served with Maine potatoes and broccoli with a sweet blueberry dish for dessert, would provide a powerhouse of Omega 3s, antioxidants, protein, and other nutrients.

Potatoes are still Maine's primary agricultural product. In recent years, Maine produced 1.79 billion pounds of potatoes valued at just under $100 million. Nearly 65 percent of Maine's potatoes are processed into chips and fries, and McDonald's restaurants in Maine serve only Maine potatoes. But demand has been dropping steadily for the round, white fresh potatoes that make up 15 percent of Maine's harvest from 65,000 acres of farms. Some growers are diversifying into unusual boutique varieties, aiming for niche markets. Still, schools in Aroostook County (known in Maine simply as "The County") still close for a few weeks each fall so children can help with the potato harvest as they have traditionally.

Broccoli, despite the dislike harbored for the vegetable by George H. W. Bush, former president and longtime Maine summer resident, is Maine's and "The County's" second-biggest agricultural crop. Acreage for broccoli growing increased from 284 acres in 1982 to 3,182 acres in recent years. Maine now ranks as the third-largest broccoli producer in the United States.

Blueberries

The state's favorite berry falls somewhere between wild harvest and agriculture. The smaller, low-bush blueberries, sweeter than the large, high-bush, cultivated varieties, grow wild in Maine, but the industry "encourages" them by burning fields, as Native Americans did centuries ago, and by applying pesticides—which they did not. Maine is the largest producer of wild blueberries in the world, harvesting half of the state's 60,000 acres of blueberry fields annually. Less than 1 percent of the wild crop is sold fresh, while 99 percent of blueberries are frozen. Some frozen berries are later canned.

Recent statistics show a total of 80.4 million pounds of blueberries valued at $28.5 million were harvested in Maine, although the industry generates nearly three times that for the state economy. Besides serving as a delicious ingredient in muffins, pies, ice cream, jam, cakes, wine, pancakes, and a wide range of other gourmet items, blueberries are now considered to provide an important antioxidant that may help prevent cancer.

Maple Syrup

Maple syrup is another Maine food product derived from a "wild" source. Producers, predominantly in Somerset County, tap maple trees in early spring, harvesting up to 60 gallons of sap from one big, healthy tree. Forty gallons of sap are needed to produce one gallon of the sweet stuff. Although Maine's output of maple syrup is a distant second to Vermont's, it is climbing each year and topped 290,000 gallons in 2004.

Major Corporations

Governor after governor of Maine has tried to shorten the economic gap between Maine's diverse regions. Southern Maine, nearer the urban center of greater Boston, is more populous with more diversity of jobs, many more people, and the sandy beaches that attract a multitude of tourists. The north has fewer people, little industry, and generally lower wages, except for the paper industry. The central region lies between the two in every respect. There are a few more population centers and a little more industry. Efforts to stimulate economic development in the less developed areas have experienced fluctuating degrees of success that largely mirror the state of the U.S. economy.

Bath Iron Works, which builds and repairs large ships, mainly for the Navy, has been Maine's biggest single employer for many years. In recent decades, cutbacks in military shipbuilding have reduced its production and therefore its work force. L. L. Bean, famous worldwide through its catalogs as a supplier of outdoor gear and sportswear, still keeps its Freeport store open seven days a week, 24 hours a day, as it has since it first opened. When L. L. Bean founded his emporium, the store provided access for hunters and anglers heading north at all hours. Now the late-night shoppers tend to be summer folks avoiding daytime crowds or simply proving to themselves the store is open at 3 A.M. The credit-card giant MBNA moved to Maine in 1993 and quickly developed a huge presence that included huge donations to libraries, museums, schools, hospitals, and small nonprofits. Recently, the company cut back its work force and shut all its facilities except that in Belfast, and its days are probably numbered.

As one local official told me: "Everyone complains that there are no jobs, but whenever an opportunity comes along, no one wants to risk changing the lifestyle." And that's a conundrum that's bound to continue for at least the foreseeable future.

The People

Maine's population didn't top the one-million mark until 1970. Thirty years later, according to the 2000 census, the state had 1,274,923 residents. Along the coast, Cumberland County, comprising the Greater Portland area, has the highest head count.

Despite the longstanding presence of several substantial ethnic groups, plus four Native American tribes (about 1 percent of the population), diversity is a relatively recent phenomenon in Maine, and the population is about 95 percent Caucasian. A steady influx of refugees, beginning after the Vietnam War, forced the state to address diversity issues, and it continues to do so today.

Natives and "People from Away"

People who weren't born in Maine aren't natives. Even people who *were* may experience close scrutiny of their credentials. In Maine, there are natives and *natives*. Every day, the obituary pages describe Mainers who have barely left the houses in which they were born—even in which their grandparents were born. We're talking roots!

Along with this kind of heritage comes a whole vocabulary all its own—lingo distinctive to Maine or at least New England. (For help in translation, see the *Glossary*.)

Part of the "native" picture is the matter of "native" produce. Hand-lettered signs sprout everywhere during the summer advertising native corn, native peas, even—believe it or not—native ice. In Maine, homegrown is well grown.

"People from away," on the other hand, are those whose families haven't lived here year-round for a generation or more. But people from away (also called flatlanders) exist all over Maine, and they have come to stay, putting down roots of their own and altering the way the state is run, looks, and *will* look. Senators Snowe and Collins are natives, but Governor King came from away, as did most of his cabinet members. You'll find other flatlanders as teachers, corporate executives, artists, retirees, writers, town selectmen, and even lobstermen.

In the 19th century, arriving flatlanders were mostly "rusticators" or "summer complaints"—summer residents who lived well, often in enclaves, and never set foot in the state off-season. They did, however, pay property taxes, contribute to causes, and provide employment for local residents. Another 19th-century wave of people from away came from the bottom of the economic ladder: Irish escaping the potato famine and French Canadians fleeing poverty in Québec. Both groups experienced subtle and overt anti-Catholicism but rather quickly assimilated into the mainstream, taking jobs in mills and factories and becoming staunch American patriots.

The late 1960s and early 1970s brought bunches of "back-to-the-landers," who scorned plumbing and electricity and adopted retro ways of life. Although a few pockets of diehards still exist, most have changed with the times and adopted contemporary mores (and conveniences).

Today, technocrats arrive from away with computers, faxes, cell phones, and other high-tech gear and "commute" via the Internet and modern electronics. Maine has played a national leadership role in telecommunications reform—thanks to the university system's early push for installation of state-of-the-art fiber optics.

Native Americans

In Maine, the *real* natives are the Wabanaki (People of the Dawn)—the Micmac, Maliseet, Penobscot, and Passamaquoddy tribes of the eastern woodlands. Many live in or near three reservations, near the headquarters for their tribal governors. The Passamaquoddies are at Pleasant Point, in Perry, near Eastport, and at Indian Township, in Princeton, near Calais. The Penobscots are based on Indian Island, in Old Town, near Bangor. Other Native American population clusters—known as "off-reservation Indians"—are the Aroostook Band of Micmacs, based in Presque Isle, and the Houlton Band of Maliseets, in Littleton, near Houlton.

In 1965, Maine became the first state to establish a Department of Indian Affairs, but just five years later the Passamaquoddy and Penobscot tribes initiated a 10-year-long land-claims case involving 12.5 million Maine acres (about two-thirds of the state) weaseled from the Indians by Massachusetts in 1794. In late 1980, a landmark agreement, signed by President Jimmy Carter, awarded the tribes $80.6 million in reparations. Despite this, the tribes still struggle to provide jobs on the reservations and to increase the overall standard of living. A 2003 referendum to allow the tribes to build a casino was defeated. The latest attempt to increase jobs and money is a controversial plan to bring a liquified natural gas port to tribal lands in Perry.

One of the true success stories of the tribes is the revival of traditional arts as businesses. The Maine Indian Basketmakers Association has an active apprenticeship program, and two renowned basket makers—Mary Gabriel and Clara Keezer—have achieved National Heritage Fellowships. Several well-attended annual summer festivals—in Bar Harbor, Grand Lake Stream, and Perry—highlight Indian traditions

The Maine Indian Basketmakers Alliance's Native American Festival takes place on the College of the Atlantic grounds in Bar Harbor every July.

© TOM NANGLE

American festival and an extensive Franco American research collection.

African Americans

Although Maine's African American population is small, the state has had an African American community since the 17th century; by the 1764 census, there were 322 slaves and free blacks in the District of Maine. Segregation remained the rule, however, so in the 19th century, blacks established their own parish, the Abyssinian Church, in Portland. Efforts are under way to restore the long-closed church as an African American cultural center and gathering place for Greater Portland's black community. For researchers delving into "Maine's black experience," the University of Southern Maine, in Portland, houses the African-American Archive of Maine, a significant collection of historic books, letters, and artifacts donated by Gerald Talbot, the first African American to serve in the Maine legislature.

and heighten awareness of Native American culture. Basket making, canoe building, and traditional dancing are all parts of the scene. The splendid Abbe Museum in Bar Harbor features Indian artifacts, interactive displays, historic photographs, and special programs. Gift shops have begun adding Native American jewelry and baskets to their inventories.

Acadians and Franco Americans

Within about three decades of their 1755 expulsion from Nova Scotia in *le grand dérangement,* Acadians had established new communities and new lives in northern Maine's St. John Valley. Gradually, they explored farther into central and southern coastal Maine and west into New Hampshire. The Acadian diaspora has profoundly influenced Maine and its culture, and it continues to do so today. Along the coast, French is spoken on the streets of Biddeford, where there's an annual Franco

Finns

Finns came to Maine in several 19th-century waves, primarily to work the granite quarries on the coast and on offshore islands and the slate quarries in Monson, near Greenville. Finnish families clustered near the quarries in St. George and on Vinalhaven and Hurricane Islands—all with landscapes similar to those of their homeland. Today, names such as Laukka, Lehtinen, Hamalainen, and Harjula are interspersed among the Yankee names in the Mid-Coast region.

Russians, Ukrainians, and Byelorussians

Arriving after World War II, Slavic immigrants established a unique community in Richmond, just inland from Bath. Only a tiny nucleus remains today, along with an onion-domed church, but a stroll through the local cemetery hints at the extent of the original colony.

The Newest Arrivals: Refugees from War

War has been the impetus for the more recent

arrival of Asians, Africans, Central Americans, and Eastern Europeans. Most have settled in the Portland area, making that city the state's center of diversity. Vietnamese and Cambodians began settling in Maine in the mid-1970s. A handful of Afghanis who fled the Soviet-Afghan conflict also ended up in Portland. Somalis, Ethiopians, and Sudanese fled their war-torn countries in the early to mid-1990s, and Bosnians and Kosovars arrived in the last half of the 1990s. With every new conflict comes a new stream of immigrants—world citizens are becoming Mainers, and Mainers are becoming world citizens.

Culture

Mainers are an independent lot, many exhibiting the classic Yankee characteristics of dry humor, thrift, and ingenuity. Those who can trace their roots back at least a generation or two in the state and have lived here through the duration can call themselves natives; everyone else, no matter how long they've lived here, is "from away."

Mainers react to outsiders depending upon how those outsiders treat them. Treat a Mainer with a condescending attitude, and you'll receive a cold shoulder at best. Treat a Mainer with respect, and you'll be welcome, perhaps even invited in to share a mug of coffee. Mainers are wary of outsiders and often with good reason. Many outsiders move to Maine because they fall in love with its independence and rural simplicity, and then they demand that the farmer stop spreading that stinky manure on his farmlands, or they insist that the town initiate garbarge pickup, or they build a glass-and-timber McMansion in the midst of white clapboard historical homes.

In most of Maine, money doesn't impress folks. The truth is, that lobsterman in the old truck and the well-worn work clothes might be sitting on a small fortune. Or living on it. Perhaps nothing has caused more troubles between natives and newcomers than the rapidly increasing value of land and the taxes that go with that. For many visitors, Maine real estate is a bargain they can't resist.

If you want real insight into Maine character, listen to a CD or watch a video by one Maine master humorist, Tim Sample. As he often says, "Wait a minute; it'll sneak up on you."

FINE ART

In 1850, in a watershed moment for Maine landscape painting, Hudson River School artist par excellence Frederic Edwin Church (1826–1900) vacationed on Mount Desert Island. Influenced by the luminist tradition of such contemporaries as Fitz Hugh Lane (1804–1865), who summered in Castine, Church accurately but romantically depicted the dramatic tableaux of Maine's coast and woodlands that even today attract slews of admirers.

By the 1880s, however, impressionism had become the style du jour and was being practiced by a coterie of artists who collected around Charles Herbert Woodbury (1864–1940) in Ogunquit. His program made Ogunquit the best-known summer art school in New England. After Hamilton Easter Field established another art school in town, modernism soon asserted itself. Among the artists who took up summertime Ogunquit residence was Walt Kuhn (1877–1949), a key organizer of New York's 1913 landmark Armory Show of modern art.

Meanwhile, a bit farther south, impressionist Childe Hassam (1859–1935), part of writer Celia Thaxter's circle, produced several hundred works on Maine's remote Appledore Island, in the Isles of Shoals off Kittery, and illustrated Thaxter's *An Island Garden.*

Another artistic summer colony found its niche in 1903, when Robert Henri (born Robert Henry Cozad, 1865–1929), charismatic leader of the Ashcan School of realist/modernists, visited Monhegan Island, about 11 miles offshore. Artists who followed him there included Rockwell Kent (1882–1971),

© HILARY NANGLE

The Ogunquit Museum of American Art is a treasure both inside and out, with an outstanding permanent collection and grounds salted with sculptures.

Edward Hopper (1882–1967), George Bellows (1882–1925), and Randall Davey (1887–1964). Among the many other artists associated with Monhegan images are William Kienbusch (1914–1980), Reuben Tam (1916–1991), and printmakers Leo Meissner (1895–1977) and Stow Wengenroth (1906–1978).

But colonies were of scant interest to other notables, who chose to derive their inspiration from Maine's stark natural beauty and work mostly in their own orbits. Among these are genre painter Eastman Johnson (1824–1906); romantic realist Winslow Homer (1836–1910), who lived in Maine for 27 years and whose studio in Prouts Neck (Scarborough) still overlooks the surf-tossed scenery he so often depicted; pointillist watercolorist Maurice Prendergast (1858–1924); John Marin (1870–1953), a cubist who painted Down East subjects, mostly around Deer Isle and Addison (Cape Split); Lewiston native Marsden Hartley (1877–1943), who first showed his abstractionist work in New York in 1909

and later worked in Berlin; Fairfield Porter (1907–1975), whose family summered on Great Spruce Head Island, in East Penobscot Bay; Andrew Wyeth (b. 1917), whose reputation as a romantic realist in the late 20th century surpassed that of his illustrator father, N. C. Wyeth (1882–1945).

On a parallel track was sculptor Louise Nevelson (1899–1988), raised in a poor Russian-immigrant family in Rockland and far better known outside her home state for her monumental wood sculptures slathered in black or gold. Two other noted sculptors with Maine connections were William Zorach (1887–1966) and Gaston Lachaise (1882–1935), both of whom lived in Georgetown, near Bath.

Today, Maine has no major community known exclusively for its summer art colony. Sure, there are artistic clusters here and there, united by the urge for creative networking and moral support—especially when threatened with reduced government subsidy. Among these artistic pockets, all close to the ocean, are the Kennebunks, Portland, Monhegan Island, Rockland, Blue Hill, Deer Isle, Gouldsboro, and Eastport.

Year-round or seasonal Maine residents with national (and international) reputations include Lincolnville's Neil Welliver and Alex Katz, North Haven's Eric Hopkins, Deer Isle's Karl Schrag, Eustis's Marguerite Robichaux, Tenants Harbor's Jamie Wyeth (third generation of the famous family), Kennebunk's Edward Betts, Port Clyde's William Thon, and Cushing's Lois Dodd and Alan Magee.

The state's most prestigious summer art program—better known in Manhattan than in Maine—is the highly selective Skowhegan School of Painting and Sculpture (Box 449, Skowhegan 04976, 207/474-9345; off-season 200 Park Ave. S, New York, NY 10003, 212/529-0505), founded in 1946. From well over 1,000 applicants, 65 young artists are chosen each year to spend nine weeks (mid-June–mid-August) on the school's 300-acre lakeside campus in East Madison. An evening lecture series is open to the public.

The two best collections of Maine art are at the **Portland Museum of Art** (7 Congress Sq., Portland, 207/775-6148) and the **Farnsworth Art Museum and Wyeth Center** (16 Museum St., Rockland, 207/596-6457). The Farnsworth, in fact, focuses only on Maine art, primarily from the 20th century. In 1996, both museums saw their already-impressive holdings greatly enhanced when philanthropic collector Elizabeth Noyce bequeathed her comprehensive Maine collection to them. The Farnsworth is the home of the Wyeth Center, featuring the works of three generations of Wyeths.

The **Ogunquit Museum of American Art,** appropriately, also has a very respectable Maine collection (in a spectacular setting). Other Maine paintings, not always on exhibit, are at the Bowdoin College Museum of Art, in Brunswick; Bates College Museum of Art, in Lewiston; and Colby College Museum of Art, in Waterville. Colby has a huge collection of works by painter Alex Katz.

CRAFTS

Any survey of Maine art, however brief, must include the significant role of crafts in the state's artistic tradition. As with painters, sculptors, and writers, craftspeople have gravitated to Maine—most notably since the establishment in 1950 of the **Haystack Mountain School of Crafts.** Started in the Belfast area, the school put down roots on Deer Isle in 1960. Each summer, internationally famed artisans—sculptors, glassmakers, weavers, jewelers, potters, papermakers, and printmakers—become the faculty for the unique school, which has weekday classes and 24-hour studio access for adult students on its handsome 40-acre campus. Many students and teachers have been unable to resist the area's inspired and inspiring scenery and have settled here.

DOWN EAST LITERATURE

Maine's first big-name writer was probably the early 17th-century French explorer Samuel de Champlain (1570–1635), who scouted the Maine coast, established a colony in 1604 near present-day Calais, and lived to describe in detail his experiences. Several decades after Champlain's forays, English naturalist John Josselyn visited Scarborough and in the 1670s published the first two books accurately describing Maine's flora and fauna (aptly describing, for example, blackflies as "not only a pesterment but a plague to the country").

Today, Maine's best-known author lives not on the coast but just inland in Bangor—Stephen King (b. 1947), wizard of the weird. Many of his dozens of horror novels and stories are set in Maine, and several have been filmed for the big screen here. King and his wife, Tabitha, also an author, are avid fans of both education and team sports and have generously distributed their largesse among schools and teams in their hometown as well as other parts of the state.

Chroniclers of the Great Outdoors

John Josselyn was perhaps the first practitioner of Maine's strong naturalist tradition in American letters, but the Pine Tree State's rugged scenic beauty and largely unspoiled environment have given rise to many ecologically and environmentally concerned writers.

The 20th century saw the arrival in Maine of crusader Rachel Carson (1907–1964), whose 1962 wake-up call, *Silent Spring,* was based partly on Maine observations and research. The Rachel Carson National Wildlife Refuge, headquartered in Wells and comprising 10 chunks of environmentally sensitive coastal real estate, covers nearly 3,500 acres between Kittery Point and the Mid-Coast region.

The tiny town of Nobleboro, near Damariscotta, drew nature writer Henry Beston (1888–1968), author of, among other things, *The Outermost House* (about Cape Cod); his *Northern Farm* lyrically chronicles a year in Maine. Beston's wife, Elizabeth Coatsworth (1893–1986), wrote more than 90 books—including *Chimney Farm,* about their life in Nobleboro.

Fannie Hardy Eckstorm (1865–1946), born in Brewer to Maine's most prosperous fur trader, graduated from Smith College and became a noted expert on Maine (and specifically Native American) folklore. Among her extensive writings, *Indian Place-Names of the Penobscot Valley and the Maine Coast,* published in 1941, remains a sine qua non for researchers.

The out-of-doors and inner spirits shaped Cape Rosier adoptees Helen and Scott Nearing, whose 1954 *Living the Good Life* became the bible of Maine's back-to-the-landers.

Classic Writings on the State

Historical novels, such as *Arundel,* were the specialty of Kennebunk native Kenneth Roberts (1885–1957), but Roberts also wrote *Trending into Maine,* a potpourri of Maine observations and experiences (the original edition was illustrated by N. C. Wyeth). Kennebunkport's Booth Tarkington (1869–1946), author of the *Penrod* novels and *The Magnificent Ambersons,* described 1920s Kennebunkport in *Mary's Neck,* published in 1932.

A little subgenre of sociological literary classics comprises astute observations (mostly by women) of daily life in various parts of the state. Some are fiction, some nonfiction, some barely disguised romans à clef. Probably the best-known chronicler of such observations is Sarah Orne Jewett (1849–1909), author of *The Country of the Pointed Firs,* a fictional 1896 account of "Dunnet's Landing" (actually Tenants Harbor); her ties, however, were in the South Berwick area, where she spent most of her life. Also in South Berwick, Gladys Hasty Carroll (1904–1999) scrutinized everyday life in her hamlet, Dunnybrook, in *As the Earth Turns* (a title later "borrowed" and tweaked by a soap-opera producer). Lura Beam (1887–1978) focused on her childhood in the Washington County village of Marshfield in *A Maine Hamlet,* published in 1957, while Louise Dickinson Rich (1903–1972) entertainingly described her coastal Corea experiences in *The Peninsula,* after first having chronicled her rugged wilderness existence in *We Took to the Woods.* Ruth Moore (1903–1989), born on Gott's Island, near Acadia National Park, published her first book at the age of 40. Her tales, recently brought back into print, have earned her a whole new, appreciative audience. Elisabeth Ogilvie (b. 1917) came to Maine in 1944 and lived for many years on remote Ragged Island, transformed into "Bennett's Island" in her fascinating "tide trilogy": *High Tide at Noon, Storm Tide,* and *The Ebbing Tide.* Ben Ames Williams (1887–1953), the token male in this roundup of perceptive observers, in 1940 produced *Come Spring,* an epic tale of hardy pioneers founding the town of Union, just inland from Rockland.

Seldom recognized for her Maine connection, antislavery crusader Harriet Beecher Stowe (1811–1896) lived in Brunswick in the mid-19th century, where she wrote *The Pearl of Orr's Island,* a folkloric novel about a tiny nearby fishing community.

Mary Ellen Chase was a Maine native, born in Blue Hill in 1887. She became an English professor at Smith College in 1926 and wrote about 30 books, including some about the Bible as literature. She died in 1973.

Two books do a creditable job of excerpting literature from throughout Maine—something of a daunting task. The most comprehensive is *Maine Speaks: An Anthology of Maine Literature,* published in 1989 by the Maine Writers and

MAINE FOOD SPECIALTIES

Everyone knows Maine is the place for lobster, but there are quite a few other foods that you should sample before you leave.

For a few weeks in May, right around Mother's Day (the second Sunday in May), a wonderful delicacy starts sprouting along Maine woodland streams: **fiddleheads,** the still-furled tops of the ostrich fern (*Matteuccia struthiopteris*). Tasting vaguely like asparagus, fiddleheads have been on May menus ever since Native Americans taught the colonists to forage for the tasty vegetable. Don't go fiddleheading unless you're with a pro, though; the lookalikes are best left to the woods critters. If you find them on a restaurant menu, indulge.

As with fiddleheads, we owe thanks to Native Americans for introducing us to **maple syrup,** one of Maine's major agricultural exports. The syrup comes in four different colors/flavors (from light amber to extra dark amber), and inspectors strictly monitor syrup quality. The best syrup comes from the sugar or rock maple, *Acer saccharum*. On Maine Maple Sunday (usually the fourth Sunday in March), several dozen syrup producers open their rustic sugarhouses to the public for "sugaring-off" parties – to celebrate the sap harvest and share the final phase in the production process. Wood smoke billows from the sugarhouse chimney while everyone inside gathers around huge kettles used to boil down the watery sap. (A single gallon of syrup starts with 30–40 gallons of sap.) Finally, it's time to sample the syrup every which way – on pancakes and waffles, in tea, on ice cream, in puddings, in muffins, even just drizzled over snow. Most producers also have containers of syrup for sale. For a list of participating sugarhouses, contact the Maine Department of Agriculture (207/287-3491, www.getrealmaine.com).

The best place for Maine maple syrup is atop pancakes made with Maine **wild blueberries.** Packed with antioxidants and all kinds of good-for-you stuff, these flavorful berries are prized by bakers because they retain their form and flavor when cooked. Much smaller than the cultivated versions, wild blueberries are also raked, not picked. Although most of the Down East barren barons harvest their crops for the lucrative wholesale market, a few growers let you pick your own blueberries in mid-August. Contact the Wild Blueberry Commission (207/581-1475) or the state Department of Agriculture for locations, recipes, and other wild-blueberry information, or log on to the website of the Wild Blueberry Association of North America (www.wildblueberries.com).

The best place to simply *appreciate* blueberries is Machias, site of the renowned annual Blueberry Festival, held the third weekend in August. While harvesting is under way in the surrounding fields, you can stuff your face with blueberry-everything – muffins, jam, pancakes, ice cream, pies. Plus you can collect blueberry-logo napkins, T-shirts, fridge magnets, pottery, and jewelry.

Another don't miss while in Maine is Maine-made **ice cream.** Skip the overpriced Ben and Jerry's outlets. Locally made ice cream is fresher and better and often comes in an astounding range of flavors. The big name in the state is Gifford's, with regional companies being Shain's and Round Top. All beat the out-of-state competition by a long shot. Even better are some of the one-of-a-kind dairy bars and farm stands.

Whenever you get a chance, shop at a **farmers market.** Their biggest asset is serendipity – you never know what you'll find. Everything is locally grown and often organic. Herbs, unusual vegetables, seedlings, baked goods, meat, free-range chicken, goat cheese, herb vinegars, berries, exotic condiments, smoked salmon, maple syrup, honey, and jams are just a few of the possibilities. For a list of all the markets (including those in inland areas), contact the Maine Department of Agriculture.

Of course, agricultural fairs also celebrate the bounty of the land, none more so than the Maine Organic Farmers and Gardeners Association's annual **Common Ground Fair,** held annually the third weekend in September. It's a must for any foodie.

Publishers Alliance. *The Quotable Moose: A Contemporary Maine Reader,* edited by Wesley McNair and published in 1994 by the University Press of New England, focuses on 20th-century authors.

A World of Her Own

For Marguerite Yourcenar (1903–1987), Maine provided solitude and inspiration for subjects ranging far beyond the state's borders. Yourcenar was a longtime Northeast Harbor resident and the first woman elected to the prestigious Académie Française. Her house, now a shrine to her work, is open to the public by appointment in summer.

Essayists, Critics, and Humorists Native and Transplanted

Maine's best-known essayist is and was E. B. White (1899–1985), who bought a farm in tiny Brooklin in 1933 and continued writing for *The New Yorker. One Man's Meat,* published in 1944, is one of the best collections of his wry, perceptive writings. His legions of admirers also include two generations raised on his classic children's stories *Stuart Little, Charlotte's Web,* and *The Trumpet of the Swan.*

Writer and critic Doris Grumbach (b. 1918), who settled in Sargentville, not far from Brooklin but far from her New York ties, wrote two particularly wise works from the perspective of a Maine transplant: *Fifty Days of Solitude* and *Coming into the End Zone.*

Maine's best contemporary exemplar of humorous writing is the late John Gould (1908–2003), whose life in rural Friendship has provided grist for many a tale. Gould's hilarious columns in the *Christian Science Monitor* and his steady book output have made him the icon of Maine humor.

Pine Tree Poets

Born in Portland, Henry Wadsworth Longfellow (1807–1882) is Maine's most famous poet; his marine themes clearly stem from his seashore childhood (in "My Lost Youth," he wistfully rhapsodized, "Often I think of the beautiful town/That is seated by the sea…").

Widely recognized in her own era, poet Celia Thaxter (1835–1894) held court on Appledore Island in the Isles of Shoals, welcoming artists, authors, and musicians to her summer salon. Today, she's best known for *An Island Garden,* published in 1894 and detailing her attempts at horticultural TLC in a hostile environment.

Edna St. Vincent Millay (1892–1950) had connections to Camden, Rockland, and Union and described a stunning Camden panorama in "Renascence."

Whitehead Island, near Rockland, was the birthplace of Wilbert Snow (1883–1977), who went on to become president of Connecticut's Wesleyan University. His 1968 memoir, *Codline's Child,* makes fascinating reading.

A longtime resident of York, May Sarton (1912–1995) approached cult status as a guru of feminist poetry and prose—and as an articulate analyst of death and dying during her terminal illness.

Among respected Maine poets today are Philip Booth (b. 1925), a resident of Castine; William Carpenter (b. 1940), of Stockton Springs; and Appleton's Kate Barnes (b. 1932), named Maine's Poet Laureate from 1996 to 1999. Although she comes by her acclaim legitimately, Barnes is also genetically disposed, being the daughter of writers Henry Beston and Elizabeth Coatsworth.

Maine Lit for Little Ones

Besides E. B. White's children's classics, *Stuart Little, Charlotte's Web,* and *The Trumpet of the Swan,* America's kids were also weaned on books written and illustrated by Maine island summer resident Robert McCloskey (b. 1914), notably *Time of Wonder, One Morning in Maine,* and *Blueberries for Sal.* Neck-and-neck in popularity is prolific Walpole illustrator-writer Barbara Cooney (1917–1999), whose award-winning titles included *Miss Rumphius, Island Boy,* and *Hattie and the Wild Waves.* Cooney produced more than 100 books, and it seems as if everyone has a different favorite.

Maine can also lay partial claim to Kate Douglas Wiggin (1856–1923), author of the eternally popular *Rebecca of Sunnybrook Farm;* she spent summers at Quillcote, in Hollis, just west of Portland.

ESSENTIALS

Getting There

Maine has two major airports, two major bus networks, a toll highway, limited Amtrak service, an international ferry, and some ad hoc local transportation systems that fill in the gaps.

BY AIR

Maine's major airline gateway is **Portland International Jetport** (PWM; 207/774-7301, www.portlandjetport.org), although visitors headed farther north sometimes prefer **Bangor International Airport** (BGR; 207/947-0384, www.flybangor.com). The "international" in their names is a bit misleading. Charter flights from Europe often stop at Bangor for refueling and customs clearance, and sometimes bad

weather also diverts flights there. Boston's Logan Airport is the nearest airport with direct flights from Europe and other worldwide destinations.

You'll undoubtedly want to fly into Bangor if you're going from Bar Harbor and Acadia National Park northeast along the coast, or anywhere north, period. But Portland is the more logical airport choice if you're visiting southern Maine—the beaches, Portland, or the coastal towns up to Damariscotta. If your destination is the Camden/Rockport area, which is equidistant between the two airports, your choice is a toss-up. Being on the coast, the Portland airport is more subject to fog shutdowns than Bangor, but many Bangor flights originate (or

© HILARY NANGLE

© HILARY NANGLE

Flying to a remote destination via floatplane can be far faster and less bumpy than driving.

stop) in Boston, where fog delays can afflict Logan Airport even more.

Increasingly popular choices for bargain hunters are **Southwest Airlines** (800/435-9792), which operates economical flights into Manchester, New Hampshire, and **JetBlue** (800/538-2583), which services Portland. Ground transportation is available between Manchester and the Portland Jetport.

All the airlines increase their flight frequency during the summer to accommodate stepped-up demand.

Airlines serving Portland and/or Bangor are **AirTran** (800/433-7300), **Continental** (800/523-3273), **Delta** (800/221-1212), **Jet Blue** (800/538-2583), **Northwest** (800/225-2525), **United Express** (800/864-8331), and **US Airways** (800/428-4322).

Portland Jetport Facilities

Portland's amenities include a newsstand/gift shop, coffee shop, restaurant/lounge, restrooms, large waiting area, ATM, and plenty of coin- and card-operated telephones. Avis, Bud-

get, Hertz, and National car-rental agencies have offices in the terminal; nearby Alamo runs a shuttle. A business center in the gate area has Internet access. Visitor information is dispensed from a desk (not always staffed, unfortunately) between the gates and the baggage-claim area. Baggage-handling offices surround the luggage carousels. Airlines are responsible for luggage, so if you have a problem, contact a representative from your airline. If you have an emergency, contact the airport manager (207/773-8462).

Ground Transportation: The **Explorer** (207/774-9891 or 800/377-4457, www.portland explorer.org) buses link all Portland transportation hubs—the airport, Portland Transportation Center, Vermont Transit terminal, Scotia Prince Ferry, and Casco Bay Lines—with hotels on the route. Portland's **Metro** bus line (207/774-0351) provides scheduled service throughout the city. **Taxis** are available outside baggage claim.

Bangor Airport Facilities

Bangor's airport has scaled-down versions

of Portland's facilities but all the necessary amenities: Avis, Budget, Hertz, National and Alamo rental cars (with Enterprise and Thrifty nearby); newsstand/gift shop; and waiting area with restrooms and phones. If you need help, contact the airport manager (207/947-0384).

Ground Transportation: Bangor Area Transportation (BAT; 207/882-4670, www.bgrme.org) buses connect the airport to downtown Bangor. Buses run Monday through Saturday. **West's Coastal Connection** (207/546-2823 or 800/596-2823, www.westbusservice.com) has scheduled service along Route 1 to Calais. **Cyr Bus Line** (207/827-2335 or 800/244-2335, www.cyrbustours.com) has scheduled service between Bangor and Limestone.

Regional Airports

Airports accessible via US Airways/Business Express from Boston are **Hancock County Airport** (BHB; 207/667-7329, www.bhbairport.com) near Bar Harbor, **Knox County Regional Airport** (RKD; 207/594-4131, http://knoxcounty.midcoast.com) at Owls Head, near Rockland and Camden, **Augusta State Airport** (AUG; 207/626-2306, www.augustaairport.org), and **Northern Maine Regional Airport** (PQI; 207/764-2550, www.flypresqueisle.com) in Aroostook County. Colgan Air is the local affiliate of US Airways Express at these airports.

Boston Logan Airport

If you fly into Boston (BOS), you easily can get to Maine via rental car (all majors at the airport, but it's not pleasant to navigate Logan in a rental car) and Concord Trailways bus (easiest and least-expensive option). You'll need to connect to North Station to take Amtrak's Downeaster train. Another option is **Mermaid Transportation** (800/696-2463, www.gomermaid.com), which operates the best van service between Boston and Portland. Pickup and dropoff, by reservation only, are at Portland Jetport and Logan airport. Mermaid also provides daily van service between Manchester, New Hampshire, and the Portland Jetport.

BY CAR

The major highway access to Maine from the south is **I-95,** which roughly parallels the coast until Bangor, before shooting up to Houlton. Other busy access points are **Route 1,** also from New Hampshire, exiting the state in Calais at the New Brunswick province border; **Route 302,** from North Conway, New Hampshire, entering Maine at Fryeburg; **Route 2,** from Gorham, New Hampshire, to Bethel, **Route 201,** entering from Québec province, just north of Jackman, and a couple of crossing points from New Brunswick into Aroostook and Washington Counties in northeastern Maine.

BY BUS

Concord Trailways (800/639-3317, www.concordtrailways.com) departs downtown Boston (South Station Transportation Center) and Logan Airport for Portland almost hourly from the wee hours of the morning until late at night, making pickups at all Logan airline terminals (lower level). Most of the buses continue directly to Bangor. The Portland bus terminal is the Portland Transportation Center, Thompson Point Road, just west of I-295. If you're headed for downtown Portland from the bus terminal, board the Metro city bus at the terminal and show your Concord Trailways bus ticket to receive a free trip.

Three daily nonexpress buses continue from Portland along the coast as far as Searsport and then head inland to the Trailways terminal in Bangor.

BY RAIL

Amtrak's Downeaster (800/872-7245, www.thedowneaster.com) makes five daily round-trip runs between Boston's North Station and Portland's Transportation Center, with stops in Wells, Saco, and seasonally in Old Orchard Beach (May 1 to October 31). The Wells Regional Transportation Center is staffed for information, has restrooms, ATM, and a climate-controlled waiting area. There's seasonal

© HILARY NANGLE

Ferries connect from Portland, Rockland, and Mount Desert Island to offshore islands.

trolley service to the beach. Taxis are on-site. The Saco station is near downtown and on the Tri-Town Shuttlebus route; taxis are available on-site. The Old Orchard Beach station is adjacent to the chamber of commerce and steps from the beach. From the Portland station, Portland's Metro municipal bus service will take you gratis to downtown Portland; just show your Amtrak ticket stub.

BY FERRY

An oceangoing car-and-passenger ferry **The Cat** (877/359-3760, www.catferry.com) links Portland and Bar Harbor with Yarmouth, in western Nova Scotia, Canada, with up to two daily trips from one port or the other between early June and mid-October. When making plans, remember that Yarmouth is on Atlantic time—an hour later than Maine's eastern time. Check for the current operating schedule and fees, but expect a 5.5-hour journey when departing from Portland, three hours from Bar Harbor. The ferry carries up to 900 passengers and 240 cars. Because of maritime law, the ferry can't operate between Portland and Bar Harbor without a stop in Canada.

Getting Around

By Bus

Ground transportation exists in Maine, but it's far from adequate. For instance, only two long-distance bus companies cover the state, and only one covers coastal Maine. There's no smoking on the buses.

Concord Trailways (800/639-3317, www .concordtrailways.com) has the most exten-

sive bus network, with routes designed to assist students, island ferry passengers, and day-trippers. Buses from Boston's Logan Airport stop in downtown Portland and follow a mostly coastal route through Brunswick, Bath, Wiscasset, Damariscotta, Waldoboro, Rockland, Camden, Belfast, and Searsport, ending in Bangor, and then follow the same route in reverse. (During the school year, the route also includes Bowdoin College in Brunswick and the University of Maine campus in Orono.)

Once-a-day buses to and from Calais coordinate with the Bangor bus schedules. The Calais line, stopping in Ellsworth, Gouldsboro, Machias, and Perry (near Eastport), is operated by **West's Coastal Connection** (207/546-2823 or 800/596-2823, www.westbusservice.com). Flag stops along the route are permitted (see the regional chapters for information).

Cyr Bus Line (207/827-2335 or 800/244-2335, www.cyrbustours.com) has scheduled service between Bangor and Limestone, with stops in Old Town, Orono, Howland, Medway, Sherman, Oakfield, Houlton, Mars Hill, Presque Isle, and Caribou.

Portland, South Portland, and Bangor have **city bus service,** with some wheelchair-accessible vehicles. A number of smaller communities have established **local shuttle** **vans** or **trolley-buses,** but most of the latter are seasonal.

By Car

No matter how much time and resourcefulness you summon, you'll never really be able to appreciate Maine without a car. The state has more than 22,000 miles of paved (mostly two-lane) roads and countless miles of unpaved country roads and logging routes (used by giant timber trucks). Down every little peninsula jutting into the Atlantic lies a picturesque village or park or ocean view. Inland, roads wind over the hills and through the woods. Even I-95, the state's major artery, boasts scenic vistas that bring photographers to a screeching halt. (Of course, a radar-equipped cop or a moose can deliver the same result for any driver.)

Note that the interstate can be a bit confusing to motorists; it's important to consult a

CAN YOU GET THERE FROM HERE?

Countless names for Maine cities, towns, villages, rivers, lakes, and streams have Native American origins; some are variations on French; and a few have German derivations. Below are some pronunciations to give you a leg up when requesting directions along the Maine coast.

Arundel – Uh-RUN-d'l
Bangor – BANG-gore
Bethel – BETH-l
Bremen – BREE-m'n
Calais – CAL-us
Carmel – CAR-m'l
Castine – Kass-TEEN
Damariscotta – dam-uh-riss-COTT-uh
Harraseeket – Hare-uh-SEEK-it
Hebron – HE-brun
Isle au Haut – i'll-a-HO, I'LL-a-ho (subject to plenty of dispute, depending on whether or not you live in the vicinity)
Katahdin – Kuh-TA-din
Kokadjo – Ko-KAD-joe
Lubec – Loo-BECK
Machias – Muh-CHIGH-us

Maranacook – Muh-RAN-uh-cook
Matinicus – Muh-TIN-i-cuss
Medomak – Muh-DOM-ick
Megunticook – Muh-GUN-tuh-cook
Monhegan – Mun-HE-gun
Mount Desert – Mount Duh-ZERT (subject to dispute; some say Mount DEZ-ert)
Narraguagus – Nare-uh-GWAY-gus
Naskeag – NASS-keg
Passagassawakeag – Puh-sag-gus-uh-WAH-keg
Passamaquoddy – Pass-uh-muh-QUAD-dee
Pemaquid – PEM-a-kwid
Piscataquis – Piss-CAT-uh-kwiss
Saco – SOCK-oh
Schoodic – SKOO-dick
Skowhegan – Skow-HE-gun
Steuben – Stew-BEN
Topsham – TOPS-'m
Umbagog – Um-BAY-gog
Wiscasset – Wiss-CASS-it
Woolwich – WOOL-itch
Wytopitlock – Wit-a-PIT-luck

map and pay close attention to the green directional signs to avoid heading off in the wrong direction. Between York and Augusta, I-95 is the same as the Maine Turnpike, regulated by The Maine Turnpike Authority (877/682-9433 or 800/675-7453 travel conditions, www.maineturnpike.com). I-295 splits from I-95 in Portland and heads up the coast to Brunswick before veering inland and rejoining I-95 in Gardiner. Service areas are infrequent on the turnpike and interstate and are not on both sides of the highway, so stop when you see one; don't wait for the next one. All exit numbers along I-95 reflect distance in miles from the border. Exits on I-295 reflect distance from where it splits from I-95 just south of Portland at Exit 44. Between Kittery, at the New Hampshire border, and Houlton, at the Canadian one, lie 305 miles of I-95, with the last toll at Augusta.

The Maine Department of Transportation (800/877-9171, www.state.me.us/mdot) has general road information on its website and also operates the Explore Maine site (www.exploremaine.org), which has information on all forms of transportation in Maine. For real-time information on road conditions, weather, construction, and major delays, dial 511 in Maine, 866/282-7578 from out of state, or visit www.511maine.gov. Information is available in both English and French.

Maximum speed on I-95 and the Maine Turnpike is 65 mph—55 mph on some stretches. In snow, sleet, or dense fog, the limit drops to 45 mph; only rarely does the highway close. On other highways, the speed limit is usually 55 mph in rural areas and posted in built-up areas.

Two lanes wide from Kittery in the south to Fort Kent at the top, U.S. Route 1 is the state's most congested road, particularly in July and August. Mileage distances can be extremely deceptive, since it will take you much longer than anticipated to get from point A to point B. If you ask anyone about distances, chances are good that you'll receive an answer in hours rather than miles. Plan accordingly. If you're trying to make time, it's best to take the Maine Turnpike or I-95;

if you want to see Maine, take U.S. 1 and lots of little offshoots.

That said, bear in mind that the Maine Turnpike south of Portland becomes megacongested on summer weekends, and especially summer *holiday* weekends. More than 300,000 vehicles use the turnpike on Memorial Day, Fourth of July, and Labor Day weekends. Worst times on the turnpike are 4–8 P.M. Friday (northbound), 11 A.M.–2 P.M. Saturday (southbound; most weekly cottage rentals run from Saturday noon to Saturday noon), and 3–7 P.M. Sunday (southbound). On three-day holiday weekends, avoid heading southbound between 3 and 7 P.M. on Monday.

Rental cars are available at the Portland, Bangor, and most smaller airports. All the major chains are represented—Alamo, Avis, Budget, Hertz, National, Thrifty, even Rent-a-Wreck. If you're planning to arrive on a July or August weekend, or a summer holiday weekend, call well ahead for a reservation or you may be out of luck.

Almost all **gas stations** in Maine are self-serve (pumps are marked Self; at those marked Full, an attendant will pump the gas for you), and many now allow you to pay at the pump with a credit card. (Many also have ATMs, but you'll usually have to pay a bank surcharge.)

Important Driving Regulations: Seat belts are mandatory in Maine. You cannot be stopped for not wearing one, but if you're stopped for any other reason, you can be fined if you're not buckled in. Maine allows right turns at red lights after you stop and check for oncoming traffic. In rare cases, you'll see a No Turn on Red sign—in which case, heed it. *Never* pass a stopped school bus in either direction. Wait until the bus's red lights have stopped flashing and all children are well off the road. Maine law also requires drivers to turn on their car's headlights any time the windshield wipers are operating.

Roadside Assistance: Since Maine is enslaved to the automobile, it's not a bad idea for vacationers to carry membership in AAA in case of breakdowns, flat tires, and other car crises. Contact your nearest AAA office or AAA Northern New England (425 Marginal Way, Portland 04101, 207/780-6800 or 800/482-7497, www.aaanne.com). The emergency road service number is 800/222-4357.

Hitchhiking
Even though Maine's public transportation network is woefully inadequate, and the crime rate is one of the lowest in the nation, it's still risky to hitchhike or pick up hitchhikers.

Tips for Travelers

VISAS AND OFFICIALDOM
Since 9/11, security has been excruciatingly tight for foreign visitors, with customs procedures in flux. For current rules, visit www.usa .gov/visitors/arriving.shtml and www.dhs.gov/ xtrvlsec. It's crucial to plan well ahead, pack diligently, and have all necessary paperwork. It's also wise to make two sets of copies of all paperwork, one to carry separately on your trip and another left with a trusted friend or relative at home.

SMOKING
Maine now has laws banning smoking in restaurants, bars, and lounges as well as enclosed areas of public places, such as shopping malls. Only a handful of B&Bs and country inns permit smoking, and more and more motels, hotels, and resorts are limiting the number of rooms where smoking is permitted. Many accommodations have instituted high fines for anyone who smokes in a nonsmoking room.

ACCOMMODATIONS, FOOD, AND ALCOHOL
Accommodations
For most accommodation listings, rates are quoted for peak season, which is usually July and August but may extend through foliage (mid-October); for alpine ski destinations, peak season usually runs between late December and mid-March. Rates drop, often dramatically, in the shoulder and off-season at accommodations that remain open. Especially during peak season, many accommodations require a two- or three-night minimum.

For the best rates, be sure to check Internet specials and to ask about packages. Many accommodations also provide discounts for members of travel clubs such as AAA, to seniors and the military, and other such groups.

Unless otherwise noted, accommodations have private baths.

Food
Days and hours of operation listed for places serving food are for peak season. These do change often, sometimes even within a season, and it's not uncommon for a restaurant to close early on a quiet night. To avoid disappointment, call before making a special trip.

Alcohol
As in the rest of the country, Maine's minimum drinking age is 21 years—and bar owners, bartenders, and serving staff can be held legally accountable for serving underage imbibers. Owners and employees also may be held liable for accidents caused by *legal* drinkers. Stiff anti-drunken-driving efforts in Maine (including random roadblocks, license revocation or suspension, hefty fines, and jail terms) have reduced but by no means halted the fatalities. If your blood alcohol level is 0.08 percent or higher, you are legally considered to be operating under the influence.

TIME ZONE
All of Maine is in the eastern time zone—the same as New York, Washington, D.C., Philadelphia, and Orlando, Florida. Eastern standard time (EST) runs from the last Sunday

in October to the first Sunday in April; eastern daylight time (EDT), one hour later, prevails otherwise. Surprising to many first-time visitors is how early the sun rises in the morning and how early it sets at night in midsummer.

If your itinerary also includes Canada, remember that the provinces of New Brunswick and Nova Scotia are on Atlantic time—one hour later than eastern— so if it's noon in Maine, it's 1 P.M. in these provinces.

Health and Safety

There's too much to do in Maine, and too much to see, to spend even a few hours laid low by illness or mishap. Be sensible—get enough sleep, wear sunscreen and appropriate clothing, know your limits and don't take foolhardy risks, heed weather and warning signs, carry water and snacks while hiking, don't overindulge in food or alcohol, always tell someone where you're going, and watch your step. If you're traveling with children, quadruple your caution.

MEDICAL CARE
In the event of an emergency, dial 911.

Southern Coast
York Hospital (15 Hospital Dr., York, emergency room 207/351-2157); **Wells Urgent Care** (109 Sanford Rd., Wells, 207/646-5211, 8 A.M.–7 P.M.); **Kennebunk Walk-In Clinic** (24 Portland Rd., Rte. 1, Kennebunk, 207/985-6027); **Southern Maine Medical Center** (Rte. 111, Biddeford, 207/283-7000, emergency 207/283-7100).

Greater Portland
Maine Medical Center (22 Bramhall St., Portland, emergency 207/871-2381); **Mercy Hospital** (144 State St., Portland, emergency 207/879-3265).

Mid-Coast
Mid-Coast Hospital (Bath Rd., Cooks Corner, Brunswick, 207/729-0181); **Parkview Hospital** (329 Maine St., a mile south of Bowdoin College, Brunswick, 207/373-2000); **St. Andrews Hospital and**
Healthcare Center (3 St. Andrews La., Boothbay Harbor, 207/633-2121); **Miles Memorial Hospital** (Bristol Rd., Rte. 130, Damariscotta, 207/563-1234).

Penobscot Bay
Penobscot Bay Medical Center (Rte. 1, Rockport, 207/596-8000); **Waldo County General Hospital** (118 Northport Ave., Belfast, 207/338-2500 or 800/649-2536).

Blue Hill and Deer Isle
Blue Hill Memorial Hospital (57 Water St., Blue Hill, 207/374-3400, emergency 207/374-2836, www.bhmh.org).

Acadia Region
Maine Coast Memorial Hospital (50 Union St., Ellsworth 04605, 207/664-5311 or 888/645-8829, emergency room 207/664-5340, www.mainehospital.org); **Mount Desert Island Hospital** (10 Wayman La., Bar Harbor, 207/288-5081, www.mdihospital.org).

Down East
Down East Community Hospital (Upper Court St., Rte. 1A, Machias, 207/255-3356); **Regional Medical Center at Lubec** (43 S. Lubec Rd., Lubec, 207/733-5541); **Eastport Health Care** (Boynton St., 207/853-6001); **Calais Regional Hospital** (50 Franklin St., Calais, 207/454-7521).

Aroostook
Houlton Regional Hospital (20 Hartford St., Houlton 04730, 207/532-9471); **A. R. Gould Memorial Hospital** (140 Academy St., Rte. 10,

Presque Isle, emergency room 207/768-4100); **Cary Medical Center** (163 Van Buren Rd., Caribou, 207/498-1234); **Northern Maine Medical Center** (143 E. Main St./Rte. 1, Fort Kent, 207/834-3155).

Maine Highlands

Millinocket Regional Hospital (200 Somerset St., Millinocket, 207/723-5161); **Charles A. Dean Memorial Hospital,** Pritham Ave., Greenville, 207/695-2223); **Mayo Regional Hospital** (75 W. Main St., Dover-Foxcroft, 207/564-8401); **Eastern Maine Medical Center** (489 State St., Bangor, 207/973-7000, emergency room 207/973-8000); **St. Joseph Hospital** (360 Broadway, Bangor, 207/262-1000).

Kennebec River Valley

MaineGeneral Medical Center (6 E. Chestnut St., Augusta, emergency room 207/626-1206); **MaineGeneral Medical Center** (149 North St., Waterville, emergency room 207/872-1300); **Redington-Fairview General Hospital** (Fairview Ave., Rte. 104, Skowhegan, 207/474-5121); **Jackman Region Health Center** (Main St., Rte. 201, Jackman, 207/668-2691).

Western Lakes and Mountains

Franklin Memorial Hospital (111 Franklin Health Commons, Farmington, emergency room 207/779-2250); **Rangeley Region Health Center** (Dallas Hill Rd., Rangeley, 207/864-3303); **The Bethel Family Health Center** (Railroad St., Bethel, 207/824-2193 or 800/287-2292); **Rumford Hospital** (420 Franklin St., Rumford, 207/369-1000, emergency room 364-4581); **Western Maine Mountain Clinic** (South Ridge Base Area, Sunday River, 207/824-4900); **Stephens Memorial Hospital** (181 Main St., Norway, 207/743-5933); **Northern Cumberland Memorial Hospital** (Hospital Dr., Bridgton, 207/647-6000); **Central Maine Medical Center** (300 Main St., Lewiston, 207/795-0111); **St. Mary's Regional Medical Center** (Campus Ave., Lewiston, emergency room 207/777-8120).

AFFLICTIONS
Lyme Disease

A bacterial infection that causes severe arthritis-like symptoms, Lyme disease (named after the Connecticut town where it was first identified in 1975) has been documented in Maine since 1986. Health officials monitor the situation carefully and issue cautionary warnings during prime tick season—mid-May into August. Atlanta's Centers for Disease Control and Prevention (www.cdc.gov) has cited the wooded, marshy areas of Maine's southernmost counties, York and Cumberland, as the highest-risk areas. From there northward along the coast to Mount Desert Island, the risk is considered low to moderate.

Lyme disease is spread by bites from tiny deer ticks (not the larger dog ticks; they don't carry it), which feed on the blood of deer, mice, songbirds, and humans. Symptoms include joint pain, extreme fatigue, chills, a stiff neck, headache, and a distinctive ringlike rash. Except for the rash, which occurs in about 80

If you're traveling with a pet, be sure to check it as well as yourself for ticks.

percent of victims, the symptoms mimic those of other ailments, such as the flu, so the disease is hard to diagnose. The rash, which expands gradually and usually is not painful, may appear from three days to a month after a bite. If left untreated, Lyme disease eventually can cause heart and neurological problems and debilitating arthritis. Preventive measures are essential. If you suspect you've been exposed, seek medical assistance.

The best advice is to take precautions: Wear a long-sleeved shirt and long pants, and tuck the pant legs into your socks. Light-colored clothing makes the ticks easier to spot. Buy tick repellent at a supermarket or convenience store and use it liberally on your legs. Spray it around your cuffs and beltline. While you're hiking, try to keep to the center of trails, away from long grasses. After any hike, check for ticks—especially behind the knees, and in the armpits, navel, and groin. Monitor children carefully. If you find a tick or suspect you have been bitten, head for the nearest hospital emergency room. If you spot a tick on you (or anyone else), remove it with tweezers and save it for analysis. Not all deer ticks are infected.

Rabies

Incidents of rabies—a life-threatening, nerve-attacking disease for which there is no cure unless treated immediately—have increased dramatically in Maine since 1994. No human has ever survived a case of rabies, and the disease is horrible, so *do not* approach, or let any child approach, any of the animals known to transmit it: raccoons, skunks, squirrels, bats, and foxes. Domestic dogs are required to have biennial rabies inoculations, thus providing a front line of defense for humans. If you're bitten by any animal, especially one acting suspiciously, head for the nearest hospital emergency room. For statewide information about rabies, contact the Maine Disease Control Administration in Augusta (207/287-3591).

Allergies (in the Land of Bees and Lobster)

If your medical history includes extreme aller-gies to shellfish or bee sting, you know the risks of eating a lobster or wandering around a wild-flower meadow. However, if you come from a landlocked area and are new to crustaceans, you might not be aware of the potential hazard. Statistics indicate that less than 2 percent of adults have a severe shellfish allergy, but for those victims, the reaction can set in quickly. Immediate treatment is needed to keep the airways open. If you have a history of severe allergic reactions to *anything,* be prepared when you come to the Maine coast dreaming of lobster feasts. Ask your doctor for a prescription for EpiPen (epinephrine), a preloaded, single-use syringe containing 0.3 mg of the drug—enough to tide you over until you can get to a hospital.

Seasickness

Samuel Butler, the 19th-century author of *Erewhon,* wrote, "How holy people look when they are sea-sick." And he wasn't kidding. Seasickness conjures visions of the pearly gates and an overwhelming urge for instant salvation. Fortunately, even though the ailment seems to last forever, it's only temporary—depending on where you are, what remedies you have, and how your system responds. If you're planning to do any boating in Maine—particularly sailing—you'll want to be prepared. (Being prepared in fact may keep you from succumbing, since fear of seasickness just about guarantees you'll get it.)

Seasickness allegedly stems from an inner-ear imbalance caused by boat motion, but researchers have had difficulty explaining why some people on a vessel become violently ill and others have no problem at all.

To prevent seasickness, try to stay in good shape. Get enough sleep and food, and keep your clothing warm and dry (not easy, of course, on a heeling sailboat). Some veteran sailors swear by salted crackers, sips of water, and bites of fresh ginger. If you start feeling queasy, keep your eyes on the horizon and stay as far away as possible from odors from the engine, the galley, the head, and other seasick passengers. If you become seasick, keep sipping water to prevent dehydration.

Dramamine, Marezine, and Bonine, taken several hours before a boat trip, have long been the preventives of choice. They do cause drowsiness, but anyone who's been seasick will tell you he'd rather be drowsy. Another popular preventive is the scopolamine patch (available by prescription under the trademark Transderm Scop; not advised for pregnant women, the elderly, or children), which gradually releases medication into the bloodstream for up to three days. Discuss the minor side effects with the physician who gives you the prescription, and read directions and cautions carefully before using.

And some people swear by the pressure bracelet, which operates somewhat on the principle of acupressure, telling your brain to ignore the fact that you're not on terra firma. Great success has been reported with these prophylactics in the last decade. Before embarking, especially if the weather is at all iffy, go ahead and put on a patch or a bracelet. Any such preventive measure also improves your mental attitude, relieving anxiety.

Sunstroke

Since Maine lies between 43° and 48° north latitude, sunstroke is not a major problem, but don't push your luck by spending an entire day frying on the beach in southern coastal Maine. Not only do you risk sunstroke and dehydration, but you're also asking for skin cancer down the road. Early in the season, slather yourself, and especially children, with plenty of PABA-free sunblock. (PABA can cause skin rashes and eruptions, even on people not abnormally sensitive.) Depending on your skin tone, use sun protection factor (SPF) 15 or higher. If you're in the water a long time, slather on some more. Start with 15–30 minutes of solar exposure and increase gradually each day. If you don't get it right, watch for symptoms of sunstroke: fever, profuse sweating, headache, nausea or vomiting, extreme thirst, and sometimes hallucinations. To treat someone with sunstroke, find a breezy spot and place a cold, wet cloth on the victim's forehead. Change the cloth frequently so it stays cold. Offer lots of liquids—strong tea or coffee, fruit juice, water, and soft drinks (no alcohol).

Hypothermia and Frostbite

Wind and weather can shift dramatically in Maine, especially at higher elevations, creating prime conditions for contracting hypothermia and frostbite. At risk are hikers, swimmers, canoeists, kayakers, sailors, skiers, even cyclists.

When body temperature plummets below the normal 97° to 98.6°F, hypothermia is likely to set in. Symptoms include disorientation, a flagging pulse rate, prolonged shivering, swelling of the face, and cool skin. Quick action is essential to prevent shock and keep body temperature from dropping into the 80s, where cardiac arrest can occur. Emergency treatment begins with removal of as much wet clothing as possible without causing further exposure. Wrap the victim in anything dry—blankets, sleeping bag, clothing, towels, even large plastic trash bags—to keep body heat from escaping. Be sure the neck and head are covered. Or practice the buddy system—climb into a sleeping bag with the victim and provide skin contact. Do not rub the skin, apply hot water, or elevate the legs. If he or she is conscious, offer high-sugar snacks and nonalcoholic hot drinks (but, again, no alcohol; it dilates blood vessels and disrupts the warming process). As quickly as possible, transport the victim to a hospital emergency room.

When extremities begin turning blue or gray, with red blotches, frostbite may be setting in. As with hypothermia, add warmth slowly but do not rub frostbitten skin. Offer snacks and warm, nonalcoholic liquids.

Even during the height of summer, be on the alert for mild hypothermia when children stay in the ocean too long. Bouncing in and out of the water, kids become preoccupied, refuse to admit they are cold, and fall prey to wind chill.

To prevent hypothermia and frostbite, dress in layers and remove or add them as needed. Wool, waterproof nylon (such as Gore-Tex), and synthetic fleece (such as Polartec) are the best fabrics for repelling dampness. Polyester fleece lining wicks excess moisture away from your body. If you plan to buy a down jacket, be sure it has a waterproof shell; down will just suck up the moisture from snow and rain. Especially in winter, always cover your head, since body heat escapes quickly through the head; a ski mask will protect ears and nose. Wear wool- or fleece-lined gloves and wool socks.

Special Considerations During Hunting Season

During Maine's fall hunting season (October to Thanksgiving weekend)—and especially during the November deer season—walk or hike only in wooded areas marked No Hunting, No Trespassing, or Posted. And even if an area *is* closed to hunters, don't decide to explore the woods during deer or moose season without wearing a "hunter orange" (read: eye-popping fluorescent) jacket or vest. If you take your dog along, be sure it, too, wears an orange vest. Deer

hunters are required to wear two items of orange clothing—a hat and usually a vest. Orange gear is available in sporting-goods stores, hardware stores, and some supermarkets and convenience stores. Hunting is illegal on Sundays.

During hunting season, moose and deer are on the move and made understandably skittish by the hunters invading their turf. Moose are primarily found inland, but deer are everywhere, and even the occasional moose strays into coastal Maine. At night, particularly in wooded areas, these huge creatures often end up alongside or in the roads, so ratchet up your defensive-driving skills. Reduce your normal speed, use high beams when there's no oncoming traffic, and remain extra-alert. In a moose-vs.-car encounter, no one wins, and human fatalities are common. An encounter between a deer and a car may be less dangerous to humans (although the deer usually dies), but some damage is inevitable.

Information and Services

MONEY
Currency

Since Maine's Down East Coast borders Canada, don't be surprised to see a few Canadian coins mixed in with American ones when you receive change from a purchase. In such cases, Canadian and U.S. quarters are equivalent, although the exchange rate is in fact drastically different. Most services (including banks) will accept a handful of Canadian coins at par, but you'll occasionally spot No Canadian Currency signs.

If you need to exchange foreign currency—other than Canadian dollars—do it at or near border crossings or in Portland. In small communities, such transactions are more complicated; you may end up spending more time and money than necessary.

Banks and Automated Teller Machines

Typical banking hours are 9 A.M.–3 P.M. weekdays, occasionally with later hours on Friday.

Drive-up windows at many banks tend to open as much as an hour earlier and stay open an hour or so after lobbies close. Some banks also maintain Saturday morning hours. But as long as you have an automated teller machine (ATM) or debit card or a credit card, you can go anywhere in Maine at any time and withdraw money from your personal checking, savings, or credit-card account.

Credit Cards/Travelers Checks

Bank credit cards have become so preferred and so prevalent that it's nearly impossible to rent a car or check into a hotel without one (the alternative is payment in advance or a hefty cash deposit). MasterCard and Visa are most widely accepted in Maine, and Discover and American Express are next most popular; Carte Blanche, Diners Club, and EnRoute (Canadian) lag far behind. Be aware, however, that small restaurants (including lobster pounds), shops, and B&Bs off the beaten track might not accept credit cards or nonlocal personal checks; you may need to settle your account with cash or travelers check.

Taxes

Maine charges a 5 percent sales tax on items such as gifts, snacks, books, clothing, and video rentals, and a 7 percent tax on all bar, restaurant, and lodging bills. Bear in mind, especially when making reservations by phone, that restaurants and lodgings usually do *not* include the 7 percent tax when quoting their prices. A whopping 10 percent tax is added to car-rental rates.

Tipping

The longtime restaurant tipping standard—15 percent of the total bill—still prevails in most of Maine. One exception is Portland, where a big-city 20 percent rate isn't unusual in the upscale restaurants. Of course, the restaurant tip always should depend on the quality of the service. If you've ever worked in a restaurant, you know how much tips are appreciated—but they need to be earned. Don't penalize a waitperson for the kitchen's mistakes or incompetence, but do reduce the tip if the service is sloppy. If for any reason you don't tip, do let a host or hostess know the reason, so you're not just considered chintzy.

Taxi drivers expect a 15 percent tip; airport porters expect at least $1 per bag, depending on the difficulty of the job. If a porter simply unloads a suitcase from a car, $0.50 is plenty; if he has to escort you to a ticket counter—and especially if he arranges for speedier service—a dollar per bag is appropriate.

The usual tip for housekeeping services in accommodations is $1–2 per person, per night, depending upon the level of service. It's not necessary to tip at B&Bs if the owners do the housekeeping.

Some accommodations add a 10- to 15-percent service fee to rates.

TOURISM INFORMATION AND MAPS
Maine Tourism Association

The Maine Tourism Association (325 Water St., Hallowell, Maine 04347, 207/623-0363, www.mainetourism.com) publishes the free, annual magazine-style guidebook *Maine Invites You,* which details sights throughout the state and provides listings of chambers of commerce and other info helpful for travelers. Call, write, or visit the website to request a copy and a state map.

State Visitors Information Centers

The Maine Tourism Association operates state visitors information centers in Calais, Fryeburg (May–October), Hampden, Houlton, Kittery, and Yarmouth. These are excellent places to visit to stock up on brochures, pick up a map, ask advice, and use restrooms.

Maine Online

The Maine Office of Tourism has established an award-winning website: www.visitmaine .com. You'll find chamber of commerce addresses, articles, photos, information on lodgings, and access to a variety of Maine tourism businesses. But hundreds of other Maine pages are also up and running, so surf away. You can use the website to request a free state map and copy of *Maine Invites You.* The state's toll-free information hotline is 888/MAINE-45 (888/624-6345).

Local Chambers of Commerce and Tourism Offices

Tourism is Maine's second-largest source of revenue, so almost every community of any size has some kind of information office, varying from York's mansionlike quarters to tiny log cabins. Information on these is listed in the destination chapters.

Maps

Peek in any Mainer's car, and you're likely to see a copy of *The Maine Atlas and Gazetteer,* published by DeLorme Mapping Company, in Yarmouth. Despite an oversize format inconvenient for hiking and kayaking, this 96-page paperbound book just about guarantees that you won't get lost (and if you're good at map reading, it can get you out of a lot of traffic jams). Scaled at one-half inch to the mile, it's meticulously compiled from aerial photographs, satellite images, U.S. Geological Survey maps, GPS readings, and timber-company maps, and it is revised annually. It details back roads and dirt roads and shows elevation, boat ramps, public lands, campgrounds and picnic areas, and trail heads. DeLorme products are available nationwide in book and map stores, but you can also order direct (800/452-5931, www.delorme.com). The atlas is $19.95 and shipping is $4 (Maine residents need to add 5 percent sales tax).

The Maine Tourism Association also publishes a free state map, but it is in no way as detailed as DeLorme's map book.

COMMUNICATIONS AND MEDIA
Postal and Shipping Services

Post offices in Maine cities and towns are open six days a week, usually 8 A.M.–5 P.M. Monday–Saturday, although Saturday service in small communities typically is 8 A.M.–noon.

Cities and large towns have strategically placed Express Mail, UPS, and Federal Express boxes. To contact Federal Express, call 800/463-3339; to contact UPS, call 800/742-5877. Other national/international delivery services available in Maine are Airborne Express (800/247-2676) and DHL (800/225-5345). Ask locally about businesses that provide packing and shipping services.

If you expect to receive mail while visiting Maine, have your correspondents address it to you c/o General Delivery in the town or city where you expect to be and mark it "Hold for arrival on [your estimated arrival date]." Be sure to give them that post office's correct zip code (every post office has a national zip code directory; overseas residents can check with the nearest U.S. embassy or consulate, or log on to www.usps.com).

Area Code

Maine still has only one telephone area code, 207. To call long distance in state and out of state, dial 1 plus the area code before the number. For directory assistance, dial 411.

Toll-Free Calling

Any number with an area code of 800, 888, 877, 866, 855, 844, 833, or 822 is toll free.

Cell Phones

When you're on vacation, a ringing telephone should be the absolute last thing you want to think about, but needs do arise, and cellular phones have become a fact of life. Transmission towers are now sprinkled everywhere in Maine; only a few pockets—mostly down peninsulas and in remote valleys and hollows—are out of cellular-phone range. (Keep in mind, however, that if you're planning to hike or camp in Baxter State Park, even in a cabin, you won't be allowed to use your phone or any other kind of electronic equipment. Baxter authorities work hard—and effectively—to maintain the park's "forever wild" philosophy.)

Internet Access

Internet access is widely available at libraries and coffeehouses. Most hotels and many inns and B&Bs also offer Internet access; many provide dataports or Wi-Fi.

RESOURCES

Glossary

To help you translate some of the lingo off the beaten track (e.g., country stores and county fairs, farmstands and flea markets), here's a sampling of local terms and expressions.

alewives herring

ayuh yes

barrens as in "blueberry barrens"; fields where wild blueberries grow

beamy wide (as in a boat or a person)

beans shorthand for the traditional Saturday-night meal, which always includes baked beans

blowdown a forest area leveled by wind

blowing a gale very windy

camp a vacation house (small or large), usually on freshwater and/or in the woods

chance serendipity or luck (as in "open by appointment or by chance")

chicken dressing chicken manure

chowder (pronounced "chowdah") soup made with lobster, clams, or fish, or a combination thereof; lobster version sometimes called lobster stew

chowderhead mischief or troublemakers, usually interchangeable with idiot

coneheads tourists (because of their presumed penchant for ice cream)

cottage a vacation house (anything from a bungalow to a mansion), usually on salt water

culch (also cultch) "stuff"; the contents of attics, basements, and some flea markets

cull a discount lobster, usually minus a claw

cunnin' cute (usually describing a baby or small child)

dinner (pronounced "dinnah") the noon meal

dinner pail lunch box

dite a very small amount

dooryard the yard near a house's main entrance

Down East with the prevailing wind; the old coastal sailing route from Boston to Nova Scotia

downcellar in the basement

dry-ki driftwood, usually remnants from the logging industry

ell a residential structural section that links a house and a barn; formerly a popular location for the "summer kitchen," to spare the house from woodstove heat

exercised upset; angry

fiddleheads unopened ostrich-fern fronds, a spring delicacy

finest kind top quality; good news; an expression of general approval; also, a term of appreciation

flatlander a person not from Maine, often but not exclusively someone from the Midwest

floatplane a small plane equipped with pontoons for landing on water; the same aircraft often becomes a skiplane in winter

flowage a water body created by damming, usually beaver handiwork (also called "beaver flowage")

frappe a thick drink containing milk, ice cream, and flavored syrup, as opposed to a milk shake, which does not include ice cream (but beware: a frappe offered in other parts of the United States is an ice-cream sundae topped with whipped cream!)

from away not native to Maine

galamander a wheeled contraption formerly used to transport quarry granite to building sites or to boats for onward shipment

gore a sliver of land left over from inaccurate boundary surveys. Maine has several gores; Hibberts Gore, for instance, has a population of one.

got done quit a job; was let go

harbormaster local official who monitors water traffic and assigns moorings; often a very political job

hardshell lobster that hasn't molted yet (more scarce, thus more pricey in summer)

hod wooden "basket" used for carrying clams

ice-out the departure of winter ice from ponds, lakes, rivers, and streams; many communities have ice-out contests, awarding prizes for guessing the exact time of ice-out, in April or May

Italian long soft bread roll sliced on top and filled with peppers, onions, tomatoes, sliced meat, black olives, and sprinkled with olive oil, salt, and pepper; veggie versions available

jimmies chocolate sprinkles, like those on an ice-cream cone

lobster car a large floating crate for storing lobsters

Maine Guide a member of the Maine Professional Guides Association, trained and tested for outdoor and survival skills; also called Registered Maine Guide

market price restaurant menu term for "the going rate," usually referring to the price of lobster or clams

molt what a lobster does when it sheds its shell for a larger one; the act of molting is called ecdysis (as a stripper is an ecdysiast)

money tree a collection device for a monetary gift

mud season mid-March to mid-April, when back roads and unpaved driveways become virtual tank traps

nasty neat extremely meticulous

near stingy

notional stubborn, determined

off island the mainland, to an islander

place another word for a house (as in "Herb Pendleton's place")

pot trap, as in "lobster pot"

public landing see "town landing"

rake hand tool used for harvesting blueberries

rusticator a summer visitor, particularly in bygone days

scooch (or scootch) to squat; to move sideways

sea smoke heavy mist rising off the water when the air temperature suddenly becomes much colder than the ocean temperature

select a lobster with claws intact

Selectmen the elected men and women who handle local affairs in small communities; the First Selectman chairs meetings. In some towns, "people from away" have tried to propose substituting a gender-neutral term, but in most cases the effort has failed.

shedder a lobster with a new (soft) shell; generally occurs in July and August (more common then, thus less expensive than hardshells)

shire town county seat

shore dinner the works: chowder, clams, lobster, and sometimes corn on the cob, too; usually the most expensive item on a menu

short a small, illegal-size lobster

slumgullion tasteless food; a mess

slut a poor housekeeper

slut's wool dust balls found under beds, couches, and so on

snapper an undersize, illegal lobster

softshell see "shedder"

soda cola, root beer, and so on (often referred to as "pop" in other parts of the country

some very (as in "some hot")

spleeny overly sensitive

steamers clams (before or after they are steamed)

sternman a lobsterman's helper (male or female)

summer complaint a tourist

supper (pronounced "suppah") evening meal, eaten by Mainers around 5 or 6 P.M. (as opposed to flatlanders and summer people, who eat dinner between 7 and 9 P.M.)

tad slightly; a little bit

thick-o'-fog zero-visibility fog

to home at home

tomalley a lobster's green insides; considered a delicacy by some

town landing shore access; often a park or a parking lot, next to a wharf or boat-launch ramp

upattic in the attic

Whoopie! Pie the trademarked name for a high-fat, calorie-laden, cakelike snack that only kids and dentists could love

wicked cold! frigid

wicked good! excellent

williwaws uncomfortable feeling

Suggested Reading

DESCRIPTION AND TRAVEL

Arlen, A. *Maine Sporting Camps: A Year-Round Guide to Vacationing at Traditional Hunting and Fishing Lodges.* 3d ed. Woodstock, VT: Countryman Press, 2003. A survey of more than 90 Maine sporting camps; the only book on the subject.

Batignani, K. W., *Maine's Coastal Cemeteries: A Historic Tour.* Camden, ME: Down East Books, 2004. A guide to 35 cemeteries with intriguing histories, unusual epitaphs, and notable carvings.

Bumsted, L. *Hot Showers! Maine Coast Lodgings for Kayakers and Sailors.* 2d ed. Brunswick, ME: Audenreed Press, 2000. Excellent, well-researched resource for anyone cruising the shoreline and yearning for alternatives to a sleeping bag. It offers some information on kayak access (but also see the *Recreation* section).

Calhoun, C. C., and T. M. Szelog. *Maine.* 4th ed. New York: Fodor's Travel Publications, Compass American Guides, 2000. Entertaining, literate prose; outstanding photography.

Curtis, W., and T. Seymour. *Maine: Off the Beaten Path.* 8th ed. Old Saybrook, CT: Globe Pequot Press, 2008. Introduction to offbeat and unexpected locales; a good supplementary guide for would-be explorers.

Dwelley, M. J. *Spring Wildflowers of New England.* 2d ed. Camden, ME: Down East Books, 2000. Back in print after several years, this beautifully illustrated gem is an essential guide for exploring spring woodlands.

Dwelley, M. J. *Summer and Fall Wildflowers of New England.* 2d ed. Camden, ME: Down East Books, 2004. Flowers are grouped by color; more than 700 lovely colored-pencil drawings simplify identification.

Karlin, L., and R. Sawyer-Fay. *Gardens Maine Style.* Camden, ME: Down East Books, 2001. A beautiful book depicting and describing private and some public gardens.

The Maine Atlas and Gazetteer. Yarmouth, ME: DeLorme, updated annually. You'll be hard put to get lost if you're carrying this essential volume; 70 full-page (oversize format) topographical maps with GPS grids.

Morrison, P. M. *The Guide to Maine Golf Courses.* Camden, ME: Down East Books, 2000. Useful, descriptive information about Maine golf courses built before publication.

Nangle, H. *Moon Coastal Maine.* 3rd ed. Emeryville, CA: Avalon Travel Publishing, 2008. A Maine native and veteran travel writer is the ideal escort for exploring the coast.

Pierson, E. C., J. E. Pierson, and P. D. Vickery. *A Birder's Guide to Maine.* Camden, ME: Down East Books, 1981. An expanded version of *A Birder's Guide to the Coast of Maine.* No ornithologist, novice or expert, should explore Maine without this valuable guide.

Taft, H., J. Taft, and C. Rindlaub. *A Cruising Guide to the Maine Coast.* 5th ed. Peaks

Island, ME: Diamond Pass Publishing, 2007. Don't even consider cruising the coast without this volume.

Thompson, W. B., et al. *A Collector's Guide to Maine Mineral Localities.* 3d ed. Augusta, ME: Maine Geological Survey, 1998. For amateur rock hounds, details on and directions to abandoned quarries and other sites.

Vietze, A. *Insiders' Guide to the Maine Coast.* 2d ed. Guilford, CT: Globe Pequot Press, 2004. Longtime *Down East* magazine editor Andy Vietze, who really *is* an insider, shares the results of his zillions of explorations.

LITERATURE, ART, AND PHOTOGRAPHY

Bennett, D. *Allagash: Maine's Wild and Scenic River.* Camden, ME: Down East Books, 1994. Elegant portrait of the Allagash Wilderness Waterway by a veteran Maine naturalist.

Curtis, J., W. Curtis, and F. Lieberman. *Monhegan: The Artists' Island.* Camden, ME: Down East Books, 1995. Fascinating island history interspersed with landscape and seascape paintings and drawings by more than 150 artists, including Bellows, Henri, Hopper, Kent, Porter, Tam, and Wyeth.

Maine Speaks: An Anthology of Maine Literature. Brunswick, ME: Maine Writers and Publishers Alliance, 1989.

McNair, W., ed. *The Maine Poets: An Anthology of Verse.* Camden, ME: Down East Books, 2003. McNair's selection of best works by Maine's finest poets.

Middleton, D., and B. Morrison. *The Photographers Guide to the Maine Coast.* Woodstock, VT: Countryman Press, 2004. Find out where to go, how to get there, when to go, and how to take perfect photos.

Silliker, B. *Wild Maine: Discoveries of a Maine Wildlife Photographer.* Camden, ME: Down East Books, 2004. Stories and superb nature photography by Maine's best-known wildlife photographer—who died unexpectedly in 2003.

Spectre, P. H. *Passage in Time.* New York: W. W. Norton, 1991. A noted marine writer cruises the coast aboard traditional windjammers; gorgeous photos complement the colorful text.

Thoreau, H. D. *The Maine Woods.* New York: Penguin Books, 1988 ed. [orig. pub. 1864]. A Maine classic, first published two years after the author's death; mid-19th-century exploration of Maine's wilderness around Greenville, Chesuncook, Katahdin, and more.

Van Riper, F. *Down East Maine: A World Apart.* Camden, ME: Down East Books, 1998. Maine's Washington County, captured with incredible insight and compassion by a master photographer and insightful wordsmith.

Villani, R. *Forever Wild: Maine's Magnificent Baxter State Park.* Camden, ME: Down East Books, 1991. Spectacular photos of Baxter in every season, taken by an accomplished professional.

LOBSTER AND LIGHTHOUSES

Caldwell, W. *Lighthouses of Maine.* Camden, ME: Down East Books, 1986. A historical tour of Maine's lighthouses, with the emphasis on history, legends, and lore.

Corson, T. *The Secret Life of Lobsters.* New York: HarperCollins, 2004. Everything you wanted—or perhaps didn't want—to know about lobster.

Hartnett, R., and P. D. Bachelder. *Maine Lighthouse Map and Guide.* Howes Cave, NY: Hartnett House Map Publishers, 2000. An illustrated map and guide providing directions on how to find all Maine beacons as well as brief histories.

Thompson, C. *Maine Lighthouses: A Pictorial*

Guide. 3d ed. Mount Desert, ME: CatNap Publications, 2001. What they look like, how to find them, and a bit of background detail.

HISTORY

Acadian Culture in Maine. Washington, DC: National Park Service, North Atlantic Region, 1994. A project report on Acadians and their traditions in the Upper St. John Valley.

Duncan, R. F., E. G. Barlow, K. Bray, K., and C. Hanks. *Coastal Maine: A Maritime History.* Woodstock, VT: Countrymen Press, 2002. Updated version of the classic work.

Isaacson, D., ed. *Maine: A Guide "Down East."* 2d ed. n.p.: Maine League of Historical Societies and Museums, 1970. Revised version of the Depression-era WPA guidebook. Still interesting for background reading.

Jaster, R. S. *Russian Voices on the Kennebec: The Story of Maine's Unlikely Colony.* Orono: University of Maine Press, 1999. A riveting account of the founding of a Russian-speaking colony in Richmond, Maine, in the 1950s. Superb historical photographs.

Judd, R. W., E. A. Churchill, and J. W. Eastman, eds. *Maine: The Pine Tree State from Prehistory to the Present.* Orono: University of Maine Press, 1995. The best available Maine history, with excellent historical maps.

Paine, L. P. *Down East: A Maritime History of Maine.* Gardiner, ME: Tilbury House, 2000. A noted maritime historian provides an enlightening introduction to the state's seafaring tradition.

MEMOIRS

Dawson, L. B. *Saltwater Farm.* Westford, ME: Impatiens Press, 1993. Witty, charming stories of growing up on the Cushing peninsula.

Greenlaw, L. *The Lobster Chronicles: Life on a Very Small Island.* New York: Hyperion, 2002. Swordfishing boat Captain Linda Greenlaw's account of returning to life on Isle au Haut after weathering the *The Perfect Storm.*

Hamlin, H. *Nine Mile Bridge: Three Years in the Maine Woods.* Yarmouth and Frenchboro, ME: Islandport Press, 2005 [orig. pub. 1945]. Hamlin's experiences as a teacher at a remote lumber camp near the headwaters of the Allagash, where her husband was a game warden.

Lunt, D. L. *Hauling by Hand: The Life and Times of a Maine Island.* Frenchboro, ME: Islandport Press, 1999. A sensitive history of Frenchboro (a.k.a. Long Island), eight miles offshore, written by an eighth-generation islander, now a journalist.

Peavey, E. *Maine and Me: 10 Years of Down East Adventures.* Camden, ME: 2004. A collection of essays and articles by a writer for *Down East* magazine.

Wass, P. B. *Lighthouse in My Life: The Story of a Maine Lightkeeper's Family.* Camden, ME: Down East Books, 1987. Offshore adventures, growing up on Libby Island, near Machias.

NATURAL HISTORY

Bennett, D. *Maine's Natural Heritage: Rare Species and Unique Natural Features.* Camden, ME: Down East Books, 1988. A dated book that examines both the special ecology of the state and how it's threatened.

Conkling, P. W. *Islands in Time: A Natural and Cultural History of the Islands of the Gulf of Maine.* 2d ed. Camden, ME: Down East Books, and Rockland, ME: Island Institute, 1999. A thoughtful overview by the president of Maine's Island Institute.

Kendall, D. L. *Glaciers and Granite: A Guide to Maine's Landscape and Geology.* Unity, ME: North Country Press, 1993. Explains why Maine looks the way it does.

Maine's Ice Age Trail Down East Map and Guide. Orono: University of Maine Press, 2007. Also available online at http://ice agetrail.umaine.ecu. Information on 46 glacial sites.

RECREATION
Hiking and Walking

AMC Maine Mountain Guide. 9th ed. Boston: Appalachian Mountain Club Books, 2005. The definitive statewide resource for going vertical. In a handy small format. (AMC has eliminated Acadia National Park and expanded its separate guide on Acadia's peaks.)

Chunn, C. *50 Hikes in the Maine Mountains: Day Hikes and Overnights from the Rangeley Lakes to Baxter State Park.* 3d ed. Woodstock, VT: Countryman Press/Backcountry, 2002. Well-researched and well-written guide (complements the Gibson guide below).

Clark, Stephen. *Katahdin: A Guide to Baxter State Park and Katahdin.* Clark Books, 2003.

Cobscook Trails: A Guide to Walking Opportunities around Cobscook Bay and the Bold Coast. 2d ed. Whiting, ME: Quoddy Regional Land Trust, 2000. Essential handbook for exploring this part of the Down East Coast. Excellent maps.

Collins, J., and J. E. McCarthy. *Nature Walks in Southern Maine.* Boston: Appalachian Mountain Club Books, 1996. Easy walks, mostly horizontal, and good natural-history commentary. Maps are primitive but do the job.

Gibson, J. *50 Hikes in Coastal and Southern Maine.* 3d ed. Woodstock, VT: Countryman Press/Backcountry Guides, 2001. Well-researched, detailed resource by a veteran hiker.

Roberts, P. *On the Trail in Lincoln County.*

Newcastle/Damariscotta, ME: Lincoln County Publishing, 2003. A great guide to more than 60 walks in preserves from Wiscasset through Waldoboro, with detailed directions to trailheads.

Ronan, Ray, ed. *Appalachian Trail Guide to Maine.* Maine Appalachian Trail Club, 2004.

Seymour, T. *Hiking Maine.* 2d ed. Helena, MT: Falcon Press, 2002. Helpful—especially for less-well-known hikes in the Mid-Coast Region. Not as comprehensive, statewide, as the Gibson hiking guide or the *AMC Maine Mountain Guide.*

Wiser, Marita. *Hikes in and around Maine's Lake Region.* Peregrine Outfitters, 2004.

Paddling

AMC River Guide: Maine. 3d ed. Boston: Appalachian Mountain Club Books, 2002. Detailed guide to canoeing or kayaking Maine's large and small rivers.

The Maine Island Trail: Stewardship Handbook and Guidebook. Rockland, ME: Maine Island Trail Association, updated annually. Available only with MITA membership (annual dues $45), providing access to dozens of islands along the watery trail.

Miller, D. *Kayaking the Maine Coast: A Paddler's Guide to Day Trips from Kittery to Cobscook.* 2nd ed. Woodstock, VT: Countryman Press/Backcountry Guides, 2006. A well-researched volume by a veteran kayaker. With her book and a copy of *Hot Showers!* (see *Description and Travel*), you're all set.

Wilson, A., and J. Hayes. *Quiet Water Canoe Guide, Maine: Best Paddling Lakes and Ponds for All Ages.* 2d ed. Boston: Appalachian Mountain Club Books, 2005. Comprehensive handbook, with helpful maps, for inland paddling.

Bicycling

Stone, H. *25 Bicycle Tours in Maine: Coastal and Inland Rides from Kittery to Caribou.* 3d ed. Woodstock, VT: Countryman Press/Backcountry Guides, 1998.

ACADIA NATIONAL PARK/MOUNT DESERT ISLAND

Abrell, D. *A Pocket Guide to the Carriage Roads of Acadia National Park.* 2nd ed. Camden, ME: Down East Books, 1995.

Brechlin, E. D. *A Pocket Guide to Paddling the Waters of Mount Desert Island.* Camden, ME: Down East Books, 1996.

Gillmore, R. *Great Walks of Acadia National Park and Mount Desert Island.* Rev. ed. Goffstown, NH: Great Walks, 1994.

Helfrich, G. W., and G. O'Neil. *Lost Bar Harbor.* Camden, ME: Down East Books, 1982. Fascinating collection of historic photographs of classic, turn-of-the-century "cottages," many obliterated by Bar Harbor's Great Fire of 1947.

Minutolo, A. *A Pocket Guide to Biking on Mount Desert Island.* Camden, ME: Down East Books, 1996.

Monkman, J., and M. Monkman. *Discover Acadia National Park: A Guide to the Best Hiking, Biking, and Paddling.* Boston: Appalachian Mountain Club Books, 2000. A comprehensive guide to well-chosen hikes, bike trips, and paddling routes, accompanied by an excellent pullout map.

Nangle, H. *Moon Acadia National Park.* 2nd ed. Emeryville, CA: Avalon Travel Publishing, 2006. Examines the region from Blue Hill through the Schoodic Peninsula in depth.

Roberts, A. R. *Mr. Rockefeller's Roads.* Camden, ME: Down East Books, 1990. The story behind Acadia's scenic carriage roads, written by the granddaughter of John D. Rockefeller (who created them).

St. Germain, T. A., Jr. *A Walk in the Park: Acadia's Hiking Guide.* 10th ed. Bar Harbor, ME: Parkman Publications, 2004. The best Acadia National Park hiking guide, in a handy Michelin-type vertical format. Part of the proceeds go to Friends of Acadia's Acadia Trails Forever campaign.

Internet Resources

GENERAL INFORMATION

State of Maine
www.maine.gov

Everything you wanted to know about Maine and then some, with links to all government departments and Maine-related sites. Among other information on this site is info on accessible arts and recreation.

Maine Office of Tourism
www.visitmaine.com

The biggest and most useful of all Maine-related tourism sites, with sections for where to visit, where to stay, things to do, trip planning, packages, calendar of events, and a search capabilities. Also lodging specials and a comprehensive calendar of events.

Maine Tourism Association
www.mainetourism.com

Find lodging, camping, restaurants, attractions, services, and more as well as links for weather, foliage, transportation planning, and chambers of commerce.

Maine Information
www.maine.info

A privately operated site with a mother lode of links handy for vacation planners.

Portland Papers
www.mainetoday.com

Home site for Maine's largest newspaper has current news as well as extensive information on travel, outdoor activities, entertainment, and sports.

Maine Emergency Management Association
www.state.me.us/mema/weather/weather.htm

Five-day weather forecasts broken down by 32 zones.

Island Institute
www.islandinstitute.org

The institute serves as a clearinghouse/advocate for Maine's islands; the website provides links to the major year-round islands.

TRANSPORTATION

Maine Department of Transportation
www.exploremaine.org

An invaluable site for trip planning, with information on and links to airports, rail service, bus service, automobile travel, and ferries, as well as links to other key travel-planning sites.

Maine Department of Transportation
www.511maine.gov

Provides real-time information about major delays, accidents, road construction, and weather conditions. You can get the same info and more by dialing 511 in-state.

Portland Maine Transportation Page
www.transportme.com

Provides information on all modes of transit to, from, and within Portland. You can connect to bus, train, and airport information, including schedules.

PARKS AND RECREATION

Department of Conservation, Maine Bureau of Parks and Lands
www.maine.gov/doc/parks

Information on state parks, public reserved lands, and state historic sites, details on facilities such as campsites, picnic areas, and boat launches. Make state campground reservations online.

Acadia National Park
www.nps.gov/acad

Information on all sections of Acadia National Park. Make ANP campground reservations online.

Baxter State Park
www.baxterstateparkauthority.com

Everything you need for planning a trip to Baxter.

Maine Audubon
www.maineaudubon.org

Information about Maine Audubon's eco-sensitive headquarters in Falmouth and all of the organization's environmental centers statewide. Activity and program schedules are included.

North Maine Woods
www.northmainewoods.org

Essential information for venturing into the privately owned North Woods.

Maine Department of Inland Fisheries and Wildlife
www.state.me.us/ifw

Info on wildlife, hunting, fishing, snowmobiling, and boating.

The Nature Conservancy
www.nature.org/wherewework/northamerica/states/maine

Information about Maine preserves, field trips, and events.

Maine Land Trust Network
www.mltn.org

Maine has dozens of land trusts statewide managing lands that provide opportunities for hiking, walking, canoeing, kayaking, and other such activities.

Healthy Maine Walks
www.healthymainewalks.com

Lists places for walking statewide.

Maine Island Trail Association
www.mita.org

Information about the association and its activities along with membership details.

Maine Professional Guides Association
www.maineguides.org

Find licensed and Registered Maine Guides for sporting adventures, including sea kayaking, hunting, fishing, and recreation (such as canoeing trips and wildlife safaris).

Maine Association of Sea Kayaking Guides and Instructors
www.maineseakayakguides.com

Information and links to about two dozen members who meet state requirements to lead commercial trips.

Bicycle Coalition of Maine
www.bikemaine.org

Tons of information for bicyclists, including routes, shops, events, organized rides, and much more.

Golf Maine
www.golfme.com

Lists member courses, stay-and-play packages, and golf links statewide.

Maine Birding
www.mainebirding.net

A must-visit site for anyone interested in learning more about birding in Maine, including news, checklists, events, forums, trips, and more.

Maine Windjammer Association
www.sailmainecoast.com

Windjammer schooners homeported in Rockland, Camden, and Rockport belong to this umbrella organization; links to the websites of all the vessels for online and phone information and reservations.

Raft Maine
www.raftmaine.com

Links to outfitters operating on Maine's Kennebec, Dead, and Penobscot Rivers.

Ski Maine
www.skimaine.com

The go-to source for information on alpine skiing in Maine.

L. L. Bean
www.llbean.com

The mega-outdoor retailer not only sells equipment but also offers courses.

ARTS AND ENTERTAINMENT

Music
www.mainemusic.org

Comprehensive site covering almost everything having to do with music in the state, from performances and festivals to musicians, composers, and instrument makers.

Maine Fiber Arts
www.mainefiberarts.org

Everything you wanted to know about fiber artists, farms producing fiber, fiber-related events and festivals, fiber-arts teachers, fiber-arts exhibitions, and more.

Maine Archives and Museums
www.mainemuseums.org

Information on and links to museums, archives, historical societies, and historic sites in Maine.

Maine Art Museum Trail
www.maineartmuseums.org

Information on art museums with significant collections statewide, including Ogunquit Museum of Art (Ogunquit); Portland Museum of Art (Portland); Bowdoin College Museum of Art (Brunswick); and Farnsworth Art Museum (Rockland).

Maine Maritime Heritage Trail
www.maritimemaine.org

Information about and links to maritime museums, boatbuilding schools, lighthouses, historic homes, fishing, naval history, forts, historic sites, and much more.

SHOPPING

Maine Antiques Dealers Association
www.maineantiques.org

Lists member dealers statewide by location and specialty and provides information on upcoming antiques events.

Maine Antiquarian Booksellers Association
www.mainebooksellers.org

Lists independent shops that specialize in used, antiquarian, and rare books.

ACCOMMODATIONS

Maine Innkeepers Association
www.maineinns.com

Lodging search for member motels, hotels, inns, and B&Bs statewide and lodging specials.

Maine Campground Owners Association
www.campmaine.com

Find private campgrounds statewide.

FOOD AND DRINK

Maine Restaurant Association
www.mainerestaurant.com

Statewide trade organization site provides searchable listings of member restaurants by name or location.

Maine Department of Agriculture
www.getrealmaine.com

Information on all things agricultural, including fairs, farmers markets, farm vacations, places to buy Maine foods, berry- and apple-picking sites, and more.

Maine Lobster Promotion Council
www.mainelobsterpromo.com

All lobster, all the time, with links for ordering Maine lobster and organizing your own lobster bake, plus recipes for preparing lobster in more ways than you ever thought possible.

Wild Blueberry Association of North America
www.wildblueberries.com

Information on blueberries as well as numerous recipes.

Index

Acknowledgments

For Amy and Griff, two people who embodied the spirit of Maine and died untimely, tragic deaths within days of each other in June 2006. Knowing each enriched my life.

Although I've lived in Maine since childhood (yes, I will always be a "from away"), and have traveled extensively for both work and pleasure, every time I revisit a place, I find something new or changed, sometimes subtly, other times dramatically. Restaurants open and close. Outfitters change their offerings. B&Bs are sold. New trails are cut. Museums expand. Hotels renovate. And on it goes. Which all goes to say, I couldn't have done this without the help of many people, who served as additional eyes and ears.

I'll start with Kathleen Brandes, who wrote the original editions of this book and whose friendship I valued and whose work and dedication I respected long before I began working on this edition. My appreciation for her meticulous research, her ability to capture a place or a person with a quick turn of phrase, and her dead-on accuracy has no bounds. I'm also grateful for her update on the Baxter State Park section of this book.

More thank-yous are due the folks at Avalon Travel who shepherded me through the process, Bill Newlin, Rebecca Browning, Kevin McLain, and most especially my editor, Kathryn Ettinger. Also thank you to Nicole Schultz, Kevin Anglin, Erin Van Rheenen, Dylan Wooters, and the many other behind-the-scenes Avalon staffers who worked on this book.

Special thank-yous, too, to those who sat down with me and shared local info, sheltered me along the way, fed me, helped with arrangements, verified information, called me with updates, or simply encouraged me: Bill and Cathy Shamel, Maureen Hart, Valerie Kidney, Jan Meiners and Joyce Morrel, Kathryn Rubeor, Alan Furth, Ben and Sonja Walter-Sundaram, Roy Kasindorf and Helene Harton, Darrin Kelly, Don Jalbert and Javier Montesinos, Risteen Masters, Mary and Don Hartley, Jack Burke and Julie Van de Graaf, Traci Klepper, Marti Mayne, Cathy Keating and Deb Bush, Bob Smith, Ellen Chandler, Abbe Levin, Rob Blood, Bruce Jackson, Jean Ginn Marvin, Patricia and Ken Mason, Gary Dominguez, Greg and Heather Burke, Kathryn Weare, Chip Gray, Barbara Whitten, Matt Polstein, Sheila Grant, Roger Merchant, Lynn and Harry Anderson, Linda and Dennis Bortis, Ruth and Dan McLaughlin, Chris and Tracey Anderson, Carolann Ouellette, Bill and Nancy White, Steve White, Wende Gray, Darlene and Jenna Ginsburg, Roger Beaudoin, Betsey Golan, Dina Jackson, John Farra, Barbara and Tim Rogers, Sarah Wills and Steve Viega, Elaine Abel, and most especially Nancy Marshall, Charlene Williams, and Rose Whitehorse, of Nancy Marshall Communications. I couldn't have done this, without all of your help and support.

I save my biggest thanks for my husband, Tom, who drove me everywhere and didn't complain (too much) when I made him backtrack two or three times along the same stretch of road, while seeking an elusive address; who waited patiently while I visited practically every restaurant, inn, and B&B from Kittery to Fort Kent and Fryeburg to Calais; who let me order for him in restaurants; who tackled research projects; and who supported me in every way possible throughout the entire process, all while shooting photographs for the book. I couldn't have done it without him.

And to you, dear reader, thank you for using this book to plan your visit to Maine. Do me a favor, will you? Give me feedback to help make the next edition will be even better. Contact me at Hilary@HilaryNangle.com, and link to my blog for updates on this book.

www.moon.com

For helpful advice on planning a trip, visit www.moon.com for the **TRAVEL PLANNER** and get access to useful travel strategies and valuable information about great places to visit. When you travel with Moon, expect an experience that is uncommon and truly unique.

MAP SYMBOLS

Expressway	**C** Highlight	✈ Airfield	⚓ Golf Course
Primary Road	○ City/Town	✈ Airport	**P** Parking Area
Secondary Road	◉ State Capital	▲ Mountain	▰ Archaeological Site
Unpaved Road	⊛ National Capital	✦ Unique Natural Feature	⌖ Church
Trail	★ Point of Interest		⌖ Gas Station
Ferry	• Accommodation	⤵ Waterfall	
Railroad	▾ Restaurant/Bar	▲ Park	Glacier
Pedestrian Walkway	■ Other Location	⬒ Trailhead	Mangrove
Stairs	▲ Campground	⛷ Skiing Area	Reef
			Swamp

CONVERSION TABLES

°C = (°F - 32) / 1.8
°F = (°C x 1.8) + 32
1 inch = 2.54 centimeters (cm)
1 foot = 0.304 meters (m)
1 yard = 0.914 meters
1 mile = 1.6093 kilometers (km)
1 km = 0.6214 miles
1 fathom = 1.8288 m
1 chain = 20.1168 m
1 furlong = 201.168 m
1 acre = 0.4047 hectares
1 sq km = 100 hectares
1 sq mile = 2.59 square km
1 ounce = 28.35 grams
1 pound = 0.4536 kilograms
1 short ton = 0.90718 metric ton
1 short ton = 2,000 pounds
1 long ton = 1.016 metric tons
1 long ton = 2,240 pounds
1 metric ton = 1,000 kilograms
1 quart = 0.94635 liters
1 US gallon = 3.7854 liters
1 Imperial gallon = 4.5459 liters
1 nautical mile = 1.852 km

MOON MAINE

Avalon Travel
a member of the Perseus Books Group
1700 Fourth Street
Berkeley, CA 94710, USA
www.moon.com

Editor and Series Manager: Kathryn Ettinger
Copy Editor: Karen Gaynor Bleske
Graphics Coordinator: Nicole Schultz
Production Coordinator: Nicole Schultz
Cover Designer: Nicole Schultz
Map Editor: Kevin Anglin
Cartographers: Kat Bennett, Chris Markiewicz
Proofreader: Jamie Andrade
Indexer: Judy Hunt

ISBN-10: 1-56691-783-2
ISBN-13: 978-1-56691-783-4
ISSN: 1096-9551

Printing History
1st Edition – 1998
4th Edition – May 2008
5 4 3 2 1

Text © 2008 by Kathleen M. Brandes and
Hilary Nangle.
Maps © 2008 by Avalon Travel.
All rights reserved.

Some photos and illustrations are used by permission
and are the property of the original copyright
owners.

Front cover photo: pair of moose in shallow mountain
    lake, Franklin County © Randy M. Ury / CORBIS
Title page: wooden dinghies at Brooklin harbor docks
    © Hilary Nangle
Photos on pages 6 and 7 © Hilary Nangle; photo on
    page 8 © Tom Nangle

Printed in the U.S. by RR Donnelley

KEEPING CURRENT

If you have a favorite gem you'd like to see included in the next edition, or see anything
that needs updating, clarification, or correction, please drop us a line. Send your
comments via email to feedback@moon.com, or use the address above.

ABOUT THE AUTHOR

Hilary Nangle

Despite brief out-of-state interludes for college, grad school, and a stint as a ski bum, Hilary Nangle couldn't resist the pull of Maine. She grew up on the coast in Cape Elizabeth, spending much of each winter skiing in the western mountains. When she worked for a whitewater rafting company and was licensed as a Registered Maine Whitewater Guide on the Kennebec, she began exploring the central and northern regions of the state, and a sense of wanderlust was ignited. When she tired of her parents asking when she was going to get a *real* job, she drew on her writing skills, working as an editor for the pro ski tour, managing editor for a food trade publication, features editor for a daily newspaper, and as a freelance writer/editor.

Hilary never tires of exploring Maine, always seeking out the off-beat and quirky, and rarely resisting the invitation of a back road. To her husband's dismay, she inherited her grandmother's shopping gene and can't pass a used bookstore, artisans' gallery, or antiques shop without browsing. She's equally curious about food and has never met a lobster she didn't like. She still divides her year between the coast and the mountains, residing with her husband, photographer Tom Nangle, and an oversized dog, Bernie, both of whom share her passions for long walks and Maine-made ice cream. To learn more about Hilary, please visit her website, www.HilaryNangle.com.

THE CURE FOR THE COMMON TRIP

Moon Handbooks give you the tools to make your own choices, with

- Can't-miss sights, activities, restaurants, and accommodations, marked with 🌙

- Suggestions on how to plan a trip that's perfect for you, including:
  Best of Maine
  Lighthouses, Lobster, and L. L. Bean
  Maine off the Beaten Track
  Special Trails for Special Interests
  Recreation Milestones
  Destination Dining Tour

- 27 detailed and easy-to-use maps

- The firsthand experience and unique perspective of author Hilary Nangle

"America's finest travel guidebook series . . . extensively researched, engagingly written, intelligently indexed, and packed with helpful maps and sidebars."

—*MONEY* MAGAZINE